Collins
ESSENTIAL ROAD ATLAS
BRITAIN

Collins

Published by Collins
An imprint of HarperCollins Publishers
Westerhill Road, Bishopbriggs,
Glasgow G64 2QT

www.harpercollins.co.uk

MIX
Paper from responsible sources
FSC C007454

FSC™ is a non-profit international organisation established to promote the responsible management of the world's forests. Products carrying the FSC label are independently certified to assure consumers that they come from forests that are managed to meet the social, economic and ecological needs of present and future generations, and other controlled sources.

Find out more about HarperCollins and the environment at
www.harpercollins.co.uk/green

Conter

C000005982

Route plannin

Route planning	
Restricted moto	
Motorway services information	
Orbital motorway maps - M25 & Birmingham	xii-xiii
Risk rating of Britain's motorways and A roads	xiv-xv
Distance chart	xvi

Urban approach maps (1 mile to 1 inch)   1-32

Symbols used on maps / Locator map	1
Plymouth	2
Bournemouth	3
Southampton & Portsmouth	4-5
Swansea	6
Cardiff & Newport	7
Bristol	8
Milton Keynes	9
London	10-13
West Midlands	14-15
Coventry	16
Leicester	17
Derby & Nottingham	18-19
Stoke-on-Trent	20
Sheffield	21
Merseyside	22-23
Greater Manchester	24-25
Leeds & Bradford	26-27
Newcastle upon Tyne & Sunderland	28
Middlesbrough	29
Glasgow	30-31
Edinburgh	32

Street maps   33-91

Symbols used on maps /		Hastings	75
Locator map	33	Hereford	75
Birmingham	34-35	Hull	76
Edinburgh	36-37	Inverness	76
Glasgow	38-39	Leicester	77
Leeds	40-41	Lincoln	77
Liverpool	42-43	Middlesbrough	78
London	44-45	Milton Keynes	78
Manchester	46-47	Newcastle upon Tyne	79
Birmingham index	48	Norwich	79
Edinburgh index	49	Nottingham	80
Glasgow index	51	Oxford	80
Leeds index	52	Perth	81
Liverpool index	54	Plymouth	81
London index	56	Portsmouth	82
Manchester index	60	Reading	82
Aberdeen	63	Salisbury	83
Bath	63	Scarborough	83
Blackpool	64	Sheffield	84
Bournemouth	64	Southampton	84
Bradford	65	Stoke-on-Trent	85
Brighton	65	Stratford-upon-Avon	85
Bristol	66	Sunderland	86
Cambridge	66	Swansea	86
Canterbury	67	Swindon	87
Cardiff	67	Torquay	87
Carlisle	68	Watford	88
Cheltenham	68	Weston-super-Mare	88
Chester	69	Winchester	89
Coventry	69	Windsor	89
Derby	70	Worcester	90
Dover	70	York	90
Dundee	71		
Durham	71	**Airport plans**	
Eastbourne	72	Birmingham International	91
Exeter	72	Gatwick	91
Folkestone	73	Glasgow	91
Gloucester	73	Heathrow	91
Guildford	74	Manchester	91
Harrogate	74	Stansted	91

Road maps   92-279

Symbols used on maps & key to map pages	92-93
England, Wales & Southern Scotland (3.2 miles to 1 inch)	94-253
Northern Scotland (4.2 miles to 1 inch)	254-279

Index   280-318

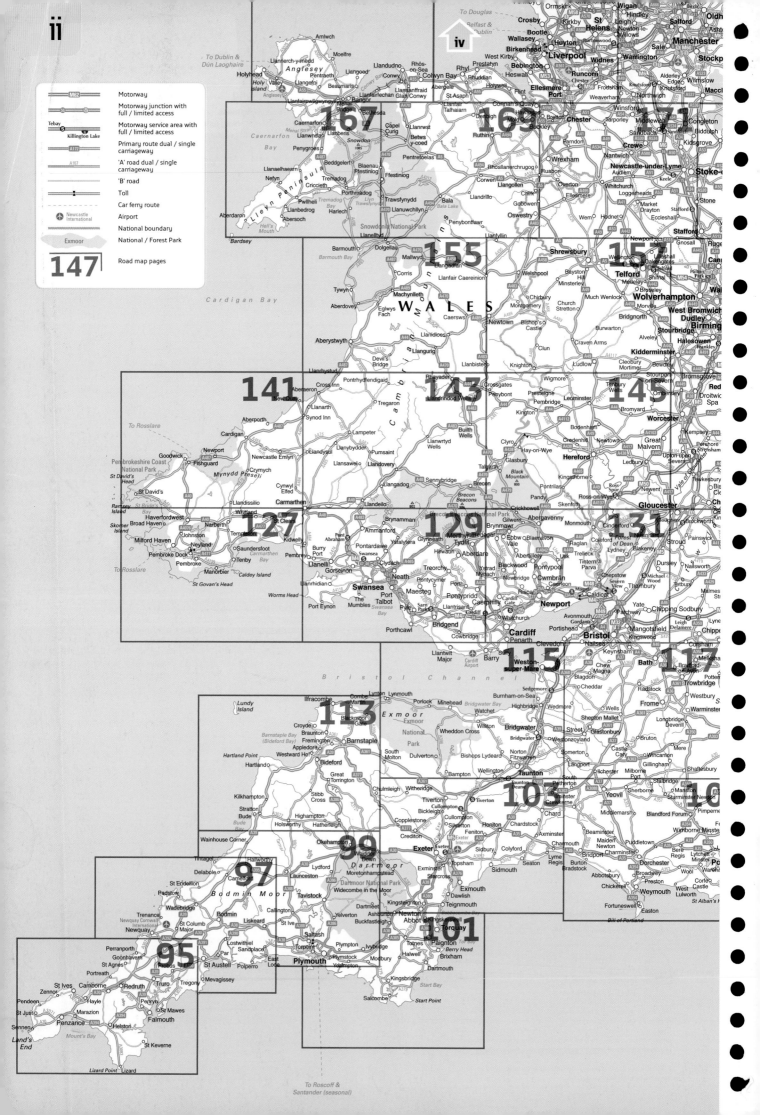

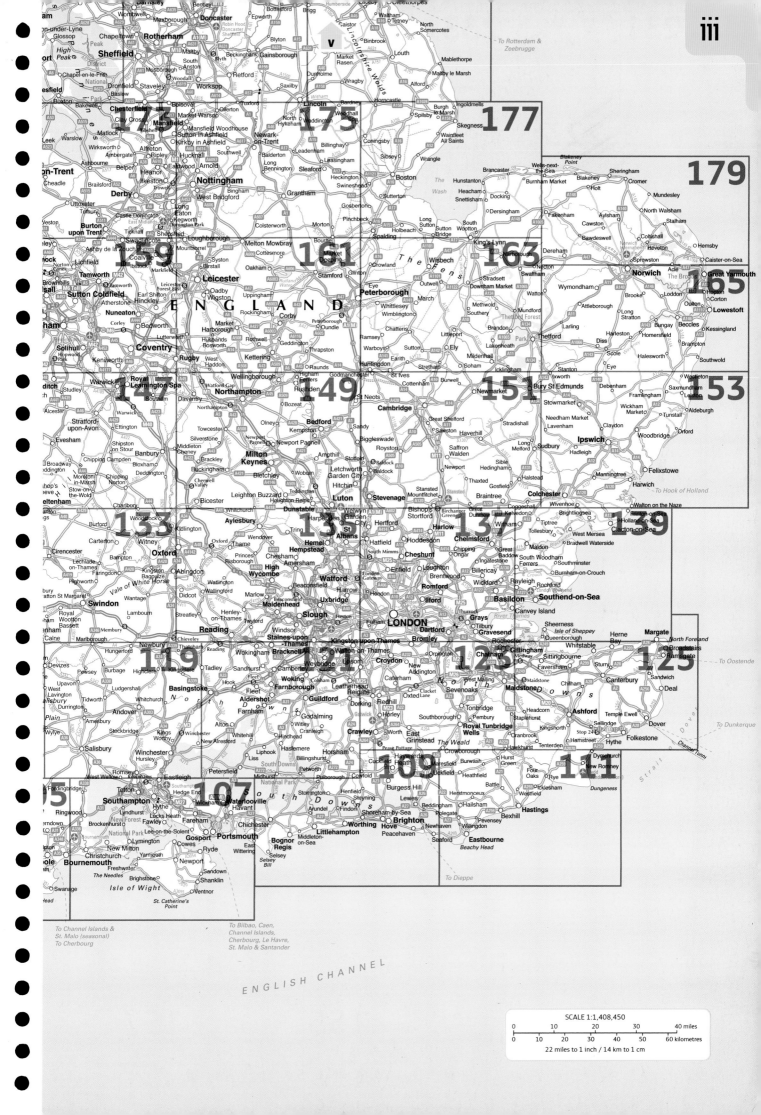

SCALE 1:1,408,450

0   10   20   30   40 miles

0   10   20   30   40   50   60 kilometres

22 miles to 1 inch / 14 km to 1 cm

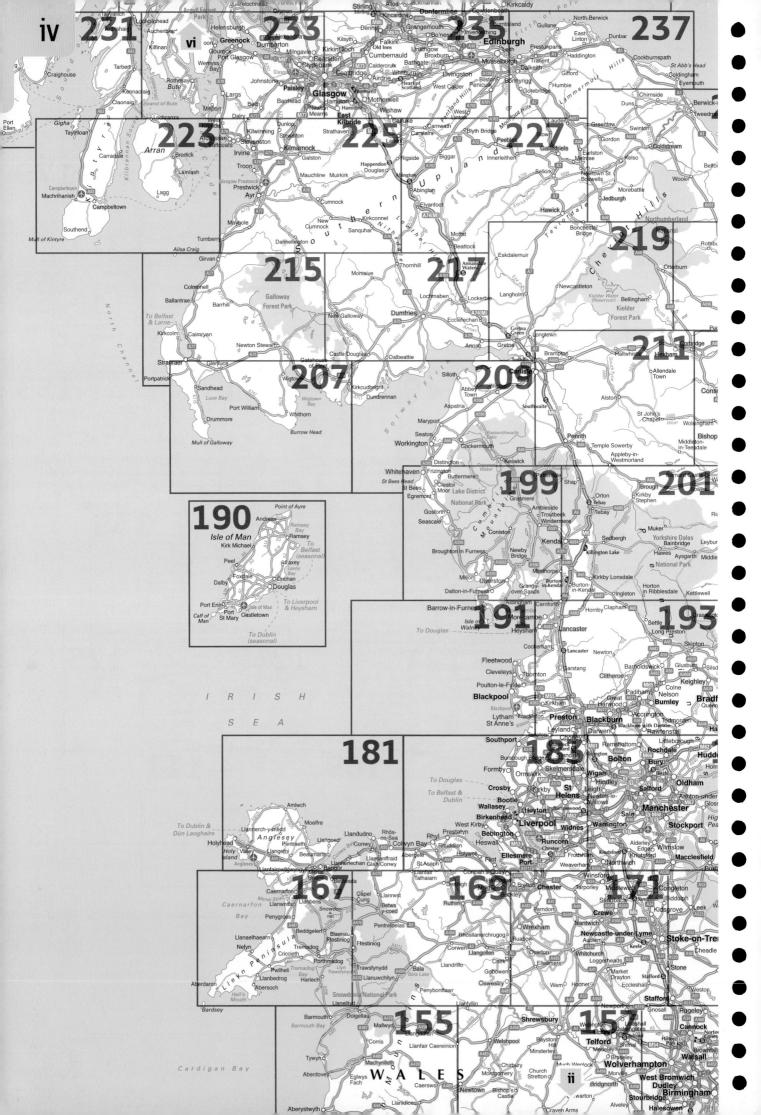

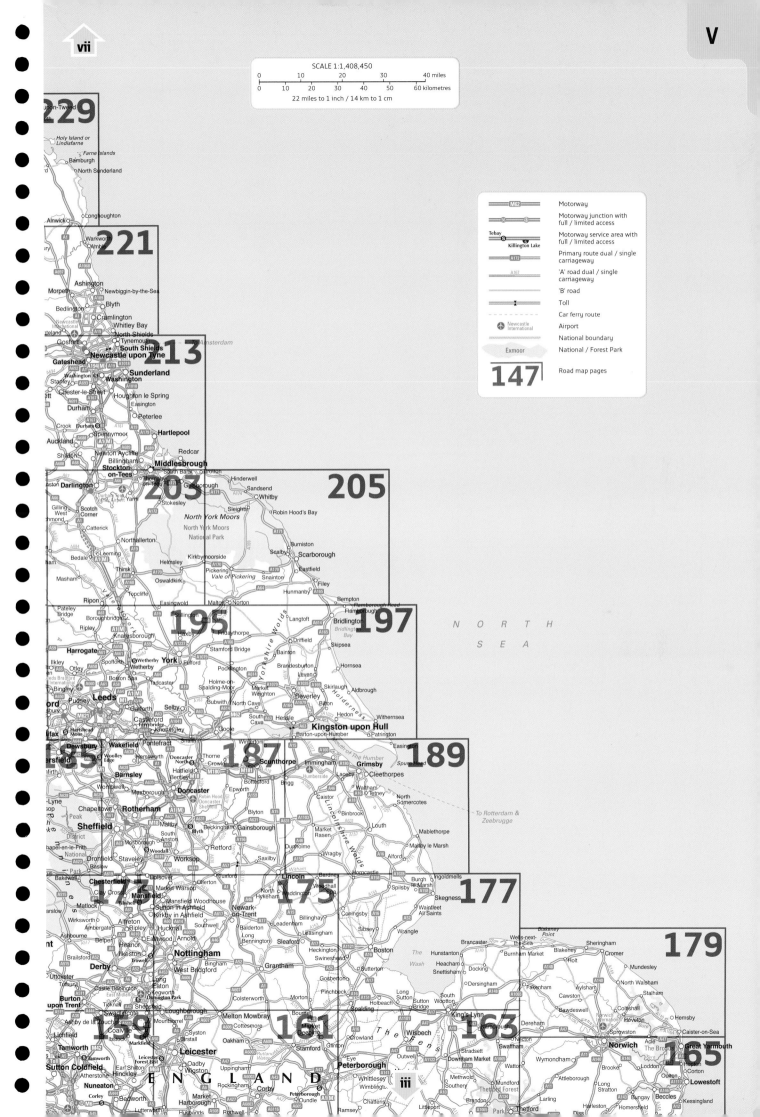

271 · **273**

263 · **265**

WESTERN ISLES

255 · **257**

247 · **249** · SCO...

239 · **241**

231 · **233** · **225**

223 · **215**

ATLANTIC OCEAN

North Harris · South Harris · North Uist · South Uist · Benbecula · Barra · Lewis

Northwest Highlands · Sutherland · Easter Ross · Wester Ross · Knoydart · Skye · Rum · Muck · Eigg · Coll · Tiree · Mull · Iona · Colonsay · Jura · Islay · Arran · Kintyre · Argyll

Cape Wrath · Durness · Tongue · Bettyhill · Strathy Point · Dounreay · Forsinard · Kinlochbervie · Scourie · Laxford Bridge · Ben Hope 927 · Altnaharra · Kinbrace · Point of Stoer · Unapool · Lochinver · Elphin · Ledmore · Lairg · Brora · Golspie · Invercassley · Pittentrail · Bonar Bridge · Ardgay · Dornoch · Tarbat Ness · Portmahomack · Tain · Hill of Fearn · Balintore · Alness · Invergordon · Cromarty · Garve · Dingwall · Black Isle · Rosemarkie · Nairn · Strathpeffer · Conon Bridge · Fortrose · Ardersier · Muir of Ord · Beauly · Inverness · Dores · Grantown-on-Spey · Dulnain Bridge · Carrbridge · Drumnadrochit · Tomatin · Boat of Garten · Aviemore · Foyers · Invermoriston · Fort Augustus · Monadhliath Mountains · Kingussie · Kincraig · Newtonmore · Laggan · Ben Macdui 1309 · Cairngorms · Spean Bridge · Roybridge · Dalwhinnie · Glenfinnan · Fort William · Ben Nevis 1345 · Invergarry · Kinlochleven · Rannoch Station · Spittal of Glenshee · Blair Atholl · Kinloch Rannoch · Pitlochry · Grandtully · Aberfeldy · Salen · Strontian · Ballachulish · Glen Coe · Bidean nam Bian 1150 · Appin · Rannoch Moor · Ben Lawers · Kenmore · Bridge of Orchy · Ben More 966 · Oban · Taynuilt · Tyndrum · Lochearnhead · Killin · Comrie · Methven · Crianlarich · Dalmally · Loch Lomond & The Trossachs National Park · Strathyre · Crieff · Kilmelford · Inveraray · Ben Lomond 974 · Arrochar · Lochgoilhead · Callander · Doune · Dunblane · Bridge of Allan · Dollar · Kilmartin · Garelochhead · Queen Elizabeth Forest Park · Aberfoyle · Stirling · Alloa · Clackmannan · Lochgilphead · Auchenbreck · Helensburgh · Drymen · Kincardine · Denny · Ardrishaig · Kilfinan · Dunoon · Greenock · Dumbarton · Milngavie · Kilsyth · Kirkintilloch · Falkirk · Linlithgow · Tarbert · Kennacraig · Rothesay · Bute · Wemyss Bay · Port Glasgow · Johnstone · Paisley · Glasgow · Clydebank · Bearsden · Cumbernauld · Coatbridge · Airdrie · Bathgate · Whitburn · Kennacraig · Claonaig · Largs · Beith · Barrhead · Hamilton · Motherwell · Wishaw · Carluke · Claonaig · Millport · Dalry · Newton Mearns · East Kilbride · Lanark · Carstairs · Gigha · Tayinloan · West Kilbride · Ardrossan · Saltcoats · Kilwinning · Stevenston · Dunlop · Stewarton · Strathaven · Rigside · Carradale · Brodick · Irvine · Troon · Kilmarnock · Galston · Mauchline · Muirkirk · Douglas · Abington · Machrihanish · Campbeltown · Lamlash · Lagg · Glasgow Prestwick · Prestwick · Ayr · Cumnock · Kirkconnel · Sanquhar · Southend · Mull of Kintyre · Maybole · New Cumnock · Dalmellington · Turnberry · Girvan · Ailsa Craig · Thornhill · Moniaive · Colmonell · Ballantrae · Barrhill · Galloway Forest Park

Butt of Lewis · Port of Ness · Barvas · Tolsta Head · Carloway · Stornoway · Portnaguran · Miabhig · Garrynahine · Great Bernera · Loch a' Tuath · Scarp · Loch Langavat · Kebock Head · Tarbert · Scalpay · Shiant Islands · Rubha Reidh · Aultbea · An Teallach 1062 · Poolewe · Gairloch · Loch Maree · Kinlochewe · Torridon · Liathach 1054 · Achnasheen · Shieldaig · Loch Fannich · Loch Monar · Pabbay · Northton · Berneray · Leverburgh · Rodel · Lochmaddy · Rubha Hunish · Uig · Loch Snizort · Monach Islands · The Storr 719 · Loch Dunvegan · Dunvegan · Borve · Portree · Raasay · Rona · Bracadale · Sligachan · Cuillin Hills · Bla Bheinn 928 · Soay · Elgol · Loch Eishort · Loch Hourn · Ardvasar · Sound of Sleat · Mallaig · Morar · Loch Morar · Arisaig · Sound of Arisaig · Glen Shiel · Loch Arkaig · Loch Quoich · Glen Garry · Loch Lochy · Lochboisdale · Eriskay · Canna · Kilchoan · Tobermory · Salen · Lochaline · Loch Linnhe · Craignure · Ulva · Pennyghael · Fionnphort · Loch Awe · Luing · Scarba · Scalasaig · Oronsay · Craobh · Tayvallich · Port Askaig · Craighouse · Portnahaven · Bowmore · Loch Indaal · Port Ellen · Mull Of Oa

Sound of Raasay · Inner Sound · Stromeferry · Lochcarron · Kyle of Lochalsh · Dornie · Broadford · Kyleakin · Glen Cannich · Glen Affric · Glen Albyn · Glen Moriston · Glen Garry · Loch Garry

Castlebay · Vatersay · Pabaigh · Mingulay

Legend

M62	Motorway
	Motorway junction with full / limited access
Tebay S / Killington Lake S	Motorway service area with full / limited access
A172	Primary route dual / single carriageway
A167	'A' road dual / single carriageway
	'B' road
	Toll
	Car ferry route
Newcastle International	Airport
	National boundary
Exmoor	National / Forest Park
147	Road map pages

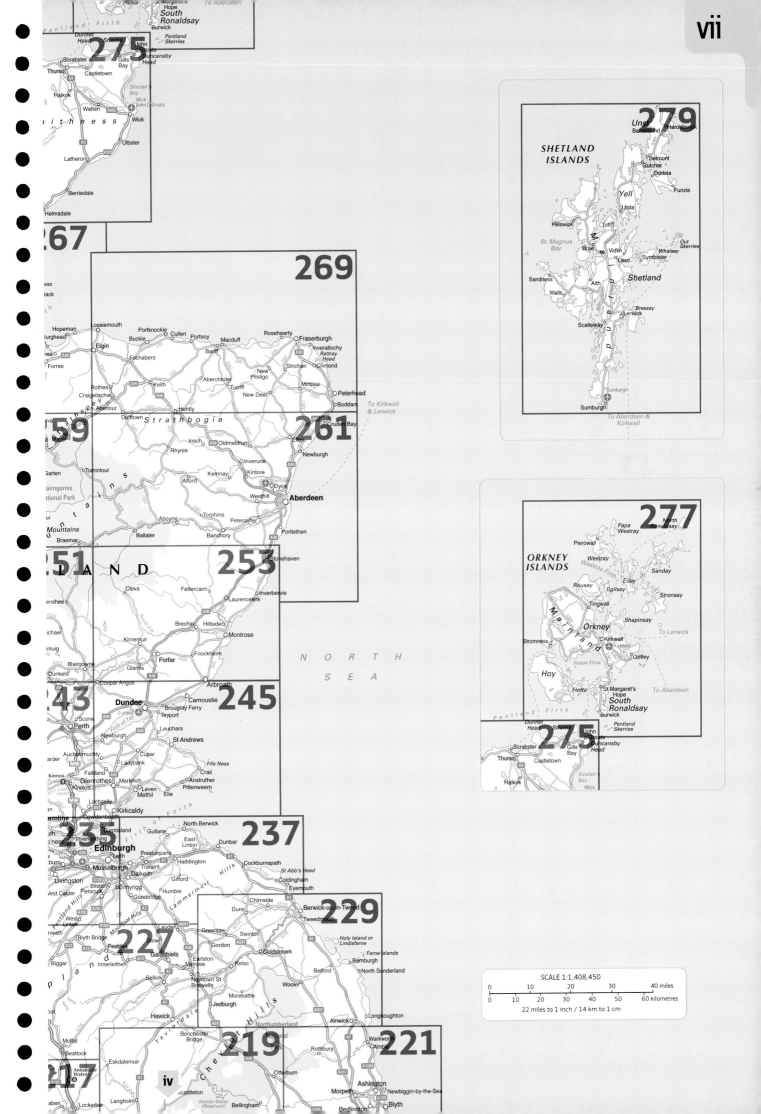

SCALE 1:1,408,450

0 — 10 — 20 — 30 — 40 miles

0 — 10 — 20 — 30 — 40 — 50 — 60 kilometres

22 miles to 1 inch / 14 km to 1 cm

Restricted motorway junctions

A1(M) LONDON TO NEWCASTLE

②
Northbound : No access
Southbound : No exit
③
Southbound : No access
⑤
Northbound : No exit
Southbound : No access
: No exit
④1
Northbound : No exit to M62 Eastbound
④3
Northbound : No exit to M1 Westbound
Dishforth
Southbound : No access from A168 Eastbound
57
Northbound : No access
: Exit only to A66(M) Northbound
Southbound : Access only from A66(M) Southbound
: No exit
65
Northbound : No access from A1
Southbound : No exit to A1

A3(M) PORTSMOUTH

①
Northbound : No exit
Southbound : No access
④
Northbound : No access
Southbound : No exit

A38(M) BIRMINGHAM

Victoria Road
Northbound : No exit
Southbound : No access

A48(M) CARDIFF

Junction with M4
Westbound : No access from M4 ㉙ Eastbound
Eastbound : No exit to M4 ㉙ Westbound
29A
Westbound : No exit to A48 Eastbound
Eastbound : No access from A48 Westbound

A57(M) MANCHESTER

Brook Street
Westbound : No exit
Eastbound : No access

A58(M) LEEDS

Westgate
Southbound : No access
Woodhouse Lane
Westbound : No exit

A64(M) LEEDS

Claypit Lane
Eastbound : No access

A66(M) DARLINGTON

Junction with A1(M)
Northbound : No access from A1(M) Southbound
: No exit
Southbound : No access
: No exit to A1(M) Northbound

A74(M) LOCKERBIE

⑱
Northbound : No access
Southbound : No exit

A167(M) NEWCASTLE

Campden Street
Northbound : No exit
Southbound : No access
: No exit

M1 LONDON TO LEEDS

②
Northbound : No exit
Southbound : No access
④
Northbound : No exit
Southbound : No access
6A
Northbound : Access only from M25 ㉑
: No exit
Southbound : No access
: Exit only to M25 ㉑
⑦
Northbound : Access only from A414
: No exit
Southbound : No access
: Exit only to A414

M1 LONDON TO LEEDS (continued)

⑰
Northbound : No access
: Exit only to M45
Southbound : Access only from M45
: No exit
⑲
Northbound : Exit only to M6
Southbound : Access only from M6
21A
Northbound : No access
Southbound : No exit
23A
Northbound : No access from A453
Southbound : No exit to A453
24A
Northbound : No exit
Southbound : No access
35A
Northbound : No access
Southbound : No exit
④3
Northbound : No access
: Exit only to M621
Southbound : No exit
: Access only from M621
④8
Northbound : No exit to A1(M) Southbound
Access only from A1(M) Northbound
Southbound : Exit only to A1(M) Southbound
: No access

M2 ROCHESTER TO CANTERBURY

①
Westbound : No exit to A2 Eastbound
Eastbound : No access from A2 Westbound

M3 LONDON TO WINCHESTER

⑧
Westbound : No access
Eastbound : No exit
⑩
Northbound : No access
Southbound : No exit
⑬
Southbound : No exit to A335 Eastbound
: No access
⑭
Westbound : No access
Eastbound : No exit

M4 LONDON TO SWANSEA

①
Westbound : No access from A4 Eastbound
Eastbound : No exit to A4 Westbound
②
Westbound : No access from A4 Eastbound
: No exit to A4 Eastbound
Eastbound : No access from A4 Westbound
: No exit to A4 Westbound
㉑
Westbound : No access from M48 Eastbound
Eastbound : No exit to M48 Westbound
㉓
Westbound : No exit to M48 Eastbound
Eastbound : No access from M48 Westbound
㉕
Westbound : No access
Eastbound : No exit
25A
Westbound : No access
Eastbound : No exit
㉙
Westbound : No access
: Exit only to A48(M)
Eastbound : Access only from A48(M) Eastbound
: No exit
38
Westbound : No access
39
Westbound : No exit
Eastbound : No access
: No exit
④1
Westbound : No exit
Eastbound : No access
④2
Westbound : No exit to A48
Eastbound : No access from A48

M5 BIRMINGHAM TO EXETER

⑩
Northbound : No exit
Southbound : No access
11A
Northbound : No access from A417 Eastbound
Southbound : No exit to A417 Westbound

M6 COVENTRY TO CARLISLE

Junction with M1
Northbound : No access from M1 ⑲ Southbound
Southbound : No exit to M1 ⑲ Northbound
3A
Northbound : No access from M6 Toll
Southbound : No exit to M6 Toll
④
Northbound : No exit to M42 Northbound
: No access from M42 Southbound
Southbound : No exit to M42
: No access from M42 Southbound
4A
Northbound : No access from M42 ⑧
Northbound
: No exit
Southbound : No access
: Exit only to M42 ⑧
⑤
Northbound : No access
Southbound : No exit
10A
Northbound : No access
: Exit only to M54
Southbound : Access only from M54
: No exit
11A
Northbound : No exit to M6 Toll
Southbound : No access from M6 Toll
㉔
Northbound : No exit
Southbound : No access
㉕
Northbound : No access
Southbound : No exit
㉚
Northbound : Access only from M61 Northbound
: No exit
Southbound : No access
: Exit only to M61 Southbound
31A
Northbound : No access
Southbound : No exit

M6 Toll BIRMINGHAM

T1
Northbound : Exit only to M42
: Access only from A4097
Southbound : No exit
: Access only from M42 Southbound
T2
Northbound : No exit
: No access
Southbound : No access
T5
Northbound : No exit
Southbound : No access
T7
Northbound : No access
Southbound : No exit
T8
Northbound : No access
Southbound : No exit

M8 EDINBURGH TO GLASGOW

⑧
Westbound : No access from M73 ②
Southbound
: No access from A8 Eastbound
: No access from A89 Eastbound
Eastbound : No access from A89 Westbound
: No exit to M73 ② Northbound
⑨
Westbound : No exit
Eastbound : No access
⑬
Westbound : Access only from M80
Eastbound : Exit only to M80
⑭
Westbound : No exit
Eastbound : No access
⑯
Westbound : No access
Eastbound : No exit
⑰
Eastbound : Access only from A82,
not central Glasgow
: Exit only to A82,
not central Glasgow
⑱
Westbound : No access
Eastbound : No access
⑲
Westbound : Access only from A814 Eastbound
Eastbound : Exit only to A814 Westbound,
not central Glasgow

M8 EDINBURGH TO GLASGOW (cont)

⑳
Westbound : No access
Eastbound : No exit
㉑
Westbound : No exit
Eastbound : No access
㉒
Westbound : No access
: Exit only to M77 Southbound
Eastbound : Access only from M77 Northbound
: No exit
㉓
Westbound : No access
Eastbound : No exit
25A
Eastbound : No access
Westbound : No access
㉖
Westbound : No access
Eastbound : No exit
28A
Westbound : No access
Eastbound : No exit

M9 EDINBURGH TO STIRLING

②
Westbound : No exit
Eastbound : No access
③
Westbound : No exit
Eastbound : No access
⑥
Westbound : No access
Eastbound : No exit
⑧
Westbound : No access
Eastbound : No exit

M11 LONDON TO CAMBRIDGE

④
Northbound : No access from A1400 Westbound
: No exit
Southbound : No access
: No exit to A1400 Eastbound
⑤
Northbound : No access
Southbound : No exit
8A
Northbound : No access
Southbound : No exit
⑨
Northbound : No access
Southbound : No exit
⑬
Northbound : No access
Southbound : No exit
⑭
Northbound : No access from A428 Eastbound
: No exit to A428 Westbound
: No exit to A1307
Southbound : No access from A428 Eastbound
: No access from A1307
: No exit

M20 LONDON TO FOLKESTONE

②
Westbound : No exit
Eastbound : No access
③
Westbound : No access
: Exit only to M26 Westbound
Eastbound : Access only from M26 Eastbound
: No exit
11A
Westbound : No exit
Eastbound : No access

M23 LONDON TO CRAWLEY

⑦
Northbound : No exit to A23 Southbound
Southbound : No access from A23 Northbound
10A
Southbound : No access from B2036
Northbound : No exit to B2036

Restricted motorway junctions are shown on the maps as:

M25 LONDON ORBITAL MOTORWAY
(1B)
Clockwise : No access
Anticlockwise : No exit
(5)
Clockwise : No exit to M26 Eastbound
Anticlockwise : No access from M26 Westbound
Spur of M25 (5)
Clockwise : No access from M26 Westbound
Anticlockwise : No exit to M26 Eastbound
(19)
Clockwise : No access
Anticlockwise : No exit
(21)
Clockwise : No access from M1 (6A) Northbound
: No exit to M1 (6A) Southbound
Anticlockwise : No access from M1 (6A) Northbound
: No exit to M1 (6A) Southbound
(31)
Clockwise : No exit
Anticlockwise : No access

M26 SEVENOAKS
Junction with M25 (5)
Westbound : No exit to M25 Anticlockwise
: No exit to M25 spur
Eastbound : No access from M25 Clockwise
: No access from M25 spur
Junction with M20
Westbound : No access from M20 (3) Eastbound
Eastbound : No exit to M20 (3) Westbound

M27 SOUTHAMPTON TO PORTSMOUTH
(4) West
Westbound : No exit
Eastbound : No access
(4) East
Westbound : No access
Eastbound : No exit
(10)
Westbound : No access
Eastbound : No exit
(12) West
Westbound : No exit
Eastbound : No exit
(12) East
Westbound : No access from A3
Eastbound : No exit

M40 LONDON TO BIRMINGHAM
(3)
Westbound : No access
Eastbound : No exit
(7)
Eastbound : No access
(8)
Northbound : No access
Southbound : No exit
(13)
Northbound : No access
Southbound : No exit
(14)
Northbound : No exit
Southbound : No access
(16)
Northbound : No exit
Southbound : No access

M42 BIRMINGHAM
(1)
Northbound : No exit
Southbound : No access
(7)
Northbound : No access
: Exit only to M6 Northbound
Southbound : Access only from M6 Northbound
: No exit
(7A)
Northbound : No access
: Exit only to M6 Eastbound
Southbound : No access
: No exit
(8)
Northbound : Access only from M6 Southbound
: No exit
Southbound : Access only from M6 Southbound
: Exit only to M6 Northbound

M45 COVENTRY
Junction with M1
Westbound : No access from M1 (17) Southbound
Eastbound : No exit to M1 (17) Northbound
Junction with A45
Westbound : No exit
Eastbound : No access

M48 CHEPSTOW
M4
Westbound : No exit to M4 Eastbound
Eastbound : No access from M4 Westbound

M49 BRISTOL
(18A)
Northbound : No access from M5 Southbound
Southbound : No access from M5 Northbound

M53 BIRKENHEAD TO CHESTER
(11)
Northbound : No access from M56 (15) Eastbound
: No exit to M56 (15) Westbound
Southbound : No access from M56 (15) Eastbound
: No exit to M56 (15) Westbound

M54 WOLVERHAMPTON TO TELFORD
Junction with M6
Westbound : No access from M6 (10A) Southbound
Eastbound : No exit to M6 (10A) Northbound

M56 STOCKPORT TO CHESTER
(1)
Westbound : No access from M60 Eastbound
: No access from A34 Northbound
Eastbound : No exit to M60 Westbound
: No exit to A34 Southbound
(2)
Westbound : No access
Eastbound : No exit
(3)
Westbound : No exit
Eastbound : No access
(4)
Westbound : No access
Eastbound : No exit
(7)
Westbound : No access
Eastbound : No exit
(8)
Westbound : No exit
Eastbound : No access
(9)
Westbound : No exit to M6 Southbound
Eastbound : No access from M6 Northbound
(15)
Westbound : No access
: No access from M53 (11)
Eastbound : No exit
: No exit to M53 (11)

M57 LIVERPOOL
(3)
Northbound : No exit
Southbound : No access
(5)
Northbound : Access only from A580 Westbound
: No exit
Southbound : No access
: Exit only to A580 Eastbound

M58 LIVERPOOL TO WIGAN
(1)
Westbound : No access
Eastbound : No exit

M60 MANCHESTER
(2)
Westbound : No exit
Eastbound : No access
(3)
Westbound : No access from M56 (1)
: No access from A34 Southbound
: No exit to A34 Northbound
Eastbound : No access from A34 Southbound
: No exit to M56 (1)
: No exit to A34 Northbound
(4)
Westbound : No access
Eastbound : No exit to M56

M60 MANCHESTER *(continued)*
(5)
Westbound : No access from A5103 Southbound
: No exit to A5103 Southbound
Eastbound : No access from A5103 Northbound
: No exit to A5103 Northbound
(14)
Westbound : No access from A580
: No exit to A580 Eastbound
Eastbound : No access from A580 Westbound
: No exit to A580
(16)
Westbound : No access
Eastbound : No exit
(20)
Westbound : No access
Eastbound : No exit
(22)
Westbound : No access
(25)
Westbound : No access
(26)
Eastbound : No access
: No exit
(27)
Westbound : No exit
Eastbound : No access

M61 MANCHESTER TO PRESTON
(2)
Northbound : No access from A580 Eastbound
: No access from A666
Southbound : No exit to A580 Westbound
(3)
Northbound : No access from A580 Eastbound
: No access from A666
Southbound : No exit to A580 Westbound
Junction with M6
Northbound : No exit to M6 (30) Southbound
Southbound : No access from M6 (30) Northbound

M62 LIVERPOOL TO HULL
(23)
Westbound : No exit
Eastbound : No access
(32A)
Westbound : No exit to A1(M) Southbound

M65 BURNLEY
(9)
Westbound : No exit
Eastbound : No access
(11)
Westbound : No access
Eastbound : No exit

M66 MANCHESTER TO EDENFIELD
(1)
Northbound : No access
Southbound : No exit
Junction with A56
Northbound : Exit only to A56 Northbound
Southbound : Access only from A56 Southbound

M67 MANCHESTER
(1)
Westbound : No exit
Eastbound : No access
(2)
Westbound : No access
Eastbound : No exit

M69 COVENTRY TO LEICESTER
(2)
Northbound : No exit
Southbound : No access

M73 GLASGOW
(1)
Northbound : No access from A721 Eastbound
Southbound : No exit to A721 Eastbound
(2)
Northbound : No access from M8 (8) Eastbound
Southbound : No exit to M8 (8) Westbound

M74 GLASGOW
(1A)
Westbound : No exit to M8 Kingston Bridge
Eastbound : No access from M8 Kingston Bridge
(3)
Westbound : No access
Eastbound : No exit
(3A)
Westbound : No exit
Eastbound : No access

M74 GLASGOW *(continued)*
(7)
Northbound : No exit
Southbound : No access
(9)
Northbound : No access
: No exit
(10)
Southbound : No exit
(11)
Northbound : No exit
Southbound : No access
(12)
Northbound : Access only from A70 Northbound
Southbound : Exit only to A70 Southbound

M77 GLASGOW
Junction with M8
Northbound : No exit to M8 (22) Westbound
Southbound : No access from M8 (22) Eastbound
(4)
Northbound : No exit
Southbound : No access
(6)
Northbound : No exit to A77
Southbound : No access from A77
(7)
Northbound : No access
: No exit
(8)
Northbound : No access
Southbound : No access

M80 STIRLING
(4A)
Northbound : No access
Southbound : No exit
(6A)
Northbound : No exit
Southbound : No access
(8)
Northbound : No access from M876
Southbound : No exit to M876

M90 EDINBURGH TO PERTH
(1)
Northbound : No exit to A90
(2A)
Northbound : No access
Southbound : No exit
(7)
Northbound : No exit
Southbound : No access
(8)
Northbound : No access
Southbound : No exit
(10)
Northbound : No access from A912
: No exit to A912 Southbound
Southbound : No access from A912 Northbound
: No exit to A912

M180 SCUNTHORPE
(1)
Westbound : No exit
Eastbound : No access

M606 BRADFORD
Straithgate Lane
Northbound : No access

M621 LEEDS
(2A)
Northbound : No exit
Southbound : No access
(5)
Northbound : No access
Southbound : No exit
(6)
Northbound : No exit
Southbound : No access

M876 FALKIRK
Junction with M80
Westbound : No exit to M80 (8) Northbound
Eastbound : No access from M80 (8) Southbound
Junction with M9
Westbound : No access
Eastbound : No exit

Motorway services information

All motorway service areas have fuel, food, toilets, disabled facilities and free short-term parking

For further information on motorway services providers:
Moto   www.moto-way.com   RoadChef   www.roadchef.com   Welcome Break   www.welcomebreak.co.uk
Euro Garages   www.eurogarages.com   Extra   www.extraservices.co.uk   Westmorland   www.westmorland.com

Motorway	Junction	Service provider	Service name	Fuel supplier	Information	Accommodation	Conference facilities	Showers	M&S Simply Food	Costa Coffee	Starbucks	Burger King	KFC	McDonalds	Wimpy
A1(M)	1	Welcome Break	South Mimms	BP	•	•	•	•			•	•	•	•	
	10	Extra	Baldock	Shell		•	•	•		•	•		•	•	
	17	Extra	Peterborough	Shell	•	•	•	•					•	•	
	34	Moto	Blyth	Esso	•	•	•	•	•	•					
	46	Moto	Wetherby	BP	•	•	•	•	•				•		
	61	RoadChef	Durham	Total	•	•	•	•		•					
	64	Moto	Washington	BP	•	•									
A74(M)	16	RoadChef	Annandale Water	BP	•	•									
	22	Welcome Break	Gretna Green	BP	•	•					•	•	•		
M1	2-4	Welcome Break	London Gateway	Shell	•	•	•	•							
	11-12	Moto	Toddington	BP		•		•	•	•					
	14-15	Welcome Break	Newport Pagnell	Shell	•	•				•	•	•			
	15A	RoadChef	Northampton	BP	•					•			•		
	16-17	RoadChef	Watford Gap	BP	•	•				•			•		
	21-21A	Welcome Break	Leicester Forest East	BP	•	•	•	•		•	•	•			
	22	Euro Garages	Markfield	BP	•	•		•							
	23A	Moto	Donington Park	BP	•	•	•	•	•	•					
	25-26	Moto	Trowell	BP	•	•	•	•	•	•					
	28-29	RoadChef	Tibshelf	Shell	•	•		•		•			•		
	30-31	Welcome Break	Woodall	Shell	•	•	•	•		•	•	•			
	38-39	Moto	Woolley Edge	BP	•	•									
M2	4-5	Moto	Medway	BP		•		•	•	•					
M3	4A-5	Welcome Break	Fleet	Shell	•	•	•	•		•	•	•			
	8-9	Moto	Winchester	Shell	•	•		•		•					
M4	3	Moto	Heston	BP	•	•	•	•		•					
	11-12	Moto	Reading	BP	•	•	•	•	•	•					
	13	Moto	Chieveley	BP	•	•			•	•					
	14-15	Welcome Break	Membury	BP	•	•				•	•	•			
	17-18	Moto	Leigh Delamere	BP	•	•	•	•		•					
	23A	RoadChef	Magor	Esso	•	•		•					•		
	30	Welcome Break	Cardiff Gate	Total	•						•	•			
	33	Moto	Cardiff West	Esso	•	•			•	•					
	36	Welcome Break	Sarn Park	Shell		•			•	•					
	47	Moto	Swansea	BP	•	•				•					
	49	RoadChef	Pont Abraham	Texaco	•					•					
M5	3-4	Moto	Frankley	BP		•		•	•	•					
	8	RoadChef	Strensham (South)	BP	•					•			•		
	8	RoadChef	Strensham (North)	Texaco	•	•		•					•		
	11-12	Westmorland	Gloucester	Texaco					•						
	13-14	Welcome Break	Michaelwood	BP	•	•				•	•	•			
	19	Welcome Break	Gordano	Shell	•	•		•		•	•	•			
	21-22	RoadChef	Sedgemoor (South)	Total	•	•		•		•			•		
	21-22	Welcome Break	Sedgemoor (North)	Shell	•	•		•		•	•	•			
	24	Moto	Bridgwater	BP	•	•				•					
	25-26	RoadChef	Taunton Deane	Shell	•	•				•					
	27	Moto	Tiverton	Shell	•	•				•					
	28	Extra	Cullompton	Shell	•	•				•					
	29-30	Moto	Exeter	BP	•	•		•	•	•					
M6 Toll	T6-T7	RoadChef	Norton Canes	BP	•	•		•		•					

Motorway	Junction	Service provider	Service name	Fuel supplier	Information	Accommodation	Conference facilities	Showers	M&S Simply Food	Costa Coffee	Starbucks	Burger King	KFC	McDonalds	Wimpy
M6	3-4	Welcome Break	Corley	Shell	•	•		•		•	•	•			
	10-11	Moto	Hilton Park	BP	•	•		•	•	•					
	14-15	RoadChef	Stafford (South)	Esso	•	•	•	•		•			•		
	14-15	Moto	Stafford (North)	BP	•	•		•	•	•					
	15-16	Welcome Break	Keele	Shell	•	•				•	•	•			
	16-17	RoadChef	Sandbach	Esso		•				•					
	18-19	Moto	Knutsford	BP	•	•		•	•	•					
	27-28	Welcome Break	Charnock Richard	Shell	•	•		•		•	•	•			
	32-33	Moto	Lancaster	BP		•		•	•	•					
	35A-36	Moto	Burton-in-Kendal (N)	BP				•		•					
	36-37	RoadChef	Killington Lake (S)	BP	•	•				•					
	38-39	Westmorland	Tebay	Total	•	•	•								
	41-42	Moto	Southwaite	BP	•	•		•	•	•					
	44-45	Moto	Todhills	BP/Shell	•										
M8	4-5	BP	Heart of Scotland	BP			•	•	•						
M9	9	Moto	Stirling	BP	•	•				•					
M11	8	Welcome Break	Birchanger Green	Shell	•	•	•	•		•	•	•			
M18	5	Moto	Doncaster North	BP	•	•	•	•		•					
M20	8	RoadChef	Maidstone	Esso	•	•		•		•			•		
	11	Stop 24	Stop 24	Shell	•	•		•		•			•	•	
M23	11	Moto	Pease Pottage	BP	•			•	•	•					
M25	5-6	RoadChef	Clacket Lane	Total	•			•		•			•		
	9-10	Extra	Cobham	Shell		•	•		•		•		•	•	
	23	Welcome Break	South Mimms	BP	•	•	•	•		•	•	•			
	30	Moto	Thurrock	Esso	•	•		•	•	•					
M27	3-4	RoadChef	Rownhams	Esso	•	•				•					
M40	2	Extra	Beaconsfield	Shell	•	•	•		•		•		•	•	
	8	Welcome Break	Oxford	BP	•	•		•		•	•				
	10	Moto	Cherwell Valley	Esso	•	•	•	•		•					
	12-13	Welcome Break	Warwick	BP	•	•	•	•		•	•	•			
M42	2	Welcome Break	Hopwood Park	Shell	•			•		•	•	•			
	10	Moto	Tamworth	Esso	•	•		•	•	•					
M48	1	Moto	Severn View	BP	•	•		•		•					
M54	4	Welcome Break	Telford	Shell	•	•				•					
M56	14	RoadChef	Chester	Shell	•	•				•			•		
M61	6-7	Euro Garages	Rivington	BP		•	•	•			•	•			
M62	7-9	Welcome Break	Burtonwood	Shell	•					•	•	•			
	18-19	Moto	Birch	BP	•	•	•	•	•	•					
	25-26	Welcome Break	Hartshead Moor	Shell	•	•	•	•		•	•	•			
	33	Moto	Ferrybridge	Esso	•	•		•	•	•					
M65	4	Extra	Blackburn with Darwen	Shell	•	•	•	•		•				•	
M74	4-5	RoadChef	Bothwell (South)	BP	•	•		•		•					
	5-6	RoadChef	Hamilton (North)	BP	•	•		•		•					
	11-12	Cairn Lodge	Happendon	Shell						•	•				
	12-13	Welcome Break	Abington	Shell	•	•		•		•					
M80	6-7	Shell	Old Inns	Shell											
M90	6	Moto	Kinross	BP	•	•		•		•			•		

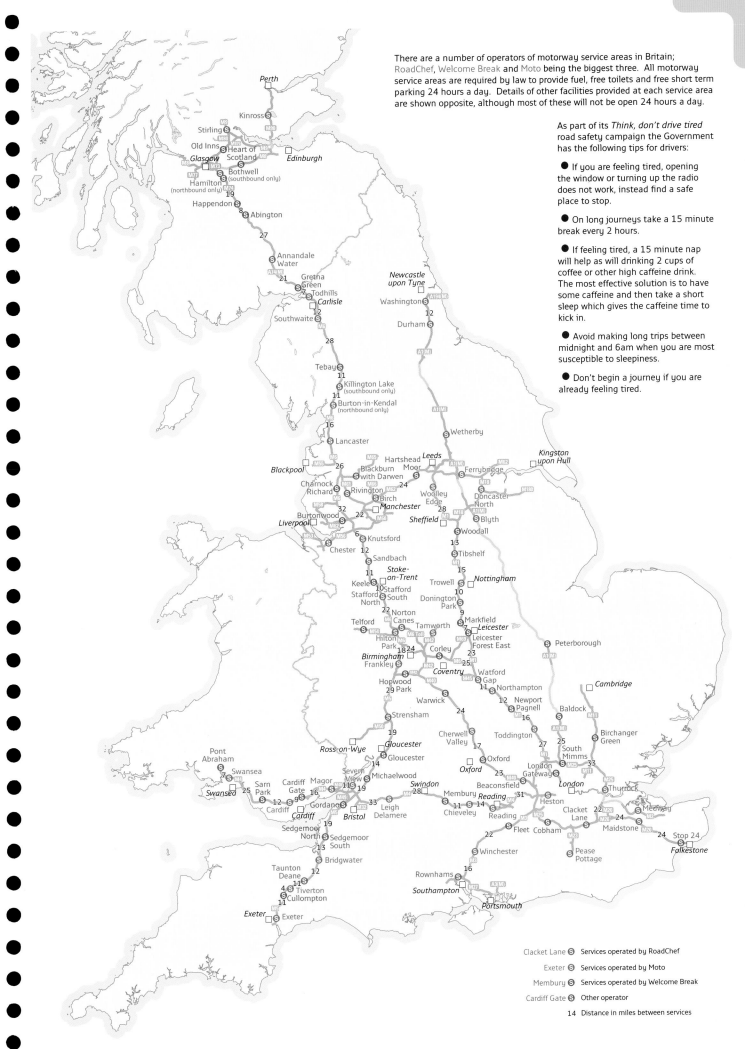

There are a number of operators of motorway service areas in Britain; RoadChef, Welcome Break and Moto being the biggest three. All motorway service areas are required by law to provide fuel, free toilets and free short term parking 24 hours a day. Details of other facilities provided at each service area are shown opposite, although most of these will not be open 24 hours a day.

As part of its *Think, don't drive tired* road safety campaign the Government has the following tips for drivers:

● If you are feeling tired, opening the window or turning up the radio does not work, instead find a safe place to stop.

● On long journeys take a 15 minute break every 2 hours.

● If feeling tired, a 15 minute nap will help as will drinking 2 cups of coffee or other high caffeine drink. The most effective solution is to have some caffeine and then take a short sleep which gives the caffeine time to kick in.

● Avoid making long trips between midnight and 6am when you are most susceptible to sleepiness.

● Don't begin a journey if you are already feeling tired.

Clacket Lane Ⓢ Services operated by RoadChef
Exeter Ⓢ Services operated by Moto
Membury Ⓢ Services operated by Welcome Break
Cardiff Gate Ⓢ Other operator
14 Distance in miles between services

M25 orbital map

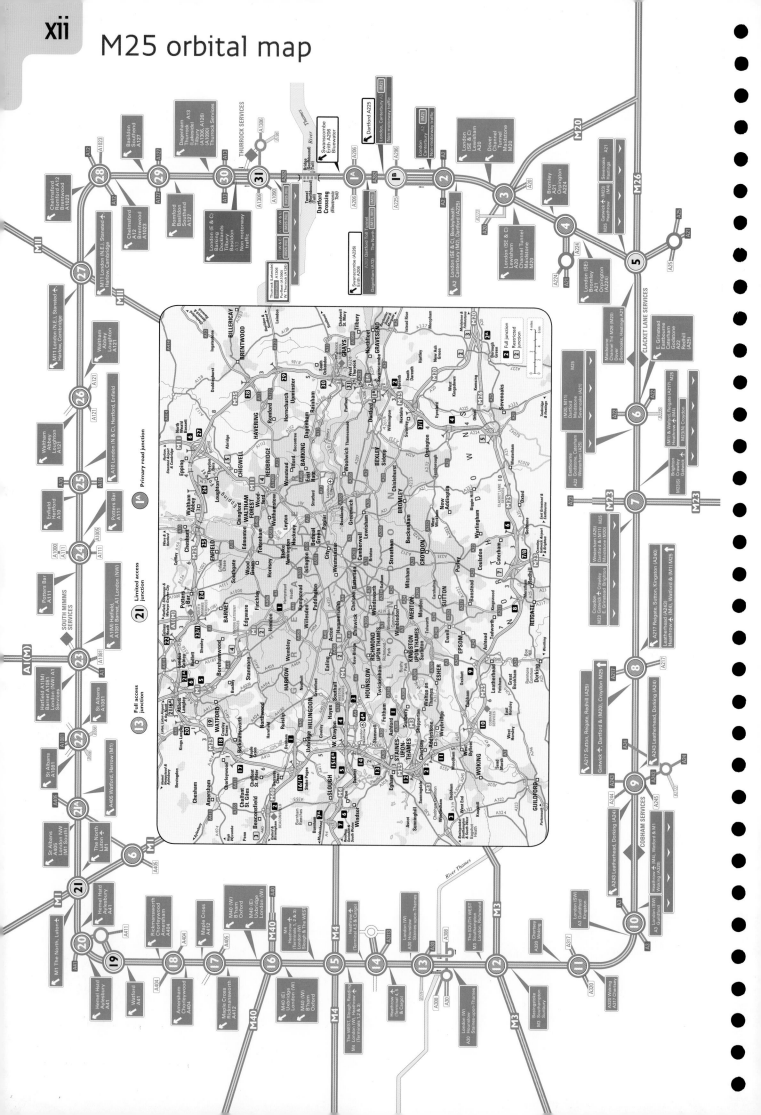

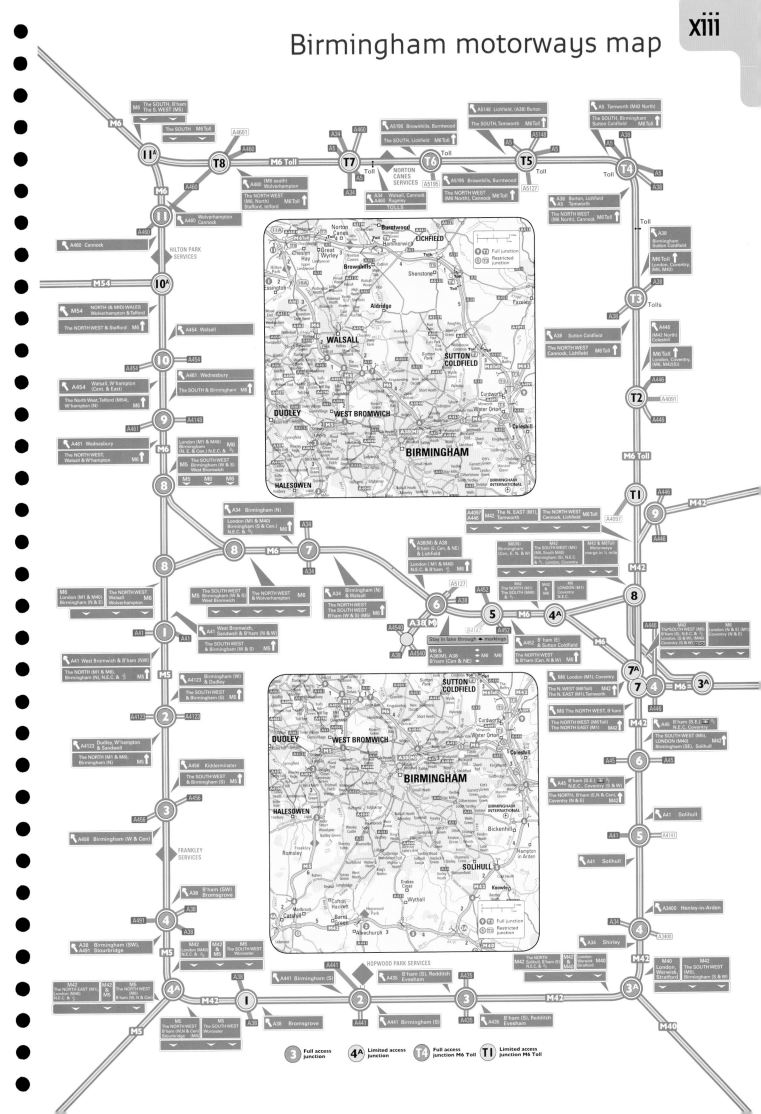

Risk rating of Britain's motorways and A roads

EuroRAP

This map shows the statistical risk of death or serious injury occurring on Britain's motorway and A road network for 2012-2014. Covering 44,500km in total, the British EuroRAP network represents just 10% of Britain's road network but carries 56% of the traffic and half of Britain's road fatalities.

The risk is calculated by comparing the frequency of road crashes resulting in death and serious injury on every stretch of road with how much traffic each road is carrying. For example, if there are 20 crashes on a road carrying 10,000 vehicles a day, the risk is 10 times higher than if the road has the same number of crashes but carries 100,000 vehicles.

Some of the roads shown have had improvements made to them recently, but during the survey period the risk of a fatal or serious injury crash on the black road sections was 23 times higher than on the safest (green) roads.

For more information on the Road Safety Foundation go to **www.roadsafetyfoundation.org.**

For more information on the statistical background to this research, visit the EuroRAP website at **www.eurorap.org.**

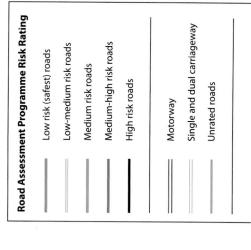

Road Assessment Programme Risk Rating

- Low risk (safest) roads
- Low-medium risk roads
- Medium risk roads
- Medium-high risk roads
- High risk roads

- Motorway
- Single and dual carriageway
- Unrated roads

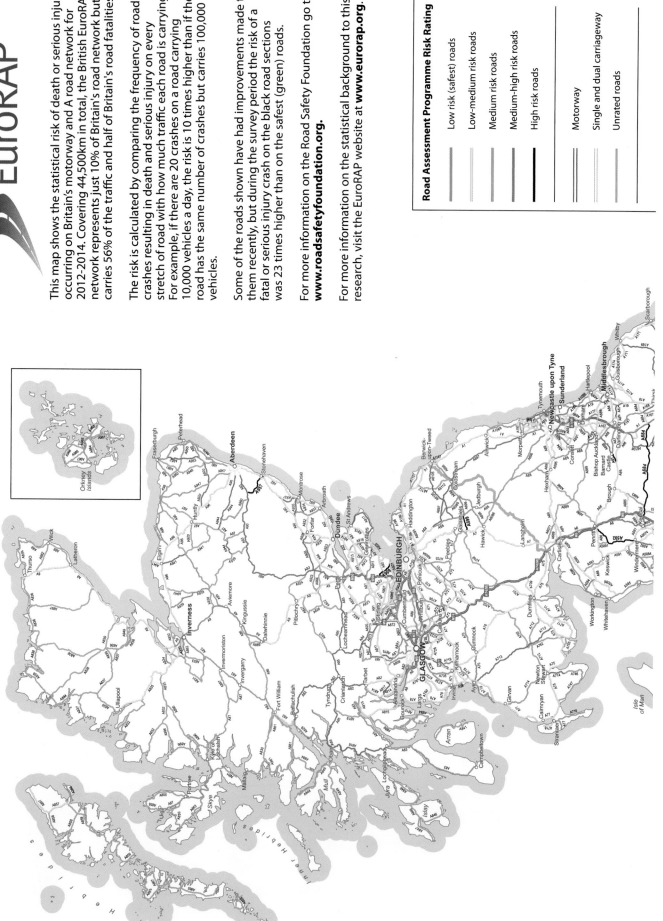

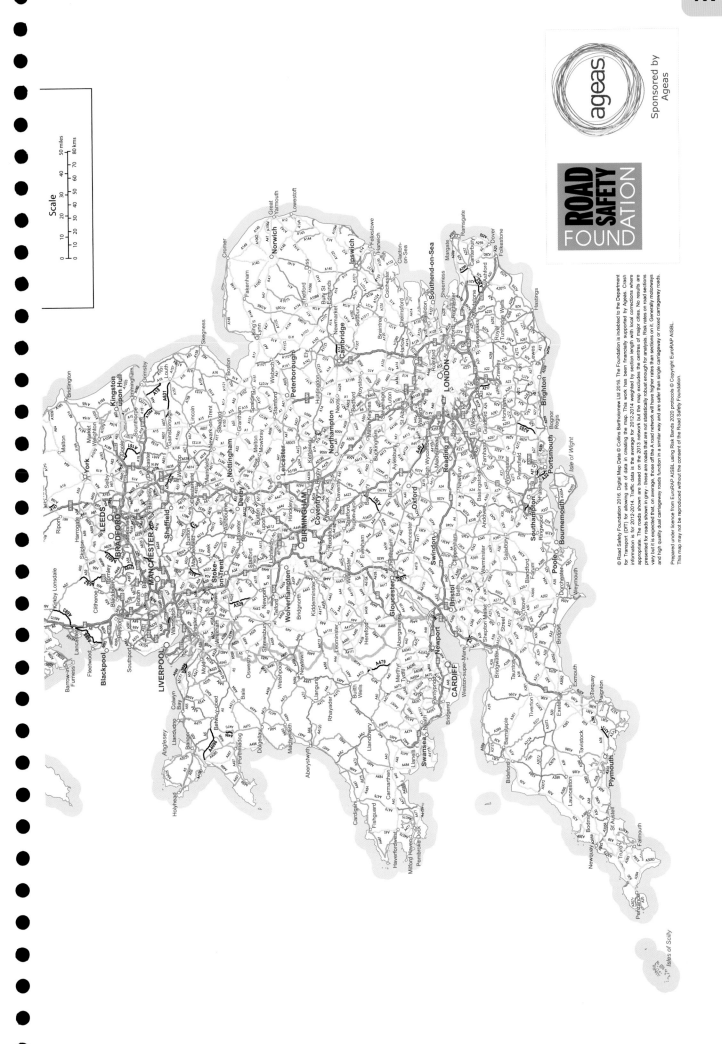

Distance chart

Distances between two selected towns in this table are shown in miles and kilometres.
In general, distances are based on the shortest routes by classified roads.

Distance in kilometres

Distance in miles

Symbols used on the map

Blue place of interest symbols e.g ★ are listed on page 93

Motorway junction with full / limited access

Motorway service area — MARKFIELD SERVICES

M6 Toll — Toll motorway

A316 — Primary route dual / single carriageway / junction / service area

A4054 — 'A' road dual / single carriageway

B7078 — 'B' road dual / single carriageway

Minor road dual / single carriageway

Restricted access road

Road proposed or under construction

Road tunnel

Roundabout

Toll / One way street

Level crossing

National Trail / Long Distance Route — Hadrian's Wall Path

Fixed safety camera / fixed average-speed safety camera. Speed shown by number within camera, a V indicates a variable limit.

Park and Ride site operated by bus / rail (runs at least 5 days a week)

Car ferry with destination — Dublin 8 hrs

Foot ferry with destination — West Cowes P ¼ hr

Airport

Railway line / Railway tunnel / Light railway line

Railway station / Light rail station

London Underground / London Overground stations

Glasgow Subway station

Extent of London congestion charging zone

Notable building

Hospital

Spot height (in metres) / Lighthouse — 362 ▲

Built up area

Woodland / Park

National Park

Heritage Coast

BRISTOL — County / Unitary Authority boundary and name

SEE PAGE 68 — Area covered by street map

Locator map

Urban approach maps	
Birmingham	14-15
Bournemouth	3
Bradford	26-27
Bristol	8
Cardiff	7
Coventry	16
Derby	18-19
Edinburgh	32
Glasgow	30-31
Greater Manchester	24-25
Leeds	26-27
Leicester	17
Liverpool	22-23
London	10-13
Manchester	24-25
Merseyside	22-23
Middlesbrough	29
Milton Keynes	9
Newcastle upon Tyne	28-29
Newport	7
Nottingham	18-19
Plymouth	2
Portsmouth	4-5
Sheffield	21
Southampton	4-5
Stoke-on-Trent	20
Sunderland	28-29
Swansea	6
West Midlands	14-15

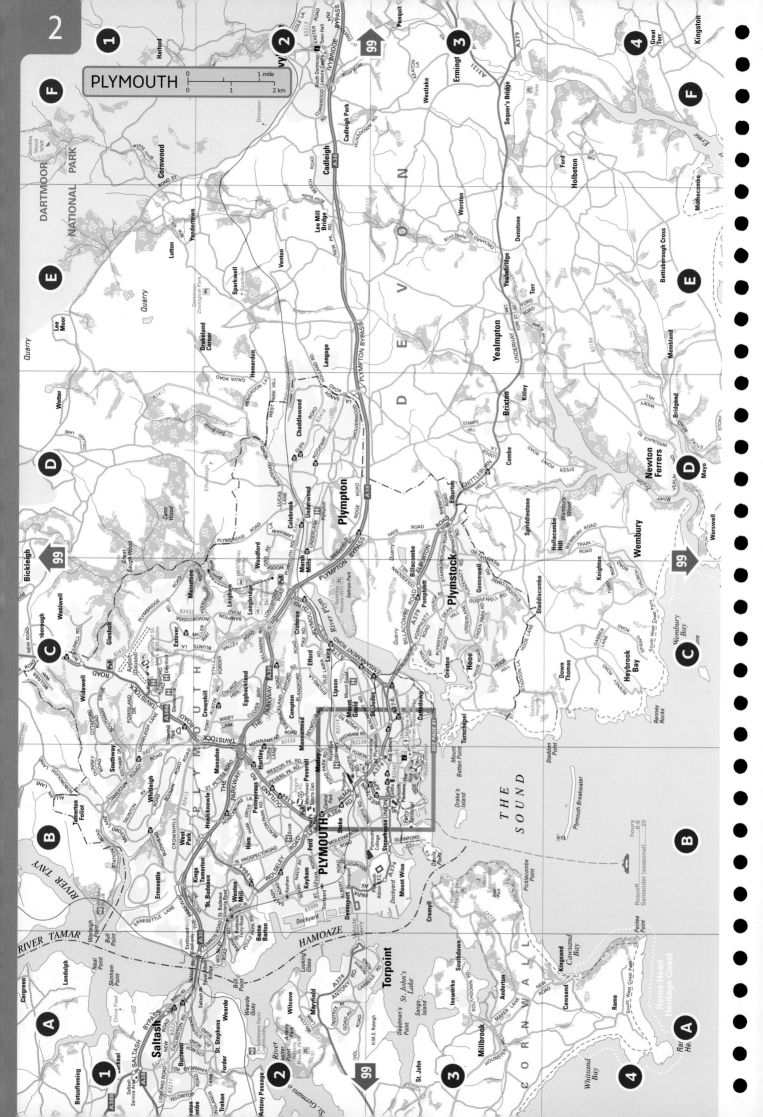

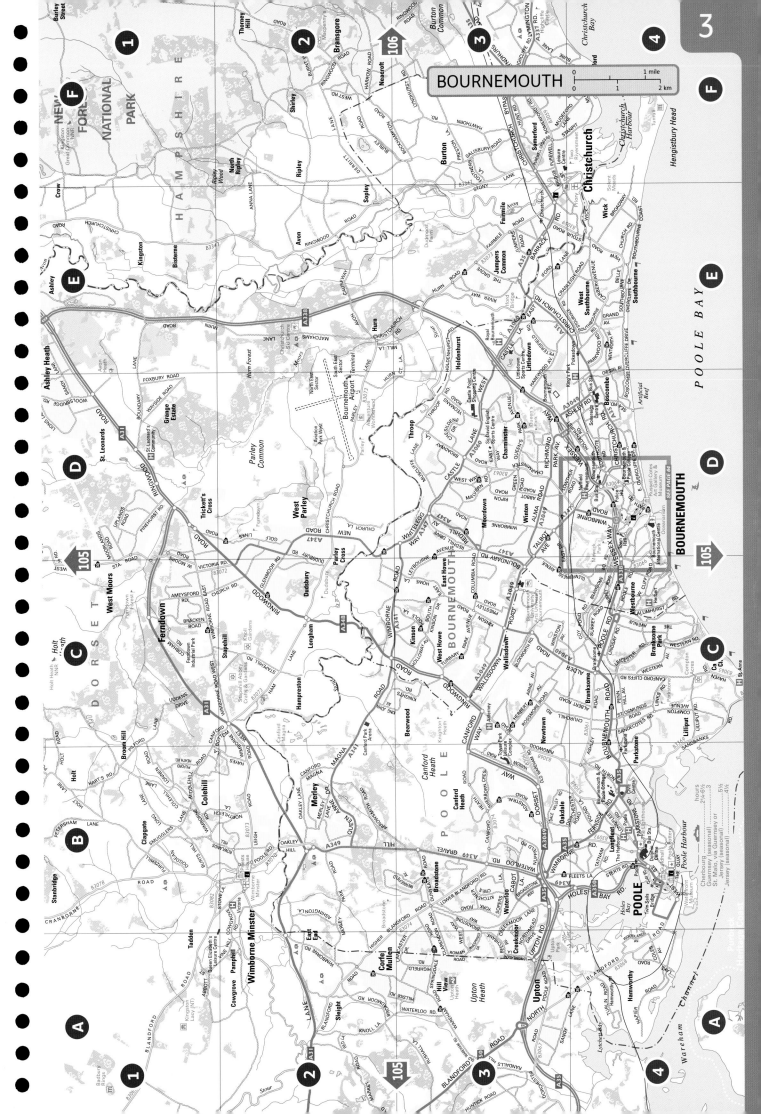

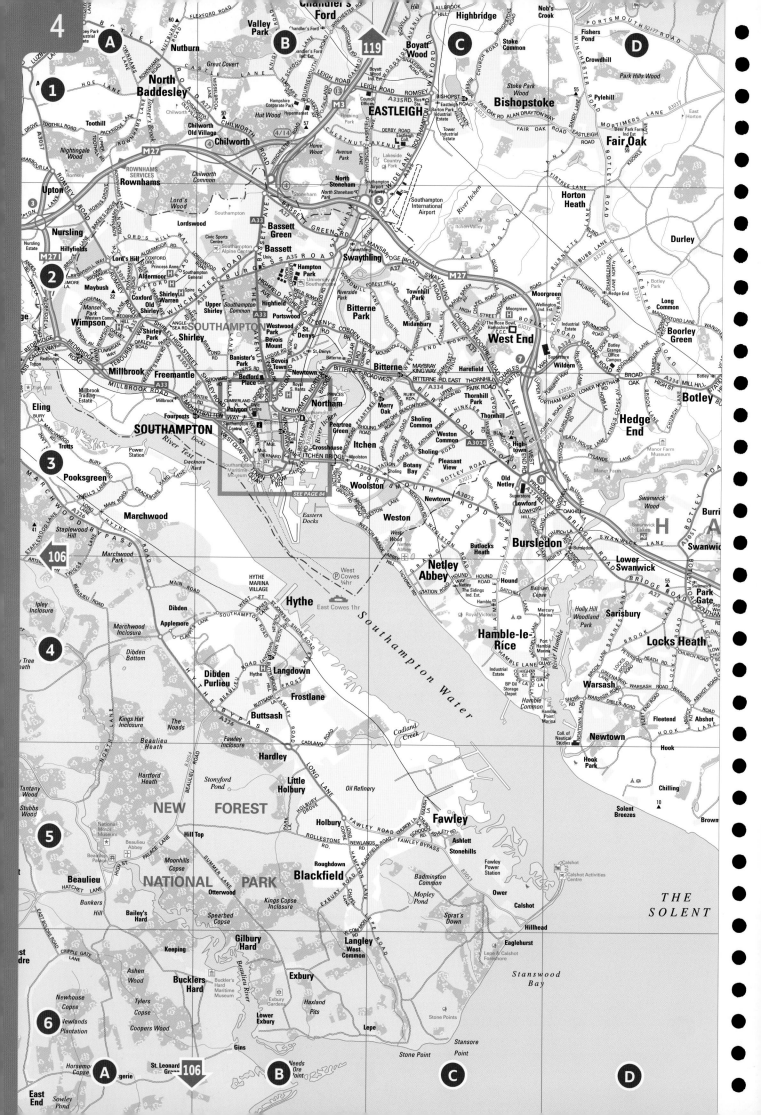

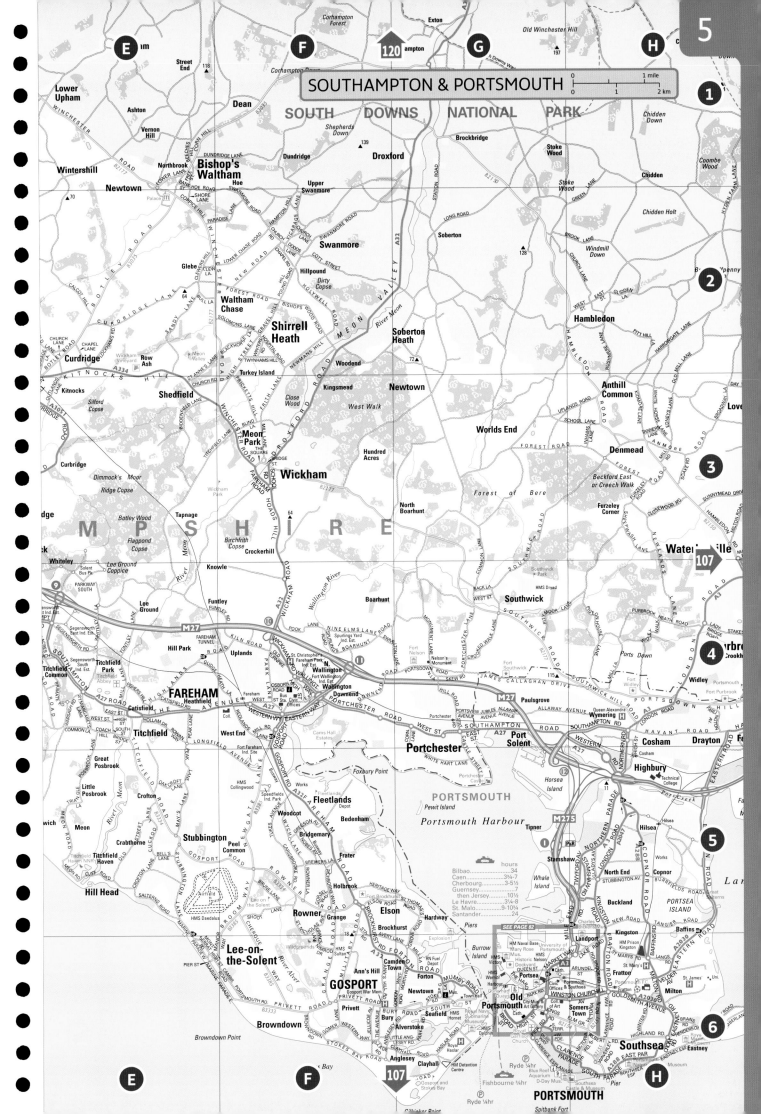

CARDIFF & NEWPORT

BRISTOL CHANNEL

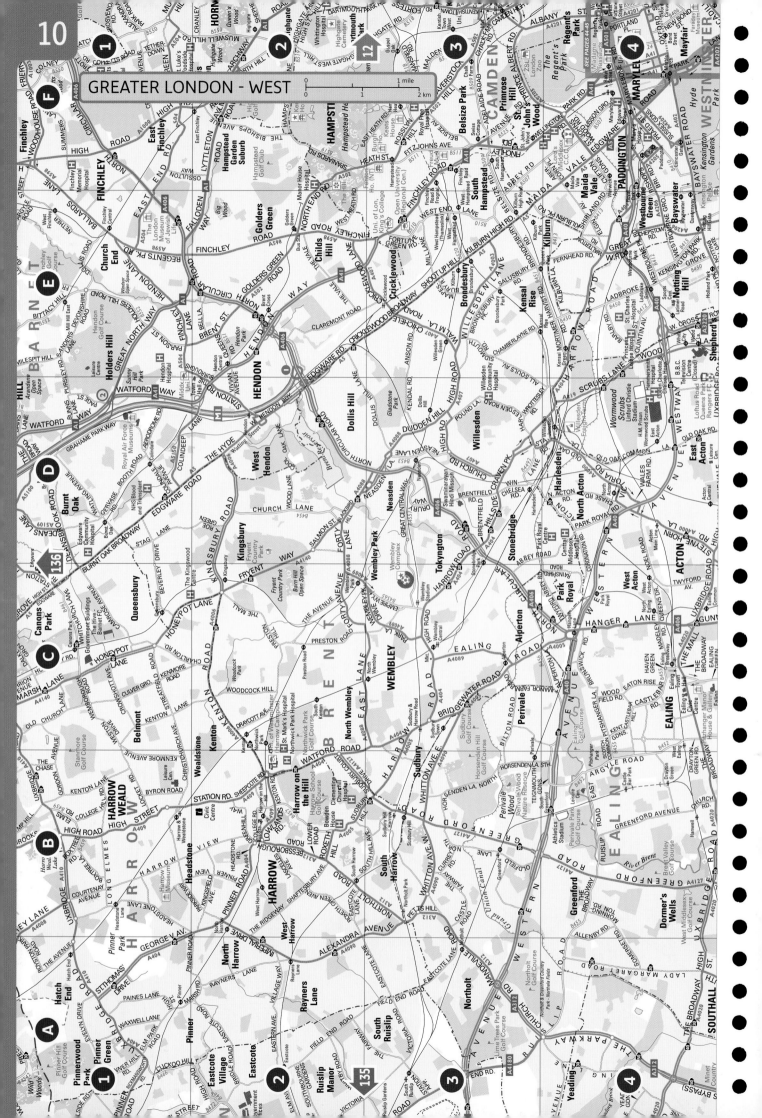

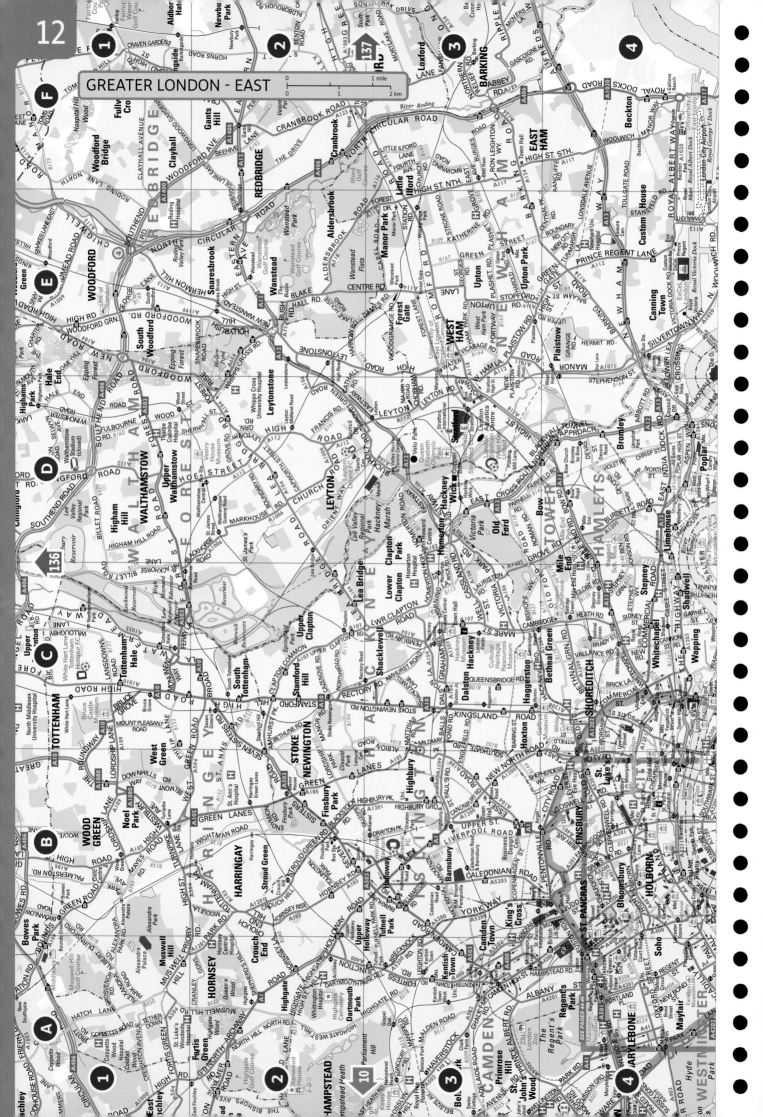

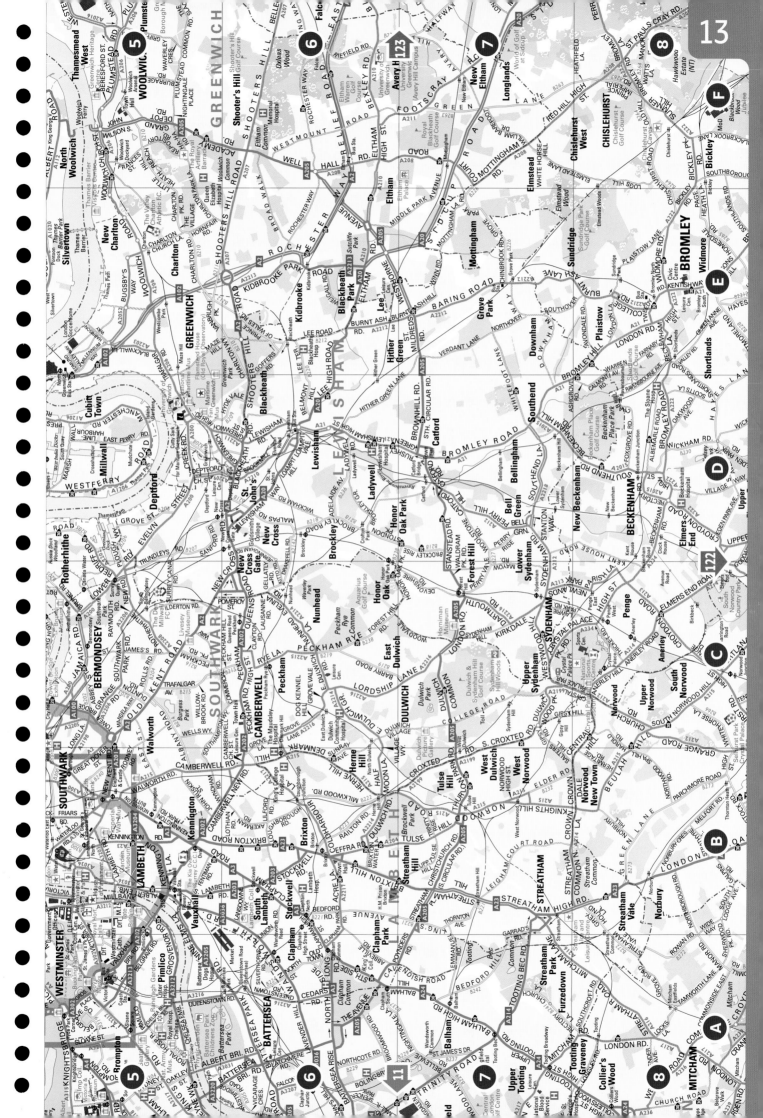

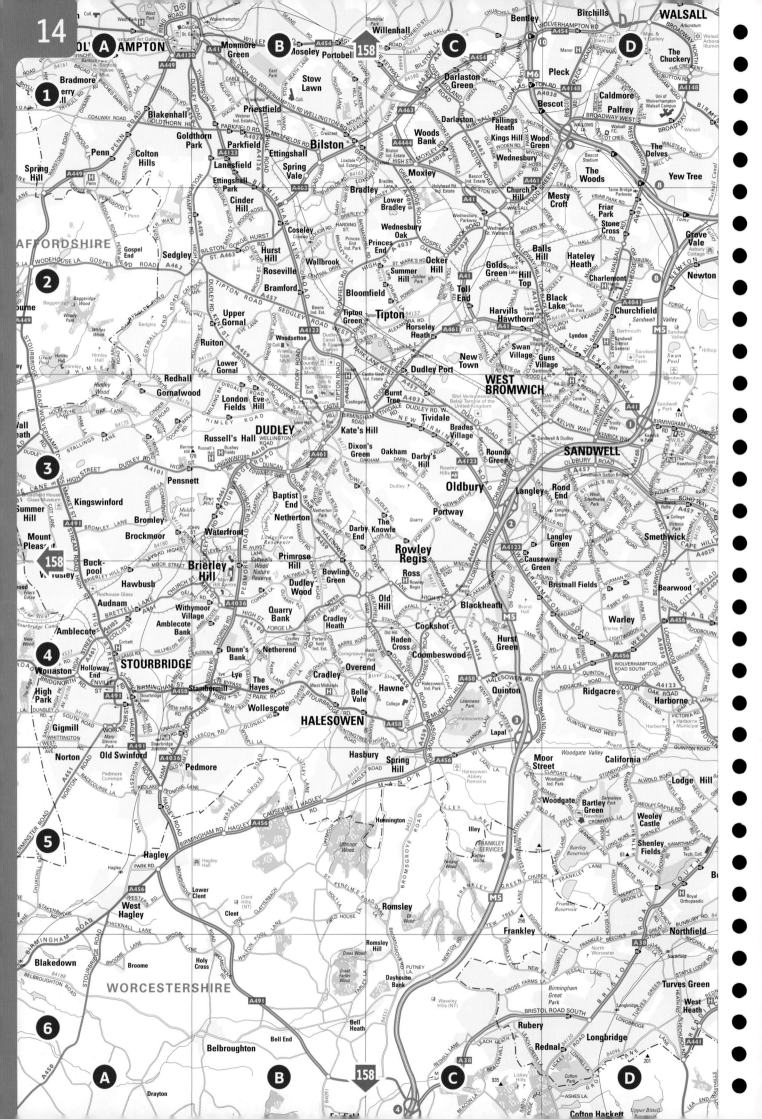

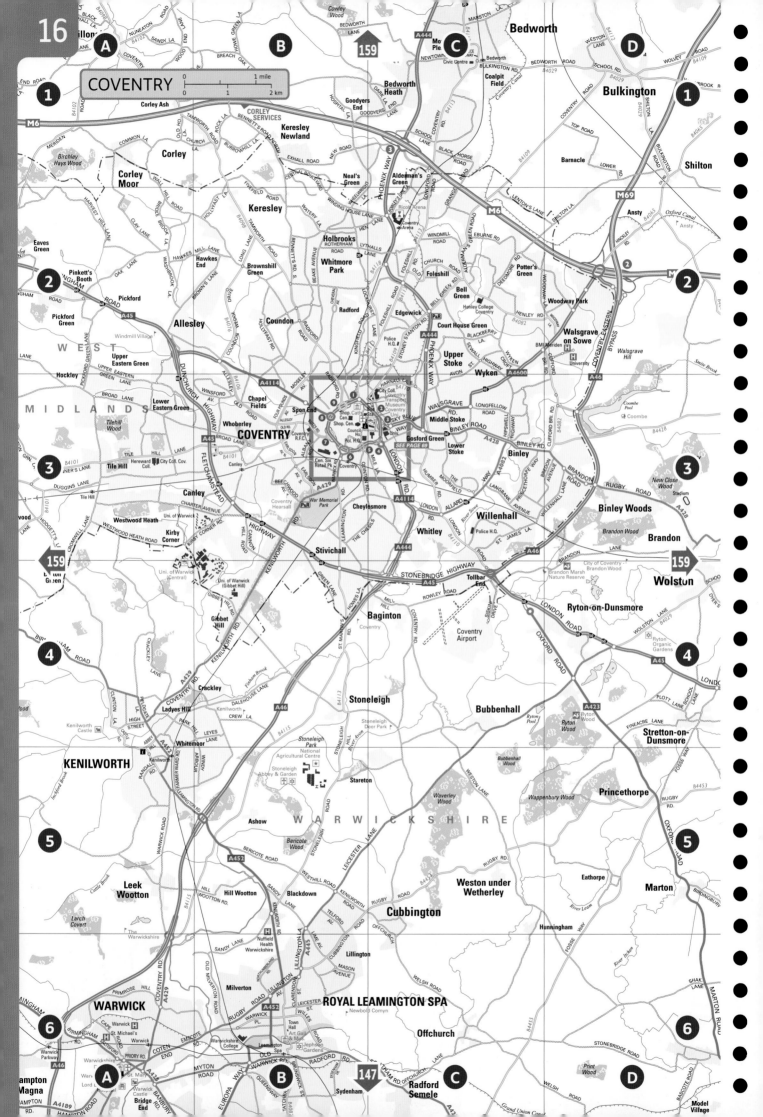

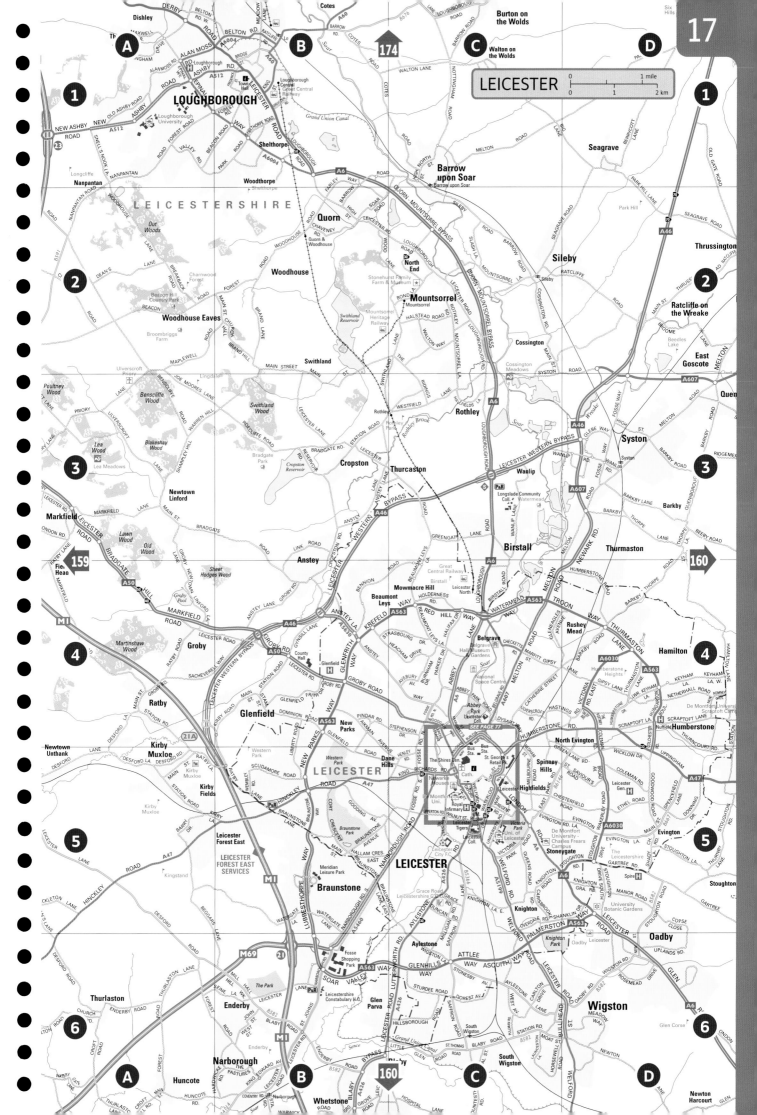

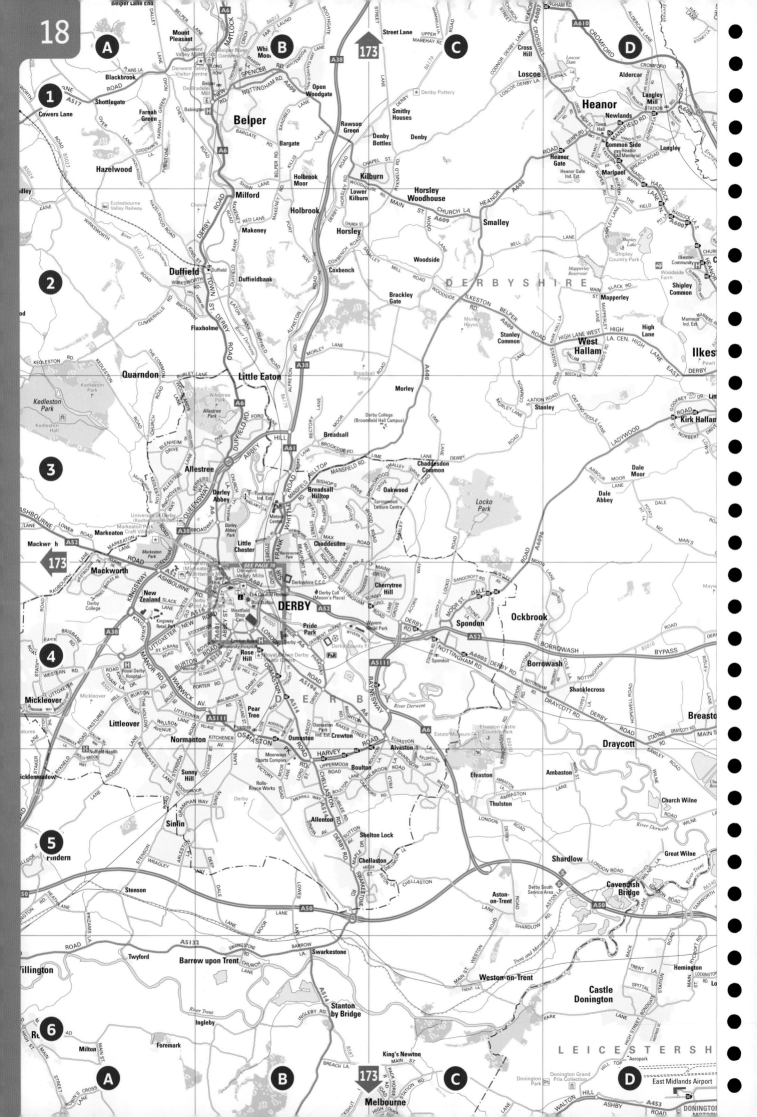

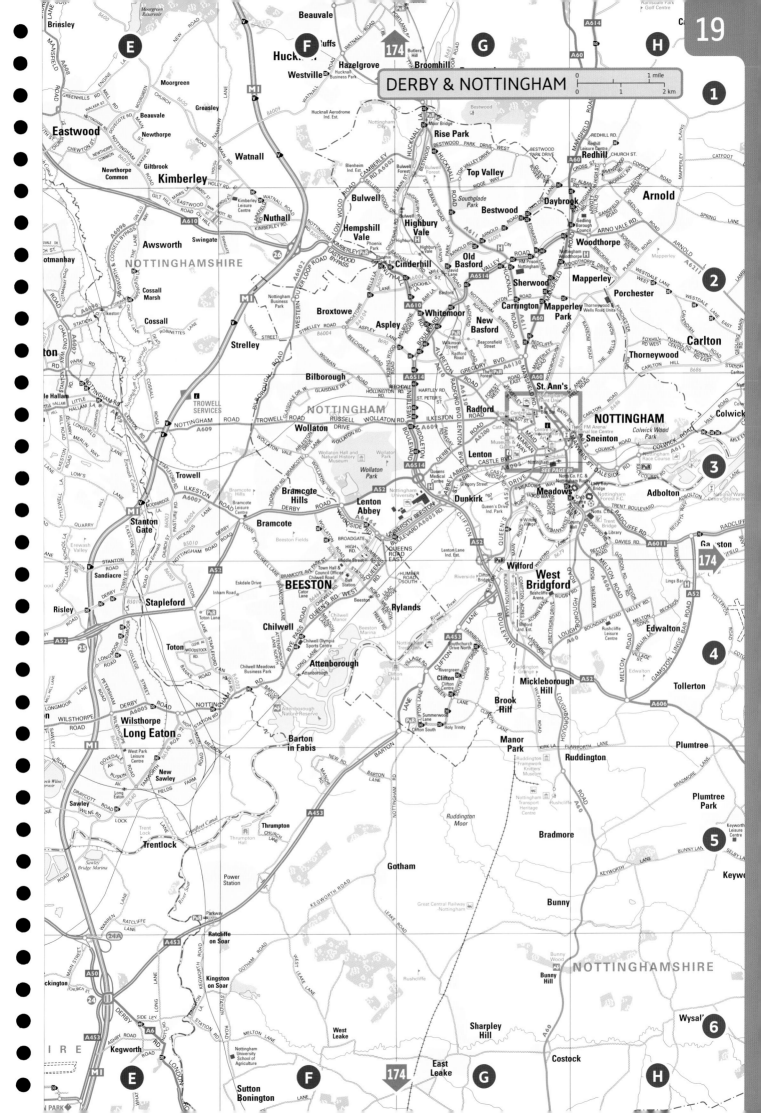

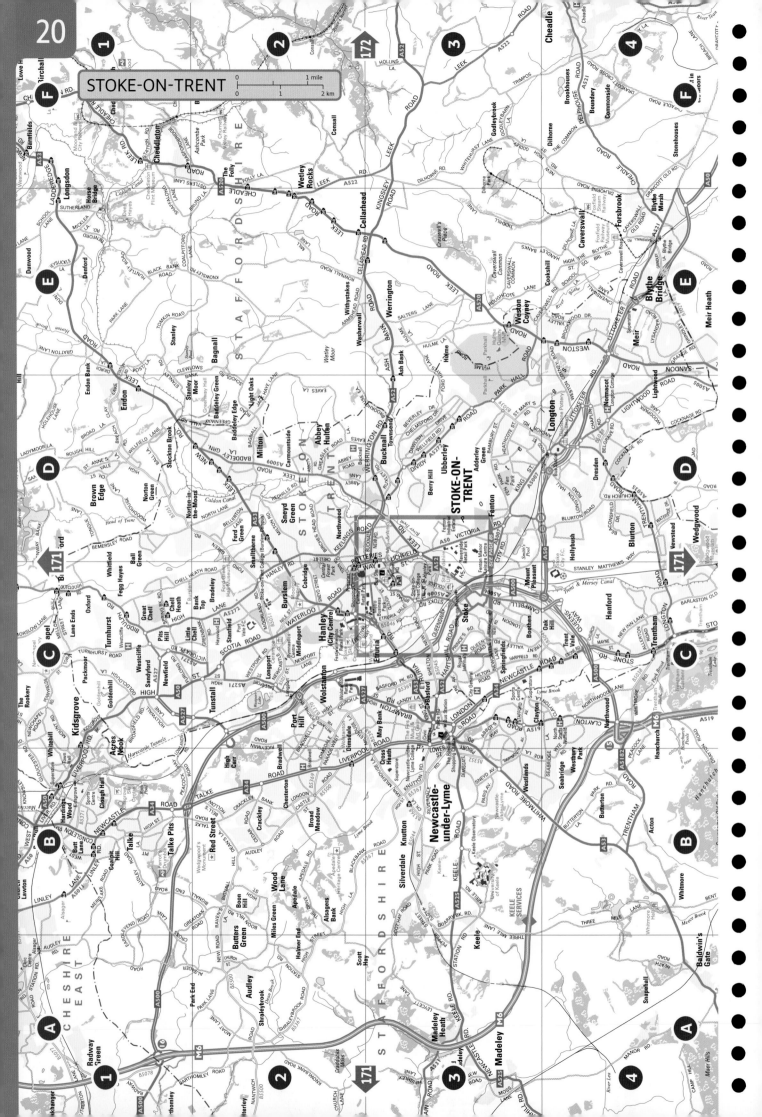

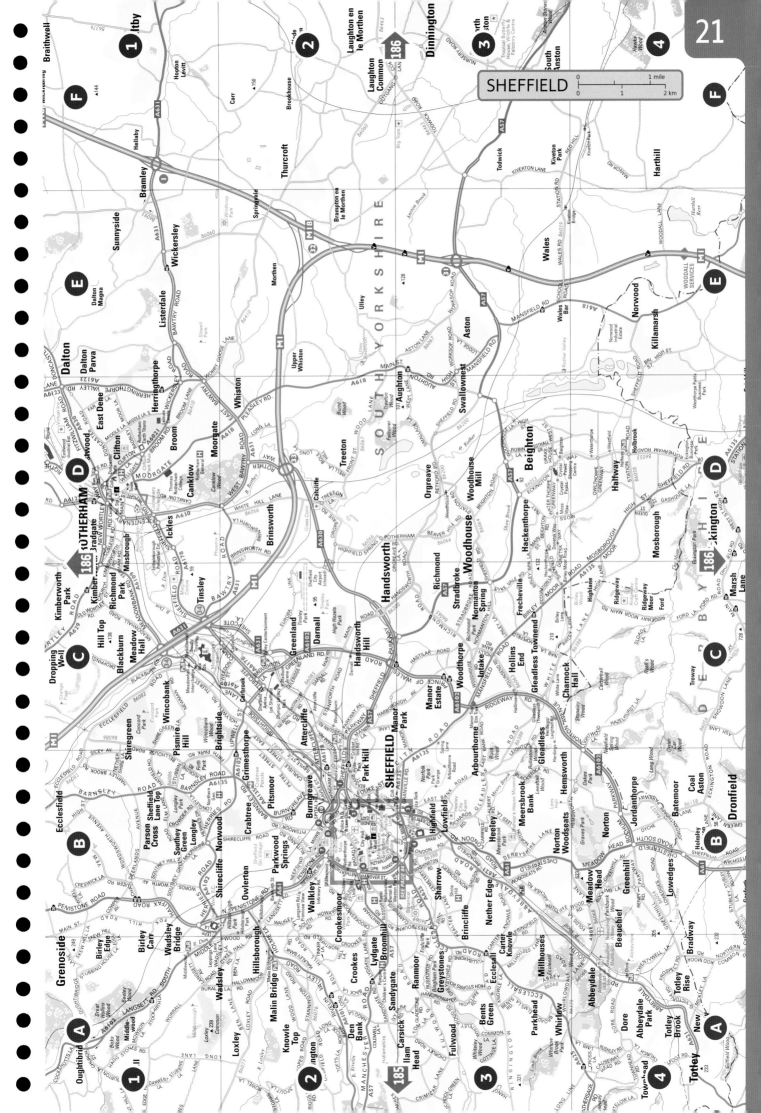

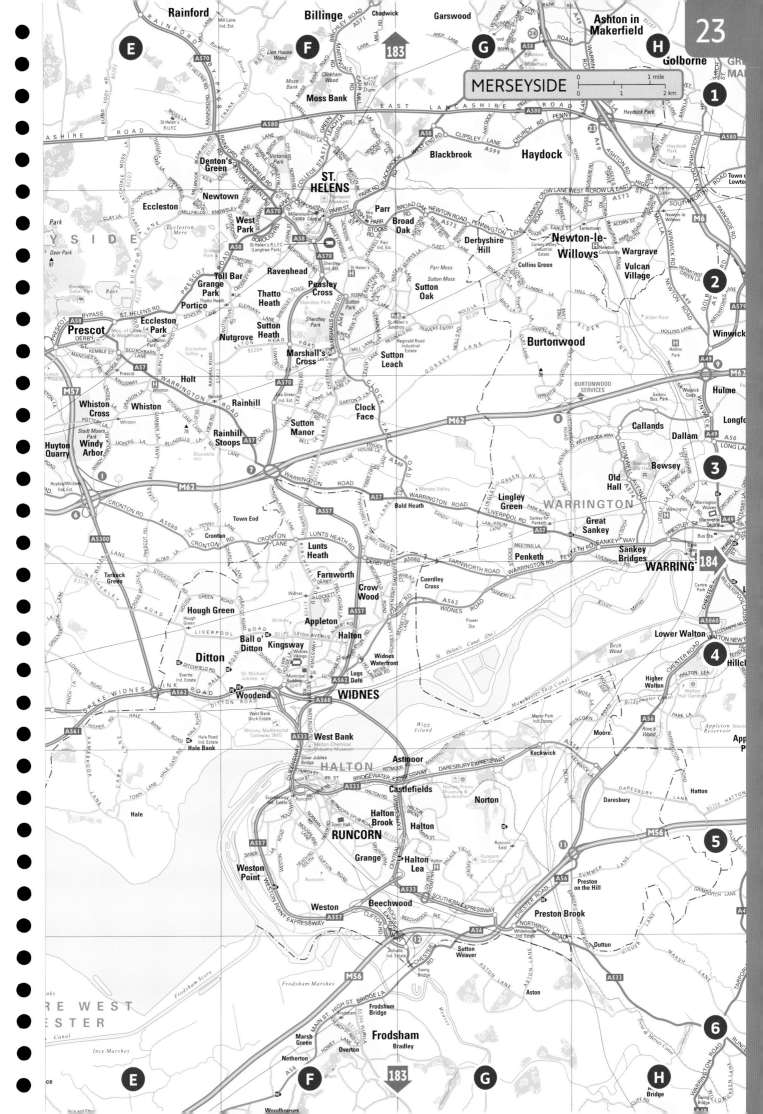

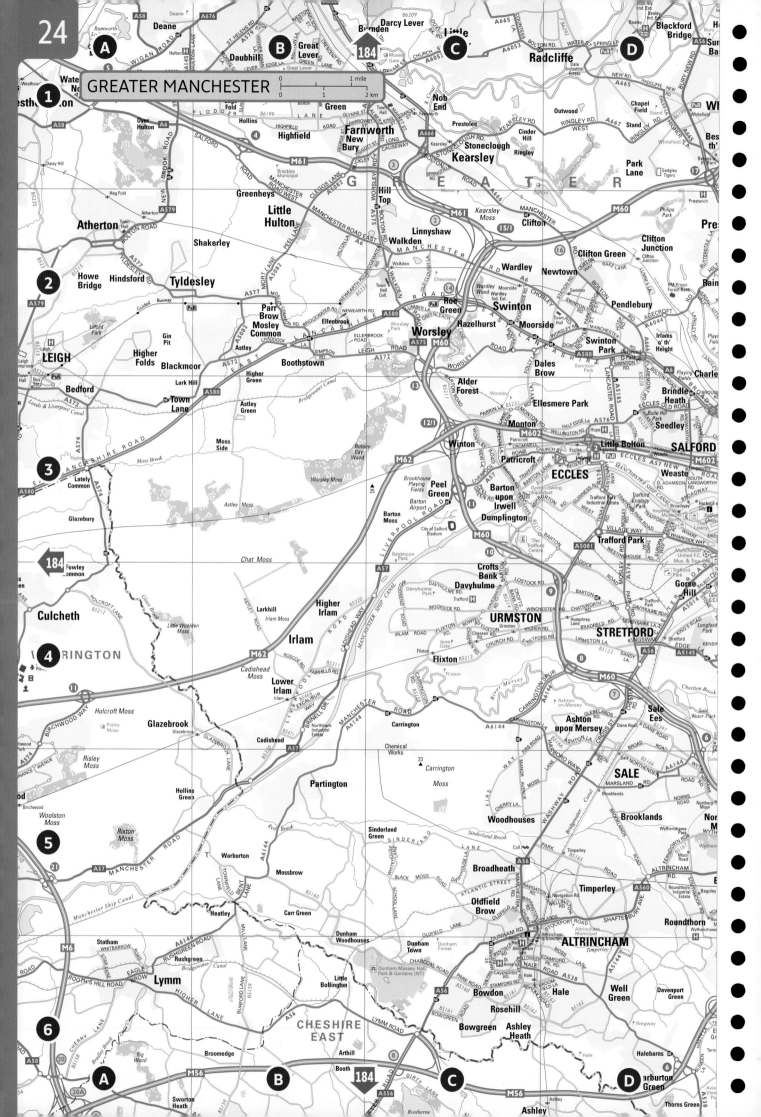

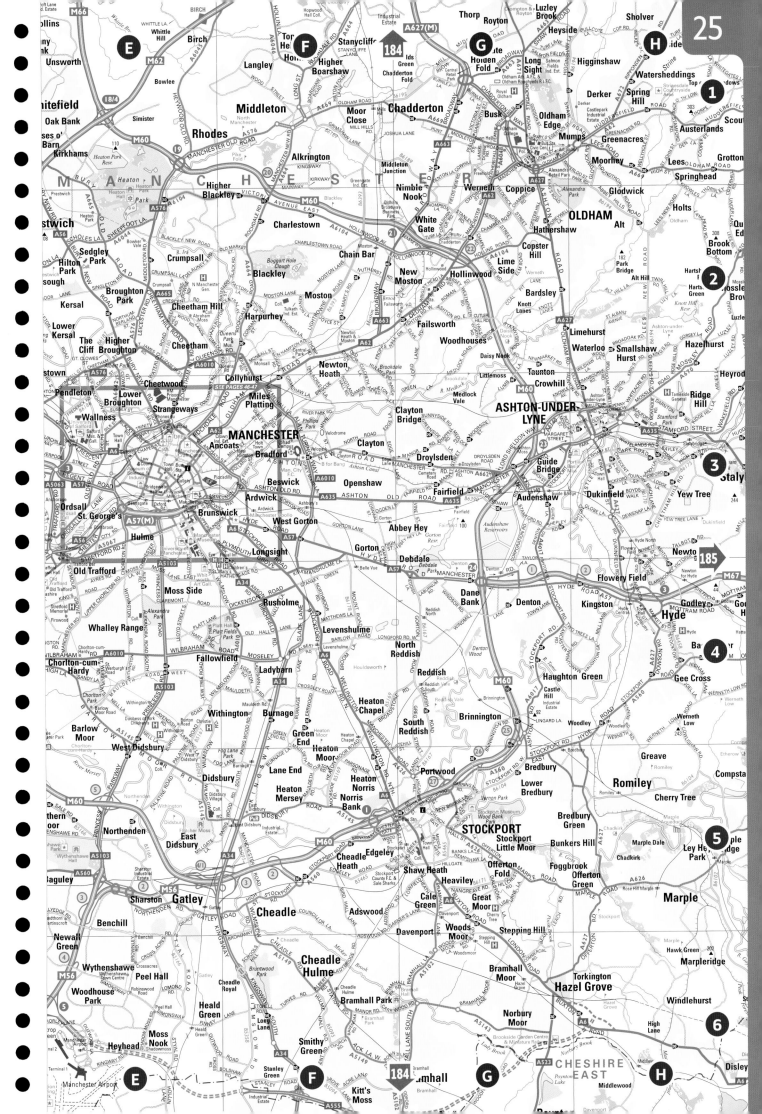

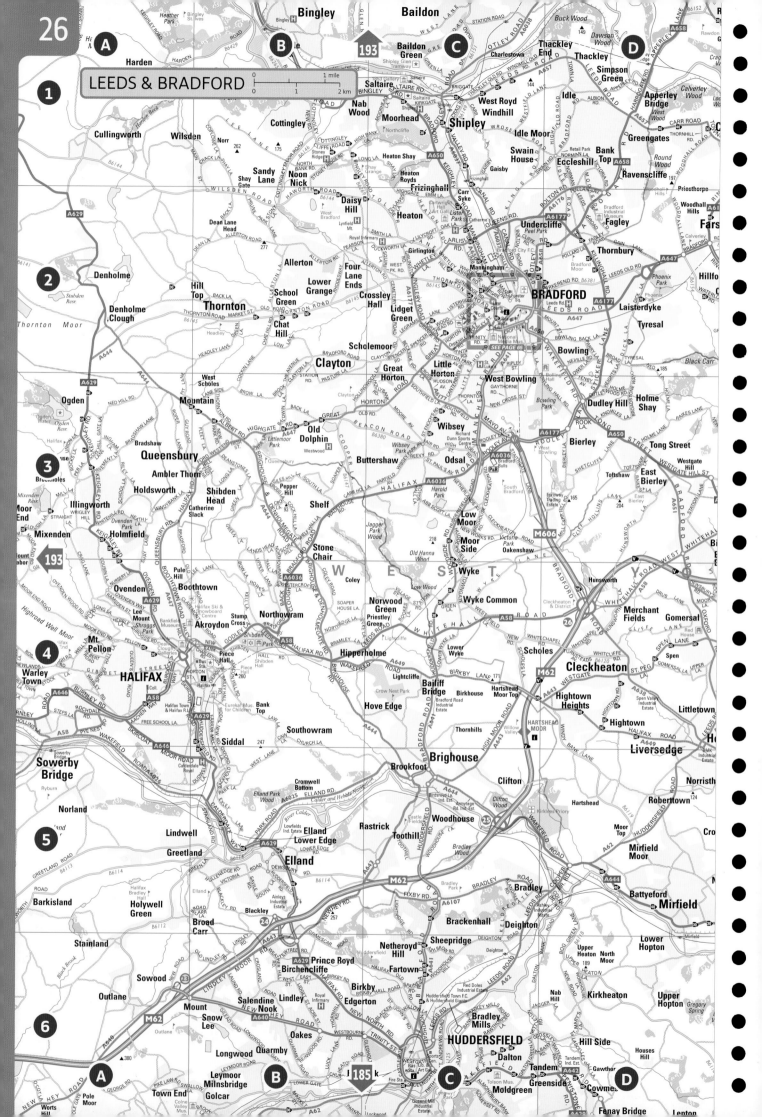

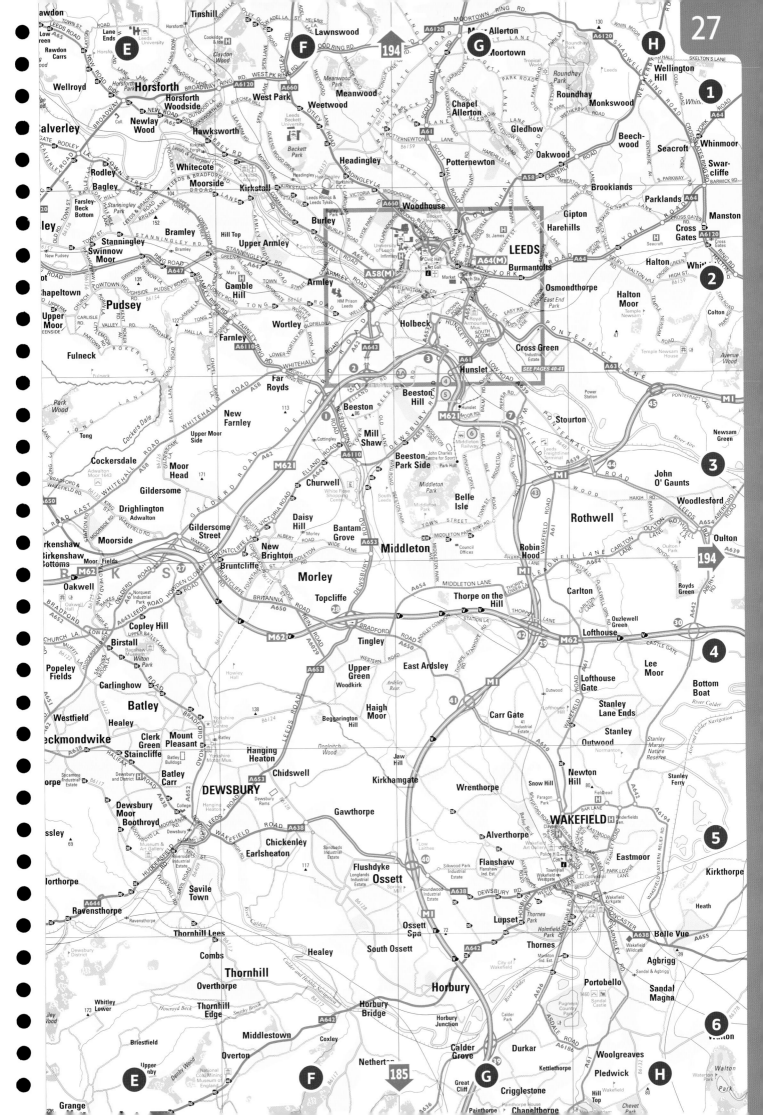

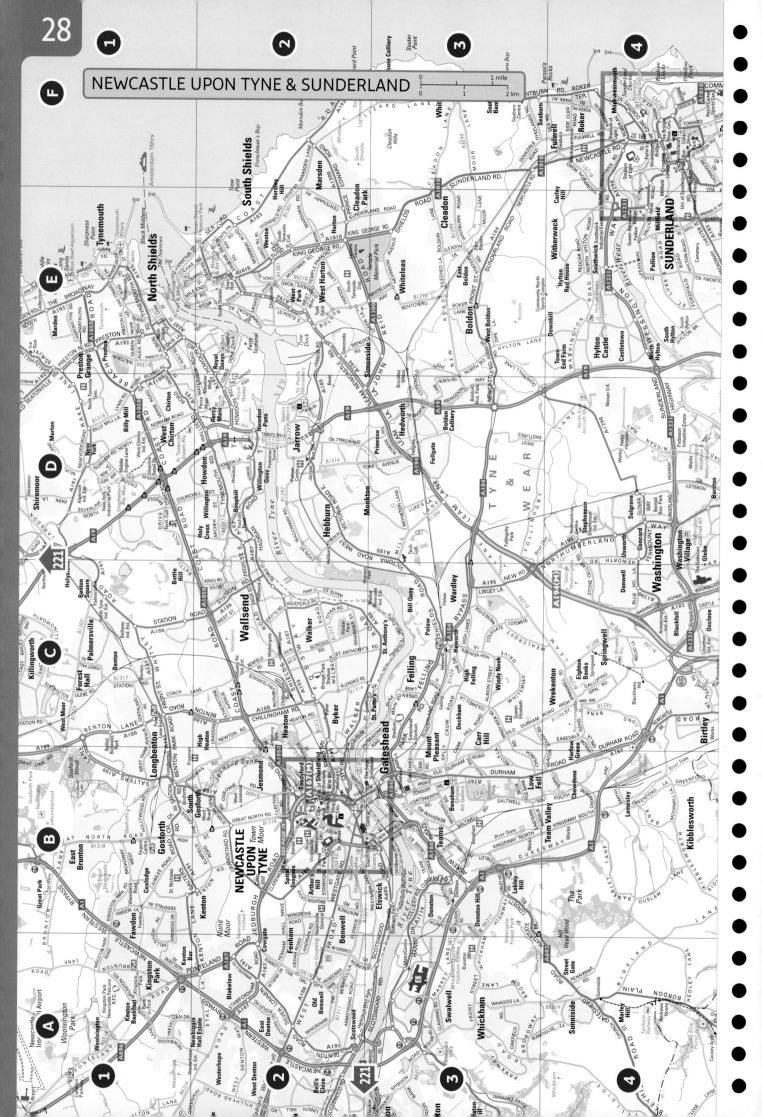

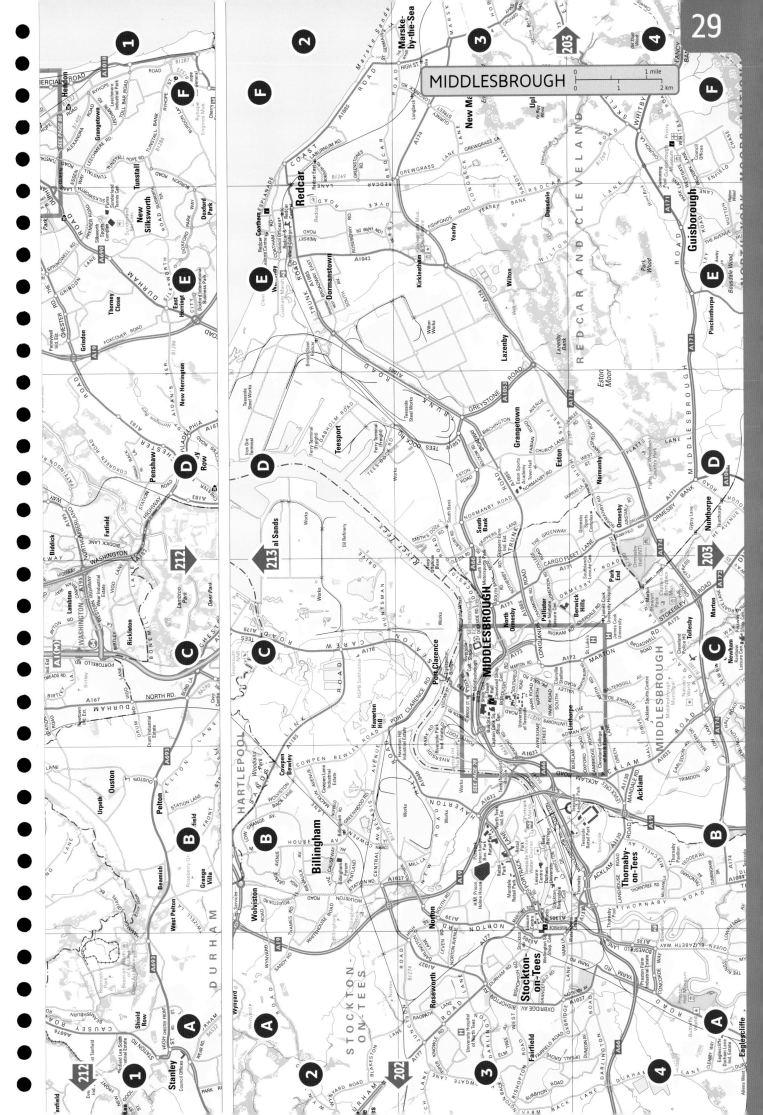

MIDDLESBROUGH

0   1 mile
0   1   2 km

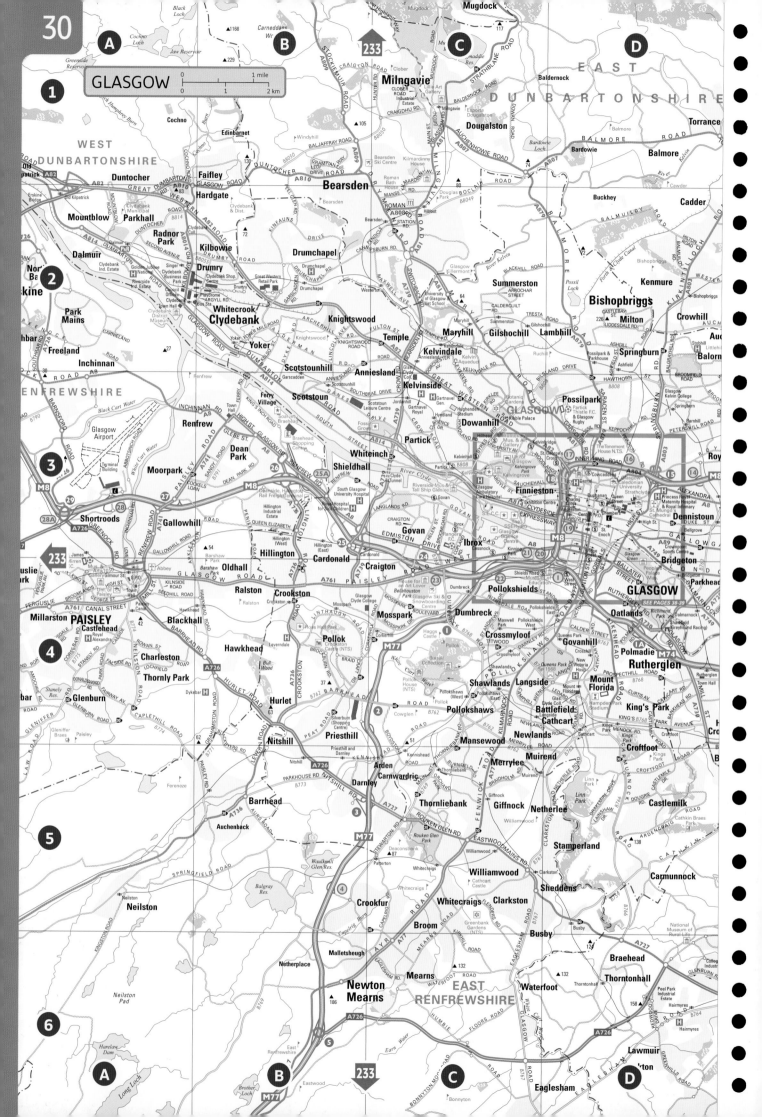

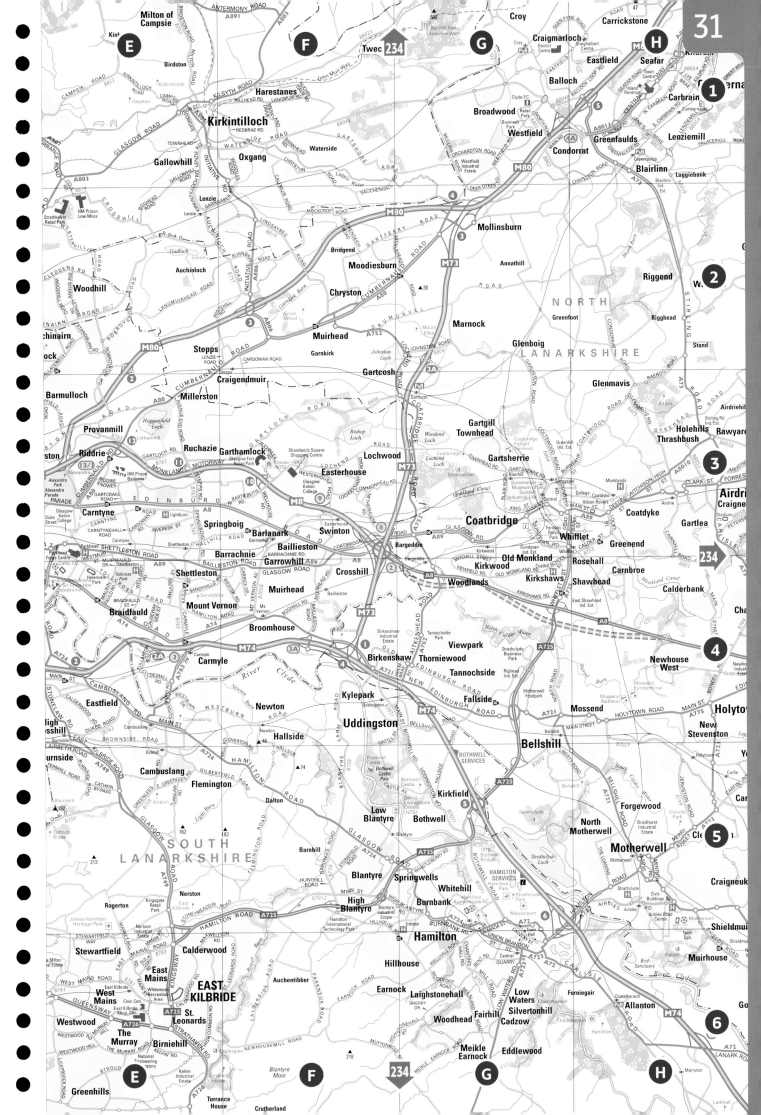

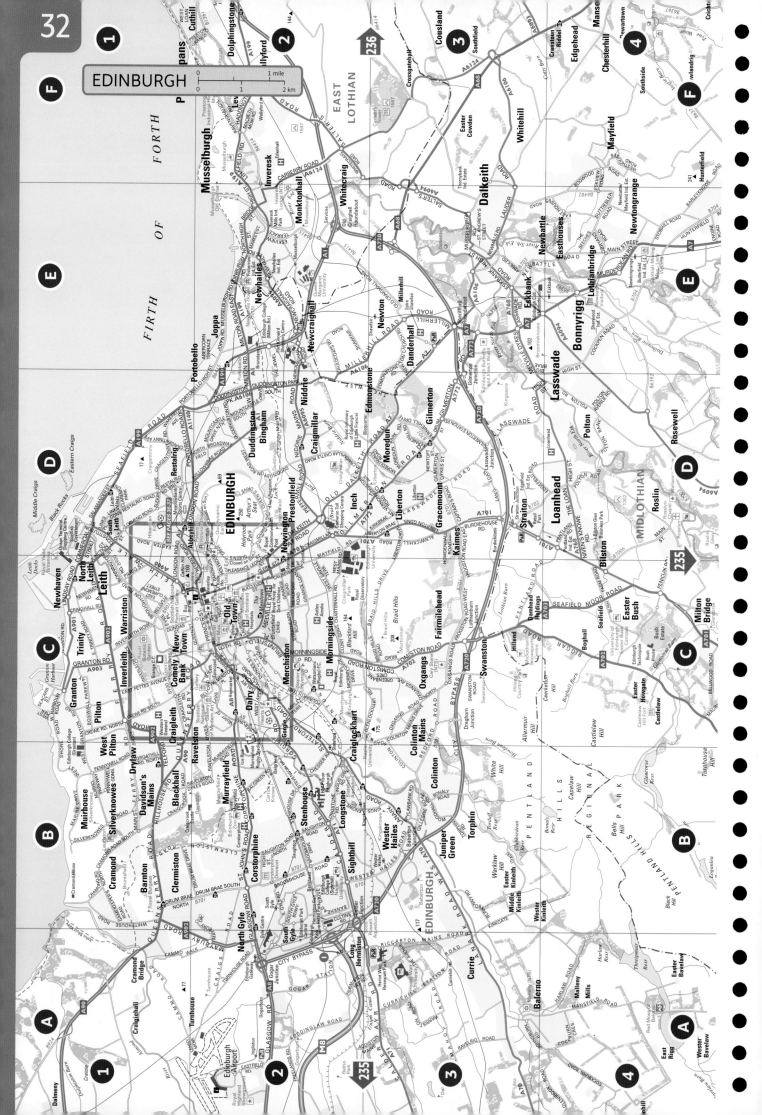

Symbols used on the map

Symbol	Description
M8	Motorway
A4 ❶	Primary route dual / single carriageway / Junction
A40	'A' road dual / single carriageway
B507	'B' road dual / single carriageway
Toll	Other road dual / single carriageway / Toll
→— 7	One way street / Orbital route
·	Access restriction
	Pedestrian street
	Street market
	Minor road / Track
FB	Footpath / Footbridge
	Road under construction
≠	Main / other National Rail station
	London Underground / Overground station
Ⓛ	Light Rail / Station

Symbol	Description
🚌	Bus / Coach station
P&R	Park and Ride site - rail operated (runs at least 5 days a week)
	Extent of London congestion charging zone
Dublin 8hrs ⊖	Vehicle / Pedestrian ferry
P P	Car park
Ⓤ	Theatre
🏨	Major hotel
ⓓ	Public House
Pol	Police station
Lib	Library
PO	Post Office
ℹ ℹ	Visitor information centre (open all year / seasonally)
🚻	Toilet

Symbol	Description
⊐JAPAN	Embassy
📽 📽	Cinema
✚ +	Cathedral / Church
☾ ✡ ■ Mormon	Mosque / Synagogue / Other place of worship
	Leisure & tourism
	Shopping
	Administration & law
	Health & welfare
	Education
	Industry / Office
	Other notable building
	Park / Garden / Sports ground
	Cemetery

Locator map

Street maps			
Aberdeen	63	Leeds index	52
Bath	63	Leicester	77
Birmingham	34-35	Lincoln	77
Birmingham index	48	Liverpool	42-43
Blackpool	64	Liverpool index	54
Bournemouth	64	London	44-45
Bradford	65	London index	56
Brighton	65	Manchester	46-47
Bristol	66	Manchester index	60
Cambridge	66	Middlesbrough	78
Canterbury	67	Milton Keynes	78
Cardiff	67	Newcastle upon Tyne	79
Carlisle	68	Norwich	79
Cheltenham	68	Nottingham	80
Chester	69	Oxford	80
Coventry	69	Perth	81
Derby	70	Plymouth	81
Dover	70	Portsmouth	82
Dundee	71	Reading	82
Durham	71	Salisbury	83
Eastbourne	72	Scarborough	83
Edinburgh	36-37	Sheffield	84
Edinburgh index	49	Southampton	84
Exeter	72	Stoke-on-Trent	85
Folkestone	73	Stratford-upon-Avon	85
Glasgow	38-39	Sunderland	86
Glasgow index	51	Swansea	86
Gloucester	73	Swindon	87
Guildford	74	Torquay	87
Harrogate	74	Watford	88
Hastings	75	Weston-super-Mare	88
Hereford	75	Winchester	89
Hull (Kingston upon Hull)	76	Windsor	89
Inverness	76	Worcester	90
Leeds	40-41	York	90

Airport plans	
Birmingham International	91
Gatwick	91
Glasgow	91
Heathrow	91
Manchester	91
Stansted	91

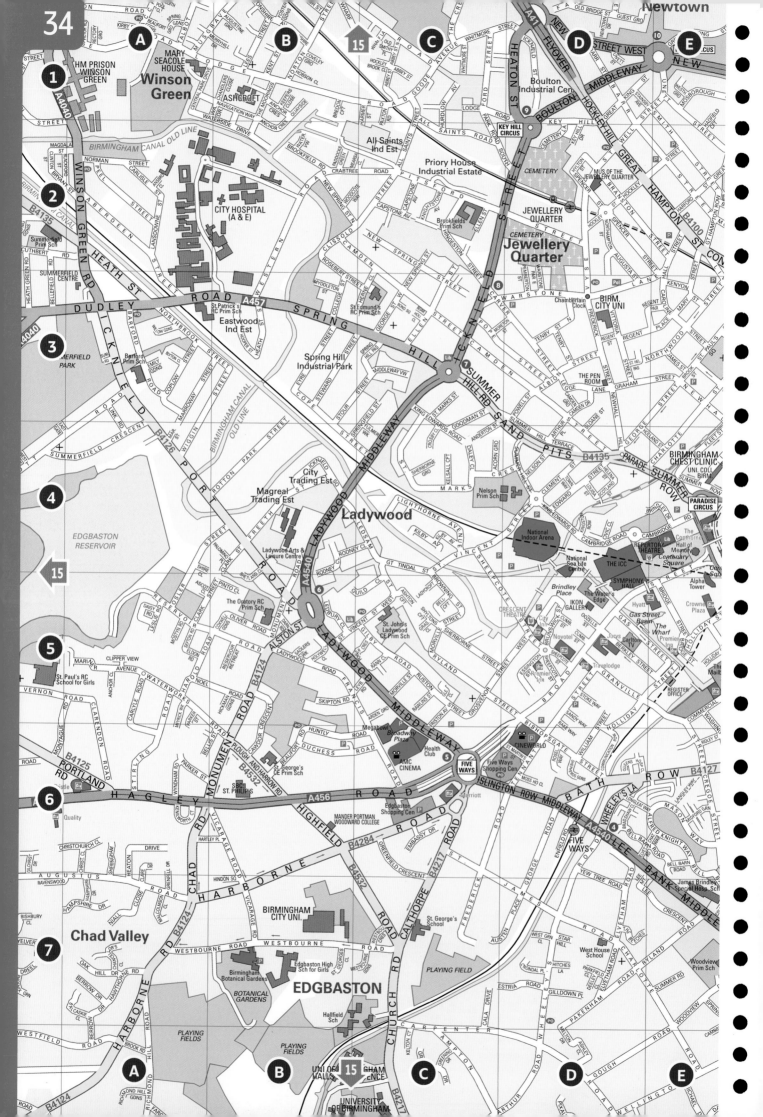

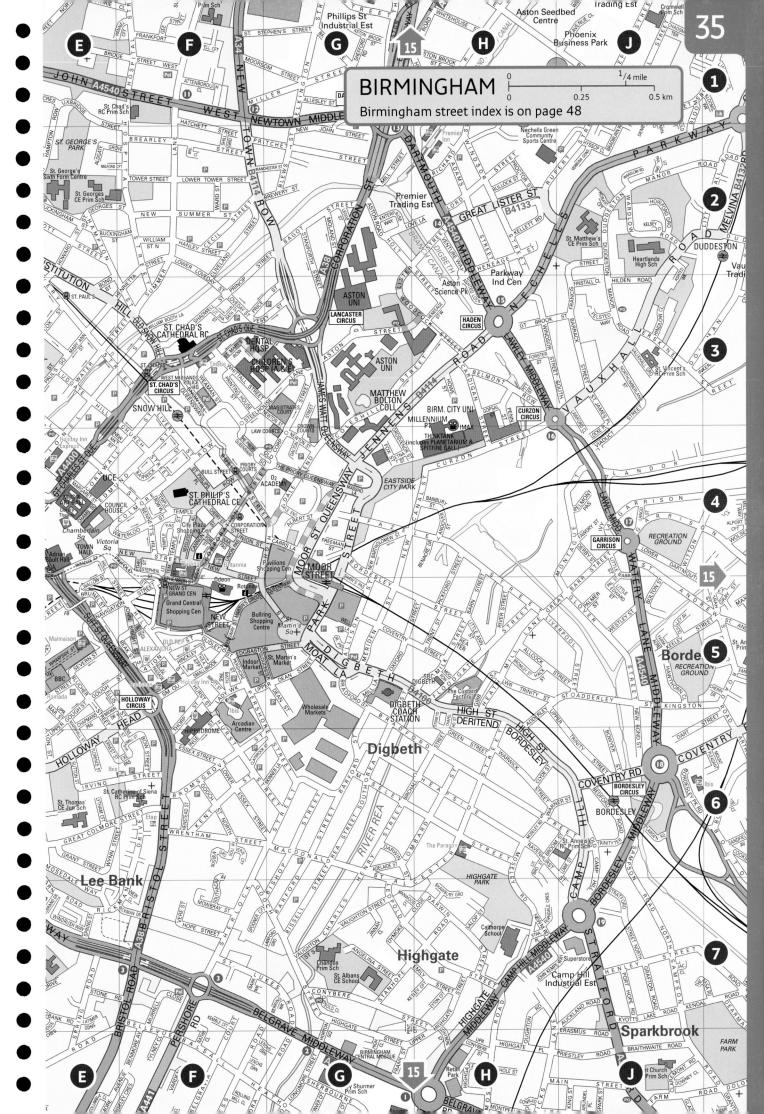

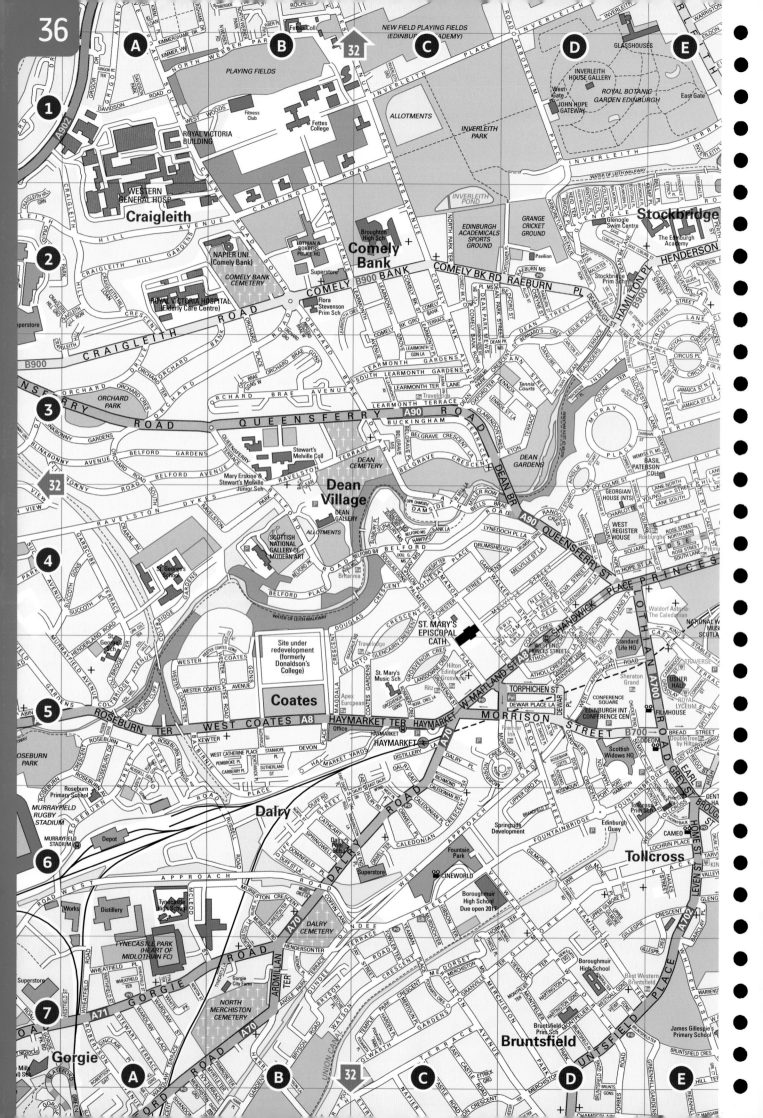

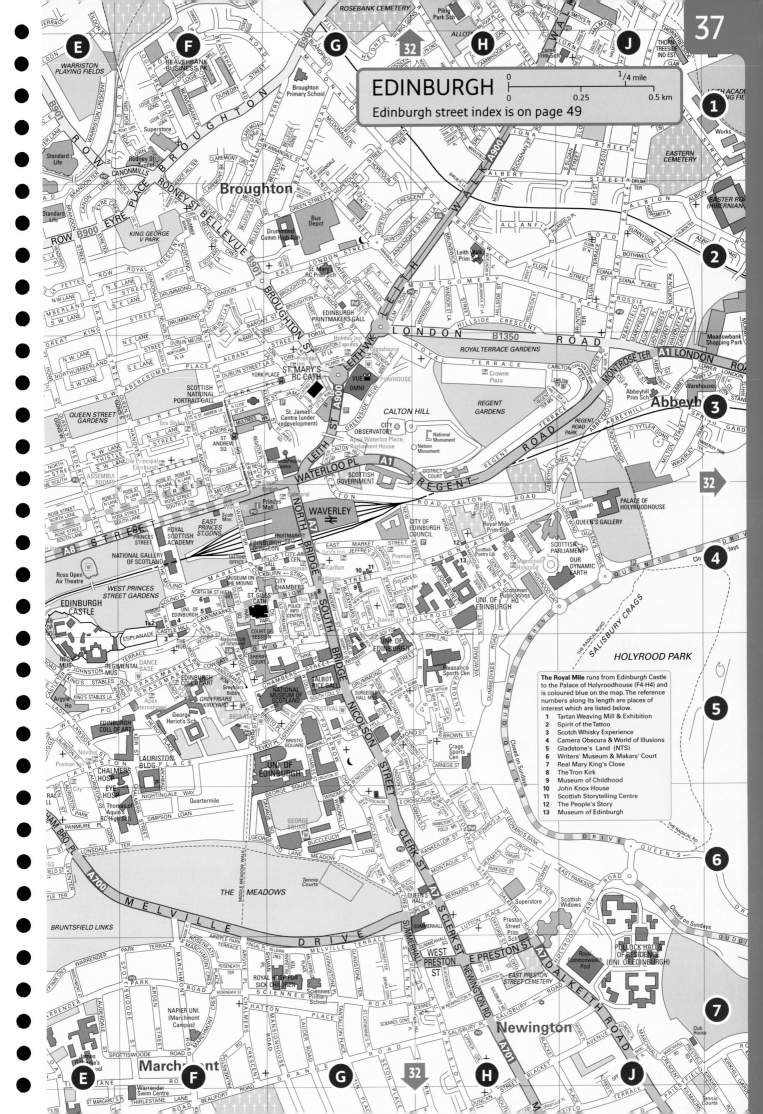

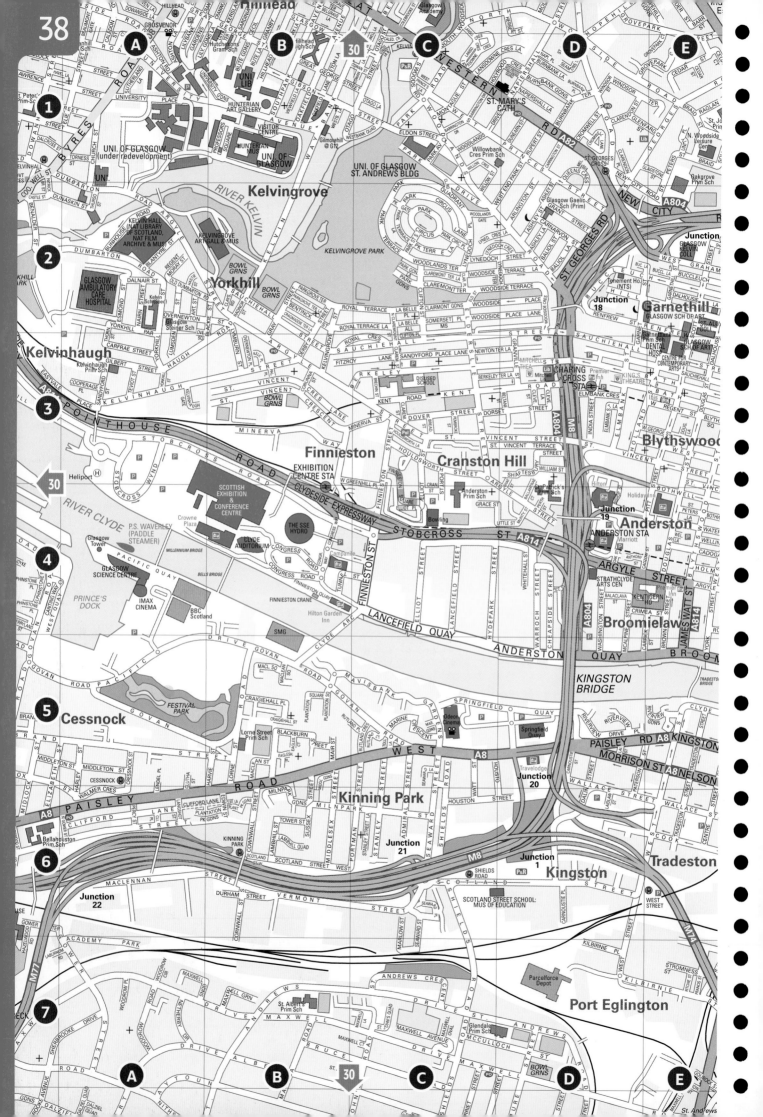

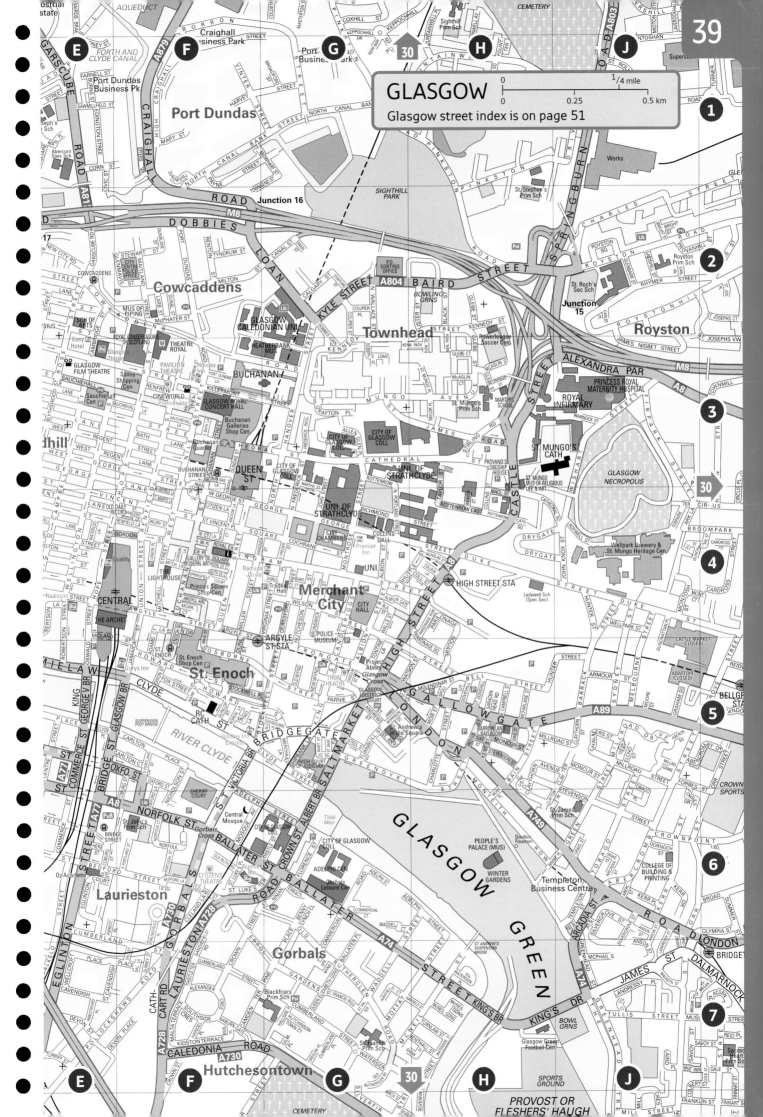

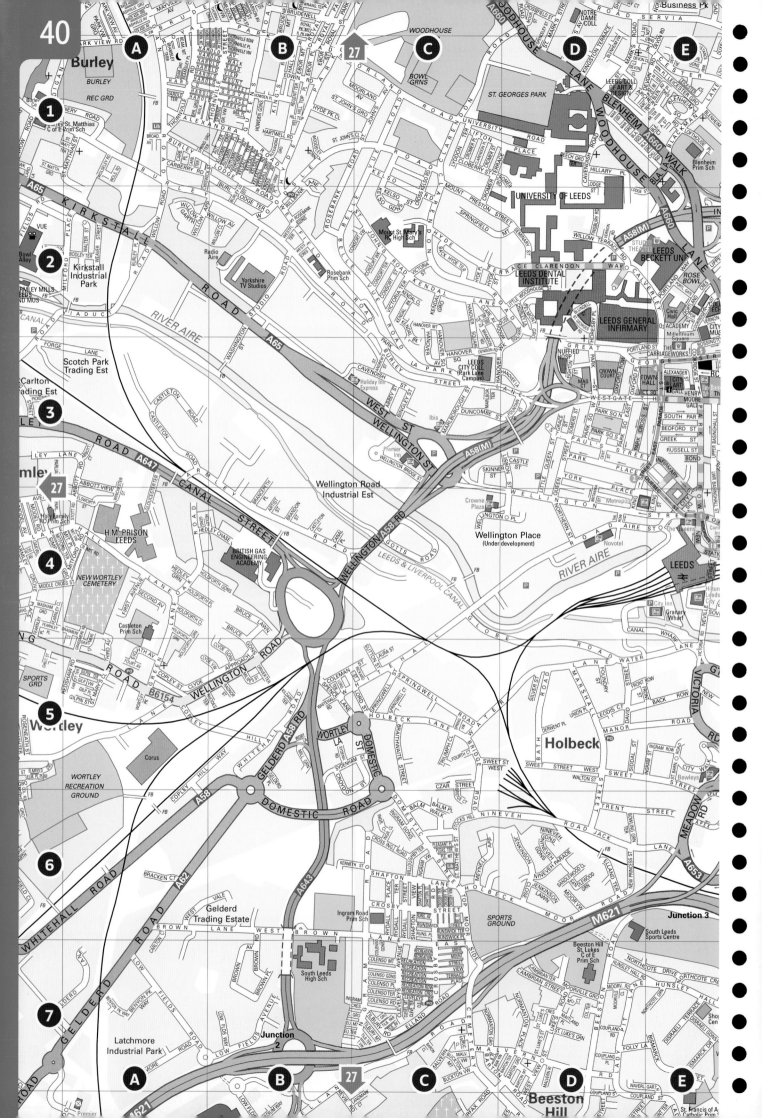

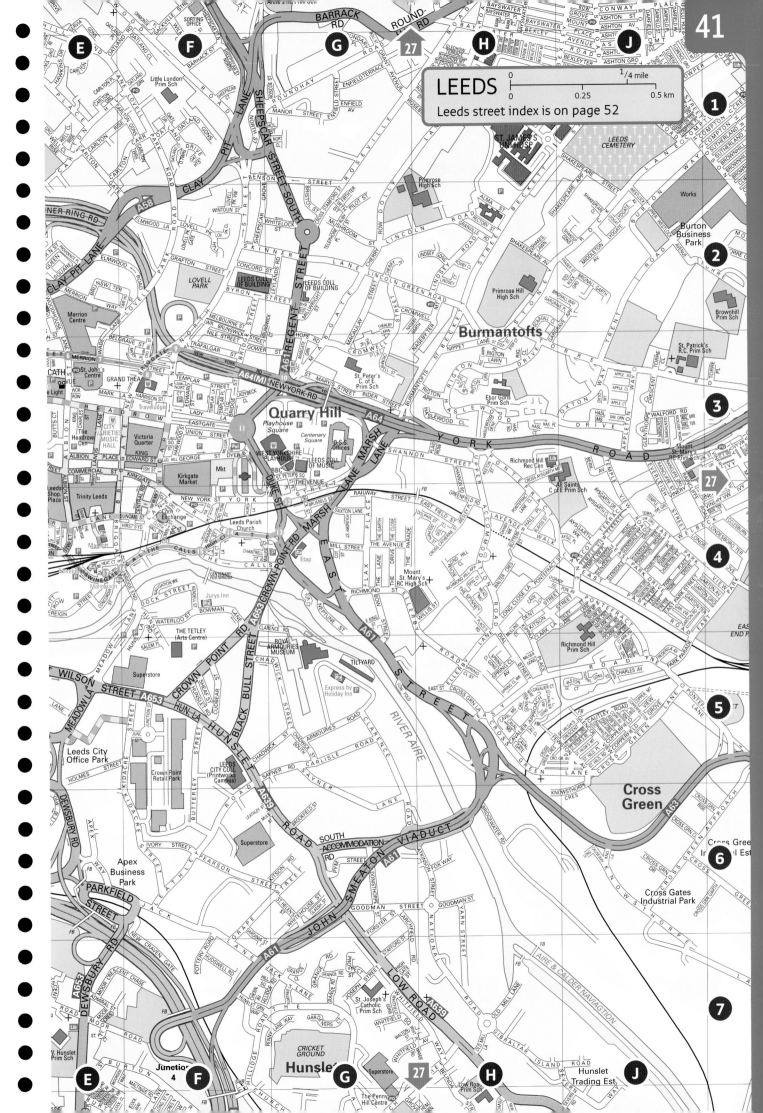

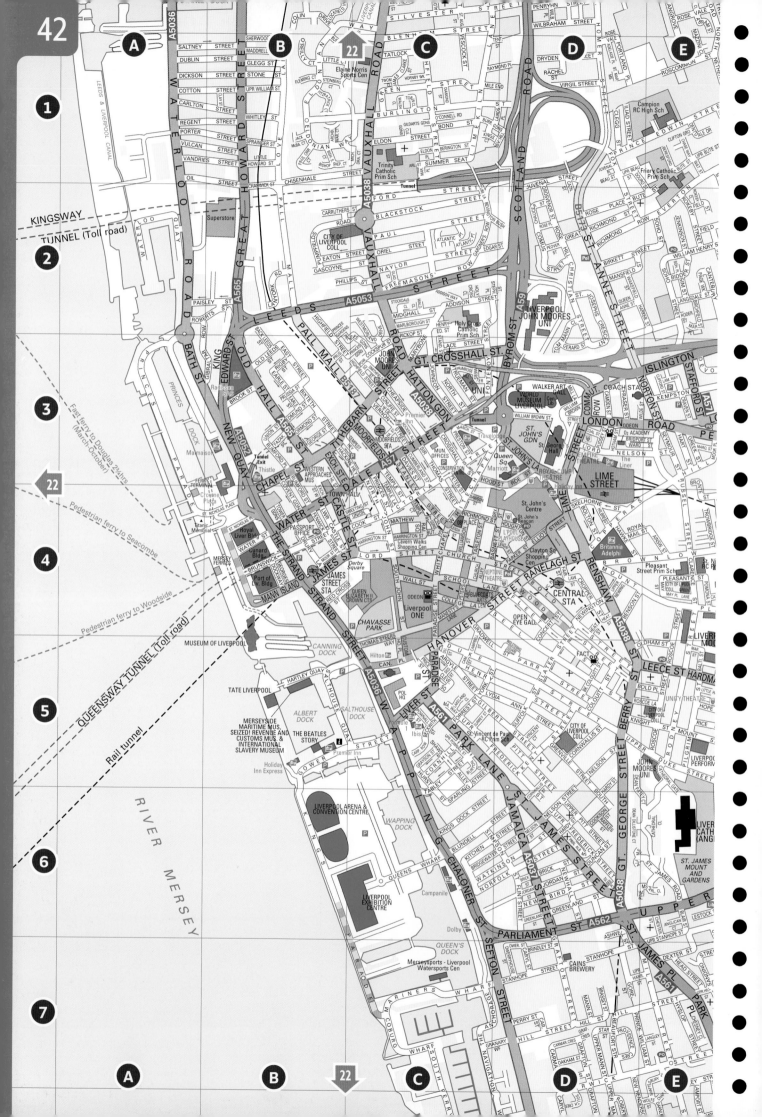

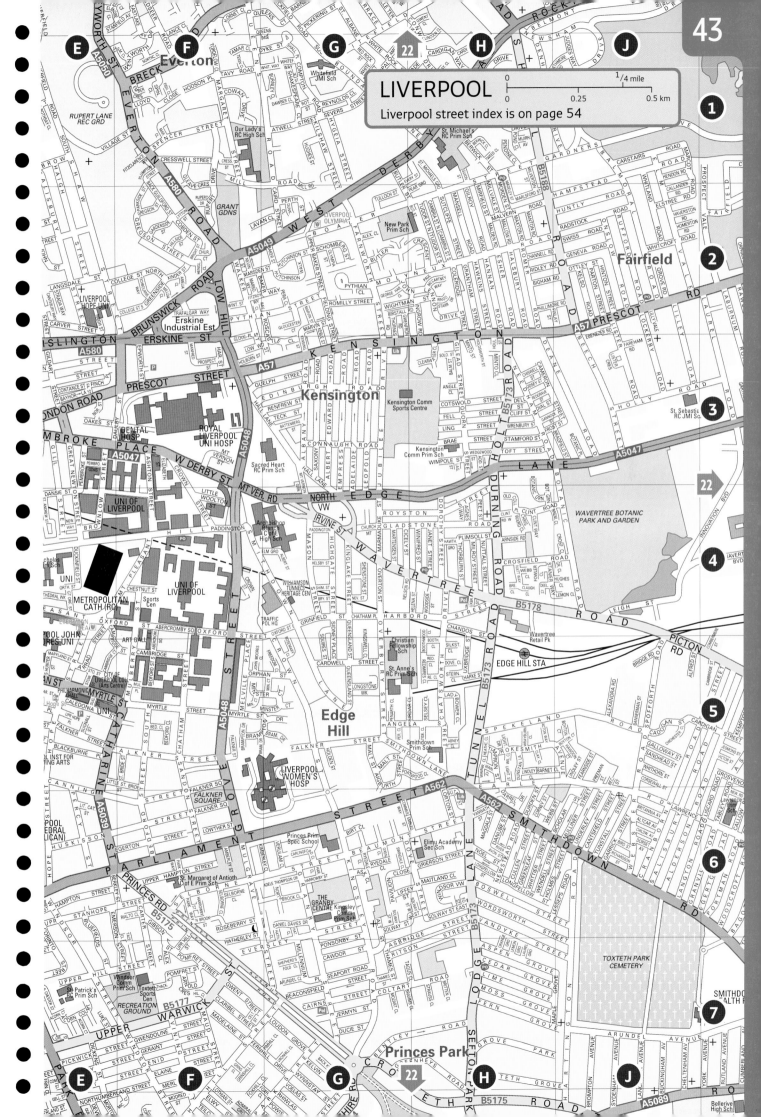

LIVERPOOL

Liverpool street index is on page 54

0   0.25   0.5 km
1/4 mile

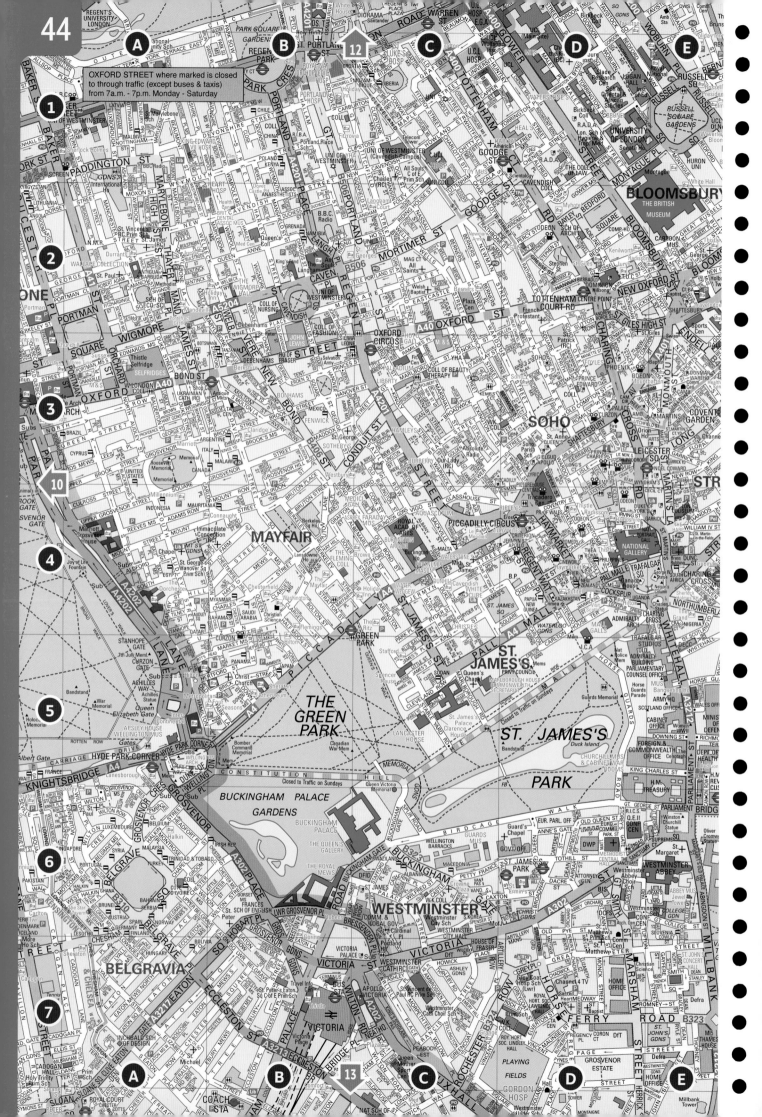

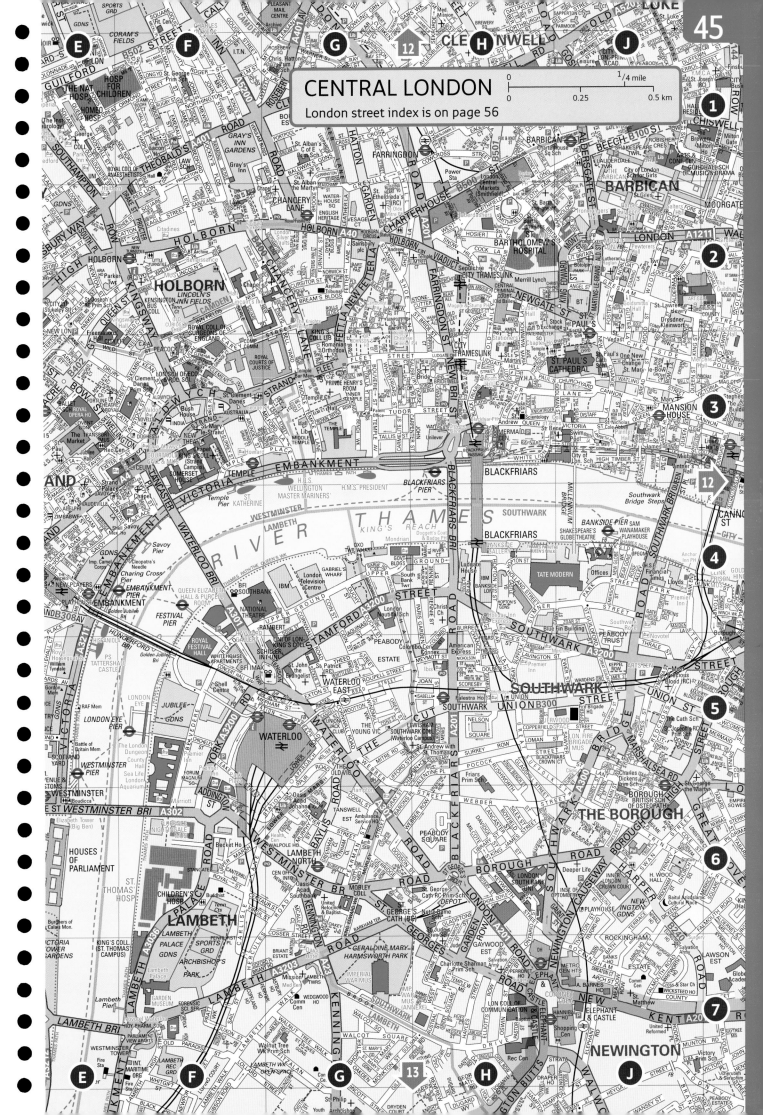

London street index is on page 56

CENTRAL LONDON

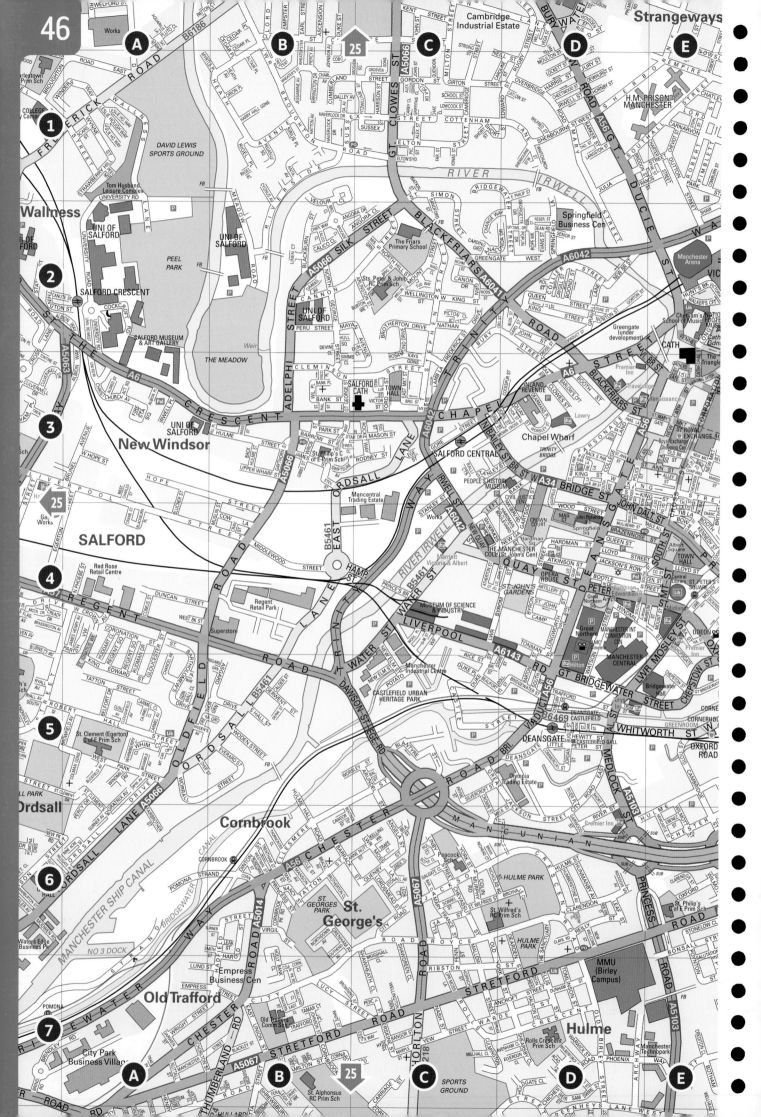

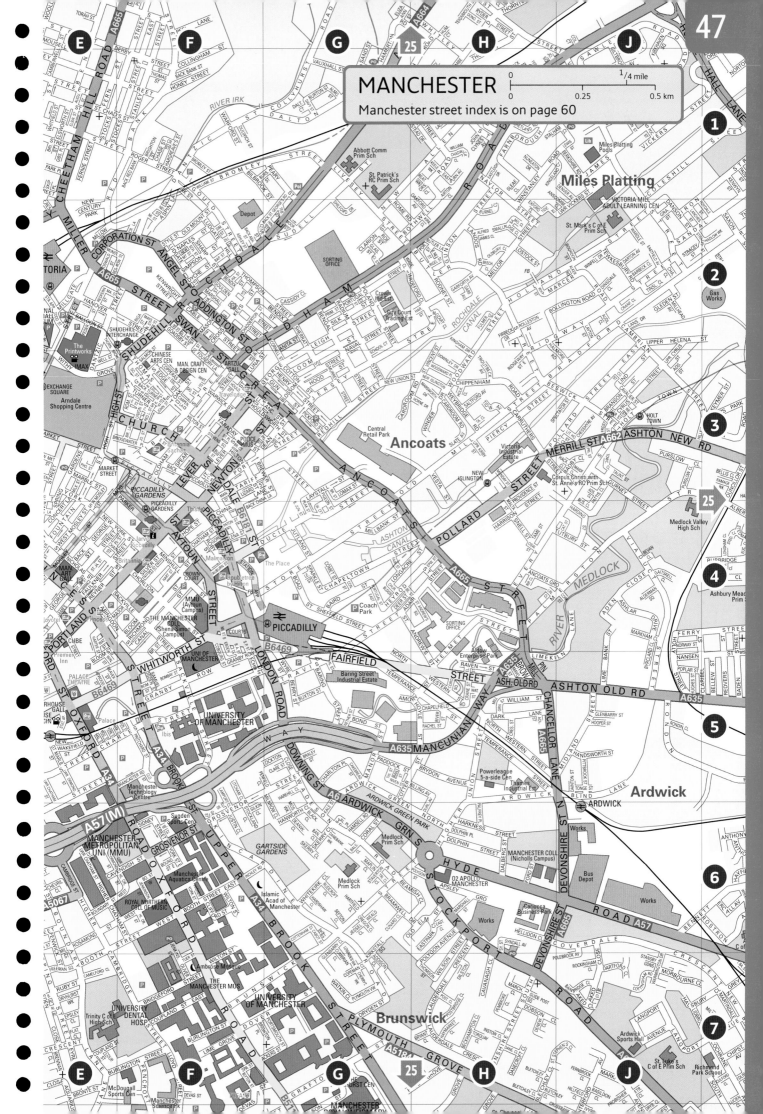

MANCHESTER
Manchester street index is on page 60

Indexes to street maps

General abbreviations

All	Alley	Chyd	Churchyard	Embk	Embankment	La	Lane	Pl	Place	W	West
App	Approach	Circ	Circus	Est	Estate	Lo	Lodge	Rd	Road	Wf	Wharf
Arc	Arcade	Clo	Close	Flds	Fields	Mans	Mansions	Ri	Rise	Wk	Walk
Av/Ave	Avenue	Cor	Corner	Gdn	Garden	Mkt/Mkts	Market/Markets	S	South	Yd	Yard
Bdy	Broadway	Cres	Crescent	Gdns	Gardens	Ms	Mews	Sq	Square		
Bldgs	Buildings	Ct	Court	Grd	Ground	N	North	St	Street		
Br/Bri	Bridge	Ctyd	Courtyard	Grn	Green	Par	Parade	St.	Saint		
Cen	Central, Centre	Dr	Drive	Gro	Grove	Pas	Passage	Ter	Terrace		
Ch	Church	E	East	Ho	House	Pk	Park	Twr	Tower		

Place names are shown in bold type

Birmingham street index

A
Abbey St **34** C1
Abbey St N **34** C1
Aberdeen St **34** A2
Acorn Gro **34** C4
Adams St **35** H2
Adderley St **35** H5
Adelaide St **35** G6
Albert St **35** G4
Albion St **34** D3
Alcester St **35** G7
Aldgate Gro **35** E2
Alfred Knight Way **34** E6
Allcock St **35** H5
Allesley St **35** G1
Allison St **35** G5
All Saints Rd **34** C1
All Saints St **34** C2
Alston St **34** B5
Anchor Cl **34** A5
Anchor Cres **34** B1
Anderton St **34** C4
Angelina St **35** G7
Ansbro Cl **34** A2
Arden Gro **34** C5
Arthur Pl **34** D4
Ascot Cl **34** A5
Ashted Lock **35** H3
Ashted Wk **35** J2
Ashton Cft **34** C5
Aston **35** H1
Aston Br **35** G1
Aston Brook St **35** G1
Aston Brook St E **35** H1
Aston Expressway **35** G2
Aston Rd **35** H1
Aston St **35** G3
Attenborough Cl **35** F1
Auckland Rd **35** J7
Augusta St **34** D2
Augustine Gro **34** B1
Austen Pl **34** C7
Autumn Gro **34** E1
Avenue Cl **35** J1
Avenue Rd **35** H1

B
Bacchus Rd **34** A1
Bagot St **35** G2
Balcaskie Cl **34** A7
Banbury St **35** G4
Barford Rd **34** A3
Barford St **35** G6
Barn St **35** H5
Barrack St **35** J3
Barrow Wk **35** F7
Barr St **34** D1
Bartholomew Row **35** G4
Bartholomew St **35** G4
Barwick St **35** F4
Bath Pas **35** F5
Bath Row **34** D6
Bath St **35** F3
Beak St **35** F5
Beaufort Gdns **34** A1
Beaufort Rd **34** B6
Bedford Rd **35** J6
Beeches, The **34** D7
Belgrave Middleway **35** F7
Bell Barn Rd **34** D6
Bellcroft **34** C5
Bellevue **35** F7
Bellis St **34** A6
Belmont Pas **35** J4
Belmont Row **35** H3
Benacre Dr **35** H4
Bennett's Hill **35** F4
Benson Rd **34** A1
Berkley St **34** D5
Berrington Wk **35** G7
Birchall St **35** G6
Bishopsgate St **34** D5
Bishop St **35** G7
Bissell St **35** G7
Blews St **35** G2
Bloomsbury St **35** J2
Blucher St **35** E5
Blyton Cl **34** A3
Boar Hound Cl **34** C3
Bodmin Gro **35** J1
Bolton St **35** J5
Bond Sq **34** C3
Bond St **35** E3
Bordesley **35** J5
Bordesley Circ **35** J6
Bordesley Middleway **35** J7
Bordesley Pk Rd **35** J6
Bordesley St **35** G4
Boulton Middleway **34** D1
Bow St **35** F6
Bowyer St **35** J6
Bracebridge St **35** G1
Bradburn Way **35** J2
Bradford St **35** G5
Branston St **34** D2
Brearley Cl **35** F2
Brearley St **35** F2
Bredon Cft **34** B1
Brewery St **35** G2
Bridge St **34** E5
Bridge St W **35** E1
Brindley Dr **34** D4
Brindley Pl **34** D5
Bristol St **35** F7
Broad St **34** D6
Broadway Plaza **34** C6
Bromley St **35** H5
Bromsgrove St **35** F6
Brookfield Rd **34** B2
Brook St **34** E3
Brook Vw Cl **34** E1
Broom St **35** H6
Brough Cl **35** J1
Browning St **34** C5
Brownsea Dr **35** E5
Brunel St **35** E5
Brunswick St **34** D5
Buckingham St **35** E2
Bullock St **35** H2
Bull St **35** F4

C
Cala Dr **34** C7
Calthorpe Rd **34** C7
Cambridge Rd **34** D4
Camden Dr **34** D3
Camden Gro **34** D3
Camden St **34** B2
Camp Hill **35** J7
Camp Hill Middleway **35** H7
Cannon St **35** F4
Capstone Av **34** C2
Cardigan St **35** H3
Carlisle St **34** A2
Carlyle Rd **34** A5
Caroline St **34** E3
Carpenter Rd **34** C7
Carrs La **35** G4
Carver St **34** C3
Cawdor Cres **34** B6
Cecil St **35** F2
Cemetery La **34** D2
Centenary Sq **34** E4
Central Pk Dr **34** A1
Central Sq **34** E5
Chad Rd **34** A7
Chadsmoor Ter **35** J1
Chad Valley **34** A7
Chamberlain Sq **35** E4
Chancellor's Cl **34** A7
Chandlers Cl **34** B1
Chapel Ho St **35** H5
Chapmans Pas **35** E5
Charles Henry St **35** G7
Charlotte Rd **34** D7
Charlotte St **34** E4
Chatsworth Way **34** E6
Cheapside **35** G6
Cherry St **35** F4
Chester St **35** H1
Chilwell Cft **35** F1
Christchurch Cl **34** A6
Church Rd **34** C7
Church St **35** F3
Civic Cl **34** D4
Clare Dr **34** A7
Clarendon Rd **34** A5
Clark St **34** A5
Claybrook St **35** F6
Clement St **34** D4
Clipper Vw **34** A5
Clissold Cl **35** G7
Clissold St **34** B2
Cliveland St **35** F3
Clyde St **35** H6
Colbrand Gro **35** E7
Coleshill St **35** G4
College St **34** B3
Colmore Circ **35** F3
Colmore Row **35** F4
Commercial St **34** E5
Communication Row **34** D6
Constitution Hill **34** E2
Conybere St **35** G7
Cope St **34** B3
Coplow St **34** A3
Cornwall St **35** E4
Corporation St **35** F4
Coveley Gro **34** B1
Coventry Rd **35** J6
Coventry St **35** G5
Cox St **35** E3
Coxwell Gdns **34** B5
Crabtree Rd **34** B2
Cregoe St **34** E6
Crescent, The **34** C1
Crescent Av **34** C1
Cromwell St **35** J1
Crondal Pl **34** D7
Crosby Cl **34** C4
Cumberland St **34** D5
Curzon Circ **35** H3
Curzon St **35** H4

D
Daisy Rd **34** A5
Dale End **35** G4
Daley Cl **34** C4
Dalton St **35** G4
Darnley Rd **34** B5
Dartmouth Circ **35** G1
Dartmouth Middleway **35** G2
Dart St **35** J6
Darwin St **35** G6
Dean St **35** G5
Deeley Cl **34** D7
Denby Cl **35** J2
Derby St **35** J4
Devonshire Av **34** B1
Devonshire St **34** B1
Digbeth **35** G6
Digbeth **35** G5
Dollman St **35** J3
Dover St **34** B1
Duchess Rd **34** B6
Duddeston Manor Rd **35** J2
Dudley St **35** F5
Dymoke Cl **35** G7

E
Edgbaston **34** B7
Edgbaston St **35** F5
Edmund St **35** E4
Edward St **34** D4
Eldon Rd **34** A5
Elkington St **35** G1
Ellen St **34** C3
Ellis St **35** E5
Elvetham Rd **34** D7
Embassy Dr **34** C6
Emily Gdns **34** A3
Emily St **35** G7
Enfield Rd **34** D6
Enterprise Way **35** G2
Ernest St **35** E6
Erskine St **35** J3
Essex St **35** F6
Essington St **34** D5
Estria Rd **34** C7
Ethel St **35** F4
Exeter Pas **35** F6
Exeter St **35** F6
Eyre St **34** B3
Eyton Cft **35** H7

F
Farmacre **35** J5
Farm Cft **34** D1
Farm St **34** D1
Fawdry St **35** J4
Fazeley St **35** G4
Felsted Way **35** J3
Ferndale Cres **35** H7
Finstall Cl **35** J3
Five Ways **34** C6
Fleet St **34** E4
Floodgate St **35** H5
Florence St **35** E6
Ford St **34** C1
Fore St **35** F4
Forster St **35** H3
Foster Gdns **34** B1
Fox St **35** G4
Francis Rd **34** B5
Francis St **35** J3
Frankfort St **35** F1
Frederick Rd **34** C7
Frederick St **34** D3
Freeman St **35** G4
Freeth St **34** B4
Friston Av **34** C6
Fulmer Wk **34** C4

G
Garrison Circ **35** J4
Garrison La **35** J4
Garrison St **35** J4
Gas St **34** D5
Gas St Basin **34** E5
Geach St **35** F1
Gee St **35** F1
George Rd **34** D7
George St **34** D4
George St W **34** C3
Gibb St **35** H5
Gilby Rd **34** C5
Gilldown Pl **34** D7
Glebeland Cl **34** C5
Gloucester St **35** F5
Glover St **35** J5
Gooch St **35** F7
Gooch St N **35** F6
Goode Av **34** C1
Goodman St **34** C4
Gopsal St **35** H3
Gough St **35** E5
Grafton Rd **35** J7
Graham St **34** D3
Grant St **35** E6
Granville St **34** D5
Graston Cl **34** C5
Great Barr St **35** H5
Great Brook St **35** H3
Great Charles St Queensway **35** E4
Great Colmore St **34** E6
Great Hampton Row **34** E2
Great Hampton St **34** D2
Great King St **34** D1
Great King St N **34** E1
Great Lister St **35** H2
Great Tindal St **34** C4
Greenfield Cres **34** C6
Green St **35** H6
Grenfell Dr **34** A7
Grosvenor St **35** G4
Grosvenor St W **34** C5
Guest Gro **34** D1
Guild Cl **34** B5
Guild Cft **35** F1
Guthrie Cl **35** E1

H
Hack St **35** H5
Hadfield Cft **34** E2
Hagley Rd **34** A6
Hall St **34** E3
Hampshire Dr **34** A7
Hampton St **35** E2
Hanley St **35** F2
Hanwood Cl **35** G7
Harborne Rd **34** A7
Harford St **34** E2
Harmer St **34** C2
Harold Rd **34** A5
Hartley Pl **34** A6
Hatchett St **35** F1
Hawthorn Cl **35** J5
Hawthorne Rd **34** A7
Heath Mill La **35** H5
Heath St S **34** B3
Heaton Dr **34** A7
Heaton St **34** D1
Helena St **34** D4
Heneage St **35** H2
Heneage St W **35** H3
Henley St **35** J7
Henrietta St **35** F3
Henstead St **35** F6
Herne Cl **34** C3
Hickman Gdns **34** B5
Highfield Rd **34** B6
Highgate **35** H7
Highgate St **35** G7
High St **35** G4
Hilden Rd **35** J3
Hill St **35** E4
Hinckley St **35** F5
Hindlow Cl **35** J3
Hindon Sq **34** B7
Hingeston St **34** C2
Hitches La **34** D7
Hobart Cft **35** J2
Hobson Cl **34** B1
Hockley Brook Cl **34** B1
Hockley Cl **35** F1
Hockley Hill **34** D1
Hockley St **34** D2
Holland St **34** D4
Holliday Pas **34** E5
Holliday St **34** E5
Holloway Circ **35** F5
Holloway Head **35** E6
Holt St **35** G2
Holywell Cl **34** B5
Hooper St **34** B3
Hope St **35** F7
Hospital St **35** F1
Howard St **35** E2
Howe St **35** H3
Howford Gro **35** J2
Hubert St **35** H1
Hunter's Vale **34** D1
Huntly Rd **34** B6
Hurdlow Av **34** C2
Hurst St **35** F5
Hylton St **34** D2
Hyssop Cl **35** J2

I
Icknield Port Rd **34** A3
Icknield Sq **34** B4
Icknield St **34** C3
Inge St **35** F6
Inkerman St **35** J3
Irving St **35** E6
Islington Row Middleway **34** C6
Ivy La **35** J4

J
Jackson Cl **35** J7
James St **34** E3
James Watt Queensway **35** G3
Jennens Rd **35** G4
Jewellery Quarter **34** D2
Jinnah Cl **35** G7
John Bright St **35** F5
John Kempe Way **35** H7

K
Keeley St **35** J5
Keepers Cl **34** B1
Kellett Rd **35** H2
Kelsall Cft **34** C4
Kelsey Cl **35** J2
Kemble Cft **35** F7
Kendal Rd **35** J7
Kenilworth Ct **34** A6
Kent St **35** F6
Kent St N **34** B1
Kenyon St **34** E3
Ketley Cft **35** G7
Key Hill **34** D2
Key Hill Dr **34** D2
Kilby Av **34** C4
King Edwards Rd **34** D4
Kingston Rd **35** J5
Kingston Row **34** D4
Kirby Rd **34** A1
Knightstone Av **34** C2
Kyotts Lake Rd **35** J7

L
Ladycroft **34** C5
Ladywell Wk **35** F5
Ladywood **34** C4
Ladywood Middleway **34** B5
Ladywood Rd **34** B5
Lancaster Circ **35** G3
Landor St **35** J4
Langdon St **35** J4
Lansdowne St **34** A2
Latimer Gdns **35** E7
Lawden Rd **35** J6
Lawford Cl **35** J3
Lawford Gro **35** G7
Lawley Middleway **35** H3
Ledbury Cl **34** B5
Ledsam St **34** C4
Lee Bk **35** E7
Lee Bk Middleway **34** D6
Lee Cres **34** D7
Lee Mt **34** D7
Lees St **34** B1
Legge La **34** D3
Legge St **35** G2
Lennox St **35** E1
Leopold St **35** G7
Leslie Rd **34** A5
Leyburn Rd **34** C5
Lighthorne Av **34** C4
Link Rd **34** A3
Lionel St **34** E4
Lister St **35** G3
Little Ann St **35** H5
Little Barr St **35** J4
Little Broom St **35** H6
Little Edward St **35** J5
Little Francis Grn **35** J2
Little Shadwell St **35** F3
Liverpool St **35** H5
Livery St **35** F3
Locke Pl **35** J4
Lodge Rd **34** A1
Lombard St **35** G6
Longleat Way **34** D6
Lord St **35** H2
Louisa St **34** D4
Loveday St **35** F3
Love La **35** G2
Lower Dartmouth St **35** J4
Lower Essex St **35** F6
Lower Loveday St **35** F2
Lower Severn St **35** F5
Lower Temple St **35** F4

Street	Grid	Street	Grid	Street	Grid	Street	Grid	Street	Grid	Street	Grid
Lower Twr St	35 F2	New Canal St	35 G4	Pinfold St	35 E4	St. Lukes Rd	35 F7	Stoke Way	34 D5	Vittoria St	34 D3
Lower Trinity St	35 H5	Newhall Hill	34 D3	Pinto Cl	34 B5	St. Marks Cres	34 C4	Stone Rd	35 E7	Vyse St	34 D3
Lowe St	35 J6	Newhall St	34 E3	Pitsford St	34 C2	St. Marks St	34 C3	Stone Yd	35 H5		
Ludgate Hill	35 E3	Newhope Cl	35 F7	Pitt St	35 H3	St. Martin's Circ		Stour St	34 B3	**W**	
Lytham Cft	35 E6	New John St	35 G2	Plough & Harrow Rd	34 B6	Queensway	35 F5	Stratford Pl	35 H7	Walter St	35 J1
		New John St W	34 E1	Pool St	35 G1	St. Martin's Sq	35 G5	Stratford Rd	35 J7	Wardlow Rd	35 J2
M		New Mkt St	35 E4	Pope St	34 C3	St. Martin's St	34 D6	Stratford St N	35 J7	Ward St	35 F2
Macdonald St	35 G6	New Moseley Rd	35 H7	Port Hope Rd	35 J7	St. Mary's Row	35 F3	Suffolk St		Warner St	35 H6
Malcolmson Cl	34 A7	New Spring St	34 C2	Powell St	34 D3	St. Paul's Sq	34 E3	Queensway	35 E5	Warstone La	34 C3
Manchester St	35 F2	New Spring St N	34 B2	Power Cres	34 C5	St. Phillips Pl	35 F4	Sugden Gro	35 F6	Warstone Par E	34 D2
Margaret St	35 E4	New St	35 F4	Price St	35 F3	St. Stephen's St	35 F1	Summer Cft	35 F1	Warwick Pas	35 F4
Mariner Av	34 A5	New Summer St	35 F2	Princip St	35 F3	St. Vincent St	34 C4	Summerfield Rd	34 A3	Warwick St	35 H6
Marroway St	34 A3	Newton St	35 G4	Printing Ho St	35 F3	St. Vincent St W	34 B5	Summer Hill Rd	34 C3	Washington St	34 E5
Marshall St	35 E5		34 E1	Priory		Salop St	35 H7	Summer Hill St	34 D4	Waterloo St	35 E4
Mary Ann St	35 E3	**Newtown**		Queensway, The	35 G4	Sampson Rd	35 J7	Summer Hill Ter	34 D3	Waterside Dr	34 A1
Mary St	34 E3	Newtown Dr	34 D1	Pritchett St	35 F2	Sampson Rd N	35 J6	Summer La	35 F3	Waterside Vw	34 B2
Mason Way	34 E6	Newtown Middleway	35 F1	Proctor St	35 H2	Sand Pits	34 C3	Summer Rd	34 E7	Water St	35 E3
Masshouse La	35 G4	New Town Row	35 F1			Sandy Way	34 D5	Summer Row	34 E4	Waterworks Rd	34 A5
Mearse Cl	34 C2	Niall Cl	34 A7	**Q**		Scotland St	34 D4	Sutton St	35 E6	Watery La Middleway	35 J4
Melton Dr	34 D7	Noel Rd	34 A5	Quayside	34 B1	Sefton Rd	34 A5	Swallow St	35 E5	Weaman St	35 F3
Meredith Pool Cl	34 A1	Norman St	34 A2	Queens Hosp Cl	34 D6	Severn St	35 E5			Well La	35 G5
Meriden St	35 G5	Northampton St	34 D2	Quigley Av	35 J5	Shadwell St	35 F3	**T**		Well St	35 D2
Merryhill Dr	34 A1	Northbrook St	34 A3			Shawbury Gro	35 H7	Talbot St	34 A1	Westbourne Cres	34 C7
Meyrick Wk	34 A6	Northumberland St	35 J3	**R**		Shaw's Pas	35 G4	Temple Pas	35 F4	Westbourne Gdns	34 B7
Middleway Vw	34 C3	Northwood St	34 D3	Radnor St	34 B1	Sheepcote St	34 C4	Temple Row	35 F4	Westbourne Rd	34 A7
Midford Grn	34 E6	Norton St	34 B1	Radshaw Cl	34 D6	Shefford Rd	35 G1	Temple Row W	35 F4	Western Rd	34 B3
Milford Cft	35 E2	Nova Scotia St	35 G4	Rake Way	34 D5	Shepherds Gdns	34 D6	Temple St	35 F4	West Grn Cl	34 D7
Milk St	35 H5	Nursery Rd	34 D1	Rann Cl	34 C5	Sherborne Gro	34 C4	Tenby St	34 D3	Westhorpe Gro	34 E1
Miller St	35 F1			Ravenhurst St	35 H6	Sherborne St	34 C5	Tenby St N	34 D3	Westley St	35 J5
Mill La	35 G5	**O**		Rawlins St	34 C5	Sheringham	34 A6	Tennant St	34 D6	Wharf, The	34 E5
Mill St	35 G2	Oak Hill Dr	34 A7	Rea St	35 G6	Sherlock St	35 F7	Theatre App	35 F5	Wharf La	34 C1
Milton St	35 F1	Old Br St	34 D1	Rea St S	35 G6	Shetland Cl	34 B5	Theresa Rd	35 J7	Wharfside St	35 E5
Moat La	35 G5	Old Camp Hill	35 J6	Rea Ter	35 H5	Shillcock Gro	35 F2	Thomas St	35 G1	Wharf St	34 B1
Moland St	35 G2	Old Smithy Pl	34 C1	Rectory Gro	34 A1	Shire Cl	34 A4	Thorp St	35 F6	Wheeler St	35 E1
Montague St	35 J4	Old Snow Hill	35 F3	Regent Par	34 D3	Shyltons Cft	34 C5	Tower St	35 F2	Wheeley's La	34 D6
Monument Rd	34 B6	Old Sq	35 F4	Regent Pl	34 D3	Skinner La	35 G6	Townsend Way	34 D4	Whitehouse St	35 H1
Moore's Row	35 H5	Oliver Rd	34 B5	Regent St	34 D3	Skipton Rd	34 B5	Trent St	35 H5	Whitmore St	34 C1
Moorings, The	34 B1	Oliver St	35 J1	Reservoir Retreat	34 B5	Sloane St	35 D4	Trinity Ter	35 J6	Whittall St	35 F3
Moorsom St	35 F1	Oozells St	34 D5	Reservoir Rd	34 A5	Smallbrook				Wiggin St	34 A4
Moor St Queensway	35 G4	Orchid Dr	35 E1	Richard St	35 H2	Queensway	35 F5	**U**		William Booth La	35 F3
Moreton St	34 C3	Orwell Pas	35 G5	Rickman Dr	35 E7	Smith St	35 F1	Unett St	34 E1	William Henry St	35 J1
Morville St	34 C5	Osler St	34 A5	Ridley St	34 E6	Snow Hill Queensway	35 F3	Union Pas	35 F4	William St	34 D6
Mosborough Cres	34 E1	Oxford St	35 G5	River St	35 H5	Soho Pool Way	34 B1	Union St	35 F4	William St N	35 F2
Mosedale Way	35 E6			Rocky La	35 J1	Southacre Av	35 F7	Upper Dean St	35 F5	Willow Gdns	34 A3
Moseley Rd	35 H6	**P**		Rodney Cl	34 B4	South Rd	35 J7	Upper Gough St	35 E6	Windmill St	35 F6
Moseley St	35 G6	Paddocks Grn	34 B2	Rosebery St	34 B2	Spencer St	34 D2	Upper Marshall St	35 E5	Windrush Way	35 E7
Moss Ho Cl	34 D6	Pakenham Rd	34 D7	Roseland Way	34 D6	Spooner Cft	35 F7	Upper Trinity St	35 H5	Windsor St	35 H2
Mostyn Rd	34 A5	Palmer St	35 J5	Rotton Pk St	34 B4	Springbank Rd	34 E7	Uxbridge St	35 E1	Windsor St S	35 H3
Mott St	34 E2	Palomino Pl	34 B4	Rupert St	35 H2	Springfield St	34 B4			**Winson Grn**	34 A1
Mowbray St	35 F7	Pannel Cft	35 F1	Ruston St	34 C5	Spring Gro Gdns	34 A1	**V**		Witton St	35 J4
Murrell Cl	35 F7	Parade	34 D4	Ryland Rd	34 D7	Spring Hill	34 B3	Vaughton St	35 G7	Woodcock St	35 G3
Musgrave Rd	34 A1	Paradise Circ	34 E4	Ryland St	34 C5	Spring Hill Pas	34 C3	Vaughton St S	35 G7	Woodcote Way	34 B2
Myddleton St	34 B3	Paradise St	35 E4			Spring St	35 E7	Vauxhall Gro	35 J3	Woodview Dr	34 E7
		Parker St	34 A6	**S**		Stainsby Av	34 D1	Vauxhall Rd	35 J3	Wrentham St	35 F6
N		Parkfield Cl	34 D7	Sadlers Wk	34 B5	Stanhope Rd	35 G7	Venture Way	35 H2	Wrottesley St	35 F5
Navigation St	35 E5	Park Rd	34 C1	St. Andrew's Rd	35 J4	Staniforth St	35 G2	Verbena Gdns	35 J2	Wyndham Rd	34 A6
Navigation Way	34 B1	Park Rd S	34 C1	St. Chad's Queensway	35 F3	Star Hill	34 D7	Vere St	35 F7	Wynn St	35 E6
Nechells Parkway	35 H3	Park St	35 G5	St. Georges Cl	34 B7	Station St	35 F5	Vernolds Cft	35 F6		
Needless All	35 F4	Paxton Rd	34 C2	St. Georges St	35 E2	Steelhouse La	35 F3	Vesey St	35 F3	**Y**	
Nelson St	34 D4	Peel St	34 A2	St. Helen's Pas	34 D3	Stephenson Pl	35 F5	Viaduct St	35 J4	Yew Tree Rd	34 D6
New Bartholomew St	35 G4	Pemberton St	34 D2	St. James Pl	35 J3	Stephenson St	35 F4	Vicarage Rd	34 E4		
Newbold Cft	35 J1	Penn St	35 H3	St. James Rd	34 C6	Steward St	34 B3	Victoria Sq	34 B6		
New Bond St	35 J5	Pershore St	35 F5	St. Jude's Pas	35 F5	Stirling Rd	34 A6	Victor Rd	34 A1		
		Pickford St	35 H5								

Edinburgh street index

Street	Grid	Street	Grid	Street	Grid	Street	Grid	Street	Grid	Street	Grid
A		Archibald Pl	37 F6	Belgrave Cres La	36 C3	Brandon Ter	37 E2	Buckingham Ter	36 C3	Castle Ter	36 E4
Abbeyhill	37 J3	Arden St	37 F7	Belgrave Ms	36 C3	Bread St	36 E5			Cathcart Pl	36 B6
Abbeyhill	37 J3	Ardmillan Pl	36 B7	Belgrave Pl	36 C3	Bridge Pl	36 D2	**C**		Cathedral La	37 G3
Abbeyhill Cres	37 H4	Ardmillan Ter	36 B7	Bellevue	37 F2	Briery Bauks	37 H5	Caledonian Cres	36 C6	Causewayside	37 H7
Abbey La	37 J3	Argyle Pk Ter	37 F7	Bellevue Cres	37 F2	Brighton St	37 G5	Caledonian Pl	36 C6	Chalmers Cres	37 F7
Abbeymount	37 J3	Argyle Pl	37 F7	Bellevue Gdns	37 G1	Bristo Pl	37 F5	Caledonian Rd	36 C6	Chalmers St	37 F5
Abbey Strand	37 J4	Arthur St	37 H1	Bellevue Gro	37 G2	Bristo Port	37 F5	Calton Hill	37 G3	Chambers St	37 F5
Abbey St	37 J3	Arthur St La	37 H1	Bellevue La	37 F2	Brougham Pl	37 E6	Calton Rd	37 G3	Chapel St	37 G5
Abercromby Pl	37 F3	Atholl Cres	36 D5	Bellevue Pl	37 F2	Brougham St	36 E6	Cambridge Av	37 H1	Charles St	37 G5
Admiral Ter	36 D7	Atholl Cres La	36 D5	Bellevue Rd	37 G2	**Broughton**	37 F1	Cambridge Gdns	37 H1	Charlotte La	36 D4
Ainslie Pl	36 D3	Avondale Pl	36 D1	Bellevue St	37 G2	Broughton Mkt	37 F3	Cambridge St	36 E5	Charlotte Sq	36 D4
Albany La	37 F2			Bellevue Ter	37 F2	Broughton Pl	37 G2	Campbell's Cl	37 H4	Chester St	36 C4
Albany St	37 F3	**B**		Bell Pl	36 E1	Broughton Pl La	37 G2	Candlemaker Row	37 F5	Cheyne St	36 D2
Albany St La	37 F3	Back Dean	36 B4	Bells Brae	36 C4	Broughton Rd	37 F1	Canning St	36 D5	Chuckie Pend	36 D5
Albert St	37 H1	Bakehouse Cl	37 H4	Bell's Mills	36 B4	Broughton St	37 G2	Canning St La	36 D5	Circus Gdns	36 E3
Albion Gdns	37 J2	Balbirnie Pl	36 A5	Bernard Ter	37 H6	Broughton St La	37 G3	Canongate	37 G4	Circus La	36 E3
Albion Pl	37 J2	Balmoral Pl	36 D1	Blacket Av	37 H7	Brown's Cl	37 H4	Canon La	37 E2	Circus Pl	36 E3
Albion Rd	37 J2	Bank St	37 F4	Blacket Pl	37 H7	Brown St	37 H5	Canonmills	37 E1	Claremont Bk	37 F2
Albion Ter	37 J2	Barclay Pl	36 E7	Blackfriars St	37 G4	Brunswick Rd	37 H2	Canon St	37 E1	Claremont Cres	37 F1
Alfred Pl	37 J7	Barony Pl	37 F2	Blackwood Cres	37 H7	Brunswick St	37 H2	Carberry Pl	36 B5	Claremont Gro	37 F1
Allanfield	37 H2	Beaverbank Pl	37 F1	Blair St	37 G4	Brunswick St La	37 H2	Carlton St	36 D3	Clarence St	36 E2
Allanfield Pl	37 H2	Beaverhall Rd	37 F1	Blandfield	37 G1	Brunton Ter	37 J3	Carlton Ter	37 H3	Clarendon Cres	36 C3
Allan St	36 D2	Bedford St	36 D2	Boat Grn	37 F1	Bruntsfield Av	36 D7	Carlton Ter Brae	37 J3	Clerk St	37 G6
Alva Pl	37 J3	Belford Av	36 A3	Boroughloch	37 G6	Bruntsfield Cres	36 E7	Carlton Ter La	37 H3	**Coates**	36 B5
Alva St	36 D4	Belford Br	36 C4	Boroughloch Sq	37 G6	Bruntsfield Gdns	36 D7	Carlton Ter Ms	37 H3	Coates Cres	36 D5
Angle Pk Ter	36 B7	Belford Gdns	36 A3	Borthwick Pl	36 B5	Bruntsfield Ter	36 D7	Carlton Wynd	37 H4	Coates Gdns	36 C5
Annandale St	37 G1	Belford Ms	36 C4	Bothwell St	37 J2	Bryson Rd	36 B7	Carlyle Pl	37 J3	Cochran Ter	37 G2
Annandale St La	37 G2	Belford Pk	36 B4	Bowmont Pl	37 H6	Buccleuch Pl	37 G6	Carnegie St	37 H5	Cockburn St	37 F4
Ann St	36 D3	Belford Pl	36 B4	Boyd's Entry	37 G4	Buccleuch St	37 G6	Carrington Rd	36 B2	Coffin La	36 B6
Arboretum Av	36 D2	Belford Rd	36 B4	Brandfield St	36 D6	Buccleuch Ter	37 G6	Castle Hill	37 F4	Collins Pl	36 D2
Arboretum Pl	36 D1	Belgrave Cres	36 C3	Brandon St	37 E2	Buchanan St	37 H1	Castle St	36 E4	Coltbridge Av	36 A5

St. James Pl	37 G3	Silvermills	36 E2
St. James Sq	37 G3	Simon Sq	37 G5
St. John's Hill	37 H5	Simpson Loan	37 F6
St. John St	37 H4	Sinclair Cl	36 A7
St. Leonard's Bk	37 H6	Sinclair Gdns	36 A7
St. Leonard's Hill	37 H6	Sinclair Pl	36 A7
St. Leonard's La	37 H6	Sloan St	37 J1
St. Leonard's St	37 H6	Smithfield St	36 A7
St. Mary's St	37 G4	South Br	37 G4
St. Patrick Sq	37 G6	South Charlotte St	36 E4
St. Stephen Pl	36 D2	South Clerk St	37 H6
St. Stephen St	36 D3	South Coll St	37 G5
St. Vincent St	36 E2	South E Circ Pl	36 E3
Salisbury Ms	37 H7	South Gray's Cl	37 G4
Salisbury Pl	37 H7	South Learmonth Av	36 C3
Salisbury Rd	37 H7	South Learmonth Gdns	36 C3
Saunders St	36 D3	South Lorne Pl	37 J1
Saxe Coburg Pl	36 D2	South Oxford St	37 H7
Saxe Coburg St	36 D2	South St. Andrew St	37 F3
Sciennes	37 G7	South St. David St	37 F3
Sciennes Gdns	37 G7	South Sloan St	37 J1
Sciennes Hill Pl	37 G7	Spence St	37 J7
Sciennes Ho Pl	37 G7	Spey St	37 H1
Sciennes Pl	37 G7	Spey St La	37 H1
Sciennes Rd	37 F7	Spey Ter	37 H1
Scotland St	37 F2	Spittal St	36 E5
Semple St	36 D5	Spottiswoode Rd	37 E7
Seton Pl	37 G7	Spottiswoode St	37 F7
Shandwick Pl	36 D5	Spring Gdns	37 J3
Shaw's Pl	37 H1	Springwell Pl	36 B6
Shaw's St	37 H1	Stafford St	36 D4
Shaw's Ter	37 H1	Stanhope Pl	36 B5
Shrub Pl La	37 H1	Stanhope St	36 B5
Sienna Gdns	37 G7		

Stevenlaw's Cl	37 G4	Tytler Gdns	37 J3
Stewart Ter	36 A7	**U**	
Stockbridge	36 E2	Union St	37 G2
Succoth Gdns	36 A4	Upper Bow	37 F4
Succoth Pl	36 A4	Upper Coltbridge Ter	36 A4
Summer Bk	37 F2	Upper Damside	36 C4
Summerhall	37 G6	Upper Dean Ter	36 D3
Summerhall Sq	37 H7	Upper Gilmore Pl	36 D6
Sunbury Ms	36 C4	Upper Gilmore Ter	36 D6
Sunbury Pl	36 C4	Upper Gray St	37 H7
Sunbury St	36 C4	Upper Gro Pl	36 D6
Sunnyside	37 J2	**V**	
Sutherland St	36 B5	Valleyfield St	36 E6
Sylvan Pl	37 G7	Veitch's Sq	36 D2
T		Victoria St	37 F5
Tantallon Pl	37 G7	Viewcraig Gdns	37 H4
Tarvit St	36 E6	Viewcraig St	37 H5
Tay St	36 C7	Viewforth	36 C6
Temple Pk Cres	36 C7	Viewforth Gdns	36 D7
Terrars Cft	37 H6	Viewforth Sq	36 D7
Teviotdale Pl	36 D1	Viewforth Ter	36 D7
Teviot Pl	37 F5	**W**	
Thirlestane Rd	37 E7	Walker St	36 C4
Thistle Pl	36 C7	Wardlaw Pl	36 A7
Thistle St	37 E3	Wardlaw St	36 A7
Thistle St N E La	37 F3	Warrender Pk Cres	36 E7
Thistle St N W La	37 E3	Warrender Pk Rd	36 E7
Thistle St S W La	37 E3	Warrender Pk Ter	37 E7
Thornybauk	36 E6	Warriston Cres	37 E1
Torphichen St	36 D5	Warriston Rd	37 E1
Tron Sq	37 G4	Washington La	36 B6
Tynecastle La	36 B7		
Tynecastle Ter	36 A7		

Waterloo Pl	37 G3	West Port	37 E5
Watson Cres	36 B7	West Preston St	37 H7
Waverley Br	37 F4	West Register St	37 F3
Waverley Pk	37 J3	West Register St La	37 F3
Waverley Pk Ter	37 J3	West Richmond St	37 G5
Waverley Pl	37 J3	West Scotland St La	37 F2
Wellington St	37 H2	West Silvermills La	36 E2
Wemyss Pl	36 E3	West Tollcross	36 E6
Wemyss Pl Ms	36 D3	West Wds	36 A1
West Adam St	37 G5	Wheatfield Pl	36 A7
West Annandale St	37 F1	Wheatfield Rd	36 A7
West App Rd	36 D5	Wheatfield St	36 A7
West Bow	37 F5	Wheatfield Ter	36 A7
West Bryson Rd	36 B7	Whitehouse Ln	36 E7
West Castle Rd	36 C7	White Pk	36 A7
West Catherine Pl	36 B5	William St	36 C5
West Coates	36 A5	William St N E La	36 D4
West Coll St	37 G5	William St N W La	36 D4
West Crosscauseway	37 G6	William St S E La	36 D4
West End Pl	36 C6	William St S W La	36 D5
Wester Coates Av	36 A5	Windmill La	37 G6
Wester Coates Gdns	36 A5	Windmill St	37 G6
Wester Coates Pl	36 B5	Windsor St	37 H2
Wester Coates Rd	36 B5	Windsor St La	37 H2
Wester Coates Ter	36 A5	**Y**	
Westfield St	36 A7	Yeaman Pl	36 C6
Westhall Gdns	36 D7	York La	37 G3
West Maitland St	36 C5	York Pl	37 F3
West Mill La	36 C4	Young St	36 D4
West Montgomery Pl	37 H2	Young St La N	36 E4
West Newington Pl	37 H7	Young St La S	36 E4
West Nicolson St	37 G5		
West Norton Pl	37 J3		
West Pk Pl	36 C6		

Glasgow street index

A

Abbotsford Pl	39 E7	Binnie Pl	39 H6
Abercromby Dr	39 J5	Bishop St	38 D4
Abercromby Sq	39 J5	Blackburn St	38 B5
Abercromby St	39 J6	Blackfriars St	39 G4
Academy Pk	38 A7	Blackie St	38 B3
Adams Ct La	39 F5	Black St	39 H2
Adelphi St	39 F6	Blantyre St	38 A2
Admiral St	38 C6	**Blythswoodhill**	
Aird's La	39 G5	Blythswood Sq	38 E3
Albert Br	39 G6	Blythswood St	38 E4
Albert Dr	38 B7	Bothwell La	38 E4
Albion Gate	39 G4	Bothwell La (Hillhead)	38 C1
Albion St	39 G5	Bothwell St	38 E4
Alexander Cres	39 F7	Braid Sq	38 E1
Alexandra Par	39 J3	Braid St	38 E1
Allen Glen Pl	39 G3	Breadalbane St	38 C3
Anchor La	39 F4	Brechin St	38 C3
Anderston	38 E4	Bridgegate	39 F5
Anderston Quay	38 C5	Bridge St	39 E6
Anson St	39 J7	Bridgeton Cross	39 J6
Anthony St	38 D4	Bright St	39 J2
Arcadia Pl	39 J6	Broadford St	39 G1
Arcadia St	39 J6	Broomielaw	38 E5
Argyle St	39 F4	Broompark Dr	39 J4
Argyll Arc	39 F4	Brown St	38 E5
Ark La	39 J4	Bruce Rd	38 B7
Arlington St	38 D2	Brunswick St	39 G4
Armour St	39 J5	Buccleuch La	38 E2
Arthur St	38 A2	Buccleuch St	38 D2
Ashley La	38 D2	Buchanan St	39 F4
Ashley St	38 D2	Bunhouse Rd	38 A2
Ashton La	38 A1	Burnbank Gdns	38 D1
Ashton Rd	38 A1	Burnbank La	38 D1
Auchentoshan Ter	39 J1	Burnbank Pl	38 D1
		Burnbank Ter	38 D1
B		Burns St	39 E1
Bain St	39 H5	Bute Gdns	38 B1
Baird St	39 H2	Bute La	38 B1
Balaclava St	38 D4		
Baliol La	38 D2	**C**	
Baliol St	38 D2	Cadogan St	38 E4
Ballantrae Ct	38 D4	Cadzow St	38 D4
Ballater Pl	39 G7	Caledonian Cres	38 C1
Ballater St	39 F6	Caledonia Rd	39 F7
Bank St	38 B1	Caledon La	38 A1
Barrack St	39 J5	Caledon St	38 A1
Barrington Dr	38 C1	Calgary St	39 G2
Bath La	38 D3	Cambridge St	39 E3
Bath St	38 D3	Camden Ter	39 F7
Beaumont Gate	38 A1	Canal St	39 G2
Bedford La	39 F6	Candleriggs	39 G5
Bedford St	39 E6	Cardwell St	38 E7
Bell St	39 G4	Carfrae St	38 A3
Beltane St	38 D3	Carlton Ct	39 E5
Benny Lynch Ct	39 G6	Carlton Pl	39 F5
Benthall St	39 G7	Carnarvon St	38 D2
Bentinck St	38 B2	Carnoustie Pl	38 D6
Berkeley St	38 C3	Carnoustie St	38 D6
Berkeley Ter La	38 C3	Carrick St	38 E5
		Carrington St	38 D1

Castle St	39 H4	Cooperage Pl	38 A3
Cathcart Rd	39 F7	Corn St	39 E1
Cathedral Sq	39 H4	Cornwall St S	38 B7
Cathedral St	39 F3	Corunna St	38 B3
Cavendish Pl	39 E7	Couper Pl	39 G2
Cavendish St	39 E7	Couper St	39 G2
Cecil St	38 B1	Cowan La	38 C1
Cedar Ct	38 E1	Cowan St	38 B1
Cedar St	38 E1	**Cowcaddens**	38 E1
Centre St	38 E6	Cowcaddens Rd	39 E2
Cessnock	38 A5	Cownall St	38 B6
Chalmers St	39 J5	Cragmaddie Ter La	38 B2
Charles St	39 J2	Craighall Rd	39 F1
Charlotte St	39 H5	Craigiehall Pl	38 B5
Cheapside St	38 D5	Craigiehall St	38 B5
Chisolm St	39 G5	**Cranston Hill**	38 C3
Church St	38 A2	Cranston St	38 C4
Circus Dr	39 J4	Cressnock St	38 A5
Citizen La	39 F4	Crimea St	38 D4
Civic St	39 E2	Cromwell La	38 D1
Clairmont Gdns	38 C2	Cromwell St	38 D1
Claremont Pl	38 C2	Crownpoint Rd	39 J6
Claremont St	38 C3	Crown St	39 F7
Claremont Ter	38 C2	Cumberland Pl	39 G7
Claremont Ter La	38 C2	Cumberland St	39 E6
Clarendon Pl	38 D1		
Clarendon St	38 D1	**D**	
Clayslaps Rd	38 B2	Dale Path	39 J7
Claythorn Av	39 H6	Dalhouse St	38 E3
Claythorn Circ	39 H5	Dalhousie La	38 E2
Claythorn Pk	39 H6	Dalintober St	38 D6
Claythorn St	39 J5	Dalmarnock Rd	39 J7
Claythorn Ter	39 J5	Dalnair St	38 A2
Cleland La	39 F6	Derby St	38 B3
Cleland St	39 F6	Devon Pl	39 E7
Cleveland La	38 D3	Devon St	39 E7
Cleveland St	38 D3	Dixon St	39 F5
Clifford La	38 A6	Dobbies Ln	39 F2
Clifford Pl	38 A6	Dobbie's Ln Pl	39 G3
Clifford St	38 A6	Dornoch St	39 J6
Cliff Rd	38 C1	Dorset St	38 C3
Clifton Pl	38 C3	Douglas La	38 E3
Clifton St	38 C2	Douglas St	38 E4
Clutha St	38 A6	Dover St	38 C3
Clyde Arc	38 B5	Drake St	39 J6
Clyde Pl	38 B5	Drury St	39 F4
Clydeside Expressway	38 B4	Drygate	39 H4
Clyde St	39 F5	Duke St	39 H4
Cobden Rd	39 J1	Dunblane St	39 F2
Coburg St	39 E6	Dunchattan Pl	39 J5
Cochrane St	39 G4	Dunchattan St	39 J4
College La	39 H4	Dundashill	39 F1
College St	39 G4	Dundas La	39 F3
Collins St	39 H4	Dundas St	39 F3
Commerce St	39 E5	Dunearn St	38 D1
Commercial Ct	39 G6	Dunlop St	39 F5
Commercial Rd	39 G7	Durham St	38 B6
Congress Rd	38 B4		
Congress Way	38 B4	**E**	
Cook St	38 E6	Eaglesham Ct	38 B5

Eaglesham Pl	38 B5	Glasgow Br	39 F5
Eagle St	39 F1	Glassford St	39 G4
Earlston Av	39 J2	Glebe Ct	39 H3
Earlston Pl	39 J2	Glebe St	39 H2
East Bath La	39 F3	Glenbarr St	39 J2
East Campbell St	39 H5	Glenfarg St	38 D1
Edington St	39 E1	Glenmavis St	39 E2
Edwin St	38 B6	Gloucester St	38 D6
Eglinton Ct	39 F6	Goosedubbs	39 G5
Elcho St	39 J5	**Gorbals**	39 G7
Elderslie St	38 C2	Gorbals St	39 F7
Eldon St	38 C1	Gordon La	39 F4
Elie St	38 A1	Gordon St	39 F4
Elliot Pl	38 C4	Gourock St	38 E7
Elliot St	38 C4	Govan Rd	38 A5
Elmbank Cres	38 D3	Grace St	38 C4
Elmbank St	38 D3	Grafton Pl	39 G3
Elmbank St La	38 D3	Graham Sq	39 J5
Errol Gdns	39 F6	Graignestock St	39 J6
Esmond St	38 A2	Granby La	38 B1
Eton La	38 B1	Grant St	38 D2
Exchange Pl	39 F4	Granville St	38 D3
		Gray St	38 B3
F		Great Dovehill	39 H5
Falfield St	38 E7	Great George St	38 B1
Farnell St	39 E1	Green, The	39 J7
Finnieston	38 B3	Greendyke St	39 G5
Finnieston Quay	38 B4	Greenhead St	39 J6
Finnieston Sq	38 C3	Green St	39 J6
Finnieston St	38 C4	Grovepark Ct	38 D1
Firpark St	39 J3	Grovepark Gdns	38 D1
Firpark Ter	39 J4		
Fitzroy La	38 B3	**H**	
Florence St	39 G6	Hallside Pl	39 G7
Forbes Dr	39 J6	Handel Pl	39 F7
Forbes St	39 J5	Hanover St	39 F4
Fountainwell Av	39 H1	Harley St	38 A6
Fountainwell Dr	39 H1	Harvey St	39 F1
Fountainwell Pl	39 H1	Harvie St	38 B5
Fountainwell Rd	39 H1	Hastie St	38 A2
Fountainwell Sq	39 H1	Haugh Rd	38 A3
Fountainwell Ter	39 H1	Hayfield Ct	39 G7
Fox St	39 F5	Hayfield St	39 G7
Francis St	38 E7	Herbertson St	39 E6
		High Craighall Rd	39 F1
G		High St	39 G5
Gadshill St	39 J2	Hillhead St	38 B1
Gallowgate	39 H5	Hill St	38 D2
Garnethill	38 E2	Holland St	38 D3
Garnethill St	38 E2	Holm St	38 E4
Garnet St	38 D3	Holyrood Cres	38 C1
Garscube Rd	39 E2	Holyrood Quad	38 D1
Garth St	39 G4	Hopehill Rd	38 D1
George Sq	39 F4	Hope St	39 E4
George St	39 G4	Houldsworth La	38 C3
Gibson St	39 H5	Houldsworth St	38 C3
Gibson St (Hillhead)	38 B1	Houston Pl	38 C5
Gilbert St	38 A3	Houston St	38 C6
Gilmour Pl	39 G7	Howard St	39 F5
Gladstone St	38 D1	Hunter St	39 H5

Leeds street index

Aysgarth Dr 41 J4
Aysgarth Pl 41 J4
Aysgarth Wk 41 J4

B
Back Ashville Av 40 A1
Back Hyde Ter 40 C2
Back Row 40 E5
Balm Pl 40 C6
Balm Wk 40 C6
Bank St 41 E4
Baron Cl 40 C7
Barrack St 41 F1
Barran Ct 41 H1
Barton Gro 40 D7
Barton Mt 40 D7
Barton Pl 40 C7
Barton Rd 40 C7
Barton Ter 40 D7
Barton Vw 40 C7
Bath Rd 40 D5
Bayswater Vw 41 H1
Beamsley Gro 40 A1
Beamsley Mt 40 A1
Beamsley Pl 40 A1
Beamsley Ter 40 A1
Beckett St 41 H3
Bedford St 40 E3
Beech Gro Ter 40 D1
Belgrave St 41 E3
Belinda St 41 H7
Belle Vue Rd 40 B2
Bell St 41 G3
Belmont Gro 40 D2
Benson St 41 F1
Benyon Pk Way 40 A7
Berking Av 41 J3
Bertrand St 40 C6
Bexley Av 41 H1
Bexley Gro 41 J1
Bexley Mt 41 H1
Bexley Pl 41 H1
Bexley Rd 41 J1
Bexley Ter 41 J1
Bingley St 40 C3
Bishopgate St 40 E4
Bismarck Dr 40 E7
Bismarck St 40 E7
Black Bull St 41 F5
Blackman La 40 E1
Blandford Gdns 40 D1
Blandford Gro 40 D1
Blayds St 41 H4
Blayd's Yd 41 E4
Blenheim Av 40 E1
Blenheim Ct 40 E1
Blenheim Cres 40 E1
Blenheim Gro 40 E1
Blenheim Sq 40 E1
Blenheim Vw 40 D1
Blenheim Wk 40 D1
Blundell St 40 D2
Boar La 40 E4
Bodley Ter 40 A2
Bond St 40 E3
Boundary Pl 41 G1
Boundary St 41 G1
Bourse, The 41 E4
Bowling Grn Ter 40 D6
Bowman La 41 F4
Bow St 41 G4
Bracken Ct 40 A6
Braithwaite St 40 C5
Brancepeth Pl 40 B4
Brandon Rd 40 C2
Brandon St 40 B4
Branksome Pl 40 B1
Brick St 41 G4
Bridge Ct 40 C5
Bridge End 41 E4
Bridge Rd 40 C5
Bridge St 41 F3
Bridgewater Rd 41 H6
Briggate 41 E4
Brignall Garth 41 J2
Brignall Way 41 H2
Bristol St 41 G2
Britannia St 40 D4
Broadway Av 40 A1
Brookfield St 41 G6
Brown Av 40 B7
Brown La E 40 B6
Brown La W 40 A6
Brown Pl 40 B7
Brown Rd 40 B7
Bruce Gdns 40 B4
Bruce Lawn 40 B4
Brunswick Ct 41 F3
Brunswick Ter 41 E2
Brussels St 41 G4
Buckton Cl 40 C7
Buckton Mt 40 C7
Buckton Vw 40 C7
Burley 40 A1

Burley Lo Pl 40 B2
Burley Lo Rd 40 A1
Burley Lo St 40 B2
Burley Lo Ter 40 B1
Burley Pl 40 A2
Burley Rd 40 A1
Burley St 40 C3
Burmantofts 41 H3
Burmantofts St
Burton Row 41 E7
Burton St 41 E7
Burton Way 41 J2
Butterfield St 41 H4
Butterley St 41 F6
Butts Ct 41 E3
Byron St 41 F2

C
Cain Cl 41 H4
Call La 41 F4
Calls, The 41 F4
Calverley St 40 D2
Cambrian St 40 D7
Cambrian Ter 40 D7
Canal Pl 40 B4
Canal St 40 A3
Canal Wf 40 D4
Carberry Pl 40 A1
Carberry Rd 40 A1
Carberry Ter 40 A1
Carlisle Rd 41 G5
Carlton Carr 41 E1
Carlton Ct 40 A7
Carlton Gdns 41 E1
Carlton Gate 41 E1
Carlton Gro 41 E1
Carlton Hill 41 E1
Carlton Pl 41 E1
Carlton Ri 41 E1
Carlton Twrs 41 F1
Carlton Vw 41 E1
Castle St 40 D3
Castleton Cl 40 B4
Castleton Rd 40 A3
Cautley Rd 41 J5
Cavalier App 41 H5
Cavalier Cl 41 H5
Cavalier Ct 41 H5
Cavalier Gdns 41 H5
Cavalier Gate 41 H5
Cavalier Ms 41 H5
Cavalier Vw 41 H5
Cavendish Rd 40 D1
Cavendish St 40 C3
Cemetery Rd 40 C7
Central Rd 41 F4
Central St 40 D3
Chadwick St 41 F5
Chadwick St S 41 G5
Chantrell Ct 41 F4
Charles Av 41 J5
Charlton Gro 41 J4
Charlton Pl 41 J4
Charlton Rd 41 J4
Charlton St 41 J4
Cherry Pl 41 G2
Cherry Row 41 G2
Chesney Av 41 F7
Chiswick St 40 A2
Chorley La 40 D2
Churchill Gdns 40 E1
Church La 41 F4
City Sq 40 E4
City Wk 40 E5
Claremont Av 40 C2
Claremont Gro 40 C2
Claremont Vw 40 C2
Clarence Rd 41 G5
Clarendon Pl 40 C1
Clarendon Rd 40 C1
Clarendon Way 40 D2
Clark Av 41 J4
Clark Cres 41 J4
Clark Gro 41 J5
Clark La 41 H5
Clark Mt 41 J4
Clark Rd 41 J5
Clark Row 41 J5
Clark Ter 41 J4
Clark Vw 41 J5
Clay Pit La 41 E2
Cleveleys Av 40 C7
Cleveleys Mt 40 C7
Cleveleys Rd 40 C7
Cleveleys St 40 C7
Cleveleys Ter 40 C7
Cloberry St 40 C1
Close, The 41 G4
Cloth Hall St 41 F4
Clyde App 40 A5
Clyde Gdns 40 B5
Clyde Vw 40 A5
Coleman St 40 B5
Colenso Gdns 40 C7

Colenso Mt 40 C7
Colenso Pl 40 C7
Colenso Rd 40 C7
Colenso Ter 40 C7
Colville Ter 40 D7
Commercial St 41 E3
Compton Av 41 J1
Compton Cres 41 G3
Compton Gro 41 J1
Compton Mt 41 J1
Compton Pl 41 J1
Compton Rd 41 J2
Compton St 41 H4
Compton Ter 41 J1
Compton Vw 41 J1
Concordia St 41 E4
Concord St 41 F2
Consort St 40 C2
Consort Ter 40 C2
Consort Vw 40 B2
Consort Wk 40 C2
Constance Gdns 40 E1
Constance Way 40 E1
Cookridge St 40 E3
Copley Hill 40 A5
Copley Hill Way 40 A6
Copley St 40 A5
Copperfield Av 41 J5
Copperfield Cres 41 J5
Copperfield Gro 41 J5
Copperfield Mt 41 J5
Copperfield Pl 41 J5
Copperfield Row 41 J5
Copperfield Ter 41 J5
Copperfield Vw 41 J5
Copperfield Wk 41 J5
Copperfiield Dr 41 J5
Cotton St 41 G4
Coupland Pl 40 D7
Coupland Rd 40 D7
Cowper Av 41 J1
Cowper Cres 41 J1
Cowper Pl 41 J1
Cromer Pl 40 C1
Cromer Rd 40 C1
Cromer St 40 C1
Cromer Ter 40 C2
Cromwell Mt 41 G2
Cromwell St 41 G3
Crosby Pl 40 C6
Crosby Rd 40 C7
Crosby St 40 C6
Crosby Ter 40 C6
Crosby Vw 40 C6
Cross Aysgarth Mt 41 H4
Cross Belgrave St 41 F3
Cross Catherine St 41 H4
Cross Grn 41 F5
Cross Grn App 41 J6
Cross Grn Av 41 H5
Cross Grn Cl 41 J6
Cross Grn Cres 41 H5
Cross Grn Dr 41 J6
Cross Grn Garth 41 J6
Cross Grn La 41 H5
Cross Grn Ri 41 J6
Cross Grn Way 41 J6
Cross Ingram Rd 40 C6
Cross Kelso Rd 40 C2
Cross Mitford Rd 40 A4
Cross Stamford St 41 G2
Cross York St 41 F4
Crown Ct 41 F4
Crown Pt Rd 41 F5
Crown St 41 F4
Croydon St 40 B5
Cudbear St 41 F5
Czar St 40 C5

D
Danby Wk 41 H4
David St 40 D5
Dene Ho Ct 40 E1
Denison Rd 40 C3
Dent St 41 H4
Derwent Pl 40 D5
Devon Cl 40 D1
Devon Rd 40 D1
Dewsbury Rd 41 E6
Dial St 41 H5
Disraeli Gdns 40 E7
Disraeli Ter 40 E7
Dock St 41 F4
Dolly La 41 G2
Dolphin Ct 41 H4
Dolphin St 41 H4
Domestic Rd 40 B6
Domestic St 40 C5
Donisthorpe St 41 H6
Drive, The 41 G4
Driver Ter 40 B5
Dudley Way 40 A5
Duke St 41 F4
Duncan St 41 E4

Duncombe St 40 C3
Duxbury Ri 40 E1
Dyer St 41 F3

E
East Fld St 41 E3
Eastgate 41 F3
East King St 41 G4
East Par 40 E3
East Pk Dr 41 J4
East Pk Gro 41 J4
East Pk Mt 41 J4
East Pk Par 41 J4
East Pk Pl 41 J4
East Pk Rd 41 J4
East Pk St 41 J4
East Pk Ter 41 J4
East Pk Vw 41 J4
East St 41 G4
Easy Rd 41 H5
Ebor Mt 40 B1
Ebor Pl 40 B1
Ebor St 40 B1
Edgware Av 41 H1
Edgware Gro 41 H1
Edgware Mt 41 H1
Edgware Pl 41 H1
Edgware Row 41 H1
Edgware St 41 H1
Edgware Ter 41 H1
Edgware Vw 41 H1
Edward St 41 F3
Edwin Rd 40 B1
Eighth Av 40 A5
Elland Rd 40 C7
Elland Ter 40 D6
Ellerby La 41 H5
Ellerby Rd 41 G4
Elmtree La 41 G7
Elmwood La 41 F2
Elmwood Rd 41 E2
Elsworth St 40 A4
Enfield Av 41 G1
Enfield St 41 G1
Enfield Ter 41 G1
Euston Gro 40 B7
Euston Mt 40 B7
Euston Ter 40 B7
Everleigh St 41 J3

F
Far Cft Ter 40 A5
Fewston Av 41 H5
Fewston Ct 41 H5
Finsbury Rd 40 D2
First Av 40 A4
Firth St 41 G2
Firth Ter 41 G2
Fish St 41 F3
Flax Pl 41 G4
Florence Av 41 J1
Florence Gro 41 J1
Florence Mt 41 J1
Florence Pl 41 J1
Florence St 41 J1
Folly La 40 D7
Forster St 41 G6
Foundry St (Holbeck) 40 C5
Foundry St (Quarry Hill) 41 G4
Fountain St 40 D3
Fourteenth Av 40 A5
Fourth Ct 40 C5
Fox Way 41 H6
Fraser St 41 J2
Frederick Av 41 J5
Front Row 40 D5
Front St 40 D5

G
Gardeners Ct 40 D5
Gargrave App 40 E1
Gargrave Pl 40 E1
Garth, The 41 G4
Garton Av 41 J4
Garton Gro 41 J4
Garton Rd 41 J4
Garton Ter 41 J4
Garton Vw 41 J4
Gelderd Pl 40 B5
Gelderd Rd 40 A7
George St 41 F3
Gibraltar Island Rd 41 H7
Gilpin Pl 40 A5
Gilpin St 40 A5
Gilpin Ter 40 A5
Gilpin Vw 40 A5
Glasshouse St 41 G6
Gledhow Mt 41 H1
Gledhow Pl 41 H1
Gledhow Rd 41 H1
Gledhow Ter 41 H1

Glencoe Vw 41 J5
Glensdale Gro 41 J4
Glensdale Mt 41 J4
Glensdale Rd 41 J4
Glensdale St 41 J4
Glensdale Ter 41 J4
Glenthorpe Av 41 J3
Glenthorpe Cres 41 J3
Glenthorpe Ter 41 J3
Gloucester Ter 40 C4
Goodman St 41 G6
Gotts Rd 40 C4
Gower St 41 F3
Grace St 40 D3
Grafton St 41 F2
Grange Cl 41 G7
Grange Rd 41 G7
Grant Av 41 G2
Granville Rd 41 H5
Grape St 40 B1
Grasmere Cl 40 A5
Grassmere Rd 40 A5
Great George St 40 D3
Great Wilson St 40 E5
Greek St 40 E3
Greenfield Rd 41 H4
Green La 40 A5
Grosvenor Hill 41 E1

H
Hall Gro 40 B1
Hall La 40 A4
Hall Pl 41 H4
Hanover Av 40 C2
Hanover La 40 D3
Hanover Mt 40 C2
Hanover Sq 40 C2
Hanover Wk 40 C3
Harewood St 41 F3
Harold Av 40 A1
Harold Gro 40 A1
Harold Mt 40 A1
Harold Pl 40 A1
Harold Rd 40 A1
Harold St 40 A1
Harold Ter 40 A1
Harold Vw 40 A1
Harold Wk 40 A1
Harper St 41 F4
Harrison St 41 F3
Hartwell Rd 40 B1
Haslewood Cl 41 H3
Haslewood Ct 41 H3
Haslewood Dene 41 H3
Haslewood Dr 41 H3
Haslewood Ms 41 J3
Haslewood Pl 41 H3
Haslewood Sq 41 H3
Hawkins Dr 41 E1
Headrow, The 40 D3
Heaton's Ct 41 E4
Hedley Chase 40 A4
Hedley Gdns 40 A4
Hedley Grn 40 A4
High 40 D7
High Ct 41 F4
High Ct La 41 F4
Hillary Pl 40 D1
Hillidge Rd 41 F7
Hillidge Sq 41 F7
Hill Top Pl 40 B1
Hill Top St 40 B1
Hirst's Yd 41 F4
Holbeck 40 D5
Holbeck La 40 C5
Holbeck Moor Rd 40 C6
Holdforth Cl 40 A4
Holdforth Gdns 40 A4
Holdforth Grn 40 A4
Holdforth Pl 40 A4
Holmes St 41 E5
Holroyd St 41 G1
Hope Rd 41 G3
Howden Gdns 40 B1
Howden Pl 40 B1
Hudson Rd 41 J1
Hudswell Rd 41 F7
Hunslet 41 G7
Hunslet Grn Way 41 F7
Hunslet Hall Rd 40 E7
Hunslet La 41 F5
Hunslet Rd 41 F4
Hyde Pk Cl 40 B1
Hyde Pk Rd 40 B1
Hyde Pl 40 C2
Hyde St 40 C2
Hyde Ter 40 C2

I
Infirmary St 40 E3
Ingram Cl 40 C6
Ingram Cres 40 B7

Ingram Gdns 40 C6
Ingram Rd 40 C7
Ingram Row 40 E5
Ingram St 40 E5
Ingram Vw 40 C6
Inner Ring Rd 40 E2
Ivory St 41 F6

J
Jack La 40 D6
Jenkinson Cl 40 D6
Jenkinson Lawn 40 D6
John Smeaton Viaduct 41 G6
Joseph St 41 G7
Junction St 41 F5

K
Keeton St 41 H3
Kelsall Av 40 B1
Kelsall Gro 40 B2
Kelsall Pl 40 B1
Kelsall Rd 40 B1
Kelsall Ter 40 B1
Kelso Gdns 40 C1
Kelso Rd 40 C1
Kelso St 40 C2
Kendal Bk 40 C2
Kendal Cl 40 C2
Kendal Gro 40 C2
Kendal La 40 C2
Kendell St 41 F4
Kenneth St 40 B6
Kepler Gro 41 H1
Kepler Mt 41 H1
Kepler Ter 41 H1
Kidacre St 41 F5
Kildare Ter 40 B5
King Charles St 41 E3
King Edward St 41 F3
Kings Av 40 B2
King's Rd 40 B1
Kingston Ter 40 D1
King St 40 D4
Kippax Pl 41 H4
Kirkgate 41 F4
Kirkstall Rd 40 A2
Kitson Rd 41 G6
Kitson St 41 H4
Knowsthorpe Cres 41 H5
Knowsthorpe La 41 J6

L
Ladybeck Cl 41 F3
Lady La 41 F3
Lady Pit La 40 D7
Lands La 41 E3
Lane, The 41 G4
Larchfield Rd 41 G6
Latchmore Rd 40 A7
Laura St 40 C5
Lavender Wk 41 H4
Leathley Rd 41 F6
Leathley St 41 F6
Leicester Cl 40 E1
Leicester Gro 40 E1
Leicester Pl 40 D1
Leighton St 40 D3
Leodis Ct 40 D5
Leylands Rd 41 G2
Lifton Pl 40 C1
Lincoln Grn Rd 41 G2
Lincoln Rd 41 G2
Lindsey Ct 41 H2
Lindsey Gdns 41 H2
Lindsey Rd 41 H2
Lisbon St 40 D3
Little King St 40 E4
Little Queen St 40 D4
Little Woodhouse St 40 D2
Livinia Gro 40 E1
Lodge St 40 D1
Lofthouse Pl 40 E1
Londesboro Gro 41 J4
Long Causeway 41 H6
Long Cl La 41 H4
Lord St 40 C5
Lord Ter 40 B5
Lovell Pk Cl 41 F2
Lovell Pk Gate 41 F2
Lovell Pk Hill 41 F2
Lovell Pk Rd 41 F2
Lovell Pk Vw 41 F2
Lower Basinghall St 40 E3
Lower Brunswick St 40 B1
Low Flds Av 40 B7
Low Flds Rd 40 A7
Low Flds Way 40 B7
Low Fold 41 G5
Low Rd 41 G7
Low Whitehouse Row 41 G6
Ludgate Hill 41 F3
Lyddon Ter 40 C1
Lydgate 41 J2

Street	Ref	Street	Ref
Lydia St	41 F3	Nile St	41 F3
M		Nineveh Gdns	40 D6
Mabgate	41 G3	Nineveh Par	40 D6
Mabgate Grn	41 G3	Nineveh Rd	40 C6
Macaulay St	41 G3	Nippet La	41 H3
Maitland Pl	40 D7	Normanton Gro	40 C7
Maltings Rd	41 F7	Normanton Pl	40 D7
Malvern Gro	40 D7	Nortech Cl	41 G1
Malvern Ri	40 D7	Northcote Cres	40 E7
Malvern Rd	40 C7	Northcote Dr	40 D7
Malvern St	40 C7	Northcote Grn	40 D7
Malvern Vw	40 C7	North Ct	41 F3
Manor Rd	40 D5	Northern St	40 D4
Manor St	41 G1	North St	41 F3
Mark La	41 E3	**O**	
Marlborough Gdns	40 D1	Oak Rd	40 A4
Marlborough Gro	40 D1	Oatland Cl	41 F1
Marlborough St	40 C3	Oatland Ct	41 F1
Marlborough Twrs	40 C3	Oatland Dr	41 F1
Marshall St	40 D5	Oatland Gdns	41 F1
Marsh La	41 G4	Oatland Grn	41 F1
Maude St	41 F4	Oatland Hts	41 F1
May Ter	41 H5	Oatland La	41 E1
Meadowcroft Ms	41 H4	Oatland Rd	41 E1
Meadow La	41 E5	Oatland Twrs	41 F1
Meadow Rd	40 E6	O'Grady Sq	41 H4
Melbourne St	41 F2	Old Mill La	41 H7
Merrion Pl	41 F3	Oval, The	41 G7
Merrion St	41 E3	Oxford Pl	40 D3
Merrion Way	41 E2	Oxford Row	40 D3
Meynell App	40 C6	Oxley St	41 J4
Middleton Av	41 J2	Oxton Mt	41 J3
Milford Pl	40 A2	Oxton Way	41 J3
Millgarth St	41 F3	**P**	
Mill Grn	40 B5	Parade, The	41 G4
Mill Hill	41 E4	Park Cross St	40 D3
Mill St	41 G4	Parkfield St	41 E6
Millwright St	41 G2	Park La	40 C3
Milner Gdns	41 H5	Park Par	41 J5
Milnes St	40 B5	Park Pl	40 D3
Mitford Rd	40 A4	Park Row	40 E3
Mitford Vw	40 A4	Park Sq E	40 D3
Moor Cres	41 E7	Park Sq N	40 D3
Moor Cres Chase	41 E7	Park Sq S	40 D3
Moorland Av	40 B1	Park Sq W	40 D3
Moorland Rd	40 B1	Park St	40 D3
Moor Rd	41 E7	Park Vw Rd	40 A1
Moorside Maltings	41 E7	Pearson St	41 F6
Moor Vw	40 D6	Penny La Way	41 F7
Moorvile Cl	40 D7	Pilot St	41 G2
Moorville Ct	40 D7	Pitt Row	41 E4
Moorville Gro	40 D7	Place's Rd	41 H4
Moorville Rd	40 D7	Plaid Row	41 H3
Mount Preston St	40 C2	Playhouse Sq	41 G3
Mulberry St	41 F6	Pleasant Mt	40 C6
Mullins Ct	41 H5	Pleasant Pl	40 C6
Mushroom St	41 G2	Pleasant Ter	40 C6
N		Pontefract Av	41 J4
Naseby Garth	41 G2	Pontefract La	41 H3
Naseby Ter	41 H3	Pontefract La Cl	41 H4
National Rd	41 H6	Pontefract St	41 H4
Navigation Wk	41 F4	Portland Cres	40 E2
Neptune St	41 G4	Portland Gate	40 E2
Neville St	40 E4	Portland St	40 D3
New Briggate	41 F3	Portland Way	40 E2
New Craven Gate	41 F6	Pottery Rd	41 F7
New La	40 E5	Prosper St	41 G7
New Mkt St	41 F4	Providence Pl	41 E2
New Princess St	40 D6	Pym St	41 G6
New Sta St	40 E4	**Q**	
New York Rd	41 G3	**Quarry Hill**	41 G3
New York St	41 F4	Quebec St	40 D3
Nickleby Rd	41 J3		

Street	Ref	Street	Ref
Queen Sq	41 E2	St. Luke's Cres	40 D7
Queens Rd	40 B1	St. Luke's Grn	40 D7
Queen St	40 D4	St. Luke's Rd	40 D7
R		St. Luke's St	40 D7
Radnor St	40 B5	St. Mark's Av	40 D1
Railway St	41 G4	St. Mark's Rd	40 D1
Raincliffe Gro	41 J3	St. Mark's St	40 D1
Raincliffe Rd	41 J3	St. Mary's Cl	40 A5
Raincliffe St	41 J3	St. Mary's St	41 G3
Recreation Cres	40 C7	St. Matthew's St	40 C6
Recreation Gro	40 C7	St. Matthias St	40 A1
Recreation Mt	40 C7	St. Matthias Ter	40 A1
Recreation Pl	40 C7	St. Paul's St	40 D3
Recreation Row	40 C7	St. Peter's Ct	41 E7
Recreation St	40 C7	St. Peter's Pl	41 G3
Recreation Ter	40 C7	St. Peter's Sq	41 G3
Recreation Vw	40 C7	St. Stephen's Ct	41 H3
Rectory St	41 H2	St. Stephen's Rd	41 H3
Redshaw Rd	40 A5	Salem Pl	41 F5
Regent St	41 G3	Sandlewood Cl	40 D6
Regent Ter	40 B1	Sandlewood Grn	40 D6
Rhodes Ter	41 J3	Sardinia St	41 F6
Richmond Hill App	41 H4	Saville Gro	41 J3
Richmond Hill Cl	41 H4	Saxton La	41 G4
Richmond St	41 G4	Sayner La	41 G5
Rickard St	40 C5	Sayner Rd	41 F5
Rider St	41 G3	Scargill Cl	41 H2
Rigton App	41 H3	Scarth Av	41 J1
Rigton Cl	41 H3	Second Av	40 A4
Rigton Dr	41 H3	Seminary St	40 D2
Rigton Grn	41 H3	Severn Way	41 H7
Rigton Lawn	41 H3	Shafton La	40 C6
Rigton Ms	41 H3	Shafton Pl	40 C6
Rillbank La	40 B2	Shafton St	40 C6
Roscoe St	41 G1	Shafton Vw	40 C6
Rosebank Gdns	40 B2	Shakespeare App	41 H2
Rosebank Rd	40 B2	Shakespeare Av	41 H2
Rosebud Wk	41 G1	Shakespeare Cl	41 J2
Roseville Rd	41 G1	Shakespeare Gdns	41 J2
Roseville St	41 H1	Shakespeare Lawn	41 H2
Rossington St	40 E3	Shakespeare St	41 J1
Roundhay Rd	41 G1	Shannon Rd	41 H3
Roxby Cl	41 H2	Shannon St	41 G3
Royal Pk Av	40 B1	Sheaf St	41 F5
Royal Pk Gro	40 B1	Sheepscar Ct	41 F1
Royal Pk Rd	40 A1	Sheepscar Gro	41 F2
Royal Pk Ter	40 B1	Sheepscar St N	41 F1
Ruby St	41 G2	Sheepscar St S	41 F1
Runswick Av	40 C6	Siddal St	40 D5
Runswick Pl	40 C6	Sidney St	41 F3
Runswick St	40 C6	Silver St	40 D5
Runswick Ter	40 C6	Skinner La	41 F2
Russell St	40 E3	Skinner St	40 C3
Rydall Pl	40 C6	Somers St	40 D3
Rydall St	40 C6	South Accommodation Rd	41 G6
Rydall Ter	40 C6	South Par	40 E3
S		Sovereign St	40 E4
Sackville St	41 F1	Spence La	40 B5
St. Andrew's St	40 C3	Spenceley St	40 D1
St. Barnabas Rd	40 E5	Spinney, The	41 H4
St. Georges Rd	40 D2	Spinneyfield Ct	41 H4
St. Helen's St	41 G6	Spring Cl Av	41 H5
St. Hilda's Av	41 J5	Spring Cl Gdns	41 H5
St. Hilda's Cres	41 H5	Spring Cl St	41 H5
St. Hilda's Gro	41 J5	Spring Cl Wk	41 H5
St. Hilda's Mt	41 J5	Springfield Mt	40 C2
St. Hilda's Pl	41 J5	Spring Gro Ter	40 A1
St. Hilda's Rd	41 J5	Spring Gro Vw	40 B1
St. John's Av	40 C1	Spring Gro Wk	40 A1
St. John's Cl	40 B1	Springwell Ct	40 C5
St. John's Gro	40 B1	Springwell Rd	40 C5
St. John's Rd	40 B2	Springwell St	40 C5
St. Luke's Cescent	40 D7	Springwell Vw	40 C5
		Stafford St	41 G7

Street	Ref	Street	Ref
Stanley Av	41 J1	Victoria Rd	40 E5
Stanley Pl	41 J1	Victoria Sq	40 D3
Stanley Rd	41 J1	Victoria St	40 C2
Stanley Ter	41 J1	Victoria Ter	40 C2
Stocks Hill	40 C6	Village Ter	40 A1
Stoney Rock Gro	41 J2	Vinery Mt	41 J4
Stoney Rock La	41 H2	Vinery Pl	41 J4
Stott Rd	40 A4	Vinery St	41 J3
Studio Rd	40 B2	Vinery Ter	41 J4
Sutton St	40 C5	**W**	
Sweet St	40 D5	Wade La	41 E3
Sweet St W	40 C5	Walford Gro	41 J3
Swinegate	40 E3	Walford Rd	41 J3
Sydenham Rd	40 B5	Walford Ter	41 J3
Sydenham St	40 B5	Walter Cres	41 H4
T		Walter St	40 A2
Telephone Pl	41 G2	Walton St	40 D5
Templar La	41 F3	Washington St	40 B3
Templar Pl	41 F3	Water La	40 C5
Templar St	41 F3	Waterloo Rd	41 G7
Temple Vw Gro	41 J4	Waterloo St	41 F4
Temple Vw Pl	41 J4	Waverley Garth	40 D7
Temple Vw Rd	41 J3	Weaver St	40 A2
Temple Vw Ter	41 J4	Welbeck Rd	41 J4
Thealby Cl	41 G3	Well Cl Ri	41 E1
Thealby Lawn	41 G2	Wellington Br St	40 C3
Thealby Pl	41 G3	Wellington Pl	40 C4
Third Av	40 A5	Wellington Rd	40 B4
Thirsk Row	40 D4	Wellington St	40 D4
Thoresby Pl	40 D3	Wesley Pl	41 H4
Thornleigh Gdns	41 J5	Westfield Cres	40 B2
Thornleigh Gro	41 J5	Westfield Rd	40 B2
Thornleigh Mt	41 J5	Westfield Ter	40 B2
Thornleigh St	41 J5	Westgate	40 D3
Thornleigh Vw	41 J5	Westlock Av	41 J2
Thornville Pl	40 B1	West St	40 C3
Thornville Rd	40 A1	West Vale	40 A6
Thornville Row	40 B1	Wharf St	41 F4
Thornville St	40 B1	Whitehall Rd	40 B5
Thornville Vw	40 B1	Whitehouse St	41 G7
Tilbury Av	40 C7	Whitelock St	41 F2
Tilbury Gro	40 C7	Whitfield Av	41 G7
Tilbury Mt	40 C7	Whitfield Gdns	41 G7
Tilbury Par	40 C7	Whitfield Pl	41 G7
Tilbury Rd	40 C7	Whitfield Sq	41 G7
Tilbury Ter	40 C7	Whitfield Way	41 G7
Tilbury Vw	40 C7	Willis St	41 H4
Tong Rd	40 A5	Willoughby Ter	40 C6
Top Moor Side	40 C6	Willow App	40 A2
Torre Cl	41 J3	Willow Av	40 A2
Torre Dr	41 J2	Willow Cl	40 B2
Torre Rd	41 H3	Willow Garth	40 A2
Tower Ho St	41 F2	Willow Rd	40 A2
Trafalgar St	41 F3	Willow Ter Rd	40 D2
Trent Rd	41 J3	Wilmington St	41 F1
Trent St	40 D6	Winchester St	40 A4
Trinity St	41 E3	Winfield Gro	40 E1
Triumph Cl	40 C5	Winfield Pl	40 E1
Turlow Ct	41 G4	Winfield Ter	40 E1
U		Wintoun St	41 F2
Union Pl	40 D5	Wolseley Rd	40 A1
Union St	41 F3	Woodhouse La	40 D1
University Rd	40 C1	Woodhouse Sq	40 D3
Upper Accommodation Rd	41 H3	Woodsley Grn	40 B1
Upper Basinghall St	40 E3	Woodsley Rd	40 B2
Upper N St	40 E2	Wormald Row	41 E3
Upper Westlock Av	41 J2	Wortley La	40 B5
V		Wortley Pk	40 A5
Vernon Rd	40 D2	**Y**	
Vernon St	40 E2	Yarn St	41 H6
Vicar La	41 F3	York Pl	40 D3
		York Rd	41 H3
		York St	41 F4

Liverpool street index

Street	Ref	Street	Ref
A		Arrad St	43 E5
Abercromby Sq	43 F4	Arundel Av	43 J7
Abney Cl	43 H5	Arundel Cl	43 G7
Acorn Ct	43 E7	Asbridge St	43 G7
Acton Way	43 H5	Ashton St	43 F3
Adderley St	43 H3	Ashwell St	42 D6
Addison St	42 C2	Askham Cl	43 G6
Addison Way	42 C2	Aspen Gro	43 H7
Adelaide Pl	42 D1	Atlantic Pt	42 C2
Adelaide Rd	43 G4	Atwell St	43 G1
Adele Thompson Dr	43 F6	**B**	
Agnes Way	43 H4	Back Colquitt St	42 D5
Aigburth St	43 G5	Back Guildford St	43 F1
Ainsworth St	42 E4	Back Kelvin Gro	43 G7
Albany Rd	43 G3	Back Leeds St	42 B2
Albert Edward Rd	43 G3	Baker St	43 G2
Albert St	43 G4	Baker Way	43 F2
Alderson Rd	43 J6	Balmoral Rd	43 J1
Alexandra Cl	43 G2		

Street	Ref	Street	Ref
Alexandra Rd	43 J5	Balm St	43 H3
Alex Cl	43 F7	Baltimore St	42 E5
Alfred Ms	42 D6	Bannerman St	43 J5
Alfred St	43 J5	Barnet Cl	43 H5
Altcar Av	43 J6	Basnett St	42 C4
Alt St	43 G6	Bath St	42 A3
Amberley St	43 F6	Battenberg St	43 G3
Amelia Cl	43 F2	Bayhorse La	43 E3
Amethyst Cl	43 G1	Beaconsfield St	43 G7
Anchorage, The	42 C7	Beaufort St	43 D7
Angela St	43 G5	Beaumont St	43 G6
Anglezark Cl	43 H3	Beau St	42 D1
Anglican Ct	42 E6	Beckwith St	42 C5
Archbishop Warlock Ct	42 B1	Bective St	43 J5
Argyle St	42 C5	Bedford Cl	43 F5
Arley St	42 C1	Bedford St S	43 F6
Arnold Cres	43 F7	Beech St	43 J3
Arnside Rd	43 H4	Benson St	42 D4
		Bentley Rd	43 G7

Street	Ref	Street	Ref
Beresford St	42 E1	Blackstock St	42 C2
Berington St	42 C1	Blair St	42 E6
Berkley St	43 E6	Blenheim St	42 C1
Berry St	42 D5	Bluefields St	43 E6
Berwick Cl	43 H1	Blundell St	42 C6
Berwick St	43 H1	Boaler St	43 G2
Bevington Bush	42 C2	Bold Pl	42 D5
Bevington Hill	42 C1	Bold St	42 D4
Bidder St	42 E2	Bolton St	42 D4
Bigham Rd	43 H2	Bond St	42 C1
Birchfield St	42 E2	Boothwood Cl	43 H5
Bird St	43 J6	Boswell St	43 H6
Birkett St	42 D2	Botanic Grn	43 H3
Birstall Rd	43 G2	Botanic Pl	43 J3
Birt Cl	43 G6	Botanic Rd	43 J3
Bishop Sheppard Ct	42 B1	Boundary La	43 G1
Bixteth St	42 B3	Boyton Ct	43 J5
Blackburne Pl	43 E5	Bradfield St	43 H3
		Brae St	43 H3

Brahms Cl — 43 G7
Brampton Dr — 43 F5
Brassey St — 42 D7
Breames Cl — 43 H4
Breck Rd — 43 F1
Bremner Cl — 43 H4
Brick St — 42 D6
Bridge Rd — 43 J5
Bridgewater St — 42 C6
Bridport St — 42 D3
Bright St — 43 F2
Brindley St — 42 D7
Britannia Av — 43 J6
Britten Cl — 43 H7
Bronte St — 42 E3
Brook St — 42 B3
Brownlow Hill — 42 D4
Brownlow St — 43 E4
Brow Side — 43 E1
Brunswick Rd — 43 F3
Brunswick St — 42 B4
Bryges St — 43 G4
Brythen St — 42 C4
Burlington St — 42 C1
Burnley Cl — 43 G1
Burroughs Gdns — 42 C1
Burrows Ct — 42 B1
Burton Cl — 42 C5
Bute St — 42 D2
Bute St (Edge Hill) — 43 H6
Butler Cres — 43 G2
Butler St — 43 G1
Button St — 42 C4
Byrom St — 42 D3

C
Cadogan St — 43 J5
Caird St — 43 G2
Cairns St — 43 G7
Caledonia St — 43 E5
Callander Rd — 43 J2
Cambria St N — 43 H2
Cambria St S — 43 H2
Cambridge Ct — 43 E5
Cambridge St — 43 E4
Camden St — 42 D3
Cameo Cl — 43 G1
Cameron St — 43 H3
Campbell St — 42 C5
Canada Boul — 42 B4
Canning Pl — 42 C4
Canning St — 43 E5
Cantebury St — 42 E2
Canterbury Way — 43 E2
Cantsfield St — 43 J6
Cardigan St — 43 J5
Cardigan Way — 43 H1
Cardwell St — 43 G5
Carlingford Cl — 43 G6
Carlton St — 42 A1
Carmarthen Cres — 42 D7
Carpenters Row — 42 C5
Carruthers St — 42 B2
Carstairs Rd — 43 J1
Carter St — 43 F6
Carver St — 43 E2
Caryl St — 42 D7
Castle St — 42 B4
Catharine St — 43 F5
Cathedral Cl — 42 E6
Cathedral Gate — 42 E5
Cathedral Wk — 42 E4
Cawdor St — 43 G7
Cazneau St — 42 D1
Cedar Gro — 43 H7
Celtic St — 43 F7
Chadwick St — 42 B2
Chaloner St — 42 C6
Chandos St — 43 H4
Channell Rd — 43 H2
Chapel St — 42 B4
Chase Way — 42 E1
Chatham Pl — 43 G4
Chatham St — 43 F5
Chatsworth Dr — 43 H5
Chaucer St — 42 D2
Cheapside — 42 C3
Chesney Cl — 42 E7
Chesterfield St — 42 E6
Chester St — 42 E7
Chestnut St — 43 F4
Chichester Cl — 43 J5
Childwall Av — 43 J6
Chisenhale St — 42 B1
Chiswell St — 43 H3
Christian St — 42 D2
Chris Ward Cl — 43 H4
Church All — 42 C4
Church Mt — 43 G4
Church St — 42 C4
Churton Ct — 43 F2
Cicely St — 43 G4
Clarence St — 42 E4
Claribel St — 43 F7

Claughton Cl — 43 H4
Claypole Cl — 43 H5
Clay St — 42 B1
Clearwater Cl — 43 H3
Clegg St — 42 D1
Clement Gdns — 42 C1
Cleveland Sq — 42 C5
Clifford St — 42 E3
Clifton Gro — 43 H3
Clint Rd — 42 E1
Clint Rd W — 43 H4
Clint Way — 43 H4
Coal St — 42 D3
Cobden St — 43 F2
Coburg Wf — 42 B3
Cockspur St — 42 C3
Coleridge St — 43 H2
College La — 42 C4
College St N — 43 E2
College St S — 43 F2
Colquitt St — 42 D5
Coltart Rd — 43 G7
Comberme St — 43 E7
Commerce Way — 43 G6
Commutation Row — 42 D3
Compton Rd — 43 G1
Comus St — 42 D2
Concert St — 42 D5
Connaught Rd — 43 G3
Contance St — 43 E3
Cookson St — 42 D6
Cook St — 42 C4
Copperas Hill — 42 D4
Corinto St — 42 E6
Corney St — 43 H6
Cornhill — 42 C5
Cornwallis St — 42 D5
Corsewall St — 43 J5
Cotswold St — 43 H3
Cotton St — 42 A1
Covent Gdn — 42 B3
Cowan Dr — 43 F1
Cranborne Rd — 43 J6
Craven St — 42 E3
Cresswell St — 43 F1
Cropper St — 42 D4
Crosfield Cl — 43 J4
Crosfield Rd — 43 H4
Crosshall St — 42 C3
Crown St — 43 F3
Croxteth Gro — 43 H7
Croxteth Rd — 43 G7
Crump St — 42 D6
Cullen St — 43 H6
Cumberland St — 42 C3
Cunliffe St — 42 C3
Custom Ho Pl — 42 C5

D
Dale St — 42 B4
Daniel Davies Dr — 43 G6
Dansie St — 43 E4
Danube St — 43 H6
Darrel Dr — 43 H6
Daulby St — 43 F3
Davies St — 42 C3
Dawber Cl — 43 G1
Dawson St — 42 C4
Dean Dillistone Ct — 42 D6
Deane Rd — 43 H3
Dean Patey Ct — 42 D5
Deeley Cl — 43 H4
Dell St — 43 H3
Denham Dr — 43 H1
Denham Way — 43 H1
Dentdale Dr — 42 E1
Devon St — 42 E3
Dexter St — 42 E7
Dial St — 43 H3
Diamond St — 42 C1
Dickens St — 42 E7
Dickson St — 42 A1
Dombey St — 43 E7
Dorothy St — 43 H4
Dorrit St — 43 E7
Dorset Av — 43 J6
Douro St — 42 D1
Dove St — 43 H5
Dovestone Cl — 43 G6
Drury La — 42 B4
Dryden St — 42 D1
Dublin St — 42 A1
Ducie St — 43 G7
Duckinfield St — 43 E4
Duke St — 42 C5
Duncan St — 42 D6
Dunkeld Cl — 43 G2
Dunstan La — 43 H5
Durden St — 43 H6
Durning Rd — 43 H3
Dwerryhouse St — 43 H4
Dyke St — 43 H5

E
Earle Rd — 42 D1
Earle St — 42 C1
East St — 42 C5
Eaton St — 42 E3
Ebenezer Rd — 43 H3
Eden St — 42 E1
Edgar St — 43 H4
Edge Hill — 43 H4
Edge La — 43 H4
Edinburgh Rd — 42 D3
Edmund St — 43 F2
Egerton St — 42 C7
Elaine St — 42 C3
Eldonian Way — 43 H2
Eldon Pl — 42 C4
Eldon St — 43 E2
Elizabeth St — 43 F2
Elliot St — 42 D5
Elm Gro — 43 G7
Elm Vale — 43 E7
Elstree Rd — 43 J5
Ember Cres — 43 G6
Embledon St — 43 H3
Emerson St — 42 D3
Empress Rd — 43 G1
Enid St — 42 D2
Epworth St — 42 D5
Erin Cl — 43 G3
Erskine St — 43 E3
Esher Rd — 42 D6
Eversley St — 42 C4
Everton Brow — 42 D4
Everton Rd — 42 E6
Every St — 43 H6
Exchange St E — 42 C5
Exchange St W — 42 D5

F
Fairclough St — 42 A1
Fairfield — 42 B3
Falkland St — 43 F1
Falkner Sq — 43 J6
Falkner St — 42 E3
Fareham Rd — 43 F1
Farnworth St — 42 D4
Fazakerley St — 43 J4
Fearnside St — 43 H4
Fell St — 42 C3
Fenwick St — 43 F3
Fern Gro — 43 H7
Fernhill Dr — 43 F7
Fielding St — 43 G2
Field St — 42 D6
Finch Pl — 43 H6
Finlay St — 42 C3
Fishguard Cl — 42 C3
Fitzclarence Way — 42 C5
Fitzpatrick Ct — 43 H1
Fitzroy Way — 43 H1
Fleet St — 42 B4
Fleming Ct — 43 G6
Flint St — 43 E4
Fontenoy St — 43 H6
Ford St — 43 H6
Forrest St — 43 F3
Fowler Cl — 42 C3
Foxhill Cl — 43 G1
Fox St — 42 D1
Fraser St — 42 D6
Freedom Cl — 43 H3
Freeman St — 42 D5
Freemasons' Row — 43 H4
Frost St — 43 H3

G
Galloway St — 42 E1
Gannock St — 42 E3
Gardenside St — 42 E7
Gardners Dr — 43 H3
Gardner's Row — 42 C1
Garrick St — 43 E7
Gascoyne St — 42 A1
Geneva Rd — 43 E7
George Harrison Cl — 43 H4
George Dockway — 43 E7
George St — 43 J6
Geraint St — 42 D1
Gerard St — 43 H5
Gibraltar Row — 43 G6
Gibson St — 42 B4
Gilbert St — 42 D1
Gildarts Gdns — 42 A1
Gildart St — 43 G7
Gilead St — 43 E4
Gill St — 42 C5
Gilroy Rd — 42 D6
Gladstone Rd — 43 G2
Gladstone St — 43 H5
Gleave Cres — 43 H6
Glegg St — 43 H3
Gloucester Ct — 43 G2
Gloucester Pl — 43 F1
Gore St — 42 D7
Gower St — 42 D7
Gradwell St — 43 H6
Grafton Cres — 42 B3
Grafton St — 42 B3
Granary Wf — 42 B2
Granby St — 43 J3
Grantham St — 43 H6
Granville Rd — 42 C2
Grayson St — 42 C5
Great Crosshall St — 43 G4
Great George Pl — 43 G3
Great George St — 43 F3
Great Howard St — 43 E6
Great Nelson St — 43 F7
Great Newton St — 42 B1
Great Orford St — 42 C1
Great Richmond St — 42 C1
Greek St — 43 F3
Greenheys Rd — 42 D4
Greenland St — 43 F4
Green La — 43 J1
Greenleaf St — 43 J2
Greenside — 43 F1
Green St — 43 G6
Gregson St — 43 E6
Grenville St S — 43 G4
Gresley Cl — 43 F7
Grierson St — 43 F3
Grinfield St — 42 E7
Grinshill Cl — 43 F3
Grosvenor St — 43 H2
Grove Pk — 43 H7
Grove Rd — 42 E2
Grove St — 43 F1
Guelph St — 43 G1
Guion St — 42 B3
Gwendoline St — 42 B3
Gwenfron Rd — 42 D4
Gwent St — 43 J2

H
Hackins Hey — 43 E3
Haigh St — 43 F6
Hale St — 42 C3
Hall La — 43 F3
Halsbury Rd — 43 G2
Hampstead Rd — 43 J3
Hampton St — 43 J5
Hannan Rd — 43 H3
Hanover St — 42 B4
Harbord St — 43 H7
Hardman St — 43 F7
Hardy St — 43 G2
Harewood St — 42 E2
Harker St — 43 E3
Harke St — 43 H2
Harper St — 43 F1
Harrington St — 43 F1
Harrowby Cl — 42 B1
Harrowby St — 43 F2
Hartley Quay — 42 D4
Hart St — 42 B1
Hatherley Cl — 42 D6
Hatherley St — 42 C3
Hatton Gdn — 42 C2
Haverston Rd — 42 C5
Hawdon Ct — 43 H4
Hawke St — 43 F7
Hawkins St — 42 D1
Hawthorn Gro — 42 D3
Head St — 43 G5
Heathcote Cl — 43 J5
Heathfield St — 42 C2
Helena St — 43 H3
Helsby St — 43 G4
Hendon Rd — 43 J1
Henglers Cl — 43 F2
Henry Edward St — 42 C2
Henry St — 42 C5
Hewitts Pl — 42 C2
Highfield St — 42 B2
Highgate St — 43 G4
High St — 42 B3
Hilbre St — 42 D4
Hillaby Cl — 43 F7
Hillside St — 43 F2
Hill St — 42 D7
Hinton St — 43 F7
Hockenhall All — 42 D3
Hodson Pl — 42 B3
Holborn St — 43 F6
Holden St — 43 G5
Holdsworth St — 43 H3
Holly Rd — 43 J3
Holmes St — 43 H6
Holt Rd — 43 H3
Holy Cross Cl — 43 H2
Homerton Rd — 43 J2
Hood St — 42 C2
Hope Pl — 43 F1
Hope St — 42 B1
Hornby Wk — 42 C1
Hotham St — 43 F3
Houghton St — 42 D7
Houlton St — 42 B5
Hughes Cl — 42 C4
Hughes St — 42 D7
Huntly Rd — 42 D6
Hurst St — 42 C7
Huskisson St — 43 G6
Hutchinson St — 43 H2
Hutchinson Wk — 43 J6
Hygeia St — 42 C5
Hyslop St — 42 C3

I
Iliad St — 42 B2
Ingrow Rd — 42 D1
Innovation Bvd — 43 E3
Irvine St — 43 E4
Islington — 42 D2
Ivatt Way — 42 E3

J
Jack McBain Ct — 42 E4
Jade Rd — 43 H6
Jamaica St — 43 F2
James Clarke St — 42 C1
James St — 43 F2
Janet St — 42 D5
Jasmine Cl — 43 J4
Jenkinson St — 43 H6
Jermyn St — 43 G4
Jet Cl — 43 F7
John Lennon Dr — 42 D1
John Moores Cl — 43 H7
Johnson St — 43 J2
John St — 43 F6
Jordan St — 43 F3
Jubilee Dr — 43 H1
Judges Dr — 43 F7
Judges Way — 43 G2
Juvenal Pl — 43 F7
Juvenal St — 43 G7

K
Keble St — 43 E1
Kelso Rd — 42 C3
Kelvin Gro — 43 F3
Kempston St — 43 H2
Kenley Cl — 43 J2
Kensington — 43 E6
Kensington — 43 H2
Kensington St — 42 C5
Kent St — 43 G4
Kilshaw St — 42 E5
Kimberley Cl — 42 D6
Kinder St — 43 G1
King Edward St — 42 D2
Kinglake St — 43 H5
Kings Dock St — 43 F3
Kingsley Rd — 42 C4
Kings Par — 43 G6
Kingsway Ct — 43 F6
Kingswell Cl — 43 G4
Kitchen St — 42 E3
Knight St — 43 G6

L
Lace St — 43 J2
Ladybower Cl — 43 J5
Laggan St — 43 H3
Lairds Pl — 42 C1
Lakeland Cl — 42 C5
Lambert Way — 42 E7
Lamport St — 42 E7
Lance Cl — 42 D4
Langley St — 43 H4
Langsdale St — 43 G4
Langton Rd — 43 J1
Lanyork Rd — 43 F2
Laurel Gro — 42 C2
Lavan Cl — 42 C5
Lawrence Rd — 42 C3
Lawton St — 42 B2
Laxey St — 43 G4
Leece St — 42 B3
Leeds St — 42 D4
Leigh St — 43 F7
Leigh St (Edge Hill) — 43 F2
Lemon Cl — 42 D7
Lemon Gro — 43 J2
Leopold Rd — 42 C3
Lesseps Rd — 43 F1
Lestock St — 43 F3
Liffey St — 43 G5
Lightwood Dr — 43 H3
Lightwood St — 43 J3
Lilley Rd — 43 H6
Lilly Vale — 43 H3
Lime Gro — 43 H7
Limekiln La — 43 J2
Lime St — 42 C3
Lincoln Cl — 42 D4
Lindley Cl — 43 H1
Lindley St — 43 J5
Ling St — 43 H3
Lister Cres — 43 J3
Lister Rd — 43 J2
Little Catherine St — 43 E6
Little Ct — 42 B1
Little Hardman St — 42 E5
Little Howard St — 42 B1
Little St. Bride St — 42 C2
Little Woolton St — 43 E5
Liver St — 42 C5
Lloyd Cl — 43 F1
Lockerby Rd — 43 H7
Lodge La — 43 H7
London Rd — 42 D3
Longfellow St — 43 H6
Longstone Wk — 43 G5
Lord Nelson St — 42 D3
Lord St — 42 C4
Lorton St — 43 H6
Lothian St — 43 F7
Loudon Gro — 43 G7
Love La — 42 B1
Lower Castle St — 42 B4
Low Hill — 43 F2
Lowther St — 43 F6
Low Wd St — 43 F3
Luke St — 43 E7
Lyceum Pl — 42 D4
Lydia Ann St — 42 C5
Lytton St — 43 F2

M
Maddrell St — 42 B1
Madelaine St — 43 F7
Madeley St — 43 H1
Magdala St — 43 H6
Maitland Cl — 43 H6
Malden Rd — 43 H2
Mallow Rd — 43 H2
Malt St — 43 G5
Malvern Rd — 43 H2
Manchester St — 42 C3
Manesty's La — 42 C4
Manfred St — 43 F3
Mann Island — 42 B4
Mann St — 42 D7
Mansell Rd — 43 H2
Mansfield St — 42 D2
Manton Rd — 43 H2
Maple Gro — 43 H7
Marathon Cl — 43 F1
Marcot Rd — 43 J1
Margaret St — 43 F1
Mariners Wf — 42 C7
Maritime Pl — 42 E2
Maritime Way — 42 C5
Marlborough St — 42 C2
Marlsford St — 43 H2
Marmaduke St — 43 G4
Marquis St — 42 E3
Marsden St — 43 F2
Marsden Way — 43 F2
Marshall Pl — 42 C1
Martensen St — 43 G4
Marvin St — 43 G2
Marybone — 42 C3
Maryland St — 43 E5
Mason St — 43 G4
Mathew St — 42 C4
Maud St — 43 F7
Maxton Rd — 43 H2
Mayfair Cl — 43 H1
May Pl — 42 E4
May St — 42 E4
Melda Cl — 43 F2
Melville Pl — 43 F5
Merlin St — 43 F7
Michael Dragonette Ct — 42 C1
Midghall St — 42 C2
Mile End — 42 C1
Millennium Pl — 43 G7
Mill La — 42 D4
Mill Rd — 43 F1
Mill St — 42 E7
Millvale St — 43 H1
Milroy St — 43 H4
Milverton St — 43 H1
Minshull St — 43 F4
Minster Ct — 43 F5
Minto Cl — 43 H3
Minto St — 43 H3
Mirfield St — 43 H2
Molyneux Rd — 43 G2
Montgomery Way — 43 H1
Moorfields — 42 C3
Moor Pl — 42 E3
Moor St — 42 B4
Morden St — 43 H1
Moss Gro — 43 H7
Mount Pleasant — 42 D4
Mount St — 42 E5

Mount Vernon Grn 43 G3
Mount Vernon Rd 43 F4
Mount Vernon St 43 F3
Mozart Cl 43 G7
Muirhead Av 43 H1
Mulberry Pl 43 F5
Mulberry St 43 F5
Mulgrave St 43 F6
Mulliner St 43 J6
Myrtle St 43 E5

N
Navigation Wf 42 C7
Naylor St 42 C2
Needham Rd 42 H3
Nelson Rd 43 G4
Nelson St 42 D6
Netherfield Rd S 42 E1
Nevin St 43 F2
Nevison St 43 G4
New Bird St 42 D6
New Grey Rock Cl 43 G1
Newhall St 42 D6
New Henderson St 42 D7
Newington 42 D4
New Quay 42 B3
New Red Rock Vw 43 G1
Newsham Dr 43 H1
Newstead Rd 43 H6
Newton Way 43 E4
Noel St 43 H6
Norfolk St 42 C6
Norman St 43 E3
Northbrook Cl 43 G6
North Brook St 43 F6
Northcote Cl 43 F1
North John St 42 C3
North St 42 C3
North Vw 43 G4
Norton St 42 D3
Norwood Gro 43 H1
Nuttall St 43 H4

O
Oakes St 43 E3
Oakham St 42 D7
O'Connell Rd 42 C1
Odsey St 43 H3
Oil St 42 A1
Old Coll Pl 43 H4
Old Hall St 42 B3
Oldham St 42 D5
Old Leeds St 42 B3
Olympia St 43 G2
Onslow Rd 43 J2
Opal Cl 43 G1
Orange Gro 43 H7
O'Reilly Ct 42 B1
Oriel Steet 42 C2
Ormond St 42 B3
Orphan St 43 F5
Orthes St 43 E4
Ottley St 43 J2
Overbury St 43 G4
Overton St 43 G4
Oxendale Cl 43 G6
Oxford St 43 E4
Oxford St E 43 G4

P
Paddington 43 F4
Page Wk 42 E2
Paisley St 42 A2
Pall Mall 42 B2
Paradise St 42 C5

Parker St 42 D4
Park La 42 C5
Park Pl 42 E7
Park Rd 43 E7
Parkside St 43 F2
Park Way 43 F6
Parliament Cl 42 E6
Parliament St 42 D6
Parr St 42 D5
Parton St 43 J2
Paul
  McCartney Way 43 H2
Paul Orr Ct 42 B1
Paul St 42 C2
Pavilion Cl 43 G6
Pear Gro 43 H2
Pearl Way 43 G1
Peet St 43 H4
Pembroke Gdns 43 E3
Pembroke Pl 43 E3
Pembroke St 43 E4
Penarth Cl 43 G5
Pendine Cl 43 H1
Penlinken Dr 43 H1
Penvalley Cres 43 H1
Peover St 42 D2
Pera Cl 43 G2
Percy St 43 E6
Perrygate Cl 43 G5
Perry St 42 D7
Perth St 43 G2
Peter's Arcade 42 C4
Peter St 42 C3
Phillimore Rd 43 H2
Pickop St 42 C3
Pickwick St 43 E7
Picton Rd 43 J5
Pilgrim St 42 E5
Pimhill Cl 43 G7
Pine Ms 42 E6
Pinetop Cl 43 H1
Pitt St 42 D5
Pleasant St 42 E4
Plimsoll St 43 H4
Plumpton St 43 F1
Pomfret St 43 F7
Pomona St 42 E4
Pond Cl 43 H1
Ponsonby St 43 G7
Porter St 42 A1
Portland Pl 42 D1
Portwood Cl 43 G5
Pownall Sq 42 C3
Pownall St 42 C5
Prescot Rd 43 J2
Prescot St 43 F3
Preston St 42 C3
Price St 42 C5
Primrose Hill 42 C3
Prince Albert Ms 42 D6
Prince Edwin St 42 D1
Princes Av 43 F6
Princes Gdns 42 B2
Princes Par 42 A3
Princes Pk 43 G7
Princes Rd 43 F6
Princes St 42 C3
Prince William St 42 D7
Prospect St 43 F3
Providence Cres 43 H2
Prussia St 42 B3
Pudsey St 42 D3
Pumpfields Rd 42 B2
Pythian Cl 43 G2
Pythian St 43 F2

Q
Queen Anne St 42 D2
Queensland St 43 G4
Queens Sq 42 D3
Queens Wf 42 C6
Quorn St 43 H3

R
Rachel St 42 D1
Radstock Rd 43 J2
Raffles St 42 D6
Rainford Gdns 42 C4
Rainford Sq 42 C4
Ranelagh St 42 D4
Raven Cl 43 F2
Raymond Pl 42 C1
Red Cross St 42 B4
Redgrave St 43 H3
Redmires Cl 43 H5
Red Rock St 43 G1
Regent St 43 A1
Renfrew St 43 G3
Renshaw St 42 D4
Reservoir St 43 F1
Reynolds Cl 43 G1
Rialto Cl 43 F6
Rice St 43 E5
Richardson St 43 J6
Richmond Row 42 D2
Richmond St 42 C4
Ridley Rd 43 H2
Rigby St 42 B3
Ringo Starr Dr 43 H2
Ritson St 43 G7
River Avon St 43 H6
Roberts St 42 A2
Roderick St 42 E2
Rodney St 42 E5
Roe St 42 D3
Rokeby Cl 42 E2
Rokeby St 42 E2
Rokesmith Av 43 H5
Romer Rd 43 H2
Romilly St 43 G2
Roscastle Cl 43 G2
Roscoe La 42 D5
Roscoe St 42 E5
Roscommon St 42 D1
Roseberry St 43 F6
Rose Hill 42 D2
Rosemary Cl 43 G4
Rose Pl 42 D2
Rothsay Cl 42 E1
Rothwell St 43 G1
Royal Mail St 42 D4
Royston St 43 G4
Rufford Rd 43 J2
Rumford Pl 42 B3
Rumford St 42 B3
Rupert Dr 43 F2
Russel St 42 E3
Ryedale Cl 43 G6

S
St. Andrew St 42 E4
St. Anne St 42 D2
St. Bride St 43 F5
St. James Pl 42 D6
St. James Rd 42 E6
St. James St 42 D6
St. John's La 42 D3
St. Josephs Cres 42 D2
St. Martins Ms 42 D1
St. Michaels Gro 43 H1
St. Nicholas Pl 42 A4

St. Stephen's Pl 42 C2
Salisbury Rd 43 J6
Salisbury St 42 E1
Salthouse Quay 42 B5
Saltney St 42 A1
Sandhead St 43 J5
Sandino St 42 E7
Sandon St 43 F5
Saxon Cl 43 G1
Saxony Rd 43 G3
Scholar St 43 J6
Schomberg St 43 G2
School La 42 C4
Scotland Rd 42 D2
Seaport Rd 43 G7
Seddon St 42 C6
Seel St 42 C4
Sefton Pk Rd 43 H7
Sefton St 42 C6
Selborne Cl 43 F6
Selborne St 43 F6
Selsey Cl 43 H5
Severs St 43 G1
Seymour St 42 E3
Shakespeare Cl 43 G1
Shallcross Pl 43 G1
Shaws All 42 C5
Shaw St 43 E1
Sheil Rd 43 H1
Shenstone St 43 G4
Shepherd's Fold Cl 43 G7
Sherwood St 42 B1
Shimmin St 43 G4
Sidney Pl 43 G4
Silkstone Cl 43 H5
Simpson St 42 C6
Sim St 42 E2
Sirdar Cl 43 H5
Sir Thomas St 42 C3
Skelhorne St 42 D4
Slater St 42 D5
Smithdown La 43 F4
Smithdown Rd 43 H6
Smithfield St 42 C3
Soho Pl 42 E2
Soho St 42 E2
Solomon St 43 H3
Solway St E 43 H6
Solway St W 43 G6
South Chester St 42 E7
Southern Cres 42 D7
South Ferry Quay 42 C7
South Hunter St 43 E5
South John St 42 C4
Sparling St 42 C6
Spekeland Rd 43 H5
Spencer St 43 F1
Spindle Cl 43 F1
Spofforth Rd 43 J5
Sprainger St 42 B1
Springfield 42 D2
Squires St 43 G4
Stafford St 42 E3
Stamford St 43 H3
Standish St 42 C3
Stanhope St 42 D7
Stanier Way 43 H4
Stanley St 42 C3
Star St 42 D7
Steinberg Ct 42 B1
Sterndale Cl 43 H5
Stockdale Cl 42 C2
Stone St 42 B1
Stowell St 43 E5
Strada Way 43 E2
Strand, The 42 B4

Strand St 42 B4
Strathmore Rd 43 H1
Strauss Cl 43 H7
Suffolk St 42 D5
Sugnall St 43 E5
Summer Seat 42 C1
Surrey St 42 C5
Sutcliffe St 43 H2
Sweeting St 42 B4
Swindale Cl 43 G6
Swiss Rd 43 J2

T
Tabley St 42 C6
Tace Cl 43 F6
Tagus Cl 43 G7
Tamar Cl 43 F1
Tarleton St 42 C4
Tatlock St 42 C1
Tavy Rd 43 F1
Teck St 43 G3
Teign St 43 F1
Tempest Hey 42 B3
Temple Ct 42 C4
Temple La 42 C3
Temple St 42 C3
Tenterden St 42 C1
Thackeray Pl 43 F7
Thames St 43 G7
Thomas St Way 42 C5
Thorburn St 43 H4
Thornes Rd 43 G2
Tichbourne Way 43 F2
Tideswell Cl 43 H5
Timpron St 43 H5
Titchfield St 42 C1
Tithebarn St 42 B3
Tobin Cl 42 C1
Toft St 43 H3
Tom Mann Cl 42 D3
Tordelow Cl 43 F1
Tower Gdns 42 B4
Trafalgar Way 43 F2
Trowbridge St 42 E4
Trueman St 42 C3
Tudor St N 43 H2
Tudor St S 43 H2
Tulloch St 43 G2
Tunnel Rd 43 H5
Tunstall St 43 J6
Tweed Cl 43 H1
Twomey Cl 42 C1

U
Underley St 43 J6
Union Ct 42 C4
Union St 42 B3
Upper Baker St 43 G2
Upper Beau St 42 D1
Upper Bute St 42 E1
Upper Duke St 42 D5
Upper Frederick St 42 C5
Upper Hampton St 43 F6
Upper Harrington St 42 D7
Upper Hill St 43 E7
Upper Hope Pl 43 E5
Upper Mann St 42 D7
Upper Mason St 43 G4
Upper Newington 42 D4
Upper Parliament St 42 D6
Upper Pitt St 42 D6
Upper Pownall St 42 C5
Upper Stanhope St 43 E6
Upper Warwick St 43 E7
Upper William St 42 B1
Uxbridge St 43 H5

V
Vandries St 42 A1
Vandyke St 43 H6
Vauxhall Rd 42 C2
Vernon St 42 C3
Verulam Cl 43 G6
Victoria St 42 C4
Village St 43 E1
Vincent Ct 42 D5
Vining St 43 F7
Virgil St 42 D1
Voelas St 43 G7
Vronhill Cl 43 G7
Vulcan St 42 A1

W
Wainwright Cl 43 H5
Wakefield St 42 D2
Waldron Cl 42 C2
Walker St 43 F2
Wall St 42 C4
Walsh Cl 42 C1
Wapping 42 C5
Ward St 42 D3
Warwick St 42 E7
Waterloo Quay 42 A2
Water St 42 B4
Watkinson St 42 C6
Watmough St 42 E1
Wavertree Bvd 43 K4
Wavertree Rd 43 G4
Webb Cl 43 H4
Webb St 43 H6
Webster Rd 43 J6
Webster St 42 C3
Wedgewood St 43 H3
Wendell St 43 H6
Wentworth Dr 43 F1
West Derby Rd 43 G2
West Derby St 43 F3
Westmorland Dr 42 C2
Whitcroft Rd 43 J2
Whitechapel 42 C4
Whitefield Rd 43 G1
Whitefield Way 43 G1
White Rock Ct 43 G1
White Rock St 43 G1
Whithorn St 43 J5
Whitland Rd 43 J1
Whitley St 42 B1
Whittier St 43 H6
Wightman St 43 G2
Wilde St 42 D3
Wilfer Cl 43 H5
William Brown St 42 D3
William Henry St 42 E2
Williamson St 42 C4
Wimpole St 43 H3
Windsor St 43 E6
Windsor Vw 43 H6
Winifred St 43 H4
Winter St 43 F2
Wolstenholme Sq 42 D5
Woodside St 43 H4
Wood St 42 D4
Wordsworth St 43 H6
Wrayburn Cl 43 H5
Wrenbury St 43 H3
Wynnstay St 43 G7

Y
Yanwath St 43 H6
York St 42 C5

London street index

A
Abbey Orchard St SW1 44 D6
Abingdon St SW1 44 E6
Achilles Way W1 44 A5
Adam & Eve Ct W1 44 C2
Adams Row W1 44 A4
Adam St WC2 45 E4
Addington St SE1 45 F6
Addle Hill EC4 45 H3
Adelaide St WC2 44 E4
Adeline Pl WC1 44 D2
Adelphi Ter WC2 45 E4
Agar St WC2 44 E4
Air St W1 44 C4
Alaska St SE1 45 G5
Albany W1 44 C4
Albany Ctyd W1 44 C4

Albemarle St W1 44 B4
Albemarle Way EC1 45 H1
Albert Barnes Ho SE1 45 J7
Albion Pl EC1 45 H1
Albion Way EC1 45 H1
Aldburgh Ms W1 44 A2
Aldermanbury EC2 45 J2
Aldermanbury Sq EC2 45 J2
Aldersgate St EC1 45 J2
Aldford St W1 44 A4
Aldwych WC2 45 F3
Alfred Ms W1 44 D1
Alfred Pl WC1 44 D1
All Souls Pl W1 44 B2
Ambassador's Ct SW1 44 C5
Ambrosden Av SW1 44 C7
Amen Cor EC4 45 H3
Amen Ct EC4 45 H2

America St SE1 45 J5
Andrew Borde St WC2 44 D2
Andrewes Ho EC2 45 J2
Andrews Crosse WC2 45 G3
Angel Ct SW1 44 C5
Angel St EC1 45 J2
Apothecary St EC4 45 H3
Apple Tree Yd SW1 44 C5
Apsley Way W1 44 A5
Aquinas St SE1 45 G4
Archer St W1 44 D3
Arches, The WC2 45 E4
Archibald Ms W1 44 A4
Arch St SE1 45 J7
Argyll St W1 44 C2
Aria Ho WC2 45 E2
Arlington St SW1 44 C4
Arne St WC2 45 E3

Arneway St SW1 44 D7
Arrol Ho SE1 45 J7
Artillery Mans SW1 44 D6
Artillery Pl SW1 44 D7
Artillery Row SW1 44 D7
Arundel Gt Ct WC2 45 F3
Arundel St WC2 45 F3
Ashentree Ct EC4 45 G3
Ashland Pl W1 44 A1
Ashley Gdns SW1 44 C7
Ashley Pl SW1 44 C7
Astbury Ho SE11 45 G7
Audley Sq W1 44 A4
Austral St SE11 45 H7
Ave Maria La EC4 45 H3
Avery Row W1 44 B3
Avonmouth St SE1 45 J6
Avon Pl SE1 45 J6

Aybrook St W1 44 A2
Aylesbury St EC1 45 H1
Ayres St SE1 45 J5

B
Babmaes St SW1 44 D4
Back Hill EC1 45 G1
Bainbridge St WC1 44 D2
Baker's Ms W1 44 A2
Baker's Row EC1 45 G1
Baker's Yd EC1 45 G1
Balcombe St NW1 44 A1
Balderton St W1 44 A3
Baldwin's Gdns EC1 45 G1
Balfour Ms W1 44 A4
Balfour Pl W1 44 A4
Baltic St E EC1 45 J1
Baltic St W EC1 45 J1
Banbury Ct WC2 44 E3

Bank End SE1 45 J4
Banks Ho SE1 45 J7
Bankside SE1 45 J4
Bankside Lofts SE1 45 H4
Banner St EC1 45 J1
Barbican EC2 45 J2
Barbican, The EC2 45 J1
Barbon Cl WC1 45 E1
Barge Ho St SE1 45 G4
Barkham Ter SE1 45 G6
Barley Mow Pas EC1 45 H2
Barlow Pl W1 44 B4
Barnard's Inn EC1 45 G2
Barons Pl SE1 45 G6
Barrett St W1 44 A3
Barter St WC1 45 E2
Bartholomew Cl EC1 45 J2
Bartholomew Pl EC1 45 J2

Bartlett Ct EC4 **45** G2
Bartletts Pas EC4 **45** G2
Barton St SW1 **44** E6
Bastion Highwalk EC2 **45** J2
Bateman's Bldgs W1 **44** D3
Bateman St W1 **44** D3
Bath Ct EC1 **45** G1
Bath Ter SE1 **45** J7
Bayley St W1 **44** D2
Baylis Rd SE1 **45** G6
Beak St W1 **44** C3
Bear All EC4 **45** H2
Bear Gdns SE1 **45** J4
Bear La SE1 **45** H4
Bear St WC2 **44** D3
Beauchamp St EC1 **45** G2
Beaumont Ms W1 **44** A1
Beaumont St W1 **44** A1
Bedford Av WC1 **44** D2
Bedfordbury WC2 **44** E3
Bedford Ct WC2 **44** E4
Bedford Pl WC1 **44** E1
Bedford Row WC1 **45** F1
Bedford Sq WC1 **44** D2
Bedford St WC2 **44** E3
Bedford Way WC1 **44** D1
Bedlam Ms SE11 **45** G7
Beech St EC2 **45** J1
Beeston Pl SW1 **44** B7
Belgrave Ms N SW1 **44** A6
Belgrave Ms S SW1 **44** A6
Belgrave Ms W SW1 **44** A6
Belgrave Pl SW1 **44** A6
Belgrave Sq SW1 **44** A6
Belgrave Yd SW1 **44** B7
Belgravia SW1 **44** A7
Bell Wf La EC4 **45** J4
Bell Yd WC2 **45** G3
Belvedere Bldgs SE1 **45** H6
Belvedere Pl SE1 **45** H6
Belvedere Rd SE1 **45** F5
Benjamin St EC1 **45** H1
Bennet's Hill EC4 **45** H3
Bennet St SW1 **44** C4
Bennetts Yd SW1 **44** D7
Bentinck Ms W1 **44** A2
Bentinck St W1 **44** A2
Berkeley Sq W1 **44** B4
Berkeley St W1 **44** B4
Bernard St WC1 **44** E1
Berners Ms W1 **44** C2
Berners Pl W1 **44** C2
Berners St W1 **44** C2
Berwick St W1 **44** D3
Betterton St WC2 **44** E3
Bingham Pl W1 **44** A1
Binney St W1 **44** A3
Birdcage Wk SW1 **44** C6
Bird St W1 **44** A3
Bishop's Ct EC4 **45** H2
Bishop's Ct WC2 **45** G2
Bishops Ter SE11 **45** G7
Bittern St SE1 **45** J6
Blackburne's Ms W1 **44** A3
Blackfriars Br EC4 **45** H3
Blackfriars Br SE1 **45** H3
Blackfriars Ct EC4 **45** H3
Black Friars La EC4 **45** H3
Blackfriars Pas EC4 **45** H3
Blackfriars Rd SE1 **45** H6
Bleeding Heart Yd EC1 **45** G2
Blenheim St W1 **44** B3
Bloomfield Pl W1 **44** B3
Bloomsbury WC1 **44** D2
Bloomsbury Ct WC1 **45** E2
Bloomsbury Pl WC1 **45** E1
Bloomsbury Sq WC1 **45** E1
Bloomsbury St WC1 **44** D2
Bloomsbury Way WC1 **44** E2
Blore Ct W1 **44** D3
Blue Ball Yd SW1 **44** C5
Bolsover St W1 **44** B1
Bolt Ct EC4 **45** G3
Bolton St W1 **44** B4
Book Ms WC2 **44** D3
Booth La EC4 **45** J3
Booth's Pl W1 **44** C2
Borough, The SE1 **45** J6
Borough High St SE1 **45** H4
Borough Rd SE1 **45** H6
Borough Sq SE1 **45** J6
Boscobel Pl SW1 **44** A7
Boswell Ct WC1 **45** E1
Boswell St WC1 **45** E1
Boundary Row SE1 **45** H5
Bourchier St W1 **44** D3
Bourdon Pl W1 **44** B3
Bourdon St W1 **44** B3
Bourlet Cl W1 **44** C2
Bourne Est EC1 **45** G1
Bouverie St EC4 **45** G3

Bow Chyd EC4 **45** J3
Bow La EC4 **45** J3
Bow St WC2 **45** E3
Boyce St SE1 **45** F5
Boyfield St SE1 **45** H6
Boyle St W1 **44** C3
Brackley St EC1 **45** J1
Brad St SE1 **45** G5
Bread St EC4 **45** J3
Bream's Bldgs EC4 **45** G2
Bressenden Pl SW1 **44** D6
Brewer's Grn SW1 **44** D6
Brewers Hall Gdns EC2 **45** J2
Brewer St W1 **44** C3
Briant Est SE1 **45** G7
Briant Ho SE1 **45** F7
Brick Ct EC4 **45** G3
Brick St W1 **44** B5
Bride Ct EC4 **45** H3
Bride La EC4 **45** H3
Bridewell Pl EC4 **45** H3
Bridford Ms W1 **44** B1
Bridge Pl SW1 **44** B7
Bridge St SW1 **44** E6
Bridgewater Sq EC2 **45** J1
Bridgewater St EC2 **45** J1
Bridle La W1 **44** C3
Brinton Wk SE1 **45** H5
Briset St EC1 **45** H1
Britton St EC1 **45** H1
Broadbent St W1 **44** B3
Broad Ct WC2 **45** E3
Broad Sanctuary SW1 **44** D6
Broadstone Pl W1 **44** A2
Broad Wk W1 **44** A4
Broadwall SE1 **45** G4
Broadway SW1 **44** D6
Broadwick St W1 **44** C3
Broad Yd EC1 **45** H1
Brockham St SE1 **45** J6
Broken Wf EC4 **45** J3
Bromley Pl W1 **44** C1
Brook Dr SE11 **45** G7
Brooke's Ct EC1 **45** G1
Brookes Mkt EC1 **45** G1
Brooke St EC1 **45** G2
Brook's Ms W1 **44** B3
Brook St W1 **44** B3
Brown Hart Gdns W1 **44** A3
Browning Ms W1 **44** B2
Brownlow Ms WC1 **45** F1
Brownlow St WC1 **45** F2
Brunswick Sq WC1 **45** E1
Bruton La W1 **44** B4
Bruton Pl W1 **44** B4
Bruton St W1 **44** B4
Brydges Pl WC2 **44** E4
Buckingham Arc WC2 **45** E4
Buckingham Gate SW1 **44** C6
Buckingham Ms SW1 **44** C6
Buckingham Pl SW1 **44** C6
Buckingham St WC2 **45** E4
Buckley St SE1 **45** G5
Bucknall St WC2 **44** D2
Bull Inn Ct WC2 **45** E4
Bulstrode Pl W1 **44** A2
Bulstrode St W1 **44** A2
Burdett St SE1 **45** G6
Burgon St EC4 **45** H3
Burleigh St WC2 **45** F3
Burlington Arc W1 **44** C4
Burlington Gdns W1 **44** C4
Burrell St SE1 **45** H4
Burrows Ms SE1 **45** H5
Bury Pl WC1 **45** E2
Bury St SW1 **44** C4
Butler Pl SW1 **44** D6
Byng Pl WC1 **44** D1
Bywell Pl W1 **44** C2

C

Cadogan La SW1 **44** A7
Cahill St EC1 **45** J1
Caleb St SE1 **45** J5
Cambridge Circ WC2 **44** D3
Candover St W1 **44** C2
Cannon St EC4 **45** J3
Canon Row SW1 **44** E6
Canterbury Ho SE1 **45** F6
Canvey St SE1 **45** H4
Capener's Cl SW1 **44** A6
Capper St WC1 **44** C1
Carburton St W1 **44** B1
Carey La EC2 **45** J2
Carey St WC2 **45** F3
Carlisle La SE1 **45** F7
Carlisle Pl SW1 **44** C7
Carlisle St W1 **44** D3
Carlos Pl W1 **44** A4
Carlton Gdns SW1 **44** D5
Carlton Ho Ter SW1 **44** D5
Carlton St SW1 **44** D4

Carmelite St EC4 **45** G3
Carnaby St W1 **44** C3
Carpenter St W1 **44** B4
Carrington St W1 **44** B5
Carteret St SW1 **44** D6
Carter La EC4 **45** H3
Carthusian St EC1 **45** J1
Carting La WC2 **45** E4
Castle Baynard St EC4 **45** H3
Castlebrook Cl SE11 **45** H7
Castle La SW1 **44** C6
Castle Yd SE1 **45** H4
Cathedral Piazza SW1 **44** C7
Cathedral Wk SW1 **44** C6
Catherine Pl SW1 **44** C6
Catherine St WC2 **45** F3
Catherine Wheel Yd SW1 **44** C5
Catton St WC1 **45** F2
Cavendish Ms N W1 **44** B1
Cavendish Ms S W1 **44** B2
Cavendish Pl W1 **44** B2
Cavendish Sq W1 **44** B2
Caxton St SW1 **44** C6
Cecil Ct WC2 **44** D4
Centaur St SE1 **45** F6
Centrepoint WC1 **44** D2
Chadwick St SW1 **44** D7
Chancel St SE1 **45** H4
Chancery La WC2 **45** G2
Chandos Pl WC2 **44** E4
Chandos St W1 **44** B2
Chapel Pl W1 **44** B3
Chapel St SW1 **44** A6
Chaplin Cl SE1 **45** G5
Chapone Pl W1 **44** D3
Chapter Ho Ct EC4 **45** J3
Charing Cross SW1 **44** D4
Charing Cross Rd WC2 **44** D2
Charles II St SW1 **44** D4
Charles St W1 **44** B4
Charlotte Ms W1 **44** C1
Charlotte Pl W1 **44** C2
Charlotte St W1 **44** C1
Charterhouse, The EC1 **45** H1
Charterhouse Bldgs EC1 **45** H1
Charterhouse Ms EC1 **45** H1
Charterhouse Sq EC1 **45** H1
Charterhouse St EC1 **45** G2
Cheapside EC2 **45** J3
Chenies Ms WC1 **44** D1
Chenies St WC1 **44** D1
Chequer St EC1 **45** J1
Cherry Tree Wk EC1 **45** J1
Chesham Cl SW1 **44** A7
Chesham Ms SW1 **44** A6
Chesham Pl SW1 **44** A7
Chesham St SW1 **44** A7
Cheshire Ct EC4 **45** G3
Chester Cl SW1 **44** A6
Chesterfield Gdns W1 **44** B4
Chesterfield Hill W1 **44** B4
Chesterfield St W1 **44** B4
Chester Ms SW1 **44** B6
Chester Sq SW1 **44** B7
Chester Sq Ms SW1 **44** B7
Chester St SW1 **44** A6
Chicheley St SE1 **45** F5
Chichester Rents WC2 **45** G2
Chiltern St W1 **44** A1
Ching Ct WC2 **44** E3
Chiswell St EC1 **45** J1
Chitty St W1 **44** C1
Christ Ch Pas EC1 **45** H2
Church Entry EC4 **45** H3
Church Pl SW1 **44** C4
Churchyard Row SE11 **45** H7
Clare Mkt WC2 **45** F3
Clarges Ms W1 **44** B4
Clarges St W1 **44** B4
Clarke's Ms W1 **44** A1
Clement's Inn WC2 **45** F3
Clement's Inn Pas WC2 **45** F3
Clennam St SE1 **45** J5
Clerkenwell EC1 **45** H1
Clerkenwell Grn EC1 **45** G1
Clerkenwell Rd EC1 **45** G1
Cleveland Ms W1 **44** C1
Cleveland Pl SW1 **44** C4
Cleveland Row SW1 **44** C5
Cleveland St W1 **44** C1
Clifford's Inn Pas EC4 **45** G3
Clifford St W1 **44** C4
Clink St SE1 **45** J4
Clipstone Ms W1 **44** C1
Clipstone St W1 **44** B1
Cliveden Pl SW1 **44** A7

Cloak La EC4 **45** J3
Cloth Ct EC1 **45** H2
Cloth Fair EC1 **45** H2
Cloth St EC1 **45** J1
Coach & Horses Yd W1 **44** B3
Coburg Cl SW1 **44** C7
Cock La EC1 **45** H2
Cockpit Steps SW1 **44** D6
Cockpit Yd WC1 **45** F1
Cockspur Ct SW1 **44** D4
Cockspur St SW1 **44** D4
Coin St SE1 **45** G4
Cole St SE1 **45** J6
Coley St WC1 **45** F1
College Hill EC4 **45** J3
College Ms SW1 **44** E6
College St EC4 **45** J3
Collinson St SE1 **45** J6
Collinson Wk SE1 **45** J6
Colnbrook St SE1 **45** H7
Colombo St SE1 **45** H5
Colonnade WC1 **44** E1
Colville Pl W1 **44** C2
Computer Pass EC2 **45** J2
Concert Hall App SE1 **45** F5
Conduit Ct WC2 **44** E3
Conduit St W1 **44** B3
Cons St SE1 **45** G5
Constitution Hill SW1 **44** B5
Conway Ms W1 **44** C1
Conway St W1 **44** C1
Cooper Cl SE1 **45** G6
Copeland Ho SE11 **45** F7
Copperfield St SE1 **45** H5
Coptic St WC1 **44** E2
Coral St SE1 **45** G6
Coram St WC1 **44** E1
Cork St W1 **44** C4
Cork St Ms W1 **44** C4
Corner Ho St WC2 **44** E4
Cornwall Rd SE1 **45** G4
Cosmo Pl WC1 **45** E1
Cosser St SE1 **45** G6
Cottesloe Ms SE1 **45** G6
County St SE1 **45** J7
Covent Gdn WC2 **45** E3
Covent Gdn Mkt WC2 **45** E3
Coventry St W1 **44** D4
Cowcross St EC1 **45** H1
Cowley St SW1 **44** E6
Craigs Ct SW1 **44** E4
Cramer St W1 **44** A2
Cranbourn St WC2 **44** D3
Crane Ct EC4 **45** G3
Cranfield Row SE1 **45** G6
Craven Pas WC2 **44** E4
Craven St WC2 **44** E4
Crawford Pas EC1 **45** G1
Creed La EC4 **45** H3
Crescent Row EC1 **45** J1
Cripplegate St EC2 **45** J1
Cromwell Twr EC2 **45** J1
Cross Keys Cl W1 **44** A2
Cross Keys Sq EC1 **45** J2
Crown Ct EC2 **45** J3
Crown Ct WC2 **45** E3
Crown Office Row EC4 **45** G3
Crown Pas SW1 **44** C5
Cubitts Yd WC2 **45** E3
Culross St W1 **44** A4
Cursitor St EC4 **45** G2
Curzon Gate W1 **44** A5
Curzon Sq W1 **44** A5
Curzon St W1 **44** A5
Cut, The SE1 **45** G5
Cypress Pl W1 **44** C1

D

Dacre St SW1 **44** D6
Dane St WC1 **45** F2
Dansey Pl W1 **44** D3
Dante Pl SE11 **45** H7
Dante Rd SE11 **45** H7
D'Arblay St W1 **44** C3
Dartmouth St SW1 **44** D6
Davidge St SE1 **45** H6
Davies Ms W1 **44** B3
Davies St W1 **44** B3
Dean Bradley St SW1 **44** E7
Deanery Ms W1 **44** A4
Deanery St W1 **44** A4
Dean Farrar St SW1 **44** D6
Dean Ryle St SW1 **44** E7
Deans Ct EC4 **45** H3
Deans Ms W1 **44** B2
Dean Stanley St SW1 **44** E7
Dean St W1 **44** D2
Dean's Yd SW1 **44** D6
Dean Trench St SW1 **44** E7
Denman St W1 **44** D4
Denmark Pl WC2 **44** D2
Denmark St WC2 **44** D3

Derby Gate SW1 **44** E5
Derby St W1 **44** A5
Dering St W1 **44** B3
Devereux Ct WC2 **45** G3
Devonshire Cl W1 **44** B1
Devonshire Ms N W1 **44** B1
Devonshire Ms S W1 **44** B1
Devonshire Ms W W1 **44** B1
Devonshire Pl W1 **44** A1
Devonshire Pl Ms W1 **44** A1
Devonshire Row Ms W1 **44** B1
Devonshire St W1 **44** A2
De Walden St W1 **44** A2
Diadem Ct W1 **44** D3
Dickens Ms EC1 **45** H1
Dickens Sq SE1 **45** J6
Disney Pl SE1 **45** J5
Disney St SE1 **45** J5
Distaff La EC4 **45** J3
Doby Ct EC4 **45** J3
Dodson St SE1 **45** G6
Dolben St SE1 **45** H5
Dombey St WC1 **45** F1
Doon St SE1 **45** G5
Dorrington St EC1 **45** G1
Dorrit St SE1 **45** J5
Dorset Bldgs EC4 **45** H3
Dorset Ms SW1 **44** B6
Dorset Ri EC4 **45** H3
Doughty Ms WC1 **45** F1
Dover St W1 **44** B4
Dover Yd W1 **44** B4
Downing St SW1 **44** E5
Down St W1 **44** B5
Down St Ms W1 **44** B5
Doyce St SE1 **45** J5
D'Oyley St SW1 **44** A7
Drake St WC1 **45** F2
Draper Ho SE1 **45** H7
Drury La WC2 **45** E3
Dryden St WC2 **45** E3
Duchess Ms W1 **44** B2
Duchess St W1 **44** B2
Duchy Pl SE1 **45** G4
Duchy St SE1 **45** G4
Duck La W1 **44** D3
Dufferin St EC1 **45** J1
Dufour's Pl W1 **44** C3
Dugard Way SE11 **45** H7
Duke of Wellington Pl SW1 **44** A5
Duke of York St SW1 **44** C4
Duke's Ms W1 **44** A2
Duke St SW1 **44** C4
Duke St W1 **44** A2
Duke's Yd W1 **44** A3
Duncannon St WC2 **44** E4
Dunns Pas WC1 **45** E2
Dunstable Ms W1 **44** A1
Durham Ho St WC2 **45** E4
Dyer's Bldgs EC1 **45** G2
Dyott St WC1 **44** E2

E

Eagle Ct EC1 **45** H1
Eagle Pl SW1 **44** C4
Eagle St WC1 **45** F2
Earlham St WC2 **44** D3
Earnshaw St WC2 **44** D2
Easley's Ms W1 **44** A2
Eastcastle St W1 **44** C2
East Harding St EC4 **45** G2
East Pas EC1 **45** H1
East Poultry Av EC1 **45** H2
Eaton Gate SW1 **44** A7
Eaton La SW1 **44** B7
Eaton Ms N SW1 **44** A7
Eaton Ms S SW1 **44** A7
Eaton Ms W SW1 **44** A7
Eaton Pl SW1 **44** A7
Eaton Row SW1 **44** B6
Eaton Sq SW1 **44** B6
Eaton Ter SW1 **44** A7
Eaton Ter Ms SW1 **44** A7
Ebury Ms SW1 **44** B7
Ebury Ms E SW1 **44** B7
Ebury St SW1 **44** B7
Eccleston Br SW1 **44** B7
Eccleston Ms SW1 **44** A7
Eccleston Pl SW1 **44** B7
Eccleston St SW1 **44** B7
Edwards Ms W1 **44** A3
Elba Pl SE17 **45** J7
Elephant & Castle SE1 **45** H7
Elephant Rd SE17 **45** J7
Elizabeth Ct SW1 **44** D7
Elizabeth St SW1 **44** A7
Ellington Ho SE1 **45** J6
Elliotts Row SE11 **45** H7
Elm Ct EC4 **45** G3
Elm St WC1 **45** F1
Elverton St SW1 **44** D7

Ely Ct EC1 **45** G2
Ely Pl EC1 **45** G2
Embankment Pier WC2 **45** F4
Embankment Pl WC2 **45** E4
Emerald St WC1 **45** F1
Emerson St SE1 **45** J4
Emery Hill St SW1 **44** C7
Emery St SE1 **45** G6
Endell St WC2 **44** E2
Errol St EC1 **45** J1
Essex Ct EC4 **45** G3
Essex St WC2 **45** G3
Euston Rd NW1 **44** B1
Evelyn Yd W1 **44** D2
Ewer St SE1 **45** J5
Excel Ct WC2 **44** D4
Exchange Ct WC2 **45** E4
Exeter St WC2 **45** E3
Exton St SE1 **45** G5
Eyre St Hill EC1 **45** G1

F

Falconberg Ct W1 **44** D2
Falconberg Ms W1 **44** D2
Falcon Ct EC4 **45** G3
Falmouth Rd SE1 **45** J6
Fann St EC1 **45** J1
Fann St EC2 **45** J1
Fareham St W1 **44** D2
Farm St W1 **44** B4
Farnham Pl SE1 **45** H5
Farringdon La EC1 **45** G1
Farringdon St EC4 **45** H2
Faulkner's All EC1 **45** H1
Ferrybridge Ho SE11 **45** F7
Fetter La EC4 **45** G3
Field Ct WC1 **45** F2
Fisher St WC1 **45** F2
Fitzalan St SE11 **45** G7
Fitzhardinge St W1 **44** A2
Fitzmaurice Pl W1 **44** B4
Fitzroy Ct W1 **44** C1
Fitzroy Ms W1 **44** C1
Fitzroy Sq W1 **44** C1
Fitzroy St W1 **44** C1
Fives Ct SE11 **45** H7
Flaxman Ct W1 **44** D3
Fleet St EC4 **45** G3
Flitcroft St WC2 **44** D2
Floral St WC2 **44** E3
Florin Ct EC1 **45** J1
Foley St W1 **44** C2
Fore St EC2 **45** J2
Fortune St EC1 **45** J1
Forum Magnum Sq SE1 **45** F5
Foster La EC2 **45** J2
Foubert's Pl W1 **44** C3
Fountain Ct EC4 **45** G3
Fountain Sq SW1 **44** B7
Fox & Knot St EC1 **45** H1
Francis St SW1 **44** C7
Frazier St SE1 **45** G6
Friars Cl SE1 **45** H5
Friar St EC4 **45** H3
Friary Ct SW1 **44** C5
Friday St EC4 **45** J3
Frith St W1 **44** D3
Fulwood Pl WC1 **45** F2
Furnival St EC4 **45** G2
Fynes St SW1 **44** D7

G

Gabriel's Wf SE1 **45** G4
Gage St WC1 **45** E1
Galen Pl WC1 **45** E2
Gambia St SE1 **45** H5
Ganton St W1 **44** C3
Garbutt Pl W1 **44** A1
Garden Row SE1 **45** H7
Gardners La EC4 **45** J3
Garlick Hill EC4 **45** J3
Garrick St WC2 **44** E3
Garrick Yd WC2 **44** E3
Gate Ho Sq SE1 **45** J4
Gate St WC2 **45** F2
Gaunt St SE1 **45** H6
Gayfere St SW1 **44** E7
Gaywood Est SE1 **45** H7
Gaywood St SE1 **45** H7
Gees Ct W1 **44** A3
George Ct WC2 **45** E4
George Mathers Rd SE11 **45** H7
George Yd W1 **44** A3
Geraldine St SE11 **45** H7
Gerald Ms SW1 **44** A7
Gerald Rd SW1 **44** A7
Gerrard Pl W1 **44** D3
Gerrard St W1 **44** D3
Gerridge St SE1 **45** G6
Gilbert Pl WC1 **44** E2
Gilbert St W1 **44** A3

Gildea St W1 44 B2
Gillingham Row SW1 44 C7
Gillingham St SW1 44 B7
Giltspur St EC1 45 H2
Gladstone St SE1 45 H6
Glasshill St SE1 45 H5
Glasshouse St W1 44 C4
Glasshouse Yd EC1 45 J1
Globe St SE1 45 J6
Globe Yd W1 44 B3
Godliman St EC4 45 J3
Golden Jubilee Br SE1 45 F5
Golden Jubilee Br WC2 45 E4
Golden La EC1 45 J1
Golden La Est EC1 45 J1
Golden Sq W1 44 C3
Goldsmith St EC2 45 J2
Goodge Pl W1 44 C2
Goodge St W1 44 C2
Goodwins Ct WC2 44 E3
Gordon Sq WC1 44 D1
Gosfield St W1 44 C1
Goslett Yd WC2 44 D3
Goswell Rd EC1 45 J1
Gough Sq EC4 45 G2
Gower Ms WC1 44 D2
Grafton Ms W1 44 C1
Grafton St W1 44 B4
Grafton Way W1 44 C1
Grafton Way WC1 44 C1
Granby Pl SE1 45 G6
Grand Av EC1 45 H1
Grange Ct WC2 45 F3
Grantham Pl W1 44 B5
Granville Pl W1 44 A3
Grape St WC2 44 E2
Gray's Inn WC1 45 F1
Gray's Inn Pl WC1 45 F2
Gray's Inn Sq WC1 45 G1
Gray St SE1 45 G6
Gray's Yd W1 44 A3
Great Arthur Ho EC1 45 J1
Great Castle St W1 44 B2
Great Chapel St W1 44 D2
Great Coll St SW1 44 E6
Great Dover St SE1 45 J6
Great George St SW1 44 D6
Great Guildford St SE1 45 J4
Great James St WC1 45 F1
Great Marlborough St W1 44 C3
Great New St EC4 45 G2
Great Ormond St WC1 45 E1
Great Peter St SW1 44 D7
Great Portland St W1 44 B1
Great Pulteney St W1 44 C3
Great Queen St WC2 45 E3
Great Russell St WC1 44 D2
Great St. Thomas Apostle EC4 45 J3
Great Scotland Yd SW1 44 E5
Great Smith St SW1 44 D6
Great Suffolk St SE1 45 H5
Great Sutton St EC1 45 H1
Great Titchfield St W1 44 C2
Great Trinity La EC4 45 J3
Great Turnstile WC1 45 F2
Great Windmill St W1 44 D3
Greek Ct W1 44 D3
Greek St W1 44 D3
Green Arbour Ct EC1 45 H2
Greencoat Pl SW1 44 C7
Greencoat Row SW1 44 C7
Greenham Cl SE1 45 G6
Greenhill's Rents EC1 45 H1
Green's Ct W1 44 D3
Greenwell St W1 44 B1
Greet St SE1 45 G5
Grenville St WC1 45 E1
Gresham St EC2 45 J2
Gresse St W1 44 D2
Greville St EC1 45 G2
Greycoat Pl SW1 44 D7
Greycoat St SW1 44 D7
Greyfriars Pas EC1 45 H2
Greystoke Pl EC4 45 G2
Grindal St SE1 45 G6
Groom Pl SW1 44 A6
Grosvenor Cotts SW1 44 A7
Grosvenor Cres SW1 44 A6
Grosvenor Cres Ms SW1 44 A6
Grosvenor Est SW1 44 D7
Grosvenor Gdns SW1 44 B6
Grosvenor Gdns Ms E SW1 44 B6
Grosvenor Gdns Ms N SW1 44 B7
Grosvenor Gdns Ms S SW1 44 B7

Grosvenor Hill W1 44 B3
Grosvenor Pl SW1 44 A6
Grosvenor Sq W1 44 A3
Grosvenor St W1 44 B3
Grotto Pas W1 44 A1
Groveland Ct EC4 45 J3
Guildhall Yd EC2 45 J2
Guildhouse St SW1 44 C7
Guilford Pl WC1 45 F1
Guilford St WC1 45 E1
Gunpowder Sq EC4 45 G2
Gutter La EC2 45 J2

H
Half Moon Ct EC1 45 J2
Half Moon St W1 44 B4
Halkin Arc SW1 44 A6
Halkin Ms SW1 44 A6
Halkin Pl SW1 44 A6
Halkin St SW1 44 A6
Hallam Ms W1 44 B1
Hallam St W1 44 B1
Hamilton Ms W1 44 B5
Hamilton Pl W1 44 A5
Ham Yd W1 44 D3
Hand Ct WC1 45 F2
Hanging Sword All EC4 45 G3
Hanover Pl WC2 45 E3
Hanover Sq W1 44 B3
Hanover St W1 44 B3
Hanson St W1 44 C1
Hanway Pl W1 44 D2
Hanway St W1 44 D2
Hare Ct EC4 45 G3
Hare Pl EC4 45 G3
Harewood Pl W1 44 B3
Harley Pl W1 44 B2
Harley St W1 44 B1
Harmsworth Ms SE11 45 H7
Harp All EC4 45 H2
Harper Rd SE1 45 J6
Harpur Ms WC1 45 F1
Harpur St WC1 45 F1
Hat & Mitre Ct EC1 45 H1
Hatfields SE1 45 G4
Hatton Gdn EC1 45 G1
Hatton Pl EC1 45 G1
Hatton Wall EC1 45 G1
Haunch of Venison Yd W1 44 B3
Hay Hill W1 44 B4
Hayles St SE11 45 H7
Haymarket SW1 44 D4
Haymarket Arc SW1 44 D4
Hayne St EC1 45 H1
Hay's Ms W1 44 B4
Hayward's Pl EC1 45 H1
Headfort Pl SW1 44 A6
Heddon St W1 44 C3
Hedger St SE11 45 H7
Hen & Chicken Ct EC4 45 G3
Henrietta Pl W1 44 B3
Henrietta St WC2 45 E3
Herald's Pl SE11 45 H7
Herbal Hill EC1 45 G1
Hercules Rd SE1 45 F7
Herrick St SW1 44 D7
Hertford St W1 44 B4
High Holborn WC1 45 E2
High Timber St EC4 45 J3
Hills Pl W1 44 C3
Hill St W1 44 A4
Hind Ct EC4 45 G3
Hinde St W1 44 A2
Hindon Ct SW1 44 C7
Hobart Pl SW1 44 B6
Holbein Pl SW1 44 A7
Holborn EC1 45 G2
Holborn WC2 45 F2
Holborn Circ EC1 45 G2
Holborn Pl WC1 45 F2
Holborn Viaduct EC1 45 G2
Holland St SE1 45 H4
Hollen St W1 44 D2
Holles St W1 44 B2
Holmes Ter SE1 45 G5
Holsworthy Sq WC1 45 F1
Holyoak Rd SE11 45 H7
Honey La EC2 45 J3
Hood Ct EC4 45 G3
Hop Gdns WC2 44 E4
Hopkins St W1 44 C3
Hopton's Gdns SE1 45 H4
Hopton St SE1 45 H4
Hornbeam Cl SE11 45 G7
Horse & Dolphin Yd W1 44 D3
Horseferry Rd SW1 44 D7
Horse Guards Av SW1 44 E5
Horse Guards Rd SW1 44 D5
Horsemongers Ms SE1 45 J6
Horse Ride SW1 44 D5

Hosier La EC1 45 H2
Houghton St WC2 45 F3
Howick Pl SW1 44 C7
Howland Ms E W1 44 C1
Howland St W1 44 C1
Hudson's Pl SW1 44 B7
Huggin Ct EC4 45 J3
Huggin Hill EC4 45 J3
Hulme Pl SE1 45 J6
Hungerford Br SE1 45 E4
Hungerford Br WC2 45 E4
Hungerford La WC2 44 E4
Huntley St WC1 44 C1
Hunt's Ct WC2 44 D4
Hutton St EC4 45 G3
Hyde Pk Cor W1 44 A5

I
India Pl WC2 45 F3
Ingestre Pl W1 44 C3
Ingram Cl SE11 45 F7
Inigo Pl WC2 44 E3
Inner Temple La EC4 45 G3
Invicta Plaza SE1 45 H4
Ireland Yd EC4 45 H3
Irving St WC2 44 D4
Isaac Way SE1 45 J5
Isabella St SE1 45 H5
Ivybridge La WC2 45 E4

J
Jacob's Well Ms W1 44 A2
James St W1 44 A2
James St WC2 45 E3
Jermyn St SW1 44 C4
Jerusalem Pas EC1 45 H1
Jervis Ct W1 44 B3
Joan St SE1 45 H5
Jockey's Flds WC1 45 F1
Johanna St SE1 45 G6
John Adam St WC2 45 E4
John Carpenter St EC4 45 H3
John Milton Pass EC2 45 J3
John Princes St W1 44 B2
John's Ms WC1 45 F1
John St WC1 45 F1
Jones St W1 44 B4
Jubilee Mkt Hall WC2 45 E3
Juxon St SE11 45 F7

K
Kean St WC2 45 F3
Keeley St WC2 45 F3
Kell St SE1 45 H6
Kemble St WC2 45 F3
Kemp's Ct W1 44 C3
Kendall Pl W1 44 A2
Kennet Wf La EC4 45 J3
Kennington Rd SE1 45 G6
Kennington Rd SE11 45 G7
Kenrick Pl W1 44 A1
Keppel Row SE1 45 J5
Keppel St WC1 44 D1
Keyworth Pl SE1 45 H6
Keyworth St SE1 45 H6
King Charles St SW1 44 D5
King Edward St EC1 45 J2
King Edward Wk SE1 45 G6
Kinghorn St EC1 45 J2
King James Ct SE1 45 H6
King James St SE1 45 H6
Kingly Ct W1 44 C3
Kingly St W1 44 C3
Kings Bench St SE1 45 H5
Kings Bench Wk EC4 45 G3
Kingscote St EC4 45 H3
King's Ms WC1 45 F1
Kings Pl SE1 45 J6
King's Reach Twr SE1 45 G4
King's Scholars' Pas SW1 44 C7
King St EC2 45 J3
King St SW1 44 C5
King St WC2 44 E3
Kingsway WC2 45 F2
Kinnerton St SW1 44 A6
Kirby St EC1 45 G1
Kirkman Pl W1 44 D2
Kirk St WC1 45 F1
Knightrider St EC4 45 J3

L
Lambeth SE1 45 F7
Lambeth Br SE1 45 E7
Lambeth Br SW1 45 E7
Lambeth Hill EC4 45 J3
Lambeth Palace Rd SE1 45 F7
Lambeth Pier SE1 45 E7
Lambeth Rd SE1 45 F7
Lambeth Rd SE11 45 F7
Lambeth Twrs SE11 45 G7
Lambeth Wk SE1 45 F7

Lambeth Wk SE11 45 F7
Lambs Conduit Pas WC1 45 F1
Lamb's Conduit St WC1 45 F1
Lamlash St SE11 45 H7
Lamp Office Ct WC1 45 F1
Lancashire Ct W1 44 B3
Lancaster Pl WC2 45 F3
Lancaster St SE1 45 H6
Lanesborough Pl SW1 44 A5
Langham Pl W1 44 B2
Langham St W1 44 B2
Langley Ct WC2 44 E3
Langley St WC2 44 E3
Lansdowne Row W1 44 B4
Lansdowne Ter WC1 45 E1
Lant St SE1 45 J5
Lauderdale Twr EC2 45 J1
Launcelot St SE1 45 G6
Lavington St SE1 45 H5
Lawrence La EC2 45 J3
Laystall St EC1 45 G1
Laytons Bldgs SE1 45 J5
Lazenby Ct WC2 44 E3
Leake St SE1 45 F5
Leather La EC1 45 G2
Lees Pl W1 44 A3
Leicester Ct WC2 44 D3
Leicester Pl WC2 44 D3
Leicester Sq WC2 44 D4
Leicester St WC2 44 D3
Leigh Hunt St SE1 45 J5
Leigh Pl EC1 45 G1
Leopards Ct EC1 45 G1
Leo Yd EC1 45 H1
Lewisham St SW1 44 D6
Lexington St W1 44 C3
Library St SE1 45 H6
Lily Pl EC1 45 G1
Limeburner La EC4 45 H3
Lincoln's Inn WC2 45 F2
Lincoln's Inn Flds WC2 45 F2
Lindsey St EC1 45 H1
Lisle St WC2 44 D3
Litchfield St WC2 44 D3
Little Argyll St W1 44 C3
Little Britain EC1 45 J2
Little Chester St SW1 44 A6
Little Coll St SW1 44 E6
Little Dean's Yd SW1 44 E6
Little Dorrit Ct SE1 45 J5
Little Essex St WC2 45 G3
Little George St SW1 44 E6
Little Newport St WC2 44 D3
Little New St EC4 45 G2
Little Portland St W1 44 C2
Little Russell St WC1 44 E2
Little St. James's St SW1 44 C5
Little Sanctuary SW1 44 D6
Little Smith St SW1 44 D6
Little Titchfield St W1 44 C2
Little Trinity La EC4 45 J3
Little Turnstile WC1 45 F2
Livonia St W1 44 C3
Lollard St SE11 45 F7
Loman St SE1 45 H5
Lombard La EC4 45 G3
London Cen Mkts EC1 45 H1
London Rd SE1 45 H6
London Silver Vaults WC2 45 G2
London Trocadero, The W1 44 D4
London Wall EC2 45 J2
Long Acre WC2 44 E3
Long La EC1 45 H1
Longridge Ho SE1 45 J7
Long's Ct WC2 44 D3
Longstone Ct SE1 45 J6
Longville Rd SE11 45 H7
Long Yd WC1 45 F1
Lord N St SW1 44 E7
Love La EC2 45 J2
Lover's Wk W1 44 A4
Lower Belgrave St SW1 44 B7
Lower Grosvenor Pl SW1 44 B6
Lower James St W1 44 C3
Lower John St W1 44 C3
Lower Marsh SE1 45 G6
Lower Rd SE1 45 G5
Lowndes Cl SW1 44 A7
Lowndes Ct W1 44 C3
Lowndes Pl SW1 44 A7
Ludgate Bdy EC4 45 H3
Ludgate Circ EC4 45 H3
Ludgate Hill EC4 45 H3
Ludgate Sq EC4 45 H3

Lumley Ct WC2 45 E4
Lumley St W1 44 A3
Luxborough St W1 44 A1
Lyall Ms SW1 44 A7
Lyall Ms W SW1 44 A7
Lyall St SW1 44 A7
Lygon Pl SW1 44 B7

M
McAuley Cl SE1 45 G6
Macclesfield St W1 44 D3
McCoid Way SE1 45 J6
Macfarren Pl NW1 44 A1
Macklin St WC2 45 E2
Mac's Pl EC4 45 G2
Maddox St W1 44 B3
Magpie All EC4 45 G3
Maiden La SE1 45 J4
Maiden La WC2 45 E4
Maidstone Bldgs Ms SE1 45 J5
Malet Pl WC1 44 D1
Malet St WC1 44 D1
Mall, The SW1 44 C5
Maltravers St WC2 45 F3
Manchester Ms W1 44 A2
Manchester Sq W1 44 A2
Manchester St W1 44 A2
Mandeville Pl W1 44 A2
Manette St W1 44 D3
Mansfield Ms W1 44 B2
Mansfield St W1 44 B2
Maple Pl W1 44 C1
Maple St W1 44 C1
Margaret Ct W1 44 C2
Margaret St W1 44 B2
Marigold All SE1 45 H4
Market Ct W1 44 C2
Market Ms W1 44 B5
Market Pl W1 44 C2
Marlborough Ct W1 44 C3
Marlborough Rd SW1 44 C5
Marshall St W1 44 C3
Marshalsea Rd SE1 45 J5
Marsham St SW1 44 D7
Martin Ho SE1 45 J6
Martlett Ct WC2 45 E3
Marylebone High St W1 44 A1
Marylebone La W1 44 B3
Marylebone Ms W1 44 B2
Marylebone Pas W1 44 C2
Marylebone St W1 44 A2
Masons Arms Ms W1 44 B3
Mason's Yd SW1 44 C4
Matthew Parker St SW1 44 D6
Matthews Yd WC2 44 E3
Maunsel St SW1 44 D7
Mayfair W1 44 B4
Mayfair Pl W1 44 B4
Mays Ct WC2 44 E4
Meadow Row SE1 45 J7
Mead Row SE1 45 G6
Meard St W1 44 D3
Medway St SW1 44 D7
Melbourne Pl WC2 45 F3
Memel Ct EC1 45 J1
Memel St EC1 45 J1
Mepham St SE1 45 F5
Mercer St WC2 44 E3
Merrick Sq SE1 45 J6
Metro Cen Hts SE1 45 J7
Meymott St SE1 45 H5
Middlesex Pas EC1 45 H2
Middle St EC1 45 J1
Middle Temple EC4 45 G3
Middle Temple La EC4 45 G3
Middleton Pl W1 44 C2
Midford Pl W1 44 C1
Milcote St SE1 45 H6
Milford La WC2 45 F3
Milk St EC2 45 J3
Millbank SW1 44 E7
Millbank Ct SW1 44 E7
Millennium Br EC4 45 J3
Millennium Br SE1 45 J3
Miller Wk SE1 45 G5
Millman Ms WC1 45 F1
Millman St WC1 45 F1
Mill St W1 44 B3
Milroy Wk SE1 45 H4
Minera Ms SW1 44 A7
Mint St SE1 45 J5
Mitre Ct EC2 45 J2
Mitre Rd SE1 45 G5
Monck St SW1 44 D7
Monkton St SE11 45 G7
Monkwell Sq EC2 45 J2
Monmouth St WC2 44 E3
Montague Cl SE1 45 J4
Montague Pl WC1 44 D1
Montague St EC1 45 J2
Montague St WC1 44 E1

Montreal Pl WC2 45 F3
Montrose Pl SW1 44 A6
Moor St W1 44 D3
Morley St SE1 45 G6
Morpeth Ter SW1 44 C7
Mortimer Mkt WC1 44 C1
Mortimer St W1 44 C2
Morton Pl SE1 45 G7
Morwell St WC1 44 D2
Mount Pleasant WC1 45 F1
Mount Row W1 44 B4
Mount St W1 44 A4
Mount St Ms W1 44 B4
Moxon St W1 44 A2
Munton Rd SE17 45 J7
Murphy St SE1 45 G6
Museum St WC1 44 E2

N
Nag's Head Ct EC1 45 J1
Nassau St W1 44 C2
Neal St WC2 44 E3
Neal's Yd WC2 44 E3
Neathouse Pl SW1 44 C7
Nelson Sq SE1 45 H5
Newall Ho SE1 45 J6
New Bond St W1 44 B3
New Br St EC4 45 H3
Newburgh St W1 44 C3
New Burlington Ms W1 44 C3
New Burlington Pl W1 44 C3
New Burlington St W1 44 C3
Newbury St EC1 45 J2
Newcastle Cl EC4 45 H2
New Cavendish St W1 44 B1
New Change EC4 45 J3
New Compton St WC2 44 D3
New Fetter La EC4 45 G2
Newgate St EC1 45 H2
New Globe Wk SE1 45 J4
Newington SE1 45 J7
Newington Causeway SE1 45 H7
New Inn Pas WC2 45 F3
New Kent Rd SE1 45 J7
Newman Pas W1 44 C2
Newman's Row WC2 45 F2
Newman St W1 44 C2
Newman Yd W1 44 C2
Newnham Ter SE1 45 G6
New N St WC1 45 F1
New Oxford St WC1 44 D2
Newport Ct WC2 44 D3
Newport Pl WC2 44 D3
New Row WC2 44 E3
New Sq WC2 45 F2
New St Sq EC4 45 G2
Newton St WC2 45 E2
New Turnstile WC1 45 F2
Nicholson St SE1 45 H5
Nightingale Ms SE11 45 G7
Noble St EC2 45 J2
Noel St W1 44 C3
Norfolk Row SE1 45 F7
Norris St W1 44 D4
North Audley St W1 44 A3
North Cres WC1 44 D1
Northington St WC1 45 F1
North Ms WC1 45 F1
Northumberland Av WC2 44 E4
Northumberland St WC2 44 E4
Norwich St EC4 45 G2
Nottingham Ct WC2 44 E3
Nottingham Pl W1 44 A1
Nottingham St W1 44 A1
Nottingham Ter NW1 44 A1

O
Oakden St SE11 45 G7
Oakey La SE1 45 G6
Oat La EC2 45 J2
Odhams Wk WC2 45 E3
Ogle St W1 44 C1
Old Bailey EC4 45 H3
Old Barrack Yd SW1 44 A5
Old Bond St W1 44 C4
Old Brewers Yd WC2 44 E3
Old Bldgs WC2 45 G2
Old Burlington St W1 44 C3
Oldbury Pl W1 44 A1
Old Cavendish St W1 44 B2
Old Compton St W1 44 D3
Old Fish St Hill EC4 45 J3
Old Fleet La EC4 45 H2
Old Gloucester St WC1 45 E1
Old Mitre Ct EC4 45 G3
Old N St WC1 45 F1

Old Palace Yd SW1 44 E6
Old Paradise St SE11 45 F7
Old Pk La W1 44 A5
Old Pye St SW1 44 D6
Old Queen St SW1 44 D6
Old Seacoal La EC4 45 H2
Old Sq WC2 45 F2
O'Meara St SE1 45 J5
Onslow St EC1 45 G1
Ontario St SE1 45 H7
Orange St WC2 44 D4
Orange Yd W1 44 D3
Orchard St W1 44 A3
Orde Hall St WC1 45 F1
Orient St SE11 45 H7
Ormond Cl WC1 45 E1
Ormond Ms WC1 45 E1
Ormond Yd SW1 44 C4
Osnaburgh St NW1 44 B1
Ossington Bldgs W1 44 A1
Oswin St SE11 45 H7
Outer Circle NW1 44 A1
Oxendon St SW1 44 D4
Oxford Circ Av W1 44 C3
Oxford St W1 44 C2
Oxo Twr Wf SE1 45 G4

P

Paddington St W1 44 A1
Pageantmaster Ct EC4 45 H3
Page St SW1 44 D7
Palace Pl SW1 44 C6
Palace St SW1 44 C6
Pall Mall SW1 44 C5
Pall Mall E SW1 44 D4
Palmer St SW1 44 D6
Pancras La EC4 45 J3
Panton St SW1 44 D4
Panyer All EC4 45 J3
Paris Gdn SE1 45 H4
Park Cres W1 44 B1
Park Cres Ms E W1 44 B1
Park Cres Ms W W1 44 B1
Parker Ms WC2 45 E2
Parker St WC2 45 E2
Park La W1 44 A5
Park Pl SW1 44 C5
Park Sq Ms NW1 44 B1
Park St SE1 45 J4
Park St W1 44 A3
Parliament Sq SW1 44 E6
Parliament St SW1 44 E6
Parliament Vw Apts SE1 45 F7
Passing All EC1 45 H1
Pastor St SE11 45 H7
Paternoster Row EC4 45 J3
Paternoster Sq EC4 45 H3
Paul's Wk EC4 45 H3
Peabody Est EC1 45 J1
Peabody Est SE1 45 G5
Peabody Est SW1 44 C7
Peabody Sq SE1 45 H6
Peabody Trust SE1 45 J5
Pearman St SE1 45 G6
Pear Pl SE1 45 G5
Pear Tree Ct EC1 45 G1
Pemberton Row EC4 45 G2
Pembroke Cl SW1 44 A6
Penhurst Pl SE1 45 F7
Pepper St SE1 45 J5
Percy Ms W1 44 D2
Percy Pas W1 44 C2
Percy St W1 44 D2
Perkin's Rents SW1 44 D6
Perkins Sq SE1 45 J4
Perrys Pl W1 44 D2
Peters Hill EC4 45 J3
Peter's La EC1 45 H1
Peter St W1 44 C3
Petty France SW1 44 C6
Phipp's Ms SW1 44 B7
Phoenix St WC2 44 D3
Piccadilly W1 44 B5
Piccadilly Arc SW1 44 C4
Piccadilly Circ W1 44 D4
Piccadilly Pl W1 44 C4
Pickering Pl SW1 44 C5
Pickwick St SE1 45 J6
Picton Pl W1 44 A3
Pilgrim St EC4 45 H3
Pineapple Ct SW1 44 C6
Pitt's Head Ms W1 44 A5
Playhouse Yd EC4 45 H3
Plaza Shop Cen, The W1 44 C2
Pleydell Ct EC4 45 G3
Pleydell St EC4 45 G3
Plough Pl EC4 45 G2
Plumtree Ct EC4 45 G2
Pocock St SE1 45 H5
Poland St W1 44 C3
Pollen St W1 44 B3
Polperro Ms SE11 45 G7
Pontypool Pl SE1 45 H5
Pooles Bldgs EC1 45 G1
Poppins Ct EC4 45 H3
Porter St SE1 45 J4
Portland Ms W1 44 C3
Portland Pl W1 44 B1
Portman Ms S W1 44 A3
Portman St W1 44 A3
Portpool La EC1 45 G1
Portsmouth St WC2 45 F3
Portugal St WC2 45 F3
Powis Pl WC1 45 E1
Pratt Wk SE11 45 F7
Price's St SE1 45 H5
Priest Ct EC2 45 J2
Primrose Hill EC4 45 G3
Prince's Arc SW1 44 C4
Princes Pl SW1 44 C4
Princess St SE1 45 H7
Princes St W1 44 B3
Princeton St WC1 45 F1
Printers Inn Ct EC4 45 G2
Printer St EC4 45 G2
Procter St WC1 45 F2
Providence Ct W1 44 A3
Prudent Pas EC2 45 J2
Puddle Dock EC4 45 H3

Q

Quadrant Arc W1 44 C4
Quality Ct WC2 45 G2
Queen Anne Ms W1 44 B2
Queen Anne's Gate SW1 44 D6
Queen Anne St W1 44 B2
Queenhithe EC4 45 J3
Queen's Head Pas EC4 45 J2
Queen Sq WC1 45 E1
Queen Sq Pl WC1 45 E1
Queen St EC4 45 J3
Queen St W1 44 B4
Queen St Pl EC4 45 J4
Queen's Wk SW1 44 C5
Queen's Wk, The SE1 45 F5
Queens Yd WC1 44 C1
Queen Victoria St EC4 45 H3
Quilp St SE1 45 J5

R

Ramillies Pl W1 44 C3
Ramillies St W1 44 C3
Rathbone Pl W1 44 D2
Rathbone St W1 44 C2
Raymond Bldgs WC1 45 F1
Ray St EC1 45 G1
Ray St Br EC1 45 G1
Redcross Way SE1 45 J5
Red Lion Ct EC4 45 G2
Red Lion Sq WC1 45 F2
Red Lion St WC1 45 F1
Red Lion Yd W1 44 A4
Red Pl W1 44 A3
Reeves Ms W1 44 A4
Regency Pl SW1 44 D7
Regency St SW1 44 D7
Regent Pl W1 44 C3
Regent St SW1 44 D4
Regent St W1 44 B2
Remnant St WC2 45 F2
Renfrew Rd SE11 45 H7
Rennie St SE1 45 H4
Rex Pl W1 44 A4
Richardson's Ms W1 44 C1
Richbell Pl WC1 45 F1
Richmond Bldgs W1 44 D3
Richmond Ms W1 44 D3
Richmond Ter SW1 44 E5
Ridgmount Gdns WC1 44 D1
Ridgmount Pl WC1 44 D1
Ridgmount St WC1 44 D1
Riding Ho St W1 44 C2
Risborough St SE1 45 H5
Rising Sun Ct EC1 45 H2
River Ct SE1 45 H4
Robert Adam St W1 44 A2
Roberts Ms SW1 44 A7
Robert St WC2 45 E4
Rochester Row SW1 44 C7
Rochester St SW1 44 D7
Rockingham Est SE1 45 J7
Rockingham St SE1 45 J7
Rodney Pl SE17 45 J7
Rodney Rd SE17 45 J7
Roger St WC1 45 F1
Rolls Bldgs EC4 45 G2
Rolls Pas EC4 45 G2
Romilly St W1 44 D3
Romney Ms W1 44 A1
Romney St SW1 44 D7
Roscoe St EC1 45 J1
Rose All SE1 45 J4
Rose & Crown Ct EC2 45 J2
Rose & Crown Yd SW1 44 C4
Rosebery Av EC1 45 G1
Rosebery Sq EC1 45 G1
Rose St EC4 45 H2
Rose St WC2 44 E3
Rotary St SE1 45 H6
Rotherham Wk SE1 45 H5
Rotten Row SW1 44 A5
Roupell St SE1 45 G5
Royal Arc W1 44 C4
Royal Ms, The SW1 44 B6
Royal Opera Arc SW1 44 D4
Royal St SE1 45 F6
Royalty Ms W1 44 D3
Rugby St WC1 45 F1
Rupert Ct W1 44 D3
Rupert St W1 44 D3
Rushworth St SE1 45 H5
Russell Ct SW1 44 C5
Russell Sq WC1 44 E1
Russell St WC2 45 E3
Russia Row EC2 45 J3
Rutherford St SW1 44 D7
Rutland Pl EC1 45 J1
Ryder Ct SW1 44 C4
Ryder St SW1 44 C4
Ryder Yd SW1 44 C4

S

Sackville St W1 44 C4
Saddle Yd W1 44 B4
Saffron Hill EC1 45 G1
Saffron St EC1 45 G1
Sail St SE11 45 F7
St. Albans Ct EC2 45 J2
St. Albans St SW1 44 D4
St. Alphage Gdn EC2 45 J2
St. Andrew's Hill EC4 45 H3
St. Andrew St EC4 45 G2
St. Anne's Ct W1 44 D3
St. Ann's La SW1 44 D6
St. Ann's St SW1 44 D6
St. Anselm's Pl W1 44 B3
St. Brides Av EC4 45 H3
St. Bride St EC4 45 H2
St. Christopher's Pl W1 44 A2
St. Clement's La WC2 45 F3
St. Cross St EC1 45 G1
St. Ermin's Hill SW1 44 D6
St. Georges Circ SE1 45 H6
St. Georges Ct EC4 45 H2
St. Georges Ms SE1 45 G6
St. Georges Rd SE1 45 G6
St. George St W1 44 B3
St. Giles High St WC2 44 D2
St. Giles Pas WC2 44 D3
St. James's SW1 44 D5
St. James's Ct SW1 44 C6
St. James's Mkt SW1 44 D4
St. James's Palace SW1 44 C5
St. James's Pk SW1 44 D5
St. James's Pl SW1 44 C5
St. James's Sq SW1 44 C4
St. James's St SW1 44 C4
St. John's La EC1 45 H1
St. John's Path EC1 45 H1
St. John's Pl EC1 45 H1
St. John's Sq EC1 45 H1
St. John St EC1 45 H1
St. Margaret's Ct SE1 45 J5
St. Margaret's St SW1 44 E6
St. Martin's La WC2 44 E3
St. Martin's-le-Grand EC1 45 J2
St. Martin's Ms WC2 44 E4
St. Martin's Pl WC2 44 E4
St. Martin's St WC2 44 D4
St. Mary's Gdns SE11 45 G7
St. Mary's Wk SE11 45 G7
St. Matthew St SW1 44 D7
St. Olaves Gdns SE11 45 G7
St. Paul's Chyd EC4 45 H3
St. Vincent St W1 44 A2
Salisbury Ct EC4 45 H3
Salisbury Sq EC4 45 G3
Sanctuary, The SW1 44 D6
Sanctuary St SE1 45 J6
Sandell St SE1 45 G5
Sandland St WC1 45 F2
Saperton Wk SE11 45 F7
Sardinia St WC2 45 F3
Savile Row W1 44 C3
Savoy Bldgs WC2 45 F4
Savoy Ct WC2 45 E4
Savoy Hill WC2 45 F4
Savoy Pl WC2 45 E4
Savoy Row WC2 45 F3
Savoy St WC2 45 F3
Savoy Way WC2 45 F4
Sawyer St SE1 45 J5
Scala St W1 44 C1
Scoresby St SE1 45 H5
Scotland Pl SW1 44 E4
Scovell Cres SE1 45 J6
Scovell Rd SE1 45 J6
Secker St SE1 45 G5
Sedding St SW1 44 A7
Sedley Pl W1 44 B3
Sekforde St EC1 45 H1
Serjeants Inn EC4 45 G3
Serle St WC2 45 F2
Sermon La EC4 45 J3
Seymour Ms W1 44 A2
Shaftesbury Av W1 44 D3
Shaftesbury Av WC2 44 D3
Shakespeare Twr EC2 45 J1
Shavers Pl SW1 44 D4
Sheffield St WC2 45 F3
Shelton St WC2 44 E3
Shepherd Mkt W1 44 B4
Shepherd's Pl W1 44 A3
Shepherd St W1 44 B5
Sheraton St W1 44 D3
Sherlock Ms W1 44 A1
Sherwood St W1 44 C3
Shoe La EC4 45 G2
Shorts Gdns WC2 44 E3
Short St SE1 45 G5
Shropshire Pl WC1 44 C1
Sicilian Av WC1 45 E2
Sidford Pl SE1 45 F7
Silex St SE1 45 H6
Silk St EC2 45 J1
Silver Pl W1 44 C3
Silvester St SE1 45 J6
Skinners La EC4 45 J3
Slingsby Pl WC2 44 E3
Smart's Pl WC2 45 E2
Smeaton Ct SE1 45 J7
Smithfield St EC1 45 H2
Smith's Ct W1 44 C3
Smith Sq SW1 44 E7
Smokehouse Yd EC1 45 H1
Snow Hill EC1 45 H2
Snow Hill Ct EC1 45 H2
Soho W1 44 C3
Soho Sq W1 44 D2
Soho St W1 44 D2
Southampton Bldgs WC2 45 G2
Southampton Pl WC1 45 E2
Southampton Row WC1 45 E1
Southampton St WC2 45 E3
South Audley St W1 44 A4
South Cres WC1 44 D2
South Eaton Pl SW1 44 A7
South Molton La W1 44 B3
South Molton St W1 44 B3
South Sq WC1 45 G2
South St W1 44 A4
Southwark SE1 45 H5
Southwark Br EC4 45 J4
Southwark Br SE1 45 J4
Southwark Br Rd SE1 45 H6
Southwark St SE1 45 H4
Spanish Pl W1 44 A2
Spenser St SW1 44 C6
Spring Gdns SW1 44 D4
Spur Rd SE1 45 G5
Spur Rd SW1 44 C6
Stable Yd SW1 44 C5
Stable Yd Rd SW1 44 C5
Stacey St WC2 44 D3
Stafford Pl SW1 44 C6
Stafford St W1 44 C4
Staining La EC2 45 J2
Stamford St SE1 45 G5
Stangate SE1 45 F6
Stanhope Gate W1 44 A4
Stanhope Row W1 44 B5
Staple Inn WC1 45 G2
Staple Inn Bldgs WC1 45 G2
Star Yd WC2 45 G2
Station App SE1 45 F5
Stedham Pl WC1 44 E2
Stephen Ms W1 44 D2
Stephen St W1 44 D2
Stew La EC4 45 J3
Stillington St SW1 44 C7
Stone Bldgs WC2 45 F2
Stonecutter St EC4 45 H2
Stones End St SE1 45 J6
Store St WC1 44 D2
Storey's Gate SW1 44 D6
Strand WC2 44 E4
Strand WC2 44 E4
Strand La WC2 45 F3
Stratford Pl W1 44 B3
Stratton St W1 44 B4
Streatham St WC1 44 D2
Strutton Grd SW1 44 D6
Stukeley St WC1 45 E2
Stukeley St WC2 45 E2
Sturge St SE1 45 J5
Sudrey St SE1 45 J6
Suffolk Pl SW1 44 D4
Suffolk St SW1 44 D4
Sullivan Rd SE11 45 G7
Summers St EC1 45 G1
Sumner St SE1 45 H4
Surrey Row SE1 45 H5
Surrey St WC2 45 F3
Sutton La EC1 45 H1
Sutton Row W1 44 D2
Sutton's Way EC1 45 J1
Sutton Wk SE1 45 F5
Swallow Pl W1 44 B3
Swallow St W1 44 C4
Swan St SE1 45 J6
Swiss Ct W1 44 D4
Sycamore St EC1 45 J1

T

Tachbrook Ms SW1 44 C7
Tallis St EC4 45 G3
Tanswell Est SE1 45 G6
Tanswell St SE1 45 G6
Tarn St SE1 45 J7
Tavistock St WC2 45 E3
Telford Ho SE1 45 J7
Temple Av EC4 45 G3
Temple La EC4 45 G3
Temple Pl WC2 45 F3
Temple W Ms SE11 45 H7
Tenison Ct W1 44 C3
Tenison Way SE1 45 G5
Tenterden St W1 44 B3
Terminus Pl SW1 44 B7
Thavies Inn EC1 45 G2
Thayer St W1 44 A2
Theed St SE1 45 G5
Theobald's Rd WC1 45 F1
Thirleby Rd SW1 44 C7
Thomas Doyle St SE1 45 H6
Thorney St SW1 44 E7
Thornhaugh Ms WC1 44 D1
Thornhaugh St WC1 44 D1
Thrale St SE1 45 J5
Three Barrels Wk EC4 45 J4
Three Cups Yd WC1 45 F2
Three Kings Yd W1 44 B3
Tilney St W1 44 A4
Tiverton St SE1 45 J7
Took's Ct EC4 45 G2
Torrington Pl WC1 44 C1
Torrington Sq WC1 44 D1
Tothill St SW1 44 D6
Tottenham Ct Rd W1 44 C1
Tottenham Ms W1 44 C1
Tottenham St W1 44 C2
Toulmin St SE1 45 J6
Tower Ct WC2 44 E3
Tower Royal EC4 45 J3
Tower St WC2 44 D3
Trafalgar Sq SW1 44 D4
Trafalgar Sq WC2 44 D4
Trebeck St W1 44 B4
Treveris St SE1 45 H5
Trig La EC4 45 J3
Trinity Ch Sq SE1 45 J6
Trinity St SE1 45 J6
Trio Pl SE1 45 J6
Trump St EC2 45 J3
Trundle St SE1 45 J5
Tudor St EC4 45 G3
Tufton St SW1 44 D6
Turk's Head Yd EC1 45 H1
Turnagain La EC4 45 H2
Turnmill St EC1 45 G1
Tweezer's All WC2 45 G3
Twyford Pl WC2 45 F2
Tyler's Ct W1 44 D3

U

Ufford St SE1 45 G5
Ulster Pl NW1 44 B1
Ulster Ter NW1 44 B1
Union Jack Club SE1 45 G5
Union St SE1 45 H5
University St WC1 44 C1
Upper Belgrave St SW1 44 A6
Upper Brook St W1 44 A4
Upper Grosvenor St W1 44 A4
Upper Grd SE1 45 G4
Upper James St W1 44 C3
Upper John St W1 44 C3
Upper Marsh SE1 45 F6
Upper St. Martin's La WC2 44 E3
Upper Tachbrook St SW1 44 C7
Upper Thames St EC4 45 H3
Upper Wimpole St W1 44 B1

V

Valentine Pl SE1 45 H5
Valentine Row SE1 45 H6
Vandon Pas SW1 44 C6
Vandon St SW1 44 C6
Vane St SW1 44 C7
Vauxhall Br Rd SW1 44 C7
Vere St W1 44 B3
Vernon Pl WC1 45 E2
Verulam Bldgs WC1 45 F1
Verulam St WC1 45 G1
Vesage Ct EC1 45 G2
Victoria Embk EC4 45 F4
Victoria Embk SW1 45 E5
Victoria Embk WC2 45 F4
Victoria Pl SW1 44 B7
Victoria Sq SW1 44 B6
Victoria Sta SW1 44 B7
Victoria St SW1 44 C7
Vigo St W1 44 C4
Villiers St WC2 44 E4
Vincent Sq SW1 44 C7
Vincent St SW1 44 D7
Vine Hill EC1 45 G1
Vine St W1 44 C4
Vine St Br EC1 45 G1
Vine Yd SE1 45 J5
Vintners Ct EC4 45 J3
Virgil St SE1 45 F6
Viscount St EC1 45 J1

W

Waithman St EC4 45 H3
Walcot Sq SE11 45 G7
Walcott St SW1 44 C7
Walkers Ct W1 44 D3
Wallis All SE1 45 J5
Wallside EC2 45 J2
Walnut Tree Wk SE11 45 G7
Walworth Rd SE1 45 J7
Walworth Rd SE17 45 J7
Wardens Gro SE1 45 J5
Wardour Ms W1 44 C3
Wardour St W1 44 D3
Wardrobe Ter EC4 45 H3
Warner St EC1 45 G1
Warner Yd EC1 45 G1
Warren Ms W1 44 C1
Warren St W1 44 B1
Warwick Ct WC1 45 F2
Warwick Ho St SW1 44 D4
Warwick La EC4 45 H3
Warwick Pas EC4 45 H2
Warwick Row SW1 44 B6
Warwick Sq EC4 45 H2
Warwick St W1 44 C3
Warwick Yd EC1 45 J1
Watergate EC4 45 H3
Watergate Wk WC2 45 E4
Waterhouse Sq EC1 45 G2
Waterloo Br SE1 45 F4
Waterloo Br WC2 45 F4
Waterloo Pl SW1 44 D4
Waterloo Rd SE1 45 G5
Waterloo Sta SE1 45 G5
Water St WC2 45 F3
Watling Ct EC4 45 J3
Watling St EC4 45 J3
Waverton St W1 44 A4
Webber Row SE1 45 G6
Webber St SE1 45 G5
Wedgwood Ho SE11 45 G7
Wedgwood Ms W1 44 D3
Weighhouse St W1 44 A3
Welbeck St W1 44 B2
Welbeck Way W1 44 B2
Well Ct EC4 45 J3
Weller St SE1 45 J5
Wellington St WC2 45 E3
Wells Ms W1 44 C2
Wells St W1 44 C2
Wesley St W1 44 A2
West Cen St WC1 44 E2
West Eaton Pl SW1 44 A7
West Eaton Pl Ms SW1 44 A7
West Halkin St SW1 44 A6
West Harding St EC4 45 G2
Westminster SW1 44 C6
Westminster Br SE1 45 E6
Westminster Br SW1 45 E6
Westminster Br Rd SE1 45 F6
Westminster Gdns SW1 44 E7
Westmoreland St W1 44 A2
West One Shop Cen W1 44 A3
West Poultry Av EC1 45 H2
West Smithfield EC1 45 H2

West Sq SE11 **45** H7
West St WC2 **44** D3
Weymouth Ms W1 **44** B1
Weymouth St W1 **44** A2
Wheatley St W1 **44** A2
Whetstone Pk WC2 **45** F2
Whichcote St SE1 **45** G5
Whitcomb St WC2 **44** D4
Whitefriars St EC4 **45** G3
Whitehall SW1 **44** E4
Whitehall Ct SW1 **44** E5
Whitehall Gdns SW1 **44** E5
Whitehall Pl SW1 **44** E5

White Hart St EC4 **45** H2
White Horse All EC1 **45** H1
White Horse Ms SE1 **45** G6
White Horse St W1 **44** B5
White Lion Hill EC4 **45** H3
White Lyon Ct EC2 **45** J1
Whitfield Pl W1 **44** C1
Whitfield St W1 **44** D2
Whitgift St SE11 **45** F7
Whittlesey St SE1 **45** G5
Whitworth Ho SE1 **45** J7
Wickstead Ho SE1 **45** J7
Wigmore Pl W1 **44** B2

Wigmore St W1 **44** A3
Wilcox Pl SW1 **44** C7
Wild Ct WC2 **45** F2
Wild St WC2 **45** E3
Wilfred St SW1 **44** C6
William IV St WC2 **44** E4
Willoughby St WC1 **44** E2
Willow Pl SW1 **44** C7
Wilton Cres SW1 **44** A6
Wilton Ms SW1 **44** A6
Wilton Pl SW1 **44** A6
Wilton Rd SW1 **44** B7
Wilton Row SW1 **44** A6

Wilton St SW1 **44** B6
Wilton Ter SW1 **44** A6
Wimpole Ms W1 **44** B1
Wimpole St W1 **44** B2
Wincott St SE11 **45** G7
Windmill St W1 **44** D2
Windmill Wk SE1 **45** G5
Windsor Pl SW1 **44** C7
Wine Office Ct EC4 **45** G2
Winnett St W1 **44** D3
Winsley St W1 **44** C2
Woburn Sq WC1 **44** D1
Wollaston Cl SE1 **45** J7

Woodstock Ms W1 **44** A2
Woodstock St W1 **44** B3
Wood St EC2 **45** J3
Wootton St SE1 **45** G5

Y
Yarmouth Pl W1 **44** B5
York Bldgs WC2 **45** E4
York Gate NW1 **44** A1
York Pl WC2 **45** E4
York Rd SE1 **45** F5
Yorkshire Grey Yd WC1 **45** F2

York Ter E NW1 **44** A1
York Ter W NW1 **44** A1

Z
Zoar St SE1 **45** J4

Manchester street index

A
Abingdon St **47** E4
Academy Wk **46** D7
Ackers St **47** F7
Acton Sq **46** A3
Adair St **47** G4
Addington St **47** F2
Addison Cl **47** G7
Adelphi St **46** B3
Aden Cl **47** J4
Adlington St **47** H5
Adstone Cl **47** J3
Adswood St **47** J3
Airton Cl **47** H1
Aked Cl **47** J7
Albion Pl **46** A3
Albion St **46** D5
Albion Way **46** A3
Alderman Sq **47** J4
Aldred St **46** A3
Alexander Gdns **46** C1
Alexandra St **47** H2
Alfred James Cl **47** H2
Alker Rd **47** J2
Alley St **46** E3
Almond St **47** G1
Altair Pl **46** B1
Amory St **47** G5
Anaconda Dr **46** C2
Ancoats **47** G3
Ancoats Gro **47** H4
Ancroft St **46** C7
Angela St **46** C6
Angel St **47** F2
Angora Cl **46** B2
Angora Dr **46** B2
Anita St **47** G3
Anne Nuttall St **46** B6
Anscombe Cl **47** H1
Antares Av **46** B1
Apsley Gro **47** H6
Aquarius St **47** E7
Archway **46** D7
Ardwick **47** J5
Ardwick Grn N **47** G5
Ardwick Grn S **47** G5
Arlington St **46** C2
Arnott Cres **46** E7
Artillery St **46** D4
Arundel St **46** C5
Asgard Dr **46** B5
Asgard Grn **46** B5
Ashlar Dr **47** J4
Ashley St **47** F2
Ashton New Rd **47** J3
Ashton Old Rd **47** H5
Aspin La **47** F2
Atherton St **46** C4
Atkinson St **46** D4
Atwood St **47** E5
Auburn St **47** F4
Audlem Cl **47** J2
Augustus St **47** E1
Avenham Cl **46** D7
Aytoun St **47** F4

B
Back Acton St **47** F4
Back Ashley St **47** F2
Back Bk St **47** F1
Back Br St **46** D3
Back China La **47** F4
Back Coll Land **46** D3
Back George St **47** E4
Back Hampson St **47** H1
Back Hulme St **46** B3
Back Junct St **47** G4
Back Piccadilly **47** F3
Back Pool Fold **46** E3
Back Red Bk **47** F1
Back St. George's Rd **47** G2
Back S Par **46** D3
Back Thomas St **47** F3

Back Turner St **47** F3
Badby Cl **47** J3
Bainbridge Cl **47** J7
Baird St **47** G4
Bale St **46** E4
Balloon St **47** E2
Balmforth St **46** C5
Balsam Cl **47** G6
Bangor St **46** C7
Bankmill Cl **47** G6
Bank Pl **46** B3
Bank St **46** B3
Baptist St **47** F2
Barbeck Cl **47** J2
Baring St **47** G5
Barker St **46** D1
Barlow Pl **47** G6
Barlow's Cft **46** D3
Barnett Dr **46** C2
Barrack St **46** B6
Barrhill Cl **46** C6
Barrow St **46** B3
Barton St **46** D5
Basildon Cl **47** J7
Beamish Cl **47** G6
Beattock St **46** C6
Beaufort St **46** C5
Beaver St **47** E5
Beckhampton Cl **47** H7
Bednal Av **47** J1
Beechcroft Cl **47** H2
Belfort Dr **46** A5
Bendix St **47** F2
Bengal St **47** G2
Bennett St **47** J6
Bentinck St **46** B6
Bent St **47** E1
Berkshire Rd **47** J1
Berry St **47** G5
Beswick Row **47** E2
Beswick St **47** H3
Betley St **47** G4
Bevan Cl **47** J4
Bilbrook St **47** F1
Billing Av **47** G5
Binns Pl **47** G3
Birchin La **47** F3
Birchvale Cl **46** D6
Birt St **47** H1
Bishopsgate **46** E4
Blackburn Pl **46** A4
Blackburn St **46** B2
Blackfriars Rd **46** C2
Blackfriars St **46** D3
Blackhill Cl **47** G6
Blackley St **46** B7
Blacklock St **46** E1
Blantyre St **46** C5
Bletchley Cl **47** H7
Blind La **47** J5
Blisworth Cl **47** J3
Bloom St **47** F4
Blossom St **46** D2
Blossom St (Ancoats) **47** G3
Blucher St **46** A4
Blyton St **47** F7
Boad St **47** G4
Bollington Rd **47** H2
Bombay St **47** F5
Bond St **47** G5
Bonsall St **46** E7
Boond St **46** D2
Booth St **46** E4
Booth St (Salford) **46** D3
Booth St E **47** F6
Booth St W **47** E7
Bootle St **46** D4
Botham Cl **47** E7
Bothwell Rd **47** G2
Boundary La **47** E6
Boundary St E **47** F6
Boundary St W **47** E6
Bourdon St **47** J2

Bow La **46** E4
Bow St **46** D4
Brackley Av **46** B6
Bradford Rd **47** H3
Bradleys Ct **47** F3
Braley St **47** G5
Bramble Av **46** A5
Bramwell Dr **47** G6
Brancaster Rd **47** F5
Branson St **47** J3
Brazennose St **46** D4
Brazil St **47** F5
Brennan Cl **47** E7
Brewer St **47** F3
Brian Redhead Ct **46** C6
Brickley St **47** E1
Brick St **47** F3
Briddon St **46** D1
Bridgeford St **47** F7
Bridge St **46** D3
Bridge St W **46** D3
Bridgewater Pl **47** E3
Bridgewater St **46** D5
Bridgewater St (Salford) **46** C1
Bridgewater Viaduct **46** D5
Briggs St **46** C2
Brighton Pl **47** F7
Brighton St **47** F1
Brindle Pl **47** E7
Brocade Cl **46** B2
Brock St **47** G3
Bromley St **47** F1
Bronte St **47** E7
Brook St **47** F5
Brotherton Cl **46** B6
Brotherton Dr **46** C2
Browfield Av **46** A5
Brown Cross St **46** C3
Browning St **46** B7
Browning St (Salford) **46** C3
Brown St **46** E4
Brunel Av **46** A3
Brunswick **47** G7
Brunswick St **47** F7
Bryant Cl **47** H7
Brydon Av **47** H5
Buckfield Av **46** A5
Bugle St **46** D5
Bunsen St **47** F3
Burlington St **47** E7
Burnell Cl **47** H2
Burstock St **47** F1
Burton St **47** G1
Burton Wk **46** B2
Bury St **46** C2
Butler La **47** H2
Butler St **47** H2
Butter La **46** D3
Buxton St **47** G5
Byrcland Cl **47** J5
Byron St **46** D4

C
Cable St **47** F2
Cabot St **47** G6
Cakebread St **47** G5
Calder St **46** B5
Calico Cl **46** B2
Camberwell St **47** E1
Cambrian St **47** J2
Cambridge St **46** E5
Cambridge St (Salford) **46** D3
Camelford Cl **47** E7
Cameron St **46** D5
Canal St **47** F4
Cannon St **46** B2
Canon Ct **46** E3
Canon Grn Dr **46** C2
Cardroom Rd **47** G3
Carey Cl **46** C1

Carib St **46** D7
Carmel Av **46** A5
Carmel Cl **46** A5
Carnarvon St **46** E1
Caroline St **46** C1
Carpenters La **47** F3
Carriage St **46** C7
Carruthers St **47** H3
Cassidy Cl **47** G2
Castle St **46** C5
Caterham St **47** J4
Cathedral Gates **46** E3
Cathedral St **46** E3
Cathedral Yd **46** E3
Catlow La **47** F3
Catlow St **46** D1
Cavalier St **47** J3
Cavanagh Cl **47** H7
Cavell St **47** F3
Cavendish St **46** E6
Cawdor St **46** B6
Caxton St **46** D3
Caygill St **46** D2
Cedar Pl **46** B1
Central St **46** E4
Century St **46** D5
Chadderton St **47** F2
Chain St **47** F3
Chancel Av **46** A5
Chancellor La **47** H5
Chancery La **46** E4
Change Way **46** C2
Chapelfield Rd **47** H5
Chapel St **46** C3
Chapeltown St **47** G4
Chapel Walks **46** E3
Charles St **47** E5
Charley Av **46** B1
Charlotte St **46** E4
Charlton Pl **47** G5
Charnley Cl **47** J2
Charter St **46** D1
Chase St **47** F1
Chatford Cl **46** C1
Chatham St **47** F4
Chatley St **47** H7
Cheapside **46** E3
Cheetham Hill Rd **47** E2
Cheetwood St **46** D1
Chepstow St **46** E5
Cherryton Wk **47** G7
Chesshyre Av **47** J3
Chester Rd **46** B6
Chester St **46** E6
Chevassut St **46** C6
Cheviot St **46** C2
Chevril Cl **47** E6
Chichester Rd **46** D7
Chiffon Way **46** B2
China La **47** F4
Chippenham Rd **47** H3
Chorlton Rd **46** C7
Chorlton St **46** E4
Chorlton St (Old Trafford) **46** A7
Christchurch Av **46** A3
Churchgate Bldgs **47** G4
Church St **47** F3
Cinder St **47** G3
Cipher St **47** G2
City Rd **46** B7
City Rd E **46** D6
Clarence St **46** E4
Clarendon St **46** D6
Clare St **47** G5
Clarion St **47** G2
Clayburn Rd **46** D6
Cleminson St **46** B3
Cleworth St **46** B6
Clifford St **47** F6
Clifton Gro **46** B7
Clifton St **46** B7
Clive St **47** F2

Cloak St **47** F5
Cloughfield Av **46** A5
Clowes St **46** D3
Cobourg St **47** F4
Coburg Av **46** B1
Cockcroft Rd **46** A2
Cockspur St **46** D3
Coleshill St **47** J1
Colin Murphy Rd **46** C6
College Land **46** D3
Collier St **46** D5
Collier St (Salford) **46** D2
Collingham St **47** F1
Collyhurst Rd **47** G1
Colman Gdns **46** A5
Comet St **47** G4
Commercial St **46** D5
Comus St **46** A4
Concert La **47** E4
Congou St **47** G4
Cooper St **46** E4
Coop St **47** F3
Copeman Cl **46** D7
Copperas St **47** F3
Coral St **46** E4
Cork St **47** J4
Cornbrook **46** B6
Cornbrook Ct **46** B7
Cornbrook Gro **46** B7
Cornbrook Pk Rd **46** B6
Cornbrook St **46** B7
Cornell St **47** G2
Coronation Sq **47** H5
Coronation St **46** A4
Corporation St **46** E3
Cottenham La **46** C1
Cottenham St **47** G6
Cotter St **47** G5
Cotton St **47** G3
Cottingham Rd **47** J7
Coupland St **47** E7
Coupland St E **47** F7
Coverdale Cres **47** H6
Cowan St **47** J3
Cowburn St **46** E1
Cow La **46** B4
Crabbe St **47** F1
Cranbourne St **46** A4
Crane St **47** H5
Cranfield Cl **47** J2
Craven St **46** B4
Crediton Cl **46** E7
Cresbury St **47** H5
Crescent, The **46** A2
Cross Keys St **47** F2
Crossley Ct **47** J3
Cross St **46** E4
Cross St (Salford) **46** D3
Crown La **47** F2
Crown St **46** C5
Crown St (Salford) **46** C2
Culmington Cl **46** C7
Cumberland St **46** B1
Cumbrian Cl **47** G6
Cunard Cl **47** G6
Cygnus Av **46** B1
Cyrus St **47** J3

D
Dainton St **47** J5
Daintry Cl **46** D6
Dalberg St **47** H6
Dale St **47** F3
Dalley Av **46** B1
Dalton Ct **47** G1
Dalton St **47** G1
Damask Av **46** B2
Danebank Wk **47** G6
Danecroft Cl **47** H7
Danson St **47** J2
Dantzic St **47** E3

Dark La **47** H5
Dartford Cl **47** J7
Darton Av **47** J2
Darwen St **46** A7
Davy St **47** G1
Dawson St **46** B5
Dean Rd **46** D2
Deansgate **46** D4
Dean St **47** F3
Deanwater Cl **47** G6
Dearden St **46** D6
Dearmans Pl **46** D3
Deer St **47** G4
Denewell Cl **47** H7
Denver Av **47** J1
Derby St **47** E1
Derwent St **46** B5
Devas St **47** F7
Devine Cl **46** B2
Devonshire St **47** H7
Devonshire St N **47** J6
Devonshire St S **47** H7
Dewhurst St **46** D1
Dickinson St **46** E4
Dilston Cl **47** H7
Dinsdale Cl **47** J2
Dinton St **46** B6
Dobson St **46** B6
Dolefield **46** D3
Dolphin Pl **47** H6
Dolphin St **47** H6
Donald St **47** F5
Dorsey St **47** F3
Dover St **47** F7
Downing St **47** G5
Downley Dr **47** H3
Drayton Wk **46** B7
Droitwich Rd **47** H1
Dryden St **47** G7
Dryhurst Wk **47** E7
Ducie St **47** F4
Duke Pl **46** C5
Duke St **46** C5
Duke St (Salford) **46** D2
Dulwich St **47** F1
Duncan St **46** A4
Dun Cl **46** B3
Dunham St **46** D7
Dunlop St **46** D3
Durant St **47** F2
Durling Av **47** H6
Dutton St **46** E1
Dyche St **47** F2
Dyer St **46** A5

E
Eagle St **47** F2
Eastburn Av **47** H1
Eastfield Av **47** J2
Eastleigh Dr **47** H1
East Mkt St **46** C3
East Newton St **47** H2
Eastnor Cl **46** B7
East Ordsall La **46** B4
Eastpark Cl **47** H6
East Philip St **46** D1
East Union St **46** B7
Ebden St **47** F4
Ebenezer St **46** E6
Echo St **47** F5
Eden Cl **46** E7
Edgehill St **47** F3
Edge St **47** F3
Edward St **46** D1
Egerton Rd **46** C5
Egerton St **46** C3
Elbe St **47** H5
Eliza St **46** C7
Ellesmere St **46** B6
Ellis St **46** D7
Elsworth St **47** E1
Elton St **46** C1
Elton's Yd **46** C1

Elverdon Cl 46 D7
Empire St 46 E1
Empress St 46 A7
Encombe Pl 46 B3
Epping St 46 E6
Epsley Cl 47 E7
Epworth St 47 H4
Errington Dr 46 B1
Erskine St 46 C7
Essex St 46 E4
Essex Way 46 C7
Etruria St 47 J7
Evans St 46 D2
Everard St 46 B5
Every St 47 H4
Exford Cl 47 H2
Eyre St 47 E7

F
Fairbrother St 46 A6
Fairfield St 47 G5
Fair St 47 G4
Falkland Av 47 J1
Faraday St 47 F3
Farnborough Rd 47 H1
Farrell St 46 C1
Farwood Cl 46 B7
Faulkner St 47 E4
Federation St 47 E2
Fennel St 46 E2
Fenn St 46 C7
Fenwick St 47 E6
Ferdinan St 47 H1
Fernbrook Cl 47 J7
Fernie St 47 E1
Fernleigh Dr 46 B7
Fern St 47 E1
Ferry St 47 J4
Filby Wk 47 J1
Firbeck Dr 47 H2
Firefly Cl 46 B3
Fire Sta Sq 46 A3
Fir St 47 H1
Fitzwilliam St 46 C1
Flatley Cl 47 E7
Flora Dr 46 C1
Ford St 47 H6
Ford St (Salford) 46 C3
Foundry La 47 F3
Fountain St 47 E4
Four Yards 46 E4
Frances St 47 G6
Francis St 46 D1
Frederick St 46 C3
Freeman Sq 47 E7
Freya Gro 46 A5
Frobisher Cl 47 J7
Frost St 47 J3
Fulmer Dr 47 H2

G
Gaitskell Cl 47 J4
Galgate Cl 46 C6
Garden La 46 D3
Garden St 46 D2
Garden Wall Cl 46 A5
Garforth Av 47 H2
Gartside St 46 D4
Garwood St 46 D6
Gateaton St 46 E3
Gaythorn St 46 B3
George Leigh St 47 F3
George St 47 E4
Georgette Dr 46 D2
Gibbs St 46 B3
Gibson Pl 47 E1
Girton St 46 C1
Glasshouse St 47 G2
Gleden St 47 J2
Glenbarry Cl 47 G7
Glenbarry St 47 J5
Gloucester St 46 E5
Gloucester St (Salford) 46 A5
Goadsby St 47 F2
Gold St 47 F4
Gordon St 46 C1
Gore St 47 F4
Gore St (Salford) 46 C3
Gorton St 46 D2
Goulden St 47 F2
Gould St 47 F1
Grafton St 47 G7
Granby Row 47 F5
Granshaw St 47 J2
Gratrix Av 46 A6
Grear Ducie St 46 E2
Great Ancoats St 47 F3
Great Bridgewater St 46 D5
Great Clowes St 46 C1
Great Ducie St 46 D1
Great George St 46 B3
Great Jackson St 46 C5
Great John St 46 C4

Great Marlborough St 47 E5
Greek St 47 F6
Greengate W 46 C2
Grenham Av 46 B6
Griffiths Cl 46 C1
Groom St 47 F6
Grosvenor Gdns 46 C1
Grosvenor Sq 46 C1
Grosvenor St 47 F6
Guide Post Sq 47 H7
Gunson St 47 H2
Gun St 47 G3
Gurner Av 46 A6
Gurney St 47 J3

H
Hackleton Cl 47 J3
Hadfield St 46 B7
Half St 46 D2
Hall St 46 E4
Halmore Rd 47 H2
Halsbury Cl 47 J7
Halston St 46 D7
Hamerton Rd 47 G1
Hamilton Gro 46 B7
Hamilton St 46 B7
Hampson St 47 H1
Hamsell Rd 47 G6
Handsworth St 47 J5
Hanging Ditch 46 E3
Hanover St 47 E2
Hanworth Cl 47 G6
Harding St 47 J4
Hardman Sq 46 D4
Hardman St 46 D4
Hardshaw Cl 47 G6
Harehill Cl 47 G5
Hare St 47 F3
Hargreave's St 47 F1
Harkness St 47 H6
Harold St 46 B7
Harnett St 47 H2
Harrison St 47 H4
Harrison St (Salford) 46 C1
Harris St 46 D1
Harry Hall Gdns 46 B1
Harter St 47 E4
Hartfield Cl 47 G6
Hart St 47 F4
Hatter St 47 F2
Hatton Av 46 B1
Haverlock Dr 46 B1
Haymarket Cl 47 H7
Heath Av 46 B1
Helga St 47 H1
Hellidon Cl 47 H6
Helmet St 47 H5
Henry St 47 G3
Henry St (Old Trafford) 46 A7
Hewitt St 46 D5
Heyrod St 47 G4
Higher Ardwick 47 H6
Higher Cambridge St 47 E6
Higher Chatham St 47 E6
Higher Ormond St 47 F6
Higher Oswald St 47 F6
Higher York St 47 F6
High St 47 E3
Hillcourt St 47 F6
Hillfield Cl 47 J7
Hillkirk St 47 J3
Hilton St 47 F3
Hinton St 47 G2
Hodson St 46 C2
Holdgate Cl 46 D7
Holkham Cl 47 H3
Holland St 47 H2
Holly Bk Cl 46 B6
Holly St 47 J4
Holt Town 47 J3
Honey St 47 F1
Hood St 47 G3
Hooper St 47 J5
Hope St 47 F4
Hope St (Salford) 46 A3
Hornby St 46 D1
Hornchurch St 46 C7
Horne Dr 47 H3
Houldsworth St 47 F3
Hoyle St 47 H5
Huddart Cl 46 A5
Hughes St 47 J3
Hull Sq 46 B2
Hulme
Hulme Ct 46 D7
Hulme Hall Rd 46 B5
Hulme Pl 46 B3
Hulme St 46 D6
Hulme St (Salford) 46 B3
Humberstone Av 46 D6
Hunmanby Av 46 D6
Hunt's Bk 46 E2

Hyde Gro 47 G7
Hyde Pl 47 H7
Hyde Rd 47 H6
Hyde St 46 C7

I
Inchley Rd 47 F6
Instow Cl 47 H7
Ionas St 46 C1
Irk St 47 F1
Iron St 47 J2
Irwell Pl 46 A3
Irwell St 46 D1
Irwell St (Salford) 46 C3
Islington Way 46 B3

J
Jackson Cres 46 C6
Jackson's Row 46 D4
James Henry Av 46 A4
James St 46 D4
James St (Salford) 46 B3
Jenkinson St 47 F6
Jersey St 47 G3
Jerusalem Pl 46 D4
Jessamine Av 46 B1
Jessel Cl 47 G6
Joddrell St 46 D4
John Clynes Av 47 H1
John Dalton St 46 D3
Johnson Sq 47 H1
Johnson St 46 B7
Johnson St (Salford) 46 C3
John St 47 F3
John St (Lower Broughton) 46 C1
John St (Salford) 46 D2
Joiner St 47 F3
Jordan St 46 D5
Joynson Av 46 B1
Julia St 46 D1
Jury St 46 D1
Justin Cl 47 F6
Jutland St 47 G4

K
Kale St 47 G6
Kays Gdns 46 C3
Keele Wk 47 H1
Kelling Wk 46 C6
Kelvin St 47 F3
Kennedy St 46 E4
Kenwright St 47 F2
Kincardine Rd 47 F6
King Edward St 46 A5
Kingham Dr 47 H2
Kingsfold Av 47 H1
Kingsland Cl 47 H1
King St 46 D3
King St (Salford) 46 D2
King St W 46 D3
Kirkgate Cl 47 H2
Kirkhaven Sq 47 J1
Kirkstall Sq 47 G7
Kirkwood Dr 47 H1

L
Lackford Dr 47 H1
Lamb La 46 C3
Lamport Cl 47 F5
Lanchester St 47 J2
Landos Rd 47 H2
Langholme Cl 46 C6
Langport Av 47 J7
Langston St 46 D1
Lanstead Dr 47 J2
Lauderdale Cres 47 H7
Laystall St 47 G3
Layton St 47 H2
Leaf St 46 D6
Leak St 46 B6
Ledburn Ct 46 C6
Left Bk 46 C4
Lena St 47 F4
Leslie Hough Way 46 A1
Lever St 47 F3
Lewis St 47 J1
Leycroft St 47 G4
Lidbrook Wk 47 J7
Lime Bk St 47 H3
Lime Gro 47 F7
Limekiln La 47 H5
Linby St 46 C6
Lind St 47 J3
Linen Ct 46 B2
Linsley St 46 D2
Linton Cl 47 H4
Litcham Cl 47 F5
Little Ancoats St 47 F3
Little Holme St 47 J3
Little John St 46 C4
Little Lever St 47 F3
Little Nelson St 47 F2
Little Peter St 46 D5

Little Pit St 47 G3
Little Quay St 46 D4
Liverpool Rd 46 C4
Livesey St 47 G1
Lizard St 47 F3
Lloyd St 46 D4
Lloyd St N 47 F7
Lockett St 46 D1
Lockton Cl 47 G5
Lomax St 47 G3
London Rd 47 F4
Longacre St 47 G4
Long Millgate 46 E2
Longworth St 46 D4
Loom St 47 G3
Lordsmead St 46 C6
Lord St 46 E1
Lostock St 47 H2
Lowcock St 46 C1
Lower Byrom St 46 C4
Lower Chatham St 47 E6
Lower Mosley St 46 D5
Lower Moss La 46 C6
Lower Ormond St 47 E5
Lower Vickers St 47 J2
Lowndes Wk 47 G6
Loxford St 46 E6
Lucy St 46 B7
Ludgate Hill 47 F2
Ludgate St 47 F2
Luna street 47 F3
Lund St 46 A7
Lupton St 46 C3
Lyceum Pl 47 E6

M
Maidford Cl 47 J3
Maich St 47 E4
Makin St 47 E5
Mallard St 47 E5
Mallow St 46 C6
Malta St 47 H3
Malt St 46 B6
Malvern St 46 B7
Manchester St 46 A7
Mancunian Way 46 C6
Mangle St Street 47 F3
Manson Av 46 B6
Maplin Cl 47 G6
Marble St 47 E3
Marcer Rd 47 H2
Marchmont Cl 47 H7
Market St 46 E3
Markfield Av 47 J7
Markham Cl 47 J4
Marple St 46 C7
Marsden St 46 E3
Marshall St 47 F2
Marshall St (Ardwick) 47 H6
Marsworth Dr 47 H3
Mary France St 46 C6
Mary St 46 D1
Mason St 46 F2
Mason St (Salford) 46 C3
Massey St 46 B3
Mayan Av 46 B2
Mayes St 47 E2
Mayo St 47 H5
Mays St 47 F2
Meadow Rd 46 B1
Medlock St 46 D5
Melbourne St 46 C6
Mellor St 47 H2
Melville St 46 C3
Merrill St 47 H3
Middlewood St 46 B4
Midland St 47 G3
Miles Platting 47 J2
Milk St 46 D6
Millbank St 47 G4
Millbeck St 46 C6
Miller St 46 E2
Mill Grn St 47 H5
Millhall Cl 46 C7
Millhead Av 47 J2
Millow St 47 E2
Milnrow Cl 47 F5
Milton St 46 C1
Mincing St 47 F2
Minshull St 47 F4
Minshull St S 47 F4
Mistletoe Grn 46 C2
Moorhead St 47 G3
Morbourne Cl 47 J7
Mosley St 47 E4
Mosscott Wk 47 G5
Mosshall Cl 46 C7
Moulton St 46 D1
Mouncey St 47 E5
Mount Carmel Cres 46 A5
Mount St 46 E4
Mount St (Salford) 46 C2
Mozart Cl 47 H2

Mullberry St 46 D4
Munday St 47 H3
Munster St 46 C4
Murrey St 47 G1
Museum St 47 F3
Muslin St 46 B4
Myrtle Pl 46 A1

N
Nancy St 46 B6
Nansen St 47 J5
Naples St 47 F2
Nash St 46 C7
Nathan Dr 46 D4
Naval St 47 G3
Naylor St 47 H1
Neild St 47 G5
Neill St 47 H2
Nelson St 46 C1
Nether St 47 G5
New Allen St 47 G2
Newbeck St 47 F2
New Br St 46 D2
Newcastle St 46 E6
New Cath St 46 E3
New Century Park 47 E2
Newcombe St 46 E1
New Elm St 46 C4
New Gartside St 46 D4
New Islington 47 H3
New Mkt 46 E3
New Mkt St 46 E3
New Mt St 47 F2
New Quay St 46 C4
Newton St 47 F3
New Union St 47 G3
New Vine St 46 D6
New Wakefield St 46 E5
New Welcome St 46 D6
New Windsor 46 A3
New York St 47 E4
Nicholas St 47 E4
Nine Acre Dr 46 A6
Niven St 47 H2
North Bailey St 46 C3
Northdown Av 46 B6
North George St 46 B2
North Hill St 46 C2
North Phoebe St 46 A4
North Star Dr 46 B3
Northumberland Cl 46 A7
Northumberland Cres 46 A7
North Western St 47 G5
North W Services Rd 46 D3
Norton St 46 D2
Norway St 47 J4
Nuneaton Dr 47 H1
Nuttall St 46 A7

O
Oakford Av 47 G1
Oak St 47 F3
Old Bk St 46 E3
Old Birley St 46 D7
Oldbury Cl 47 H2
Old Elm St 47 G6
Oldfield Rd 46 A5
Oldham Rd 47 F3
Oldham St 47 F2
Old Medlock St 46 C4
Old Mill St 47 G3
Old Mt St 47 F2
Old Trafford 47 H2
Old York St 46 C6
Oliver St 47 F7
Ordsall Dr 46 A6
Ordsall La 46 A5
Oregon Cl 47 G6
Orion Pl 46 B1
Ormsgill St 46 D7
Orsett Cl 47 H1
Osborne St 47 G1
Oswald St 47 E2
Oswald St (Ancoats) 47 H4
Overbridge Rd 46 D1
Oxford Rd 47 E5
Oxford St 46 E4

P
Paddock St 47 G5
Palfrey Pl 47 H6
Pall Mall 46 E4
Palmerston St 47 H4
Parish Vw 46 A4
Parker St 47 F3
Park Pl 46 E1
Park St 46 E1
Park St (Salford) 46 B3
Parsonage 46 D3
Parsonage La 46 D3
Parsonage Way 46 A5
Paton St 47 F4
Pattishall Cl 47 J4

Peak St 47 G3
Peary St 47 G1
Peel Mt 46 A1
Pegasus Sq 46 B1
Pembroke Cl 47 H7
Pencroft Way 47 F7
Penfield Cl 47 F5
Percy Dr 46 A6
Percy St 46 C7
Peru St 46 B2
Peter St 46 D4
Phoenix St 47 E3
Phoenix Way 47 F3
Piccadilly 47 F3
Pickford St 46 G3
Picton Cl 46 C2
Picton St 46 C1
Piercy Av 46 B1
Piercy St 47 H3
Pigeon St 47 G3
Pimblett St 46 E1
Pine St 47 E4
Pin Mill Brow 47 H5
Pittbrook St 47 J5
Plymouth Gro 47 G7
Plymouth Vw 47 G7
Pochin St 47 J1
Poland St 47 G2
Polebrook Av 47 H7
Police St 46 D3
Pollard St 47 H4
Pollard St E 47 H3
Polygon Av 47 H7
Polygon St 47 G6
Pomona Strand 46 A6
Poplar St 47 J5
Poplin Dr 46 D2
Portland St 47 E5
Portsmouth St 47 G7
Port St 47 F3
Portugal St 47 G2
Portugal St E 47 G4
Postal St 47 G3
Postbridge Cl 47 H7
Potato Wf 46 C5
Poynton St 46 E6
Price St 47 J3
Primrose St 47 G2
Prince's Br 46 C4
Princess Rd 46 D6
Princess St 46 E4
Princess St (Cornbrook) 46 B6
Pritchard St 47 F5
Providence St 47 H4
Pryme St 46 C5
Purslow Cl 47 J3

Q
Quay St 46 C4
Quay St (Salford) 46 D3
Queen St 46 D4
Queen St (Salford) 46 D2
Quenby St 46 C6
Quendon Av 46 C1

R
Rachel St 47 H5
Radium St 47 G2
Ralli Cts 46 C3
Randerson St 47 G5
Rankin Cl 46 D7
Raven St 47 H5
Reather Wk 47 H1
Red Bk 47 E2
Redfern St 47 E2
Redhill St 47 G3
Red Lion St 47 F3
Regent Sq 46 A5
Reilly St 46 D6
Reservoir St 46 D2
Reyner St 47 E4
Rial Pl 47 E7
Ribston St 46 C7
Rice St 46 C5
Richmond St 47 F4
Richmond St (Salford) 46 C2
Ridgefield 46 D3
Ridgeway St E 47 H3
Ridgway St 47 H3
Riga St 47 F2
Rigel Pl 46 B1
Rigel St 47 H2
Rimworth Dr 47 H1
Ringstead Dr 47 G1
Ripley Cl 47 H4
River Pl 46 D5
Riverside 46 B2
River St 46 D6
River St (Ardwick) 47 H5
Robert St 46 E1
Roby St 47 F4
Rochdale Rd 47 F2

Rockdove Av 46 D6
Rocket Way 46 C3
Rockingham Cl 47 J7
Rodney St 47 H2
Rodney St (Salford) 46 C3
Roe St 47 G2
Roger St 47 F1
Rolla St 46 D2
Rolleston Av 47 H2
Rolls Cres 46 C7
Roman St 47 F3
Rome Rd 47 G2
Rondin Cl 47 J5
Rondin Rd 47 J5
Rope Wk 46 D2
Rosamond Dr 46 C3
Rosamond St W 47 E6
Rosewell Cl 47 J1
Rostron Av 47 J6
Rowendale St 46 D5
Royce Rd 46 C6
Roydale St 47 J2
Royds Cl 47 J7
Ruby St 47 E7
Rudcroft Cl 47 G6
Rudman Dr 46 A5
Rugby St 46 D1
Runcorn St 46 B6

S
Sackville St 47 E4
Sagar St 46 D1
St. Andrew's Sq 47 H4
St. Andrew's St 47 G4
St. Ann's Sq 46 D3
St. Ann St 46 D3
St. Bartholomew's Dr 46 A4
St. Chad's St 47 E1
St. Clement's Dr 46 A5
St. George's 46 B6
St. Ignatius Wk 46 A5
St. James's Sq 46 E4
St. James St 47 E4
St. John St 46 D4
St. Mary's Gate 46 E3
St. Mary's
   Parsonage 46 D3
St. Mary's St 46 C3
St. Nicholas Rd 46 C6
St. Philip's St 46 B3
St. Simon St 46 C1
St. Stephen's Cl 47 H7
St. Stephen St 46 C3
St. Thomas St 47 F1
St. Vincent St 47 H3
St. Wilfrids St 46 C6
Salford 46 A4
Salmon St 47 F3
Saltford Av 47 H3
Salutation St 46 E7
Samouth Cl 47 H2
Sam Swire St 46 D7
Samuel Ogden St 47 F5
Sanctuary, The 46 D7
Sandal St 47 J2
Sandford St 46 C1
Sand St 47 G1
Sawley Rd 47 J1
Scarsdale St 46 A1
School Ct 47 G3
School St 47 F2
School St (Salford) 46 C1
Scotporth Cl 47 G6
Sefton Cl 47 G6
Senior St 46 D2
Seymour Cl 46 A7
Sharp St 47 F2
Shaw Cres 46 E2
Shawgreen Cl 46 C6
Shawheath Cl 46 C6
Shearsby Cl 46 D7
Sheffield St 47 G4
Sherborne St 46 D1
Sherbourne St W 46 D1
Sherratt St 47 G2
Shetland Rd 47 H1
Shilford Dr 47 G2
Shortcroft St 46 D5
Short St 47 F3
Short St (Salford) 46 C1
Shrewsbury St 46 B7
Shudehill 47 F3
Sidney St 47 F6
Sidney St (Salford) 46 C3
Silkin Cl 47 F6
Silk St 47 G2
Silk St (Salford) 46 B2
Silvercroft St 46 C5
Silver St 47 F4
Simeon St 47 F2
Simms Cl 46 B3
Simpson St 47 F2
Sirius Pl 46 B1
Skerry Cl 47 G6

Skip Pl 47 E1
Slate Av 47 H3
Sleaford Cl 47 H1
Smallridge Cl 47 H2
Smith St 46 A6
Smithy La 46 D3
Snell St 47 H4
Soar St 47 F3
Sorrel St 46 C6
Southall St 46 D4
Southall St
   (Strangeways) 46 D1
Southend Av 46 B7
Southern St 46 D5
Southgate 46 D3
South Hall St 46 B5
South King St 46 D3
Southmill St 46 E4
South Pump St 47 F4
South W Services Rd 46 C4
Sparkle St 47 G4
Spaw St 46 C3
Spear St 47 F3
Spectator St 47 H3
Springfield La 46 D2
Springfield Sq 46 D4
Spring Gdns 47 E4
Spruce St 46 C7
Stalham Cl 47 H1
Stanley Rd 46 B7
Stanley St 47 F1
Stanley St (Salford) 46 C4
Stansby Gdns 47 J7
Station App (for
   Oxford Road
   Station) 47 E5
Station App (for
   Piccadilly Station) 47 F4
Staverton Cl 47 G6
Stephen St 46 E1
Stevenson Pl 47 F3
Stevenson Sq 47 F3
Stevenson St 46 B3
Stockland Cl 47 F6
Stockport Rd 47 H6
Stocks St 47 E1
Stocks St E 47 E1
Stonall Av 46 C6
Stonelow Cl 46 E6
Stone St 46 C5
Store St 47 F4
Stracey St 47 J2
Strawberry Hill 46 A1
Stretford Rd 46 B7
Style St 47 F2
Sudbury Cl 46 B7
Sudell St 47 G2
Sussex St 46 B1
Swan St 47 F2
Swiftsure Av 46 B3
Syndall Av 47 H6
Syndall St 47 H6

T
Talgarth Rd 47 G1
Tamar Ct 46 B7
Tame St 47 H4
Tariff St 47 F3
Tasle All 46 D4
Tatton St 46 B6
Tatton St (Salford) 46 A5
Taunton St 47 J3
Tavery Cl 47 H3
Tebutt St 47 G2
Teer St 47 J3
Temperance St 47 G5
Tewkesbury Rd 47 J2
Thirsk St 47 G5
Thomas St 47 F3
Thompson St 47 F2
Thompson St
   (Strangeways) 46 D1
Thomson St 47 H7
Thor Grn 46 B5
Thornage Dr 47 H1
Thorncross Cl 46 B6
Thornden Rd 47 J1
Thornley Brow 47 E2
Thornton St 47 H1
Tib La 46 E4
Tib St 47 F3
Tideswell Av 47 H2
Tidworth Av 47 H3
Tinsley Cl 47 J2
Tivoli St 46 D4
Todd St 47 E2
Tomlinson St 46 D7
Tonge St 47 J5
Tonman St 46 D4
Torquay Cl 47 H7
Towcester Cl 47 J3
Town Hall La 46 E3
Trafford Bk Rd 46 A7

Trafford Ct 46 C6
Trafford Pl 46 B7
Trafford St 46 D5
Travis St 47 G5
Trentham St 46 B6
Trinity Way 46 B5
Tristam Cl 47 G6
Troutbeck Av 47 H3
Trumpet St 46 D5
Tudbury Way 46 C2
Tuer St 47 F7
Turner St 47 F3
Turner St
   (Old Trafford) 46 A6
Tutbury St 47 H4
Twillbrook Dr 46 D2

U
Union St 47 F3
Union St (Ardwick) 47 H5
University Rd 46 A2
University Rd W 46 A2
Upper Brook St 47 F6
Upper Cyrus St 47 J3
Upper Helena St 47 J2
Upper Kirby St 47 H3
Upper Moss La 46 C7
Upper Wf St 46 B3

V
Varley St 47 J1
Vauxhall St 47 G1
Velour Cl 46 B1
Vesta St 47 H3
Viaduct St 47 J4
Viaduct St (Salford) 46 D2
Vickers St 47 J1
Victoria Br St 46 D3
Victoria Sta App 46 E2
Victor St 47 G1
Victor St (Salford) 46 C3
Virgil St 46 B6

W
Wadeford Cl 47 G2
Wadeson Rd 47 G5
Wadlow Cl 46 C2
Walker's Cft 46 E2
Wallness 46 A1
Wallness La 46 A1
Warde St 46 C7
Wardle St 47 J2
Warford St 47 F1
Warmington Dr 47 J7
Warwick St 47 F3
Warwick St (Hulme) 46 D7
Waterloo St 47 E4
Water St 46 B5
Water St (Ardwick) 47 H5
Watkin Cl 47 G7
Watkin St 46 C1
Watson St 46 D5
Weald Cl 47 G6
Weir St 46 D7
Welland Cl 46 B7
Wellhead Cl 46 E7
Wellington Grn 46 C7
Wellington St 46 C2
Well St 47 E3
West Bk St 46 A4
West Charles St 46 A3
West Crown Av 46 A4
West Hope St 46 A3
West King St 46 C2
Westminster St 46 B6
West Mosley St 47 E4
Weston St 47 J3
West Pk St 46 A5
Weybridge Rd 47 H3
Whalley St 47 H2
Wheater's Cres 46 B1
Wheater's St 46 B1
Wheater's Ter 46 B1
Whimberry Cl 46 A5
Whitchurch St 46 D1
Whitekirk Cl 47 G6
White St 46 B7
Whitfield St 47 E1
Whittle's Cft 47 G4
Whittle St 47 F3
Whitworth St 47 F5
Whitworth St W 46 D5
Wilberforce Cl 46 D7
Wilfred St 46 D1
William Chadwick Cl 47 H1
Williamson St 47 F1
William St 47 H5
Wilmott St 46 E6
Wilson St 47 H7
Wilton Pl 46 B3
Wilton St 47 F6
Winder Dr 47 H3
Windmill Av 46 A5
Windmill St 46 D4

Winfell Dr 47 J2
Winscombe Dr 47 H1
Winser St 47 E5
Winstanley Rd 47 H2
Withy Gro 47 E3
Woden's Av 46 A5
Woden St 46 B5
Woodlark Cl 46 B3
Wood St 46 D4
Woodward Pl 47 H3
Woodward St 47 H3
Woollam Pl 46 C4
Worrall St 46 A5
Worsley St 46 B5
Worsley St (Salford) 46 D3
Wright St 46 A7
Wroe St 46 B3
Wyatt Av 46 A5
Wynne St 46 A1
Wyre St 47 G5

Y
Yew St 46 C7
Yorkshire St 46 D3
York St 47 E3
York St (Hulme) 46 C6
York St (off Charles
   Street) 47 E5
York St E 47 F6

Z
Zion Cres 46 D7

ABERDEEN

Tourist Information Centre: 23 Union Street
Tel: 01224 269180

Albert Quay	C3	Hutcheon Street	B2
Albert Street	B2	Justice Mill Lane	B3
Albury Road	B3	King's Crescent	C1
Albyn Place	A3	King Street	C1
Argyll Place	A2	Langstane Place	B3
Ashgrove Road	A1	Leadside Road	B2
Ashgrove Road West	A1	Leslie Terrace	B1
Ash-hill Drive	A1	Links Road	C2
Ashley Road	A3	Linksfield Road	C1
Back Hilton Road	A1	Loch Street	B2
Baker Street	B2	Maberly Street	B2
Beach Boulevard	C2	Market Street	C3
Bedford Place	B1	Menzies Road	C3
Bedford Road	B1	Merkland Road East	C1
Beechgrove Terrace	A2	Mid Stocket Road	A2
Belgrave Terrace	A2	Mile-end Avenue	A2
Berryden Road	B1	Miller Street	C2
Blaikie's Quay	C3	Mount Street	B2
Bon-Accord Street	B3	Nelson Street	C2
Bonnymuir Place	A2	North Esplanade East	C3
Bridge Street	B2	North Esplanade West	C3
Brighton Place	A3	Orchard Street	C1
Cairncry Road	A1	Osborne Place	A3
Canal Road	B1	Palmerston Road	C3
Carden Place	A3	Park Road	C1
Carlton Place	A3	Park Street	C2
Cattofield Place	A1	Pittodrie Place	C1
Causewayend	B1	Pittodrie Street	C1
Chapel Street	B2	Powis Place	B1
Claremont Street	A3	Powis Terrace	B1
Clifton Road	A1	Queens Road	A3
College Bounds	B1	Queens Terrace	A3
College Street	C3	Regent Quay	C2
Commerce Street	C2	Rosehill Crescent	A1
Commercial Quay	C3	Rosehill Drive	A1
Constitution Street	C2	Rosemount Place	A2
Cornhill Drive	A1	Rose Street	B2
Cornhill Road	A1	Rubislaw Terrace	B3
Cornhill Terrace	A1	St. Swithin Street	A3
Cotton Street	C2	Schoolhill	B2
Cromwell Road	A3	Seaforth Road	C1
Desswood Place	A3	Sinclair Road	C3
Devonshire Road	A3	Skene Square	B2
Elmbank Terrace	B1	Skene Street	B2
Esslemont Avenue	B2	South Crown Street	B3
Ferryhill Road	B3	South Esplanade West	C3
Fonthill Road	B3	Spital	C1
Forest Road	A3	Springbank Terrace	B3
Forest Avenue	A3	Spring Gardens	B2
Fountainhall Road	A2	Stanley Street	A3
Froghall Terrace	B1	Sunnybank Road	B1
Gallowgate	C2	Sunnyside Road	B1
George Street	B1	Union Glen	B3
Gillespie Crescent	A1	Union Grove	A3
Gladstone Place	A3	Union Street	B3
Golf Road	C1	Urquhart Road	C2
Gordondale Road	A2	Victoria Bridge	C3
Great Southern Road	B3	Victoria Road	C3
Great Western Road	A3	Walker Road	C3
Guild Street	C3	Waterloo Quay	C2
Hamilton Place	A2	Waverley Place	B3
Hardgate	B3	Well Place	C3
Hilton Drive	A1	Westburn Drive	A1
Hilton Place	A1	Westburn Road	A2
Hilton Street	A1	West North Street	C2
Holburn Road	B3	Whitehall Place	A2
Holburn Street	B3	Whitehall Road	A2
Holland Street	B1	Willowbank Road	B3

ABERDEEN

0   500 yds
0   500m

Appears on main
map page 261

BATH

Tourist Information Centre: Abbey Chambers, Abbey Churchyard
Tel: 0906 711 2000

Ambury	A3	Pierrepont Street	B3
Archway Street	C3	Pulteney Gardens	C3
Argyle Street	B2	Pulteney Mews	C1
Avon Street	A2	Pulteney Road	C2
Barton Street	A2	Queen Street	A2
Bath Street	B2	Quiet Street	A1
Bathwick Hill	C1	Rossiter Road	B3
Beau Street	B2	Royal Crescent	A1
Bennett Street	A1	St. James's Parade	A2
Bridge Street	B2	St. John's Road	B1
Broad Quay	A3	St. Marks Road	B3
Broad Street	B1	Sawclose	A2
Broadway	C3	Southgate Street	B3
Brock Street	A1	Spring Crescent	C3
Chapel Row	A2	Stall Street	B2
Charles Street	A2	Sutton Street	C1
Charlotte Street	A1	Sydney Place	C1
Cheap Street	B2	The Circus	A1
Claverton Street	B3	Union Street	B2
Corn Street	A3	Upper Borough Walls	A2
Daniel Street	C1	Walcot Street	B1
Darlington Street	C1	Wells Road	A3
Dorchester Street	B3	Westgate Buildings	A2
Edward Street	C1	Westgate Street	A2
Excelsior Street	C3	Wood Street	A1
Ferry Lane	C2	York Street	B2
Gay Street	A1		
George Street	A1		
Grand Parade	B2		
Great Pulteney Street	C1		
Green Park Road	A2		
Green Street	B1		
Grove Street	B1		
Henrietta Gardens	C1		
Henrietta Mews	C1		
Henrietta Road	B1		
Henrietta Street	B1		
Henry Street	B2		
High Street	B2		
Holloway	A3		
James Street West	A2		
John Street	A1		
Kingsmead East	A2		
Kingsmead Square	A2		
Lansdown Road	A1		
Laura Place	B1		
Lime Grove	C2		
Lime Grove Gardens	C2		
Lower Borough Walls	A2		
Lower Bristol Road	A3		
Magdalen Avenue	A3		
Manvers Street	B3		
Milk Street	A2		
Milsom Street	B1		
Monmouth Place	A1		
Monmouth Street	A2		
Newark Street	B3		
New Bond Street	B2		
New King Street	A2		
New Orchard Street	B2		
New Street	A2		
North Parade	B2		
North Parade Road	C2		
Old King Street	A1		
Orange Grove	B2		
Paragon	B1		

BATH

0   200 yds
0   200m

Appears on main
map page 117

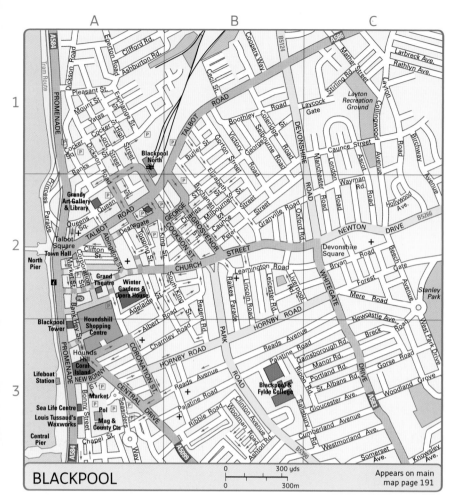

Tourist Information Centre: Festival House, Promenade
Tel: 01253 478222

Abingdon Street	A2	Manor Road	C3
Adelaide Street	A2	Market Street	A2
Albert Road	A3	Mather Street	C1
Ascot Road	C1	Mere Road	C2
Ashburton Road	A1	Milbourne Street	B2
Ashton Road	B3	Mount Street	A1
Bank Hey Street	A2	New Bonny Street	A3
Banks Street	A1	Newcastle Avenue	C2
Beech Avenue	C2	Newton Drive	C2
Birchway Avenue	C1	Oxford Road	B2
Bonny Street	A3	Palatine Road	B3
Boothley Road	B1	Park Road	B3
Breck Road	C3	Peter Street	B2
Bryan Road	C2	Pleasant Street	A1
Buchanan Street	B2	Portland Road	C3
Butler Street	B1	Princess Parade	A2
Caunce Street	B2/C1	Promenade	A1
Cecil Street	B1	Queens Square	A2
Central Drive	A3	Queen Street	A2
Chapel Street	A3	Rathlyn Avenue	C1
Charles Street	B2	Reads Avenue	B3
Charnley Road	A3	Regent Road	B2
Church Street	B2	Ribble Road	B3
Clifford Road	A1	Ripon Road	B3
Clifton Street	A2	St. Albans Road	C3
Clinton Avenue	B3	Salisbury Road	C3
Cocker Square	A1	Seasiders Way	A3
Cocker Street	A1	Selbourne Road	B1
Coleridge Road	B1	Somerset Avenue	C3
Collingwood Avenue	C1	South King Street	B2
Cookson Street	B2	Stirling Road	C1
Coopers Way	B1	Talbot Road	A2/B1
Coronation Street	A3	Talbot Square	A2
Corporation Street	A2	Topping Street	A2
Cumberland Avenue	C3	Victory Road	B1
Deansgate	A2	Wayman Road	C2
Devonshire Road	B1	Westmorland Avenue	C3
Devonshire Square	C2	West Park Drive	C2
Dickson Road	A1	Whitegate Drive	C2/C3
Egerton Road	A1	Woodland Grove	C3
Elizabeth Street	B1	Woolman Road	B3
Exchange Street	A1	Yates Street	A1
Forest Gate	C2		
Gainsborough Road	B3		
George Street	B2/B1		
Gloucester Avenue	C3		
Gorse Road	C3		
Gorton Street	B1		
Granville Road	B2		
Grosvenor Street	B2		
High Street	A1		
Hollywood Avenue	C2		
Hornby Road	A3		
Hounds Hill	A3		
King Street	A2		
Knowsley Avenue	C3		
Larbreck Avenue	C1		
Laycock Gate	C1		
Layton Road	C1		
Leamington Road	B2		
Leicester Road	B2		
Lincoln Road	B2		
Liverpool Road	B2		
London Road	C1		
Lord Street	A1		
Manchester Road	C1		

BLACKPOOL

0 — 300 yds
0 — 300m

Appears on main
map page 191

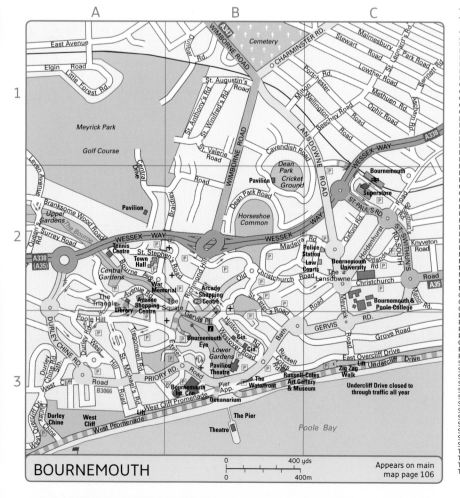

Tourist Information Centre: Westover Road
Tel: 0845 051 1700

Ascham Road	C1	Undercliff Drive	C3
Avenue Road	A2	Wellington Road	C1
Bath Road	B3	Wessex Way	A2/C1
Beechey Road	C1	West Cliff Promenade	A3
Bennett Road	C1	West Cliff Road	A3
Bourne Avenue	A2	West Hill Road	A3
Braidley Road	B2	West Overcliff Drive	A3
Branksome Wood Road	A2	West Promenade	A3
Cavendish Road	B1	Westover Road	B3
Central Drive	A1	Wimborne Road	B2
Charminster Road	B1		
Christchurch Road	C2		
Cotlands	C2		
Dean Park Road	B2		
Dunbar Road	B1		
Durley Chine	A3		
Durley Chine Road	A3		
Durley Chine Road South	A3		
Durley Road	A3		
East Avenue	A1		
East Overcliff Drive	C3		
Elgin Road	A1		
Exeter Road	B3		
Gervis Place	B3		
Gervis Road	C3		
Grove Road	C3		
Hinton Road	B3		
Holdenhurst Road	C2		
Knyveton Road	C2		
Lansdowne Road	B1		
Leven Avenue	A1		
Little Forest Road	A1		
Lowther Road	C1		
Madeira Road	B2		
Malmesbury Park Road	C1		
Manor Road	C2		
Methuen Road	C1		
Meyrick Road	C2		
Milton Road	B1		
Old Christchurch Road	B2		
Ophir Road	C1		
Oxford Road	C2		
Pier Approach	B3		
Poole Hill	A3		
Portchester Road	C1		
Priory Road	A3		
Queen's Road	A2		
Richmond Hill	B2		
Russell Cotes Road	B3		
St. Augustin's Road	B1		
St. Anthony's Road	B1		
St. Leonard's Road	C1		
St. Michael's Road	A3		
St. Pauls' Road	C2		
St. Peter's Road	B2		
St. Stephen's Road	A2		
St. Swithun's Road	C2		
St. Swithun's Road South	C2		
St. Valerie Road	B1		
St. Winifred's Road	B1		
Stewart Road	C1		
Surrey Road	A2		
The Lansdowne	B2		
The Square	B2		
The Triangle	A2		
Tregonwell Road	A3		

BOURNEMOUTH

0 — 400 yds
0 — 400m

Appears on main
map page 106

Tourist Information Centre: Britannia House, Broadway
Tel: 01274 433678

Akam Road	A1	John Street	A2
Ann Place	A3	Kirkgate	B2
Ashgrove	A3	Leeds Road	C2
Balme Street	B1	Little Horton Lane	A3
Bank Street	B2	Lower Kirkgate	B2
Baptist Place	A1	Lumb Lane	A1
Barkerend Road	C1	Manchester Road	B3
Barry Street	A2	Manningham Lane	A1
Bolling Road	C3	Mannville Terrace	A3
Bolton Road	C1	Manor Row	B1
Brearton Street	A1	Melbourne Place	A3
Bridge Street	B2	Midland Road	B1
Britannia Street	B3	Moody Street	C3
Broadway	B2	Morley Street	A3
Burnett Street	C2	Neal Street	A3
Caledonia Street	B3	Nelson Street	B3
Canal Road	B1	North Parade	B1
Captain Street	C1	North Street	C1
Carlton Street	A2	North Wing	C1
Carter Street	C3	Nuttall Road	C1
Centenary Square	B2	Otley Road	C1
Chain Street	A1	Paradise Street	A1
Channing Way	B2	Park Road	B3
Chapel Street	C2	Peckover Street	B2
Charles Street	B2	Prince's Way	B2
Cheapside	B2	Prospect Street	C3
Chester Street	A3	Radwell Drive	A3
Churchbank	C2	Rawson Place	B1
Claremont	C1	Rawson Road	A1
Croft Street	B3	Rebecca Street	A1
Darfield Street	A1	Rouse Fold	C3
Darley Street	B1	Russell Street	A3
Drake Street	B2	Salem Street	B1
Drewton Road	A1	Sawrey Place	A3
Dryden Street	C3	Sedgwick Close	A1
Duke Street	B1	Sharpe Street	B3
Dyson Street	A1	Shipley Airedale Road	C1
East Parade	C2	Simes Street	A1
Edmund Street	A3	Snowden Street	A1
Edward Street	C3	Sunbridge Road	A1
Eldon Place	A1	Sylhet Close	A1
Fairfax Street	C3	Ternhill Grove	B3
Filey Street	C2	Tetley Street	A2
Fitzwilliam Street	C3	The Tyrls	B2
Fountain Street	A1	Thornton Road	A2
George Street	C2	Trafalgar Street	A1
Godwin Street	B2	Trinity Road	A3
Gracechurch Street	A1	Tumbling Hill Street	A2
Grafton Street	A3	Valley Road	B1
Grattan Road	A2	Vaughan Street	A1
Great Horton Road	A3	Vicar Lane	C2
Grove Terrace	A3	Vincent Street	A2
Guy Street	C3	Wakefield Road	C3
Hall Ings	B2	Wapping Road	C1
Hall Lane	C3	Water Lane	A2
Hallfield Road	A1	Westgate	A1
Hamm Strasse	B1	Wigan Street	A2
Hammerton Street	C2		
Hanover Square	A1		
Harris Street	C2		
Heap Lane	C1		
Houghton Place	A1		
Howard Street	B2		
Hustlergate	B2		
Ivegate	B2		
James Street	B2		

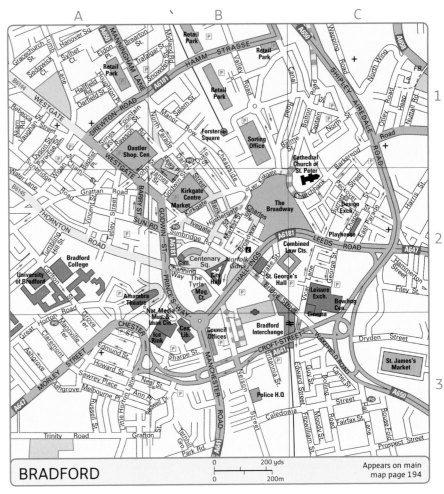

BRADFORD

200 yds
200m

Appears on main
map page 194

Tourist Information Centre: Royal Pavilion Shop,
4-5 Pavilion Buildings   Tel: 01273 290337

Addison Road	A1	Southover Street	C2
Albion Hill	C2	Springfield Road	B1
Beaconsfield Road	B1	Stafford Road	A1
Brunswick Square	A2	Stanford Road	B1
Buckingham Place	B1	Sussex Street	C2
Buckingham Road	B2	Terminus Road	B2
Carlton Hill	C2	The Lanes	B3
Cheapside	B2	The Upper Drive	A1
Church Street	B2	Trafalgar Street	B2
Churchill Square	B3	Union Road	C1
Clifton Hill	A2	Upper Lewes Road	C1
Clyde Road	B1	Upper North Street	A2
Davigdor Road	A1	Upper Rock Gardens	C3
Ditchling Rise	B1	Viaduct Road	B1
Ditchling Road	C1	Victoria Road	A2
Dyke Road	B2	Waterloo Street	A2
Dyke Road Drive	B1	Wellington Road	C1
Eastern Road	C3	West Drive	C2
Edward Street	C3	West Street	B3
Elm Grove	C1	Western Road	A2
Fleet Street	B2	Wilbury Crescent	A1
Florence Road	B1	York Avenue	A2
Freshfield Road	C3	York Place	C2
Furze Hill	A2		
Gloucester Road	B2		
Grand Junction Road	B3		
Hamilton Road	B1		
Hanover Street	C2		
Highdown Road	A1		
Holland Road	A2		
Hollingdean Road	C1		
Howard Place	B1		
Islingword Road	C1		
John Street	C2		
King's Road	A3		
Lansdowne Road	A2		
Lewes Road	C1		
London Road	B1		
Lyndhurst Road	A1		
Madeira Drive	C3		
Marine Parade	C3		
Montefiore Road	A1		
Montpelier Road	A2		
New England Road	B1		
New England Street	B1		
Nizells Avenue	A1		
Norfolk Terrace	A2		
North Road	B2		
North Street	B2		
Old Shoreham Road	A1		
Old Steine	C3		
Park Crescent Terrace	C1		
Park Street	C2		
Port Hall Road	A1		
Preston Circus	B1		
Preston Road	B1		
Preston Street	A3		
Prince's Crescent	C1		
Queen's Park Road	C2		
Queen's Road	B2		
Richmond Place	C2		
Richmond Road	C1		
Richmond Street	C2		
Richmond Terrace	C2		
St. James's Street	C3		
Somerhill Road	A2		

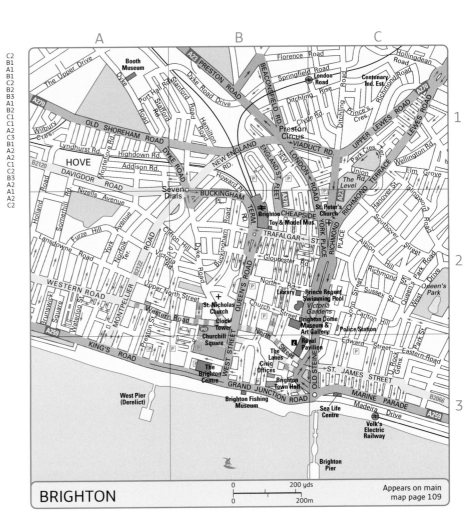

BRIGHTON

200 yds
200m

Appears on main
map page 109

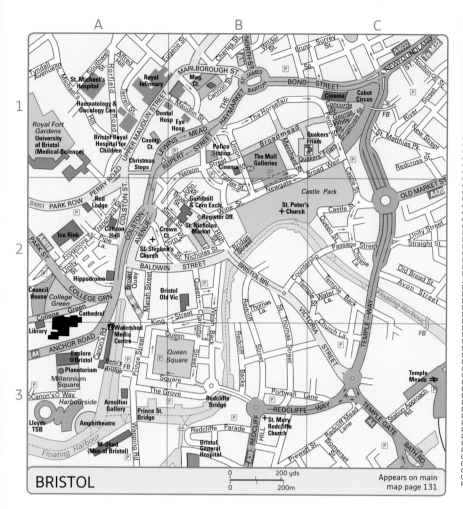

BRISTOL

0   200 yds
0   200m

Appears on main
map page 131

Tourist Information Centre: E Shed 1, Canons Road
Tel: 0906 711 2191

Alfred Hill	A1	Redcliffe Bridge	B3
Anchor Road	A3	Redcliffe Parade	B3
Avon Street	C2	Redcliff Hill	B3
Baldwin Street	A2	Redcliff Mead Lane	C3
Bath Road	C3	Redcliff Street	B2
Bond Street	B1	Redcross Street	C1
Bridge Street	B2	River Street	C1
Brigstowe Street	C1	Rupert Street	A1
Bristol Bridge	B2	St. James Barton	B1
Broadmead	B1	St. Matthias Park	C1
Broad Quay	A2	St. Michael's Hill	A1
Broad Street	B2	St. Nicholas Street	B2
Broad Weir	C1	St. Thomas Street	B2
Brunswick Square	B1	Small Street	A2
Cannon Street	B1	Somerset Street	C3
Canon's Road	A3	Southwell Street	A1
Canon's Way	A3	Station Approach Road	C3
Castle Street	C2	Straight Street	C2
Charles Street	B1	Surrey Street	C1
Cheese Lane	C2	Temple Back	C2
Christmas Steps	A1	Temple Gate	C3
Church Lane	C2	Temple Street	B2
College Green	A2	Temple Way	C2
Colston Avenue	A2	Terrell Street	A1
Colston Street	A2	The Grove	A3
Concorde Street	C1	The Haymarket	B1
Corn Street	C1	The Horsefair	B1
Countership	B2	Thomas Lane	B2
Eugene Street	A1	Trenchard Street	A2
Fairfax Street	B1	Tyndall Avenue	A1
Frogmore Street	A2	Union Street	B1
George White Street	C1	Unity Street	A2
High Street	B2	Unity Street	C2
Horfield Road	A1	Upper Maudlin Street	A1
Houlton Street	C1	Victoria Street	B2
John Street	B2	Wapping Road	A3
King Street	A2	Water Lane	C2
Lewins Mead	A1	Welsh Back	B2
Lower Castle Street	C1	Wilder Street	B1
Lower Maudlin Street	B1	Wine Street	B2
Marlborough Street	B1		
Marsh Street	A2		
Merchant Street	B1		
Nelson Street	B1		
Newfoundland Street	C1		
Newgate	B2		
New Street	C1		
North Street	B1		
Old Bread Street	C2		
Old Market Street	C2		
Park Row	A2		
Park Street	A2		
Passage Street	C2		
Penn Street	C1		
Pero's Bridge	A3		
Perry Road	A2		
Pipe Lane	A2		
Portwall Lane	B3		
Prewett Street	B3		
Prince Street	A3		
Prince Street Bridge	C1		
Quakers' Friars	B1		
Queen Charlotte Street	B2		
Queen Square	A3		
Queen Street	C2		
Redcliff Backs	B3		

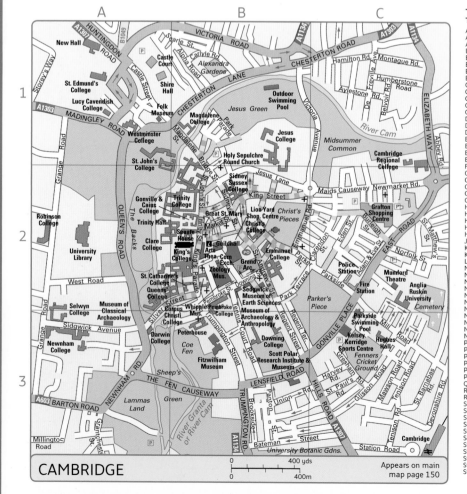

CAMBRIDGE

0   400 yds
0   400m

Appears on main
map page 150

Tourist Information Centre: Wheeler Street
Tel: 0871 226 8006

Adam and Eve Street	C2	Tenison Road	C3
Alpha Road	B1	Tennis Court Road	B2
Aylestone Road	C1	Trinity Street	B2
Barton Road	A3	Trumpington Road	B3
Bateman Street	B3	Trumpington Street	B3
Belvior Road	C1	Union Road	B3
Brookside	B3	Victoria Avenue	B1
Burleigh Street	C2	Victoria Road	B1
Carlyle Road	B1	West Road	A2
Castle Street	A1		
Chesterton Lane	B1		
Chesterton Road	B1		
Clarendon Street	C2		
De Freville Avenue	C1		
Devonshire Road	C3		
Downing Street	B2		
East Road	C2		
Eden Street	C2		
Elizabeth Way	C1		
Emmanuel Road	B2		
Fen Causeway, The	A3		
Glisson Road	C3		
Gonville Place	C3		
Granchester Street	A3		
Grange Road	A3		
Gresham Road	C3		
Hamilton Road	C1		
Harvey Road	C3		
Hills Road	C3		
Humberstone Road	C1		
Huntingdon Road	A1		
Jesus Lane	B2		
King's Parade	B2		
King Street	B2		
Lensfield Road	B3		
Madingley Road	A1		
Magdalene Bridge Street	B1		
Maids Causeway	C2		
Market Street	B2		
Mawson Road	C3		
Millington Road	A3		
Mill Road	C3		
Montague Road	C1		
Newmarket Road	C2		
Newnham Road	A3		
Norfolk Street	C2		
Panton Street	B3		
Parker Street	B2		
Park Parade	B1		
Parkside	C2		
Park Terrace	B2		
Pembroke Street	B2		
Queen's Road	A2		
Regent Street	B2		
Regent Terrace	B2		
St. Andrew's Street	B2		
St. Barnabas Road	C3		
St. John's Street	B2		
St. Matthew's Street	C3		
St. Paul's Road	C3		
Searce Street	A1		
Sidgwick Avenue	A3		
Sidney Street	B2		
Silver Street	A3		
Station Road	C3		
Storey's Way	A1		

Tourist Information Centre: 18 The High Street
Tel: 01227 862162

Best Lane	B2	Watling Street	B2
Borough Northgate	B1	Whitehall Gardens	A2
Broad Street	C1	Whitehall Road	A2
Burgate	B2	Wincheap	A3
Castle Row	A3	York Road	A3
Castle Street	A3		
College Road	C1		
Cossington Road	C3		
Craddock Road	C1		
Dover Street	C2		
Edgar Road	C1		
Ersham Road	C3		
Forty Acres Road	A1		
Gordon Road	A3		
Havelock Street	C1		
Hawk's Lane	B2		
High Street	B2		
Ivy Lane	C2		
King Street	B1		
Kirby's Lane	A1		
Lansdown Road	B3		
Longport	C2		
Lower Bridge Street	C2		
Lower Chantry Lane	C2		
Marlowe Avenue	B3		
Martyrs' Field Road	A3		
Mead Way	A2		
Military Road	C1		
Monastery Street	C2		
New Dover Road	C3		
North Holmes Road	C1		
North Lane	A1		
Nunnery Fields	C3		
Oaten Hill	C3		
Old Dover Road	C3		
Orchard Street	A1		
Oxford Road	B3		
Palace Street	B2		
Pin Hill	A3		
Pound Lane	A1		
Puckle Lane	C3		
Rheims Way	A2		
Rhodaus Town	B3		
Roper Road	A1		
Rose Lane	B2		
St. Dunstan's Street	A1		
St. George's Lane	B2		
St. George's Place	C2		
St. George's Street	B2		
St. Gregory's Road	C1		
St. Margarets Street	B2		
St. Peter's Lane	B1		
St. Peter's Place	A2		
St. Peter's Street	A1		
St. Radigund's Street	B1		
St. Stephen's Road	B1		
Simmonds Road	A3		
Station Road East	A3		
Station Road West	A1		
Stour Street	A2		
The Causeway	B1		
The Friar's	B2		
Tourtel Road	C1		
Tudor Road	A3		
Union Street	C1		
Upper Bridge Street	B3		

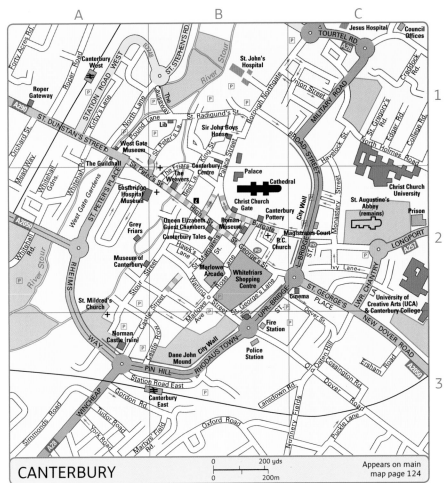

CANTERBURY

0 — 200 yds
0 — 200m

Appears on main map page 124

Tourist Information Centre: The Old Library, Trinity Street
Tel: 029 2087 3573

Adam Street	C3	Moira Terrace	C2
Albany Road	C1	Moy Road	C1
Allerton Street	A3	Museum Avenue	B1
Arran Place	C1	Neville Street	A2
Arran Street	C1	Newport Road	C2
Basil Place	B1	Newport Road Lane	C2
Bedford Street	C1	Ninian Park Road	A3
Boulevard de Nantes	B2	North Road	A1
Bridge Street	B3	Oxford Lane	C2
Brook Street	A3	Park Grove	B2
Bute Street	B3	Park Place	B1
Bute Terrace	B3	Park Street	B3
Castle Street	A2	Partridge Road	C1
Cathays Terrace	B1	Penarth Road	B3
Cathedral Road	A2	Pendyris Street	A3
Celerity Drive	C3	Pitman Street	A2
Central Link	C3	Planet Street	C2
Charles Street	B2	Queen Street	B2
Churchill Way	C2	Rhymney Street	B1
City Road	C1	Richmond Road	B1
Clare Road	A3	Richmond Road	C1
Clare Street	A2	Ryder Street	A2
Claude Road	C1	St. Mary Street	B3
Coburn Street	B1	St. Peters Street	C2
College Road	B2	Salisbury Road	B1
Colum Road	A1	Schooner Way	C3
Corbett Road	B1	Senghennydd Road	B1
Cornwall Street	A3	Stafford Road	A3
Cottrell Road	C1	Strathnairn Street	C1
Cowbridge Road East	A2	Stuttgarter Strasse	B2
Craddock Street	A3	Taffs Mead Embankment	B3
Craiglee Drive	C3	Talbot Street	A2
Croft Street	C1	Thesiger Street	B1
Crwys Road	B1	The Parade	C1
Cyfartha Street	C1	The Walk	C1
De Burgh Street	A2	Tudor Street	A3
Despenser Street	A3	Tyndall Street	C3
Duke Street	B2	Wedmore Road	A3
Dumfries Place	C2	Wells Street	A3
Ellen Street	C3	West Grove	C2
Elm Street	C1	Westgate Street	B2
Fanny Street	B1	Windsor Place	B2
Fitzhamon Embankment	A3	Windsor Road	C2
Flora Street	B1	Wood Street	B3
Glossop Road	C2	Woodville Road	B1
Gordon Road	C1	Wordsworth Avenue	C2
Greyfriars Road	B2	Working Street	B2
Hamilton Street	A2	Wyeverne Road	B1
Harriet Street	B1		
Herbert Street	C3		
High Street	B2		
Hirwain Street	B1		
Keppoch Street	C1		
Kingsway	B2		
Lewis Street	A2		
Longcross Street	C2		
Maindy Road	A1		
Mardy Street	A3		
Mark Street	A2		
Merches Gardens	A3		
Merthyr Street	B1		
Meteor Street	C2		
Mill Lane	B3		
Minny Street	B1		
Miskin Street	B1		
Moira Place	C2		

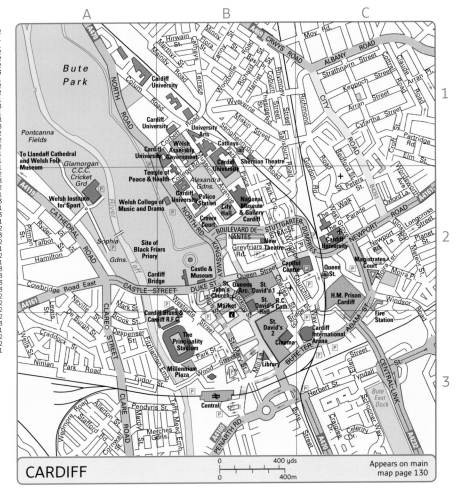

CARDIFF

0 — 400 yds
0 — 400m

Appears on main map page 130

Carlisle   Cheltenham

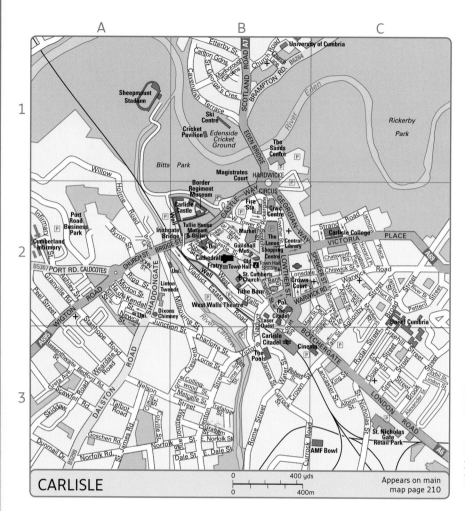

Tourist Information Centre: Old Town Hall, Green Market
Tel: 01228 598596

Abbey Street	B2	Lancaster Street	C3
Aglionby Street	C2	Lime Street	B3
Albion Street	C3	Lindon Street	C3
Alexander Street	C3	Lismore Place	C2
Alfred Street	C2	Lismore Street	C2
Ashley Street	A2	London Road	C3
Bank Street	B2	Lonsdale	B2
Bassenthwaite Street	A3	Lorne Crescent	B3
Bedford Road	A3	Lorne Street	B3
Botchergate	B3	Lowther Street	B2
Brampton Road	B1	Marlborough Gardens	B1
Bridge Lane	A2	Mary Street	B3
Bridge Street	A2	Metcalfe Street	B3
Broad Street	C2	Milbourne Street	B2
Brook Street	C3	Morton Street	A2
Brunswick Street	C2	Myddleton Street	C2
Byron Street	A2	Nelson Street	A3
Caldcotes	A2	Newcastle Street	A2
Carlton Gardens	B1	Norfolk Road	A3
Castle Street	B2	Norfolk Street	A3
Castle Way	B2	Peel Street	A2
Cavendish Terrace	B1	Petteril Street	C2
Cecil Street	C2	Port Road	A2
Charlotte Street	B3	Portland Place	C3
Chatsworth Square	C2	Rickergate	B2
Chiswick Street	C2	Rigg Street	A2
Church Lane	B1	River Street	C2
Church Road	B1	Robert Street	B3
Church Street	A2	Rome Street	B3
Clifton Street	A3	Rydal Street	C3
Close Street	C3	St. George's Crescent	B1
Collingwood Street	B3	St. James Road	A3
Colville Street	A3	St. Nicholas Street	C3
Crown Street	B3	Scawfell Road	A3
Currock Road	B3	Scotch Street	B2
Currock Street	B3	Scotland Road	B1
Dale Street	B3	Shaddongate	A2
Denton Street	B3	Silloth Street	A2
Dunmail Drive	A3	Skiddaw Road	A3
East Dale Street	B3	Spencer Street	C2
East Norfolk Street	B3	Stanhope Road	A2
Eden Bridge	B1	Strand Road	C2
Edward Street	C3	Sybil Street	C3
Elm Street	B3	Tait Street	C3
English Street	B2	Talbot Road	A3
Etterby Street	B1	Trafalgar Street	B3
Finkle Street	B2	Viaduct Estate Road	B2
Fisher Street	B2	Victoria Place	C2
Fusehill Street	C3	Victoria Viaduct	B3
Georgian Way	B2	Warwick Road	B2
Goschen Road	A3	Warwick Square	C2
Graham Street	B3	Water Street	B3
Granville Road	A2	Weardale Road	A3
Greta Avenue	A3	West Tower Street	B2
Grey Street	C3	West Walls	B2
Hardwicke Circus	B1	Westmorland Street	B3
Hart Street	C2	Wigton Road	A2
Hartington Place	C2	Willow Holme Road	A1
Hawick Street	A2		
Howard Place	C2		
Infirmary Street	A2		
James Street	B3		
John Street	A2		
Junction Street	A2		
Kendal Street	A2		
King Street	C3		

CARLISLE

0   400 yds

0   400m

Appears on main
map page 210

Tourist Information Centre: 77 Promenade
Tel: 01242 522878

Albany Road	A3	Portland Street	B2
Albert Road	C1	Prestbury Road	C1
Albion Street	B2	Princes Road	A3
All Saints Road	C2	Priory Street	C3
Andover Road	A3	Promenade	B2
Arle Avenue	A1	Rodney Road	B2
Ashford Road	A3	Rosehill Street	C3
Bath Parade	B2	Royal Well Road	B2
Bath Road	B3	St. George's Place	B2
Bayshill Road	A2	St. George's Road	A2
Berkeley Street	B2	St. James Street	B2
Brunswick Street	B1	St. Johns Avenue	B2
Carlton Street	C2	St. Margaret's Road	B1
Central Cross Drive	C1	St. Paul's Road	B1
Christchurch Road	A2	St. Paul's Street North	B1
Churchill Drive	C3	St. Paul's Street South	B1
Clarence Road	B1	St. Stephen's Road	A3
College Lawn	B3	Sandford Mill Road	C3
College Road	B3	Sandford Road	B3
Cranham Road	C3	Sherborne Street	C2
Douro Road	A2	Southgate Drive	C3
Dunalley Street	B1	Strickland Road	C3
Eldon Road	C2	Suffolk Road	A3
Evesham Road	C1	Suffolk Square	A3
Fairview Road	C2	Sun Street	A1
Folly Lane	B1	Swindon Road	A1
Gloucester Road	A2	Sydenham Road	C2
Grafton Road	A3	Sydenham Villas Road	C3
Hales Road	C3	Tewkesbury Road	A1
Hanover Street	B1	Thirlestaine Road	B3
Hayward's Road	C3	Tivoli Road	A3
Henrietta Street	B2	Townsend Street	A1
Hewlett Road	C2	Vittoria Walk	B3
High Street	B1	Wellington Road	C1
Honeybourne Way	A1	West Drive	B1
Hudson Street	B1	Western Road	A2
Imperial Square	B2	Whaddon Road	C1
Keynsham Road	B3	Winchcombe Street	B2
King Alfred Way	C3	Windsor Street	C1
King's Road	C2		
Lansdown Crescent	A3		
Lansdown Road	A3		
London Road	C3		
Lypiatt Road	A3		
Malvern Road	A2		
Market Street	A1		
Marle Hill Parade	B1		
Marle Hill Road	B1		
Millbrook Street	A1		
Montpellier Spa Road	B3		
Montpellier Street	A3		
Montpellier Terrace	A3		
Montpellier Walk	A3		
New Street	A2		
North Place	B2		
North Street	B2		
Old Bath Road	C3		
Oriel Road	B2		
Overton Road	A2		
Painswick Road	A3		
Parabola Road	A2		
Park Place	A3		
Park Street	A1		
Pittville Circus	C1		
Pittville Circus Road	C2		
Pittville Lawn	C1		

CHELTENHAM

0   300 yds

0   300m

Appears on main
map page 146

Tourist Information Centre: Town Hall, Northgate Street
Tel: 0845 647 7868

Bath Street	C2	Queen's Park Road	B3
Bedward Row	A2	Queen's Road	C1
Black Diamond Street	B1	Queen Street	B2
Black Friars	A3	Raymond Street	A1
Bold Square	B2	Russel Street	C2
Boughton	C2	St. Anne Street	B1
Bouverie Street	A1	St. George's Crescent	C3
Bridge Street	B2	St. John's Road	C3
Brook Street	B1	St. John Street	B2
Canal Street	A1	St. Martins Way	A1
Castle Drive	A3	St. Oswalds Way	B1
Charles Street	B1	St. Werburgh Street	B2
Cheyney Road	A1	Seller Street	C2
Chichester Street	A1	Sibell Street	C1
City Road	C2	Souter's Lane	B3
City Walls Road	A2	Stanley Street	A2
Commonhall Street	A2	Station Road	C1
Cornwall Street	B1	Steam Mill Street	C2
Crewe Street	C1	Talbot Street	B1
Cuppin Street	A3	The Bars	C2
Dee Hills Park	C2	The Groves	B3
Dee Lane	C2	Trafford Street	B1
Deva Terrace	C2	Union Street	B2
Duke Street	B3	Upper Northgate Street	A1
Eastgate Street	B2	Vicar's Lane	B2
Edinburgh Way	C3	Victoria Crescent	C3
Egerton Street	B1	Victoria Place	B2
Elizabeth Crescent	C3	Victoria Road	A1
Foregate Street	B2	Walker Street	C1
Forest Street	B2	Walpole Street	A1
Francis Street	C1	Walter Street	B1
Frodsham Street	B2	Watergate Street	A2
Garden Lane	A1	Water Tower Street	A2
George Street	B1	Weaver Street	A2
Gloucester Street	B1	White Friars	A3
Grey Friars	A3	York Street	B2
Grosvenor Park Terrace	C2		
Grosvenor Road	A3		
Grosvenor Street	A3		
Handbridge	B3		
Hoole Road	B1		
Hoole Way	B1		
Hunter Street	A2		
King Street	A2		
Leadworks Lane	C2		
Lightfoot Street	C1		
Louise Street	A1		
Love Street	B2		
Lower Bridge Street	B3		
Lower Park Road	C3		
Mill Street	C2		
Milton Street	B1		
Newgate Street	B2		
Nicholas Street	A2		
Nicholas Street Mews	A2		
Northern Pathway	C3		
Northgate Avenue	B1		
Northgate Street	A2		
Nun's Road	A3		
Old Dee Bridge	B3		
Pepper Street	B3		
Phillip Street	C1		
Prince's Avenue	C1		
Princess Street	A2		
Queen's Avenue	C1		
Queen's Drive	C3		

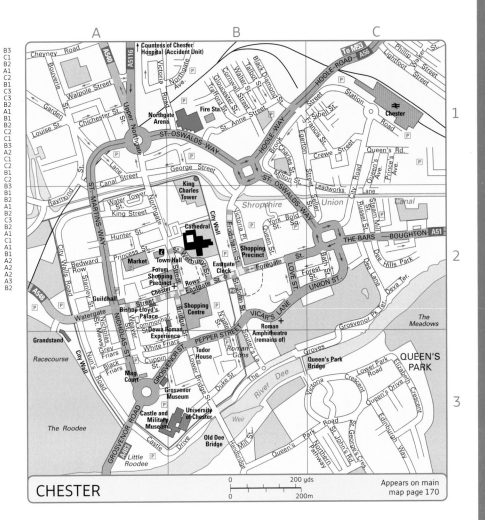

CHESTER

0 ____ 200 yds
0 ____ 200m

Appears on main map page 170

Tourist Information Centre: St. Michael's Tower, Coventry Cathedral   Tel: 024 7622 5616

Abbott's Lane	A1	New Union Street	B2
Acacia Avenue	C3	Norfolk Street	A2
Albany Road	A3	Oxford Street	C2
Alma Street	C2	Park Road	B3
Asthill Grove	B3	Parkside	B3
Barker's Butts Lane	A1	Primrose Hill Street	C1
Barras Lane	A2	Priory Street	B2
Berry Street	C1	Puma Way	B3
Bishop Street	B1	Quarryfield Lane	C3
Blythe Road	C1	Queen's Road	A3
Bond Street	A2	Queen Street	C1
Bramble Street	C2	Queen Victoria Road	A2
Bretts Close	C1	Quinton Road	B3
Broadway	A3	Radford Road	A1
Burges	B2	Raglan Street	C2
Butts Road	A2	Regent Street	A3
Cambridge Street	C1	Ringway Hill Cross	A2
Canterbury Street	C1	Ringway Queens	A2
Clifton Street	C1	Ringway Rudge	
Colchester Street	C1	A2	
Cornwall Road	C3	Ringway St. Johns	B3
Corporation Street	B2	Ringway St. Nicholas	B1
Coundon Road	A1	Ringway St. Patricks	B3
Coundon Street	A1	Ringway Swanswell	B1
Cox Street	C2	B2	
Croft Road	A2	Ringway Whitefriars	C2
Drapers Fields	B1	St. Nicholas Street	B1
Earl Street	B2	Sandy Lane	B1
East Street	C2	Seagrave Road	C3
Eaton Road	B3	Silver Street	B1
Fairfax Street	B2	Sky Blue Way	C2
Far Gosford Street	C2	South Street	C2
Foleshill Road	B1	Spencer Avenue	A3
Fowler Road	A1	Spon Street	A2
Gordon Street	A3	Srathmore Avenue	C3
Gosford Street	C2	Stoney Road	B3
Greyfriars Road	A2	Stoney Stanton Road	B1
Gulson Road	C2	Swanswell Street	B1
Hales Street	B2	The Precinct	B2
Harnall Lane East	C1	Tomson Avenue	A1
Harnall Lane West	B1	Trinity Street	B2
Harper Road	C2	Upper Hill Street	A2
Harper Street	B2	Upper Well Street	B2
Hertford Street	B2	Vauxhall Street	C2
Hewitt Avenue	A1	Vecquaray Street	C2
High Street	B2	Victoria Street	C1
Hill Street	A2	Vine Street	C1
Holyhead Road	A2	Warwick Road	A3
Hood Street	C2	Waveley Road	A2
Howard Street	B1	Westminster Road	A3
Jordan Well	B2	White Street	B1
King William Street	C1	Windsor Street	A2
Lamb Street	B2	Wright Street	C1
Leicester Row	B1		
Leigh Street	C1		
Little Park Street	B3		
London Road	C3		
Lower Ford Street	C2		
Market Way	B2		
Meadow Street	A2		
Michaelmas Road	A3		
Middleborough Road	A1		
Mile Lane	B3		
Mill Street	A1		
Minster Road	A2		
Much Park Street	B2		

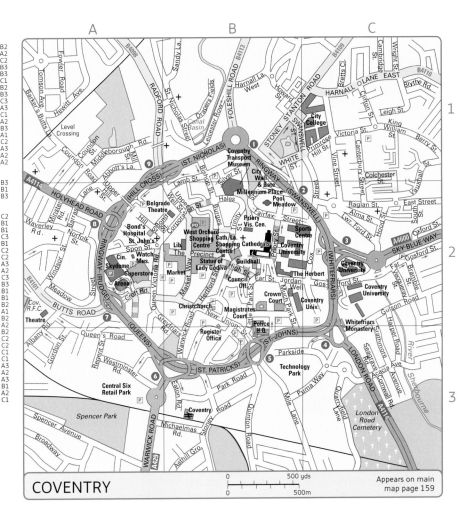

COVENTRY

0 ____ 500 yds
0 ____ 500m

Appears on main map page 159

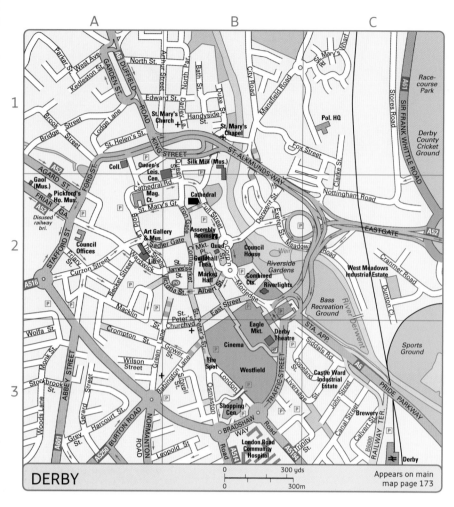

DERBY

Scale: 0 300 yds / 0 300m

Appears on main map page 173

Tourist Information Centre: Assembly Rooms, Market Place
Tel: 01332 643411

Street	Ref	Street	Ref
Abbey Street	A3	Railway Terrace	C3
Agard Street	A1	Sadler Gate	B2
Albert Street	B2	St. Alkmunds Way	B1
Arthur Street	A1	St. Helen's Street	A1
Babington Lane	A3	St. James Street	B2
Bath Street	B1	St. Mary's Gate	A2
Becket Street	A2	St. Mary's Wharf Road	C1
Bold Lane	A2	St. Peter's Churchyard	B3
Bradshaw Way	B3	St. Peter's Street	B2
Bridge Street	A1	Siddals Road	C3
Brook Street	A1	Sir Frank Whittle Road	C1
Burton Road	A3	Sitwell Street	B3
Calvert Street	C3	Stafford Street	A2
Canal Street	C3	Station Approach	C2
Cathedral Road	A2	Stockbrook Street	A3
City Road	B1	Stores Road	C1
Clarke Street	C2	The Strand	A2
Copeland Street	B3	Traffic Street	B3
Cornmarket	B2	Trinity Street	B3
Corporation Street	B2	Victoria Street	A2
Cranmer Road	C2	Wardwick	A2
Crompton Street	A3	West Avenue	A1
Curzon Street	A2	Wilson Street	A3
Darley Lane	B1	Wolfa Street	A3
Derwent Street	B2	Woods Lane	A3
Duffield Road	A1		
Duke Street	B1		
Dunton Close	C2		
Eastgate	C2		
East Street	B2		
Edward Street	A1		
Exeter Street	B2		
Ford Street	A2		
Fox Street	B1		
Friar Gate	A2		
Friary Street	A2		
Full Street	B2		
Garden Street	A1		
Gerard Street	A3		
Gower Street	B3		
Green Lane	A3		
Grey Street	A3		
Handyside Street	B1		
Harcourt Street	A3		
Iron Gate	B2		
John Street	C3		
Kedleston Street	A1		
King Street	A1		
Leopold Street	A3		
Liversage Street	B3		
Lodge Lane	A1		
London Road	B3		
Macklin Street	A2		
Mansfield Road	B1		
Market Place	B2		
Meadow Road	B2		
Monk Street	A3		
Morledge	B2		
Normanton Road	A3		
North Parade	B1		
North Street	A1		
Nottingham Road	C2		
Osmaston Road	B3		
Parker Street	A1		
Pride Parkway	C3		
Queen Street	B1		

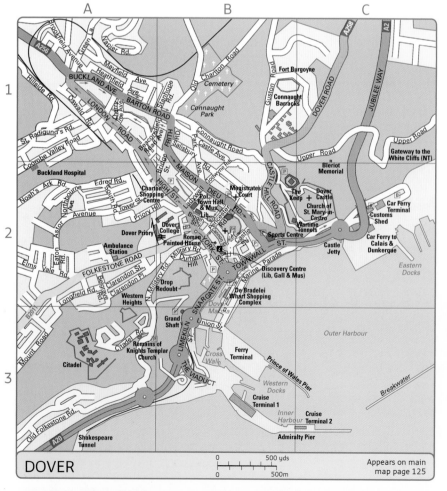

DOVER

Scale: 0 500 yds / 0 500m

Appears on main map page 125

Tourist Information Centre: Dover Museum, Market Square
Tel: 01304 201066

Street	Ref
Astor Avenue	A2
Barton Road	A1
Beaconsfield Avenue	A1
Beaconsfield Road	A1
Belgrave Road	A2
Biggin Street	B2
Bridge Street	B2
Brookfield Avenue	A1
Buckland Avenue	A1
Cannon Street	B2
Canons Gate Road	B2
Castle Avenue	B1
Castle Hill Road	B2
Castle Street	B2
Cherry Tree Avenue	A1
Citadel Road	A3
Clarendon Place	A2
Clarendon Street	A2
Connaught Road	B1
Coombe Valley Road	A2
Dover Road	C1
Durham Hill	B2
Eaton Road	A2
Edred Road	A2
Elms Vale Road	A2
Folkestone Road	A2
Frith Road	B1
Godwyne Road	B2
Green Lane	A1
Guston Road	B1
Heathfield Avenue	A1
High Street	B2
Hillside Road	A1
Jubilee Way	C1
Ladywell	B2
Limekiln Street	B3
London Road	A1
Longfield Road	A2
Maison Dieu Road	B2
Marine Parade	B2
Mayfield Avenue	A1
Military Road	B2
Mount Road	A3
Napier Road	A2
Noah's Ark Road	A2
Northbourne Avenue	A2
North Military Road	A2
Old Charlton Road	B1
Old Folkestone Road	A3
Oswald Road	A2
Park Avenue	B1
Pencester Road	B2
Priory Hill	A2
St. Radigund's Road	A1
Salisbury Road	B1
Snargate Street	B3
South Road	A2
Stanhope Road	B1
The Viaduct	B3
Tower Street	A2
Townwall Street	B2
Union Street	B3
Upper Road	C1
York Street	B2

Tourist Information Centre: 16 City Square
Tel: 01382 527527

Adelaide Place	A1	South Marketgait	B3
Albany Terrace	A1	South Tay Street	A3
Albert Street	C2	Strathmartine Road	B1
Alexander Street	B1	Tannadice Street	B1
Ann Street	B2	Tay Road Bridge	B3
Arbroath Road	C2	Trades Lane	B2
Arklay Street	C1	Upper Constitution Street	A1
Arklay Terrace	C1	Victoria Road	B2
Arthurstone Terrace	C2	Victoria Street	C2
Barrack Road	A2	Ward Road	A2
Blackness Road	A2	West Marketgait	A2
Blinshall Street	A2	West Port	A2
Brewery Lane	A2	William Street	C2
Brook Street	A2		
Broughty Ferry Road	C2		
Brown Street	A2		
Bruce Street	A1		
Byron Street	A1		
Canning Street	B1		
City Square	B3		
Clepington Road	C1		
Constitution Road	B2		
Constitution Street	B1		
Court Street	C1		
Cowgate Street	B2		
Dens Road	B1		
Douglas Street	A2		
Dudhope Street	A1		
Dudhope Terrace	C1		
Dundonald Street	C1		
Dura Street	C2		
East Dock Street	C2		
East Marketgait	B2		
Fairbairn Street	B1		
Greenmarket	B3		
Guthrie Street	A2		
Hawkhill	A2		
High Street	B3		
Hill Street	B1		
Hilltown	B1		
Kenmore Terrace	A1		
Killin Avenue	A1		
Kinghorne Road	A1		
King Street	B2		
Larch Street	A2		
Law Crescent	A1		
Lawside Avenue	A1		
Law Street	A1		
Leng Street	A1		
Lochee Road	A2		
Lower Princes Street	C2		
Mains Road	B1		
Main Street	B1		
Meadowside	B2		
Morgan Street	C2		
Murraygate	B2		
Nelson Street	B2		
Nethergate	A3		
North Marketgait	A2		
Perth Road	A3		
Polepark Road	A2		
Princes Street	C2		
Riverside Drive	A3		
Roseangle	A3		
Rosebank Road	B2		
Seagate	B2		

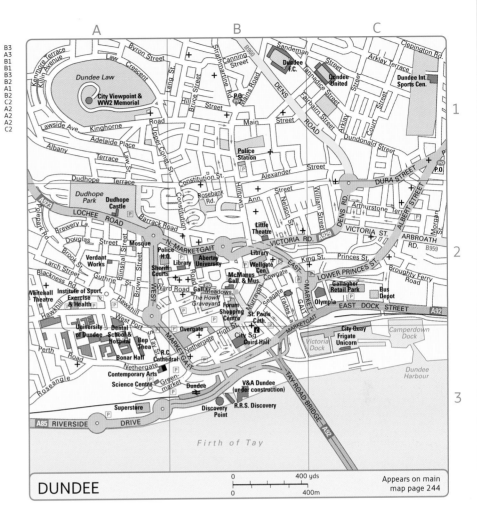

DUNDEE

0   400 yds
0   400m

Appears on main
map page 244

Tourist Information: Telephone Service
Tel: 03000 262626

Aykley Heads	A1
Church Street	B3
Clay Lane	A3
Claypath	B2
Crossgate	B2
Crossgate Peth	A3
Darlington Road	A3
Dryburn Road	A1
Durham Road	A1
Fieldhouse Lane	A1
Framwelgate	B2
Framwelgate Peth	B1
Framwelgate Waterside	B2
Gilesgate	C2
Great North Road	A1
Green Lane	C2
Grove Street	B3
Hallgarth Street	C3
Hawthorn Terrace	A2
Leazes Road	B2
Margery Lane	B3
Market Place	B2
Millburngate Bridge	B2
Newcastle Road	A1
New Elvet	B2
North Bailey	B2
North End	A1
North Road	B2
Old Elvet	C2
Pity Me Bypass	A1
Potters Bank	A3
Quarryheads Lane	B3
Providence Row	B2
Redhills Lane	A2
St. Monica Grove	A2
Sidegate	B2
Silver Street	B2
South Bailey	B3
South Road	B3
South Street	B3
Southfield Way	A1
Stockton Road	B3
Sutton Street	B2
The Avenue	A3
Toll House Road	A2
Western Hill	A2
Whinney Hill	C3
Whitesmocks	A1

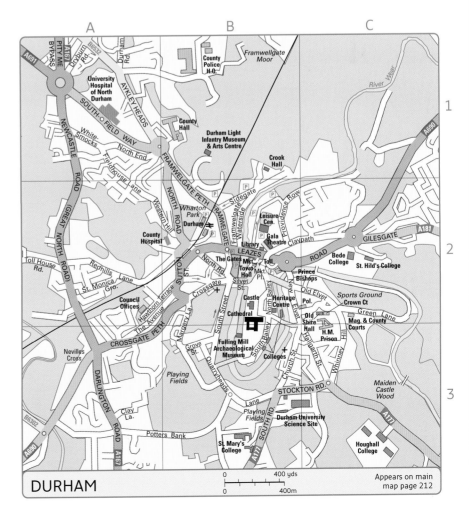

DURHAM

0   400 yds
0   400m

Appears on main
map page 212

Edinburgh street map on pages 36-37

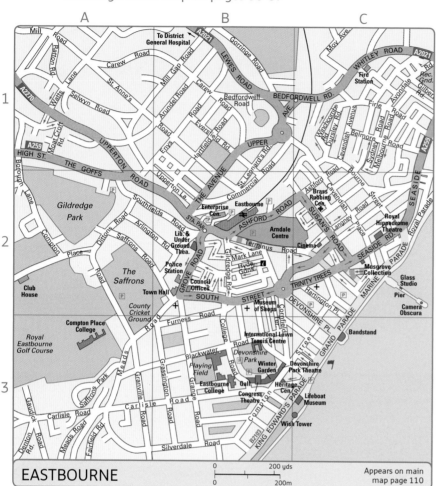

EASTBOURNE

0 ___ 200 yds
0 ___ 200m

Appears on main map page 110

Tourist Information Centre: 3 Cornfield Road
Tel: 01323 415415

Street	Grid	Street	Grid
Arlington Road	A2	The Avenue	B2
Arundel Road	B1	The Goffs	A1
Ashford Road	B2/C2	Trinity Trees	C2
Avondale Road	C1	Upper Avenue	B1
Bedfordwell Road	B1	Upperton Lane	B2
Belmore Road	C1	Upperton Road	A1
Blackwater Road	B3	Watts Lane	A1
Borough Lane	A1	Whitley Road	A1
Bourne Street	C2	Willingdon Road	A1
Carew Road	A1/B1	Winchcombe Road	C1
Carlisle Road	A3		
Cavendish Avenue	C1		
Cavendish Place	C2		
College Road	B3		
Commercial Road	B2		
Compton Place Road	A2		
Compton Street	B3		
Cornfield Terrace	B2		
Denton Road	A3		
Devonshire Place	B2		
Dittons Road	A2		
Dursley Road	C2		
Enys Road	B1		
Eversfield Road	B1		
Fairfield Road	A3		
Firle Road	C1		
Furness Road	B3		
Gaudick Road	A3		
Gilbert Road	C1		
Gildredge Road	B2		
Goringe Road	B1		
Grand Parade	C3		
Grange Road	B3		
Grassington Road	B3		
Grove Road	B2		
Hartfield Road	B1		
Hartington Place	C2		
High Street	A1		
Hyde Gardens	B2		
King Edward's Parade	B3		
Langney Road	C2		
Lewes Road	B1		
Marine Parade	C2		
Mark Lane	B2		
Meads Road	A3		
Melbourne Road	C1		
Mill Gap Road	A1		
Mill Road	A1		
Moat Croft Road	A1		
Moy Avenue	C1		
Ratton Road	A1		
Royal Parade	C2		
Saffrons Park	A3		
Saffrons Road	A2		
St. Anne's Road	A1		
St. Leonard's Road	B2		
Seaside	C2		
Seaside Road	C2		
Selwyn Road	A1		
Silverdale Road	B3		
South Street	B2		
Southfields Road	A2		
Station Parade	B2		
Susan's Road	C2		
Sydney Road	C2		
Terminus Road	B2		

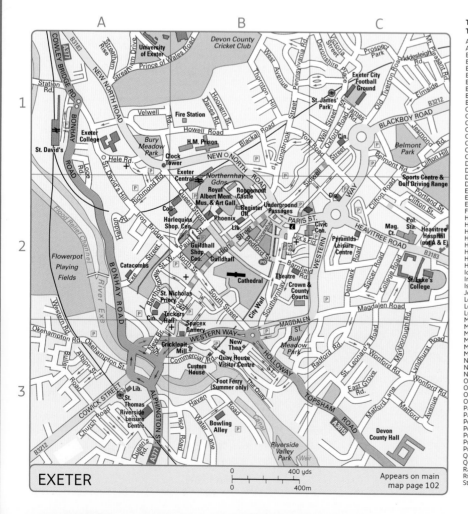

EXETER

0 ___ 400 yds
0 ___ 400m

Appears on main map page 102

Tourist Information Centre: Dix's Field
Tel: 01392 665700

Street	Grid	Street	Grid
Albion Street	A3	St. James' Road	C1
Alphington Street	A3	St. Leonard's Road	C3
Barnfield Road	B2	Sidwell Street	B2
Bartholomew Street West	A2	Southernhay East	B2
Bedford Street	B2	South Street	B2
Belmont Road	C1	Spicer Road	C2
Blackboy Road	C1	Station Road	A1
Blackall Road	B1	Streatham Drive	A1
Bonhay Road	A2	Streatham Rise	A1
Buller Road	A3	The Quay	B3
Church Road	A3	Thornton Hill	B1
Clifton Hill	C1	Topsham Road	B3
Clifton Road	C2	Velwell Road	A1
Clifton Street	C2	Victoria Street	C1
College Road	C2	Water Lane	B3
Commercial Road	B3	Well Street	C1
Cowick Street	A3	West Avenue	B1
Cowley Bridge Road	A1	Western Road	A2
Danes Road	B1	Western Way	C2
Denmark Road	C2	Wonford Road	C3
Devonshire Place	C1	York Road	B1
Dix's Field	B2		
East Grove Road	C3		
Elmside	C1		
Exe Street	A2		
Fore Street	B2		
Haldon Road	A2		
Haven Road	B3		
Heavitree Road	C2		
Hele Road	A1		
High Street	B2		
Holloway Street	B3		
Hoopern Street	B1		
Howell Road	B1		
Iddesleigh Road	C1		
Iron Bridge	A2		
Isca Road	B3		
Jesmond Road	C1		
Longbrook Street	B1		
Looe Road	A1		
Lyndhurst Road	C3		
Magdalen Road	C2		
Magdalen Street	B3		
Marlborough Road	C3		
Matford Avenue	C3		
Matford Lane	C3		
Mount Pleasant Road	C1		
New Bridge Street	A3		
New North Road	A1/B1		
North Street	B2		
Okehampton Road	A3		
Okehampton Street	A3		
Old Tiverton Road	C1		
Oxford Road	C1		
Paris Street	B2		
Paul Street	B2		
Pennsylvania Road	B1		
Portland Street	C2		
Prince of Wales Road	A1		
Princesshay	B2		
Prospect Park	C1		
Queen's Road	A3		
Queen Street	B2		
Radford Road	C3		
Richmond Road	A2		
St. David's Hill	A1		

Tourist Information Centre: Discover Folkestone, 20 Bouverie Place. Tel: 01303 258594

Alder Road	B2
Archer Road	C2
Bathurst Road	A2
Beatty Road	C1
Black Bull Road	B2
Bournemouth Road	B2
Bouverie Road West	A3
Bradstone Road	B2
Broadfield Road	A2
Broadmead Road	B2
Brockman Road	B2
Canterbury Road	C1
Castle Hill Avenue	B3
Cheriton Gardens	B3
Cheriton Road	A2/B2
Cherry Garden Avenue	A1
Christ Church Road	B3
Churchill Avenue	B1
Clifton Crescent	A3
Coniston Road	A1
Coolinge Road	B2
Cornwallis Avenue	A2
Dawson Road	B2
Dixwell Road	A3
Dolphins Road	B1
Dover Hill	C1
Dover Road	C1
Downs Road	B1
Earles Avenue	A3
Foord Road	B2
Godwyn Road	A3
Grimston Avenue	A3
Grimston Gardens	A3
Guildhall Street	B2
Guildhall Street North	B2
Harbour Way	C2
Hill Road	C1
Ivy Way	C1
Joyes Road	C1
Linden Crescent	B2
Links Way	A1
Lower Sandgate Road	A3
Lucy Avenue	A1
Manor Road	B3
Marine Parade	B3
Marshall Street	C1
Mead Road	B2
Old High Street	C3
Park Farm Road	B1
Pavilion Road	B2
Radnor Bridge Road	C2
Radnor Park Avenue	A2
Radnor Park Road	B2
Radnor Park West	A2
Sandgate Hill	A3
Sandgate Road	B3
Shorncliffe Road	A2
Sidney Street	C2
The Leas	B3
The Stade	C3
The Tram Road	C2
Tontine Street	C2
Turketel Road	A3
Tyson Road	C1
Wear Bay Crescent	C2
Wear Bay Road	C1

Westbourne Gardens	A3
Wingate Road	B1
Wood Avenue	C1
Wilton Road	A2

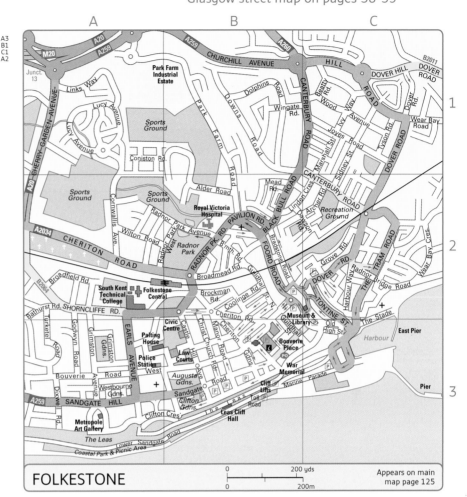

FOLKESTONE

| 0 | 200 yds |
| 0 | 200m |

Appears on main map page 125

Tourist Information Centre: 28 Southgate Street Tel: 01452 396572

Adelaide Street	B3
Alexandra Road	B1
Alfred Street	C2
Alma Place	A3
Alvin Street	B1
Archdeacon Street	A1
Argyll Road	C1
Askwith Road	C3
Barnwood Road	C1
Barton Street	B2
Black Dog Way	B1
Bristol Road	A3
Brunswick Road	B2
Bruton Way	B2
Calton Road	B3
Castle Meads Way	A1
Cecil Road	A3
Cheltenham Road	C1
Churchill Road	A3
Clifton Road	A3
Conduit Street	B3
Coney Hill Road	C3
Dean's Way	B1
Denmark Road	B1
Derby Road	B2
Estcourt Road	B1
Eastern Avenue	C3
Eastgate Street	B2
Frampton Road	A3
Gouda Way	A1
Great Western Road	B2
Greyfriars	B2
Hatherley Road	B3
Heathville Road	B1
Hempsted Lane	A2
Henry Road	B1
High Street	B3
Hopewell Street	B3
Horton Road	C2
Howard Street	B3
India Road	C2
King Edward's Avenue	B3
Kingsholm Road	B1
Lansdown Road	B1
Linden Road	A3
Llanthony Road	A2
London Road	B1
Lower Westgate Street	A1
Marlborough Road	C3
Merevale Road	C1
Metz Way	B2
Midland Road	B3
Millbrook Street	B2
Myers Road	C2
Northgate Street	B2
Oxford Road	B2
Oxstalls Lane	C1
Painswick Road	C3
Park Road	B2
Parkend Road	B2
Pitt Street	B1
Quay Street	A2
Regent Street	B3
Robinson Road	A3
Ryecroft Street	B3
St. Ann Way	A3

St. Oswald's Road	A1
Secunda Way	A3
Severn Road	A2
Seymour Road	A3
Southgate Street	A2
Spa Road	A2
Stanley Road	B3
Station Road	B2
Stroud Road	A3
The Quay	A2
Tredworth Road	B3
Trier Way	A3
Upton Street	B3
Vicarage Road	C1
Victoria Street	B2
Wellington Street	B2
Westgate Street	A1
Weston Road	A3
Wheatstone Road	B3
Willow Avenue	C3
Worcester Street	B1

GLOUCESTER

| 0 | 500 yds |
| 0 | 500m |

Appears on main map page 132

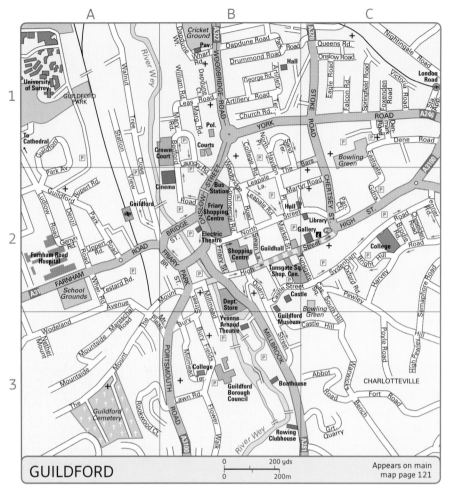

GUILDFORD

0 ___ 200 yds
0 ___ 200m

Appears on main map page 121

Tourist Information Centre: 155 High Street
Tel: 01483 444333

Abbot Road	C3	Portsmouth Road	B3
Artillery Road	B1	Poyle Road	C3
Artillery Terrace	B1	Quarry Street	B2
Bedford Road	B1	Queens Road	C1
Bridge Street	B2	Rookwood Court	A3
Bright Hill	C2	Rupert Road	A2
Brodie Road	C2	Sand Terrace	B1
Bury Fields	B3	Semaphore Road	C3
Bury Street	B3	South Hill	C2
Castle Hill	C3	Springfield Road	C1
Castle Square	C2	Station Approach	C1
Castle Street	B2	Station View	A1
Chertsey Street	C1	Stoke Road	C1
Cheselden Road	C2	Swan Lane	B2
Commercial Road	B2	Sydenham Road	C2
Dapdune Court	B1	Testard Road	A2
Dapdune Road	B1	The Bars	B2
Dapdune Wharf	B1	The Mount	A3
Dene Road	C1	Tunsgate	C2
Denmark Road	C1	Upperton Road	A2
Denzil Road	A2	Victoria Road	C1
Drummond Road	B1	Walnut Tree Close	A1
Eagle Road	C1	Warwicks	C3
Eastgate Gardens	C1	Wharf Road	B1
Falcon Road	C1	Wherwell Road	A2
Farnham Road	A2	William Road	B1
Flower Walk	B3	Wodeland Avenue	A3
Fort Road	C3	Woodbridge Road	B1
Foxenden Road	C1	York Road	B1
Friary Bridge	B2		
Friary Street	B2		
Genyn Road	A2		
George Road	B1		
Great Quarry	C3		
Guildford Park Avenue	A1		
Guildford Park Road	A2		
Harvey Road	C2		
Haydon Place	B1		
High Pewley	C3		
High Street	B2/C2		
Laundry Road	B1		
Lawn Road	B3		
Leap Lane	B2		
Leas Road	B1		
Ludlow Road	A2		
Mareschal Road	A3		
Margaret Road	B1		
Market Street	B2		
Martyr Road	B2		
Mary Road	B1		
Millbrook	B3		
Millmead	B2		
Millmead Terrace	B3		
Mount Pleasant	A3		
Mountside	A3		
Nether Mount	A3		
Nightingale Road	C1		
North Place	B1		
North Street	B2		
Onslow Road	C1		
Onslow Street	B2		
Oxford Road	C2		
Pannells Court	C2		
Park Road	B1		
Park Street	B2		
Pewley Hill	C2		

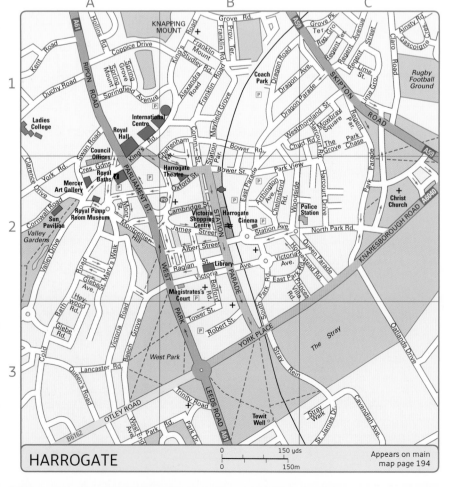

HARROGATE

0 ___ 150 yds
0 ___ 150m

Appears on main map page 194

Tourist Information Centre: Royal Baths, Crescent Road
Tel: 01423 537300

Ainsty Road	C1	Regent Grove	C1
Albert Street	B2	Regent Parade	C1
Alexandra Road	B1	Regent Street	C1
Arthington Avenue	B2	Regent Terrace	C1
Beech Grove	A3	Ripon Road	A1
Belford Road	B2	Robert Street	B3
Bower Road	B1	St. James Drive	C3
Bower Street	B2	St. Mary's Walk	A3
Cambridge Street	B2	Skipton Road	C1
Cavendish Avenue	C3	South Park Road	B3
Chelmsford Road	B2	Springfield Avenue	A1
Cheltenham Mount	B1	Spring Grove	A1
Chudleigh Road	C1	Spring Mount	A1
Clarence Drive	A2	Station Avenue	B2
Claro Road	C1	Station Parade	B2
Cold Bath Road	A3	Stray Rein	B3
Commercial Street	B1	Stray Walk	C3
Coppice Drive	A1	Studley Road	B1
Cornwall Road	A2	Swan Road	A2
Crescent Gardens	A2	The Grove	C1
Dragon Avenue	B1	Tower Street	B3
Dragon Parade	B1	Trinity Road	B3
Dragon Road	B1	Valley Drive	A2
Duchy Road	A1	Victoria Avenue	B2
East Parade	B2	Victoria Road	A3
East Park Road	B2	West End Avenue	A3
Franklin Mount	B1	West Park	B2
Franklin Road	B1	Woodside	B2
Gascoigne Crescent	C1	York Place	B3
Glebe Avenue	A2	York Road	A2
Glebe Road	A3		
Grove Park Terrace	C1		
Grove Road	B1		
Harcourt Drive	C2		
Harcourt Road	C1		
Heywood Road	A3		
Hollins Road	A1		
Homestead Road	B2		
James Street	B2		
Kent Road	A1		
King's Road	A2		
Knaresborough Road	C3		
Lancaster Road	A3		
Leeds Road	B3		
Lime Grove	C1		
Lime Street	C1		
Mayfield Grove	B1		
Montpellier Hill	A2		
Montpellier Street	A2		
Mowbray Square	C1		
North Park Road	C2		
Oatlands Drive	C3		
Otley Road	A3		
Oxford Street	B2		
Park Chase	C1		
Park Drive	B3		
Park Parade	C2		
Park View	B2		
Parliament Street	A2		
Princes Villa Road	B2		
Providence Terrace	B1		
Queen Parade	C2		
Queen's Road	A3		
Raglan Street	B2		
Regent Avenue	C1		

Tourist Information Centre: Aquila House, 2 Breeds Place
Tel: 01424 451111

Albert Road	B3
All Saints Street	C2
Amherst Road	A2
Ashburnham Road	A1
Ashford Road	A1
Ashford Way	A1
Baldslow Road	B2
Beaconsfield Road	B1
Bembrook Road	C2
Bohemia Road	A2
Braybrooke Road	B2
Broomsgrove Road	C1
Cambridge Road	A3
Castle Hill Road	B3
Castle Street	B3
Chiltern Drive	C1
Church Road	A3
Collier Road	C2
Cornwallis Terrace	A3
Croft Road	C2
De Cham Road	A3
Denmark Place	B3
Downs Road	B1
East Parade	C3
Elphinstone Road	B1
Eversfield Place	A3
Falaise Road	A3
Farley Bank	C1
Fearon Road	B1
Fellows Road	C1
Frederick Road	C1
Freshwater Avenue	A1
George Street	C3
Harold Place	B3
Harold Road	C2
High Street	C2
Hillside Road	A1
Hoad's Wood Road	B1
Hughenden Road	B1
Laton Road	B1
Linley Drive	B1
Linton Road	A2
Lower Park Road	A2
Magdalen Road	A3
Malvern Way	C1
Marine Parade	C3
Milward Road	B2
Mount Pleasant Road	B1
Old London Road	C2
Park Avenue	A1
Park Crescent	A1
Park View	A1
Park Way	A1
Parker Road	B1
Parkstone Road	A1
Pelham Place	B3
Priory Avenue	B2
Priory Road	C2
Queen's Road	B2
Robertson Street	B3
Rock-a-Nore Road	C3
St. George's Road	C2
St. Helen's Down	B1
St. Helen's Park Road	B2
St. Helen's Road	A1
St. John's Road	A3

St. Margaret's Road	A3
St. Mary's Road	B2
St. Mary's Terrace	B2
St. Thomas's Road	C2
Thanet Way	A1
The Bourne	C2
Upper Park Road	A2
Vicarage Road	B2
Warrior Square	A3
Wellington Road	B2
White Rock	A3
Woodbrook Road	B1
Wykeham Road	A2

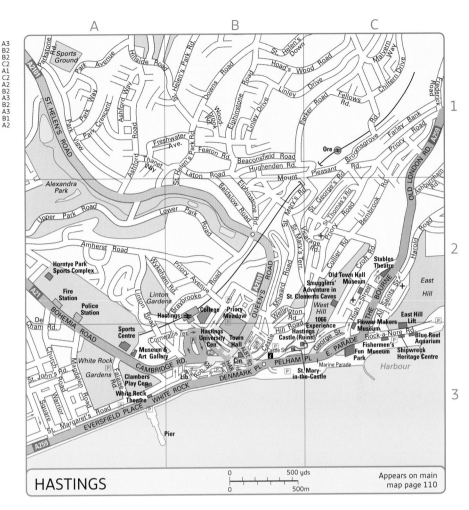

HASTINGS

0   500 yds
0   500m

Appears on main map page 110

Tourist Information Centre: Town Hall, St. Owen Street
Tel: 01432 268430

Aubrey Street	B2
Barrs Court Road	C1
Barton Road	A2
Barton Yard	A2
Bath Street	C2
Belmont Avenue	A3
Berrington Street	B2
Bewell Street	B2
Blackfriars Street	B1
Blueschool Street	B1
Brewers Passage	B2
Bridge Street	B2
Broad Street	B2
Canonmoor Street	A1
Cantilupe Street	C2
Castle Street	B2
Catherine Street	B1
Central Avenue	C2
Church Street	B2
Commercial Road	C1
Commercial Street	B2
Coningsby Street	B1
East Street	B2
Edgar Street	B1
Eign Gate	B2
Eign Street	A2
Ferrers Street	B2
Friars Street	A2
Gaol Street	C2
Green Street	C3
Grenfell Road	C3
Greyfriars Avenue	A3
Greyfriars Bridge	B2
Grove Road	C3
Harold Street	C3
High Street	B2
High Town	B2
King Street	B2
Kyrle Street	C2
Maylord Street	B2
Mill Street	C3
Monkmoor Street	C1
Moorfield Street	A1
Moor Street	A1
Mostyn Street	A1
Nelson Street	C3
Newmarket Street	B1
Park Street	C3
Penhaligon Way	A1
Plough Lane	A1
Portland Street	A1
Quay Street	B2
Ryeland Street	A2
St. Guthiac Street	C3
St. James Road	C3
St. Martin's Avenue	B3
St. Martin's Street	B3
St. Owen Street	C2
Station Approach	C1
Station Road	A2
Stonebow Road	C1
Symonds Street	C2
The Atrium	B1
Turner Street	C3
Union Street	B2
Union Walk	C1

Vaughan Street	C2
Victoria Street	A2
West Street	B2
Widemarsh Street	B2
Wye Street	B3

HEREFORD

0   250 yds
0   250m

Appears on main map page 145

HULL (KINGSTON UPON HULL)

0 — 300 yds
0 — 300m

Appears on main map page 196

Tourist Information Centre: 1 Paragon Street
Tel: 01482 300300

Adelaide Street	A3
Albion Street	A2
Alfred Gelder Street	B2
Anlaby Road	A2
Anne Street	A2
Beverley Road	A1
Bond Street	B2
Brunswick Avenue	A1
Caroline Street	B1
Carr Lane	A2
Castle Street	B2
Charles Street	B1
Charterhouse Lane	B1
Church Street	C2
Citadel Way	C2
Clarence Street	C2
Cleveland Street	C1
Dansom Lane	C1
English Street	A3
Ferensway	A2
Francis Street	B1
Freetown Way	A1
Garrison Road	C2
George Street	B2
Great Union Street	C1
Green Lane	B1
Guildhall Road	B2
Hessle Road	A3
High Street	C1
Hyperion Street	C1
Jameson Street	A2
Jarratt Street	B1
Jenning Street	B1
King Edward Street	A2
Kingston Street	A3
Liddell Street	A1
Lime Street	B1
Lister Street	A3
Lowgate	B2
Market Place	B2
Myton Street	A2
New Cleveland Street	C1
New George Street	B1
Norfolk Street	A1
North Bridge	B1
Osborne Street	A2
Pilots Way	C3
Porter Street	A3
Princes Dock Street	B2
Prospect Street	A1
Queen Street	B3
Reform Street	B1
St. Lukes Street	A2
St. Mark Street	C1
Scale Lane	B2
Scott Street	B1
Scott Street Bridge	B1
South Bridge Road	C2
Spring Bank	A1
Spring Street	A2
Spyvee Street	C1
Waterhouse Lane	A2
Wellington Street West	A3
William Street	A3
Witham	C1
Worship Street	B1
Wright Street	A1

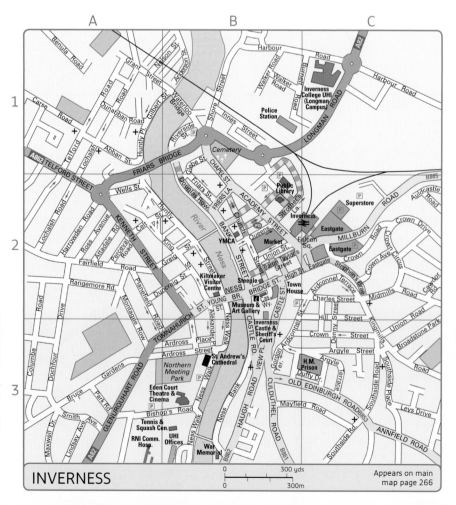

INVERNESS

0 — 300 yds
0 — 300m

Appears on main map page 266

Tourist Information Centre: Castle Wynd
Tel: 01463 252401

Abban Street	A1	Lochalsh Road	A1
Academy Street	B2	Longman Road	C1
Alexander Place	B2	Maxwell Drive	A3
Anderson Street	B1	Mayfield Road	B3
Ardconnel Street	B3	Midmills Road	C2
Ardconnel Terrace	C2	Millburn Road	C2
Ardross Place	B3	Montague Row	A2
Ardross Street	B3	Muirfield Road	C3
Argyle Street	C3	Nelson Street	A1
Argyle Terrace	C3	Ness Bank	B3
Attadale Road	A2	Ness Bridge	B2
Auldcastle Road	C2	Ness Walk	B3
Bank Street	B2	Old Edinburgh Road	B3
Baron Taylor's Street	B2	Park Road	A3
Benula Road	A1	Perceval Road	A2
Bishop's Road	A3	Planefield Road	A2
Bridge Street	B2	Queensgate	B2
Broadstone Park	C3	Rangemore Road	A2
Bruce Gardens	A3	Riverside Street	B1
Burnett Road	C1	Ross Avenue	A2
Carse Road	A1	Shore Street	B1
Castle Road	B2	Smith Avenue	A3
Castle Street	B2	Southside Place	C3
Castle Wynd	B2	Southside Road	C3
Cawdor Road	C2	Stephen's Brae	C2
Celt Street	A2	Strother's Lane	B2
Chapel Street	B1	Telford Road	A1
Charles Street	C2	Telford Street	A1
Church Street	B2	Tomnahurich Street	A3
Columba Road	A3	Union Road	C3
Crown Avenue	C2	Union Street	B2
Crown Circus	C2	View Place	B3
Crown Drive	C2	Walker Road	B1
Crown Road	C2	Waterloo Bridge	B1
Crown Street	C3	Wells Street	A2
Culduthel Road	B3	Young Street	B2
Denny Street	C3		
Dochfour Drive	A3		
Douglas Row	B1		
Duffy Drive	B3		
Duncraig Street	A2		
Eastgate	C2		
Fairfield Road	A2		
Falcon Square	B2		
Friars Bridge	A1		
Friars Lane	B2		
Friars Street	B2		
Gilbert Street	A1		
Glebe Street	B1		
Glen Urquhart Road	A3		
Gordon Terrace	B3		
Grant Street	A1		
Greig Street	A2		
Harbour Road	B1		
Harrowden Road	A2		
Haugh Road	B3		
High Street	B2		
Hill Street	C2		
Hontly Place	A1		
Huntly Street	A2		
Innes Street	B1		
Kenneth Street	A2		
Kingsmills Road	C2		
King Street	A2		
Leys Drive	C3		
Lindsay Avenue	A3		

Liverpool street map on pages 42-43, London street map on pages 44-45

Tourist Information Centre: 7-9 Every Street, Town Hall Square
Tel: 0844 888 5181

Abbey Street	B1	Market Place South	B2
Albion Street	B2	Market Street	B2
All Saints Road	A2	Mill Lane	A3
Aylestone Road	B3	Millstone Lane	B2
Bassett Street	A1	Montreal Road	C1
Bath Lane	A2	Morledge Street	C2
Bedford Street North	C1	Narborough Road	B3
Belgrave Gate	B1	Narborough Road North	A2
Bell Lane	C1	Nelson Street	C3
Belvoir Street	B2	Newarke Close	A3
Braunstone Gate	A2	Newarke Street	B2
Burgess Street	B1	Northgate Street	A1
Burleys Way	B1	Ottawa Way	C1
Byron Street	B1	Oxford Street	B2
Cank Street	B2	Pasture Lane	A1
Castle Street	A2	Peacock Lane	B2
Charles Street	C2	Pocklingtons Walk	B2
Christow Street	C1	Prebend Street	C3
Church Gate	B1	Princess Road East	C3
Clarence Street	C1	Pringle Street	A1
Clyde Street	C1	Queen Street	C2
College Street	C2	Regent Road	B3
Colton Street	C2	Regent Street	C3
Conduit Street	C2	Repton Street	A1
Crafton Street East	C1	Rutland Street	C2
Cravan Street	A1	Samuel Street	C2
De Montfort Street	C3	Sanvey Gate	A1
Deacon Street	B3	Saxby Street	C3
Dryden Street	B1	Slater Street	A1
Duns Lane	A2	Soar Lane	A1
Dunton Street	A1	South Albion Street	C2
Eastern Boulevard	A3	Southampton Street	C2
Friar Lane	B2	Sparkenhoe Street	C2
Friday Street	B1	St. George Street	C2
Frog Island	A1	St. George's Way	C2
Gallowtree Gate	B2	St. John's Street	B1
Gaul Street	A3	St. Margaret's Way	A1
Glebe Street	C2	St. Matthew's Way	C1
Gotham Street	C3	St. Nicholas Circle	A2
Granby Street	B2	Swain Street	C2
Grange Lane	B3	Swan Street	A1
Grasmere Street	A3	Taylor Road	C1
Great Central Street	A1	Thames Street	B1
Halford Street	B2	The Gateway	A3
Havelock Street	B3	The Newarke	A2
Haymarket	B1	Tigers Way	B3
High Street	B2	Tower Street	B3
Highcross Street	A1	Tudor Road	A1
Hobart Street	C2	Ullswater Street	A3
Horsfair Street	B2	University Road	C3
Humberstone Gate	B2	Upperton Road	A3
Humberstone Road	C1	Vaughan Way	A1
Infirmary Road	B3	Vestry Street	C2
Jarrom Street	A3	Walnut Street	A3
Jarvis Street	A2	Waterloo Way	C3
Kamloops Crescent	C1	Welford Road	B2
Kent Street	C1	Wellington Street	B2
King Richard's Road	A2	West Street	B3
King Street	B2	Western Boulevard	A3
Lancaster Road	B3	Western Road	A3
Lee Street	B1	Wharf Street North	C1
Lincoln Street	C2	Wharf Street South	C1
London Road	C3	Wilberforce Road	A3
Loseby Lane	B2	Windermere Street	A3
Lower Brown Street	B2	Woodboy Street	C1
Manitoba Road	C1	Yeoman Street	B2
Mansfield Street	B1	York Road	B2

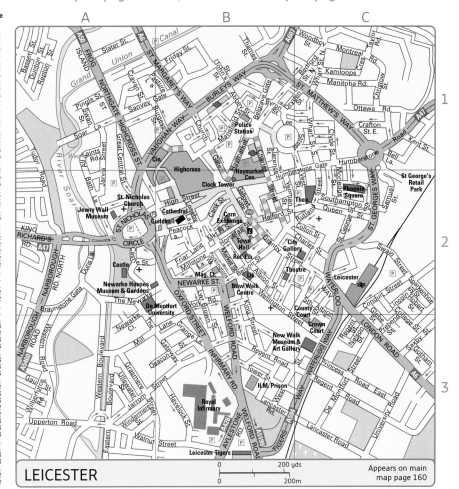

LEICESTER

0   200 yds
0   200m

Appears on main map page 160

Tourist Information Centre: 9 Castle Hill
Tel: 01522 545458

Alexandra Terrace	A2	Spa Road	C3
Baggholme Road	C2	St. Anne's Road	C2
Bailgate	B1	St. Giles Avenue	C1
Beaumont Fee	B2	St. Mark Street	B3
Beevor Street	A3	St. Mary's Street	B3
Brayford Way	A3	St. Rumbold Street	B2
Brayford Wharf North	A2	Stamp End	C3
Broadgate	B2	Steep Hill	B2
Broadway	B1	The Avenue	A2
Bruce Road	C1	Tritton Road	A3
Burton Road	A1	Union Row	B2
Canwick Road	B3	Upper Lindum Street	C2
Carholme Road	A2	Upper Long Leys Road	A1
Carline Road	A1	Vere Street	B1
Carr Street	A2	Vine Street	C2
Cheviot Street	C2	Waterside North	B3
Church Lane	B1	Waterside South	B3
Clasketgate	B2	West Parade	A2
Croft Street	B2	Westgate	B1
Cross Street	B3	Wigford Way	B2
Curle Avenue	C1	Wilson Street	A1
Drury Lane	B2	Winn Street	C2
East Gate	B2	Wragby Road	C1
Firth Road	A3	Yarborough Road	A1
George Street	C3		
Great Northern Terrace	B3		
Greetwell Close	C1		
Greetwell Road	C2		
Gresham Street	A2		
Hampton Street	A2		
Harvey Street	A2		
High Street	B3		
John Street	C2		
Langworthgate	B1		
Lee Road	C1		
Lindum Road	B2		
Lindum Terrace	C2		
Long Leys Road	A1		
Mainwaring Road	C1		
Mill Road	A1		
Milman Road	C2		
Monks Road	C2		
Monson Street	B3		
Moor Street	A2		
Mount Street	A1		
Nettleham Road	B1		
Newland	A2		
Newland Street West	A2		
Newport	B1		
Northgate	B1		
Orchard Street	A2		
Pelham Bridge	B3		
Portland Street	B3		
Portland Street	B3		
Pottergate	B2		
Queensway	C1		
Rasen Lane	B1		
Richmond Road	A2		
Ripon Street	B3		
Rope Walk	A3		
Rosemary Lane	B2		
Ruskin Avenue	C1		
Saltergate	B2		
Sewell Road	C2		
Silver Street	B2		
Sincil Bank	B3		

LINCOLN

0   200 yds
0   200m

Appears on main map page 187

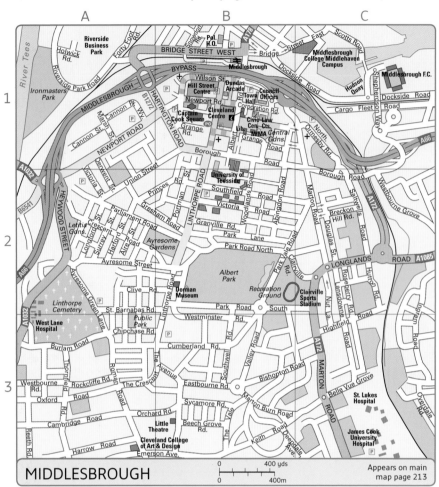

MIDDLESBROUGH

0	400 yds
0	400m

Appears on main
map page 213

Tourist Information Centre: Town Hall, Albert Road
Tel: 01642 729700

Abingdon Road	B2	Roman Road	A3
Aire Street	A2	Roseberry Road	C2
Albert Road	B1	Saltwells Road	C2
Ayresome Green Lane	A2	Scotts Road	C1
Ayresome Street	A2	Sheperdson Way	C1
Beech Grove Road	B3	Snowdon Road	B1
Belle Vue Grove	C3	Southfield Road	B2
Bishopton Road	B3	Southwell Road	B3
Borough Road	B1/C3	St. Barnabas Road	A2
Breckon Hill Road	C2	Surrey Street	A2
Bridge Street East	B1	Sycamore Road	B3
Bridge Street West	B1	The Avenue	B3
Burlam Road	A3	The Crescent	A3
Cambridge Road	A3	The Vale	B3
Cannon Park Way	A1	Thornfield Road	A3
Cannon Street	A1	Union Street	A2
Cargo Fleet Road	C1	Valley Road	B3
Chipchase Road	A3	Victoria Road	B2
Clairville Road	B2	Victoria Street	A1
Clive Road	A2	Westbourne Grove	C2
Corporation Road	B1	Westbourne Road	A3
Crescent Road	A2	Westminster Road	B3
Cumberland Road	B3	Wilson Street	B1
Deepdale Avenue	B3	Woodlands Road	B2
Derwent Street	A1		
Dockside Road	B1/C1		
Douglas Street	C2		
Eastbourne Road	B3		
Emerson Avenue	B3		
Forty Foot Road	A1		
Grange Road	B1		
Granville Road	B2		
Gresham Road	A2		
Harford Street	A2		
Harrow Road	A3		
Hartington Road	A1		
Heywood Street	A2		
Highfield Road	C3		
Holwick Road	A1		
Hudson Quay	C1		
Hutton Road	C2		
Ingram Road	C2		
Keith Road	B3		
Lansdowne Road	C2		
Linthorpe Road	B3		
Longford Street	A2		
Longlands Road	C2		
Marsh Street	A1		
Marton Burn Road	B3		
Marton Road	C2/C3		
Newport Road	A1/B1		
North Ormesby Road	C1		
Nut Lane	C2		
Orchard Road	A3		
Overdale Road	C3		
Oxford Road	A3		
Park Lane	B2		
Park Road North	B2		
Park Road South	B2		
Park Vale Road	B2		
Parliament Road	A2		
Portman Street	B2		
Princes Road	A2		
Reeth Road	A3		
Riverside Park Road	A1		
Rockcliffe Road	A3		

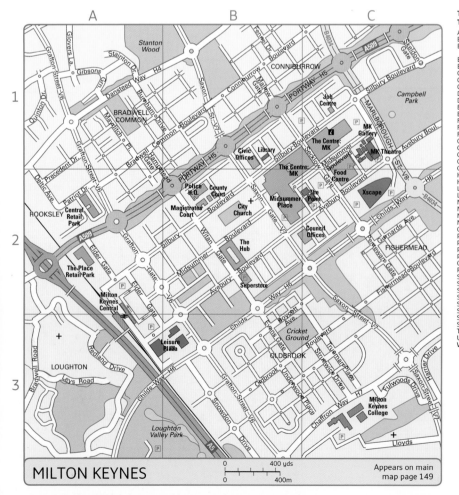

MILTON KEYNES

0	400 yds
0	400m

Appears on main
map page 149

Tourist Information Centre: Silbury Arcade
Tel: 01908 688293

Avebury Boulevard	B2/C1
Boycott Avenue	B3
Bradwell Common	
Boulevard	A1
Bradwell Road	A3
Burnham Drive	A1
Chaffron Way	C3
Childs Way	A3/C2
Conniburrow Boulevard	B1
Dansteed Way	A1
Deltic Avenue	A2
Elder Gate	A2
Evans Gate	B3
Fennel Drive	B1
Fishermead Boulevard	C2
Fulwoods Drive	C3
Gibsons Green	A1
Glovers Lane	A1
Grafton Gate	A2
Grafton Street	A1/B3
Gurnards Avenue	C2
Hampstead Gate	A1
Harrier Drive	C3
Leys Road	A3
Lloyds	C3
Mallow Gate	B1
Marlborough Street	C1
Mayditch Place	A1
Midsummer Boulevard	B2/C1
Oldbrook Boulevard	B3
Patriot Drive	A2
Pentewan Gate	C2
Portway	B2/C1
Precedent Drive	A2
Quinton Drive	A1
Redland Drive	A3
Saxon Gate	B2
Saxon Street	B1/C3
Secklow Gate	C1
Silbury Boulevard	B2/C1
Skeldon Gate	C1
Snowdon Drive	B3
Stainton Drive	A1
Strudwick Drive	C3
Trueman Place	C3
Underwood Place	B3
Witan Gate	B2

Tourist Information Centre: 8-9 Central Arcade
Tel: 0191 277 8000

Albert Street	C2	Pitt Street	A2
Ancrum Street	A1	Portland Road	C1
Argyle Street	C2	Portland Terrace	C1
Askew Road	C3	Pottery Lane	A3
Barrack Road	A1	Quarryfield Road	C3
Barras Bridge	B1	Quayside	C3
Bath Lane	A2	Queen Victoria Road	B1
Bigg Market	B2	Railway Street	A3
Blackett Street	B2	Redheugh Bridge	A3
Byron Street	C1	Richardson Road	A1
Chester Street	C1	Rye Hill	A3
City Road	C2	St. James Boulevard	A3
Claremont Road	B1	St. Mary's Place	B1
Clarence Street	C2	St. Thomas Street	B1
Clayton Street	B2	Sandyford Road	B1/C1
Clayton Street West	A3	Scotswood Road	A3
Corporation Street	A2	Skinnerburn Road	B3
Coulthards Lane	C3	South Shore Road	C3
Crawhall Road	C2	Stanhope Street	A2
Dean Street	B2	Starbeck Avenue	C1
Diana Street	A2	Stodart Street	C1
Elswick East Terrace	A3	Stowell Street	A2
Eskdale Terrace	C1	Strawberry Place	A2
Essex Close	A3	Summerhill Grove	A2
Falconar Street	C1	Swing Bridge	B3
Forth Banks	B3	The Close	B3
Forth Street	A3	Tyne Bridge	C3
Gallowgate	A2	Union Street	C2
Gateshead Highway	C3	Warwick Street	C1
George Street	A3	Wellington Street	A2
Gibson Street	C2	West Street	C3
Grainger Street	B2	Westgate Road	A2
Grantham Road	C1	Westmorland Road	A3
Grey Street	B2	Windsor Terrace	B1
Hanover Street	B3	York Street	A2
Hawks Road	C3		
Helmsley Road	C1		
High Street	C3		
Hillgate	C3		
Howard Street	C2		
Hunters Road	A1		
Ivy Close	A3		
Jesmond Road	C1		
Jesmond Road West	B1		
John Dobson Street	B2		
Kelvin Grove	C1		
Kyle Close	A3		
Lambton Street	C3		
Mansfield Street	A2		
Maple Street	A3		
Maple Terrace	A3		
Market Street	B2		
Melbourne Street	C2		
Mill Road	C3		
Neville Street	A3		
New Bridge Street	C2		
Newgate Street	B2		
Northumberland Road	B1		
Northumberland Street	B1		
Oakwellgate	C3		
Orchard Street	B3		
Oxnam Crescent	A1		
Park Terrace	B1		
Percy Street	B2		
Pilgrim Street	B2		
Pipewellgate	B3		

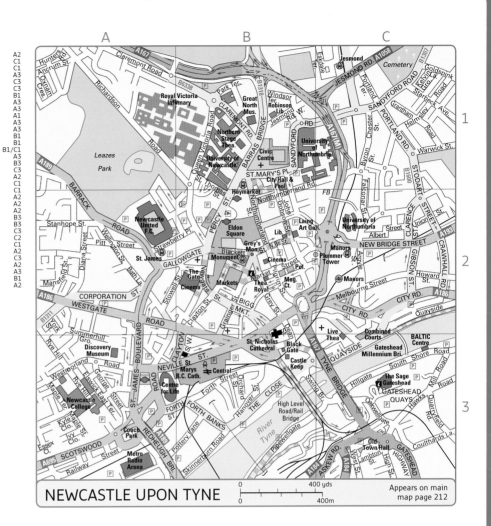

NEWCASTLE UPON TYNE

0   400 yds
0   400m

Appears on main map page 212

Tourist Information Centre: The Forum, Millennium Plain
Tel: 01603 213999

Albion Way	C3	Queens Road	B3
All Saints Green	B3	Rampant Horse Street	B2
Ashby Street	B3	Recorder Road	C2
Bakers Road	A1	Red Lion Street	B2
Bank Plain	B2	Riverside	C3
Barker Street	A1	Riverside Road	C2
Barn Road	A2	Rosary Road	C2
Barrack Street	B1	Rose Lane	B2
Bedford Street	B2	Rouen Road	B3
Ber Street	B3	Rupert Street	A3
Bethel Street	A2	Russell Street	A1
Bishopbridge Road	C2	St. Andrew's Street	B2
Bishopgate	C2	St. Augustine's Street	A1
Botolph Street	B1	St. Benedict's Street	A2
Brazen Gate	B3	St. Crispin's Road	A1
Britannia Road	C1	St. Faiths Lane	B2
Brunswick Road	A3	St. George's Street	B1
Bullclose Road	B1	St. Giles Street	A2
Canary Way	C3	St. James Close	C1
Carrow Hill	C3	St. Leonards Road	C2
Carrow Road	C3	St. Martin's Road	A1
Castle Meadow	B2	St. Stephen's Road	A3
Chapel Field Road	A2	St. Stephen's Street	B3
Chapelfield North	A2	Silver Road	B1
City Road	B3	Silver Street	B1
Clarence Road	C3	Southwell Road	B3
Colegate	B1	Surrey Street	B3
Coslany Street	A2	Sussex Street	A1
Cowgate	B1	Theatre Street	A2
Dereham Road	A2	Thorn Lane	B3
Duke Street	B1	Thorpe Road	C2
Earlham Road	A2	Tombland	B2
Edward Street	B1	Trinity Street	A3
Elm Hill	B2	Trory Street	A2
Fishergate	B1	Union Street	A3
Gas Hill	C1	Unthank Road	A3
Grapes Hill	A2	Vauxhall Street	A3
Grove Avenue	A3	Victoria Street	A3
Grove Road	A3	Wensum Street	B1
Grove Walk	A3	Wessex Street	A3
Gurney Road	C1	Westwick Street	A1
Hall Road	B3	Wherry Road	C3
Hardy Road	C3	Whitefriars	B1
Heathgate	C1	Wodehouse Street	B1
Heigham Street	A1	York Street	A3
Horns Lane	B3		
Ipswich Road	A3		
Ketts Hill	C1		
King Street	B3		
Koblenz Avenue	C3		
Lothian Street	A1		
Lower Clarence Road	C2		
Magdalen Street	B1		
Magpie Road	B1		
Market Avenue	B2		
Marlborough Road	B1		
Mountergate	B2		
Mousehold Street	C1		
Newmarket Road	A3		
Newmarket Street	A3		
Oak Street	A1		
Orchard Street	A1		
Palace Street	B2		
Pitt Street	B1		
Pottergate	A2		
Prince of Wales Road	B2		

NORWICH

0   400 yds
0   400m

Appears on main map page 178

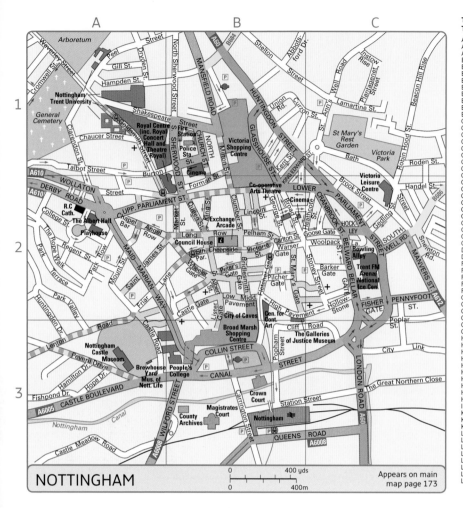

NOTTINGHAM

| 0 | 400 yds |
| 0 | 400m |

Appears on main map page 173

Tourist Information Centre: 1-4 Smithy Row
Tel: 0844 477 5678

Abbotsford Drive	B1	Maid Marian Way	A2
Albert Street	B2	Mansfield Road	B1
Angel Row	A2	Manvers Street	C2
Barker Gate	C2	Market Street	B2
Bath Street	C1	Middle Pavement	B2
Beacon Hill Rise	C1	Milton Street	B1
Bellar Gate	C2	Mount Street	A2
Belward Street	C2	North Church Street	B1
Bridlesmith Gate	B2	North Sherwood Street	B1
Broad Street	B2	Park Row	A2
Brook Street	C1	Park Terrace	A2
Burton Street	A1	Park Valley	A2
Canal Street	B3	Peel Street	A1
Carlton Street	B2	Pelham Street	B2
Carrington Street	B3	Pennyfoot Street	C2
Castle Boulevard	A3	Peveril Drive	A3
Castle Gate	B2	Pilcher Gate	B2
Castle Meadow Road	A3	Plantagenet Street	C1
Castle Road	A3	Popham Street	B3
Chapel Bar	A2	Poplar Street	C2
Chaucer Street	A1	Queens Road	B3
Cheapside	B2	Queen Street	B2
City Link	C3	Regent Street	A2
Clarendon Street	A1	Robin Hood Street	C1
Cliff Road	B3	Roden Street	C1
Clumber Street	B2	St. Ann's Well Road	C1
College Street	A2	St. James Street	A2
Collin Street	B3	St. Mary's Gate	B2
Cranbrook Street	C2	St. Peter's Gate	B2
Cromwell Street	A1	Shakespeare Street	A1
Curzon Street	B1	Shelton Street	B1
Derby Road	A2	Sneinton Road	C2
Dryden Street	A1	South Parade	B2
Fisher Gate	C2	South Sherwood Street	B1
Fishpond Drive	A3	Southwell Road	C2
Fletcher Gate	B2	Station Street	B3
Forman Street	B2	Stoney Street	C2
Friar Lane	A2	Talbot Street	A1
Gedling Street	C2	The Great Northern Close	C3
George Street	B2	The Rope Walk	A2
Gill Street	A1	Union Road	B1
Glasshouse Street	B1	Upper Parliament Street	A2
Goldsmith Street	A1	Victoria Street	B2
Goose Gate	C2	Warser Gate	B2
Hamilton Drive	A3	Waverley Street	A1
Hampden Street	A1	Wheeler Gate	B2
Handel Street	C2	Wilford Street	A3
Heathcote Street	B2	Wollaton Street	A2
High Pavement	B2	Woolpack Lane	C2
Hockley	C2		
Hollowstone	C2		
Hope Drive	A3		
Huntingdon Drive	A2		
Huntingdon Street	B1		
Instow Rise	C1		
Kent Street	B1		
King Edward Street	B2		
King Street	B2		
Lamartine Street	C1		
Lenton Road	A3		
Lincoln Street	B2		
Lister Gate	B3		
London Road	C3		
Long Row	B2		
Low Pavement	B2		
Lower Parliament Street	B2		

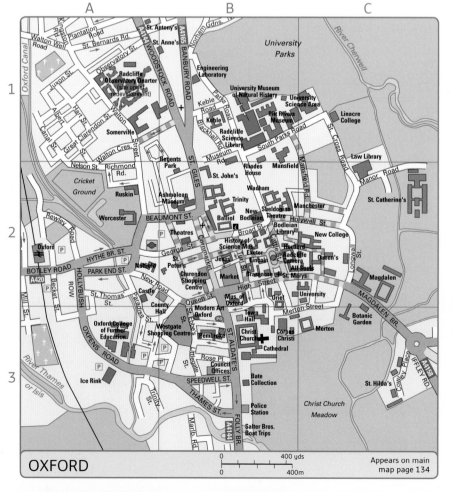

OXFORD

| 0 | 400 yds |
| 0 | 400m |

Appears on main map page 134

Tourist Information Centre: 15-16 Broad Street
Tel: 01865 686430

Albert Street	A1
Banbury Road	B1
Beaumont Street	A2
Becket Street	A2
Blackhall Road	B1
Botley Road	A2
Broad Street	B2
Canal Street	A1
Cattle Street	B2
Cornmarket	B2
Cowley Place	C3
Folly Bridge	B3
George Street	A2
Great Clarendon Street	A1
Hart Street	A1
High Street	B2
Hollybush Row	A2
Holywell Street	B2
Hythe Bridge Street	A2
Iffley Road	C3
Juxon Street	A1
Keble Road	B1
Kingston Road	A1
Littlegate Street	B3
Longwall Street	C2
Magdalen Bridge	C2
Manor Road	C1
Mansfield Road	C1
Marlborough Road	B3
Merton Street	B3
Mill Street	A2
Museum Road	B1
Nelson Street	A2
New Road	A2
Norham Gardens	B1
Observatory Street	A1
Oxpens Road	A3
Paradise Street	A2
Park End Street	A2
Parks Road	B1
Plantation Road	A1
Queen Street	B2
Rewley Road	A2
Richmond Road	A2
Rose Place	B3
St. Aldate's	B3
St. Bernards Road	A1
St. Cross Road	C1
St. Ebbe's Street	B3
St. Giles	B1
St. Thomas' Street	A2
South Parks Road	B1
Speedwell Street	B3
Thames Street	B3
Trinity Street	A3
Turl Street	B2
Walton Crescent	A1
Walton Street	A1
Walton Well Road	A1
Woodstock Road	A1

Perth

Tourist Information Centre: Lower City Mills, West Mill Street
Tel: 01738 450600

Abbot Crescent	A3
Abbot Street	A3
Albany Terrace	A1
Atholl Street	B1
Balhousie Street	B1
Barossa Place	B1
Barossa Street	B1
Barrack Street	B1
Bowerswell Road	C2
Caledonian Road	B2
Canal Street	B2
Cavendish Avenue	A3
Charlotte Street	B1
Clyde Place	A3
Darnhall Drive	A3
Dundee Road	C2
Dunkeld Road	A1
Edinburgh Road	B3
Feus Road	A1
Friar Street	A3
George Street	C2
Glasgow Road	A2
Glover Street	A2
Gowrie Street	C1
Gray Street	A2
Graybank Road	A2
Hay Street	B1
High Street	B2
Isla Road	C1
Jeanfield Road	A2
King's Place	B3
King James Place	B3
King Street	B2
Kinnoull Street	B1
Kinnoull Terrace	C2
Knowelea Place	A3
Leonard Street	B2
Lochie Brae	C1
Long Causeway	A1
Main Street	C1
Manse Road	C2
Marshall Place	B3
Melville Street	B1
Mill Street	B2
Milne Street	B2
Murray Crescent	A3
Needless Road	A3
New Row	B2
North Methven Street	B1
Park Place	A3
Perth Bridge	C1
Pickletullum Road	A2
Pitcullen Terrace	C1
Pitheavlis Crescent	A3
Princes Street	C3
Priory Place	B3
Queen Street	A3
Queens Bridge	C2
Raeburn Park	A3
Riggs Road	A2
Rose Crescent	A2
Rose Terrace	B1
St. Catherines Road	A1
St. John Street	C2
St. Leonard's Bank	B3
Scott Street	B2

Shore Road	C3
South Methven Street	B2
South Street	B2
Strathmore Street	C1
Stuart Avenue	A3
Tay Street	C2
Victoria Street	B2
Watergate	C2
Whitefriars Crescent	A2
Whitefriars Street	A2
William Street	B2
Wilson Street	A3
Young Street	A3
York Place	A2

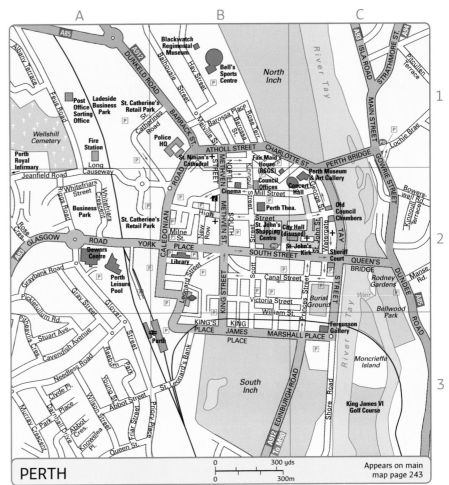

PERTH

0   300 yds
0   300m

Appears on main
map page 243

Plymouth

Tourist Information Centre: Plymouth Mayflower Centre,
3-5 The Barbican Tel: 01752 306330

Alexandra Road	C1
Alma Road	A1
Armada Street	B2
Armada Way	B2
Ashford Road	C1
Barbican Approach	C3
Beaumont Road	C2
Beechwood Avenue	B1
Belgrave Road	C1
Bretonside	B2
Buckwell Street	B3
Camden Street	B2
Cattledown Road	C3
Cecil Street	A2
Central Park Avenue	A1
Charles Street	B2
Citadel Road	A3
Clarence Place	A2
Cliff Road	A3
Clifton Place	B1
Clovelly Road	C3
Cobourg Street	B2
Coleridge Road	C1
Connaught Avenue	C1
Cornwall Street	B2
Dale Road	B1
De-La-Hay Avenue	A1
Desborough Road	C2
Drake Circus	B2
East Street	A3
Ebrington Street	B2
Elliot Street	A3
Embankment Road	C2
Exeter Street	B2
Ford Park Road	B1
Furzehill Road	C1
Gdynia Way	C3
Glen Park Avenue	B1
Grand Parade	A3
Greenbank Avenue	C2
Greenbank Road	C1
Grenville Road	C2
Harwell Street	A2
Hill Park Crescent	B1
Hoe Road	B3
Houndiscombe Road	B1
James Street	B2
King Street	A2
Knighton Road	C2
Lipson Hill	C1
Lipson Road	C2
Lisson Grove	C1
Lockyer Street	B3
Looe Street	B2
Madeira Road	B3
Manor Road	A2
Martin Street	A3
Mayflower Street	B2
Millbay Road	A3
Mount Gould Road	C1
Mutley Plain	B1
New George Street	A2
North Cross	B2
North Hill	B2
North Road East	B2
North Road West	A2

North Street	B2
Notte Street	B3
Oxford Street	A2
Pentillie Road	B1
Ponsonby Road	A1
Princess Street	B3
Queen's Road	C1
Royal Parade	B2
Salisbury Road	C2
Saltash Road	A1
Seaton Avenue	B1
Seymour Avenue	C2
Southside Street	B3
Stoke Road	A2
Stuart Road	A1
Sutton Road	C2
Sydney Street	A2
Teats Hill Road	C3
The Crescent	A3
Tothill Avenue	C2
Tothill Road	C2
Union Street	A2
Vauxhall Street	B3
West Hoe Road	A3
Western Approach	A2
Whittington Street	A1
Wilton Street	A2
Wyndham Street	A2

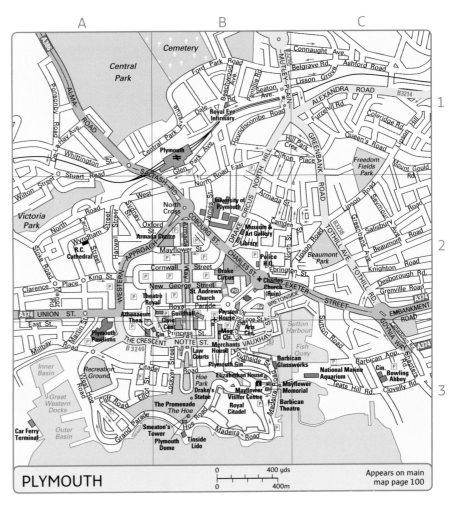

PLYMOUTH

0   400 yds
0   400m

Appears on main
map page 100

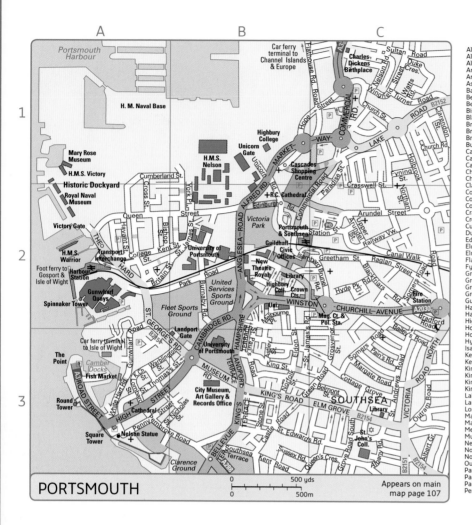

PORTSMOUTH

0 500 yds
0 500m

Appears on main map page 107

Street	Grid	Street	Grid
Albany Road	C3	Penny Street	A3
Albert Grove	C3	Queen's Crescent	C3
Alfred Road	B2	Queen Street	A2
Anglesea Road	B2	Raglan Street	C2
Arundel Street	C2	Railway View	C2
Astley Street	B3	St. Andrews Road	C3
Bailey's Road	C2	St. Edward's Road	B3
Bellevue Terrace	B3	St. George's Road	A2
Belmont Street	C3	St. James Road	B3
Bishop Street	A1	St. James Street	B2
Blackfriars Road	C2	St. Paul's Road	B3
Bradford Road	C2	St. Thomas's Street	A3
Britain Street	A2	Somers Road	C2
Broad Street	A3	Southsea Terrace	B3
Burnaby Road	B2	Station Street	C2
Cambridge Road	B3	Stone Street	B3
Canal Walk	C2	Sultan Road	C1
Castle Road	B3	Sussex Street	B3
Church Road	C1	The Hard	A2
Church Street	C1	Turner Road	C1
Clarendon Street	C1	Unicorn Road	B1
College Street	A2	Upper Arundel Street	C2
Commercial Road	B2	Victoria Road North	C3
Cottage Grove	C3	Warblington Street	A3
Crasswell Street	C1	Watts Road	C1
Cross Street	A1	White Hart Road	A3
Cumberland Street	A1	Wingfield Street	C1
Duke Crescent	C1	Winston Churchill Avenue	B2
Edinburgh Road	B2	York Place	B2
Eldon Street	B3		
Elm Grove	C3		
Flathouse Road	C1		
Fyning Street	C1		
Green Road	B3		
Greetham Street	C2		
Grosvenor Street	C3		
Grove Road South	C3		
Gunwharf Road	A3		
Hampshire Terrace	B3		
Havant Street	A2		
High Street	A3		
Holbrook Road	B1		
Hope Street	B1		
Hyde Park Road	C2		
Isambard Brunel Road	B2		
Kent Road	B3		
Kent Street	A1		
King Charles Street	A3		
King's Road	B3		
King's Terrace	B3		
King Street	B3		
Lake Road	C1		
Landport Terrace	B3		
Lombard Street	A3		
Margate Road	C3		
Market Way	B1		
Melbourne Place	B2		
Museum Road	B3		
Nelson Road	C1		
Norfolk Street	B3		
Northam Street	C2		
Outram Road	C3		
Pain's Road	C3		
Paradise Street	C2		
Park Road	B2		
Pembroke Road	A3		

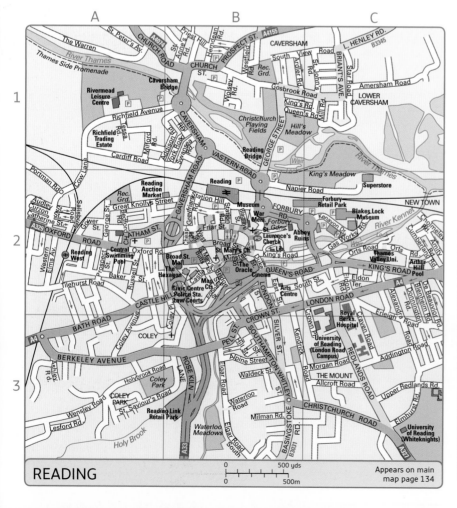

READING

0 500 yds
0 500m

Appears on main map page 134

Street	Grid	Street	Grid
Addington Road	C3	Lesford Road	A3
Addison Road	A1	London Road	C2
Alexandra Road	C2	London Street	B2
Allcroft Road	C3	Lower Henley Road	C1
Alpine Street	B3	Mill Road	C1
Amersham Road	C1	Milford Road	A1
Amity Road	A2	Milman Road	B3
Ardler Road	B1	Minster Street	B2
Ashley Road	A3	Morgan Road	C3
Audley Street	A2	Napier Road	B2
Baker Street	A2	Orts Road	C2
Basingstoke Road	B3	Oxford Road	A2
Bath Road	A3	Pell Street	B3
Bedford Road	A2	Portman Road	A1
Berkeley Avenue	A3	Priest Hill	B1
Blagrave Street	B2	Prospect Street Caversham	B1
Blenheim Road	C2	Prospect Street Reading	A2
Briant's Avenue	C1	Queen's Road Caversham	B1
Bridge Street	B2	Queen's Road Reading	B2
Broad Street	B2	Richfield Avenue	A1
Cardiff Road	A1	Rose Kiln Lane	B3
Castle Hill	A2	Russell Street	A2
Castle Street	B2	St. Anne's Road	B1
Catherine Street	A2	St. John's Road	C1
Caversham Road	B2	St. Mary's Butts	B2
Chatham Street	A2	St. Peters Avenue	A1
Cheapside	B2	St. Saviours Road	A3
Cholmeley Road	C2	Silver Street	B3
Christchurch Road	C3	South Street	B2
Church Road	A1	Southampton Street	B3
Church Street	B1	South View Road	B1
Coley Avenue	A3	Star Road	C1
Coley Place	B2	Station Hill	B2
Cow Lane	A1	Station Road	B2
Craven Road	C3	Swansea Road	B1
Crown Place	C2	Tessa Road	A1
Crown Street	B3	The Warren	A1
Cumberland Road	C2	Tilehurst Road	A2
Curzon Street	A2	Upper Redlands Road	C3
De Beauvoir Road	C2	Vastern Road	B1
Donnington Road	C2	Waldelk Street	B3
Duke Street	B2	Waterloo Road	B3
East Street	B2	Wensley Road	A3
Eldon Road	C2	Western Elms Avenue	A2
Eldon Terrace	C2	Westfield Road	B1
Elgar Road	B3	West Street	B2
Elgar Road South	B3	Whitley Street	B3
Elmhurst Road	C3	Wolsey Road	B1
Erleigh Road	C2	York Road	B1
Fobney Street	B2		
Forbury Road	B2		
Friar Street	B2		
Gas Work Road	B2		
George Street Caversham	B1		
George Street Reading	B2		
Gosbrook Road	B1		
Gower Street	A2		
Great Knollys Street	A2		
Greyfriars Road	B2		
Hemdean Road	B1		
Hill Road	B3		
Holybrook Road	A3		
Kenavon Drive	C2		
Kendrick Road	B3		
King's Road Caversham	B1		
King's Road Reading	B2		

Tourist Information Centre: Fish Row
Tel: 01722 342860

Albany Road	B1
Ashley Road	A1
Avon Terrace	A1
Barnard Street	C2
Bedwin Street	B1
Belle Vue Road	B1
Bishops Walk	B3
Blackfriars Way	C3
Blue Boar Row	B2
Bourne Avenue	C1
Bourne Hill	C1
Bridge Street	B2
Brown Street	B2
Butcher Row	B2
Carmelite Way	B3
Castle Street	B2
Catherine Street	B2
Chipper Lane	B2
Churchfields Road	A2
Churchill Way East	C2
Churchill Way North	B1
Churchill Way South	C3
Churchill Way West	A1
Clifton Road	A1
College Street	C1
Crane Bridge Road	A2
Crane Street	B2
De Vaux Place	B3
Devizes Road	A1
Elm Grove Road	C2
Endless Street	B1
Estcourt Road	C1
Exeter Street	B3
Fairview Road	C1
Fisherton Street	A2
Fowlers Hill	C2
Fowlers Road	C2
Friary Lane	C3
Gas Lane	A1
Gigant Street	C2
Greencroft Street	C1
Hamilton Road	B1
High Street	B2
Ivy Street	B2
Kelsey Road	C1
Laverstock Road	C2
Manor Road	C1
Marsh Lane	A1
Meadow Road	A1
Milford Hill	C2
Milford Street	B2
Mill Road	A2
Millstream Approach	B1
Minster Street	B2
New Canal	B2
New Street	B2
North Walk	B3
Park Street	C1
Pennyfarthing Street	B2
Queens Road	B1
Rampart Road	C2
Rollestone Street	B1
St. Ann Street	C3
St. John's Street	B2
St. Marks Road	C1
St. Paul's Road	A1
Salt Lane	B2
Scots Lane	B2
Silver Street	B2
Southampton Road	C3
Swaynes Close	B1
Tollgate Road	C2
Trinity Street	C2
Wain-a-long Road	C1
West Walk	B3
Wilton Road	A1
Winchester Street	B2
Windsor Road	A2
Wyndham Road	B1
York Road	A1

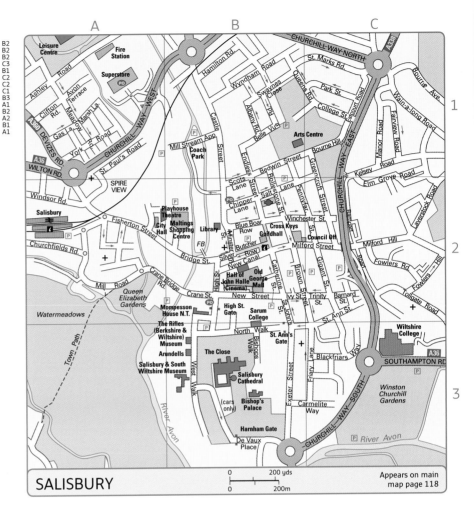

SALISBURY

0   200 yds
0   200m

Appears on main map page 118

Tourist Information Centre: Brunswick Shopping Centre,
Unit 15a, Westborough Tel: 01723 383636

Aberdeen Walk	B2
Albion Road	B3
Ashville Avenue	A2
Avenue Road	A3
Belmont Road	B3
Candler Street	A2
Castle Road	B2
Chatsworth Gardens	A1
Columbus Ravine	A2
Commercial Street	A3
Cross Street	B2
Dean Road	A2
Eastborough	B2
Esplanade	B3
Falconers Rd	B2
Falsgrave Road	A3
Foreshore Road	B2
Franklin Street	A2
Friargate	B2
Friarsway	B2
Garfield Road	A2
Gladstone Road	A2
Gladstone Street	A2
Gordon Street	A2
Grosvenor Road	B3
Highfield	A3
Hoxton Road	A2
Longwestgate	C2
Manor Road	A2
Marine Drive	C1
Mayville Avenue	A2
Moorland Road	A1
New Queen Street	B1
Newborough	B2
North Marine Road	B1
North Street	B2
Northstead Manor Drive	A1
Northway	A2
Norwood Street	A2
Oak Road	A3
Peasholm Crescent	A1
Peasholm Drive	A1
Peasholm Road	A1
Prince Of Wales Terrace	B3
Princess Street	C2
Prospect Road	A2
Queen Street	B2
Queen's Parade	B1
Raleigh Street	A2
Ramshill Road	B3
Roscoe Street	A3
Rothbury Street	A2
Royal Albert Drive	B1
Royal Avenue	B3
Sandside	C2
Seamer Road	A3
St. James Road	A3
St. John's Avenue	A3
St. John's Road	A3
St. Thomas Street	B2
Tollergate	B1
Trafalgar Road	A1
Trafalgar Square	B1
Trafalgar Street West	A2
Trinity Road	A3
Valley Bridge Parade	B3
Valley Bridge Road	B2
Valley Road	A3
Vernon Road	B2
Victoria Park Mount	A1
Victoria Road	A3
Victoria Street	B2
West Street	B3
Westborough	A3
Westbourne Grove	B3
Westover Road	A3
Westwood	B3
Westwood Road	A3
Weydale Avenue	A1
Wykeham Street	A3

SCARBOROUGH

0   400 yds
0   400m

Appears on main map page 204

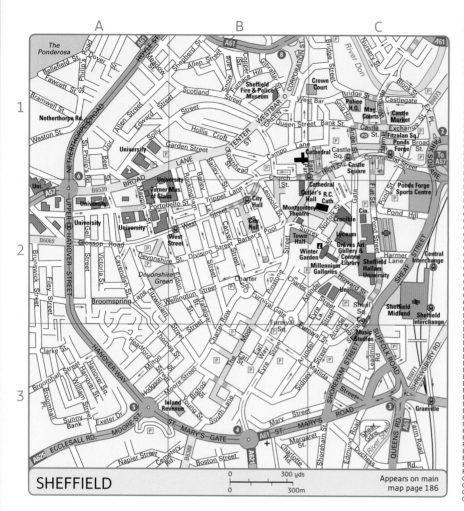

SHEFFIELD

0   300 yds
0   300m

Appears on main map page 186

Tourist Information Centre: Winter Garden, 90 Surrey Street
Tel: 0114 221 1900

Allen Street	B1	Hanover Square	A3
Angel Street	C1	Hanover Street	A3
Arundel Gate	B2	Hanover Way	A3
Arundel Lane	C3	Harmer Lane	C2
Arundel Street	B3	Haymarket	C1
Bailey Lane	B1	Headford Street	A3
Bailey Street	B1	High Street	C1
Bank Street	C1	Hodgson Street	A3
Barker's Pool	B2	Hollis Croft	B1
Beet Street	A1	Howard Street	C2
Bellefield Street	A1	Hoyle Street	A1
Bishop Street	B3	Leadmill Road	C3
Blonk Street	C1	Leopold Street	B2
Boston Street	B3	Mappin Street	A2
Bower Street	B1	Margaret Street	B3
Bramwell Street	A1	Mary Street	B3
Bridge Street	C1	Matilda Street	C3
Broad Lane	A2	Meadow Street	A1
Broad Street	C1	Milton Street	A3
Broomhall Street	A3	Moore Street	A3
Broomhall Place	A3	Napier Street	A3
Broomspring Lane	A2	Netherthorpe Road	A1
Brown Street	C3	Norfolk Street	C1
Brunswick Street	A2	Nursery Street	C1
Campo Lane	B1	Pinstone Street	B2
Carver Street	B2	Pond Hill	C2
Castle Square	C1	Pond Hill	C2
Castle Street	C1	Pond Street	C2
Castlegate	C1	Portobello Street	A2
Cavendish Street	A2	Queen Street	B1
Cemetery Road	A3	Queens Road	C3
Charles Street	B2/C2	Rockingham Street	B2
Charlotte Road	B3	St. Mary's Gate	B3
Charter Row	B3	St. Mary's Road	B3
Charter Square	B2	St. Philip's Road	A1
Church Street	B1	Scotland Street	B1
Clarke Street	A3	Sheaf Gardens	C3
Commercial Street	C1	Sheaf Square	C2
Copper Street	B1	Sheaf Street	C2
Corporation Street	B1	Shepherd Street	B1
Devonshire Street	A2	Shoreham Street	C3
Division Street	B2	Shrewsbury Road	C3
Dover Street	A1	Sidney Street	B3
Duchess Road	C3	Snig Hill	C1
Earl Street	B3	Snow Lane	B1
Earl Way	B3	Solly Street	A1
East Parade	C1	South Lane	B3
Ecclesall Road	A3	Spring Street	B1
Edmund Road	C3	Suffolk Road	C3
Edward Street	A1	Sunny Bank	A3
Eldon Street	B2	Surrey Street	B2
Exchange Street	C1	Tenter Street	B1
Exeter Drive	A3	The Moor	B3
Eyre Lane	C2	Thomas Street	A3
Eyre Street	B3	Townhead Street	B1
Farm Road	C3	Trafalgar Street	B2
Fawcett Street	A1	Trippet Lane	B2
Filey Street	A2	Upper Allen Street	A1
Fitzwilliam Street	A2	Upper Hanover Street	A2
Flat Street	C1	Victoria Street	A2
Furnace Hill	B1	Waingate	C1
Furnival Gate	B2	Wellington Street	B2
Furnival Square	B2	West Bar	B1
Furnival Street	B2	West Street	B2
Garden Street	A1	Westbar Green	B1
Gell Street	A2	Weston Street	A1
Gibraltar Street	B1	William Street	A3
Glossop Road	A2	Young Street	B3

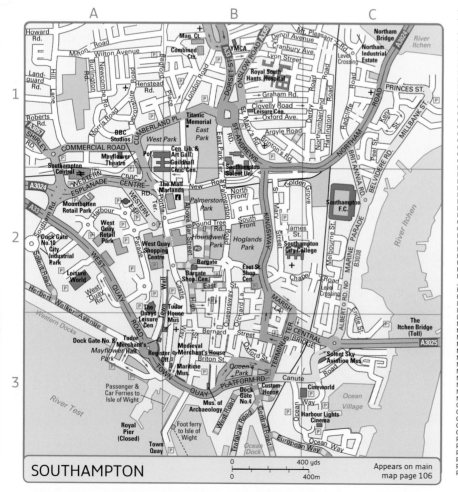

SOUTHAMPTON

0   400 yds
0   400m

Appears on main map page 106

Tourist Information Centre: 9 Civic Centre Road
Tel: 023 8083 3333

Above Bar Street	B2	Queensway	B3
Albert Road North	C3	Radcliffe Road	C1
Argyle Road	B1	Roberts Road	A1
Bedford Place	A1	St. Andrews Road	B1
Belvidere Road	C2	St. Mary's Road	B1
Bernard Street	B3	St. Mary Street	B2
Brintons Road	B1	Shirley Road	A1
Britannia Road	C1	Solent Road	A2
Briton Street	B3	Southern Road	A2
Burlington Road	A1	South Front	B2
Canute Road	B3	Terminus Terrace	B3
Castle Way	B2	Town Quay	A3
Central Bridge	B3	Trafalgar Road	B3
Central Road	B3	West Quay Road	A2
Chapel Road	B2	West Road	B3
Civic Centre Road	A2	Western Esplanade	A2
Clovelly Road	B1	Wilton Avenue	A1
Commercial Road	A1		
Cranbury Avenue	B1		
Cumberland Place	B1		
Denzil Avenue	B1		
Derby Road	C1		
Devonshire Road	A1		
Dorset Street	B1		
East Park Terrace	B1		
East Street	B2		
Endle Street	C2		
European Way	B3		
Golden Grove	B2		
Graham Road	B1		
Harbour Parade	A2		
Hartington Road	C1		
Henstead Road	A1		
Herbert Walker Avenue	A2		
High Street	B2		
Hill Lane	A1		
Howard Road	A1		
James Street	B2		
Kent Street	C1		
Kingsway	B2		
Landguard Road	A1		
London Road	B1		
Lyon Street	B1		
Marine Parade	C2		
Marsh Lane	B2		
Melbourne Street	C2		
Millbank Street	C1		
Milton Road	A1		
Morris Road	A1		
Mount Pleasant Road	B1		
Newcombe Road	A1		
New Road	B2		
Northam Road	C1		
North Front	B2		
Northumberland Road	C1		
Ocean Way	B3		
Onslow Road	B1		
Orchard Lane	B3		
Oxford Avenue	B1		
Oxford Street	B3		
Palmerston Road	B2		
Peel Street	C1		
Platform Road	B3		
Portland Terrace	A2		
Pound Tree Road	B2		
Princes Street	C1		

Tourist Information Centre: The Potteries Museum & Art Gallery, Bethesda Street   Tel: 01782 236000

Albion Street	B1	Snow Hill	B2
Ashford Street	B2	Stafford Street	B1
Avenue Road	B2	Station Road	B3
Aynsley Road	B2	Stoke	B3
Bedford Road	B2	Stoke Road	B3
Bedford Street	A2	Stone Street	A3
Belmont Road	A1	Stuart Road	C2
Beresford Street	B2	Sun Street	B1
Berry Hill Road	C2	The Parkway	B2
Boon Avenue	A3	Trentmill Road	C2
Botteslow Street	C1	Victoria Road	C2
Boughey Road	B3	Warner Street	B1
Broad Street	B1	Waterloo Road	C1
Bucknall New Road	C1	Wellesley Street	B2
Bucknall Old Road	C1	Wellington Road	C1
Cauldon Road	B2	West Avenue	A3
Cemetery Road	A2	Westland Street	A3
Church Street	B3	Yoxall Avenue	A3
Clough Street	A1		
College Road	B2		
Commercial Road	C1		
Copeland Street	B3		
Dewsbury Road	C3		
Eagle Street	C1		
Eastwood Road	C1		
Elenora Street	B3		
Etruria Road	A1		
Etruria Vale Road	A1		
Etruscan Street	A2		
Festival Way	A1		
Forge Lane	A1		
Garner Street	A2		
Glebe Street	B3		
Greatbatch Avenue	A3		
Hanley	B1		
Hartshill Road	A3		
Hill Street	A3		
Honeywall	A3		
Howard Place	B2		
Ivy House Road	C1		
Leek Road	B3		
Lichfield Street	C1		
Liverpool Road	B3		
Lordship Lane	B3		
Lytton Street	B3		
Manor Street	C3		
Marsh Street	B1		
Newlands Street	B2		
North Street	A2		
Old Hall Street	B1		
Oxford Street	A3		
Parliament Row	B1		
Potteries Way	B1		
Potters Way	C1		
Prince's Road	A3		
Quarry Avenue	A3		
Quarry Road	A3		
Queen's Road	A3		
Queensway	A2		
Rectory Road	B2		
Regent Road	B2		
Richmond Street	A3		
Ridgway Road	B2		
Seaford Street	B2		
Shelton New Road	A2		
Shelton Old Road	A3		

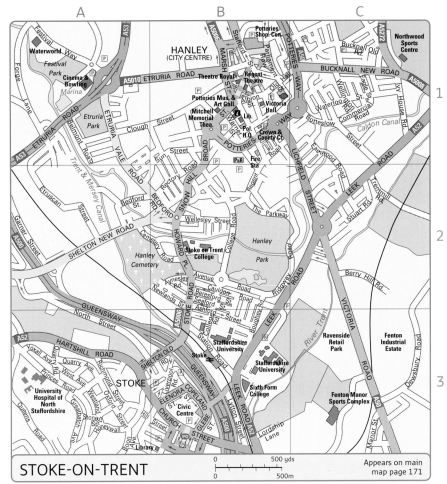

STOKE-ON-TRENT

0   500 yds
0   500m

Appears on main
map page 171

**Tourist Information Centre: Bridgefoot
Tel: 01789 264293**

Albany Road	A2	Swan's Nest Lane	C2
Alcester Road	A1	The Waterways	A1
Arden Street	A1	Tiddington Road	C2
Avonside	B3	Trinity Street	B3
Banbury Road	C2	Tyler Street	B1
Bancroft Place	C2	Union Street	B2
Birmingham Road	A1	Warwick Court	B1
Brewery Street	B1	Warwick Crescent	C1
Bridgefoot	C2	Warwick Road	C1
Bridge Street	B2	Waterside	B2
Bridgeway	C2	Welcombe Road	C1
Bridgetown Road	C3	Westbourne Grove	A2
Broad Street	A3	Western Road	A1
Broad Walk	A3	West Street	A3
Bull Street	A3	Wharf Road	A1
Chapel Lane	B2	Windsor Street	B2
Chapel Street	B2	Wood Street	B2
Cherry Orchard	A3		
Chestnut Walk	A2		
Church Street	B2		
Clopton Bridge	C2		
Clopton Road	B1		
College Lane	B3		
College Street	B3		
Ely Street	B2		
Evesham Place	A3		
Evesham Road	A3		
Great William Street	B1		
Greenhill Street	A2		
Grove Road	A2		
Guild Street	B1		
Henley Street	B1		
High Street	B2		
Holtom Street	A3		
John Street	B1		
Kendall Avenue	B1		
Maidenhead Road	B1		
Mansell Street	A1		
Meer Street	B2		
Mill Lane	B3		
Mulberry Street	B1		
Narrow Lane	A3		
New Street	B3		
Old Town	B3		
Old Town Square	A3		
Old Tramway Walk	C3		
Orchard Way	A3		
Payton Street	B1		
Red Lion Court	B2		
Rother Street	A2		
Ryland Street	B3		
St. Andrews Crescent	A2		
St. Gregory's Road	B1		
Sanctus Drive	A3		
Sanctus Road	A3		
Sanctus Street	A3		
Sandfield Road	A3		
Scholar's Lane	A2		
Seven Meadow Road	A3		
Shakespeare Street	B1		
Sheep Street	B2		
Shipston Road	C3		
Shottery Road	A2		
Shrieve's Walk	B2		
Southern Lane	B3		
Station Road	A1		

STRATFORD-UPON-AVON

0   500 yds
0   500m

Appears on main
map page 147

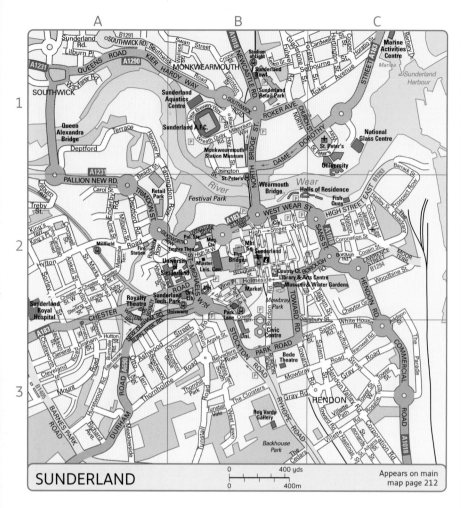

SUNDERLAND

0   400 yds
0   400m

Appears on main
map page 212

Tourist Information Centre: 50 Fawcett Street
Tel: 0191 553 2000

Abbotsford Grove	B3	Lime Street	A2
Addison Street	C3	Livingstone Road	B2
Aiskell Street	A2	Lumley Road	A2
Argyle Street	B3	Matamba Terrace	A2
Ashwood Street	A3	Milburn Street	A2
Azalea Terrace South	B3	Millennium Way	B1
Barnes Park Road	A3	Moor Terrace	C2
Barrack Street	C1	Mount Road	A3
Beach Street	A2	Mowbray Road	B3
Beechwood Terrace	A3	New Durham Road	A3
Belvedere Road	B3	Newcastle Road	B1
Black Road	B1	North Bridge Street	B2
Borough Road	B2/C2	Otto Terrace	A3
Bramwell Road	C3	Pallion New Road	A2
Brougham Street	B2	Park Lane	B2
Burdon Road	B3	Park Road	B3
Burn Park Road	A3	Peel Street	B3
Burnaby Street	A3	Prospect Row	C2
Burnville Road	A3	Queens Road	A1
Carol Street	A2	Raby Road	A2
Chatsworth Street	A3	Railway Row	A2
Chaytor Grove	C2	Roker Avenue	B1/C1
Chester Road	A2	Rosalie Terrace	C3
Chester Street	A2	Ryhope Road	B3
Church Street East	C2	St. Albans Street	C3
Church Street North	B1	St. Leonards Street	C3
Cleveland Road	A3	St. Marks Road	A2
Commercial Road	C3	St. Mary's Way	B2
Cooper Street	C1	St. Michaels Way	B2
Coronation Street	C2	St. Peter's Way	C1
Corporation Road	C3	Salem Road	C3
Cousin Street	C2	Salem Street	C3
Cromwell Street	A2	Salisbury Street	B2
Crozier Street	B1	Sans Street	C2
Dame Dorothy Street	B1	Selbourne Street	B1
Deptford Road	A2	Silksworth Row	A2
Deptford Terrace	A2	Sorley Street	A2
Durham Road	A3	Southwick Road	A1
Easington Street	B1	Southwick Road	B1
Eden House Road	A3	Stewart Street	A3
Eglinton Street	B1	Stockton Road	B3
Enderby Road	A2	Suffolk Street	C3
Farringdon Row	A1	Sunderland Road	A1
Forster Street	C1	Swan Street	B1
Fox Street	A3	Tatham Street	C2
Fulwell Road	B1	The Cedars	B3
General Graham Street	A3	The Cloisters	B3
Gladstone Street	B1	The Parade	C3
Gray Road	B3/C3	The Quadrant	C2
Hanover Place	A/1	The Royalty	A2
Hartington Street	C1	Thornhill Park	B3
Hartley Street	C2	Thornhill Terrace	B3
Hastings Street	C3	Thornholme Road	A3
Hay Street	B1	Toward Road	B2/C3
Hendon Road	C2	Tower Street	C3
Hendon Valley Road	C3	Tower Street West	C3
High Street East	C2	Trimdon Street	A2
High Street West	B2	Tunstall Road	B3
Holmeside	B2	Tunstall Vale	B3
Horatio Street	C1	Vaux Brewery Way	B1
Hurstwood Road	A3	Villette Road	C3
Hutton Street	A3	Vine Place	B2
Hylton Road	A2	Wallace Street	B1
Hylton Street	A2	West Lawn	B3
Jackson Street	A3	West Wear Street	B2
James William Street	C2	Western Hill	A2
Kenton Grove	B1	Wharncliffe Street	A2
Kier Hardy Way	A1	White House Road	C3
King's Place	A2	Woodbine Street	C2
Lawrence Street	C2	Wreath Quay Road	B1

SWANSEA

0   500 yds
0   500m

Appears on main
map page 128

Tourist Information Centre: Plymouth Street
Tel: 01792 468321

Aberdyberthi Street	C1	Mount Pleasant	B2
Albert Row	B3	Mumbles Road	A3
Alexandra Road	B2	Neath Road	C1
Argyle Street	A3	Nelson Street	B3
Baptist Well Place	B1	New Cut Road	C2
Baptist Well Street	B1	New Orchard Street	B1
Beach Street	A3	Nicander Parade	A2
Belgrave Lane	A3	Norfolk Street	A2
Belle Vue Way	B2	North Hill Road	B1
Berw Road	A1	Orchard Street	B2
Berwick Terrace	B1	Oxford Street	A3
Bond Street	A3	Oystermouth Road	A3
Brooklands Terrace	A2	Page Street	B2
Brunswick Street	A3	Pant-y-Celyn Road	A2
Brynymor Crescent	A3	Park Terrace	B1
Brynymor Road	A3	Pedrog Terrace	A1
Burrows Place	C3	Penlan Crescent	A2
Cambrian Place	C3	Pentre Guinea Road	C1
Carig Crescent	A1	Pen-y-Craig Road	A1
Carlton Terrace	B2	Picton Terrace	B2
Carmarthen Road	B1	Powys Avenue	A1
Castle Street	B2	Princess Way	B2
Clarence Terrace	B3	Quay Parade	C2
Colbourne Terrace	B1	Rhondda Street	A2
Constitution Hill	A2	Rose Hill	A2
Creidiol Road	A1	St. Elmo Avenue	C1
Cromwell Street	A2	St. Helen's Avenue	A3
Cwm Road	C1	St. Helen's Road	A3
De La Beche Street	B2	St. Mary Street	B2
Delhi Street	C2	Singleton Street	B3
Dillwyn Street	B3	Somerset Place	C3
Dyfatty Street	B1	South Guildhall Road	A3
Dyfed Avenue	A2	Strand	C2
Earl Street	C1	Taliesyn Road	A2
East Burrows Road	C3	Tan-y-Marian Road	A2
Eigen Crescent	A1	Tegid Road	A1
Emlyn Road	A1	Teilo Crescent	A1
Fabian Way	C2	Terrace Road	A2
Fairfield Terrace	A2	The Kingsway	B2
Ffynone Drive	A2	Townhill Road	A1
Ffynone Road	A2	Trawler Road	B3
Foxhole Road	C1	Villiers Street	C1
Glamorgan Street	B3	Vincent Street	A3
Gors Avenue	A1	Walter Road	A3
Granagwen Road	B1	Watkin Street	B2
Grove Place	B2	Waun-Wen Road	B1
Gwent Road	A1	Wellington Street	B3
Gwili Terrace	A1	West Way	B3
Hanover Street	A2	Westbury Street	A3
Heathfield	B2	Western Street	A3
Hewson Street	A2	William Street	B3
High Street	B2	Windmill Terrace	C1
High View	B1	York Street	C3
Islwyn Road	A1		
Kilvey Road	C1		
Kilvey Terrace	C2		
King Edward's Road	A3		
King's Road	C2		
Llangyfelach Road	B1		
Long Ridge	B1		
Mackworth Street	C2		
Maesteg Street	C1		
Mansel Street	A2		
Mayhill Road	A1		
Milton Terrace	B2		
Morris Lane	C2		

Tourist Information Centre: Central Library, Regent Circus
Tel: 01793 466454

Albion Street	A3	Upham Road	C3
Bath Road	B3	Victoria Road	C2
Beatrice Street	B1	Westcott Place	A3
Beckhampton Street	C2	Western Street	C3
Birch Street	A2	William Street	A3
Bridge Street	B2	York Road	C2
Broad Street	C1		
Canal Walk	B2		
Caulfield Road	C1		
Church Place	A2		
Cirencester Way	C1		
Clifton Street	B3		
Commercial Road	B2		
County Road	C1		
Cricklade Street	C3		
Curtis Street	B2		
Dean Street	A2		
Drove Road	C3		
Eastcott Hill	B3		
Edmund Street	B2		
Elmina Road	C1		
Euclid Street	C2		
Faringdon Road	A2		
Farnsby Street	B2		
Fleet Street	B2		
Fleming Way	C1		
Gladstone Street	C1		
Goddard Avenue	B3		
Great Western Way	A1		
Grosvenor Road	A3		
Groundwell Road	C2		
Hawksworth Way	A1		
High Street	C3		
Holbrook Way	B2		
Hythe Road	B3		
Islington Street	B2		
Jennings Street	A2		
Kemble Drive	A1		
Kent Road	B3		
Kingshill Street	A3		
Lansdown Road	B3		
Manchester Road	B1		
Market Street	B2		
Milford Street	B2		
Milton Road	B2		
Morris Street	A1		
Newburn Crescent	A2		
Newcombe Drive	A1		
North Star Avenue	B1		
Ocotal Way	C1		
Okus Road	A3		
Park Lane	A2		
Penzance Drive	A2		
Plymouth Street	C2		
Princes Street	C2		
Queen Street	B2		
Radnor Street	A3		
Redcliffe Street	A2		
Regent Street	B2		
Rodbourne Road	A1		
Rosebery Street	C1		
Spring Gardens	C2		
Stafford Street	B3		
Station Road	B1		
Swindon Road	B3		
The Parade	B2		

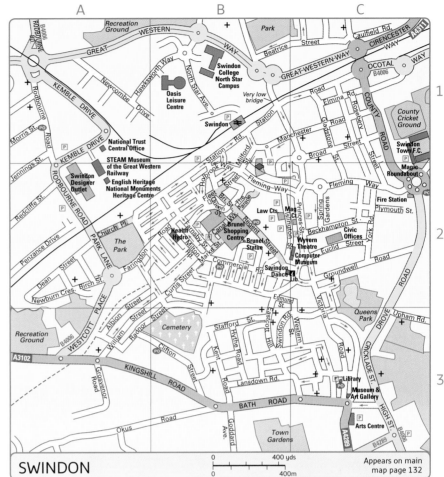

SWINDON

0   400 yds
0   400m

Appears on main
map page 132

Tourist Information Centre: 5 Vaughan Parade
Tel: 01803 211211

Abbey Road	B2	Thurlow Road	B1
Ash Hill Road	B1	Tor Hill Road	B2
Avenue Road	A2	Torbay Road	A3
Bampfylde Road	A2	Torwood Gardens Road	C3
Barton Road	A1	Torwood Street	C3
Belgrave Road	A2	Union Street	B2
Belmont Road	C1	Upton Hill	B1
Braddons Hill Road East	C2	Upton Road	A1
Bridge Road	A2	Vanehill Road	C3
Bronshill Road	B1	Victoria Parade	C3
Brunswick Square	B1	Walnut Road	A3
Carlton Road	C1	Warbro Road	C1
Cary Parade	C3	Warren Road	B2
Cedars Road	C2	Windsor Road	C1
Chestnut Avenue	A2		
Cockington Lane	A3		
Croft Road	B2		
Crownhill Park	A1		
Dunmere Road	C1		
East Street	A1		
Ellacombe Church Road	C1		
Ellacombe Road	B1		
Falkland Road	A2		
Falkland Road	A2		
Fleet Street	B2		
Forest Road	B1		
Goshen Road	A2		
Hatfield Road	B1		
Hennapyn Road	A3		
Higher Warberry Road	C2		
Hillesdon Road	C2		
Kenwyn Road	C1		
Lower Warberry Road	C2		
Lucius Street	A2		
Lymington Road	B1		
Mallock Road	A2		
Market Street	B2		
Marnham Road	C1		
Meadfoot Lane	C3		
Meadfoot Road	C3		
Middle Warberry Road	C2		
Mill Lane	A2		
Newton Road	A1		
Old Mill Road	A2		
Old Mill Road	A3		
Parkfield Road	B1		
Parkhill Road	C3		
Prince's Road	C2		
Princes Road East	C2		
Quinta Road	C1		
Rathmore Road	A3		
Reddenhill Road	C1		
Rosehill Road	C2		
Sanford Road	A3		
Seaway Lane	A3		
Shedden Hill	B2		
Sherwell Lane	A2		
Solsbro Road	A3		
South Street	A2		
St. Lukes Road	B2		
St. Marychurch Road	B2		
St. Michael's Road	A1		
Stitchill Road	C2		
Strand	C3		
Teignmouth Road	A1		
The King's Drive	A2		

TORQUAY

0   400 yds
0   400m

Appears on main
map page 101

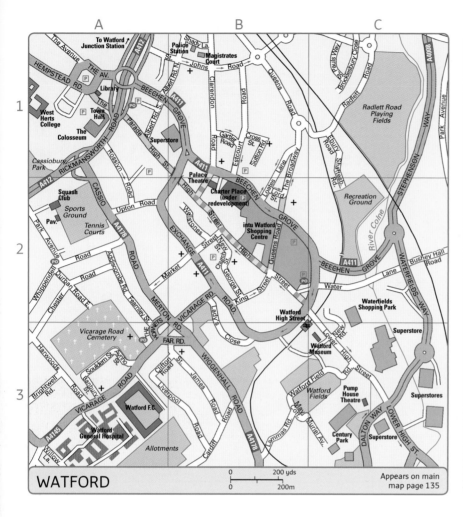

WATFORD

Addiscombe Road	A2
Albert Road North	A1
Albert Road South	A1
Aynho Street	A3
Banbury Street	A3
Beechen Grove	A1/C2
Brightwell Road	A3
Brocklesbury Close	C1
Bushey Hall Road	C2
Cardiff Road	B3
Cassio Road	A2
Chester Road	A2
Church Street	B2
Clarendon Road	B1
Clifton Road	A3
Cross Street	B1
Dalton Way	C3
Durban Road East	A2
Ebury Road	C1
Estcourt Road	B1
Exchange Road	A2
Farraline Road	A3
Fearnley Street	A2
Garlet Road	B1
George Street	B2
Harwoods Road	A3
Hempsted Road	A1
High Street	A1/B2
King Street	B2
Lady's Close	B2
Lammas Road	B3
Liverpool Road	A3
Loates Lane	B2
Lord Street	B2
Lower High Street	C3
Market Street	A2
May Cottages	B3
Merton Road	A2
Muriel Avenue	B3
New Road	C3
New Street	B2
Park Avenue	C1
Park Avenue	A2
Queens Road	B1/B2
Radlett Road	C1
Rickmansworth Road	A2
Rosslyn Road	A1
Shaftesbury Road	C1
Souldern Street	A3
St. James Road	B3
St. Johns Road	A1
St. Pauls Way	C1
Stephenson Way	C2
Sutton Road	B1
The Avenue	A1
The Broadway	B2
The Hornets	A3
The Parade	A1
Upton Road	A2
Vicarage Road	A3/B2
Water Lane	C2
Waterfields Way	C2
Watford Field Road	B3
Wellstones	B2
Whippendell Road	A2
Wiggenhall Road	B3
Willow Lane	A3

0 200 yds
0 200m

Appears on main
map page 135

Tourist Information Centre: Winter Gardens, Royal Parade
Tel: 01934 417117

Addicott Road	B3	Stafford Road	C2
Albert Avenue	B3	Station Road	B2
Alexandra Parade	B2	Sunnyside Road	B3
Alfred Street	B2	Swiss Road	C2
All Saints Road	B1	The Centre	B2
Amberey Road	C3	Trewartha Park	C1
Arundell Road	B1	Upper Church Road	A1
Ashcombe Gardens	C1	Walliscote Road	B3
Ashcombe Road	C2	Waterloo Street	B2
Atlantic Road	A1	Whitecross Road	B3
Baker Street	B2	Winterstoke Road	C3
Beach Road	B3		
Beaconsfield Road	B2		
Birnbeck Road	A1		
Boulevard	B2		
Brendon Avenue	C1		
Bridge Road	C2		
Brighton Road	B3		
Bristol Road	B1		
Carlton Street	B2		
Cecil Road	B1		
Clarence Road North	B3		
Clarendon Road	C2		
Clevedon Road	B3		
Clifton Road	B3		
Drove Road	C3		
Earlham Grove	C2		
Ellenborough Park North	B3		
Ellenborough Park South	B3		
Exeter Road	B3		
George Street	B2		
Gerard Road	B2		
Grove Park Road	B1		
High Street	B2		
Highbury Road	A1		
Hildesheim Bridge	B2		
Hill Road	C1		
Jubilee Road	B2		
Kenn Close	C3		
Kensington Road	C3		
Knightstone Road	A1		
Langford Road	C3		
Lewisham Grove	C2		
Locking Road	C2		
Lower Bristol Road	C1		
Lower Church Road	A1		
Manor Road	C1		
Marchfields Way	C3		
Marine Parade	B3		
Meadow Street	B2		
Milton Road	C2		
Montpelier	B1		
Neva Road	B2		
Norfolk Road	C3		
Oxford Street	B2		
Queen's Road	B1		
Rectors Way	C3		
Regent Street	B2		
Ridgeway Avenue	B3		
Royal Crescent	A1		
St. Paul's Road	B3		
Sandford Road	C2		
Severn Road	B3		
Shrubbery Road	A1		
South Road	A1		
Southside	B1		

WESTON-SUPER-MARE

0 400 yds
0 400m

Appears on main
map page 115

Tourist Information Centre: Guildhall, High Street
Tel: 01962 840500

Alison Way	A1	St. Peter Street	B2
Andover Road	A1	St. Swithun Street	B3
Archery Lane	A2	St. Thomas Street	B3
Bar End Road	C3	Saxon Road	B1
Barfield Close	C3	Silver Hill	B2
Beaufort Road	A3	Southgate Street	A3
Beggar's Lane	C2	Staple Gardens	B2
Blue Ball Hill	C2	Station Road	A1
Bridge Stret	C2	Step Terrace	A2
Broadway	B2	Stockbridge Road	A1
Canon Street	B3	Sussex Street	A2
Chesil Street	C3	Swan Lane	B1
Christchurch Road	A3	Symond's Street	B3
City Road	A1	Tanner Street	B2
Clifton Hill	A2	The Square	B2
Clifton Road	A1	Tower Street	A2
Clifton Terrace	A2	Union Street	C2
Colebrook Street	B2	Upper Brook Street	B2
College Street	B3	Upper High Street	A2
College Walk	B3	Wales Street	C2
Compton Road	A3	Water Lane	C2
Cranworth Road	A1	Wharf Hill	C3
Culver Road	B3	Worthy Lane	A1
Domum Road	C3		
Durngate	C2		
East Hill	C3		
Eastgate Street	C2		
Easton Lane	C1		
Ebden Road	C1		
Edgar Road	A3		
Elm Road	A1		
Fairfield Road	A1		
Friarsgate	B2		
Gordon Road	B1		
Great Minster Street	B2		
Hatherley Road	A1		
High Street	B2		
Hyde Abbey Road	B1		
Hyde Close	B1		
Hyde Street	B1		
Jewry Street	B2		
King Alfred Place	B1		
Kingsgate Street	B3		
Little Minster Street	B2		
Lower Brook Street	B2		
Magdalen Hill	C2		
Market Lane	B2		
Middle Brook Street	B2		
Middle Road	A2		
Milland Road	C3		
North Walls	A1		
Parchment Street	B2		
Park Avenue	B1		
Peninsula Square	A2		
Portal Road	C3		
Quarry Road	C3		
Romans' Road	A3		
Romsey Road	A2		
St. Catherine's Road	C3		
St. Cross Road	A3		
St. George's Street	B2		
St. James Lane	A2		
St. James Villas	A3		
St. John's Street	C2		
St. Michael's Road	A3		
St. Paul's Hill	A1		

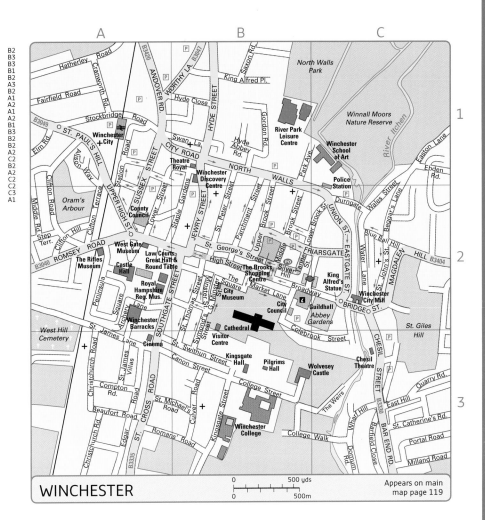

WINCHESTER

0   500 yds
0   500m

Appears on main
map page 119

Tourist Information Centre: Old Booking Hall, Central Station
Tel: 01753 743900

Adelaide Square	C3
Albert Street	A2
Alexandra Road	B3
Alma Road	B2/B3
Arthur Road	B2
Barry Avenue	B1
Bexley Street	B2
Bolton Avenue	B3
Bolton Crescent	B3
Bolton Road	B3
Bulkeley Avenue	A3
Castle Hill	C2
Charles Street	B2
Clarence Crescent	B2
Clarence Road	A2
College Crescent	A3
Dagmar Road	B2
Datchet Road	C1
Frances Road	B3
Goslar Way	A2
Goswell Road	B2
Green Lane	A2
Grove Road	B2
Helston Lane	A2
High Street (Eton)	B1
High Street (Windsor)	C2
Imperial Road	A3
King Edward VII Avenue	C1
Kings Road	C3
Meadow Lane	B1
Mill Lane	A1
Osborne Road	B3
Oxford Road	B2
Park Street	C2
Parsonage Lane	A2
Peascod Street	B2
Peel Close	A3
Princess Avenue	A3
Romney Lock Road	C1
St. Leonards Road	B3
St. Marks Road	B2
Sheet Street	C2
South Meadow Lane	B1
Springfield Road	A3
Stovell Road	A1
Thames Street	C1
The Long Walk	C3
Upcroft	A3
Vansittart Road	B2
Victoria Street	B2
Victor Road	B3
Westmead	A2
Windsor & Eton Relief Road	A2
York Avenue	A3
York Road	A3

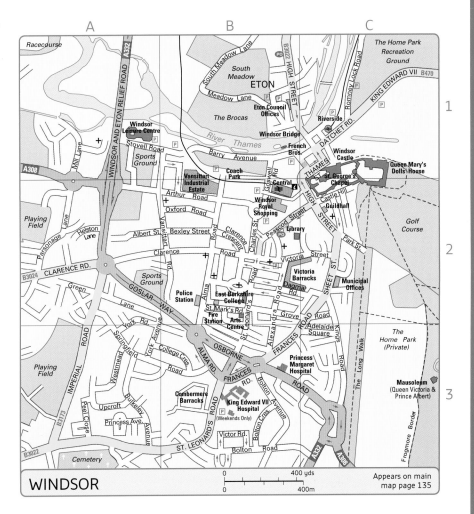

WINDSOR

0   400 yds
0   400m

Appears on main
map page 135

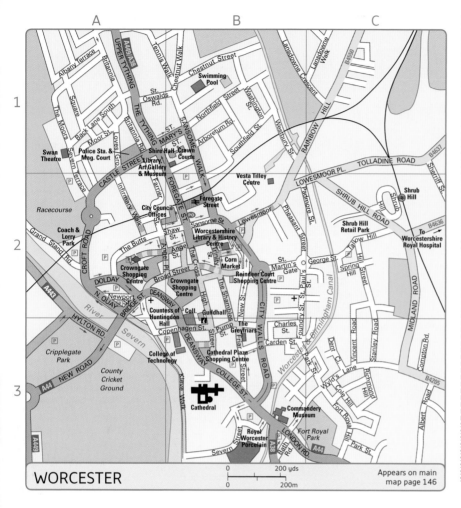

Tourist Information Centre: The Guildhall, High Street
Tel: 01905 726311

Albany Terrace	A1	Sherriff Street	C1
Albert Road	C3	Shrub Hill	C2
Angel Place	A2	Shrub Hill Road	C2
Angel Street	B2	Sidbury	B3
Arboretum Road	B1	Southfield Street	B1
Back Lane South	A1	Spring Hill	C2
Bath Road	B3	Stanley Road	C3
Bridge Street	A2	Tallow Hill	C2
Britannia Road	A1	Tennis Walk	A1
Britannia Square	A1	The Butts	A2
Broad Street	A2	The Cross	B2
Carden Street	B3	The Moors	A1
Castle Street	A2	The Shambles	B2
Charles Street	B3	The Tything	A1
Chestnut Street	B1	Tolladine Road	C1
Chestnut Walk	B1	Trinity Street	B2
City Walls Road	B2	Upper Tything	A1
Cole Hill	C3	Vincent Road	C3
College Street	B3	Washington Street	B1
Compton Road	C3	Westbury Street	B1
Copenhagen Street	A3	Wyld's Lane	C3
Croft Road	A2		
Deansway	A2		
Dent Close	C3		
Dolday	A2		
Farrier Street	A2		
Foregate Street	B2		
Fort Royal Hill	C3		
Foundry Street	B3		
Friar Street	B3		
George Street	C2		
Grand Stand Road	A2		
High Street	B2		
Hill Street	C2		
Hylton Road	A2		
Infirmary Walk	A2		
Kleve Walk	B3		
Lansdowne Crescent	B1		
Lansdowne Walk	C1		
London Road	B3		
Loves Grove	A1		
Lowesmoor	B2		
Lowesmoor Place	B2		
Midland Road	C3		
Moor Street	A1		
Newport Street	A2		
New Road	A3		
New Street	B2		
Northfield Street	B1		
North Quay	A2		
Padmore Street	B2		
Park Street	B3		
Park Street	C3		
Pheasant Street	B3		
Pump Street	B3		
Rainbow Hill	B1		
Richmond Hill	C3		
St. Martin's Gate	B2		
St. Mary's Street	A1		
St. Oswalds Road	A1		
St. Paul's Street	B2		
Sansome Street	B2		
Sansome Walk	B1		
Severn Street	B3		
Severn Terrace	A1		
Shaw Street	A2		

WORCESTER

Appears on main map page 146

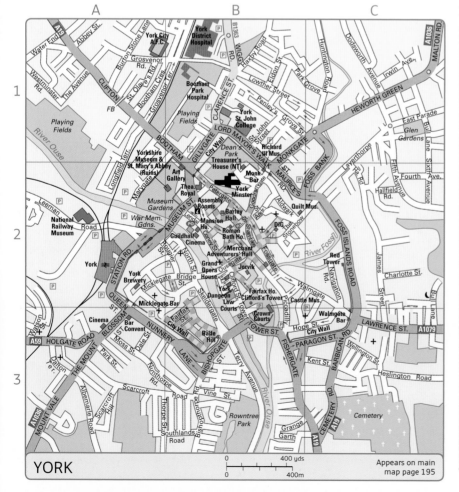

Tourist Information Centre: 1 Museum Street
Tel: 01904 550099

Abbey Street	A1	Paragon Street	B3
Albermarle Road	A3	Park Grove	B1
Aldwark	B2	Park Street	A3
Barbican Road	C3	Penley's Grove Street	B1
Bishopthorpe Road	B3	Petergate	B2
Bishopgate Street	B3	Piccadilly	B2
Blossom Street	A3	Queen Street	A2
Bootham	A1	Rougier Street	A2
Bootham Crescent	A1	St. Andrewgate	B2
Bridge Street	B2	St. John Street	B1
Bull Lane	C1/C2	St. Maurice's Road	B2
Burton Stone Lane	A1	St. Olave's Road	A1
Cemetery Road	C3	Scarcroft Hill	A3
Charlotte Street	C2	Scarcroft Road	A3
Church Street	B2	Shambles	B2
Clarence Street	B1	Sixth Avenue	C1
Clifford Street	B2	Skeldergate	B2
Clifton	A1	Southlands Road	A3
Coney Street	B2	Station Road	A2
Dale Street	A3	Terry Avenue	B3
Dalton Terrace	A3	The Avenue	A1
Dodsworth Avenue	C1	The Mount	A3
East Parade	C1	The Stonebow	B2
Eldon Street	B1	Thorpe Street	A3
Fairfax Street	B3	Tower Street	B2
Fifth Avenue	C1	Vine Street	B3
Fishergate	B3	Walmgate	B2
Foss Bank	C2	Water End	A1
Fossgate	B2	Watson Street	A3
Foss Islands Road	C2	Wellington Street	C3
Fourth Avenue	C1	Westminster Road	A1
Gillygate	B1	Wigginton Road	B1
Goodramgate	B2		
Grange Garth	B3		
Grosvenor Road	A1		
Grosvenor Terrace	A1		
Hallfield Road	C2		
Haxby Road	B1		
Heslington Road	C3		
Heworth Green	C1		
Holgate Road	A3		
Hope Street	B3		
Huntington Road	C1		
Irwin Avenue	C1		
James Street	B2		
Kent Street	C3		
Lawrence Street	C3		
Layerthorpe	C2		
Leeman Road	A2		
Lendal	B2		
Longfield Terrace	A2		
Lord Mayor's Walk	B1		
Lowther Street	B1		
Malton Road	C1		
Marygate	A2		
Maurices Road	B2		
Micklegate	A2		
Monkgate	B1		
Moss Street	A3		
Mount Vale	A3		
Museum Street	B2		
Navigation Road	C2		
North Street	B2		
Nunnery Lane	A3		
Nunthorpe Road	A3		
Ousegate	B2		

YORK

Appears on main map page 195

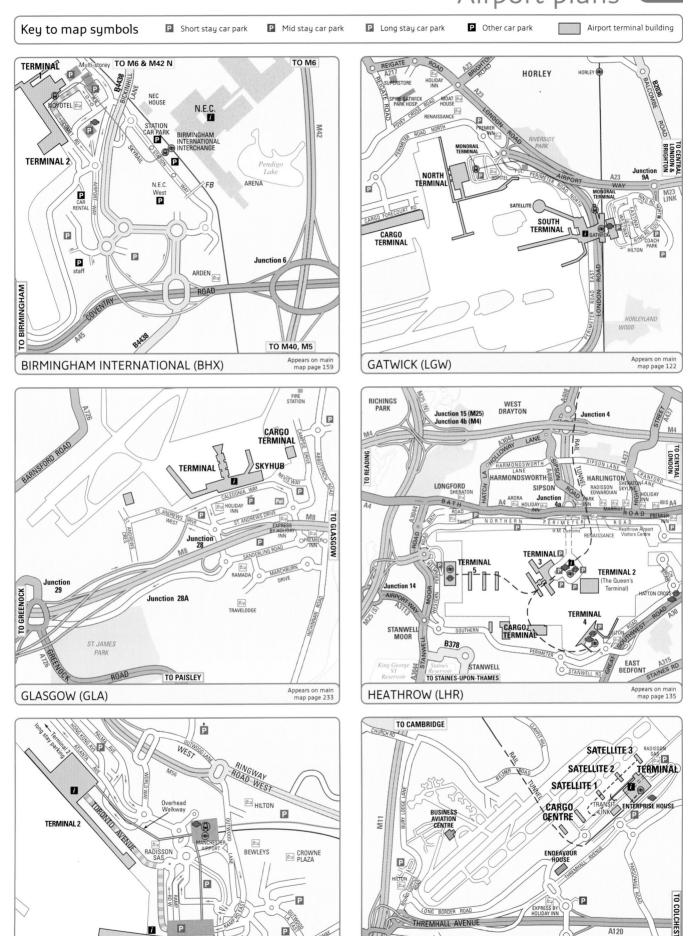

Key to map symbols

🅿 Short stay car park 🅿 Mid stay car park 🅿 Long stay car park 🅿 Other car park ▭ Airport terminal building

BIRMINGHAM INTERNATIONAL (BHX)
Appears on main map page 159

GATWICK (LGW)
Appears on main map page 122

GLASGOW (GLA)
Appears on main map page 233

HEATHROW (LHR)
Appears on main map page 135

MANCHESTER (MAN)
Appears on main map page 184

STANSTED (STN)
Appears on main map page 150

Symbols used on the map

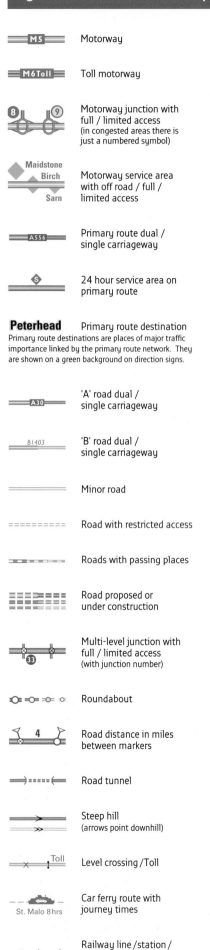

M5	Motorway
M6Toll	Toll motorway
8 ... 9	Motorway junction with full / limited access (in congested areas there is just a numbered symbol)
Maidstone / Birch / Sarn	Motorway service area with off road / full / limited access
A556	Primary route dual / single carriageway
S	24 hour service area on primary route
Peterhead	Primary route destination

Primary route destinations are places of major traffic importance linked by the primary route network. They are shown on a green background on direction signs.

A30	'A' road dual / single carriageway
B1403	'B' road dual / single carriageway
	Minor road
	Road with restricted access
	Roads with passing places
	Road proposed or under construction
33	Multi-level junction with full / limited access (with junction number)
	Roundabout
4	Road distance in miles between markers
	Road tunnel
	Steep hill (arrows point downhill)
Toll	Level crossing / Toll
St. Malo 8hrs	Car ferry route with journey times
	Railway line / station / tunnel
Wales Coast Path	National Trail / Long Distance Route

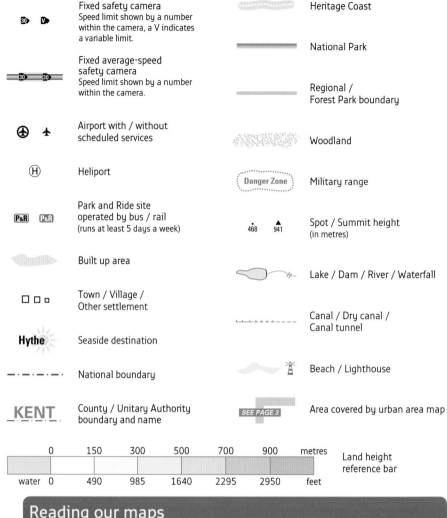

30 V	Fixed safety camera Speed limit shown by a number within the camera, a V indicates a variable limit.
30 ... 30	Fixed average-speed safety camera Speed limit shown by a number within the camera.
✈ ✈	Airport with / without scheduled services
H	Heliport
P&R P&R	Park and Ride site operated by bus / rail (runs at least 5 days a week)
	Built up area
□ □ ▫	Town / Village / Other settlement
Hythe	Seaside destination
— · — · —	National boundary
KENT	County / Unitary Authority boundary and name

	Heritage Coast
	National Park
	Regional / Forest Park boundary
	Woodland
Danger Zone	Military range
·468 ▲941	Spot / Summit height (in metres)
	Lake / Dam / River / Waterfall
	Canal / Dry canal / Canal tunnel
⌂	Beach / Lighthouse
SEE PAGE 3	Area covered by urban area map

metres	0	150	300	500	700	900	metres
	water						
feet	0	490	985	1640	2295	2950	feet

Land height reference bar

Reading our maps

Safety Camera
The number inside the camera shows the speed limit at the camera location.

Multi-level junctions
Non-motorway junctions where slip roads are used to access the main roads.

Distances
Blue numbers give distances in miles between junctions shown with a blue marker.

Park & Ride
Sites are shown that operate at least 5 days a week. Bus operated sites have a yellow symbol and rail operated sites a pink symbol.

Motorway service area

World Heritage site
Places of interest defined by UNESCO as special on a world scale.

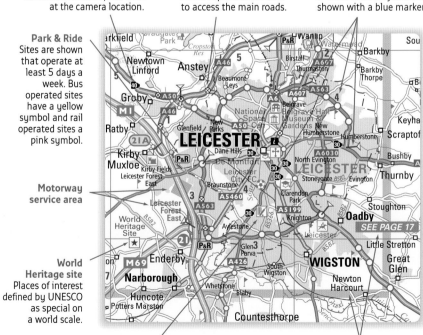

Places of interest
Blue symbols indicate places of interest. See the section at the bottom of the page for the different types of feature represented on the map.

More detailed maps
Green boxes indicate busy built-up-areas. More detailed mapping is available.

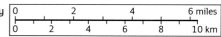
Places of interest

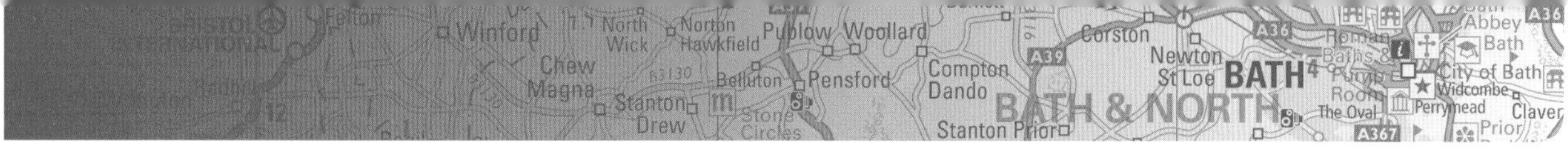

A selection of tourist detail is shown on the mapping. It is advisable to check with the local tourist information centre regarding opening times and facilities available.

Any of the following symbols may appear on the map in maroon ★ which indicates that the site has World Heritage status.

i	Tourist information centre (open all year)
i	Tourist information centre (open seasonally)
�🏛	Ancient monument
🐟	Aquarium
🌉	Aqueduct / Viaduct
🌳	Arboretum
⚔ 1643	Battlefield
⚑	Blue flag beach
▲ 🚐	Camp site / Caravan site
🏰	Castle
🕳	Cave
🌲	Country park
🏏	County cricket ground
🍶	Distillery
✝	Ecclesiastical feature
🏟	Event venue
🐄	Farm park
❀	Garden
⛳	Golf course
🏠	Historic house
⚓	Historic ship
⚽	Major football club
£	Major shopping centre / Outlet village
⌛	Major sports venue
🏎	Motor racing circuit
🚵	Mountain bike trail
🏛	Museum / Art gallery
🐦	Nature reserve (NNR indicates a National Nature Reserve)
🏇	Racecourse
🚂	Rail Freight Terminal
⛷ 🎿	Ski slope (artificial / natural)
🐾	Spotlight nature reserve (Best sites for access to nature)
🚂	Steam railway centre / preserved railway
🏄	Surfing beach
🎡	Theme park
🎓	University
🍇	Vineyard
🐘	Wildlife park / Zoo
📷	Wildlife Trust nature reserve
★	Other interesting feature
(NT) (NTS)	National Trust / National Trust for Scotland property

Map scale

A scale bar appears at the bottom of every page to help with distances.

0		2		4		6 miles
0	2	4	6	8		10 km

England, Wales & Southern Scotland are at a scale of 1:200,000 or 3.2 miles to 1 inch Northern Scotland is at a scale of 1:263,158 or 4.2 miles to 1 inch.

Map pages

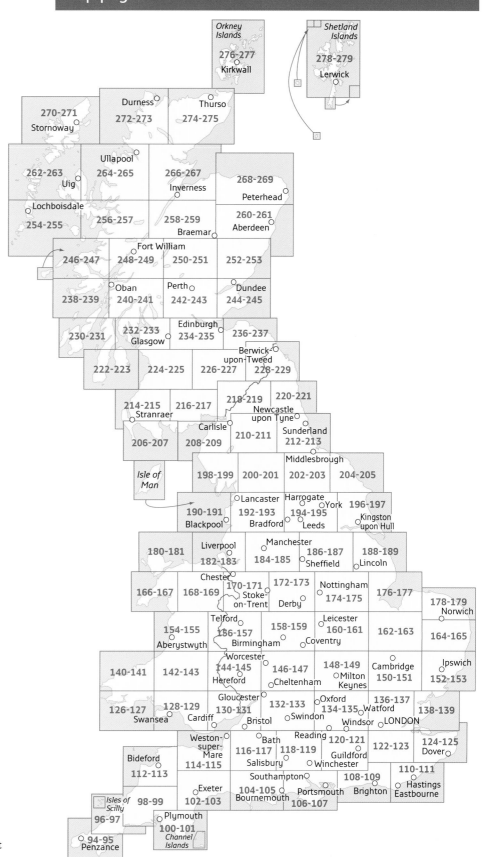

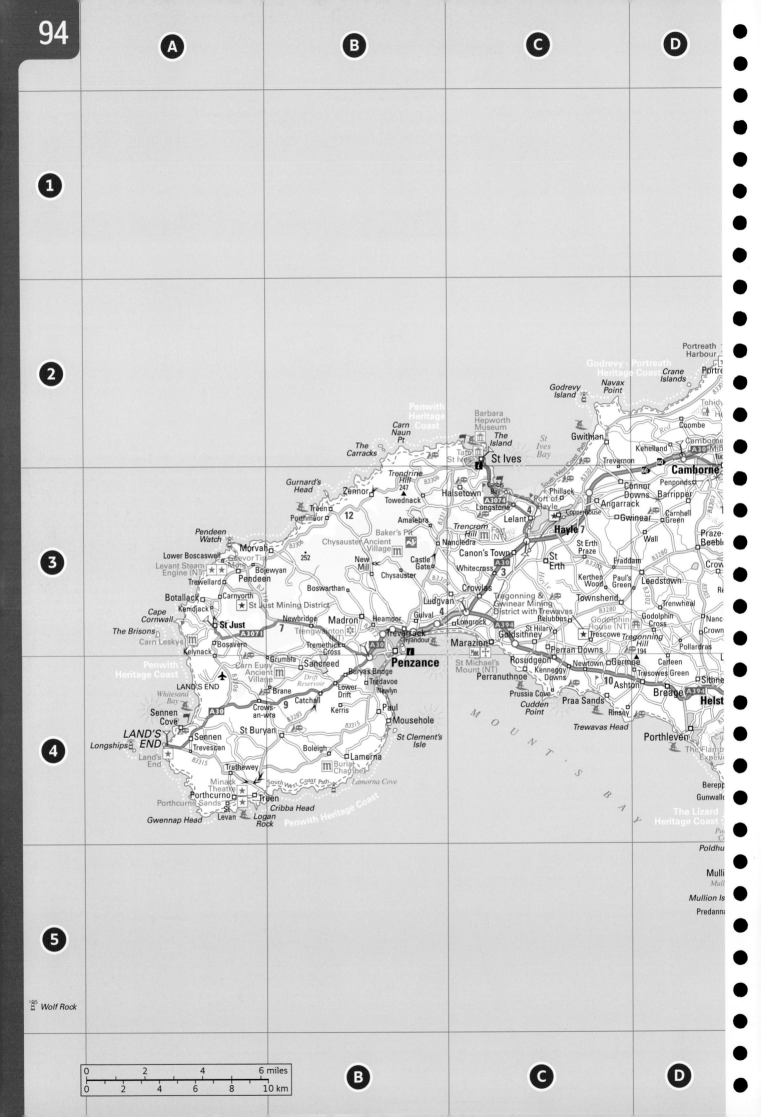

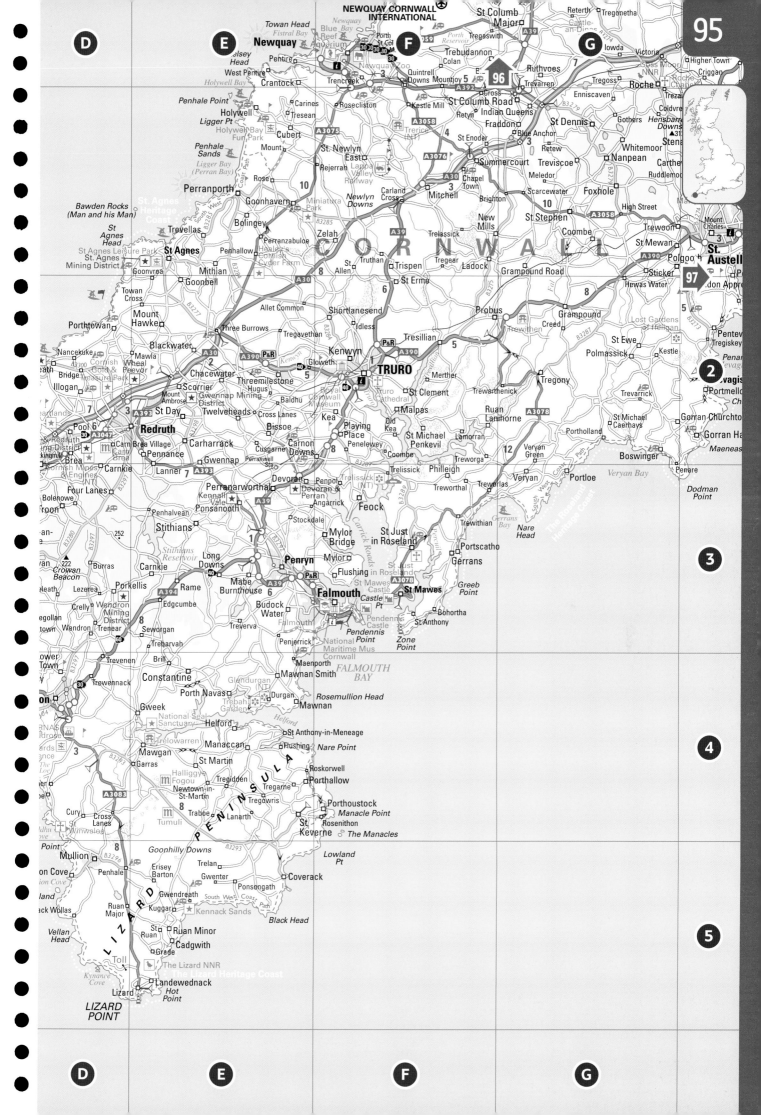

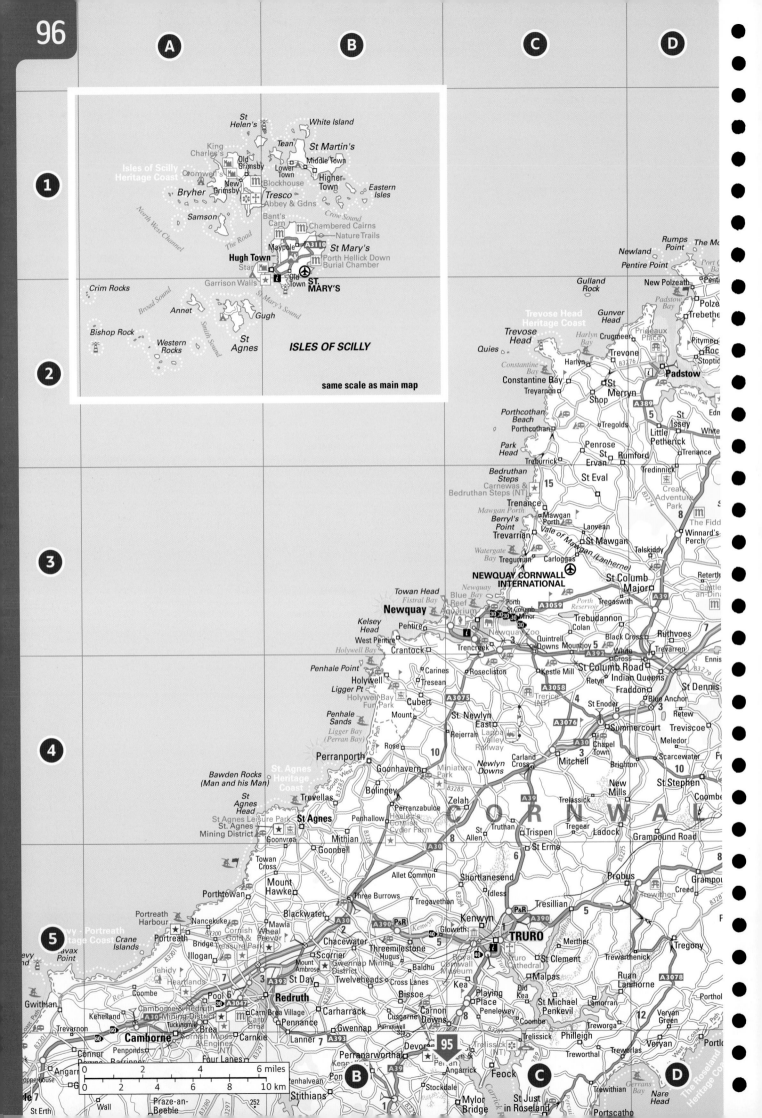

A   B   C   D

1

2

St Helen's
White Island
Tean
St Martin's
King Charles's
Cromwell's   Old Grimsby   Middle Town
New Grimsby   Lower Town   Higher Town
Blockhouse   Town
Bryher   Tresco   Eastern Isles
Abbey & Gdns
Samson   Bant's Carn   Crow Sound
Chambered Cairns
Nature Trails
Maypole   St Mary's
Hugh Town   Porth Hellick Down Burial Chamber
Star
Garrison Walls   Old Town   ST. MARY'S
Isles of Scilly Heritage Coast
North West Channel
The Road
St Mary's Sound
Crim Rocks
Broad Sound
Annet   Gugh
Bishop Rock   Western Rocks   St Agnes   Smith Sound
ISLES OF SCILLY

same scale as main map

Rumps Point   The Mo
Newland   Port
Pentire Point   Pent
Gulland Rock   New Polzeath   Polze
Trebethe
Trevose Head Heritage Coast   Gunver Head   Padstow Bay
Trevose Head   Harlyn Bay   Crugmeer   Prideaux Place   Pitym
Quies   Constantine Bay   Harlyn   Trevone   Roc
Constantine Bay   St Merryn   Stoptic
Treyarnon   Shop   Padstow
Porthcothan Beach   Tregolds   St Issey   Edn
Porthcothan   Penrose   Little   White
St Ervan   Rumford   Petherick
Park Head   Treburrick   Trenance
Tredinnick
Bedruthan Steps   St Eval   Crealy Adventure Park
Carnewas & Bedruthan Steps (NT)   15
Trenance
Mawgan Porth   Winnard's
Mawgan Porth   Lanvean   The Fidd   Perch
Berryl's Point   Vale of Mawgan (Lanhernel)   St Mawgan   Talskiddy
Trevarrian   Tregurrian   Carloggas
Watergate Bay   NEWQUAY CORNWALL INTERNATIONAL   St Columb Major   Reterth   7
Castle an-Dina

3

Towan Head   Newquay   Porth   Porth Reservoir   Tregaswith
Fistral Bay   Blue Bay   St Columb   A3059   Trebudannon
Newquay   Aquarium   Minor   Colan   Black Cross   Ruthvoes
Kelsey Head   Pentire   30 30   30   Quintrell Downs   Mountjoy   5   Indian Queens   St Dennis
West Pentire   Newquay Zoo   3   Retyn   Trevarren   Enni
Holywell Bay   Crantock   Trencreek   A3058   Fraddon   Blue Anchor
Penhale Point   Carines   Rosecliston   Kestle Mill   Trerice   4   St Enoder   Retew
Holywell   Tresean   A3075   (NT)   A3076   Summercourt   Treviscoe
Ligger Pt   Cubert   St Newlyn   Lappa   A30   Chapel   Scarcewater
Holywell Bay Fun Park   Mount   East   Valley   Carland   Meledor
Penhale Sands   Rejerrah   Railway   3   Town   10
Ligger Bay   Rose   Cross   Mitchell   Brighton   St Stephen
(Perran Bay)   Newlyn   New   Coombe
Perranporth   Goonhavern   Downs   Mills
Bawden Rocks   Miniature   Carland Cross   Trelassick
(Man and his Man)   Bolingey   Park   Zelah   A39   Tregear   Ladock   Grampound Road
St Agnes Heritage Coast   B3285   CORNWALL   Truthan   Trispen
St Agnes Head   Trevellas   Peranzabuloe   Tregavethan   St Erme   Probus   Grampou
St Agnes Leisure Park   Healey's Cornish Cyder Farm   8   St Allen   Creed   Trewithen
St. Agnes Mining District   St Agnes   Penhallow   Truthan   Idless   5   B3275
Goonvrea   Mithian   Shortlanesend   Fal
Goonbell   Allet Common   Kenwyn   A390   Treal

4

5

Portreath Harbour   Nancekuke   Mawla   Three Burrows   A30   P&R   Kenwyn   A390   Merther   Tregony
Crane Islands   Portreath   Wheal Peevor   Blackwater   P&R   Gloweth   TRURO   Trewarthenick
Portreath   Cornish Gold &   Chacewater   Threemilestone   Hugus   Truro Museum   St Clement   Ruan
Illogan   Treasure Park   Scorrier   Baldhu   40   Cathedral   Malpas   Lanihorne
Tehidy   Mount   Gwennap Mining   Cross Lanes   Old   Trelissick   Portho
Gwithian   Headlands   Ambrose   District   Bissoe   Kea   Kea   (NT)   A3078
Coombe   St Day   Twelveheads   Playing   St Michael   Porth
Camborne & Redruth   Pool   Redruth   Carharrack   Carnon   Place   Penkevil   Lamorran
Kehelland   Mining District   Carn   Cusgarne   Downs   St   Coombe   Veryan   12
Trevarnon   Tuckingmill   Brea Village   Pennance   Gwennap   Perranwell Sta   8   Penelewey   Old   Trewornan   Green
Camborne   Brea   Carnkie   Lanner   A393   Sta   Feock   Kea   Trelissick   Philleigh   Treworlas   Veryan
Connor   Penponds   Cornish Mines   Four Lanes   7   Perranarworthal   Devor   95   Trelissick   Veryan
Downs   Barripper   & Engines   Kenw   (NT)   Gerrans   Nare
Angar   Angarrick   Feock   Bay   Head
Me 7   Wall   Praze-an-Beeble   3297   252   Stithians   Stockdale   St Just in Roseland   Portscatho
Copperhouse   Mylor Bridge   Trewithian   Portholl
Gwithan   Penhalvean   Pon   1   Angarrick   Trewithen

0   2   4   6 miles
0   2   4   6   8   10 km

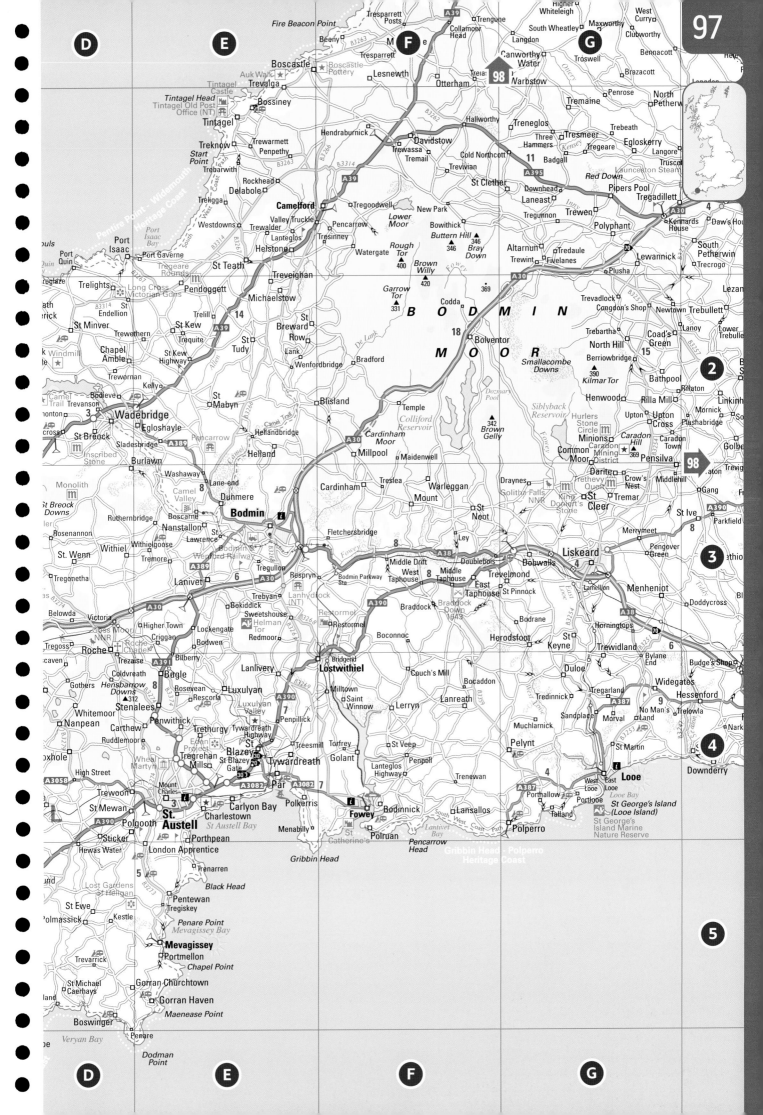

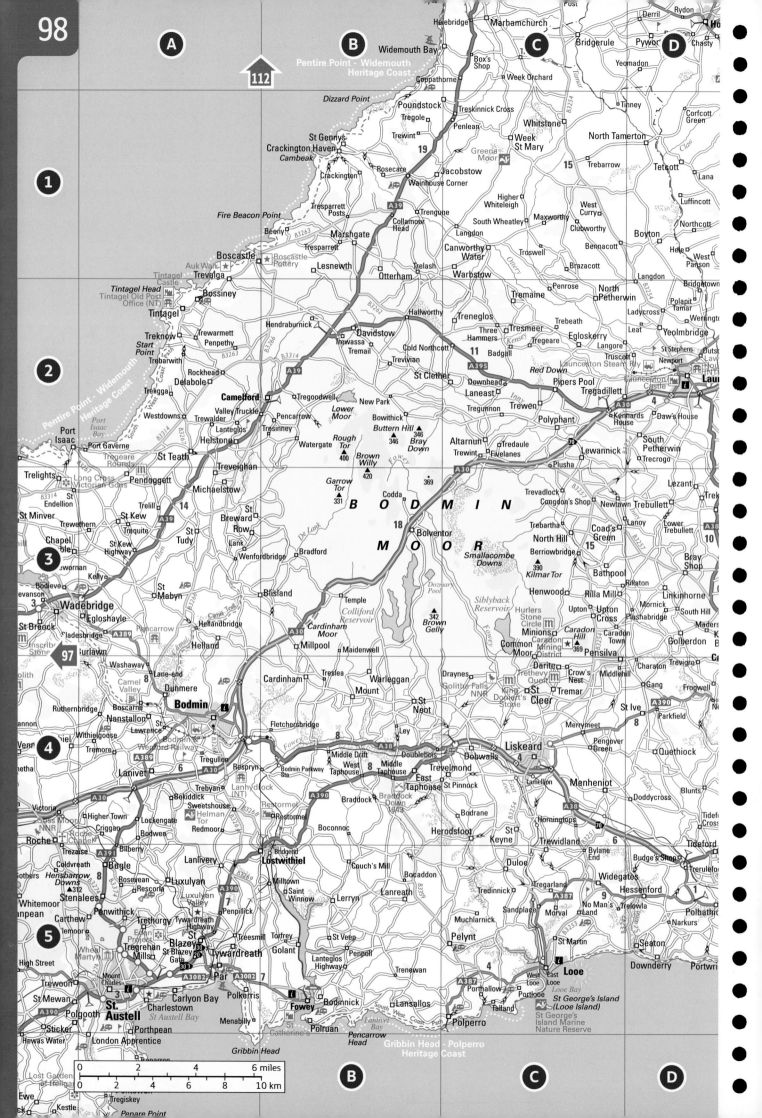

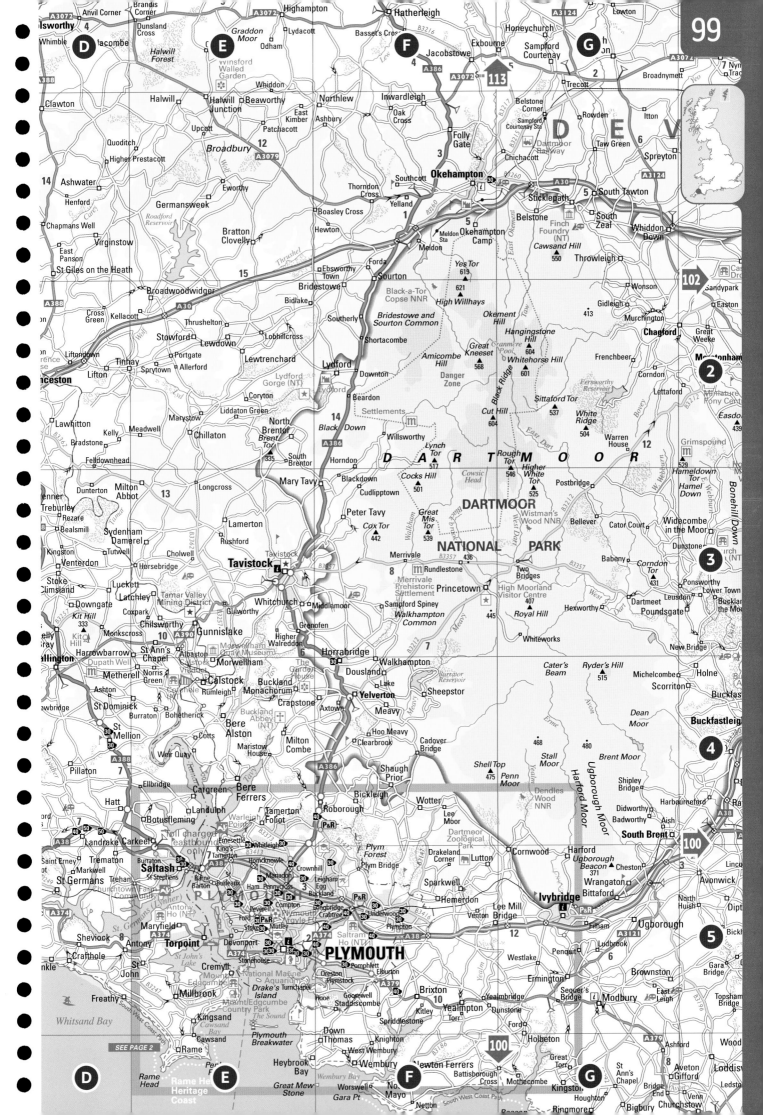

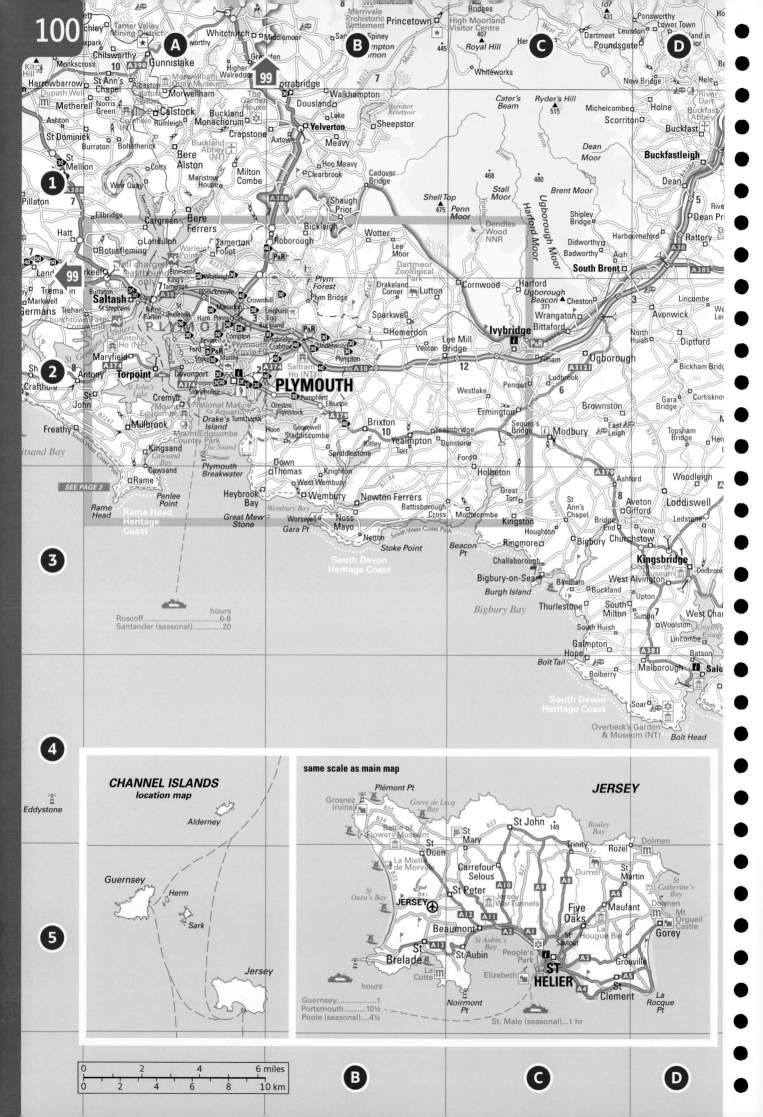

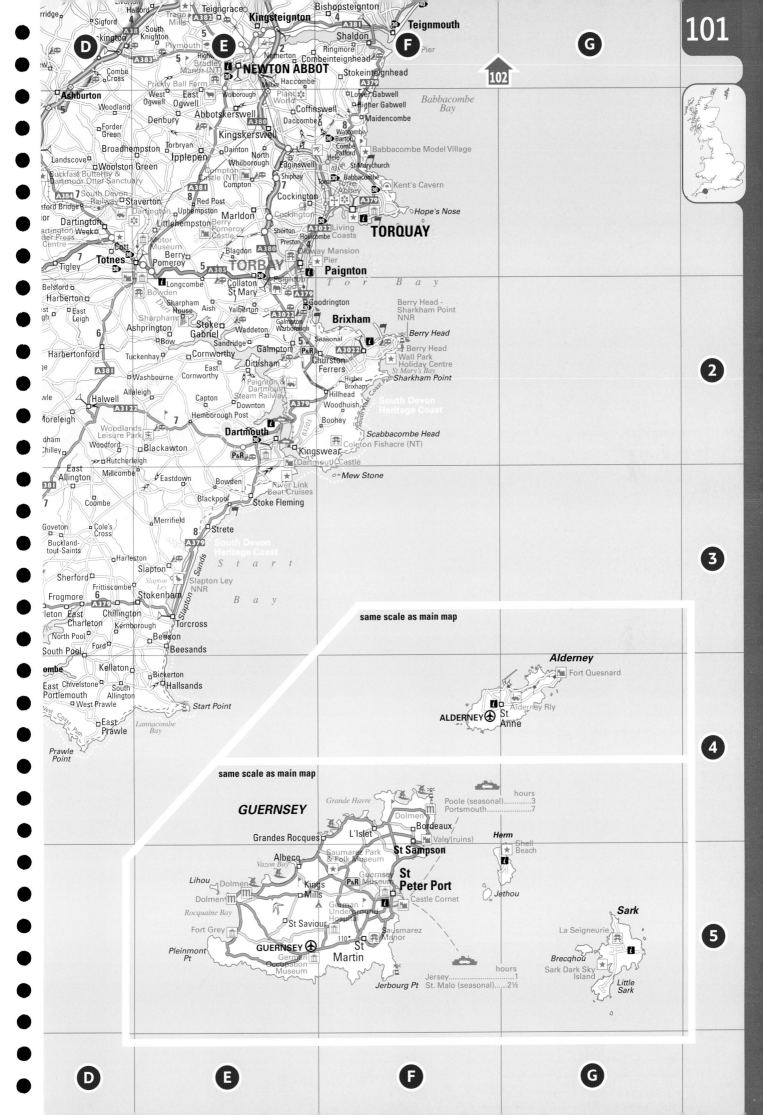

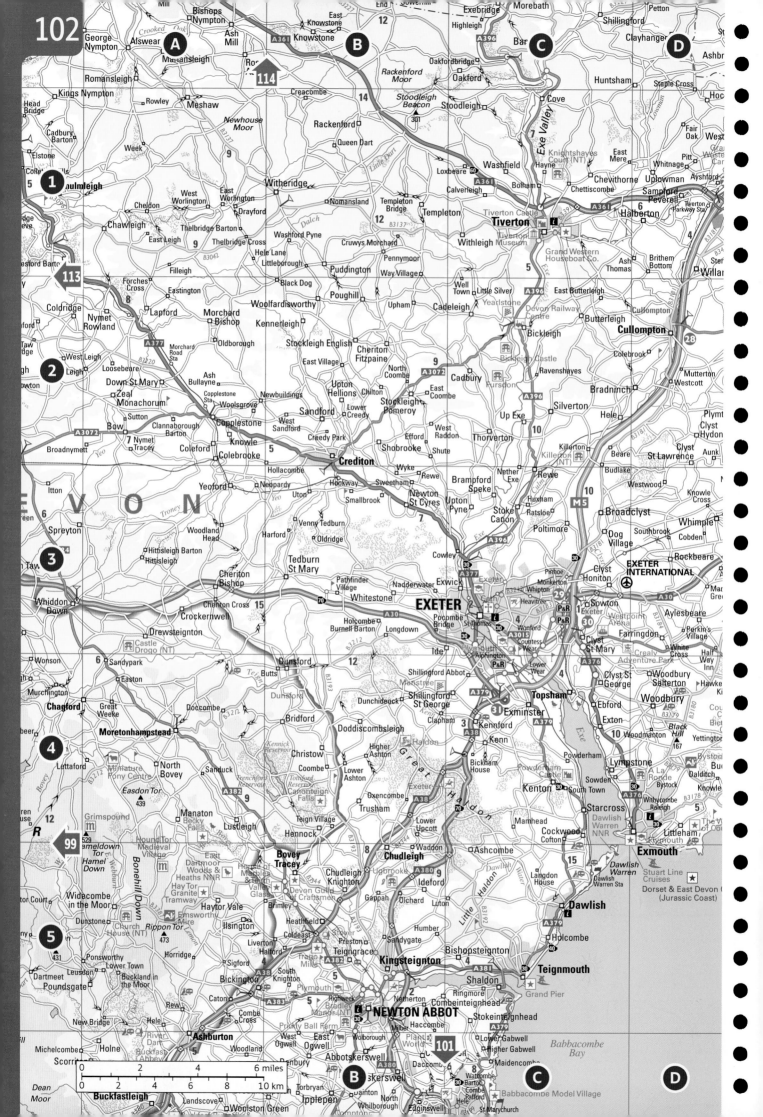

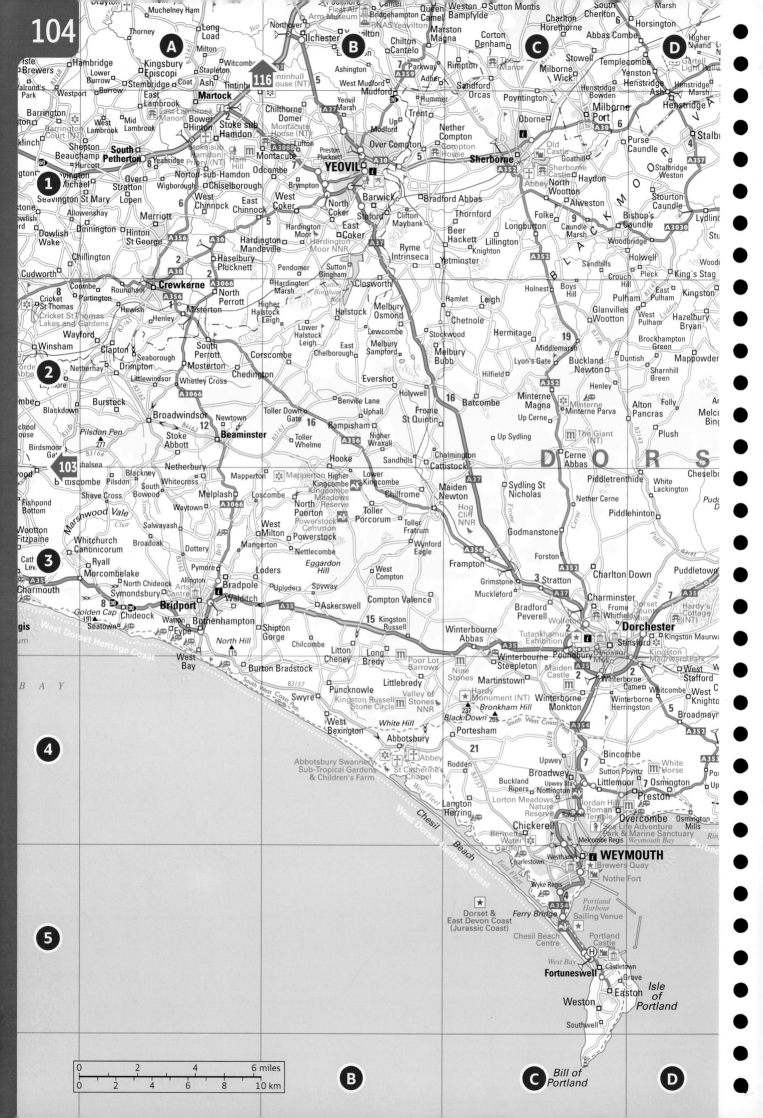

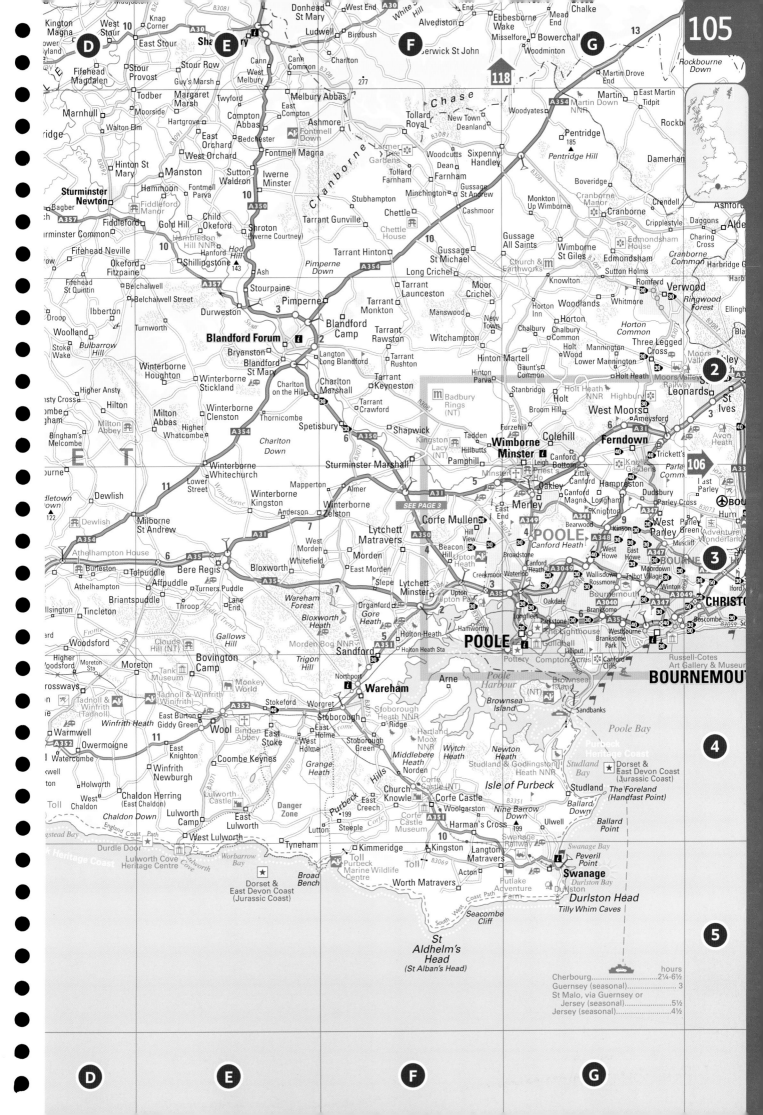

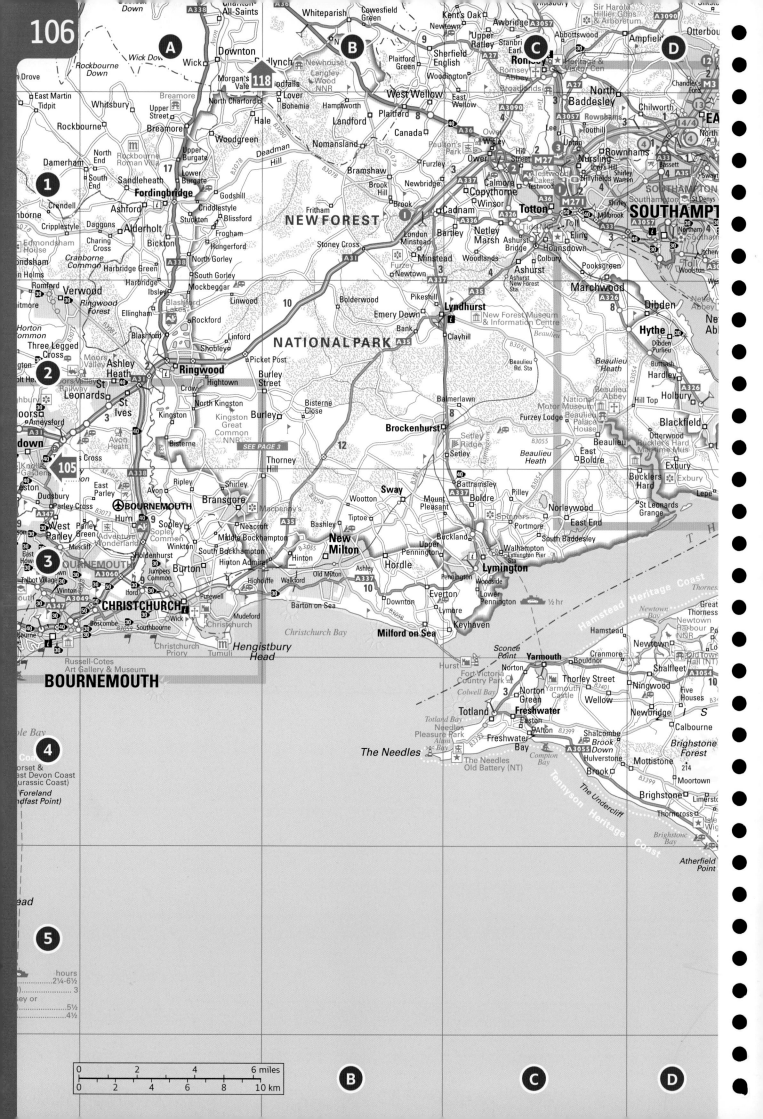

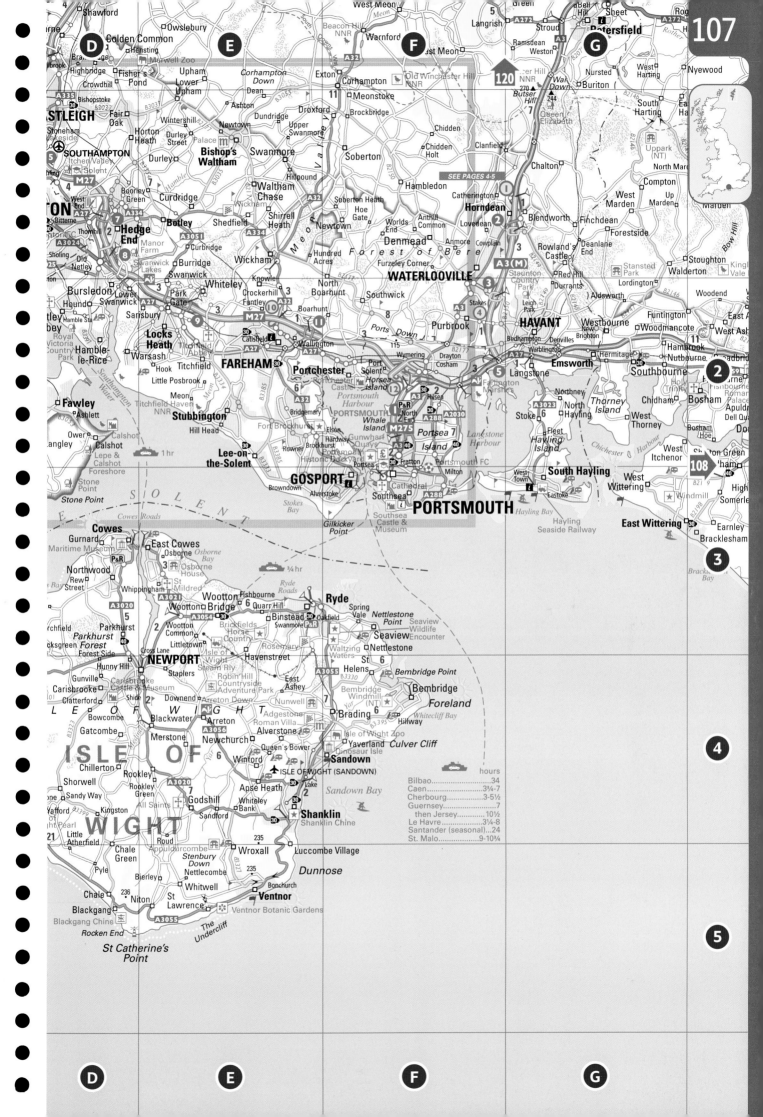

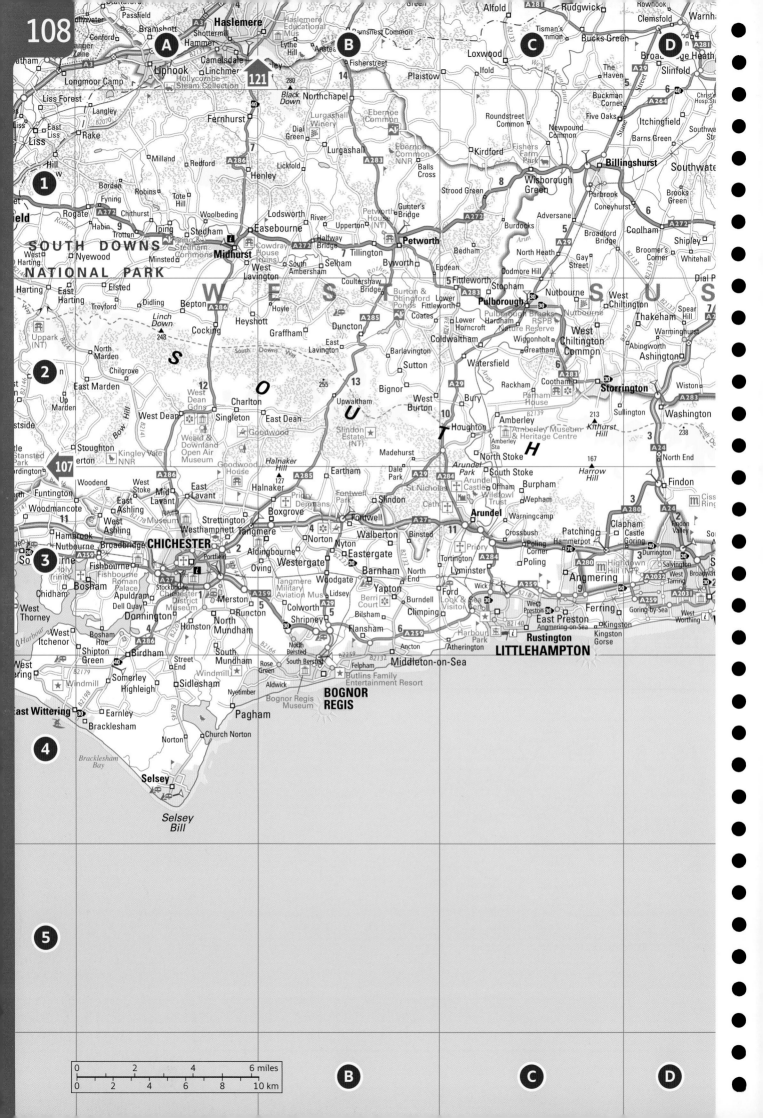

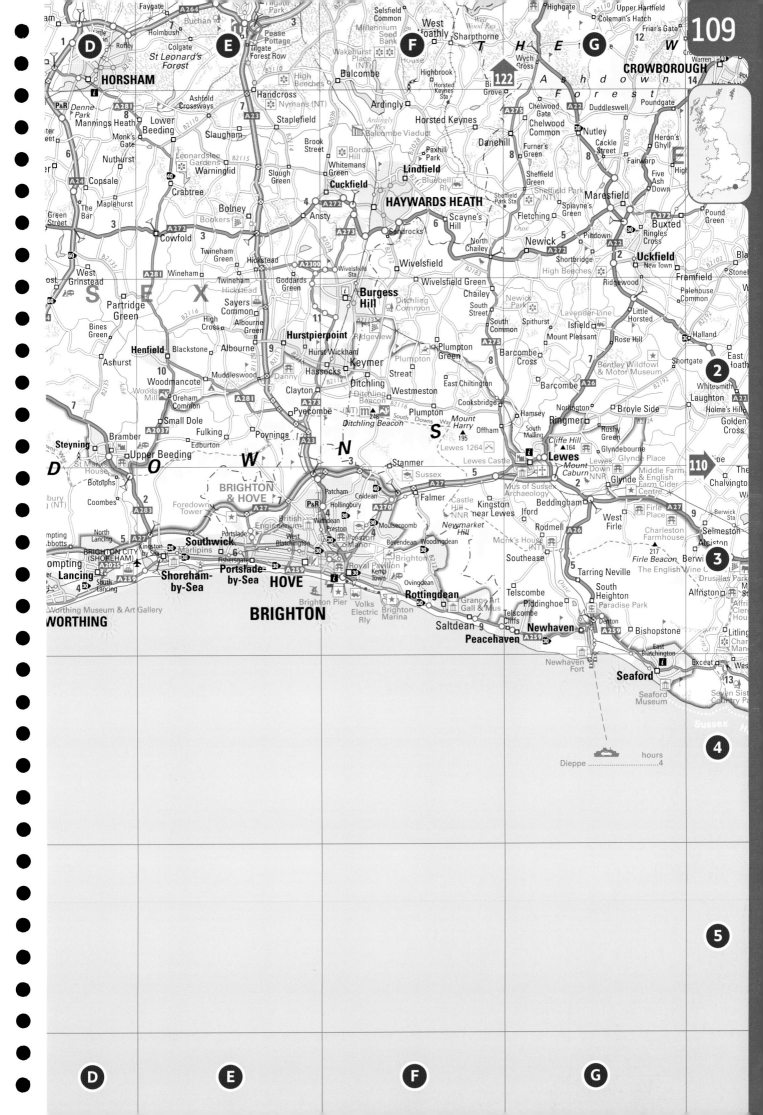

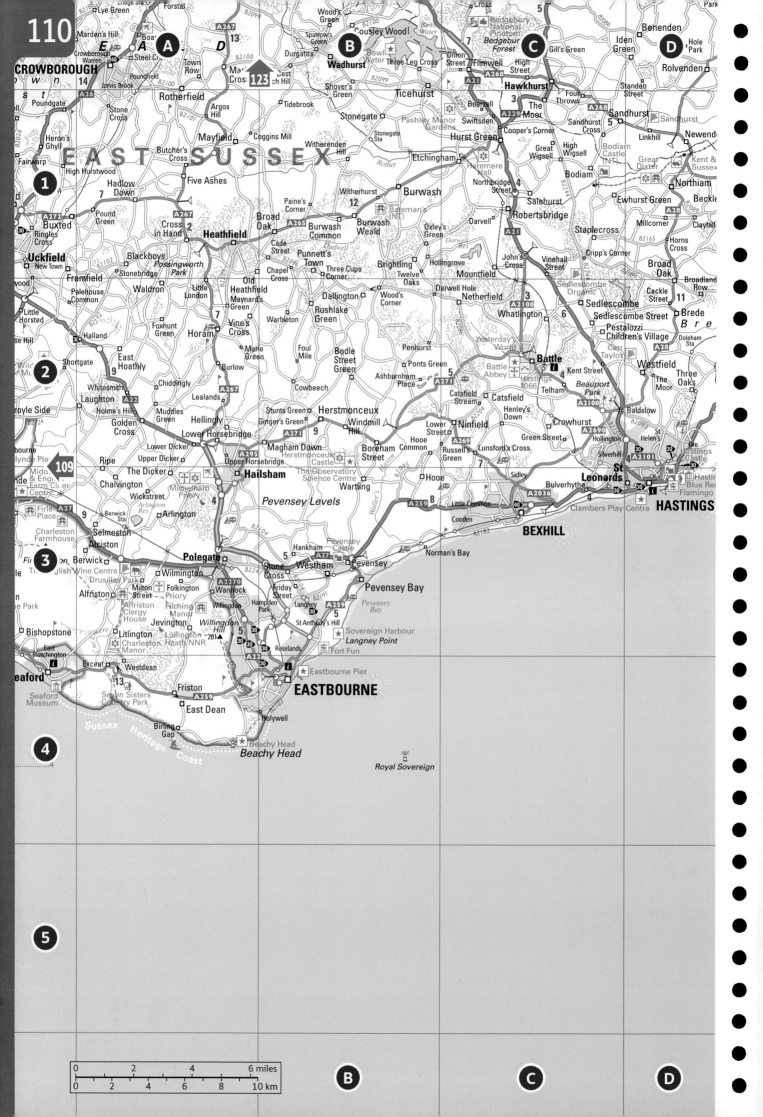

Channel Tunnel terminal maps

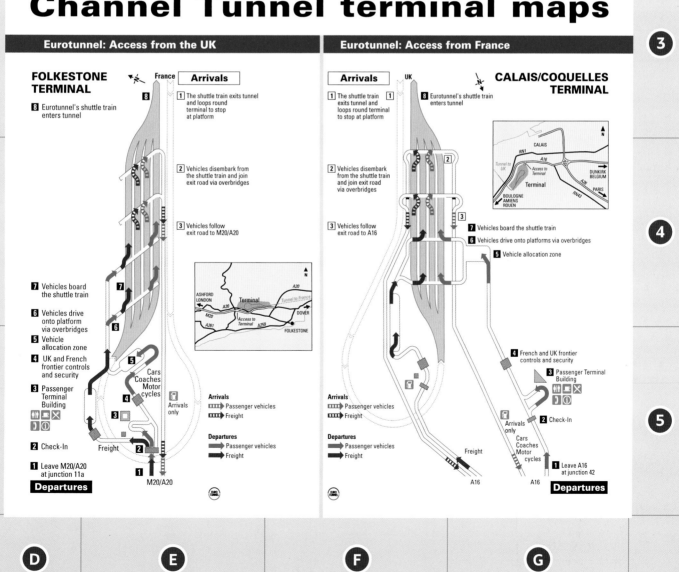

Eurotunnel: Access from the UK

FOLKESTONE TERMINAL

France

Arrivals

8 Eurotunnel's shuttle train enters tunnel

1 The shuttle train exits tunnel and loops round terminal to stop at platform

2 Vehicles disembark from the shuttle train and join exit road via overbridges

3 Vehicles follow exit road to M20/A20

7 Vehicles board the shuttle train

6 Vehicles drive onto platform via overbridges

5 Vehicle allocation zone

4 UK and French frontier controls and security

3 Passenger Terminal Building

2 Check-In

1 Leave M20/A20 at junction 11a

Departures

ASHFORD LONDON
A20
Terminal
Tunnel to France
M20
Access to Terminal
A259
DOVER
A261
FOLKESTONE

Cars Coaches Motor cycles

Freight

Arrivals only

M20/A20

Arrivals
▭▭▭ Passenger vehicles
▭▭▭ Freight

Departures
➡ Passenger vehicles
➡ Freight

Eurotunnel: Access from France

Arrivals

UK

CALAIS/COQUELLES TERMINAL

N

1 The shuttle train exits tunnel and loops round terminal to stop at platform

8 Eurotunnel's shuttle train enters tunnel

2 Vehicles disembark from the shuttle train and join exit road via overbridges

3 Vehicles follow exit road to A16

N
CALAIS
RN1
A16
Tunnel to UK
Access to Terminal
Terminal
DUNKIRK BELGIUM
A26
PARIS
BOULOGNE AMIENS ROUEN
RN43

7 Vehicles board the shuttle train

6 Vehicles drive onto platforms via overbridges

5 Vehicle allocation zone

4 French and UK frontier controls and security

3 Passenger Terminal Building

2 Check-In

Arrivals only

Cars Coaches Motor cycles

Freight

1 Leave A16 at junction 42

A16

A16

Arrivals
▭▭▭ Passenger vehicles
▭▭▭ Freight

Departures
➡ Passenger vehicles
➡ Freight

Departures

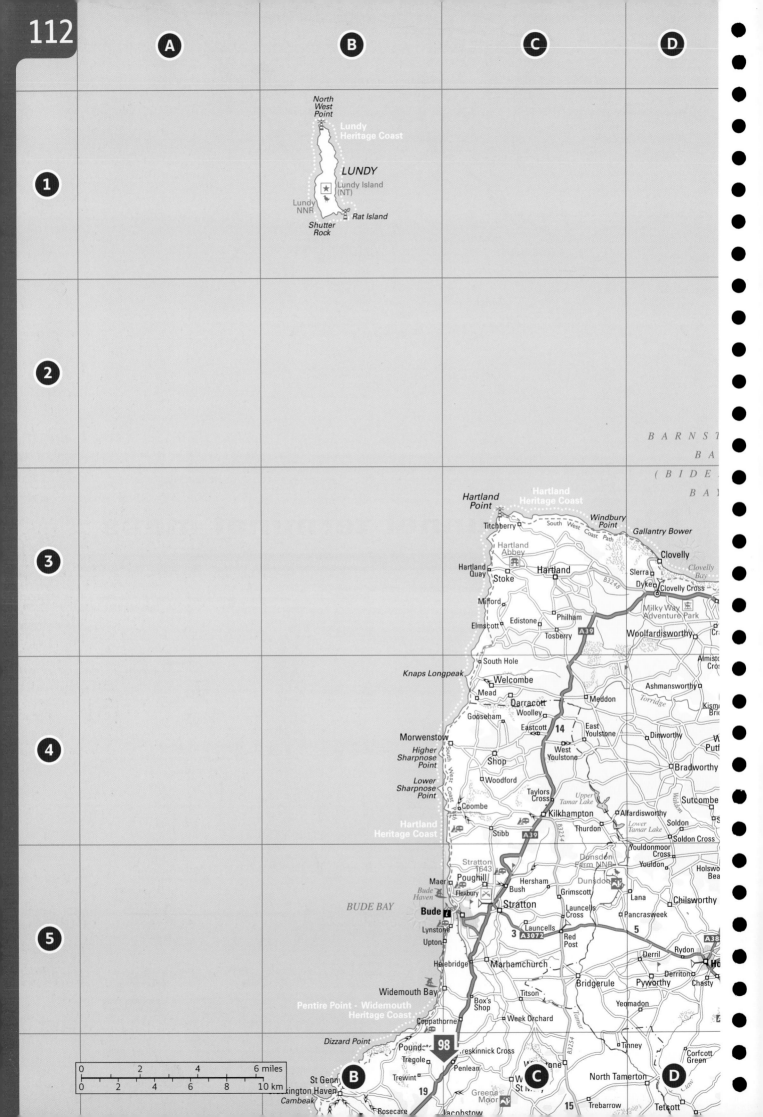

A B C D

1

2

3

4

5

North West Point

Lundy Heritage Coast

LUNDY

Lundy Island (NT)

Lundy NNR

Shutter Rock

Rat Island

BARNST
BA
(BIDE
BAY

Hartland Point

Hartland Heritage Coast

Titchberry

South West Coast Path

Windbury Point

Gallantry Bower

Clovelly

Clovelly Bay

Hartland Abbey

Hartland Quay

Stoke

Hartland

Slerra

Dyke

Clovelly Cross

Milford

Milky Way Adventure Park

Elmscott

Edistone

Philham

B3248

Woolfardisworthy

Cr

Tosberry

A39

South Hole

Almisto

Cro

Knaps Longpeak

Welcombe

Ashmansworthy

Torridge

Mead

Darracott

Meddon

Kism

Bri

Gooseham

Woolley

Eastcott

14

East Youlstone

Dinworthy

Morwenstow

W
Puth

Higher Sharpnose Point

South West Coast Path

Shop

West Youlstone

Bradworthy

Lower Sharpnose Point

Woodford

Upper Tamar Lake

Su

Sutcombe

Taylors Cross

Lower Tamar Lake

Coombe

Kilkhampton

Alfardisworthy

Soldon

Weldon

Hartland Heritage Coast

Stibb

A39

B3254

Thurdon

Soldon Cross

Youldonmoor Cross

Youldon

Dunsdon Farm NNR

Holsw

Bea

Stratton 1643

Poughill

Hersham

Bush

Dunsdon

Maer

Bude Haven

Flexbury

Grimscott

Lana

Chilsworthy

BUDE BAY

Bude

Stratton

Launcells Cross

Pancrasweek

Lynstone

Launcells

Red Post

5

A38

Upton

3

A3072

Derril

Rydon

Helebridge

Marhamchurch

Bridgerule

Derriton

Ho

Pyworthy

Chasty

Widemouth Bay

Titson

Yeomadon

Pentire Point - Widemouth Heritage Coast

Box's Shop

Week Orchard

Tinney

Corfcott Green

Dizzard Point

Coppathorne

98

reskinnick Cross

W
St I

Tamar

B3254

North Tamerton

Tetcott

0 2 4 6 miles
0 2 4 6 8 10 km

St Genn

B

Poundst

Tregole

Penlean

C

D

kington Haven

Cambeak

Trewint

19

Greena Moor

15

Trebarrow

Rosecare

Jacobstow

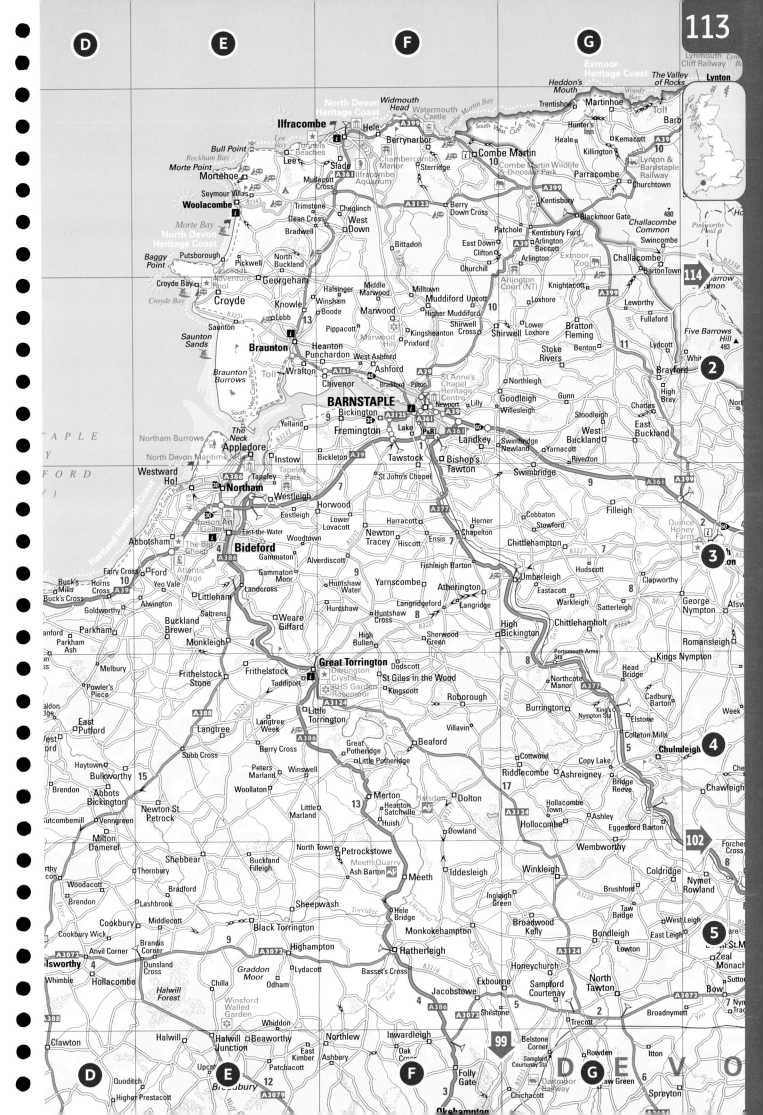

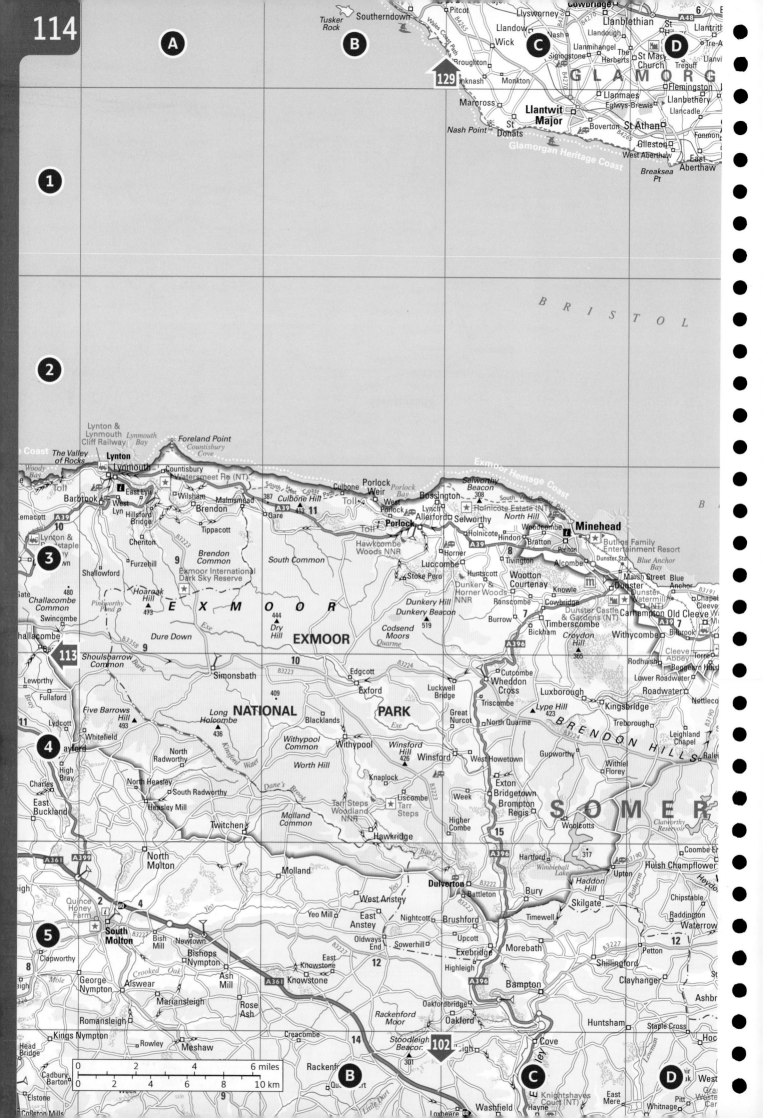

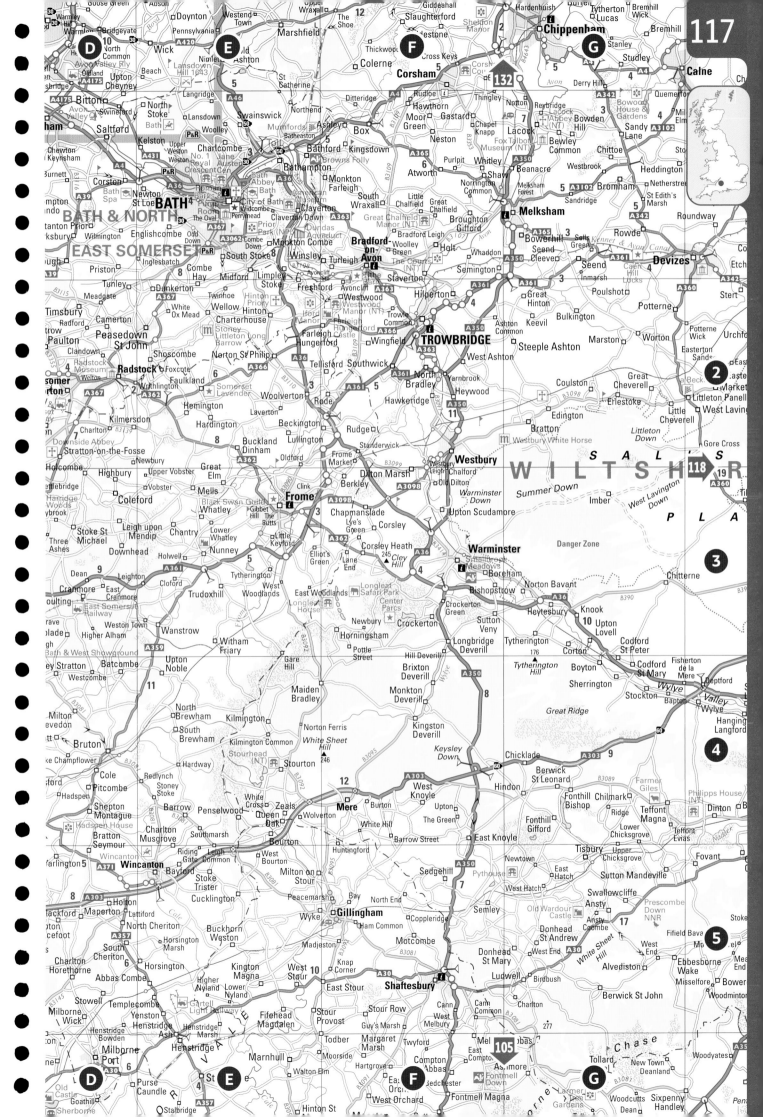

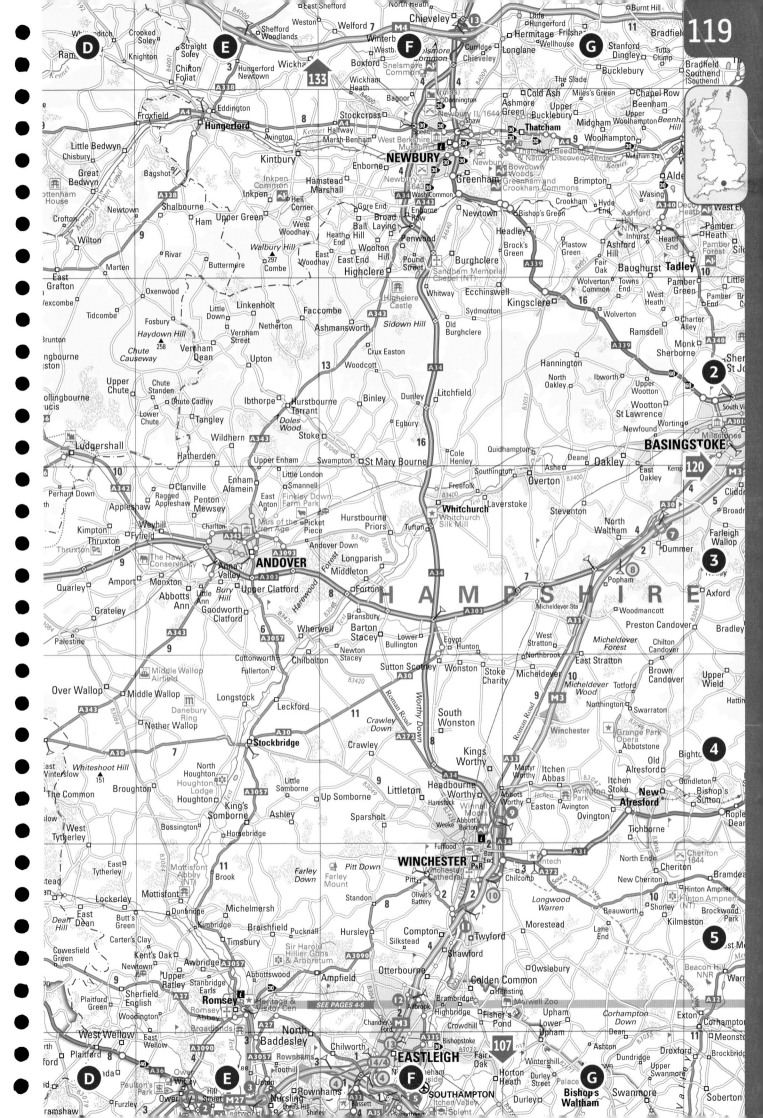

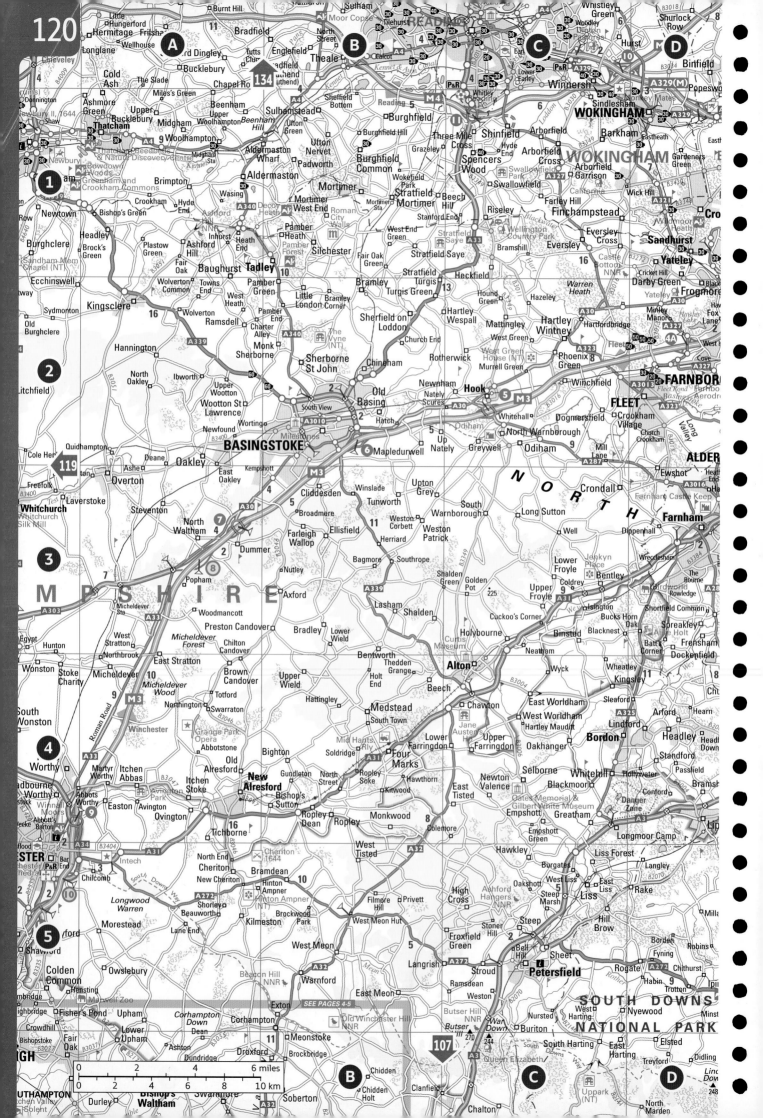

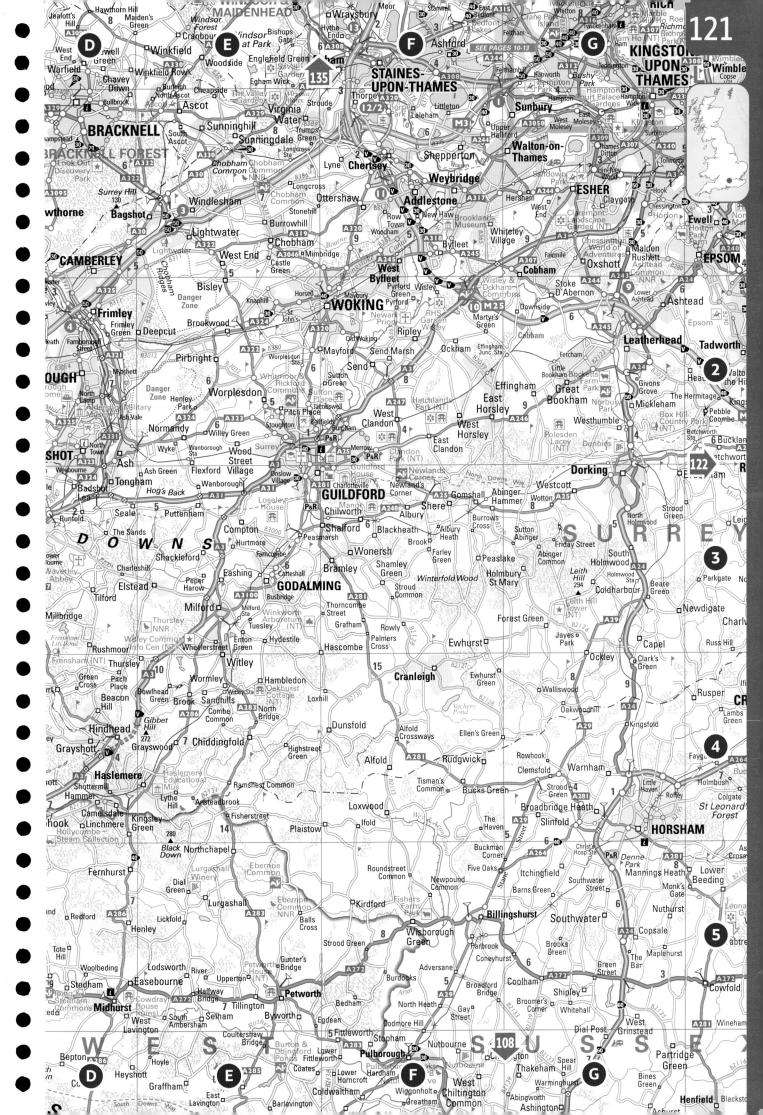

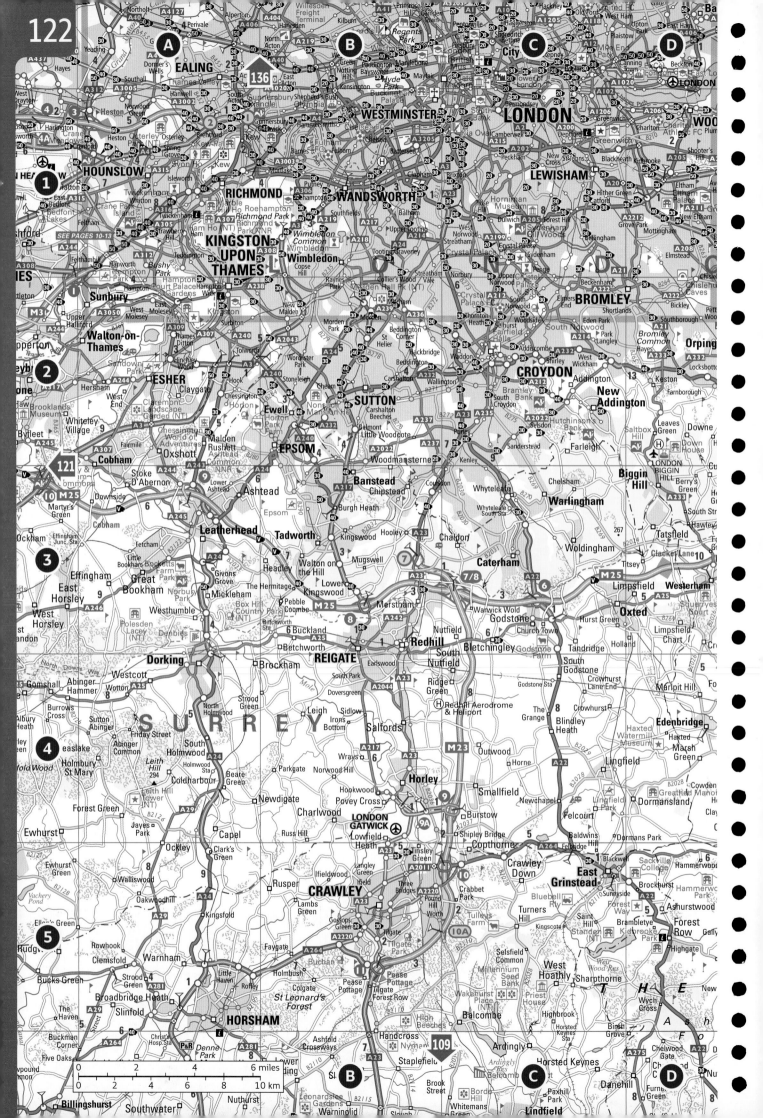

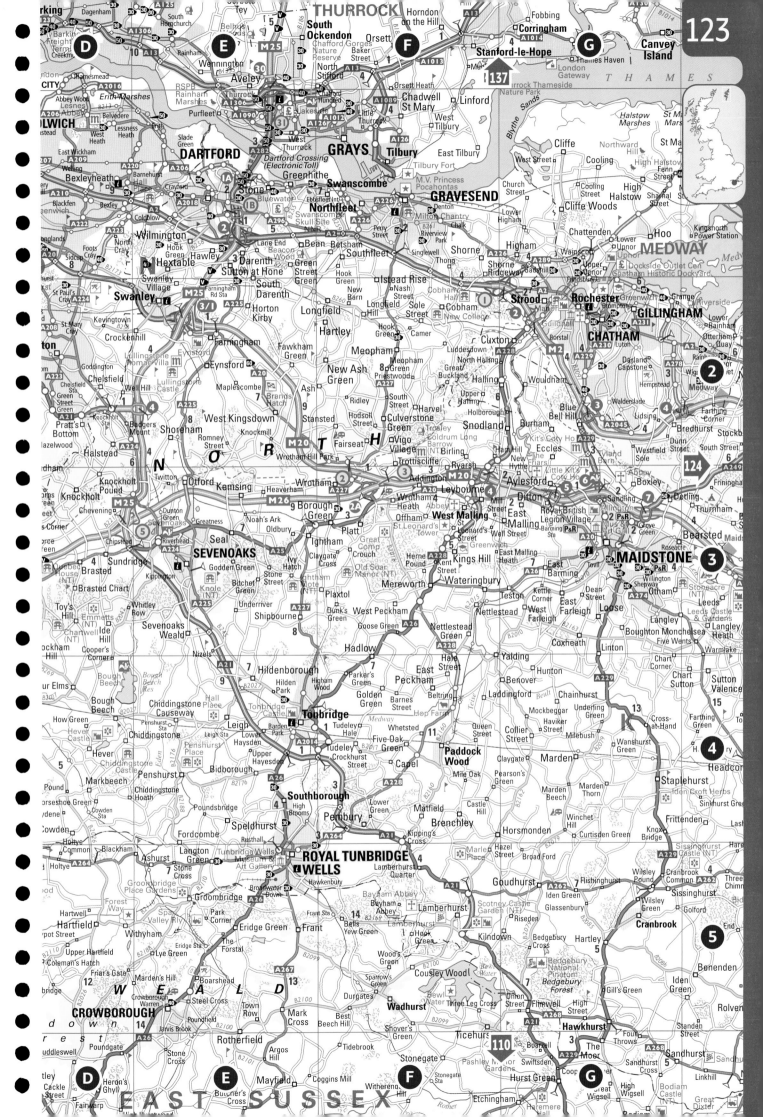

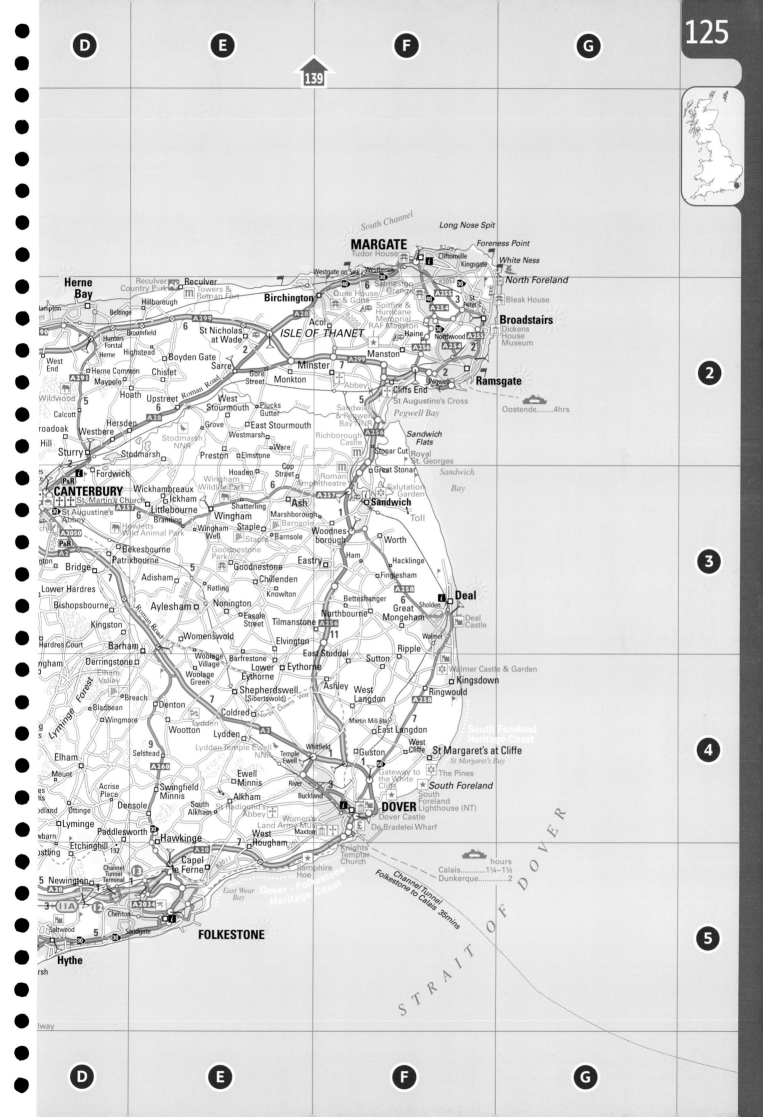

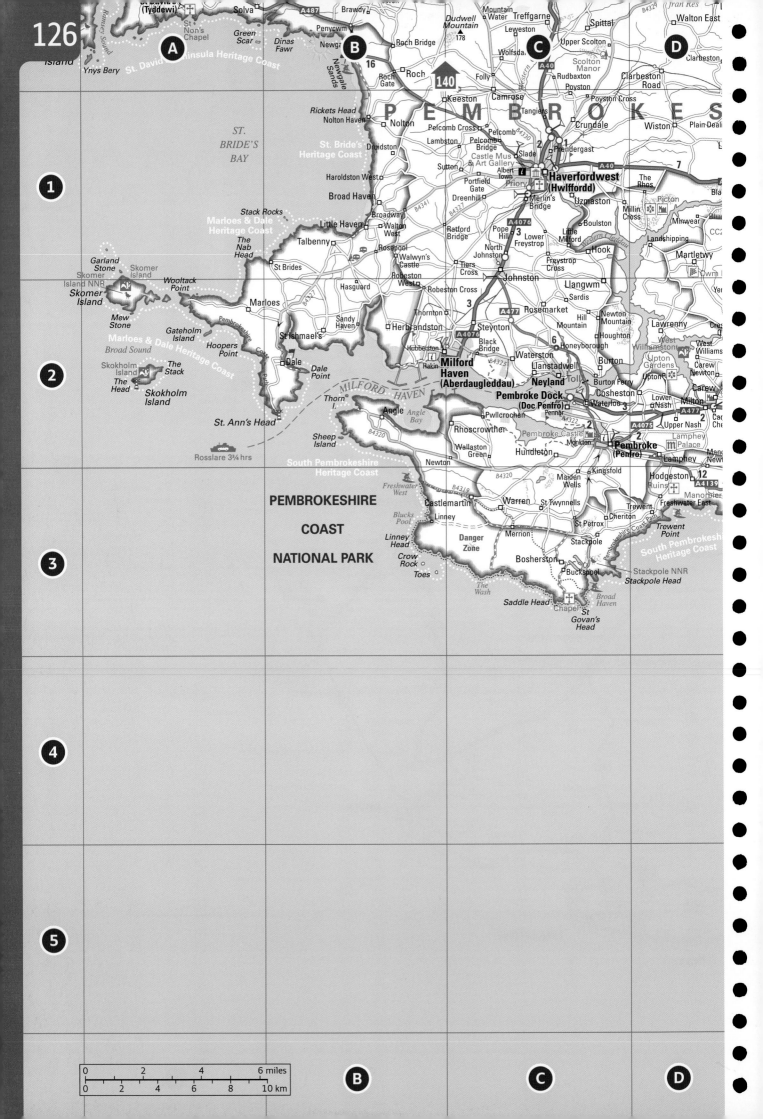

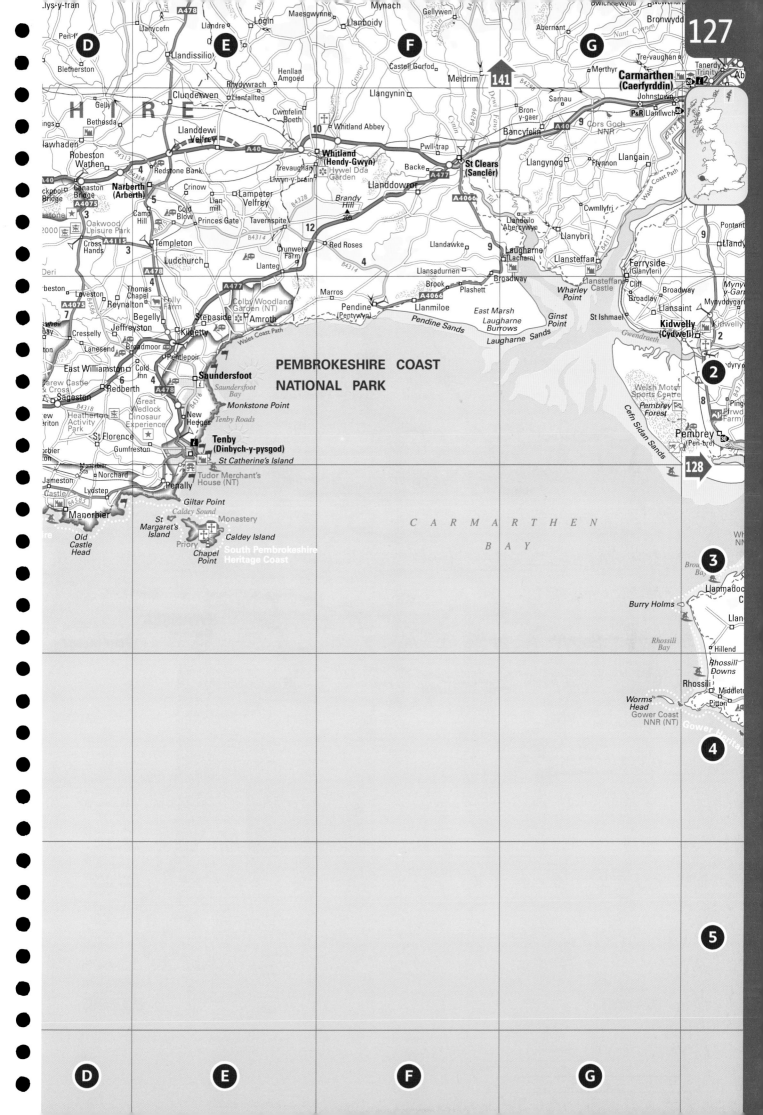

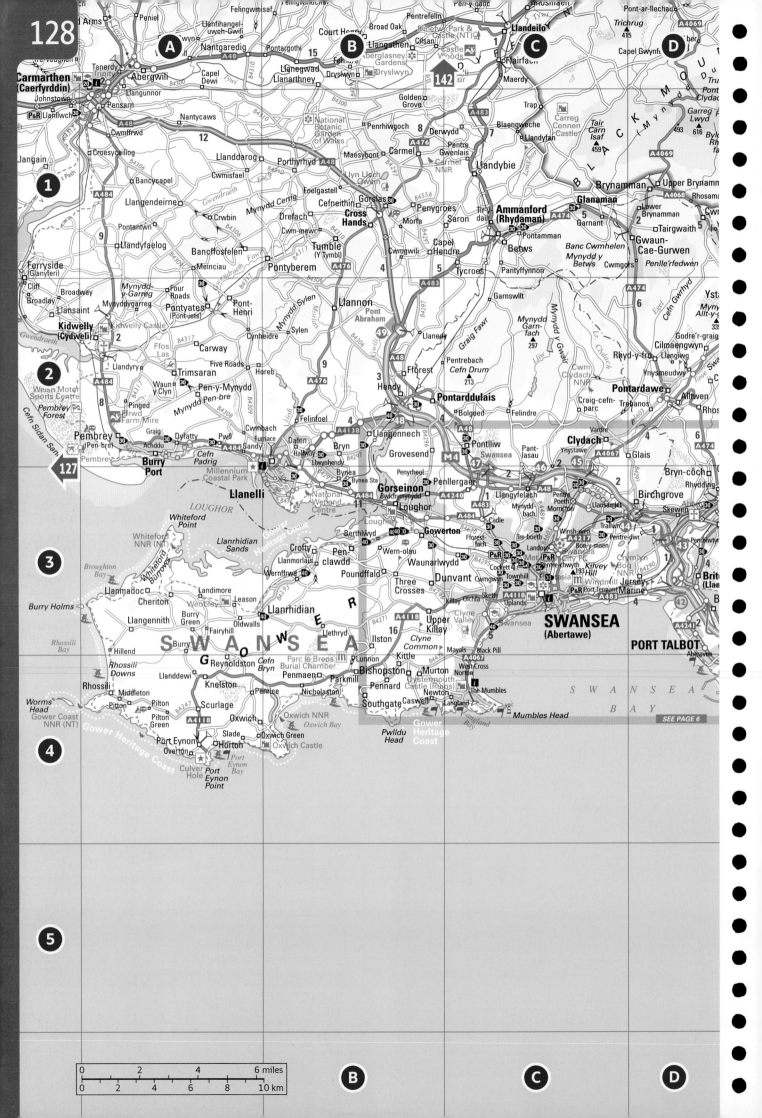

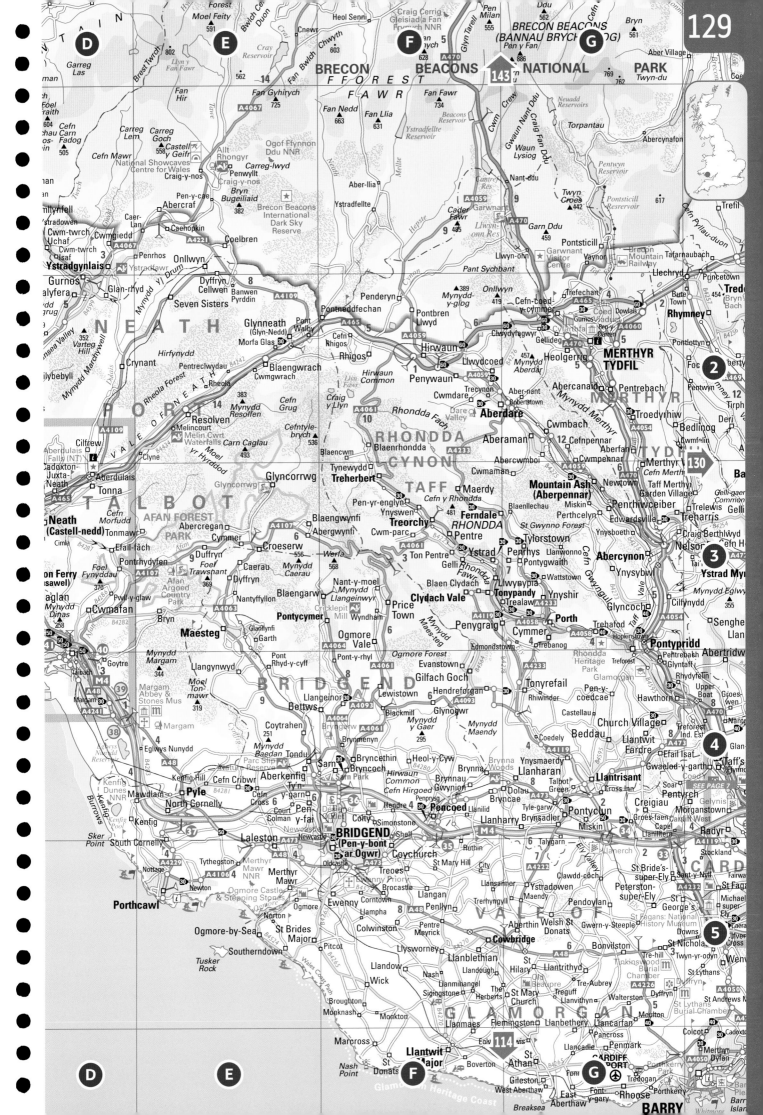

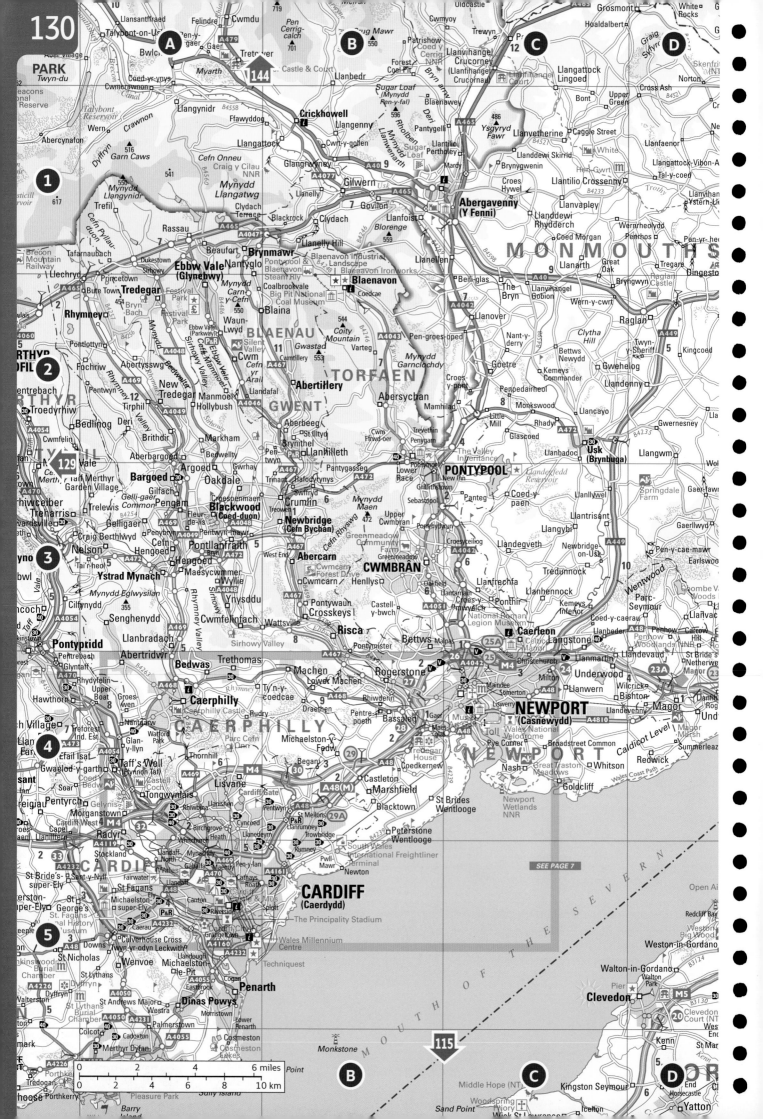

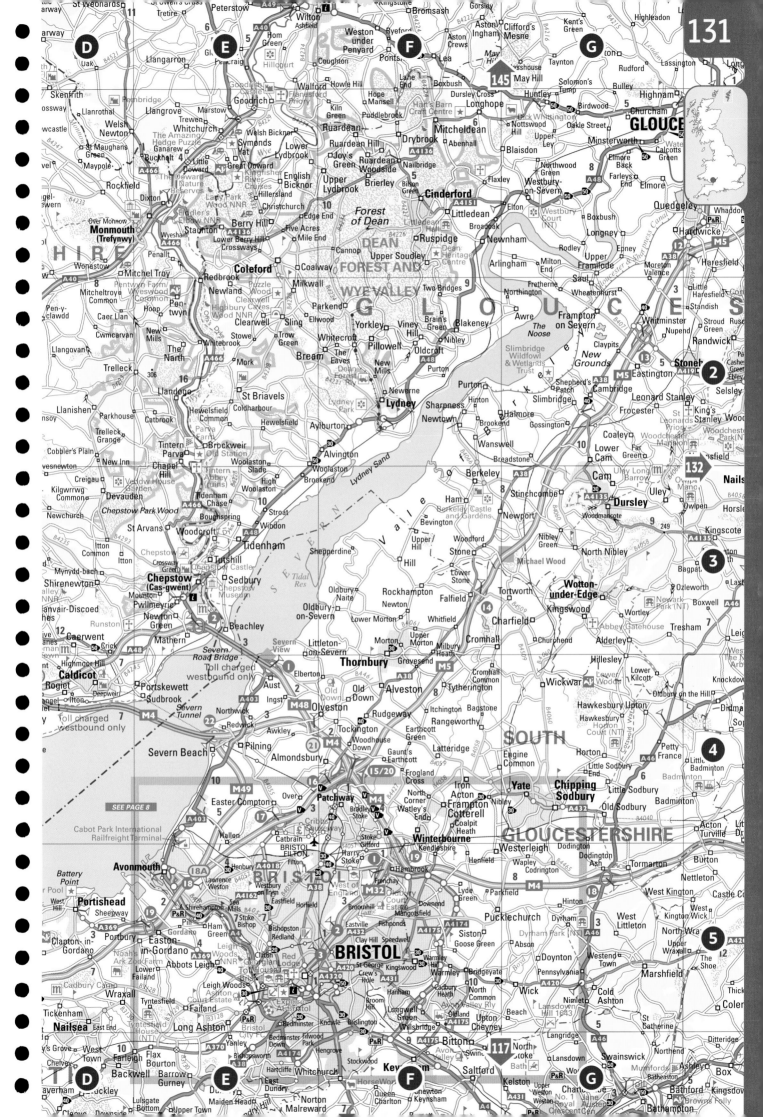

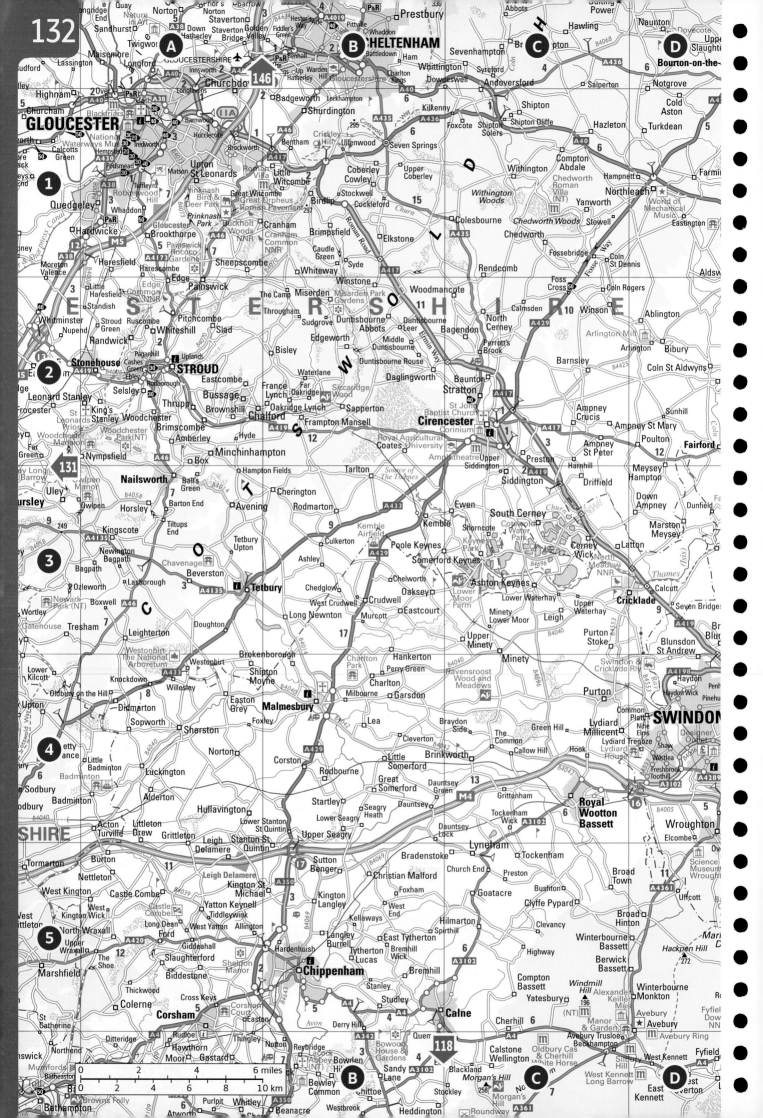

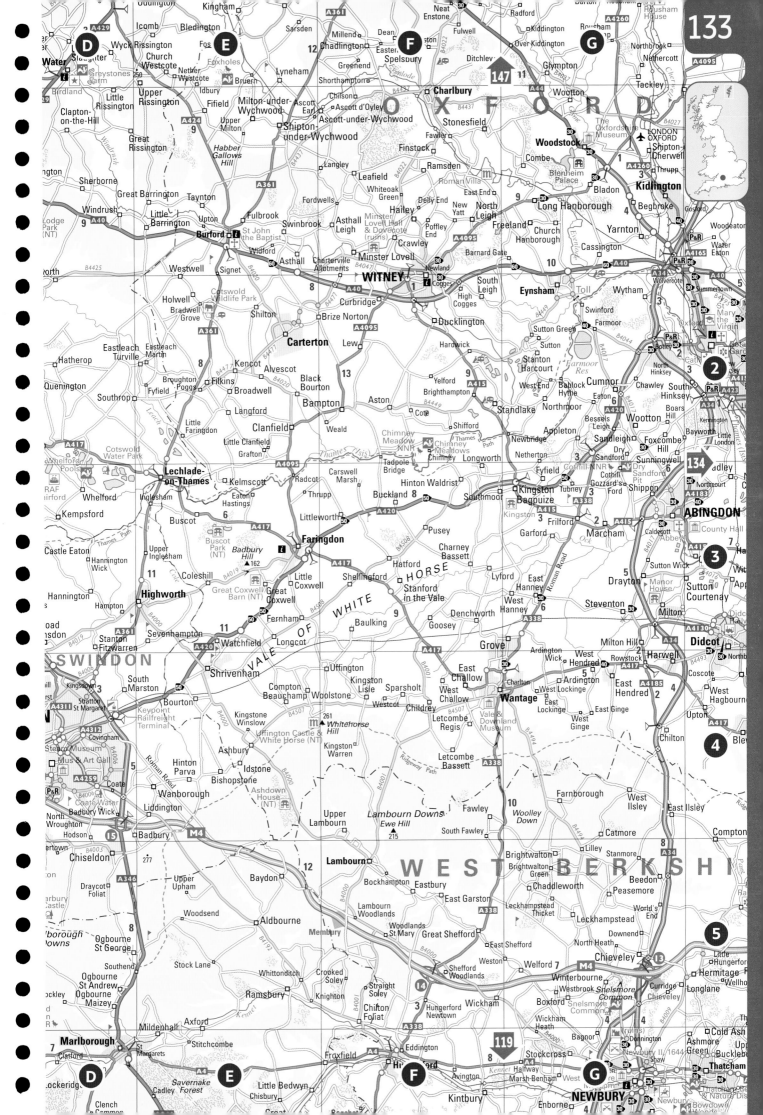

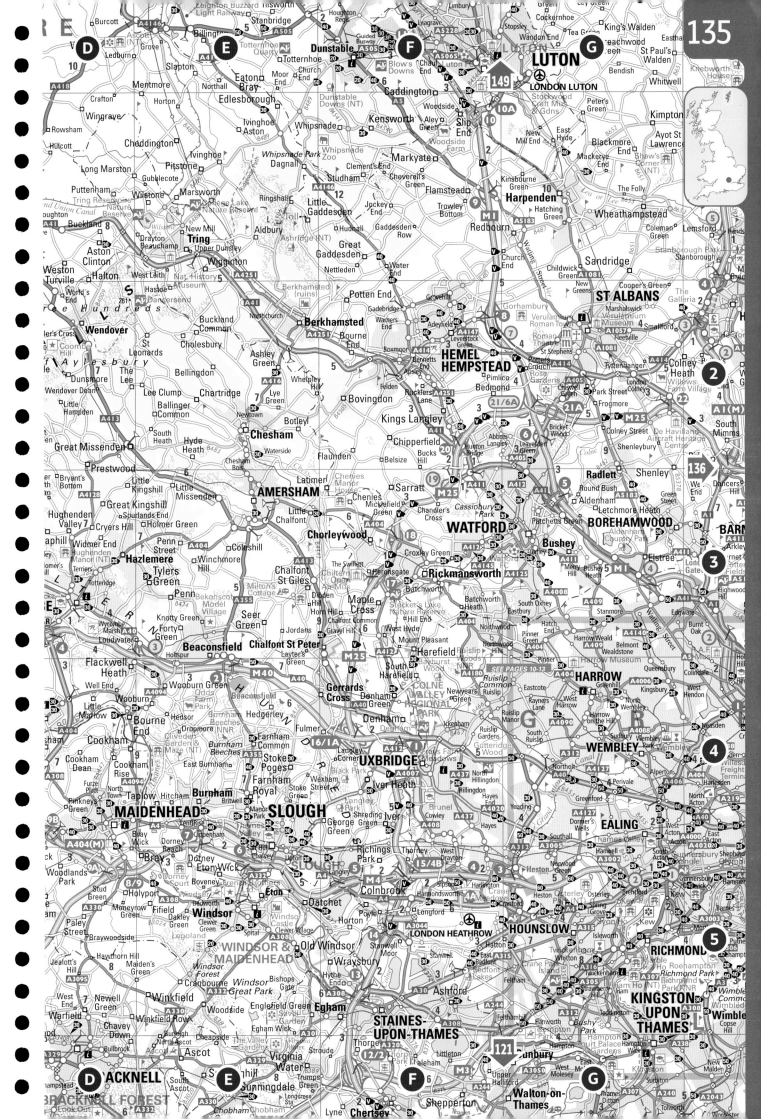

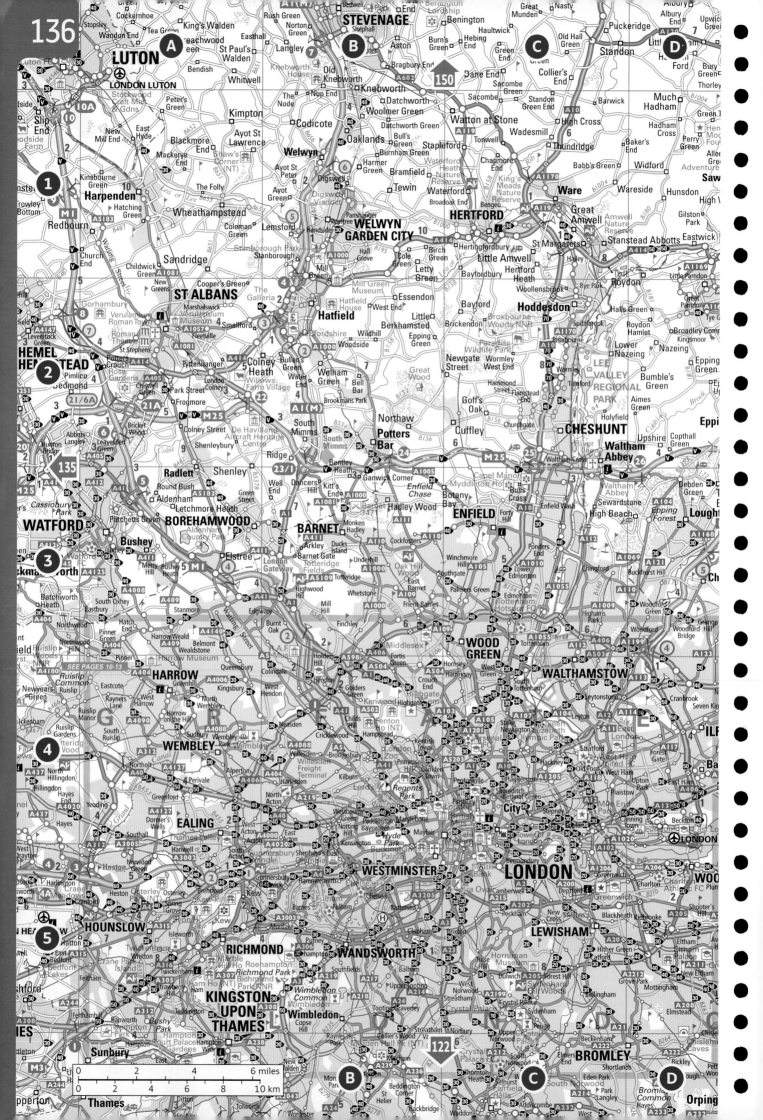

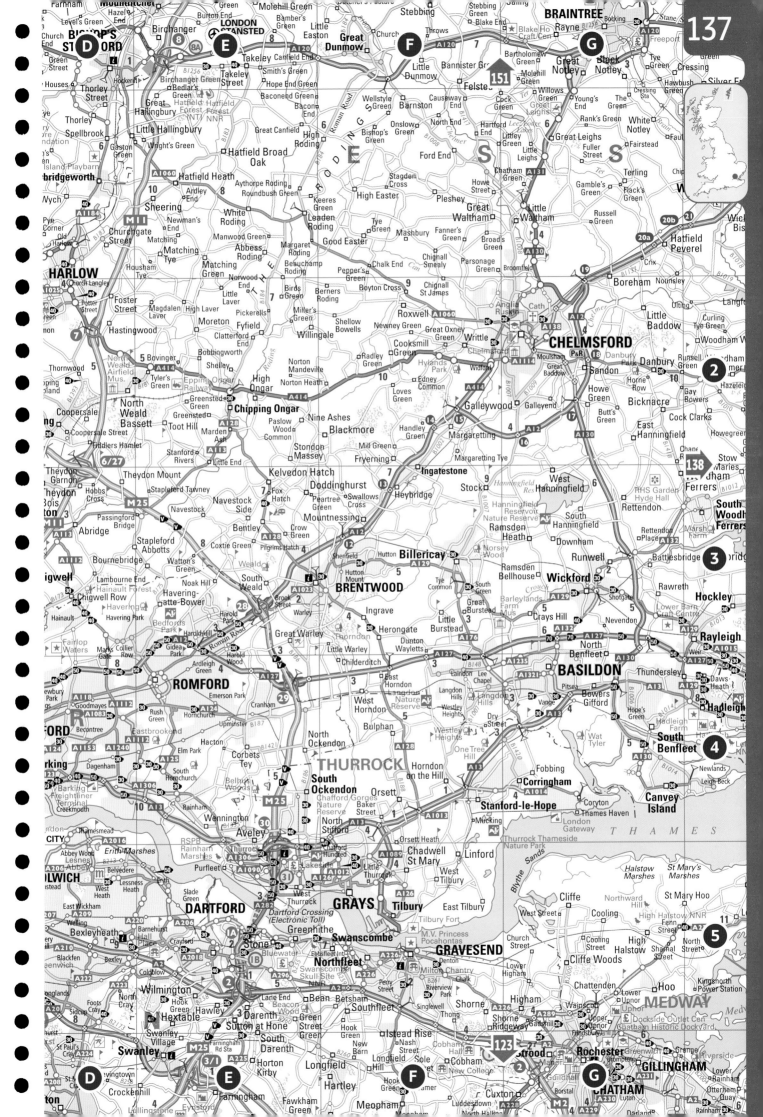

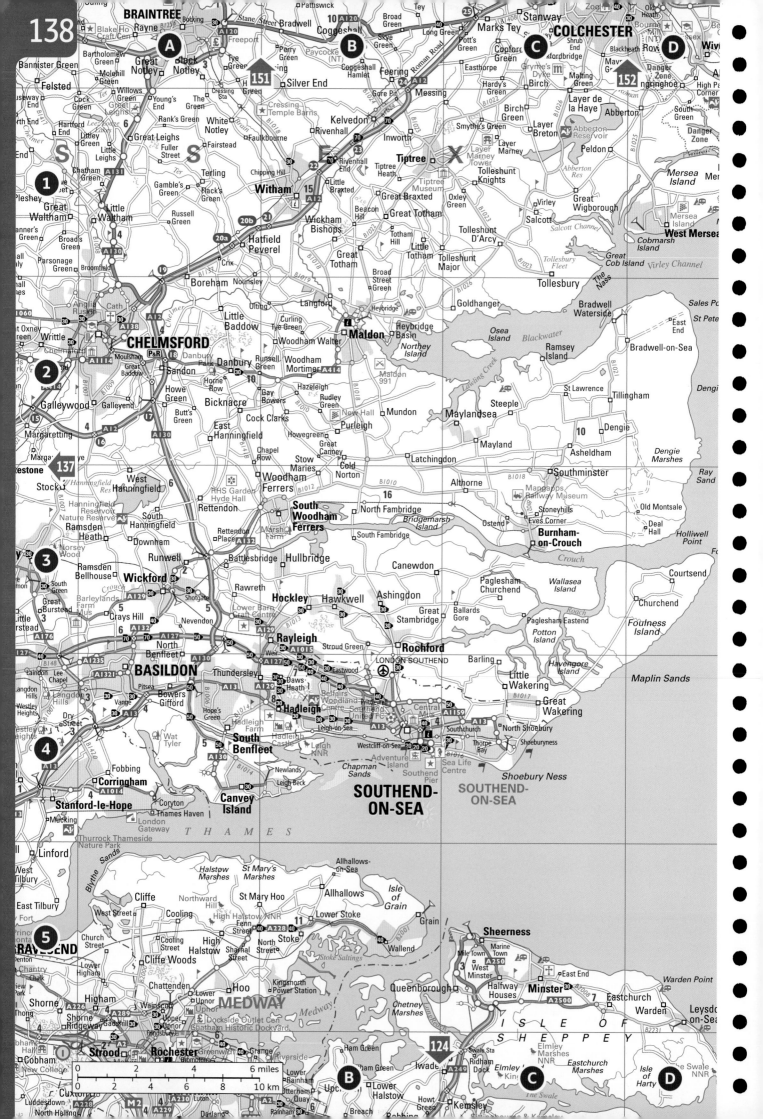

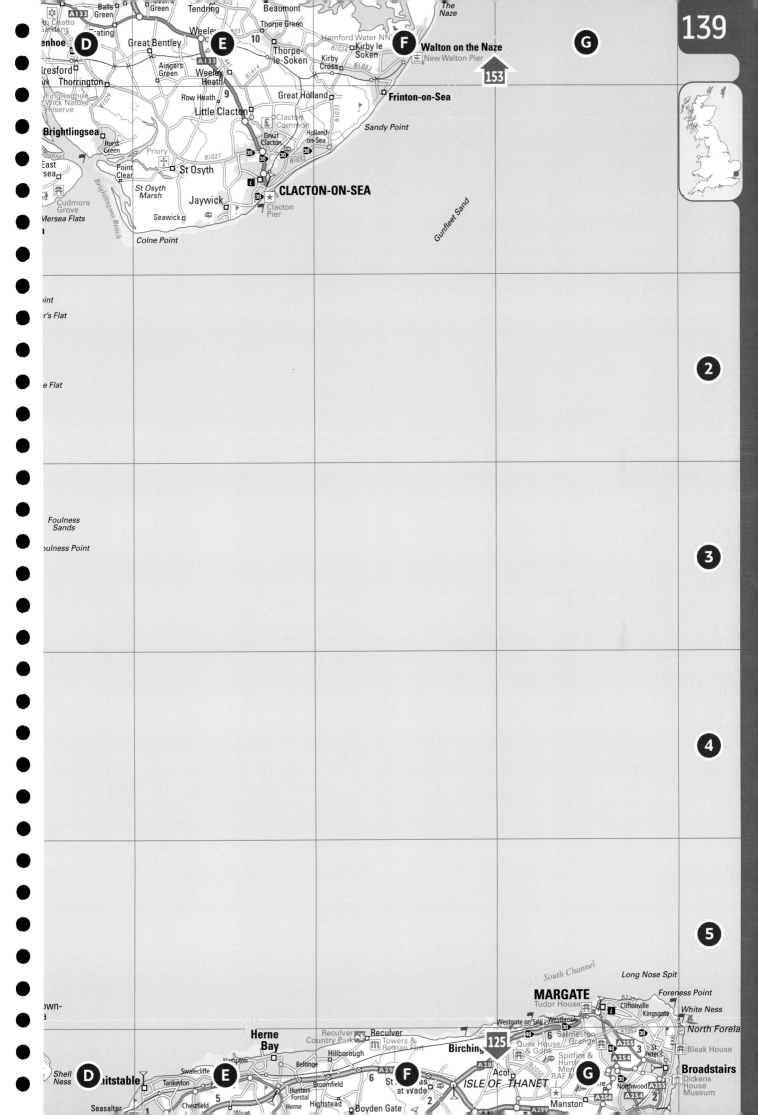

D

Balls
Green
Chatto
Gardens
A133
Weeley
Tendring
Beaumont
The
Naze

enhoe
Great Bentley
eating

E

Thorpe Green
10
Hamford Water NN
Kirby le
Soken
B1034
Kirby
Cross

F

Walton on the Naze
New Walton Pier
153

Aingers
Green
Weeley
Heath
A133
Thorpe-
le-Soken
B1414
441

G

lresford
ark
Thorrington
Row Heath
9
Great Holland
B1032
Frinton-on-Sea

Fingringhoe
Wick Nature
Reserve
B1029
Little Clacton
Holland-
on-Sea
Sandy Point

Brightlingsea
Hurst Green
Priory
Clacton
Common
Great
Clacton
B1027
30
30

East
ersea
Point
Clear
St Osyth
30
30
B1033
Gunfleet Sand

Cudmore
Grove
St Osyth
Marsh
Jaywick
30
CLACTON-ON-SEA
Clacton
Pier

Mersea Flats
Seawick
Colne Point

oint

r's Flat

2

e Flat

Foulness
Sands

3

oulness Point

4

South Channel
Long Nose Spit

5

MARGATE
Tudor House
Foreness Point
White Ness
Cliftonville
Kingsgate
North Forela

own-

Westgate on Sea
Westbrook
40
6
Salmeston
Grange
B2052
30
3
St
Peter's
Bleak House

Shell
Ness

D

hitstable
Tankerton

Herne
Bay
Swalecliffe
Reculver
Country Park
Reculver
Towers &
Roman Fort

E

Hillborough
Birching
125
Quex House
& Gdns
Spitfire &
Hurri
Mem
RAF M

F

Broadstairs
Dickens
House
Museum
A255

Seasalter
Chestfield
Hampton
Beltinge
Broomfield
Hunters
Forstal
Herne
Highstead
Boyden Gate
5
6
A29
A28
St as
at vvade
Acol
ISLE OF THANET
Manston
A299
A2050

G

Northwood
A254
A256
2
Northwood
30
2

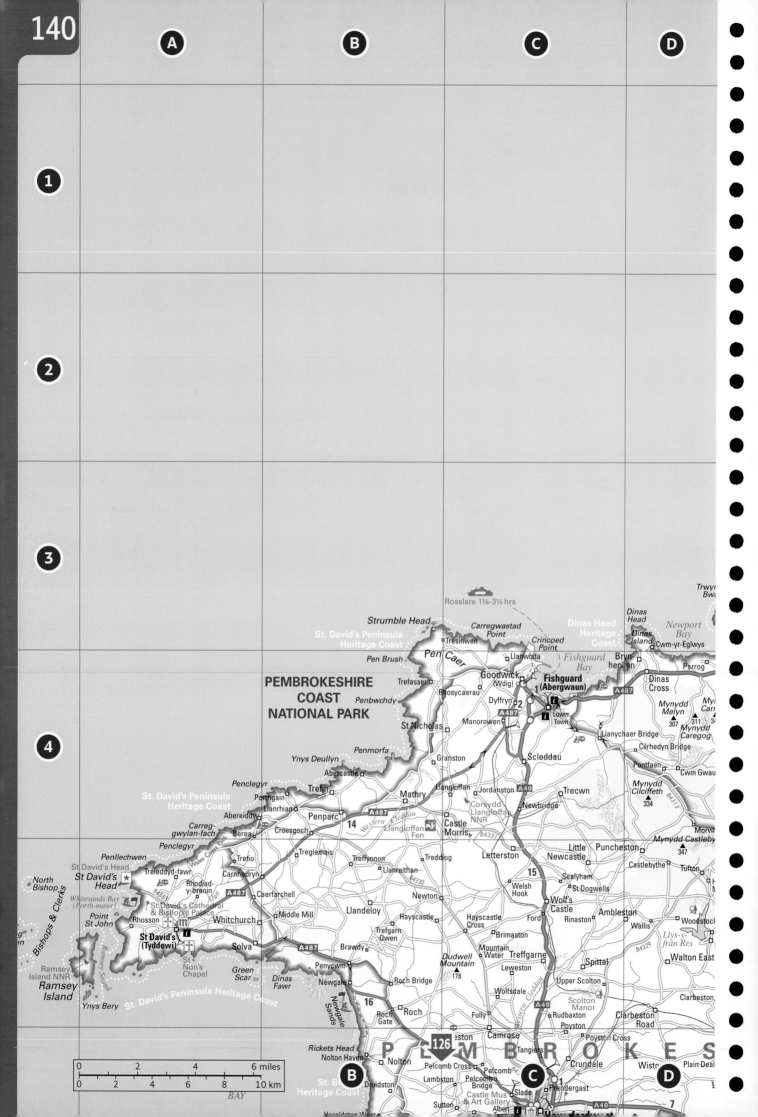

A   B   C   D

1

2

3

4

Rosslare 1¾-3½ hrs

Strumble Head
Carregwastad Point
Crincoed Point
St. David's Peninsula
Heritage Coast
Tresinwen
Pen Brush   *Pen Caer*   Llanwnda
Dinas Head
Heritage Coast
Dinas Head
Newport Bay
Dinas Island
Cwm-yr-Eglwys

PEMBROKESHIRE
COAST
NATIONAL PARK
Trefasser   Goodwick (Wdig)   *Fishguard Bay*   **Fishguard (Abergwaun)**   Bryn-henllan
Penbwchdy   Rhosycaerau   Dyffryn   Lower Town   A487   Dinas Cross
St Nicholas   Manorowen   Llanychaer Bridge   Mynydd Melyn
Penmorfa   Granston   Scleddau   Cilrhedyn Bridge   307   Mynydd Caregog
Ynys Deullyn   Pontfaen   Cwm Gwau
Penclegyr   Abercastle   Llangloffan   Jordanston   A40   Trecwn   Mynydd Cilciffeth
St. David's Peninsula   Trefin   Mathry   Corsydd   Newbridge   334
Heritage Coast   Porthgain   Llangloffan   Castle   B4331
Llanrhian   Penparc   14   Llangloffan NNR   Morris
Carreg-   Berea   Croesgoch   Western Cleddau   Little   Puncheston   Mynydd Castlebythe
gwylan-fach   Fen   Newcastle   347
Penclegyr   Trefio   Treglemais   Treffynnon   Treddiog   Letterston   Castlebythe
Penllechwen   Carnhedryn   Llanreithan   15   Sealyham   Tufton
St David's Head   Treleddyd-fawr   Newton   Welsh   St Dogwells
St David's Head   Hook   Wolf's   Ambleston
North   Rhodiad-   Caerfarchell   Hayscastle   Ford   Castle   Wallis   Woodstock
Bishops   y-brenin   A487   Middle Mill   Hayscastle   Rinaston
Whitesands Bay   Cross   Llys-y-frân Res
(Porth-mawr)   Llandeloy   Brimaston
Point   Rhosson   Whitchurch   Trefgarn   Mountain   Treffgarne   B4329   Walton East
St John   St David's Cathedral   Owen   Water   Spittal
& Bishop's Palace   Brawdy   Upper Scolton
St David's   Solva   A487   Dudwell   Leweston   Clarbeston
(Tyddewi)   Mountain   Scolton   Clarbeston
St   Penycwm   178   Wolfsdale   Manor   Road
Ramsey   Non's   Green   Roch Bridge   A40
Island NNR   Chapel   Scar   Newgale   Rudbaxton
**Ramsey   Dinas   16   Roch   Folly   Poyston
Island   Fawr   Gate   Camrose   Poyston Cross
Ynys Bery   St. David's Peninsula Heritage Coast   Newgale Sands   126   Tangiers   Crundale   Wisto   Plain-Deal
Rickets Head   P E M B R O K E S   Prendergast   7
Nolton Haven   Nolton   Pelcomb Cross   Slade   A40
St B   Druidston   Lambston   Pelcomb   Castle Mus
Heritage Coast   Bridge   & Art Gallery
BAY   Sutton   Albert

0   2   4   6 miles
0   2   4   6   8   10 km

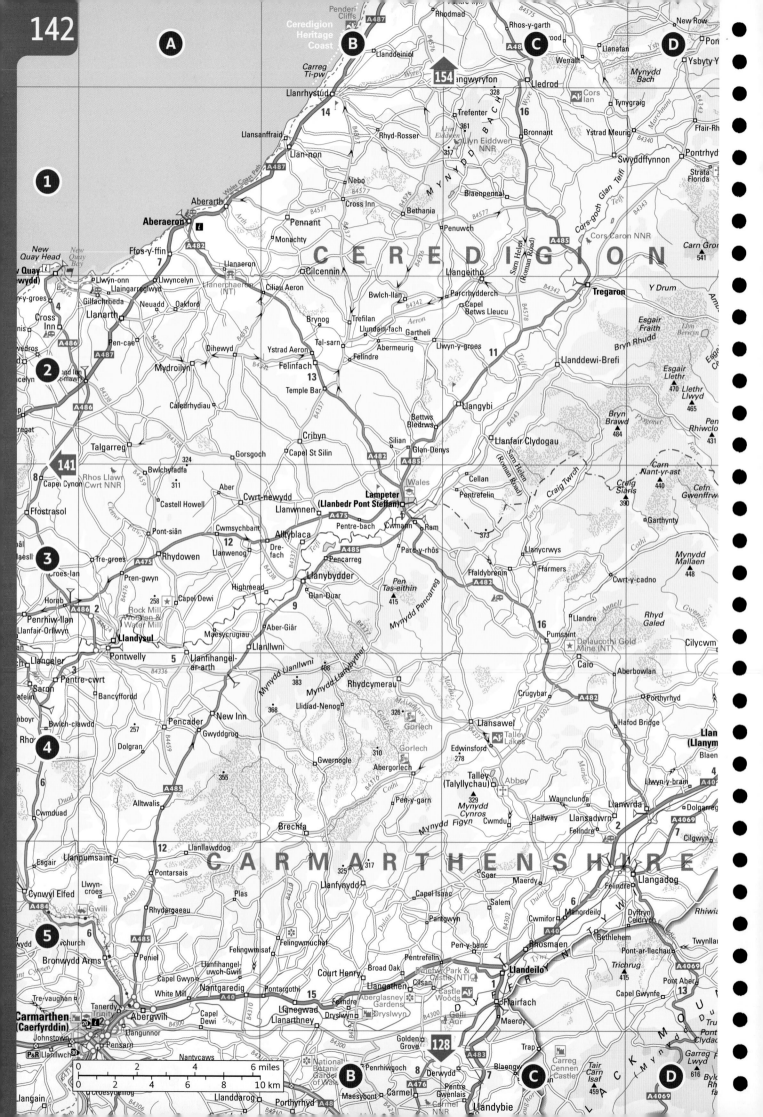

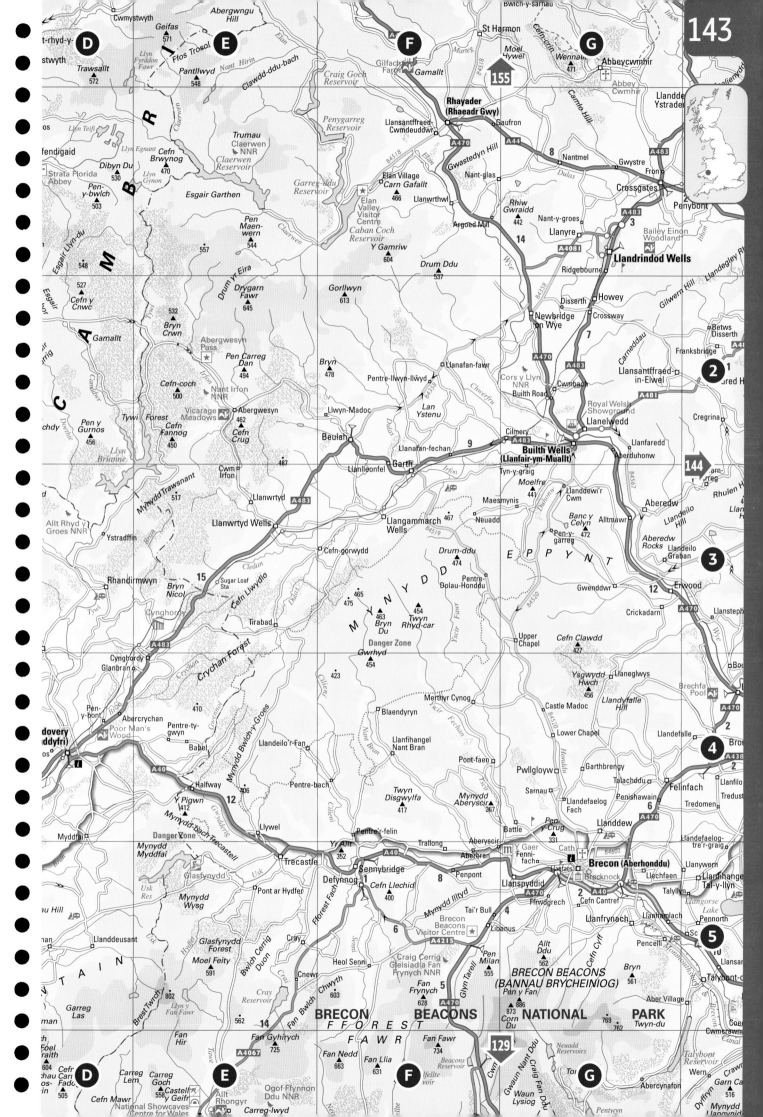

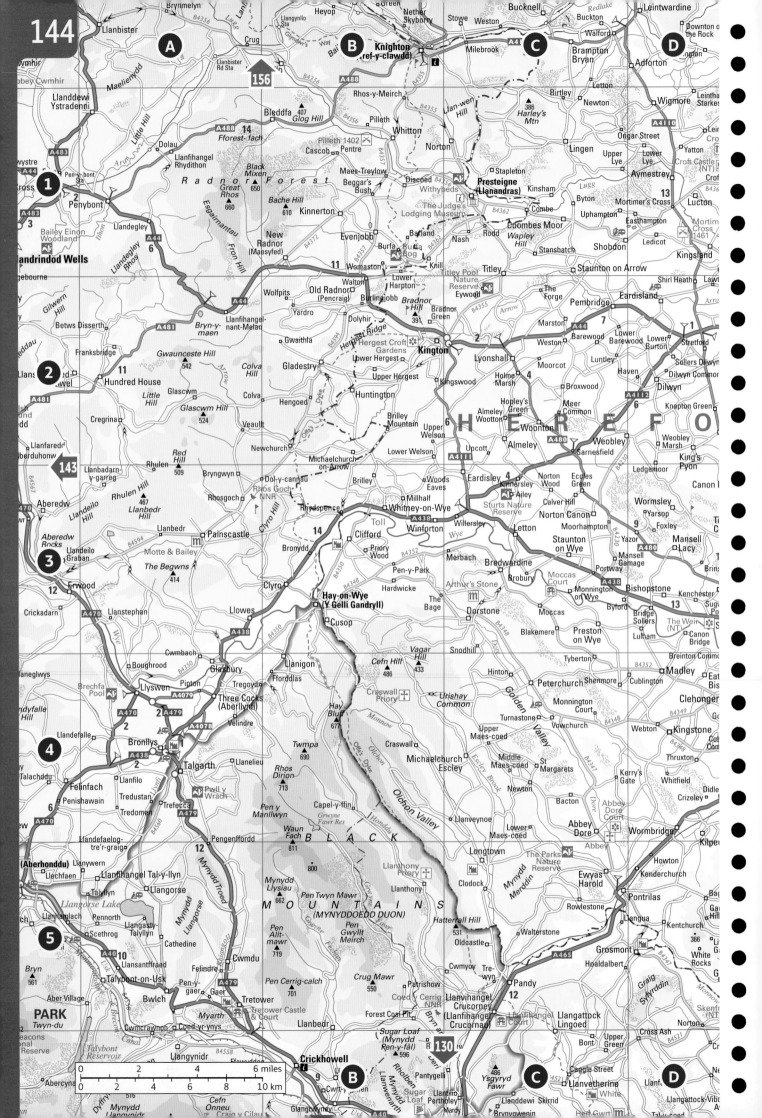

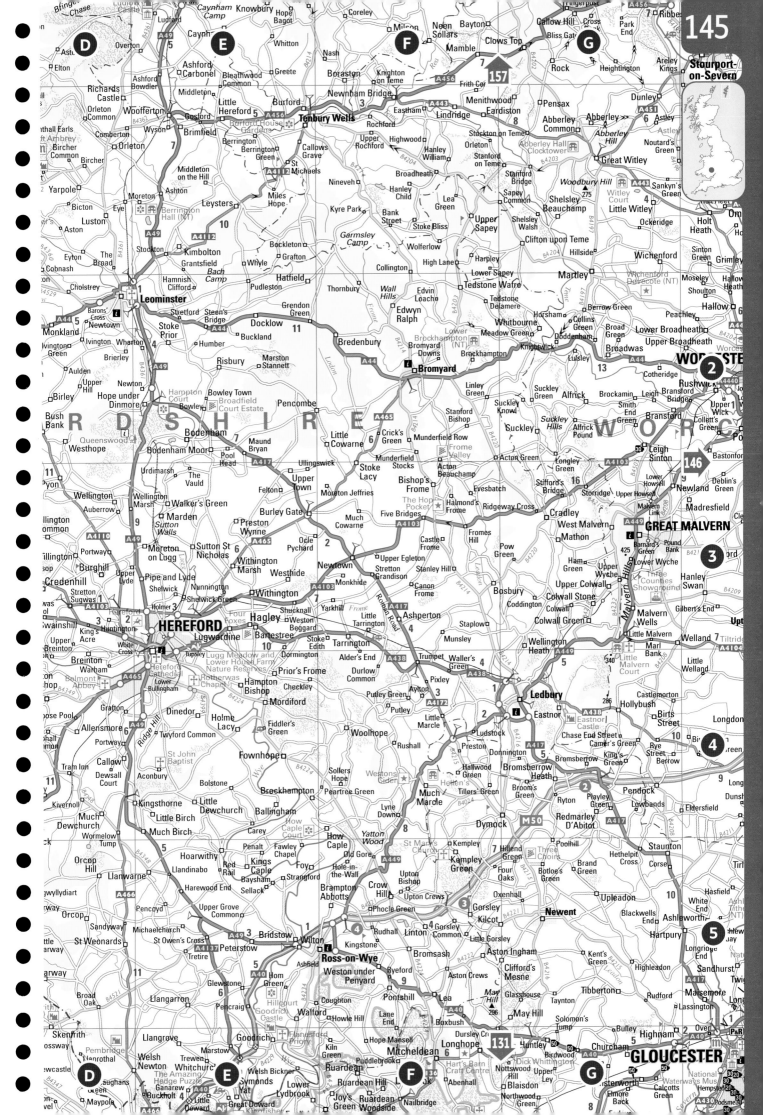

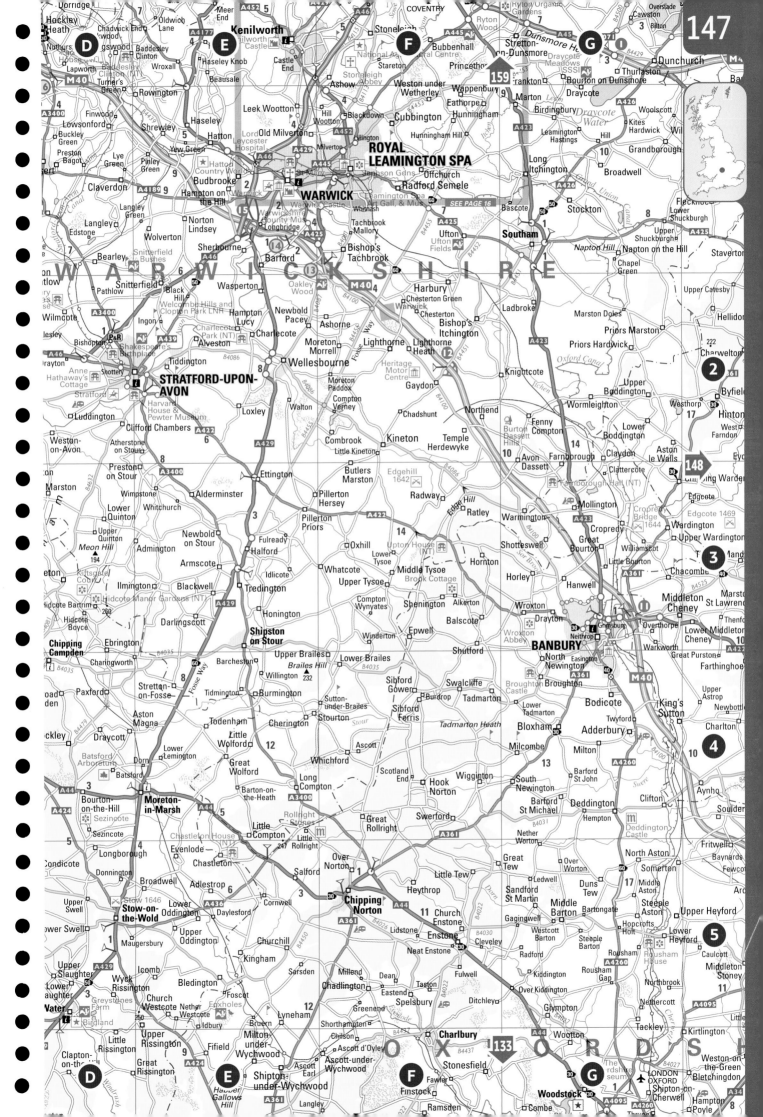

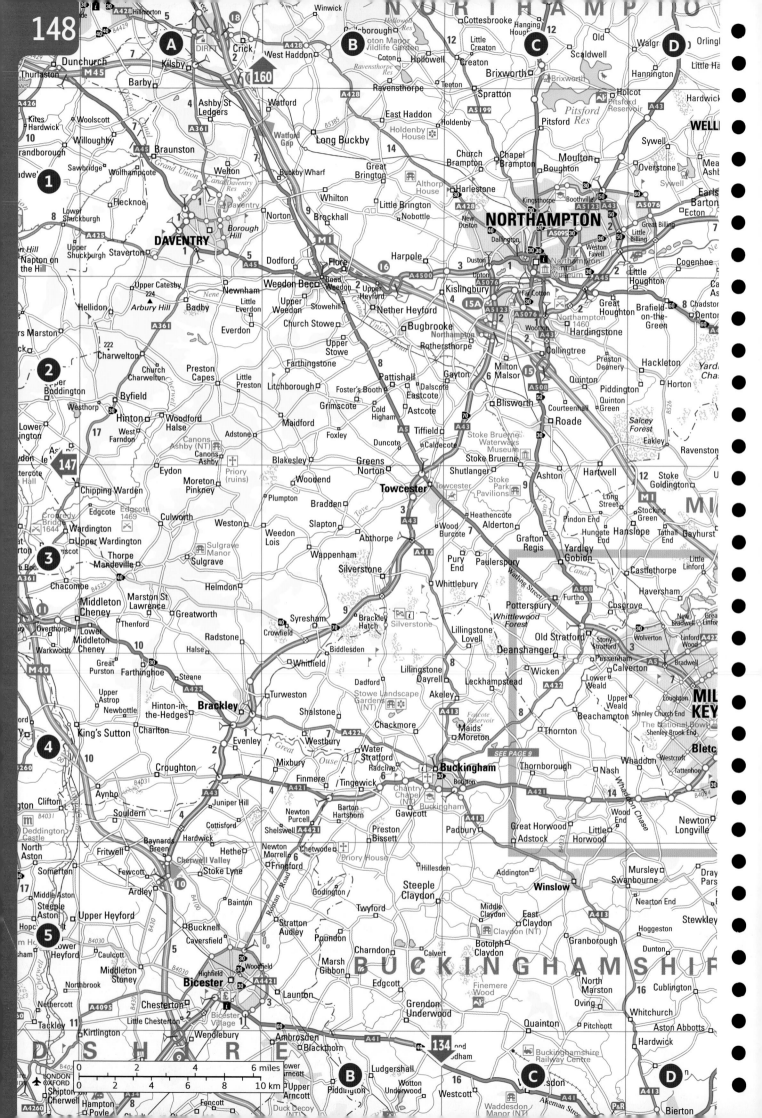

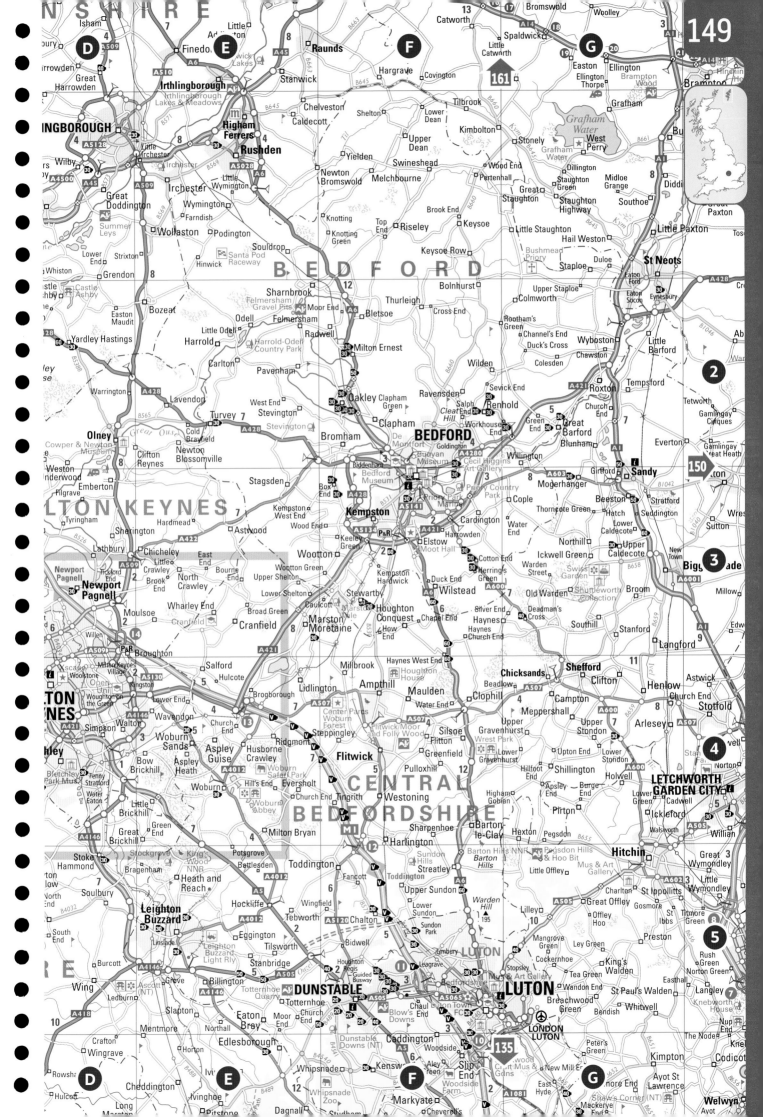

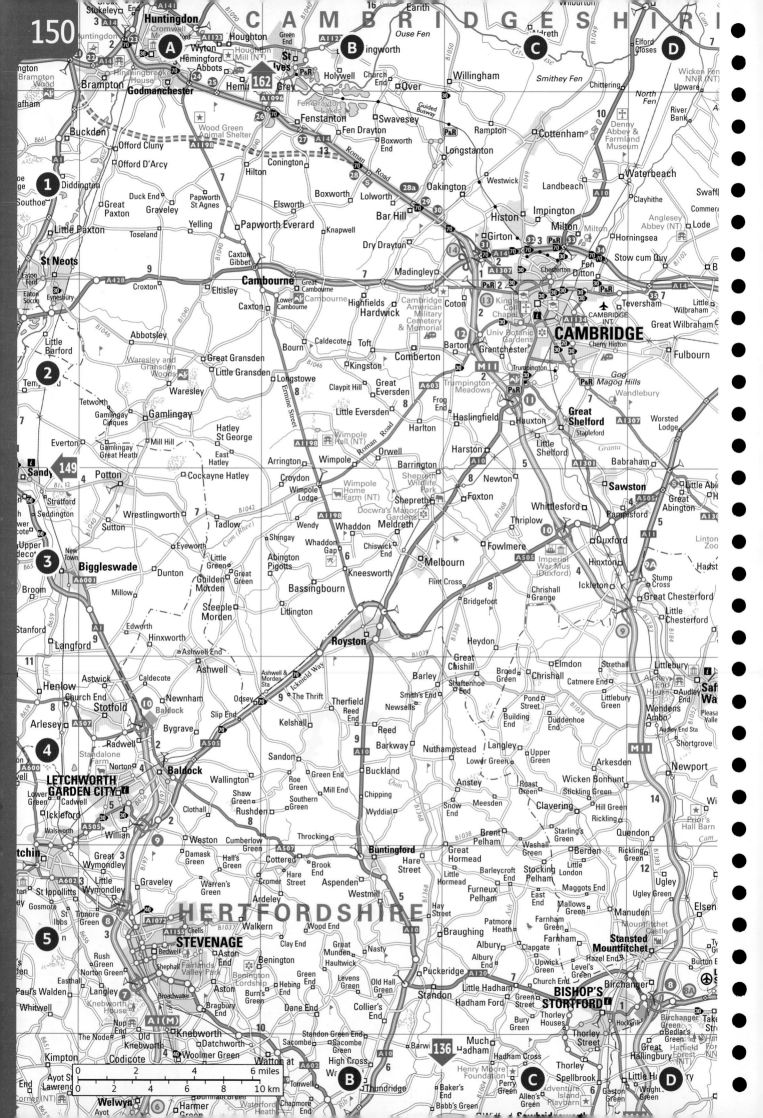

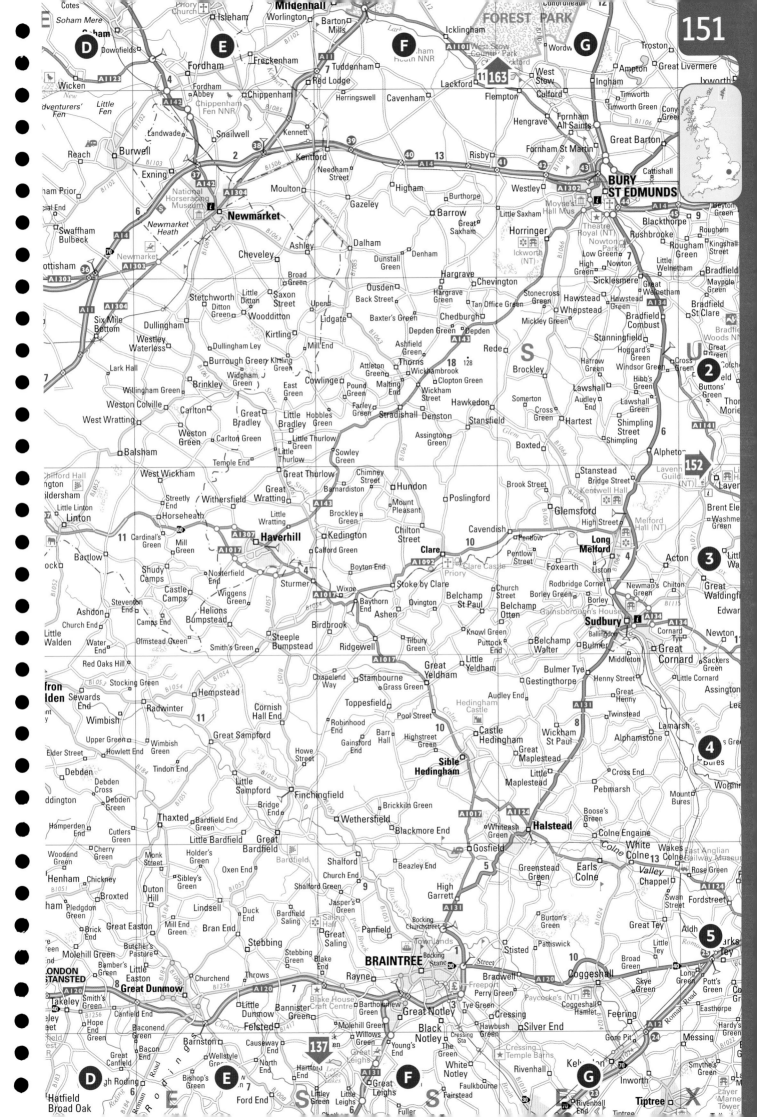

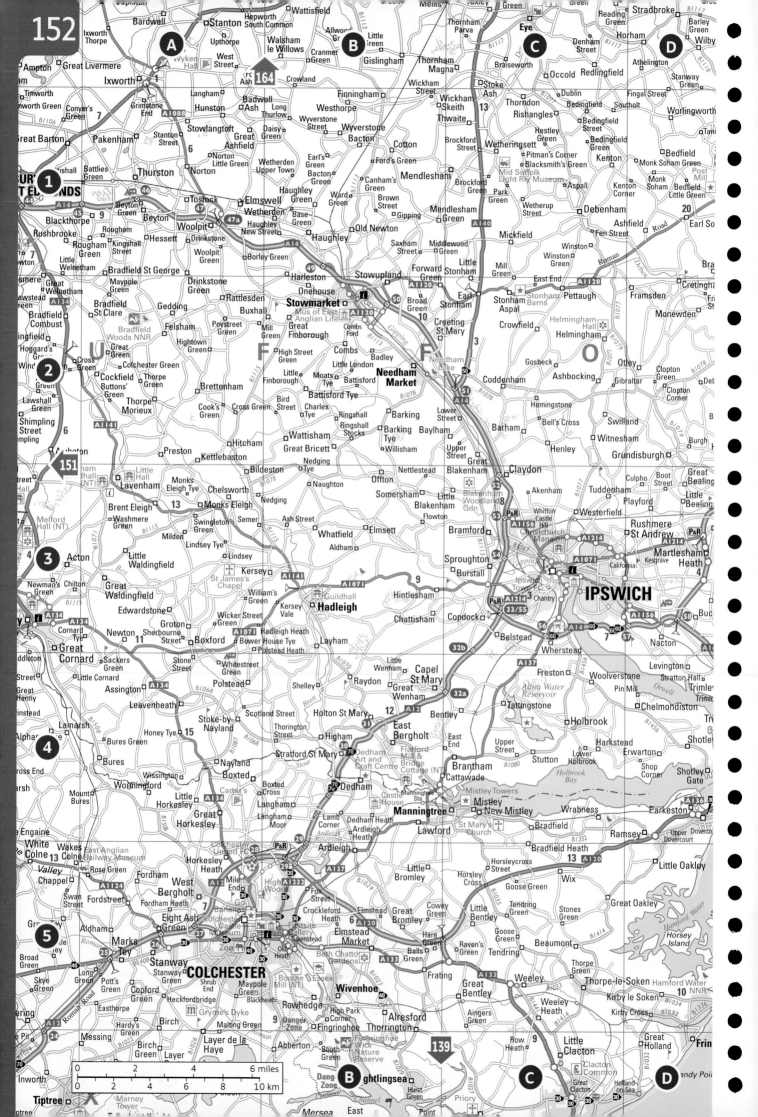

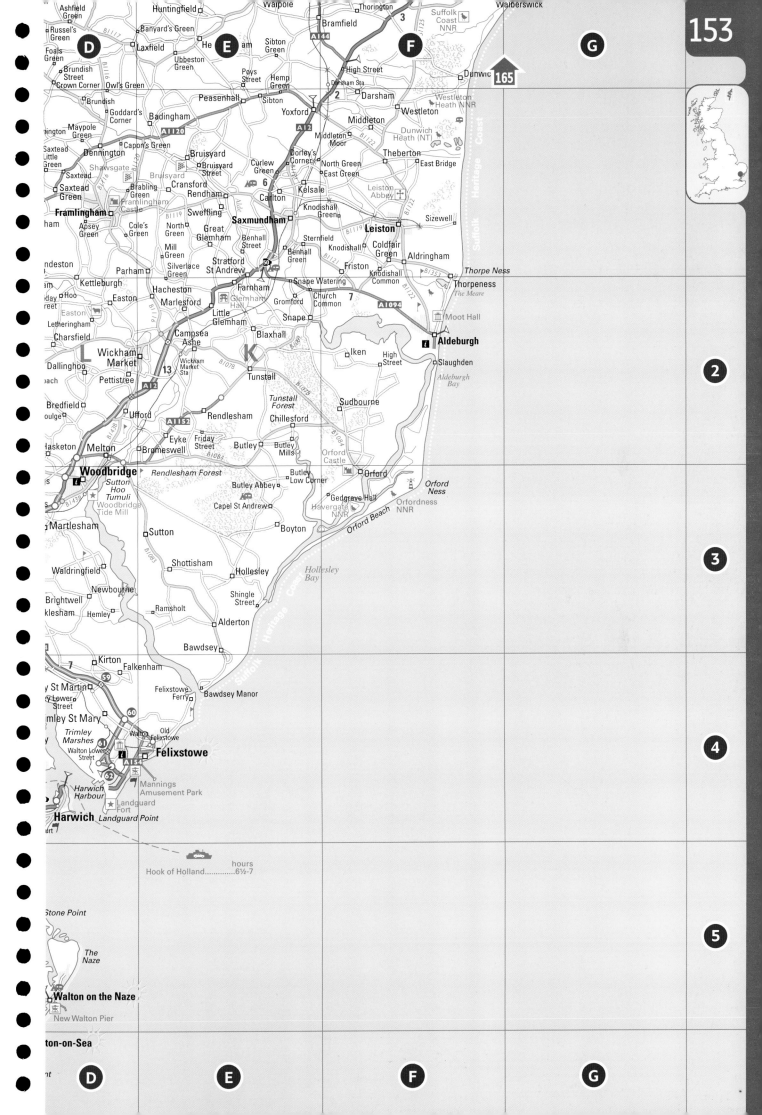

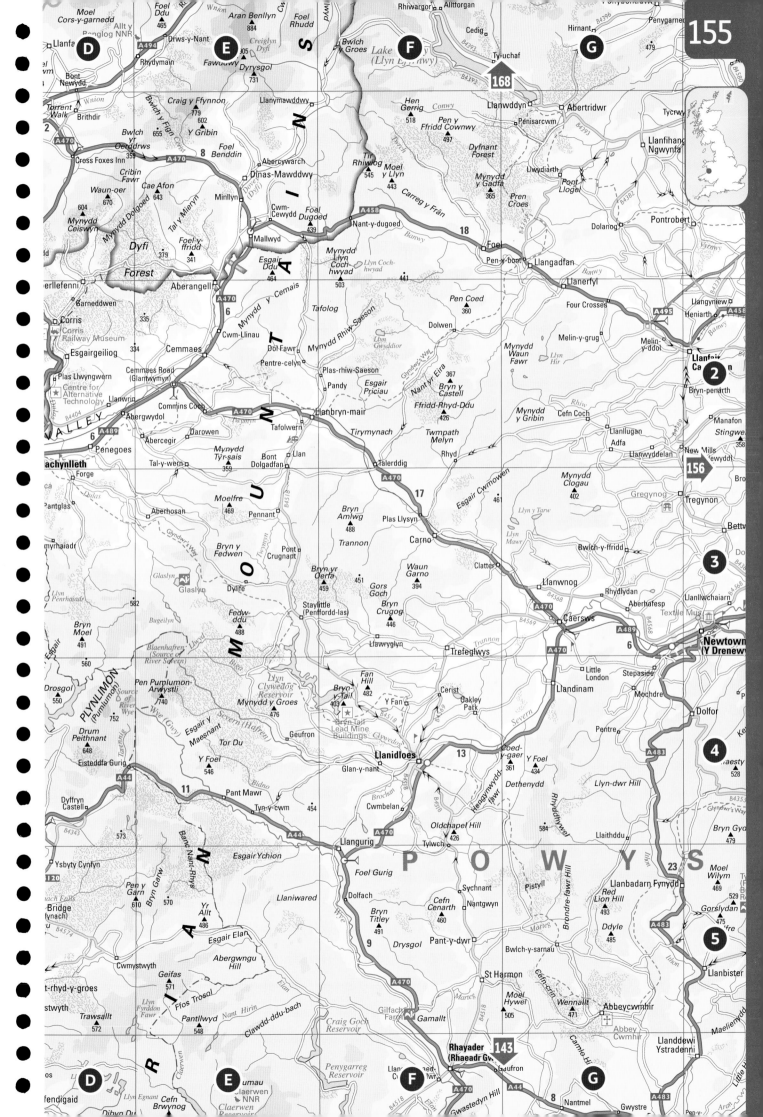

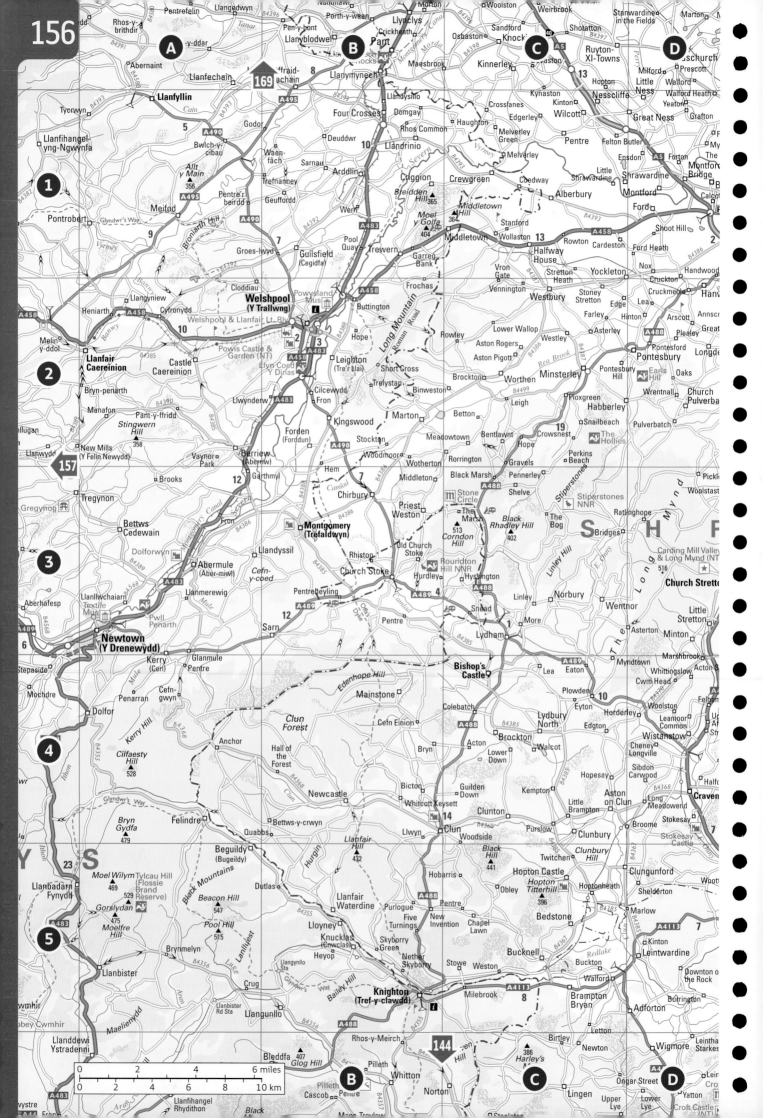

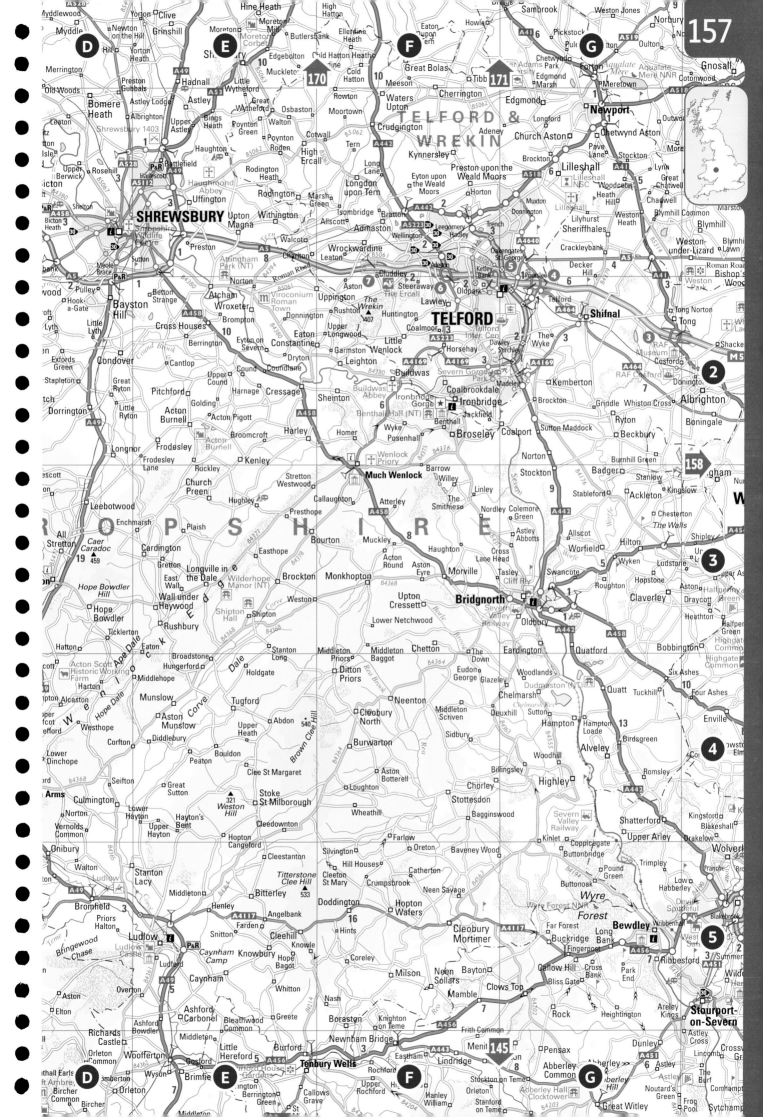

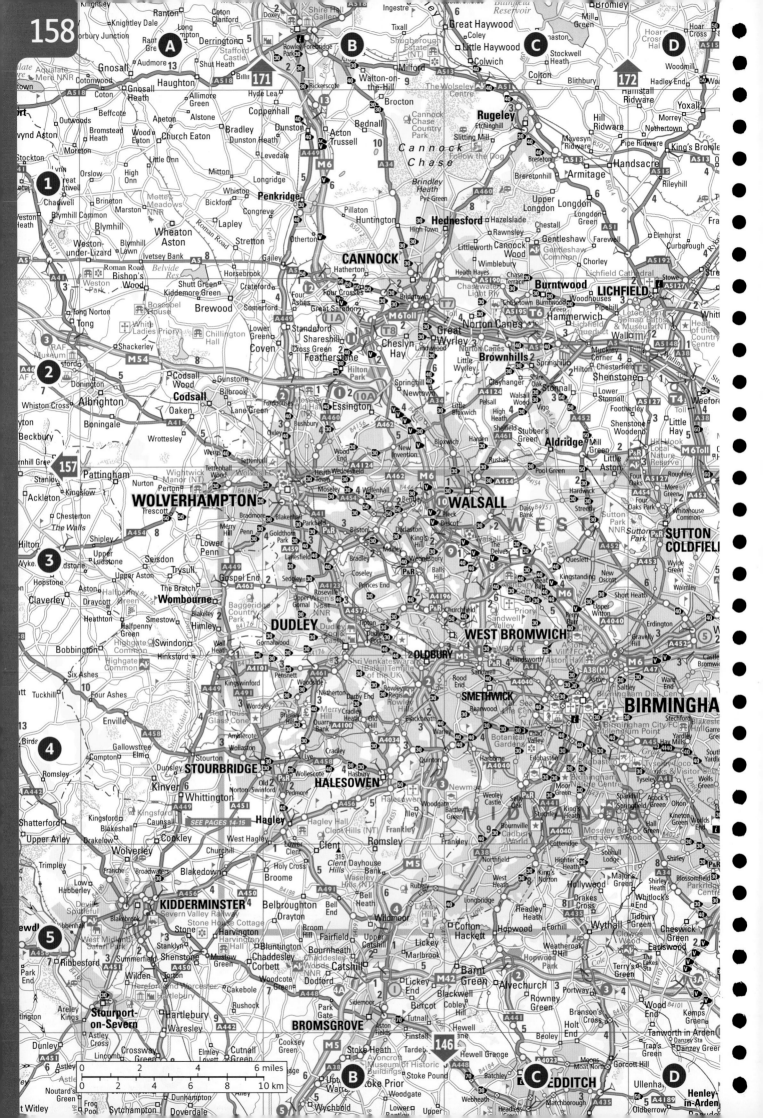

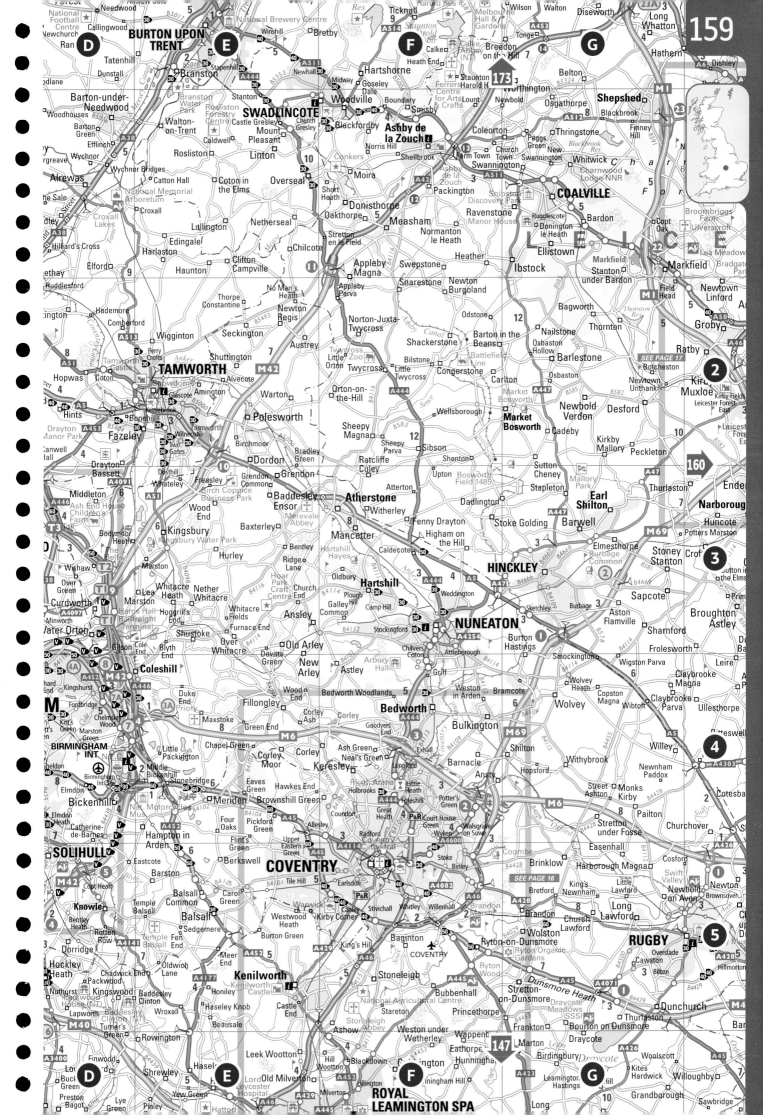

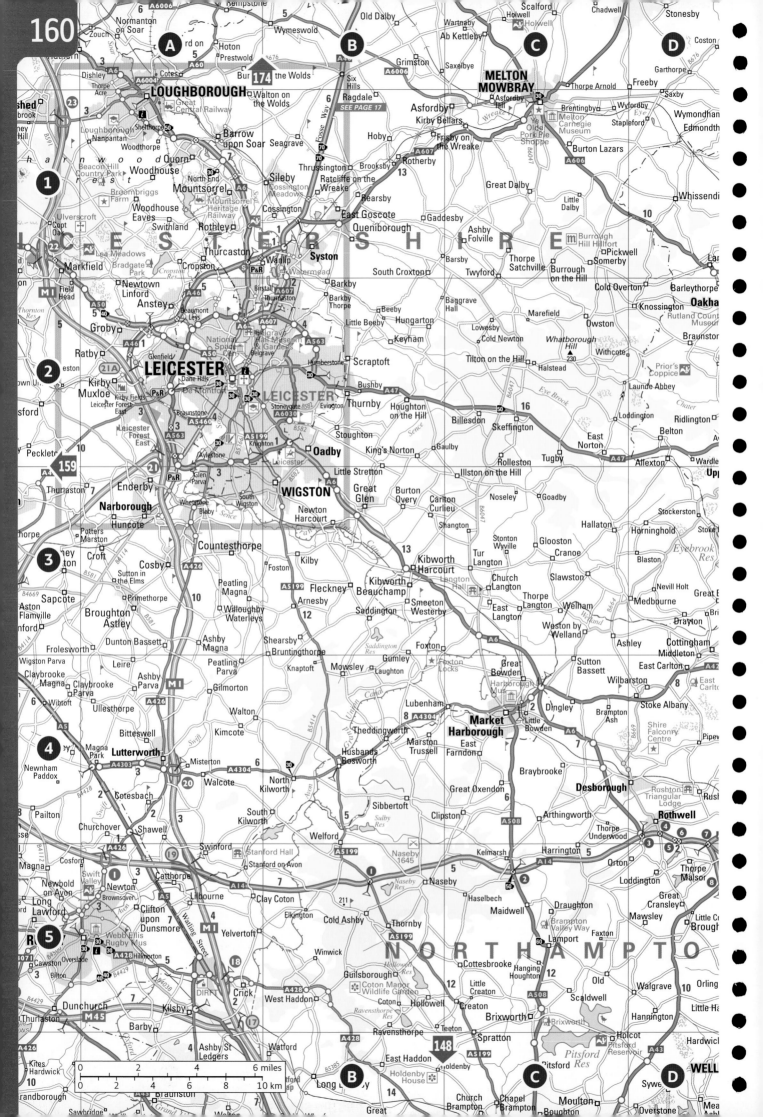

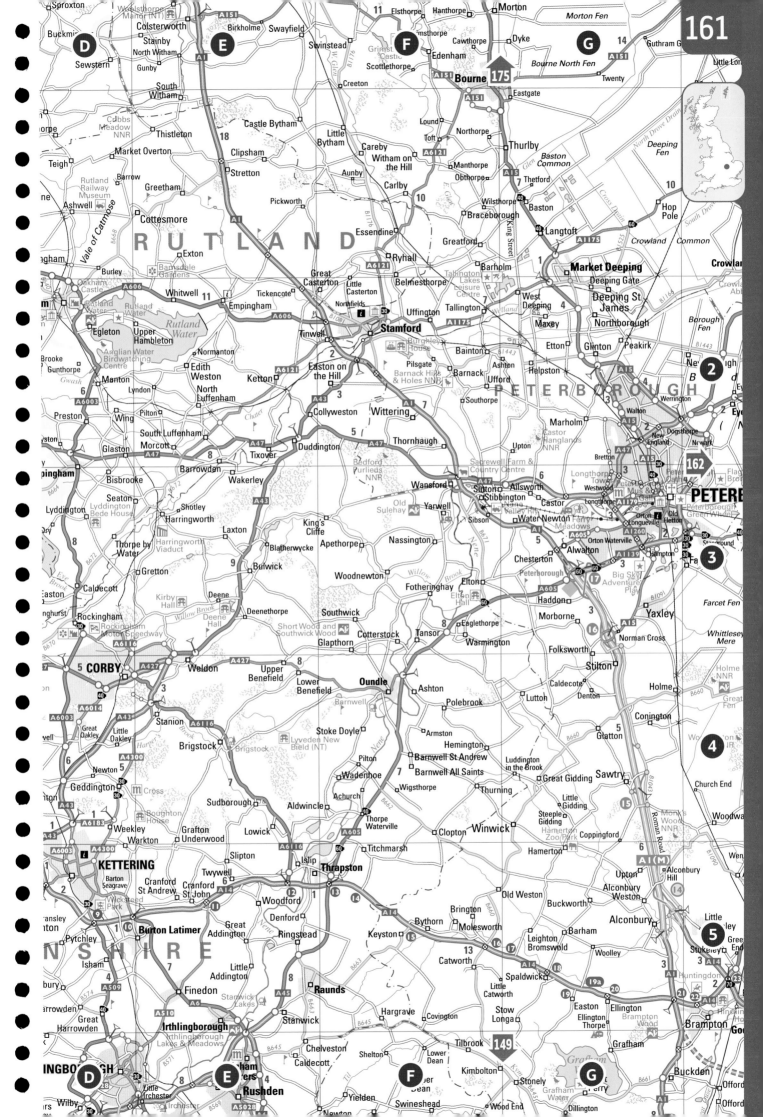

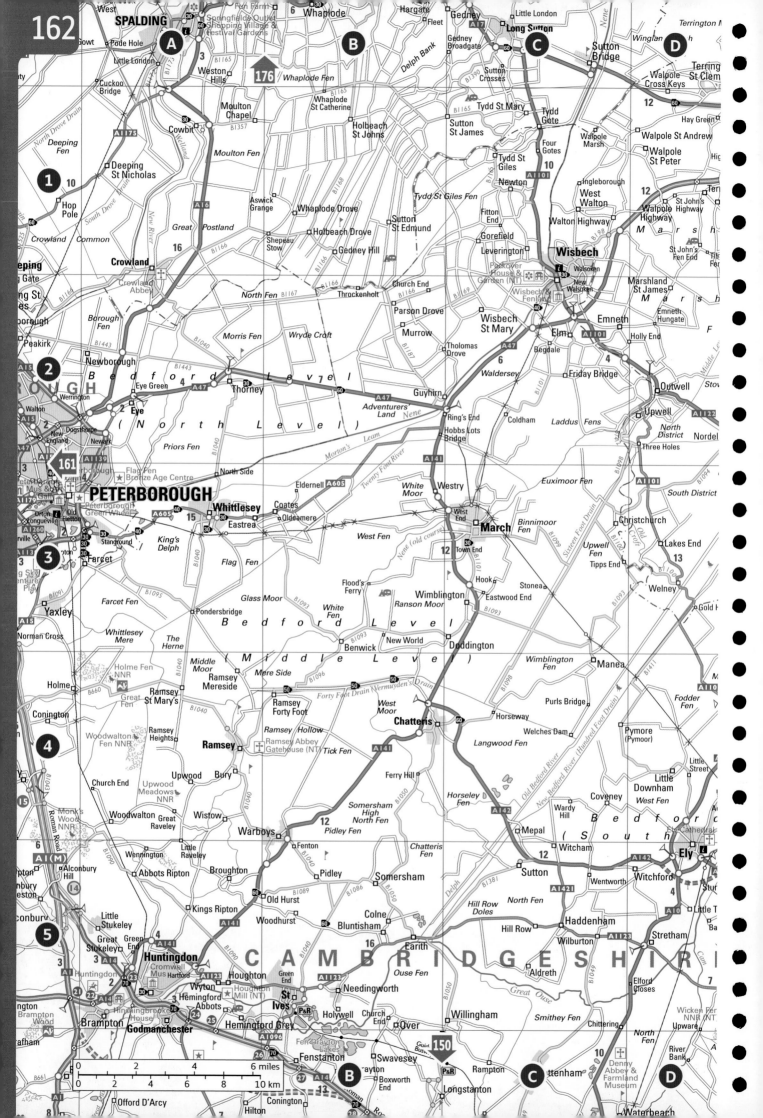

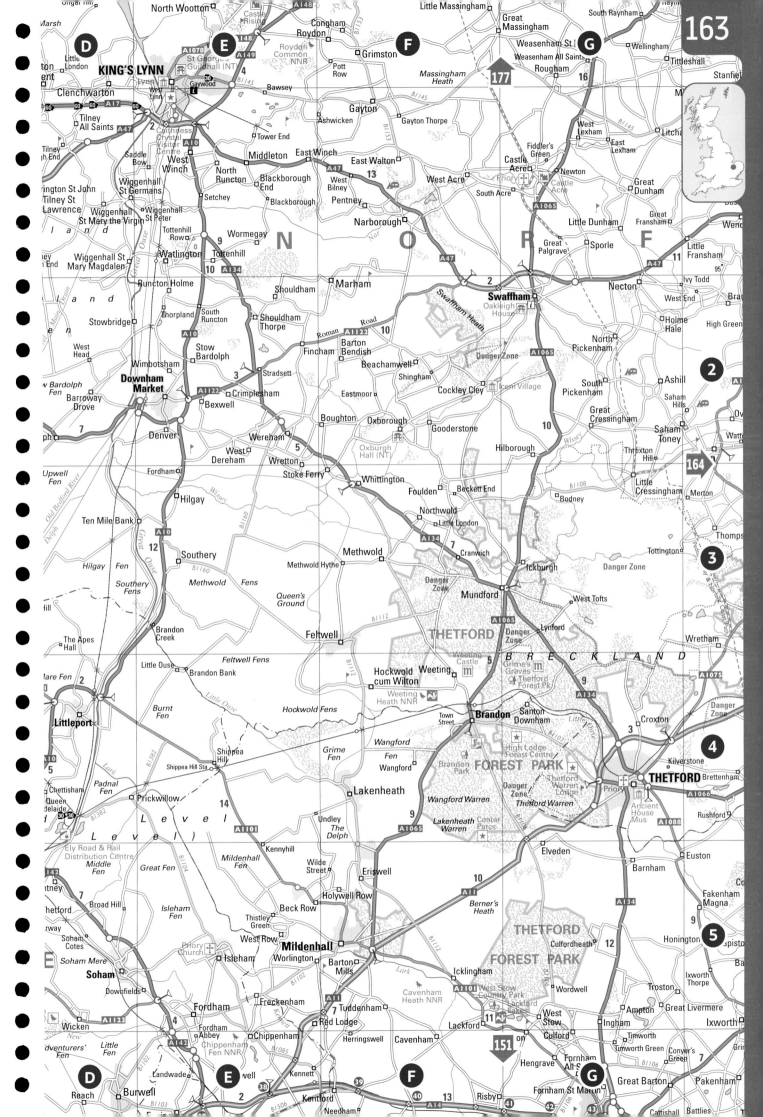

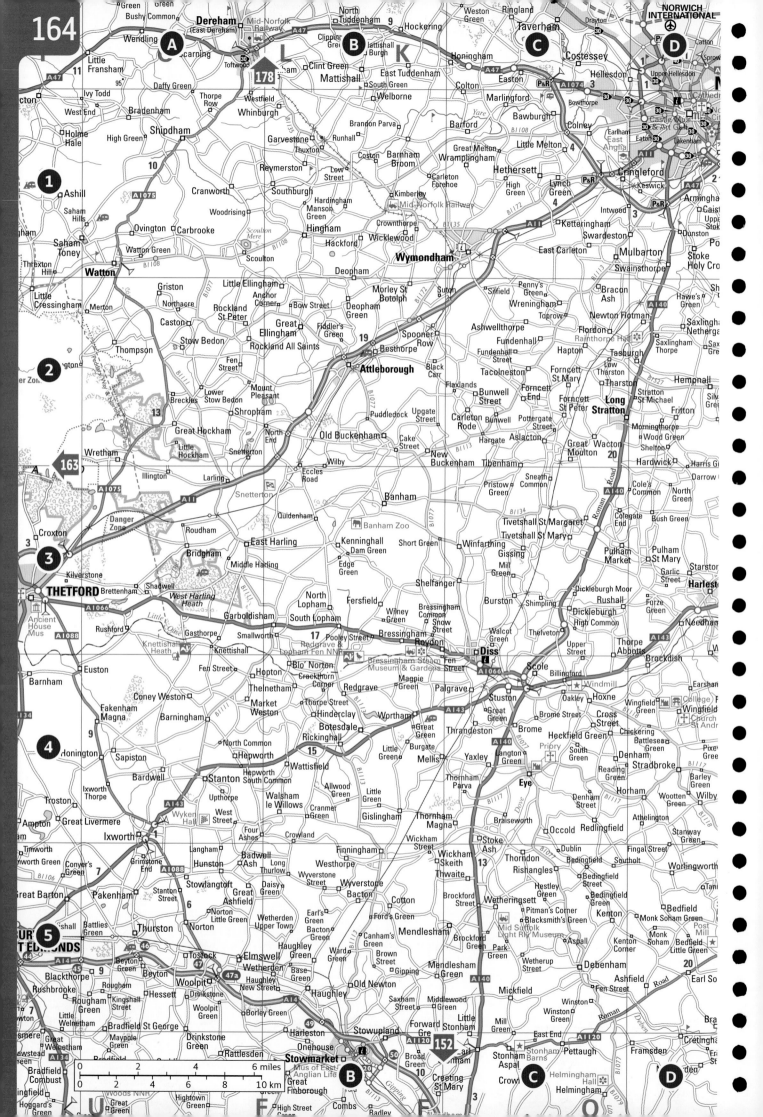

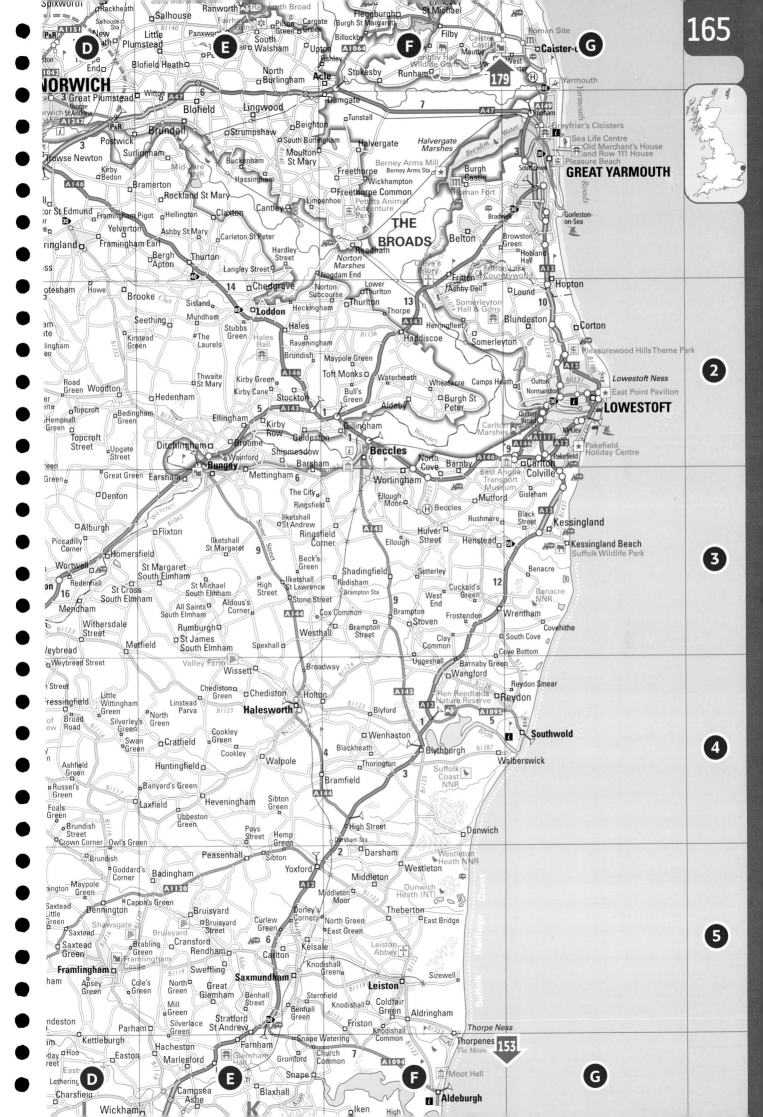

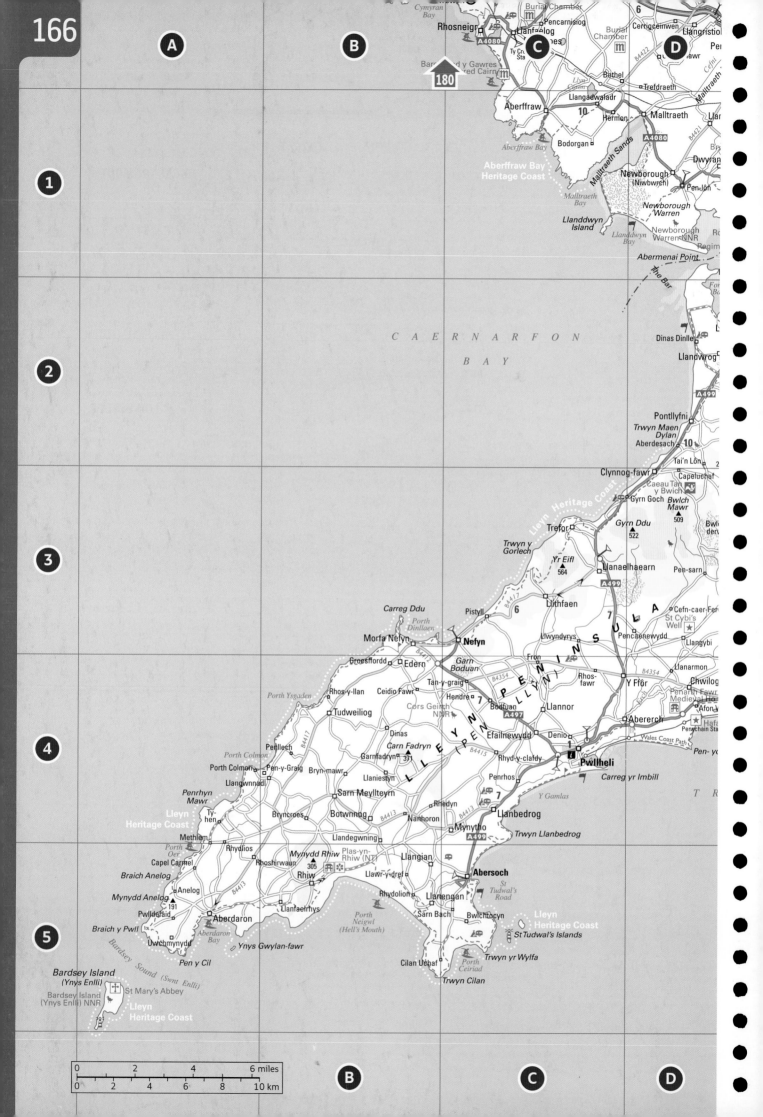

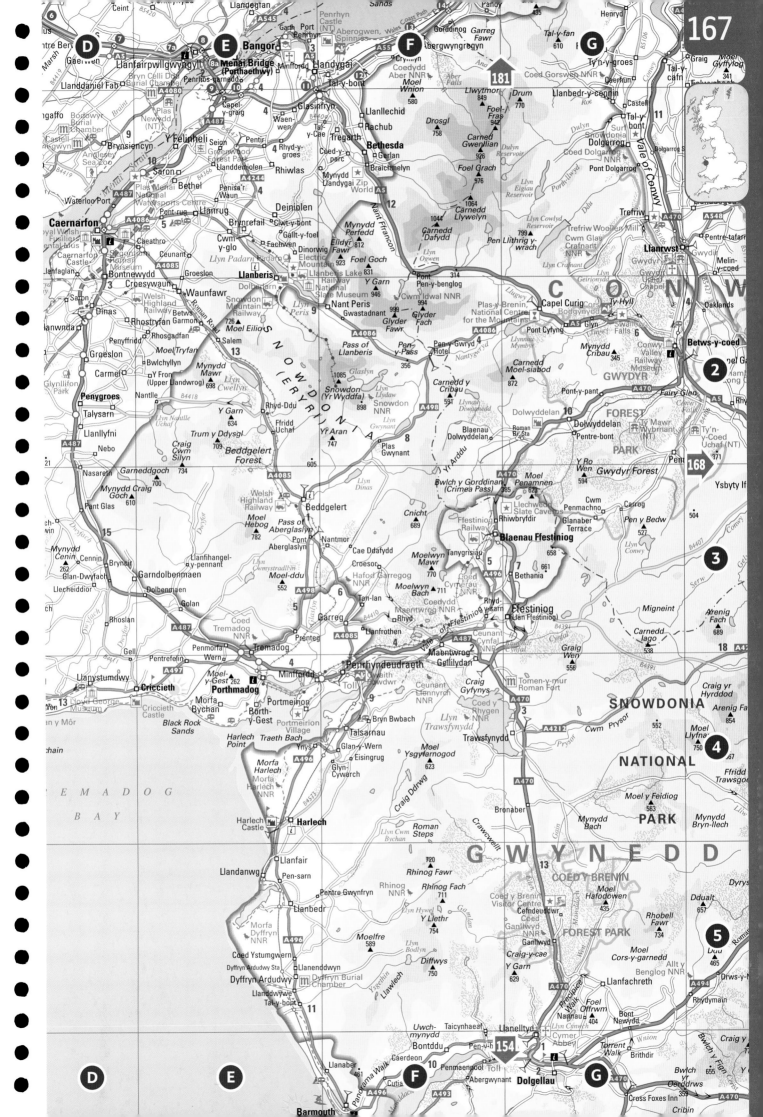

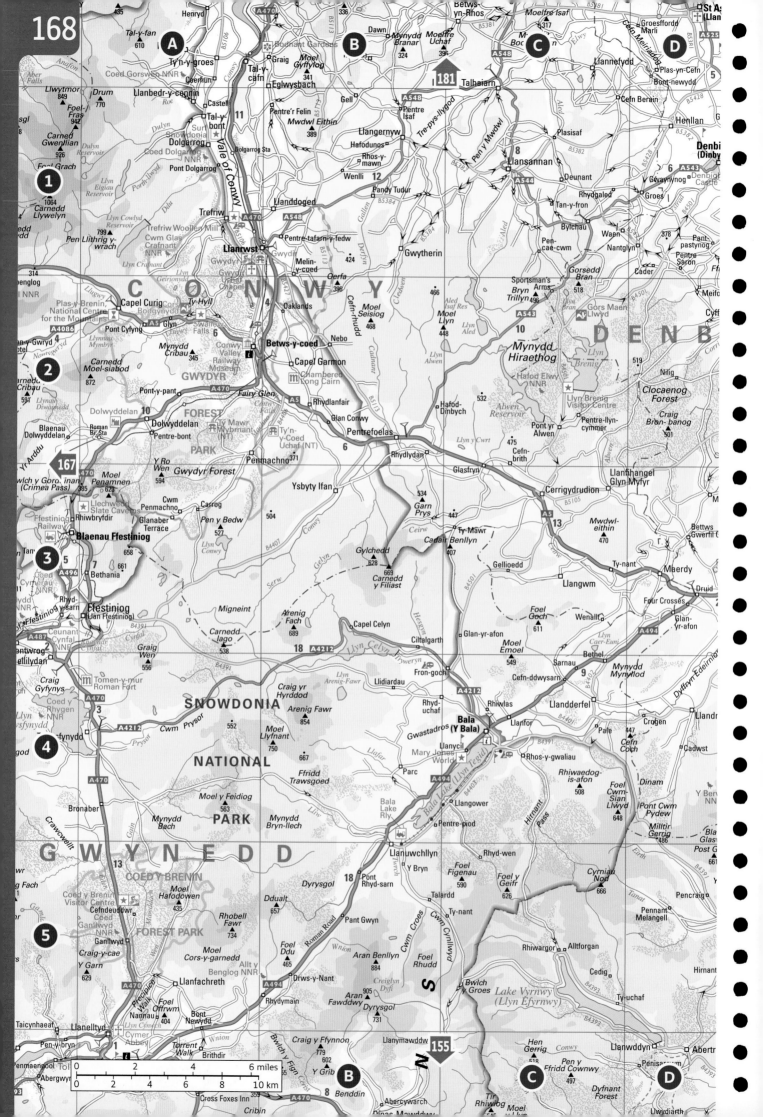

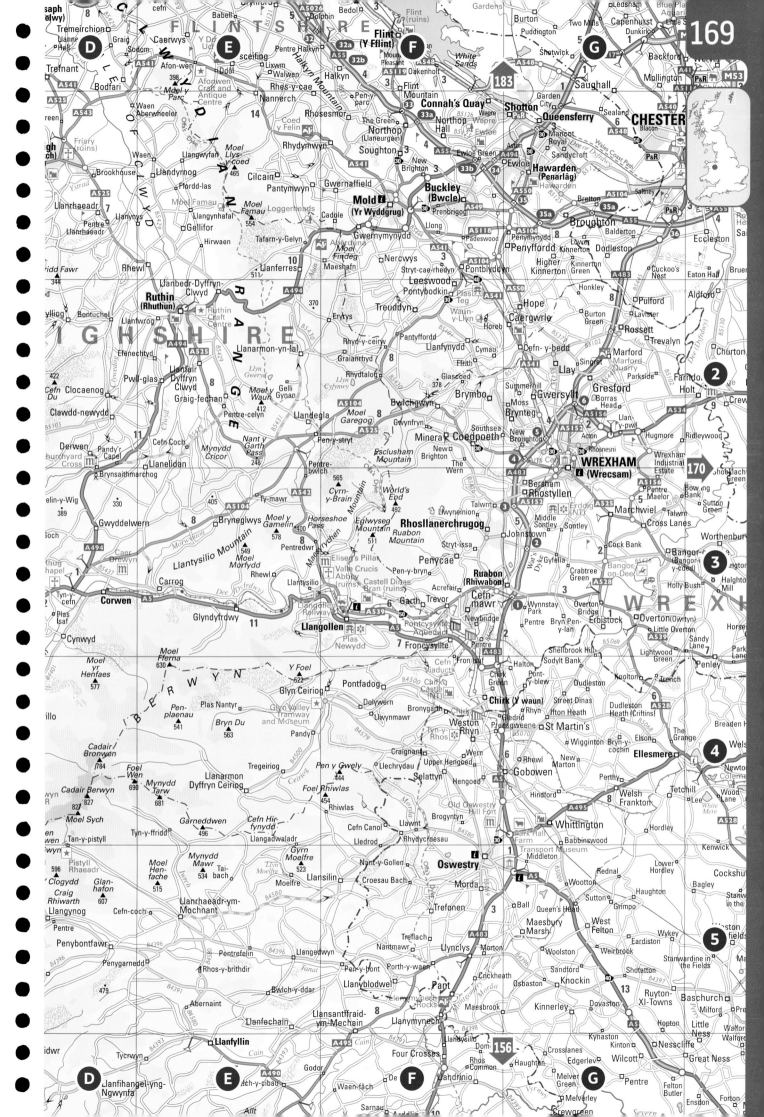

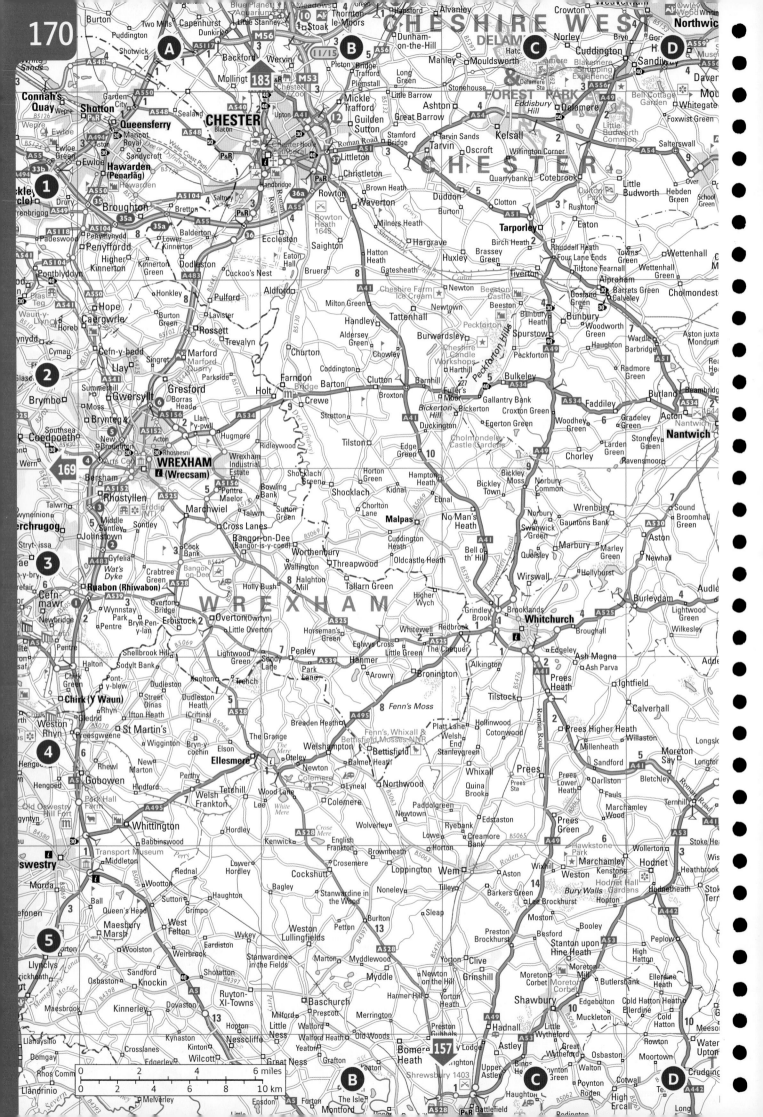

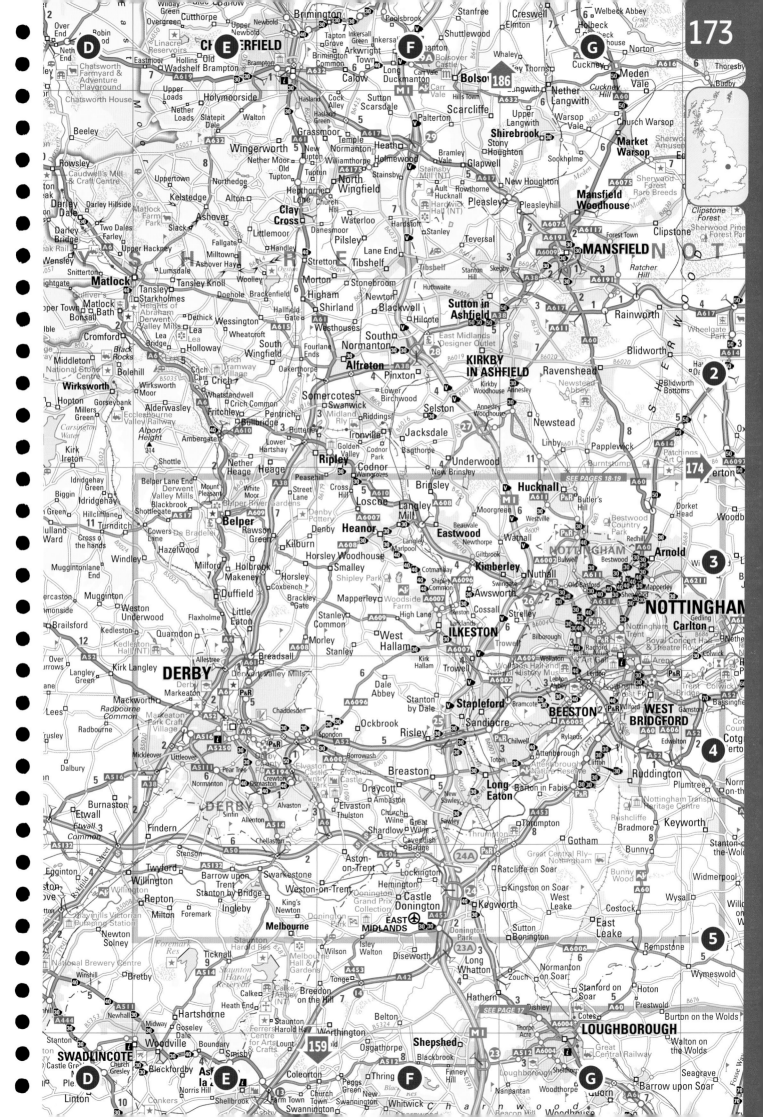

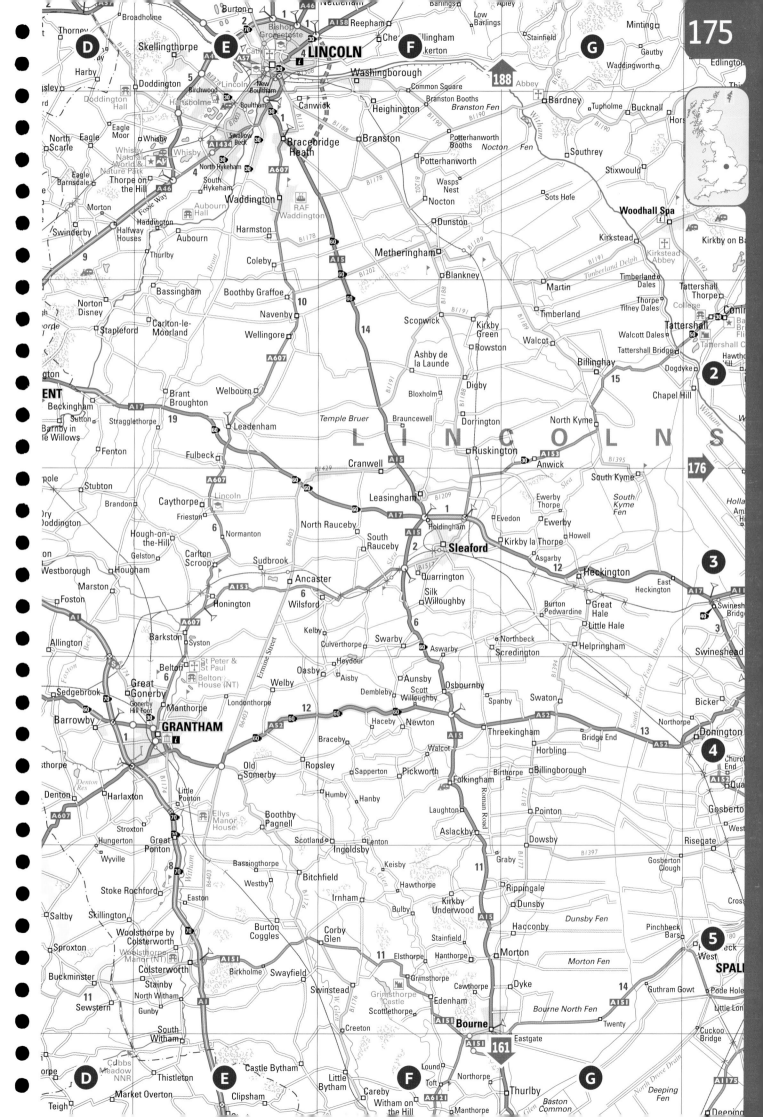

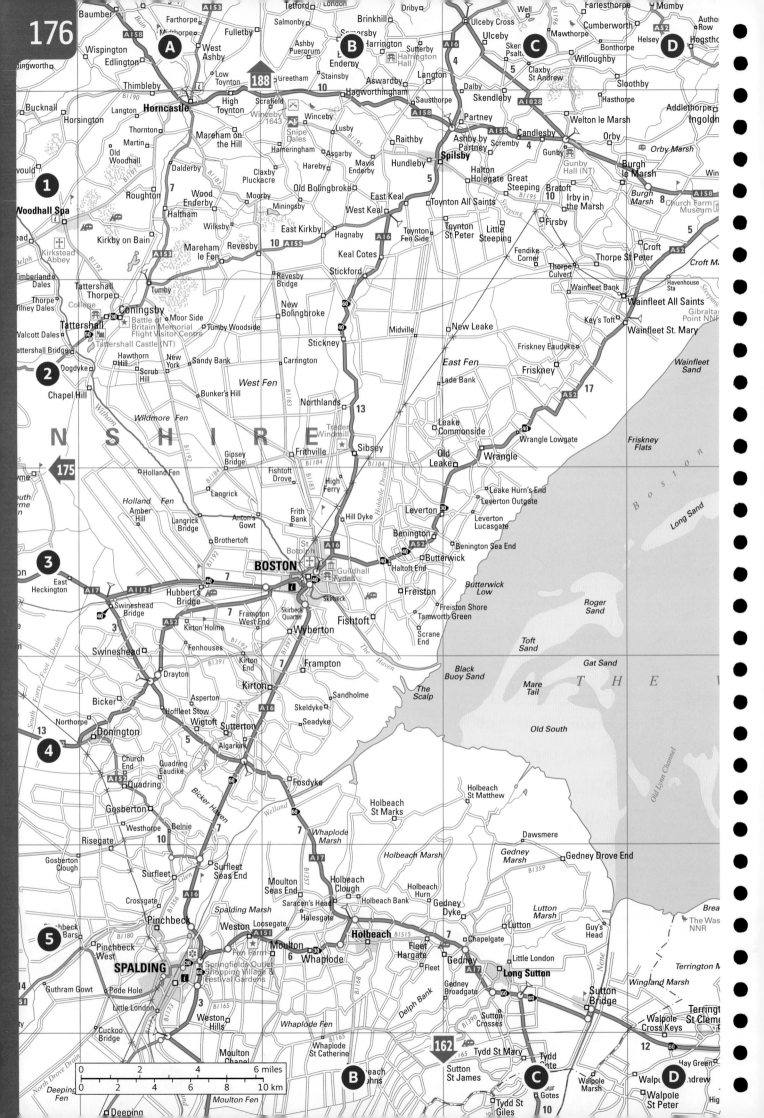

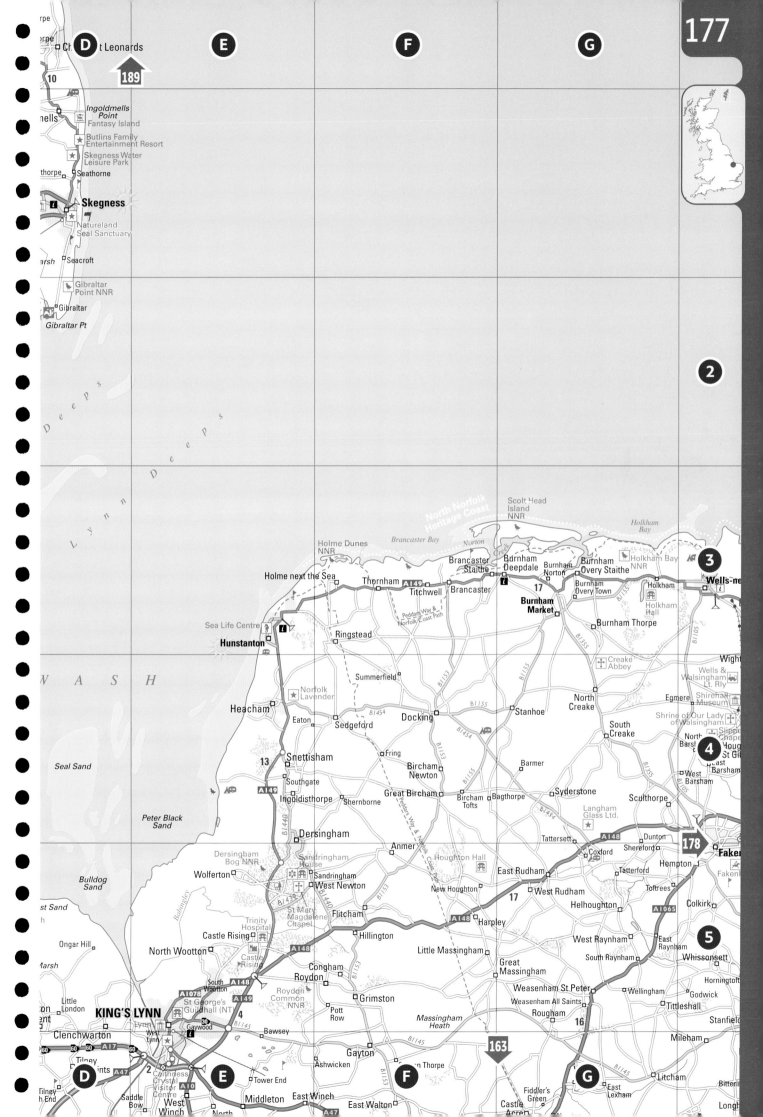

D **Ch—t Leonards** E F G

189

10

Ingoldmells Point
Fantasy Island
nells
Butlins Family
Entertainment Resort
Skegness Water
Leisure Park

thorpe
Seathorne

Skegness
Natureland
Seal Sanctuary

rsh
Seacroft

Gibraltar
Point NNR

Gibraltar
Gibraltar Pt

2

D e e p s

L y n n   D e e p s

North Norfolk
Heritage Coast
Scolt Head
Island
NNR
Holkham
Bay

Holme Dunes
NNR
Brancaster Bay
Norton
Creek

Holme next the Sea
Thornham
A149
Brancaster
Staithe
Burnham
Deepdale
Burnham
Norton
Burnham
Holkham Bay
NNR
Holkham

3

Wells-ne

Titchwell
Brancaster
17
Burnham
Overy Town
Holkham
Hall

Sea Life Centre
Ringstead
**Burnham
Market**
Burnham Thorpe

Hunstanton

Peddars Way &
Norfolk Coast Path

Burnham
Overy Staithe

W A S H

Summerfield
B1153
Creake
Abbey
Wight
Wells &
Walsingham
Lt. Rly
Egmere Shirehall
Museum

Norfolk
Lavender
Heacham
B1454
Stanhoe
North
Creake
Shrine of Our Lady
of Walsingham

Eaton
Sedgeford
Docking
B1155
South
Creake
North
Bars
Slipper
Chapel
Houg
St Gil

Seal Sand

13
Snettisham
Fring
Bircham
Newton
B1155
Barmer
Syderstone
West
Barsham
East
Barsham

A149
Southgate
Great Bircham
Bircham
Tofts
Bagthorpe
Sculthorpe

Ingoldisthorpe
Shernborne
Peddars Way & Norfolk Coast Path
Langham
Glass Ltd.

Peter Black
Sand
B1440
Dersingham
Anmer
Tattersett
A148
Dunton
Shereford
178

Faker

Dersingham
Bog NNR
Sandringham
House
Houghton Hall
East Rudham
Coxford
Hempton
Fakenh

Bulldog
Sand
Wolferton
Sandringham
West Newton
New Houghton
17
West Rudham
Toftrees
A1065
Colkirk

St Mary
Magdalene
Chapel
Helhoughton

st Sand
h
Trinity
Hospital
Flitcham
West Raynham
East
Raynham
5

Ongar Hill
Castle Rising
Hillington
Little Massingham
South Raynham
Whissonsett

North Wootton
Castle
Rising
A148
Great
Massingham
Horningtoft

Marsh
South
Wootton
A148
Congham
Roydon
Weasenham St Peter
Wellingham
Godwick

KING'S LYNN
A1078
A149
Roydon
Common
NNR
Grimston
Weasenham All Saints
Rough am
16
Tittleshall

Clenchwarton
St George's
Guildhall (NT
Pott
Row
*Massingham
Heath*
163
Stanfield

West
Lynn
Gaywood
Bawsey
B1145
Gayton
Mileham

Tilney
ints
A17
Caithness
Crystal
Visitor
Centre
A10
Ashwicken
Bitterin
Litcham

Tilney
h End
A47
West
Winch
Middleton
East Winch
East Walton
Fiddler's
Green
East
Lexham
Longh

D E Tower End F G
Saddle
Bow
North
Castle
Acre

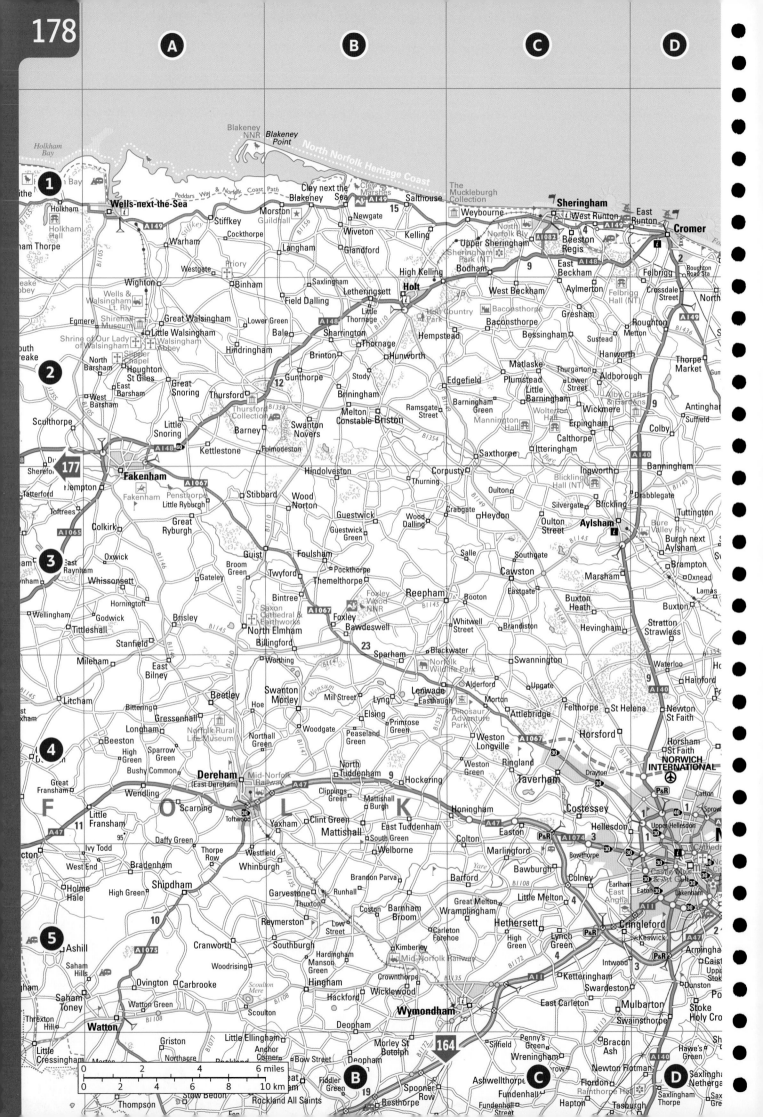

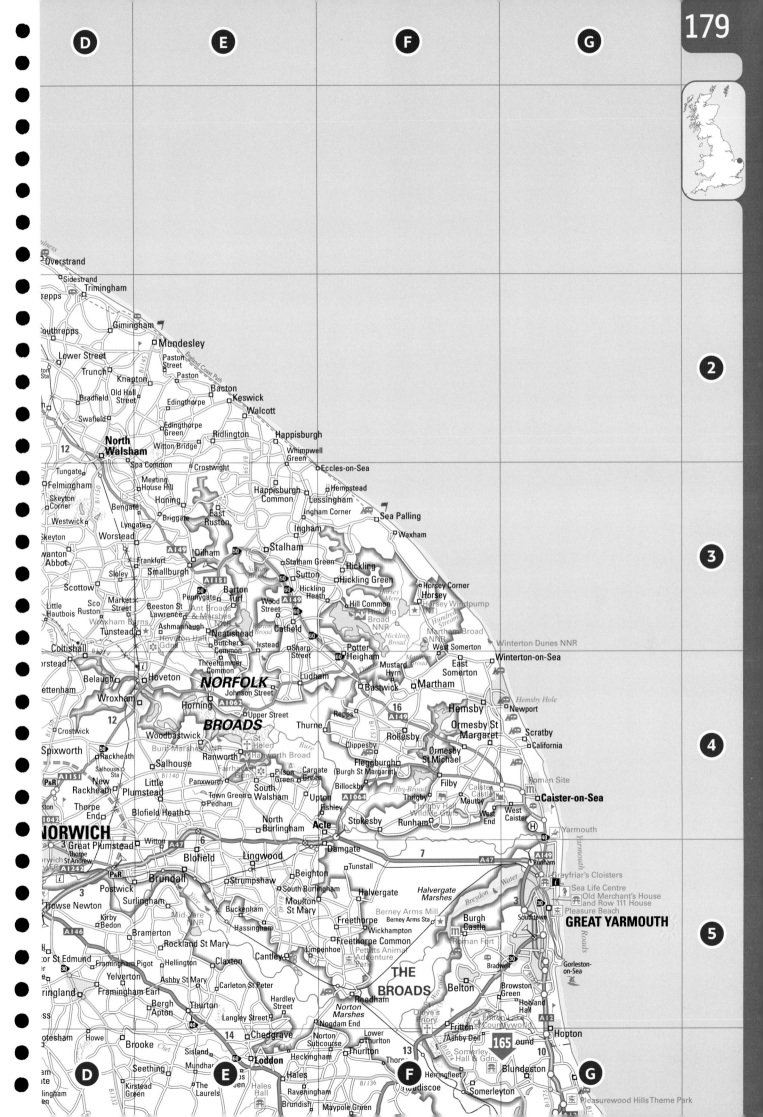

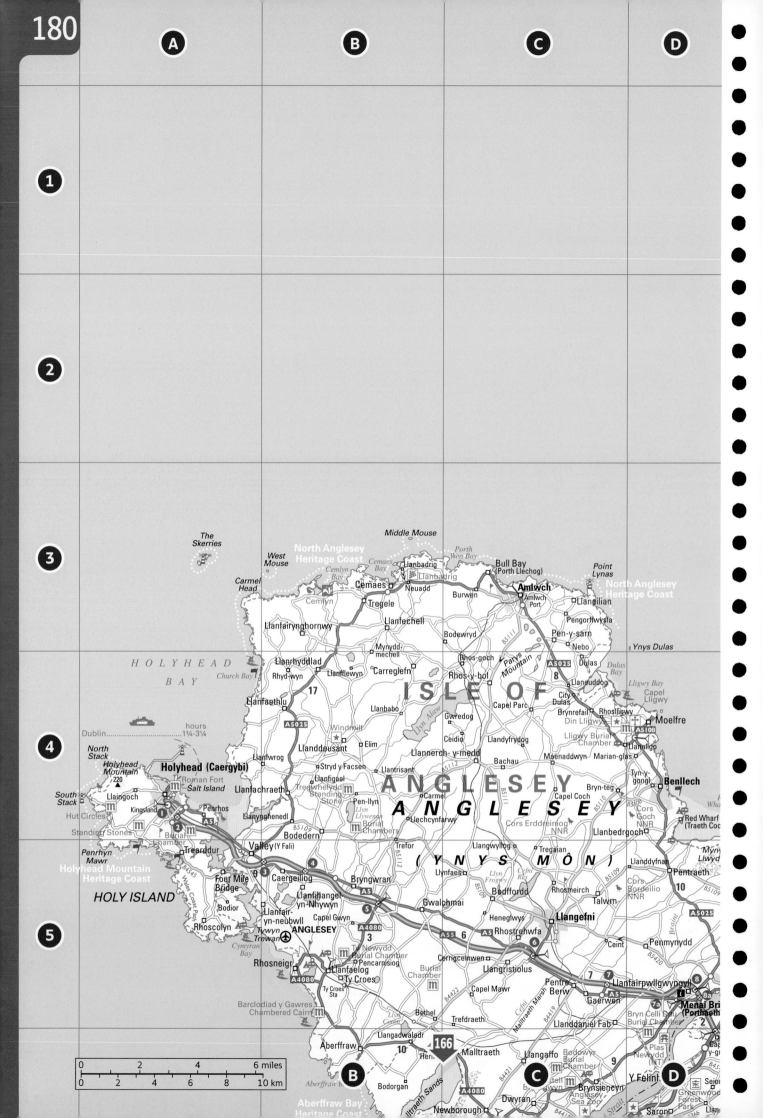

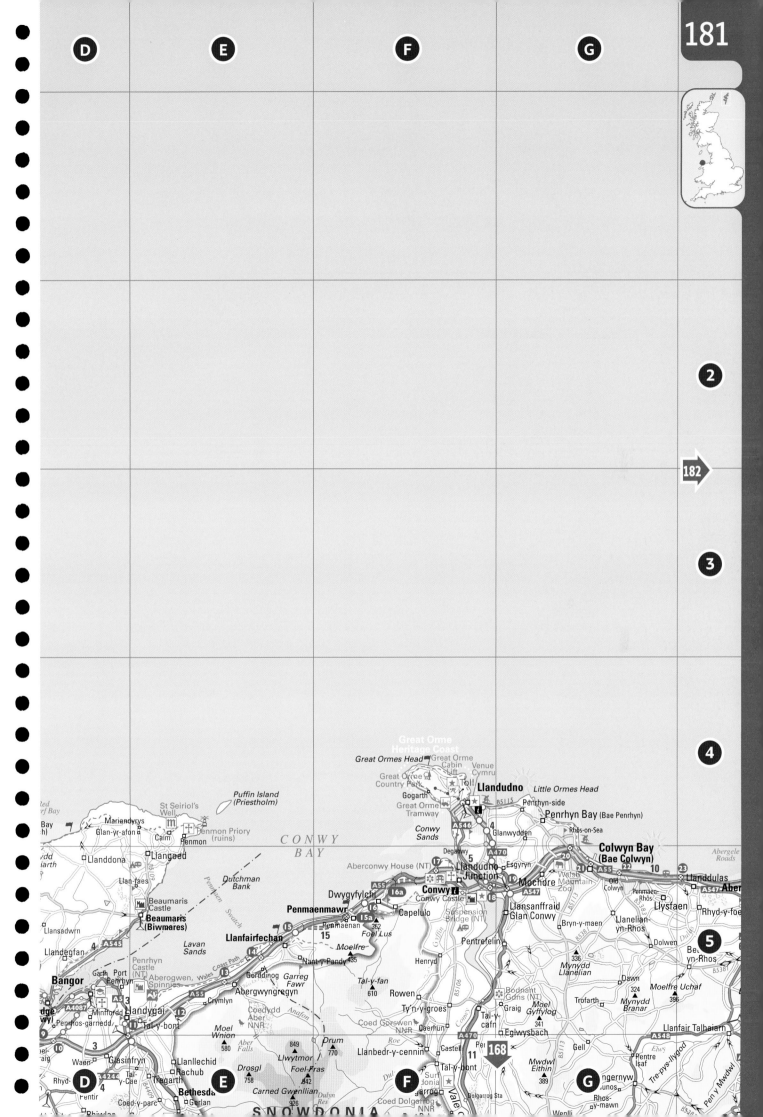

D E F G

182

2

3

4

Great Orme Heritage Coast

Great Ormes Head Great Orme Cabin Lift Venue Cymru

Great Orme Country Park Toll **Llandudno** Little Ormes Head

Gogarth Great Orme Tramway

Penrhyn-side

St Seiriol's Well Puffin Island (Priestholm) Penrhyn Bay (Bae Penrhyn)

Mariandyrys Penmon Priory (ruins) Conwy Sands Rhos-on-Sea

Glan-yr-afon Caim Penmon C O N W Y Glanwydden Abergele Roads

Red Surf Bay Llanddona Llangoed B A Y Deganwy Esgyryn Colwyn Bay (Bae Colwyn)

Rhyd Garth Llan-faes Dutchman Bank Aberconwy House (NT) Llandudno Junction Mochdre 10 Llanddulas

Beaumaris Castle Conwy Llansanffraid Glan Conwy Old Colwyn Penmaen-Rhos Aber

Llansadwrn **Beaumaris (Biwmares)** Dwygyfylchi Conwy Castle Bryn-y-maen Llanelian-yn-Rhos Llysfaen

Llandegfan Suspension Bridge (NT) Rhyd-y-foe

Llangefni **Penmaenmawr** Capelulo Liansanffraid Pentrefelin Dolwen Ben yn-Rhos

Bangor Penrhyn Castle (NT) **Llanfairfechan** Penmaenan Foel Lus Henryd Mynydd Llanelian Dawn Moelfre Uchaf

Garth Port Aberogwen Wales Coast Path Nant-y-Pandy Moelfre Trofarth Mynydd Branar

Spinnies Goddinog Garreg Fawr Tal-y-fan Rowen Bodnant Gdns (NT) Moel Gyffylog Llanfair Talhaiarn

Minffordd Llandygai Tal-y-bont Crymlyn Abergwyngregyn Graig Tal-y-cafn Trofarth Gell Pentre Isaf

Glasinfryn Coedydd Aber NNR Coed Gorswen NNR Caerhûn Eglwysbach Mwdwl Eithin

Llanllechid Moel Wnion Drum Coed Dolgarrog Llanbedr-y-cennin Castell Pel Tre-pys-llyod

Rachub Aber Falls Llwytmor Roe Sarn Dolgarrog Sta Pen y Mwdwl

Bethesda Drosgl Foel-Fras Ty-n-y-bont Rhos-mawn

Carned Gwenllian Dulyn Res

Gerlan S N O W D O N I A

A   B   C   D

1

2

181

3

Liverpool
(Birkenhead) to   hours
Belfast..................8
Douglas.......4¼ (Nov-March)
Liverpool to   hours
Douglas........2¾ (March-Oct)
Dublin..................8

L I V E R P O O L

B A Y

Ainsdale San

Formby

4

*West
Hoyle
Bank*

Welsh Channel

Point of
Ayr

East
Hoyle
Bank

Meols
Sta

A553

Hoylake

Manor Road Sta
Hoylake Sta

Royal
Liverpool

Hilbre Island

Red
Rocks
Marsh

West
Kirby
Sta

West Kirby

Grange

Caldy

Frankby

Irby
Hil

A540

Thurstaston

Dawpool
Bank

Talacre

Llawndy

Mostyn Bank

Flynnongroyw

Pen-y-ffordd

A548

Mostyn Quay

Prestatyn
Sands
Holiday
Centre

Prestatyn

Gronant

Gwespyr

Llanasa

Gyrn

Glan-y-don

Trelogan

Mostyn

Llannerch-y-Môr

Holywell Bank

Sky
Tower

A548

Efrith

A547

Gwaenysgor

Axton

Whitford
(Chwitffordd)

A5151

Greenfield Valley
Greenfield
(Maes-Glas)

St Winefride's Holy Well & Chap

Rhyl

SeaQuarium

Rhyl Sun Centre

Meliden
(Gallt Melyd)

Gop
Hill 8

Trelawnyd

Maen
Achwyfaen

Basingwerk
Abbey

A5026

Carmel

Whelston

30

Kinmel Bay
(Bae Cinmel)

B5119

2

Tan-yr-
allt

Dyserth

Ochr-
y-foel

Lloc

Gorsedd

Pantasaph
Friary

Pantasaph

Bagillt
Bank

Holywell (Treffynnon)

Bagillt

A548

Towyn

Plas
Uchaf

A525

Bodrhyddan
Hall

Roman

Road

Babell

Dolphin

Bedol

Abergele
Roads

Wales Coast Path

A548

Morfa
Rhuddlan

Rhuddlan

Rhuddlan
Cae & Twt Hll

Marian
Cwm

Helyg

Calcoed

Brynford

Pantasaph

Flin
(

wyn Bay
Colwyn)

10

23

Llanddulas

23a

Pensarn

5

Llwyd

6

Pengwern

B5429

Rhuallt

29

30

31

Pen-y-
cefn

A55

A5026

32a

Flint
(Y Fflint)

Penrhyn)

22

Abergele

A547

24

St George

24a

Bodelwyddan

27a

28

Caerwys

Ysceifiog

Lixwm

Halkyn

32b

Mount Pleasant

A5119

Oak

Llysfaen

Rhyd-y-foel

A55

525

26

27

**St Asaph
(Llanelwy)**

Tremeirchion

Graig

Sodom

Afon-wen

Moel
y Parc

Ddôl

Walwen

F L I N T S H I R E

Pentre Halkyn

Halkyn

Flin

Oak

elian
Rhos

Penmaen
Rhôs

Betws
yn-Rhos

6

Moelfre Isaf

B5381

317

Mynydd
Bodrochwyn

Cefn Meiriadog

B538

Groesffordd
Marli

Llannerch
Hall

B525

Llanverth

Caerwys

Y Dôl
Uchaf

A541

Pentre Halkyn

B5121

Mount Pleasant

A55

32b

Rhes-y-cae

The Green

Flin

Dawn

324

Moelfre Uchaf

396

Llannefydd

Plas-yn-Cefn

Bont-newydd

Trefnant

A541
Bodfari

Afonwen
Craft and
Antique
Centre

14

Coed
y Felin

Rhosesmor

rthop

Mynydd
Branar

Llanfair Talhaiarn

A548

Cefn
Berain

B525

Henllan

B5382

168

eeler

Nannerch

The Green
urgain

Pentre
Isaf

Tre-pys-llydog

A544

Green

A543

Friary
(ruins)

VALE OF CLWYD

Llangwyfan

Llys-y-coed

Rhydymwyn

Ne

nyw

Elwy

0   2   4   6 miles

0 2 4 6 8 10 km

B

**Denbigh
(Dinbych)**

A543

Llansannan

Waen

Llangwyfan

C

Moel
Llys-y-coed

D

ough

30

Bright

A B C D

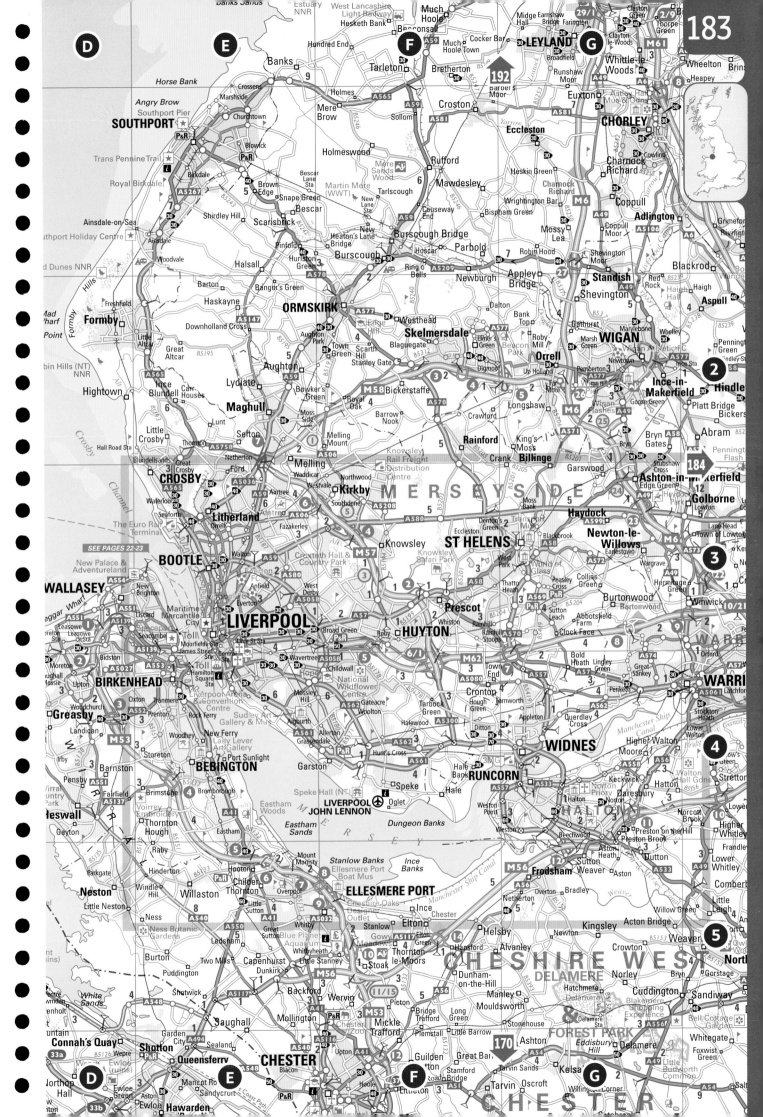

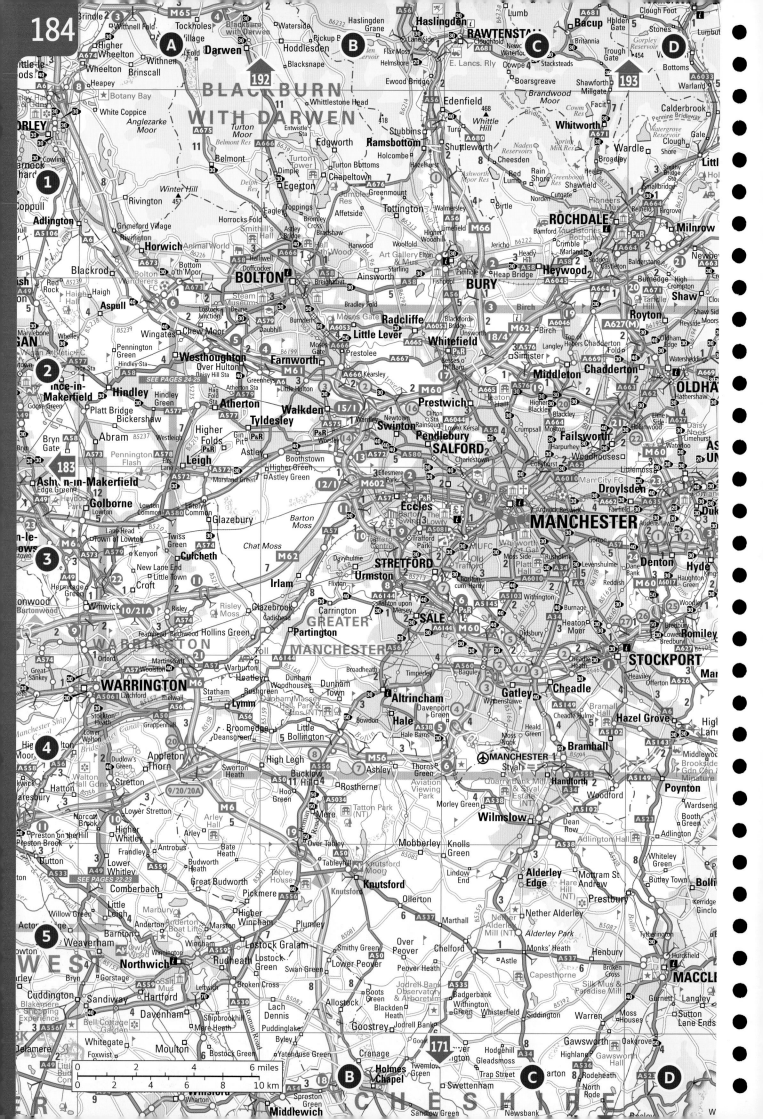

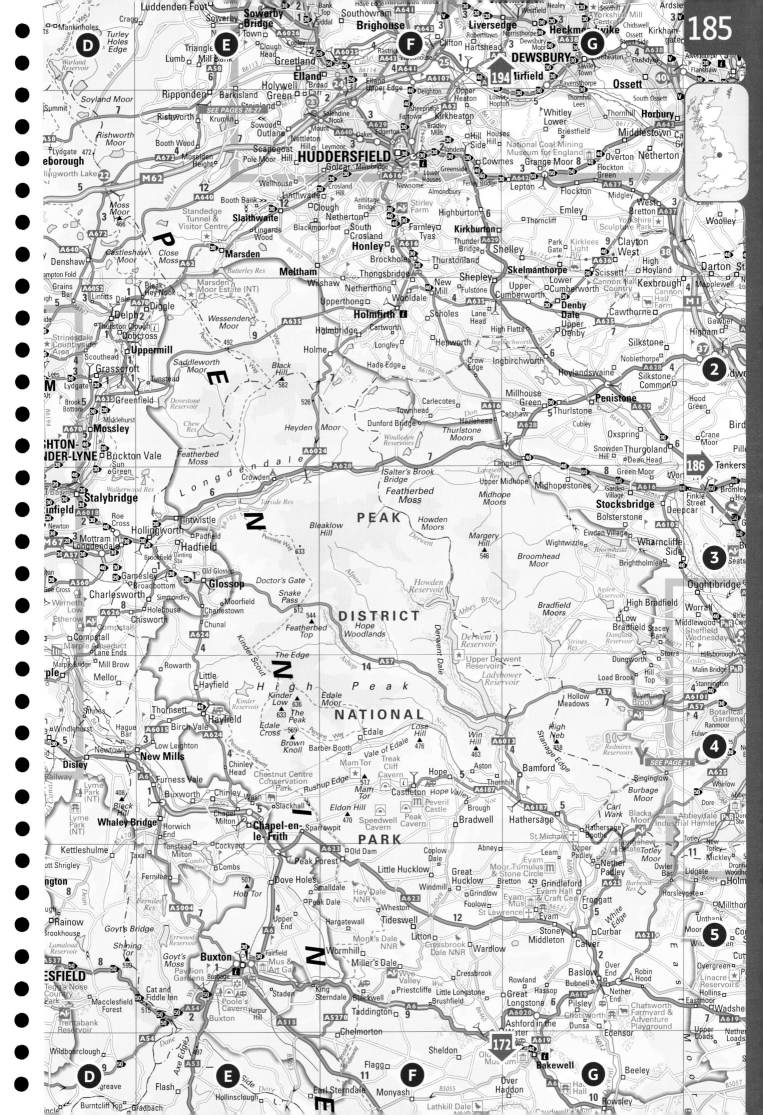

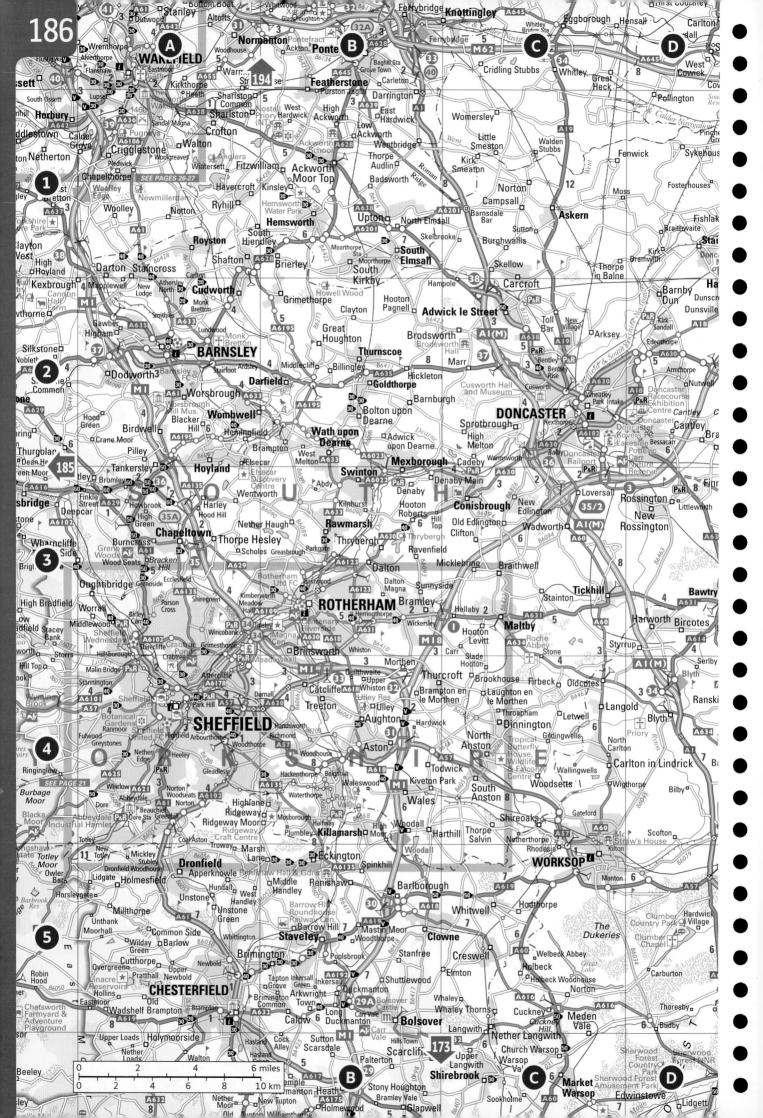

D   **E**   **F**   **G**

Holmpton

Out
Newton

7

Weeton

197

Easington

Skeffling

*Skeffling
Clays*

Kilnsea

Spurn Heritage
Coast

*Kilnsea
Clays*

Spurn NNR

Spurn Point
Nature Reserve

*Spurn
Head*

Spurn Head

2

s Coast Light Rly
s
Centre

Marshchapel

Donna
Nook

Donna
Nook

Eskham

Wragholme

Donna Nook NNR

Grainthorpe

Meals

North Somercotes

Ludney

Church
End

Skidbrooke
North End

Conisholme

South
Somercotes

A1031

Saltfleet

3

enham St Mary

South
Somercotes
Fen Houses

Skidbrooke

Yarburgh

Alvingham

Saltfleetby
St Clements

North
Cockerington

Saltfleetby
All Saints

12

Saltfleetby -
Theddlethorpe NNR

ton
ner

South
Cockerington

Saltfleetby
St Peter

Theddlethorpe St Helen

ddington

Grimoldby

Theddlethorpe
All Saints

Stewton

B1200

Manby

A1031

Little
Carlton

Great
Carlton

Great Eau

A157

Legbourne

North
Reston

Gayton
le Marsh

A1104

i

Mablethorpe

4

Little
Cawthorpe

South
Reston

4

Trusthorpe

Muckton

Authorpe

11

Tothill

Strubby

3

Thorpe

A52

Sutton on Sea

Withern

A157

Maltby
le Marsh

H

Sutton
le Marsh

Sandilands

Woodthorpe

Beesby

Hagnaby

6

Hannah

ell

Claythorpe

Saleby

A16

Belleau

Aby

Greenfield

Markby

A52

8

White
Pit

Swaby

A111

Thorestorpe

Asserby
The Grange

5

sgate

South
Thoresby

Ailby

Bilsby

Thurlby

Huttoft

Anderby Creek

Ketsby

Rigsby

Alford

B1449

Anderby

5

th Ormsby

Calceby

Haugh

3

Bilsby Field

Driby

A1104

Well

Farlesthorpe

Mumby

Authorpe
Row

Brinkhill

Ulceby Cross

Mawthorpe

B1196

Cumberworth

mersby

Sutterby

Ulceby

Helsey

Hogsthorpe

Chapel St Leonards

Harrington

A16

Skendleby
Psalter

Bonthorpe

erby

Harrington
Hall

4

Langton

Dalby

Claxby
St Andrew

Willoughby

Aswardby

5

Skendleby

Sloothby

10

agworthingham

Sausthorpe

A1028

Welton
le Marsh

Hasthorpe

A52

Partney

Addlethorpe

Ingoldmells

177

A158

Scremby

sby

Ingoldmells Point

Fantasy Island

B195

hby

A16

Gunby

Orby

*Orby
Marsh*

Butlins
Family Entertainment Resort

Spilsby

Ashby by
Partney

Gunby
Hall (NT)

Skegness Water Leisure Park

Mavis
Enderby

Hundleby

Halton
olgate

gh le Marsh

Winthorpe

Seathorne

D   **E**   **F**   **G**

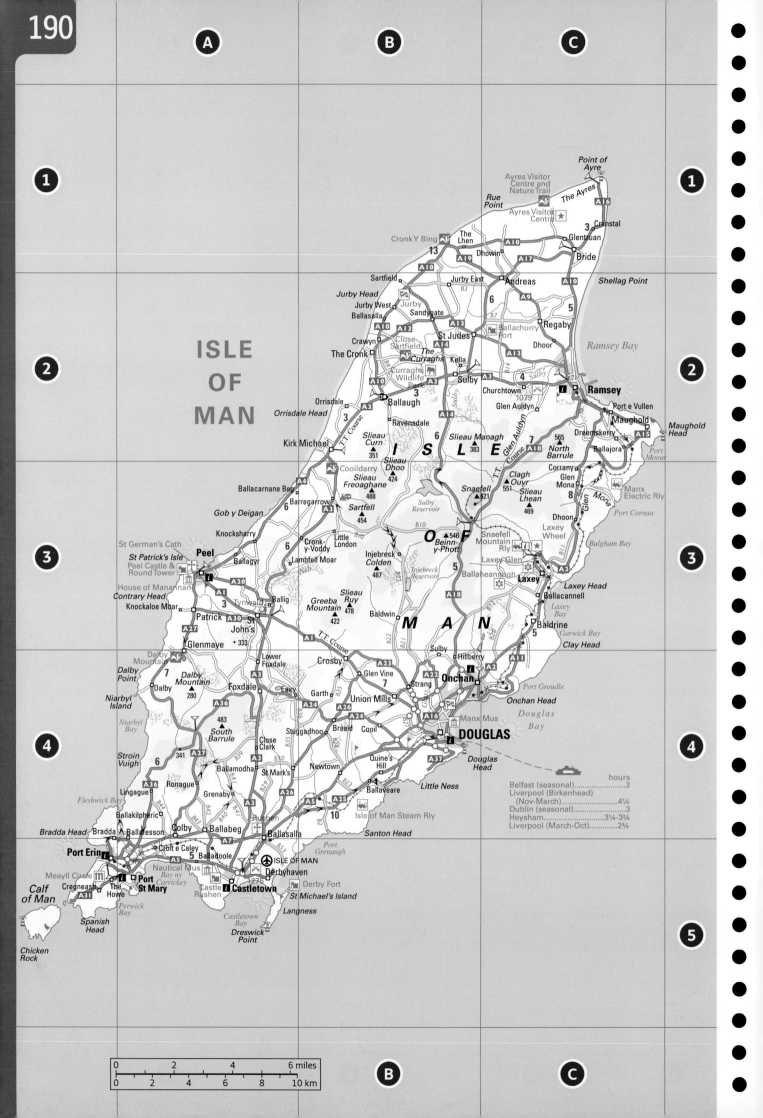

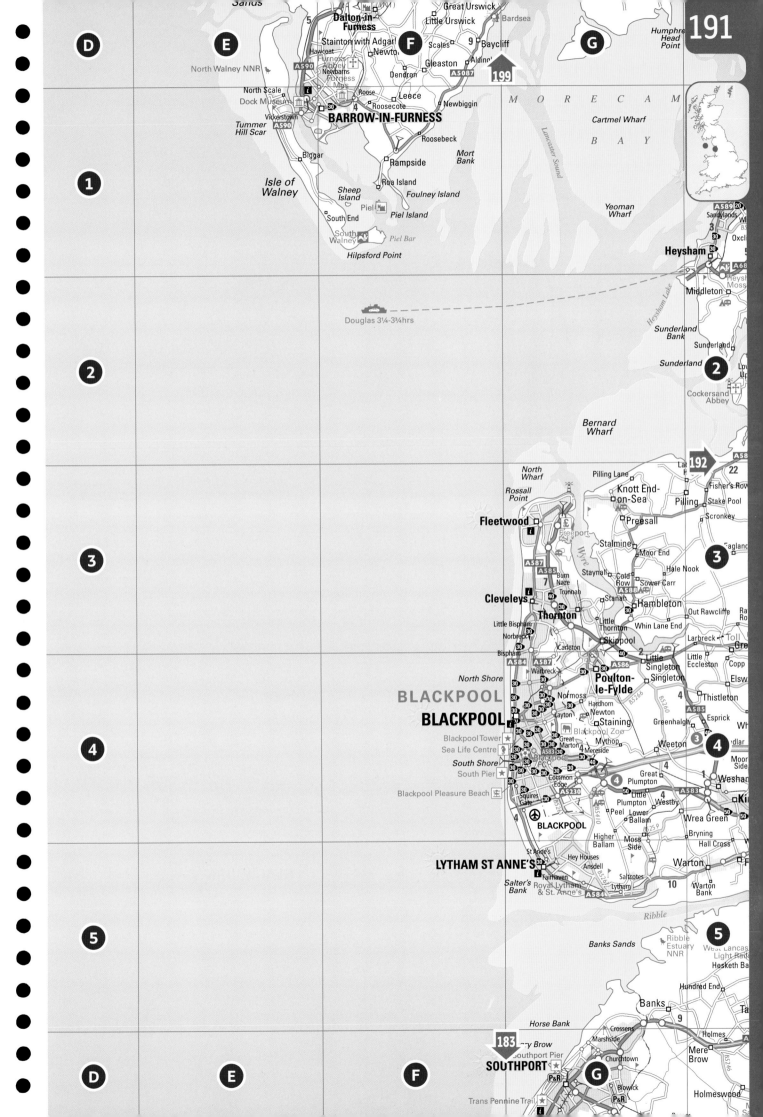

Sands

Great Urswick
Dalton-in-Furness
Little Urswick
Bardsea

Stainton with Adgarley
Newton
Scales
9 Baycliff

Hawcoat
Gleaston
Aldingham

Furness
Abbey
North Walney NNR
Dendron

Furness
Mbs
Newbarns

North Scale
Roose
Leece

Dock Museum
Roosecote
Newbiggin

BARROW-IN-FURNESS
4
Roosecote

Tummer
Hill Scar
Vickerstown

Biggar
Rooseback

Rampside
Mort
Bank

Isle of
Walney
Roa Island

Sheep
Island
Foulney Island

Piel
South End

South
Walney
Piel Island

Hilpsford Point
Piel Bar

M O R E C A M

B A Y

Cartmel Wharf

Lancaster Sound

Yeoman
Wharf

Humphre
Head
Point

Sandylands

Oxcl

Heysham

Heysh
Moss

Middleton

Douglas 3¼-3¾hrs

Heysham Lake

Sunderland
Bank

Sunderland

Sunderland
2

Cockersand
Abbey

Bernard
Wharf

North
Wharf
Pilling Lane
192
22

Rossall
Point
Knott End-
on-Sea
Fisher's Row

Fleetwood
Preesall
Pilling
Stake Pool

Freeport
Stalmine
Scronkey

A587
Moor End
Eagland

A585
Staynall
Hale Nook

7
Burn
Naze
Cold
Row
Sower Carr

Trunnah
Stanah
Hambleton

Cleveleys
40
Little
Thornton
Out Rawcliffe
Ra
Ro

Thornton
Skippool
Whin Lane End

Little Bispham
Carleton
Larbreck
Toll
Gre

Norbreck
Little
Singleton
Little
Eccleston
Copp

Bispham
A586
Singleton
Elswi

North Shore
Warbreck
Poulton-
le-Fylde
Thistleton

BLACKPOOL
Normoss
BS7366
4

BLACKPOOL
Hardhorn
Newton
Greenhalgh
Esprick
Wh

Blackpool Tower
Layton
Staining
Weeton

Sea Life Centre
Great
Marton
Blackpool Zoo
Mythop
3
4

South Shore
Mereside
Great
Plumpton
Wesha

South Pier
Common
Edge
4
Moor
Side

Blackpool Pleasure Beach
Squires
Gate
A5230
50
Little
Plumpton
Westby
4
Ki

4
BLACKPOOL
Peel
Lower
Ballam
Wrea Green

Higher
Ballam
Moss
Side
Bryning
Hall Cross

St Anne's
Hey Houses
Warton

LYTHAM ST ANNE'S
Fairhaven
Ansdell
Saltcotes
Warton
Bank

Salter's
Bank
Royal Lytham
& St. Anne's
A584
Lytham
10

Ribble

Banks Sands
Ribble
Estuary
NNR
West Lancas
Light Rai
Hesketh Ba

Hundred End

Banks

Horse Bank
Crossens
Marshside
Holmes

183
Brow
Mere
Brow

Southport Pier
Churchtown
Holmeswood

SOUTHPORT
P&R
Blowick
P&R

Trans Pennine Trail

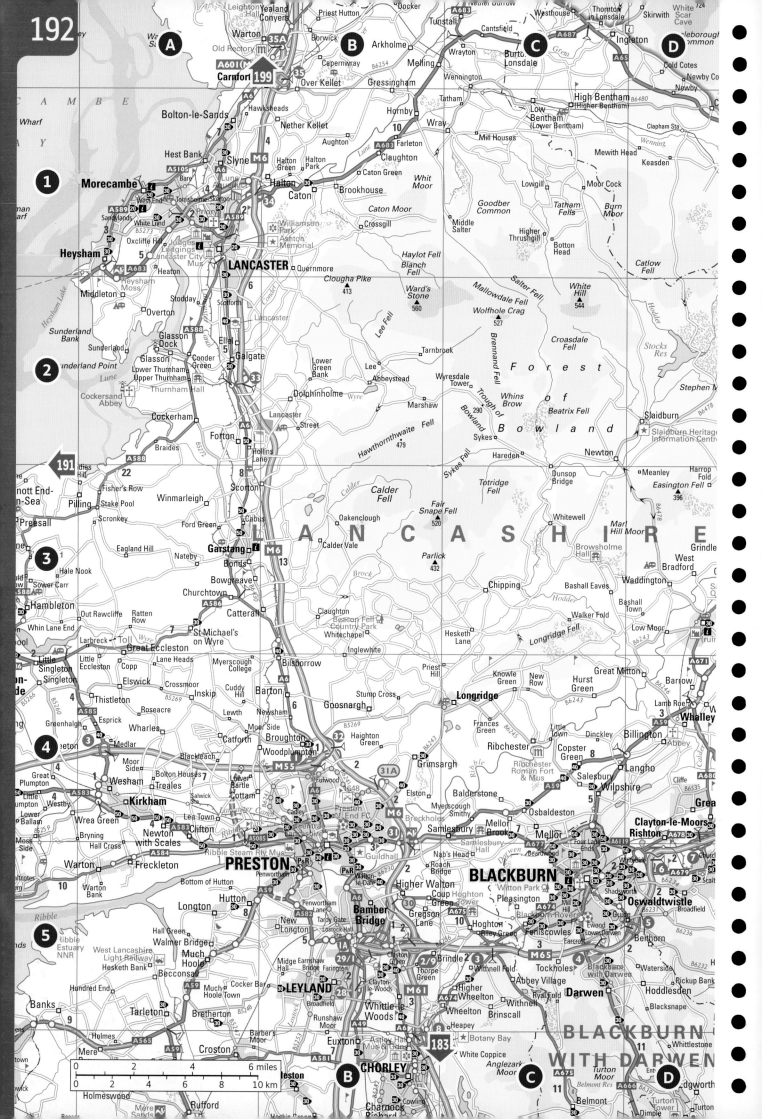

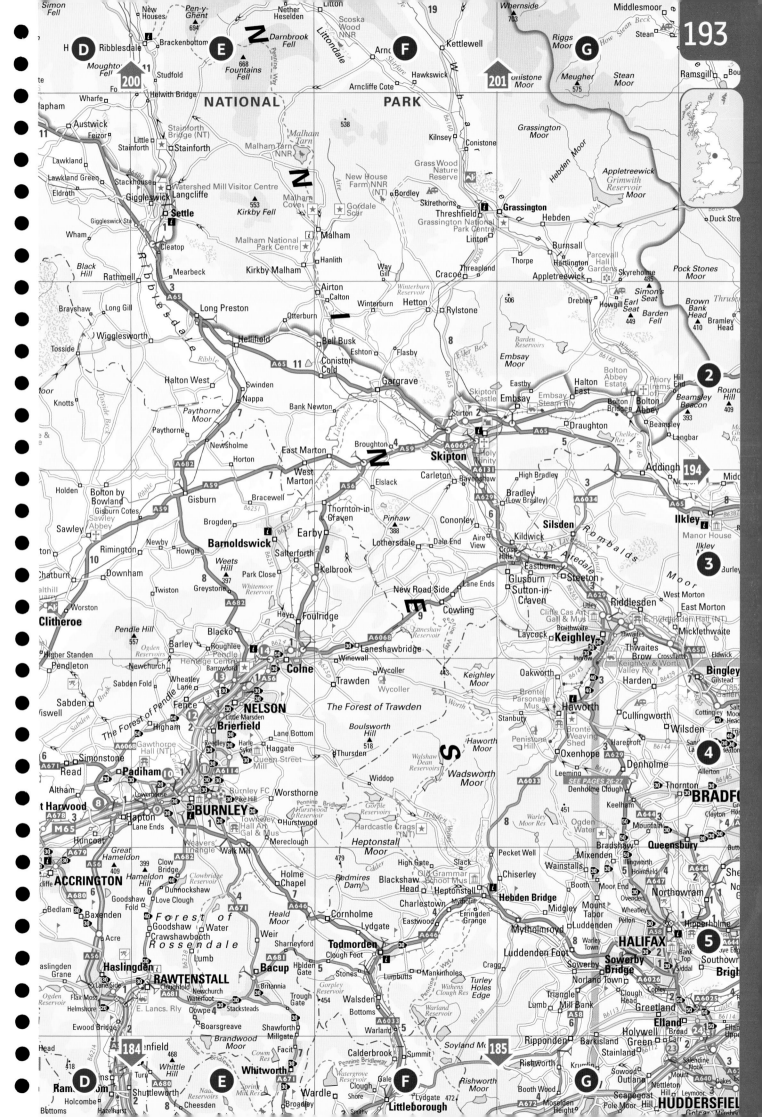

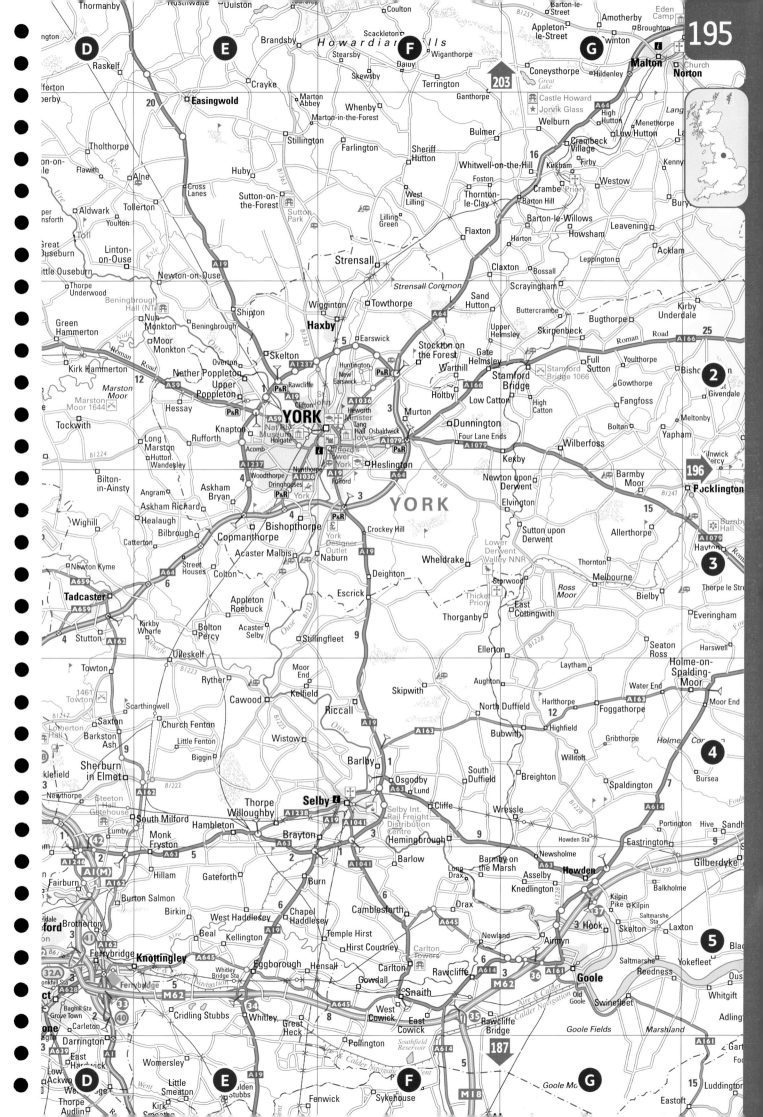

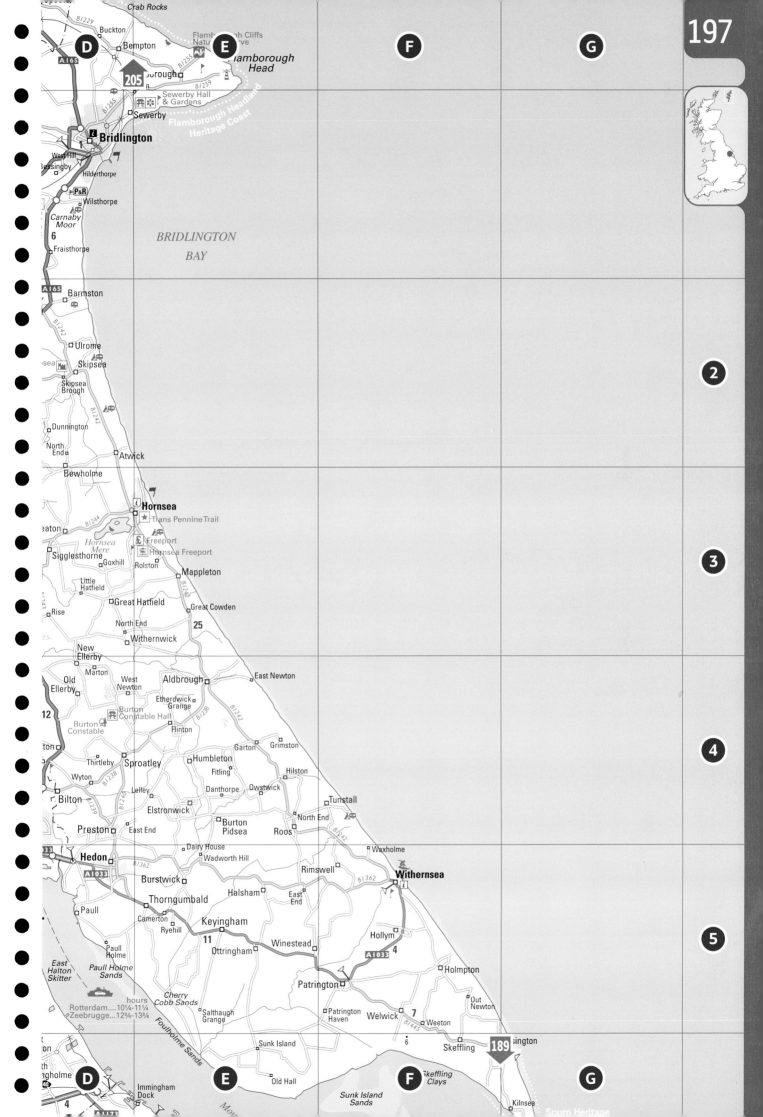

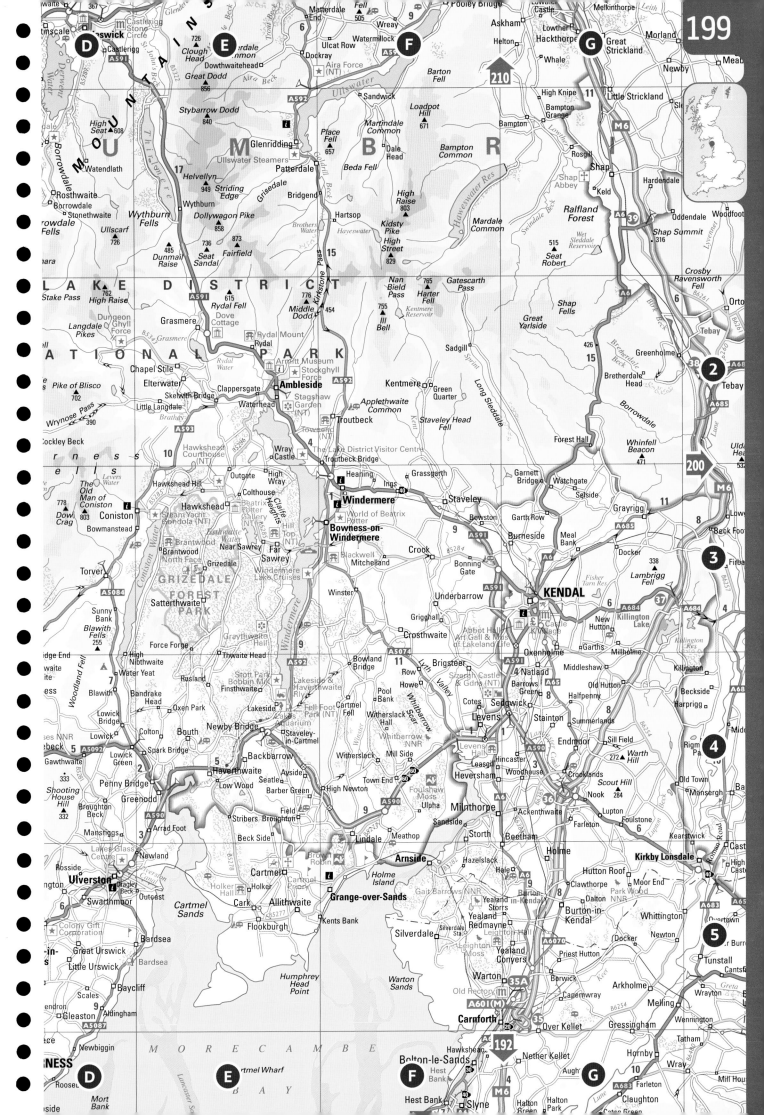

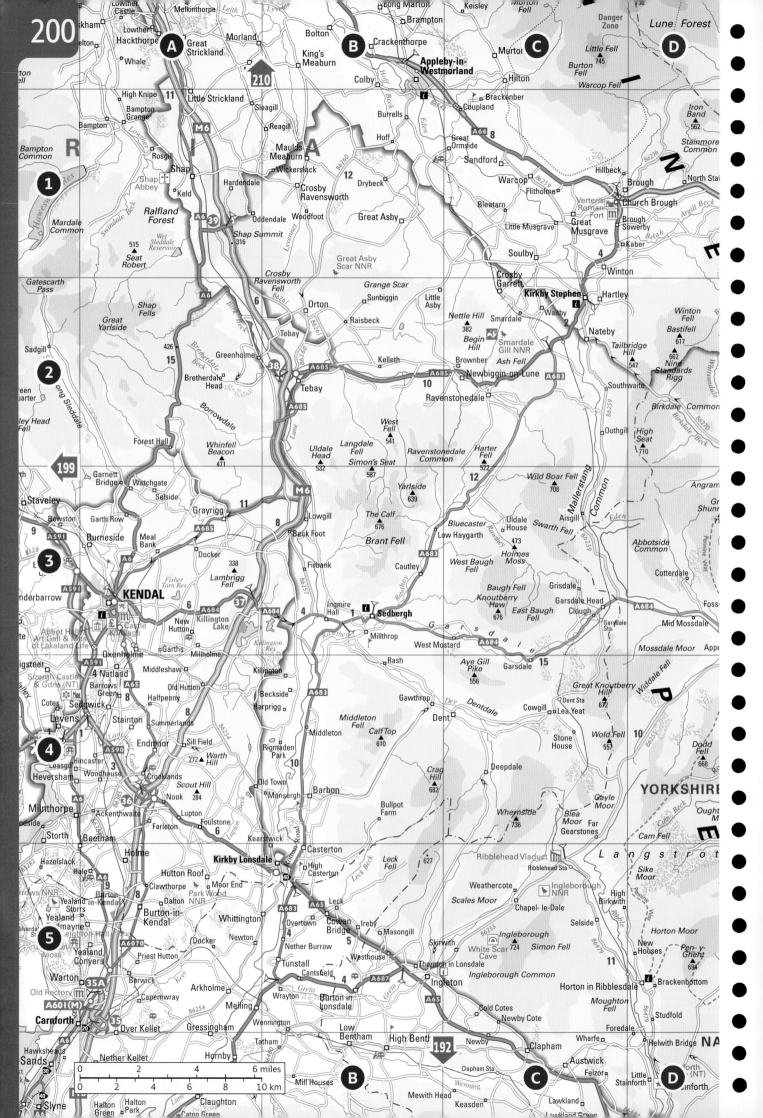

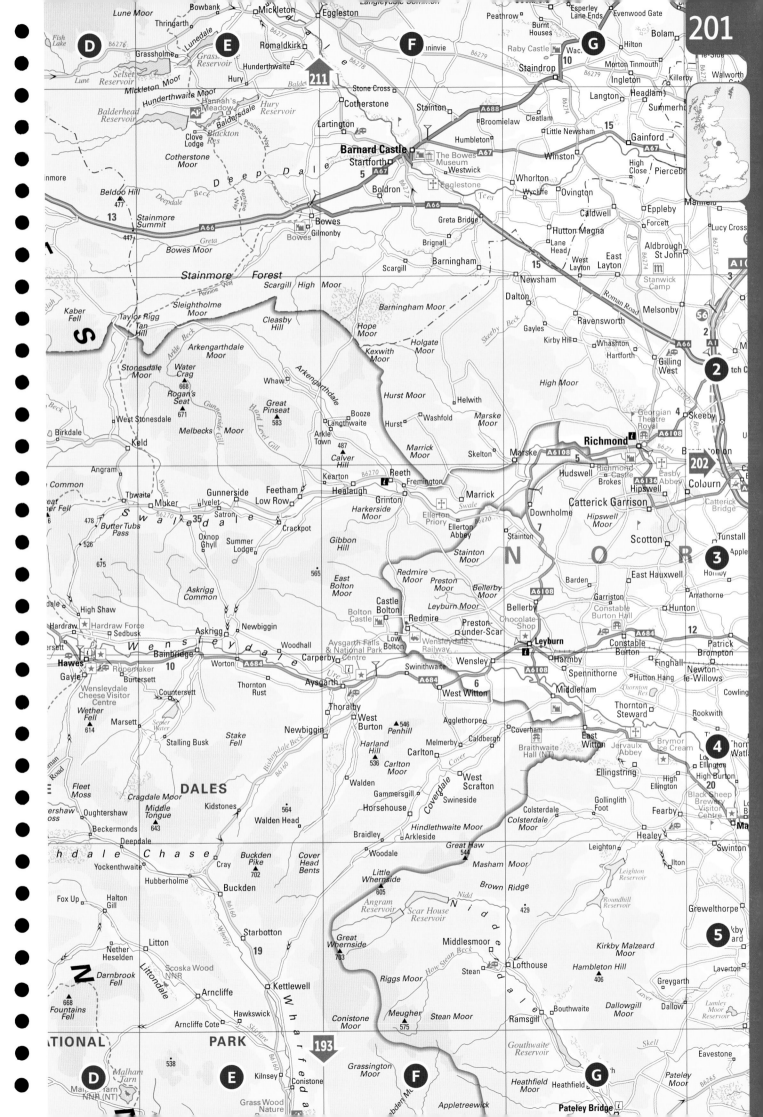

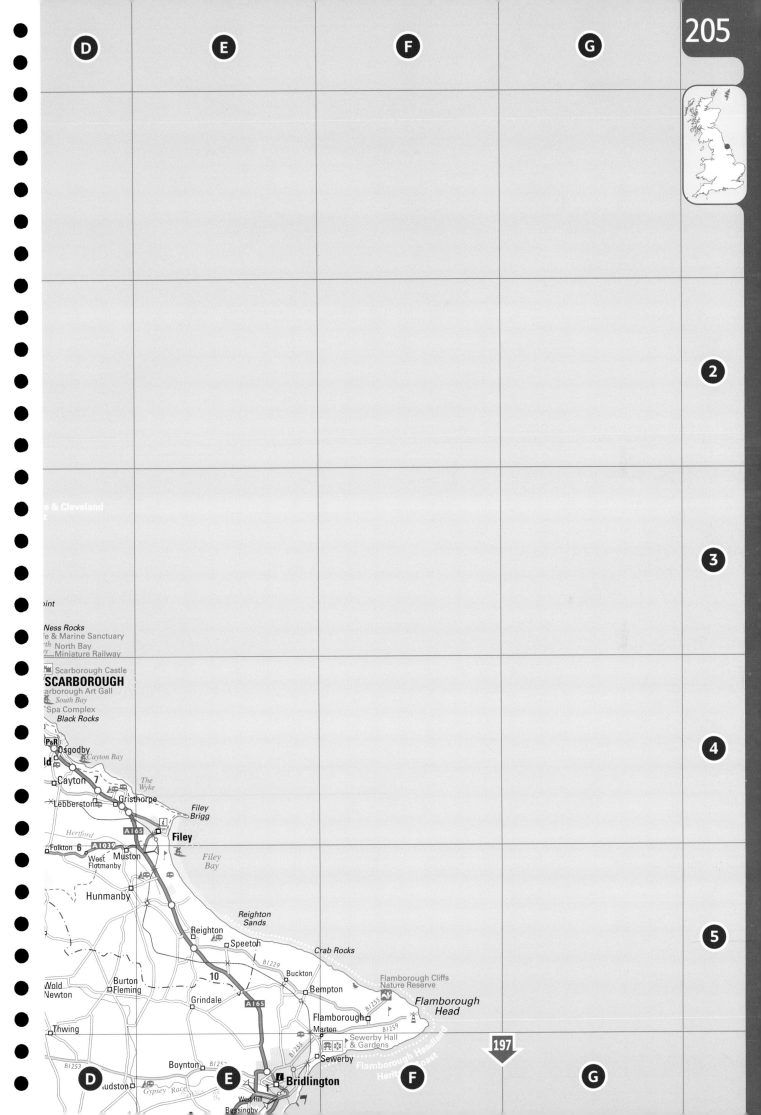

D E F G

2

3

e & Cleveland
t

Ness Rocks
e & Marine Sanctuary
North Bay
Miniature Railway

Scarborough Castle
SCARBOROUGH
carborough Art Gall
South Bay
Spa Complex
Black Rocks

P&R
Osgodby
ld *Cayton Bay*
Cayton **7**
Lebberston Gristhorpe
The Wyke
Filey Brigg
Hertford A165
Folkton **6** A1039 **Filey**
West Muston
Flotmanby *Filey Bay*

Hunmanby

Reighton Sands
Reighton
Speeton
Crab Rocks
B1229
10
Wold Burton Buckton
Newton Fleming Bempton
A165
Grindale Flamborough Cliffs
Nature Reserve
Thwing *Flamborough Head*
Flamborough
Marton B1259
Sewerby Hall
& Gardens
B1253 Boynton B1255
Sewerby *Flamborough Headland Herit*
D E Sewerby
B1253 **Bridlington**
udston *Gypsy Race* F **197** G
West Hill
Bessingby

4

5

D E F G

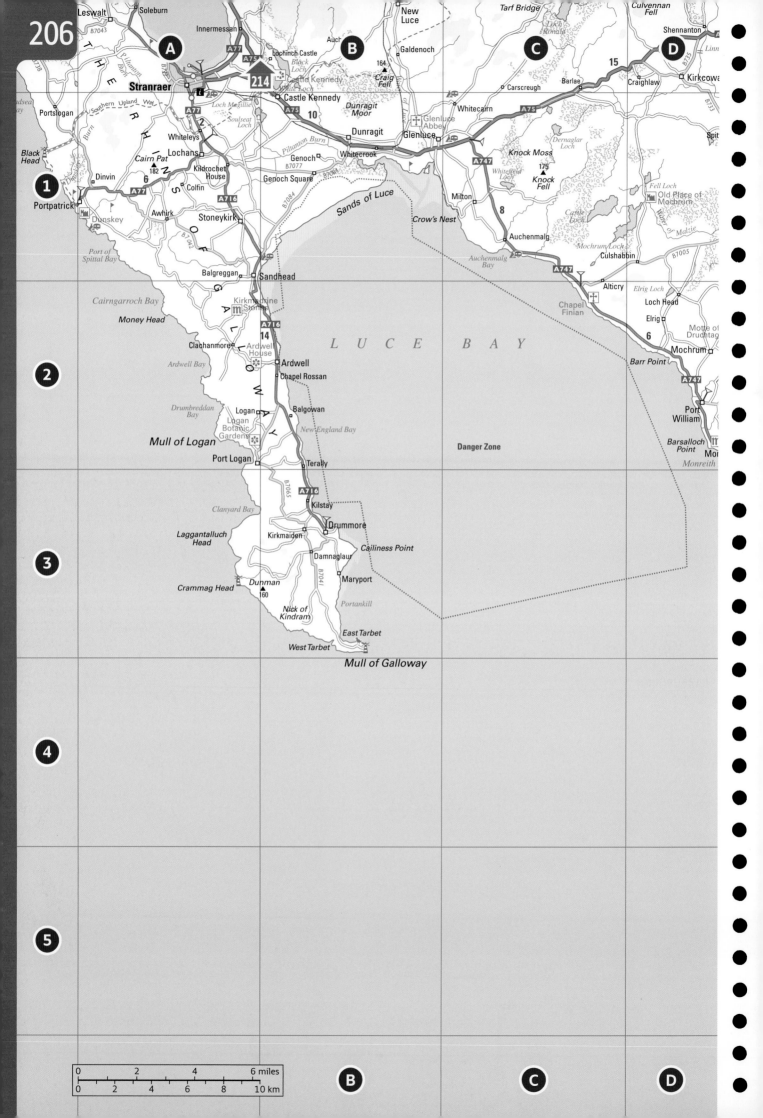

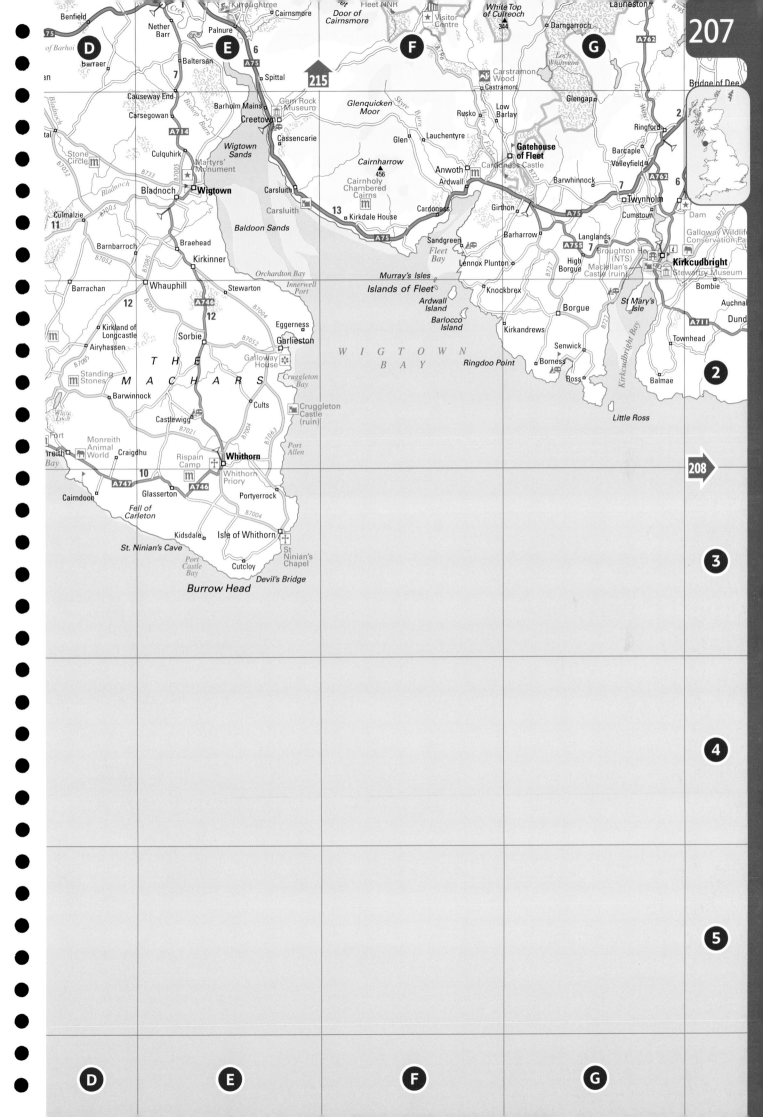

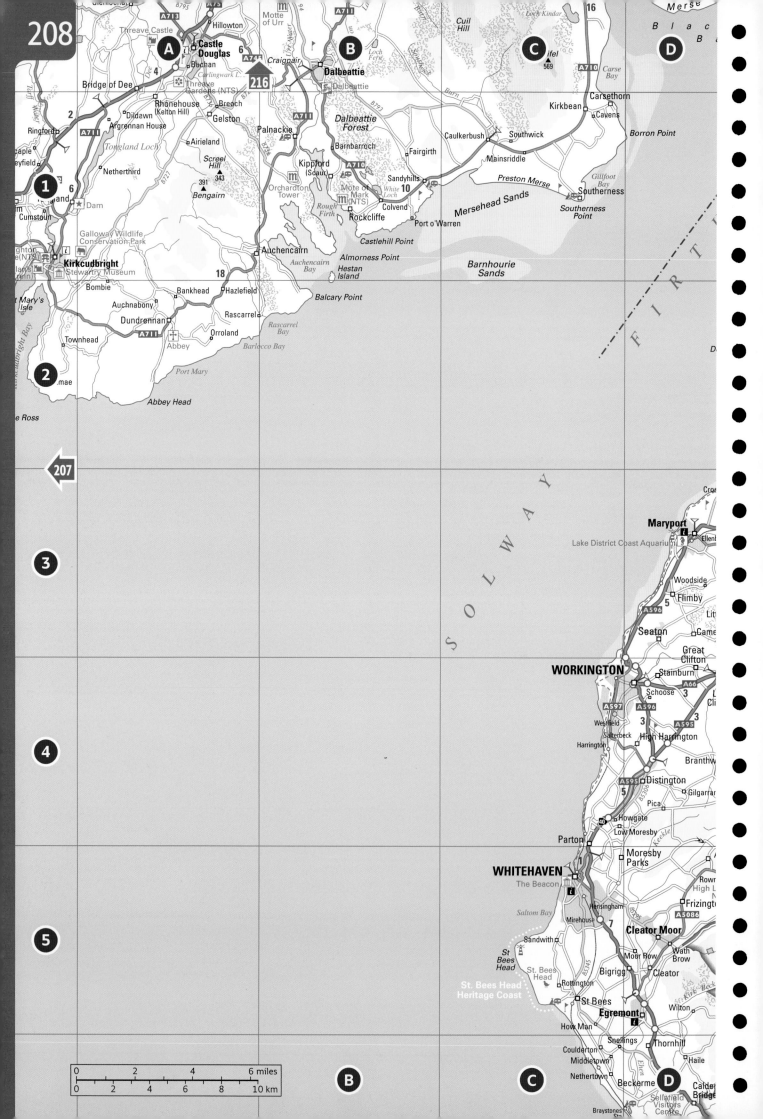

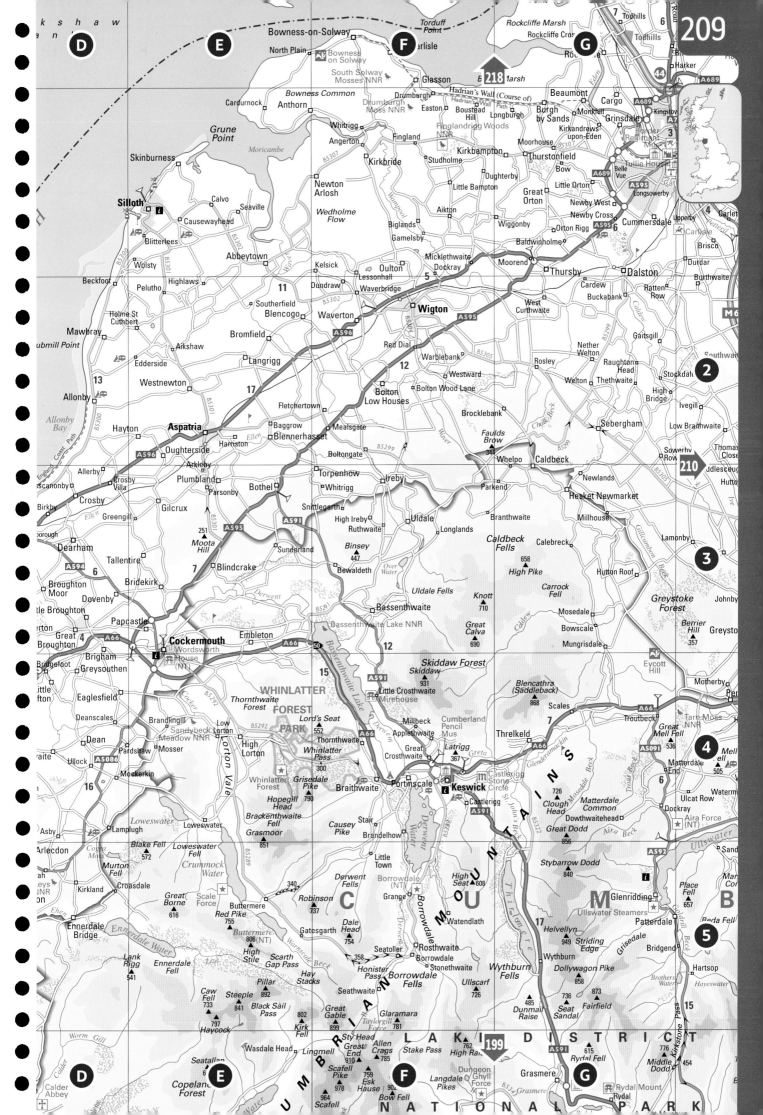

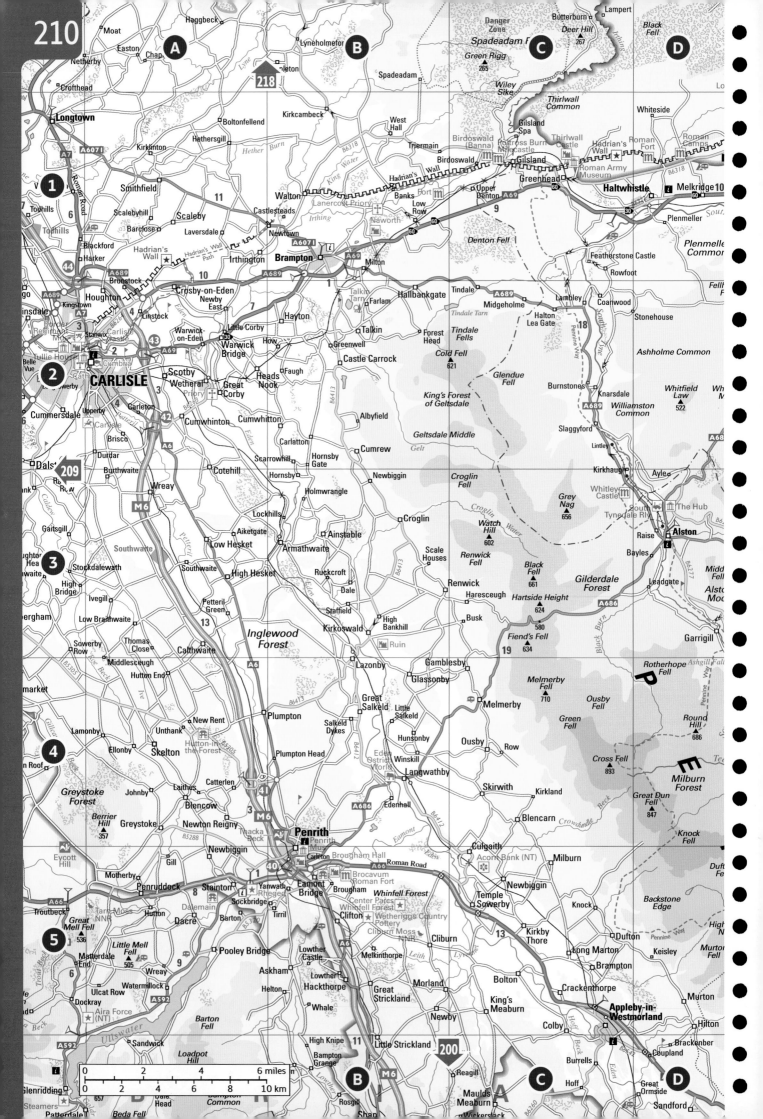

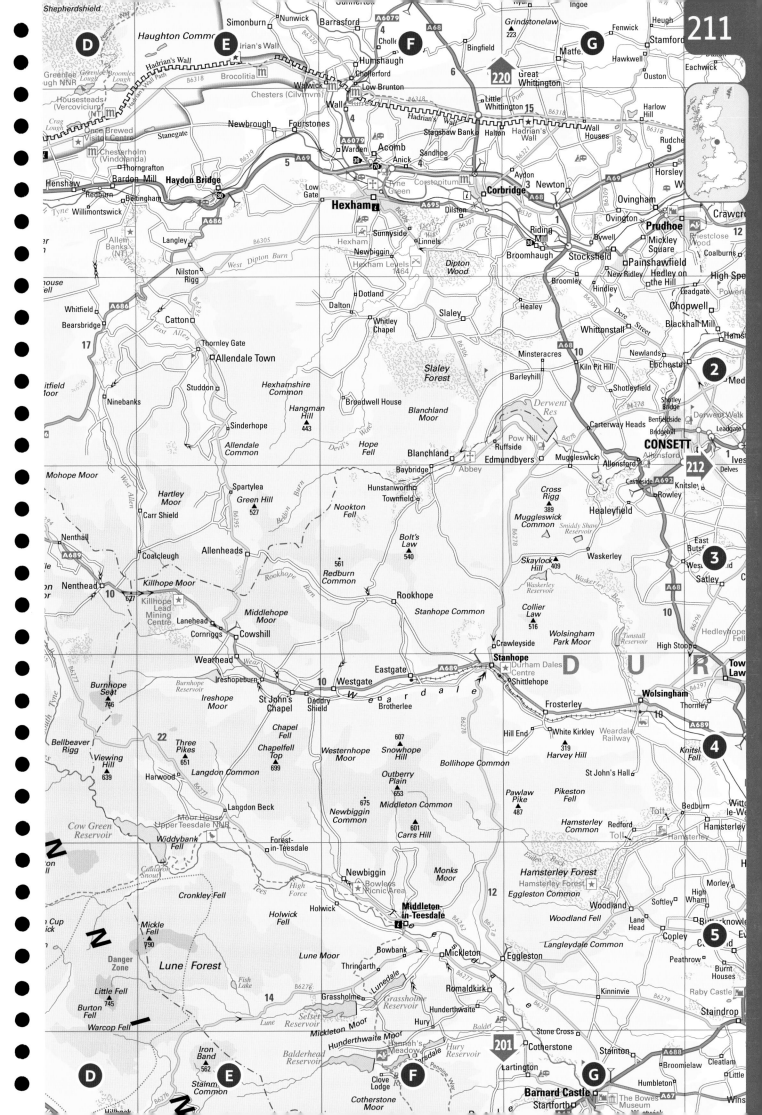

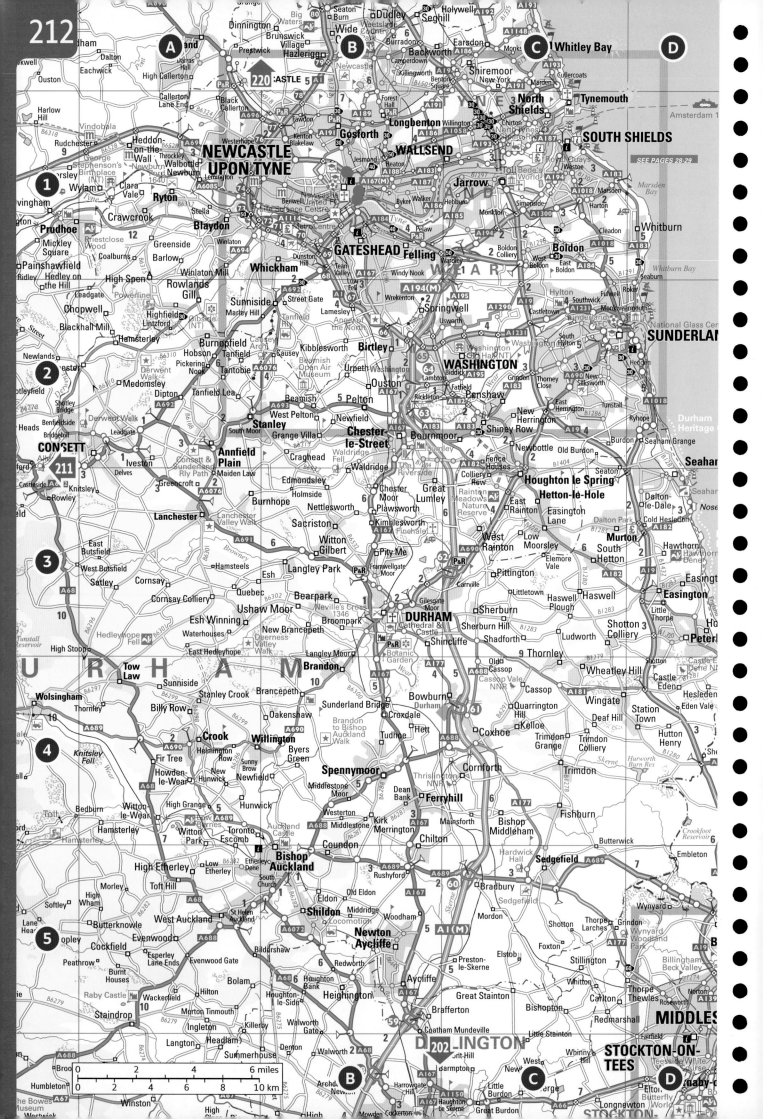

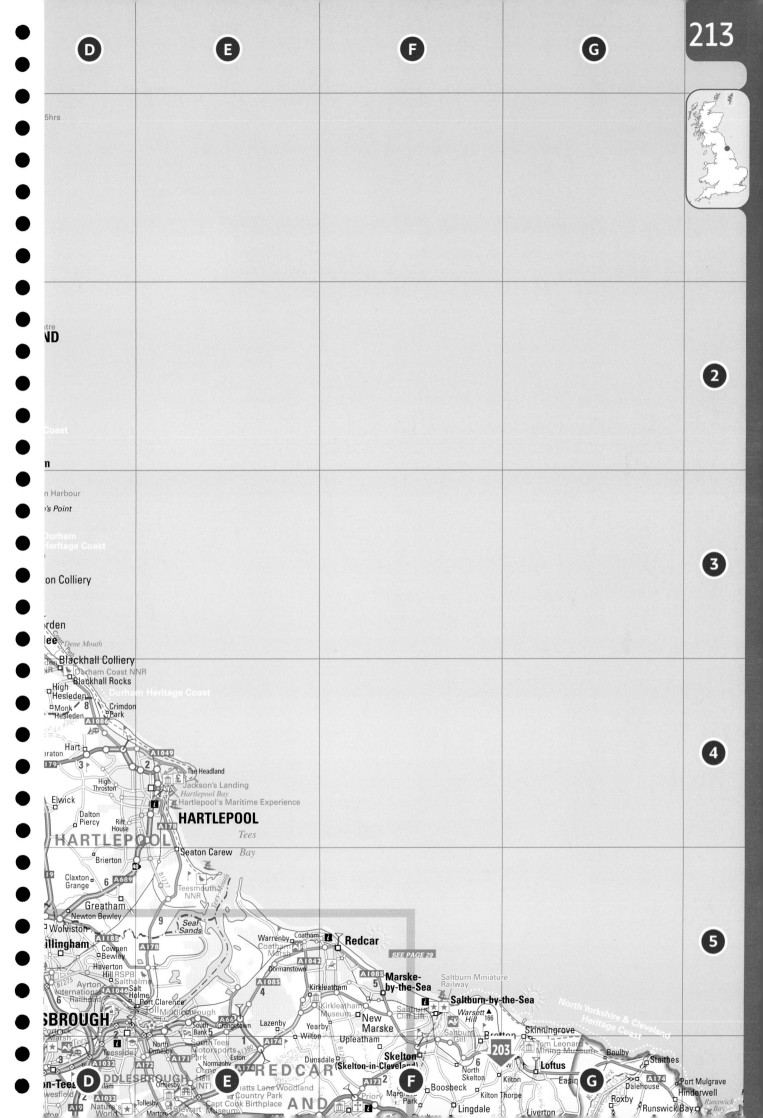

D
E
F
G

2

3

4

5hrs

Coast

Harbour

's Point

Durham
Heritage Coast

on Colliery

rden

lee · *Castle Dene Mouth*

Blackhall Colliery
NNR · Durham Coast NNR
Blackhall Rocks
High
Hesleden
Monk 8 · Crimdon
Hesleden · Park

Durham Heritage Coast

A1086

eraton · Hart

A1049

A179 · 3 · 2 · *The Headland*
High · Jackson's Landing
Throston · *Hartlepool Bay*
Elwick · Hartlepool's Maritime Experience

Dalton · Rift
Piercy · House
HARTLEPOOL
A1032 · *Tees*

HARTLEPOOL · Brierton · Seaton Carew · *Bay*

19 · 40
Claxton · 6 · A689
Grange · B1277

Greatham · Teesmouth
Newton Bewley · NNR · *Tees Mouth*

Wolviston · 9 · *Seal*
A1185 · *Sands*

illingham · Cowpen · Coatham · *i* · **Redcar**
Bewley · Warrenby
A178 · Coatham · A1042
Haverton · Marsh
Ayrton · Hill · RSPB · Dormanstown
International · A1046 · Saltholme · A1085 · **Marske-**
Railroad · Salt · Port Clarence · Kirkleatham · 5 · **by-the-Sea** · Saltburn Miniature
6 · Holme · Kirkleatham · Railway
A174 · Saltburn · **Saltburn-by-the-Sea**
SBROUGH · Toll · Middlesbrough · Museum · Cliff Lift · *i*
South · A66 · Grangetown · New · *Warsett* · North Yorkshire & Cleveland
2 · South Bank · 5 · Lazenby · Yearby · Marske · *Hill* · 166 · Heritage Coast
i · North · South Tees · Wilton · Upleatham · Saltburn · Brotton · Skinningrove
3 · Ormesby · Motorsports · 1 · A174 · Gill · **203** · Tom Leonard · Boulby
A1032 · Park · Normanby · Eston · Dunsdale · **Skelton** · Mining Museum · Staithes
A172 · **(Skelton-in-Cleveland)** · W · **Loftus**
n-Tees · D · E · Hall · **REDCAR** · F · North · Kilton · Easin · G · Dalehouse · Hinderwell
A19 · Nature's · (NT) · atts Lane Woodland · 2 · Skelton · Boosbeck · Kilton Thorpe · Roxby · Runswick Bay
World · Tollesby · Country Park · Margrove · Lingdale · Liverton · *Runswick*
Marton · Capt Cook Birthplace · Park · *Bay*
Museum

SEE PAGE 29

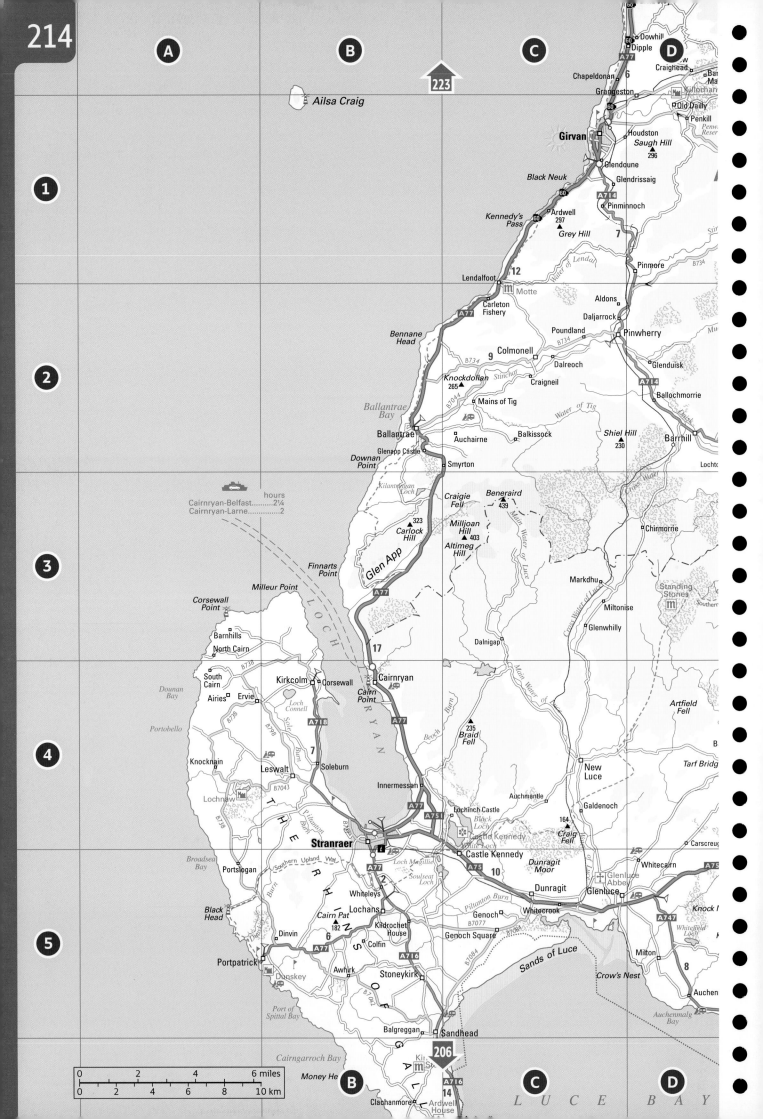

A · **B** · **C** · **D**

223

Ailsa Craig

Dowhill
Dipple
Craighead
Chapeldonan
Grangeston
Killochan
Old Daily
Penkill
Girvan
Houdston
Saugh Hill
296
Glendoune
Black Neuk
Glendrissaig
Kennedy's Pass
Ardwell
297
Pinminnoch
Grey Hill
7
Pinmore
Lendalfoot
12
Water of Lendal
B734
Motte
Aldons
Carleton Fishery
Daljarrock
Bennane Head
Poundland
Pinwherry
Colmonell
B734
Dalreoch
Glenduisk
9
Knockdollian
Stinchar
Craigneil
265
Ballochmorrie
Ballantrae Bay
Mains of Tig
Water of Tig
Balkissock
Shiel Hill
Ballantrae
Auchairne
230
Barrhill
Glenapp Castle
Smyrton
Downan Point
Lochto
Kilantringan Loch
Craigie Fell
Beneraird
439
hours
Cairnryan-Belfast..........2¼
Cairnryan-Larne.............2
323
Milljoan Hill
Chirmorrie
Carlock Hill
403
Finnarts Point
Glen App
Altimeg Hill
Milleur Point
Markdhu
Standing Stones
Corsewall Point
17
Miltonise
A77
Dalnigap
Glenwhilly
Barnhills
North Cairn
LOCH
Cairnryan
South Cairn
B738
Airies
Ervie
Kirkcolm
Corsewall
Cairn Point
Artfield Fell
Dounan Bay
Loch Connell
235
Braid Fell
Portobello
A718
Knocknain
7
Soleburn
Innermessan
Tarf Bridg
Leswalt
B7043
Auchmantle
New Luce
Lochnaw
B738
A77
Lochinch Castle
Galdenoch
Broadsea Bay
Stranraer
Castle Kennedy
164
Carscreu
Portslogan
A77
Black Loch
Craig Fell
Castle Kennedy
Whitecairn
A75
Black Head
Whiteleys
2
10
Dunragit Moor
Glenluce
Lochans
Genoch
Dunragit
Abbey
Cairn Pat
Kildrochet House
Whitecrook
Glenluce
Dinvin
6
182
Colfin
Genoch Square
A747
Knock
Portpatrick
A77
Awhirk
A716
B7084
Whitefield Loch
Milton
Stoneykirk
8
Dunskey
Port of Spittal Bay
Balgreggan
Sandhead
Auchen
Cairngarroch Bay
206
Auchenmalg Bay
0   2   4   6 miles
0 2 4 6 8 10 km
Money He
14
Clachanmore
Ardwell House
L U C E   B A Y

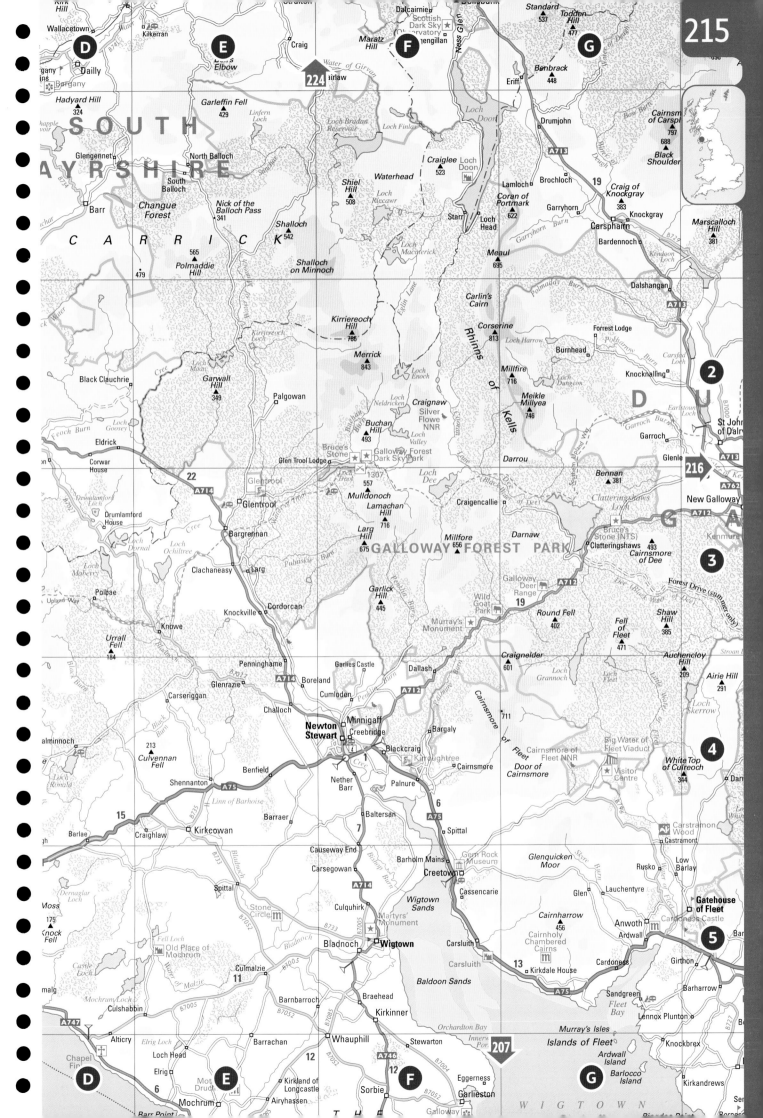

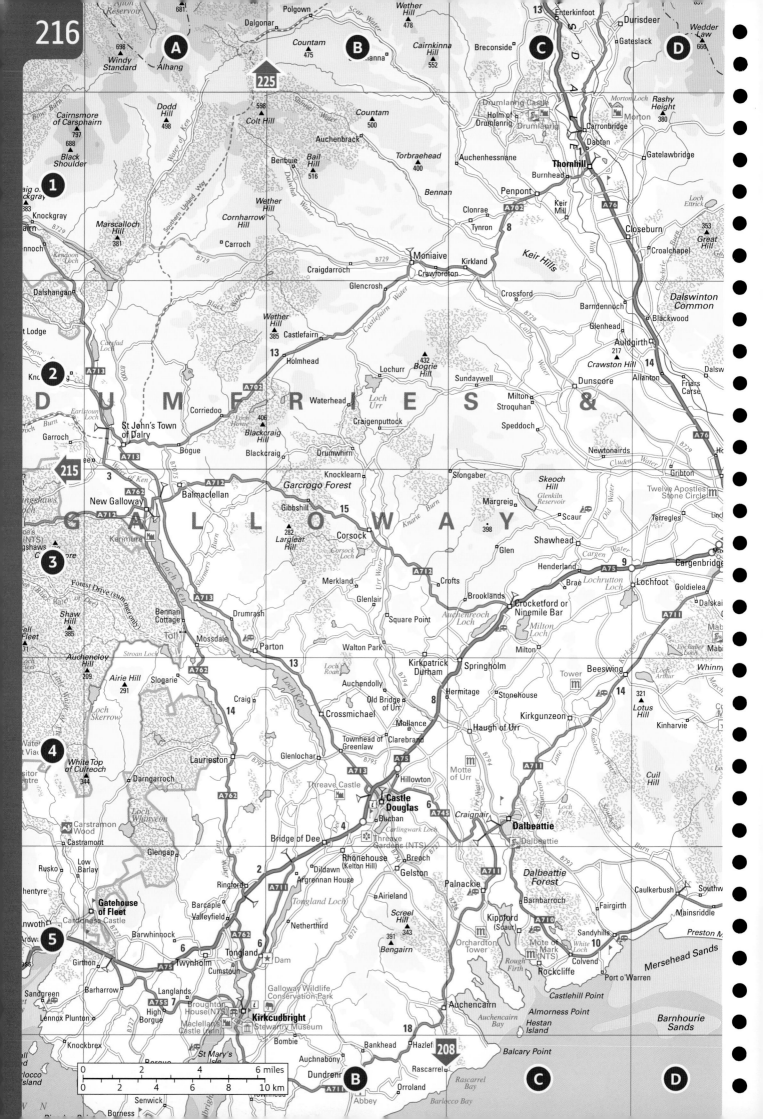

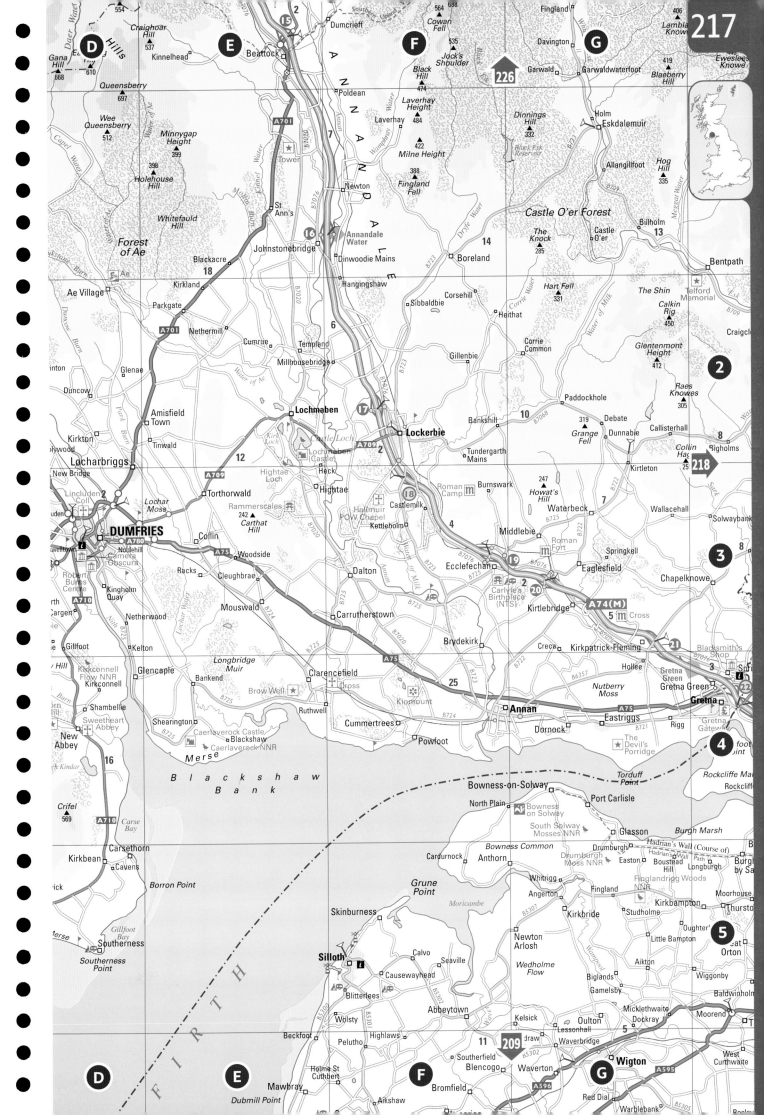

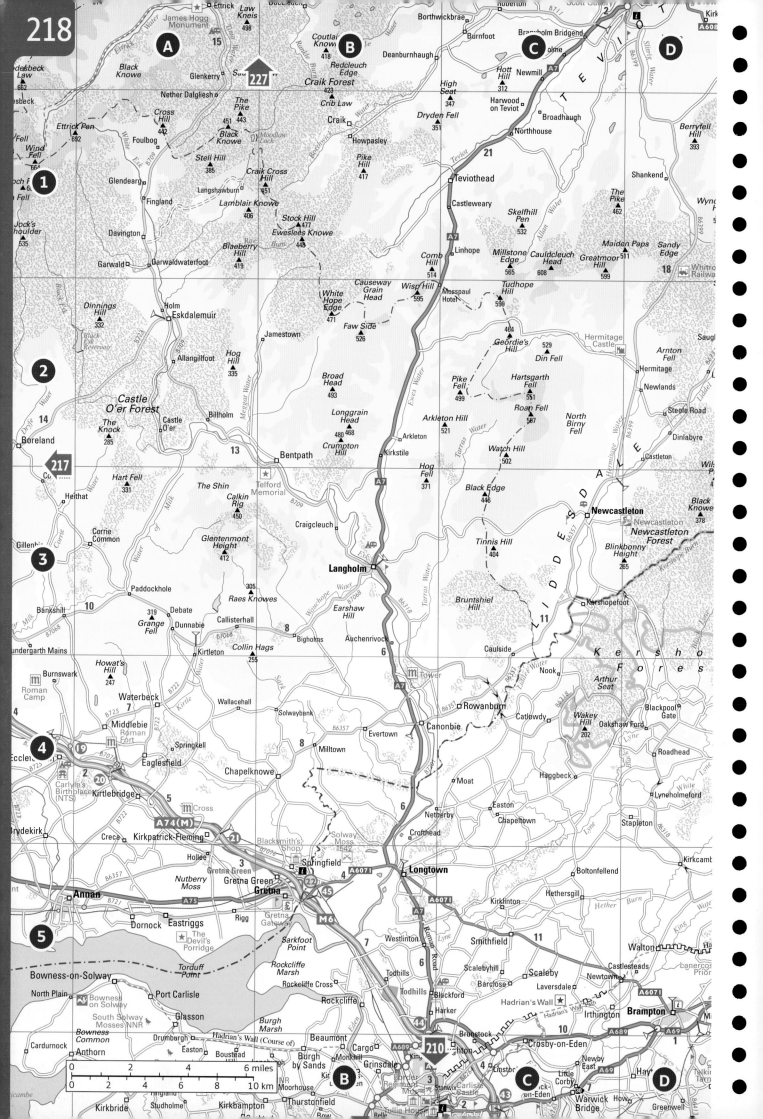

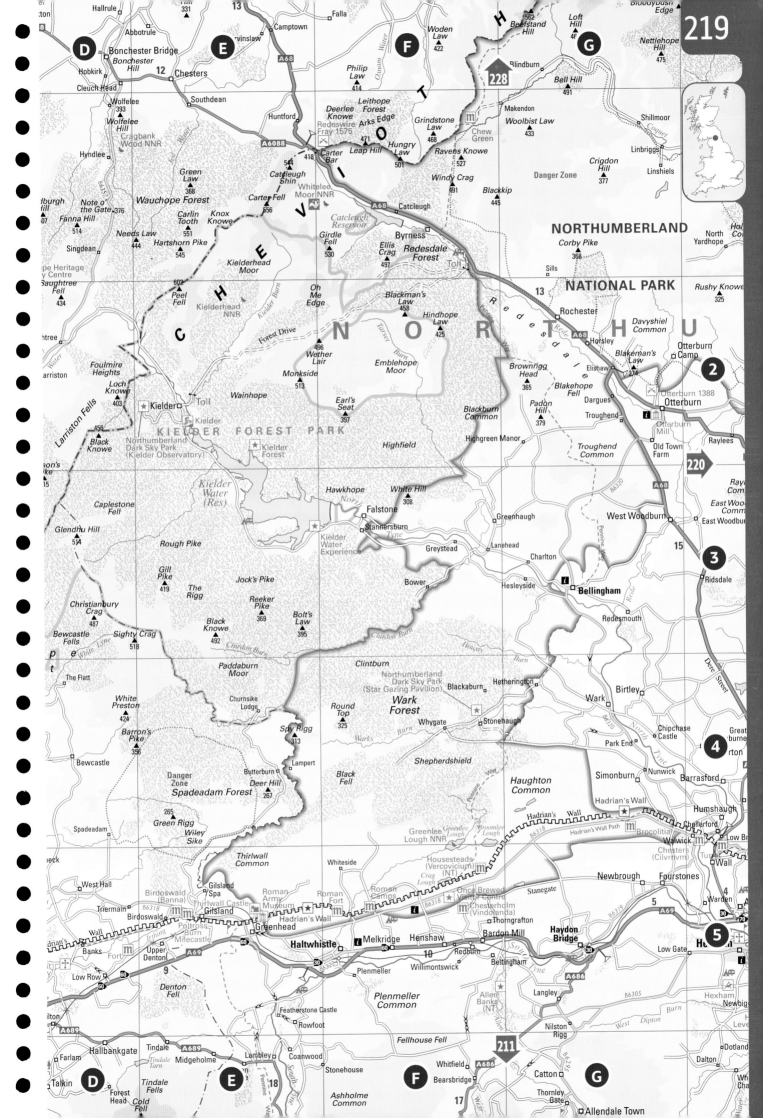

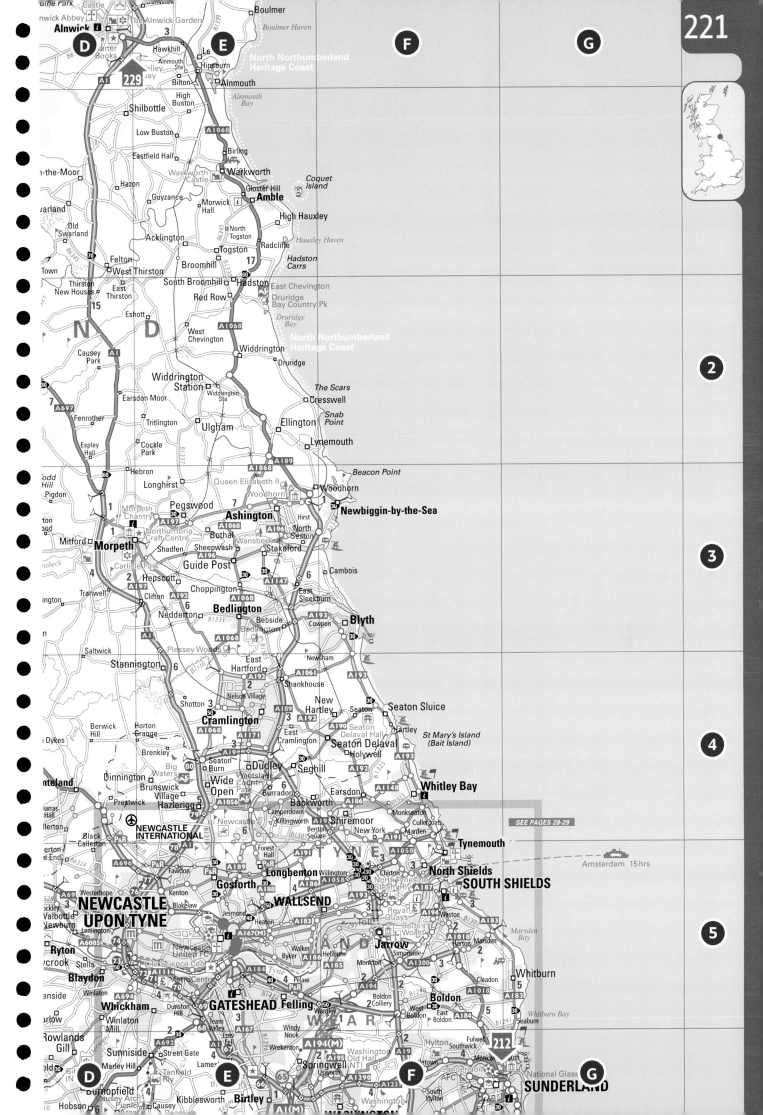

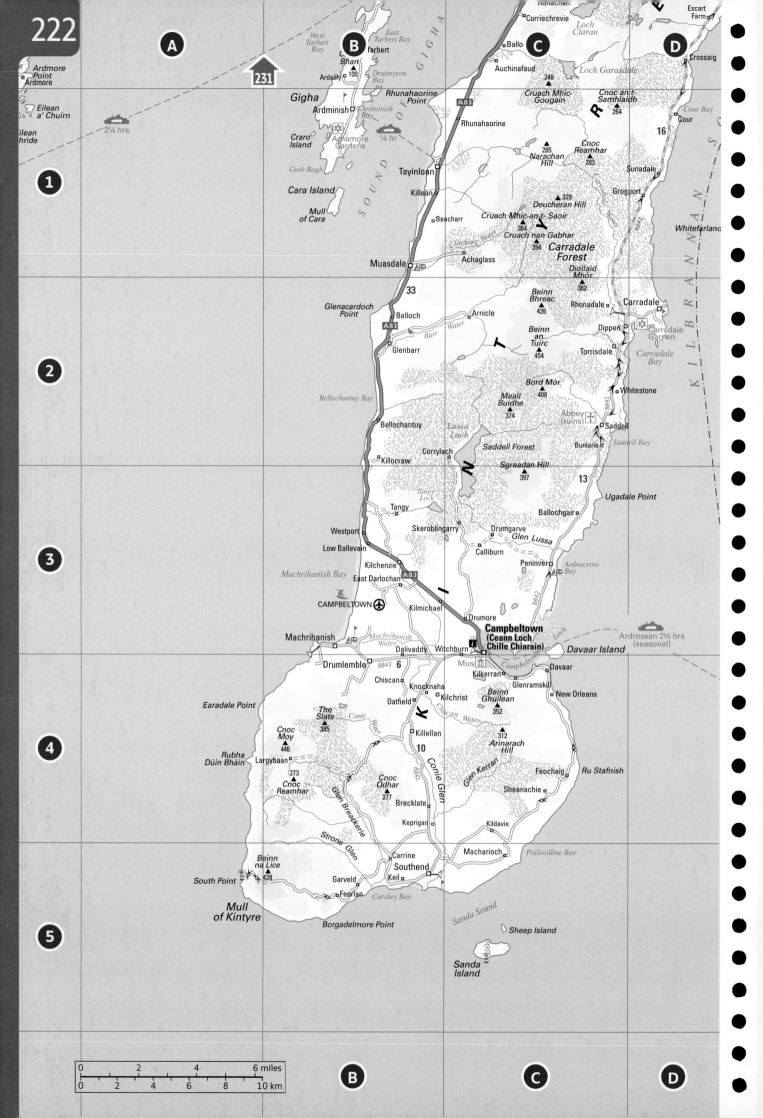

Ardmore
Point
Ardmore

Eilean
a' Chuirn

Eilean
Bhride

2¼ hrs

West
Tarbert
Bay

East
Tarbert Bay

Tarbert

Bhan
100

Ardailly

Druimyeon
Bay

Rhunahaorine
Point

Gigha

Ardminish

Ardminish
Bay

¼ hr

Craro
Island

Achamore
Gardens

Grob Bagh

Cara Island

Mull
of Cara

SOUND OF GIGHA

Ronachan

Corriechrevie

Ballo

Auchinafaud

Loch
Ciaran

Loch Garasdale

Escart
Farm

Crossaig

A83

Rhunahaorine

248

Cruach Mhic-
Gougain

Cnoc an t-
Samhlaidh

264

Cour Bay

Cour

16

Tayinloan

Killean

Beacharr

285

Narachan
Hill

Cnoc
Reamhar
203

Sunadale

Grogport

329

Deucheran Hill

Cruach Mhic-an-t- Saoir

364

Cruach nan Gabhar

354

Carradale
Forest

Diollaid
Mhòr
362

Whitefarlane

Muasdale

33

Glenacardoch
Point

Belloch

A83

Glenbarr

Arnicle

Beinn
Bhreac
426

Rhonadale

Carradale

Dippen

Beinn
an
Tuirc
454

Torrisdale

Carradale
Garden

Carradale
Bay

Bellochantuy Bay

Bellochantuy

Killocraw

Corrylach

Lussa
Loch

Bord Mòr
408

Meall
Buidhe
374

Saddell Forest

Sgreadan Hill
397

Abbey
(ruins)

Whitestone

Saddell

Bunlarie

Saddell Bay

13

Tangy

Skeroblingarry

Tangy
Loch

Drumgarve

Glen Lussa

Callibun

Ugadale Point

Ballochgair

Westport

Low Ballevain

Kilchenzie

A83

East Darlochan

Machrihanish Bay

Peninver

Ardnacross
Bay

CAMPBELTOWN

Kilmichael

Drumore

Campbeltown
(Ceann Loch
Chille Chiarain)

Davaar Island

Ardrossan 2⅔ hrs
(seasonal)

Machrihanish

Machrihanish
Water

Dalivaddy

Witchburn

Mus

Davaar

Drumlemble

B843

6

Chiscan

Knocknaha

Kilchrist

Kilkerran

Glenramskil

New Orleans

Earadale Point

The
Slate
385

Oatfield

Conie

Killean

Beinn
Ghuilean
352

Cnoc
Moy
446

Water

312

Arinarach
Hill

Rubha
Dùin Bhàin

Largybaan

273

Cnoc
Reamhar

10

Cnoc
Odhar
277

Brecklate

Glen Kerran

Chiscan Water

Feochaig

Sheanachie

Ru Stafnish

Strone Glen

Kildavie

Keprigan

Glen Breackerie

Conie Glen

B842

Macharioch

Polliwilline Bay

Beinn
na Lice
428

Carrine

Southend

South Point

Garveld

Keil

Fenrlan

Carskey Bay

Sanda Sound

Sheep Island

Mull
of Kintyre

Borgadelmore Point

Sanda
Island

KILBRANNAN SOUND

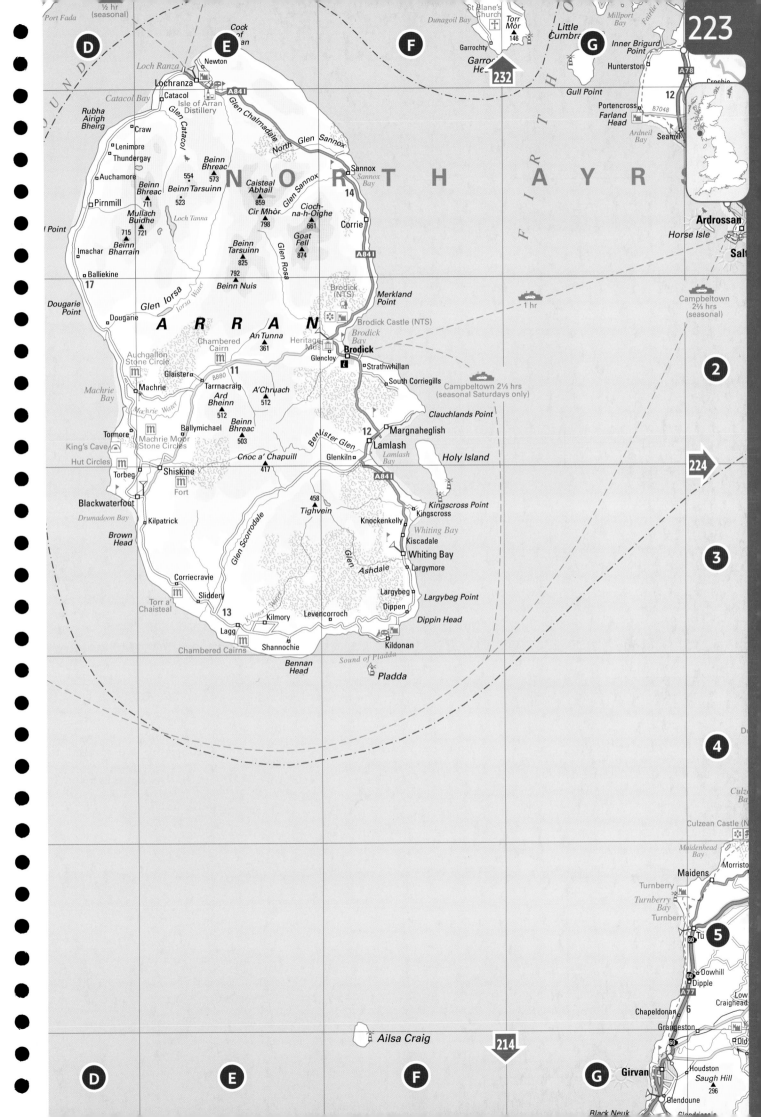

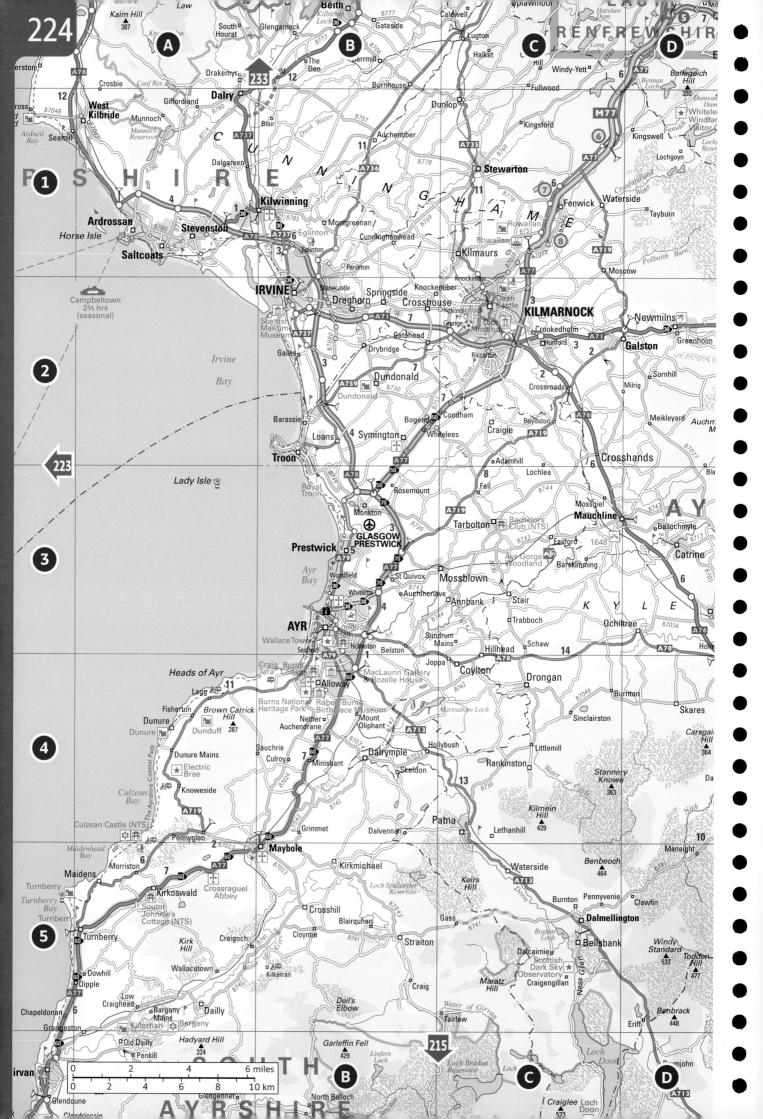

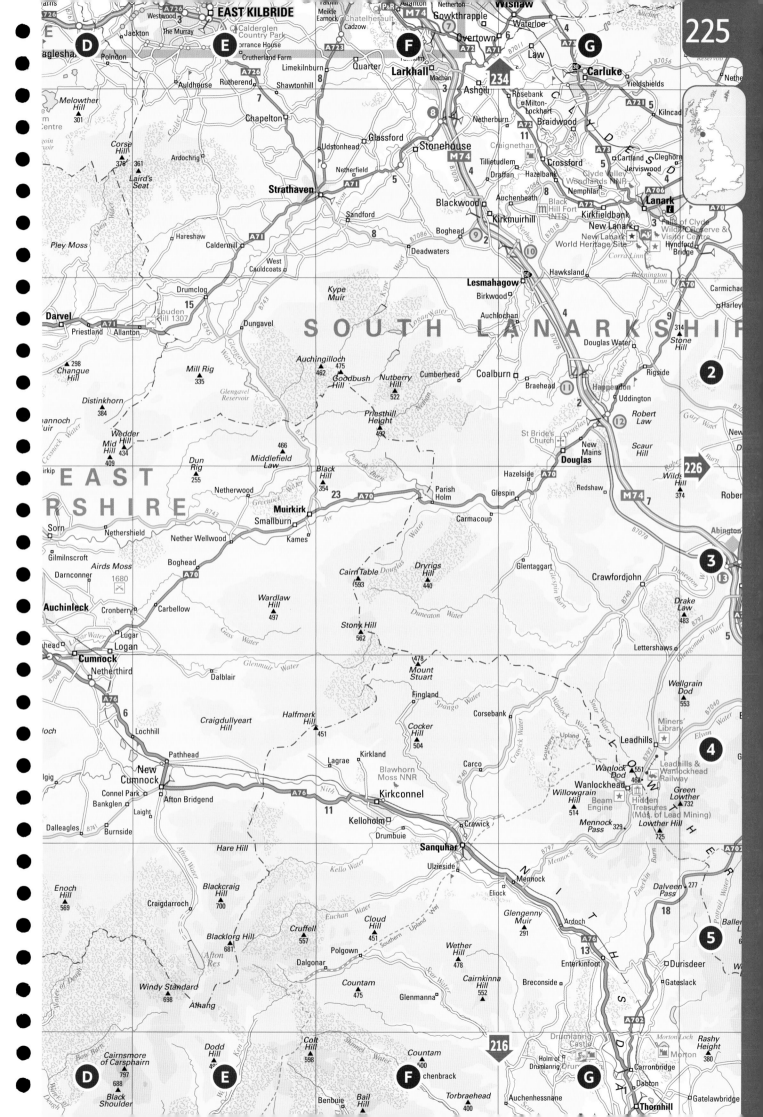

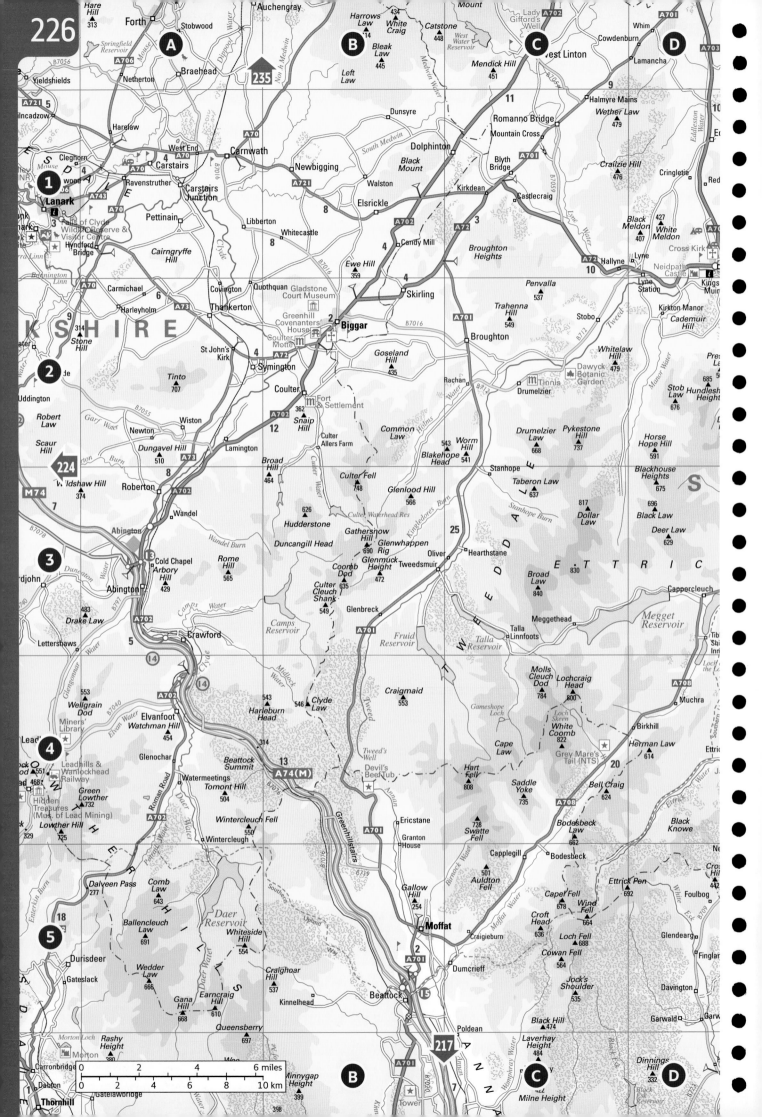

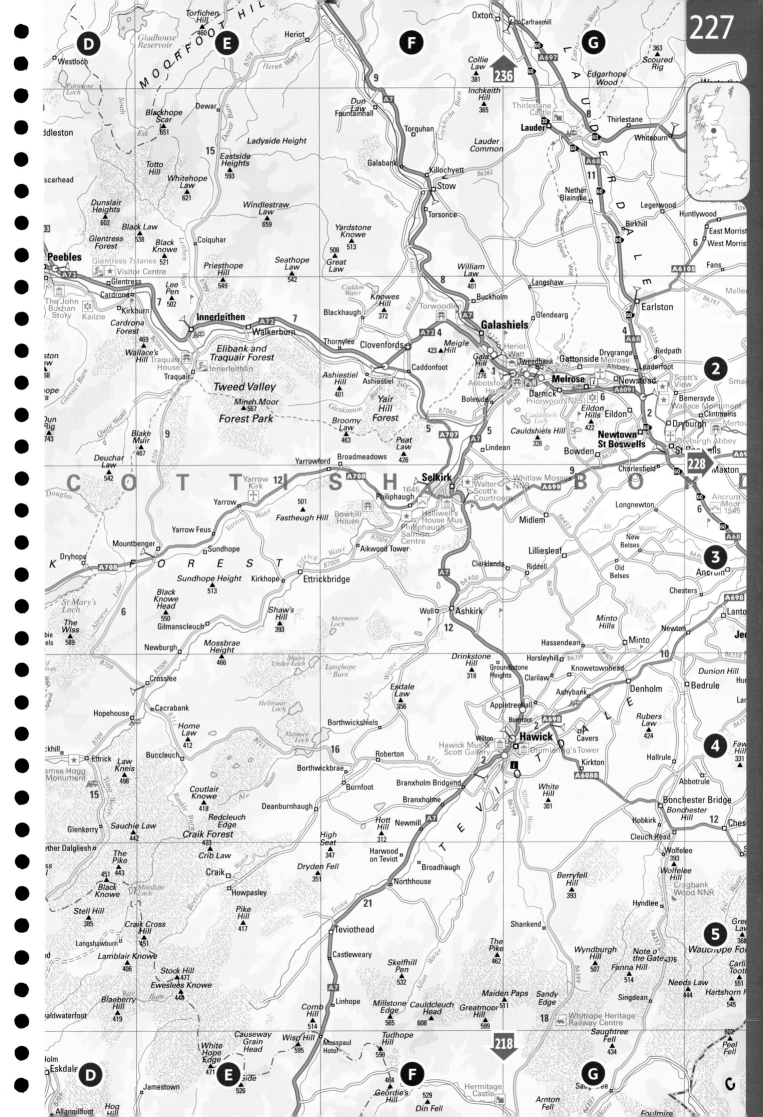

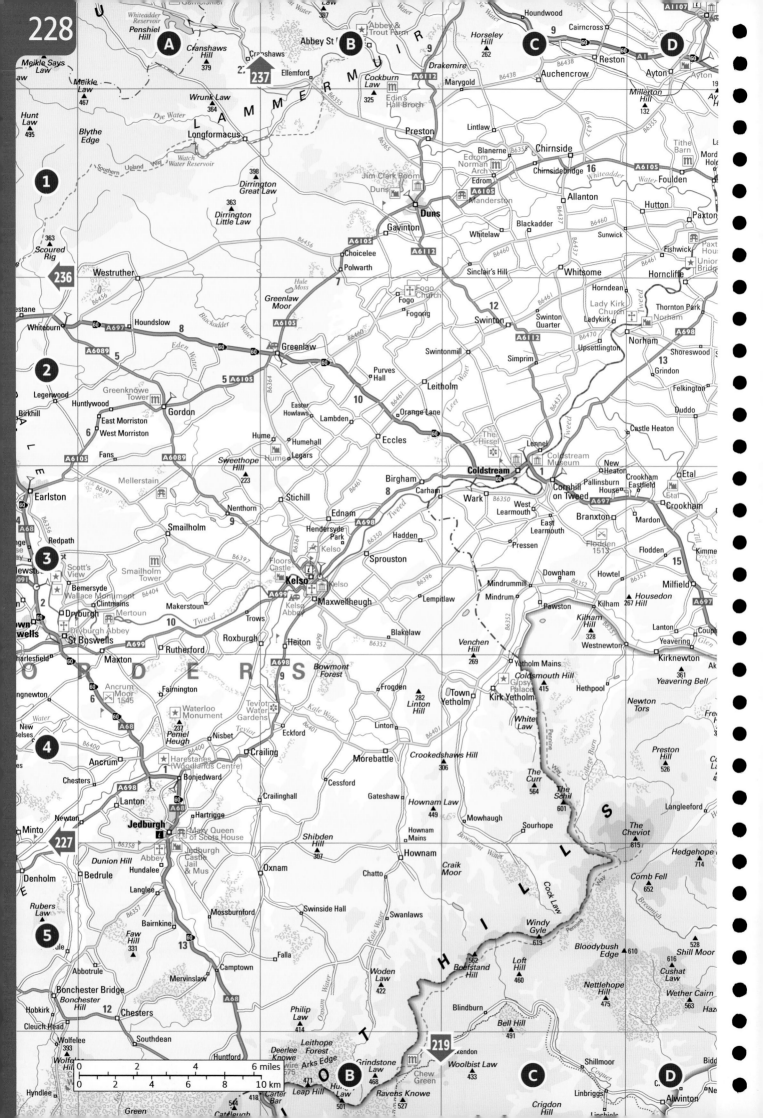

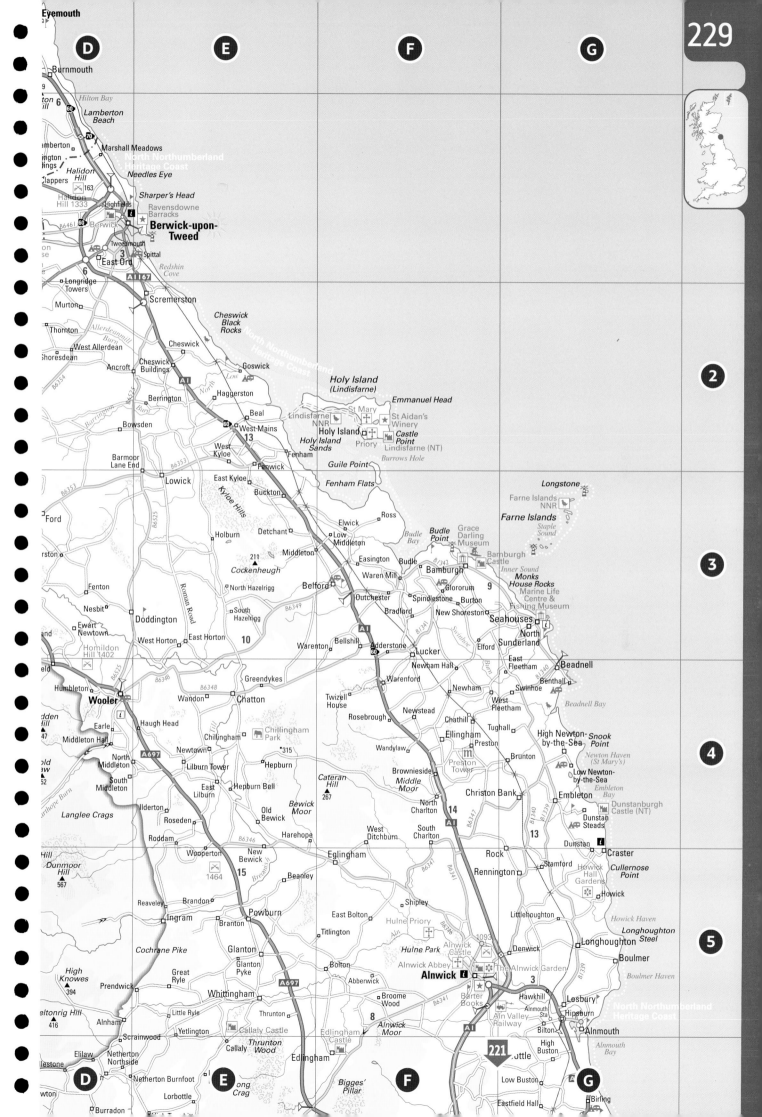

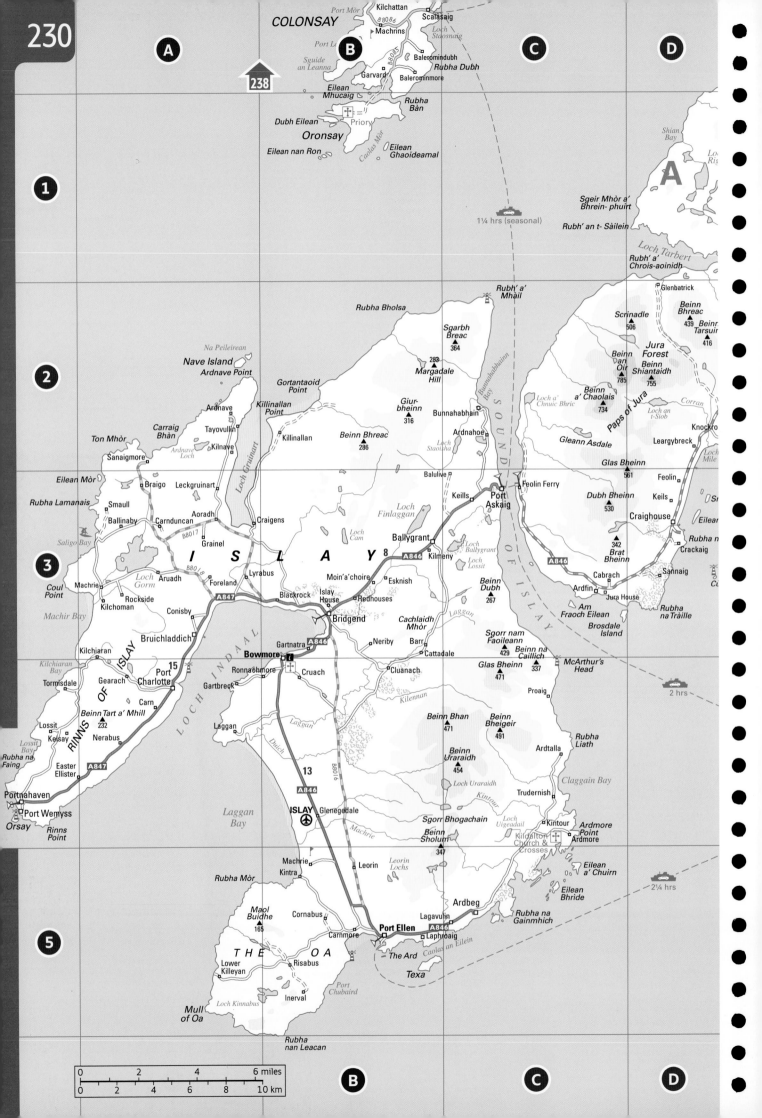

COLONSAY

Port Mòr · Kilchattan
B8086 · Scalasaig
Machrins
Loch Staosnaig
Port L...
Garvard · Baleromindubh
Balerominmore · Rubha Dubh
Eilean Mhucaig
Rubha Bàn
Priory
Dubh Eilean
Oronsay
Eilean nan Ron · Eilean Ghaoideamal
Caolas Mòr

Shian Bay
Loch Rig...

A

Sgeir Mhòr a' Bhrein- phuirt
Rubh' an t- Sàilein
1¼ hrs (seasonal)
Loch Tarbert
Rubh' a' Chrois-aoinidh

Rubh' a' Mhàil
Rubha Bholsa
Glenbatrick
Scrinadle · 506
Beinn Bhreac · 439 · Beinn Tarsuir · 416
Sgarbh Breac · 364
Beinn an Oir · 785 · **Jura Forest**
Beinn Shiantaidh · 755
Margadale Hill · 283
Na Peileirean
Beinn a' Chaolais · 734
Paps of Jura
Loch an t-Siob
Corran
Nave Island
Ardnave Point
Gortantaoid Point
Killinallan Point
Giurbheinn · 316
Bunnahabhain
Loch a' Chnuic Bhric
Ardnave
Carraig Bhàn
Tayovullin
Killinallan
Beinn Bhreac · 286
Ardnahoe
Gleann Asdale
Leargybreck
Knockro...
Loch Mile...
Ton Mhòr
Kilnave
Loch Gruinart
Ardnave Loch
Sanaigmore
Loch Staoisha
Glas Bheinn · 561
Feolin
Eilean Mòr
Braigo · Leckgruinart
Keills
Port Askaig · Feolin Ferry
Dubh Bheinn · 530
Keils
Rubha Lamanais
Smaull
Aoradh
Craigens
Loch Finlaggan
Sr...
Ballinaby · Carnduncan
Grainel
ISLAY
8 · A846 · Kilmeny
Craighouse
Saligo Bay
B8017
Lyrabus
Moin'a'choire
Loch Cam
Loch Ballygrant
Ballygrant
Loch Lossit
Brat Bheinn · 342
Rubha n...
Crackaig
Coul Point
B80..
Aruadh
Foreland
Blackrock
Esknish
Loch Gorm
Machrie
Ardfin
Jura House
Sannaig
Rockside
Kilchoman
Conisby
A847
Islay House · Redhouses
Beinn Dubh · 267
Am Fraoch Eilean
Rubha na Tràille
Machir Bay
Bridgend
Cachlaidh Mhòr
Brosdale Island
RINNS OF ISLAY
Bruichladdich
Neriby · Barr
Sgorr nam Faoileann · 429
Kilchiaran
Gartnatra · A846
Cattadale
Beinn na Caillich
McArthur's Head
Kilchiaran Bay
Bowmore
Cruach
Cluanach
Glas Bheinn · 471
2 hrs
Port Charlotte · 15
Ronnachmore
Gearach
Gartbreck
Tormisdale
Carn
Laggan
Kilennan
Proaig
Lossit
Beinn Tart a' Mhill · 232
Beinn Bhan · 471
Beinn Bheigeir · 491
Lossit Bay · Kelsay
Nerabus
Laggan
13
Beinn Uraraidh · 454
Rubha Liath
Ardtalla
Rubha na Faing
A847
Duich
A846
B8016
Loch Uraraidh
Trudernish
Easter Ellister
Claggain Bay
Portnahaven
ISLAY
Glenegedale
Kintour
Port Wemyss
Laggan Bay
Machrie
Sgorr Bhogachain
Loch Uigeadail
Kintour
Orsay
Rinns Point
Ardmore Point
Machrie
Leorin
Leorin Lochs
Beinn Sholum · 347
Kildalton Church & Crosses
Ardmore
Rubha Mòr
Kintra
2¼ hrs
Maol Buidhe · 165
Cornabus
Eilean a' Chuirn
Lower Killeyan
THE OA
Carnmore
Ardbeg
Eilean Bhride
Risabus
Lagavulin
Rubha na Gainmhich
Inerval
Port Ellen
Laphroaig
Mull of Oa
Loch Kinnabus
The Ard
Texa
Port Chubaird
Caolas an Eilein
Rubha nan Leacan

0 · 2 · 4 · 6 miles
0 · 2 · 4 · 6 · 8 · 10 km

B · **C** · **D**

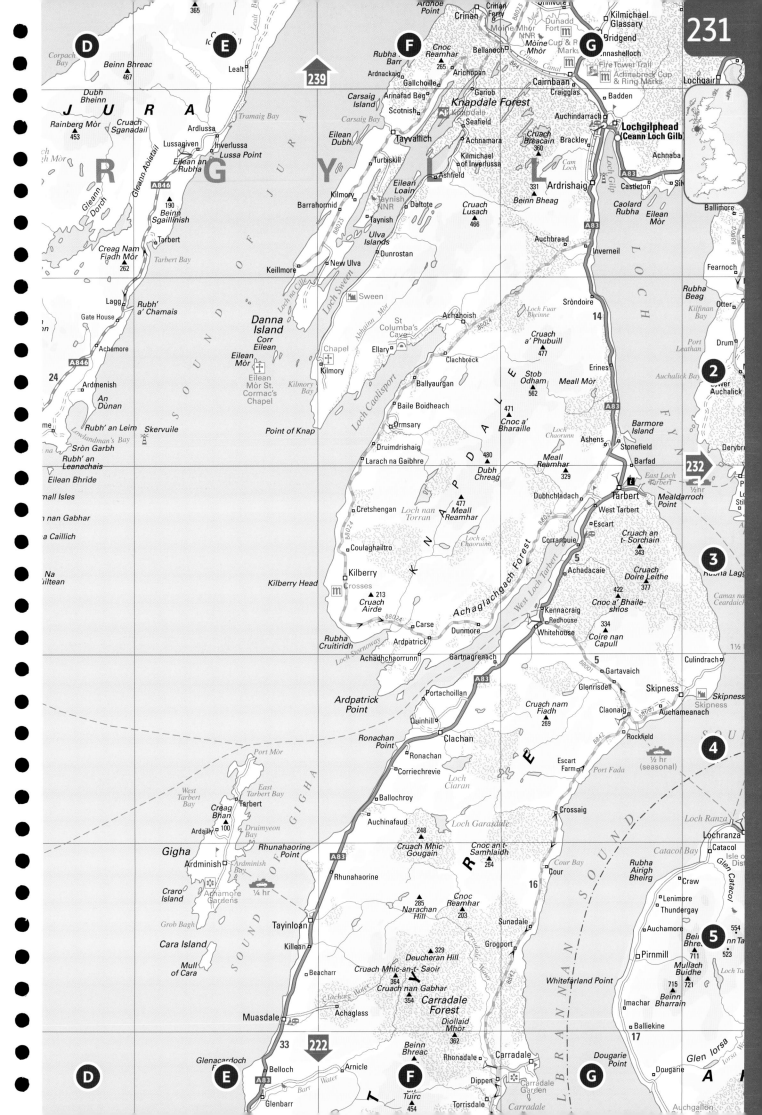

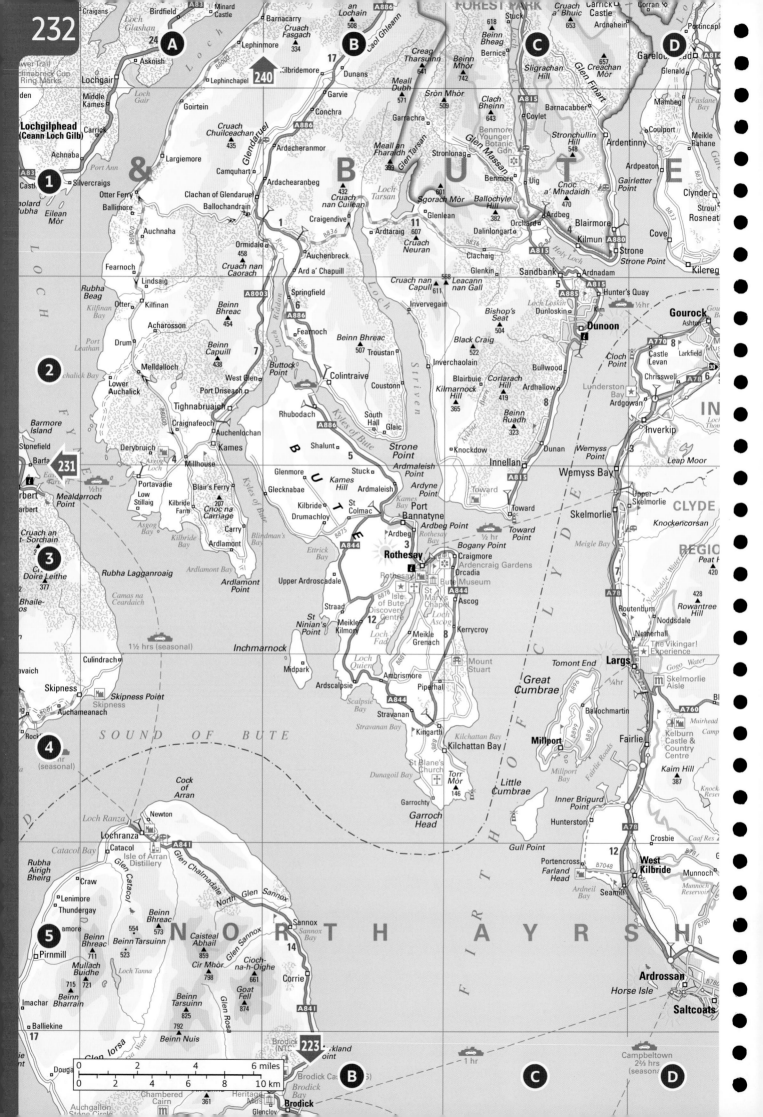

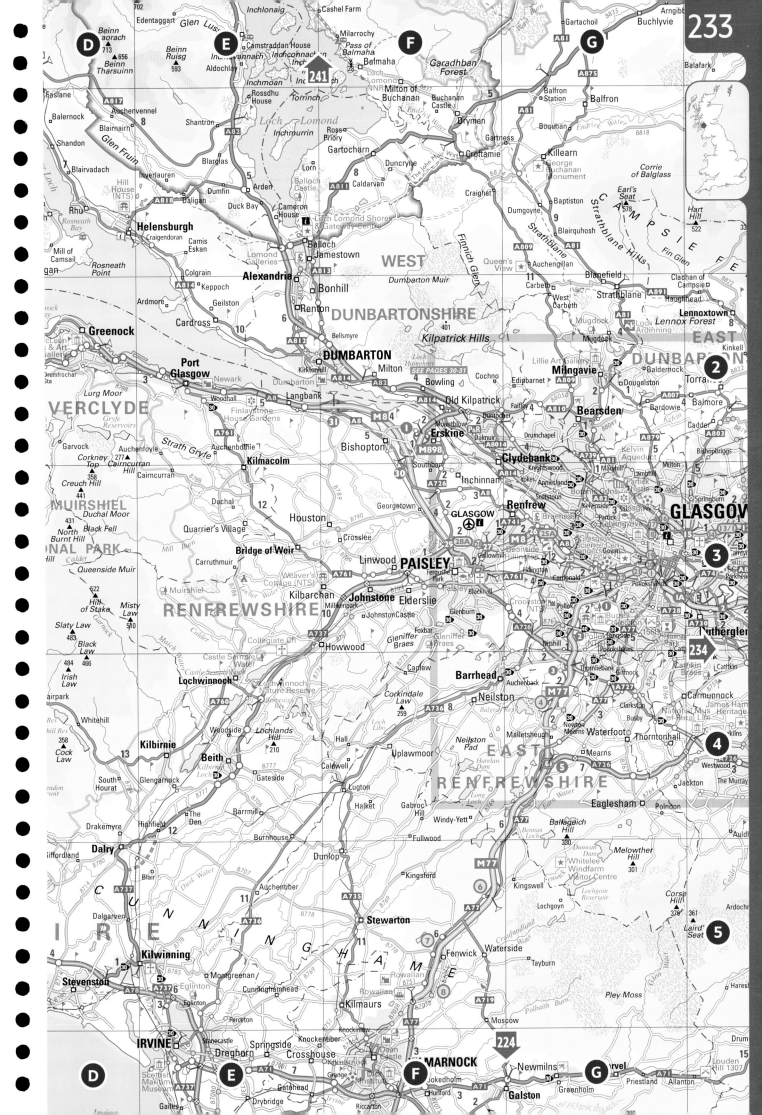

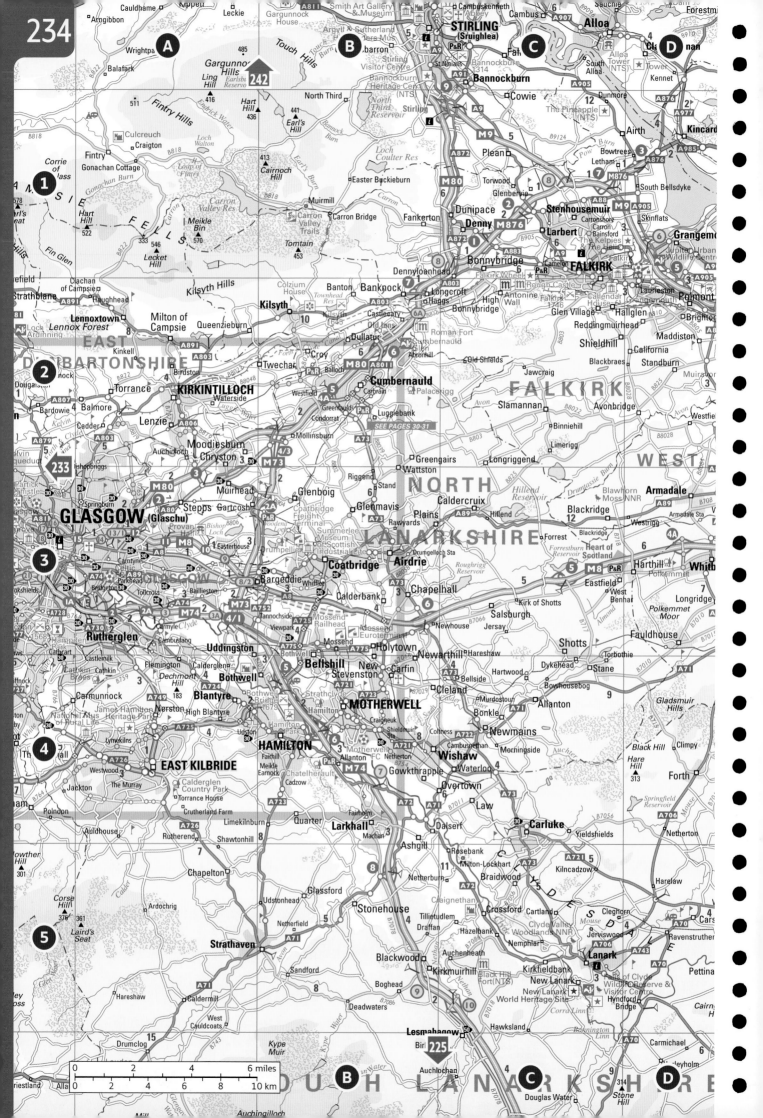

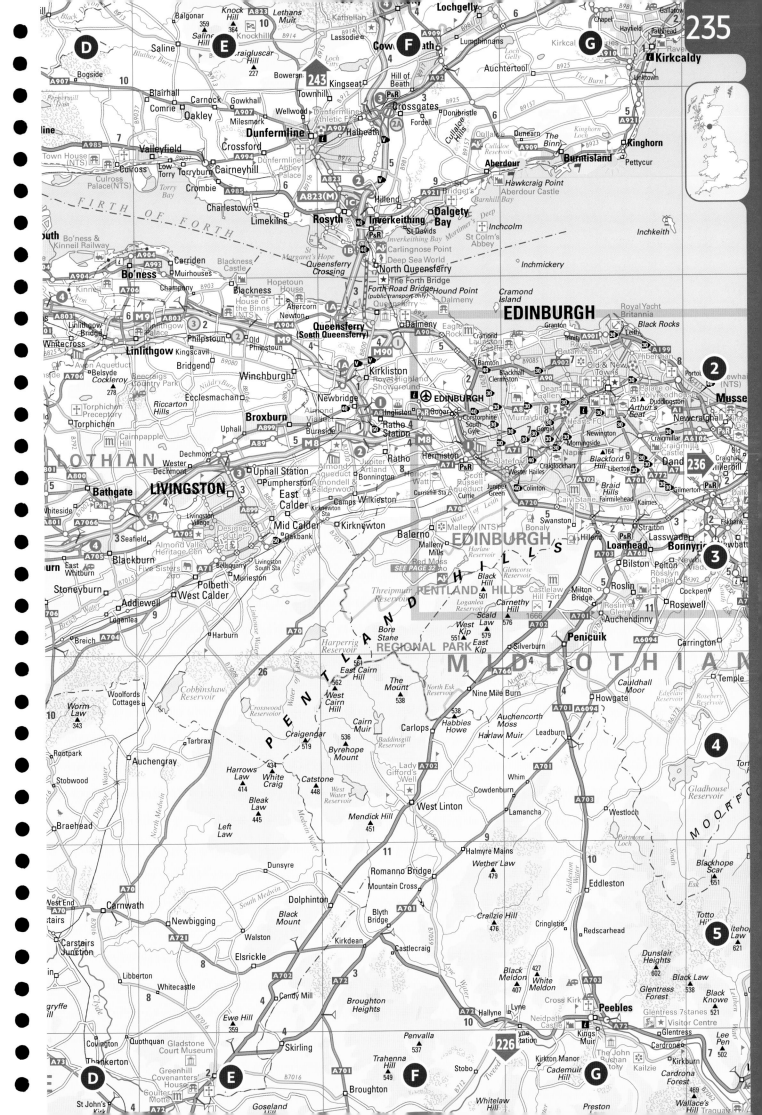

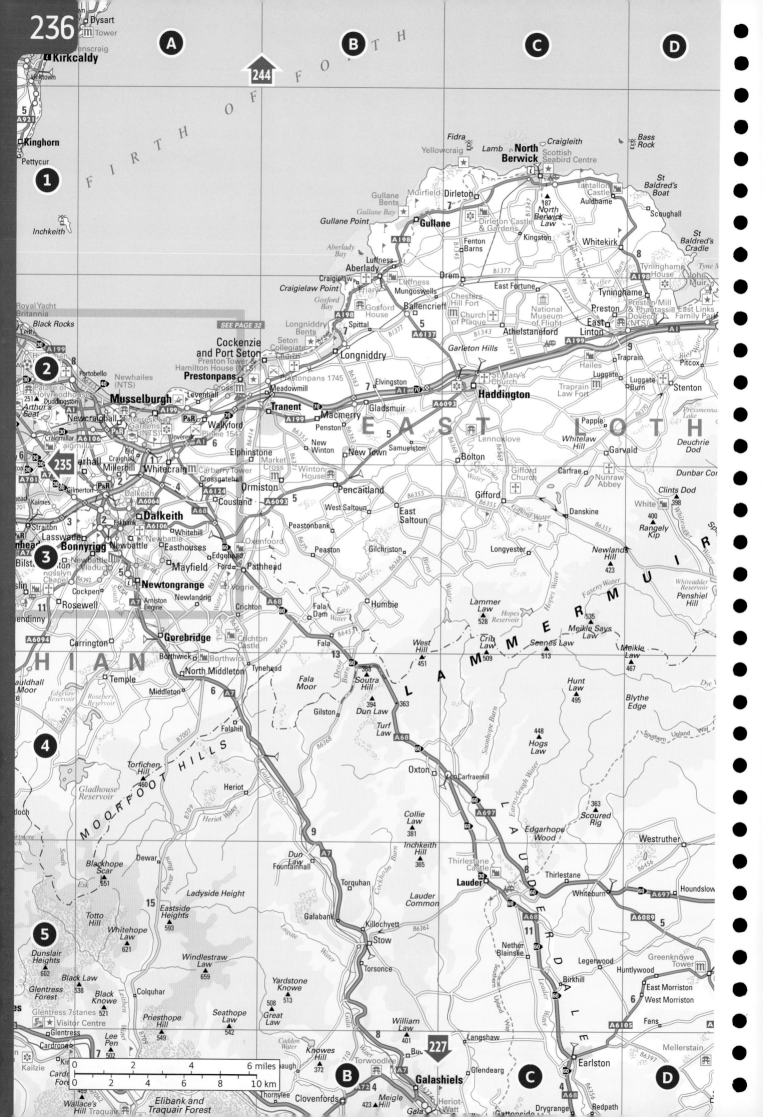

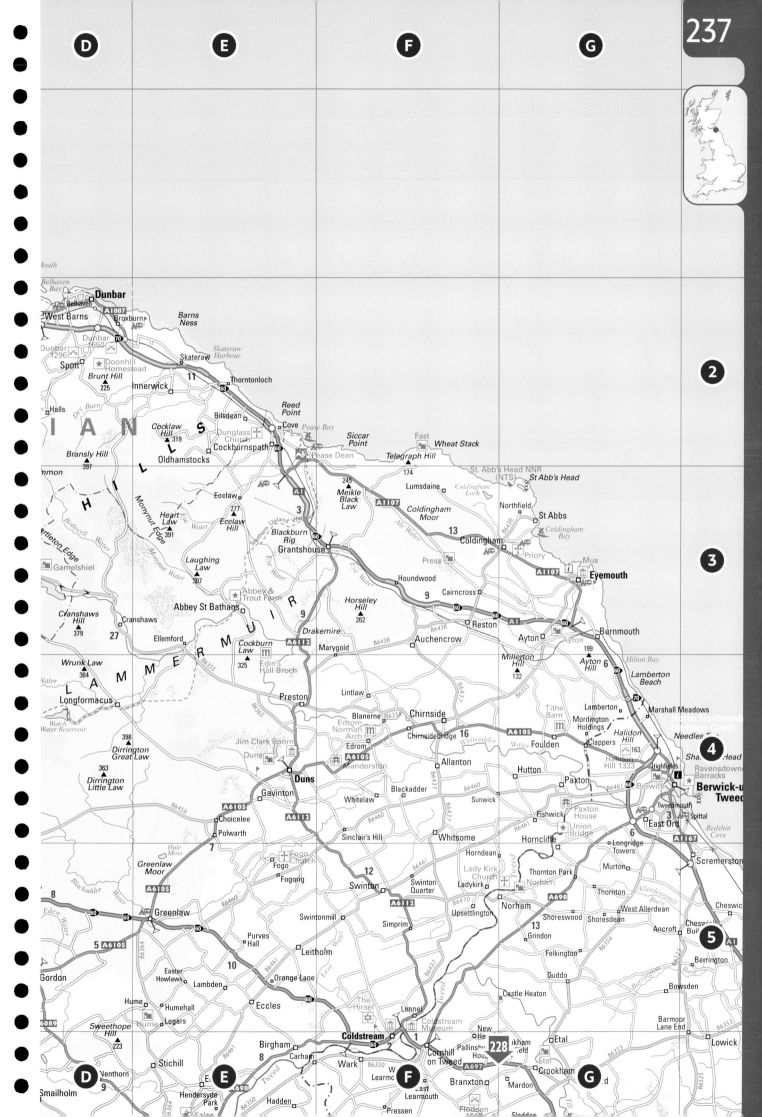

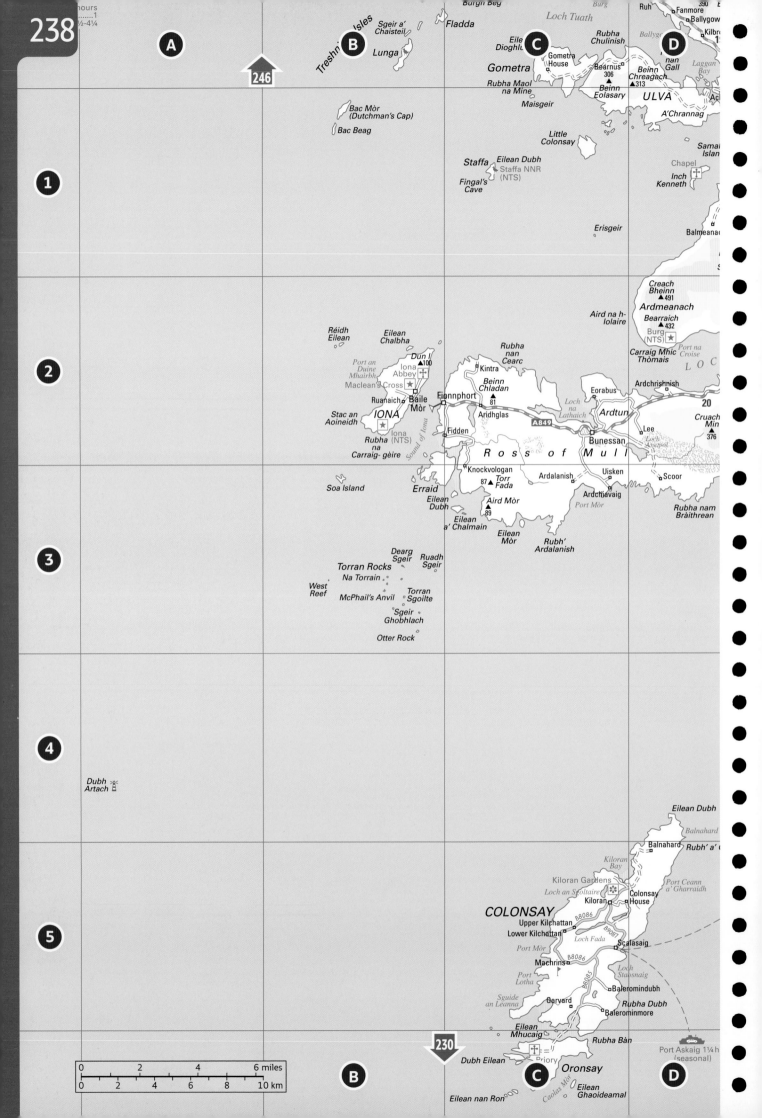

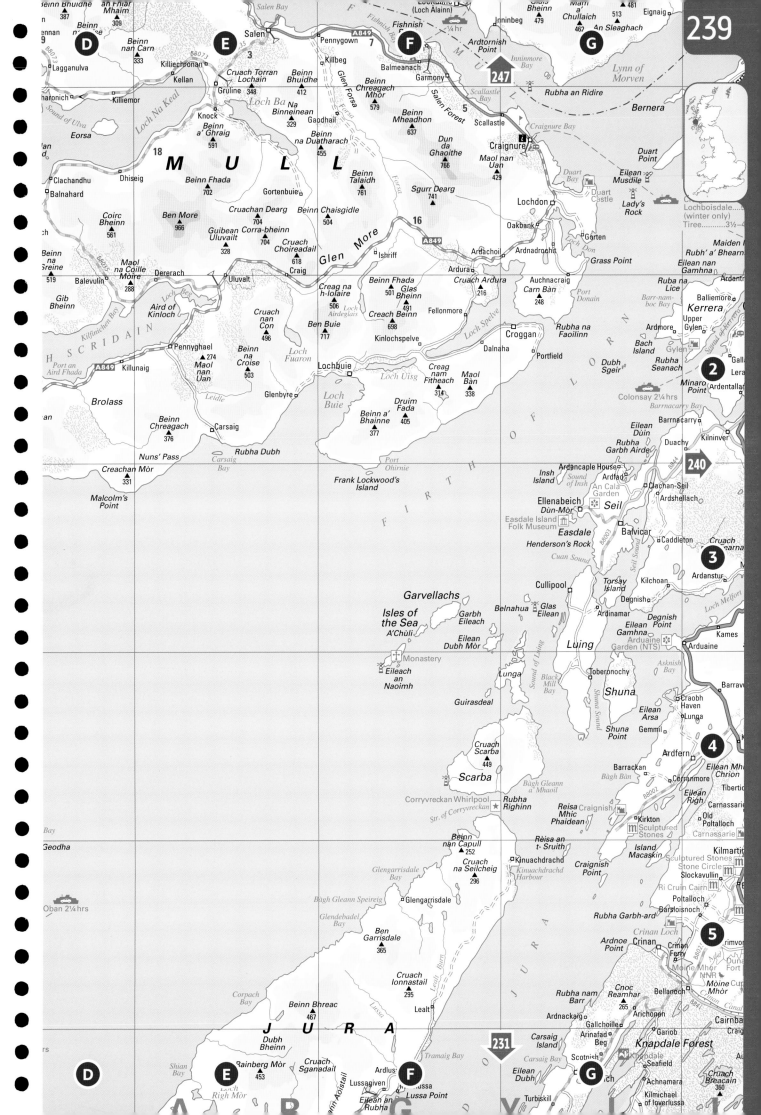

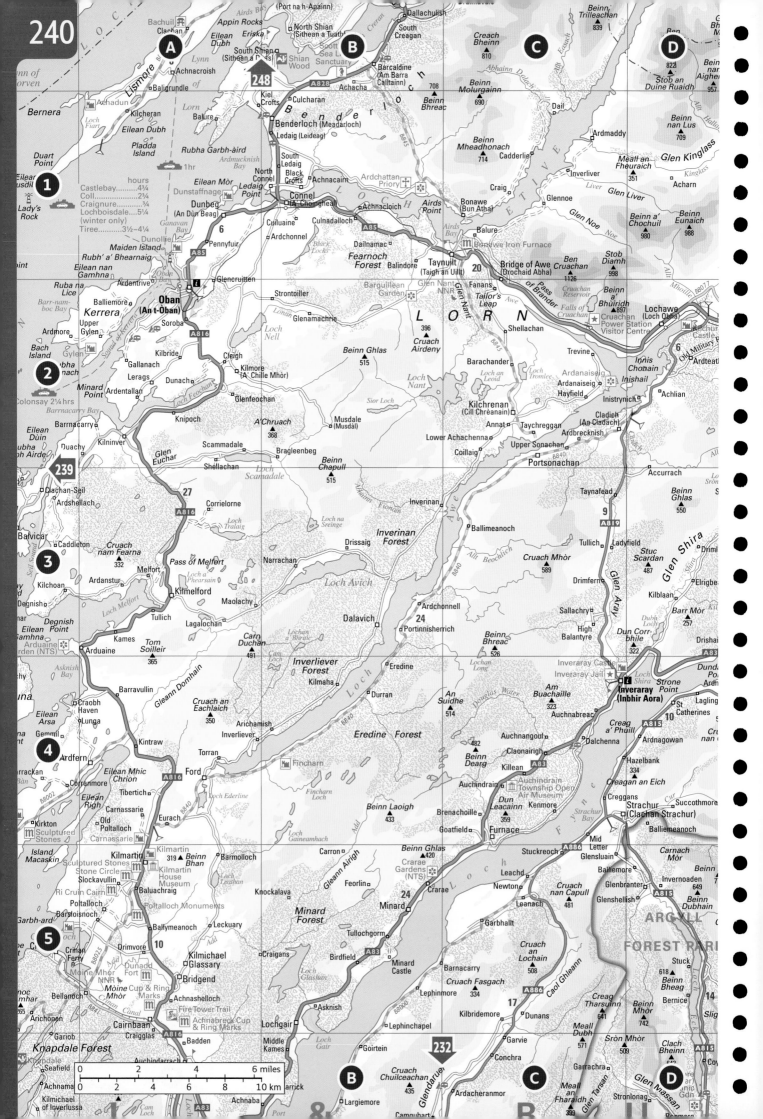

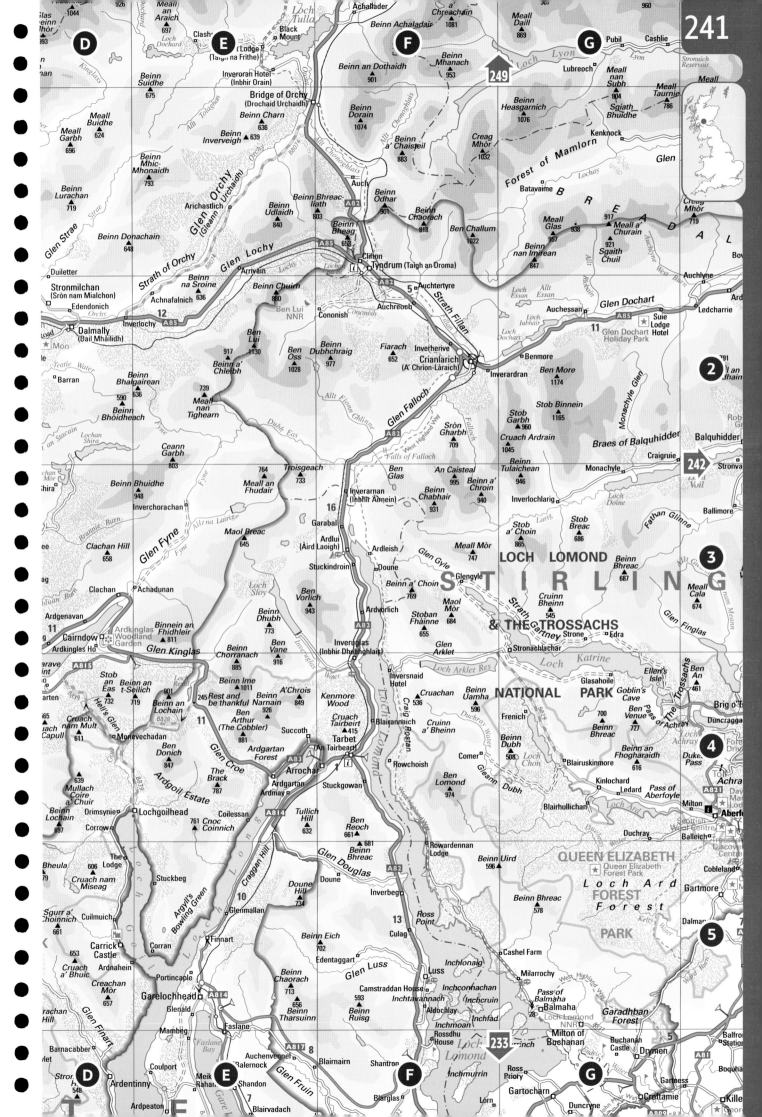

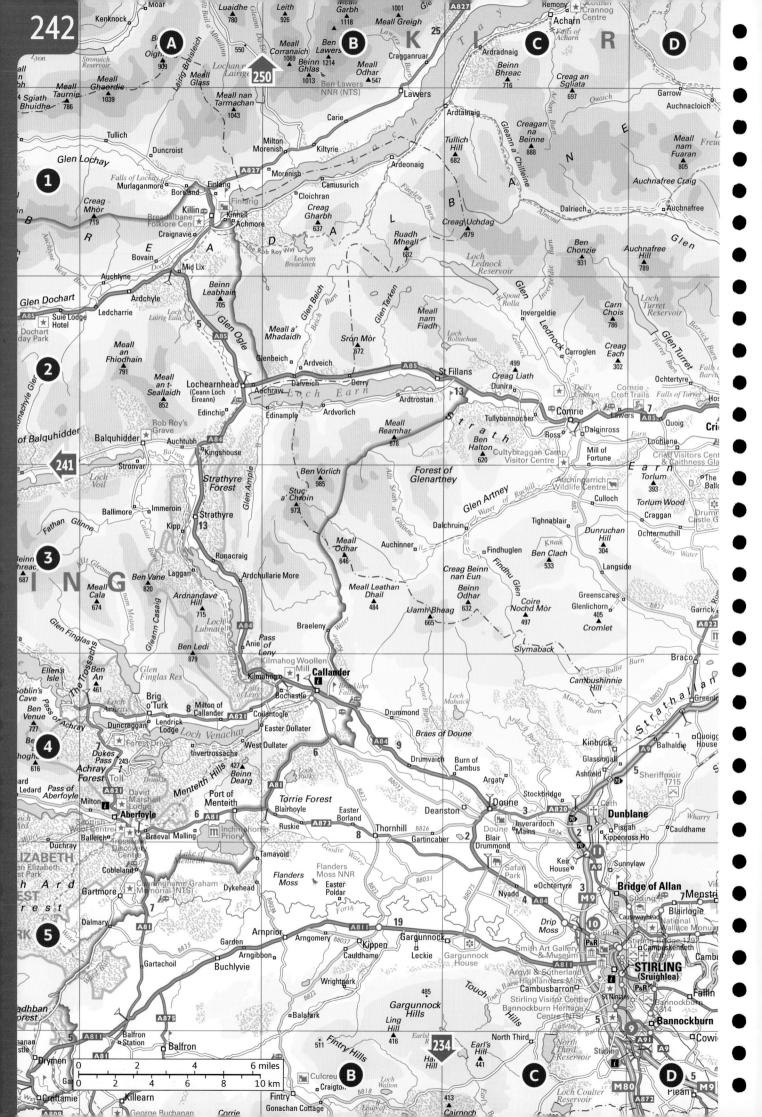

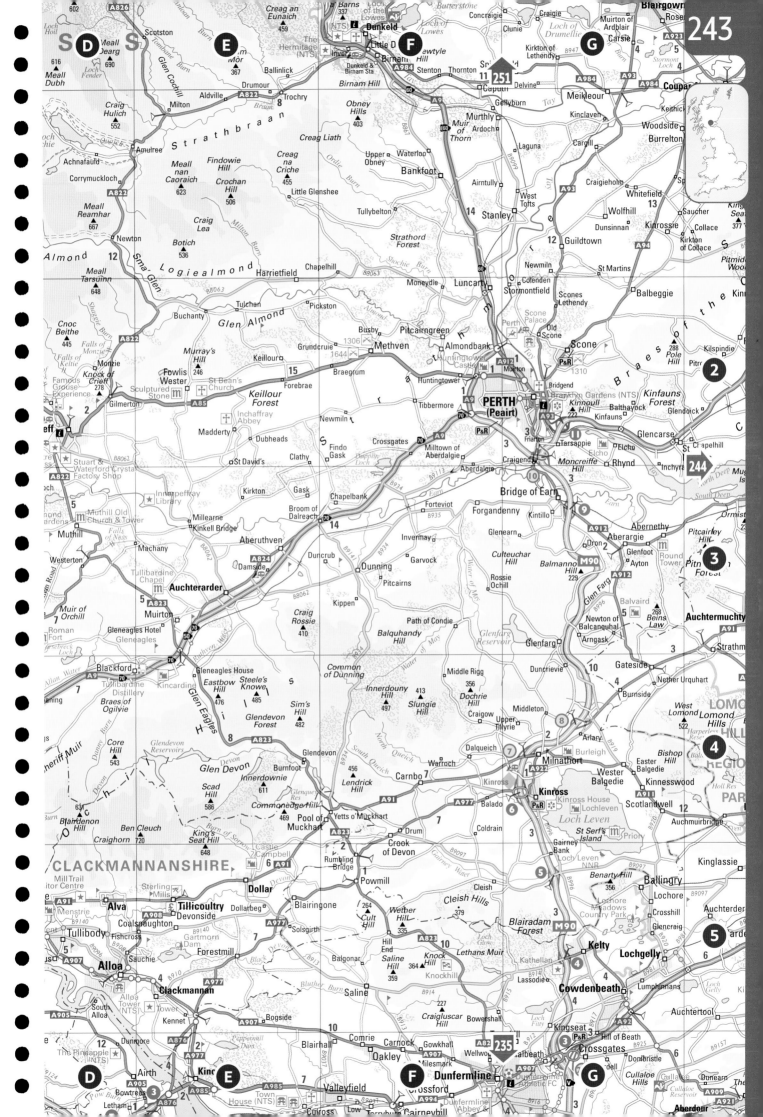

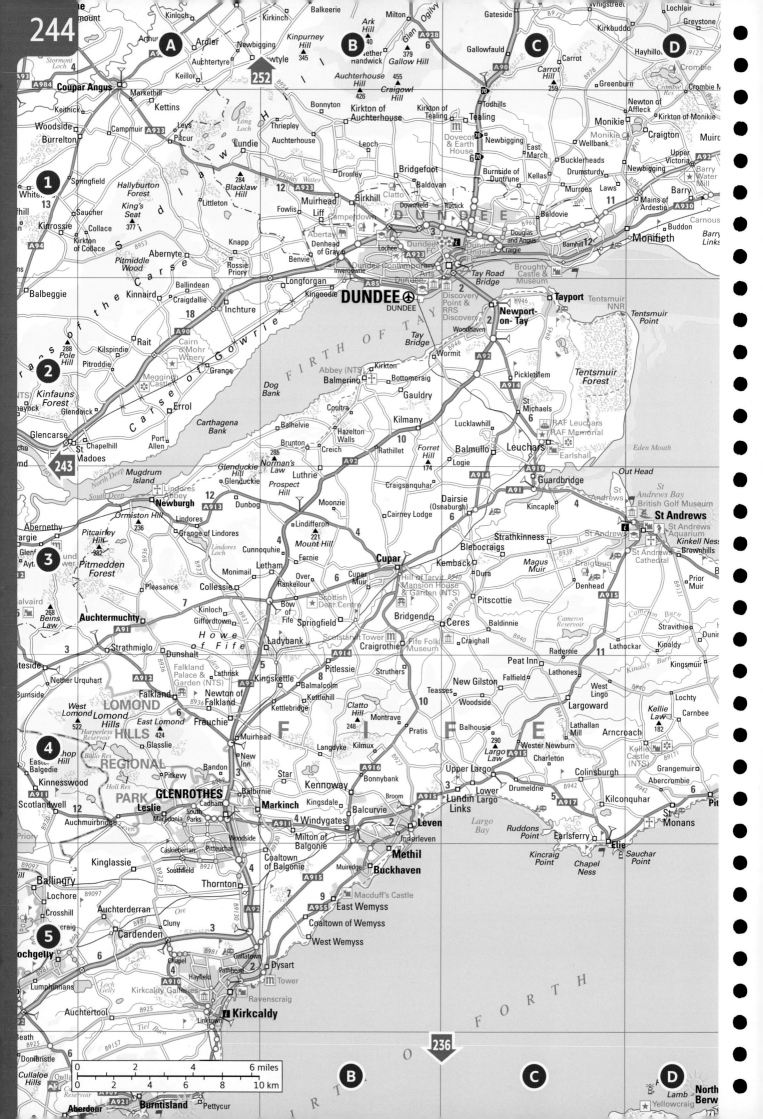

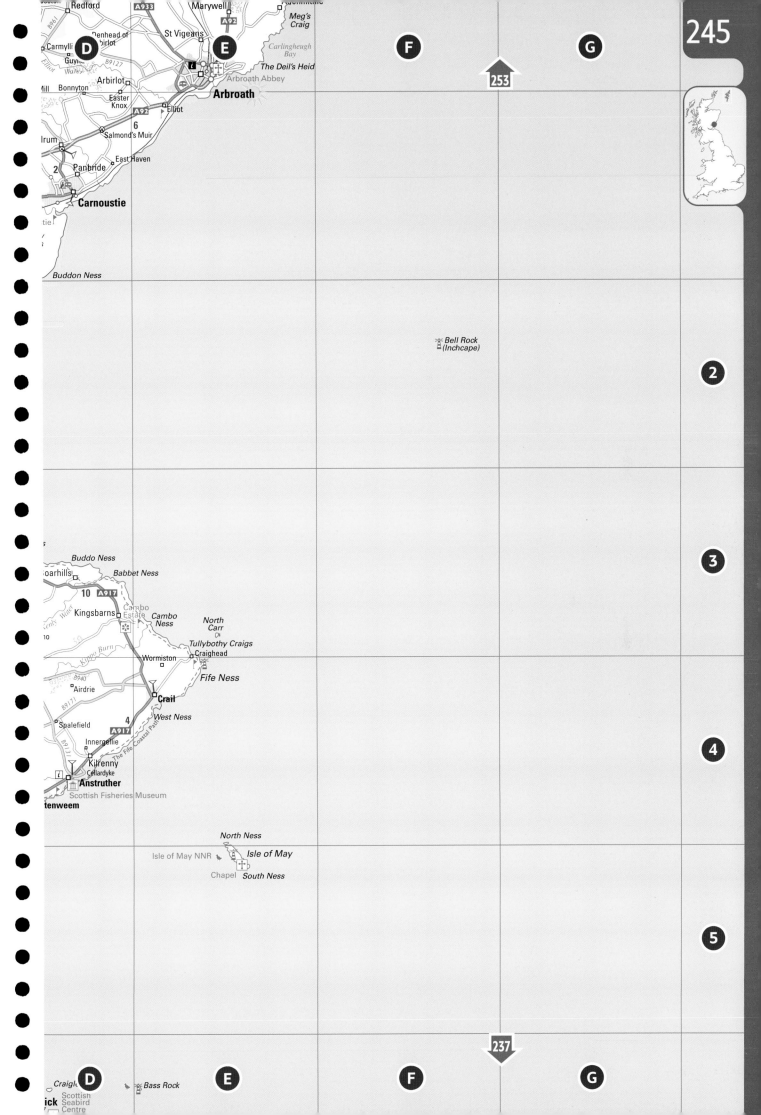

Redford
Marywell
Meg's Craig
Carmylli
Denhead of birlot
St Vigeans
Carlingheugh Bay
Guyli
Arbirlot
Bonnyton
The Deil's Heid
Arbroath Abbey
Arbroath
Easter Knox
Elliot
Salmond's Muir
East Haven
Panbride
Carnoustie
Buddon Ness

F

G

253

2

Bell Rock
(Inchcape)

3

Buddo Ness
oarhills
Babbet Ness
Kingsbarns
Cambo Estate
Cambo Ness
North Carr
Tullybothy Craigs
Wormiston
Craighead
Fife Ness
Airdrie
Crail
West Ness
Spalefield
Innergellie
The Fife Coastal Path
Kilrenny
Cellardyke
Anstruther
Scottish Fisheries Museum
tenweem

4

North Ness
Isle of May NNR
Isle of May
Chapel
South Ness

5

237

D

E

Craigl
Bass Rock
ick
Scottish Seabird Centre

A B C D

1

255

Rubha Sgor an t-Snidhe

ival 528 Ainshval 781 Sgurr nan Gillean 764

Rubha nam Meirleach

SOUND OF RUM

Rubha an Fhasaidh

Beinn Tigh

Sound of Eigg

same scale as main map

Point COLL

Gunna Caolas Bàn Port a' Mhurain

Urvaig

Miodar

Sgeir Bharrach Salum Bay Salum Caolas Rubha Dubh

Vaul 4 Ruaig

The Green Clachan Mòr Balephetrish Bay Balephetrish Hill B8069 Brock

Hough Bay Kilkenneth T I R E E Kenovay 5 Gott Bay

Rubha Liath Soa

Eilean nan Each Gòdag

Rubh' Leam na Làraich Beinn Airein 137 Port Mòr

Muck

2

B8068 3 B8065 5

Moss Crossapoll TIREE Scarinish

Sandaig Heylipoll 2 B8065 Baugh Heanish

Barrapoll 3

hours
Coll.....................1
Oban........3½-4¼

Sanna Point

Sanna Bay

Point of Ardnamurchan Portuairk Grigadale Port Min

A R

B8067 Balemartine

Balephuil Mannal

Rinn Thorbhais Hynish

Hynish Centre,
'The story of
Skerryvore Lighthouse'

3

Eag na Maoile Eilean Mòr

Rubha Mòr

Rubh' a' Bhinnein B8072 Bousd Rubha Sgor-Innis Sorisdale

5 Loch Fada Bagh na Coille

Torastan

Cliad Bay Arnabost

Grishipoll B8071 ★ Coll Dark Sky Island

Grishipoll Bay Clabhach 2 Loch Cliad B8021 73

Ballyhaugh Ben Hogh 2

Hogh Bay 104 Totamore Arinagour

Totronald C O L L Loch Eatharna

Sorne Point

Quinish Point

4

Port Mine Feall Bay Arileod Acha 5 B8070 Oban 2¾ hrs

Calgary Point Uig Gorton Eilean Ornsay Tiree 1 hr

Gunna Caolas Bàn Crossapol Crossapol Bay Soa Friesland Bay Rubha Fasachd

Urvaig Port a' Mhurain

Caliach Point Sunipol Port na Bà Langamull Croig

Quinish

Mornish Cruach Sleibhe 166 Calgary Frachadil 5 Dervaig B8073

Rubha nan Oirean ★ Calgary Art in Nature

Carn Mòr 342 Cruachan Ceann a' Ghairbh 261 Beinn nan Clach-corra

5

Miodar Salum Caolas Rubha Dubh

Ruaig T I R E E Port Bàn

Rubha Liath So

hours
Coll.....................1
Oban........3½-4¼

Calgary Bay Treshnish Point Treshnish Ensay

191 ▲ Beinn Duill Cruachan Odhar 256 Burg Tostarie Kilninian

Cnoc an da Chinn 390

Cairn na Burgh More Cairn na Burgh Beg

Treshnish Isles Sgeir a' Chaisteil Fladda

Sgeir a' Chaisteil Lunga

Rubh' a' Chaoil Rubh' an t-Suibhein Port Burg Normann's Ruh Fanmore Ballygow

Eilean Dioghlum Rubha Chulinish Rubha nan Gall Ballygown Bay Laggan Bay Kilbre

Gometra House Bèarnus 306 Beinn Chreagach Beinn Eolasary

Gometra Rubha Maol na Mine Maisgeir A'Chrannag

Loch Tuath Beinn Chreagach ▲313 U L V A Ac

238

Bac Mòr (Dutchman's Cap)

B C D

Little Colonsay Samal Island

Staffa Eilean Dubh Chapel

0 2 4 6 miles
0 2 4 6 8 10 km

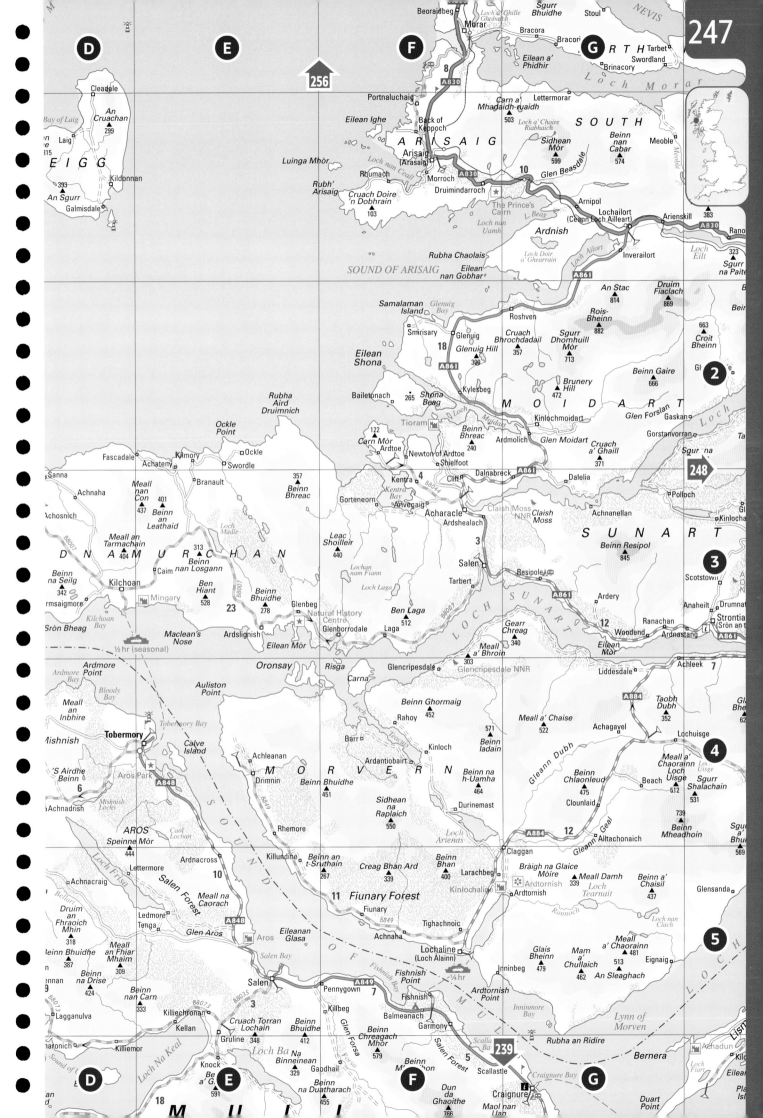

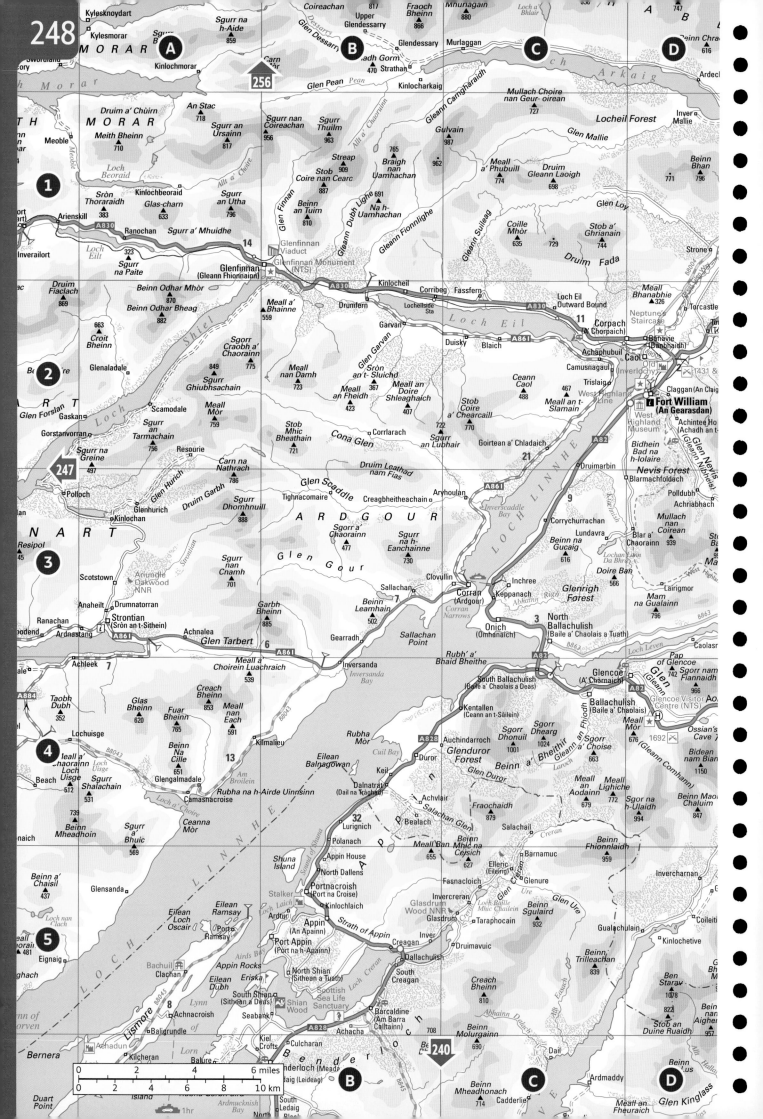

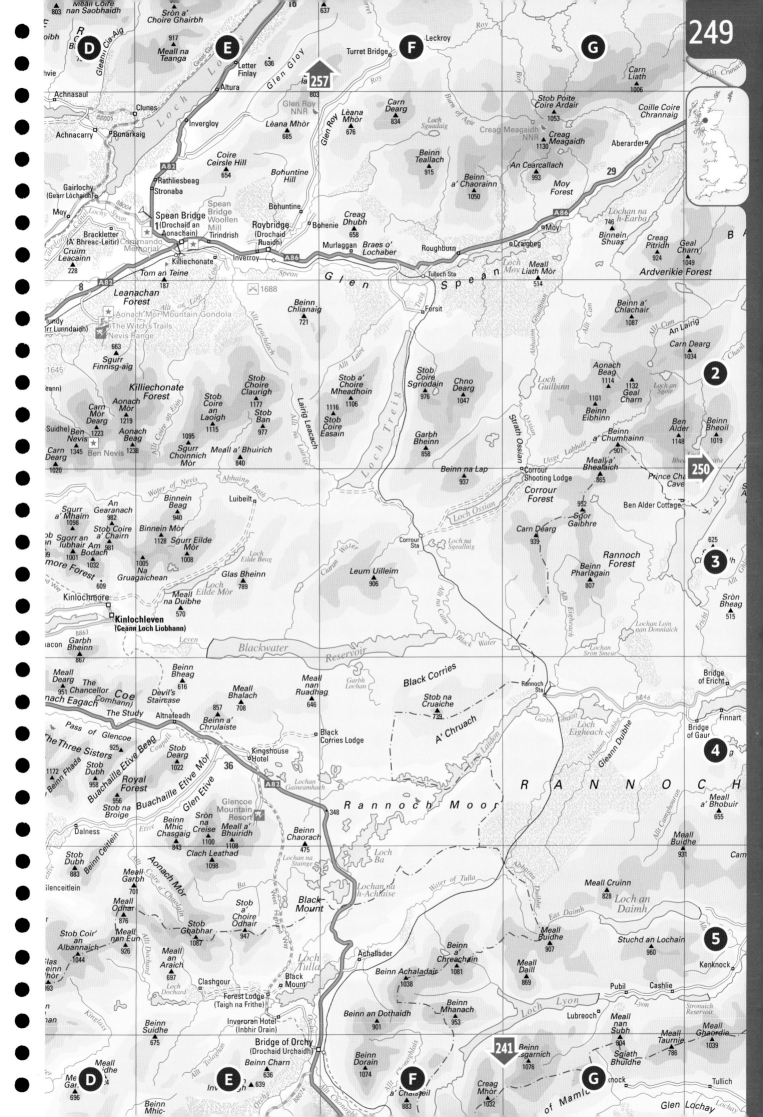

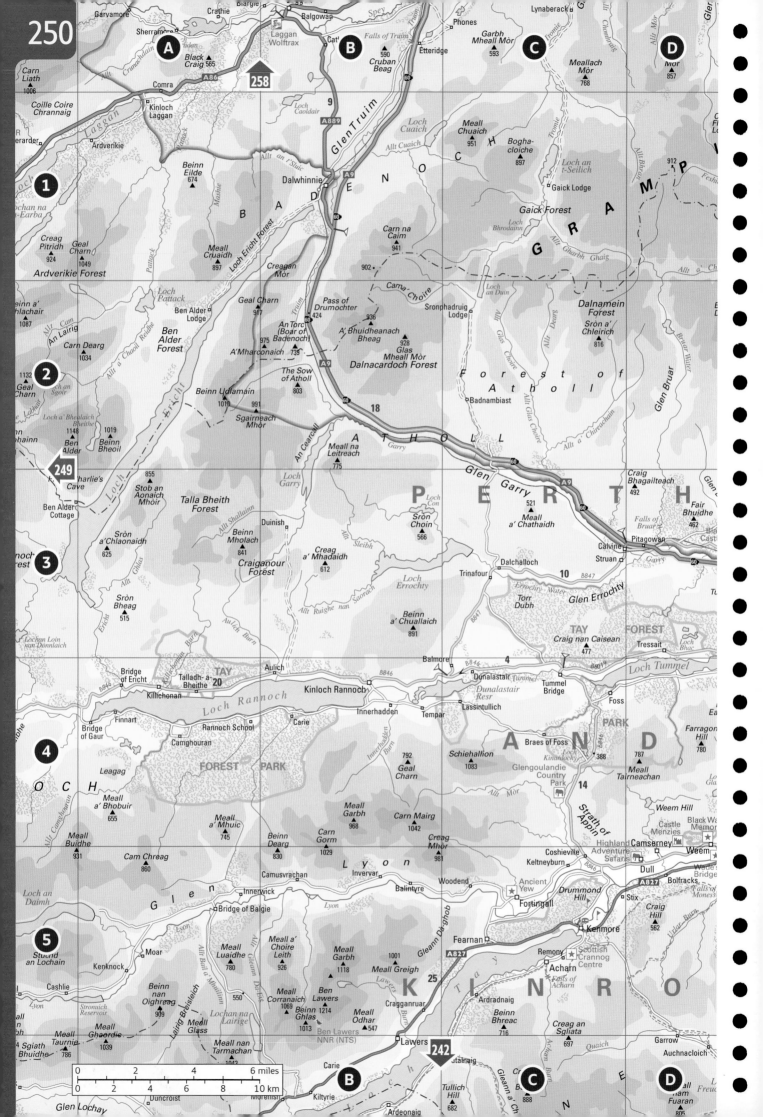

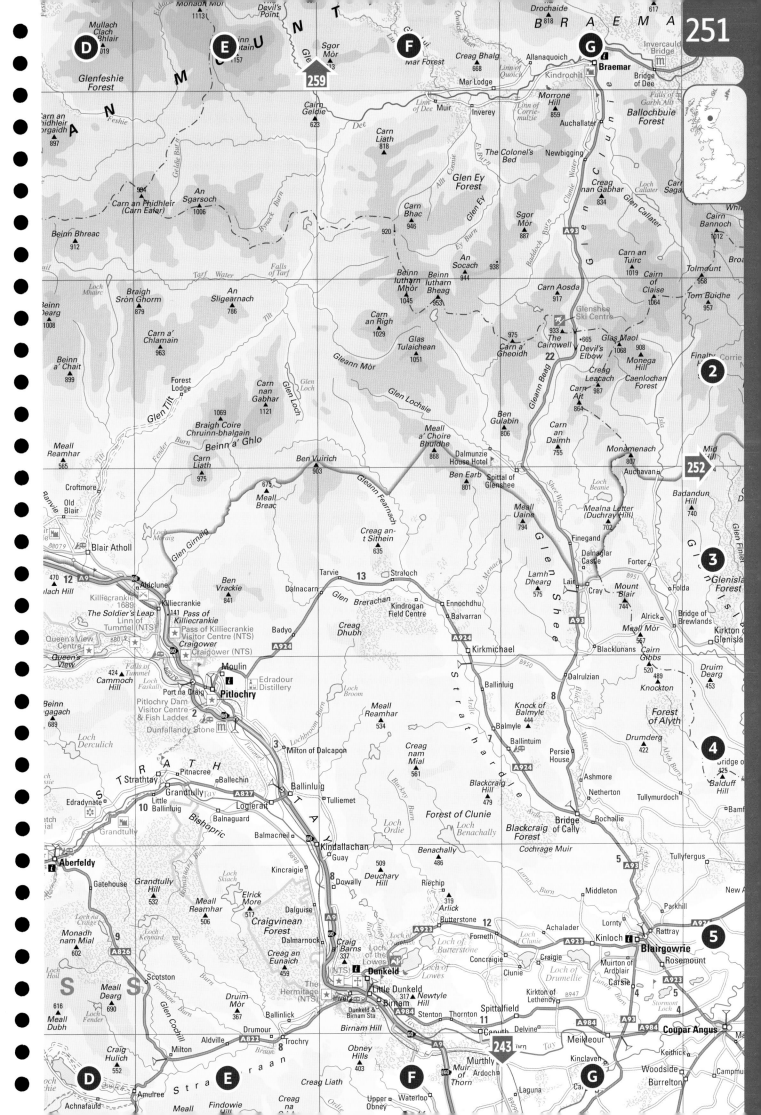

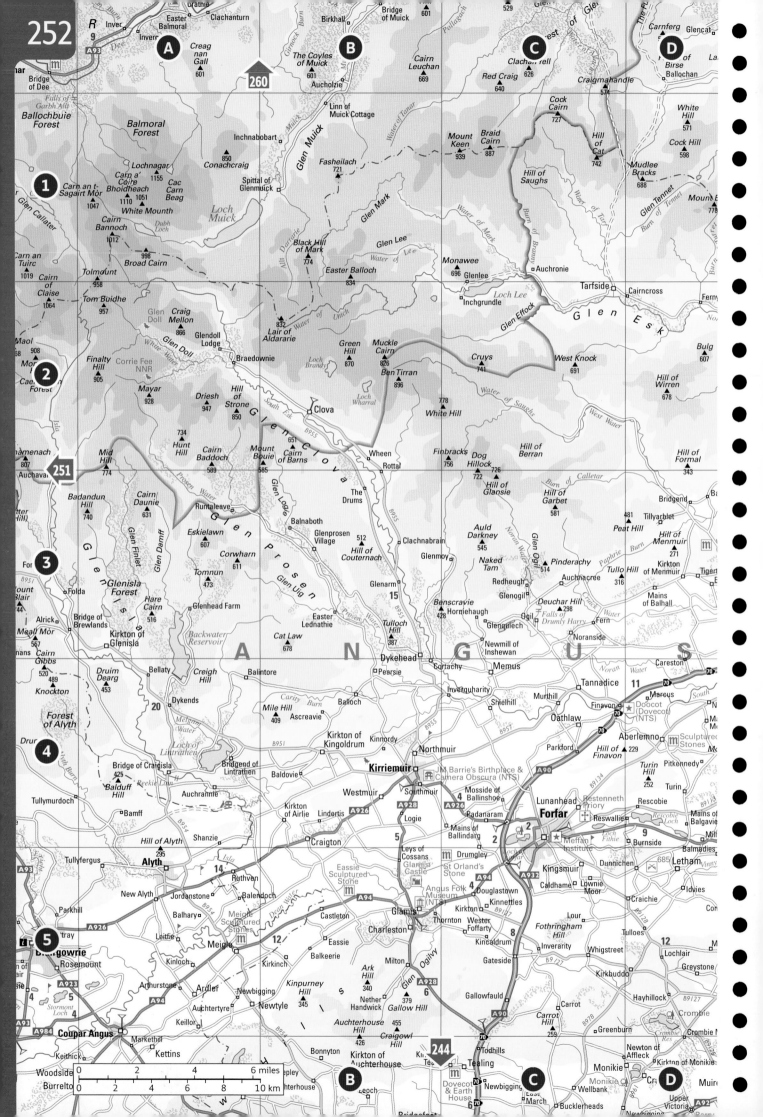

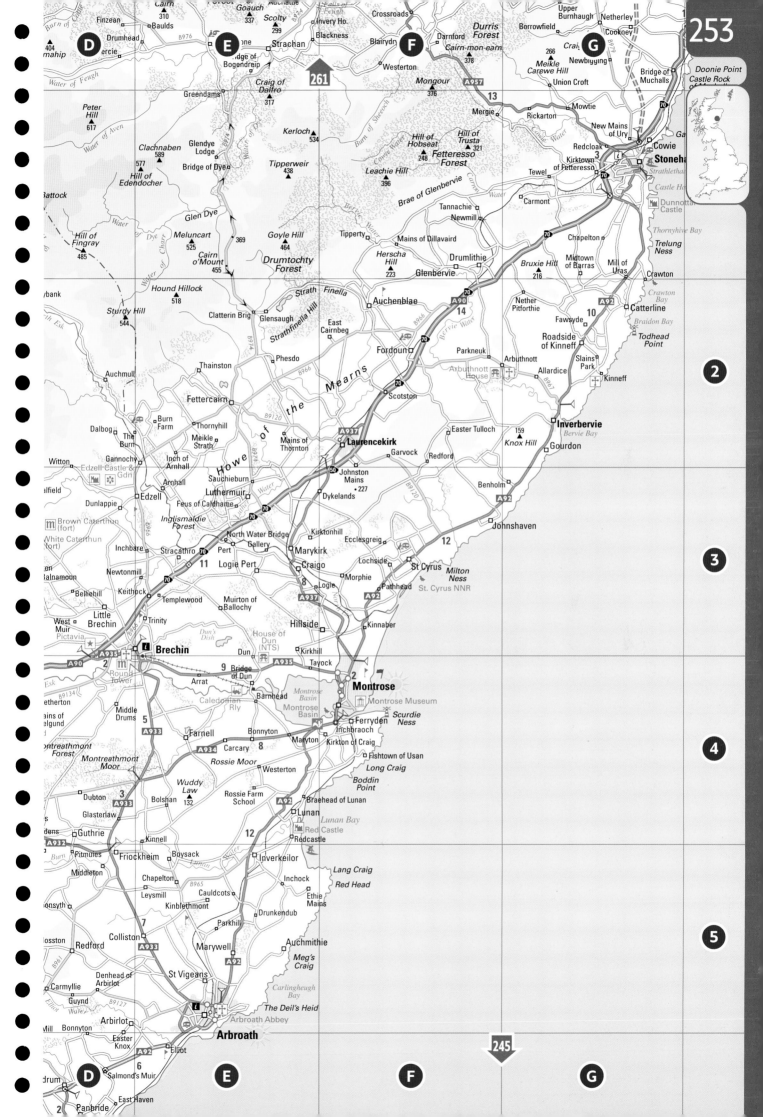

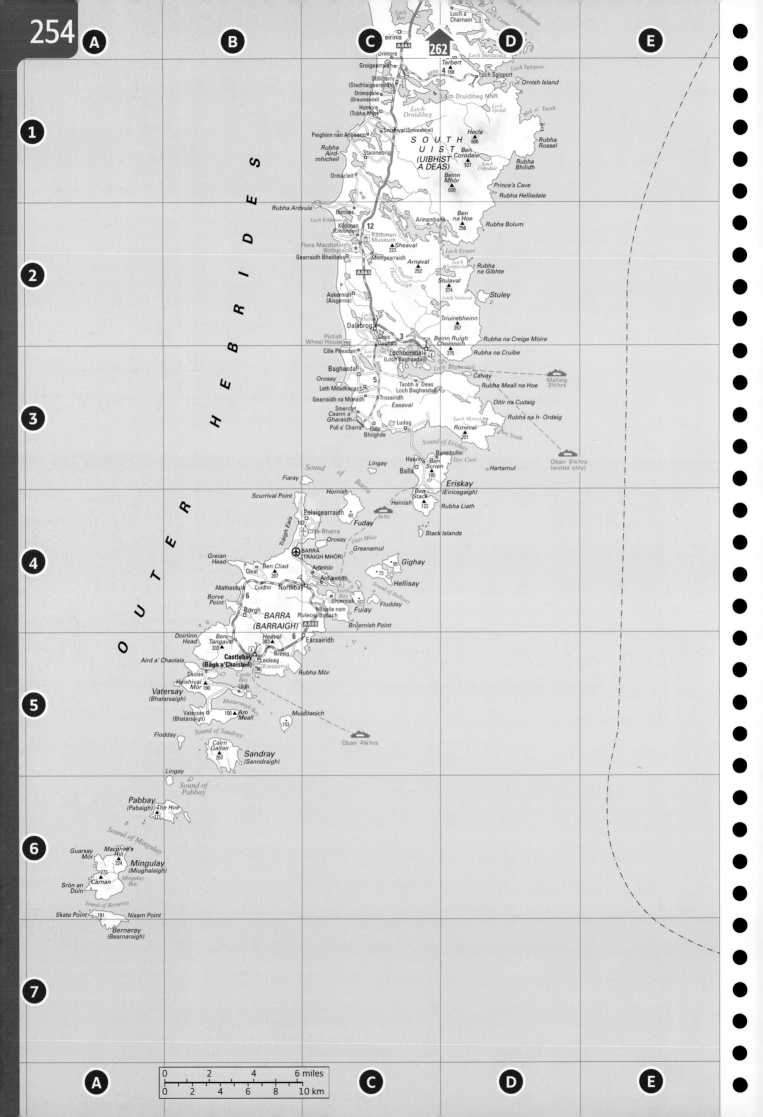

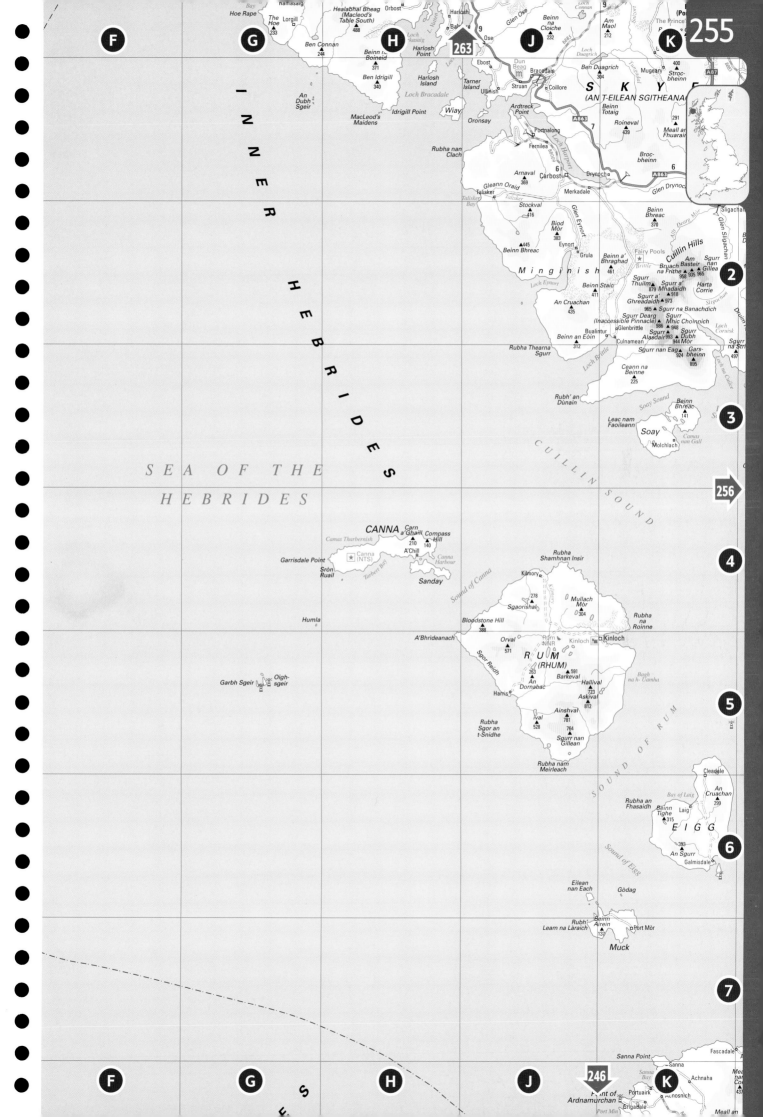

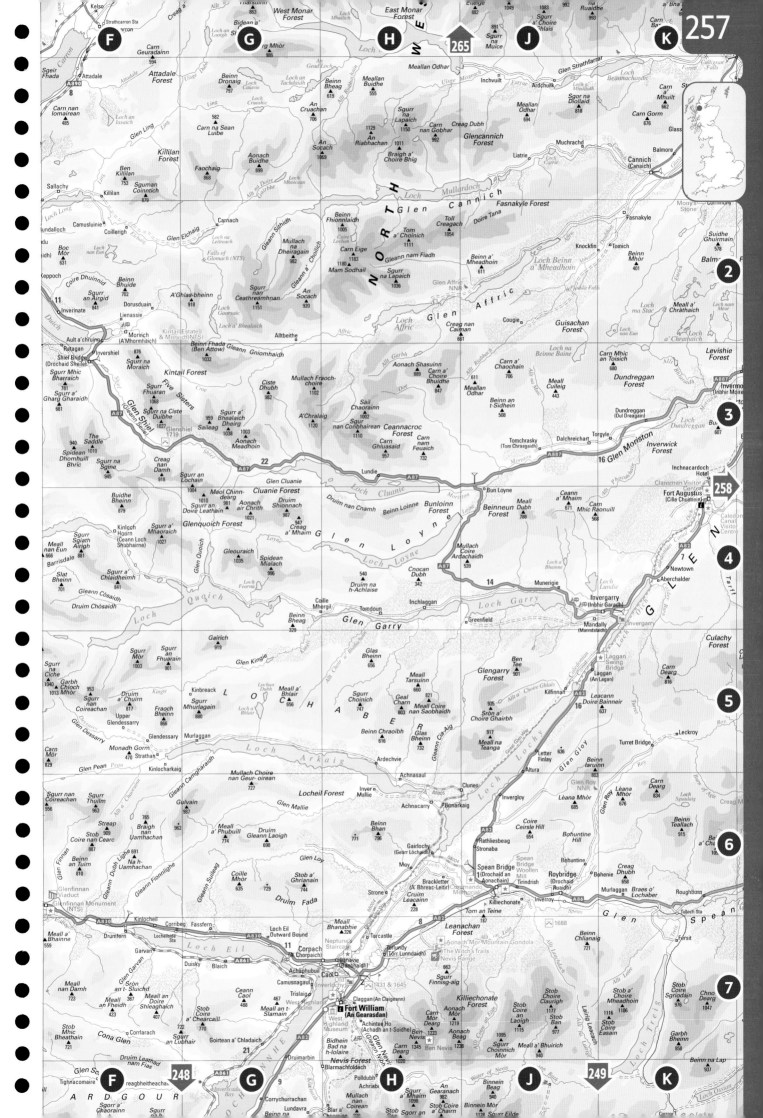

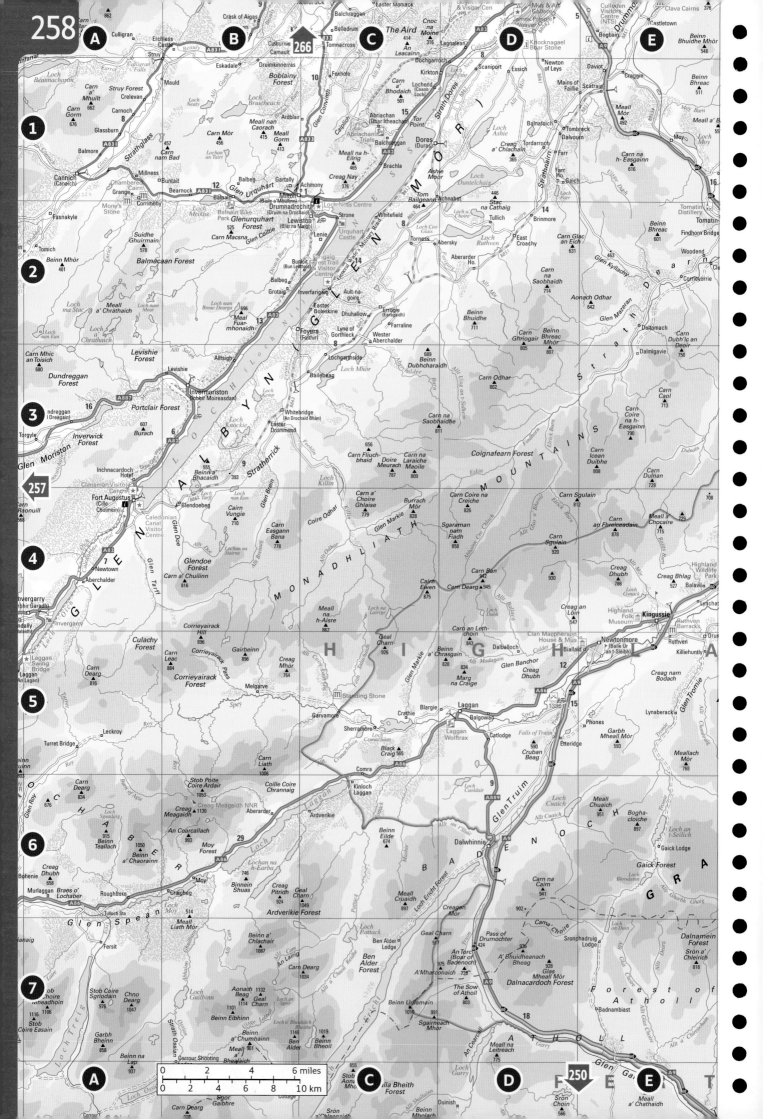

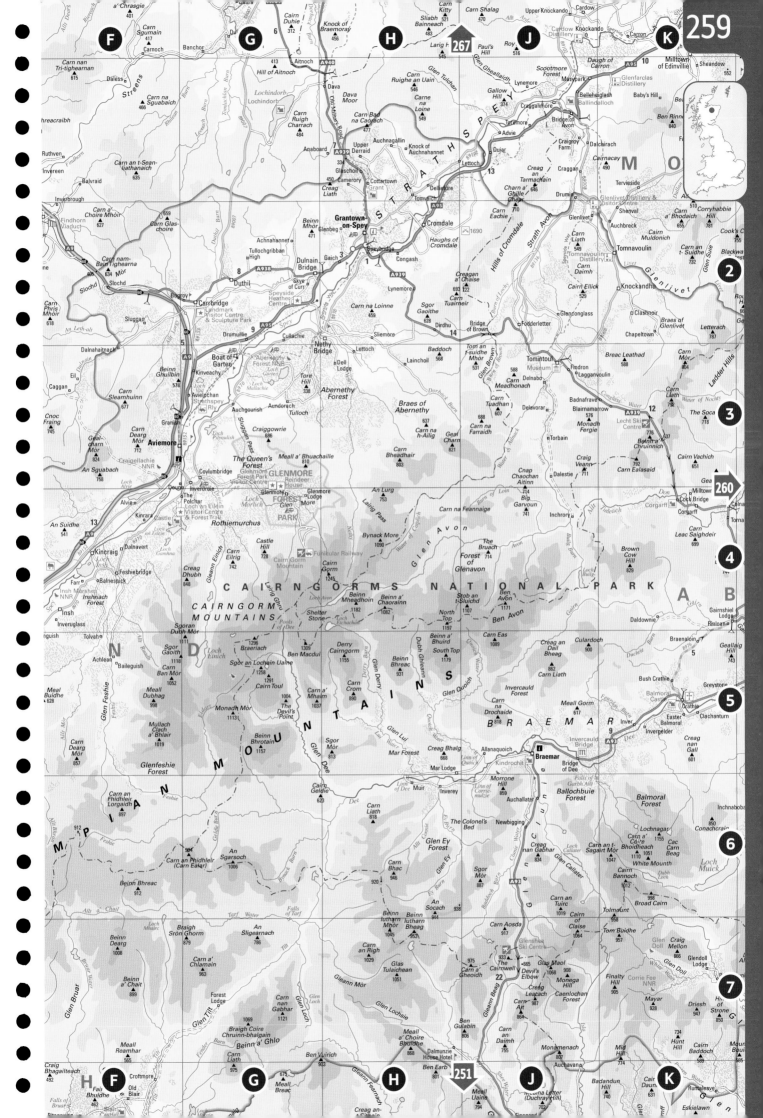

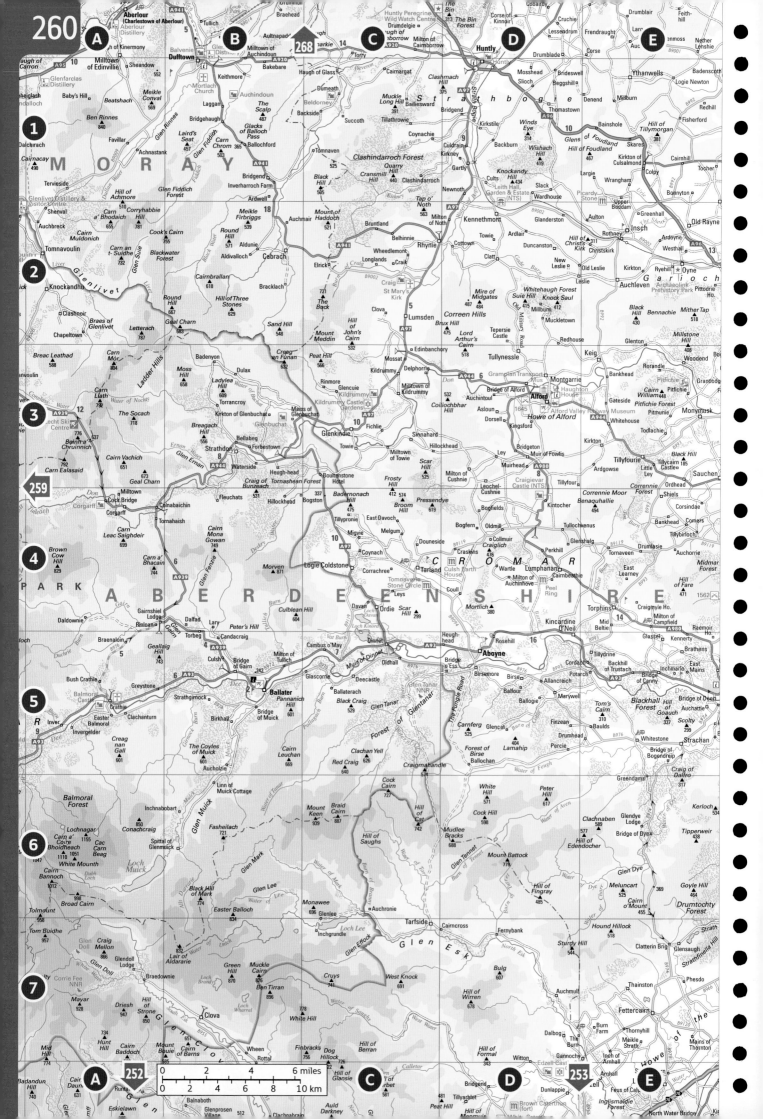

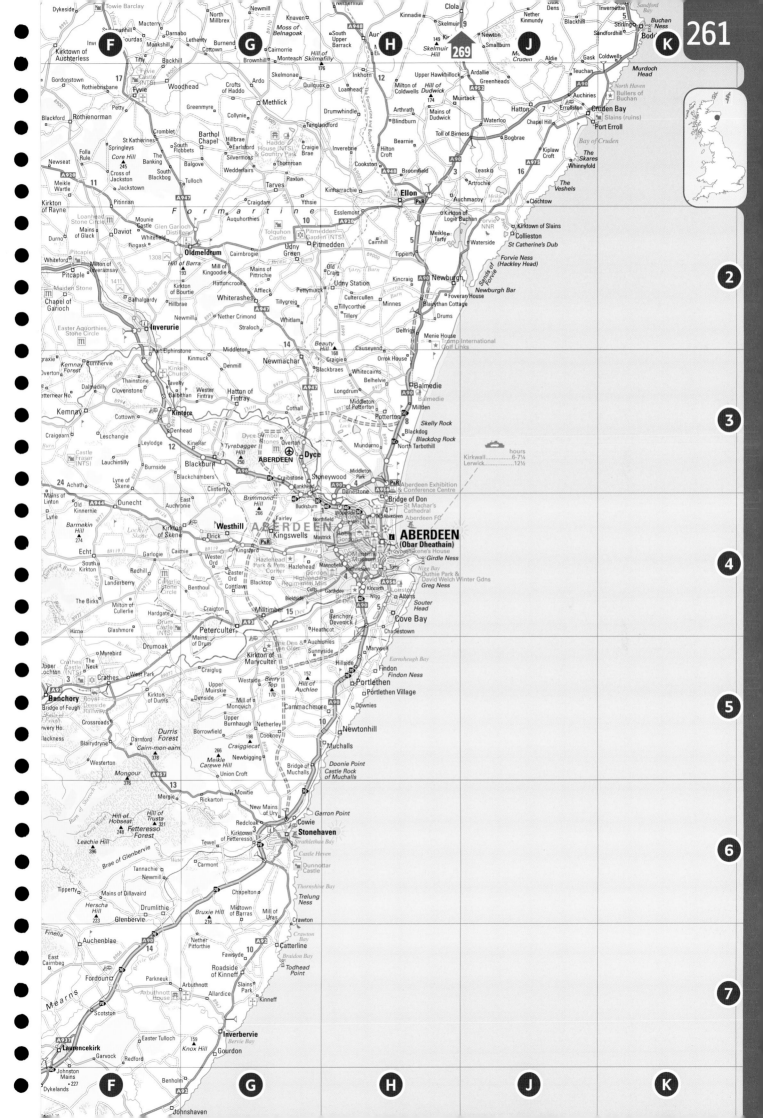

A B C D E

1

2

3

NA H-EILEANAN SIAR
(WESTERN ISLES)

4

5

6

7

Haskeir
Eagach

Haskeir
Island

Taransay Glorigs

Aird Vanish
Rubha Sgeirigin

Rubha Màs a' Chnuic
Toe Head

Shillay

Chaipaval
339
365

Tràigh na Cleavag

Northton
(Taobh Tuath)

Sound of Shillay

Beinn
a'
Chàrnain
196

Pabbay

Carminish
Islands

Baile-na-Cill

Quinish

Ensay

Killegray

Sound of Pabbay

Berneray
(Eilean Bhearnaraigh)

Massacamber

SOUND

Groay

Boreray

Borgh

Borve
Hill
85

Ruisigearraidh

OF

1hr

Caolas a' Mhòrain

HARRIS

Huilish Point

Veilish Point

Valley

Griminis
Point

Scolpaig

A865

Balelone
(Baile Lìon)

Baile Mhartainn

Manish Point
Tigh a' Gearraidh

Hogha Gearraidh

Causamul

Aird an
Rùnair

Baile Raghaill

Valley
Strand

Malaclen

Loch
Hosta

Rosta

NORTH UIST
(UIBHIST A TUATH)

Sollas
(Solas)

12

Middlequarter
(Ceathramh
Meadhanach)

Grenitote
(Greinetobht)

Trumaisgearraidh

Loch nan
Geireann

Oronsay

Lingay

Port nan Long

Baile Mhic Phail

Beinn Mhòr

3

190

Maari
180
171

Crogary
Mòr

A865

4

Blàthaisbhal

Aird Thormaid

Stromay

Keallasay
Mòr

Keallasay
Beg

Hermetray

Leac
na Hoe

Scarts Rock

Lochportain

Sound

of

Berneray

Otternish

Rubha Port Scolpaig

Knockintorran
(Cnoc an Torrain)

Deasker

Rubha Raouill

Huskeiran

Shillay

Ceann Iar

Hearnish

Stockay

Monach
Islands
NNR
Scrot Mòr

Ceann Ear

Monach Islands
(Heisker Islands)

Sound of Monach

Ceann
a' Bhaigh

Cladach Chnoc a Lìn

8

Balemore
(Baile Mòr)

Oitir
Mhòr

Cladach Chìrcebost

Kirkibost
Island

Cladach a' Chaplais

Clachan-a-Luib

Carnach

Marrival
230

Loch
Fada

Loch
Scadavay

Loch
nan Eun

Loch
na Bharpa

Langais

Loch
Huna

Clachan-a-Luib

Locheport
(Lochaphort)

A865

Teanamachar

Samhla

Loch
Skealtar

Lochmaddy
(Loch na Madadh)

Loch na Madadh

North
Lee

8

A867

South
Lee
250

Loch
Scadavay

Loch
Hunder

Loch Euphoirt

Saighdinis

Loch
Obisary

Rubha Mhic
Gille- mhicheil

Eigneig Mhòr

Baleshare
(Bhaleshear)

Teampull na
Trionaid

Carinish
(Càirinis)

5

Loch
Caravat

Eaval
347

Eigneig Bheag

Cladach a' Bhale Shear

Baile Glas

Oitir
Mhòr

4

Grimsay
(Griomsaigh)

Bàgh Mòr

Eilean
Flodaigh

Ceannaridh

Beinn a'
Chàrnain
115

Floddaybeg

Floddaymore

Ronay
(Ronaigh)

BENBECULA (BALIVANICH)

Balivanich
(Baile a' Mhanaich)

Aird

Uachdar

Gramisdale
(Gramasdail)

Eorran

Beinn
Rodagrich
99

Rubha na
Rodagrich

Baile nan Cailleach

Griminish
(Griminis)

6

A865

Rueval
124

Loch
Olavat

BENBECULA
(BEINN NA FAOGHLA)

Torlum

Loch
Uisgebhagh

Loch
Olavat

Uiskevagh
(Uisgebhagh)

Linaclate
(Lìonacleit)

Gualann

Creagorry
(Creag Ghoraidh)

B891

Hacklet
(Haclait)

Rubha Cam
nan Gall

Hornish Point

Ardivachar
Point

Baile
Gharbhaidh

Carnan

Iochdar

Wiay

Aird a' Mhachair

Clachan

Bualadubh

Peter's Port
(Port Pheadair)

102

Bàgh
nam
Faoileann

7

A865

Geirinis

Loch
Bee

Loch a Charnain

Loch Carnan

Drimore

Loch
Sgioport

Ornish Island

Loch
Sheilavaig

A C D E

0   2   4   6 miles

0   2   4   6   8   10 km

254

Drimsdale
(Dreumasdal)

Loch Druidibeg
NNR

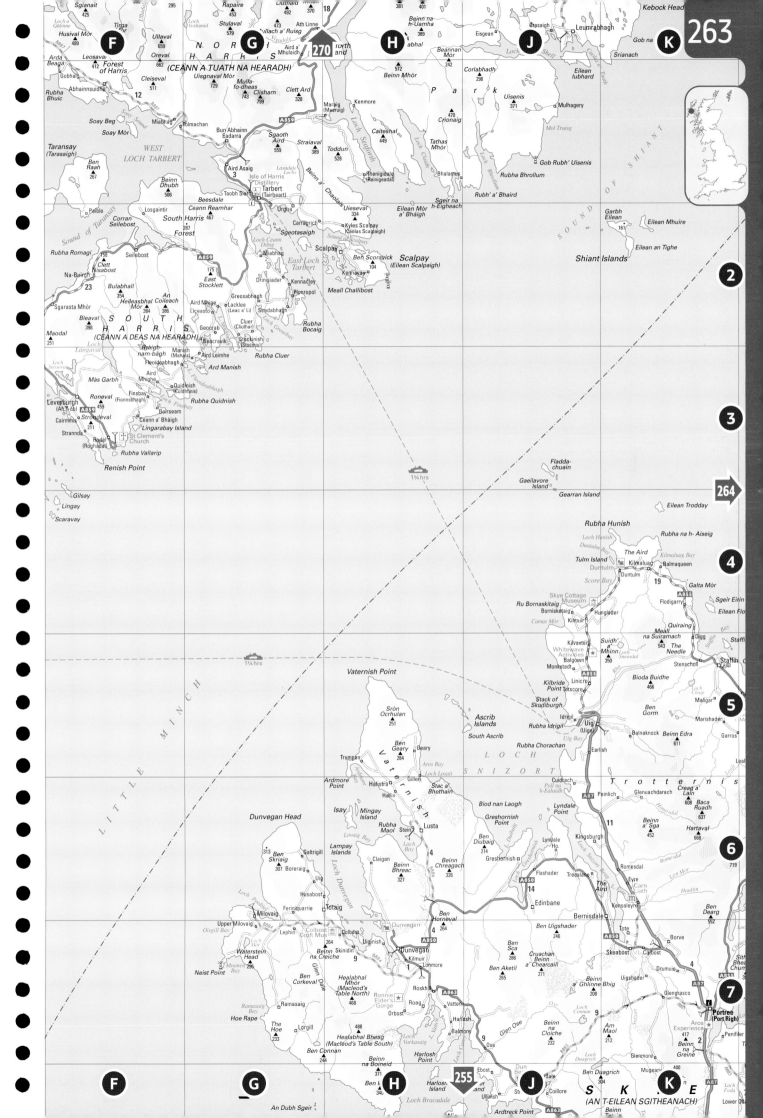

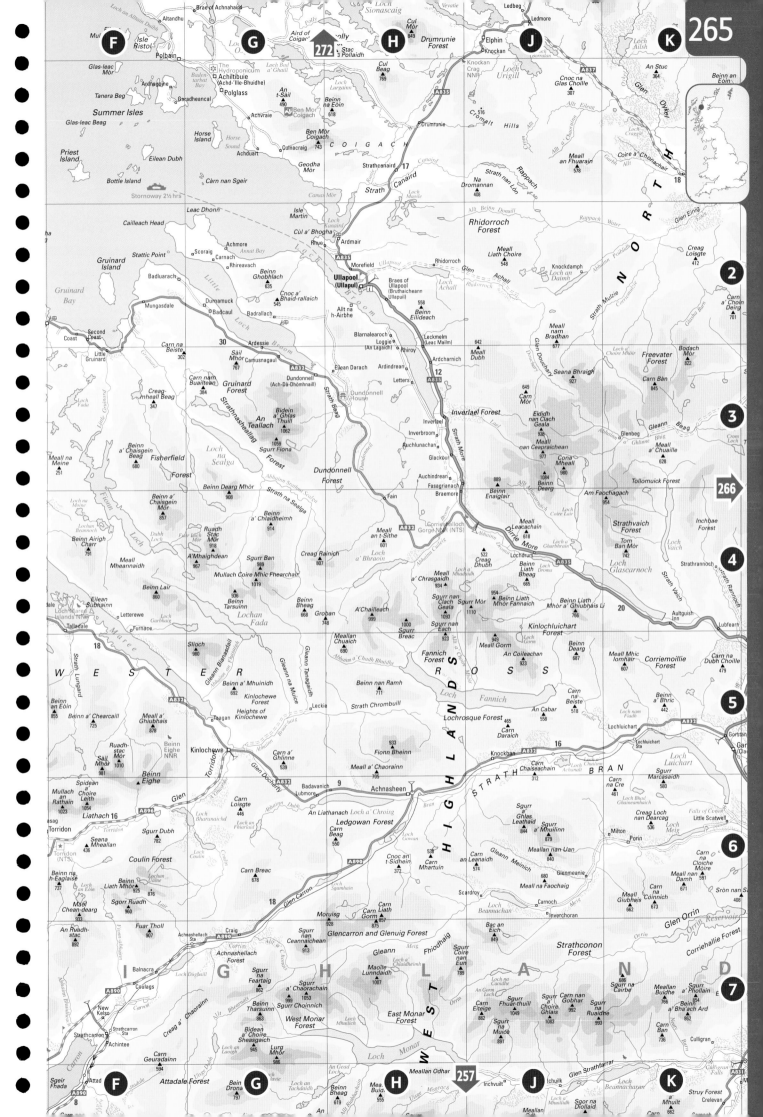

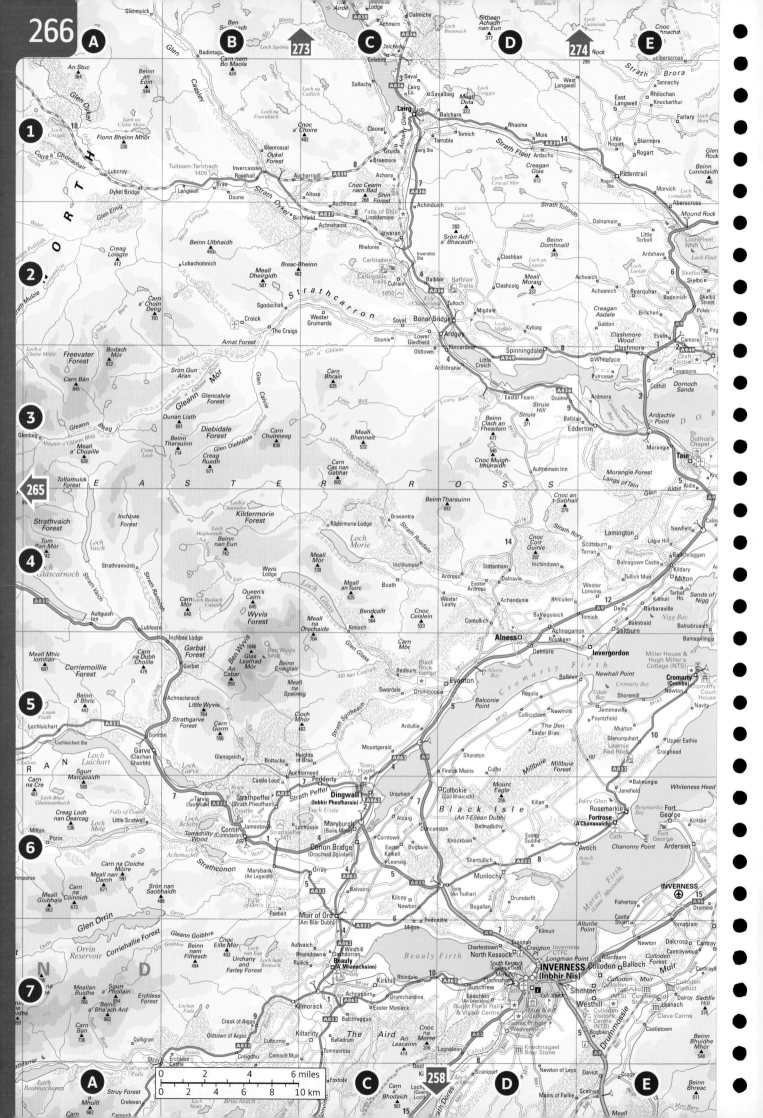

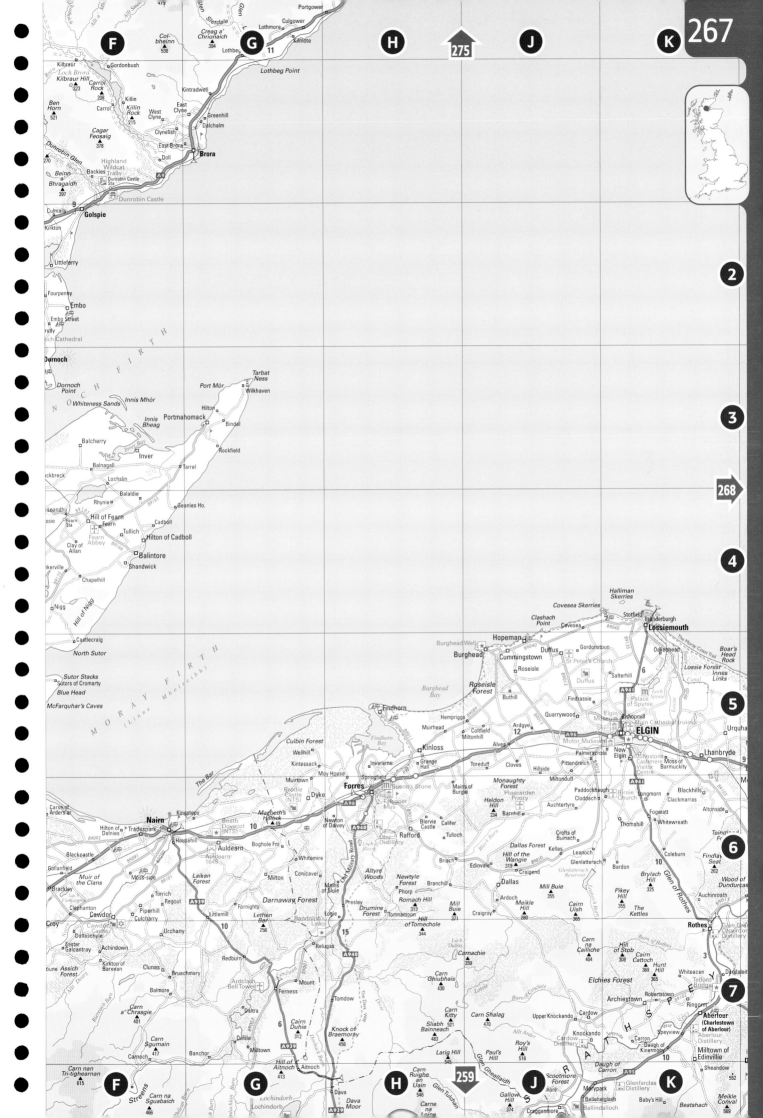

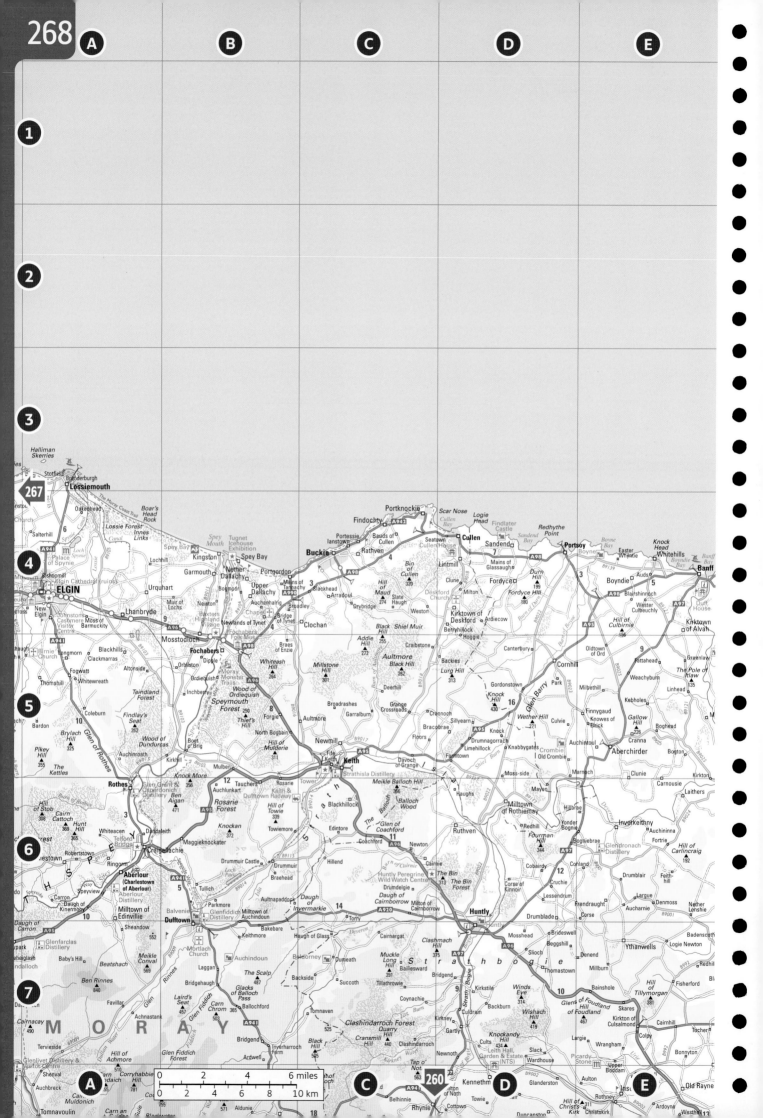

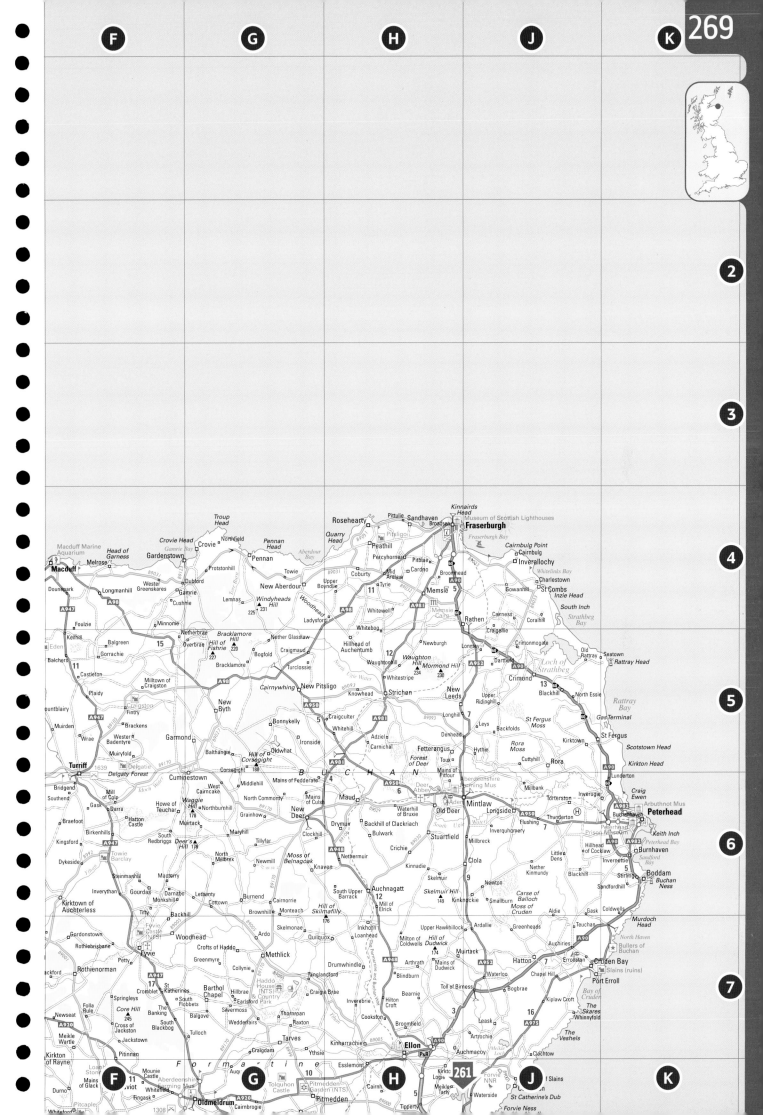

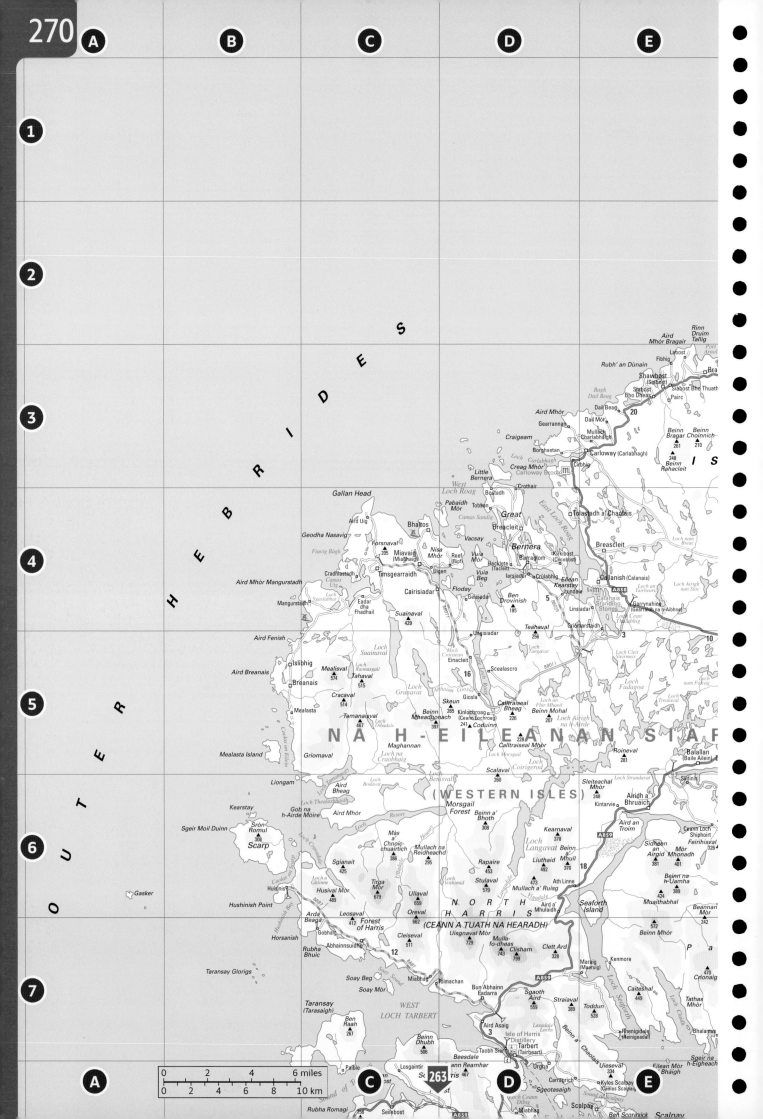

A B C D E

1

2

3

HEBRIDES

Rinn Druim Tallig
Aird Mhòr Bragair
Port Arnol
Rubh' an Dùnain
Labost
Fibhig
Shawbost (Siabost)
Bra
Bagh Dail Beag
Siabost Bho Thuath
Siabost Bho Dheas
Pairc
Aird Mhòr
Dail Beag
Gearrannan
Dail Mòr
Craigeam
Mullach Charlabhaigh
Beinn Bragar 261
Beinn Choinnich 210
Borghastan
Loch Carlabhagh
Carloway (Carlabhagh)
248
Beinn Rahacleit
IS
Creag Mhòr
Carloway Broch
Cirbhig
Little Bernera
Crothair
Bostadh

4

Gallan Head
West Loch Roag
Great Breacleit
Tolastadh a' Chaolais
Aird Uig
Pabaidh Mòr
Camas Sandig
Bhaltos
Geodha Nasavig
Forsnaval
Vacsay
Bernera
Breascleit
Loch nam Breac
Fiavig Bàgh
Miavaig (Miabhaig) 205
Nisa Mhòr
Reef (Riof)
Vuia Mòr
Barraglom
Kirkibost (Circebost)
Cradhlastadh
Timsgearraidh
Uigen
Vuia Beg
Iarsiadar
Crùlabhig
Eilean Kearstay
Callanish (Calanais)
Camas Uig
Aird Mhòr Mangurstadh
Cairisiadar
Floday
Gelsiadar
Jundale
Loch Airigh nan Sloc
Loch Sgaslabhal
Eadar dha Fhadhail
Ben Drovinish 185
Linsiadar
Calanais Standing Stones
Garrynahine (Gearraidh na h-Aibhne)
Mangurstadh
Suainaval 429
Teahaval 256
Griomarstaidh
Loch Cean Thulabhig
3
10

5

Aird Fenish
Loch Suainaval
Loch Croistean
Einacleit
Loch Tungavat
Loch Cleit Steirmeis
Islibhig
Mealisval 574
Loch Raonaxgail
Tahaval 515
16
Scealascro
Loch Fadagoa
Loch nam Fuacag
Aird Breanais
Breanais
Ahainn Giosla
Loch Grunavat
Giosla
Calltraiseal Bheag
Loch Trealaval
Cracaval 514
Skeun 265
Kinlochroag (Ceann Lochroag)
Beinn Mohal 207
Loch Airigh na h-Airde
Mealasta
Tamanaisval 467
Beinn Mheadhonach 397
241 Coduinn
226
Balallan (Baile Ailein)
NA H-EILEANAN SIAR
Maghannan
Calltraiseal Mhòr 228
Roineval 281
Mealasta Island
Griomaval
Loch na Craobhaig
Loch Morsgail
Loch Coirigerod
Loch Strandavat
Sildinis
Scalaval 260
Benisval
(WESTERN ISLES)
Sleiteachal Mhòr 248
Liongam
Aird Bheag
Loch Bodavat
Airidh a' Bhruaich
Kearstay
Gob na h-Airde Mòire
Aird Mhòr
Loch Resort
Morsgail Forest
Beinn a' Bhoth 308
Kintarvie
Aird an Troim
Ceann Loch Shiphoirt
Sgeir Moil Duinn
Sròn Romul 308
Màs a' Chnoic-chuairtich 386
Mullach na Reidheachd 295
Kearnaval 378
Loch Langavat
Sidhean an Airigid 381
Mòr Mhonadh 401
Feirihisval 326

6

Scarp
Sgianait 425
Rapaire 453
Beinn Mhuil
Liuthaid 492
370
18
Aird an Troim
Gasker
Loch a Ghlinne
Loch Voshimid
Stulaval 579
Kearnaval
Ath Linne
Beinn na h-Uamha 389
Huisinis
Husival Mòr 489
Tirga Mòr 679
Ullaval 659
Mullach a' Ruisg 473
Muaithabhal 424
Hushinish Point
Leosaval
Oreval 662
NORTH HARRIS
Aird a' Mhulaidh
Seaforth Island
Beannan Mòr 242
Arda Beaga
Forest of Harris
(CEANN A TUATH NA HEARADH)
Beinn Mhòr 572
Horsanish
Gobhaig
Cleiseval 511
Uisgnaval Mòr 729
Mulla-fo-dheas 743
Clisham 799
Clett Ard 328
Maraig (Maarig)
Kenmore
Crìonaig 470
Rubha Bhuic
Abhainnsuidhe
12
Taransay Glorigs
Soay Beg
Miabhag
Tolmachan
Bun Abhainn Eadarra
Sgaoth Aird 559
Straiaval 389
Toddun 528
Caiteshal 449
Tathas Mhòr

7

Soay Mòr
WEST LOCH TARBERT
Laxdale Lochs
Rhenigidale (Reinigeadal)
Taransay (Tarasaigh)
Ben Raah 267
Aird Asaig
Isle of Harris Distillery
Beinn a' Chaolais
Uieseval 334
Beinn Dhubh 506
Taobh Siar
Tarbert (Tairbeart)
Beesdale
Eilean Mòr h-Eigheach
Sgeir na h-Eigheach
Paible
Losgaintir
ann Reamhar 467
263
Urgha
Carraprich
Kyles Scalpay
Caolas Scalpay

A

0 2 4 6 miles
0 2 4 6 8 10 km

C
ost
ris
Lochganvir
D
Sgeotasaigh
Scalpay
A859
E
Ben Scoravick Scalpay

Rubha Romagi
Seilebost
158
Miabhag

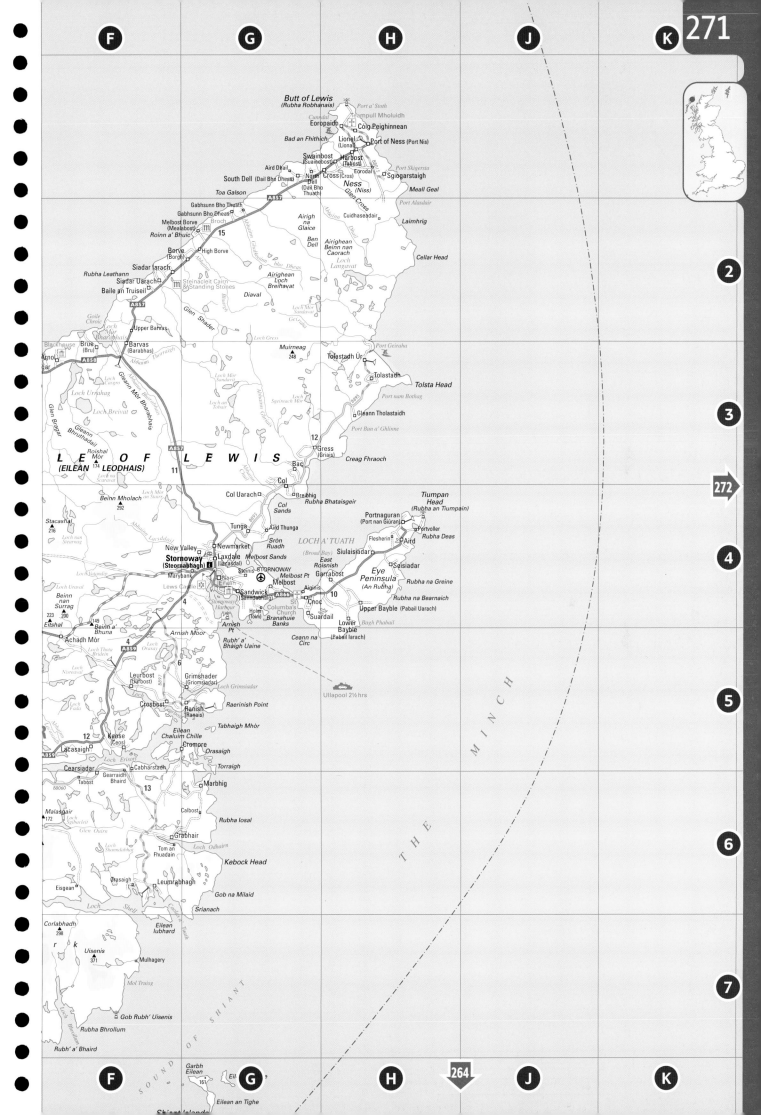

Butt of Lewis
(Rubha Robhanais)
Port a' Stoth
Cunndal
Teampull Mholuidh
Eoropaidh
Còig Peighinnean
Bad an Fhithich
Lionel
(Lional)
Port of Ness (Port Nis)
Swainbost
(Suainebost)
Harbost
(Tabost)
Aird Dhail
Port Skigersta
Erodal
South Dell (Dail Bho Dheas)
North
Dell
Cross (Cros)
Sgiogarstaigh
Toa Galson
(Dail Bho
Thuath)
Ness
(Niss)
Meall Geal
Gabhsunn Bho Thuath
Port Alasdair
Gabhsunn Bho Dheas
Broch
Cuidhaseadair
Laimhrig
Melbost Borve
(Mealabost)
15
Airigh
na
Glaice
Airighean
Beinn nan
Caorach
Roinn a' Bhuic
Ben
Dell
Cellar Head
Borve
(Borgh)
High Borve
Loch
Langavat
Siadar Iarach
Airighean
Loch
Breihavat
Rubha Leathann
Siadar Uarach
Steinacleit Cairn
& Standing Stones
Baile an Truiseil
Diaval

Glen Shader

Upper Barvas
Loch
Gress

Brue
(Bru)
Blackhouse
Barvas
(Barabhas)
Muirneag
248
Tolastadh Ùr
Arnol
gar
Loch
Urrahag
Loch Mòr
Sandavat
Tolastadh
Loch Breivat
Tolsta Head
Gleann Mòr Bharabhais
Port nam Bothag
Glen Bragar
Loch an
Tobair
Gleann
Bhruthadail
Gleann Tholastaidh
Roishal
Mòr
174
Loch
Sgeireach Mòr
Port Bun a' Ghlinne
L E   O F   L E W I S
(EILEAN   LEODHAIS)
11
Gress
(Griais)
Creag Fhraoch
Bac
Loch na
Scaravat
Beinn Mholach
292
Col
Col Uarach
Breibhig
Col
Sands
Rubha Bhataisgeir
Tiumpan
Head
(Rubha an Tiumpain)
Stacashal
216
Loch nan
Stearnag
Tunga
Aird Thunga
Sròn
Ruadh
Portnaguran
(Port nan Giùran)
Portvoller
New Valley
Newmarket
LOCH A' TUATH
(Broad Bay)
Siulaisiadar
Flesherin
Aird
Rubha Deas
Stornoway
(Steornabhagh)
Laxdale
(Lacasdal)
Melbost Sands
East
Roisnish
Seisiadar
Marybank
Steinis
STORNOWAY
Melbost Pt
Garrabost
Eye
Peninsula
(An Rubha)
Rubha na Greine
Loch Sunndin
Loch Uraval
Sandwick
(Sanndabhaig)
Melbost
Aiginis
Rubha na Bearnaich
Beinn
nan
Surrag
223
200
Lews Castle
Cnoc
10
Upper Bayble (Pabail Uarach)
Eltshal
149
Beinn a'
Bhuna
Holm
(Tolm)
Columba's
Church
Suardail
Lower
Bayble
(Pabail Iarach)
Bagh Phabail
Achadh Mòr
4
Sandwick
Branahuie
Banks
Arnish
Pt
Arnish Moor
Rubh' a'
Bhàigh Uaine
Ceann na
Circ
Loch
Nisreaval
Loch Thota
Brideim
4
6
Leurbost
(Liurbost)
Grimshader
(Griomsiadar)
Loch Grimsiadar
Ullapool 2½ hrs
Loch
Fada
Crosbost
Ranish
(Ranais)
Raerinish Point
THE   MINCH
12
Keose
(Ceos)
Eilean
Chaluim Chille
Tabhaigh Mhòr
Lacasaigh
Cromore
Orasaigh
Cearsiadar
Cabharstadh
Torraigh
Gearraidh
Bhaird
Tabost
13
Marbhig
58060
Malasgair
172
Loch
Sgibacleit
Calbost
Rubha Iosal
Glen Ouirn
Grabhair
Loch
Shaundabhag
Tom an
Fhuadain
Loch Odhairn
Kebock Head
Orasaigh
Leumrabhagh
Gob na Milaid
Eisgean
Srianach
Loch Shell
Corlabhadh
298
Eilean
Iubhard
r   k
Uisenis
371
Mulhagery
Mol Truisg
THE   SOUND   OF   SHIANT
Gob Rubh' Uisenis
Rubha Bhrollum
Rubh' a' Bhaird
Garbh
Eilean
161
Eilean an Tighe
Shiant Islands

272
264

A857
A858
A859
A866
B895
B8060

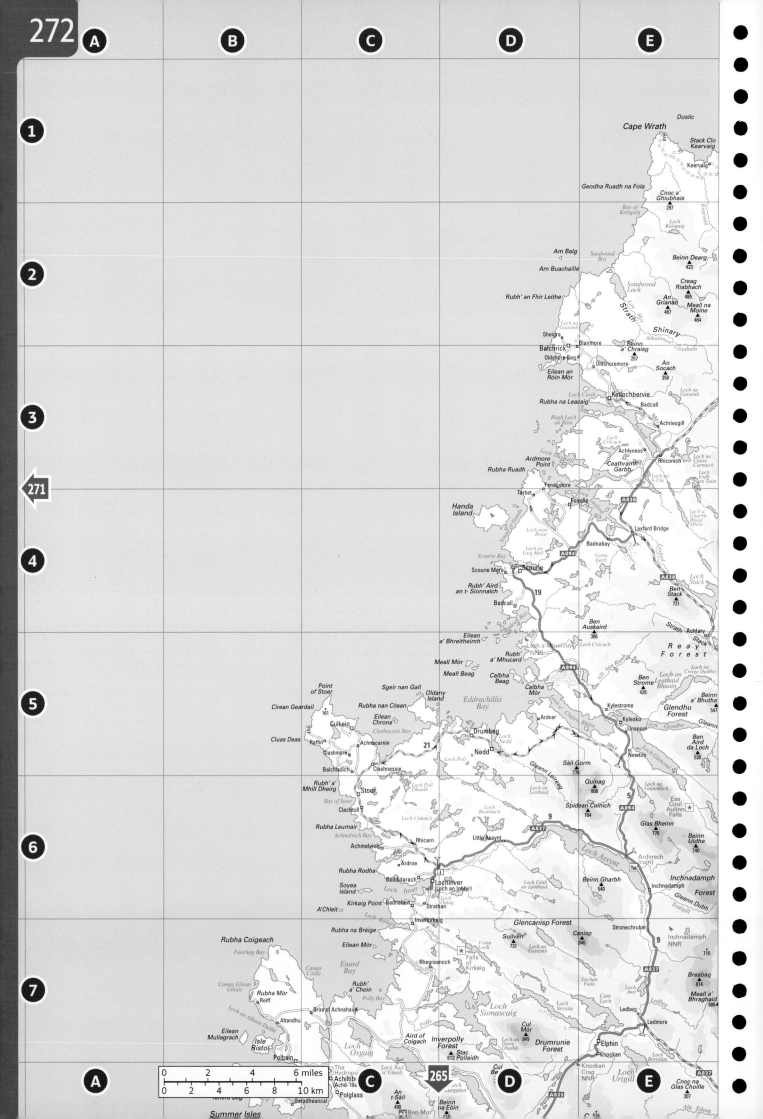

A **B** **C** **D** **E**

1

2

3

271

4

5

6

7

Cape Wrath Duslic
Stack Clo Kearvaig
Kearvaig

Geodha Ruadh na Fola
Cnoc a' Ghiubhais
297
Bay of Keisgaig
Loch Keisgaig

Am Balg *Sandwood Bay*
Beinn Dearg 423
Am Buachaille *Sandwood Loch*
Creag Riabhach 485
Rubh' an Fhir Leithe
An Grianan 467
Meall na Moine 464
Strath Shinary
Loch na Gainimh
Sheigra Blairmore
Balchrick **Beinn a' Chraisg** 257
Oldshòre Beg
Oldshoremore
An Socach 358
Eilean an Ròin Mòr
Loch Clash
Kinlochbervie
Rubha na Leacaig Badcall
Loch na Gainimh
Achriesgill
Bàgh Loch an Ròin
Achlyness
Loch Crocach
Rhiconich
Loch na Claise Carnaich
Ardmore Point
Ceathramh Garbh
Rubha Ruadh
Fanagmore
Loch na h-Ula
Tàrbet
Foindle
A838
Loch a' Gharbh Rhaid Mhòir
Handa Island
Laxford Bridge
Loch nam Breac
A894
Badnabay
Loch Stack
Scourie Bay
Gorm Loch
Ben Stack 721
Scourie Mgre Scourie
Rubh' Aird an t- Sionnaich
19
Strath Achfary
Badcall
Ben Auskaird 386
Reay Forest
Eilean a' Bhreitheimh
Loch a' Mhuilinn NNR
Meall Mòr
Rubh' a' Mhucard
Loch Crocach
Ben Strome 426
Loch an Leathaid Bhuain
Meall Beag
A894
Beinn a' Bhutha 547
Calbha Beag
Kylestrome
Glendhu Forest
Point of Stoer
Sgeir nan Gall
Oldany Island
Calbha Mòr
Kylesku
Gleann
Cirean Geardail 161
Rubha nan Còsan
Eddrachillis Bay
Ardvar
Unapool
Ben Aird da Loch 530
Cluas Deas
Eilean Chrona
Clashnessie Bay
Ardvreck (ruin)
Raffin
Culkein
Achmacarnin
Drumbeg
Newton
Eas Coul Aulinn Falls
Clashmore
Nedd
5
Loch Nedd
Balchladich
Clashnessie
Loch Poll
Sàil Gorm 776
Gleann Leireag
Quinag 808
Loch na Gainmhich
Rubh' a' Mhill Dheirg
Stoer
Loch Poll Dhaidh
Loch an Leathaid
Spidean Coinich 764
A894
5
Bay of Stoer
Clachtoll
Loch Beannach
9
A837
Glas Bheinn 775
Beinn Uidhe 740
Rubha Leumair
Loch Crocach
Achmelvich Bay
Rhicarn
Little Assynt
Loch Assynt
Ardvrech (ruin)
Achmelvich
Inver
Inchnadamph Forest
Rubha Rodha
Ardroe
Baddidarach
Beinn Gharbh 540
Inchnadamph
Soyea Island
Lochinver (Loch an Inbhir)
Loch Fèith an Leothaid
Gleann Dubh
Kirkaig Point
Badnaban
Strathan
Loch Druing
Tralgill
A'Chleit
Loch Kirkaig
Inverkirkaig
Glencanisp Forest
Stronechrubie
Rubha na Brèige
Glencanisp Forest
Canisp 846
Inchnadamph NNR
Rubha Coigeach
Eilean Mòr
Rhegreanoch
Sùlven 731
9
715
Feochag Bay
Enard Bay
Fionn Loch
Loch na Gainmh
Camas Coille
Rhegreanoch
Falls of Kirkaig
A837
Breabag 814
Camas Eilean Ghlais
Rubh' a' Choin
Polly Bay
Lochan Fada
Meall a' Bhraghaid 688
Rubha Mòr
Reiff
Brae of Achnahaird
Loch Veyatie
Ledbeg
Eilean Mullagrach
Altandhu
Loch an Allltan Dubh
Loch Sionascaig
Cam Loch
Ledmore
Isle Ristol
Aird of Coigach
Cul Mòr 849
Loch Awe
Polbain
Loch Osgaig
Inverpolly Forest
Cul Beg
Drumrunie Forest
Elphin
Knockan

The Hydropo
Achiltib
Achd-'Ille
An t-Sàil 490
Beinn na Eoin
Knockan Crag NNR
A835
Loch Urigill
A837
Cnoc na Glas Choille 307

0 2 4 6 miles
0 2 4 6 8 10 km

Summer Isles
Tanera Beg
Garadheancal
Polglass
Ben Mor

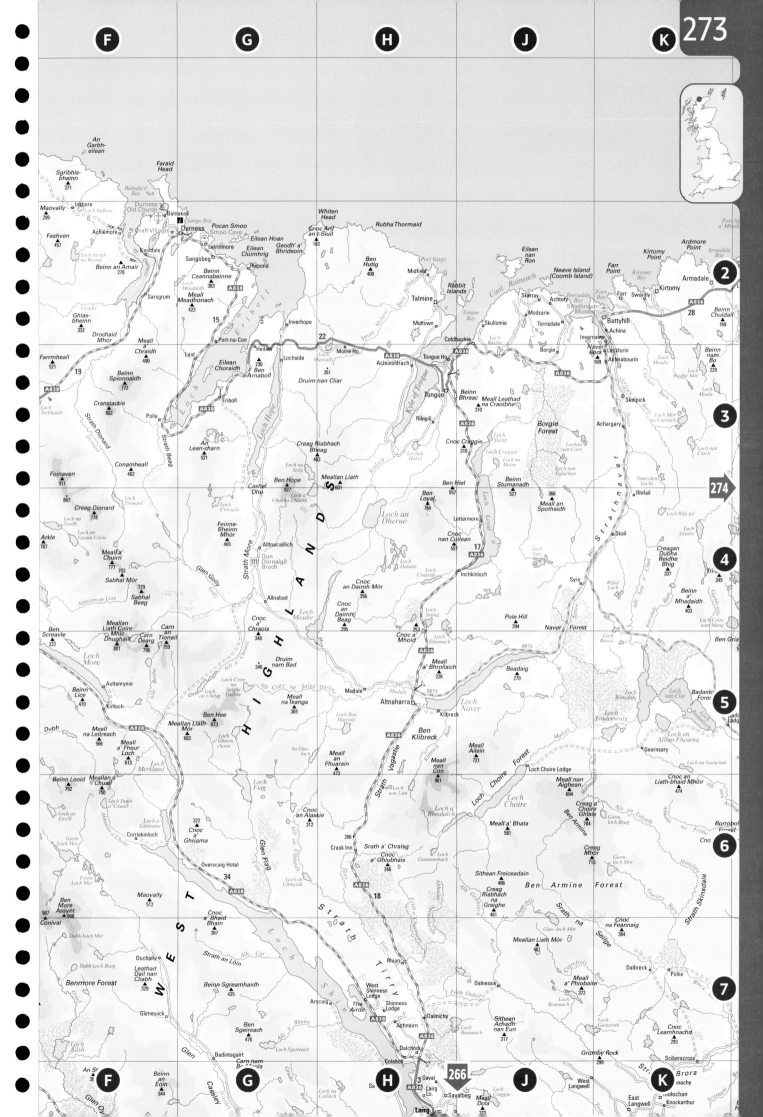

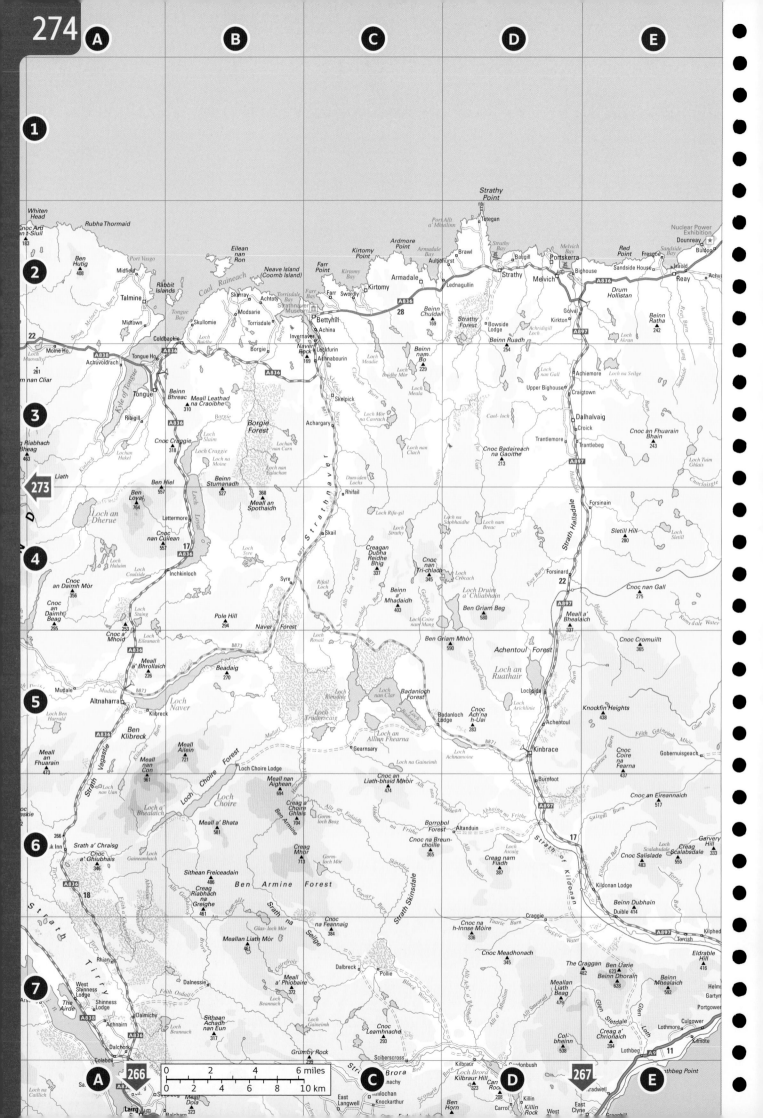

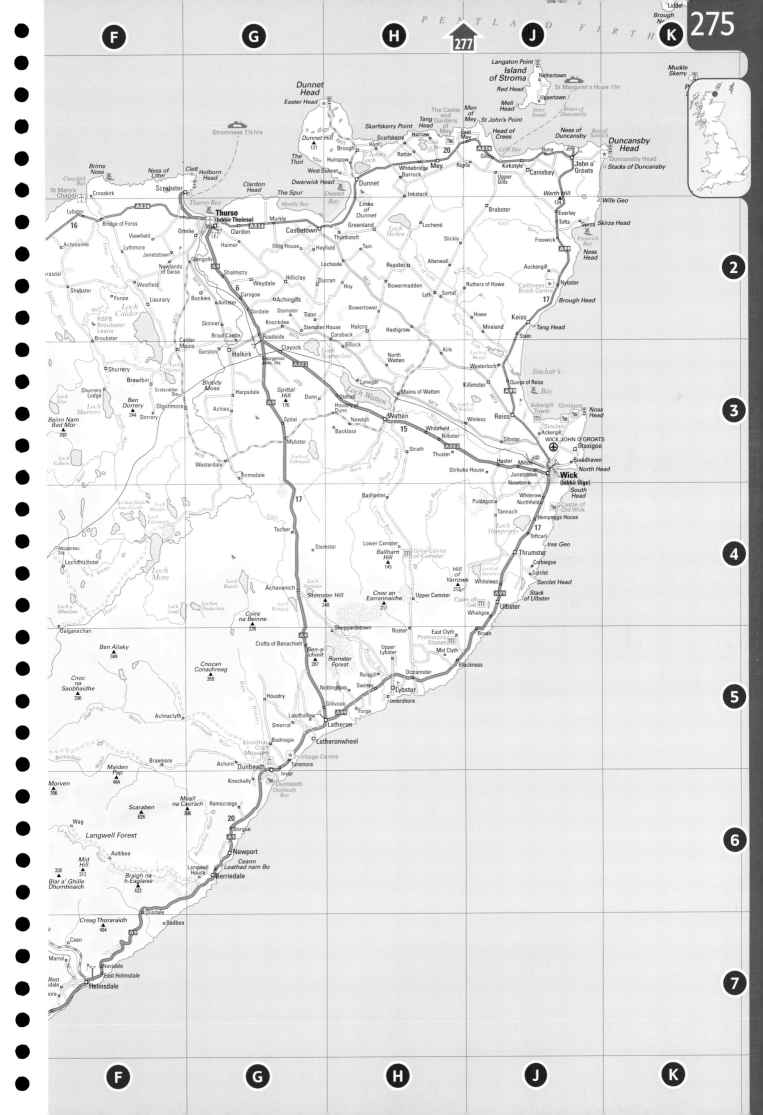

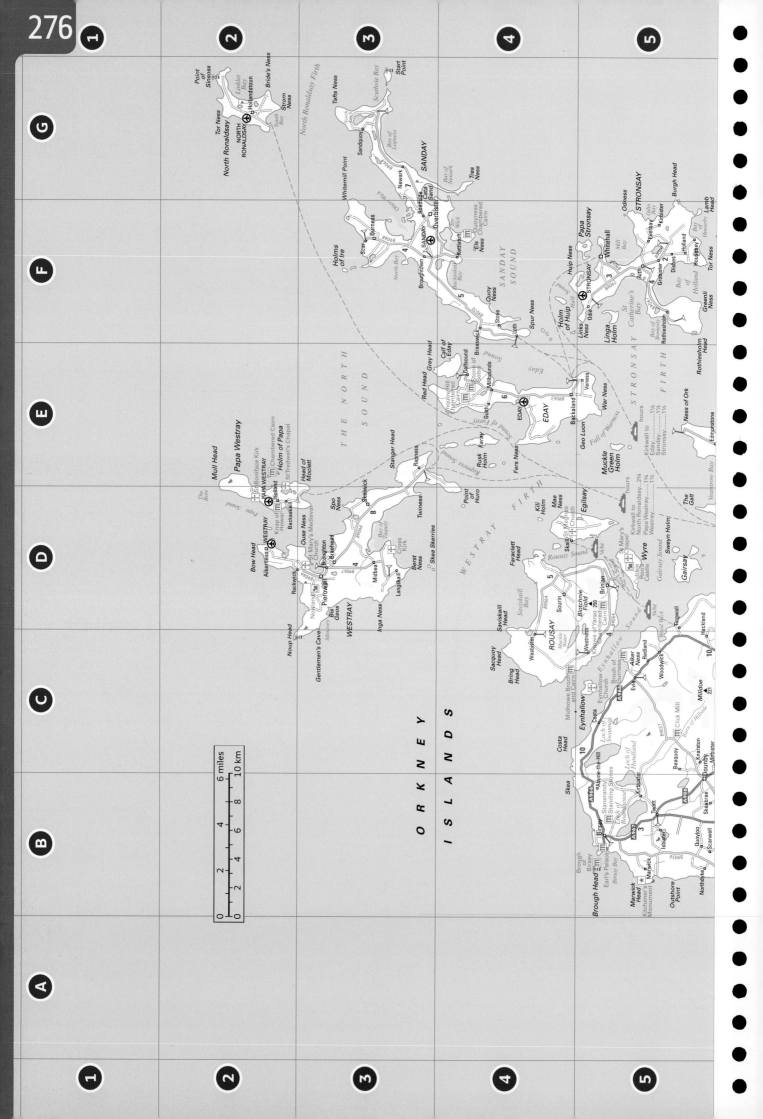

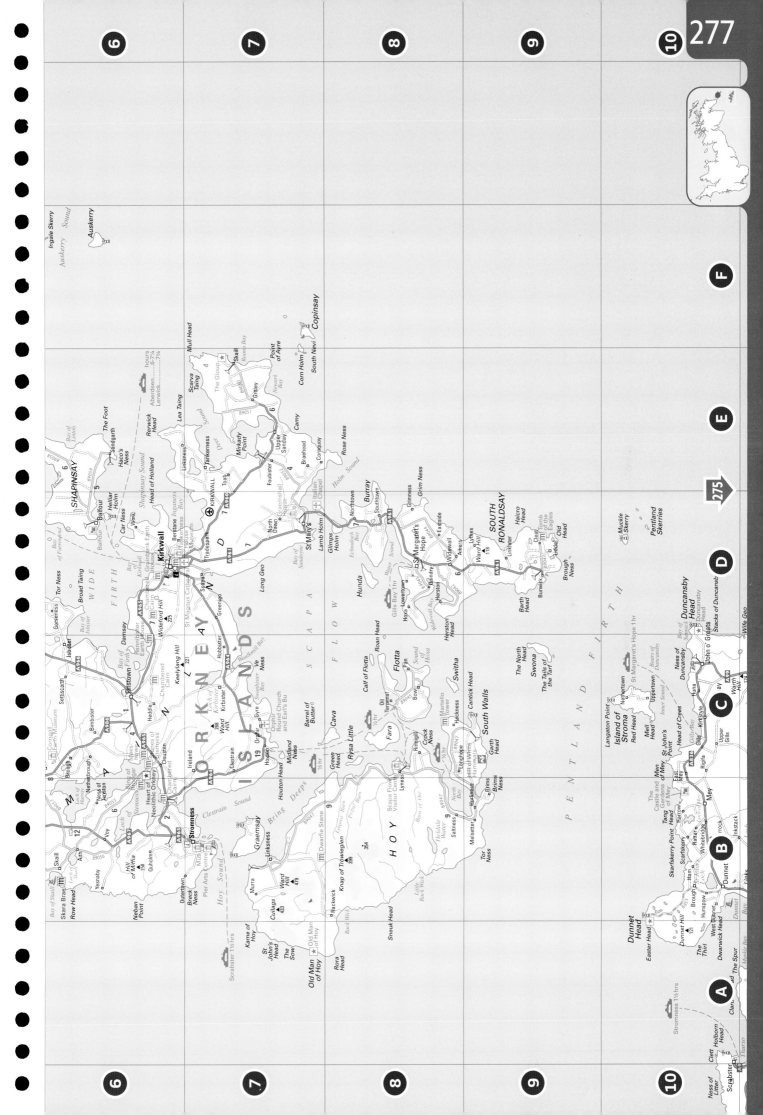

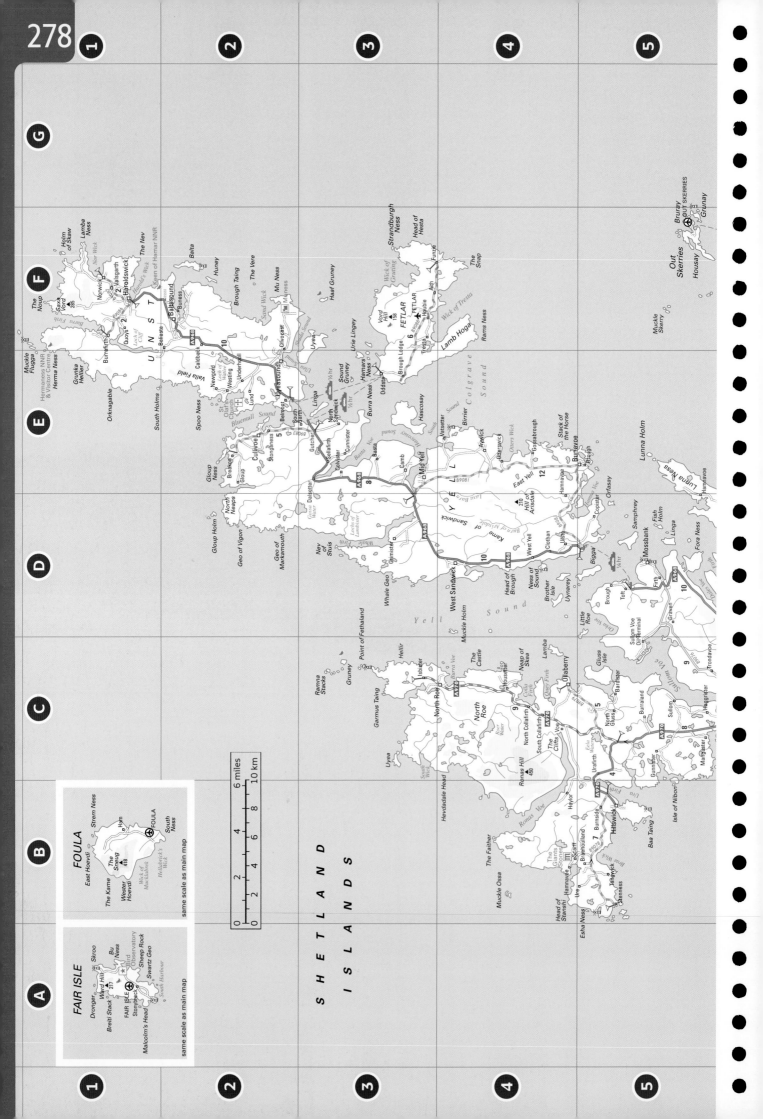

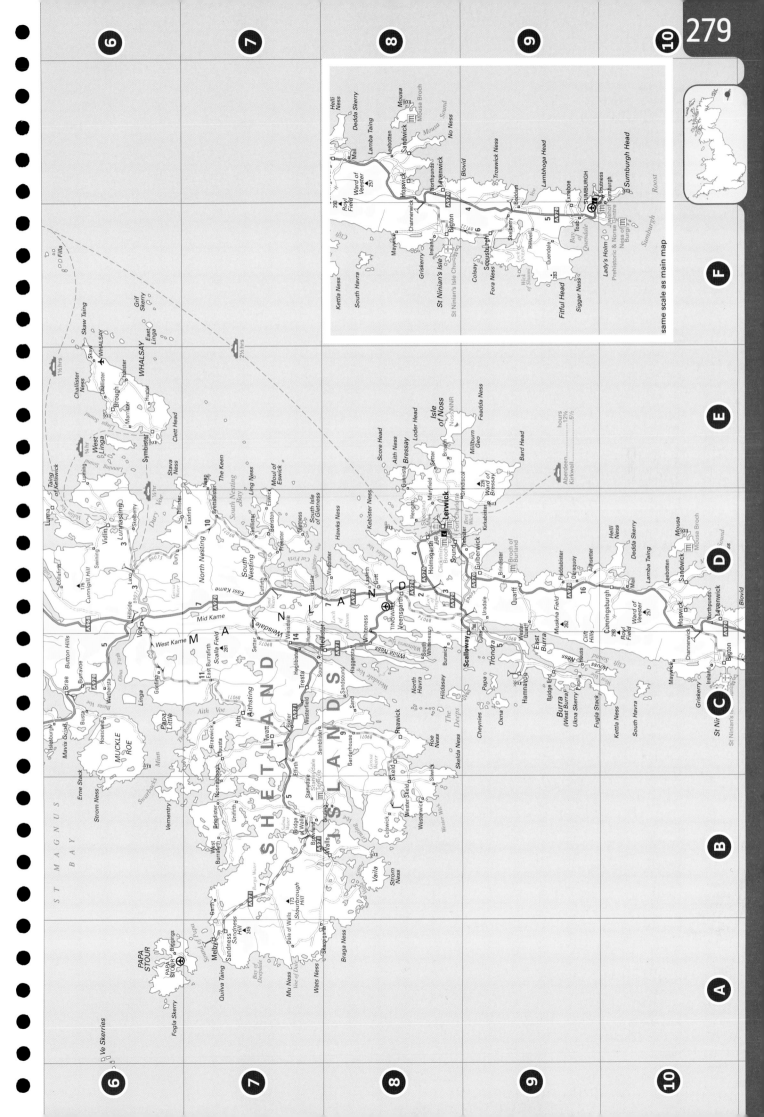

Place and place of interest names are followed by a **page number** and a grid reference in black type. The feature can be found on the map somewhere within the grid square shown.

Where two or more places have the same name the abbreviated *county* or *unitary authority* names are shown to distinguish between them. A list of these abbreviated names appears below.

A selection of the most popular places of interest are shown within the index in blue type. Their postcode information is supplied after the county names to aid integration with satnav systems.

1	Bath & North East Somerset
2	Blaenau Gwent
3	Bournemouth
4	Bracknell Forest
5	Bridgend
6	Bristol
7	Caerphilly
8	Cardiff
9	Clackmannanshire
10	Darlington
11	Dundee
12	East Dunbartonshire
13	East Renfrewshire
14	Glasgow
15	Halton
16	Hartlepool
17	Inverclyde
18	Luton
19	Merthyr Tydfil
20	Middlesbrough
21	Monmouthshire
22	Neath Port Talbot
23	Newport
24	North Lanarkshire
25	Plymouth
26	Poole
27	Portsmouth
28	Reading
29	Redcar And Cleveland
30	Renfrewshire
31	Rhondda Cynon Taff
32	Slough
33	South Gloucestershire
34	Southampton
35	Stockton-on-tees
36	Telford & Wrekin
37	Torfaen
38	Vale Of Glamorgan
39	Warrington
40	West Dunbartonshire
41	Windsor & Maidenhead
42	Wokingham

A&B	Argyll & Bute
Aber	Aberdeenshire
B&H	Brighton & Hove
B&NESom	Bath & North East Somerset
B'burn	Blackburn with Darwen
B'pool	Blackpool
BGwent	Blaenau Gwent
Bed	Bedford
Bourne	Bournemouth
BrackF	Bracknell Forest
Bucks	Buckinghamshire
Caerp	Caerphilly
Cambs	Cambridgeshire
Carmar	Carmarthenshire
CenBeds	Central Bedfordshire
Cere	Ceredigion
Chanl	Channel Islands
ChesE	Cheshire East
ChesW&C	Cheshire West & Chester
Corn	Cornwall
Cumb	Cumbria
D&G	Dumfries & Galloway
Darl	Darlington
Denb	Denbighshire
Derbys	Derbyshire
Dur	Durham
EAyr	East Ayrshire
EDun	East Dunbartonshire
ELoth	East Lothian
ERenf	East Renfrewshire
ERid	East Riding of Yorkshire
ESuss	East Sussex
Edin	Edinburgh
Falk	Falkirk
Flints	Flintshire
Glas	Glasgow
Glos	Gloucestershire
GtLon	Greater London
GtMan	Greater Manchester
Gwyn	Gwynedd
Hants	Hampshire
Hart	Hartlepool
Here	Herefordshire
Herts	Hertfordshire
High	Highland
Hull	Kingston upon Hull
Invcly	Inverclyde
IoA	Isle of Anglesey
IoM	Isle of Man
IoS	Isles of Scilly
IoW	Isle of Wight
Lancs	Lancashire
Leic	Leicester
Leics	Leicestershire
Lincs	Lincolnshire
MK	Milton Keynes
MTyd	Merthyr Tydfil
Med	Medway
Mersey	Merseyside
Middl	Middlesbrough
Midlo	Midlothian

Mon	Monmouthshire
Na H-E. Siar	Na H-Eileanan Siar (Western Isles)
N'hants	Northamptonshire
N'umb	Northumberland
NAyr	North Ayrshire
NELincs	North East Lincolnshire
NLan	North Lanarkshire
NLincs	North Lincolnshire
NPT	Neath Port Talbot
NSom	North Somerset
NYorks	North Yorkshire
Norf	Norfolk
Nott	Nottingham
Notts	Nottinghamshire
Ork	Orkney
Oxon	Oxfordshire

P&K	Perth & Kinross
Pembs	Pembrokeshire
Peter	Peterborough
Plym	Plymouth
Ports	Portsmouth
R&C	Redcar & Cleveland
RCT	Rhondda Cynon Taff
Read	Reading
Renf	Renfrewshire
Rut	Rutland
S'end	Southend-on-Sea
SAyr	South Ayrshire
SGlos	South Gloucestershire
SLan	South Lanarkshire
SYorks	South Yorkshire

ScBord	Scottish Borders
Shet	Shetland
Shrop	Shropshire
Slo	Slough
Som	Somerset
Soton	Southampton
Staffs	Staffordshire
Stir	Stirling
Stock	Stockton-on-Tees
Stoke	Stoke-on-Trent
Suff	Suffolk
Surr	Surrey
Swan	Swansea
Swin	Swindon
T&W	Tyne & Wear
Tel&W	Telford & Wrekin
Thur	Thurrock

VGlam	Vale of Glamorgan
W&M	Windsor & Maidenhead
W'ham	Wokingham
WBerks	West Berkshire
WDun	West Dunbartonshire
WLoth	West Lothian
WMid	West Midlands
WSuss	West Sussex
WYorks	West Yorkshire
Warks	Warwickshire
Warr	Warrington
Wilts	Wiltshire
Worcs	Worcestershire
Wrex	Wrexham

1853 Gallery *WYorks*
BD18 3LA **26** C1

A
Ab Kettleby **174** C5
Ab Lench **146** C2
Abbas Combe **117** E5
Abberley **145** G1
Abberley Common **145** G1
Abberton *Essex* **138** D1
Abberton *Worcs* **146** B2
Abberwick **229** F5
Abbess Roding **137** E1
Abbey Dore **144** C4
Abbey Hulton **171** G3
Abbey St. Bathans **237** E3
Abbey Village **192** C5
Abbey Wood **137** D5
Abbeycwmhir **155** G5
Abbeydale **186** A4
Abbeystead **192** B2
Abbeytown **209** E1
Abbotrule **228** A5
Abbots Bickington **113** D4
Abbots Bromley **172** B5
Abbots Langley **135** F2
Abbots Leigh **131** E5
Abbots Morton **146** C2
Abbots Ripton **162** A4
Abbot's Salford **146** C2
Abbots Worthy **119** F4
Abbotswood **119** E5
Abbotsbury **104** B4
Abbotsbury Swannery,
Subtropical Gardens &
Children's Farm *Dorset*
DT3 4JG **104** B4
Abbotsfield Farm **183** G3
Abbotsham **113** E3
Abbotskerswell **101** E1
Abbotsley **150** A2
Abbotstone **119** G4
Abbotts Ann **119** E3
Abbott's Barton **119** F4
Abbottswood **119** E5
Abdon **157** E4
Abdy **186** B3
Abenhall **131** F1
Aber **142** A3
Aber Village **144** A5
Aberaeron **142** A1
Aberaman **129** G2
Aberangell **155** E2
Aber-Arad **141** G3
Aberarder **249** G1
Aberarder House **258** D2
Aberargie **243** G3
Aberarth **142** A1
Aber-banc **141** G3
Aberbargoed **130** A2
Aberbeeg **130** B2
Aberbowlan **142** C4
Aberbran **143** F5
Abercanaid **129** G2
Abercarn **130** B3
Abercastle **140** B4
Abercegir **155** E2
Aberchalder **257** K4
Aberchirder **268** E5
Abercorn **235** E2
Abercraf **129** E1
Abercregan **129** E3
Abercrombie **244** D4
Abercychan **143** D4
Abercwmboi **129** G2
Abercych **141** F3
Abercynafon **129** G1
Abercynon **129** G3
Abercywarch **155** E1
Aberdalgie **243** F2
Aberdare **129** F2
Aberdaron **166** A5
Aberdeen (Obar Dheathain)
261 H4
Aberdeen Airport **261** G3
Aberdeen Art Gallery *AB10*
1FQ **63** Aberdeen
Aberdeen Exhibition &
Conference Centre
Aberdeen AB23 8BL
261 H3
Aberdesach **166** D2
Aberdour **235** F1
Aberdovey (Aberdyfi)
154 C3
Aberduhonw **143** G2
Aberedw **143** G3
Abereiddy **140** A4
Abererch **166** C4
Aberfan **129** G2
Aberfeldy **251** D5
Aberffraw **166** C1
Aberffrwd **154** C5
Aberford **194** D4
Aberfoyle **242** A4
Abergavenny (Y Fenni)
130 B1
Abergele **182** A5
Aber-Giâr **142** B3
Abergorlech **142** B4
Abergwesyn **143** E2
Abergwili **142** A5
Abergwydol **155** D2
Abergwynant **154** C1
Abergwynfi **129** E3
Abergwyngregyn **181** E5
Abergynolwyn **154** C2
Aberhafesp **155** G3
Aberhosan **155** E3
Aberkenfig **129** E4
Aberlady **236** B1
Aberlemno **252** D4
Aberllefenni **155** D2
Aber-Ilia **129** F1
Aberlour (Charlestown of
Aberlour) **267** K7
Abermad **154** B5
Abermeurig **142** B2
Abermule (Aber-miwl)
156 A3
Abernaint **169** E5
Abernant *Carmar* **141** G5
Aber-nant *RCT* **129** G2
Abernethy **243** G3
Abernyte **244** A1
Aberporth **141** F2
Abercross **266** E2

Abersky **258** C2
Abersoch **166** C5
Abersychan **130** B2
Aberthin **129** G5
Abertillery **130** B2
Abertridwr *Caerp* **130** A4
Abertridwr *Powys* **155** G1
Abertysswg **130** A2
Aberuthven **243** E3
Aberyscir **143** F5
Aberystwyth **154** B4
Aberystwyth Arts Centre
Cere SY23 3DE **154** B4
Abhainnsuidhe **270** C7
Abingdon **133** G3
Abinger Common **121** G3
Abinger Hammer **121** F3
Abington **226** A3
Abington Pigotts **150** B3
Abingworth **108** D2
Ablington *Glos* **132** D2
Ablington *Wilts* **118** C3
Abney **185** F5
Above Church **172** B2
Aboyne **260** D5
Abram **184** A2
Abriachan (Obar Itheachan)
258 C1
Abridge **137** D3
Abronhill **234** B2
Abson **131** G5
Abthorpe **148** B3
Abune-the-Hill **276** B5
Aby **189** E5
Acaster Malbis **195** E3
Acaster Selby **195** E3
Accrington **193** D5
Accurrach **240** D1
Acha **246** A4
Achachork **263** K7
Achadacaie **231** G3
Achadh Mòr **271** F5
Achadh-chaorrunn **231** F4
Achadunan **241** E3
Achagavel **247** G4
Achaglass **231** F5
Achahoish **231** F2
Achalader **251** G5
Achallader **249** G3
Achamore **231** D2
Achandunie **266** D4
Achany **266** C1
Achaphubuil **248** C2
Acharacle **247** F3
Achargary **274** C3
Acharn *A&B* **240** D1
Acharn *P&K* **250** C5
Acharonich **239** D1
Acharosson **232** A2
Achateny **247** E2
Achath **261** F3
Achavanich **275** G4
Achdduu **128** A2
Achduart **265** G1
Achentoul **274** D5
Achfary **272** E5
Achgarve **264** E2
Achiemore *High* **273** F2
Achiemore *High* **274** D3
Achies **275** G3
A'Chill **255** H4
Achiltibuie (Achd-'Ille-
Bhuidhe) **265** G1
Achina **274** C2
Achindown **267** F7
Achinduich **266** C2
Achingills **275** G3
Achintee **184** B1
Achintee House (Achadh
an t-Suidhe) **248** D2
Achintraid **256** E1
Achlean **259** F5
Achleanan **247** E4
Achleek **247** G4
Achlian **240** D2
Achlyness **272** E3
Achmelvich **272** C6
Achmony **258** C1
Achmore *High* **256** E1
Achmore *High* **265** E1
Achmore *Stir* **242** A1
Achnaba **232** A1
Achnabat **258** C1
Achnabourin **274** C3
Achnacairn **240** B1
Achnacarnin **272** C5
Achnacarry **249** D1
Achnaclerach **266** B5
Achnacloich *A&B* **240** B1
Achnacloich *High* **256** B4
Achnaclyth **275** F5
Achnacraig **247** D5
Achnacroish **248** A5
Achnadrish **246** D4
Achnafalnich **241** E2
Achnafauld **243** D1
Achnagarron **266** C7
Achnagarron **266** D4
Achnaha *High* **247** F5
Achnaha *High* **247** D3
Achnahanat **266** C2
Achnahannet **259** G2
Achnairn **273** H7
Achnalea **248** A3
Achnamara **231** F1
Achnanellan **247** G3
Achnasaul **249** D1
Achnasheen **265** H6
Achnashelloch **240** A5
Achnastank **259** K1
Achorn **275** G5
Achosnich *High* **266** E2
Achosnich *High* **246** D3
Achreamie **275** F2
Achriabhach **248** D3
Achriesgill **272** E3
Achtoty **273** J2
Achurch **161** F4
Achuvoldrach **273** H3
Achvaich **266** E2
Achvarasdal **274** C3
Achvlair **248** A4
Achvraie **265** G1
Ackenthwaite **199** G4
Ackergill **275** J3
Acklam *Middl* **203** D1
Acklam *NYorks* **195** G1
Ackleton **157** G3

Acklington **221** E1
Ackton **194** D5
Ackworth Moor Top **186** B1
Acle **179** F4
Acock's Green **158** D4
Acol **125** F2
Acomb *N'umb* **211** F1
Acomb *York* **195** E2
Aconbury **145** E4
Acre **193** D5
Acrefair **169** F3
Acrise Place **125** D4
Acton *ChesE* **170** D2
Acton *Dorset* **105** F5
Acton *GtLon* **136** A4
Acton *Shrop* **156** C4
Acton *Staffs* **171** F3
Acton *Suff* **151** G3
Acton *Worcs* **146** A1
Acton *Wrex* **170** A2
Acton Beauchamp **145** F2
Acton Bridge **183** G5
Acton Burnell **157** E2
Acton Green **145** F2
Acton Pigott **157** E2
Acton Round **157** F3
Acton Scott **157** D4
Acton Trussell **158** B1
Acton Turville **132** A4
Adamhill **224** C2
Adbaston **171** E5
Adber **116** C5
Adderbury **147** G4
Adderley **171** D3
Adderstone **229** F3
Addiewell **235** D3
Addingham **193** G3
Addington *Bucks* **148** C5
Addington *GtLon* **122** C2
Addington *Kent* **123** F3
Addiscombe **122** C2
Addlestone **121** F1
Addlethorpe **176** D1
Adel **194** B4
Adeney **157** G1
Adeyfield **135** F2
Adfa **155** G2
Adforton **156** D5
Adisham **125** E3
Adlestrop **147** E5
Adlingfleet **196** A5
Adlington *ChesE* **184** D4
Adlington *Lancs* **183** G1
Admaston *Staffs* **172** B5
Admaston *Tel&W* **157** F1
Admington **147** E3
Adsborough **115** F5
Adscombe **115** E4
Adstock **148** C4
Adstone **148** A2
Adventure Island *S'end*
SS1 1EE **138** B4
Adversane **121** F5
Advie **259** J1
Adwalton **194** B5
Adwell **134** B3
Adwick le Street **186** C2
Adwick upon Dearne
186 B2
Adziel **269** H5
Ae Village **217** D2
Afan Argoed Country Park
NPT SA13 3HG **129** E3
Affetside **184** B1
Affleck **261** G2
Affpuddle **105** E3
Afon Wen **166** D4
Afon-wen **182** C5
Afton **106** C4
Afton Bridgend **225** E4
Agglethorpe **201** F4
Aigburth **183** E4
Aiginis **271** G4
Aike **196** C3
Aikerness **276** D2
Aikers **277** D8
Aiketgate **210** A3
Aikton **209** F1
Aikwood Tower **227** F3
Ailby **189** E5
Ailey **144** C3
Ailsworth **161** G3
Aimes Green **136** D2
Aimster **275** G2
Ainderby Quernhow
202 C4
Ainderby Steeple **202** C3
Aingers Green **152** C5
Ainsdale **183** E1
Ainsdale-on-Sea **183** E1
Ainstable **210** B3
Ainsworth **184** B1
Ainthorpe **203** G2
Aintree **183** E3
Aird *Na H-E. Siar* **262** C6
Aird *Na H-E. Siar* **271** H4
Aird a' Mhachair **262** C7
Aird a' Mhulaidh **270** D6
Aird Asaig **270** D7
Aird Dhail **271** G1
Aird Leimhe **263** G3
Aird Mhige **263** F3
Aird Mhighe **263** F3
Aird of Sleat **256** B4
Aird Thunga **271** G4
Aird Uig **270** C4
Airdrie *Fife* **245** D4
Airdrie *NLan* **234** B3
Aire View **193** F3
Airidh a' Bhruaich **270** E6
Airieland **216** B5
Airies **214** A4
Airigh-drishaig **256** C1
Airmyn **195** G5
Airntully **243** F1
Airor **256** D4
Airth **234** C1
Airton **193** F2

Airyhassen **207** D2
Aisby *Lincs* **187** F3
Aisby *Lincs* **175** F4
Aisgill **200** D3
Aish *Devon* **100** C1
Aish *Devon* **101** D3
Aisholt **115** E4
Aiskew **202** B4
Aislaby *NYorks* **204** B3
Aislaby *NYorks* **203** G4
Aislaby *Stock* **202** D1
Aisthorpe **187** G4
Aith *Ork* **277** B6
Aith *Ork* **276** F5
Aith *Shet* **279** C7
Aith *Shet* **279** F5
Aithsetter **279** D9
Aitnoch **259** G1
Akeld **229** D4
Akeley **148** C4
Akenham **152** C3
Albaston **99** E3
Albecq **101** E5
Alberbury **156** C1
Albert Park *TS1* 3LB
78 Middlesbrough
Albert Town **126** C1
Albourne **109** E2
Albourne Green **109** E2
Albrighton *Shrop* **158** A2
Albrighton *Shrop* **157** D1
Alburgh **165** D3
Albury *Herts* **150** C5
Albury *Oxon* **134** B2
Albury *Surr* **121** F3
Albury End **150** C5
Albury Heath **121** F3
Albyfield **210** B2
Alcaig **266** C6
Alcaston **157** D4
Alcester **146** C2
Alciston **110** A3
Alcombe **114** C3
Alconbury **161** G5
Alconbury Hill **161** G5
Alconbury Weston **161** G5
Aldborough *Norf* **178** C2
Aldborough *NYorks*
194 D1
Aldbourne **133** E5
Aldbrough **197** E4
Aldbrough St. John **202** B1
Aldbury **135** E1
Aldclune **251** E3
Aldeburgh **153** F2
Aldeby **165** F2
Aldenham **136** A3
Alderbury **118** C5
Alderford **178** C4
Alderholt **106** A1
Alderley **131** G3
Alderley Edge **184** C5
Aldermaston **119** G5
Aldermaston Wharf **120** B1
Alderminster **147** E3
Alderney **101** G4
Alderney Airport **101** F4
Alder's End **145** F4
Aldersey Green **170** B2
Aldershot **121** D2
Alderton *Glos* **146** B4
Alderton *N'hants* **148** C3
Alderton *Suff* **153** E3
Alderton *Wilts* **132** A4
Alderwasley **173** D2
Aldfield **194** B1
Aldford **170** B2
Aldham *Essex* **152** A5
Aldham *Suff* **152** B3
Aldie *Aber* **269** J6
Aldie *High* **266** E3
Aldingbourne **108** B3
Aldingham **199** D5
Aldington *Kent* **124** C5
Aldington *Worcs* **146** C3
Aldivalloch **260** B2
Aldochlay **241** F5
Aldons **214** C2
Aldous's Corner **165** E3
Aldreth **162** C5
Aldridge **158** C2
Aldringham **153** F1
Aldsworth *Glos* **133** D2
Aldsworth *WSuss* **107** G2
Aldunie **260** B2
Aldville **243** E1
Aldwark *Derbys* **172** D2
Aldwark *NYorks* **195** D1
Aldwick **108** B4
Aldwincle **161** F4
Aldworth **134** A5

Allanton *ScBord* **237** F4
Allanton *SLan* **234** B4
Allardice **253** G2
Allbrook **119** F5
Allen End **159** D3
Allenheads **211** E3
Allen's Green **137** D1
Allensford **211** G2
Allensford Country Park
Dur DH8 9BA **211** G2
Allensmore **145** D4
Allenton **173** E4
Aller **116** B5
Allerby **209** D3
Allercombe **102** D3
Allerford **114** C3
Allerston **204** B4
Allerthorpe **195** G3
Allerton *Mersey* **183** F4
Allerton *WYorks* **194** A4
Allerton Bywater **194** D5
Allerton Mauleverer **194** D2
Allesley **159** E4
Allestree **173** E4
Allet Common **96** B5
Allexton **160** D2
Allgreave **171** G1
Allhallows **124** A1
Allhallows-on-Sea **124** A1
Alligin Shuas **264** E6
Allimore Green **158** A1
Allington *Dorset* **104** A3
Allington *Lincs* **175** D3
Allington *Lincs* **176** A3
Allington *Wilts* **118** D4
Allington *Wilts* **118** B1
Allington *Wilts* **132** A5
Allithwaite **199** E5
Allnabad **273** G5
Allonby **209** D2
Allostock **184** B5
Alloway **224** B4
Allowenshay **103** G1
Allscot **157** G3
Allscott **157** F1
Allt na h-Airbhe **265** H2
Alltachonaich **247** G4
Alltbeithe **257** G2
Alltforgan **168** C5
Alltmawr **143** G3
Alltnacaillich **273** G4
Allt-nan-sùugh **257** F1
Alltsigh **258** B3
Alltwalis **142** A4
Alltwen **128** D2
Alltyblaca **142** B3
Allwood Green **164** B4
Almeley **144** C2
Almeley Wootton **144** C2
Almer **105** E2
Almington **171** E4
Alminstone Cross **113** D3
Almondbank **243** F2
Almondbury **185** F1
Almondell & Calderwood
Country Park *WLoth*
EH52 5PE **235** E3
Alne **195** D1
Alness **266** D5
Alnham **229** D5
Alnmouth **229** G5
Alnwick **229** F5
Alnwick Garden, The *N'umb*
NE66 1YU **229** F5
Alperton **136** A4
Alphamstone **151** G4
Alpheton **151** G2
Alphington **102** C3
Alport **172** D1
Alpraham **170** C2
Alresford **152** B5
Alrewas **159** D1
Alrick **251** G3
Alsager **171** E3
Alsagers Bank **171** F3
Alsop en le Dale **172** C2
Alston *Cumb* **210** D3
Alston *Devon* **103** G2
Alston Sutton **116** B2
Alstone *Glos* **146** B4
Alstone *Som* **116** A3
Alstone *Staffs* **158** A1
Alstonefield **172** C2
Alswear **114** A5
Alt **184** D2
Altandhu **272** B7
Altanduin **274** D6
Altarnun **97** G1
Altass **266** C1
Altens **261** H4
Alterwall **275** H2
Altham **193** D4
Althorne **138** C3
Althorp House *N'hants*
NN7 4HQ **148** B1
Althorpe **187** F2
Alticry **215** D5
Altnafeadh **249** E4
Altnaharra **273** H5
Altofts **194** C5
Alton *Derbys* **173** E1
Alton *Hants* **120** C4
Alton *Staffs* **172** B3
Alton Barnes **118** C1
Alton Pancras **104** D2
Alton Priors **118** C1
Alton Towers Leisure Park
Staffs ST10 4DB **172** B3
Alton Water Reservoir *Suff*
IP9 2RY **152** C4
Altonside **267** K6
Altrincham **184** B4
Altura **249** J5
Alva **243** D5
Alvanley **183** F5
Alvaston **173** E4
Alvechurch **158** C5
Alvecote **159** E2
Alvediston **118** A5
Alveley **157** G4
Alverdiscott **113** F3
Alverstoke **107** F3
Alverstone **107** E4
Alverthorpe **194** C5
Alverton **174** C3

Alves **267** J5
Alvescot **133** E2
Alveston *SGlos* **131** F4
Alveston *Warks* **147** E2
Alvie **259** F4
Alvingham **189** D3
Alvington **131** F2
Alwalton **161** G3
Alweston **104** C1
Alwington **113** E3
Alwinton **220** B1
Alwoodley **194** C3
Alwoodley Gates **194** C3
Alyth **252** A5
Amalebra **94** B3
Ambaston **173** F3
Amber Hill **176** A3
Ambergate **173** E2
Amberley *Glos* **132** A2
Amberley *WSuss* **108** C2
Amble **221** E1
Amblecote **158** A4
Ambleston **140** D5
Ambleston **140** D5
Ambrismore **232** B4
Ambrosden **134** B1
Amcotts **187** F2
Amersham **135** E3
Amerton **171** G5
Amerton Farm *Staffs*
ST18 0LA **171** G5
Amesbury **118** C3
Ameysford **105** G2
Amington **159** E2
Amisfield Town **217** E2
Amlwch **180** C3
Amlwch Port **180** C3
Ammanford
(Rhydaman) **128** C1
Amotherby **203** G5
Ampfield **119** E5
Ampleforth **203** E5
Ampleforth College **203** E5
Ampney Crucis **132** C2
Ampney St. Mary **132** C2
Ampney St. Peter **132** C2
Amport **119** E3
Ampthill **149** F4
Ampton **163** G5
Amroth **127** E2
Amulree **243** D1
Anaboard **259** H1
Anaheilt **248** A1
Ancaster **175** E3
Anchor **156** A4
Anchor Corner **164** B2
Ancroft **237** G5
Ancrum **228** A4
Ancton **108** B3
Anderby **189** F5
Anderby Creek **189** F5
Andersea **116** A4
Andersfield **115** F4
Anderson **105** E2
Anderton **184** A5
Anderton Boat Lift
ChesW&C
CW9 6FW **184** A5
Andover **119** E3
Andover Down **119** E3
Andoversford **132** C1
Andreas **190** C2
Anelog **166** A5
Anfield **183** E3
Angarrack **94** C3
Angarrick **95** E3
Angelbank **157** E4
Angerton **209** F1
Angle **126** B2
Anglers Country
Park *WYorks*
WF4 2EB **186** A1
Angler's Retreat **154** D3
Anglesey
(Ynys Môn) **180** B4
Anglesey Abbey *Cambs*
CB25 9EJ **150** D1
Anglesey Airport **180** B5
Angmering **108** C3
Angmering-on-Sea **108** C3
Angram *NYorks* **195** E3
Angram *NYorks* **201** D3
Anick **211** F1
Anie **242** A3
Animal World & Butterfly
House *GtMan*
BL1 5UG **184** A1
Ankerville **267** F4
Anlaby **196** C5
Anmer **177** F5
Anmore **107** F1
Anna Valley **119** E3
Annan **217** F4
Annaside **198** B4
Annat *A&B* **240** C2
Annat *High* **264** E6
Annbank **224** C3
Annesley **173** F2
Annesley
Woodhouse **173** F2
Annfield Plain **212** A2
Anniesland **233** G3
Annscroft **157** D2
Ansdell **191** G5
Ansford **116** D4
Ansley **159** F3
Anslow **172** C5
Anslow Gate **172** C5
Ansteadbrook **121** E4
Anstey *Herts* **150** C4
Anstey *Leics* **160** A2
Anstruther **245** E4
Ansty *Warks* **159** F4
Ansty *Wilts* **118** A5
Ansty *WSuss* **109** E1
Ansty Coombe **118** A5
Ansty Cross **105** D2
Anthill Common **107** F1
Anthorn **209** E1
Antingham **179** D2
Anton's Gowt **176** A3
Antony **99** D5
Antrobus **184** A5
Anvil Corner **113** D5
Anvil Green **124** D4

Anwick **175** G2
Anwoth **215** G5
Aonach Mòr Mountain
Gondola & Nevis Range
Ski Centre *High*
PH33 6SW **249** D2
Aoradh **230** A3
Apethorpe **161** F3
Apeton **158** A1
Apley **188** B3
Apperknowle **186** A5
Apperley **146** A4
Apperley Bridge **194** A4
Appersett **201** D3
Appin (An Apainn) **248** B5
Appin House **248** B5
Appleby **187** G1
Appleby Magna **159** F1
Appleby Parva **159** F2
Appleby-in-
Westmorland **210** C5
Applecross **264** D7
Appledore *Devon* **113** E2
Appledore *Devon* **103** D1
Appledore *Kent* **111** E1
Appledore Heath **124** B5
Appleford **134** A3
Appleshaw **119** E3
Applethwaite **209** F4
Appleton *Halton* **183** G4
Appleton *Oxon* **133** G2
Appleton Roebuck **195** E3
Appleton Thorn **184** A4
Appleton Wiske **202** D2
Appleton-le-Moors **203** G4
Appleton-le-Street **203** G5
Appletreehall **227** G4
Appletreewick **193** G2
Appley **115** D5
Appley Bridge **183** G2
Apse Heath **107** E4
Apsey Green **153** D1
Apsley **135** F2
Apsley End **149** G4
Apuldram **108** A3
Arbeia Roman Fort &
Museum *T&W*
NE33 2BB **28** E1
Arbirlot **253** D5
Arborfield **120** C1
Arborfield Cross **120** C1
Arborfield Garrison **120** C1
Arbourthorne **186** A4
Arbroath **253** E5
Arbuthnott **253** F2
Archdeacon
Newton **202** B1
Archiestown **267** K7
Arclid **171** E1
Ard a' Chapuill **232** B1
Ardacheranbeg **232** B1
Ardacheranmor **232** B1
Ardachoil **239** G1
Ardachu **266** D1
Ardailly **231** E4
Ardalanish **238** C3
Ardallie **261** J1
Ardanaiseig **240** C2
Ardaneaskan **256** E1
Ardanstur **240** A3
Ardantrive **240** A2
Ardarroch **264** E7
Ardbeg *A&B* **232** B3
Ardbeg *A&B* **230** C5
Ardbeg *A&B* **232** C1
Ardblair **258** C1
Ardbrecknish **240** C2
Ardcharnich **265** H3
Archiavaig **238** C3
Ardchonnel **240** B1
Ardchonnell **240** B3
Ardchrishnish **238** C3
Ardchronie **266** D3
Archuilk **257** J1
Ardchullarie More **242** A3
Archyle **242** A2
Arddlin **156** B1
Ardechvie **257** H5
Ardeley **150** B5
Ardelve **256** E2
Arden **233** E1
Ardencaple House **239** G3
Ardens Grafton **146** D2
Ardentallan **240** A2
Ardentinny **232** C1
Ardeonaig **242** B1
Ardersier **266** E6
Ardery **247** G3
Ardessie **265** G3
Ardfad **239** G3
Ardfern **240** A4
Ardfin **230** C3
Ardgartan **241** E4
Ardgay **266** D2
Ardgenavan **241** D3
Ardgour (Corran) **248** C3
Ardgowan **232** D2
Ardgowse **260** D3
Ardgye **267** J5
Ardhallow **232** C2
Ardheslaig **264** D6
Ardiecow **268** D4
Ardinamar **239** G3
Ardindrean **265** H3
Ardingly **109** E1
Ardington **133** G4
Ardington Wick **133** G4
Ardintoul **256** E2
Ardkinglas House **241** D3
Ardlair **260** D2
Ardlamont **232** A3
Ardleigh **152** B5
Ardleigh Green **137** E4
Ardleigh Heath **152** B4
Ardleish **241** F3
Ardler **252** A5
Ardley **148** A4
Ardley End **137** E1
Ardlui (Aird Laoigh) **241** F3
Ardlussa **231** E1
Ardmaddy **240** C1
Ardmair **265** H2
Ardmaleish **232** B3
Ardmay **241** E4
Ardmenish **231** D2
Ardmhôr **254** C4
Ardminish **231** E5

Ardmolich 247 G2
Ardmore A&B 230 C4
Ardmore A&B 239 G2
Ardmore A&B 233 E2
Ardmore High 266 E3
Ardnackaig 239 G5
Ardnacross 247 E5
Ardnadam 232 C1
Ardnadrochit 239 G1
Ardnagoine 265 F1
Ardnagowan 240 D4
Ardnahein 241 D5
Ardnahoe 230 C2
Ardnarff 256 E1
Ardnastang 248 A3
Ardnave 230 A2
Ardno 241 D4
Ardo 261 G1
Ardoch D&G 225 G5
Ardoch Moray 267 J6
Ardoch P&K 243 F1
Ardochrig 234 A5
Ardoyne 260 E2
Ardpatrick 231 F3
Ardpeaton 232 D1
Ardradnaig 250 C5
Ardrishaig 231 G1
Ardroe 272 C6
Ardross 266 D4
Ardrossan 232 D5
Ardscalpsie 232 B4
Ardshave 266 E2
Ardshealach 247 F3
Ardshellach 239 G3
Ardsley 186 A2
Ardslignish 247 E3
Ardtalla 230 C4
Ardtalnaig 242 C1
Ardtaraig 232 B1
Ardteatle 240 D2
Ardtoe 247 F2
Ardtornish 247 G5
Ardtrostan 242 B2
Ardtur 248 B5
Arduaine 240 A3
Ardullie 266 C5
Ardura 239 F1
Ardvar 272 D5
Ardvasar 256 C4
Ardveenish 254 C4
Ardveich 242 B2
Ardverikie 250 A1
Ardvorlich A&B 241 F3
Ardvorlich P&K 242 B2
Ardwall 215 G5
Ardwell D&G 206 B2
Ardwell Moray 260 B1
Ardwell SAyr 214 C1
Ardwick 184 C3
Areley Kings 158 A5
Arford 120 D4
Argaty 242 C4
Argoed 130 A3
Argoed Mill 143 F1
Argos Hill 110 A1
Argrennan House 216 B5
Argyll & Sutherland Highlanders Museum Stir FK8 1EH 242 C5
Arichamish 240 B4
Arichastlich 241 E1
Arichonan 239 G5
Aridhglas 238 C2
Arienskill 247 G1
Arileod 246 A4
Arinacrinachd 264 D6
Arinafad Beg 231 F1
Arinagour 246 B4
Arinambane 254 C2
Arisaig (Àrasaig) 247 F1
Arivegaig 247 F3
Arkendale 194 C1
Arkesden 150 C4
Arkholme 199 G5
Arkle Town 201 F2
Arkleby 209 E3
Arkleside 201 F4
Arkleton 218 B2
Arkley 136 B3
Arksey 186 C2
Arkwright Town 186 B5
Arlary 243 G4
Arle 146 B5
Arlecdon 208 D5
Arlesey 149 G4
Arleston 157 F1
Arley 184 A4
Arlingham 131 G1
Arlington Devon 113 G1
Arlington ESuss 110 A3
Arlington Glos 132 D2
Arlington Beccott 113 G1
Armadale High 274 C2
Armadale High 256 C4
Armadale WLoth 234 D3
Armathwaite 210 B3
Arminghall 179 D5
Armitage 158 C1
Armitage Bridge 185 F1
Armley 194 B4
Armscote 147 E3
Armshead 171 G3
Armston 161 F4
Armthorpe 186 D2
Arnabost 246 B3
Arnaby 198 C4
Arncliffe 201 E5
Arncliffe Cote 201 E5
Arncroach 244 D4
Arne 105 F4
Arnesby 160 B3
Arngask 243 G3
Arngibbon 242 B5
Arngomery 242 B5
Arnhall 253 E3
Arnicle 222 C2
Arnipol 247 G1
Arnisdale (Arnasdal) 256 E3
Arnish 264 B7
Arniston Engine 236 A3
Arnol 271 F3
Arnold ERid 196 D3
Arnold Notts 173 G3
Arnolfini Gallery BS1 4QA 66 Bristol
Arnprior 242 B5
Arnside 199 F5
Aros Experience High IV51 9EU 263 K7
Arowry 170 B4
Arrad Foot 199 E4
Arradoul 268 C4
Arram 196 C3
Arran 223 E2
Arras 196 B3
Arrat 253 E4
Arrathorne 202 B3
Arreton 107 E4
Arrington 150 B2
Arrivain 241 E1
Arrochar 241 F4
Arrow 146 C2
Arscaig 273 H7
Arscott 156 D2
Arthington 194 B3
Arthingworth 160 C4
Arthog 154 C1
Arthrath 261 H1
Arthurstone 252 A5
Artrochie 261 J1
Aruadh 230 A3
Arundel 108 C3
Arundel Castle WSuss BN18 9AB 108 C3
Arundel Cathedral (R.C.) WSuss BN18 9AY 108 C3
Aryhoulan 248 C3
Asby 209 D4
Ascog 232 C3
Ascot 121 E1
Ascott 147 F4
Ascott d'Oyley 133 F1
Ascott Earl 133 E1
Ascott-under-Wychwood 133 F1
Ascreavie 252 B4
Asenby 202 D5
Asfordby 160 C1
Asfordby Hill 160 C1
Asgarby Lincs 176 B1
Asgarby Lincs 175 G3
Ash Dorset 105 E1
Ash Kent 125 E3
Ash Kent 123 F2
Ash Som 116 B5
Ash Surr 121 D2
Ash Barton 113 F5
Ash Bullayne 102 A2
Ash Green Surr 121 E3
Ash Green Warks 159 F4
Ash Magna 170 C4
Ash Mill 114 A5
Ash Parva 170 C4
Ash Priors 115 E5
Ash Street 152 B3
Ash Thomas 102 D1
Ash Vale 121 D2
Ashampstead 134 A5
Ashbocking 152 C2
Ashbourne 172 C3
Ashbrittle 115 D5
Ashburnham Place 110 B2
Ashburton 101 D1
Ashbury Devon 99 F1
Ashbury Oxon 133 E4
Ashby 187 F2
Ashby by Partney 176 C1
Ashby cum Fenby 188 C2
Ashby de la Launde 175 F2
Ashby de la Zouch 159 F1
Ashby Dell 165 F2
Ashby Folville 160 C1
Ashby Hill 188 C2
Ashby Magna 160 A3
Ashby Parva 160 A4
Ashby Puerorum 188 D5
Ashby St. Ledgers 148 A1
Ashby St. Mary 179 E5
Ashchurch 146 B4
Ashcombe Devon 102 C5
Ashcombe NSom 116 A1
Ashcott 116 B4
Ashdon 151 D3
Ashe 119 G3
Asheldham 138 C2
Ashen 151 F3
Ashenden 124 A5
Ashendon 134 C1
Ashens 231 G2
Ashfield A&B 231 F1
Ashfield Here 145 E5
Ashfield Stir 242 C4
Ashfield Suff 152 D1
Ashfield Green Suff 165 D4
Ashfield Green Suff 151 F2
Ashfold Crossways 109 E1
Ashford Devon 100 C3
Ashford Devon 113 F2
Ashford Hants 106 A1
Ashford Kent 124 C4
Ashford Surr 135 F5
Ashford Bowdler 157 E5
Ashford Carbonel 157 E5
Ashford Hill 119 G1
Ashford in the Water 185 F5
Ashgill 234 B4
Ashiestiel 227 F2
Ashill Devon 103 D1
Ashill Norf 163 G2
Ashill Som 103 G1
Ashingdon 138 B3
Ashington N'umb 221 E3
Ashington Som 116 C5
Ashington WSuss 108 D2
Ashkirk 227 F3
Ashlett 107 D2
Ashleworth 146 A5
Ashleworth Quay 146 A5
Ashley Cambs 151 E1
Ashley ChesE 184 B4
Ashley Devon 113 G4
Ashley Glos 132 B3
Ashley Hants 119 E4
Ashley Hants 106 B3
Ashley Kent 125 F4
Ashley N'hants 160 C3
Ashley Staffs 171 E4
Ashley Wilts 117 F1
Ashley Down 131 E5
Ashley Green 135 E2
Ashley Heath Dorset 106 A2
Ashley Heath Staffs 171 E4
Ashmanhaugh 179 E3
Ashmansworth 119 F2
Ashmansworthy 112 D4
Ashmolean Museum Oxon OX1 2PH 80 Oxford
Ashmore Dorset 105 F1
Ashmore P&K 251 G4
Ashmore Green 119 G1
Ashorne 147 F2
Ashover 173 E1
Ashover Hay 173 E1
Ashow 159 F5
Ashperton 145 F3
Ashprington 101 E2
Ashreigney 113 G4
Ashridge Estate Herts HP4 1LX 135 E1
Ashtead 121 G2
Ashton ChesW&C 170 C1
Ashton Corn 94 D4
Ashton Corn 99 D4
Ashton Hants 107 E1
Ashton Here 145 E1
Ashton Invcly 232 D2
Ashton N'hants 161 F4
Ashton N'hants 148 C3
Ashton Peter 161 G2
Ashton Common 117 F2
Ashton Court Estate NSom BS41 9JN 8 B3
Ashton Keynes 132 C3
Ashton under Hill 146 B4
Ashton upon Mersey 184 B3
Ashton-in-Makerfield 183 G3
Ashton-under-Lyne 184 D3
Ashurst Hants 106 C1
Ashurst Kent 123 E5
Ashurst WSuss 109 D2
Ashurst Bridge 106 C1
Ashurstwood 122 D5
Ashwater 99 D1
Ashwell Herts 150 A4
Ashwell Rut 161 D1
Ashwell End 150 A3
Ashwellthorpe 164 C2
Ashwick 116 D3
Ashwicken 163 F1
Ashybank 227 G4
Askam in Furness 198 D5
Askern 186 C1
Askernish (Aisgernis) 254 C2
Askerswell 104 B3
Askett 134 D2
Askham Cumb 210 B5
Askham Notts 187 E5
Askham Bryan 195 E3
Askham Richard 195 E3
Asknish 240 B5
Askrigg 201 E3
Askwith 194 A3
Aslackby 175 F4
Aslacton 164 C2
Aslockton 174 C3
Asloun 260 D3
Aspall 152 C1
Aspatria 209 E2
Aspenden 150 B5
Asperton 176 A4
Aspley Guise 149 E4
Aspley Heath 149 E4
Aspull 184 A2
Asselby 195 G5
Asserby 189 E5
Assington 152 A4
Assington Green 151 F2
Astbury 171 F1
Astcote 148 B2
Asterby 188 C5
Asterley 156 C2
Asterton 156 D3
Asthall 133 E1
Asthall Leigh 133 F1
Astle 184 C5
Astley GtMan 184 B2
Astley Shrop 157 E1
Astley Warks 159 F4
Astley Worcs 145 G1
Astley Abbotts 157 G3
Astley Bridge 184 B1
Astley Cross 146 A1
Astley Green 184 B3
Astley Lodge 157 E1
Aston ChesE 170 D3
Aston ChesW&C 183 G5
Aston Derbys 185 F4
Aston Derbys 172 C4
Aston Flints 170 A1
Aston Here 157 D5
Aston Here 145 D1
Aston Herts 150 A5
Aston Oxon 133 F2
Aston Shrop 170 C5
Aston Shrop 158 A3
Aston Staffs 171 E3
Aston SYorks 186 B4
Aston Tel&W 157 F2
Aston W'ham 134 C4
Aston WMid 158 C4
Aston Abbotts 148 D5
Aston Botterell 157 F4
Aston Cantlow 146 D2
Aston Clinton 135 D1
Aston Crews 145 F5
Aston Cross 146 B4
Aston End 150 A5
Aston Eyre 157 F3
Aston Fields 146 B1
Aston Flamville 159 G3
Aston Heath 183 G5
Aston Ingham 145 F5
Aston juxta Mondrum 171 D2
Aston le Walls 147 G2
Aston Magna 147 D4
Aston Munslow 157 E4
Aston on Carrant 146 B4
Aston on Clun 156 C4
Aston Pigott 156 C2
Aston Rogers 156 C2
Aston Rowant 134 C3
Aston Sandford 134 C2
Aston Somerville 146 C4
Aston Subedge 146 D3
Aston Tirrold 134 A4
Aston Upthorpe 134 A4
Aston-by-Stone 171 G4
Aston-on-Trent 173 F5
Astwick 150 A4
Astwood 149 E3
Astwood Bank 146 C1
Aswarby 175 F3
Aswardby 189 D5
Aswick Grange 162 B1
Atch Lench 146 C2
Atcham 157 E2
Ath Linne 270 D6
Athelhampton 105 D3
Athelington 164 D4
Athelney 116 A5
Athelstaneford 236 C2
Atherington Devon 113 F3
Atherington WSuss 108 C3
Athersley North 186 A2
Atherstone 159 F3
Atherstone on Stour 147 E2
Atherton 184 A2
Atlow 172 D3
Attadale 257 F1
Attenborough 173 G4
Attenborough Nature Reserve Notts NG9 6DY 19 F4
Atterby 187 G3
Attercliffe 186 A4
Atterley 157 F3
Atterton 159 F3
Attingham Park Shrop SY4 4TP 157 E1
Attleborough Norf 164 B2
Attleborough Warks 159 F3
Attlebridge 178 C4
Attleton Green 151 F2
Atwick 197 D2
Atworth 117 F1
Auberrow 145 D3
Aubourn 175 E1
Auch 241 F1
Auchairne 214 C2
Auchallater 251 G1
Auchameanach 231 G4
Auchamore 231 G5
Aucharnie 268 E6
Aucharrigill 266 B1
Auchattie 260 E5
Auchavan 251 G3
Auchbraad 231 G1
Auchbreck 259 K2
Auchenback 233 G4
Auchenblae 253 F2
Auchenbothie 233 E2
Auchenbrack 216 B1
Auchenbreck 232 B1
Auchencairn 216 B5
Auchencrow 237 F3
Auchendinny 235 G3
Auchendolly 216 B4
Auchenfoyle 233 E2
Auchengillan 233 G1
Auchengray 235 D4
Auchenhalrig 268 B4
Auchenheath 234 C5
Auchenhessnane 216 C1
Auchenlochan 232 A2
Auchenmalg 214 D5
Auchenrivock 218 B3
Auchentiber 233 E5
Auchenvennel 233 D1
Auchessan 241 G2
Auchgourish 259 G3
Auchinafaud 231 F4
Auchincruive 224 B3
Auchindarrach 231 G1
Auchindarroch 248 C4
Auchindrain 240 C4
Auchindrean 265 H3
Auchininna 268 E6
Auchinleck 224 D3
Auchinloch 234 A2
Auchinner 242 B3
Auchinroath 267 K6
Auchintoul Aber 260 D3
Auchintoul Aber 268 E5
Auchintoul High 266 C2
Auchiries 261 J1
Auchleven 260 E2
Auchlochan 225 G2
Auchlunachan 265 H3
Auchlunies 261 G5
Auchlunkart 268 B6
Auchlyne 242 A2
Auchmacoy 261 H1
Auchmair 260 B2
Auchmantle 214 C4
Auchmithie 253 E5
Auchmuirbridge 244 A4
Auchmull 253 D2
Auchnabony 208 A2
Auchnabreac 240 C4
Auchnacloich 242 D1
Auchnacraig 239 G1
Auchnacree 252 C3
Auchnafree 242 D1
Auchnagallin 259 H1
Auchnagatt 269 H6
Auchnaha 232 A1
Auchnangoul 240 C4
Aucholzie 260 B5
Auchorrie 260 E4
Auchrannie 252 A4
Auchraw 242 A2
Auchreoch 241 F2
Auchronie 252 C1
Auchterarder 243 E3
Auchtercairn 264 E4
Auchterderran 244 A5
Auchterhouse 244 B1
Auchtermuchty 244 A3
Auchterneed 266 B6
Auchtertool 244 A5
Auchtertyre Angus 252 A5
Auchtertyre (Uachdar Thire) High 256 E2
Auchtertyre Moray 267 J6
Auchtertyre Stir 241 F2
Auchtubh 242 A2
Auckengill 275 J2
Auckley 186 D2
Audenshaw 184 D3
Audlem 171 D3
Audley 171 E2
Audley End Essex 150 D4
Audley End Essex 151 G4
Audley End Suff 151 G2
Audmore 171 F5
Auds 268 E4
Aughton ERid 195 G4
Aughton Lancs 183 E2
Aughton Lancs 192 B1
Aughton SYorks 186 B4
Aughton Wilts 118 D2
Aughton Park 183 F2
Auldearn 267 G6
Aulden 145 D2
Auldgirth 216 D2
Auldhame 236 C1
Auldhouse 234 A4
Aulich 250 B4
Ault a'chruinn 257 F2
Ault Hucknall 173 F1
Aultanrynie 273 F5
Aultbea (An t-Allt Beithe) 264 E3
Aultgrishan 264 D3
Aultguish Inn 265 K4
Aultibea 275 F6
Aultiphurst 274 D2
Aultmore 268 C5
Ault-na-goire 258 C2
Aultnamain Inn 266 D3
Aultnapaddock 268 B6
Aulton 260 E2
Aultvaich 266 C7
Aultvoulin 256 D4
Aunby 161 F1
Aundorach 259 G3
Aunk 102 D2
Aunsby 175 F4
Auquhorthies 261 G2
Aust 131 E4
Austerfield 187 D3
Austrey 159 E2
Austwick 193 D1
Authorpe 189 E4
Authorpe Row 189 F5
Avebury 132 D5
Avebury Trusloe 118 B1
Aveley 137 E4
Avening 132 A3
Averham 174 C2
Avery Hill 136 D5
Aveton Gifford 100 C3
Aviation Viewing Park GtMan M90 1QX 25 E6
Avielochan 259 G3
Aviemore 259 F3
Avington Hants 119 G4
Avington WBerks 119 E1
Avoch 266 D6
Avon 106 A3
Avon Dassett 147 G2
Avon Heath Country Park Dorset BH24 2DA 3 E1
Avon Valley Railway SGlos BS30 6HD 8 E4
Avonbridge 234 D2
Avoncliff 117 F2
Avonmouth 131 E5
Avonwick 100 D2
Awbridge 119 E5
Awhirk 214 B5
Awkley 131 E4
Awliscombe 103 E2
Awre 131 G2
Awsworth 173 F3
Axbridge 116 B2
Axford Hants 120 B3
Axford Wilts 133 E5
Axminster 103 F3
Axmouth 103 F3
Axton 182 C4
Axtown 100 B1
Aycliffe 212 B5
Aydon 211 G1
Aylburton 131 F2
Ayle 210 D3
Aylesbeare 102 D3
Aylesbury 134 D1
Aylesby 188 C2
Aylesford 123 G3
Aylesham 125 E3
Aylestone 160 A2
Aylmerton 178 C2
Aylsham 178 C3
Aylton 145 F4
Aymestrey 144 D1
Aynho 148 A4
Ayot Green 136 B1
Ayot St. Lawrence 136 A1
Ayot St. Peter 136 B1
Ayr 224 B3
Aysgarth 201 F4
Aysgarth Falls & National Park Centre NYorks DL8 3TH 201 F4
Ayshford 102 D1
Ayside 199 E4
Ayston 161 D2
Aythorpe Roding 137 E1
Ayton P&K 243 G3
Ayton ScBord 237 G3
Aywick 278 E4
Azerley 202 B5

B

Babbacombe 101 F1
Babbacombe Model Village Torbay TQ1 3LA 101 F1
Babbinswood 170 A4
Babb's Green 136 C1
Babcary 116 C5
Babel 143 E4
Babell 182 C5
Babeny 99 G3
Bablock Hythe 133 G2
Babraham 150 D2
Babworth 187 D4
Baby's Hill 259 K1
Bac 271 G3
Bachau 180 C4
Back of Keppoch 247 F1
Back Street 151 F2
Backaland 276 E4
Backaskaill 276 D2
Backbarrow 199 E4
Backburn 260 D1
Backe 127 F1
Backfolds 269 J5
Backford 183 F5
Backhill 261 F1
Backhill of Clackriach 269 H6
Backhill of Trustach 260 E5
Backies High 267 F1
Backies Moray 268 D5
Backlass 275 H3
Backside 260 C1
Backwell 116 B1
Backworth 221 E4
Bacon End 137 E1
Baconend Green 137 E1
Baconsthorpe 178 C2
Bacton Here 144 C4
Bacton Norf 179 E2
Bacton Suff 152 B1
Bacton Green 152 B1
Bacup 193 E5
Badachro 264 D4
Badanloch Lodge 274 C5
Badavanich 265 H6
Badbea 275 F7
Badbury 133 D4
Badbury Wick 133 D4
Badby 148 A2
Badcall High 272 D4
Badcall High 272 E3
Badcaul 265 G2
Baddeley Green 171 G2
Badden 231 G1
Baddesley Clinton 159 D5
Baddesley Clinton Warks B93 0DQ 159 D5
Baddesley Ensor 159 E3
Baddidarach 272 C6
Badenscoth 261 F1
Badenyon 260 B3
Badgall 97 G1
Badger 157 G3
Badgerbank 184 C5
Badgers Mount 123 D2
Badgeworth 132 B1
Badgworth 116 A2
Badicaul 256 D2
Badingham 153 E1
Badintagairt 273 G7
Badlesmere 124 C3
Badley 152 B2
Badlipster 275 H4
Badluarach 265 F2
Badminton 132 A4
Badnaban 272 C6
Badnabay 272 E4
Badnafrave 259 K3
Badnagie 275 G5
Badnambiast 250 C2
Badninish 266 E2
Badrallach 265 G2
Badsey 146 C3
Badshot Lea 121 D3
Badsworth 186 B1
Badwell Ash 152 A1
Badworthy 100 C1
Badyo 251 E3
Bag Enderby 189 D5
Bagber 105 D1
Bagby 203 D4
Bagendon 132 C2
Baggeridge Country Park Staffs DY3 4HB 14 A2
Bagginswood 157 F4
Baggrave Hall 160 B2
Baggrow 209 E2
Bàgh Mòr 262 D6
Baghasdal 254 C3
Bagillt 182 D5
Baginton 159 F5
Baglan 128 D3
Bagley Shrop 170 B5
Bagley Som 116 B3
Bagmore 120 B3
Bagnall 171 G2
Bagnor 119 F1
Bagpath 132 A3
Bagshot Surr 121 E1
Bagshot Wilts 119 E1
Bagstone 131 F4
Bagthorpe Norf 177 F4
Bagthorpe Notts 173 F2
Baguley 184 C4
Bagworth 159 G2
Bagwyllydiart 144 D5
Baildon 194 A4
Baile an Truiseil 271 F2
Baile Boidheach 231 F2
Baile Gharbhaidh 262 C7
Baile Glas 262 D6
Baile Mhartainn 262 C4
Baile Mhic Phail 262 D4
Baile Mòr 238 B2
Baile nan Cailleach 262 C6
Baile Raghaill 262 C5
Bailebeag 258 C3
Baileguish 259 F5
Baile-na-Cille 262 D3
Bailetonach 247 F2
Bailiesward 260 C1
Bailiff Bridge 194 A5
Baillieston 234 A3
Bainbridge 201 E3
Bainsford 234 C1
Bainshole 260 E1
Bainton ERid 196 B2
Bainton Oxon 148 A5
Bainton Peter 161 F2
Bairnkine 228 A5
Bakebare 260 B1
Baker Street 137 F4
Baker's End 136 C1
Bakewell 172 D1
Bala (Y Bala) 168 C4
Balachuirn 264 B7
Balado 243 F4
Balafark 242 B5
Balaldie 267 F4
Balallan (Baile Ailein) 270 E5
Balavil 258 E4
Balbeg High 258 B1
Balbeg High 258 B2
Balbeggie 243 G2
Balbirnie 244 A4
Balbithan 261 F3
Balblair High 266 E5
Balblair High 266 C2
Balblair High 266 E3
Balby 186 C2
Balcharn 266 C1
Balcherry 267 F3
Balchers 269 F5
Balchladich 272 C5
Balchraggan High 266 C7
Balchraggan High 258 C1
Balchrick 272 D3
Balcombe 122 C5
Balcurvie 244 B4
Baldernock 233 G2
Baldersby 202 C5
Baldersby St. James 202 C5
Balderstone GtMan 184 D1
Balderstone Lancs 192 C4
Balderton ChesW&C 170 A1
Balderton Notts 174 D2
Baldhu 96 B5
Baldinnie 244 C3
Baldock 150 A4
Baldon Row 134 A2
Baldovan 244 B1
Baldovie Angus 252 B4
Baldovie Dundee 244 C1
Baldrine 190 C3
Baldslow 110 C2
Baldwin 190 B3
Baldwinholme 209 G1
Baldwin's Gate 171 E3
Baldwins Hill 122 C5
Bale 178 B2
Balelone (Baile Lion) 262 C4
Balemartine 246 A2
Balemore (Baile Mòr) 262 C5
Balendoch 252 A5
Balephuil 246 A2
Balerno 235 F3
Balernock 233 D1
Baleromindubh 238 C5
Baleromninmore 238 C5
Baleshare (Bhaleshear) 262 C5
Balevulin 239 D2
Balfield 252 D3
Balfour Aber 260 D5
Balfour Ork 277 D6
Balfron 233 G1
Balfron Station 233 G1
Balgonar 243 F5
Balgove 261 G1
Balgowan D&G 206 B2
Balgowan High 258 D5
Balgown 263 J5
Balgreen 269 F5
Balgreggan 214 B5
Balgy 264 E6
Balhaldie 242 D4
Balhalgardy 261 F2
Balham 136 B5
Balhary 252 A5
Balhelvie 244 B2
Balhousie 244 C4
Baliasta 278 F2
Baligill 274 D2
Baligrundle 248 A5
Balindore 240 B1
Balintore Angus 252 A4
Balintore High 267 F4
Balintraid 266 E4
Balintyre 250 B5
Balivanich (Baile a'Mhanaich) 262 C6
Balkeerie 252 B5
Balkholme 195 G5
Balkissock 214 C2
Ball 170 A5
Ball Haye Green 171 G2
Ball Hill 119 F1
Balla 254 C3
Ballabeg 190 A4
Ballacannell 190 C3
Ballacarnane Beg 190 A3
Ballachulish (Baile a'Chaolais) 248 C4
Balladoole 190 A5
Ballafesson 190 A4
Ballagyr 190 A3
Ballajora 190 C2
Ballakilpheric 190 A4
Ballamodha 190 A4
Ballantrae 214 B2
Ballards Gore 138 C3
Ballasalla IoM 190 A4
Ballasalla IoM 190 B2
Ballater 260 B5
Ballaterach 260 C5
Ballaugh 190 B2
Ballaveare 190 B4
Ballchraggan 266 E4
Ballechin 251 E4
Balleich 242 A4
Ballencrieff 236 B2
Ballidon 172 D2
Balliekine 231 G5
Balliemeanoch 240 D4
Balliemore A&B 240 D5
Balliemore A&B 240 A2
Ballig 190 A3
Ballimeanoch 240 C3
Ballimore A&B 232 A1
Ballimore Stir 242 A3
Ballinaby 230 A3
Ballindean 244 A2
Ballingdon 151 G3
Ballinger Common 135 E2
Ballingham 145 E4
Ballingry 243 G5
Ballinlick 251 E5
Ballinluig P&K 251 E4
Ballinluig P&K 251 F4
Ballintuim 251 G4
Balloch Angus 252 B4
Balloch High 266 E7
Balloch NLan 234 B2
Balloch WDun 233 E1
Ballochan 260 D5
Ballochandrain 232 A1
Ballochford 260 B1
Ballochgair 222 C3
Ballochmartin 232 C4
Ballochmorrie 214 D2
Ballochmyle 224 D3
Ballochroy 231 F4

Ballogie 260 D5
Balls Cross 121 E5
Balls Green *Essex* 152 B5
Ball's Green *Glos* 132 A3
Balls Hill 158 B3
Ballyaurgan 231 F2
Ballygown 246 D5
Ballygrant 230 B3
Ballyhaugh 246 A4
Ballymeanoch 240 A5
Ballymichael 223 E2
Balmacara
(Baile Mac Ara) 256 E2
Balmaclellan 216 A3
Balmacneil 251 E4
Balmadies 253 D5
Balmae 207 G2
Balmaha 241 G5
Balmalcolm 244 B4
Balmaqueen 263 K4
Balmeanach *A&B* 247 F5
Balmeanach *A&B* 238 D1
Balmedie 261 H3
Balmedie Country Park
Aber AB23 8XG 261 H3
Balmer Heath 170 B4
Balmerino 244 B2
Balmerlawn 106 C2
Balminnoch 215 D4
Balmore *EDun* 234 A2
Balmore *High* 267 F7
Balmore *High* 257 K1
Balmore *High* 263 H7
Balmore *P&K* 250 C4
Balmullo 244 C2
Balmungie 266 E6
Balmyle 251 F4
Balnaboth 252 B3
Balnabruaich 266 E4
Balnacra 265 F7
Balnafoich 258 D1
Balnagall 267 F3
Balnagown Castle 266 E4
Balnaguard 251 E4
Balnaguisich 266 D4
Balnahard *A&B* 238 D5
Balnahard *A&B* 239 D1
Balnain 258 B1
Balnakeil 273 F2
Balnaknock 263 K5
Balnamoon 252 D3
Balnapaling 266 E5
Balnespick 259 F4
Balquhidder 242 A2
Balsall 159 E5
Balsall Common 159 E5
Balsall Heath 158 C4
Balscote 147 F3
Balsham 151 D2
Baltasound 278 F2
Balterley 171 E2
Balterley Heath 171 E2
Baltersan 215 F4
Balthangie 269 G5
Balthayock 243 G2
Baltonsborough 116 C4
Baluachraig 240 A5
Balulive 230 C3
Balure *A&B* 240 C1
Balure *A&B* 240 A1
Balvaird 266 C6
Balvarran 251 F3
Balvicar 239 G3
Balvraid *High* 256 E3
Balvraid *High* 259 F1
Bamber Bridge 192 B5
Bamber's Green 151 D5
Bamburgh 229 F3
Bamburgh Castle *N'umb*
NE69 7DF 229 F3
Bamff 252 A4
Bamford *Derbys* 185 G4
Bamford *GtMan* 184 C1
Bampton *Cumb* 199 G1
Bampton *Devon* 114 C5
Bampton *Oxon* 133 F2
Bampton Grange 199 G1
Banavie
(Banbhaidh) 248 D2
Banbury 147 G3
Banbury Museum *Oxon*
OX16 2PQ 147 G4
Bancffosfelen 128 A1
Banchor 267 G7
Banchory 261 F5
Banchory Devenick 261 H4
Bancycapel 128 A1
Bancyfelin 127 G1
Bancyffordd 142 A4
Bandon 244 A4
Bandrake Head 199 E4
Banff 268 E4
Bangor 181 D5
Bangor-on-Dee (Bangor-is-y-coed) 170 A3
Bangor's Green 183 E2
Banham 164 B3
Banham Zoo *Norf*
NR16 2HE 164 B3
Bank 106 B2
Bank End 198 C4
Bank Newton 193 F2
Bank Street 145 F1
Bank Top *Lancs* 183 G2
Bank Top *WYorks* 194 A5
Bankend 217 E4
Bankfoot 243 F1
Bankglen 225 D4
Bankhead *Aber* 260 E3
Bankhead *Aber* 260 E4
Bankhead
Aberdeen 261 G3
Bankhead *D&G* 208 A2
Bankland 116 A5
Banknock 234 B2
Banks *Cumb* 210 B1
Banks *Lancs* 191 G5
Bankshill 217 F2
Banningham 178 D3
Bannister Green 151 E5
Bannockburn 242 D5
Banstead 122 B3
Bantam Grove 194 B5
Bantham 100 C3
Banton 234 B2
Banwell 116 A2
Banwen Pyrddin 129 E2
Banyard's Green 165 E4
Bapchild 124 B2
Baptiston 233 G1
Bapton 118 A4
Bar End 119 F5
Bar Hill 150 B1
Barachander 240 C2
Barassie 224 B2
Barbaraville 266 E4
Barber Booth 185 F4
Barber Green 199 E4
Barber's Moor 183 F1
Barbican Arts & Conference
Centre *GtLon*
EC2Y 8DS 45 J1
Barbon 200 B4
Barbridge 170 D2
Barbrook 114 A3
Barby 160 A5
Barcaldine (Am Barra Calltainn) 248 B5
Barcaple 216 A5
Barcheston 147 E4
Barclose 210 A1
Barcombe 109 G2
Barcombe Cross 109 G2
Barden 202 A3
Barden Park 123 E4
Bardennoch 215 G1
Bardfield End Green 151 E4
Bardfield Saling 151 E5
Bardister 278 C5
Bardney 175 G1
Bardon *Leics* 159 G1
Bardon *Moray* 267 K6
Bardon Mill 211 D1
Bardowie 233 G2
Bardsea 199 D5
Bardsey 194 C3
Bardsey Island
(Ynys Enlli) 166 A5
Bardwell 164 A4
Bare 192 A1
Barewood 144 C2
Barfad 231 G3
Barford *Norf* 178 C5
Barford *Warks* 147 E1
Barford St. John 147 G4
Barford St. Martin 118 B4
Barford St. Michael 147 G4
Barfrestone 125 E3
Bargaly 215 F4
Bargany Mains 224 A5
Bargeddie 234 A3
Bargoed 130 A3
Bargrennan 215 E3
Barham *Cambs* 161 G5
Barham *Kent* 125 E3
Barham *Suff* 152 C2
Barharrow 216 A5
Barholm 161 F1
Barholm Mains 215 F5
Barkby 160 B2
Barkby Thorpe 160 B2
Barkers Green 170 C5
Barkestone-le-Vale 174 C4
Barkham 120 C1
Barking *GtLon* 136 D4
Barking *Suff* 152 B2
Barking Tye 152 B2
Barkisland 193 G5
Barkston 175 E3
Barkston Ash 195 D4
Barkway 150 B4
Barlae 215 D4
Barland 144 B1
Barlaston 171 F4
Barlavington 108 B2
Barlborough 186 B5
Barlby 195 F4
Barlestone 159 G2
Barley *Herts* 150 B4
Barley *Lancs* 193 E3
Barley Green 164 D4
Barleycroft End 150 C5
Barleyhill 211 G2
Barleythorpe 160 D2
Barling 138 C4
Barlings 188 A5
Barlow *Derbys* 186 A5
Barlow *NYorks* 195 F5
Barlow *T&W* 212 A1
Barmby Moor 195 G3
Barmby on the
Marsh 195 F5
Barmer 177 G4
Barmolloch 240 A5
Barmoor Lane End 229 E3
Barmouth
(Abermaw) 154 C1
Barmpton 202 C1
Barmston 197 D2
Barnaby Green 165 F4
Barnacabber 232 C1
Barnacarry 240 B5
Barnack 161 F2
Barnacle 159 F4
Barnamuc 248 C5
Barnard Castle 201 F1
Barnard Gate 133 G1
Barnardiston 151 F3
Barnard's Green 145 G3
Barnbarroch *D&G* 215 E5
Barnbarroch *D&G* 216 C5
Barnburgh 186 B2
Barnby 165 F3
Barnby Dun 186 D2
Barnby in
the Willows 175 D2
Barnby Moor 187 D4
Barndennoch 216 C2
Barne Barton 100 A2
Barnehurst 137 E5
Barnes 136 B5
Barnes Street 123 F4
Barnet 136 B3
Barnet Gate 136 B3
Barnetby le Wold 188 A2
Barney 178 A2
Barnham *Suff* 163 G5
Barnham *WSuss* 108 B3
Barnham Broom 178 B5
Barnhead 253 E4
Barnhill *ChesW&C* 170 B2
Barnhill *Dundee* 244 C1
Barnhill *Moray* 267 J6
Barnhills 214 A3
Barningham *Dur* 201 F1
Barningham *Suff* 164 A4
Barningham Green 178 C2
Barnoldby le Beck 188 C2
Barnoldswick 193 E3
Barns Green 121 G5
Barnsdale Bar 186 C1
Barnsley *Glos* 132 C2
Barnsley *SYorks* 186 A2
Barnsole 125 E3
Barnstaple 113 F2
Barnston *Essex* 137 F1
Barnston *Mersey* 183 D4
Barnstone 174 C4
Barnt Green 158 C5
Barnton *ChesW&C* 184 A5
Barnton *Edin* 235 F2
Barnwell All Saints 161 F4
Barnwell Country Park
N'hants
PE8 5PB 161 F4
Barnwell St. Andrew 161 F4
Barnwood 132 A1
Barons' Cross 145 D2
Barr *A&B* 230 B3
Barr *High* 247 F4
Barr *SAyr* 215 D1
Barr *Som* 115 E5
Barr Hall 151 F4
Barra (Barraigh) 254 B4
Barra (Tràigh Mhòr)
Airport 254 B4
Barrachan 207 D2
Barrackan 239 G4
Barraer 215 E4
Barraglom 270 D4
Barrahormid 231 F1
Barran 241 D2
Barrapoll 246 A2
Barrasford 220 B4
Barravullin 240 A4
Barregarrow 190 B3
Barrets Green 170 C2
Barrhead 233 F4
Barrhill 214 D2
Barrington *Cambs* 150 B3
Barrington *Som* 103 G1
Barripper 94 D3
Barrisdale 256 E4
Barrmill 233 E4
Barrnacarry 240 A2
Barrock 275 H1
Barrow *Glos* 146 A5
Barrow *Lancs* 192 D4
Barrow *Rut* 161 D1
Barrow *Shrop* 157 F2
Barrow *Som* 117 E4
Barrow *Som* 116 C3
Barrow *Suff* 151 F1
Barrow Gurney 116 C1
Barrow Hann 196 C5
Barrow Haven 196 C5
Barrow Hill 186 B5
Barrow Nook 183 F2
Barrow Street 117 F4
Barrow upon
Humber 196 C5
Barrow upon Soar 160 A1
Barrow upon Trent 173 E5
Barroway Drove 163 D2
Barrowby 175 D4
Barrowcliff 204 D4
Barrowden 161 E2
Barrowford 193 E4
Barrow-in-Furness 191 F1
Barrows Green 199 G4
Barry *Angus* 244 D1
Barry *VGlam* 115 E1
Barry Island Pleasure
Park *VGlam*
CF62 5TR 115 E1
Barsby 160 B1
Barsham 165 E3
Barskimming 224 C3
Barsloisnoch 240 A5
Barston 159 E5
Barter Books,
Alnwick *N'umb*
NE66 2NP 229 F5
Bartestree 145 E3
Barthol Chapel 261 G1
Bartholomew Green 151 F5
Barthomley 171 E2
Bartley 106 C1
Bartley Green 158 C4
Bartlow 151 D3
Barton *Cambs* 150 C2
Barton *ChesW&C* 170 B2
Barton *Cumb* 210 A5
Barton *Glos* 146 C5
Barton *Lancs* 192 B4
Barton *Lancs* 183 E2
Barton *NYorks* 202 B2
Barton *Oxon* 134 A2
Barton *Torbay* 101 F1
Barton *Warks* 146 D2
Barton Bendish 163 F2
Barton End 132 A3
Barton Green 159 D1
Barton Hartshorn 148 B4
Barton Hill 195 G1
Barton in Fabis 173 G4
Barton in the Beans 159 F2
Barton Mills 163 F5
Barton on Sea 106 B3
Barton St. David 116 C4
Barton Seagrave 161 D5
Barton Stacey 119 F3
Barton Town 113 G1
Barton Turf 179 E3
Bartongate 147 G5
Barton-le-Clay 149 F4
Barton-le-Street 203 G5
Barton-le-Willows 195 G1
Barton-on-
the-Heath 147 E4
Barton-under-
Needwood 159 D1
Barton-upon-
Humber 196 C5
Barvas
(Barabhas) 271 F3
Barway 162 D5
Barwell 159 G3
Barwhinnock 216 A5
Barwick *Herts* 136 C1
Barwick *Som* 104 B1
Barwick in Elmet 194 C4
Barwinnock 207 D2
Baschurch 170 B5
Bascote 147 G1
Base Green 152 B1
Basford Green 171 G2
Bashall Eaves 192 C3
Bashall Town 192 D3
Bashley 106 B3
Basildon *Essex* 137 G4
Basildon *WBerks* 134 B5
Basingstoke 120 B2
Baslow 185 G5
Bason Bridge 116 A3
Bassaleg 130 B4
Bassenthwaite 209 F3
Basset's Cross 113 F5
Bassett 106 D1
Bassingbourn 150 B3
Bassingfield 174 B4
Bassingham 175 E2
Bassingthorpe 175 E5
Basta 278 E3
Baston 161 G1
Bastonford 146 A2
Bastwick 179 F4
Batavaime 241 G1
Batch 116 A2
Batchley 146 C1
Batchworth 135 F3
Batchworth Heath 135 F3
Batcombe
Dorset 104 C2
Batcombe *Som* 117 D4
Bate Heath 184 A5
Bath 117 E1
Bath Abbey *B&NESom*
BA1 1LT 63 Bath
Bathampton 117 E1
Bathealton 115 D5
Batheaston 117 E1
Bathford 117 E1
Bathgate 235 D3
Bathley 174 C2
Bathpool *Corn* 97 G2
Bathpool *Som* 115 F5
Bathway 116 C2
Batley 194 B5
Batsford 147 D4
Batson 100 D4
Battersby 203 E2
Battersea 136 B5
Battersea Cats & Dogs
Home *GtLon*
SW8 4AA 13 A5
Battersea Park Children's
Zoo *GtLon*
SW11 4NJ 13 A5
Battisborough
Cross 100 C3
Battisford 152 B2
Battisford Tye 152 B2
Battle *ESuss* 110 C2
Battle *Powys* 143 G4
Battle Abbey *ESuss*
TN33 0AD 110 C2
Battledown 146 B5
Battlefield 157 E1
Battlesbridge 137 G3
Battlesden 149 E5
Battlesea Green 164 D4
Battleton 114 C5
Battlies Green 152 A1
Battramsley 106 C3
Batt's Corner 120 D3
Bauds of Cullen 268 C4
Baugh 246 B2
Baughton 146 A3
Baughurst 119 G1
Baulds 260 E5
Baulking 133 F3
Baumber 188 C5
Baunton 132 C2
Baveney Wood 157 F5
Baverstock 118 B4
Bawburgh 178 C5
Bawdeswell 178 B3
Bawdrip 116 A4
Bawdsey 153 E3
Bawdsey Manor 153 E4
Bawsey 163 E1
Bawtry 187 D3
Baxenden 193 D5
Baxterley 159 E3
Baxter's Green 151 F2
Baxters Highland
Village *Moray*
IV32 7LD 268 B4
Bay 117 F5
Baybridge 211 F3
Baycliff 199 D5
Baydon 133 E5
Bayford *Herts* 136 C2
Bayford *Som* 117 E5
Bayfordbury 136 C1
Bayham Abbey 123 F5
Bayles 210 D3
Baylham 152 C2
Baynards Green 148 A5
Baysham 145 E5
Bayston Hill 157 D2
Bayswater 136 B4
Baythorn End 151 F3
Bayton 157 F5
Bayworth 134 A2
Beach *High* 247 G4
Beach *SGlos* 131 G5
Beachampton 148 C4
Beachamwell 163 F2
Beacharr 231 E5
Beachley 131 E3
Beacon *Devon* 103 E2
Beacon *Devon* 103 F2
Beacon Fell Country
Park *Lancs*
PR3 2NL 192 B3
Beacon Hill *Dorset* 105 F3
Beacon Hill *Essex* 138 B1
Beacon Hill *Surr* 121 D4
Beacon Hill Country Park
Leics LE12 8SR 17 A2
Beacon Park,
Up Holland *Lancs*
WN8 7RU 183 G2
Beacon's Bottom 134 C3
Beaconsfield 135 E3
Beacravik 263 G2
Beadlam 203 F4
Beadlow 149 G4
Beadnell 229 G4
Beaford 113 F4
Beal *N'umb* 229 E2
Beal *NYorks* 195 E5
Bealach 248 B4
Beale Park *WBerks*
RG8 9NH 134 B5
Bealsmill 99 D3
Beambridge 170 D2
Beamhurst 172 B4
Beaminster 104 A2
Beamish 212 B2
Beamish, North of England
Open Air Museum
Dur DH9 0RG 29 A1
Beamsley 193 G2
Bean 137 E5
Beanacre 118 A1
Beanley 229 E5
Beaquoy 276 C5
Beardon 99 F2
Beardwood 192 C5
Beare 102 C2
Beare Green 121 G3
Bearley 147 D1
Bearnie 261 H1
Bearnock 258 B1
Bearnus 246 C5
Bearpark 212 B3
Bearsbridge 211 D2
Bearsden 233 G2
Bearsted 123 G3
Bearstone 171 E4
Bearwood *Poole* 105 G3
Bearwood *WMid* 158 C4
Beatles Story
Mersey L3 4AD 42 B5
Beattock 226 B5
Beauchamp Roding 137 E1
Beauchief 186 A4
Beaudesert 147 D1
Beaufort 130 A1
Beaulieu 106 C2
Beaulieu: National Motor
Museum, Abbey & Palace
House *Hants*
SO42 7ZN 4 A5
Beauly (A' Mhanachainn)
266 C7
Beaumaris (Biwmares)
181 E5
Beaumont *Chanl* 100 C5
Beaumont *Cumb* 209 G1
Beaumont *Essex* 152 C5
Beaumont Hill 202 B1
Beaumont Leys 160 A2
Beausale 159 E5
Beauvale 173 F3
Beauworth 119 G5
Beaver Green 124 B4
Beaworthy 99 E1
Beazley End 151 F5
Bebington 183 E4
Bebside 221 E3
Beccles 165 F2
Beccles Heliport 165 F3
Becconsall 192 A5
Beck Foot 200 B3
Beck Hole 204 B2
Beck Row 163 E5
Beck Side *Cumb* 198 D4
Beck Side *Cumb* 199 E4
Beckbury 157 G2
Beckenham 122 C2
Beckering 188 B4
Beckermet 198 B2
Beckermonds 201 D4
Beckett End 163 F3
Beckfoot *Cumb* 198 C2
Beckfoot *Cumb* 209 D2
Beckford 146 B4
Beckhampton 118 B1
Beckingham *Lincs* 175 D2
Beckingham *Notts* 187 E4
Beckington 117 F2
Beckley *ESuss* 111 D1
Beckley *Oxon* 134 A1
Beck's Green 165 E3
Beckside 200 B4
Beckton 136 D4
Beckwithshaw 194 B2
Becontree 137 D4
Bedale 202 B4
Bedburn 211 G4
Bedchester 105 E1
Beddau 129 G4
Beddgelert 167 E3
Beddingham 109 G3
Beddington 122 B2
Beddington Corner 122 B2
Bedfield 152 D1
Bedfield Little
Green 152 D1
Bedford 149 F3
Bedgebury Cross 123 G5
Bedgrove 134 D1
Bedham 121 F5
Bedhampton 107 G2
Bedingfield 152 C1
Bedingfield Green 152 C1
Bedingfield Street 152 C1
Bedingham Green 165 D2
Bedlam *Lancs* 193 D5
Bedlam *NYorks* 194 B1
Bedlar's Green 150 D5
Bedlington 221 E3
Bedlinog 129 G2
Bedminster 131 E5
Bedmond 135 F2
Bednall 158 B1
Bedol 182 D5
Bedrule 228 A5
Bedstone 156 C5
Bedwas 130 A4
Bedwell 150 A5
Bedwellty 130 A2
Bedworth 159 F4
Bedworth
Woodlands 159 F4
Beeby 160 B2
Beech *Hants* 120 B4
Beech *Staffs* 171 F4
Beech Hill 120 B1
Beechingstoke 118 B2
Beechwood 183 G4
Beecraigs Country
Park *WLoth*
EH49 6PL 235 D2
Beedon 133 G5
Beeford 196 D2
Beeley 173 D1
Beelsby 188 C2
Beenham 119 G1
Beeny 98 B1
Beer 103 F4
Beer Hackett 104 C1
Beercrocombe 116 A5
Beesands 101 E3
Beesby *Lincs* 189 E4
Beesby *NELincs* 188 C3
Beeson 101 E3
Beeston *CenBeds* 149 G3
Beeston *ChesW&C* 170 C2
Beeston *Norf* 178 A4
Beeston *Notts* 173 G4
Beeston *WYorks* 194 B4
Beeston Regis 178 C1
Beeston
St. Lawrence 179 E3
Beeswing 216 C4
Beetham *Cumb* 199 F5
Beetham *Som* 103 F1
Beetley 178 A4
Beffcote 158 A1
Began 130 B4
Begbroke 133 G1
Begdale 162 C2
Begelly 127 E2
Beggar's Bush 144 B1
Beggearn Huish 114 D4
Beggshill 260 D1
Beguildy (Bugeildy) 156 A5
Beighton *Norf* 179 E5
Beighton *SYorks* 186 B4
Beili-glas 130 C2
Beith 233 E4
Bekesbourne 125 D3
Bekonscot Model Village
Bucks HP9 2PL 135 E3
Belaugh 179 D4
Belbroughton 158 B5
Belchalwell 105 D2
Belchalwell Street 105 D2
Belchamp Otten 151 G3
Belchamp St. Paul 151 F3
Belchamp Walter 151 G3
Belchford 188 C5
Belfield 184 D1
Belford 229 F3
Belgrave 160 A2
Belhaven 237 D2
Belhelvie 261 H3
Belhinnie 260 C2
Bell Bar 136 B2
Bell Busk 193 F2
Bell End 158 B5
Bell Heath 158 B5
Bell Hill 120 C5
Bell o' th' Hill 170 C3
Bellabeg 260 B3
Belladrum 266 C7
Bellanoch 240 A5
Bellaty 252 A4
Belle Isle 194 C5
Belle Vue 209 G1
Belleau 189 E5
Belleheiglash 259 J1
Bellerby 202 A3
Bellever 99 G3
Bellfields 121 E2
Belliehill 253 D3
Bellingdon 135 E2
Bellingham *GtLon* 136 C5
Bellingham *N'umb* 220 A3
Belloch 222 B2
Bellochantuy 222 B2
Bell's Cross 152 C2
Bells Yew Green 123 F5
Bellsbank 224 C5
Bellshill *N'umb* 229 F3
Bellshill *NLan* 234 B3
Bellside 234 C4
Bellsmyre 233 F2
Bellsquarry 235 E3
Belluton 116 D1
Belmaduthy 266 D6
Belmesthorpe 161 F1
Belmont *B'burn* 184 A1
Belmont *GtLon* 122 B2
Belmont *GtLon* 136 A3
Belmont *Shet* 278 E2
Belnie 176 A4
Belowda 97 D3
Belper 173 E3
Belper Lane End 173 E3
Belsay 220 D4
Belsford 101 D2
Belsize 135 F2
Belstead 152 C3
Belston 224 B3
Belstone 99 G1
Belstone Corner 99 G1
Belsyde 235 D2
Belthorn 192 D5
Beltinge 125 D2
Beltingham 211 D1
Beltoft 187 F2
Belton *Leics* 173 F5
Belton *Lincs* 175 E4
Belton *NLincs* 187 E2
Belton *Norf* 179 F5
Belton *Rut* 160 D2
Belton House *Lincs*
NG32 2LS 175 E4
Beltring 123 F4
Belvedere 137 D5
Belvoir 174 D4
Bembridge 107 F4
Bemersyde 227 G2
Bemerton 118 C4
Bempton 205 E5
Ben Alder Cottage 249 G3
Ben Alder Lodge 250 A2
Ben Rhydding 194 A3
Benacre 165 G3
Benbecula (Beinn na
Faoghla) 262 D6
Benbecula (Balivanich)
Airport 262 C6
Benbuie 216 B1
Benderloch
(Meadarloch) 240 B1
Bendish 149 G5
Benenden 124 A5
Benfield 215 E4
Benfieldside 211 G2
Bengate 179 E3
Bengeo 136 C1
Bengeworth 146 C3
Benhall 146 B5
Benhall Green 153 E1
Benhall Street 153 E1
Benholm 253 G3
Beningbrough 195 E2
Benington *Herts* 150 A5
Benington *Lincs* 176 B3
Benington Sea End 176 C3
Benllech 180 D4
Benmore *A&B* 232 C1
Benmore *Stir* 241 G2
Bennacott 98 C1
Bennan Cottage 216 A3
Bennett End 134 C3
Bennetts End 135 F2
Benniworth 188 C4
Benover 123 G4
Benson 134 B3
Benston 279 D7
Benthall *N'umb* 229 G4
Benthall *Shrop* 157 F2
Bentham 132 B1
Benthoul 261 G4
Bentlawnt 156 C2
Bentley *ERid* 196 C4
Bentley *Essex* 137 E3
Bentley *Hants* 120 C3
Bentley *Suff* 152 C4
Bentley *SYorks* 186 C2
Bentley *Warks* 159 E3
Bentley *WMid* 158 B3
Bentley *WYorks* 194 B4
Bentley Heath
Herts 136 B3
Bentley Heath
WMid 159 D5
Bentley Rise 186 C2
Benton 113 G2
Benton Square 221 F4
Bentpath 218 B2
Bentworth 120 B3
Benvie 244 B1
Benville Lane 104 B2
Benwell 212 B1
Benwick 162 B3
Beoley 146 C1
Beoraidbeg 256 C5
Bepton 108 A2
Berden 150 C5
Bere Alston 100 A1
Bere Ferrers 100 A1
Bere Regis 105 E3
Berea 140 A4
Berepper 95 D4
Bergh Apton 179 E5
Berinsfield 134 A3
Berkeley 131 F3
Berkhamsted 135 E2
Berkley 117 F3
Berkswell 159 E5
Bermondsey 136 C5
Bernera 256 E2
Berneray (Eilean
Bhearnaraigh) 262 E3
Berners Roding 137 F2
Bernice 240 D5
Bernisdale 263 K6
Berrick Prior 134 B3
Berrick Salome 134 B3
Berriedale 275 G6
Berriew (Aberriw) 156 A2
Berrington
N'umb 229 E2
Berrington *Shrop* 157 E2
Berrington *Worcs* 145 E1
Berrington Green 145 E1
Berrowbridge 97 G2
Berrow *Som* 115 F2
Berrow *Worcs* 145 G4
Berrow Green 145 G2
Berry Cross 113 E4
Berry Down Cross 113 F1
Berry Hill *Glos* 131 E1
Berry Hill *Pembs* 141 D3
Berry Pomeroy 101 E1
Berryhillock 268 D4
Berrynarbor 113 F1
Berry's Green 122 D3
Bersham 170 A3
Berstane 277 D6
Berthlŵyd 128 B3
Berwick 110 A3
Berwick Bassett 132 D5
Berwick Hill 221 D4
Berwick St. James 118 B4
Berwick St. John 118 A5
Berwick St. Leonard 118 A4
Berwick-upon-
Tweed 237 G4
Bescar 183 E1
Bescot 158 C3
Besford *Shrop* 170 C5
Besford *Worcs* 146 B3
Bessacarr 186 D2
Bessels Leigh 133 G2
Besses o' th' Barn 184 C2
Bessingby 197 D1
Bessingham 178 C2
Best Beech Hill 123 F5
Besthorpe *Norf* 164 B2
Besthorpe *Notts* 174 D1
Bestwood 173 G3
Bestwood Country Park
Notts NG6 8UF 19 G1
Beswick *ERid* 196 C3
Beswick *GtMan* 184 C3
Betchworth 122 B3
Bethania *Cere* 142 B1
Bethania *Gwyn* 168 A3
Bethel *Gwyn* 167 E1
Bethel *Gwyn* 168 C4
Bethel *IoA* 180 B5
Bethersden 124 B5
Bethesda *Gwyn* 167 F1
Bethesda *Pembs* 127 D1
Bethlehem 142 C5
Bethnal Green 136 C4
Betley 171 E3
Betley Common 171 E3
Betsham 137 F5
Betteshanger 125 F3
Bettiscombe 103 G3
Bettisfield 170 B4
Betton *Shrop* 156 C2
Betton *Shrop* 171 D4
Betton Strange 157 E2
Bettws *Bridgend* 129 F4

Bettws Newport 130 B3
Bettws Bledrws 142 B2
Bettws Cedewain 156 A3
Bettws Gwerfil
 Goch 168 B2
Bettws Newydd 130 C2
Bettyhill 274 C1
Betws 278 C1
Betws Disserth 144 A2
Betws Garmon 167 E2
Betws Ifan 141 G3
Betws-y-coed 168 A2
Betws-yn-Rhos 182 A5
Beulah Cere 141 F3
Beulah Powys 143 F2
Bevendean 109 F3
Bevercotes 187 D5
Beverley 196 B5
Beverston 132 A3
Bevington 131 F3
Bewaldeth 209 F3
Bewcastle 219 D4
Bewdley 157 G5
Bewerley 194 A1
Bewholme 197 D2
Bewl Water ESuss
 TN8 3JH 123 F5
Bewley Common 118 A1
Bexhill 110 C3
Bexley 137 D5
Bexleyheath 137 D5
Bexwell 163 E2
Beyton 152 A1
Beyton Green 152 A1
Bhalamus 270 E7
Bhaltos 270 C4
Biallaid 258 C5
Bibury 132 D2
Bicester 148 A5
Bickenhall 103 F1
Bickenhill 159 D4
Bicker 176 A4
Bickershaw 184 A2
Bickerstaffe 183 F2
Bickerton
 ChesW&C 170 C2
Bickerton Devon 101 E4
Bickerton N'umb 220 B1
Bickerton NYorks 195 D2
Bickford 158 A1
Bickham 114 C3
Bickham Bridge 100 D2
Bickham House 102 C4
Bickington Devon 113 F3
Bickington Devon 102 A5
Bickleigh Devon 100 B1
Bickleigh Devon 102 C3
Bickleton 113 F2
Bickley 122 C2
Bickley Moss 170 C3
Bickley Town 170 C3
Bicknacre 137 G2
Bicknoller 115 E4
Bicknor 124 A3
Bickton 106 A1
Bicton Here 145 D1
Bicton Shrop 156 D1
Bicton Shrop 156 B4
Bicton Heath 157 D1
Bicton Park Gardens
 Devon EX9 7BJ 103 D4
Bidborough 123 E4
Biddenden 124 A5
Biddenden Green 124 A4
Biddenham 149 F3
Biddestone 132 A5
Biddick 212 C2
Biddisham 116 A2
Biddlesden 148 B3
Biddlestone 220 B1
Biddulph 171 F2
Biddulph Moor 171 G2
Bideford 113 E3
Bidford-on-Avon 146 D2
Bidlake 99 E2
Bidston 183 D3
Bidwell 149 F5
Bielby 195 G3
Bieldside 261 G4
Bierley IoW 107 E5
Bierley WYorks 194 A4
Bierton 134 D1
Big Pit National Coal
 Museum Torfaen
 NP4 9XP 130 B2
Big Sand 264 D4
Big Sheep, The Devon
 EX39 5AP 113 E3
Big Sky Adventure Play
 Peter PE2 7BU 161 G3
Bigbury 100 C3
Bigbury-on-Sea 100 C3
Bigby 188 A2
Bigert Mire 198 C2
Biggar Cumb 191 E1
Biggar SLan 226 B2
Biggin Derbys 173 D3
Biggin Derbys 172 C2
Biggin NYorks 195 E4
Biggin Hill 122 D3
Biggin Hill Airport 122 D2
Biggings 279 A6
Biggleswade 149 G3
Bigholms 218 B3
Bighouse 274 D2
Bighton 120 B4
Biglands 209 F1
Bignor 108 B2
Bigrigg 208 D5
Bigton 279 C10
Bilberry 97 E4
Bilborough 173 G3
Bilbrook Som 114 D3
Bilbrook Staffs 158 A2
Bilbrough 195 E3
Bilbster 275 H3
Bilby 186 D4
Bildershaw 212 A5
Bildeston 152 A3
Billericay 137 F3
Billesdon 160 C2
Billesley 146 D2
Billholm 218 A2
Billingborough 175 G4
Billinge 183 G3
Billingford Norf 164 C4
Billingford Norf 178 B3

Billingham 213 D5
Billinghay 175 G2
Billingley 186 B2
Billingshurst 121 F5
Billingsley 157 G4
Billington CenBeds 149 E5
Billington Lancs 192 D4
Billington Staffs 171 F5
Billister 279 D6
Billockby 179 F4
Billy Row 212 A4
Bilsborrow 192 B4
Bilsby 189 E5
Bilsby Field 189 E5
Bilsborough 107 D5
Bilsby 189 E5
Bilsdean 237 E2
Bilsham 108 B3
Bilsington 124 C5
Bilson Green 131 F1
Bilsthorpe 174 B1
Bilsthorpe Moor 174 B2
Bilston Midlo 235 G3
Bilston WMid 158 B3
Bilstone 159 F2
Bilting 124 C4
Bilton ERid 197 D4
Bilton N'umb 229 G5
Bilton NYorks 194 C2
Bilton Warks 159 G5
Bilton-in-Ainsty 195 D3
Bimbister 277 C6
Binbrook 188 C3
Bincombe 104 C4
Bindal 267 G3
Bindon 115 E5
Binegar 116 D3
Bines Green 109 D2
Binfield 134 C4
Binfield Heath 134 C5
Bingfield 220 B4
Bingham 174 C4
Bingham's
 Melcombe 105 D2
Bingley 194 A4
Bings Heath 157 E1
Binham 178 A2
Binley Hants 119 F2
Binley WMid 159 F5
Binniehill 234 C2
Binsoe 202 B5
Binstead 107 E3
Binsted Hants 120 C3
Binsted WSuss 108 B3
Binton 146 D2
Bintree 178 B3
Binweston 156 C2
Birch Essex 152 A5
Birch GtMan 184 C2
Birch Cross 172 C4
Birch Green Essex 138 C1
Birch Green Herts 136 B1
Birch Grove 109 G1
Birch Heath 170 C1
Birch Vale 185 E4
Birch Wood 103 F1
Bircham Newton 177 F4
Bircham Tofts 177 F4
Birchanger 150 D5
Bircher 145 D1
Bircher Common 145 D1
Birchfield 266 B2
Birchgrove Cardiff 130 A4
Birchgrove Swan 128 D3
Birchington 125 F2
Birchmoor 159 E2
Birchover 172 D1
Birchwood Lincs 175 E1
Birchwood Warr 184 A3
Bircotes 186 D3
Bird Street 152 B2
Birdbrook 151 F3
Birdbush 118 A5
Birdfield 240 B5
Birdforth 203 D5
Birdham 108 A3
Birdingbury 147 G1
Birdland, Bourton-on-
 the-Water Glos
 GL54 2BN 147 D5
Birdlip 132 B1
Birdoswald 210 C1
Birds Green 137 E2
Birdsall 196 A1
Birdsgreen 157 G4
Birdsmoor Gate 103 G2
Birdston 234 A2
Birdwell 186 A2
Birdwood 131 G1
Birdworld, Farnham Hants
 GU10 4LD 120 D3
Birgham 228 B3
Birichen 266 E2
Birkby Cumb 209 D3
Birkby NYorks 202 C3
Birkdale Mersey 183 E1
Birkdale NYorks 201 D2
Birkenhead 183 E4
Birkenhills 269 F6
Birkenshaw 194 B5
Birkhall 260 B5
Birkhill Angus 244 B1
Birkhill ScBord 236 B5
Birkhill ScBord 226 D4
Birkholme 175 E5
Birkin 195 E5
Birks 194 B5
Birkwood 225 G2
Birley 145 D2
Birley Carr 186 A3
Birling Kent 123 F2
Birling N'umb 221 E1
Birling Gap 110 A4
Birlingham 146 B3
Birmingham 158 C4
Birmingham Botanical
 Gardens WMid
 B15 3TR 34 B7
Birmingham City Museum
 & Art Gallery WMid
 B3 3DH 35 A4
Birmingham International
 Airport 159 D4
Birnam 251 F5
Birsay 276 B5 Birse
 260 D5
Birsemore 260 D5
Birstall 160 A2
Birstall Smithies 194 B5
Birstwith 194 B2

Birthorpe 175 G4
Birtle 184 C1
Birtley Here 144 C1
Birtley N'umb 220 A4
Birtley T&W 212 B2
Birts Street 145 G4
Birtsmorton 146 A4
Bisbrooke 161 D3
Biscathorpe 188 C4
Bish Mill 114 A5
Bisham 135 D4
Bishampton 146 B2
Bishop Auckland 212 B5
Bishop Burton 196 B3
Bishop Middleham 212 C4
Bishop Monkton 194 C1
Bishop Norton 187 G3
Bishop Thornton 194 B1
Bishop Wilton 195 G2
Bishopbridge 188 A3
Bishopbriggs 234 A2
Bishopmill 267 K5
Bishops Cannings 118 B1
Bishop's Castle 156 C4
Bishop's Caundle 104 C1
Bishop's Cleeve 146 B5
Bishop's Frome 145 F3
Bishops Gate 135 E5
Bishop's Green
 Essex 137 F1
Bishop's Green
 Hants 119 G1
Bishop's Hull 115 F5
Bishop's Itchington 147 F2
Bishops Lydeard 115 E5
Bishop's Norton 146 A5
Bishops Nympton 114 A5
Bishop's Offley 171 E5
Bishop's Stortford 150 C5
Bishop's Sutton 120 B4
Bishop's Tachbrook 147 F1
Bishop's Tawton 113 F2
Bishop's Waltham 107 E1
Bishop's Wood 158 A2
Bishopsbourne 125 D3
Bishopsteignton 102 C5
Bishopston Bristol 131 E5
Bishopston Swan 128 B4
Bishopstone Bucks 135 D1
Bishopstone ESuss 109 G3
Bishopstone Here 144 D3
Bishopstone Swin 133 E4
Bishopstone Wilts 118 B5
Bishopstrow 117 F3
Bishopswood 103 F1
Bishopsworth 116 C1
Bishopthorpe 195 E3
Bishopton Darl 212 C5
Bishopton NYorks 202 B5
Bishopton Renf 233 F2
Bishopton Warks 147 D2
Bishton 130 C4
Bisley Glos 132 B2
Bisley Surr 121 E2
Bispham 191 G4
Bispham Green 183 F1
Bissoe 96 B5
Bisterne 106 A2
Bisterne Close 106 B2
Bitchet Green 123 E3
Bitchfield 175 E5
Bittadon 113 F1
Bittaford 100 C2
Bittering 178 A4
Bitterley 157 E5
Bitterne 107 D1
Bitteswell 160 A4
Bitton 117 D1
Bix 134 C4
Bixter 279 C7
Blaby 160 A3
Black Bourton 133 E2
Black Bridge 126 C2
Black Callerton 212 A1
Black Carr 164 B2
Black Clauchrie 215 D2
Black Corries Lodge 249 E4
Black Country Living
 Museum WMid
 DY1 4SQ 14 B2
Black Crofts 240 B1
Black Cross 96 D3
Black Dog 102 B2
Black Heddon 220 C4
Black Hill 147 E2
Black Marsh 156 C2
Black Moor 194 B3
Black Mount 249 E4
Black Notley 151 F5
Blackacre 217 E1
Blackadder 237 F4
Blackawton 101 E2
Blackborough
 Devon 103 D2
Blackborough Norf 163 E1
Blackborough End 163 E1
Blackboys 110 A1
Blackbraes Aber 261 G3
Blackbraes Falk 234 D2
Blackbrook Derbys 173 E3
Blackbrook Leics 159 G1
Blackbrook Mersey 183 G3
Blackbrook Staffs 171 E4
Blackburn Aber 261 G3
Blackburn B'burn 192 C5
Blackburn NSom 195 G1
Blackburn WLoth 235 D3
Blackbushe 120 C2
Blackcastle 267 F6
Blackchambers 261 F3
Blackcraig D&G 215 F4
Blackcraig D&G 216 B2
Blackden Heath 184 B5

Blackdown Devon 99 F3
Blackdown Dorset 103 G2
Blackdown Warks 147 F1
Blacker Hill 186 A2
Blackfen 137 D5
Blackfield 106 D2
Blackford Aber 261 F1
Blackford Cumb 218 B5
Blackford P&K 243 D4
Blackford Som 116 B2
Blackford Som 116 B3
Blackford Bridge 184 C2
Blackfordby 159 F1
Blackgang Chine
 IoW PO38 2HN 107 D5
Blackhall Edin 235 G2
Blackhall Renf 233 F3
Blackhall Colliery 213 D4
Blackhall Mill 212 A2
Blackhall Rocks 213 D4
Blackham 123 E5
Blackhaugh 227 F2
Blackheath Essex 152 B5
Blackheath GtLon
 136 C5
Blackheath Suff 165 F4
Blackheath Surr 121 F3
Blackheath WMid
 158 B4
Blackhill Aber 269 J5
Blackhill Aber 269 J6
Blackhillock 268 C6
Blackhills 267 K6
Blackland 118 B1
Blacklands 118 B4
Blackleach 192 A4
Blackley 184 C2
Blacklunans 251 G3
Blackmill 129 F4
Blackmoor Hants 120 C4
Blackmoor Som 103 E1
Blackmoor Gate 113 G1
Blackmoorfoot 185 E1
Blackmore 137 F2
Blackmore End
 Essex 151 F4
Blackmore End
 Herts 136 A1
Blackness Aber 260 E5
Blackness Falk 235 D2
Blackness High 275 H5
Blackness 120 C3
Blackney 104 A3
Blackno 96 C3
Blackpole 146 A2
Blackpool B'pool 191 G4
Blackpool Devon 101 E3
Blackpool Airport 191 G4
Blackpool Bridge 127 D1
Blackpool Gate 218 D4
Blackpool Piers B'pool
 FY4 1BB 191 G4
Blackpool Pleasure
 Beach B'pool
 FY4 1PL 191 G4
Blackpool Tower
 FY1 4BJ 64 Blackpool
Blackpool Zoo
 B'pool FY3 8PP 191 G4
Blackridge 234 C3
Blackrock A&B 230 B3
Blackrock Mon 130 B1
Blackrod 184 A1
Blackshaw 217 E4
Blackshaw Head 193 F5
Blacksmith's Green 152 C1
Blacksnape 192 D5
Blackstone 109 E2
Blackthorn 134 B1
Blackthorpe 152 A1
Blacktoft 196 A5
Blacktop 261 G4
Blacktown 130 B4
Blackwater Corn 96 B5
Blackwater Hants 120 D2
Blackwater IoW 107 E4
Blackwater Norf 178 B3
Blackwater Som 103 F1
Blackwaterfoot 223 E3
Blackwell Darl 202 B1
Blackwell Derbys 185 F5
Blackwell Derbys 173 F2
Blackwell Warks 147 E3
Blackwell Worcs 158 B5
Blackwell WSuss 122 C5
Blackwells End 145 G5
Blackwood (Coed-duon)
 Caerp 130 A3
Blackwood D&G 216 D2
Blackwood SLan 234 B5
Blackwood Hill 171 G2
Blacon 170 A1
Bladbean 125 D4
Bladnoch 215 F5
Bladon 133 G1
Blaen Clydach 129 F3
Blaenannerch 141 F3
Blaenau
 Dolwyddelan 167 F2
Blaenau Ffestiniog 167 F3
Blaenavon 130 B2
Blaenawey 130 B1
Blaencelyn 141 G2
Blaencwm 129 F2
Blaendyryn 143 F4
Blaenffos 141 E4
Blaengarw 129 F3
Blaengeuffordd 154 C4
Blaengweche 128 C1
Blaengwrach 129 E2
Blaengwynfi 129 E3
Blaenllechau 129 G3
Blaenos 143 D4
Blaenpennal 142 C1
Blaenplwyf 154 B5
Blaenporth 141 F3
Blaenrhondda 129 F2
Blaenwaun 141 F5
Blaen-y-coed 141 G5
Blagdon NSom 116 C2
Blagdon Torbay 101 E1
Blagdon Hill 103 F1
Blaguegate 183 F2
Blaich 248 C2
Blaina 130 A2
Blair 233 E5
Blair Atholl 251 D3

Blair Castle P&K
 PH18 5TL 251 D3
Blair Drummond 242 C5
Blair Drummond Safari &
 Adventure Park Stir
 FK9 4UR 242 C5
Blairannaich 241 F4
Blairbuie 232 C2
Blairgowrie 251 G5
Blairhall 235 E1
Blairhoyle 242 B4
Blairhullichan 241 G4
Blairingone 243 E5
Blairkip 224 D2
Blairlogie 242 D5
Blairmore A&B 232 C1
Blairmore High 266 E1
Blairmore High 272 D3
Blairnairn 233 D1
Blairnamarrow 259 K3
Blairpark 232 D4
Blairquhan 224 B5
Blairquhosh 233 G1
Blair's Ferry 232 A3
Blairshinnoch 268 E4
Blairvadach 233 D1
Blairydryne 261 F5
Blairythan Cottage 261 H2
Blaisdon 131 G1
Blake End 151 F5
Blake House Craft
 Centre Essex
 CM77 6RA 151 F5
Blakebrook 158 A5
Blakedown 158 A5
Blakelaw ScBord 228 B3
Blakelaw T&W 212 B1
Blakeley 158 A3
Blakelow 171 D2
Blakemere 144 C3
Blakemere Shopping
 Experience ChesW&C
 CW8 2EB 183 G5
Blakeney Glos 131 F2
Blakeney Norf 178 B1
Blakenhall
 ChesE 171 E3
Blakenhall WMid 158 B3
Blakeshall 158 A4
Blakesley 148 B2
Blakewell 113 F2
Blanchland 211 F2
Bland Hill 194 B2
Blandford Camp 105 F2
Blandford Forum 105 E2
Blandford St. Mary 105 E2
Blanefield 233 G2
Blanerne 237 F4
Blankney 175 F1
Blantyre 234 A4
Blar a' Chaorainn 248 D3
Blargie 258 D5
Blarglas 233 E1
Blarmachfoldach 248 C3
Blarnalearoch 265 H2
Blashford 106 A2
Blaston 160 D3
Blathaisbhal 262 D4
Blatherwycke 161 E3
Blawith 199 D4
Blaxhall 153 E2
Blaxton 187 D2
Blaydon 212 A1
Bleadney 116 B3
Bleadon 116 A2
Bleak Hey Nook 185 E2
Blean 124 D2
Bleasby Lincs 188 B4
Bleasby Notts 174 C3
Bleasby Moor 188 B4
Bleatarn 200 C1
Bleathwood
 Common 145 E1
Blebocraigs 244 C3
Bleddfa 144 B1
Bledington 147 E5
Bledlow 134 C2
Bledlow Ridge 134 C3
Blencarn 210 C4
Blencogo 209 E2
Blencow 210 A4
Blendworth 107 G1
Blenheim Palace Oxon
 OX20 1PX 133 G1
Blennerhasset 209 E2
Blervie Castle 267 H6
Bletchingdon 134 A1
Bletchingley 122 C3
Bletchley MK 149 D4
Bletchley Shrop 170 D4
Bletherston 141 D5
Bletsoe 149 F2
Blewbury 134 A4
Blickling 178 C3
Blickling Hall Norf
 NR11 6NF 178 C3
Blidworth 173 G2
Blidworth Bottoms 173 G2
Blindburn Aber 261 H1
Blindburn N'umb 228 C3
Blindcrake 209 E3
Blindley Heath 122 C4
Blisland 97 E2
Bliss Gate 157 G5
Blissford 106 A1
Blisworth 148 C2
Blithbury 172 B5
Blitterlees 209 E1
Blo' Norton 164 B4
Blockley 147 D4
Blofield 179 E5
Blofield Heath 179 E4
Blore 172 C3
Blossomfield 158 D5
Blount's Green 172 B4
Blowick 183 E1
Bloxham 147 G4
Bloxholm 175 F2
Bloxwich 158 B3
Bloxworth 105 E3
Blubberhouses 194 A2
Blue Anchor Corn 96 D4
Blue Anchor Som 114 D3
Blue Bell Hill 123 G2
Blue Planet Aquarium,
 Ellesmere Port
 ChesW&C
 CH65 9LF 183 F5

Blue Reef Aquarium
 ESuss TN34 3DW
 75 Hastings
Blue Reef Aquarium,
 Newquay Corn
 TR7 1DU 96 C3
Blue Reef Aquarium,
 Southsea Ports
 PO5 3PB 5 G6
Blue Reef Aquarium,
 Tynemouth T&W
 NE30 4JF 28 E1
Bluebell Railway WSuss
 TN22 3QL 109 F1
Bluewater 137 E5
Blundellsands 183 E3
Blundeston 165 G2
Blunham 149 G2
Blunsdon
 St. Andrew 132 D4
Bluntington 158 A5
Bluntisham 162 B5
Blunts 98 D4
Blurton 171 F3
Blyborough 187 G3
Blyford 165 F4
Blymhill 158 A1
Blymhill Common 157 G1
Blymhill Lawn 158 A1
Blyth N'umb 221 F3
Blyth Notts 186 D4
Blyth Bridge 235 F5
Blyth End 159 E3
Blythburgh 165 F4
Blythe Bridge 171 G3
Blythe Marsh 171 G3
Blyton 187 F3
Boarhills 245 D3
Boarhunt 107 F2
Boars Hill 133 G2
Boarsgreave 193 E5
Boarshead 123 E5
Boarstall 134 B1
Boarzell 110 C1
Boasley Cross 99 F1
Boat o' Brig 268 B5
Boat of Garten 259 G3
Boath 266 C4
Bobbing 124 A2
Bobbington 158 A3
Bobbingworth 137 E2
Bocaddon 97 F4
Bochastle 242 B4
Bocketts Farm Park
 Surr KT22 9BS 121 G2
Bockhampton 133 E3
Bocking 151 F5
Bocking
 Churchstreet 151 F5
Bockleton 145 E1
Boconnoc 97 F3
Boddam Aber 269 K6
Boddam Shet 279 F9
Bodden 116 D3
Boddington 146 A5
Bodedern 180 B4
Bodelwyddan 182 B5
Bodenham Here 145 E2
Bodenham Wilts 118 C5
Bodenham Moor 145 E2
Bodesbeck 226 C5
Bodewryd 180 C3
Bodfari 182 B5
Bodffordd 180 C5
Bodfuan 166 C4
Bodham 178 C1
Bodiam 110 C1
Bodiam Castle ESuss
 TN32 5UA 110 C1
Bodicote 147 G4
Bodieve 97 D2
Bodinnick 97 F4
Bodior 180 A5
Bodle Street Green 110 B2
Bodleian Library
 Oxon OX1 3BG
 80 Oxford
Bodmin 97 E3
Bodnant Garden Conwy
 LL28 5RE 181 G5
Bodney 163 G3
Bodorgan 166 C1
Bodrane 97 G3
Bodsham 124 D4
Bodwen 97 E3
Bodymoor Heath 159 D3
Bogallan 266 D6
Bogbain 266 E7
Bogbrae 261 J1
Bogbuie 266 C6
Bogend 224 B2
Bogfields 260 D4
Bogfold 269 F5
Boghall Aber 268 C5
Boghall SLan 234 B5
Boghole Farm 267 G6
Bogmoor 268 B4
Bogniebrae 268 D6
Bognor Regis 108 B4
Bograxie 261 F3
Bogroy 259 G2
Bogside 243 E5
Bogston 260 B4
Bogton 268 E5
Bogue 216 A2
Bohemia 106 B1
Bohenie 249 E1
Bohetherick 100 A1
Bohortha 95 F3
Bohuntine 249 E1
Boirseam 263 F3
Bojewyan 94 A3
Bokiddick 97 E3
Bolam Dur 212 A5
Bolam N'umb 220 C3
Bolam Lake Country
 Park N'umb
 NE20 0HE 220 C3
Boldon 212 C1
Boldon Colliery 212 C1
Boldre 106 C3
Boldron 201 F1
Bole 187 E4

Bolehill 173 D2
Boleigh 94 B4
Bolenowe 95 D3
Boleside 287 F2
Bolfracks 250 D5
Bolgoed 128 C2
Bolham Devon 102 C1
Bolham Notts 187 E4
Bolham Water 103 E1
Bolingey 96 B4
Bollington 184 D5
Bolney 109 E1
Bolnhurst 149 F2
Bolshan 253 E4
Bolsover 186 B5
Bolsterstone 185 G3
Bolstone 145 E4
Boltby 203 D4
Bolter End 134 C3
Bolton Cumb 210 C5
Bolton ERid 236 C2
Bolton ERid 195 G2
Bolton GtMan 184 B2
Bolton N'umb 229 F5
Bolton Abbey 193 G2
Bolton Abbey Estate
 NYorks
 BD23 6EX 193 G2
Bolton Bridge 193 G2
Bolton by Bowland 193 D3
Bolton Houses 192 A4
Bolton Low Houses 209 F2
Bolton Museum &
 Art Gallery GtMan
 BL1 1SE 184 B2
Bolton Percy 195 E3
Bolton Priory NYorks
 BD23 6EX 193 G2
Bolton upon
 Dearne 186 B2
Bolton Wood Lane 209 F2
Boltonfellend 210 A1
Boltongate 209 F2
Bolton-le-Sands 192 A1
Bolton-on-Swale 202 B3
Bolventor 97 F1
Bombie 208 A2
Bomere Heath 157 D1
Bonar Bridge 266 D2
Bonawe (Bun Atha) 240 C1
Bonby 188 A1
Boncath 141 F4
Bonchester Bridge 227 G4
Bonchurch 107 E5
Bondleigh 113 G5
Bonds 192 A3
Bonehill 159 D2
Bo'ness 235 D1
Bonhill 233 E2
Boningale 158 A2
Bonjedward 228 A4
Bonkle 234 C4
Bonning Gate 199 F3
Bonnington Edin 235 F3
Bonnington Kent 124 C5
Bonnybank 244 B4
Bonnybridge 234 C1
Bonnykelly 269 G5
Bonnyrigg 236 A3
Bonnyton Aber 260 E1
Bonnyton Angus 245 D1
Bonnyton Angus 253 E4
Bonnyton Angus 244 B1
Bonsall 173 D2
Bont 130 C1
Bont Dolgadfan 155 E2
Bont Newydd 168 A5
Bontddu 154 C1
Bont-goch (Elerch) 154 C4
Bonthorpe 189 E5
Bont-newydd
 Conwy 182 B5
Bontnewydd Gwyn 167 D1
Bontuchel 169 D2
Bonvilston 129 G5
Bon-y-maen 128 C3
Boode 113 F2
Boohay 101 F2
Booker 134 D3
Booley 170 C5
Boor 264 E3
Boorley Green 107 E1
Boosbeck 203 F1
Boose's Green 151 G4
Boot 198 C2
Boot Street 152 D3
Booth 193 G5
Booth Bank 185 E1
Booth Green 184 D4
Booth Wood 185 E1
Boothby Graffoe 175 E2
Boothby Pagnell 175 E4
Boothstown 184 B2
Boothville 148 C1
Booton 178 C3
Boots Green 184 B5
Booze 201 F2
Boquhan 233 G1
Boraston 157 F5
Bordeaux 101 G4
Borden Kent 124 A2
Borden WSuss 120 D5
Bordley 193 F1
Bordon 120 C4
Boreham Essex 137 G2
Boreham Wilts 117 F3
Boreham Street 110 B2
Borehamwood 136 A3
Boreland D&G 217 E2
Boreland D&G 215 E4
Boreland Stir 242 A1
Boreley 146 A1
Boreraig 263 G6
Borgh Na H-E. Siar 262 E3
Borgh Na H-E. Siar 254 B4
Borghastan 270 D3
Borgie 273 J3
Borgue D&G 207 G2
Borgue High 275 G5
Borley 151 G3
Borley Green Essex 151 G3
Borley Green Suff 152 A1
Bornais 254 C2
Borness 207 G2
Borniskitaig 263 J4
Borough Green 123 F3

Boroughbridge **194** C1
Borras Head **170** A2
Borrowash **173** F4
Borrowby *NYorks* **203** G1
Borrowby *NYorks* **202** D4
Borrowdale **209** F5
Borrowfield **261** G5
Borstal **123** G2
Borth **154** C4
Borthwick **236** A4
Borthwickbrae **227** F4
Borthwickshiels **227** F4
Borth-y-Gest **167** E4
Borve *High* **263** K7
Borve (Borgh)
    Na H-E. Siar **271** G2
Borwick **199** G5
Borwick Rails **198** C5
Bosavern **94** A3
Bosbury **145** F3
Boscarne **97** E3
Boscastle **98** A1
Boscastle Pottery *Corn*
    PL35 0HE **98** B1
Boscombe *Bourne* **106** A3
Boscombe *Wilts* **118** D4
Bosham **108** A3
Bosham Hoe **108** A3
Bosherston **126** C3
Bosley **171** G1
Bossall **195** G1
Bossiney **97** E1
Bossingham **125** D4
Bossington *Hants* **119** E4
Bossington *Som* **114** B3
Bostadh **270** D4
Bostock Green **171** D1
Boston **176** B3
Boston Spa **194** D3
Boswarthan **94** B3
Boswinger **97** D5
Bosworth Battlefield
    Country Park *Leics*
    CV13 0AD **159** G2
Botallack **94** A3
Botanic Garden
    Oxon OX1 4AZ
    80 Oxford
Botany Bay **136** C3
Botany Bay *Lancs*
    PR6 9AF **184** A1
Botcheston **159** G2
Botesdale **164** B4
Bothal **221** E3
Bothamsall **187** D5
Bothel **209** E3
Bothenhampton **104** A3
Bothwell **234** B4
Botley *Bucks* **135** E2
Botley *Hants* **107** E1
Botley *Oxon* **133** G2
Botloe's Green **145** G5
Botolph Claydon **148** C5
Botolphs **109** D3
Botolph's Bridge **124** D5
Bottacks **266** B5
Bottesford *Leics* **174** D4
Bottesford *NLincs* **187** F2
Bottisham **150** D1
Bottlesford **118** C2
Bottom Boat **194** C5
Bottom of Hutton **192** A5
Bottom o'th'Moor **184** A1
Bottomcraig **244** B2
Bottoms **193** E5
Botton Head **192** C1
Botusfleming **100** A1
Botwnnog **166** B4
Bough Beech **123** D4
Boughrood **144** A4
Boughspring **131** E3
Boughton *N'hants* **148** C1
Boughton *Norf* **163** F2
Boughton *Notts* **174** B1
Boughton Aluph **124** C4
Boughton Lees **124** C4
Boughton Malherbe **124** A4
Boughton
    Monchelsea **123** G3
Boughton Street **124** C3
Boulby **203** G1
Bouldnor **106** C4
Bouldon **157** E4
Boulge **153** D2
Boulmer **229** G5
Boulston **126** C1
Boultenstone Hotel **260** C3
Boultham **175** E1
Boundary *Derbys* **159** F1
Boundary *Staffs* **171** G3
Bourn **150** B2
Bourne **175** F5
Bourne End *Bucks* **135** D4
Bourne End
    CenBeds **149** E3
Bourne End *Herts* **135** F2
Bournebridge **137** E3
Bournemouth **105** G3
Bournemouth
    Airport **106** A3
Bournemouth International
    Centre BH2 5BH **64**
Bournemouth
Bournheath **158** B5
Bournmoor **212** C2
Bournville **158** C4
Bourton *Bucks* **148** C4
Bourton *Dorset* **117** E4
Bourton *NSom* **116** A1
Bourton *Oxon* **133** E4
Bourton *Shrop* **157** E3
Bourton *Wilts* **118** B1
Bourton on
    Dunsmore **159** G5
Bourton-on-the-Hill **147** D4
Bourton-on-
    the-Water **147** D5
Bousd **246** B2
Boustead Hill **209** F1
Bouth **199** E4
Bouthwaite **202** A5
Bovain **242** A1
Boveney **135** E5
Boveridge **105** G1
Boverton **114** C1
Bovey Tracey **102** B5
Bovingdon **135** F2
Bovinger **137** E2

Bovington Camp **105** E4
Bow *Cumb* **209** G1
Bow *Devon* **102** A2
Bow *Devon* **101** E2
Bow *Ork* **277** C8
Bow Brickhill **149** E4
Bow of Fife **244** B3
Bow Street *Cere* **154** C4
Bow Street *Norf* **164** B2
Bowbank **211** F5
Bowburn **212** C4
Bowcombe **107** D4
Bowd **103** E3
Bowden *Devon* **101** E3
Bowden *ScBord* **227** G2
Bowden Hill **118** A1
Bowdon **184** B4
Bower **219** F3
Bower Hinton **104** A1
Bower House Tye **152** A3
Bowerchalke **118** B5
Bowerhill **118** A1
Bowermadden **275** H2
Bowers **171** F4
Bowers Gifford **137** G4
Bowershall **243** F5
Bowertower **275** H2
Bowes **201** E1
Bowgreave **192** A3
Bowhousebog **234** C4
Bowithick **97** F1
Bowker's Green **183** F2
Bowland Bridge **199** F4
Bowley **145** E2
Bowley Town **145** E2
Bowlhead Green **121** E4
Bowling *WDun* **233** F2
Bowling *WYorks* **194** A4
Bowling Bank **170** A3
Bowlish **116** B3
Bowmanstead **199** E3
Bowmore **230** B3
Bowness-on-
    Solway **218** A5
Bowness-on-
    Windermere **199** F3
Bowood House &
    Gardens *Wilts*
    SN11 0LZ **118** A1
Bowscale **209** G3
Bowsden **237** G5
Bowside Lodge **274** D2
Bowston **199** F3
Bowthorpe **178** C5
Bowtrees **234** D1
Box *Glos* **132** A2
Box *Wilts* **117** F1
Box End **149** F3
Boxbush *Glos* **131** G1
Boxbush *Glos* **145** F5
Boxford *Suff* **152** A3
Boxford *WBerks* **133** G5
Boxgrove **108** B3
Boxley **123** G3
Boxmoor **135** F2
Box's Shop **112** C5
Boxted *Essex* **152** A4
Boxted *Suff* **151** G2
Boxted Cross **152** A4
Boxwell **132** A3
Boxworth **150** B1
Boxworth End **150** B1
Boyden Gate **125** E2
Boydston **224** C2
Boylestone **172** C4
Boyndie **268** E4
Boynton **196** D1
Boys Hill **104** C2
Boysack **253** E5
Boyton *Corn* **98** D1
Boyton *Suff* **153** E3
Boyton *Wilts* **118** A4
Boyton Cross **137** F2
Boyton End **151** F3
Bozeat **149** E2
Braaid **190** B4
Braal Castle **275** G2
Brabling Green **153** D1
Brabourne **124** D4
Brabourne Lees **124** C4
Brabster **275** J2
Bracadale **255** J1
Braceborough **161** F1
Bracebridge Heath **175** E1
Braceby **175** F4
Bracewell **193** E3
Brachla **258** C1
Brackenber **200** C1
Brackenbottom **200** D5
Brackenfield **173** E2
Brackens **269** F5
Bracklach **260** B2
Bracklamore **269** G5
Bracklesham **108** A4
Brackletter (A' Bhreac-
    Leitir) **249** D1
Brackley *A&B* **231** G1
Brackley *High* **267** F6
Brackley *N'hants* **148** A4
Brackley Gate **173** E3
Brackley Hatch **148** B3
Bracknell **121** D1
Braco **242** D4
Bracobrae **268** D5
Bracon Ash **164** C2
Bracora **256** D5
Bracorina **256** D5
Bradbourne **172** D2
Bradbury **212** C5
Bradda **190** A4
Bradden **148** B3
Braddock **97** F3
Bradenham *Bucks* **134** D3
Bradenham *Norf* **178** A5
Bradenstoke **132** C5
Bradfield *Devon* **103** D2
Bradfield *Essex* **152** C4
Bradfield *Norf* **179** D2
Bradfield *WBerks* **134** B5
Bradfield Combust **151** G2
Bradfield Green **171** D2
Bradfield Heath **152** C5
Bradfield St. Clare **152** A2
Bradfield St. George **152** A1
Bradfield Southend
    (Southend) **134** A5
Bradford *Corn* **97** F2
Bradford *Derbys* **172** D1

Bradford *Devon* **113** E5
Bradford *N'umb* **229** F3
Bradford *N'umb* **220** C4
Bradford *WYorks* **194** A4
Bradford Abbas **104** B1
Bradford Cathedral
    Church of St. Peter
    WYorks BD1 4EH
    65 Bradford
Bradford Leigh **117** F1
Bradford Peverell **104** C3
Bradford-on-Avon **117** F1
Bradford-on-Tone **115** E5
Bradgate Park *Leics*
    LE6 0HE **17** B3
Bradiford **113** F2
Brading **107** F4
Bradley *ChesW&C* **183** G5
Bradley *Derbys* **172** D3
Bradley *Hants* **120** B3
Bradley *NELincs* **188** C2
Bradley (Low Bradley)
    NYorks **193** G3
Bradley *Staffs* **158** A1
Bradley *WMid* **158** B3
Bradley Fold **184** B2
Bradley Green
    Warks **159** E2
Bradley Green
    Worcs **146** B1
Bradley in the
    Moors **172** B3
Bradley Mills **185** F1
Bradley Stoke **131** F4
Bradmore *Notts* **173** G4
Bradmore *WMid* **158** A3
Bradney **116** A4
Bradninch **102** D2
Bradnop **172** B2
Bradnor Green **144** B2
Bradpole **104** A3
Bradshaw *GtMan* **184** B1
Bradshaw *WYorks* **193** G4
Bradstone **99** D2
Bradwall Green **171** E1
Bradwell *Derbys* **185** F4
Bradwell *Devon* **113** E1
Bradwell *Essex* **151** G5
Bradwell *MK* **148** D4
Bradwell *Norf* **179** G5
Bradwell Grove **133** E2
Bradwell Waterside **138** C2
Bradwell-on-Sea **138** D2
Bradworthy **112** D4
Brae *D&G* **216** C3
Brae *High* **266** B1
Brae *Shet* **279** C6
Brae of Achnahaird **272** C7
Braeantra **266** C4
Braedownie **252** A2
Braefoot **269** F6
Braegrum **243** F2
Braehead *D&G* **215** F5
Braehead *Glas* **233** G3
Braehead *Moray* **268** B6
Braehead *Ork* **277** E7
Braehead *Ork* **276** D3
Braehead *SLan* **225** G2
Braehead *SLan* **235** D4
Braehead of Lunan **253** E4
Braehoulland **278** B5
Braelangwell **266** C2
Braeleny **242** B3
Braemar **259** J5
Braemore *High* **266** C1
Braemore *High* **275** F5
Braemore *High* **265** H4
Braenaloin **259** K5
Braes of Enzie **268** B5
Braes of Foss **250** C4
Braes of Ullapool
    (Bruthaichean Ullapuil)
    265 K2
Braeswick **276** F4
Braeval **242** A4
Braewick **279** C7
Brafferton *Darl* **212** B5
Brafferton *NYorks* **202** D5
Brafield-on-the-
    Green **148** D2
Bragar **270** E3
Bragbury End **150** A5
Bragenham **149** E5
Bragleenbeg **240** B2
Braichmelyn **167** F1
Braides **192** A2
Braidley **201** F4
Braidwood **234** C5
Braigo **230** A3
Brailsford **173** D3
Brain's Green **131** F2
Braintree **151** F5
Braiseworth **164** C4
Braishfield **119** E5
Braithwaite *Cumb* **209** F4
Braithwaite
    SYorks **186** D1
Braithwaite
    WYorks **193** G3
Braithwell **186** C3
Bramber **109** D2
Brambletye **122** D5
Brambridge **119** F5
Bramcote *Notts* **173** G4
Bramcote *Warks* **159** G4
Bramdean **120** B5
Bramerton **179** D5
Bramfield *Herts* **136** B1
Bramfield *Suff* **165** E4
Bramford **152** C3
Bramhall **184** C4
Bramham **194** C3
Bramhope **194** B3
Bramley *Hants* **120** B3
Bramley *Surr* **121** F3
Bramley *SYorks* **186** B3
Bramley Corner **120** B2
Bramley Head **194** A2
Bramley Vale **173** F1
Bramling **125** E3
Brampford Speke **102** C3
Brampton *Cambs* **162** A5
Brampton *Cumb* **210** B1
Brampton *Cumb* **210** B3
Brampton *Derbys* **186** A5
Brampton *Lincs* **187** F5
Brampton *Norf* **178** D3
Brampton *Suff* **165** F3
Brampton *SYorks* **186** B2

Brampton Abbotts **145** F5
Brampton Ash **160** C4
Brampton Bryan **156** C5
Brampton en le
    Morthen **186** B4
Brampton Street **165** F3
Brampton Valley Way
    Country Park *N'hants*
    NN6 9DG **160** C5
Bramshall **172** B4
Bramshaw **106** B1
Bramshill **120** C1
Bramshott **120** D4
Bramwell **116** B5
Bran End **151** E5
Branault **247** E3
Brancaster **177** F3
Brancaster Staithe **177** F3
Brancepeth **212** B4
Branchill **267** H6
Brand Green **145** G5
Brandelhow **209** F4
Brandon *Devon* **114** A3
Brandon *Devon* **113** D4
Brandon *Devon* **113** D5
Brandon *Dur* **212** B4
Brandon *Lincs* **175** E3
Brandon *N'umb* **229** E5
Brandon *Suff* **163** F4
Brandon *Warks* **159** G5
Brandon Bank **163** E3
Brandon Creek **163** E3
Brandon Parva **178** B5
Brandon Park *Suff*
    IP27 0SU **163** F4
Brandon to Bishop
    Auckland Walk *Dur*
    DH7 7RJ **212** B4
Brandsby **203** E5
Brandy Wharf **188** A3
Brane **94** B3
Branksome **105** G3
Branksome Park **105** G3
Bransbury **119** F3
Bransby **187** F5
Branscombe **103** E4
Bransford **145** G2
Bransford Bridge **146** A2
Bransgore **106** A3
Bransholme **196** D4
Branson's Cross **158** C5
Branston *Leics* **174** D5
Branston *Lincs* **175** F1
Branston *Staffs* **172** D5
Branston Booths **175** F1
Brant Broughton **175** E2
Brantham **152** C4
Branthwaite *Cumb* **209** F3
Branthwaite *Cumb* **209** D4
Brantingham **196** B5
Branton *N'umb* **229** E5
Branton *SYorks* **186** D2
Brantwood **199** E3
Branxholm
    Bridgend **227** F4
Branxholme **227** F4
Branxton **228** C3
Brassey Green **170** C1
Brassington **172** D2
Brasted **123** D3
Brasted Chart **123** D3
Brathens **260** E5
Bratoft **176** C1
Bratton *Som* **114** C3
Bratton *Tel&W* **157** F1
Bratton *Wilts* **118** A2
Bratton Clovelly **99** E1
Bratton Fleming **113** G2
Bratton Seymour **117** D5
Braughing **150** B5
Brauncewell **175** F2
Braunston *N'hants* **148** A1
Braunston *Rut* **160** D2
Braunstone **160** A2
Braunton **113** E2
Brawby **203** G5
Brawdy **140** B5
Brawith **203** E2
Brawl **274** D2
Brawlbin **275** F3
Bray **135** E5
Bray Shop **98** D3
Bray Wick **135** D5
Braybrooke **160** C4
Braydon Side **132** C4
Brayford **113** G2
Brayshaw **193** E3
Braythorn **194** B3
Brayton **195** F4
Braywoodside **135** D5
Brazacott **98** C1
Brea **96** A5
Breach *Kent* **125** D4
Breach *Kent* **124** A2
Breachwood Green **149** G5
Breacleit **270** D4
Breaden Heath **170** B4
Breadsall **173** E4
Breadstone **131** G2
Breage **94** D4
Breakon **278** E2
Bream **131** F2
Breamore **106** A1
Brean **115** F2
Breanais **270** B5
Brearton **194** C1
Breascleit **270** E4
Breaston **173** F4
Brechfa **142** B4
Brechin **253** E3
Brecklate **222** B4
Breckles **164** A2
Brecon
    (Aberhonddu) **143** G5
Brecon Beacons International
    Dark Sky Reserve
    Carmar./Powys **129** E1
Brecon Beacons Visitor
    Centre *Powys*
    LD3 8ER **143** F5
Breconside **225** G3
Bredbury **184** D3

Brede **110** D2
Bredenbury **145** F2
Bredfield **153** D2
Bredgar **124** A2
Bredhurst **123** G2
Bredon **146** B4
Bredon's Hardwick **146** B4
Bredon's Norton **146** B4
Bredwardine **144** C3
Breedon on the Hill **173** F5
Breibhig **271** G4
Breich **235** D3
Breightmet **184** B2
Breighton **195** G4
Breinton **145** D4
Breinton Common **145** D4
Bremhill **132** B5
Bremhill Wick **132** B5
Brenachoille **240** C4
Brenchley **123** F4
Brendon *Devon* **114** A3
Brendon *Devon* **113** D4
Brendon *Devon* **113** D5
Brenkley **221** E4
Brent Eleigh **152** A3
Brent Knoll **116** A2
Brent Pelham **150** C4
Brentford **136** A5
Brentingby **160** C1
Brentwood **137** E3
Brenzett **111** F1
Brenzett Green **111** F1
Breoch **216** B5
Brereton **158** C1
Brereton Green **171** E1
Brereton Heath **171** F1
Breretonhill **158** C1
Bressay **279** E8
Bressingham **164** B3
Bressingham Common **164** B3
Bressingham Steam
    Museum & Gardens
    Norf IP22 2AA **164** B3
Bretby **173** D5
Bretford **159** G5
Bretforton **146** C3
Bretherdale Head **199** G2
Bretherton **192** A5
Brettabister **279** D7
Brettenham *Norf* **164** A3
Brettenham *Suff* **152** A2
Bretton *Derbys* **185** F5
Bretton *Flints* **170** A1
Bretton *Peter* **161** G2
Brevig **254** B5
Brewood **158** A2
Briach **267** H6
Briantspuddle **105** E3
Brick End **151** D5
Brickendon **136** C2
Bricket Wood **136** A2
Brickfields Horse Country
    IoW PO33 3TH **107** E3
Brickkiln Green **151** F4
Bricklehampton **146** B3
Bride **190** C1
Bridekirk **209** E3
Bridell **141** E3
Bridestones **171** G1
Bridestowe **99** F1
Brideswell **260** D1
Bridford **102** B4
Bridge *Corn* **96** A5
Bridge *Kent* **125** D3
Bridge End *Cumb* **198** D4
Bridge End *Devon* **100** C3
Bridge End *Essex* **151** E4
Bridge End *Lincs* **175** G4
Bridge End *Shet* **279** C9
Bridge Hewick **202** C5
Bridge o'Ess **260** D5
Bridge of Alford **260** D3
Bridge of Allan **242** C5
Bridge of Avon **259** J1
Bridge of
    Bogendreip **260** E5
Bridge of
    Brewlands **251** G3
Bridge of Brown **259** J2
Bridge of Cally **251** G4
Bridge of Canny **260** E5
Bridge of Craigisla **252** A4
Bridge of Dee *Aber* **259** J5
Bridge of Dee *Aber* **260** E5
Bridge of Dee *D&G* **216** B4
Bridge of Don **261** H4
Bridge of Dun **253** E4
Bridge of Dye **253** E1
Bridge of Earn **243** G3
Bridge of Ericht **250** A4
Bridge of Feugh **260** E5
Bridge of Forss **275** F2
Bridge of Gairn **260** B5
Bridge of Gaur **250** A4
Bridge of Muchalls **261** H5
Bridge of Muick **260** B5
Bridge of Orchy (Drochaid
    Urchaidh) **241** E1
Bridge of Tynet **268** B4
Bridge of Walls **279** B7
Bridge of Weir **233** E3
Bridge Reeve **113** G4
Bridge Sollers **144** D3
Bridge Street **151** G3
Bridge Trafford **183** F5
Bridgefoot *Angus* **244** B1
Bridgefoot *Cambs* **150** C3
Bridgefoot *Cumb* **209** D4
Bridgehampton **116** C5
Bridgehaugh **260** B1
Bridgehill **211** F2
Bridgemary **107** E2
Bridgemere **171** E3
Bridgend *A&B* **230** B3
Bridgend *A&B* **240** A5
Bridgend *Aber* **260** D1
Bridgend *Aber* **269** F6
Bridgend *Angus* **252** D3
Bridgend (Pen-y-bont ar
    Ogwr) *Bridgend* **129** E5
Bridgend *Corn* **97** F4
Bridgend *Cumb* **199** F1
Bridgend *Fife* **244** B3
Bridgend *Moray* **260** B1
Bridgend *P&K* **243** G2

Bridgend *WLoth* **235** E2
Bridgend of
    Lintrathen **252** A4
Bridgerule **112** C5
Bridges **156** C3
Bridgeton *Aber* **260** D3
Bridgeton *Glas* **234** A3
Bridgetown *Corn* **98** D2
Bridgetown *Som* **114** C4
Bridgewater Hall,
    Manchester *GtMan*
    M2 3WS **46** Manchester
Bridgeyate **131** F5
Bridgham **164** A3
Bridgnorth **157** G3
Bridgnorth Cliff
    Railway *Shrop*
    WV16 4AH **157** G3
Bridgtown **158** B2
Bridgwater **115** F4
Bridlington **197** D1
Bridport **104** A3
Bridstow **145** E5
Brierfield **193** E4
Brierley *Glos* **131** F1
Brierley *Here* **145** D2
Brierley *SYorks* **186** B1
Brierley Hill **158** B4
Brierton **213** D5
Briestfield **185** G1
Brig o'Turk **242** A4
Brigg **188** A2
Briggate **179** E3
Briggswath **204** B2
Brigham *Cumb* **209** D3
Brigham *ERid* **196** C2
Brighouse **194** A5
Brighstone **106** D4
Brightgate **173** D2
Brighthampton **133** F2
Brightholmlee **185** G3
Brightling **110** B1
Brightlingsea **139** D1
Brighton *B&H* **109** F3
Brighton *Corn* **96** D4
Brighton Centre, The
    B&H BN1 2GR
    65 Brighton
Brighton City (Shoreham)
    Airport **109** D3
Brighton Museum &
    Art Gallery *B&H*
    BN1 1EE **65** Brighton
Brighton Pier *B&H*
    BN2 1TW **65** Brighton
Brightons **234** D2
Brightwalton **133** G5
Brightwalton Green **133** G5
Brightwell **152** D3
Brightwell Baldwin **134** B3
Brightwell
    Upperton **134** B3
Brightwell-cum-
    Sotwell **134** A3
Brignall **201** F1
Brigsley **188** C2
Brigsteer **199** F4
Brigstock **161** E4
Brill *Bucks* **134** B1
Brill *Corn* **95** E4
Brilley **144** B3
Brilley Mountain **144** B2
Brimaston **140** C5
Brimfield **145** E1
Brimington **186** B5
Brimington
    Common **186** B5
Brimley **102** B5
Brimpsfield **132** B1
Brimpton **119** G1
Brims **277** B9
Brimscombe **132** A2
Brimstage **183** E4
Brinacory **256** D5
Brindham **116** B3
Brindister *Shet* **279** D9
Brindister *Shet* **279** B7
Brindle **192** B5
Brindley Ford **171** F2
Brineton **158** A1
Bringhurst **160** D3
Brington **161** F5
Brinian **276** D5
Briningham **178** B2
Brinkhill **189** D5
Brinkley *Cambs* **151** E2
Brinkley *Notts* **174** C2
Brinklow **159** G5
Brinkworth **132** C4
Brinmore **258** D2
Brinscall **192** B5
Brinsea **116** B1
Brinsley **173** F3
Brinsop **144** D3
Brinsworth **186** B3
Brinton **178** B2
Brisco **210** A2
Brisley **178** A3
Brislington **131** F5
Brissenden Green **124** B5
Bristol **131** E5
Bristol Cathedral
    BS1 5TJ **66** Bristol
Bristol City Museum &
    Art Gallery *Bristol*
    BS8 1RL **8** B3
Bristol Filton
    Airport **131** E4
Bristol International
    Airport **116** C1
Bristol Zoo *Bristol*
    BS8 3HA **8** B3
Briston **178** B2
Britannia **193** E5
Britford **118** C5
Brithdir *Caerp* **130** A2
Brithdir *Gwyn* **155** D1
Brithem Bottom **102** D1
British Empire &
    Commonwealth Museum
    BS1 6QH **66** Bristol
British Library
    (St. Pancras) *GtLon*
    NW1 2DB **12** B4
British Museum *GtLon*
    WC1B 3DG **44** E2
Briton Ferry
    (Llansawel) **128** D3

Britwell **135** E4
Britwell Salome **134** B3
Brixham **101** F2
Brixton *Devon* **100** B2
Brixton *GtLon* **136** C5
Brixton Deverill **117** F4
Brixworth **160** C5
Brixworth Country Park
    N'hants
    NN6 9DG **160** C5
Brize Norton **133** E2
Broad Alley **146** A1
Broad Blunsdon **133** D3
Broad Campden **147** D4
Broad Carr **185** E1
Broad Chalke **118** B5
Broad Ford **123** G5
Broad Green
    Cambs **151** E2
Broad Green
    CenBeds **149** E3
Broad Green *Essex* **151** G5
Broad Green *Essex* **150** C4
Broad Green
    Mersey **183** F3
Broad Green *Suff* **152** B2
Broad Green *Worcs* **145** G2
Broad Haven **126** B1
Broad Hill **163** D5
Broad Hinton **132** D5
Broad Laying **119** F1
Broad Marston **146** D3
Broad Oak *Carmar* **142** B5
Broad Oak *Cumb* **198** C3
Broad Oak *ESuss* **110** D2
Broad Oak *ESuss* **110** B1
Broad Oak *Here* **145** D5
Broad Road **165** D3
Broad Street *ESuss* **111** D2
Broad Street *Kent* **124** A3
Broad Street *Kent* **124** C2
Broad Street *Wilts* **118** C2
Broad Street Green **138** C2
Broad Town **132** C5
Broadbottom **185** D3
Broadbridge **108** A3
Broadbridge Heath **121** G4
Broadclyst **102** C3
Broadfield *Lancs* **192** B5
Broadfield *Lancs* **192** B5
Broadford (An t-Ath
    Leathann) **256** D2
Broadford Airport **256** C2
Broadford Bridge **121** F5
Broadgate **198** C4
Broadhaugh **227** F4
Broadhaven **275** J3
Broadheath *GtMan* **184** B4
Broadheath *Worcs* **145** F1
Broadhembury **103** E2
Broadhempston **101** E1
Broadholme **187** F5
Broadlam Row **110** D2
Broadlay **127** G2
Broadley *Lancs* **184** C1
Broadley *Moray* **268** B4
Broadley Common **136** D2
Broadmayne **104** D4
Broadmeadows **227** F2
Broadmere **120** B3
Broadmoor **127** D2
Broadnymett **102** A2
Broadoak *Dorset* **104** A3
Broadoak *Glos* **131** F1
Broadoak *Kent* **125** D2
Broadoak End **136** C1
Broadrashes **268** C5
Broad's Green **137** F2
Broadsea **269** H4
Broadstairs **125** F2
Broadstone *Poole* **105** G3
Broadstone *Shrop* **157** E4
Broadstreet
    Common **130** C4
Broadwas **145** G2
Broadwater *Herts* **150** A5
Broadwater *WSuss* **108** D3
Broadwater Down **123** E5
Broadwaters **158** A5
Broadway *Carmar* **127** G2
Broadway *Carmar* **127** F1
Broadway *Pembs* **126** B1
Broadway *Som* **103** G1
Broadway *Suff* **165** E4
Broadway *Worcs* **146** D4
Broadwell *Glos* **147** E5
Broadwell *Oxon* **133** E2
Broadwell *Warks* **147** G1
Broadwell House **211** F2
Broadwey **104** C4
Broadwindsor **104** A2
Broadwoodkelly **113** G5
Broadwoodwidger **99** E2
Brobury **144** C3
Brocastle **129** F5
Brochel **264** B7
Brochloch **215** G1
Brock **246** B2
Brockamin **145** G2
Brockbridge **107** F1
Brockdish **164** D4
Brockenhurst **106** B2
Brockford Green **152** C1
Brockford Street **152** C1
Brockhall **148** B1
Brockham **121** G3
Brockhampton
    Glos **146** C5
Brockhampton
    Glos **146** B5
Brockhampton
    Here **145** E4
Brockhampton
    Here **145** F2
Brockhampton
    Green **104** D2
Brockholes **185** F1
Brockholes *Lancs* PR5 0AG
    192 B4
Brockhurst *Hants* **107** E2
Brockhurst *WSuss* **122** D5
Brocklebank **209** G2
Brocklesby **188** B1
Brockley *NSom* **116** A1
Brockley *Suff* **151** G2
Brockley Green **151** F3
Brock's Green **119** F1
Brockton *Shrop* **157** E3
Brockton *Shrop* **157** G2

Brockton *Shrop* 156 C2
Brockton *Shrop* 156 C4
Brockton *Tel&W* 157 G1
Brockweir 131 E2
Brockwood Park 120 B5
Brocton 158 B1
Brodick 223 F2
Brodsworth 186 C2
Brogborough 149 E4
Brogden 193 E3
Broguntyn 169 F4
Broken Cross
ChesE 184 C5
Broken Cross
ChesE 184 A5
Brokenborough 132 B4
Brokes 202 B3
Bromborough 183 E4
Brome *Suff* 164 C4
Brome Street 164 C4
Bromeswell 153 E2
Bromfield *Cumb* 209 E2
Bromfield *Shrop* 157 D5
Bromham *Bed* 149 F2
Bromham *Wilts* 118 A1
Bromley *GtLon* 122 D2
Bromley *SYorks* 186 A3
Bromley Cross 184 B1
Bromley Green 124 B5
Brompton *Med* 123 G2
Brompton *NYorks* 202 C3
Brompton *NYorks* 204 C4
Brompton *Shrop* 157 E2
Brompton on Swale 202 B3
Brompton Ralph 115 D4
Brompton Regis 114 C4
Bromsash 145 F5
Bromsberrow 145 G4
Bromsberrow
Heath 145 G4
Bromsgrove 158 B5
Bromstead Heath 158 A1
Bromyard 145 F2
Bromyard Downs 145 F2
Bronaber 168 A4
Brondesbury 136 B4
Brongest 141 G3
Bronington 170 B4
Bronllys 144 A4
Bronnant 142 C1
Brontë Weaving Shed
WYorks
BD22 8EP 193 G4
Bronwydd Arms 142 A5
Bronydd 144 B3
Bron-y-gaer 127 G1
Bronygarth 169 F4
Brook *Carmar* 127 F2
Brook *Hants* 106 B1
Brook *Hants* 119 E5
Brook *IoW* 106 C4
Brook *Kent* 124 C5
Brook *Surr* 121 E4
Brook *Surr* 121 F3
Brook Bottom 185 D2
Brook End *Bed* 149 F1
Brook End *Herts* 150 B5
Brook End *MK* 149 E3
Brook End *Worcs* 146 A3
Brook Hill 106 B1
Brook Street *Essex* 137 E3
Brook Street *Kent* 124 B5
Brook Street *Suff* 152 B3
Brook Street *WSuss* 109 F1
Brooke *Norf* 165 D2
Brooke *Rut* 160 D2
Brookend *Glos* 131 E3
Brookend *Glos* 131 F2
Brookfield 185 E3
Brookhampton 134 B3
Brookhouse *ChesE* 184 D5
Brookhouse *Denb* 169 D1
Brookhouse *Lancs* 192 B1
Brookhouse *SYorks* 186 C4
Brookhouse Green 171 F1
Brookhouses 171 G2
Brookland 111 E1
Brooklands *D&G* 216 C3
Brooklands *Shrop* 170 C3
Brooklands Museum *Surr*
KT13 0QN 121 F1
Brookmans Park 136 B2
Brooks 156 A3
Brooks Green 121 G5
Brooksby 160 B1
Brookside Miniature
Railway *ChesE*
SK12 1BZ 25 G6
Brookthorpe 132 A1
Brookwood 121 E2
Broom *CenBeds* 149 G3
Broom *Fife* 244 B4
Broom *Warks* 146 C2
Broom Green 178 A3
Broom Hill *Dorset* 105 G2
Broom Hill *Worcs* 158 B5
Broom of Dalreach 243 F3
Broomcroft 157 E2
Broome *Norf* 165 E2
Broome *Shrop* 156 D4
Broome *Worcs* 158 B5
Broome Wood 229 F5
Broomedge 184 B4
Broomer's Corner 121 G5
Broomfield *Aber* 261 H1
Broomfield *Essex* 137 G1
Broomfield *Kent* 125 D2
Broomfield *Kent* 124 A3
Broomfield *Som* 115 F4
Broomfleet 196 A5
Broomhall Green 170 D3
Broomhaugh 211 G1
Broomhead 269 H4
Broomhill *Bristol* 131 F5
Broomhill *N'umb* 221 E1
Broomielaw 201 F1
Broomley 211 G1
Broompark 212 B3
Broom's Green 145 G4
Brora 267 G1
Broseley 157 F2
Brotherlee 211 F4
Brothertoft 176 A3
Brotherton 195 D5
Brotton 203 F1
Broubster 275 F2
Brough *Cumb* 200 C1

Brough *Derbys* 185 F4
Brough *ERid* 196 B5
Brough *High* 275 H1
Brough *Notts* 174 D4
Brough *Ork* 277 C6
Brough *Shet* 279 E8
Brough *Shet* 278 D5
Brough *Shet* 279 E6
Brough *Shet* 278 E5
Brough Lodge 278 E3
Brough Sowerby 200 C1
Broughall 170 C3
Brougham 210 B5
Brougham Hall *Cumb*
CA10 2DE 210 B5
Broughton *Bucks* 134 D1
Broughton *Cambs* 162 A5
Broughton *Flints* 170 A1
Broughton *Hants* 119 E4
Broughton *Lancs* 192 B4
Broughton *MK* 149 D3
Broughton *N'hants* 160 D5
Broughton *NLincs* 187 G2
Broughton *NYorks* 203 G5
Broughton *NYorks* 193 F2
Broughton *Ork* 276 D3
Broughton *Oxon* 147 G4
Broughton *ScBord* 226 C2
Broughton *VGlam* 129 F5
Broughton Astley 160 A3
Broughton Beck 199 D4
Broughton Gifford 117 F1
Broughton Green 146 B1
Broughton Hackett 146 B2
Broughton in
Furness 198 D4
Broughton Mills 198 D3
Broughton Moor 209 D3
Broughton Poggs 133 E2
Broughtown 276 F2
Broughton in
Furness 198 D4
Broughty Ferry 244 C1
Browland 279 B7
Brown Candover 119 G4
Brown Edge *Lancs* 183 E1
Brown Edge *Staffs* 171 G2
Brown Heath 170 B1
Brown Lees 171 F2
Brown Street 152 B1
Brownber 200 C2
Browndown 107 E3
Brownheath 170 B5
Brownhill 269 G6
Brownhills *Fife* 244 D3
Brownhills *WMid* 158 C2
Brownieside 229 F4
Brownlow 171 F1
Brownlow Heath 171 F1
Brown's Bank 170 D3
Brownsea Island *Dorset*
BH13 7EE 105 G4
Brownshill 132 A2
Brownshill Green 159 F4
Brownsover 160 A5
Brownston 100 C2
Browston Green 179 F5
Broxa 204 C3
Broxbourne 136 C2
Broxburn *ELoth* 237 D2
Broxburn *WLoth* 235 E2
Broxholme 187 G5
Broxted 151 D5
Broxton 170 B2
Broxwood 144 C2
Broyle Side 109 G2
Bruachmary 267 F7
Bruan 275 J5
Bruera 170 B1
Bruern 147 E5
Bruernish 254 C4
Bruichladdich 230 A3
Bruisyard 153 E1
Bruisyard Street 153 E1
Brumby 187 G1
Brund 172 C1
Brundall 179 E5
Brundish *Norf* 165 E2
Brundish *Suff* 153 D1
Brundish Street 153 D1
Brunstane 210 A2
Brunswick Village 221 E4
Bruntingthorpe 160 B3
Bruntland 260 C2
Brunton *Fife* 244 B2
Brunton *N'umb* 229 G4
Brunton *Wilts* 118 D2
Brushfield 185 F5
Brushford *Devon* 113 G5
Brushford *Som* 114 C5
Bruton 117 D4
Bryanston 105 E2
Bryant's Bottom 135 D3
Brydekirk 217 F3
Brymbo 169 F2
Brymor Ice Cream *NYorks*
HG4 4PG 202 A4
Brympton 104 B1
Bryn *Caerp* 130 A3
Bryn *Carmar* 128 B2
Bryn *ChesW&C* 184 A5
Bryn *GtMan* 183 G2
Bryn *NPT* 129 E3
Bryn *Shrop* 156 B4
Bryn Bach Country
Park *BGwent*
NP22 3AY 130 A2
Bryn Gates 183 G2
Bryn Pen-y-lan 170 A3
Brynamman 128 D1
Brynberian 141 E4
Bryncae 129 F4
Bryncethin 129 F4
Bryncir 167 D3
Bryncoch *Bridgend* 129 F4
Bryn-côch *NPT* 128 D3
Bryncroes 166 B4
Bryncrug 154 C2
Bryneglwys 169 E3
Brynford 182 C5
Bryngwran 180 B5
Bryngwyn *Mon* 130 C2
Bryngwyn *Powys* 144 A3
Bryn-henllan 140 D4
Brynhoffnant 141 G2
Bryning 192 A4
Brynithel 130 B2
Brynmawr *BGwent* 130 A1

Bryn-mawr *Gwyn* 166 B4
Brynmelyn 156 A5
Brynmenyn 129 F4
Brynna 129 F4
Brynnau Gwynion 129 F4
Brynog 142 B2
Bryn-penarth 156 A2
Brynrefail *Gwyn* 167 E1
Brynrefail *IoA* 180 C4
Brynsadler 129 G4
Brynsaithmarchog 169 D2
Brynsiencyn 167 D1
Bryn-teg *IoA* 180 C4
Brynteg *Wrex* 170 A2
Bryn-y-cochin 170 A4
Brynygwenin 130 C1
Bryn-y-maen 181 G5
Buaile nam Bodach 254 C4
Bualadubh 262 C7
Bualintur 255 K2
Bualnaluib 264 E3
Bubbenhall 159 F5
Bubnell 185 G5
Bubwith 195 G4
Buccleuch 227 E4
Buchan 216 B4
Buchanan Castle 233 F1
Buchanhaven 269 K6
Buchanty 243 E2
Buchlyvie 242 A5
Buckabank 209 G2
Buckby Wharf 148 B1
Buckden *Cambs* 149 G1
Buckden *NYorks* 201 E5
Buckenham 179 E5
Buckerell 103 E2
Buckfast 100 D1
Buckfast Abbey *Devon*
TQ11 0EE 100 D1
Buckfastleigh 100 D1
Buckhaven 244 B5
Buckholm 227 F2
Buckholt 131 E1
Buckhorn Weston 117 E5
Buckhurst Hill 136 D3
Buckie 268 C4
Buckies 275 G2
Buckingham 148 B4
Buckingham Palace *GtLon*
SW1A 1AA 44 B6
Buckland *Bucks* 135 D1
Buckland *Devon* 100 D3
Buckland *Glos* 146 C4
Buckland *Hants* 106 C3
Buckland *Here* 145 E2
Buckland *Herts* 150 B4
Buckland *Kent* 125 F4
Buckland *Oxon* 133 F3
Buckland *Surr* 122 B3
Buckland Brewer 113 E3
Buckland Common 135 E2
Buckland Dinham 117 E2
Buckland Filleigh 113 E5
Buckland in the
Moor 102 A3
Buckland
Monachorum 100 A1
Buckland Newton 104 C2
Buckland Ripers 104 C4
Buckland St. Mary 103 F1
Buckland-tout-
Saints 101 D3
Bucklebury 134 A5
Bucklerheads 244 C1
Bucklers Hard 106 D3
Bucklesham 152 D3
Buckley (Bwcle) 169 F1
Buckley Green 147 D1
Bucklow Hill 184 B4
Buckman Corner 121 G5
Buckminster 175 D5
Bucknall *Lincs* 175 G1
Bucknall *Oxon* 148 A5
Bucknell *Shrop* 156 C5
Buckridge 157 G5
Buck's Cross 112 D3
Bucks Green 121 F4
Bucks Hill 135 F2
Bucks Horn Oak 120 D3
Buck's Mills 113 D3
Bucksburn 261 G4
Buckspool 126 C3
Buckton *ERid* 205 E5
Buckton *Here* 156 C5
Buckton *N'umb* 229 E3
Buckton Vale 185 D2
Buckworth 161 G5
Budbrooke 147 E1
Buddon 244 D1
Bude 112 C5
Budge's Shop 98 D5
Budlake 102 C2
Budleigh Salterton 103 D4
Budock Water 95 E3
Budworth Heath 184 A5
Buerton 171 D3
Bugbrooke 148 B2
Buglawton 171 F1
Bugle 97 E4
Bugthorpe 195 G2
Building End 150 C4
Buildwas 157 F2
Builth Road 143 G2
Builth Wells (Llanfair-
ym-Muallt) 143 G2
Bulby 175 F5
Bulcote 174 B3
Buldoo 274 E2
Bulford 118 C3
Bulford Camp 118 C3
Bulkeley 170 C2
Bulkington *Warks* 159 F4
Bulkington *Wilts* 118 A2
Bulkworthy 112 D4
Bull Bay
(Porth Llechog) 180 C3
Bull Green 124 B5
Bullbridge 173 E2
Bullbrook 121 D1
Bullen's Green 136 B2
Bulley 131 G1
Bullington 188 A5
Bullpot Farm 200 B4
Bulls Cross 136 C3
Bull's Green *Herts* 136 B1
Bull's Green *Norf* 165 F2

Bullwood 232 C2
Bulmer *Essex* 151 G3
Bulmer *NYorks* 195 F1
Bulphan 137 F4
Bulstone 103 E4
Bulverhythe 110 C3
Bulwark 269 H6
Bulwell 173 G3
Bulwick 161 E3
Bumble's Green 136 D2
Bun Abhainn
Eadarra 270 D7
Bun Loyne 257 J4
Bunacaimb 256 C5
Bunarkaig 249 D1
Bunbury 170 C2
Bunbury Heath 170 C2
Bunchrew 266 D7
Bundalloch 256 D7
Buness 278 F2
Bunessan 238 C2
Bungay 165 E3
Bunker's Hill 176 A2
Bunlarie 222 C2
Bunloit
(Bun Leothaid) 258 C2
Bunmhullin 254 C3
Bunnahabhain 230 C2
Bunny 173 G5
Buntait 257 K1
Buntingford 150 B5
Bunwell 164 C2
Bunwell Street 164 C2
Burbage *Derbys* 185 E5
Burbage *Leics* 159 G3
Burbage *Wilts* 118 D1
Burbage Common *Leics*
LE10 3DD 159 G3
Burchett's Green 134 D4
Burcombe 118 B4
Burcot *Oxon* 134 A3
Burcot *Worcs* 158 B5
Burcott 149 D5
Burdale 191 G1
Burdocks 121 F5
Burdon 212 C2
Burdrop 147 F4
Bure Valley Railway *Norf*
NR11 6BW 178 D3
Bures 152 A4
Bures Green 152 A4
Burfa 144 B1
Burford *Oxon* 133 E1
Burford *Shrop* 145 E1
Burg 246 C5
Burgate 164 B4
Burgates 120 C4
Burge End 149 G4
Burgess Hill 109 F2
Burgh 152 D2
Burgh by Sands 209 G1
Burgh Castle 179 F5
Burgh Heath 122 B3
Burgh le Marsh 176 C1
Burgh next
Aylsham 178 D3
Burgh on Bain 188 C4
Burgh St. Margaret
(Fleggburgh) 179 F4
Burgh St. Peter 165 F2
Burghclere 119 F1
Burghead 267 J5
Burghfield 120 B1
Burghfield
Common 120 B1
Burghfield Hill 120 B1
Burghill 145 D3
Burghwallis 186 C1
Burham 123 G2
Burland 170 D2
Burlawn 97 D3
Burleigh 121 E1
Burlescombe 103 D1
Burley *Hants* 106 B2
Burley *Rut* 161 D1
Burley *WYorks* 194 B4
Burley Gate 145 E3
Burley in
Wharfedale 194 A3
Burley Street 106 B2
Burley Woodhead 194 A3
Burleydam 170 D2
Burlingjobb 144 B2
Burlow 110 A2
Burlton 170 B5
Burmarsh 124 D5
Burmington 147 E4
Burn 195 E5
Burn Farm 253 E2
Burn Naze 191 G3
Burn of Cambus 242 C4
Burnage 184 C3
Burnaston 173 D4
Burnby 196 A3
Burncross 186 A3
Burndell 108 B3
Burnden 184 B2
Burnedge 184 D1
Burness 276 F3
Burneston 202 C4
Burnett 117 D1
Burnfoot *High* 274 D6
Burnfoot *P&K* 243 E4
Burnfoot *ScBord* 227 G4
Burnfoot *ScBord* 227 F4
Burnham *Bucks* 135 E4
Burnham *NLincs* 188 A1
Burnham Deepdale 177 G3
Burnham Green 136 B1
Burnham Market 177 G3
Burnham Norton 177 G3
Burnham Overy
Staithe 177 G3
Burnham Overy
Town 177 G3
Burnham Thorpe 177 G3
Burnham-on-
Crouch 138 C3
Burnham-on-Sea 116 A3
Burnhaven 269 K6
Burnhead *D&G* 215 G2
Burnhead *D&G* 216 C1
Burnhervie 261 F3
Burnhill Green 157 G2

Burnhope 212 A3
Burnhouse 233 E4
Burniston 204 D3
Burnley 193 E4
Burnmouth 237 G3
Burnopfield 212 A2
Burn's Green 150 B5
Burns National Heritage
Park *SAyr*
KA7 4PQ 224 B4
Burnsall 193 G1
Burnside *Aber* 261 F3
Burnside *Angus* 252 D4
Burnside *EAyr* 225 D4
Burnside *Fife* 243 G4
Burnside *Shet* 278 B5
Burnside *WLoth* 235 F2
Burnside of
Duntrune 244 C1
Burnstones 210 C2
Burnswark 217 F3
Burnt Hill 134 A5
Burnt Houses 212 A5
Burnt Oak 136 B3
Burnt Yates 194 B1
Burntcliff Top 171 G1
Burntisland 235 G1
Burnton *EAyr* 224 C4
Burnton *EAyr* 224 C5
Burntwood 158 C2
Burntwood Green 158 C2
Burnworthy 103 E1
Burpham *Surr* 121 F2
Burpham *WSuss* 108 C3
Burra 279 C9
Burradon *N'umb* 220 B1
Burradon *T&W* 221 E4
Burrafirth 278 F1
Burraland 278 C5
Burras 95 D3
Burraton *Corn* 100 A1
Burraton *Corn* 100 A2
Burravoe *Shet* 278 E5
Burravoe *Shet* 279 C6
Burray 277 D8
Burrell Collection
Glas G43 1AT 30 C4
Burrells 200 B1
Burrelton 244 A1
Burridge *Devon* 103 G2
Burridge *Hants* 107 E2
Burrill 202 B4
Burringham 187 F2
Burrington *Devon* 113 G4
Burrington *Here* 156 D5
Burrington *NSom* 116 B2
Burrough Green 151 E2
Burrough on the
Hill 160 C1
Burrow *Som* 114 C3
Burrow *Som* 104 A1
Burrow Bridge 116 A4
Burrowhill 121 E1
Burrows Cross 121 F3
Burry 128 A3
Burry Green 128 A3
Burry Port 128 A2
Burscough 183 F1
Burscough Bridge 183 F1
Bursea 196 A4
Burshill 196 C3
Bursledon 107 D2
Burslem 171 F3
Burstall 152 C3
Burstock 104 A2
Burston *Norf* 164 C3
Burston *Staffs* 171 G4
Burstow 122 C4
Burstwick 197 E5
Burtersett 201 D4
Burthorpe 151 F1
Burthwaite 210 A3
Burtle 116 B3
Burtle Hill 116 A3
Burton *ChesW&C* 183 E5
Burton *ChesW&C* 170 C1
Burton *Dorset* 106 A3
Burton *Lincs* 187 G5
Burton *N'umb* 229 F3
Burton *Pembs* 126 C2
Burton *Som* 115 E3
Burton *Wilts* 132 A5
Burton *Wilts* 117 F4
Burton Agnes 196 D1
Burton Bradstock 104 A4
Burton Coggles 175 E5
Burton End 150 D5
Burton Ferry 126 C2
Burton Fleming 205 D5
Burton Green
Warks 159 E5
Burton Green *Wrex* 170 A2
Burton Hastings 159 G4
Burton in Lonsdale 200 B5
Burton Joyce 174 B3
Burton Latimer 161 E5
Burton Lazars 160 C1
Burton Leonard 194 C1
Burton on the
Wolds 173 G5
Burton Overy 160 B3
Burton Pedwardine 175 G3
Burton Pidsea 197 E4
Burton Salmon 195 D5
Burton Stather 187 F1
Burton upon
Stather 187 F1
Burton upon Trent 172 D5
Burton-in-Kendal 199 G5
Burton's Green 151 G5
Burwardsley 170 C2
Burwarton 157 F4
Burwash 110 B1
Burwash Common 110 B1
Burwash Weald 110 B1
Burwell *Cambs* 151 D1
Burwell *Lincs* 189 D5
Burwen 180 C3
Burwick *Ork* 277 D9
Burwick *Shet* 279 C8
Bury *Cambs* 162 A4
Bury *GtMan* 184 C1
Bury *Som* 114 C5
Bury *WSuss* 108 C2
Bury End 146 C4
Bury Green 150 C5
Bury St. Edmunds 151 G1

Buryas Bridge 94 B4
Burythorpe 195 G1
Busbridge 121 E3
Busby *ERenf* 233 G4
Busby *P&K* 243 F2
Buscot 133 E3
Bush 112 C5
Bush Bank 145 D2
Bush Crathie 259 K5
Bush Green 164 D3
Bushbury 158 B2
Bushby 160 B2
Bushey 136 A3
Bushey Heath 136 A3
Bushley 146 A4
Bushley Green 146 A4
Bushton 132 C5
Bushy Common 178 A4
Busk 210 C3
Buslingthorpe 188 A4
Bussage 132 A2
Busta 279 C6
Butcher's Common 179 E3
Butcher's Cross 110 A1
Butcher's Pasture 151 E5
Butcombe 116 C1
Bute 232 B3
Bute Town 130 A2
Buthill 267 J5
Butleigh 116 C4
Butleigh Wootton 116 C4
Butler's Cross 134 D2
Butler's Hill 173 G3
Butlers Marston 147 F3
Butlersbank 170 C5
Butley 153 E2
Butley Low Corner 153 E3
Butley Mills 153 E3
Butley Town 184 D5
Butt Green 171 D2
Butt Lane 171 F3
Butterburn 219 E4
Buttercrambe 195 G2
Butterknowle 212 A5
Butterleigh 102 C2
Butterley 173 F2
Buttermere *Cumb* 209 E5
Buttermere *Wilts* 119 E1
Butters Green 171 F2
Buttershaw 194 A4
Butterstone 251 F5
Butterton *Staffs* 172 B2
Butterton *Staffs* 171 F3
Butterwick *Dur* 212 C5
Butterwick *Lincs* 176 B3
Butterwick *NYorks* 204 C5
Butterwick *NYorks* 203 G5
Buttington 156 B2
Buttonbridge 157 G5
Buttonoak 157 G5
Buttons' Green 152 A2
Butts 102 B4
Butt's Green *Essex* 137 G2
Butt's Green
Hants 119 D5
Buttsash 106 D2
Buxhall 152 B2
Buxted 109 G1
Buxton *Derbys* 185 E5
Buxton *Norf* 178 D3
Buxton Heath 178 C3
Buxworth 185 E4
Bwlch 144 A5
Bwlch-clawdd 141 G4
Bwlch-derwin 167 D3
Bwlchgwyn 169 F2
Bwlch-llan 142 B2
Bwlchnewydd 141 G5
Bwlchtocyn 166 C5
Bwlch-y-cibau 156 A1
Bwlch-y-ddar 169 E5
Bwlchyfadfa 142 A3
Bwlch-y-ffridd 155 G3
Bwlch-y-groes 141 F4
Bwlchyllyn 167 E2
Bwlchymynydd 128 B3
Bwlch-y-sarnau 155 G5
Byers Green 212 B4
Byfield 148 A2
Byfleet 121 F1
Byford 144 C3
Bygrave 150 A4
Byker 212 B1
Bylane End 97 G4
Bylchau 168 C1
Byley 171 E1
Bynea 128 B3
Byrness 219 F1
Bystock 102 D4
Bythorn 161 F5
Byton 144 C1
Bywell 211 G1
Byworth 121 E5

C

Cabharstadh 271 F5
Cabourne 188 B2
Cabourne Parva 188 B2
Cabrach *A&B* 230 C3
Cabrach *Moray* 260 B2
Cabus 192 A3
Cackle Street
ESuss 110 C2
Cackle Street
ESuss 109 G1
Cacrabank 227 E4
Cadbury 102 C2
Cadbury Barton 113 G4
Cadbury Heath 131 F5
Cadbury World *WMid*
B30 1JR 15 E5
Cadder 234 A2
Cadderlie 240 C1
Caddington 135 F1
Caddleton 239 G3
Cade Street 110 B1
Cadeby *Leics* 159 G2
Cadeby *SYorks* 186 C2
Cadeleigh 102 C2
Cader 168 D1
Cadgwith 95 E5

Cadham 244 A4
Cadishead 184 B3
Cadle 128 C3
Cadley *Lancs* 192 B4
Cadley *Wilts* 118 D1
Cadmore End 134 C2
Cadnam 106 B1
Cadney 188 A2
Cadole 169 F1
Cadover Bridge 100 B1
Cadoxton 115 E1
Cadoxton-Juxta-
Neath 129 D3
Cadwell 149 G4
Cadwst 168 D4
Cadzow 234 B4
Cae Ddafydd 167 F3
Caeathro 167 E1
Caehopkin 129 E1
Caen 275 F7
Caenby 188 A4
Caenby Corner 187 G4
Caer Llan 131 D2
Caerau *Bridgend* 129 E3
Caerau *Cardiff* 130 A5
Caerdeon 154 C1
Caerfarchell 140 A5
Caergeiliog 180 B5
Caergwrle 170 A2
Caerhun 181 F5
Caer-Lan 129 E1
Caerleon 130 C3
Caernarfon 167 D1
Caernarfon Castle *Gwyn*
LL55 2AY 167 D1
Caerphilly 130 A4
Caersws 155 G3
Caerwedros 141 G2
Caerwent 131 D3
Caerwys 182 C5
Caethle Farm 154 C3
Caggan 259 F2
Caggle Street 130 C1
Caim *High* 247 E3
Caim *IoA* 181 E4
Caio 142 C4
Cairisiadar 270 C4
Cairminis 263 F3
Cairnargat 260 C1
Cairnbaan 240 A5
Cairnbeathie 260 D4
Cairnbrogie 261 G2
Cairnbulg 269 J4
Cairncross *Angus* 252 D2
Cairncross *ScBord* 237 F3
Cairncurran 233 E3
Cairndoon 207 D3
Cairndow 241 D3
Cairness 269 J4
Cairney Lodge 244 B3
Cairneyhill 235 E1
Cairngorm Mountain *High*
PH22 1RB 259 G4
Cairnhill *Aber* 261 H2
Cairnhill *Aber* 260 E1
Cairnie *Aber* 261 G4
Cairnie *Aber* 268 C6
Cairnorrie 269 G6
Cairnryan 214 B4
Cairnsmore 215 F4
Caister-on-Sea 179 G4
Caistor 188 B3
Caistor St. Edmund 178 D5
Caistron 220 B1
Caithness Crystal Visitor
Centre *Norf*
PE30 4NE 163 E1
Cake Street 164 B2
Cakebole 158 A5
Calbost 271 G6
Calbourne 106 D4
Calceby 189 D5
Calcoed 182 C5
Calcot 134 B5
Calcott *Kent* 125 D2
Calcott *Shrop* 156 D1
Calcotts Green 131 G1
Calcutt 132 C3
Caldarvan 233 F1
Caldback 278 E3
Caldbeck 209 G3
Caldbergh 201 F4
Caldecote *Cambs* 150 B2
Caldecote *Cambs* 161 G4
Caldecote *Herts* 150 A4
Caldecote *N'hants* 148 B2
Caldecote Works 159 F3
Caldecott *N'hants* 149 E1
Caldecott *Oxon* 133 G3
Caldecott *Rut* 161 D3
Calder Bridge 198 B2
Calder Grove 186 A1
Calder Mains 275 F3
Calder Vale 192 B3
Calderbank 234 B3
Calderbrook 184 D1
Caldercruix 234 C3
Calderglen 234 A4
Calderglen Country Park
SLan G75 0QZ 31 E6
Caldermill 234 A5
Caldey Island 127 E3
Caldhame 252 C5
Caldicot 131 D3
Caldwell *Derbys* 159 E1
Caldwell *ERenf* 233 F4
Caldwell *NYorks* 202 A1
Caldy 182 D2
Calebreck 209 G3
Calford Green 151 E3
Calfsound 276 E4
Calgary 246 C4
Califer 267 H6
California *Falk* 234 D2
California *Norf* 179 G4
California *Suff* 152 D3
California Country Park
W'ham
RG40 4HT 120 C1
Calke 173 E5
Calke Abbey *Derbys*
DE73 7LE 173 E5
Callakille 264 C6
Callaly 220 C1
Callander 242 B4
Callanish (Calanais) 270 E4
Callaughton 157 F3

Callerton Lane End 212 A1
Calliburn 222 C3
Calligarry 256 C4
Callington 99 D4
Callingwood 172 C5
Callisterhall 218 A3
Callow 145 D4
Callow End 146 A3
Callow Hill Wilts 132 C4
Callow Hill Worcs 157 G5
Callow Hill Worcs 146 C1
Callows Grave 145 E1
Calmore 106 C1
Calmsden 132 C2
Calne 132 B5
Calow 186 B5
Calrossie 266 E4
Calshot 107 D2
Calstock 100 A1
Calstone Wellington 118 B1
Calthorpe 178 C2
Calthwaite 210 A3
Calton NYorks 193 F2
Calton Staffs 172 C2
Calveley 170 C2
Calver 185 G5
Calver Hill 144 C3
Calverhall 170 D4
Calverleigh 102 C1
Calverley 194 B4
Calvert 148 B5
Calverton MK 148 C4
Calverton Notts 174 B3
Calvine 250 C3
Calvo 209 E1
Cam 131 G3
Camasnacroise 248 A4
Camastianavaig 256 B1
Camasunary 256 B3
Camault Muir 266 C7
Camb 278 E3
Camber 111 E2
Camberley 121 D1
Camberwell 136 C5
Camblesforth 195 F5
Cambo 220 C3
Cambois 221 F3
Camborne 95 D3
Cambourne 150 B2
Cambridge Cambs 150 C2
Cambridge Glos 131 G2
Cambridge American Military Cemetery & Memorial Cambs CB23 7PH 150 B2
Cambridge International Airport 150 C2
Cambridge University Botanic Garden Cambs CB2 1JF 150 C2
Cambus 243 D5
Cambus o'May 260 C5
Cambusbarron 242 C5
Cambuskenneth 242 D5
Cambuslang 234 A3
Cambusnethan 234 C4
Camden Town 136 B4
Camel Hill 116 C5
Camel Trail Corn PL27 7AL 97 D2
Cameley 116 D2
Camelford 97 F1
Camelon 234 C1
Camelsdale 121 D4
Camer 123 F2
Cameron House 233 E1
Camerory 259 H1
Camer's Green 145 G4
Camerton B&NESom 117 D2
Camerton Cumb 208 D3
Camerton ERid 197 E5
Camghouran 250 A4
Camis Eskan 233 E1
Cammachmore 261 H5
Cammeringham 187 G4
Camore 266 E2
Camp Hill Pembs 127 E1
Camp Hill Warks 159 F3
Campbeltown (Ceann Loch Chille Chiarain) 222 C3
Campbeltown Airport 222 B3
Camperdown 221 E4
Camperdown Country Park Dundee DD2 4TF 244 B1
Campmuir 244 A1
Camps 235 F3
Camps End 151 E3
Camps Heath 165 G2
Campsall 186 C1
Campsea Ashe 153 E2
Campton 149 G4
Camptown 228 A5
Camquhart 232 A1
Camrose 140 C5
Camserney 250 D5
Camstraddan House 241 F5
Camus Croise 256 C3
Camus-luinie 257 F2
Camusnagaul High 248 C2
Camusnagaul High 265 G3
Camusrory 256 E5
Camusteel 264 D7
Camusterrach 264 D7
Camusurich 242 B1
Camusvrachan 250 B5
Canada 106 B1
Canaston Bridge 127 D1
Candacraig 260 B5
Candlesby 176 C1
Candy Mill 235 E5
Cane End 134 B5
Canewdon 138 B3
Canfield End 151 D5
Canford Bottom 105 G2
Canford Cliffs 105 G4
Canford Heath 105 G3
Canford Magna 105 G3
Canham's Green 152 B1
Canisbay 275 J1
Canley 159 F5
Cann 117 F5
Cann Common 117 F5
Canna 255 H4
Cannard's Grave 116 D3
Cannich (Canaich) 257 K1
Canning Town 136 D4
Cannington 115 F4
Cannock 158 B2
Cannock Wood 158 C1
Cannon Hall Country Park SYorks S75 4AT 185 G2
Cannon Hall Farm SYorks S75 4AT 185 G2
Cannon Hill Park WMid B13 8RD 15 E4
Cannop 131 F1
Canon Bridge 144 D3
Canon Frome 145 F3
Canon Pyon 145 D3
Canonbie 218 B4
Canons Ashby 148 A2
Canon's Town 94 C3
Canterbury Aber 268 D5
Canterbury Kent 124 D3
Canterbury Cathedral Kent CT1 2EH 67 Canterbury
Canterbury Tales, The Kent CT1 2TG 67 Canterbury
Cantley Norf 179 E5
Cantley SYorks 186 D2
Cantlop 157 E2
Canton 130 A5
Cantray 266 E7
Cantraydoune 266 E7
Cantraywood 266 E7
Cantsfield 200 B5
Canvey Island 137 G4
Canwell Hall 158 D2
Canwick 175 E1
Canworthy Water 98 C1
Caol 248 D2
Caolas A&B 246 B2
Caolas Na H-E. Siar 254 B5
Caolasnacon 248 D3
Capel Kent 123 F4
Capel Surr 121 G3
Capel Bangor 154 C4
Capel Betws Lleucu 142 C2
Capel Carmel 166 A5
Capel Celyn 168 B3
Capel Coch 180 C4
Capel Curig 168 A2
Capel Cynon 141 G3
Capel Dewi Carmar 142 A5
Capel Dewi Cere 154 C4
Capel Dewi Cere 142 A3
Capel Garmon 168 B2
Capel Gwyn Carmar 142 A5
Capel Gwyn IoA 180 B5
Capel Gwynfe 142 D5
Capel Hendre 128 B1
Capel Isaac 142 B5
Capel Iwan 141 F4
Capel le Ferne 125 E5
Capel Llanilltern 129 G4
Capel Mawr 180 C5
Capel Parc 180 C4
Capel St. Andrew 153 E3
Capel St. Mary 152 B4
Capel St. Silin 142 B2
Capel Seion 154 C5
Capel Tygwydd 141 F3
Capeluchaf 166 D3
Capelulo 181 F5
Capel-y-ffin 144 B4
Capel-y-graig 167 E1
Capenhurst 183 E5
Capernwray 199 G5
Capheaton 220 C3
Caplaw 233 F4
Capon's Green 153 D1
Cappercleuch 226 D3
Capplegill 226 C5
Capstone 123 G2
Capton Devon 101 E2
Capton Som 115 D4
Caputh 251 F5
Car Colston 174 C3
Caradon Town 97 G2
Carbellow 225 E3
Carbeth 233 G2
Carbis Bay 94 C3
Carbost High 263 K7
Carbost High 255 J1
Carbrain 234 B2
Carbrooke 178 A5
Carburton 186 D5
Carcary 253 E4
Carco 225 F4
Carcroft 186 C1
Cardenden 244 A5
Cardeston 156 C1
Cardew 209 G2
Cardiff (Caerdydd) 130 A5
Cardiff Bay Visitor Centre Cardiff CF10 4PA 7 C4
Cardiff Castle & Museum CF10 3RB 67 Cardiff
Cardiff Airport 115 D1
Cardiff Millennium Stadium CF10 1GE 67 Cardiff
Cardigan (Aberteifi) 141 E3
Cardinal's Green 151 E3
Cardington Bed 149 F3
Cardington Shrop 157 E3
Cardinham 97 F3
Cardno 269 H4
Cardonald 233 G3
Cardoness 215 G5
Cardow 267 J7
Cardrona 227 D2
Cardross 233 E2
Cardurnock 209 E1
Careby 161 F1
Careston 252 D4
Carew 126 D2
Carew Cheriton 126 D2
Carew Newton 126 D2
Carey 145 E4
Carfin 234 B4
Carfrae 236 C3
Carfraemill 236 C4
Cargate Green 179 E4
Cargen 217 D3
Cargenbridge 217 D3
Cargill 243 G1
Cargo 209 G1
Cargreen 100 A1
Carham 228 B3
Carhampton 114 D3
Carharrack 96 B5
Carie P&K 250 B4
Carie P&K 242 B1
Carines 96 B4
Carinish (Cairinis) 262 D5
Carisbrooke 107 D4
Carisbrooke Castle & Museum IoW PO30 1XY 107 D4
Cark 199 E5
Carkeel 100 A1
Carland Cross 96 C4
Carlatton 210 B2
Carlby 161 F1
Carlecotes 185 F2
Carleen 94 D4
Carleton Cumb 210 A2
Carleton Cumb 210 B5
Carleton Lancs 191 G3
Carleton NYorks 193 F3
Carleton WYorks 195 D5
Carleton Fishery 214 C2
Carleton Forehoe 178 B5
Carleton Rode 164 C2
Carleton St. Peter 179 E5
Carlin How 203 G1
Carlisle 210 A2
Carlisle Cathedral Cumb CA3 8TZ 68 Carlisle
Carlisle Park, Morpeth N'umb NE61 1YD 221 D3
Carloggas 96 C3
Carlops 235 F4
Carloway (Càrlabhagh) 270 E3
Carlton Bed 149 E2
Carlton Cambs 151 E2
Carlton Leics 159 F2
Carlton Notts 174 B3
Carlton NYorks 195 F5
Carlton NYorks 201 F4
Carlton NYorks 203 F4
Carlton Stock 212 C5
Carlton Suff 153 E1
Carlton SYorks 186 A1
Carlton WYorks 194 C5
Carlton Colville 165 G2
Carlton Curlieu 160 B3
Carlton Green 151 E2
Carlton Husthwaite 203 D5
Carlton in Lindrick 186 C4
Carlton Miniott 202 C4
Carlton Scroop 175 E3
Carlton-in-Cleveland 203 E2
Carlton-le-Moorland 175 E2
Carlton-on-Trent 174 D1
Carluke 234 C4
Carlyon Bay 97 E4
Carmacoup 225 F3
Carmarthen (Caerfyrddin) 142 A5
Carmel Carmar 128 B1
Carmel Flints 182 C5
Carmel Gwyn 167 D2
Carmel IoA 180 B4
Carmichael 226 A2
Carmont 253 G1
Carmunnock 233 G4
Carmyle 234 A3
Carmyllie 253 D5
Carn 230 A4
Carn Brea Village 96 A5
Carn Dearg 264 D4
Carnaby 196 D1
Carnach High 257 G2
Carnach High 265 G2
Carnach Na H-E. Siar 262 D5
Carnan 262 C7
Carnassarie 240 A4
Carnbee 244 D4
Carnbo 243 F4
Carndu 256 E2
Carnduncan 230 A3
Carnforth 199 F5
Carnhedryn 140 B5
Carnhell Green 94 D3
Carnichal 269 H5
Carnkie Corn 95 D3
Carnkie Corn 95 E3
Carnmore 230 B5
Carno 155 F3
Carnoch High 257 K1
Carnoch High 265 J6
Carnoch High 267 F7
Carnock 235 E1
Carnon Downs 96 C5
Carnousie 268 E5
Carnoustie 245 D1
Carntyne 234 A3
Carnwath 235 D5
Carnyorth 94 A3
Carol Green 159 E5
Carperby 201 F4
Carr 186 C3
Carr Hill 187 D3
Carr Houses 183 E2
Carr Shield 211 E3
Carr Vale 186 B5
Carradale 222 D2
Carragrich 263 G2
Carrbridge 259 G2
Carrefour Selous 100 C5
Carreglefn 180 B4
Carreg-wen 141 F3
Carrhouse 187 E2
Carrick 232 A1
Carrick Castle 241 D5
Carriden 235 E1
Carrine 222 B5
Carrington GtMan 184 B3
Carrington Lincs 176 B2
Carrington Midlo 236 A3
Carroch 216 A1
Carrog Conwy 168 A3
Carrog Denb 169 E3
Carroglen 242 C2
Carrol 267 F1
Carron A&B 240 B5
Carron Falk 234 C1
Carron Moray 267 K7
Carron Bridge 234 B1
Carronbridge 216 C1
Carronshore 234 C1
Carrot 252 C5
Carrow Hill 130 D3
Carrutherstown 217 F3
Carruthmuir 233 E3
Carrville 212 C3
Carry 232 A3
Carsaig 239 E2
Carscreugh 214 D4
Carse 231 F3
Carse of Ardersier 267 F6
Carsegowan 215 F5
Carseriggan 215 E4
Carsethorn 217 D5
Carsgoe 275 G2
Carshalton 122 B2
Carshalton Beeches 122 B2
Carsie 251 G5
Carsington 173 D2
Carsington Water Derbys DE6 1ST 172 D2
Carsluith 215 F5
Carsphairn 215 G1
Carstairs 234 D5
Carstairs Junction 235 D5
Carswell Marsh 133 F3
Carter's Clay 119 E5
Carterton 133 E2
Carterway Heads 211 G2
Carthew 97 E4
Carthorpe 202 C4
Cartington 220 C1
Cartland 234 C5
Cartmel 199 E5
Cartmel Fell 199 F4
Cartworth 185 F2
Carway 128 A2
Cascades Adventure Pool Devon EX33 1NZ 113 E2
Cascob 144 B1
Cashel Farm 241 G5
Cashes Green 132 A2
Cashlie 249 G5
Cashmoor 105 F1
Caskieberran 244 A4
Cassencarie 215 F5
Cassington 133 G1
Cassop 212 C4
Castell 168 A1
Castell Gorfod 141 F5
Castell Howell 142 A3
Castellau 129 G4
Castell-y-bwch 130 B3
Casterton 200 B5
Castle Acre 163 G1
Castle Ashby 149 D2
Castle Bolton 201 F3
Castle Bromwich 158 D4
Castle Bytham 161 E1
Castle Caereinion 156 A2
Castle Camps 151 E3
Castle Carrock 210 B2
Castle Cary 116 D4
Castle Combe 132 A5
Castle Donington 173 F5
Castle Douglas 216 B4
Castle Drogo Devon EX6 6PB 102 A3
Castle Eaton 132 D3
Castle Eden 212 D4
Castle Eden Dene National Nature Reserve Dur SR8 1NJ 212 D4
Castle End 159 E5
Castle Frome 145 F3
Castle Gate 94 B3
Castle Goring 108 D3
Castle Green 121 E1
Castle Gresley 159 E1
Castle Heaton 237 G5
Castle Hedingham 151 F4
Castle Hill Kent 123 F4
Castle Hill Suff 152 C3
Castle Howard NYorks YO60 7DA 195 G1
Castle Kennedy 214 C5
Castle Leod 266 B6
Castle Levan 232 D2
Castle Madoc 143 G4
Castle Morris 140 C4
Castle O'er 218 A2
Castle Rising 177 E5
Castle Semple Water Country Park Renf PA12 4HJ 233 E4
Castle Stuart 266 E7
Castlebay (Bàgh a'Chaisteil) 254 B5
Castlebythe 140 D5
Castlecary 234 B2
Castlecraig High 267 F5
Castlecraig ScBord 235 F5
Castlefairn 216 B2
Castleford 194 D5
Castlemartin 126 C3
Castlemilk D&G 217 F3
Castlemilk Glas 234 A4
Castlemorton 145 G4
Castlerigg 209 F4
Castleside 211 G3
Castlesteads 210 B1
Castlethorpe 148 C3
Castleton A&B 231 G1
Castleton Aber 269 F5
Castleton Angus 252 B5
Castleton Derbys 185 F4
Castleton GtMan 184 C1
Castleton Newport 130 B4
Castleton NYorks 203 F2
Castleton ScBord 218 D2
Castletown Dorset 104 C5
Castletown High 275 G2
Castletown High 266 E7
Castletown IoM 190 A5
Castletown T&W 212 C2
Castleweary 227 F5
Castlewigg 207 E2
Castley 194 B3
Caston 164 A2
Castor 161 G3
Castramont 215 G4
Caswell 128 B4
Cat & Fiddle Inn 185 E5
Catacol 232 A5
Catbrain 131 E4
Catbrook 131 E2
Catchall 94 B4
Catcleugh 219 F1
Catcliffe 186 B4
Catcott 116 A4
Caterham 122 C3
Catfield 179 E3
Catfirth 279 D7
Catford 136 C5
Catforth 192 A4
Cathays 130 A5
Cathcart 233 G3
Cathedine 144 A5
Catherine-de-Barnes 159 D4
Catherington 107 F1
Catherston Leweston 103 G3
Catherton 157 F5
Cathkin 234 A4
Catisfield 107 E2
Catlodge 258 D5
Catlowdy 218 C4
Catmere End 150 C4
Catmore 133 G4
Caton Devon 102 A5
Caton Lancs 192 B1
Caton Green 192 B1
Cator Court 99 G3
Catrine 224 D3
Catsfield 110 C2
Catsfield Stream 110 C2
Catshaw 185 G2
Catshill 158 B5
Cattadale 230 B3
Cattal 194 D2
Cattawade 152 B4
Catterall 192 B3
Catterick 202 B3
Catterick Bridge 202 B3
Catterick Garrison 202 A3
Catterlen 210 A4
Catterline 253 G2
Catterton 195 E3
Catteshall 121 E3
Catthorpe 160 A5
Cattishall 151 G1
Cattistock 104 B2
Catton N'umb 211 E2
Catton Norf 178 D4
Catton NYorks 202 C5
Catton Hall 159 E1
Catwick 196 D3
Catworth 161 F5
Caudle Green 132 B1
Caudwell's Mill & Craft Centre Derbys DE4 2EB 173 D1
Caulcott CenBeds 149 F3
Caulcott Oxon 148 A5
Cauldcots 253 E5
Cauldhame Stir 242 B5
Cauldhame Stir 242 D4
Cauldon 172 B3
Caulkerbush 216 D5
Caulside 218 C3
Caundle Marsh 104 C1
Caunsall 158 A4
Caunton 174 C1
Causeway End D&G 215 F4
Causeway End Essex 137 F1
Causeway End Lancs 183 F1
Causewayhead Cumb 209 E1
Causewayhead Stir 242 D5
Causey 212 B2
Causey Arch Picnic Area Dur NE16 5EG 28 A4
Causey Park 221 D2
Causeyend 261 H3
Cautley 200 B3
Cavendish 151 G3
Cavendish Bridge 173 F5
Cavenham 151 F1
Cavens 217 D5
Cavers 227 G4
Caversfield 148 A5
Caversham 134 C5
Caverswall 171 G3
Cawdor 267 F6
Cawkeld 196 B2
Cawkwell 188 C4
Cawood 195 E4
Cawsand 100 A3
Cawston Norf 178 C3
Cawston Warks 159 G5
Cawthorn 203 G4
Cawthorne 185 G2
Cawthorpe 175 F5
Cawton 203 F5
Caxton 150 B2
Caxton Gibbet 150 A1
Caynham 157 E5
Caythorpe Lincs 175 E3
Caythorpe Notts 174 B3
Cayton 205 D4
CC2000 Pembs SA67 8DD 127 D1
Ceallan 262 D6
Ceann a' Bhàigh Na H-E. Siar 262 C5
Ceann a' Bhàigh Na H-E. Siar 263 F3
Ceann Loch Shiphoirt 270 E6
Ceannaridh 262 D6
Cearsiadar 271 F6
Cedig 168 C5
Cefn Berain 168 C1
Cefn Canol 169 F4
Cefn Cantref 143 G5
Cefn Coch Denb 169 E2
Cefn Coch Powys 155 G2
Cefn Cribwr 129 E4
Cefn Cross 129 E4
Cefn Einion 156 B4
Cefn Hengoed 130 A3
Cefn Llwyd 154 C4
Cefn Rhigos 129 F2
Cefn-brith 168 C2
Cefn-caer-Ferch 166 D3
Cefn-coch 169 E5
Cefn-coed-y-cymmer 129 G2
Cefn-ddwysarn 168 C4
Cefndeuddwr 168 A5
Cefneithin 128 B1
Cefn-gorwydd 143 F3
Cefn-gwyn 156 A4
Cefn-mawr 169 F3
Cefnpennar 129 G2
Cefn-y-bedd 170 A2
Cefn-y-pant 141 E5
Ceidio 180 C4
Ceidio Fawr 166 B4
Ceint 180 C5
Cellan 142 C3
Cellardyke 245 D4
Cellarhead 171 G3
Cemaes 180 B3
Cemmaes 155 E2
Cemmaes Road (Glantwymyn) 155 E2
Cenarth 141 F3
Cennin 167 D3
Centre for Life T&W NE1 4EP 79 Newcastle upon Tyne
Ceramica Stoke ST6 3DS 20 C2
Ceres 244 C3
Cerist 155 F4
Cerne Abbas 104 C2
Cerney Wick 132 C3
Cerrigceinwen 180 C5
Cerrigydrudion 168 C3
Cessford 228 B4
Ceunant 167 E1
Chaceley 146 A4
Chacewater 96 B5
Chackmore 148 B4
Chacombe 147 G3
Chad Valley 158 C4
Chadderton 184 D2
Chadderton Fold 184 C2
Chaddesden 173 E4
Chaddesley Corbett 158 A5
Chaddleworth 133 G5
Chadlington 147 F5
Chadshunt 147 F2
Chadstone 149 D2
Chadwell Leics 174 C5
Chadwell Shrop 157 G1
Chadwell St. Mary 137 F5
Chadwick End 159 E5
Chaffcombe 103 G1
Chafford Hundred 137 F5
Chagford 102 A4
Chailey 109 F2
Chainhurst 123 G4
Chalbury 105 G2
Chalbury Common 105 G2
Chaldon 122 C3
Chaldon Herring (East Chaldon) 105 D4
Chale 107 D5
Chale Green 107 D4
Chalfont Common 135 F3
Chalfont St. Giles 135 E3
Chalfont St. Peter 135 F3
Chalford Glos 132 A2
Chalford Wilts 117 F3
Chalgrove 134 B3
Chalk 137 F5
Chalk End 137 F1
Challaborough 100 C3
Challacombe 113 G1
Challister 279 E6
Challoch 215 E4
Challock 124 C3
Chalmington 104 B2
Chalton CenBeds 149 F5
Chalton Hants 107 G1
Chalvey 135 E5
Chalvington 110 A3
Champany 235 E2
Chancery 154 B5
Chandler's Cross 135 F3
Chandler's Ford 119 F5
Channel Islands 100 A5
Channel's End 149 G2
Channerwick 279 D10
Chantry Som 117 E3
Chantry Suff 152 C3
Chapel 244 A5
Chapel Allerton Som 116 B2
Chapel Allerton WYorks 194 C4
Chapel Amble 97 D2
Chapel Brampton 148 C1
Chapel Chorlton 171 F4
Chapel Cleeve 114 D3
Chapel Cross 110 B1
Chapel End 149 F3
Chapel Green Warks 159 E4
Chapel Green Warks 147 G1
Chapel Haddlesey 195 E5
Chapel Hill Aber 261 J1
Chapel Hill Lincs 176 A2
Chapel Hill Mon 131 E2
Chapel Hill NYorks 194 C3
Chapel Knapp 117 F1
Chapel Lawn 156 C5
Chapel Leigh 115 E5
Chapel Milton 185 E4
Chapel of Garioch 261 F2
Chapel Rossan 206 B2
Chapel Row Essex 137 G2
Chapel Row WBerks 119 G1
Chapel St. Leonards 189 F5
Chapel Stile 199 E2
Chapel Town 96 C4
Chapelbank 243 F3
Chapeldonan 223 G5
Chapelend Way 151 F4
Chapel-en-le-Frith 185 E4
Chapelgate 176 C5
Chapelhall 234 B3
Chapelhill High 267 F4
Chapelhill P&K 244 A2
Chapelhill P&K 243 F1
Chapelknowe 218 B4
Chapel-le-Dale 200 C5
Chapelthorpe 186 A1
Chapelton Aber 253 G1
Chapelton Angus 253 E5
Chapelton Devon 113 F3
Chapelton SLan 234 A5
Chapeltown B'burn 184 B1
Chapeltown Cumb 218 C4
Chapeltown Moray 259 K2
Chapeltown SYorks 186 A3
Chapmans Well 99 D1
Chapmanslade 117 F3
Chapmore End 136 C1
Chappel 151 G5
Charaton 98 D4
Chard 103 G2
Chard Junction 103 G2
Chardleigh Green 103 G1
Chardstock 103 G2
Charfield 131 G3
Charing 124 B4
Charing Cross 106 A1
Charing Heath 124 B4
Charingworth 147 D4
Charlbury 133 F1
Charlcombe 117 E1
Charlecote 147 E2
Charles 113 G2
Charles Tye 152 B2
Charlesfield 227 G3
Charleshill 121 D3
Charleston 252 B5
Charlestown Aber 269 J4
Charlestown Aberdeen 261 H4
Charlestown Corn 97 E4
Charlestown Derbys 185 E3
Charlestown Dorset 104 C5
Charlestown Fife 235 E1
Charlestown GtMan 184 C2
Charlestown High 264 E4
Charlestown High 266 D7
Charlestown WYorks 194 A4
Charlestown WYorks 193 F5
Charlestown of Aberlour (Aberlour) 267 K7
Charlesworth 185 E3
Charleton 244 C4
Charlinch 115 F4
Charlotteville 121 F3
Charlton GtLon 136 D5
Charlton Hants 119 E3
Charlton Herts 149 G5
Charlton N'hants 148 A4
Charlton N'umb 220 A3
Charlton Oxon 133 G4
Charlton Som 117 D2
Charlton Som 116 D3
Charlton Som 115 F5
Charlton Tel&W 157 E1
Charlton Wilts 118 A5
Charlton Wilts 132 B4
Charlton Wilts 118 C2
Charlton Worcs 146 C3
Charlton WSuss 108 A2
Charlton Abbots 146 C5
Charlton Adam 116 C5
Charlton Down 104 C3
Charlton Horethorne 117 D5
Charlton Kings 146 B5
Charlton Mackrell 116 C5
Charlton Marshall 105 E2
Charlton Musgrove 117 E5
Charlton on the Hill 105 E2
Charlton-All-Saints 118 C5
Charlton-on-Otmoor 134 A1
Charltons 203 F1
Charlwood 122 B4
Charminster 104 C3
Charmouth 103 G3
Charndon 148 B5
Charney Bassett 133 F3
Charnock Richard 183 G1
Charsfield 153 D2
Chart Corner 123 G4
Chart Sutton 124 A4
Charter Alley 119 G2
Charterhouse 116 B2
Charterville Allotments 133 F2
Chartham 124 D3
Chartham Hatch 124 D3
Chartridge 135 E2
Chartwell Kent TN16 1PS 123 D3
Charvil 134 C5
Charwelton 148 A2
Chase End Street 145 G4
Chase Terrace 158 C2
Chasetown 158 C2
Chastleton 147 E5
Chasty 112 D5
Chatburn 193 D3
Chatcull 171 E4
Chatelherault Country Park SLan ML3 7UE 31 G6
Chatham 123 G2
Chatham Green 137 G1
Chatham Historic Dockyard Med ME4 4TZ 123 G2
Chathill 229 F4
Chatsworth Farmyard & Adventure Playground Derbys DE45 1PP 185 G5
Chatsworth House Derbys DE45 1PP 185 G5
Chattenden 137 G5
Chatteris 162 B4
Chattisham 152 B3
Chatto 228 B5
Chatton 229 E4
Chaul End 149 F5
Chavey Down 121 D1
Chawleigh 102 A1
Chawley 133 G2
Chawston 149 G2
Chawton 120 C4
Chazey Heath 134 B5
Cheadle GtMan 184 C4
Cheadle Staffs 172 B3
Cheadle Heath 184 C4
Cheadle Hulme 184 C4
Cheam 122 B2
Cheapside 121 E1

Chearsley 134 C1
Chebsey 171 F5
Checkendon 134 B4
Checkley ChesE 171 E3
Checkley Here 145 E4
Checkley Staffs 172 B4
Checkley Green 171 E3
Chedburgh 151 F2
Cheddar 116 B2
Cheddar Caves & Gorge Som BS27 3QF 116 B2
Cheddington 135 E1
Cheddleton 171 G2
Cheddon Fitzpaine 115 F5
Chedglow 132 B3
Chedgrave 165 E2
Chedington 104 A2
Chediston 165 E4
Chediston Green 165 E4
Chedworth 132 C1
Chedzoy 116 A4
Cheesden 184 C1
Cheeseman's Green 124 C5
Cheetham Hill 184 C2
Cheglinch 113 F1
Cheldon 102 A1
Chelford 184 C5
Chellaston 173 E4
Chells 150 A5
Chelmarsh 157 G4
Chelmondiston 152 D4
Chelmorton 172 C1
Chelmsford 137 G2
Chelmsford Cathedral Essex CM1 1TY 137 G2
Chelmsley Wood 159 D4
Chelsea 136 B5
Chelsfield 123 D2
Chelsham 122 C3
Chelston Heath 115 E5
Chelsworth 152 A3
Cheltenham 146 B5
Chelveston 149 E1
Chelvey 116 B1
Chelwood 116 D1
Chelwood Common 109 G1
Chelwood Gate 109 G1
Chelworth 132 B3
Cheney Longville 156 D4
Chenies 135 F3
Chepstow (Cas-gwent) 131 E3
Cherhill 132 C5
Cherington Glos 132 B3
Cherington Warks 147 E4
Cheriton Devon 114 A3
Cheriton Hants 119 G5
Cheriton Kent 125 D5
Cheriton Pembs 126 C3
Cheriton Swan 128 A3
Cheriton Bishop 102 A3
Cheriton Cross 102 A3
Cheriton Fitzpaine 102 B2
Cherrington 171 D3
Cherry Burton 196 B3
Cherry Green 151 D5
Cherry Hinton 150 C2
Cherry Willingham 188 A5
Chertsey 121 F1
Cheselbourne 105 D3
Chesham 135 E2
Chesham Bois 135 E2
Cheshire Farm Ice Cream, Tattenhall ChesW&C CH3 9NE 170 B2
Cheshunt 136 C2
Cheslyn Hay 158 B2
Chessington 121 G1
Chessington World of Adventures GtLon KT9 2NE 121 G1
Chestall 158 C1
Chester 170 B1
Chester Cathedral ChesW&C CH1 2HU 69 Chester
Chester Moor 212 B3
Chester Zoo ChesW&C CH2 1LH 183 F5
Chesterblade 117 D3
Chesterfield Derbys 186 A5
Chesterfield Staffs 158 D2
Chesters ScBord 228 A3
Chesters ScBord 228 A4
Chesterton Cambs 150 C1
Chesterton Cambs 161 G3
Chesterton Oxon 148 A5
Chesterton Shrop 157 G3
Chesterton Staffs 171 F3
Chesterton Warks 147 F2
Chesterton Green 147 F2
Chestfield 124 D2
Cheston 100 C2
Cheswardine 171 E5
Cheswick 229 F3
Cheswick Buildings 229 F2
Cheswick Green 158 D5
Chetnole 104 C2
Chettiscombe 102 C1
Chettisham 162 D4
Chettle 105 F1
Chetton 157 F3
Chetwode 148 B5
Chetwynd Aston 157 G1
Chetwynd Park 171 E5
Cheveley 151 E1
Chevening 123 D3
Cheverell's Green 135 F1
Chevin Forest Park WYorks LS21 3JL 194 B3
Chevington 151 F2
Chevithorne 102 C1
Chew Magna 116 C1
Chew Moor 184 A2
Chew Stoke 116 C1
Chewton Keynsham 116 D1
Chewton Mendip 116 C2
Chichacott 99 F1
Chicheley 149 E3
Chichester 108 A3
Chichester Cathedral WSuss PO19 1PX 108 A3
Chickerell 104 C4
Chickering 164 D4
Chicklade 118 A4

Chickney 151 D5
Chicksands 149 G4
Chidden 107 F1
Chidden Holt 107 F1
Chiddingfold 121 E4
Chiddingly 110 A2
Chiddingstone 123 D4
Chiddingstone Causeway 123 E4
Chiddingstone Hoath 123 D4
Chideock 104 A3
Chidham 107 G2
Chidswell 194 B5
Chieveley 133 G5
Chignall St. James 137 F2
Chignall Smealy 137 F1
Chigwell 136 D3
Chigwell Row 137 D3
Chilbolton 119 E3
Chilcomb 119 G5
Chilcombe 104 B3
Chilcompton 117 D2
Chilcote 159 E1
Child Okeford 105 E1
Childer Thornton 183 E5
Childerditch 137 F4
Childrey 133 F4
Child's Ercall 171 D5
Childswickham 146 C4
Childwall 183 F4
Childwick Green 136 A1
Chilfrome 104 B3
Chilgrove 108 A2
Chilham 124 C3
Chilhampton 118 B4
Chilla 113 E5
Chillaton 99 E2
Chillenden 125 E3
Chillerton 107 D4
Chillesford 153 E2
Chilley 101 D2
Chillingham 229 E4
Chillington Devon 101 D3
Chillington Som 103 G1
Chilmark 118 A4
Chilson Oxon 133 F1
Chilson Som 103 G2
Chilsworthy Corn 99 E3
Chilsworthy Devon 112 D5
Chilthorne Domer 104 B1
Chilton Bucks 134 B1
Chilton Devon 102 B2
Chilton Dur 212 B5
Chilton Oxon 133 G4
Chilton Suff 151 G3
Chilton Candover 119 G4
Chilton Cantelo 116 C5
Chilton Foliat 133 F5
Chilton Polden 116 A4
Chilton Street 151 F3
Chilton Trinity 115 F4
Chilvers Coton 159 F3
Chilwell 173 G4
Chilworth Hants 106 D1
Chilworth Surr 121 F3
Chimney 133 F2
Chimney Street 151 F3
Chineham 120 B2
Chingford 136 C3
Chinley 185 E4
Chinley Head 185 E4
Chinnor 134 C2
Chipchase Castle 220 A4
Chipley 115 E5
Chipnall 171 E4
Chippenham Cambs 151 E1
Chippenham Wilts 132 B5
Chipperfield 135 F2
Chipping Herts 150 B4
Chipping Lancs 192 C3
Chipping Campden 147 D4
Chipping Hill 138 B1
Chipping Norton 147 F5
Chipping Ongar 137 E2
Chipping Sodbury 131 G4
Chipping Warden 147 G3
Chipstable 114 D5
Chipstead Kent 123 D3
Chipstead Surr 122 B3
Chirbury 156 B3
Chirk (Y Waun) 169 F4
Chirk Green 169 F4
Chirmorrie 214 D3
Chirnside 237 F4
Chirnsidebridge 237 F4
Chirton T&W 212 C1
Chirton Wilts 118 B2
Chisbury 119 D1
Chiscan 222 B4
Chiselborough 104 A1
Chiseldon 133 D5
Chiserley 193 G5
Chislehampton 134 A3
Chislehurst 136 D5
Chislet 125 E2
Chiswell Green 136 A2
Chiswick 136 B5
Chiswick End 150 B3
Chisworth 185 D3 Chithurst 120 D5
Chittering 162 C5
Chitterne 118 A3
Chittlehamholt 113 G3
Chittlehampton 113 G3
Chittoe 118 A1
Chivelstone 101 D4
Chivenor 113 F2
Chobham 121 E1
Choicelee 237 E4
Cholderton 118 D3
Cholesbury 135 E2
Chollerford 220 B4
Chollerton 220 B4
Cholmondeston 170 D2
Cholsey 134 A4
Cholstrey 145 D2
Cholwell B&NESom 116 D2
Cholwell Devon 99 E3
Chop Gate 203 E3
Choppington 221 E3
Chopwell 212 A2
Chorley ChesE 170 C2
Chorley Lancs 183 G1
Chorley Shrop 157 F4

Chorley Staffs 158 C1
Chorleywood 135 F3
Chorlton 171 E2
Chorlton Lane 170 B3
Chorlton-cum-Hardy 184 C3
Chowley 170 B2
Chrishall 150 C4
Chrishall Grange 150 C3
Chriswell 232 D2
Christ Church Oxon OX1 1DP 80 Oxford
Christchurch Cambs 162 C3
Christchurch Dorset 106 A3
Christchurch Glos 131 E1
Christchurch Newport 130 C4
Christian Malford 132 B5
Christleton 170 B1
Christmas Common 134 C3
Christon 116 A2
Christon Bank 229 G4
Christow 102 B4
Christskirk 260 E2
Chryston 234 A2
Chudleigh 102 B5
Chudleigh Knighton 102 B5
Chulmleigh 113 G4
Chunal 185 E3
Church 192 D5
Church Aston 157 G1
Church Brampton 148 C1
Church Brough 200 C1
Church Broughton 172 D4
Church Charwelton 148 A2
Church Common 153 E2
Church Crookham 120 D2
Church Eaton 158 A1
Church End CenBeds 149 G4
Church End CenBeds 149 E5
Church End CenBeds 149 G4
Church End CenBeds 149 E4
Church End CenBeds 149 E4
Church End ERid 196 C2
Church End Essex 151 D3
Church End Essex 151 F5
Church End Glos 146 A4
Church End Hants 120 B2
Church End Herts 136 A1
Church End Herts 150 C1
Church End Lincs 176 A5
Church End Lincs 189 E3
Church End Warks 159 E3
Church End Wilts 132 C5
Church Enstone 147 F5
Church Fenton 195 E4
Church Green 103 E3
Church Gresley 159 E1
Church Hanborough 133 G1
Church Hill ChesW&C 170 D1
Church Hill Derbys 173 F1
Church Houses 203 F3
Church Knowle 105 F4
Church Laneham 187 F5
Church Langley 137 D2
Church Langton 160 C3
Church Lawford 159 G5
Church Lawton 171 F2
Church Leigh 172 B4
Church Lench 146 C2
Church Mayfield 172 C3
Church Minshull 171 D1
Church Norton 108 A4
Church of St. Mary-in-Castro Kent CT16 1HU 70 Dover
Church Preen 157 E3
Church Pulverbatch 156 D2
Church Stoke 156 B3
Church Stowe 148 B2
Church Street Essex 151 F3
Church Street Kent 137 G5
Church Stretton 157 D3
Church Town Leics 159 F1
Church Town Surr 122 C3
Church Village 129 G4
Church Warsop 173 G1
Church Westcote 147 E5
Church Wilne 173 F4
Churcham 131 G1
Churchdown 132 A1
Churchend Essex 138 D3
Churchend Essex 151 F5
Churchend SGlos 131 G3
Churchfield 158 C3
Churchgate 136 C2
Churchgate Street 137 D1
Churchill Devon 113 F1
Churchill Devon 103 F2
Churchill Oxon 147 E5
Churchill Worcs 146 B2
Churchill Worcs 158 A5
Churchingford 103 E1
Churchover 160 A4
Churchstanton 103 E1
Churchstow 100 D3
Churchtown Devon 113 G1
Churchtown IoM 190 C2
Churchtown Lancs 192 A3
Churchtown Mersey 183 E1
Churnsike Lodge 219 E4
Churston Ferrers 101 F2
Churt 121 D4
Churton 170 B2
Churwell 194 B5
Chute Cadley 119 E2
Chute Standen 119 E2
Chwilog 166 D4
Chyandour 94 B3
Chysauster 94 B3

Cilan Uchaf 166 B5
Cilcain 169 E1
Cilcennin 142 B1
Cilcewydd 156 B2
Cilfrew 129 D2
Cilfynydd 129 G3
Cilgerran 141 E3
Cilgwyn Carmar 142 D4
Cilgwyn Pembs 141 D4
Ciliau Aeron 142 B2
Cille Bhrighde 254 C3
Cille Pheadair 254 C3
Cilmaengwyn 128 D2
Cilmery 143 G2
Cilrhedyn 141 F4
Cilrhedyn Bridge 140 D4
Cilsan 142 B5
Ciltalgarth 168 B4
Cilwendeg 141 F4
Cilybebyll 128 D2
Cilycwm 143 D3
Cimla 129 D3
Cinderford 131 F1
Cippenham 135 E4
Cippyn 141 E3
Cirbhig 270 D3
Cirencester 132 C2
City GtLon 136 C4
City VGlam 129 F5
City Airport 136 D4
City Dulas 180 C4
City of Coventry Stadium (Coventry City F.C.) WMid CV6 6GE 16 D2
Clabhach 246 A4
Clachaig 232 C1
Clachan A&B 241 D3
Clachan A&B 248 A5
Clachan A&B 231 F4
Clachan High 256 B1
Clachan Na H-E. Siar 262 C7
Clachan Mòr 246 A2
Clachan of Campsie 234 A2
Clachan of Glendaruel 232 A1
Clachan-a-Luib 262 D5
Clachaneasy 215 E3
Clachanmore 206 A2
Clachan-Seil 239 G3
Clachbreck 231 F2
Clachnabrain 252 B3
Clachnaharry 266 D7
Clachtoll 272 C6
Clackmannan 243 E5
Clackmarras 267 K6
Clacton Pier Essex CO15 1QX 139 E1
Clacton-on-Sea 139 E1
Cladach a Bhale Shear 262 D5
Cladach a' Chaolais 262 C5
Cladach Chircebost 262 C5
Cladach Chnoc a Lin 262 C5
Cladich (An Cladach) 240 C2
Cladswell 146 C2
Claggan (An Claigeann) High 248 D2
Claggan High 247 G5
Claigan 263 H6
Claines 146 A2
Clandown 117 D2
Clanfield Hants 107 G1
Clanfield Oxon 133 E2
Clannaborough Barton 102 A2
Clanville 119 E3
Claonaig 231 G4
Claonairigh 240 C4
Claonel 266 C1
Clapgate 150 C5
Clapham Bed 149 F2
Clapham Devon 102 B4
Clapham GtLon 136 B5
Clapham NYorks 192 D1
Clapham WSuss 108 C3
Clapham Green 149 F2
Clapham Hill 124 C2
Clappers 237 G4
Clappersgate 199 E2
Clapton Som 104 A2
Clapton Som 116 D2
Clapton-in-Gordano 116 B5
Clapton-on-the-Hill 133 D1
Clapworthy 113 G3
Clara Vale 212 A1
Clarach 154 C4
Clarbeston 141 D5
Clarbeston Road 140 D5
Clarborough 187 E4
Clardon 275 G2
Clare 151 F3
Clare Castle Country Park Suff CO10 8NJ 151 F3
Clarebrand 216 B4
Claremont Landscape Garden Surr KT10 9JG 121 G1
Clarencefield 217 E4
Clarilaw 227 G2
Clark's Green 121 G4
Clarkston 233 G4
Clashban 266 D2
Clashcoig 266 D2
Clashdorran 266 C7
Clashgour 249 E5
Clashindarroch 260 C1
Clashmore High 266 E3
Clashmore High 272 C5
Clashnessie 272 C5
Clashnoir 259 K2
Clatford 118 C1
Clathy 243 F2
Clatt 260 D2
Clatter 155 F3
Clattercote 147 G3
Clatterford 107 D4
Clatterford End 137 E2
Clatterin Brig 253 E2

Clatteringshaws 215 G3
Clatworthy 115 D4
Claughton Lancs 192 B1
Claughton Lancs 192 B3
Clavelshay 115 F4
Claverdon 147 D1
Claverham 116 B1
Clavering 150 C4
Claverley 157 G3
Claverton 117 E1
Claverton Down 117 E1
Clawdd-côch 129 G5
Clawdd-newydd 169 D2
Clawfin 224 D5
Clawthorpe 199 G5
Clawton 99 D1
Claxby 188 B3
Claxby Pluckacre 176 B1
Claxby St. Andrew 189 E5
Claxton Norf 179 E5
Claxton NYorks 195 F1
Claxton Grange 213 D5
Clay Common 165 F3
Clay Coton 160 A5
Clay Cross 173 E1
Clay End 150 B5
Clay Hill 131 F5
Clay of Allan 267 F4
Claybokie 251 J1
Claybrooke Magna 159 G4
Claybrooke Parva 159 G4
Claydene 123 D4
Claydon Oxon 147 G2
Claydon Suff 152 C3
Claygate Kent 123 G4
Claygate Surr 121 G1
Claygate Cross 123 F3
Clayhanger Devon 114 D5
Clayhanger WMid 158 C2
Clayhidon 103 E1
Clayhill ESuss 110 D1
Clayhill Hants 106 C2
Clayhithe 150 D1
Clayock 275 G3
Claypit Hill 150 B2
Claypole 174 D3
Claythorpe 189 E5
Clayton Staffs 171 F3
Clayton SYorks 186 B2
Clayton WSuss 109 E2
Clayton Green 192 B5
Clayton West 185 G1
Clayton-le-Moors 192 D4
Clayton-le-Woods 192 B5
Clayworth 187 E4
Cleadale 247 D1
Cleadon 212 C1
Clearbrook 100 B1
Clearwell 131 E2
Cleasby 202 B1
Cleat Ork 277 D9
Cleat Na H-E. Siar 254 B4
Cleatlam 202 A1
Cleatop 193 E1
Cleator 208 D5
Cleator Moor 208 D5
Cleckheaton 194 A5
Clee St. Margaret 157 E4
Cleedownton 157 E4
Cleehill 157 E5
Cleestanton 157 E5
Cleethorpes 188 D2
Cleethorpes Discovery Centre NELincs DN35 0AG 188 D2
Cleeton St. Mary 157 F5
Cleeve NSom 116 B1
Cleeve Oxon 134 B4
Cleeve Hill 146 B5
Cleeve Prior 146
Cleghorn 234 C5
Clehonger 145 D4
Cleigh 240 A2
Cleish 243 F5
Cleland 234 B4
Clement's End 135 F1
Clemsfold 121 G4
Clench Common 118 C1
Clenchwarton 177 D5
Clennell 220 B1
Clent 158 B5
Clent Hills Worcs DY9 9JR 14 B5
Cleobury Mortimer 157 F5
Cleobury North 157 F4
Clephanton 267 F6
Clerklands 227 G3
Clerkenwell 127 C7
Clestrain 277 C7
Cleuch Head 227 G4
Cleughbrae 217 E3
Clevancy 132 C5
Clevedon 116 B5
Cleveland Tontine Inn 202 D3
Cleveley 147 F5
Cleveleys 191 G3
Clevelode 146 A3
Cleverton 132 B4
Clewer 116 B2
Clewer Green 135 E5
Clewer Village 135 E5
Cley Marshes Norf NR25 7SA 178 B1
Cley next the Sea 178 B1
Cliburn 210 B5
Cliddesden 120 B3
Cliff Carmar 127 G2
Cliff High 247 F3
Cliff End 111 D2
Cliff Grange 170 D4
Cliffe Lancs 192 D4
Cliffe Med 137 G5
Cliffe NYorks 195 F4
Cliffe Woods 137 G5
Clifford Here 144 B3
Clifford WYorks 194 D3
Clifford Chambers 147 D2
Clifford's Mesne 145 F5
Clifford's Tower YO1 9SA 90 York
Cliffs End 125 F2
Clifton Bristol 131 E5
Clifton CenBeds 149 G4
Clifton Cumb 210 B5
Clifton Derbys 172 C3
Clifton Devon 113 F1

Clifton Lancs 192 A4
Clifton N'umb 221 E3
Clifton Nott 173 G4
Clifton NYorks 194 A3
Clifton Oxon 147 G4
Clifton Stir 241 F1
Clifton SYorks 186 C3
Clifton Worcs 146 A3
Clifton WYorks 194 A5
Clifton York 195 E2
Clifton Campville 159 E1
Clifton Reynes 149 E2
Clifton upon Dunsmore 160 A5
Clifton upon Teme 145 G1
Cliftonville 125 F1
Climping 108 C3
Climpy 234 D4
Clink 117 E3
Clint 194 B2
Clint Green 178 B4
Clinterty 261 G3
Clintmains 228 A3
Clippesby 179 F4
Clippings Green 178 B4
Clipsham 161 E1
Clipston N'hants 160 C4
Clipston Notts 174 B4
Clipstone 173 G1
Clitheroe 192 D3
Clive 170 C5
Cliveden Garden & Maze Bucks SL6 0JA 135 E4
Clivocast 278 F2
Clixby 188 B2
Clocaenog 169 D2
Clochan 268 C4
Clochtow 261 J1
Clock Face 183 G3
Clockhill 269 G6
Cloddach 267 J6
Cloddiau 156 A2
Clodock 144 C5
Cloford 117 E3
Cloichran 242 B1
Clola 269 J6
Clonrae 216 C3
Clophill 149 F4
Clopton 161 F4
Clopton Corner 152 D2
Clopton Green Suff 151 F2
Clopton Green Suff 152 D2
Close Clark 190 A4
Closeburn 216 C2
Closworth 104 B1
Clothall 150 A4
Clothan 278 D4
Clotton 170 C1
Clough Cumb 200 C3
Clough GtMan 184 D1
Clough GtMan 184 B1
Clough WYorks 185 E1
Clough Foot 193 F5
Clough Head 193 G5
Cloughfold 193 E5
Cloughton 204 D3
Cloughton Newlands 204 D3
Clounlaid 247 G4
Clousta 279 C7
Clouston 277 C6
Clova Aber 260 C2
Clova Angus 252 B2
Clove Lodge 201 F1
Clovelly 112 D3
Clovelly Cross 112 D3
Clovelly Village Devon EX39 5TA 112 D3
Clovenfords 227 F2
Clovenstone 261 F3
Cloves 267 J5
Clovullin 248 C3
Clow Bridge 193 E5
Clowne 186 B5
Clows Top 157 G5
Cloyntie 224 B5
Cluanach 230 B4
Clubworthy 98 C1
Cluddley 157 F1
Cluer (Cliuthar) 263 G2
Clumber Country Park Notts S80 3AZ 186 D5
Clun 156 B4
Clunas 267 F7
Clunbury 156 C4
Clunderwen 127 E1
Clune High 258 E2
Clune Moray 268 D4
Clunes 249 E1
Clungunford 156 C5
Clunie Aber 268 D5
Clunie P&K 251 G5
Clunton 156 C4
Cluny 243 H1
Clutton B&NESom 116 D2
Clutton ChesW&C 170 B2
Clwt-y-bont 167 E1
Clwydfagwyr 129 G2
Clydach Mon 130 B1
Clydach Swan 128 C2
Clydach Terrace 130 A1
Clydach Vale 129 F3
Clydebank 233 F2
Clydey 141 F4
Clyffe Pypard 132 C5
Clynder 232 D1
Clyne 129 E2
Clynelish 267 F1
Clynfyw 141 F4
Clynnog-fawr 166 D3
Clyro 144 B3
Clyst Honiton 102 C3
Clyst Hydon 102 C2
Clyst St. George 102 C4
Clyst St. Lawrence 102 C2
Clyst St. Mary 102 C3
Clyst William 103 D2
Cnewr 143 E5
Cnoc 271 G4
Cnwch Coch 154 C5
Coachford 268 C6
Coad's Green 97 G2
Coal Aston 186 A5
Coalbrookdale 157 F2

Coalbrookvale 130 A2
Coalburn 225 G2
Coalburns 212 A1
Coalcleugh 211 E3
Coaley 131 G2
Coalmoor 157 F2
Coalpit Heath 131 F4
Coalport 157 G2
Coalsnaughton 243 E5
Coaltown of Balgonie 244 B5
Coaltown of Wemyss 244 B5
Coalville 159 G1
Coalway 131 E1
Coanwood 210 C2
Coast 116 B5
Coatbridge 234 B3
Coate Swin 133 D4
Coate Wilts 118 B1
Coates Cambs 162 B3
Coates Glos 132 B2
Coates Lincs 187 G4
Coates Notts 187 F4
Coates WSuss 108 B2
Coatham 213 E5
Coatham Mundeville 212 B5
Cobairdy 268 D6
Cobbaton 113 G3
Cobbler's Plain 131 D2
Cobby Syke 194 A2
Cobden 102 D3
Coberley 132 B1
Cobhall Common 145 D4
Cobham Kent 123 F2
Cobham Surr 121 G1
Cobleland 242 A5
Cobley Hill 158 C5
Cobnash 145 D1
Coburty 269 H4
Cochno 233 F2
Cock Alley 173 F1
Cock Bank 170 A3
Cock Bevington 146 C2
Cock Bridge 259 K4
Cock Clarks 138 C2
Cock Green 137 G1
Cock Marling 111 D2
Cockayne 203 F3
Cockayne Hatley 150 A3
Cockburnspath 237 E2
Cockenzie & Port Seton 236 B2
Cocker Bar 192 B5
Cockerham 192 A2
Cockermouth 209 E3
Cockernhoe 149 G5
Cockerton 202 B1
Cockett 128 C3
Cockfield Dur 212 A5
Cockfield Suff 152 A2
Cockfosters 136 B3
Cocking 108 A2
Cockington 101 E1
Cockington Country Park Torbay TQ2 6XA 101 E1
Cocklake 116 B3
Cocklaw 220 B4
Cockle Park 221 E2
Cockleford 132 B1
Cockley Cley 163 F2
Cockley Beck 198 D2
Cockpen 236 A2
Cockpole Green 134 C4
Cockshutt 170 B5
Cockthorpe 178 A1
Cockwood Devon 102 C4
Cockwood Som 115 F3
Cockyard 185 E4
Codda 97 F2
Coddenham 152 C2
Coddington ChesW&C 170 B2
Coddington Here 145 G3
Coddington Notts 174 D2
Codford St. Mary 118 A4
Codford St. Peter 118 A4
Codicote 136 B1
Codmore Hill 108 C2
Codnor 173 F3
Codnor Park 173 F2
Codrington 131 G5
Codsall 158 A2
Codsall Wood 158 A2
Coed Morgan 130 C1
Coed Ystumgwern 167 G5
Coedcae 130 B2
Coedely 129 G4
Coedkernew 130 B4
Coedpoeth 169 F2
Coedway 156 C1
Coed-y-bryn 141 G3
Coed-y-caerau 130 C3
Coed-y-paen 130 C3
Coed-y-parc 167 F1
Coed-yr-ynys 144 A5
Coelbren 129 E1
Coffinswell 101 E1
Cofton 102 C4
Cofton Hackett 158 C5
Cogan 130 A5
Cogenhoe 148 D1
Cogges 133 F2
Coggeshall 151 G5
Coggeshall Hamlet 151 G5
Coggins Mill 110 A1
Cóig Peighinnean 271 H1
Coilantogle 242 A4
Coilessan 241 E4
Coillaig 240 C2
Coille Mhorgil 257 G4
Coille-righ 257 F2
Coillore 255 J1
Coity 129 F4
Col 271 G4
Col Uarach 271 G4
Colaboll 273 H7
Colan 96 C3
Colaton Raleigh 103 D4
Colbost 263 H7
Colburn 202 B3
Colbury 106 C1

Colby Cumb 210 C5
Colby IoM 190 A4
Colby Norf 178 D2
Colchester 152 A5
Colchester Castle Museum Essex CO1 1TJ 152 A5
Colchester Green 152 A2
Colchester Zoo Essex CO3 0SL 152 A5
Colcot 115 E1
Cold Ash 119 G1
Cold Ashby 160 B5
Cold Ashton 131 G5
Cold Aston 132 D1
Cold Blow 127 E1
Cold Brayfield 149 E2
Cold Chapel 226 A3
Cold Cotes 200 C5
Cold Hanworth 188 A4
Cold Harbour 134 B4
Cold Hatton 170 D5
Cold Hatton Heath 170 D5
Cold Hesledon 212 D3
Cold Higham 148 B2
Cold Inn 127 E2
Cold Kirby 203 E4
Cold Newton 160 C2
Cold Northcott 97 G1
Cold Norton 138 B2
Cold Overton 160 D2
Cold Row 191 G3
Coldbackie 273 J2
Coldblow 137 E5
Coldean 109 F3
Coldeast 102 B5
Coldeaton 172 C2
Colden Common 119 F5
Coldfair Green 153 F1
Coldham 162 C2
Coldharbour Glos 131 E2
Coldharbour Surr 121 G3
Coldingham 237 G3
Coldrain 243 F4
Coldred 125 E4
Coldrey 120 C3
Coldridge 113 G5
Coldrife 220 C2
Coldstream 228 C3
Coldvreath 97 D4
Coldwaltham 108 C2
Coldwells 269 K6
Cole 117 D4
Cole End 159 D4
Cole Green 136 B1
Cole Henley 119 F2
Colebatch 156 C4
Colebrook 102 D2
Colebrooke 102 A2
Coleburn 267 K6
Coleby Lincs 175 E1
Coleby NLincs 187 F1
Coleford Devon 102 A2
Coleford Glos 131 E1
Coleford Som 117 D3
Colegate End 164 C3
Colehill 105 G2
Coleman Green 136 A1
Coleman's Hatch 122 D5
Colemere 170 B4
Colemore 120 C4
Colemore Green 157 G3
Colenden 243 G2
Coleorton 159 G1
Colerne 132 A5
Cole's Common 164 D3
Cole's Cross 101 D3
Cole's Green 153 D1
Colesbourne 132 C1
Colesden 149 G2
Coleshill Bucks 135 E3
Coleshill Oxon 133 E3
Coleshill Warks 159 E4
Colestocks 103 D2
Coley B&NESom 116 C2
Coley Staffs 172 B5
Colfin 214 B5
Colgate 122 B5
Colgrain 233 E2
Colindale 136 B4
Colinsburgh 244 C4
Colinton 235 G3
Colintraive 232 B2
Colkirk 178 A3
Coll 246 A4
Collace 244 A1
Collafirth 279 D6
Collamoor Head 98 B1
Collaton St. Mary 101 E1
Coll Dark Sky Island Argyll & Bute 246 B4
Collessie 244 A3
Colleton Mills 113 G4
Collett's Green 146 A2
Collier Row 137 E3
Collier Street 123 G4
Collier's End 150 B5
Collier's Wood 136 B5
Colliery Row 212 C3
Collieston 261 J2
Collin 217 E3
Collingbourne Ducis 118 D2
Collingbourne Kingston 118 D2
Collingham Notts 174 D1
Collingham WYorks 194 C3
Collington 145 F1
Collingtree 148 C2
Collins End 134 B5
Collins Green Warr 183 G3
Collins Green Worcs 145 G2
Colliston 253 E5
Colliton 103 D2
Collmuir 260 D4
Collycroft 159 F4
Collyhurst 184 C2
Collynie 261 G1
Collyweston 161 E2
Colmonell 214 C2
Colmworth 149 G2
Coln Rogers 132 C2
Coln St. Aldwyns 132 D2
Coln St. Dennis 132 C1
Colnabaichin 259 K4
Colnbrook 135 F5
Colne Cambs 162 B5
Colne Lancs 193 E4
Colne Engaine 151 G4
Colney 178 C5
Colney Heath 136 B2
Colney Street 136 A2
Colonsay 238 C5
Colonsay House 238 C5
Colony Gift Corporation Cumb LA12 0LD 199 D5
Colpy 260 E1
Colquhar 236 A5
Colsterdale 202 A4
Colsterworth 175 E5
Colston Bassett 174 C4
Colston Hall BS1 5AR 66 Bristol
Coltfield 267 J5
Colthouse 199 E3
Coltishall 179 D4
Coltness 234 C4
Colton Cumb 199 E4
Colton Norf 178 C5
Colton NYorks 195 E3
Colton Staffs 172 B5
Colton WYorks 194 C4
Colva 144 B2
Colvend 216 C5
Colvister 278 E3
Colwall 145 G3
Colwall Green 145 G3
Colwall Stone 145 G3
Colwell 220 B4
Colwich 172 B5
Colwick 174 B3
Colwinston 129 F5
Colworth 108 B3
Colwyn Bay (Bae Colwyn) 181 G5
Colyford 103 F3
Colyton 103 F3
Combe Here 144 C1
Combe Oxon 133 G1
Combe Som 116 B5
Combe WBerks 119 E1
Combe Common 121 E4
Combe Cross 102 A5
Combe Down 117 E1
Combe Florey 115 E4
Combe Hay 117 E2
Combe Martin 113 F1
Combe Martin Wildlife & Dinosaur Park Devon EX34 0NG 113 G1
Combe Pafford 101 F1
Combe Raleigh 103 E2
Combe St. Nicholas 103 G1
Combeinteignhead 102 B5
Comberbach 184 A5
Comberford 159 D2
Comberton Cambs 150 B2
Comberton Here 145 D1
Combpyne 103 F3
Combridge 172 B4
Combrook 147 F2
Combs Derbys 185 E5
Combs Suff 152 B2
Combs Ford 152 B2
Combwich 115 F3
Comer 241 F4
Comers 260 E4
Comhampton 146 A1
Comins Coch 154 C4
Commercial End 151 D1
Commins Coch 155 E2
Common Edge 191 G4
Common Moor 97 G2
Common Platt 132 D4
Common Side 186 A5
Common Square 188 A5
Commondale 203 F1
Commonside 172 D3
Compstall 185 D3
Compton Devon 101 E1
Compton Hants 119 F5
Compton Plym 100 A2
Compton Staffs 158 A4
Compton Surr 121 E3
Compton WBerks 134 A5
Compton Wilts 118 C2
Compton WSuss 107 G1
Compton WYorks 194 D3
Compton Abbas 105 E1
Compton Abdale 132 C1
Compton Bassett 132 C5
Compton Beauchamp 133 E4
Compton Bishop 116 A2
Compton Chamberlayne 118 B5
Compton Dando 116 D1
Compton Dundon 116 B4
Compton Martin 116 C2
Compton Pauncefoot 116 D5
Compton Valence 104 B3
Compton Verney 147 F2
Compton Wynyates 147 F3
Comra 258 C5
Comrie Fife 235 E1
Comrie P&K 242 C2
Conchra A&B 232 B1
Conchra High 256 E2
Concraigie 251 G5
Conder Green 192 A2
Conderton 146 B4
Condicote 146 D5
Condorrat 234 B2
Condover 157 D2
Coney Weston 164 A4
Coneyhurst 121 G5
Coneysthorpe 203 G5
Coneythorpe 194 C2
Conford 120 D4
Congash 259 H2
Congdon's Shop 97 G2
Congerstone 159 F2
Congham 177 F5
Congleton 171 F1
Congresbury 116 B1
Congreve 158 B1
Conicavel 267 G6
Coningsby 176 A2
Conington Cambs 161 G4
Conington Cambs 150 B1
Conisbrough 186 C3
Conisby 230 A3
Conisholme 189 E3
Coniston Cumb 199 E3
Coniston ERid 197 D4
Coniston Cold 193 F2
Conistone 193 F1
Conkers, Swadlincote Leics DE12 6GA 159 F1
Conland 268 E6
Connah's Quay 169 F1
Connel (A' Choingheal) 240 B1
Connel Park 225 E4
Connor Downs 94 C3
Conock 118 B2
Conon Bridge (Drochaid Sgùideil) 266 C6
Cononish 241 F2
Cononley 193 F3
Cononsyth 253 D5
Consall 171 G3
Consett 212 A2
Constable Burton 202 A3
Constantine 95 E4
Constantine Bay 96 C2
Contin (Cunndainn) 266 B6
Contlaw 261 G4
Contullich 266 D4
Conwy 181 F5
Conwy Castle Conwy LL32 8LD 181 F5
Conyer 124 B2
Conyer's Green 151 G1
Cooden 110 C3
Coodham 224 C2
Cooil 190 B4
Cookbury 113 E5
Cookbury Wick 113 D5
Cookham 135 D4
Cookham Dean 135 D4
Cookham Rise 135 D4
Cookhill 146 C2
Cookley Suff 165 E4
Cookley Worcs 158 A4
Cookley Green Oxon 134 B3
Cookley Green Suff 165 E4
Cookney 261 G5
Cook's Green 152 A2
Cooksbridge 109 F2
Cooksey Green 146 B1
Cookshill 171 G3
Cooksmill Green 137 F2
Cookston 261 H1
Coolham 121 G5
Cooling 137 G5
Cooling Street 137 G5
Coombe Corn 97 D4
Coombe Corn 112 C4
Coombe Corn 96 A5
Coombe Corn 96 C5
Coombe Devon 101 D3
Coombe Devon 102 B4
Coombe Devon 103 E3
Coombe Som 115 F5
Coombe Som 104 A2
Coombe Wilts 118 C2
Coombe Bissett 118 C5
Coombe Country Park Warks CV3 2AB 16 D3
Coombe End 114 D5
Coombe Hill 146 A5
Coombe Keynes 105 E4
Coombes 109 D3
Coombes Moor 144 C1
Cooper's Corner ESuss 110 C1
Cooper's Corner Kent 123 D4
Cooper's Green 136 A2
Coopersale 137 D2
Coopersale Street 137 D2
Cootham 108 C2
Cop Street 125 E3
Copdock 152 C3
Copford Green 152 A5
Copgrove 194 C1
Copister 278 D5
Cople 149 G3
Copley Dur 211 G5
Copley WYorks 193 G5
Coplow Dale 185 F5
Copmanthorpe 195 E3
Copmere End 171 F5
Copp 192 A4
Coppathorne 112 C5
Coppenhall 158 B1
Coppenhall Moss 171 E2
Copperhouse 94 C3
Coppicegate 157 G4
Coppingford 161 G4
Coppleridge 117 F5
Copplestone 102 A2
Coppull 183 G1
Coppull Moor 183 G1
Copsale 121 G5
Copse Hill 122 B2
Copster Green 192 C4
Copston Magna 159 G4
Copt Heath 159 D5
Copt Hewick 202 C5
Copt Oak 159 G1
Copthall Green 136 D2
Copthorne 122 C5
Copy Lake 113 G4
Copythorne 106 C1
Coralhill 269 J4
Corbets Tey 137 E4
Corbiegoe 275 J4
Corbridge 211 F1
Corby 161 D4
Corby Glen 175 F5
Cordach 260 E5
Cordorcan 215 E3
Coreley 157 F5
Corfcott Green 98 D1
Corfe 103 F1
Corfe Castle 105 F4
Corfe Castle Dorset BH20 5EZ 105 F4
Corfe Mullen 105 F3
Corfton 157 D4
Corgarff 259 K4
Corhampton 120 B5
Corley 159 F4
Corley Ash 159 E4
Corley Moor 159 E4
Corn Exchange Cambs CB2 3QB 66 Cambridge
Cornabus 230 B5
Cornard Tye 152 A3
Corndon 99 G2
Corney 198 C3
Cornforth 212 C4
Cornhill 268 D5
Cornhill on Tweed 228 C3
Cornholme 193 F5
Cornish Gold & Treasure Park Corn TR16 4HN 96 A5
Cornish Hall End 151 E4
Cornquoy 277 E7
Cornriggs 211 E3
Cornsay 212 A3
Cornsay Colliery 212 A3
Corntown High 266 C6
Corntown VGlam 129 F5
Cornwell 147 E5
Cornwood 100 C2
Cornworthy 101 E2
Corpach (A' Chorpaich) 248 D2
Corpusty 178 C3
Corrachree 260 C4
Corran A&B 241 E5
Corran High 256 E4
Corran (Ardgour) High 248 C3
Corranbuie 231 G3
Corranmore 239 G4
Corrany 190 C3
Corribeg 248 B2
Corrie 232 B5
Corrie Common 218 A3
Corriechrevie 231 F4
Corriecravie 223 E3
Corriedoo 216 A2
Corriekinloch 273 F6
Corrielorne 240 A3
Corrievorrie 258 E2
Corrimony 257 K1
Corringham Lincs 187 F3
Corringham Thur 137 G4
Corris 155 D2
Corris Uchaf 154 D2
Corrlarach 248 B2
Corrour Shooting Lodge 249 G3
Corrow 241 D4
Corry 256 C2
Corrychurrachan 248 C3
Corrylach 222 C2
Corrymuckloch 243 D1
Corsback 275 H2
Corscombe 104 B2
Corse Aber 268 E6
Corse Glos 145 G5
Corse Lawn 146 A4
Corse of Kinnoir 268 D6
Corsebank 225 G4
Corsegight 269 G5
Corsehill 217 F2
Corsewall 214 B4
Corsham 132 A5
Corsindae 260 E4
Corsley 117 F3
Corsley Heath 117 F3
Corsock 216 B3
Corston B&NESom 117 D1
Corston Wilts 132 B4
Corstorphine 235 F2
Cortachy 252 B4
Corton Suff 165 G2
Corton Wilts 118 A3
Corton Denham 116 D5
Corwar House 215 D2
Corwen 169 D3
Coryton Devon 99 E2
Coryton Thur 137 G4
Cosby 160 A3
Coscote 134 A4
Coseley 158 B3
Cosford Shrop 157 G2
Cosford Warks 160 A5
Cosgrove 148 C3
Cosham 107 F2
Cosheston 126 D2
Coshieville 250 C5
Coskills 188 A2
Cosmeston 115 E1
Cosmeston Lakes Country Park VGlam CF64 5UY 115 E1
Cossall 173 F3
Cossington Leics 160 B1
Cossington Som 116 A3
Costa 276 C5
Costessey 178 C4
Costock 173 G5
Coston Leics 174 D5
Coston Norf 178 B5
Cote Oxon 133 F2
Cote Som 116 A3
Cotebrook 170 C1
Cotehill 210 A2
Cotes Cumb 199 F4
Cotes Leics 173 G5
Cotes Staffs 171 F4
Cotesbach 160 A4
Cotford St. Luke 115 E5
Cotgrave 174 B4
Cothall 261 G3
Cotham 174 C3
Cothelstone 115 E4
Cotheridge 145 G2
Cotherstone 201 F1
Cothill 133 G3
Cotleigh 103 F2
Cotmanhay 173 F3
Coton Cambs 150 C2
Coton N'hants 160 B5
Coton Staffs 171 G4
Coton Staffs 159 D2
Coton Staffs 171 F5
Coton Clanford 171 F5
Coton Hill 171 G4
Coton in the Clay 172 C5
Coton in the Elms 159 E1
Cotonwood Shrop 170 C4
Cotonwood Staffs 171 F5
Cotswold Water Park Glos GL7 6DF 132 C3
Cotswold Wildlife Park Oxon OX18 4JP 133 E2
Cott 101 D1
Cottam Lancs 192 A4
Cottam Notts 187 F4
Cottartown 259 H1
Cottenham 150 C1
Cotterdale 200 D3
Cottered 150 B5
Cotteridge 158 C5
Cotterstock 161 F3
Cottesbrooke 160 C5
Cottesmore 161 E1
Cottingham ERid 196 C4
Cottingham N'hants 160 D3
Cottingley 194 A4
Cottisford 148 A4
Cotton Staffs 172 B3
Cotton Suff 152 B1
Cotton End 149 F3
Cottonworth 119 E4
Cottown Aber 260 D2
Cottown Aber 269 G6
Cottown Aber 261 F3
Cotts 100 A1
Cottwood 113 G4
Cotwall 157 F1
Cotwalton 171 G4
Couch's Mill 97 F4
Coughton Here 145 E5
Coughton Warks 146 C1
Cougie 257 J2
Coulaghailtro 231 F3
Coulags 265 F7
Coulby Newham 203 E1
Coulderton 198 A2
Coull 260 D4
Coulport 232 D1
Coulsdon 122 B3
Coulston 118 A2
Coulter 226 B2
Coultershaw Bridge 108 B2
Coultings 115 F3
Coulton 203 F5
Coultra 244 B2
Cound 157 E2
Coundlane 157 E2
Coundon Dur 212 B5
Coundon WMid 159 F4
Countersett 201 E4
Countess Wear 102 C3
Countesthorpe 160 A3
Countisbury 114 A3
Coup Green 192 B5
Coupar Angus 252 A5
Coupland Cumb 200 C1
Coupland N'umb 228 D3
Cour 231 G5
Court Colman 129 E4
Court Henry 142 B5
Court House Green 159 F4
Court-at-Street 124 C5
Courtauld Institute of Art Gallery GtLon WC2R 0RN 45 F3
Courteenhall 148 C2
Courtsend 138 D3
Courtway 115 F4
Cousland 236 A3
Cousley Wood 123 F5
Coustonn 232 B2
Cove A&B 232 D1
Cove Devon 102 C1
Cove Hants 120 D2
Cove High 264 E2
Cove ScBord 237 E2
Cove Bay 261 H4
Cove Bottom 165 F3
Covehithe 165 G3
Coven 158 B2
Coveney 162 C4
Covenham St. Bartholomew 188 D3
Covenham St. Mary 188 D3
Coventry 159 F5
Coventry Airport 159 F5
Coventry Cathedral WMid CV1 5AB 69 Coventry
Coventry Transport Museum WMid CV1 1JD 69 Coventry
Coverack 95 E5
Coverham 202 A4
Covesea 267 J4
Covingham 133 D4
Covington Cambs 161 F5
Covington SLan 226 A2
Cowan Bridge 200 B5
Cowbeech 110 B2
Cowbit 162 A1
Cowbridge Som 114 C3
Cowbridge VGlam 129 F5
Cowden 123 D4
Cowden Pound 123 D4
Cowdenbeath 243 G5
Cowdenburn 235 G4
Cowers Lane 173 E3
Cowes 107 D3
Cowesby 203 D4
Cowesfield Green 119 D5
Cowey Green 152 B5
Cowfold 109 E1
Cowgill 200 C4
Cowie Aber 253 G1
Cowie Stir 234 C1
Cowlam Manor 196 B1
Cowley Devon 102 C3
Cowley Glos 132 B1
Cowley GtLon 135 F4
Cowley Oxon 134 A2
Cowling Lancs 183 G1
Cowling NYorks 193 F3
Cowling NYorks 202 B4
Cowlinge 151 F2
Cowmes 185 F1
Cowpe 193 E5
Cowpen 221 E3
Cowpen Bewley 213 D5
Cowplain 107 F1
Cowsden 146 B2
Cowshill 211 E3
Cowthorpe 194 D2
Cox Common 165 E3
Coxbank 171 D3
Coxbench 173 E3
Coxbridge 116 C4
Coxford 177 G5
Coxheath 123 G3
Coxhoe 212 C4
Coxley 116 C3
Coxley Wick 116 C3
Coxpark 99 E3
Coxtie Green 137 E3
Coxwold 203 E5
Coychurch 129 F5
Coylet 232 C1
Coylton 224 C4
Coylumbridge 259 G3
Coynach 260 C4
Coynachie 260 C1
Coytrahen 129 E4
Crabbet Park 122 C5
Crabgate 178 B3
Crabtree Plym 100 B2
Crabtree SYorks 186 A4
Crabtree WSuss 109 E1
Crabtree Green 170 A3
Crackaig 230 D3
Crackenthorpe 210 C5
Crackington 98 B1
Crackington Haven 98 B1
Crackley 171 F2
Crackleybank 157 G1
Crackpot 201 E3
Crackthorn Corner 164 B4
Cracoe 193 F1
Craddock 103 D1
Cradhlastadh 270 C4
Cradley Here 145 G3
Cradley WMid 158 B4
Cradley Heath 158 B4
Crafthole 99 D5
Crafton 135 D1
Cragg 193 G5
Cragg Hill 194 B4
Craggan Moray 259 J1
Craggan P&K 242 D3
Cragganmore 259 J1
Cragganruar 250 B5
Craggie High 258 E1
Craggie High 274 D7
Craghead 212 B2
Cragside N'umb NE65 7PX 220 C1
Craibstone Aberdeen 261 G3
Craibstone Moray 268 C5
Craichie 252 D5
Craig A&B 240 C1
Craig A&B 239 E1
Craig D&G 216 A4
Craig High 264 D5
Craig High 265 G7
Craig SAyr 224 B5
Craig Berthlŵyd 129 G3
Craigans 240 A5
Craigbeg 249 G1
Craig-cefn-parc 128 C2
Craigcleuch 218 B3
Craigculter 269 H5
Craigdallie 244 A2
Craigdam 261 G1
Craigdarroch D&G 216 B1
Craigdarroch EAyr 225 E5
Craigdhu D&G 207 D2
Craigdhu High 266 B7
Craigearn 261 F3
Craigellachie 267 K7
Craigellie 269 J4
Craigencallie 215 G3
Craigend Moray 267 J6
Craigend P&K 243 G2
Craigendive 232 B1
Craigendoran 233 E1
Craigengillan 224 C5
Craigenputtock 216 B2
Craigens 230 A3
Craigglas 240 A5
Craighall 244 C3
Craighat 233 F1
Craighead Fife 245 E3
Craighead High 266 E5
Craighlaw 215 E4
Craighouse 230 D3
Craigie Aber 261 H3
Craigie Dundee 244 C1
Craigie P&K 251 G5
Craigie SAyr 224 C2
Craigie Brae 261 G1
Craigieburn 226 C5
Craigieholm 243 G1
Craigielaw 236 B2
Craiglockhart 235 G2
Craiglug 261 G5
Craigmaud 269 G5
Craigmillar 235 G2
Craigmore 232 C3
Craigmyle House 260 E4
Craignafeoch 232 A2
Craignant 169 F4
Craignavie 242 A1
Craigneil 214 C2
Craigneuk 234 B4
Craignure 239 G1
Craigo 253 E3
Craigoch 224 A5
Craigow 243 F4
Craigrothie 244 B3
Craigroy 267 J6
Craigroy Farm 259 J1
Craigruie 241 G2
Craigsanquhar 244 B3
Craigton Aberdeen 261 G4
Craigton Angus 244 D1
Craigton Angus 252 B4
Craigton High 266 D7
Craigton Stir 234 A1
Craigtown 274 D3
Craig-y-nos 129 E1
Craik Aber 260 C2
Craik ScBord 227 E5
Crail 245 E4
Crailing 228 A4
Crailinghall 228 A4
Crakehill 202 D5
Crakemarsh 172 B4
Crambe 195 G1
Crambeck Village 195 G1
Cramlington 221 E4
Cramond 235 F2
Cranage 171 E1
Cranberry 171 F4
Cranborne 105 G1
Cranbourne 135 E5
Cranbrook GtLon 136 D4
Cranbrook Kent 123 G5
Cranbrook Common 123 G5
Crane Moor 186 A2
Crane Park Island Gt Lon N1C 4PW 11 A7
Cranfield 149 E3
Cranford Devon 112 D3
Cranford GtLon 136 A5
Cranford St. Andrew 161 E5
Cranford St. John 161 E5
Cranham Glos 132 A1
Cranham GtLon 137 E4
Crank 183 G3
Cranleigh 121 F4
Cranmer Green 164 B4
Cranmore IoW 106 C4
Cranmore Som 117 D3
Cranna 268 E5
Crannoch 268 C5
Cranoe 160 C3
Cransford 153 E1
Cranshaws 237 D3
Cranstal 190 C1
Crantock 96 B3
Cranwell 175 F3
Cranwich 163 F3
Cranworth 178 A5
Craobh Haven 239 G4
Crapstone 100 B1
Crarae 240 B5
Crask Inn 273 H6
Crask of Aigas 266 B7
Craskins 260 D4
Craster 229 G5
Craswall 144 B4
Crateford 158 B2
Cratfield 165 E4
Crathes 261 F5
Crathie Aber 259 K5
Crathie High 258 C5
Crathorne 202 D2
Craven Arms 156 D4
Craw 231 G5
Crawcrook 212 A1
Crawford Lancs 183 F2
Crawford SLan 226 A3
Crawfordjohn 225 G3
Crawfordton 216 B1
Crawick 225 F4
Crawley Devon 103 F2
Crawley Hants 119 F4
Crawley Oxon 133 F1
Crawley WSuss 122 B5
Crawley Down 122 C5
Crawleyside 211 F3
Crawshawbooth 193 E5
Crawton 253 G2
Crawyn 190 B2
Cray NYorks 201 E5
Cray P&K 251 G3
Cray Powys 143 E5
Crayford 137 E5
Crayke 203 E5
Crays Hill 137 G3
Cray's Pond 134 B4
Crazies Hill 134 C4
Creacombe 102 B1
Creagan 248 B5
Creagbheitheachain 248 B3
Creagorry (Creag Ghoraidh) 262 C7
Crealy Adventure Park Devon Devon EX5 1DR 102 C3
Creamore Bank 170 C4
Creaton 160 C5
Creca 218 A4
Credenhill 145 D3
Crediton 102 B2
Creebridge 215 F4
Creech Heathfield 115 F5
Creech St. Michael 115 F5
Creed 96 D5
Creedy Park 102 B2
Creekmoor 105 F3
Creekmouth 137 D4
Creeting St. Mary 152 B2
Creeton 175 F5
Creetown 215 F5
Creggans 240 C4
Cregneash 190 A5
Cregrina 144 A2
Creich 244 B2
Creigau 131 D3
Creigiau 129 G4
Crelevan 257 K1
Crelly 95 D3
Cremyll 100 A2
Crendell 105 G1
Cressage 157 E2
Cressbrook 185 F5
Cresselly 127 D2
Cressing 151 F5
Cresswell N'umb 221 E2
Cresswell Staffs 171 G4
Cresswell Quay 127 D2
Creswell 186 C5
Cretingham 152 D2
Cretshengan 231 F3
Crewe ChesE 171 E2
Crewe ChesW&C 170 B2
Crewe Green 171 E2
Crewgreen 156 C1
Crewkerne 104 A2
Crew's Hole 131 F5
Crewton 173 E4
Crianlarich (A' Chrìon-Làraich) 241 F2
Cribbs Causeway 131 E4
Cribyn 142 B2
Criccieth 167 D4
Crich 173 E2
Crich Carr 173 E2
Crich Common 173 E2
Crich Tramway Village Derbys DE4 5DP 173 E2
Crichie 269 H6
Crichton 236 A3
Crick Mon 131 D3
Crick N'hants 160 A5
Crickadarn 143 G3
Cricket Hill 120 D1
Cricket St. Thomas 103 G2
Crickham 116 B3
Crickheath 169 F5
Crickhowell 130 B1
Cricklade 132 D3
Cricklewood 136 B4
Crickley Hill Country Park Glos GL4 8JY 132 B1
Crick's Green 145 F2
Criddlestyle 106 A1
Cridling Stubbs 195 E5
Crieff 243 D2

Crieff Visitor Centre &
  Caithness Glass *P&K*
  PH7 4HQ **243** D2
Criftins (Dudleston
  Heath) **170** A4
Criggan **97** E3
Criggion **156** B1
Crigglestone **186** A1
Crimble **184** C1
Crimchard **103** G2
Crimdon Park **213** D4
Crimond **269** J5
Crimonmogate **269** J5
Crimplesham **163** E2
Crinan **239** G5
Crinan Ferry **239** G5
Cringleford **178** C5
Cringletie **235** G5
Crinow **127** E3
Cripplestyle **105** G1
Cripp's Corner **110** C1
Crix **137** G1
Crizeley **144** D4
Croalchapel **216** D1
Croasdale **209** D5
Crock Street **103** G1
Crockenhill **123** E2
Crocker End **134** C4
Crockerhill **107** F3
Crockernwell **102** A3
Crockerton **117** F3
Crockerton Green **117** F3
Crocketford
  (Ninemile Bar) **216** C3
Crockey Hill **195** F3
Crockhurst Street **123** F4
Crockleford Heath **152** B5
Croes Hywel **130** C1
Croesau Bach **169** F5
Croeserw **129** E3
Croesgoch **140** B4
Croes-lan **141** G3
Croesor **167** F2
Croespenmaen **130** A3
Croesyceiliog
  Carmar **128** A1
Croesyceiliog
  Torfaen **130** C3
Croes-y-mwyalch **130** C3
Croes-y-pant **130** C2
Croesywaun **167** E2
Croford **115** E5
Croft *Here* **145** D1
Croft *Leics* **160** A3
Croft *Lincs* **176** D1
Croft *Warr* **184** A3
Croftamie **233** F1
Crofthead **218** B4
Croftmore **251** D3
Crofton *Wilts* **119** D1
Crofton *WYorks* **186** A1
Croft-on-Tees **202** B2
Crofts **216** B3
Crofts of Benachielt
  275 D4
Crofts of Buinach **267** J6
Crofts of Haddo **261** G1
Crofty **128** B3
Crogen **168** D4
Croggan **239** G2
Croglin **210** B3
Croick *High* **266** B2
Croick *High* **274** D3
Croig **246** D4
Crois Dughaill **254** C3
Croit e Caley **190** A5
Cromarty (Cromba) **266** E5
Crombie **235** E1
Crombie Country Park
  Angus DD5 3QL **252** D5
Crombie Mill **244** D1
Cromblet **261** F1
Cromdale **259** H2
Cromer *Herts* **150** A5
Cromer *Norf* **178** D1
Cromford **173** D2
Cromhall **131** F3
Cromhall Common **131** F4
Cromore **271** G5
Crompton Fold **185** D1
Cromwell **174** C1
Cronberry **225** E3
Crondall **120** C3
Cronk-y-Voddy **190** B3
Cronton **183** F4
Crook *Cumb* **199** F3
Crook *Dur* **212** A4
Crook of Devon **243** F4
Crooked Soley **133** F5
Crookedholm **224** C2
Crookham *N'umb* **228** D3
Crookham *WBerks* **119** G1
Crookham Eastfield **228** D3
Crookham Village **120** C2
Crooklands **199** G4
Cropredy **147** G3
Cropston **160** A1
Cropthorne **146** B3
Cropton **203** G4
Cropwell Bishop **174** B4
Cropwell Butler **174** B4
Crosbie **232** D5
Crosbost **271** F5
Crosby *Cumb* **209** D3
Crosby *IoM* **190** B4
Crosby *Mersey* **183** E3
Crosby *NLincs* **187** F1
Crosby Court **202** C3
Crosby Garrett **200** C2
Crosby
  Ravensworth **200** B1
Crosby Villa **209** D3
Crosby-on-Eden **210** A2
Croscombe **116** C3
Crosemere **170** B5
Crosland Hill **185** F1
Cross *Som* **116** B2
Cross (Cros) *Na H-E. Siar*
  271 H1
Cross Ash **130** D1
Cross Bank **145** G1
Cross End *Bed.* **149** F2
Cross End *Essex* **151** G4
Cross Foxes Inn **155** F5
Cross Gates **194** C4
Cross Green *Devon* **99** D2
Cross Green *Staffs* **158** B2

Cross Green *Suff* **152** A2
Cross Green *Suff* **151** G2
Cross Green *Suff* **151** G2
Cross Hands
  Carmar **128** B1
Cross Hands
  Pembs **127** E3
Cross Hill **173** F3
Cross Hills **193** G3
Cross Houses **157** E2
Cross in Hand **110** A1
Cross Inn *Cere* **141** G1
Cross Inn *Cere* **142** B1
Cross Inn *RCT* **129** G4
Cross Keys **132** A5
Cross Lane **107** E3
Cross Lane Head **157** G3
Cross Lanes *Corn* **96** B5
Cross Lanes *Corn* **95** D4
Cross Lanes *NYorks* **195** E1
Cross Lanes *Wrex* **170** A3
Cross of Jackston **261** F1
Cross o'th'hands **173** D3
Cross Street **164** C4
Crossaig **231** G4
Crossapol **246** A4
Crossapoll **246** A2
Cross-at-Hand **123** G4
Crossbush **108** C3
Crosscanonby **209** D3
Crossdale Street **178** D2
Crossens **183** E1
Crossflatts **194** A3
Crossford *D&G* **216** C2
Crossford *Fife* **235** E1
Crossford *SLan* **234** C5
Crossgate *Lincs* **176** A5
Crossgate *Staffs* **171** G4
Crossgatehall **236** A3
Crossgates *Fife* **235** F1
Crossgates *NYorks* **204** D4
Crossgates *P&K* **243** F2
Crossgates *Powys* **143** G2
Crossgill **192** B1
Crosshands **224** C2
Crosshill *Fife* **243** G5
Crosshill *SAyr* **224** B5
Crosshouse **224** B2
Crosskeys **130** B3
Crosskirk **275** F1
Crosslanes **156** C1
Crosslee *Renf* **233** F3
Crosslee *ScBord* **227** E4
Crossmichael **216** B4
Crossmoor **192** A4
Crossroads *Aber* **261** F5
Crossroads *EAyr* **224** C3
Crossway *Mon* **130** D1
Crossway *Powys* **143** G2
Crossway Green
  Mon **131** E3
Crossway Green
  Worcs **146** A1
Crossways *Dorset* **105** D4
Crossways *Glos* **131** E1
Crosswell **141** E4
Crostwick **179** D4
Crostwight **179** E3
Crothair **270** D4
Crouch **123** F3
Crouch End **136** B4
Crouch Hill **104** D1
Crouchers **108** B5
Croughton **148** A4
Crovie **269** G4
Crow **106** A2
Crow Edge **185** F2
Crow Green **137** E3
Crow Hill **145** F5
Crowan **94** C3
Crowborough **123** E5
Crowborough
  Warren **123** E5
Crowcombe **115** E4
Crowdecote **172** C1
Crowden **185** E3
Crowdhill **119** F5
Crowell **134** C3
Crowfield *N'hants* **148** B3
Crowfield *Suff* **152** C2
Crowhurst *ESuss* **110** C2
Crowhurst *Surr* **122** C4
Crowhurst Lane End **122** C4
Crowland *Lincs* **162** A1
Crowland *Suff* **164** B4
Crowlas **94** C3
Crowle *NLincs* **187** E1
Crowle *Worcs* **146** B2
Crowle Green **146** B2
Crowmarsh Gifford **134** B4
Crown Corner **165** D3
Crownhill **100** A2
Crownthorpe **178** B5
Crowntown **94** D3
Crow's Nest **97** G3
Crows-an-wra **94** A4
Crowsnest **156** C2
Crowthorne **120** D1
Crowton **183** G5
Croxall **159** E1
Croxby **188** B3
Croxdale **212** B4
Croxden **172** B4
Croxley Green **135** F3
Croxteth Country Park
  Mersey L12 0HB **22** C2
Croxteth Hall *Mersey*
  L12 0HB **22** C2
Croxton *Cambs* **150** A2
Croxton *NLincs* **188** A1
Croxton *Norf* **163** G4
Croxton *Staffs* **171** E4
Croxton Green **170** C2
Croxton Kerrial **174** D5
Croxtonbank **171** E4
Croy *High* **266** E7
Croy *NLan* **234** B2
Croyde **113** E1
Croyde Bay **113** E1
Croydon *Cambs* **150** B3
Croydon *GtLon* **122** C2
Cruach **230** B4
Cruchie **268** D6
Cruckmeole **156** D2
Cruckton **156** D1
Cruden Bay **261** J1

Crudgington **157** F1
Crudwell **132** B3
Crug **156** A5
Crugmeer **96** D2
Crugybar **142** C4
Crûlabhig **270** D4
Crumlin **130** B3
Crumpsall **184** C2
Crumpsbrook **157** F5
Crundale *Kent* **124** C4
Crundale *Pembs* **126** C1
Crunwere Farm **127** E3
Crutherland Farm **234** A4
Cruwys Morchard **102** B1
Crux Easton **119** F2
Crwbin **128** A1
Cryers Hill **135** D3
Crymlyn **181** E5
Crymych **141** E4
Crynant **129** D2
Crystal Palace **136** C5
Crystal Palace Park
  GtLon SE20 8DT **13** C7
Cuaig **264** D6
Cubbington **147** F1
Cubert **96** B4
Cubley **185** G2
Cublington *Bucks* **148** D5
Cublington *Here* **144** D4
Cuckfield **109** F1
Cucklington **117** E5
Cuckney **186** C5
Cuckold's Green **165** F3
Cuckoo Bridge **176** A5
Cuckoo's Corner **120** C3
Cuckoo's Nest **170** A1
Cuddesdon **134** A2
Cuddington *Bucks* **134** C1
Cuddington
  ChesW&C **183** G5
Cuddington Heath **170** B3
Cuddy Hill **192** A4
Cudham **122** D3
Cudlipptown **99** F3
Cudworth *Som* **103** G1
Cudworth *SYorks* **186** A2
Cuerdley Cross **183** G4
Cuffley **136** C3
Cuidhaseadair **271** H2
Cuidhir **254** B4
Cuidrach **263** J6
Cuilmuich **241** D5
Cuil-uaine **240** B1
Culag **241** F5
Culbo **266** D5
Culbokie
  (Cùil Bhàicidh) **266** D6
Culbone **114** B3
Culburnie **266** B7
Culcabock **266** D7
Culcharan **240** B1
Culcharry **267** F6
Culcheth **184** A3
Culdrain **260** D1
Culduie **264** D7
Culford **151** G1
Culfordheath **163** G5
Culgaith **210** C5
Culgower **274** E2
Culham **134** A3
Culindrach **232** A4
Culkein **272** C5
Culkerton **132** B3
Cullachie **259** G2
Cullen **268** D4
Cullercoats **221** F4
Cullicudden **266** D5
Culligran **265** K7
Cullingworth **193** G4
Cullipool **239** G3
Cullivoe **278** E2
Culloch **242** C3
Culloden **266** E7
Cullompton **102** D2
Culmaily **267** F2
Culmalzie **215** E5
Culmington **157** D4
Culmstock **103** E1
Culnacraig **265** G1
Culnadalloch **240** B1
Culnaknock **264** B5
Culnamean **255** K2
Culpho **152** D3
Culquhirk **215** F5
Culrain **266** C2
Culross **235** E1
Culroy **224** B4
Culsh **260** B5
Culshabbin **215** E5
Culswick **279** B8
Culter Allers Farm **226** B2
Cultercullen **261** H2
Cults *Aber* **260** D1
Cults *Aberdeen* **261** G4
Cults *D&G* **207** E2
Cultybraggan Camp Visitor
  Centre P&K PH6 2AB
  242 C3
Culverhouse Cross **130** A5
Culverstone Green **123** F2
Culverthorpe **175** F3
Culvie **268** D5
Culworth **148** A3
Culzean Castle & Country
  Park *SAyr*
  KA19 8LE **224** A4
Cumberhead **225** G2
Cumberlow Green **150** B4
Cumbernauld **234** B2
Cumberworth **189** F5
Cuminestown **269** G6
Cumloden **215** F4
Cummersdale **209** G1
Cummertrees **217** F4
Cummingstown **267** J5
Cumnock **225** D3
Cumnor **133** G2
Cumrew **210** B2
Cumrue **217** E2
Cumstoun **216** A5
Cumwhinton **210** A2
Cumwhitton **210** B2
Cundall **202** D5
Cunningsburgh **279** D10

Cunnister **278** E3
Cunnoquhie **244** B3
Cupar **244** B3
Cupar Muir **244** B3
Curbar **185** G5
Curborough **158** D1
Curbridge *Hants* **107** E1
Curbridge *Oxon* **133** F2
Curdridge **107** E1
Curdworth **159** D3
Curland **103** F1
Curlew Green **153** E1
Curling Tye Green **138** B2
Curload **116** A5
Curridge **133** G5
Currie **235** F3
Curry Mallet **116** A5
Curry Rivel **116** A5
Curteis' Corner **124** A5
Curtisden Green **123** G4
Curtisknowle **100** D2
Cury **95** D4
Cusgarne **96** B5
Cushnie **269** F4
Cushuish **115** E4
Cusop **144** B3
Cusworth **186** C2
Cutcloy **207** E3
Cutcombe **114** C4
Cutgate **184** C1
Cuthill **266** E3
Cutiau **154** C1
Cutlers Green **151** D4
Cutnall Green **146** A1
Cutsdean **146** C4
Cutsyke **194** D5
Cutthorpe **186** A5
Cutts **279** D9
Cuttyhill **269** J5
Cuxham **134** B3
Cuxton **123** G2
Cuxwold **188** B2
Cwm *BGwent* **130** A2
Cwm *Denb* **182** B5
Cwm Ffrwd-oer **130** B2
Cwm Gwaun **140** D4
Cwm Head **156** D4
Cwm Irfon **143** E3
Cwm Penmachno **168** A3
Cwm Plysgog **141** E3
Cwmafan **129** D3
Cwmaman **129** G3
Cwmann **142** B3
Cwmbach *Carmar* **141** F5
Cwmbach *Carmar* **127** F5
Cwmbach *Powys* **144** A4
Cwmbach *Powys* **143** G2
Cwmbach *RCT* **129** G2
Cwmbrân **130** B3
Cwmbrwyno **154** D4
Cwmcarn **130** B3
Cwmcarvan **131** D2
Cwm-Cewydd **155** E1
Cwm-cou **141** F3
Cwmcrawnon **130** A1
Cwmdare **129** F2
Cwmdu *Carmar* **142** C4
Cwmdu *Powys* **144** A5
Cwmduad **141** G4
Cwmerfyn **154** D4
Cwmfelin *Bridgend* **129** D1
Cwmfelin *MTyd* **129** G2
Cwmfelin Boeth **127** E1
Cwmfelin Mynach **141** F5
Cwmfelinfach **130** A3
Cwmffrwd **128** A1
Cwmgiedd **129** D1
Cwmgors **128** D1
Cwmgwili **128** B1
Cwmgwrach **129** E2
Cwmgwyn **128** C3
Cwmhiraeth **141** G4
Cwmifor **142** C5
Cwmisfael **128** A1
Cwm-Llinau **155** E2
Cwmllyfri **127** G1
Cwmllynfell **128** D1
Cwm-mawr **128** B1
Cwm-miles **141** E5
Cwm-Morgan **141** F4
Cwm-parc **129** F3
Cwmpengraig **141** G4
Cwmpennar **129** G2
Cwmsychbant **142** A3
Cwmsymlog **154** D4
Cwmtillery **130** B2
Cwm-twrch Isaf **129** D1
Cwm-twrch Uchaf **129** D1
Cwm-y-glo **167** E1
Cwmyoy **144** C5
Cwm-yr-Eglwys **140** D3
Cwmyrhaiadr **155** D3
Cwmystwyth **155** D5
Cwrt **154** C2
Cwrt-newydd **142** A3
Cwrt-y-cadno **142** C3
Cwrt-y-gollen **130** B1
Cyffylliog **169** D2
Cyfronydd **156** A2
Cymau **169** F2
Cymer *NPT* **129** E3
Cymer *RCT* **129** G3
Cyncoed **130** A4
Cynghordy **143** D4
Cynheidre **128** A2
Cynwyd **169** D3
Cynwyl Elfed **141** G5

D

Dabton **216** C1
Daccombe **101** F1
Dacre *Cumb* **210** A5
Dacre *NYorks* **194** A1
Dacre Banks **194** A1
Daddry Shield **211** E4
Dadford **148** B4
Dadlington **159** G3
Dafen **128** B2
Daffy Green **178** A5
Dagdale **172** B4
Dagenham **137** D4
Daggons **106** A1
Daglingworth **132** B2
Dagnall **135** E1
Dail **240** C1
Dail Beag **270** E3
Dail Mòr **270** E3
Dailly **224** A5

Dailnamac **240** B1
Dainton **101** E1
Dairsie (Osnaburgh) **244** C3
Dairy House **197** E5
Daisy Bank **158** C3
Daisy Green **152** B1
Dalabrog **254** C2
Dalavich **240** B3
Dalballoch **258** D5
Dalbeattie **216** C4
Dalblair **225** E4
Dalbog **253** D2
Dalby *IoM* **190** A4
Dalby *Lincs* **176** C1
Dalby *NYorks* **203** F5
Dalby Forest Drive *NYorks*
  YO18 7LT **204** B4
Dalcairnie **224** C5
Dalchalloch **250** C3
Dalchalm **267** G1
Dalchenna **240** C1
Dalchirach **259** J1
Dalchork **273** H7
Dalchreichart **257** J3
Dalchruin **242** C2
Dalcross **266** E7
Dalderby **176** A1
Daldownie **259** K4
Dale *Cumb* **210** B3
Dale *GtMan* **185** D2
Dale *Pembs* **126** B2
Dale Abbey **173** F4
Dale End *Derbys* **172** D1
Dale End *NYorks* **193** F3
Dale Head **199** F1
Dale of Walls **279** A7
Dale Park **108** B2
Dalehouse **203** G1
Dalelia **247** G3
Daless **259** F1
Dalestie **259** J3
Dalfad **260** B4
Dalganachan **275** F4
Dalgarven **233** D5
Dalgety Bay **235** F1
Dalgig **225** D4
Dalginross **242** C2
Dalgonar **225** F5
Dalguise **251** E5
Dalhalvaig **274** D3
Dalham **151** F1
Daligan **233** E1
Dalinlongart **232** C1
Dalivaddy **222** B3
Daljarrock **214** C2
Dalkeith **236** A3
Dallachulish **248** B5
Dallas **267** J6
Dallaschyle **267** F7
Dallash **215** F4
Dalleagles **225** D4
Dallinghoo **153** D2
Dallington *ESuss* **110** B2
Dallington *N'hants* **148** C1
Dallow **202** A5
Dalmadilly **261** F3
Dalmally
  (Dail Mhàilidh) **241** D2
Dalmarnock **255** F5
Dalmary **242** A5
Dalmellington **224** C5
Dalmeny **235** F2
Dalmichy **273** H7
Dalmigavie **258** D3
Dalmore **266** D5
Dalmuir **233** F2
Dalnabreck **247** G3
Dalnacarn **251** F3
Dalnaglar Castle **251** G3
Dalnaha **239** F2
Dalnahaitnach **259** F3
Dalnamain **266** E2
Dalnatrat
  (Dail na Tràghad) **248** B4
Dalnavert **259** F4
Dalnavie **266** D4
Dalness **249** D4
Dalnessie **273** J7
Dalqueich **243** F4
Dalreoch **214** C2
Dalriech **242** C1
Dalroy **266** E7
Dalry **233** D5
Dalrymple **224** B4
Dalscote **148** B2
Dalserf **234** B4
Dalsetter **278** E3
Dalshangan **215** G2
Dalskairth **216** D3
Dalston **209** G1
Dalswinton **216** D2
Dalton *Cumb* **199** G5
Dalton *D&G* **217** F3
Dalton *Lancs* **183** F2
Dalton *N'umb* **220** D4
Dalton *N'umb* **211** F2
Dalton *NYorks* **202** A2
Dalton *NYorks* **202** A3
Dalton *SYorks* **186** B3
Dalton Magna **186** B3
Dalton Piercy **213** D4
Dalton-in-Furness **198** D5
Dalton-le-Dale **212** D3
Dalton-on-Tees **202** B2
Daltote **231** F1
Daltra **267** G7
Dalveich **242** B2
Dalvennan **224** B4
Dalvourn **258** D1
Dalwhinnie **250** B1
Dalwood **103** F2
Dam Green **164** B3
Damask Green **150** A5
Damerham **106** A1
Damgate **179** E5
Damnaglaur **206** B3
Damside **243** E3
Danaway **124** A2
Danbury **137** G2
Danby **203** G2

Danby Wiske **202** C3
Dancers Hill **136** B3
Dandaleith **267** K7
Danderhall **236** A3
Dane Bank **184** D3
Dane End **150** B5
Dane Hills **160** A2
Danebridge **171** G1
Danehill **109** G1
Danesmoor **173** F1
Danestone **261** H3
Daniel's Water **124** C4
Danskine **236** C3
Danthorpe **197** E4
Danzey Green **146** D1
Darby End **158** B4
Darby Green **120** D1
Darenth **137** E5
Daresbury **183** G4
Darfield **186** B2
Dargate **124** C2
Dargues **220** A2
Darite **97** G3
Darland **123** G2
Darlaston **158** B3
Darley **194** B2
Darley Bridge **173** D1
Darley Dale **173** D1
Darley Head **194** A2
Darley Hillside **173** D1
Darlingscott **147** E3
Darlington **202** B1
Darliston **170** C4
Darlton **187** E5
Darnabo **269** F6
Darnall **186** A4
Darnconner **225** D3
Darnford **261** G5
Darngarroch **216** A4
Darnick **227** G3
Darowen **155** E2
Darra **269** F6
Darracott **112** C4
Darras Hall **221** D4
Darrington **186** B1
Darrow Green **165** D3
Darsham **153** F1
Dartfield **269** J5
Dartford **137** E5
Dartington **101** D1
Dartington Cider Press
  Centre *Devon*
  TQ9 6TQ **101** D1
Dartington Crystal Ltd.
  Devon
  EX38 7AN **113** E4
Dartmeet **99** G3
Dartmouth **101** E2
Darton **186** A1
Darvel **225** D2
Darwell Hole **110** C1
Darwen **192** C5
Datchet **135** E5
Datchworth **136** B1
Datchworth Green **136** B1
Daubhill **184** A2
Daugh of
  Kinermony **267** K7
Dauntsey **132** B4
Dauntsey Green **132** B4
Dauntsey Lock **132** B4
Dava **259** H1
Davaar **222** C4
Davan **260** C4
Davenham **184** A5
Davenport Green **184** C4
Daventry **148** A1
Daventry Country Park
  N'hants
  NN11 2JB **148** A1
David Marshall Lodge
  Stir FK8 3SX **242** A4
Davidstow **97** F1
Davington **226** D5
Daviot *Aber* **261** F2
Daviot *High* **258** E1
Davoch of Grange **268** C5
Davyhulme **184** B3
Dawley **157** F2
Dawlish **102** C5
Dawn **181** G5
Daws Heath **138** B4
Daw's House **98** D3
Dawsmere **176** B3
Day Green **171** E2
Dayhills **171** G4
Dayhouse Bank **158** B5
Daylesford **147** E5
Ddôl **182** C5
Deadman's Cross **149** G3
Deadwaters **234** B5
Deaf Hill **212** C4
Deal **125** F3
Deal Hall **138** D3
Dean *Cumb* **209** D4
Dean *Devon* **100** D1
Dean *Dorset* **105** F1
Dean *Hants* **107** E1
Dean *Oxon* **147** F5
Dean *Som* **117** D3
Dean Bank **212** B4
Dean Castle & Country
  Park *EAyr*
  KA3 1XB **224** C2
Dean Cross **113** F1
Dean Gallery *Edin*
  EH4 3DS **36** B4
Dean Head **185** G2
Dean Prior **100** D1
Dean Row **184** C4
Deane *GtMan* **184** A2
Deane *Hants* **119** G2
Deanland **105** F1
Deanlane End **107** G1
Deans Bottom **124** A2
Deanscales **209** D4
Deanshanger **148** C4
Deanston **242** C4
Dearham **209** D3
Debach **152** D2
Debate **218** A3
Debdale **151** D4
Debden **151** D4
Debden Cross **151** D4
Debden Green *Essex* **51** D4

Debden Green
  Essex **136** D3
Debenham **152** C1
Deblin's Green **146** A3
Dechmont **235** E2
Decker Hill **157** G1
Deddington **147** G4
Dedham **152** B4
Dedham Heath **152** B4
Dedworth **135** E5
Deecastle **260** C5
Deene **161** E3
Deenethorpe **161** E3
Deep, The *HU1 4DP*
  76 Kingston upon Hull
Deep Sea World, North
  Queensferry *Fife*
  KY11 1JR **235** F1
Deepcar **185** G3
Deepcut **121** E2
Deepdale *Cumb* **200** C4
Deepdale *NYorks* **201** D5
Deeping Gate **161** G2
Deeping St. James **161** G2
Deeping
  St. Nicholas **162** A1
Deepweir **131** D4
Deerhill **268** C5
Deerhurst **146** A5
Deerhurst Walton **146** A5
Deerness Valley Walk
  Dur DH7 7RJ **212** A3
Deerton Street **124** B2
Defford **146** B3
Defynnog **143** F5
Deganwy **181** F5
Degnish **239** G2
Deighton *NYorks* **202** C2
Deighton *WYorks* **185** F1
Deighton *York* **195** F3
Deiniolen **167** E1
Delabole **97** E1
Delamere **170** C1
Delavorar **259** J3
Delfrigs **261** H2
Dell Lodge **259** H3
Dell Quay **108** A3
Delliefure **259** H1
Delly End **133** F1
Delnabo **259** J3
Delny **266** E4
Delph **185** D2
Delphorrie **260** C3
Delves **212** A3
Delvine **251** G5
Dembleby **175** F4
Denaby **186** B3
Denaby Main **186** B3
Denbies Wine Estate
  Surr RH5 6AA **121** G2
Denbigh (Dinbych) **168** D1
Denbury **101** E1
Denby **173** E3
Denby Dale **185** G2
Denby Pottery *Derbys*
  DE5 8NX **18** C1
Denchworth **133** F3
Dendron **198** D5
Denend **260** E1
Denford **161** E5
Dengie **138** C2
Denham *Bucks* **135** F4
Denham *Suff* **164** C3
Denham *Suff* **151** F1
Denham Green **135** F4
Denham Street **164** C4
Denhead *Aber* **261** F3
Denhead *Aber* **269** J5
Denhead *Fife* **244** C3
Denhead of
  Arbirlot **253** D5
Denhead of Gray **244** B1
Denholm **227** G4
Denholme **193** G4
Denholme Clough **193** G4
Denio **166** C4
Denmead **107** F1
Denmill **261** G3
Denmoss **268** E6
Dennington **153** D1
Denny **234** C1
Dennyloanhead **234** C1
Denshaw **185** D1
Denside **261** G5
Densole **125** E4
Denston **151** F2
Denstone **172** B3
Dent **200** C4
Denton *Cambs* **161** G4
Denton *Darl* **202** B1
Denton *ESuss* **109** G3
Denton *GtMan* **184** D3
Denton *Kent* **125** E4
Denton *Kent* **137** F5
Denton *Lincs* **175** D4
Denton *N'hants* **148** D2
Denton *Norf* **165** D3
Denton *NYorks* **194** A3
Denton *Oxon* **134** A2
Denton's Green **183** F3
Denver **163** E2
Denville **107** G2
Denwick **229** G5
Deopham **178** B5
Deopham Green **164** B2
Depden **151** F2
Depden Green **151** F2
Deptford *GtLon* **136** C5
Deptford *Wilts* **118** B4
Derby **173** E4
Derby City Museum & Art
  Gallery *DE1 1BS*
  70 Derby
Derbyhaven **190** A5
Dereham
  (East Dereham) **178** A4
Dererach **239** E2
Deri **130** A2
Derril **112** D5
Derringstone **125** E4
Derriton **112** D5
Derry **242** D1
Derry Hill **132** B5
Derrythorpe **187** F2
Dersingham **177** E4
Dervaig **246** D4
Derwen **169** D2

Derwenlas **154** D3
Derwent Walk Country Park
  Dur NE16 3BN **28** A3
Derwydd **128** C1
Derybruich **232** A2
Desborough **160** D4
Desford **159** G2
Detchant **229** E3
Dethick **173** E2
Detling **123** G3
Deuddwr **156** B1
Deunant **168** C1
Deuxhill **157** F4
Devauden **131** D3
Devil's Bridge
  (Pontarfynach) **154** D5
Devitts Green **159** E3
Devizes **118** B1
Devon Guild of Craftsmen
  Devon
  TQ13 9AF **102** B5
Devonport **100** A2
Devonside **243** E5
Devoran **95** E3
Dewlish **105** D3
Dewsall Court **145** D4
Dewsbury **194** B5
Dewsbury Moor **194** B5
Dhiseig **239** D3
Dhoon **190** C3
Dhoor **190** C2
Dhowin **190** C1
Dhuhallow **258** C2
Dial Green **121** F3
Dial Post **109** D2
Dibden **106** D2
Dibden Hill **135** E3
Dibden Purlieu **106** D2
Dick Institute *EAyr*
  KA1 3BU **224** C2
Dickleburgh **164** C3
Dickleburgh Moor **164** C3
Didbrook **146** C4
Didcot **134** A3
Diddington **149** G1
Diddlebury **157** F4
Didley **145** D4
Didling **108** A2
Didmarton **132** A4
Didsbury **184** C3
Didworthy **100** C1
Digby **175** F2
Digg **263** K5
Diggle **185** E2
Digmoor **183** F2
Digswell **136** B1
Dihewyd **142** A2
Dildawn **216** B5
Dilham **179** E3
Dilhorne **171** G3
Dillington **149** G1
Dilston **211** F1
Dilton **144** D2
Dilton Marsh **117** F3
Dilwyn **144** D2
Dilwyn Common **144** D2
Dimple **184** B1
Dinas *Carmar* **141** F4
Dinas *Gwyn* **167** D2
Dinas *Gwyn* **166** B4
Dinas Cross **140** D4
Dinas Dinlle **166** D2
Dinas Powys **130** A5
Dinas-Mawddwy **155** E1
Dinckley **192** C4
Dinder **116** C3
Dinedor **145** E4
Dingestow **131** D1
Dingley **160** C4
Dingwall (Inbhir
  Pheofharain) **266** C6
Dinlabyre **218** D2
Dinnet **260** C5
Dinnington *Som* **104** A1
Dinnington *SYorks* **186** B4
Dinnington *T&W* **221** E4
Dinorwig **167** E1
Dinosaur Adventure Park
  Norf NR9 5JW **178** C4
Dinosaur Museum,
  Dorchester *Dorset*
  DT1 1EW **104** D3
Dinton *Bucks* **134** C1
Dinton *Wilts* **118** B4
Dinton Pastures Country
  Park *W'ham*
  RG10 0TH **134** C5
Dinvin **214** B5
Dinwoodie Mains **217** F1
Dinworthy **112** D4
Dipford **115** F5
Dippen *A&B* **222** C2
Dippen *NAyr* **223** F3
Dippenhall **120** D3
Dipple *Moray* **268** B5
Dipple *SAyr* **224** A5
Diptford **100** D2
Dipton **212** A2
Dirdhu **259** H2
Dirleton **236** C1
Discoed **144** B1
Discovery Museum
  T&W NE1 4JA
  79 Newcastle upon Tyne
Diseworth **173** F5
Dishes **276** F5
Dishforth **202** C5
Dishley **173** G5
Disley **185** D4
Diss **164** C3
Disserth **143** G2
Distington **208** D4
Ditcheat **116** D4
Ditchingham **165** E2
Ditchley **147** F5
Ditchling **109** F2
Ditteridge **117** F1
Dittisham **101** E2
Ditton *Halton* **183** F4
Ditton *Kent* **123** G3
Ditton Green **151** E2
Ditton Priors **157** F4
Dixton *Glos* **146** B4
Dixton *Mon* **131** E1
Dobcross **185** D2
Dobwalls **97** G3
Dochgarroch **258** D1

Dock Museum, Barrow-in-
  Furness *Cumb*
  LA14 2PW **191** E1
Dockenfield **120** D3
Docker *Cumb* **199** G3
Docker *Lancs* **199** G5
Docking **177** F4
Dockray *Cumb* **209** G4
Dockray *Cumb* **209** F1
Dodbrooke **100** D3
Doddenham **145** G2
Doddinghurst **137** E3
Doddington *Cambs* **162** C3
Doddington *Kent* **124** B3
Doddington *Lincs* **187** G5
Doddington *N'umb* **229** D3
Doddington *Shrop* **157** F5
Doddiscombsleigh **102** B4
Doddycross **98** D4
Dodford *N'hants* **148** B1
Dodford *Worcs* **158** B5
Dodington *SGlos* **131** G4
Dodington *Som* **115** G3
Dodington Ash **131** G5
Dodleston **170** A1
Dods Leigh **172** B4
Dodscott **113** F4
Dodworth **186** A2
Doehole **173** E2
Doffcocker **184** A1
Dog Village **102** C3
Dogdyke **176** A2
Dogmersfield **120** C2
Dogsthorpe **162** A2
Dol Fawr **155** F2
Dolanog **155** G1
Dolau *Powys* **144** A1
Dolau *RCT* **129** G4
Dolbenmaen **167** E3
Doley **171** E5
Dolfach **155** F5
Dolfor **156** A4
Dolgarreg **142** D4
Dolgarrog **168** A1
Dolgellau **154** D1
Dolgoch **154** C2
Dolgran **142** A4
Doll **267** F2
Dollar **243** E5
Dollarbeg **243** E5
Dolphin **182** C5
Dolphinholme **192** B2
Dolphinton **235** F5
Dolton **113** F4
Dolwen *Conwy* **181** G5
Dolwen *Powys* **155** F2
Dolwyddelan **168** A2
Dôl-y-bont **154** C4
Dol-y-cannau **144** A3
Dolyhir **144** B2
Dolwern **169** F4
Domgay **156** B1
Doncaster **186** C2
Doncaster Racecourse
  Exhibition Centre
  SYorks DN2 6BB **186** D2
Donhead
  St. Andrew **118** A5
Donhead St. Mary **118** A5
Donibristle **235** F1
Doniford **115** D3
Donington *Lincs* **176** A4
Donington *Shrop* **158** A3
Donington le Heath **159** G1
Donington on Bain **188** C4
Donisthorpe **159** F1
Donkey Sanctuary,
  Salcombe Regis *Devon*
  EX10 0NU **103** E4
Donna Nook **189** E3
Donnington *Glos* **147** D5
Donnington *Here* **145** G4
Donnington *Shrop* **157** E2
Donnington *Tel&W* **157** G1
Donnington *WBerks* **119** F1
Donnington *WSuss* **108** A3
Donyatt **103** G1
Dorchester *Dorset* **104** D3
Dorchester *Oxon* **134** A3
Dorchester Abbey *Oxon*
  OX10 7HH **134** A3
Dordon **159** E2
Dore **186** A4
Dores (Duras) **258** C1
Dorket Head **173** G3
Dorking **121** G3
Dorley's Corner **153** E1
Dormans Park **122** C4
Dormansland **122** C4
Dormanstown **213** E5
Dormer's Wells **136** A4
Dormington **145** E3
Dormston **146** B2
Dorn **147** E4
Dorney **135** E5
Dorney Reach **135** E5
Dornie
  (An Dòrnaidh) **256** E2
Dornoch **266** E3
Dornock **218** A5
Dorrery **275** F3
Dorridge **159** D5
Dorrington *Lincs* **175** F2
Dorrington *Shrop* **157** D2
Dorsell **260** D3
Dorsington **146** D3
Dorstone **144** C3
Dorton **134** B1
Dorusduain **257** F2
Dosthill **159** E3
Dotland **211** F2
Dottery **104** A3
Doublebois **97** F3
Dougalston **233** G2
Dougarie **223** D2
Doughton **132** A3
Douglas *IoM* **190** B4
Douglas *SLan* **225** G2
Douglas & Angus **244** C1
Douglas Water **225** G2
Douglastown **252** C5
Doulting **116** D3
Dounby **276** B5
Doune *A&B* **241** E5
Doune *A&B* **241** F3
Doune *High* **259** F3
Doune *High* **266** B1

Doune *Stir* **242** C4
Dounepark **269** F4
Douneside **260** C4
Dounie *High* **266** D3
Dounie *High* **266** C2
Dounreay **274** E2
Dousland **100** B1
Dovaston **170** A5
Dove Holes **185** E5
Dovenby **209** E3
Dovendale **188** D4
Dover **125** F4
Dovercourt **152** D4
Doverdale **146** A1
Doveridge **172** C4
Doversgreen **122** B4
Dowally **251** F5
Dowdeswell **146** C5
Dowhill **224** A5
Dowlais **129** G4
Dowlands **103** F3
Dowlish Ford **103** G1
Dowlish Wake **103** G1
Down Ampney **132** D3
Down End **116** A3
Down Hatherley **146** A5
Down St. Mary **102** A2
Down Thomas **100** B3
Downderry **98** D5
Downe **122** D2
Downend *IoW* **107** E4
Downend *SGlos* **131** F5
Downend *WBerks* **133** G5
Downfield **244** B1
Downfields **163** E5
Downgate **99** D3
Downham *Essex* **137** G3
Downham *Lancs* **193** D3
Downham *N'umb* **228** C3
Downham Market **163** E2
Downhead *Corn* **97** G1
Downhead *Som* **117** D3
Downhead *Som* **116** C5
Downholland Cross **183** E2
Downholme **202** A3
Downies **261** H5
Downley **135** D3
Downs **130** A5
Downside *NSom* **116** B1
Downside *Som* **116** D3
Downside *Som* **116** D2
Downside *Surr* **121** G2
Downton *Devon* **99** F2
Downton *Devon* **101** E2
Downton *Hants* **106** B3
Downton *Wilts* **118** C5
Downton on the
  Rock **156** D5
Dowsby **175** G5
Dowthwaitehead **209** G4
Doxey **171** F5
Doynton **131** G5
Drabblegate **178** D3
Draethen **130** B4
Draffan **234** B5
Dragley Beck **199** D5
Drakeland Corner **100** B2
Drakelow **158** A4
Drakemyre **233** D4
Drakes Broughton **146** B3
Drakes Cross **158** C5
Draughton *N'hants* **160** C5
Draughton *NYorks* **193** G2
Drax **195** F5
Draycot Foliat **133** D5
Draycote **147** G1
Draycott *Derbys* **173** F4
Draycott *Glos* **147** D4
Draycott *Shrop* **158** A3
Draycott *Som* **116** B2
Draycott *Worcs* **146** A3
Draycott in the
  Clay **172** C5
Draycott in the
  Moors **171** G4
Drayford **102** A1
Draynes **97** G3
Drayton *Leics* **160** D3
Drayton *Lincs* **176** A4
Drayton *Norf* **178** C4
Drayton *Oxon* **147** G3
Drayton *Oxon* **133** G3
Drayton *Ports* **107** F2
Drayton *Som* **116** B5
Drayton *Warks* **147** D2
Drayton *Worcs* **158** B5
Drayton Bassett **159** D2
Drayton Beauchamp
  135 E1
Drayton Manor Park *Staffs*
  B78 3TW **159** D2
Drayton Parslow **148** D5
Drayton
  St. Leonard **134** A3
Drebley **193** G2
Dreemskerry **190** C2
Dreenhill **126** C1
Drefach *Carmar* **141** G4
Drefach *Carmar* **128** B1
Dre-fach *Cere* **142** B3
Drefelin **141** G4
Dreghorn **224** B2
Drem **236** C1
Drewsteignton **102** A3
Drhy **189** D5
Driffield *ERid* **196** C2
Driffield *Glos* **132** C3
Drigg **198** B3
Drighlington **194** B5
Drimfern **240** C3
Drimlee **240** D3
Drimnin **247** E4
Drimore **262** C7
Drimpton **104** A2
Drimsdale
  (Dreumasdal) **254** C1
Drimsynie **241** D4
Drimvore **240** A5
Drinan **256** B3
Dringhouses **195** E2
Drinisiader **263** G2
Drinkstone **152** A1
Drinkstone Green **152** A1
Drishaig **241** D3
Drissaig **240** B3

Drointon **172** B5
Droitwich Spa **146** A1
Dron **243** G3
Dronfield **186** A5
Dronfield
  Woodhouse **186** A5
Drongan **224** C4
Dronley **244** B1
Droop **105** D2
Dropmore **135** E4
Droxford **107** F1
Droylsden **184** D3
Druid **168** D2
Druidston **126** B1
Druimarbin **248** C2
Druimavuic **248** C5
Druimdrishaig **231** F2
Druimindarroch **247** F1
Druimkinnerras **258** B1
Drum *A&B* **232** A4
Drum *P&K* **243** F4
Drumachloy **232** B3
Drumbeg **272** D5
Drumblade **268** D6
Drumblair **268** E6
Drumbuie *D&G* **225** F4
Drumbuie *High* **256** D1
Drumburgh **209** F1
Drumchapel **233** G2
Drumchardine **266** C7
Drumchork **264** E3
Drumclog **225** E2
Drumdelgie **268** C6
Drumderfit **266** D6
Drumeldrie **244** C4
Drumelzier **226** C2
Drumfearn **256** C3
Drumgarve **222** C3
Drumgley **252** C4
Drumguish **258** E5
Drumhead **260** E5
Drumin **259** J1
Drumine **266** E6
Drumjohn **215** G1
Drumlamford
  House **215** D3
Drumlasie **260** E4
Drumlemble **222** B4
Drumlithie **253** F1
Drummond *High* **266** D5
Drummond *Stir* **242** B4
Drummore **206** B3
Drummuir **268** B6
Drummuir Castle **268** B6
Drumnadrochit (Druim na
  Drochaid) **258** C2
Drumnagorrach **268** D5
Drumnatorran **248** A3
Drumoak **261** F4
Drumore **222** C3
Drumour **243** E1
Drumrash **216** A3
Drumrunie **265** H1
Drums **261** H2
Drumsturdy **244** C1
Drumuie **263** K7
Drumuillie **259** G2
Drumvaich **242** B4
Drumwhindle **261** H1
Drumwhirn **216** B2
Drunkendub **253** E5
Druridge **221** E2
Druridge Bay Country
  Park *N'umb*
  NE61 5BX **221** E2
Drury **169** F1
Drusillas Park *ESuss*
  BN26 5QS **110** A3
Drws-y-nant **168** B5
Dry Doddington **174** D3
Dry Drayton **150** B1
Dry Harbour **264** C6
Dry Sandford **133** G2
Dry Street **137** F4
Drybeck **200** B1
Drybridge *Moray* **268** C4
Drybridge *NAyr* **224** B2
Drybrook **131** F1
Dryburgh **227** G2
Dryhope **227** D3
Drymen **233** F1
Drymuir **269** H6
Drynoch **255** K1
Dryslwyn **142** B5
Dryton **157** E2
Duachy **240** A2
Dubford **269** F4
Dubhchladach **231** G3
Dubheads **243** E2
Dublin **152** C1
Dubton **253** D4
Duchal **233** E3
Duchray **241** G4
Duck Bay **233** E1
Duck End *Bed* **149** F3
Duck End *Cambs* **150** A1
Duck End *Essex* **151** F5
Duck Street **194** A1
Duckington **170** B2
Ducklington **133** F2
Duckmanton **186** B5
Duck's Cross **149** G2
Ducks Island **136** B3
Duddenhoe End **150** C4
Duddingston **235** G2
Duddington **161** F2
Duddlestone **115** F5
Duddleswell **109** G1
Duddo **237** F5
Duddon **170** C1
Duddon Bridge **198** C4
Dudleston **170** A4
Dudleston Heath
  (Criftins) **170** A4
Dudley *T&W* **221** E4
Dudley *WMid* **158** B3
Dudley Port **158** B3
Dudley Zoo & Castle
  WMid DY1 4QB **14** B3
Dudlow's Green **184** A4
Dudsbury **105** G3
Duffield **173** E3
Duffryn **129** E3

Dufftown **260** B1
Duffus **267** J5
Dufton **210** C5
Duggleby **196** A1
Duiar **259** J1
Duible **274** E6
Duiletter **241** D2
Duinish **250** D3
Duirinish **256** D1
Duisky **248** C2
Duke End **159** E4
Dukestown **130** A1
Dukinfield **184** D3
Dulas **180** C4
Dulax **260** B3
Dulcote **116** C3
Dulford **103** D2
Dull **250** D5
Dullatur **234** B2
Dullingham **151** E2
Dullingham Ley **151** E2
Dulnain Bridge **259** G2
Duloe *Bed* **149** G1
Duloe *Corn* **97** G4
Dulsie **267** G7
Dulverton **114** C5
Dulwich **136** C5
Dulwich Picture Gallery
  GtLon SE21 7AD **13** C7
Dumbarton **233** F2
Dumbleton **146** C4
Dumcrieff **226** C5
Dumeath **260** C1
Dumfin **233** E1
Dumfries **217** D3
Dumgoyne **233** G1
Dummer **119** G3
Dun **253** E4
Dunach **240** A2
Dunalastair **250** C4
Dunan *A&B* **232** B2
Dunan *High* **256** B2
Dunans **240** C5
Dunball **116** A3
Dunbar **237** D2
Dunbeath **275** G5
Dunbeg **240** A2
Dunblane **242** C4
Dunbog **244** A3
Dunbridge **119** E5
Duncanston *Aber* **260** D2
Duncanston *High* **266** C6
Dunchideock **102** B4
Dunchurch **159** G5
Duncote **148** B2
Duncow **217** D2
Duncraggan **242** A4
Duncrievie **243** G4
Duncroist **242** A1
Duncton **108** B2
Dundee **244** C1
Dundee Airport **244** B2
Dundee Contemporary Arts
  DD1 4DY **71** Dundee
Dundon **116** B4
Dundon Hayes **116** B4
Dundonald **224** B2
Dundonnell (Ach-Dà-
  Dhòmhnaill) **265** G3
Dundraw **209** F2
Dundreggan
  (Dul Dreagain) **257** K3
Dundrennan **208** A2
Dundridge **107** E1
Dundry **116** C1
Dunearn **235** G1
Dunecht **261** F4
Dunfermline **235** E1
Dunfield **132** D3
Dunford Bridge **185** F2
Dungate **124** B3
Dungavel **225** E2
Dungworth **185** G3
Dunham **187** D5
Dunham Massey Hall,
  Park & Gardens *GtMan*
  WA14 4SJ **24** C5
Dunham Town **184** B4
Dunham
  Woodhouses **184** B4
Dunham-on-the-
  Hill **183** F5
Dunhampton **146** A1
Dunholme **188** A5
Dunino **244** D3
Dunipace **234** C1
Dunira **242** C2
Dunkeld **251** F5
Dunkerton **117** E2
Dunkeswell **103** D2
Dunkeswick **194** C3
Dunkirk *ChesW&C* **183** E5
Dunkirk *Kent* **124** C3
Dunk's Green **123** F3
Dunlappie **253** D3
Dunley *Hants* **119** F2
Dunley *Worcs* **145** G1
Dunlop **233** F5
Dunloskin **232** C2
Dunmere **97** E3
Dunmore *A&B* **231** F3
Dunmore *Falk* **234** C1
Dunn **275** H1
Dunn Street **123** G2
Dunnabie **218** A3
Dunnet **275** H1
Dunnichen **252** D5
Dunning **243** F3
Dunnington *ERid* **197** D2
Dunnington *Warks* **146** C2
Dunnington *York* **195** D2
Dunnockshaw **193** E5
Dunollie **240** A2
Dunoon **232** C2
Dunragit **214** C5
Dunrostan **231** F1
Duns **237** E4
Duns Tew **147** G5
Dunsa **185** G5
Dunsby **175** G5
Dunscore **216** C2
Dunscroft **187** D2
Dunsdale **203** F1
Dunsden Green **134** C5
Dunsfold **121** G4
Dunsford **121** F4

Dunsford **102** B4
Dunsford *Devon* EX6 7EG
  102 B4
Dunshalt **244** A3
Dunshill **146** A4
Dunsinnan **243** G1
Dunsland Cross **113** E5
Dunsley *NYorks* **204** B1
Dunsley *Staffs* **158** A4
Dunsmore **135** D2
Dunsop Bridge **192** C2
Dunstable **149** F5
Dunstable Downs *CenBeds*
  LU6 2GY **149** F5
Dunstall **172** C5
Dunstall Green **151** F1
Dunstan **229** F4
Dunstan Steads **229** G4
Dunster **114** C4
Dunster Castle & Gardens
  Som TA24 6SL **114** C4
Dunston *Lincs* **175** F1
Dunston *Norf* **178** D5
Dunston *Staffs* **158** B1
Dunston Heath **158** B1
Dunston Hill **212** B1
Dunstone *Devon* **102** A5
Dunstone *Devon* **100** B2
Dunsville **187** D2
Dunswell **196** C4
Dunsyre **235** E5
Dunterton **99** D3
Duntisbourne
  Abbots **132** B2
Duntisbourne Leer **132** B2
Duntisbourne
  Rouse **132** B2
Duntish **104** C2
Duntocher **233** F2
Dunton *Bucks* **148** D5
Dunton *CenBeds* **150** A3
Dunton *Norf* **177** G4
Dunton Bassett **160** A3
Dunton Green **123** E3
Dunton Wayletts **137** F3
Duntulm **263** K4
Dunure **224** A4
Dunure Mains **224** A4
Dunvant **128** B3
Dunvegan **263** H7
Dunvegan Castle *High*
  IV55 8WF **263** H7
Dunwich **165** F4
Dura **244** C3
Durdar **210** A2
Durgan **95** E4
Durgates **123** F5
Durham **212** B3
Durham Cathedral
  DH1 3EH **71** Durham
Durham Dales Centre *Dur*
  DL13 2FJ **211** G4
Durham Tees Valley
  Airport **202** C1
Durinemast **247** F4
Durisdeer **225** G4
Durleigh **115** F4
Durley *Hants* **107** E1
Durley *Wilts* **118** D1
Durley Street **107** E1
Durlow Common **145** F4
Durnamuck **265** G2
Durness **273** G2
Durno **261** F2
Duror **248** B4
Durran *A&B* **240** B4
Durran *High* **275** G2
Durrants **107** G2
Durrington *Wilts* **118** C3
Durrington *WSuss* **108** C3
Dursley **131** G3
Dursley Cross **131** F1
Durston **115** F5
Durweston **105** E2
Dury **279** D6
Duston **148** C1
Duthie Park & David Welch
  Winter Gardens *Aberdeen*
  AB11 7TH **261** H4
Duthil **259** G2
Dutlas **156** B5
Duton Hill **151** E5
Dutson **98** D2
Dutton **183** G5
Duxford **150** C3
Dwygyfylchi **181** F5
Dwyran **166** D1
Dyce **261** G3
Dyfatty **128** A2
Dyffryn *Bridgend* **129** E3
Dyffryn *Pembs* **140** C4
Dyffryn *VGlam* **129** G5
Dyffryn Ardudwy **167** E5
Dyffryn Castell **155** F3
Dyffryn Ceidrych **142** D5
Dyffryn Cellwen **129** E2
Dyke *Devon* **112** D3
Dyke *Lincs* **175** G5
Dyke *Moray* **267** G6
Dykehead *Angus* **252** B3
Dykehead *NLan* **234** C5
Dykehead *Stir* **242** A5
Dykelands **253** F3
Dykends **252** A4
Dykeside **269** F6
Dylan Thomas Centre
  SA1 1RR **86** Swansea
Dylife **155** E3
Dymchurch **111** G1
Dymock **145** G4
Dyrham **131** G5
Durham Park *SGlos*
  SN14 8ER **8** F2
Dysart **244** B5
Dyserth **182** B5

E

Eachwick **220** D4
Eadar dha Fhadhail **270** C4
Eagland Hill **192** A3
Eagle **175** D1
Eagle Barnsdale **175** D1
Eagle Moor **175** D1
Eaglescliffe **202** D1
Eaglesfield *Cumb* **209** D4

Eaglesfield *D&G* **218** A4
Eaglesham **233** G4
Eaglethorpe **161** F3
Eagley **184** B1
Eairy **190** A4
Eakley **148** D2
Eakring **174** B1
Ealand **187** E1
Ealing **136** A4
Eamont Bridge **210** B5
Earby **193** F3
Earcroft **192** C5
Eardington **157** G3
Eardisland **144** D2
Eardisley **144** C3
Eardiston *Shrop* **170** A5
Eardiston *Worcs* **145** F1
Earith **162** B5
Earl Shilton **159** G3
Earl Soham **152** D1
Earl Sterndale **172** B1
Earl Stonham **152** C2
Earle **229** D4
Earlestown **183** G3
Earley **134** C5
Earlham **178** D5
Earlish **263** J5
Earls Barton **149** D1
Earls Colne **151** G5
Earl's Common **146** B2
Earl's Court **136** B5
Earl's Croome **146** A3
Earl's Green **152** B1
Earlsdon **159** F5
Earlsferry **244** C4
Earlsford **261** G1
Earlsheaton **194** B5
Earlston *ScBord* **227** G2
Earlswood *Mon* **131** D3
Earlswood *Surr* **122** B4
Earlswood *Warks* **158** D5
Earnley **108** A4
Earnshaw Bridge **192** B5
Earsairidh **254** C5
Earsdon **221** F4
Earsdon Moor **221** D2
Earsham **165** E3
Earsham Street **164** D4
Earswick **195** E2
Eartham **108** B3
Earthcott Green **131** F4
Easby **203** E2
Easdale **239** G3
Easebourne **121** D5
Easenhall **159** G5
Eashing **121** E3
Easington *Bucks* **134** B1
Easington *Dur* **212** D3
Easington *ERid* **189** D1
Easington *N'umb* **229** F3
Easington *Oxon* **134** B3
Easington *Oxon* **147** G4
Easington *R&C* **203** G1
Easington Colliery **212** D3
Easington Lane **212** C3
Easingwold **195** E1
Easole Street **125** E3
Eassie **252** B5
East Aberthaw **114** D1
East Acton **136** B4
East Allington **101** D3
East Anstey **114** B5
East Anton **119** E3
East Appleton **202** B3
East Ardsley **194** C5
East Ashey **107** E4
East Ashling **108** A3
East Auchronie **261** G4
East Ayton **204** C4
East Barkwith **188** B4
East Barming **123** G3
East Barnby **204** B1
East Barnet **136** B3
East Barsham **178** A2
East Beckham **178** C2
East Bedfont **135** F5
East Bergholt **152** B4
East Bierley **194** A5
East Bilney **178** A4
East Blatchington **109** G4
East Boldon **212** C1
East Boldre **106** C2
East Bolton **229** F5
East Bower **116** A4
East Brent **116** A2
East Bridge **153** F1
East Bridgford **174** B3
East Brora **267** G1
East Buckland **113** G2
East Budleigh **103** D4
East Burnham **135** E4
East Burra **279** C9
East Burrafirth **279** C7
East Burton **105** E4
East Butsfield **212** A3
East Butterleigh **102** C2
East Butterwick **187** F2
East Cairnbeg **253** F2
East Calder **235** E3
East Carleton **178** C5
East Carlton
  N'hants **160** D4
East Carlton
  WYorks **194** B3
East Carlton Countryside
  Park *N'hants*
  LE16 8YF **160** D4
East Chaldon (Chaldon
  Herring) **105** D4
East Challow **133** F4
East Charleton **101** D3
East Chelborough **104** B2
East Chiltington **109** F2
East Chinnock **104** A1
East Chisenbury **118** C2
East Clandon **121** F2
East Claydon **148** C5
East Clyne **267** G1
East Coker **104** B1
East Compton
  Dorset **105** E1
East Compton
  Som **116** D3
East Coombe **102** B2
East Cornworthy **101** E2
East Cottingwith **195** G3
East Cowes **107** E3

East Cowick 195 F5
East Cowton 202 C2
East Cramlington 221 E4
East Cranmore 117 D3
East Creech 105 F4
East Croachy 258 D2
East Darlochan 222 B3
East Davoch 260 C4
East Dean ESuss 110 A4
East Dean Hants 119 D5
East Dean WSuss 108 B2
East Dereham (Dereham) 178 A4
East Down 113 F1
East Drayton 187 E5
East Dundry 116 C1
East Ella 196 C5
East End ERid 197 D4
East End ERid 197 E5
East End Essex 138 D2
East End Hants 119 F1
East End Hants 106 C3
East End Herts 150 C5
East End Kent 124 A5
East End Kent 124 B1
East End MK 149 E3
East End NSom 131 D5
East End Oxon 133 F1
East End Poole 105 F3
East End Som 116 C2
East End Suff 152 C4
East End Suff 152 C2
East Farleigh 123 G3
East Farndon 160 C4
East Ferry 187 F3
East Firsby 188 A4
East Fleetham 229 G4
East Fortune 236 C2
East Garston 133 F5
East Ginge 133 G4
East Goscote 160 B1
East Grafton 119 D1
East Green Suff 153 F1
East Green Suff 151 E2
East Grimstead 118 D5
East Grinstead 122 C5
East Guldeford 111 E1
East Haddon 148 B1
East Hagbourne 134 A4
East Halton 188 B1
East Ham 136 D4
East Hanney 133 G3
East Hanningfield 137 G2
East Hardwick 186 B1
East Harling 164 A3
East Harlsey 202 D3
East Harnham 118 C5
East Harptree 116 C2
East Hartford 221 E4
East Harting 107 G1
East Hatch 118 A5
East Hatley 150 A2
East Hauxwell 202 A3
East Haven 245 D1
East Heckington 175 G3
East Hedleyhope 212 A3
East Helmsdale 275 F7
East Hendred 133 G4
East Herrington 212 C2
East Heslerton 204 C5
East Hewish 116 B1
East Hoathly 110 A2
East Holme 105 E4
East Horndon 137 F4
East Horrington 116 C3
East Horsley 121 F2
East Horton 229 E3
East Howe 105 G3
East Huntspill 116 A3
East Hyde 136 A1
East Ilsley 133 G4
East Keal 176 B1
East Kennett 118 C1
East Keswick 194 C3
East Kilbride 234 A4
East Kimber 99 E1
East Kirkby 176 B1
East Knapton 204 B5
East Knighton 105 E4
East Knowstone 114 B5
East Knoyle 117 F4
East Kyloe 229 E3
East Lambrook 104 A1
East Lancashire Railway Lancs BL9 0EY 193 E5
East Langdon 125 F4
East Langton 160 C3
East Langwell 266 E1
East Lavant 108 A3
East Lavington 108 B2
East Layton 202 A1
East Leake 173 G5
East Learmouth 228 C3
East Learney 260 E4
East Leigh Devon 102 A2
East Leigh Devon 102 A1
East Leigh Devon 101 D2
East Leigh Devon 100 C2
East Lexham 163 G1
East Lilburn 229 E4
East Linton 236 C2
East Liss 120 C5
East Lockinge 133 G4
East Looe 97 G4
East Lound 187 E2
East Lulworth 105 E4
East Lutton 196 B1
East Lydford 116 C4
East Lyn 114 A3
East Lyng 116 A5
East Mains 260 E5
East Malling 123 G3
East Malling Heath 123 F3
East March 244 C1
East Marden 108 A2
East Markham 187 E5
East Martin 105 G1
East Marton 193 F2
East Meon 120 B5
East Mere 102 C1
East Mersea 139 D1
East Mey 275 J1
East Midlands Airport 173 F5
East Molesey 121 G1
East Moor 194 C5
East Morden 105 F3
East Morriston 236 D5
East Morton 194 A3
East Ness 203 F5
East Newton 197 E4
East Norton 160 C2
East Oakley 119 G2
East Ogwell 102 B5
East Orchard 105 E1
East Ord 237 G4
East Panson 99 D1
East Parley 106 A3
East Peckham 123 F4
East Pennard 116 C4
East Point Pavilion, Lowestoft Suff NR33 0AP 165 G2
East Portlemouth 100 D4
East Prawle 101 D4
East Preston 108 C3
East Pulham 104 D2
East Putford 113 D4
East Quantoxhead 115 E3
East Rainton 212 C3
East Ravendale 188 C3
East Raynham 177 G5
East Retford (Retford) 187 E4
East Rigton 194 C3
East Rolstone 116 A1
East Rounton 202 D2
East Row 204 B1
East Rudham 177 G5
East Runton 178 D1
East Ruston 179 E3
East Saltoun 236 B3
East Shefford 133 F5
East Sleekburn 221 E3
East Somerton 179 F4
East Stockwith 187 E3
East Stoke Dorset 105 E4
East Stoke Notts 174 C3
East Stour 117 F5
East Stourmouth 125 E2
East Stratton 119 G3
East Street 116 C4
East Studdal 125 F4
East Suisnish 256 B1
East Taphouse 97 F3
East Thirston 221 D2
East Tilbury 137 F5
East Tisted 120 C4
East Torrington 188 B4
East Town 116 D3
East Tuddenham 178 B4
East Tytherley 119 D5
East Tytherton 132 B5
East Village 102 B2
East Wall 157 E3
East Walton 163 F1
East Wellow 119 E5
East Wemyss 244 B5
East Whitburn 235 D3
East Wickham 137 D5
East Williamston 127 D2
East Winch 163 E1
East Winterslow 118 D4
East Wittering 107 G3
East Witton 202 A4
East Woodburn 220 B3
East Woodhay 119 F1
East Woodlands 117 E3
East Worldham 120 C4
East Worlington 102 A1
East Youlstone 112 C4
Eastacott 113 G3
Eastbourne 110 B4
Eastbourne Pier ESuss BN21 3EL 72 Eastbourne
Eastbrook 130 A5
Eastburn ERid 196 B2
Eastburn WYorks 193 G3
Eastbury Herts 136 A3
Eastbury WBerks 133 F5
Eastby 193 G2
Eastchurch 124 B1
Eastcombe Glos 132 A2
Eastcombe Som 115 E4
Eastcote GtLon 136 A4
Eastcote N'hants 148 B2
Eastcote WMid 159 D5
Eastcott Corn 112 C4
Eastcott Wilts 118 B2
Eastcourt 132 B3
Eastdown 101 E3
Eastend 147 F5
Easter Ardross 266 D4
Easter Balgedie 243 G4
Easter Balmoral 259 K5
Easter Boleskine 258 C2
Easter Borland 242 B4
Easter Brae 266 D5
Easter Buckieburn 234 B1
Easter Compton 131 E4
Easter Drummond 258 B3
Easter Dullater 242 B4
Easter Ellister 230 A4
Easter Fearn 266 D3
Easter Galcantray 267 F7
Easter Howlaws 237 E5
Easter Kinkell 266 C6
Easter Knox 253 D5
Easter Lednathie 252 B3
Easter Moniack 266 C7
Easter Ord 261 G4
Easter Poldar 242 B5
Easter Skeld (Skeld) 279 C8
Easter Suddie 266 D6
Easter Tulloch 253 F2
Easter Whyntie 268 E4
Eastergate 108 B3
Easterhouse 234 A3
Easterton 118 B2
Easterton Sands 118 B2
Eastertown 116 A2
Eastfield Bristol 131 E5
Eastfield NLan 234 C3
Eastfield NYorks 204 D4
Eastfield Hall 221 E1
Eastgate Dur 211 F4
Eastgate Lincs 161 G1
Eastgate Norf 178 C3
Easthall 150 A5
Eastham Mersey 183 E4
Eastham Worcs 145 F1
Easthampstead 121 D1
Easthampton 144 D1
Easthaugh 178 B4
Eastheath 120 D1
Easthope 157 E3
Easthorpe Essex 152 A5
Easthorpe Leics 174 D4
Easthorpe Notts 174 C2
Easthouses 236 A3
Eastington Devon 102 A2
Eastington Glos 132 D1
Eastington Glos 131 G2
Eastleach Martin 133 E2
Eastleach Turville 133 E2
Eastleigh Devon 113 E3
Eastleigh Hants 106 D1
Eastling 124 B3
Eastmoor Derbys 186 A5
Eastmoor Norf 163 F2
Eastnor 145 G4
Eastoft 187 F1
Eastoke 107 G3
Easton Cambs 161 G5
Easton Cumb 218 C4
Easton Cumb 209 F1
Easton Devon 102 A4
Easton Dorset 104 C5
Easton Hants 119 G4
Easton IoW 106 C4
Easton Lincs 175 E5
Easton Norf 178 C4
Easton Som 116 C3
Easton Suff 153 D2
Easton Wilts 132 A5
Easton Grey 132 A4
Easton Maudit 149 D2
Easton on the Hill 161 F2
Easton Royal 118 D1
Easton-in-Gordano 131 E5
Eastrea 162 A3
Eastriggs 218 A5
Eastrington 195 G4
Eastry 125 F3
Eastside 277 D8
East-the-Water 113 E3
Eastville 131 F5
Eastwell 174 C5
Eastwick 136 D1
Eastwood Notts 173 F3
Eastwood S'end 138 B4
Eastwood SYorks 186 B3
Eastwood WYorks 193 F5
Eastwood End 162 C3
Eathorpe 147 F1
Eaton ChesE 171 F1
Eaton ChesW&C 170 C1
Eaton Leics 174 C5
Eaton Norf 178 D5
Eaton Norf 177 E4
Eaton Notts 187 E5
Eaton Oxon 133 G2
Eaton Shrop 157 E3
Eaton Shrop 156 C4
Eaton Bishop 144 D4
Eaton Bray 149 E5
Eaton Constantine 157 F2
Eaton Ford 149 G2
Eaton Hall 170 B1
Eaton Hastings 133 E3
Eaton Socon 149 G2
Eaton upon Tern 171 D5
Eaves Green 159 E4
Eavestone 194 B1
Ebberston 204 B4
Ebbesborne Wake 118 A5
Ebbw Vale (Glynebwy) 130 A2
Ebchester 212 A2
Ebdon 116 A1
Ebford 102 C4
Ebley 132 A2
Ebnal 170 B3
Ebost 255 J1
Ebrington 147 D3
Ebsworthy Town 99 F1
Ecchinswell 119 F2
Ecclaw 237 E3
Ecclefechan 217 F3
Eccles GtMan 184 B3
Eccles Kent 123 G2
Eccles ScBord 237 E5
Eccles Green 144 C3
Eccles Road 164 B2
Ecclesfield 186 A3
Ecclesgreig 253 F3
Eccleshall 171 F5
Eccleshill 194 A4
Ecclesmachan 235 E2
Eccles-on-Sea 179 F3
Eccleston ChesW&C 170 B1
Eccleston Lancs 183 G1
Eccleston Mersey 183 F3
Eccup 194 B3
Echt 261 F4
Eckford 228 B4
Eckington Derbys 186 B5
Eckington Worcs 146 B3
Ecton N'hants 148 D1
Ecton Staffs 172 B2
Edale 185 F4
Eday 276 E4
Eday Airfield 276 E4
Edburton 109 E2
Edderside 209 E2
Edderton 266 E3
Eddington 119 E1
Eddleston 235 G5
Eden Camp NYorks YO17 6RT 204 B5
Eden Park 122 C2
Eden Project Corn PL24 2SG 97 E4
Eden Vale 212 D4
Edenbridge 122 D4
Edendonich 241 D2
Edenfield 184 B1
Edenhall 210 B4
Edenham 175 F5
Edensor 185 G5
Edentaggart 241 F5
Edenthorpe 186 D2
Edern 166 B4
Edgarley 116 C4
Edgbaston 158 C4
Edgcote 148 A3
Edgcott Bucks 148 B5
Edgcott Som 114 B4
Edgcumbe 95 E3
Edge Glos 132 A2
Edge Shrop 156 C2
Edge End 131 E1
Edge Green ChesW&C 170 B2
Edge Green GtMan 183 G3
Edge Green Norf 164 B3
Edgebolton 170 C5
Edgefield 178 B2
Edgehead 236 A3
Edgeley 170 C3
Edgerley 156 C1
Edgerton 185 F1
Edgeworth 132 B2
Edginswell 101 E1
Edgmond 157 G1
Edgmond Marsh 171 E5
Edgton 156 C4
Edgware 136 B3
Edgworth 184 B1
Edinample 242 B2
Edinbanchory 260 C3
Edinbane 263 J6
Edinbarnet 233 G2
Edinburgh 235 G2
Edinburgh Airport 235 F2
Edinburgh Castle Edin EH1 2NG 37 E4
Edinburgh Zoo Edin EH12 6TS 32 B2
Edinchip 242 A2
Edingale 159 E1
Edingley 174 B2
Edingthorpe 179 E2
Edingthorpe Green 179 E2
Edington Som 116 A4
Edington Wilts 118 A2
Edintore 268 C6
Edinvale 267 J6
Edistone 112 C3
Edith Weston 161 E2
Edithmead 116 A3
Edlaston 172 C3
Edlesborough 135 E1
Edlingham 220 D1
Edlington 188 C5
Edmondsham 105 G1
Edmondsley 212 B3
Edmondstown 129 G3
Edmondthorpe 161 D1
Edmonstone 276 E5
Edmonton Corn 97 D2
Edmonton GtLon 136 C3
Edmundbyers 211 G2
Ednam 228 B3
Ednaston 172 D3
Edney Common 137 F2
Edra 241 G3
Edradynate 251 D4
Edrom 237 F4
Edstaston 170 C4
Edstone 147 D1
Edvin Loach 145 F2
Edwalton 173 G4
Edwardstone 152 A3
Edwardsville 129 G3
Edwinsford 142 C4
Edwinstowe 174 B1
Edworth 150 A3
Edwyn Ralph 145 F2
Edzell 253 E3
Efail Isaf 129 G4
Efail-fâch 129 D3
Efailnewydd 166 C4
Efailwen 141 E5
Efenechtyd 169 E2
Effingham 121 G2
Effirth 279 C7
Efflinch 159 D1
Efford 102 B2
Egbury 119 F2
Egdean 121 E5
Egdon 146 B2
Egerton GtMan 184 B1
Egerton Kent 124 B4
Egerton Forstal 124 A4
Egerton Green 170 C2
Egg Buckland 100 A2
Eggborough 195 E5
Eggerness 207 E2
Eggesford Barton 113 G4
Eggington 149 E5
Egginton 173 D5
Egglescliffe 202 D1
Eggleston 211 F5
Egham 135 F5
Egham Wick 135 E5
Egilsay 276 D5
Egleton 161 D2
Eglingham 229 F5
Eglinton 233 E5
Egloshayle 97 E2
Egloskerry 97 G1
Eglwys Cross 170 B3
Eglwys Fach 154 C3
Eglwys Nunydd 129 E4
Eglwysbach 181 G5
Eglwys-Brewis 114 D1
Eglwyswrw 141 E4
Egmanton 174 C1
Egmere 178 A2
Egremont 208 D5
Egton 204 B2
Egton Bridge 204 B2
Egypt 119 F3
Eigg 247 D1
Eight Ash Green 152 A5
Eignaig 247 G5
Eil 259 F3
Eilanreach 256 E3
Eildon 227 G2
Eilean Darach 265 H3
Eilean Donan Castle High IV40 8DX 256 E2
Eilean Shona 247 F2
Einacleit 270 D5
Eisgean 271 F6
Eisingrug 167 F4
Eisteddfa Gurig 155 D4
Elan Valley Visitor Centre Powys LD6 5HP 143 F1
Elan Village 143 F1
Elberton 131 F4
Elborough 116 A2
Elburton 100 B2
Elcho 243 G2
Elcombe 132 D4
Elder Street 151 D4
Eldernell 162 B3
Eldersfield 145 G4
Elderslie 233 F3
Eldon 212 B5
Eldrick 215 D2
Eldroth 193 D1
Eldwick 194 A3
Elemore Vale 212 C3
Elford N'umb 229 F3
Elford Staffs 159 D1
Elford Closes 162 D5
Elgin 267 K5
Elgol 256 B3
Elham 125 D4
Elie 244 C4
Elilaw 220 B1
Elim 180 B4
Eling Hants 106 C1
Eling WBerks 134 A5
Eling Tide Mill Hants SO40 9HF 4 A3
Eliock 225 G5
Elishader 263 K5
Elishaw 220 A2
Elkesley 187 D5
Elkington 160 B5
Elkstone 132 B1
Elland 194 A5
Elland Upper Edge 194 A5
Ellary 231 F2
Ellastone 172 C3
Ellbridge 100 A1
Ellel 192 A2
Ellemford 237 E3
Ellenabeich 239 G3
Ellenborough 208 D3
Ellenhall 171 F5
Ellen's Green 121 F4
Ellerbeck 202 D3
Ellerby 203 G1
Ellerdine 170 D5
Ellerdine Heath 170 D5
Elleric (Eileirig) 248 C5
Ellerker 196 B5
Ellerton ERid 195 G3
Ellerton NYorks 202 B3
Ellerton Shrop 171 E5
Ellerton Abbey 201 F3
Ellesborough 134 D2
Ellesmere 170 A4
Ellesmere Park 184 B3
Ellesmere Port 183 F5
Ellingham Hants 106 A2
Ellingham N'umb 229 F4
Ellingham Norf 165 E2
Ellingstring 202 A4
Ellington Cambs 161 G5
Ellington N'umb 221 E2
Ellington Thorpe 161 G5
Elliot 245 E1
Elliot's Green 117 E3
Ellisfield 120 B3
Ellistown 159 G1
Ellon 261 H1
Ellonby 210 A4
Ellough 165 F3
Ellough Moor 165 F3
Elloughton 196 B5
Ellwood 131 E2
Elm 162 C2
Elm Park 137 E4
Elmbridge 146 B1
Elmdon Essex 150 C4
Elmdon WMid 159 D4
Elmdon Heath 159 D4
Elmers End 122 C2
Elmer's Green 183 F2
Elmesthorpe 159 G3
Elmhurst 158 D1
Elmley Castle 146 B3
Elmley Lovett 146 A1
Elmore 131 G1
Elmore Back 131 G1
Elmscott 112 C3
Elmsett 152 B3
Elmstead Essex 152 B5
Elmstead GtLon 136 D5
Elmstead Market 152 B5
Elmstone 125 E2
Elmstone Hardwicke 146 B5
Elmswell ERid 196 B2
Elmswell Suff 152 A1
Elmton 186 C5
Elphin 272 E7
Elphinstone 236 A2
Elrick Aber 261 G4
Elrick Moray 260 C2
Elrig 206 D2
Elrigbeag 240 D3
Elsdon 220 B2
Elsecar 186 A2
Elsecar Heritage Centre SYorks S74 8HJ 186 A3
Elsenham 150 D5
Elsfield 134 A1
Elsham 188 A1
Elsing 178 B4
Elslack 193 F3
Elson Hants 107 F2
Elson Shrop 170 A4
Elsrickle 235 E5
Elstead 121 E3
Elsted 108 A2
Elsthorpe 175 F5
Elstob 212 C5
Elston Lancs 192 B4
Elston Notts 174 C3
Elstone 113 G4
Elstow 149 F3
Elstree 136 A3
Elstronwick 197 E4
Elswick 192 A4
Elsworth 150 B1
Elterwater 199 E2
Eltham 136 D5
Eltisley 150 A2
Elton Cambs 161 F3
Elton ChesW&C 183 F5
Elton Derbys 172 D1
Elton Glos 131 G1
Elton GtMan 184 B1
Elton Here 157 D5
Elton Notts 174 C4
Elton Stock 202 D1
Elton Green 183 F5
Elvanfoot 226 A4
Elvaston 173 F4
Elvaston Castle Country Park Derbys DE72 3EP 18 C4
Elveden 163 G5
Elvingston 236 B2
Elvington Kent 125 E3
Elvington York 195 G3
Elwick Hart 213 D4
Elwick N'umb 229 F3
Elworth 171 E1
Elworthy 115 D4
Ely Cambs 162 D5
Ely Cardiff 130 A5
Emberton 149 D3
Emberton Country Park MK MK46 5FJ 149 D2
Embleton Cumb 209 E3
Embleton Hart 212 D5
Embleton N'umb 229 G4
Embo 267 F2
Embo Street 267 F2
Emborough 116 D2
Embsay 193 G2
Embsay Steam Railway NYorks BD23 6AF 193 G2
Emerson Park 137 E4
Emery Down 106 B2
Emley 185 G1
Emmington 134 C2
Emneth 162 C2
Emneth Hungate 162 D2
Empingham 161 E2
Empshott 120 C4
Empshott Green 120 C4
Emsworth 107 G2
Enborne 119 F1
Enborne Row 119 F1
Enchmarsh 157 E3
Enderby 160 A3
Endmoor 199 G4
Endon 171 G2
Endon Bank 171 G2
Enfield 136 C3
Enfield Wash 136 C3
Enford 118 C2
Engine Common 131 F4
Englefield 134 B5
Englefield Green 135 E5
Englesea-brook 171 E2
English Bicknor 131 E1
English Frankton 170 B5
Englishcombe 117 E1
Enham Alamein 119 E3
Enmore 115 F4
Ennerdale Bridge 209 D5
Enniscaven 97 D4
Ennochdhu 251 F3
Ensay 246 C5
Ensdon 156 D1
Ensis 113 F3
Enson 171 G5
Enstone 147 F5
Enterkinfoot 225 G5
Enterpen 203 D2
Enton Green 121 E3
Enville 158 A4
Eolaigearraidh 254 C4
Eorabus 238 C2
Eorodal 271 H1
Eoropaidh 271 H1
Epney 131 G1
Epperstone 174 B3
Epping 137 D2
Epping Green Essex 136 D2
Epping Green Herts 136 B2
Epping Upland 136 D2
Eppleby 202 A1
Eppleworth 196 C4
Epsom 122 B2
Epwell 147 F3
Epworth 187 E2
Epworth Turbary 187 E2
Erbistock 170 A3
Erbusaig 256 D2
Erchless Castle 266 B7
Erdington 158 D3
Eredine 240 B4
Eriboll 273 G3
Ericstane 226 B4
Eridge Green 123 E5
Eriff 224 D5
Erines 231 G2
Erisey Barton 95 E5
Eriskay (Eiriosgaigh) 254 C3
Eriswell 163 F5
Erith 137 E5
Erlestoke 118 A2
Ermington 100 C2
Ernesettle 100 A1
Erpingham 178 C2
Erringden Grange 193 F5
Errogie (Earagaidh) 258 C2
Errol 244 A2
Errollston 261 J1
Erskine 233 F2
Ervie 214 A4
Erwarton 152 D4
Erwood 143 G3
Eryholme 202 C2
Eryrys 169 F2
Escart 231 G3
Escart Farm 231 G4
Escomb 212 A5
Escrick 195 F3
Esgair 141 G5
Esgairgeiliog 155 D2
Esgyryn 181 G5
Esh 212 A3
Esh Winning 212 A3
Esher 121 G1
Eshott 221 E2
Eshton 193 F2
Eskadale 258 B1
Eskbank 236 A3
Eskdale Green 198 C2
Eskdalemuir 218 A2
Eskham 189 D3
Eskish 230 B3
Esperley Lane Ends 212 A5
Espley Hall 221 D2
Esprick 192 A4
Essendine 161 F1
Essendon 136 B2
Essich 258 D1
Essington 158 B2
Esslemont 261 H2
Eston 203 E1
Eswick 279 D7
Etal 228 D3
Etchilhampton 118 B1
Etchingham 110 C1
Etchinghill Kent 125 D5
Etchinghill Staffs 158 C1
Etherdwick Grange 197 E4
Etherley Dene 212 A5
Etherow Country Park GtMan SK6 5JQ 25 H5
Ethie Mains 253 E5
Eton 135 E5
Eton Wick 135 E5
Etteridge 258 D5
Ettiley Heath 171 E1
Ettington 147 E3
Etton ERid 196 B3
Etton Peter 161 G2
Ettrick 227 D4
Ettrickbridge 227 E3
Ettrickhill 227 D4
Etwall 173 D4
Eudon George 157 F4
Eurach 240 A4
Eureka! Museum for Children WYorks HX1 2NE 26 B4
Euston 163 G5
Euxton 183 G1
Evanstown 129 F4
Evanton 266 D5
Evedon 175 F3
Evelix 266 E2
Evenjobb 144 B1
Evenley 148 A4
Evenlode 147 E5
Evenwood 212 A5
Evenwood Gate 212 A5
Everbay 276 F5
Evercreech 116 D4
Everdon 148 A2
Everingham 196 A3
Everleigh 118 D2
Everley High 275 J2
Everley NYorks 204 C4
Eversholt 149 E4
Evershot 104 B2
Eversley 120 C1
Eversley Cross 120 C1
Everthorpe 196 B4
Everton CenBeds 150 A2
Everton Hants 106 B3
Everton Mersey 183 E3
Everton Notts 187 D3
Evertown 218 B4
Eves Corner 138 C3
Evesbatch 145 F3
Evesham 146 C3
Evesham Country Park Shopping & Garden Centre Worcs WR11 4TP 146 C3
Evie 276 C5
Evington 160 B2
Ewart Newtown 229 D3
Ewden Village 185 G3
Ewell 122 B2
Ewell Minnis 125 E4
Ewelme 134 B3
Ewen 132 C3
Ewenny 129 F5
Ewerby 175 G3
Ewerby Thorpe 175 G3
Ewhurst 121 F3
Ewhurst Green ESuss 110 C1
Ewhurst Green Surr 121 F4
Ewloe 170 A1
Ewloe Green 169 F1
Ewood 192 C5
Ewood Bridge 193 D5
Eworthy 99 E1
Ewshot 120 D3
Ewyas Harold 144 C5
Exbourne 113 G5
Exbury 106 D2
Exbury Gardens Hants SO45 1AZ 4 B6
Exceat 110 A4
Exebridge 114 C5
Exelby 202 B4
Exeter 102 C3
Exeter Cathedral Devon EX1 1HS 72 Exeter
Exeter International Airport 102 C3
Exford 114 B4
Exfords Green 157 D2
Exhall Warks 146 D2
Exhall Warks 159 F4
Exlade Street 134 B4
Exminster 102 C4
Exmoor International Dark Sky Reserve Devon/Som. 114 A3
Exmouth 102 D4
Exnaboe 279 F9
Exning 151 E1
Explore-At-Bristol BS1 5DB 66 Bristol
Exton Devon 102 C4
Exton Hants 120 B5
Exton Rut 161 E1
Exton Som 114 C4
Exwick 102 C3
Eyam 185 G5
Eydon 148 A3
Eye Here 145 D1
Eye Peter 162 A2
Eye Suff 164 C4
Eye Green 162 A2
Eyemouth 237 G3
Eyeworth 150 A3
Eyhorne Street 124 A3
Eyke 153 E2
Eynesbury 149 G2
Eynort 255 J2
Eynsford 123 E2
Eynsham 133 G2
Eype 104 A3
Eyre 263 K6
Eythorne 125 E4
Eyton Here 145 D1
Eyton Shrop 156 C4
Eyton on Severn 157 E2
Eyton upon the Weald Moors 157 F1
Eywood 144 C2

F

Faccombe 119 E2
Faceby 203 D2
Fachwen 167 E1
Facit 184 C1
Faddiley 170 C2
Fadmoor 203 F4
Faebait 266 B6
Faifley 233 G2
Fail 224 C3
Failand 131 E5
Failford 224 C3
Failsworth 184 C2
Fain 265 H4
Fair Isle 278 A1
Fair Isle Airstrip 278 A1
Fair Oak Devon 102 D1
Fair Oak Hants 107 D1
Fair Oak Hants 119 G1
Fair Oak Green 120 B1
Fairbourne 154 C1
Fairburn 195 D5
Fairfield Derbys 185 E5
Fairfield GtMan 184 D3
Fairfield Kent 111 E1
Fairfield Mersey 183 D4
Fairfield Stock 202 D1
Fairfield Worcs 158 B5
Fairfield Halls, Croydon GtLon CR9 1DG 122 C2
Fairford 132 D2
Fairgirth 216 C5
Fairhaven 191 G5
Fairhill 234 B4
Fairholm 234 B4
Fairlands Valley Park Herts SG2 0BL 150 A5
Fairley 261 G4
Fairlie 232 D4
Fairlight 111 D2
Fairlight Cove 111 D2
Fairmile Devon 103 D3
Fairmile Surr 121 G1
Fairmilehead 235 G3
Fairnington 228 A4
Fairoak 171 E4
Fairseat 123 F2
Fairstead 137 G1
Fairwarp 109 G1
Fairwater 130 A5
Fairy Cross 113 E3
Fairyhill 128 A3
Fakenham 178 A3
Fakenham Magna 164 A4
Fala 236 B3
Fala Dam 236 B3
Falahill 236 A4
Faldingworth 188 A4
Falfield Fife 244 C4
Falfield SGlos 131 F3
Falin-Wnda 141 G3
Falkenham 153 D4
Falkirk 234 C2
Falkirk Wheel Falk FK1 4RS 234 C1
Falkland 244 A4
Falla 228 B5
Fallgate 173 E1
Fallin 242 D5
Falmer 109 F3
Falmouth 95 F3
Falsgrave 204 D4
Falstone 219 F3
Famous Grouse Experience, Glenturret Distillery P&K PH7 4HA 243 D2
Fanagmore 272 D4
Fanans 240 C2
Fancott 149 F5
Fangdale Beck 203 E3
Fangfoss 195 G2
Fankerton 234 B1
Fanmore 246 D5
Fanner's Green 137 F1
Fans 236 D5
Fantasy Island Lincs PE25 1RH 177 D1
Far Cotton 148 C2
Far Forest 157 G5
Far Gearstones 200 C4
Far Green 131 G2
Far Moor 183 G2
Far Oakridge 132 B2
Far Royds 194 B4
Far Sawrey 199 E3
Farcet 162 A3
Farden 157 E5
Fareham 107 E2
Farewell 158 C1
Farforth 188 D5
Faringdon 133 E3
Farington 192 B5
Farlam 210 B2
Farlary 266 E1
Farleigh NSom 116 C1
Farleigh Surr 122 C2
Farleigh Hungerford 117 F2
Farleigh Wallop 120 B3
Farlesthorpe 189 E5
Farleton Cumb 199 G4
Farleton Lancs 192 B1
Farley Derbys 173 D1
Farley Shrop 156 C2
Farley Staffs 172 B3
Farley Wilts 118 D5
Farley Green Suff 151 F2
Farley Green Surr 121 F3
Farley Hill 120 C1
Farleys End 131 G1
Farlington 195 F1
Farlow 157 F4
Farm Town 159 F1
Farmborough 117 D1
Farmcote 146 C5
Farmington 132 D1
Farmoor 133 G2
Farmtown 268 D5
Farnborough GtLon 122 D2
Farnborough Hants 121 D2
Farnborough Warks 147 G3
Farnborough WBerks 133 G4
Farnborough Street 121 D2
Farncombe 121 E3
Farndish 149 E1
Farndon ChesW&C 170 B2
Farndon Notts 174 C2
Farne Islands 229 G3
Farnell 253 E4
Farnham Dorset 105 F1
Farnham Essex 150 C5
Farnham NYorks 194 C1
Farnham Suff 153 E1
Farnham Surr 120 D3
Farnham Common 135 E4
Farnham Green 150 C5
Farnham Royal 135 E4
Farningham 123 E2
Farnley NYorks 194 B3
Farnley WYorks 194 B4
Farnley Tyas 185 F1
Farnsfield 174 B2
Farnworth GtMan 184 B2
Farnworth Halton 183 G4
Farr High 274 C2
Farr High 258 D1
Farr High 259 F4
Farr House 258 D1
Farraline 258 C2
Farringdon 102 D3
Farrington Gurney 116 D2
Farsley 194 B4
Farthing Corner 124 A2
Farthing Green 124 A4
Farthinghoe 148 A4
Farthingstone 148 B2
Farthorpe 188 C5
Fartown 185 F1
Farway 103 E3
Fasag 264 E6
Fasagrianach 265 H3
Fascadale 247 E2
Fashion Museum B&NESom BA1 2QH 63 Bath
Faslane 232 D1
Fasnacloich 248 C5
Fasnakyle 257 K2
Fassfern 248 C2
Fatfield 212 C2
Fattahead 268 E5
Faugh 210 B2
Fauldhouse 234 D3
Faulkbourne 137 G1
Faulkland 117 E2
Fauls 170 C4
Faulston 118 B5
Faversham 124 C2
Favillar 259 K1
Fawdington 202 D5
Fawdon 212 B1
Fawfieldhead 172 B1
Fawkham Green 123 E2
Fawler 133 F1
Fawley Bucks 134 C4
Fawley Hants 107 D2
Fawley WBerks 133 F4
Fawley Chapel 145 E5
Fawsyde 253 G2
Faxfleet 196 A5
Faxton 160 C5
Faygate 122 B5
Fazakerley 183 E3
Fazeley 159 E2
Fearby 202 A4
Fearn 267 F4
Fearnan 250 C5
Fearnbeg 264 D6
Fearnhead 184 A3
Fearnmore 264 D5
Fearnoch A&B 232 B2
Fearnoch A&B 232 A1
Featherstone Staffs 158 B2
Featherstone WYorks 194 D5
Featherstone Castle 210 C1
Feckenham 146 C1
Feering 151 G5
Feetham 201 E3
Feith-hill 268 E6
Feizor 193 D1
Felbridge 122 C5
Felbrigg 178 D2
Felcourt 122 C4
Felden 135 F2
Felhampton 156 D4
Felindre Carmar 142 D5
Felindre Carmar 142 B5
Felindre Carmar 141 G4
Felindre Carmar 142 C4
Felindre Cere 142 B2
Felindre Powys 156 A4
Felindre Powys 144 A5
Felindre Swan 128 C2
Felinfach Cere 142 B2
Felinfach Powys 143 G4
Felinfoel 128 B2
Felingwmisaf 142 B5
Felingwmuchaf 142 B5
Felixkirk 203 D4
Felixstowe 153 E4
Felixstowe Ferry 153 E4
Felkington 237 G5
Felldownhead 99 D2
Felling 212 B1
Fellonmore 239 F2
Felmersham 149 E2
Felmingham 179 D3
Felpham 108 B4
Felsham 152 A2
Felsted 151 E5
Feltham 136 A5
Felthamhill 136 A5
Felthorpe 178 C4
Felton Here 145 E3
Felton N'umb 221 D1
Felton NSom 116 C1
Felton Butler 156 C1
Feltwell 163 F3
Fen Ditton 150 C1
Fen Drayton 150 B1
Fen End 159 E5
Fen Street Norf 164 A2
Fen Street Norf 164 B4
Fen Street Suff 164 A4
Fen Street Suff 152 C1
Fenay Bridge 185 F1
Fence 193 E4
Fence Houses 212 C2
Fencott 134 A1
Fendike Corner 176 C1
Fenham 229 E2
Fenhouses 176 A3
Feniscowles 192 C5
Feniton 103 E3
Fenn Street 137 G5
Fenni-fach 143 G5
Fenny Bentley 172 C2
Fenny Bridges 103 E3
Fenny Compton 147 G2
Fenny Drayton 159 F3
Fenny Stratford 149 D4
Fenrother 221 D2
Fenstanton 150 B1
Fenton Cambs 162 B5
Fenton Lincs 187 F5
Fenton Lincs 175 D2
Fenton N'umb 229 D3
Fenton Notts 187 E4
Fenton Stoke 171 F3
Fenton Barns 236 C1
Fenwick EAyr 233 F5
Fenwick N'umb 220 C4
Fenwick N'umb 229 E2
Fenwick SYorks 186 C1
Feochaig 222 C4
Feock 95 F3
Feolin 230 D3
Feolin Ferry 230 C3
Feorlan 222 B5
Feorlin 240 B5
Ferens Art Gallery HU1 3RA 76 Kingston upon Hull
Ferguslie Park 233 F3
Feriniquarrie 263 G6
Fern 252 C3
Ferndale 129 F3
Ferndown 105 G2
Ferness 267 G7
Fernham 133 E3
Fernhill Heath 146 A2
Fernhurst 121 D5
Fernie 244 B3
Fernilea 255 J1
Fernilee 185 E5
Fernybank 252 D2
Ferrensby 194 C1
Ferrers Centre for Arts & Crafts Leics LE65 1RU 173 E5
Ferrindonald 256 C4
Ferring 108 C3
Ferry Hill 162 B4
Ferrybridge 195 D5
Ferryden 253 F4
Ferryhill 212 B4
Ferryside (Glanyferi) 127 G1
Fersfield 164 B3
Fersit 249 F2
Ferwig 141 E3
Feshiebridge 259 F4
Festival Park BGwent NP23 8FP 130 A2
Fetcham 121 G2
Fetlar 278 F3
Fetlar Airport 278 F3
Fetterangus 269 H5
Fettercairn 253 E2
Fetternear House 261 F3
Feus of Caldhame 253 E3
Fewcott 148 A5
Fewston 194 A2
Ffairfach 142 C5
Ffair-Rhos 142 D1
Ffaldybrenin 142 C3
Ffarmers 142 C3
Ffawyddog 130 B1
Ffestiniog (Llan Ffestiniog) 168 A3
Ffestiniog Railway Gwyn LL49 9NF 167 F3
Ffordd-las Denb 169 E1
Ffordd-las Powys 144 B4
Fforest 128 B2
Fforest-fach 128 C3
Ffostrasol 141 G3
Ffos-y-ffin 142 A1
Ffridd Uchaf 167 E2
Ffrith Denb 182 B4
Ffrith Flints 169 F2
Ffrwdgrech 143 G5
Ffynnon 127 G1
Ffynnongroyw 182 C4
Fibhig 270 E3
Fichlie 260 C3
Fidden 238 C2
Fiddington Glos 146 B4
Fiddington Som 115 F3
Fiddleford 105 E1
Fiddler's Green Glos 146 B5
Fiddler's Green Here 145 E4
Fiddler's Green Norf 163 G1
Fiddler's Green Norf 164 B2
Fiddlers Hamlet 137 D2
Field 172 B4
Field Broughton 199 E4
Field Dalling 178 B2
Field Head 159 G2
Fife Keith 268 C5
Fifehead Magdalen 117 E5
Fifehead Neville 105 D1
Fifehead St. Quintin 105 D1
Fifield Oxon 133 E1
Fifield W&M 135 E5
Fifield Bavant 118 B5
Figheldean 118 C3
Filby 179 F4
Filey 205 E4
Filgrave 149 D3
Filham 100 C2
Filkins 133 E2
Filleigh Devon 113 G3
Filleigh Devon 102 A1
Fillingham 187 G4
Fillongley 159 E4
Filmore Hill 120 B5
Filton 131 F5
Fimber 196 A1
Finavon 252 C4
Fincham 163 E2
Finchampstead 120 C1
Finchdean 107 G1
Finchingfield 151 E4
Finchley 136 B3
Findern 173 E4
Findhorn 267 H5
Findhorn Bridge 259 F2
Findhuglen 242 C3
Findo Gask 243 F2
Findochty 268 C4
Findon Aber 261 H5
Findon WSuss 108 D3
Findon Mains 266 D5
Findon Valley 108 D3
Findrassie 267 J5
Findron 259 J3
Finedon 161 E5
Finegand 251 G3
Fingal Street 164 D4
Fingask 261 F2
Fingerpost 157 G5
Fingest 134 C3
Finghall 202 A4
Fingland Cumb 209 F1
Fingland D&G 226 D5
Fingland D&G 225 F4
Finglesham 125 F3
Fingringhoe 152 B5
Finkle Street 186 A3
Finlarig 242 A1
Finmere 148 B4
Finnart A&B 241 E5
Finnart P&K 250 A4
Finney Hill 159 G1
Finningham 152 B1
Finningley 187 D3
Finnygaud 268 E5
Finsbay (Fionnsbhagh) 263 F3
Finsbury 136 C4
Finstall 158 B5
Finsthwaite 199 E4
Finstock 133 F1
Finstown 277 C6
Fintry Aber 269 F5
Fintry Stir 234 A1
Finwood 147 D1
Finzean 260 D5
Fionnphort 238 B2
Fir Tree 212 A4
Firbank 200 B3
Firbeck 186 C4
Firby NYorks 202 B4
Firby NYorks 195 G1
Firgrove 184 D1
Firs Lane 184 A2
Firsby 176 C1
Firsdown 118 D4
Firth 278 D5
Fishbourne IoW 107 E3
Fishbourne WSuss 108 A3
Fishburn 212 C4
Fishcross 243 E5
Fisherford 260 E1
Fishers Farm Park WSuss RH14 0EG 121 F5
Fisher's Pond 119 F5
Fisher's Row 192 A3
Fishersgate 109 E3
Fisherstreet 121 E4
Fisherton High 266 E6
Fisherton SAyr 224 A4
Fisherton de la Mere 118 A4
Fishguard (Abergwaun) 140 C4
Fishlake 187 D1
Fishleigh Barton 113 F3
Fishley 179 F4
Fishnish 247 F5
Fishpond Bottom 103 G3
Fishponds 131 F5
Fishpool 184 C2
Fishtoft 176 B3
Fishtoft Drove 176 B3
Fishtown of Usan 253 F4
Fishwick 237 G4
Fiskerton Lincs 188 A5
Fiskerton Notts 174 C2
Fitling 197 E4
Fittleton 118 C3
Fittleworth 108 C2
Fitton End 162 C1
Fitz 156 D1
Fitzhead 115 E5
Fitzroy 115 E5
Fitzwilliam 186 B1
Fitzwilliam Museum Cambs CB2 1RB 66 Cambridge
Fiunary 247 F5
Five Acres 131 E1
Five Ash Down 109 G1
Five Ashes 110 A1
Five Bridges 145 F3
Five Houses 106 D4
Five Lanes 130 D3
Five Oak Green 123 F4
Five Oaks Chanl 100 C5
Five Oaks WSuss 121 F5
Five Roads 128 A2
Five Turnings 156 B5
Five Wents 124 A3
Fivehead 116 A5
Fivelanes 97 G1
Flack's Green 137 G1
Flackwell Heath 135 D4
Fladbury 146 B3
Fladdabister 279 D9
Flagg 172 C1
Flambards Experience, The Corn TR13 0QA 95 D4
Flamborough 205 F5
Flamborough Cliffs Nature Reserve ERid YO15 1BJ 205 F5
Flamingo Land Theme Park NYorks YO17 6UX 203 G4
Flamingo Park, Hastings ESuss TN34 3AR 110 D3
Flamstead 135 F1
Flamstead End 136 C2
Flansham 108 B3
Flanshaw 194 C5
Flasby 193 F2
Flash 172 B1
Flashader 263 J6
Flask Inn 204 C2
Flatts Lane Woodland Country Park R&C TS6 0NN 29 D4
Flaunden 135 F2
Flawborough 174 C3
Flawith 195 D1
Flax Bourton 116 C1
Flax Moss 193 D5
Flaxby 194 C2
Flaxholme 173 E3
Flaxlands 164 C2
Flaxley 131 F1
Flaxpool 115 E4
Flaxton 195 F1
Fleckney 160 B3
Flecknoe 148 A1
Fledborough 187 F5
Fleet Hants 120 D2
Fleet Hants 107 G2
Fleet Lincs 176 B5
Fleet Air Arm Museum Som BA22 8HT 116 C5
Fleet Hargate 176 B5
Fleetville 136 A2
Fleetwood 191 G3
Fleggburgh (Burgh St. Margaret) 179 F4
Flemingston 129 G5
Flemington 234 A4
Flempton 151 G1
Fleoideabhagh 263 F3
Flesherin 271 H4
Fletchersbridge 97 F3
Fletchertown 209 F2
Fletching 109 G1
Fleuchats 260 B4
Fleur-de-lis 130 A3
Flexbury 112 C5
Flexford 121 E2
Flimby 208 D3
Flimwell 123 G5
Flint (Y Fflint) 182 D5
Flint Cross 150 C3
Flint Mountain 182 D5
Flintham 174 C3
Flinton 197 E4
Flint's Green 159 E4
Flishinghurst 123 G5
Flitcham 177 F5
Flitholme 200 C1
Flitton 149 F4
Flitwick 149 F4
Flixborough 187 F1
Flixton GtMan 184 B3
Flixton NYorks 204 D5
Flixton Suff 165 E3
Flockton 185 G1
Flockton Green 185 G1
Flodden 228 D3
Flodigarry 263 K4
Flood's Ferry 162 B3
Flookburgh 199 E5
Floors 268 C5
Flordon 164 C2
Flore 148 B1
Flotta 277 C8
Flotterton 220 C1
Flowton 152 B3
Flushdyke 194 B5
Flushing Aber 269 J6
Flushing Corn 95 F3
Flushing Corn 95 E4
Fluxton 103 D3
Flyford Flavell 146 B2
Foals Green 165 D4
Fobbing 137 G4
Fochabers 268 B5
Fochriw 130 A2
Fockerby 187 F1
Fodderletter 259 J2
Fodderty 266 C6
Foddington 116 C5
Foel 155 F1
Foelgastell 128 B1
Foggathorpe 195 G4
Fogo 237 E5
Fogorig 237 E5
Fogwatt 267 K6
Foindle 272 D4
Folda 251 G3
Fole 172 B4
Foleshill 159 F4
Folke 104 C1
Folkestone 125 E5
Folkingham 175 F4
Folkington 110 A3
Folksworth 161 G4
Folkton 205 D5
Folla Rule 261 F1
Follifoot 194 C2
Folly Dorset 104 D2
Folly Pembs 140 C5
Folly Farm, Begelly Pembs SA68 0XA 127 E2
Folly Gate 99 F1
Fonmon 115 D1
Fonthill Bishop 118 A4
Fonthill Gifford 118 A4
Fontmell Magna 105 E1
Fontmell Parva 105 E1
Fontwell 108 B3
Font-y-gary 115 D1
Foolow 185 F5
Footherley 158 D2
Foots Cray 137 D5
Forbestown 260 B3
Force Forge 199 E3
Force Green 122 D3
Forcett 202 A1
Forches Cross 102 A2
Ford A&B 240 A4
Ford Bucks 134 C2
Ford Devon 100 C2
Ford Devon 113 E3
Ford Devon 101 D3
Ford Glos 146 C5
Ford Mersey 183 E3
Ford Midlo 236 A3
Ford N'umb 229 D3
Ford Pembs 140 C5
Ford Plym 100 A2
Ford Shrop 156 D1
Ford Som 115 D5
Ford Staffs 172 B2
Ford Wilts 132 A5
Ford WSuss 108 B3
Ford End 137 F1
Ford Green 192 A3
Ford Heath 156 D1
Ford Street 103 E1
Forda 99 F1
Fordbridge 159 D4
Fordcombe 123 E4
Fordell 235 F1
Forden (Ffordun) 156 B2
Forder Green 101 D1
Fordgate 116 A4
Fordham Cambs 163 E5
Fordham Essex 152 A5
Fordham Norf 163 E3
Fordham Abbey 151 E1
Fordham Heath 152 A5
Fordhouses 158 B2
Fordingbridge 106 A1
Fordon 205 D5
Fordoun 253 F2
Ford's Green 152 B1
Fordstreet 152 A5
Fordwells 133 F1
Fordwich 125 D3
Fordyce 268 D4
Forebrae 243 E2
Forebridge 171 G5
Foredale 193 E1
Foreland 230 A3
Foremark 173 E5
Foremark Reservoir Derbys DE65 6EG 173 E5
Forest 202 B2
Forest Coal Pit 144 B5
Forest Gate 136 D4
Forest Green 121 G3
Forest Hall Cumb 199 G2
Forest Hall T&W 212 B1
Forest Head 210 B2
Forest Hill GtLon 136 C5
Forest Hill Oxon 134 A2
Forest Lane Head 194 C2
Forest Lodge (Taigh na Frithe) A&B 249 E5
Forest Lodge P&K 251 E2
Forest Row 122 D5
Forest Side 107 D4
Forest Town 173 G1
Forestburn Gate 220 C2
Forest-in-Teesdale 211 E5
Forestmill 243 E5
Forestside 107 G1
Forfar 252 C4
Forfar Loch Country Park Angus DD8 1BT 252 C4
Forgandenny 243 F3
Forge 155 D3
Forgie 268 B5
Forhill 158 C5
Formby 183 D2
Forncett End 164 C2
Forncett St. Mary 164 C2
Forncett St. Peter 164 C2
Forneth 251 F5
Fornham All Saints 151 G1
Fornham St. Martin 151 G1
Fornighty 267 G6
Forres 267 H6
Forrest 234 C3
Forrest Lodge 215 G2
Forsbrook 171 G3
Forse 275 H5
Forsie 275 F2
Forsinain 274 E4
Forsinard 274 D4
Forston 104 C3
Fort Augustus (Cille Chuimein) 257 K4
Fort Fun, Eastbourne ESuss BN22 7LQ 110 B3
Fort George 266 E6
Fort William (An Gearasdan) 248 D2
Forter 251 G3
Forteviot 243 F3
Forth 234 D4
Forthampton 146 A4
Fortingall 250 C5
Fortis Green 136 B4
Forton Hants 119 F3
Forton Lancs 192 A2
Forton Shrop 156 D1
Forton Som 103 G2
Forton Staffs 171 E5
Fortrie 268 E6
Fortrose (A'Chananaich) 266 E6
Fortuneswell 104 C5
Forty Green 135 E3
Forty Hill 136 C3
Forward Green 152 B2
Fosbury 119 E2
Foscot 147 E5
Fosdyke 176 B4
Foss 250 C4
Foss Cross 132 C2
Fossdale 201 D3
Fossebridge 132 C1
Foster Street 137 D2
Fosterhouses 186 D1
Foster's Booth 148 B2
Foston Derbys 172 C4
Foston Leics 160 B3
Foston Lincs 175 D3
Foston NYorks 195 F1
Foston on the Wolds 196 D2
Fotherby 188 D3
Fotheringhay 161 F3
Foubister 277 E7
Foul Mile 110 B2
Foula 278 B1
Foula Airstrip 278 B1
Foulbog 226 D5
Foulden Norf 163 F3
Foulden ScBord 237 G4
Foulness Island 138 D3
Foulridge 193 E3
Foulsham 178 B3
Foulstone 199 G4
Foulzie 269 F4
Fountainhall 236 B5
Four Ashes Staffs 158 B2
Four Ashes Staffs 158 A4
Four Ashes Suff 164 A4
Four Crosses Denb 168 D3
Four Crosses Powys 156 B1
Four Crosses Powys 155 G2
Four Crosses Staffs 158 B2
Four Elms 123 D4
Four Forks 115 F4
Four Gotes 162 C1
Four Lane Ends B'burn 192 C5
Four Lane Ends ChesW&C 170 C1
Four Lane Ends York 195 F2
Four Lanes 95 D3
Four Marks 120 B4
Four Mile Bridge 180 A5
Four Oaks ESuss 111 D1
Four Oaks Glos 145 F5
Four Oaks WMid 159 E4
Four Oaks WMid 158 D3
Four Oaks Park 158 D3
Four Roads 128 A2
Four Throws 110 C1
Fourlane Ends 173 E2
Fourlanes End 171 F2
Fourpenny 267 F2
Fourstones 211 E1
Fovant 118 B5
Foveran House 261 H2
Fowey 97 F4
Fowlis 244 B1
Fowlis Wester 243 E2
Fowlmere 150 C3
Fownhope 145 E4
Fox Hatch 137 E3
Fox Lane 121 D2
Fox Street 152 B5
Fox Up 201 D5
Foxbar 233 F3
Foxcombe Hill 133 G2
Foxcote Glos 132 C1
Foxcote Som 117 E2
Foxdale 190 A4
Foxearth 151 G3
Foxfield 198 D4
Foxham 132 B5
Foxhole Corn 97 D4
Foxhole High 258 C1
Foxholes 204 D5
Foxhunt Green 110 A2
Foxley Here 144 D3
Foxley N'hants 148 B2
Foxley Norf 178 B3
Foxley Wilts 132 A4
Foxt 172 B3
Foxton Cambs 150 C3
Foxton Dur 212 C5
Foxton Leics 160 B3
Foxton Locks Leics LE16 7RA 160 B4
Foxwist Green 170 D1
Foy 145 E5
Foyers (Foithir) 258 B2
Frachadil 246 C4
Fraddam 94 C3
Fraddon 96 D4
Fradley 159 D1
Fradswell 171 G4
Fraisthorpe 197 D1
Framfield 109 G1
Framingham Earl 179 D5
Framingham Pigot 179 D5
Framlingham 153 D1
Frampton Dorset 104 C3
Frampton Lincs 176 B4
Frampton Cotterell 131 F4
Frampton Mansell 132 B2
Frampton on Severn 131 G2
Frampton West End 176 A3
Framsden 152 D2
Framwellgate Moor 212 B3
France Lynch 132 B2
Frances Green 192 C4
Franche 158 A5
Frandley 184 A5
Frankby 182 D4
Frankfort 179 E3
Frankley 158 B4
Franksbridge 144 A2
Frankton 159 G5
Frant 123 E5
Fraserburgh 269 H4
Frating 152 B5
Fratton 107 F2
Freasley 159 E3
Freathy 99 D5
Freckenham 163 E5
Freckleton 192 A5
Freeby 174 D5
Freefolk 119 F3
Freehay 172 B3
Freeland 133 G1
Freester 279 D7
Freethorpe 179 F5
Freethorpe Common 179 F5
Freiston 176 B3
Freiston Shore 176 B3
Fremington Devon 113 F2
Fremington NYorks 201 F3
French Brothers Cruises W&M SL4 5JH 135 E5
Frenchay 131 F5
Frenchbeer 99 G2
Frendraught 268 E6
Frenich 241 G4
Frensham 120 D3
Fresgoe 274 E2
Freshbrook 132 D4
Freshfield 183 D2
Freshford 117 E2
Freshwater 106 C4
Freshwater Bay 106 C4
Freshwater East 126 D3
Fressingfield 165 D4
Freston 152 C4
Freswick 275 J2
Fretherne 131 G2
Frettenham 178 D4
Freuchie 244 A4
Freystrop Cross 126 C1
Friars, The, Aylesford Kent ME20 7BX 123 G3
Friars Carse 216 D2
Friar's Gate 123 D5
Friarton 243 G2

Friday Bridge 162 C2
Friday Street ESuss 110 B3
Friday Street Suff 152 D2
Friday Street Suff 153 E2
Friday Street Surr 121 G3
Fridaythorpe 196 B2
Friern Barnet 136 B3
Friesthorpe 188 A4
Frieston 175 E3
Frieth 134 C3
Frilford 133 G3
Frilsham 134 A5
Frimley 121 D2
Frimley Green 121 D2
Frindsbury 123 G2
Fring 177 F4
Fringford 148 B5
Friningham 124 A3
Frinsted 124 A2
Frinton-on-Sea 139 F1
Friockheim 253 D5
Friog 154 C1
Frisby on the
   Wreake 160 B1
Friskney 176 C2
Friskney
   Eaudyke 176 C2
Friston ESuss 110 A4
Friston Suff 153 F1
Fritchley 173 E2
Frith 124 B3
Frith Bank 176 B3
Frith Common 145 F1
Fritham 106 B1
Frithelstock 113 E4
Frithelstock
   Stone 113 E4
Frithville 176 B2
Frittenden 124 A4
Frittiscombe 101 E3
Fritton Norf 164 D2
Fritton Norf 179 F5
Fritwell 148 A5
Frizinghall 194 A4
Frizington 208 D5
Frocester 131 G2
Frochas 156 B2
Frodesley 157 E2
Frodesley Lane 157 E2
Frodingham 187 F1
Frodsham 183 G5
Frog End 150 C2
Frog Pool 145 G1
Frogden 228 B4
Froggatt 185 G5
Froghall 172 B3
Frogham 106 A1
Frogland Cross 131 F4
Frogmore Devon 101 D3
Frogmore Hants 120 D2
Frogmore Herts 136 A2
Frogwell 98 D4
Frolesworth 160 A3
Frome 117 E3
Frome Market 117 F2
Frome St. Quintin 104 B2
Frome Whitfield 104 C3
Fromes Hill 145 F3
Fron Gwyn 166 C4
Fron Powys 156 B2
Fron Powys 143 G1
Fron Powys 156 A3
Fron Isaf 169 F4
Froncysyllte 169 F3
Fron-goch 168 C4
Frostenden 165 F3
Frosterley 211 G4
Froxfield 119 E1
Froxfield Green 120 C5
Fruitmarket Gallery Edin
   EH1 1DF 37 G4
Fryerning 137 F2
Fugglestone
   St. Peter 118 C4
Fulbeck 175 E2
Fulbourn 150 D2
Fulbrook 133 E1
Fulflood 119 F5
Fulford Som 115 F5
Fulford Staffs 171 G4
Fulford York 195 F3
Fulham 136 B5
Fulking 109 E2
Full Sutton 195 G2
Fullaford 113 G2
Fuller Street 137 G1
Fuller's Moor 170 B2
Fullerton 119 E4
Fulletby 188 C5
Fulmer 135 F4
Fulmodeston 178 A2
Fulnetby 188 B5
Fulready 147 E3
Fulstone 185 F1
Fulstow 188 D3
Fulwell Oxon 147 F5
Fulwell T&W 212 C2
Fulwood Lancs 192 B4
Fulwood SYorks 186 A4
Fun Farm, Spalding Lincs
   PE12 6JU 176 A3
Fundenhall 164 C2
Fundenhall
   Street 164 C2
Funtington 108 A3
Funtley 107 E2
Funzie 278 F3
Furley 103 F2
Furnace A&B 240 C4
Furnace Carmar 128 B2
Furnace Cere 154 C3
Furnace End 159 F3
Furnace High 265 F4
Furner's Green 109 G1
Furneux Pelham 150 C5
Furnham 103 G2
Further Quarter 124 A5
Furtho 148 C3
Furzehill Devon 114 A3
Furzehill Dorset 105 G2
Furzeley Corner 107 F1
Furzey Lodge 106 C2
Furzey 106 B1
Fyfett 103 F2

Fyfield Essex 137 E2
Fyfield Glos 133 E2
Fyfield Hants 119 D3
Fyfield Oxon 133 G3
Fyfield Wilts 118 C1
Fyfield Wilts 118 C1
Fylingthorpe 204 C2
Fyning 120 D5
Fyvie 261 F1

G

Gabalfa 130 A5
Gabhsunn Bho
   Dheas 271 G2
Gabhsunn Bho
   Thuath 271 G2
Gablon 266 E2
Gabroc Hill 233 F4
Gaddesby 160 B1
Gaddesden Row 135 F1
Gadebridge 135 F2
Gadshill 137 G5
Gaer Newport 130 B4
Gaer Powys 144 A5
Gaer-fawr 130 D3
Gaerllwyd 130 D3
Gaerwen 180 C5
Gagingwell 147 G5
Gaich High 259 H2
Gaich High 258 D1
Gaick Lodge 250 C1
Gailes 224 B2
Gailey 158 B1
Gainford 202 A1
Gainsborough 187 F3
Gainsford End 151 F4
Gairloch
   (Geàrrloch) 264 D4
Gairlochy (Geàrr
   Lòchaidh) 249 D1
Gairney Bank 243 G5
Gairnshiel Lodge 259 K4
Gaitsgill 209 G2
Galabank 236 B5
Galashiels 227 F2
Galdenoch 214 C4
Gale 184 D1
Galgate 192 A2
Galhampton 116 D5
Gallaber 193 E1
Gallanach 240 A2
Gallantry Bank 170 C2
Gallatown 244 A5
Gallchoille 239 G5
Gallery 253 E3
Gallery of Modern Art,
   Glasgow Glas
   G1 3AH 39 F4
Galley Common 159 F3
Galleyend 137 G2
Galleywood 137 G2
Galloway Forest Dark Sky
   Park D & G 215 F2
Gallowfauld 252 C5
Gallowhill 233 F3
Gallows Green 172 B3
Gallowstree
   Common 134 B4
Gallowstree Elm 158 A4
Galltair 256 E2
Gallt-y-foel 167 E1
Gallypot Street 135 D5
Galmington 115 F5
Galmisdale 247 D1
Galmpton Devon 100 C3
Galmpton Torbay 101 E2
Galmpton
   Warborough 101 E2
Galphay 202 B5
Galston 224 C2
Galtrigill 263 G6
Gamble's Green 137 G1
Gamblesby 210 C4
Gamelsby 209 F1
Gamesley 185 E3
Gamlingay 150 A2
Gamlingay Cinques 150 A2
Gamlingay Great
   Heath 150 A2
Gammaton 113 E3
Gammaton Moor 113 E3
Gammersgill 201 F4
Gamrie 269 F4
Gamston Notts 187 E5
Gamston Notts 174 B4
Ganarew 131 E1
Gang 98 D4
Ganllwyd 168 A5
Gannochy 253 E2
Ganstead 197 D4
Ganthorpe 203 F5
Ganton 204 C5
Ganwick Corner 136 B3
Gaodhail 239 F1
Gappah 102 B5
Gara Bridge 100 D2
Garabal 241 F4
Garadheancal 265 F2
Garbat 266 B5
Garbhallt 240 C5
Garboldisham 164 B3
Garden 242 A5
Garden City 170 A1
Garden Village 185 G3
Gardeners Green 120 D1
Gardenstown 269 F4
Garderhouse 279 C8
Gardham 196 B3
Gare Hill 117 E3
Garelochhead 241 E5
Garford 133 G3
Garforth 194 D4
Gargrave 193 F3
Gargunnock 242 C5
Gariob 231 F1
Garlic Street 164 D3
Garlies Castle 215 F4
Garlieston 207 E2
Garlinge Green 124 D3
Garlogie 261 F4
Garmelow 171 F5
Garmond 269 G5
Garmony 247 F5
Garmouth 268 B4
Garmston 157 F2
Garndolbenmaen 167 D3
Garneddwen 155 D2

Garnett Bridge 199 G3
Garnfadryn 166 B4
Garnswllt 128 C2
Garrabost 271 H4
Garrachra 232 B1
Garralburn 268 C5
Garras 95 E4
Garreg 167 F3
Garreg Bank 156 B1
Garrets Green 159 D4
Garrick 242 D3
Garrigill 210 D3
Garriston 202 A3
Garroch 215 G2
Garrochty 232 B4
Garros 263 K5
Garrow 242 D1
Garryhorn 215 G1
Garrynahine (Gearraidh na
   h-Aibhne) 270 E4
Garsdale 200 C4
Garsdale Head 200 C3
Garsdon 132 B4
Garshall Green 171 G4
Garsington 134 A2
Garstang 192 A3
Garston 183 F4
Garswood 183 G3
Gartachoil 242 A5
Gartally 258 C4
Gartavaich 231 G4
Gartbreck 230 A4
Gartcosh 234 A3
Gartheli 142 B2
Garthmyl 156 A3
Garthynty 142 D3
Gartincaber 242 B4
Gartly 260 D1
Gartmore 242 A4
Gartnagrenach 231 F4
Gartnatra 230 B3
Gartness 233 G1
Gartocharn 233 F1
Garton 197 E4
Garton-on-the-
   Wolds 196 B1
Gartymore 275 F7
Garvald 236 C2
Garvamore 258 C5
Garvan 248 B2
Garvard 238 C5
Garve (Clachan
   Ghairbh) 265 K5
Garveld 222 B5
Garvestone 178 B5
Garvie 232 B1
Garvock Aber 253 F2
Garvock Invcly 233 D2
Garvock P&K 243 F3
Garwald 226 D5
Garwaldwaterfoot 226 D5
Garway 145 D5
Garway Hill 144 D5
Gask Aber 269 J6
Gask Aber 269 F6
Gask P&K 243 E3
Gaskan 248 A2
Gass 224 C5
Gastard 117 F1
Gasthorpe 164 A3
Gaston Green 137 E1
Gatcombe 107 D4
Gate Burton 187 F4
Gate Helmsley 195 F2
Gate House 231 D2
Gateacre 183 F4
Gateford 186 C4
Gateforth 195 E5
Gatehead 224 B2
Gatehouse 251 D5
Gatehouse of Fleet 216 A5
Gatelawbridge 216 D1
Gateley 178 A3
Gatenby 202 C4
Gatesgarth 209 E5
Gateshaw 228 B4
Gateshead 212 B1
Gatesheath 170 B1
Gateside Aber 260 E3
Gateside Angus 252 C5
Gateside Fife 243 G4
Gateside NAyr 233 E4
Gateslack 225 G5
Gathurst 183 G2
Gatley 184 C4
Gattonside 227 G2
Gatwick Airport 122 B4
Gaufron 143 F1
Gaulby 160 B2
Gauldry 244 B2
Gauntons Bank 170 C3
Gaunt's Common 105 G2
Gaunt's Earthcott 131 F4
Gautby 188 B5
Gavinton 237 E4
Gawber 186 A2
Gawcott 148 B4
Gawsworth 184 C5
Gawthrop 200 B4
Gawthwaite 199 D4
Gay Bowers 137 G2
Gay Street 121 F5
Gaydon 147 F2
Gayhurst 148 D3
Gayle 201 D4
Gayles 202 A2
Gayton Mersey 183 D4
Gayton N'hants 148 C2
Gayton Norf 163 F1
Gayton Staffs 171 G5
Gayton le Marsh 189 E4
Gayton le Wold 188 C4
Gayton Thorpe 163 F1
Gaywood 177 E5
Gazeley 151 F1

Geanies House 267 F4
Gearach 230 A4
Gearnsary 274 C5
Gearradh 248 B3
Gearraidh Bhailteas
   254 C2
Gearraidh Bhaird 271 F5
Gearraidh na
   Monadh 254 C3
Gearrannan 270 D3
Geary 263 H5
Gedding 152 A2
Geddington 161 D4
Gedgrave Hall 153 F3
Gedintailor 256 B1
Gedling 174 B3
Gedney 176 C5
Gedney Broadgate 176 C5
Gedney Drove End 176 C5
Gedney Dyke 176 C5
Gedney Hill 162 B1
Gee Cross 185 D3
Geilston 233 E2
Geirinis 262 C7
Geisiadar 270 D4
Geldeston 165 E2
Gell Conwy 168 B1
Gell Gwyn 167 D4
Gelli 219 F3
Gelli Aur Country
   Park Carmar
   SA32 8LR 142 C5
Gelli Gynan 169 E2
Gellideg 129 G2
Gellifor 169 E1
Gelligaer 130 A3
Gellilydan 167 F4
Gellioedd 168 C3
Gelly 127 D1
Gellyburn 243 F1
Gellywen 141 F5
Gelston D&G 216 B5
Gelston Lincs 175 E3
Gembling 196 D2
Gemmil 239 G4
Genoch 214 C5
Genoch Square 214 C5
Gentleshaw 158 C1
Geocrab 263 G2
George Green 135 F4
George Nympton 114 A5
Georgeham 113 E2
Georgetown 233 F3
Gerlan 167 F1
Germansweek 99 E1
Germoe 94 C4
Gerrans 95 F3
Gerrards Cross 135 F4
Gerston 275 G3
Gestingthorpe 151 G4
Geuffordd 156 B1
Geufron 155 E4
Gibbet Hill 117 E3
Gibbshill 216 B3
Gibraltar Lincs 177 D2
Gibraltar Suff 152 C2
Gibraltar Point National
   Nature Reserve Lincs
   PE24 4SU 177 D2
Gibside T&W
   NE16 6BG 212 A2
Giddeahall 132 A5
Giddy Green 105 E4
Gidea Park 137 E4
Gidleigh 99 G2
Giffnock 233 G4
Gifford 236 C3
Giffordland 233 D5
Giffordtown 244 A3
Giggleswick 193 E1
Gigha 231 E5
Gilberdyke 196 A5
Gilbert's End 146 A3
Gilchriston 236 B3
Gilcrux 209 E3
Gildersome 194 B5
Gildingwells 186 C4
Gileston 114 D1
Gilfach 130 A3
Gilfach Goch 129 F4
Gilfachrheda 142 A2
Gilgarran 208 D4
Gill 210 A5
Gillamoor 203 F4
Gillen 263 H5
Gillenbie 217 F2
Gillfoot 217 D3
Gilling East 203 F5
Gilling West 202 A2
Gillingham Dorset 117 E5
Gillingham Med 123 G2
Gillingham Norf 165 F2
Gillivoan 275 G5
Gillock 275 H3
Gillow Heath 171 F2
Gills 275 J1
Gill's Green 123 G5
Gilmanscleuch 227 E3
Gilmerton Edin 235 G3
Gilmerton P&K 243 D2
Gilmilnscroft 225 D3
Gilmonby 201 E1
Gilmorton 160 A4
Gilsland 210 C1
Gilsland Spa 210 C1
Gilson 159 D3
Gilstead 194 A4
Gilston 236 B4
Gilston Park 136 D2
Giltbrook 173 F3
Gilwern 130 B1
Gimingham 179 D2
Gin Pit 184 A2
Ginclough 185 D5
Ginger's Green 110 B2
Giosla 270 D5
Gipping 152 B1
Gipsey Bridge 176 A3
Girlsta 279 D7
Girsby 202 C2
Girtford 149 G3
Girthon 216 A5
Girton Cambs 150 C1
Girton Notts 174 D1
Girvan 214 C1
Gisburn 193 E3
Gisburn Cotes 193 E3

Gisleham 165 G3
Gislingham 164 B4
Gissing 164 C3
Gittisham 103 E3
Givons Grove 121 G2
Glackour 265 H3
Gladestry 144 B2
Gladsmuir 236 B2
Glaic 232 B2
Glais 128 D2
Glaisdale 203 G2
Glaister 223 E2
Glame 264 B7
Glamis 252 B5
Glamis Castle Angus
   DD8 1QJ 252 B5
Glan Conwy 168 B2
Glanaber Terrace 168 A3
Glanaman 128 C1
Glanbran 143 E4
Glan-Denys 142 B2
Glanderston 260 D2
Glandford 178 B1
Glan-Duar 142 B3
Glandwr NPT 129 D2
Glan-Dwyfach 167 D3
Glangrwyney 130 B1
Glanllynfi 129 E4
Glan-rhyd NPT 129 D2
Glanrhyd Pembs 141 E3
Glanton 229 E5
Glanton Pyke 229 E5
Glanvilles Wootton 104 C2
Glanwern 154 C4
Glanwydden 181 G4
Glan-y-don 182 C5
Glan-y-llyn 130 A4
Glan-y-nant 155 F4
Glan-yr-afon
   Gwyn 168 C3
Glan-yr-afon
   Gwyn 168 D3
Glan-yr-afon IoA 181 E4
Glan-y-Wern 167 F4
Glapthorn 161 F3
Glapwell 173 F1
Glasahoile 241 G4
Glasbury 144 A4
Glaschoil 259 H1
Glascoed Mon 130 C2
Glascoed Wrex 169 F2
Glascorrie 260 C5
Glascote 159 E2
Glascwm 144 A2
Glasdrum 248 C5
Glasfryn 168 C2
Glasgow (Glaschu) 233 G3
Glasgow Airport 233 F3
Glasgow Botanic
   Garden Glas
   G12 0UE 30 C3
Glasgow Prestwick
   Airport 224 B3
Glasgow Royal Concert Hall
   Glas G2 3NY 39 F3
Glasgow Science Centre
   Glas G51 1EA 38 A4
Glashmore 261 F4
Glasinfryn 167 E1
Glasnacardoch 256 C5
Glasnakille 256 B3
Glaspant 141 F4
Glaspwll 154 D3
Glassburn 257 K1
Glassel 260 E5
Glassenbury 123 G5
Glasserton 207 E3
Glassford 234 B5
Glasshouse 145 G5
Glasshouses 194 A1
Glassingall 242 C4
Glasslie 244 A4
Glasson Cumb 218 A5
Glasson Lancs 192 A2
Glasson Dock 192 A2
Glassonby 210 B4
Glasterlaw 253 D4
Glaston 161 D2
Glastonbury 116 B4
Glastonbury Abbey Som
   BA6 9EL 116 C4
Glatton 161 G4
Glazebrook 184 A3
Glazebury 184 A3
Glazeley 157 G4
Gleadless 186 A4
Gleadsmoss 171 F1
Gleann Tholastaidh
   271 H3
Gleaston 199 D5
Glecknabae 232 B3
Gledhow 194 C4
Gledrid 169 F4
Glemsford 151 G3
Glen D&G 216 C3
Glen D&G 215 G3
Glen Auldyn 190 C2
Glen Mona 190 C2
Glen Parva 160 A3
Glen Trool Lodge 215 F2
Glen Village 234 C2
Glen Vine 190 B4
Glenae 217 D2
Glenaladale 248 A2
Glenald 241 E4
Glenamachrie 240 B2
Glenapp Castle 214 B2
Glenarm 252 B3
Glenbarr 222 B2
Glenbatrick 230 D2
Glenbeg High 265 K3
Glenbeg High 259 H2
Glenbeg High 247 D3
Glenbeich 242 B2
Glenbervie Aber 253 F1
Glenbervie Falk 234 C1
Glenboig 234 B3
Glenborrodale 247 F3
Glenbranter 240 D5
Glenbreck 226 B3
Glenbrittle 255 K2
Glenburn 233 F3
Glenbyre 239 E2
Glencaple 217 D4

Glencarse 243 G2
Glencat 260 D5
Glenceitlein 248 D5
Glencloy 223 F2
Glencoe
   (A' Chàrnaich) 248 D4
Glencoe Visitor Centre
   High PH49 4LA 248 D4
Glenconglass 259 J2
Glencraig 243 G5
Glencripesdale 247 F4
Glencrosh 216 B2
Glendearg D&G 226 D5
Glendearg ScBord 227 G2
Glendessary 257 F2
Glendevon 243 E4
Glendoebeg 258 B4
Glendoick 244 A2
Glendoll Lodge 252 A2
Glendoune 214 C1
Glendrissaig 214 C1
Glenduckie 244 A3
Glenduisk 214 D2
Glendye Lodge 253 E1
Gleneagles Hotel 243 E3
Gleneagles House 243 E4
Glenearn 243 G3
Glenegedale 230 B4
Glenelg
   (Gleann Eilg) 256 E3
Glenfarg 243 G3
Glenfeochan 240 A2
Glenfield 160 A2
Glenfinnan (Gleann
   Fhionnain) 248 B1
Glenfoot 243 G3
Glengalmadale 248 A4
Glengap 216 A5
Glengarnock 233 E4
Glengarrisdale 239 F5
Glengennet 215 D1
Glengolly 275 G2
Glengrasco 263 K7
Glengyle 241 G3
Glenhead 216 C2
Glenhead Farm 252 A3
Glenhurich 248 A3
Glenkerry 227 E4
Glenkiln 223 F2
Glenkin 232 C1
Glenkindie 260 C3
Glenlair 216 B3
Glenlatterach 267 K6
Glenlean 232 B1
Glenlee Angus 252 C2
Glenlee D&G 216 A2
Glenlichorn 242 C3
Glenlivet 259 J2
Glenlochar 216 B4
Glenluce 214 C5
Glenmallan 241 E5
Glenmanna 225 G3
Glenmavis 234 B3
Glenmaye 190 A4
Glenmeanie 265 J6
Glenmore A&B 232 B1
Glenmore High 263 K7
Glenmore Lodge 259 G4
Glenmoy 252 C3
Glenmuick 273 F7
Glennoe 240 C1
Glenochar 226 A3
Glenogil 252 C3
Glenprosen
   Village 252 B3
Glenquiech 252 C3
Glenramskill 222 C4
Glenrazie 215 E3
Glenridding 209 G5
Glenrisdell 231 G4
Glenrossal 266 B1
Glenrothes 244 A4
Glensanda 248 A5
Glensaugh 253 E2
Glensgaich 266 B5
Glenshalg 260 D4
Glenshellish 240 D5
Glensluain 240 C5
Glentaggart 225 G3
Glentham 188 A3
Glenton 260 E2
Glentress 227 E2
Glentress 7stanes ScBord
   EH45 8NB 235 G5
Glentress Forest
   Visitor Centre ScBord
   EH45 8NB 235 G5
Glentrool 215 E3
Glentruan 190 C1
Glentworth 187 G4
Glenuachdarach 263 K6
Glenuig 247 F2
Glenure 248 C5
Glenurquhart 266 E5
Glenwhilly 214 C3
Glespin 225 G3
Gletness 279 D7
Glewstone 145 E5
Glinton 161 G2
Glogue 141 F4
Glooston 160 C3
Glororum 229 F3
Glossop 185 E3
Gloster Hill 221 E1
Gloucester 132 A1
Gloucester Cathedral
   Glos GL1 2LR
   73 Gloucester
Gloucester Historic
   Docks Glos GL1 2ER
   73 Gloucester
Gloucestershire
   Airport 146 A5
Gloucestershire &
   Warwickshire Railway
   Glos GL54 5DT 146 B5
Gloup 278 E2
Gloweth 96 B5
Glusburn 193 G3
Glutt Lodge 275 F5
Glympton 147 G5

Glyn 168 A2
Glyn Ceiriog 169 F4
Glynarthen 141 G3
Glyncoch 129 G3
Glyncorrwg 129 E3
Glynde 109 G3
Glyndebourne 109 G2
Glyndyfrdwy 169 E3
Glynneath
   (Glyn-Nedd) 129 E2
Glynogwr 129 F4
Glyntaff 129 G4
Gnosall 171 F5
Gnosall Heath 171 F5
Go Bananas, Colchester
   Essex CO1 1BX 152 A5
Goadby 160 C3
Goadby Marwood 174 C5
Goatacre 132 C5
Goatfield 240 C4
Goathill 104 C1
Goathland 204 B2
Goathurst 115 F4
Gobernuisgeach 274 E5
Gobhaig 270 C7
Gobowen 170 A4
Godalming 121 E3
Goddard's Corner 153 D1
Goddards Green 109 E1
Godden Green 123 E3
Goddington 123 D2
Godford Cross 103 E3
Godington 148 B5
Godleybrook 171 G3
Godmanchester 162 A5
Godmanstone 104 C3
Godmersham 124 C3
Godney 116 B3
Godolphin Cross 94 D3
Godor 156 B2
Godre'r-graig 129 D2
Godshill Hants 106 A1
Godshill IoW 107 E4
Godstone 122 C3
Godstone Farm Surr
   RH9 8LX 122 C3
Godwick 178 A3
Goetre 130 C2
Goff's Oak 136 C2
Gogar 235 F2
Goginan 154 C4
Goirtean a'
   Chladaich 248 C2
Goirtein 232 A1
Golan 167 E3
Golant 97 F4
Golberdon 98 D3
Golborne 184 A3
Golcar 185 F1
Gold Hill Cambs 162 D3
Gold Hill Dorset 105 E1
Goldcliff 130 C4
Golden Acre Park
   WYorks
   LS16 8BQ 194 B3
Golden Cross 110 A2
Golden Green 123 F4
Golden Grove 128 B1
Golden Pot 120 C3
Golden Valley
   Derbys 173 F2
Golden Valley Glos 146 B5
Goldenhill 171 F2
Golders Green 136 B4
Goldhanger 138 C2
Goldielea 216 D3
Golding 157 E2
Goldington 149 F2
Goldsborough
   NYorks 204 B1
Goldsborough
   NYorks 194 C2
Goldsithney 94 C3
Goldstone 171 E5
Goldthorn Park 158 B3
Goldthorpe 186 B2
Goldworthy 113 D3
Goleulong 2000 Lightship,
   Cardiff Cardiff
   CF10 4PA 7 C4
Golford 123 G5
Gollanfield 267 F6
Gollinglith Foot 202 A4
Golspie 267 F2
Golval 274 D2
Gomeldon 118 C4
Gomersal 194 B5
Gometra 246 C5
Gometra House 246 C5
Gomshall 121 F3
Gonachan Cottage 234 A1
Gonalston 174 B3
Gonerby Hill Foot 175 E4
Gonfirth 279 C6
Good Easter 137 F1
Gooderstone 163 F2
Goodleigh 113 G2
Goodmanham 196 A3
Goodmayes 137 D4
Goodnestone Kent 125 E3
Goodnestone Kent 124 C2
Goodrich 131 E1
Goodrington 101 E2
Goodshaw 193 E5
Goodshaw Fold 193 E5
Goodwick (Wdig) 140 C4
Goodworth Clatford 119 E3
Goodyers End 159 F4
Goole 195 G5
Goom's Hill 146 C2
Goonbell 96 B4
Goonhavern 96 B4
Goonvrea 96 B5
Goose Green Essex 152 C5
Goose Green Essex 152 C5
Goose Green
   GtMan 183 G2
Goose Green Kent 123 F4
Goose Green SGlos 131 F5
Goose Pool 145 D4
Gooseham 112 C4
Goosehill Green 146 B1
Goosewell 100 B2
Goosey 133 F3
Goosnargh 192 B4
Goostrey 184 B5

Gorcott Hill 146 C1
Gorddinog 181 E5
Gordon 236 D5
Gordonbush 267 F1
Gordonstoun 267 J5
Gordonstown Aber 268 D5
Gordonstown Aber 261 F1
Gore Cross 118 C2
Gore End 119 F1
Gore Pit 138 B1
Gore Street 125 E2
Gorebridge 236 A3
Gorefield 162 C1
Gorey 100 D5
Gorgie 235 G2
Gorgie City Farm Edin
 EH11 2LA 36 B7
Goring 134 B4
Goring Heath 134 B5
Goring-by-Sea 108 D3
Gorleston-on-Sea 179 G4
Gorllwyn 141 G4
Gornalwood 158 B3
Gorrachie 269 F5
Gorran Churchtown 97 D5
Gorran Haven 97 E5
Gors 154 C5
Gorsedd 182 C5
Gorseinon 128 B3
Gorseness 277 D6
Gorseybank 173 D2
Gorsgoch 142 A2
Gorslas 128 B1
Gorsley 145 F5
Gorsley Common 145 F5
Gorstage 184 A5
Gorstan 265 K5
Gorstanvorran 248 A2
Gorsten 239 G1
Gortenbuie 239 E1
Gorteneorn 247 F3
Gorsty Hill 172 C5
Gorton A&B 246 A4
Gorton GtMan 184 C3
Gosbeck 152 C2
Gosberton 175 G5
Gosberton Clough 175 G5
Goseley Dale 173 E5
Gosfield 151 F5
Gosford Here 145 E1
Gosford Oxon 134 A1
Gosforth Cumb 198 B2
Gosforth T&W 212 A1
Gosland Green 170 C2
Gosmore 149 G5
Gosport 107 F3
Gossabrough 278 E4
Gossington 131 G2
Gossops Green 122 B5
Goswick 229 E2
Gotham 173 G4
Gotherington 146 B5
Gothers 97 D4
Gott 279 D8
Gotton 115 F5
Goudhurst 123 G5
Goulceby 188 C5
Gourdas 269 F6
Gourdon 253 G2
Gourock 232 D2
Govan 233 G3
Goverton 174 C2
Goveton 101 D3
Govilon 130 B1
Gowanhill 269 J4
Gowdall 195 F5
Gowerton 128 B3
Gowkhall 235 E1
Gowkthrapple 234 B4
Gowthorpe 195 G2
Goxhill ERid 197 D3
Goxhill NLincs 196 D5
Goytre 129 D2
Gozzard's Ford 133 G3
Grabhair 271 F6
Graby 175 F5
Gradbach 171 G1
Grade 95 E5
Gradeley Green 170 C2
Graffham 108 B2
Grafham Cambs 149 G1
Grafham Surr 121 F3
Grafham Water Cambs
 PE28 0BH 149 G1
Grafton Here 145 D4
Grafton NYorks 194 D1
Grafton Oxon 133 E2
Grafton Shrop 156 D1
Grafton Worcs 145 E1
Grafton Worcs 146 B4
Grafton Flyford 146 B2
Grafton Regis 148 C3
Grafton Underwood 161 E4
Grafty Green 124 A4
Graianrhyd 169 F2
Graig Carmar 128 A2
Graig Conwy 181 G5
Graig Denb 182 B5
Graig-fechan 169 E2
Grain 124 A1
Grainel 230 A3
Grainhow 269 G6
Grains Bar 185 D2
Grainsby 188 A2
Grainthorpe 189 D3
Graizelound 187 E3
Gramisdale
 (Gramsdal) 262 D6
Grampound 96 D5
Grampound Road 96 D4
Granborough 148 C5
Granby 174 C4
Grand Pier, Teignmouth
 Devon
 TQ14 8BB 102 C5
Grandborough 147 G1
Grandes Rocques 101 F4
Grandtully 251 E4
Grange Cumb 209 F5
Grange EAyr 224 C2
Grange High 257 K1
Grange Med 123 G2
Grange Mersey 182 D4
Grange P&K 244 A2
Grange Crossroads 268 C5
Grange de Lings 187 G5
Grange Hall 267 H5

Grange Hill 136 D3
Grange Moor 185 G1
Grange of Lindores 244 A3
Grange Villa 212 B2
Grangemill 172 D2
Grangemouth 234 D1
Grangemuir 244 D4
Grange-over-Sands 199 F5
Grangeston 214 D1
Grangetown
 Cardiff 130 A5
Grangetown R&C 213 E5
Granish 259 G3
Gransmoor 196 D2
Granston 140 B4
Grantchester 150 C2
Grantham 175 E4
Grantley 202 B5
Grantlodge 261 F3
Granton 235 G2
Granton House 226 B5
Grantown-on-Spey 259 H2
Grantsfield 145 E1
Grantshouse 237 F3
Grappenhall 184 A4
Grasby 188 A2
Grasmere 199 E2
Grass Green 151 F4
Grasscroft 185 D2
Grassendale 183 E4
Grassgarth 199 F3
Grassholme 211 F5
Grassington 193 G1
Grassmoor 173 F1
Grassthorpe 174 C1
Grateley 119 D3
Gratwich 172 B4
Gravel Hill 135 F3
Graveley Cambs 150 A1
Graveley Herts 150 A5
Gravelly Hill 158 D3
Gravels 156 C2
Graven 278 D5
Graveney 125 D2
Gravesend 137 F5
Grayingham 187 G3
Grayrigg 199 G3
Grays 137 F5
Grayshott 121 D4
Grayswood 121 E4
Grazeley 120 B1
Greasbrough 186 B3
Greasby 183 D4
Great Aberystwyth Camera
 Obscura Cere
 SY23 2DN 154 B4
Great Abington 150 D3
Great Addington 161 E5
Great Alne 146 D2
Great Altcar 183 E2
Great Amwell 136 C1
Great Asby 200 B1
Great Ashfield 152 A1
Great Ayton 203 E1
Great Baddow 137 G2
Great Bardfield 151 E4
Great Barford 149 G2
Great Barr 158 C3
Great Barrington 133 E1
Great Barrow 170 B1
Great Barton 151 G1
Great Barugh 203 G5
Great Bavington 220 B3
Great Bealings 152 D3
Great Bedwyn 119 D1
Great Bentley 152 C5
Great Bernera 270 D4
Great Billing 148 D1
Great Bircham 177 F4
Great Blakenham 152 C2
Great Bolas 170 D5
Great Bookham 121 G2
Great Bourton 147 G3
Great Bowden 160 C4
Great Bradley 151 E2
Great Braxted 138 B1
Great Bricett 152 B2
Great Brickhill 149 E4
Great Bridgeford 171 F5
Great Brington 148 B1
Great Bromley 152 B5
Great Broughton
 Cumb 209 D3
Great Broughton
 NYorks 203 E1
Great Buckland 123 F2
Great Budworth 184 A5
Great Burdon 202 C1
Great Burstead 137 F3
Great Busby 203 E2
Great Cambourne 150 B2
Great Canfield 137 E1
Great Canney 138 B2
Great Carlton 189 E4
Great Casterton 161 F2
Great Chalfield 117 F1
Great Chart 124 B4
Great Chatwell 157 G1
Great Chell 171 F2
Great Chesterford 150 D3
Great Cheverell 118 A2
Great Chishill 150 C4
Great Clacton 139 E1
Great Clifton 208 D4
Great Coates 188 C2
Great Comberton 146 B3
Great Corby 210 A2
Great Cornard 151 G3
Great Cowden 197 E3
Great Coxwell 133 E3
Great Crakehall 202 B4
Great Cransley 160 D5
Great
 Cressingham 163 G2
Great Crosby 183 E2
Great Crosthwaite 209 F4
Great Cubley 172 C4
Great Cumbrae 232 C4
Great Dalby 160 C1
Great Doddington 149 D1
Great Doward 131 E2
Great Dunham 163 G1
Great Dunmow 151 E5
Great Durnford 118 C4
Great Easton Essex 151 E5
Great Easton Leics 160 D3
Great Eccleston 192 A3
Great Edstone 203 G4

Great Ellingham 164 B2
Great Elm 117 E3
Great Eversden 150 B2
Great Fencote 202 B3
Great Finborough 152 B2
Great Fransham 163 G1
Great Gaddesden 135 F1
Great Gidding 161 G4
Great Givendale 196 A2
Great Glemham 153 E1
Great Glen 160 B3
Great Gonerby 175 D4
Great Gransden 150 A2
Great Green
 Cambs 150 A3
Great Green Norf 165 D3
Great Green Suff 152 A2
Great Green Suff 164 C4
Great Green Suff 164 B4
Great Habton 203 G5
Great Hale 175 G3
Great Hall Hants
 SO23 8UJ
 89 Winchester
Great Hallingbury 137 E1
Great Hampden 134 D2
Great Harrowden 161 D5
Great Harwood 192 D4
Great Haseley 134 B2
Great Hatfield 197 D3
Great Haywood 172 B5
Great Heath 159 F4
Great Heck 195 E5
Great Henny 151 G4
Great Hinton 118 A2
Great Hockham 164 A2
Great Holland 139 F1
Great Horkesley 152 A4
Great Hormead 150 C4
Great Horton 194 A4
Great Horwood 148 C4
Great Houghton
 N'hants 148 C2
Great Houghton
 SYorks 186 B2
Great Hucklow 185 F5
Great Kelk 196 D2
Great Kimble 134 D2
Great Kingshill 135 D3
Great Langton 202 B3
Great Leighs 137 G1
Great Limber 188 B2
Great Linford 149 D3
Great Livermere 163 G5
Great Longstone 185 G5
Great Lumley 212 B3
Great Lyth 157 D2
Great Malvern 145 G3
Great Maplestead 151 G4
Great Marton 191 G4
Great Massingham 177 F5
Great Melton 178 C5
Great Milton 134 B2
Great Missenden 135 D2
Great Mitton 192 D4
Great Mongeham 125 F3
Great Moulton 164 C2
Great Munden 150 B5
Great Musgrave 200 C1
Great Ness 156 D1
Great Notley 151 F5
Great Nurcot 114 C4
Great Oak 130 C2
Great Oakley Essex 152 C5
Great Oakley
 N'hants 161 D4
Great Offley 149 G5
Great Orme Tramway
 Conwy
 LL30 2HG 181 F4
Great Ormside 200 C1
Great Orton 209 G1
Great Ouseburn 194 D1
Great Oxendon 160 C4
Great Oxney Green 137 F2
Great Palgrave 163 G1
Great Parndon 136 D2
Great Paxton 150 A1
Great Plumpton 191 G4
Great Plumstead 179 E5
Great Ponton 175 E4
Great Potheridge 113 F4
Great Preston 194 C5
Great Purston 148 A4
Great Raveley 162 A4
Great Rissington 133 D1
Great Rollright 147 F4
Great Ryburgh 178 A3
Great Ryle 229 E5
Great Ryton 157 D2
Great St. Mary's Church
 Cambs CB2 3PQ
 66 Cambridge
Great Saling 151 F5
Great Salkeld 210 B4
Great Sampford 151 E4
Great Sankey 183 G4
Great Saredon 158 B2
Great Saxham 151 F1
Great Shefford 133 F5
Great Shelford 150 C2
Great Smeaton 202 C2
Great Snoring 178 A2
Great Somerford 132 B4
Great Stainton 212 C5
Great Stambridge 138 C3
Great Staughton 149 G1
Great Steeping 176 C1
Great Stonar 125 F3
Great Strickland 210 B5
Great Stukeley 162 A5
Great Sturton 188 C5
Great Sutton
 ChesW&C 183 E5
Great Sutton Shrop 157 E4
Great Swinburne 220 B4
Great Tew 147 F5
Great Tey 151 G5
Great Thorness 107 D3
Great Thurlow 151 E3
Great Torr 100 C3
Great Torrington 113 F4
Great Tosson 220 C1
Great Totham
 Essex 138 B1
Great Totham
 Essex 138 B1
Great Tows 188 C3

Great Urswick 199 D5
Great Wakering 138 C4
Great Waldingfield 152 A3
Great Walsingham 178 A2
Great Waltham 137 F1
Great Warley 137 E3
Great Washbourne 146 B4
Great Weeke 102 A4
Great Welnetham 151 G2
Great Wenham 152 B4
Great Whittington 220 C4
Great Wigborough 138 C1
Great Wigsell 110 C1
Great Wilne 173 F4
Great Wishford 118 B4
Great Witcombe 132 B1
Great Witley 145 G1
Great Wolford 147 E4
Great Wratting 151 E3
Great Wymondley 150 A5
Great Wyrley 158 B2
Great Wytheford 157 E1
Great Yarmouth 179 G5
Great Yeldham 151 F4
Greatford 161 F1
Greatgate 172 B3
Greatham Hants 120 C4
Greatham Hart 213 D5
Greatham WSuss 108 C2
Greatness 123 E3
Greatstone-on-Sea 111 F1
Greatworth 148 A3
Green 169 D1
Green Cross 121 D4
Green End Bed 149 G2
Green End Bucks 149 E4
Green End Cambs 162 A5
Green End Cambs 162 B5
Green End Herts 150 B5
Green End Herts 150 B4
Green End Warks 159 E4
Green Hammerton 195 D2
Green Hill 132 C4
Green Lane 146 C1
Green Moor 185 G3
Green Ore 116 C2
Green Quarter 199 F2
Green Street ESuss 110 C2
Green Street Herts 136 A3
Green Street Herts 150 C5
Green Street Worcs 146 A3
Green Street Green
 GtLon 123 D2
Green Street Green
 Kent 137 E5
Green Tye 136 D1
Greenburn 252 C5
Greencroft 212 A3
Greendams 253 E1
Greendykes 229 E4
Greenend 147 F5
Greenfaulds 234 B2
Greenfield CenBeds 149 F4
Greenfield (Maes-Glas)
 Flints 182 C5
Greenfield GtMan 185 E2
Greenfield High 257 J4
Greenfield Lincs 189 E5
Greenfield Oxon 134 C3
Greenford 136 A4
Greengairs 234 B2
Greengates 194 A4
Greengill 209 E3
Greenhalgh 192 A4
Greenhall 260 E2
Greenham 119 F1
Greenhaugh 219 F3
Greenhead 210 C1
Greenheads 261 J1
Greenheys 184 B2
Greenhill GtLon 136 A4
Greenhill High 267 G1
Greenhill SYorks 186 A4
Greenhithe 137 E5
Greenholm 224 D2
Greenholme 199 G2
Greenhow Hill 194 A1
Greenigo 277 D7
Greenland 275 H2
Greenlands 134 C4
Greenlaw Aber 268 E5
Greenlaw ScBord 237 E5
Greenloaning 242 D4
Greenmeadow 130 B3
Greenmoor Hill 134 B4
Greenmount 184 B1
Greenmyre 261 G1
Greenock 233 D2
Greenodd 199 E4
Greens Norton 148 B3
Greenscares 242 C3
Greenside T&W 212 A1
Greenside WYorks 185 F1
Greenstead 152 B5
Greenstead Green 151 G5
Greensted 137 E2
Greensted Green 137 E2
Greenway Pembs 140 D5
Greenway Som 116 A5
Greenwell 210 B2
Greenwich 136 C5
Greenwood Forest Park,
 Y Felinheli Gwyn
 LL56 4QN 167 E1
Greet 146 C4
Greete 157 E5
Greetham Lincs 188 D5
Greetham Rut 161 E1
Greetland 193 G5
Gregson Lane 192 B5
Greinton 116 B4
Grenaby 190 A4
Grendon N'hants 149 D1
Grendon Warks 159 E3
Grendon Common 159 E3
Grendon Green 145 E2
Grendon
 Underwood 148 B5
Grenitote
 (Greinetobht) 262 D7
Grenoside 186 A3
Greosabhagh 263 G2
Gresford 170 A2
Gresham 178 C2

Greshornish 263 J6
Gress (Griais) 271 G3
Gressenhall 178 A4
Gressingham 192 A4
Greta Bridge 201 F1
Gretna 218 B5
Gretna Green 218 B5
Gretton Glos 146 C4
Gretton N'hants 161 D3
Gretton Shrop 157 E3
Grewelthorpe 202 B5
Greygarth 202 A5
Greylake 116 A4
Greys Green 134 C4
Greysouthen 209 D4
Greystead 219 F3
Greystoke 210 A4
Greystone Angus 252 D5
Greystone Lancs 193 E3
Greystones 186 A4
Greywell 120 C2
Gribthorpe 195 G4
Gribton 216 D2
Griff 159 F4
Griffithstown 130 B3
Grigadale 246 D1
Grigghall 199 F3
Grimeford Village 184 A1
Grimesthorpe 186 A3
Grimethorpe 186 B2
Griminish (Griminis) 262 C6
Grimister 278 D3
Grimley 146 A1
Grimmet 224 B4
Grimness 277 D8
Grimoldby 189 D4
Grimpo 170 A5
Grimsargh 192 B4
Grimsay
 (Griomsaigh) 262 D6
Grimsbury 147 G3
Grimsby 188 C2
Grimscote 148 B2
Grimscott 112 C5
Grimshader
 (Griomsiadar) 271 G5
Grimsthorpe 175 F5
Grimston ERid 197 E4
Grimston Leics 174 B5
Grimston Norf 177 F5
Grimstone 104 C3
Grimstone End 152 A1
Grindale 205 E5
Grindiscol 278 D3
Grindle 157 G2
Grindleford 185 G5
Grindleton 193 D3
Grindley 172 B5
Grindley Brook 170 C3
Grindlow 185 F5
Grindon N'umb 237 G5
Grindon Staffs 172 B2
Grindon Stock 212 C5
Grindon T&W 212 C2
Gringley on the Hill 187 E3
Grinsdale 209 G1
Grinshill 170 C5
Grinton 201 F3
Griomarstaidh 270 E4
Grisdale 200 C3
Grishipoll 246 A4
Gristhorpe 205 D4
Griston 164 A2
Gritley 277 E7
Grittenham 132 C4
Grittleton 132 A5
Grizebeck 198 D4
Grizedale 199 E3
Grizedale Forest Park
 Cumb LA22 0QJ 199 E3
Grobister 276 F5
Groby 160 A2
Groes 168 D1
Groes-faen 129 G4
Groesffordd 166 B4
Groesffordd Marli 182 B5
Groeslon Gwyn 167 D2
Groeslon Gwyn 167 E1
Groes-lwyd 156 B1
Groes-wen 130 A4
Grogport 231 G5
Groigearraidh 254 C1
Gromford 153 E2
Gronant 182 B4
Groombridge 123 E5
Groombridge Place Gardens
 Kent TN3 9QG 123 E5
Grosmont Mon 144 D5
Grosmont NYorks 204 B2
Grotaig 258 B2
Groton 152 A3
Groundistone
 Heights 227 F4
Grouville 100 C3
Grove Bucks 149 E5
Grove Dorset 104 C5
Grove Kent 125 E2
Grove Notts 187 E5
Grove Oxon 133 G3
Grove End 124 A2
Grove Green 123 G3
Grove Park 136 D5
Grove Town 195 D5
Grovehill 135 F2
Grovesend SGlos 131 F4
Grovesend Swan 128 B2
Gruids 266 D1
Gruinard 265 F3
Gruinart 230 A3
Grula 255 J2
Gruline 247 E5
Grumbla 94 B4
Grundcruie 243 F2
Grundisburgh 152 D2
Gruting 279 B8
Grutness 279 G10
Gualachulain 248 D5
Guardbridge 244 C3
Guarlford 146 A3
Guay 251 F5
Gubblecote 135 E1
Gubbergill 198 B3
Guernsey 101 F5
Guernsey Airport 101 E5
Guestling Green 111 D2
Guestling Thorn 111 D2
Guestwick 178 B3
Guestwick Green 178 B3
Guide 192 D5

Guide Post 221 E3
Guilden Down 156 C4
Guilden Morden 150 A3
Guilden Sutton 170 B1
Guildford 121 E3
Guildford House Gallery
 Surr GU1 3AJ
 74 Guildford
Guildtown 243 G1
Guilsborough 160 B5
Guilsfield (Cegidfa) 156 B1
Guilthwaite 186 B4
Guisborough 203 F1
Guiseley 194 A3
Guist 178 B3
Guith 276 E4
Guiting Power 146 C5
Gulberwick 279 D9
Gullane 236 B1
Gulval 94 B3
Gulworthy 99 E3
Gumfreston 127 E2
Gumley 160 B3
Gunby Lincs 175 E5
Gunby Lincs 176 C1
Gundleton 120 B4
Gunn 113 G2
Gunnersbury 136 A5
Gunnerside 201 E3
Gunnerton 220 B4
Gunness 187 F1
Gunnislake 99 E3
Gunnista 279 E8
Gunstone 158 A2
Gunter's Bridge 121 E5
Gunthorpe Norf 178 B2
Gunthorpe Notts 174 B3
Gunthorpe Rut 161 D2
Gunville 107 D4
Gunwalloe 95 D4
Gupworthy 114 C4
Gurnard 107 D3
Gurnett 184 D5
Gurney Slade 116 D3
Gurnos MTyd 129 G2
Gurnos Powys 129 D2
Gushmere 124 C3
Gussage All Saints 105 G1
Gussage St. Andrew 105 F1
Gussage St. Michael 105 F1
Guston 125 F4
Gutcher 278 E3
Guthram Gowt 175 G5
Guthrie 253 D4
Guyhirn 162 B2
Guy's Head 176 C5
Guy's Marsh 117 F5
Guyzance 221 E1
Gwaelod-y-garth 130 A4
Gwaenysgor 182 B4
Gwaithla 144 B2
Gwalchmai 180 B5
Gwastad 140 D5
Gwastadnant 167 F2
Gwaun-Cae-Gurwen 128 D1
Gwaynynog 168 D1
Gwbert 141 E3
Gweek 95 E4
Gwehelog 130 C2
Gwenddwr 143 G3
Gwendreath 95 E5
Gwennap 96 B5
Gwenter 95 E5
Gwernaffield 169 F1
Gwernesney 130 C2
Gwernogle 142 B4
Gwernymynydd 169 F1
Gwern-y-Steeple 129 G5
Gwersyllt 170 A2
Gwespyr 182 C4
Gwinear 94 C3
Gwithian 94 C2
Gwredog 180 C4
Gwrhay 130 A3
Gwyddelwern 169 D3
Gwyddgrug 142 A4
Gwynfryn 169 F2
Gwystre 143 G1
Gwytherin 168 B1
Gyfelia 170 A3
Gyrn Goch 166 D3

H
H.M.S. Belfast GtLon
 SE1 2JH 12 C4
H.M.S. Victory PO1 3PX
 82 Portsmouth
H.M.S. Warrior PO1 3QX
 82 Portsmouth
Habberley 156 C2
Habin 120 D5
Habrough 188 B1
Haccombe 102 B5
Hacconby 175 G5
Haceby 175 F4
Hacheston 153 E2
Hackbridge 122 B2
Hackenthorpe 186 B4
Hackford 178 B5
Hackforth 202 B3
Hackland 276 C5
Hacklet (Haclait) 262 D7
Hacklete (Tacleit) 270 D4
Hackleton 148 D2
Hacklinge 125 F3
Hackness NYorks 204 C3
Hackness Ork 277 C8
Hackney 136 C4
Hackthorn 187 G4
Hackthorpe 210 B5
Hacton 137 E4
Hadden 228 B3
Haddenham
 Cambs 162 C5
Haddenham Bucks 134 C2
Haddington ELoth 236 C2
Haddington Lincs 175 E1
Haddiscoe 165 F2
Haddo Country Park Aber
 AB41 7EQ 261 G1
Haddon 161 G3
Hade Edge 185 F2
Hademore 159 D2

Hadfield 185 E3
Hadham Cross 136 D1
Hadham Ford 150 C5
Hadleigh Essex 138 B4
Hadleigh Suff 152 B3
Hadleigh Castle Country
 Park Essex
 SS7 2PP 138 B4
Hadleigh Farm Essex
 SS7 2AP 138 B4
Hadleigh Heath 152 A3
Hadley Tel&W 157 F1
Hadley Worcs 146 A1
Hadley End 172 C5
Hadley Wood 136 B3
Hadlow 123 F4
Hadlow Down 110 A1
Hadnall 170 C5
Hadstock 151 D3
Hadston 221 E2
Hadzor 146 B1
Haffenden Quarter 124 A4
Hafod Bridge 142 C4
Hafod-Dinbych 168 B2
Hafodunos 168 B1
Hafodyrynys 130 B3
Haggate 193 E4
Haggbeck 218 C4
Haggersta 279 C8
Haggerston GtLon 136 C4
Haggerston N'umb 229 E2
Haggrister 278 C5
Haggs 234 B2
Hagley Here 145 E3
Hagley Worcs 158 B4
Hagnaby Lincs 176 B1
Hagnaby Lincs 189 E5
Hague Bar 185 D4
Hagworthingham 176 B1
Haigh 184 A2
Haigh Hall Country Park
 GtMan
 WN2 1PE 183 G2
Haighton Green 192 B4
Hail Weston 149 G1
Haile 198 B2
Hailes 146 C4
Hailey Herts 136 C1
Hailey Oxon 134 B4
Hailey Oxon 133 F1
Hailsham 110 A3
Haimer 275 G2
Hainault 137 D3
Hainault Forest Country
 Park Essex
 IG7 4QN 137 D3
Haine 125 F2
Hainford 178 D4
Hainton 188 B4
Haisthorpe 196 D1
Hakin 126 B2
Halam 174 B2
Halbeath 235 F1
Halberton 102 D1
Halcro 275 H3
Hale Cumb 199 G5
Hale GtMan 184 B4
Hale Halton 183 F4
Hale Hants 106 A1
Hale Surr 120 D3
Hale Bank 183 F4
Hale Barns 184 B4
Hale Nook 191 G3
Hale Street 123 F4
Hales Norf 165 E2
Hales Staffs 171 E4
Hales Green 172 C3
Hales Place 124 D3
Halesgate 176 B5
Halesowen 158 B4
Halesworth 165 E4
Halewood 183 F4
Half Way Inn 102 D3
Halford Devon 102 B5
Halford Shrop 156 D4
Halford Warks 147 E3
Halfpenny 199 G4
Halfpenny Green 158 A3
Halfway Carmar 142 C4
Halfway Carmar 128 B2
Halfway Powys 143 E4
Halfway SYorks 186 B4
Halfway WBerks 119 F1
Halfway Bridge 121 E5
Halfway House 156 C1
Halfway Houses
 Kent 124 B1
Halfway Houses
 Lincs 175 E5
Halghton Mill 170 B3
Halifax 193 G5
Halistra 263 H6
Halket 233 F4
Halkirk 275 G3
Halkyn 182 D5
Hall 233 F4
Hall Cross 192 A5
Hall Dunnerdale 198 D3
Hall Green ChesE 171 F2
Hall Green Lancs 183 E2
Hall Green WMid 158 D4
Hall Grove 136 B1
Hall of the Forest 156 B4
Halland 110 A2
Hallaton 160 C3
Hallatrow 116 D2
Hallbankgate 210 B2
Hallen 131 E4
Hallfield Gate 173 E2
Hallglen 234 C2
Hallin 263 H6
Halling 123 G2
Hallington Lincs 188 D4
Hallington N'umb 220 B4
Halliwell 184 A1
Halloughton 174 B2
Hallow 146 A2
Hallow Heath 146 A2
Hallrule 227 G4
Halls 237 D2
Halls Green Essex 136 D2
Hall's Green Herts 150 A5
Hallsands 101 E4
Hallthwaites 198 C4
Hallwood Green 145 F4
Hallworthy 97 F1
Hallyne 235 F5

Halmer End 171 E3
Halmond's Frome 145 F3
Halmore 131 F2
Halmyre Mains 235 F5
Halnaker 108 B3
Halsall 183 E1
Halse N'hants 148 A3
Halse Som 115 E5
Halsetown 94 C3
Halsham 197 E5
Halsinger 113 E2
Halstead Essex 151 G4
Halstead Kent 123 D2
Halstead Leics 160 C2
Halstock 104 B2
Halsway 115 E4
Haltemprice Farm 196 C4
Haltham 176 A1
Haltoft End 176 B3
Halton Bucks 135 D1
Halton Halton 183 G4
Halton Lancs 192 B1
Halton N'umb 211 F1
Halton Wrex 170 A4
Halton East 193 G2
Halton Green 192 B1
Halton Gill 201 D5
Halton Holegate 176 C1
Halton Lea Gate 210 C2
Halton Park 192 B1
Halton West 193 E2
Haltwhistle 210 D1
Halvergate 179 F5
Halwell 101 D2
Halwill 99 E1
Halwill Junction 99 E1
Ham Devon 103 F2
Ham Glos 131 F3
Ham Glos 146 B5
Ham GtLon 136 A5
Ham High 275 H1
Ham Kent 125 F3
Ham Plym 100 A2
Ham Shet 278 B1
Ham Som 115 F5
Ham Som 103 F1
Ham Wilts 119 E1
Ham Common 117 F5
Ham Green Here 145 G3
Ham Green Kent 124 A2
Ham Green Kent 111 D1
Ham Green NSom 131 E5
Ham Green Worcs 146 C1
Ham Hill 123 F2
Ham Hill Country Park
    Som TA14 6RW 104 A1
Ham Street 115 G2
Hambleden 134 C4
Hambledon Hants 107 F1
Hambledon Surr 121 E4
Hamble-le-Rice 107 D2
Hambleton Lancs 191 G3
Hambleton NYorks 195 E4
Hambridge 116 A5
Hambrook SGlos 131 F5
Hambrook WSuss 107 G2
Hameringham 176 B1
Hamerton 161 G5
Hamilton 234 B4
Hamlet Devon 103 E3
Hamlet Dorset 104 B2
Hammer 121 D4
Hammerpot 108 C3
Hammersmith 186 B5
Hammersmith Apollo
    GtLon W6 9QH 11 E5
Hammerwich 158 C2
Hammerwood 122 D5
Hammond Street 136 B5
Hammoon 105 E1
Hamnavoe Shet 279 C9
Hamnavoe Shet 278 D4
Hamnavoe Shet 278 B3
Hamnavoe Shet 278 D5
Hamnish Clifford 145 E2
Hamp 115 F4
Hampden Park 110 B3
Hamperden End 151 D4
Hampnett 132 D1
Hampole 186 C2
Hampreston 105 G3
Hampstead 186 B4
Hampstead
    Norreys 134 A5
Hampsthwaite 194 B2
Hampton Devon 103 G3
Hampton GtLon 121 G1
Hampton Kent 125 D2
Hampton Peter 161 G3
Hampton Shrop 157 G4
Hampton Swin 133 D3
Hampton Worcs 146 C3
Hampton Bishop 145 E4
Hampton Court Palace &
    Garden GtLon
    KT8 9AU 11 B8
Hampton Fields 132 A3
Hampton Heath 170 B3
Hampton in Arden 159 E4
Hampton Loade 157 G4
Hampton Lovett 146 A1
Hampton Lucy 147 E2
Hampton on the
    Hill 147 E1
Hampton Poyle 134 A1
Hampton Wick 121 G1
Hamptworth 106 B1
Hamsey 109 G2
Hamstall Ridware 158 D1
Hamstead 106 C3
Hamstead Marshall 119 F1
Hamsteels 185 F3
Hamsterley Dur 212 A4
Hamsterley Dur 212 A2
Hamsterley Forest Dur
    DL13 3NL 211 G5
Hamstreet 124 C5
Hamworthy 105 F3
Hanbury Staffs 172 C5
Hanbury Worcs 146 B1
Hanbury Woodend 172 C5
Hanby 175 F4
Hanchurch 171 F3
Handa Island 272 D4
Handale 203 G1
Handbridge 170 B1

Handcross 122 B5
Handforth 184 C4
Handley ChesW&C 170 B2
Handley Derbys 173 E1
Handley Green 137 F2
Handsacre 158 C1
Handside 136 B1
Handsworth SYorks 186 B4
Handsworth WMid 158 C3
Handwoodbank 156 D1
Handy Cross 135 D3
Hanford Dorset 105 E1
Hanford Stoke 171 F3
Hanging Bridge 172 C3
Hanging Houghton 160 C5
Hanging Langford 118 B4
Hangingshaw 217 E2
Hanham 131 F5
Hankelow 171 D3
Hankerton 132 B3
Hankham 110 B3
Hanley 171 F3
Hanley Castle 146 A3
Hanley Child 145 F1
Hanley Swan 146 A3
Hanley William 145 F1
Hanlith 193 F1
Hanmer 170 B4
Hannah 189 E5
Hannington Hants 119 G2
Hannington
    N'hants 160 D5
Hannington Swin 133 D3
Hannington Wick 133 D3
Hanslope 148 D3
Hanthorpe 175 F5
Hanwell GtLon 136 A4
Hanwell Oxon 147 G3
Hanwood 156 D2
Hanworth GtLon 136 A5
Hanworth Norf 178 C2
Happisburgh 179 E2
Happisburgh
    Common 179 E3
Hapsford 183 F5
Hapton Lancs 193 D4
Hapton Norf 164 C2
Harberton 101 D2
Harbertonford 101 D2
Harbledown 124 D3
Harborne 158 C4
Harborough Magna 159 G5
Harbost (Tabost) 271 H1
Harbottle 220 B1
Harbour Park Amusements,
    Littlehampton WSuss
    BN17 5LL 108 C3
Harbourneford 100 D1
Harbridge 106 A1
Harbridge Green 106 A1
Harburn 235 E3
Harbury 147 F2
Harby Leics 174 C4
Harby Notts 187 F5
Harcombe 103 E3
Harcombe Bottom 103 G3
Harden WMid 158 C2
Harden WYorks 193 G4
Hardendale 199 G1
Hardenhuish 132 B5
Hardgate Aber 261 F4
Hardgate NYorks 194 B1
Hardham 108 C2
Hardhorn 191 G4
Hardingham 178 B5
Hardingstone 148 C2
Hardington 117 E2
Hardington
    Mandeville 104 B1
Hardington Marsh 104 B2
Hardington Moor 104 B1
Hardley 106 D2
Hardley Street 179 E5
Hardmead 149 E3
Hardraw 201 D3
Hardstoft 173 F1
Hardway Hants 107 F2
Hardway Som 117 E4
Hardwick Bucks 134 D1
Hardwick Cambs 150 C2
Hardwick Lincs 187 F5
Hardwick N'hants 161 D5
Hardwick Norf 164 D2
Hardwick Oxon 133 F2
Hardwick Oxon 148 A5
Hardwick SYorks 186 B4
Hardwick WMid 158 C3
Hardwick Hall Derbys
    S44 5QJ 173 F1
Hardwick Hall Country Park,
    Sedgefield Dur
    TS21 2EH 212 C5
Hardwick Village 186 D5
Hardwicke Glos 146 B5
Hardwicke Glos 131 G5
Hardwicke Here 144 B3
Hardy's Green 152 A5
Hare Green 152 B5
Hare Hatch 134 D3
Hare Street Herts 150 B5
Hare Street Herts 150 B5
Hareby 176 B1
Harecroft 193 G4
Hareden 192 C3
Harefield 135 F3
Harehill 172 C4
Harehills 194 C4
Harehope 229 E4
Harelaw 234 D5
Haresceugh 210 C5
Haresfield 132 A1
Hareshaw NLan 234 C3
Hareshaw SLan 234 A5
Harestock 119 F4
Harewood 194 C3
Harewood End 145 E5
Harewood House WYorks
    LS17 9LG 194 C3
Harford Devon 100 C2
Harford Devon 102 B3
Hargate 164 F2
Hargatewall 185 F5
Hargrave ChesW&C 170 B1
Hargrave N'hants 161 F5
Hargrave Suff 151 F2
Hargrave Green 151 F2

Harker 218 B5
Harkstead 152 C4
Harlaston 159 E1
Harlaxton 175 D4
Harle Syke 193 E4
Harlech 167 E4
Harlech Castle Gwyn
    LL46 2YH 167 E4
Harlequin 174 B4
Harlescott 157 E1
Harlesden 136 B4
Harleston Devon 101 D3
Harleston Norf 164 D3
Harleston Suff 152 B1
Harlestone 148 C1
Harley Shrop 157 E2
Harley SYorks 186 A3
Harleyholm 226 A2
Harlington
    CenBeds 149 F4
Harlington GtLon 135 F5
Harlosh 263 H7
Harlow 136 D2
Harlow Hill 211 G1
Harlthorpe 195 G4
Harlton 150 B2
Harlyn 96 C2
Harman's Cross 105 F4
Harmby 202 A4
Harmer Green 136 B1
Harmer Hill 170 B5
Harmondsworth 135 F5
Harmston 175 E1
Harnage 157 E2
Harnham 118 C5
Harnhill 132 C2
Harold Hill 137 E3
Harold Park 137 E3
Harold Wood 137 E3
Haroldston West 126 B1
Haroldswick 278 F1
Harome 203 F4
Harpenden 136 A1
Harpford 103 D3
Harpham 196 C1
Harpley Norf 177 F5
Harpley Worcs 145 F1
Harpole 148 B1
Harprigg 200 B4
Harpsdale 275 G3
Harpsden 134 C4
Harpswell 187 G4
Harpur Hill 185 E5
Harpurhey 184 C2
Harracott 113 F3
Harrapool 256 C2
Harrietfield 243 E2
Harrietsham 124 A3
Harringay 136 C4
Harrington Cumb 208 C4
Harrington Lincs 189 D5
Harrington N'hants 160 C5
Harringworth 161 E3
Harris 255 J5
Harris Green 164 D2
Harris Museum & Art
    Gallery, Preston Lancs
    PR1 2PP 192 B5
Harriseahead 171 F2
Harriston 209 E2
Harrogate 194 C2
Harrogate International
    Centre NYorks HG1 5LA
    74 Harrogate
Harrold 149 E2
Harrop Fold 192 D3
Harrow GtLon 136 A4
Harrow High 275 H1
Harrow Green 151 G2
Harrow Museum GtLon
    HA2 6PX 10 B1
Harrow on the Hill 136 A4
Harrow Weald 136 A3
Harrowbarrow 99 E3
Harrowden 149 F3
Harrowgate Hill 202 B1
Harry Stoke 131 F5
Harston Cambs 150 C2
Harston Leics 174 D4
Harswell 196 A3
Hart 213 D4
Hartburn 220 C3
Hartest 151 G2
Hartfield ESuss 123 D5
Hartfield High 264 D7
Hartford Cambs 162 A5
Hartford Som 114 C5
Hartford End 137 F1
Hartfordbridge 120 C2
Hartforth 202 A2
Hartgrove 105 E1
Harthill ChesW&C 170 C2
Harthill NLan 234 D3
Harthill SYorks 186 B4
Hartington 172 C1
Hartington Hall 220 C3
Hartland 112 C3
Hartland Quay 112 C3
Hartlebury 158 A5
Hartlepool 213 E4
Hartlepool's Maritime
    Experience Hart
    TS24 0XZ 213 E4
Hartley Cumb 200 C2
Hartley Kent 123 F2
Hartley Kent 123 G5
Hartley N'umb 221 F4
Hartley Green 171 G5
Hartley Mauditt 120 C4
Hartley Wespall 120 B2
Hartley Wintney 120 C2
Hartlington 193 G1
Hartlip 124 A2
Hartoft End 203 G3
Harton NYorks 195 G1
Harton Shrop 157 D4
Harton T&W 212 C1
Hartpury 146 A5
Hartrigge 228 A4
Hartshead 194 A5
Hartshill 159 F3
Hartsholme Country Park
    Lincs LN6 0EY 175 E1
Hartshorne 173 E5
Hartsop 199 F1

Hartwell Bucks 134 C1
Hartwell ESuss 123 D5
Hartwell N'hants 148 C2
Hartwith 194 B1
Hartwood 234 C4
Harvel 123 F2
Harvel 123 F2
Harvington Worcs 146 C3
Harvington Worcs 158 A5
Harwell Notts 187 D3
Harwell Oxon 133 G4
Harwich 152 D4
Harwood Dur 211 E4
Harwood GtMan 184 B1
Harwood N'umb 220 C2
Harwood Dale 204 C3
Harwood on
    Teviot 227 F5
Harworth 186 D3
Hasbury 158 B4
Hascombe 121 E4
Haselbech 160 C5
Haselbury
    Plucknett 104 A1
Haseley 147 E1
Haseley Knob 159 E5
Haselor 146 C2
Hasfield 146 A5
Hasguard 126 B2
Haskayne 183 E2
Hasketon 153 D2
Hasland 173 E1
Hasland Green 173 E1
Haslemere 121 E4
Haslingden 193 D5
Haslingden Grane 193 D5
Haslingfield 150 C2
Haslington 171 E2
Hassall 171 E2
Hassall Green 171 E2
Hassall Street 124 C4
Hassendean 227 G3
Hassingham 179 E5
Hassocks 109 F2
Hassop 185 G5
Haster 275 J3
Hasthorpe 176 C1
Hastigrow 275 H2
Hastingleigh 124 C4
Hastings ESuss 110 D3
Hastings Som 103 G1
Hastings Fishermen's
    Museum ESuss
    TN34 3DW 75 Hastings
Hastingwood 137 D2
Hastoe 135 E2
Haswell 212 C2
Haswell Plough 212 C3
Hatch CenBeds 149 G3
Hatch Hants 120 B2
Hatch Beauchamp 116 A5
Hatch End 136 A3
Hatch Green 103 G1
Hatching Green 136 A1
Hatchmere 183 G5
Hatcliffe 188 C2
Hatfield Here 145 E2
Hatfield Herts 136 B2
Hatfield SYorks 187 D2
Hatfield Broad Oak 137 E1
Hatfield Heath 137 E1
Hatfield House Herts
    AL9 5NF 136 B2
Hatfield Peverel 137 G1
Hatfield
    Woodhouse 187 D2
Hatford 133 F3
Hatherden 119 E2
Hatherleigh 113 F5
Hathern 173 F5
Hatherop 133 D2
Hathersage 185 G4
Hathersage Booths 185 G4
Hathershaw 184 D2
Hatherton ChesE 171 D3
Hatherton Staffs 158 B1
Hatley St. George 150 A2
Hatt 99 D4
Hattingley 120 B4
Hatton Aber 261 J1
Hatton Derbys 172 D5
Hatton GtLon 136 A5
Hatton Lincs 188 B5
Hatton Shrop 157 D3
Hatton Warks 147 E1
Hatton Warr 183 G4
Hatton Castle 269 F6
Hatton Country World
    Warks
    CV35 8XA 147 E1
Hatton Heath 170 B1
Hatton of Fintray 261 G3
Hattoncrook 261 G2
Haugh 189 E5
Haugh Head 229 E4
Haugh of Glass 260 C1
Haugh of Urr 216 C4
Haugham 188 D4
Haughhead 234 A2
Haughley 152 B1
Haughley Green 152 B1
Haughley New
    Street 152 B1
Haughs 268 D6
Haughton ChesE 170 C2
Haughton Notts 187 D5
Haughton Powys 156 C1
Haughton Shrop 157 F3
Haughton Shrop 157 G3
Haughton Shrop 170 A5
Haughton Staffs 171 F5
Haughton Green 184 D3
Haughton le Skerne 202 C1
Haultwick 150 B5
Haunn 254 C3
Haunton 159 E1
Hauxton 150 C2
Havannah 171 F1
Havant 107 G2
Haven 144 D2
Havenstreet 107 E3
Havercroft 186 A1
Haverfordwest
    (Hwlffordd) 126 C1
Haverhill 151 E3
Haverigg 198 C5
Havering Park 137 D3
Havering-atte-
    Bower 137 E3

Haversham 148 D3
Haverthwaite 199 E4
Haverton Hill 213 D5
Haviker Street 123 G4
Havyat 116 C4
Hawarden
    (Penarlâg) 170 A1
Hawbridge 146 B3
Hawbush Green 151 F5
Hawcoat 198 D5
Hawes 201 D4
Hawe's Green 164 D2
Hawick 227 G4
Hawkchurch 103 G2
Hawkedon 151 F2
Hawkenbury Kent 123 E5
Hawkenbury Kent 124 A4
Hawkeridge 117 F2
Hawkerland 103 D4
Hawkes End 159 E4
Hawkesbury 131 G4
Hawkesbury
    Upton 131 G4
Hawkhill 229 G5
Hawkhurst 123 G5
Hawkinge 125 E4
Hawkley 120 C5
Hawkridge 114 B4
Hawkshead 199 E3
Hawkshead Hill 199 E3
Hawksheads 192 A1
Hawksland 234 A1
Hawkswick 201 E5
Hawksworth Notts 174 C3
Hawksworth
    WYorks 194 A3
Hawksworth
    WYorks 194 B4
Hawkwell Essex 138 B3
Hawkwell N'umb 220 C4
Hawley Hants 121 D2
Hawley Kent 137 E5
Hawley's Corner 122 D3
Hawling 146 C5
Hawnby 203 E4
Haworth 193 G4
Hawstead 151 G2
Hawstead Green 151 G2
Hawthorn Dur 212 D3
Hawthorn Hants 120 B4
Hawthorn RCT 129 G4
Hawthorn Wilts 117 F1
Hawthorn Hill
    BrackF 135 D5
Hawthorn Hill
    Lincs 176 A2
Hawthorpe 175 F5
Hawton 174 C2
Haxby 195 F2
Haxey 187 E2
Haxted 122 D4
Haxton 118 C3
Hay Green 162 D1
Hay Mills 158 D4
Hay Street 150 B5
Haydock 183 G3
Haydon Dorset 104 C1
Haydon Swin 132 D4
Haydon Bridge 211 E1
Haydon Wick 132 D4
Hayes GtLon 135 F4
Hayes GtLon 122 D2
Hayes End 135 F4
Hayfield A&B 240 C2
Hayfield Derbys 185 E4
Hayfield Fife 244 A5
Hayfield High 275 G2
Haygrove 115 F4
Hayhillock 252 D5
Hayle 94 C3
Hayling Island 107 G2
Haymoor Green 171 D3
Hayne 102 C1
Haynes 149 G3
Haynes Church End 149 F3
Haynes West End 149 F3
Hay-on-Wye (Y Gelli
    Gandryll) 144 B3
Hayscastle 140 B5
Hayscastle Cross 140 C5
Hayton Cumb 210 B2
Hayton Cumb 209 E2
Hayton ERid 196 A3
Hayton Notts 187 E4
Hayton's Bent 157 E4
Haytor Vale 102 A5
Haytown 113 D4
Hayward Gallery
    GtLon SE1 8XZ 45 F4
Haywards Heath 109 F1
Haywood Oaks 174 B2
Hazel End 150 C5
Hazel Grove 184 D4
Hazel Street 123 F5
Hazelbank A&B 240 C4
Hazelbank SLan 234 A5
Hazelbury Bryan 104 D2
Hazeleigh 138 B2
Hazeley 120 C2
Hazelhurst 184 B1
Hazelside 225 G3
Hazelslack 199 F5
Hazelslade 158 C1
Hazelton Walls 244 B2
Hazelwood Derbys 173 E3
Hazelwood GtLon 122 D2
Hazlefield 208 A2
Hazlehead Aber 261 G4
Hazlehead SYorks 185 F2
Hazlemere 135 D3
Hazlerigg 221 E4
Hazleton 132 C1
Hazon 221 E1
Heacham 177 E4
Head Bridge 113 G4
Headbourne
    Worthy 119 F4
Headcorn 124 A4
Headingley 194 B4
Headington 134 A2
Headlam 202 A1
Headless Cross 146 C1
Headley Hants 120 D4
Headley Hants 119 G1
Headley Surr 120 D3
Headley Down 120 D4
Headley Heath 158 C5
Headon 187 E5

Heads Nook 210 A2
Heady Hill 184 C1
Heage 173 E2
Healaugh NYorks 201 F3
Healaugh NYorks 195 E3
Heald Green 184 C4
Heale Devon 113 G1
Heale Som 116 A5
Healey Lancs 184 C1
Healey N'umb 211 G2
Healey NYorks 202 A4
Healey WYorks 194 B5
Healeyfield 211 G3
Healing 188 C1
Heamoor 94 B3
Heaning 199 F3
Heanish 246 B2
Heanor 173 F3
Heanton
    Punchardon 113 F2
Heanton Satchville 113 F4
Heap Bridge 184 C1
Heapey 192 C5
Heapham 187 F4
Hearn 120 D4
Heart of the Country
    Centre Staffs
    WS14 9QR 158 D2
Hearthstane 226 C2
Heasley Mill 114 A4
Heast 256 C3
Heath Cardiff 130 A4
Heath Derbys 173 F1
Heath WYorks 186 A1
Heath & Reach 149 E5
Heath End Derbys 173 E5
Heath End Hants 119 G1
Heath End Hants 119 F1
Heath End Surr 120 D3
Heath Hayes 158 C1
Heath Hill 157 G1
Heath House 116 B3
Heath Town 158 B3
Heathbrook 170 D5
Heathcote Derbys 172 C1
Heathcote Shrop 157 D5
Heathencote 148 C3
Heather 159 F1
Heatherton Activity Park
    Pembs
    SA70 8RJ 127 D2
Heathfield Devon 102 B5
Heathfield ESuss 110 A1
Heathfield NYorks 194 A1
Heathfield Som 115 E5
Heathrow Airport 135 F5
Heathton 158 A3
Heatley 184 B4
Heaton Lancs 192 A4
Heaton Staffs 171 G1
Heaton T&W 212 B1
Heaton WYorks 194 A4
Heaton Moor 184 C3
Heaton Park GtMan
    M25 2SW 25 E2
Heaton's Bridge 183 F1
Heaverham 123 E3
Heaviley 184 D4
Heavitree 102 C3
Hebburn 212 C1
Hebden 193 G1
Hebden Bridge 193 F5
Hebden Green 170 D1
Hebing End 150 B5
Hebron Carmar 141 E5
Hebron N'umb 221 D3
Heck 217 E2
Heckfield 120 C1
Heckfield Green 164 C4
Heckfordbridge 152 A5
Heckingham 165 E2
Heckington 175 G3
Heckmondwike 194 B5
Heddington 118 A1
Heddle 277 C6
Heddon-on-the-
    Wall 212 A1
Hedenham 165 E2
Hedge End 107 D1
Hedgerley 135 E4
Hedging 116 A5
Hedley on the Hill 211 G2
Hednesford 158 C1
Hedon 197 D5
Hedsor 135 E4
Heeley 186 A4
Heglibister 279 C7
Heighington Darl 212 B5
Heighington Lincs 175 F1
Heightington 157 G5
Heights of Brae 266 C5
Heilam 273 G3
Heisker Islands (Monach
    Islands) 262 B5
Heithat 217 F2
Heiton 228 B3
Hele Devon 113 F1
Hele Devon 102 C2
Hele Devon 98 D1
Hele Devon 102 A5
Hele Som 115 E5
Hele Torbay 101 F1
Hele Bridge 113 F5
Hele Lane 102 A1
Helebridge 112 C5
Helensburgh 233 D1
Helford 95 E4
Helhoughton 177 G5
Helions Bumpstead 151 E3
Hell Corner 119 E1
Hellaby 186 C3
Helland Corn 97 E2
Helland Som 116 A5
Hellandbridge 97 E2
Hellesdon 178 D4
Hellidon 148 A2
Hellifield 193 E2
Hellingly 110 A2
Hellington 179 E5
Hellister 279 C8
Helmdon 148 A3
Helmingham 152 C2
Helmington Row 212 A4
Helmsdale 275 F7
Helmshore 193 D5

Helmsley 203 F4
Helperby 194 D1
Helperthorpe 204 C5
Helpringham 175 G3
Helpston 161 G2
Helsby 183 F5
Helsey 189 F5
Helston 95 D4
Helstone 97 E1
Helwith Bridge 193 E1
Hem 156 B2
Hemborough Post 101 E2
Hemel Hempstead 135 F2
Hemerdon 100 B2
Hemingbrough 195 F4
Hemingby 188 C5
Hemingfield 186 A2
Hemingford Abbots 162 A5
Hemingford Grey 162 A5
Hemingstone 152 C2
Hemington Leics 173 F5
Hemington
    N'hants 161 F4
Hemington Som 117 E2
Hemley 153 D3
Hemlington 203 D1
Hemp Green 153 E1
Hempholme 196 C2
Hempnall 164 D2
Hempnall Green 164 D2
Hempriggs 267 J5
Hempriggs House 275 J4
Hempstead Essex 151 E4
Hempstead Med 123 G2
Hempstead Norf 179 F3
Hempstead Norf 178 C2
Hempsted 132 A1
Hempton Norf 178 A3
Hempton Oxon 147 G4
Hemsby 179 F4
Hemswell 187 G3
Hemswell Cliff 187 G4
Hemsworth 186 B1
Hemyock 103 E1
Henbury Bristol 131 E5
Henbury ChesE 184 C5
Henderland 216 C3
Hendersyde Park 228 B3
Hendham 100 D2
Hendon GtLon 136 B4
Hendon T&W 212 C2
Hendraburnick 97 F1
Hendre Bridgend 129 F4
Hendre Gwyn 166 C2
Hendreforgan 129 F4
Hendy 128 B2
Heneglwys 180 C5
Henfield SGlos 131 F5
Henfield WSuss 109 E2
Henford 99 D1
Hengherst 124 B5
Hengoed Caerp 130 A3
Hengoed Powys 144 B2
Hengoed Shrop 169 F4
Hengrave 151 G1
Henham 150 D5
Heniarth 156 A2
Henlade 115 F5
Henley Dorset 104 C2
Henley Shrop 157 E5
Henley Som 116 B4
Henley Som 116 A2
Henley Suff 152 C2
Henley WSuss 121 D5
Henley Corner 116 B4
Henley Park 121 E2
Henley-in-Arden 147 D1
Henley's Down 110 C2
Henllan Carmar 141 G3
Henllan Denb 168 D1
Henllan Amgoed 141 E5
Henllys 130 B3
Henlow 149 G4
Hennock 102 B4
Henny Street 151 G4
Henryd 181 F5
Henry's Moat 140 D5
Hensall 195 E5
Henshaw 211 D1
Hensingham 208 C5
Henstead 165 F3
Hensting 119 F5
Henstridge 104 D1
Henstridge Ash 104 D1
Henstridge
    Bowden 117 D5
Henstridge Marsh 117 E5
Henton Oxon 134 C2
Henton Som 116 B3
Henwood 97 G2
Heogan 279 D8
Heol Senni 143 F5
Heolgerrig 129 G2
Heol-y-Cyw 129 F4
Hepburn 229 E4
Hepburn Bell 229 E4
Hepple 220 B1
Hepscott 221 E3
Hepthorne Lane 173 F1
Heptonstall 193 F5
Hepworth Suff 164 A4
Hepworth WYorks 185 F2
Hepworth South
    Common 164 A4
Herbrandston 126 B2
Hereford 145 E3
Hereford Cathedral
    Here HR1 2NG
    75 Hereford
Heriot 236 A4
Heritage Motor Centre,
    Gaydon Warks
    CV35 0BJ 147 F2
Herm 101 G5
Hermiston 235 F2
Hermitage D&G 216 B4
Hermitage Dorset 104 C2
Hermitage ScBord 218 D2
Hermitage WBerks 134 A5
Hermitage WSuss 107 G2
Hermitage Green 184 A3
Hermon Carmar 141 G4
Hermon IoA 166 C1
Hermon Pembs 141 F4
Herne 125 D2

Herne Bay 125 D2
Herne Common 125 D2
Herne Pound 123 F3
Herner 113 F3
Hernhill 124 C2
Herodsfoot 97 G3
Herongate 137 F3
Heron's Ghyll 109 G1
Heronsgate 135 F3
Herriard 120 B3
Herringfleet 165 F2
Herring's Green 149 F3
Herringswell 151 F1
Herringthorpe 186 B3
Hersden 125 D2
Hersham Corn 112 C5
Hersham Surr 121 G1
Herstmonceux 110 B2
Herston 277 D8
Hertford 136 C1
Hertford Heath 136 C1
Hertingfordbury 136 C1
Hesket Newmarket 209 G3
Hesketh Bank 192 A5
Hesketh Lane 192 C3
Heskin Green 183 G1
Hesleden 212 D4
Hesleyside 220 A3
Heslington 195 F2
Hessay 195 E2
Hessenford 98 D5
Hessett 152 A1
Hessle 196 C5
Hest Bank 192 A1
Hester's Way 146 B5
Hestley Green 152 C1
Heston 148 A5
Heswall 183 D4
Hethe 148 A5
Hethelpit Cross 145 G5
Hetherington 220 A4
Hethersett 178 C5
Hethersgill 210 A1
Hethpool 228 C4
Hett 212 B4
Hetton 193 F2
Hetton-le-Hole 212 C3
Heugh 220 C4
Heugh-head Aber 260 B3
Heugh-head Aber 260 D5
Heveningham 165 E4
Hever 123 D4
Hever Castle & Gardens
   Kent TN8 7NG 123 D4
Heversham 199 F4
Hevingham 178 C3
Hewas Water 97 D5
Hewell Grange 146 C1
Hewell Lane 146 C1
Hewelsfield 131 E2
Hewelsfield
   Common 131 E2
Hewish NSom 116 B1
Hewish Som 104 A2
Hewood 103 G2
Heworth 195 F2
Hewton 99 F1
Hexham 211 F1
Hexham Abbey N'umb
   NE46 3NB 211 F1
Hextable 137 E5
Hexthorpe 186 C2
Hexton 149 G4
Hexworthy 99 G3
Hey 193 F2
Hey Houses 191 G5
Heybridge Essex 137 F3
Heybridge Essex 138 B2
Heybridge Basin 138 B2
Heybrook Bay 100 A3
Heydon Cambs 150 C3
Heydon Norf 178 C3
Heydour 175 F4
Heylipoll 246 A2
Heylor 278 B4
Heyop 156 B5
Heysham 192 A1
Heyshaw 194 A1
Heyshott 108 A2
Heyside 184 D2
Heytesbury 118 A3
Heythrop 147 F5
Heywood GtMan 184 C1
Heywood Wilts 117 F2
Hibaldstow 187 G2
Hibb's Green 151 G2
Hickleton 186 B2
Hickling Norf 179 F3
Hickling Notts 174 B5
Hickling Green 179 F3
Hickling Heath 179 F3
Hickstead 109 E1
Hidcote Bartrim 147 D3
Hidcote Boyce 147 D3
Hidcote Manor Garden
   Glos GL55 6LR 147 D3
High Ackworth 186 B1
High Angerton 220 C3
High Balantyre 240 C3
High Bankhill 210 B3
High Beach 136 D3
High Bentham (Higher
   Bentham) 192 C1
High Bickington 113 F3
High Birkwith 200 C5
High Blantyre 234 A4
High Bonnybridge 234 C2
High Borgue 216 A5
High Borve 271 G2
High Bradfield 185 G3
High Bradley 193 G3
High Bransholme 196 D4
High Bray 113 G2
High Bridge 209 G2
High Brooms 123 E4
High Bullen 113 F3
High Burton 202 B4
High Buston 221 E1
High Callerton 221 D4
High Casterton 200 B5
High Catton 195 G2
High Close 202 A1
High Cogges 133 F2
High Common 164 C3
High Coniscliffe 202 B1
High Crompton 184 D2
High Cross Hants 120 C5
High Cross Herts 136 C1

High Cross WSuss 109 E2
High Easter 137 F1
High Ellington 202 A4
High Entercommon 202 C2
High Ercall 157 E1
High Ferry 176 B3
High Flatts 185 G2
High Garrett 151 F5
High Gate 193 F5
High Grange 212 A4
High Green Norf 178 C5
High Green Norf 178 A4
High Green Norf 178 A5
High Green Suff 151 G1
High Green SYorks 186 A4
High Green Worcs 146 A3
High Halden 124 A5
High Halstow 137 G5
High Ham 116 B4
High Harrington 208 D4
High Harrogate 194 C2
High Hatton 170 D5
High Hauxley 221 E1
High Hawsker 204 C2
High Heath Shrop 171 D5
High Heath WMid 158 C2
High Hesket 210 A3
High Hesleden 213 D4
High Hoyland 185 G1
High Hunsley 196 B4
High Hurstwood 109 G1
High Hutton 195 G1
High Ireby 209 F3
High Kelling 178 B2
High Kilburn 203 E5
High Kingthorpe 204 B4
High Knipe 199 G1
High Lane Derbys 173 F3
High Lane GtMan 185 D4
High Lane Worcs 145 F1
High Laver 137 E2
High Legh 184 B4
High Leven 203 D1
High Littleton 116 D2
High Lodge Forest Centre
   Suff IP27 0AF 163 D4
High Lorton 209 E4
High Marishes 204 B5
High Marnham 187 F5
High Melton 186 C2
High Moor 186 B4
High Moorland Visitor
   Centre, Princetown Devon
   PL20 6QF 99 F3
High Newton 199 F4
High Newton-by-the-
   Sea 229 G4
High Nibthwaite 199 D3
High Offley 171 E5
High Ongar 137 E2
High Onn 158 A1
High Park Corner 152 B5
High Roding 137 F1
High Shaw 201 D3
High Spen 212 A1
High Stoop 212 A3
High Street Corn 97 D4
High Street Kent 123 G5
High Street Suff 153 F2
High Street Suff 165 E3
High Street Suff 165 F4
High Street Suff 151 G3
High Street Green 152 B2
High Throston 213 D4
High Town 158 B1
High Toynton 176 A1
High Trewhitt 220 C1
High Wham 212 A5
High Wigsell 110 C1
High Woods Country Park
   Essex CO4 5JR 152 B5
High Woolaston 131 E3
High Worsall 202 C2
High Wray 199 E3
High Wych 137 D1
High Wycombe 135 D3
Higham Derbys 173 E2
Higham Kent 137 G5
Higham Lancs 193 E4
Higham Suff 151 F1
Higham Suff 152 B4
Higham SYorks 186 A2
Higham Dykes 220 D4
Higham Ferrers 149 E1
Higham Gobian 149 G4
Higham on the Hill 159 F3
Higham Wood 123 F4
Highampton 113 E5
Highams Park 136 C3
Highbridge Hants 119 F5
Highbridge Som 116 A3
Highbrook 122 C5
Highburton 185 F1
Highbury 117 D3
Highclere 119 F1
Highcliffe 106 B3
Higher Alham 117 D3
Higher Ansty 105 D2
Higher Ashton 102 B4
Higher Ballam 191 G4
Higher Bentham (High
   Bentham) 192 C1
Higher Blackley 184 C2
Higher Brixham 101 F2
Higher Cheriton 103 E2
Higher Combe 114 C4
Higher Folds 184 A2
Higher Gabwell 101 F1
Higher Green 184 B3
Higher Halstock
   Leigh 104 B2
Higher Kingcombe 104 B3
Higher Kinnerton 170 A1
Higher Muddiford 113 F2
Higher Nyland 117 E5
Higher Prestacott 99 D1
Higher Standen 193 D3
Higher Tale 103 E2
Higher Thrushgill 192 C1
Higher Town Corn 97 E3
Higher Town IoS 96 B1
Higher Walreddon 99 E3
Higher Walton
   Lancs 192 B5
Higher Walton
   Warr 183 G4
Higher Wambrook 103 F2

Higher Whatcombe 105 E2
Higher Wheelton 192 C5
Higher Whiteleigh 98 C1
Higher Whitley 184 A4
Higher Wincham 184 A5
Higher Woodhill 184 B1
Higher Woodsford 105 D4
Higher Wraxall 104 C3
Higher Wych 170 B3
Highfield ERid 195 G4
Highfield NAyr 233 E4
Highfield Oxon 148 A5
Highfield SYorks 186 A4
Highfield T&W 212 A2
Highfields Cambs 150 B2
Highfields N'umb 237 G4
Highgate ESuss 122 D5
Highgate GtLon 136 B4
Highgreen Manor 220 A2
Highlane ChesE 171 F1
Highlane Derbys 186 B4
Highlaws 209 E2
Highleadon 145 G5
Highleigh Devon 114 C5
Highleigh WSuss 108 A4
Highley 157 G4
Highmead 142 B3
Highmoor Cross 134 B4
Highmoor Hill 131 D4
Highnam 131 G1
Highstead 125 E2
Highsted 124 B3
Highstreet 124 C2
Highstreet Green
   Essex 151 F4
Highstreet Green
   Surr 121 E4
Hightae 217 E3
Highter's Heath 158 C5
Hightown Hants 106 A2
Hightown Mersey 183 D2
Hightown Green 152 A2
Highway 172 C5
Highweek 102 B5
Highwood 145 F1
Highwood Hill 136 B3
Highworth 133 E3
Hilborough 163 G2
Hilcote 173 F2
Hilcott 118 C2
Hilden Park 123 E4
Hildenborough 123 E4
Hildenley 203 G5
Hildersham 150 D3
Hilderstone 171 G4
Hilderthorpe 197 D1
Hilfield 104 C2
Hilgay 163 E3
Hill SGlos 131 F3
Hill Warks 147 G1
Hill Worcs 146 B3
Hill Brow 120 C5
Hill Chorlton 171 E4
Hill Common 179 F3
Hill Cottages 203 G3
Hill Croome 146 A3
Hill Deverill 117 F3
Hill Dyke 176 B3
Hill End Dur 211 G4
Hill End Fife 243 F5
Hill End Glos 146 A4
Hill End GtLon 135 F3
Hill End NYorks 193 G2
Hill Green 150 C4
Hill Head 107 E2
Hill Houses 157 F5
Hill Mountain 126 C2
Hill of Beath 235 F1
Hill of Fearn 267 F4
Hill Ridware 158 C1
Hill Row 162 C5
Hill Side 185 F1
Hill Street 106 C1
Hill Top Hants 106 D2
Hill Top SYorks 186 B3
Hill Top SYorks 185 G4
Hill View 105 F3
Hill Wootton 147 F1
Hillam 195 E5
Hillberry 190 B4
Hillborough 125 E2
Hillbrae Aber 268 E6
Hillbrae Aber 261 F2
Hillbrae Aber 261 G1
Hillbutts 105 F2
Hillclifflane 173 D3
Hillend Aber 268 C6
Hillend Fife 235 F1
Hillend MidLo 235 G3
Hillend NLan 234 C3
Hillend Swan 128 A3
Hillend Green 145 G5
Hillersland 131 E1
Hillesden 148 B5
Hillesley 131 G4
Hillfarrance 115 E5
Hillfoot End 149 G4
Hillhead Devon 101 F2
Hillhead SAyr 224 C3
Hillhead of
   Auchentumb 269 H5
Hillhead of Cocklaw 269 J6
Hilliard's Cross 159 D1
Hilliclay 275 G2
Hillington 135 F4
Hillington Glas 233 G3
Hillington Norf 177 F5
Hillmorton 160 A5
Hillockhead Aber 260 B4
Hillockhead Aber 260 C3
Hillowton 216 B4
Hillpound 107 E1
Hill's End 149 E4
Hills Town 173 F1
Hillsborough 186 A3
Hillside Bridge 114 A3
Hillside Aber 261 H5
Hillside Angus 253 F3
Hillside Moray 267 J5
Hillside Shet 279 D6
Hillside Worcs 145 G1
Hillswick 278 B5
Hillway 107 F2
Hillwell 279 F9
Hillyfields 106 C1
Hilmarton 132 C5
Hilperton 117 F2

Hilsea 107 F2
Hilston 197 E4
Hilton Cambs 150 A1
Hilton Cumb 210 D5
Hilton Derbys 172 D4
Hilton Dur 212 A5
Hilton Dorset 105 D2
Hilton High 267 G3
Hilton Shrop 157 G3
Hilton Staffs 158 C2
Hilton Stock 203 D1
Hilton Croft 261 H1
Hilton of Cadboll 267 F4
Hilton of Delnies 267 F6
Himbleton 146 B2
Himley 158 A3
Himley Hall & Park
   WMid DY3 4DF 14 A2
Hincaster 199 G4
Hinchley Wood 121 G1
Hinckley 159 G3
Hinderclay 164 B4
Hinderton 183 E5
Hinderwell 203 G1
Hindford 170 A4
Hindhead 121 D4
Hindley GtMan 184 A2
Hindley N'umb 211 G2
Hindley Green 184 A2
Hindlip 146 A2
Hindolveston 178 B3
Hindon Som 114 C3
Hindon Wilts 118 A4
Hindringham 178 A2
Hingham 178 B5
Hinksford 158 A4
Hinstock 171 D5
Hintlesham 152 B3
Hinton Glos 131 F2
Hinton Hants 106 B3
Hinton Here 144 C4
Hinton N'hants 148 A2
Hinton SGlos 131 G5
Hinton Shrop 156 D2
Hinton Admiral 106 B3
Hinton Ampner 119 G5
Hinton Blewett 116 C2
Hinton
   Charterhouse 117 E2
Hinton Martell 105 G2
Hinton on the
   Green 146 C3
Hinton Parva
   Dorset 105 G2
Hinton Parva Swin 133 E4
Hinton St. George 104 A1
Hinton St. Mary 105 D1
Hinton Waldrist 133 F3
Hinton-in-the-
   Hedges 148 A4
Hints Shrop 157 E5
Hints Staffs 159 D2
Hinwick 149 E1
Hinxhill 124 C4
Hinxton 150 C3
Hinxworth 150 A3
Hipperholme 194 A5
Hipsburn 229 G5
Hipswell 202 A3
Hirn 261 F4
Hirnant 169 G5
Hirst 221 E3
Hirst Courtney 195 F5
Hirwaen 169 E1
Hirwaun 129 F2
Hiscott 113 F3
Histon 150 C1
Hitcham Bucks 135 E4
Hitcham Suff 152 A2
Hitchin 149 G5
Hither Green 136 C5
Hittisleigh 102 A3
Hittisleigh Barton 102 A3
Hive 196 A4
Hixon 172 B5
Hoaden 125 E3
Hoaldalbert 144 C5
Hoar Cross 172 C5
Hoar Park Craft Centre
   Warks
   CV10 0QU 159 E3
Hoarwithy 145 E5
Hoath 125 E2
Hobarris 156 C5
Hobbister 277 C7
Hobbles Green 151 F2
Hobbs Cross 137 D3
Hobbs Lots Bridge 162 B2
Hobkirk 227 G4
Hobland Hall 179 G5
Hobson 212 A2
Hoby 160 B1
Hockerill 150 C5
Hockering 178 B4
Hockerton 174 C2
Hockley 138 B3
Hockley Heath 159 D5
Hockliffe 149 E5
Hockwold cum
   Wilton 163 F4
Hockworthy 102 D1
Hoddesdon 136 C2
Hoddlesden 192 D5
Hodgehill 171 F1
Hodgeston 126 D3
Hodnet 170 D5
Hodnetheath 170 D5
Hodsoll Street 123 F2
Hodson 133 D4
Hodthorpe 186 C5
Hoe 178 A4
Hoe Gate 107 F1
Hoff 200 B1
Hoffleet Stow 176 A4
Hoggard's End 151 G2
Hoggeston 148 D5
Hoggie 268 E5
Hoggrill's End 159 E3
Hoghá Gearraidh 262 C4
Hoghton 192 C5
Hognaston 172 D2
Hogsthorpe 189 F5
Holbeach 176 B5
Holbeach Bank 176 B5
Holbeach Clough 176 B5
Holbeach Drove 162 B1
Holbeach Hurn 176 B5
Holbeach St. Johns 162 B1

Holbeach St. Marks 176 B4
Holbeach St. Matthew 176 C4
Holbeck 186 C5
Holbeck
   Woodhouse 186 C5
Holberrow Green 146 C2
Holbeton 100 C2
Holborough 123 G2
Holbrook Derbys 173 E3
Holbrook Suff 152 C4
Holbrooks 159 F4
Holburn 229 E3
Holbury 106 D2
Holcombe Devon 102 C5
Holcombe GtMan 184 B1
Holcombe Som 117 D3
Holcombe Burnell
   Barton 102 B3
Holcombe Rogus 103 D1
Holcot 148 B1
Holden 193 D3
Holden Gate 193 E5
Holdenby 148 B1
Holdenhurst 106 A3
Holder's Green 151 E5
Holders Hill 136 B4
Holdgate 157 E4
Holdingham 175 F3
Holditch 103 G2
Hole 103 E1
Hole Park 124 A5
Holehouse 185 E3
Hole-in-the-Wall 145 F5
Holford 115 E3
Holgate 195 E2
Holker 199 E5
Holkham 177 G3
Hollacombe Devon 113 D5
Hollacombe Devon 102 B2
Hollacombe Town 113 G4
Holland Ork 276 D2
Holland Ork 276 F1
Holland Surr 122 D3
Holland Fen 176 A3
Holland-on-Sea 139 E1
Hollandstoun 276 G1
Hollee 218 A5
Hollesley 153 E3
Hollicombe 101 F1
Hollingbourne 124 A3
Hollingbury 109 F3
Hollingrove 110 B1
Hollington Derbys 172 D4
Hollington ESuss 110 C2
Hollington Staffs 172 B4
Hollingworth 185 E3
Hollins 184 A3
Hollins Green 184 A3
Hollins Lane 192 A3
Hollinsclough 172 B1
Hollinwood GtMan 184 D2
Hollinwood Shrop 170 C4
Hollocombe 113 G4
Hollow Meadows 185 G4
Holloway 173 E2
Hollowell 160 B5
Holly Bush 170 B3
Holly End 162 C2
Holly Green 134 C3
Hollybush Caerp 130 A2
Hollybush EAyr 224 B4
Hollybush Worcs 145 G4
Hollyhurst 170 C3
Hollym 197 F5
Hollywater 120 D4
Hollywood 158 C5
Holm D&G 218 A2
Holm (Tolm) Na H-E. Siar
   271 G2
Holm of Drumlanrig 216 C1
Holmbridge 185 F2
Holmbury St. Mary 121 G3
Holmbush 122 B5
Holme Cambs 161 G4
Holme Cumb 199 G5
Holme NLincs 187 G2
Holme Notts 174 D2
Holme NYorks 202 C4
Holme WYorks 185 F2
Holme Chapel 193 E5
Holme Hale 163 G2
Holme Lacy 145 E4
Holme Marsh 144 C2
Holme next the Sea 177 F3
Holme on the
   Wolds 196 B3
Holme Pierrepont 174 B4
Holme St. Cuthbert 209 E2
Holme-on-Spalding-
   Moor 196 A4
Holmer 145 E3
Holmer Green 135 E3
Holmes 183 F1
Holmes Chapel 171 E1
Holme's Hill 110 A2
Holmeswood 183 F1
Holmewood 173 F1
Holmfield 193 G5
Holmfirth 185 F2
Holmhead D&G 216 B2
Holmhead EAyr 225 D3
Holmpton 197 F5
Holmrook 198 B2
Holmsgarth 279 D8
Holmside 212 B3
Holmsleigh Green 103 F2
Holmston 224 B3
Holmwrangle 210 B3
Holne 100 D2
Holnest 104 C2
Holnicote 114 C3
Holsworthy 112 D5
Holsworthy Beacon 113 D5
Holt Dorset 105 G2
Holt Norf 178 B2
Holt Wilts 117 F1
Holt Worcs 146 A1
Holt Wrex 170 B2
Holt End Hants 120 B4
Holt End Worcs 146 C1
Holt Fleet 146 A1
Holt Heath Dorset 105 G2
Holt Heath Worcs 146 A1
Holt Wood 105 G2
Holtby 195 F2
Holton Oxon 134 B2
Holton Som 117 D5

Holton Suff 165 F4
Holton cum
   Beckering 188 B4
Holton Heath 105 F3
Holton le Clay 188 C3
Holton le Moor 188 A3
Holton St. Mary 152 B4
Holtspur 135 E4
Holtye 123 D5
Holtye Common 123 D5
Holway 115 F5
Holwell Dorset 104 C1
Holwell Herts 149 G4
Holwell Leics 174 C5
Holwell Oxon 133 E2
Holwell Som 117 E3
Holwick 211 F5
Holworth 105 D4
Holy Cross 158 B5
Holy Island IoA 180 A5
Holy Island (Lindisfarne)
   N'umb 229 F2
Holy Trinity Church,
   Skipton NYorks
   BD23 1NJ 193 F2
Holy Trinity Church,
   Stratford-upon-Avon
   Warks CV37 6BG
   85 Stratford-upon-Avon
Holybourne 120 C3
Holyfield 136 C2
Holyhead
   (Caergybi) 180 A4
Holymoorside 173 E1
Holyport 135 D5
Holystone 220 B1
Holytown 234 B3
Holywell Cambs 162 B5
Holywell Corn 96 B4
Holywell Dorset 104 B2
Holywell ESuss 110 B4
Holywell (Treffynnon)
   Flints 182 C5
Holywell N'umb 221 F4
Holywell Bay Fun Park
   Corn TR8 5PW 96 B4
Holywell Green 185 E1
Holywell Lake 115 E5
Holywell Row 163 F5
Holywood 216 D2
Hom Green 145 E5
Homer 157 F2
Homersfield 165 D3
Homington 118 C5
Homore
   (Tobha Mòr) 254 C1
Honey Hill 124 D2
Honey Street 118 C1
Honey Tye 152 A4
Honeyborough 126 C2
Honeybourne 146 D3
Honeychurch 113 G5
Honicknowle 100 A2
Honiley 159 E5
Honing 179 E3
Honingham 178 C4
Honington Lincs 175 E3
Honington Suff 164 A4
Honington Warks 147 E3
Honiton 103 E2
Honkley 170 A2
Honley 185 F1
Hoo Med 137 G5
Hoo Suff 153 D2
Hoo Green 184 B4
Hoo Meavy 100 B1
Hood Green 186 A2
Hood Hill 186 A3
Hooe ESuss 110 B3
Hooe Plym 100 B2
Hooe Common 110 B2
Hook Cambs 162 C3
Hook ERid 195 G5
Hook GtLon 121 G1
Hook Hants 120 C2
Hook Hants 107 E2
Hook Pembs 126 C1
Hook Wilts 132 C4
Hook Green Kent 123 F5
Hook Green Kent 123 F2
Hook Green Kent 137 F5
Hook Green Kent 137 E5
Hook Norton 147 F4
Hook-a-Gate 157 D2
Hooke 104 B2
Hookgate 171 E4
Hookway 102 B3
Hookwood 122 B4
Hoole 170 B1
Hooley 122 B3
Hoop 131 E2
Hooton 183 E5
Hooton Levitt 186 C3
Hooton Pagnell 186 B2
Hooton Roberts 186 B3
Hop Farm, The Kent
   TN12 6PY 123 F4
Hop Pocket, The Here
   WR6 5BT 145 F3
Hop Pole 161 G1
Hope Derbys 185 F4
Hope Devon 100 C4
Hope Flints 170 A2
Hope Powys 156 B2
Hope Shrop 156 C2
Hope Staffs 172 C2
Hope Bagot 157 E5
Hope Bowdler 157 D3
Hope End Green 151 D5
Hope Mansell 131 F1
Hope under
   Dinmore 145 E2
Hopehouse 227 E3
Hopeman 267 J5
Hope's Green 137 G4
Hopesay 156 C4
Hopkinstown 129 G3
Hopley's Green 144 C2
Hopperton 194 D2
Hopsford 159 G4
Hopstone 157 G3
Hopton Derbys 173 D2
Hopton Norf 165 G2
Hopton Shrop 170 C5
Hopton Shrop 170 A5
Hopton Staffs 171 G5
Hopton Suff 164 A4

Hopton Cangeford 157 E4
Hopton Castle 156 C5
Hopton Wafers 157 F5
Hoptonheath 156 C5
Hopwas 159 D2
Hopwood 158 C5
Horam 110 A2
Horbling 175 G4
Horbury 185 G1
Horden 212 D3
Horderley 156 D4
Hordle 106 B3
Hordley 170 A4
Horeb Carmar 128 A2
Horeb Cere 141 G3
Horeb Flints 169 F2
Horfield 131 E5
Horham 164 D4
Horkesley Heath 152 A5
Horkstow 187 G1
Horley Oxon 147 G3
Horley Surr 122 B4
Horn Hill 135 F3
Hornblotton 116 C4
Hornblotton Green 116 C4
Hornby Lancs 192 B1
Hornby NYorks 202 B3
Hornby NYorks 202 C2
Horncastle 176 A1
Hornchurch 137 E4
Horncliffe 237 G5
Horndean Hants 107 G1
Horndean ScBord 237 G5
Horndon 99 F2
Horndon on the Hill 137 F4
Horne Row 137 G2
Horner 114 B3
Horniehaugh 252 C3
Horniman Museum GtLon
   SE23 3PQ 13 C7
Horning 179 E4
Horninghold 160 D3
Horninglow 172 D5
Horningsea 150 C1
Horningsham 117 F3
Horningtoft 178 A3
Horningtops 97 G3
Horns Cross Devon 113 D3
Horns Cross ESuss 110 D1
Horns Green 123 D3
Hornsbury 103 G1
Hornsby 210 B3
Hornsby Gate 210 B2
Hornsea 197 E3
Hornsea Freeport ERid
   HU18 1UT 197 E3
Hornsey 136 C4
Hornton 147 F3
Horrabridge 100 B1
Horridge 102 A5
Horringer 151 G1
Horrocks Fold 184 B1
Horse Bridge 171 G2
Horsebridge Devon 99 E3
Horsebridge Hants 119 E4
Horsebrook 158 A1
Horsecastle 116 B1
Horsehay 157 F2
Horseheath 151 E3
Horsehouse 201 F4
Horsell 121 E2
Horseman's Green 170 B3
Horsenden 134 C2
Horseshoe Green 123 D4
Horseway 162 C4
Horsey 179 F3
Horsey Corner 179 F3
Horsford 178 C4
Horsforth 194 B4
Horsham Worcs 145 G2
Horsham WSuss 121 G4
Horsham St. Faith 178 D4
Horsington Lincs 175 G1
Horsington Som 117 E5
Horsington Marsh 117 E5
Horsley Derbys 173 E3
Horsley Glos 132 A3
Horsley N'umb 211 G1
Horsley N'umb 220 C2
Horsley Cross 152 C5
Horsley Woodhouse 173 E3
Horsleycross Street 152 C5
Horsleyhill 227 G4
Horsleygate 186 A5
Horsmonden 123 F4
Horspath 134 A2
Horstead 179 D4
Horsted Keynes 109 F1
Horton Bucks 135 E1
Horton Dorset 105 G2
Horton Lancs 193 E3
Horton N'hants 148 D2
Horton SGlos 131 G4
Horton Shrop 170 B5
Horton Som 103 G1
Horton Staffs 171 G2
Horton Swan 128 A4
Horton Tel&W 157 F1
Horton W&M 135 F5
Horton Wilts 118 B1
Horton Cross 103 G1
Horton Grange 221 E4
Horton Green 170 B3
Horton Heath 107 D1
Horton in
   Ribblesdale 200 D5
Horton Inn 105 G2
Horton Kirby 123 F2
Horton Park Farm Surr
   KT19 8PT 121 G1
Horton-cum-
   Studley 134 B1
Horwich 184 A1
Horwich End 185 E4
Horwood 113 F3
Hoscar 183 F1
Hose 174 C5
Hoses 198 D3
Hosh 243 D2
Hosta 262 C4
Hoswick 279 D10
Hotham 196 A4
Hothfield 124 B4
Hoton 173 G5
Houbie 278 F3
Houdston 214 C1
Hough 171 E2

Hough Green **183** F4
Hougham **175** D3
Hough-on-the-Hill **175** E3
Houghton *Cambs* **162** A5
Houghton *Cumb* **210** A2
Houghton *Devon* **100** C3
Houghton *Hants* **119** E4
Houghton *Pembs* **126** C2
Houghton *WSuss* **108** C2
Houghton Bank **212** B5
Houghton Conquest **149** E3
Houghton le Spring **212** C1
Houghton on the
  Hill **160** B2
Houghton Regis **149** F5
Houghton St. Giles **178** A2
Houghton-le-Side **212** B5
Houlsyke **203** G2
Hound **107** E3
Hound Green **120** C2
Houndslow **236** D5
Houndsmoor **115** E5
Houndwood **237** F3
Hounsdown **106** C1
Hounslow **136** A5
House of Marbles & Teign
  Valley Glass *Devon*
  TQ13 9DS **102** B5
Housebay **276** D3
Househill **267** F6
Houses Hill **185** F1
Housesteads Roman
  Fort *N'umb*
  NE47 6NN **211** D1
Housetter **278** C4
Housham Tye **137** E1
Houss **279** C9
Houston **233** F3
Houstry **275** G5
Houstry of Dunn **275** H3
Houton **277** C7
Hove **109** E3
Hove Edge **194** A5
Hoveringham **174** B3
Hoveton **179** E4
Hovingham **203** F5
How **210** B2
How Caple **145** F4
How End **149** F5
How Green **123** D4
How Man **208** C5
Howbrook **185** G3
Howden **195** G5
Howden Clough **194** B5
Howden-le-Wear **212** A4
Howe *Cumb* **208** C4
Howe *High* **275** J2
Howe *Norf* **165** D2
Howe *NYorks* **202** C4
Howe Green **137** G2
Howe of Teuchar **269** F6
Howe Street *Essex* **137** F1
Howe Street *Essex* **151** E4
Howegreen **138** B2
Howell **175** G3
Howey **143** G2
Howgate *Cumb* **208** C4
Howgate *MidLo* **235** G4
Howgill *Lancs* **193** E3
Howgill *NYorks* **193** G2
Howick **229** G5
Howle **171** D5
Howle Hill **145** F5
Howlett End **151** D4
Howletts Wild Animal Park
  Kent CT4 5EL **125** D3
Howley **103** F2
Hownam **228** B5
Hownam Mains **228** B4
Howpasley **227** F5
Howsham *NLincs* **188** A2
Howsham *NYorks* **195** G1
Howt Green **124** A3
Howtel **228** C3
Howton **144** D5
Howwood **233** F3
Hoxa **277** D8
Hoxne **164** C4
Hoy *High* **275** H2
Hoy *Ork* **277** B8
Hoylake **182** D4
Hoyland **186** A2
Hoylandswaine **185** G2
Hoyle **108** B2
Hubberholme **201** E5
Hubberston **126** B2
Hubbert's Bridge **176** A3
Huby *NYorks* **195** E1
Huby *NYorks* **194** B3
Hucclecote **132** A1
Hucking **124** A3
Hucknall **173** G3
Huddersfield **185** F1
Huddington **146** B2
Huddlesford **158** D2
Hudnall **135** F1
Hudscott **113** G3
Hudswell **202** A3
Huggate **196** A2
Hugglescote **159** G1
Hugh Town **96** C5
Hughenden Valley **135** D3
Hughley **157** E3
Hugmore **170** A2
Hugus **96** B5
Huish *Devon* **113** F4
Huish *Wilts* **118** C1
Huish Champflower **114** D5
Huish Episcopi **116** B5
Huisinis **270** B6
Hulcote **160** A5
Hulcott **135** D1
Hull **196** B5
Hulland **172** D3
Hulland Ward **173** D3
Hullavington **132** A4
Hullbridge **138** B3
Hulme **171** G3
Hulme End **172** C2
Hulme Walfield **171** F1
Hulverstone **106** D4
Hulver Street **165** F3
Humber *Devon* **102** B5
Humber *Here* **145** E2
Humber Bridge Country
  Park *ERid*
  HU13 0LN **196** C5
Humberside Airport **188** A1

Humberston **188** D2
Humberstone **160** B2
Humberton **194** D1
Humbie **236** B3
Humbleton *Dur* **201** F1
Humbleton *ERid* **197** E4
Humbleton *N'umb* **229** D4
Humby **175** F4
Hume **237** E5
Humehall **237** E5
Hummer **104** B1
Humshaugh **220** B4
Huna **275** J1
Huncoat **193** D4
Huncote **160** A3
Hundalee **228** B3
Hundall **186** A5
Hunderthwaite **211** F5
Hundleby **176** B1
Hundleton **126** C2
Hundon **151** F2
Hundred Acres **107** E1
Hundred End **192** A5
Hundred House **144** A2
Hungarton **160** B2
Hungate End **148** C3
Hungerford *Hants* **106** A1
Hungerford *Shrop* **157** E4
Hungerford *WBerks* **119** E1
Hungerford
  Newtown **133** F5
Hungerton **175** D5
Hunglader **263** J4
Hunmanby **205** D5
Hunningham **147** F1
Hunningham Hill **147** F1
Hunny Hill **107** D4
Hunsdon **136** D1
Hunsingore **194** D2
Hunslet **194** C4
Hunsonby **210** B4
Hunspow **275** H1
Hunstanton **177** E3
Hunstanworth **211** F3
Hunston *Suff* **152** A1
Hunston *WSuss* **108** A3
Hunsworth **194** A5
Hunt End **146** C1
Hunt House **204** B3
Hunter's Inn **113** G1
Hunter's Quay **232** C2
Hunterston **232** C4
Huntford **219** E1
Huntham **116** A5
Hunthill Junction **228** B4
Huntingdon **162** A5
Huntingfield **165** E4
Huntingford **117** F4
Huntington *Here* **144** B2
Huntington *Here* **145** D3
Huntington *Staffs* **158** B1
Huntington *Tel&W* **157** E2
Huntington *York* **195** F2
Huntingtower **243** F2
Huntley **131** G1
Huntly **260** D1
Huntlywood **236** D5
Hunton *Hants* **119** F3
Hunton *Kent* **123** G4
Hunton *NYorks* **202** A3
Hunton Bridge **135** F2
Hunt's Cross **183** F4
Huntscott **114** C3
Huntsham **114** D5
Huntshaw **113** F3
Huntshaw Cross **113** F3
Huntshaw Water **113** F3
Huntspill **116** A3
Huntworth **116** A4
Hunworth **178** B2
Hurcott *Som* **116** C5
Hurcott *Som* **103** G1
Hurdley **156** B3
Hurdsfield **184** D5
Hurley *W&M* **134** D4
Hurley *Warks* **159** E3
Hurley Bottom **134** D4
Hurlford **224** C2
Hurliness **277** B9
Hurlston Green **183** E5
Hurn **106** A3
Hursley **119** F5
Hurst *NYorks* **201** F2
Hurst *W'ham* **134** C5
Hurst Green *Essex* **139** D1
Hurst Green *ESuss* **110** C1
Hurst Green *Lancs* **192** C4
Hurst Green *Surr* **122** C3
Hurst Wickham **109** E2
Hurstbourne Priors **119** F3
Hurstbourne
  Tarrant **119** E2
Hurstpierpoint **109** E2
Hurstwood **193** E4
Hurtmore **121** E3
Hurworth-on-Tees **202** C1
Hury **211** F5
Husabost **263** G6
Husbands Bosworth **160** B4
Husborne Crawley **149** E4
Husthwaite **203** E5
Hutcherleigh **101** D2
Huthwaite **173** F2
Huttoft **189** F5
Hutton *Cumb* **210** A5
Hutton *Essex* **137** F3
Hutton *Lancs* **192** B5
Hutton *NSom* **116** A2
Hutton *ScBord* **237** G4
Hutton Buscel **204** C4
Hutton Bonville **202** C2
Hutton Conyers **202** C5
Hutton Cranswick **196** C2
Hutton End **210** A4
Hutton Hang **202** A4
Hutton Henry **212** D4
Hutton Magna **202** A1
Hutton Mount **137** F3
Hutton Mulgrave **204** B2
Hutton Roof *Cumb* **199** G5
Hutton Roof *Cumb* **209** G3
Hutton Rudby **203** D2
Hutton Sessay **203** D5
Hutton Wandesley **195** E2
Hutton-le-Hole **203** E4
Huxham **102** C3

Huxham Green **116** C4
Huxley **170** C1
Huxter *Shet* **279** C7
Huxter *Shet* **279** E6
Huyton **183** F3
Hycemoor **198** B4
Hyde *Glos* **132** A2
Hyde *GtMan* **184** D3
Hyde End *W'ham* **120** C1
Hyde End *WBerks* **119** G1
Hyde Heath **135** E2
Hyde Lea **158** B1
Hydestile **121** E3
Hykeham Moor **175** E1
Hylands Park *Essex*
  CM2 8WQ **137** F2
Hyndford Bridge **234** D5
Hyndlee **227** G5
Hynish **246** A3
Hythe *Hants* **106** D2
Hythe *Kent* **125** D5
Hythe End **135** F5
Hythie **269** J5
Hyton **198** B4

I

Ianstown **268** C4
Iarsiadar **270** D4
Ibberton **105** D2
Ible **172** D2
Ibsley **106** A2
Ibstock **159** G1
Ibstone **134** C4
Ibthorpe **119** E2
Ibworth **119** G2
Icelton **116** A1
Ickburgh **163** G3
Ickenham **135** F4
Ickford **134** B2
Ickham **125** E3
Ickleford **149** G4
Icklesham **111** D2
Ickleton **150** C3
Icklingham **163** F5
Ickwell Green **149** G3
Icomb **147** E5
Idbury **147** E5
Iddesleigh **113** F5
Ide **102** C3
Ide Hill **123** D3
Ideford **102** B5
Iden **111** E1
Iden Green *Kent* **123** G5
Iden Green *Kent* **124** A5
Idle **194** A4
Idless **96** C5
Idlicote **147** E3
Idmiston **118** C4
Idridgehay **173** D3
Idridgehay Green **173** D3
Idrigil **263** J5
Idstone **133** E4
Idvies **252** D5
Iffley **134** A2
Ifield **122** B5
Ifieldwood **122** B5
Ifold **121** F4
Iford *Bourne* **106** A3
Iford *ESuss* **109** G3
Ifton **131** D4
Ifton Heath **170** A4
Ightfield **170** C4
Ightham **123** E3
Ightham Mote *Kent*
  TN15 0NT **123** E3
Iken **153** F2
Ilam **172** C2
Ilchester **116** C5
Ilderton **229** E4
Ilford **136** D4
Ilfracombe **113** F1
Ilkeston **173** F3
Ilketshall
  St. Andrew **165** E3
Ilketshall
  St. Lawrence **165** E3
Ilketshall
  St. Margaret **165** E3
Ilkley **194** A3
Illey **158** B4
Illidge Green **171** E1
Illington **164** A3
Illingworth **193** G5
Illogan **96** A5
Illston on the Hill **160** C3
Ilmer **134** C2
Ilmington **147** E3
Ilminster **103** G1
Ilsington *Devon* **102** A5
Ilsington *Dorset* **105** D3
Ilston **128** B3
Ilton *NYorks* **202** A5
Ilton *Som* **103** G1
Imachar **231** G5
Imber **118** A3
Immeroin **242** A3
Immingham **188** B1
Immingham Dock **188** C1
Imperial War Museum,
  Duxford *Cambs*
  CB22 4QR **150** C3
Imperial War Museum,
  London *GtLon*
  SE1 6HZ **45** G7
Imperial War Museum
  North *GtMan*
  M17 1TZ **24** D3
Impington **150** C1
Ince **183** F5
Ince Blundell **183** E2
Ince-in-Makerfield **183** G2
Inch Kenneth **238** D1
Inch of Arnhall **253** E2
Inchbae Lodge **266** B5
Inchbare **253** E3
Inchberry **268** B5
Inchbraoch **253** F4
Inchgrundle **252** C2
Inchindown **266** D4
Inchinnan **233** F3
Inchkinloch **273** J4
Inchlaggan **257** H4
Inchlumpie **266** C4
Inchmarlo **260** E5
Inchmarnock **232** B4
Inchnabobart **252** B1
Inchnacardoch
  Hotel **257** K3

Inchnadamph **272** E6
Inchock **253** E5
Inchree **248** C3
Inchrory **259** J4
Inchture **244** A2
Inchvuilt **257** J1
Inchyra **243** G2
Indian Queens **96** D4
Inerval **243** B5
Ingatestone **137** F3
Ingbirchworth **185** G2
Ingerthorpe **194** B1
Ingestre **171** G5
Ingham *Lincs* **187** G4
Ingham *Norf* **179** E3
Ingham *Suff* **163** G5
Ingham Corner **179** E3
Ingleborough **162** C1
Ingleby *Derbys* **173** E5
Ingleby *Lincs* **187** F5
Ingleby Arncliffe **202** D2
Ingleby Barwick **202** D1
Ingleby Cross **202** D2
Ingleby Greenhow **203** E2
Ingleigh Green **113** G5
Inglesbatch **117** E1
Inglesham **133** E3
Ingleton *Dur* **212** A5
Ingleton *NYorks* **200** B5
Inglewhite **192** B4
Ingliston **235** F2
Ingoe **220** C4
Ingoldisthorpe **177** E4
Ingoldmells **177** D1
Ingoldsby **175** F4
Ingon **147** E2
Ingram **229** E5
Ingrave **137** F3
Ingrow **193** G4
Ings **199** F3
Ingst **131** E4
Ingworth **178** C3
Inhurst **119** G1
Inistrynich **240** D2
Injebreck **190** B3
Inkberrow **146** C2
Inkersall **186** B5
Inkersall Green **186** B5
Inkhorn **261** H1
Inkpen **119** E1
Inkstack **275** H1
Inmarsh **118** A1
Innellan **232** C3
Innergellie **245** D4
Innerhadden **250** B4
Innerleithen **227** E2
Innerleven **244** B4
Innermessan **214** B4
Innerwick *ELoth* **237** E2
Innerwick *P&K* **250** A5
Inninbeg **247** F5
Innsworth **146** A5
Insch **260** E2
Insh **259** F4
Inshore **273** F2
Inskip **192** A4
Instow **113** E2
Intake **186** C2
Intech, Winchester *Hants*
  SO21 1HX **119** G5
International Centre, The,
  Telford *Tel&W*
  TF3 4JH **157** G2
Intwood **178** C5
Inver *A&B* **248** B5
Inver *Aber* **259** K5
Inver *High* **267** F3
Inver *High* **275** G5
Inver *P&K* **251** F5
Inver Mallie **248** D1
Inverailort **247** G1
Inveralligin **264** E6
Inverallochy **269** J4
Inveran **266** C2
Inveraray
  (Inbhir Aora) **240** C4
Inverardoch Mains **242** C4
Inverardran **241** F2
Inverarish **256** B1
Inverarity **252** C5
Inverarnan
  (Inbhir Àirnein) **241** F3
Inverasdale **264** E3
Inverbain **264** D6
Inverbeg **241** F4
Inverbervie **253** G2
Inverboyndie **269** F4
Invercassley **266** B1
Inverchaolain **232** B2
Invercharnan **248** D4
Inverchorachan **241** E3
Invercreran **248** C4
Inverdruie **259** G3
Inverebrie **261** H1
Invereen **258** D1
Invererne **267** H5
Inveresk **236** A2
Inverey **251** J2
Inverfarigaig **258** C2
Invergarry
  (Inbhir Garadh) **257** K4
Invergelder **259** K5
Invergeldie **242** C2
Invergloy **249** E1
Invergowrie **244** B2
Inverguseran **256** D4
Inverharroch Farm **260** B1
Inverherive **241** F2
Inverhope **273** H2
Inverie **256** D4
Inverinan **240** B3
Inverinate **257** F2
Inverkeilor **253** E5
Inverkeithing **235** F1
Inverkeithny **268** E6
Inverkip **232** C2
Inverkirkaig **272** C7
Inverlael **265** H3
Inverlauren **233** E1
Inverliever **240** A4
Inverliver **248** C5
Inverlochlarig **241** G3
Inverlochy **241** D2
Inverlussa **231** E1

Invermay **243** F3
Invermoriston (Inbhir
  Moireasdan) **258** B3
Invernaver **274** C2
Inverneil **231** G1
Inverness
  (Inbhir Nis) **266** D7
Inverness Airport **266** E6
Invernettie **269** K6
Invernoaden **240** D5
Inveroran Hotel (Inbhir
  Orain) **249** E5
Inverquharity **252** C4
Inverquhomery **269** J6
Inverroy **249** E1
Inversanda **248** B4
Invershiel **257** F3
Invershore **275** H5
Inversnaid Hotel **241** F4
Invertrossachs **242** A4
Inverugie **269** K6
Inveruglas (Inbhir
  Dhubhlais) **241** F4
Inveruglas **259** F4
Inverurie **261** F2
Invervar **250** B5
Invervegain **232** B2
Inverythan **269** F6
Inwardleigh **99** F1
Inworth **138** C1
Iochdar **262** C7
Iona **238** B2
Iping **121** D5
Ipplepen **101** E1
Ipsden **134** B4
Ipstones **172** B3
Ipswich **152** C3
Irby **183** D4
Irby Hill **183** D4
Irby in the Marsh **176** C1
Irby upon Humber **188** B2
Irchester **149** E1
Irchester Country Park
  N'hants NN29 7DL **149** E1
Ireby *Cumb* **209** F3
Ireby *Lancs* **200** B5
Ireland *Ork* **277** C7
Ireland *Shet* **279** C10
Ireland's Cross **171** E3
Ireleth **198** D5
Ireshopeburn **211** E4
Irlam **184** B3
Irnham **175** F5
Iron Acton **131** F4
Iron Cross **146** C2
Ironbridge **157** F2
Ironbridge Gorge *Tel&W*
  TF8 7DQ **157** F2
Irons Bottom **122** B4
Ironside **269** G5
Ironville **173** F2
Irstead **179** E3
Irthington **210** A1
Irthlingborough **161** E5
Irton **204** D4
Irvine **224** B2
Isauld **274** E2
Isbister *Ork* **277** C6
Isbister *Ork* **276** B5
Isbister *Shet* **279** E6
Isbister *Shet* **278** C3
Isfield **109** G2
Isham **161** D5
Ishriff **239** F1
Isington **120** C4
Island of Stroma **275** J1
Islawr-dref **154** C1
Islay **230** B4
Islay Airport **230** B4
Islay House **230** B3
Isle Abbotts **116** A5
Isle Brewers **116** A5
Isle of Bute Discovery Centre
  A&B PA20 0AH **232** B3
Isle of Lewis (Eilean
  Leodhais) **271** F3
Isle of Man **190** B3
Isle of Man Airport **190** A5
Isle of May **245** E5
Isle of Noss **279** E8
Isle of Sheppey **124** B1
Isle of Walney **191** E1
Isle of Whithorn **207** E3
Isle of Wight **107** D4
Isle of Wight Pearl *IoW*
  PO30 4DD **106** D4
Isle of Wight (Sandown)
  Airport **107** E4
Isle of Wight Zoo *IoW*
  PO36 8QB **107** F4
Isleham **163** E5
Isleornsay (Eilean
  Iarmain) **256** C3
Isles of Scilly
  (Scilly Isles) **96** B1
Islesburgh **279** C6
Islesteps **217** D3
Isleworth **136** A5
Isley Walton **173** F5
Islibhig **270** B5
Islington *N'hants* **161** E2
Islip *Oxon* **134** A1
Isombridge **157** F1
Istead Rise **123** F2
Itchen **106** D1
Itchen Abbas **119** G4
Itchen Stoke **119** G4
Itchen Valley Country Park
  Hants SO30 3HQ **4** C2
Itchingfield **121** G5
Itchington **131** F4
Itteringham **178** C2
Itton *Devon* **99** G1
Itton *Mon* **131** D3
Itton Common **131** D3
Ivegill **210** A3
Ivelet **201** E3
Iver **135** F4
Iver Heath **135** F4
Iveston **212** A2
Ivetsey Bank **158** A1
Ivinghoe **135** E1
Ivinghoe Aston **135** E1
Ivington **145** D2
Ivington Green **145** D2
Ivy Hatch **123** E3
Ivy Todd **163** G2
Ivybridge **100** C2

Ivychurch **111** F1
Iwade **124** B2
Iwerne Courtney
  (Shroton) **105** E1
Iwerne Minster **105** E1
Ixworth **164** A4
Ixworth Thorpe **164** A4

J

Jack Hill **194** A2
Jackfield **157** F2
Jacksdale **173** F2
Jackstown **261** F1
Jackton **233** G4
Jacobstow **98** B1
Jacobstowe **113** F5
Jacobswell **121** F2
James Hamilton
  Heritage Park *SLan*
  G74 5LB **31** E5
James Pringle Weavers
  of Inverness *High*
  IV2 4RB **266** D7
Jameston **126** D3
Jamestown *D&G* **218** B2
Jamestown *High* **266** B6
Jamestown *WDun* **233** E1
Janefield **266** E6
Janetstown *High* **275** F2
Janetstown *High* **275** J3
Jarrow **212** C1
Jarvis Brook **123** C1
Jasper's Green **151** F5
Jawcraig **234** C2
Jayes Park **121** G3
Jaywick **139** E1
Jealott's Hill **135** D5
Jeater Houses **202** D3
Jedburgh **228** A4
Jeffreyston **127** D2
Jemimaville **266** E5
Jephson Gardens *Warks*
  CV32 4ER **16** B6
Jericho **184** C1
Jersay **234** C3
Jersey **100** C5
Jersey Airport **100** B5
Jersey Marine **128** D3
Jerviswood **234** C5
Jesmond **212** B1
Jevington **110** A3
Jinney Ring Craft Centre,
  The *Worcs*
  B60 4BU **146** B1
Jockey End **135** F1
Jodrell Bank **184** B5
Jodrell Bank Observatory &
  Arboretum *ChesE*
  SK11 9DL **184** B5
John Muir Country Park
  ELoth
  EH42 1UW **236** D2
John o' Groats **275** J1
John's Cross **110** C1
Johnby **210** A4
Johnshaven **253** F2
Johnson Street **179** E4
Johnston **126** C1
Johnston Mains **253** F2
Johnstone **233** F3
Johnstone Castle **233** F3
Johnstonebridge **217** E1
Johnstons Cashmere Visitor
  Centre *Moray*
  IV30 4AF **267** K5
Johnstown
  Carmar **127** G1
Johnstown *Wrex* **170** A3
Joppa **224** C4
Jordans **135** E3
Jordanston **140** C4
Jordanstone **252** A5
Jorvik *YO1 9WT* **90** York
Jorvik Glass *NYorks*
  YO60 7DA **195** G1
Joy's Green **131** F1
Jumpers Common **106** A3
Juniper Green **235** F2
Juniper Hill **148** A4
Jura **231** D1
Jura House **230** C3
Jurby East **190** B2
Jurby West **190** B2

K

Kaber **200** C1
Kaimes **235** G3
Kames *A&B* **232** A2
Kames *A&B* **240** A3
Kames *EAyr* **225** E3
Kathellan *Fife*
  KY4 0JR **243** G5
Kea **96** C5
Keadby **187** F1
Keal Cotes **176** B1
Kearsley **184** B2
Kearstwick **200** B5
Kearton **201** F3
Kearvaig **272** E1
Keasden **192** D1
Kebholes **268** E5
Keckwick **183** G4
Keddington **188** D4
Keddington Corner **189** D4
Kedington **151** F3
Kedleston **173** E3
Keelby **188** B1
Keele **171** F3
Keeley Green **149** F3
Keelham **193** G4
Keenthorne **115** F4
Keeres Green **137** E1
Keeston **126** B1
Keevil **118** A2
Kegworth **173** F5
Kehelland **96** A5
Keig **260** E3
Keighley **193** G3
Keighley & Worth Valley
  Railway *WYorks*
  BD22 8NJ **193** G3
Keil *A&B* **222** B5
Keil *High* **248** B4
Keilhill **269** F5
Keillmore **231** E1
Keillor **252** A5
Keillour **243** E2
Keills **230** C3

Keils **230** D3
Keinton Mandeville **116** C4
Keir House **242** C5
Keir Mill **216** C1
Keisby **175** F5
Keiss **275** J2
Keith **268** C5
Keithick **244** A1
Keithmore **260** B1
Keithock **253** E3
Kelbrook **193** F3
Kelby **175** F3
Keld *Cumb* **199** G1
Keld *NYorks* **201** D2
Keldholme **203** G4
Keldy Castle **203** G3
Kelfield *NLincs* **187** F2
Kelfield *NYorks* **195** E4
Kelham **174** C2
Kella **190** B2
Kellacott **99** E2
Kellan **247** E5
Kellas *Angus* **244** C1
Kellas *Moray* **267** J6
Kellaton **101** D4
Kellaways **132** B5
Kelleth **200** B3
Kellethorpe **196** C2
Kelling **178** B1
Kellington **195** E5
Kelloe **212** C4
Kelloholm **225** F4
Kells **209** E5
Kelly *Corn* **97** G1
Kelly *Devon* **99** D2
Kelly Bray **99** D3
Kelmarsh **160** C5
Kelmscott **133** E3
Kelsale **153** E1
Kelsall **170** C1
Kelsay **230** A4
Kelshall **150** B4
Kelsick **209** F1
Kelso **228** B3
Kelstedge **173** E1
Kelstern **188** C3
Kelston **117** E1
Keltneyburn **250** C5
Kelton **217** D3
Kelton Hill
  (Rhonehouse) **216** B5
Kelty **243** G5
Kelvedon **138** C1
Kelvedon Hatch **137** E3
Kelvin Hall *Glas*
  G3 8AW **38** A2
Kelvingrove Art Gallery &
  Museum *Glas*
  G3 8AG **38** B2
Kelvinside **233** G3
Kelynack **94** A4
Kemacott **113** G1
Kemback **244** C3
Kemberton **157** G2
Kemble **132** B3
Kemerton **146** B4
Kemeys
  Commander **130** C2
Kemeys Inferior **130** C3
Kemnay **261** F3
Kemp Town **109** F3
Kempe's Corner **124** C4
Kempley **145** F5
Kempley Green **145** F5
Kempsey **146** A3
Kempsford **133** D3
Kempshott **119** G3
Kempston **149** F3
Kempston Hardwick **149** F3
Kempston West End **149** F3
Kempton **156** C4
Kemsing **123** E2
Kemsley **124** B2
Kenardington **124** B5
Kenchester **144** D3
Kencot **133** E2
Kendal **199** G3
Kenderchurch **144** D5
Kendleshire **131** F5
Kenfig **129** D4
Kenfig Hill **129** D4
Kenidjack **94** A3
Kenilworth **159** E5
Kenilworth Castle *Warks*
  CV8 1NE **16** A4
Kenknock *P&K* **250** A5
Kenknock *Stir* **241** G1
Kenley *GtLon* **122** C2
Kenley *Shrop* **157** E2
Kenmore *A&B* **240** C4
Kenmore *High* **264** D6
Kenmore *P&K* **250** C5
Kenmore *Na H-E. Siar*
  270 E7
Kenn *Devon* **102** C4
Kenn *NSom* **116** B1
Kennacley **263** G2
Kennacraig **231** G3
Kennavay **263** H2
Kennerleigh **102** B2
Kenneggy Downs **94** C4
Kennerleigh **102** B2
Kennerty **260** E5
Kennet **243** E5
Kennethmont **260** D2
Kennett **151** E1
Kennford **102** C4
Kenninghall **164** B3
Kennington *Kent* **124** C4
Kennington *Oxon* **134** A2
Kennoway **244** B4
Kenny **103** G1
Kennyhill **163** E5
Kennythorpe **195** G1
Kenovay **246** A2
Kensington **136** B4
Kensington Palace *GtLon*
  W8 4PX **10** E4
Kenstone **170** C5
Kensworth **135** F1
Kent & East Sussex Railway
  Kent TN30 6HE **124** A5
Kent Street *ESuss* **110** C2
Kent Street *Kent* **123** F3
Kentallen (Ceann an t-
  Sàilein) **248** C4

Kentchurch 144 D5
Kentford 151 F1
Kentisbeare 103 D2
Kentisbury 113 G1
Kentisbury Ford 113 G1
Kentish Town 136 B4
Kentmere 199 F2
Kenton Devon 102 C4
Kenton Suff 152 C1
Kenton T&W 212 B1
Kenton Corner 152 D1
Kentra 247 F3
Kents Bank 199 E5
Kent's Green 145 G5
Kent's Oak 119 E5
Kenwick 170 B4
Kenwood House GtLon
  NW3 7JR 10 F2
Kenwyn 96 C5
Kenyon 184 A3
Keoldale 273 F2
Keose (Ceòs) 271 F5
Keppanach 248 C3
Keppoch A&B 233 E2
Keppoch High 256 E2
Keprigan 222 B4
Kepwick 203 D3
Keresley 159 F4
Kernborough 101 D3
Kerrera 240 A2
Kerridge 184 D5
Kerris 94 B4
Kerry (Ceri) 156 A1
Kerrycroy 232 C3
Kerry's Gate 144 C4
Kerrysdale 264 E4
Kersall 174 C1
Kersey 152 B3
Kersey Vale 152 B3
Kershopefoot 218 C3
Kerswell 103 D2
Kerswell Green 146 A3
Kerthen Wood 94 C3
Kesgrave 152 D3
Kessingland 165 G3
Kessingland Beach 165 G3
Kestle 97 D5
Kestle Mill 96 C4
Keston 122 D2
Keswick Cumb 209 F4
Keswick Norf 178 D5
Keswick Norf 179 E2
Ketley Bank 157 F1
Ketsby 189 D5
Kettering 161 D2
Ketteringham 178 C5
Kettins 244 A1
Kettle Corner 123 G3
Kettlebaston 152 A2
Kettlebridge 244 B4
Kettlebrook 159 E2
Kettleburgh 153 D1
Kettlehill 244 B4
Kettleholm 217 F3
Kettleness 204 B1
Kettleshulme 185 D5
Kettlesing 194 B2
Kettlesing Bottom 194 B2
Kettlesing Head 194 B2
Kettlestone 178 A4
Kettlethorpe 187 F5
Kettletoft 276 F4
Kettlewell 201 E5
Ketton 161 E2
Kevingtown 123 D2
Kew 136 A5
Kewstoke 116 A1
Kexbrough 186 A2
Kexby Lincs 187 F4
Kexby York 195 G2
Key Green 171 F1
Keyham 160 B2
Keyhaven 106 C3
Keyingham 197 E5
Keymer 109 F2
Keynsham 117 D1
Key's Toft 176 C2
Keysoe 149 F1
Keysoe Row 149 F1
Keyston 161 F5
Keyworth 174 B4
Kibblesworth 212 B2
Kibworth
  Beauchamp 160 B3
Kibworth Harcourt 160 B3
Kidbrooke 136 D5
Kiddemore Green 158 A2
Kidderminster 158 A5
Kiddington 147 G5
Kidlington 133 G1
Kidmore End 134 B5
Kidnal 170 B3
Kidsdale 207 E3
Kidsgrove 171 F2
Kidstones 201 E4
Kidwelly (Cydweli) 128 A2
Kiel Crofts 240 A1
Kielder 219 E2
Kielder Forest N'umb
  NE48 1ER 219 E2
Kielder Water N'umb
  NE48 1BX 219 F3
Kilbarchan 233 F3
Kilbeg 256 C4
Kilberry 231 F3
Kilbirnie 233 E4
Kilblaan 240 D3
Kilbraur 274 D7
Kilbrennan 246 D3
Kilbride A&B 240 A2
Kilbride A&B 232 B3
Kilbride High 256 B2
Kilbride Farm 232 A3
Kilbridemore 240 B5
Kilburn Derbys 173 E3
Kilburn GtLon 136 B4
Kilburn NYorks 203 E5
Kilby 160 B3
Kilchattan Bay 232 C4
Kilchenzie 222 B3
Kilcheran 240 A1
Kilchiaran 230 A3
Kilchoan A&B 239 G3
Kilchoan High 247 D3
Kilchoman 230 A3
Kilchrenan
  (Cill Chrèanain) 240 C2
Kilchrist 222 B4

Kilconquhar 244 C4
Kilcot 145 F5
Kilcoy 266 C6
Kilcreggan 232 D1
Kildale 203 F2
Kildary 266 E4
Kildavie 222 C4
Kildermorie Lodge 266 C4
Kildonan NAyr 223 F3
Kildonan (Cilldonnain)
  Na H-E. Siar 254 C2
Kildonan Lodge 274 E6
Kildonnan 247 D1
Kildrochet House 214 B5
Kildrummy 260 C3
Kildwick 193 G3
Kilfinan 232 A2
Kilfinnan 257 J3
Kilgetty 127 E2
Kilgwrrwg Common 131 D3
Kilham ERid 196 C1
Kilham N'umb 228 C3
Kilkenneth 246 A2
Kilkenny 132 C1
Kilkerran A&B 222 C4
Kilkerran SAyr 224 B5
Kilkhampton 112 C4
Killamarsh 186 B4
Killay 128 C3
Killbeg 247 F5
Killean A&B 231 E5
Killean A&B 240 C4
Killearn 233 G1
Killellan 222 B4
Killen 266 D6
Killerby 212 A5
Killerton 102 C2
Killerton Devon
  EX5 3LE 102 C2
Killichonan 250 A4
Killiechonate 249 E1
Killiechronan 247 E5
Killiecrankie 251 E3
Killiehuntly 258 E5
Killiemor 239 D1
Killilan 257 F1
Killimster 275 J3
Killin High 267 F1
Killin Stir 242 A1
Killinallan 230 B2
Killinghall 194 B2
Killington Cumb 200 B4
Killington Devon 113 G1
Killingworth 221 E4
Killochyett 236 B5
Killocraw 222 B2
Killunaig 239 D2
Killundine 247 E5
Kilmacolm 233 E3
Kilmaha 240 B4
Kilmahog 242 B4
Kilmalieu 248 A4
Kilmaluag 246 B4
Kilmany 244 B2
Kilmarie 256 B3
Kilmarnock 224 C2
Kilmartin 240 A5
Kilmaurs 233 F5
Kilmelford 240 A3
Kilmeny 230 B3
Kilmersdon 117 D2
Kilmeston 119 F5
Kilmichael 222 B3
Kilmichael
  Glassary 240 A5
Kilmichael of
  Inverlussa 231 F1
Kilmington Devon 103 F3
Kilmington Wilts 117 E4
Kilmington
  Common 117 E4
Kilmorack 266 B7
Kilmore A&B 240 A2
Kilmore High 256 C4
Kilmory A&B 231 F1
Kilmory A&B 231 F2
Kilmory High 255 J4
Kilmory NAyr 223 E3
Kilmote 274 E7
Kilmuir High 263 H7
Kilmuir High 266 D7
Kilmuir High 266 E4
Kilmuir High 263 J4
Kilmun 232 C1
Kilmux 244 B4
Kiln Green Here 131 F1
Kiln Green W'ham 134 D5
Kiln Pit Hill 211 G2
Kilnave 230 A2
Kilncadzow 234 C5
Kilndown 123 G5
Kilnhurst 186 B3
Kilninian 246 D5
Kilninver 240 A2
Kilnsea 189 E1
Kilnsey 193 F1
Kilnwick 196 B3
Kilnwick Percy 196 A2
Kiloran 238 C5
Kilpatrick 223 E3
Kilpeck 144 D4
Kilphedir 274 E7
Kilpin 195 G5
Kilpin Pike 195 G5
Kilsby 160 A5
Kilspindie 244 A2
Kilstay 206 B3
Kilsyth 234 B2
Kiltarlity 266 C7
Kilton Notts 186 C5
Kilton R&C 203 F1
Kilton Som 115 E3
Kilton Thorpe 203 F1
Kiltyrie 242 B1
Kilvaxter 263 J5
Kilve 115 E3
Kilverstone 163 G4
Kilvington 174 D3
Kilwinning 233 E5
Kimberley Norf 178 B5
Kimberley Notts 173 G3
Kimberworth 186 B3
Kimble Wick 134 D2
Kimblesworth 212 B3
Kimbolton Cambs 149 F1

Kimbolton Here 145 E1
Kimbridge 119 E5
Kimcote 160 A4
Kimmeridge 105 F5
Kimmerston 229 D3
Kimpton Hants 119 D3
Kimpton Herts 136 A1
Kinaldy 244 D3
Kinblethmont 253 E5
Kinbrace 274 D5
Kinbreack 257 G5
Kinbuck 242 C4
Kincaldrum 252 C5
Kincaple 244 C3
Kincardine Fife 234 D1
Kincardine High 266 E3
Kincardine O'Neil 260 D5
Kinclaven 243 G1
Kincorth 261 H4
Kincraig Aber 261 H2
Kincraig High 259 F4
Kincraigie 251 E5
Kindallachan 251 E4
Kindrogan Field
  Centre 251 F3
Kinellar 261 G3
Kineton Glos 146 C5
Kineton Warks 147 F2
Kineton Green 158 D4
Kinfauns 243 G2
King Sterndale 185 E5
Kingarth 232 B4
Kingcoed 130 D2
Kingerby 188 A3
Kingham 147 E5
Kingholm Quay 217 D3
Kinghorn 235 G1
Kinglassie 244 A5
Kingoodie 244 B2
King's Acre 145 D3
King's Bank 111 D1
King's Bromley 158 D1
Kings Caple 145 E5
King's College Chapel,
  Cambridge Cambs
  CB2 1ST 150 C3
King's Coughton 146 C2
King's Green 145 G4
King's Heath 158 C4
Kings Hill Kent 123 F4
King's Hill Warks 159 F3
King's Hill WMid 158 B3
Kings Langley 135 F2
King's Lynn 177 E5
King's Meaburn 210 C5
Kings Mills 101 E5
King's Moss 183 G2
Kings Muir 227 D2
King's Newnham 159 G5
King's Newton 173 E5
King's Norton Leics 160 B2
King's Norton
  WMid 158 C5
King's Nympton 113 G4
King's Pyon 144 D2
Kings Ripton 162 A5
King's Somborne 119 E4
King's Stag 104 D1
King's Stanley 132 A2
King's Sutton 147 G4
King's Tamerton 100 A2
King's Walden 149 G5
Kings Worthy 119 F4
Kingsand 100 A2
Kingsbarns 245 D3
Kingsbridge Devon 100 D3
Kingsbridge Som 114 C4
Kingsburgh 263 J6
Kingsbury GtLon 136 A4
Kingsbury Warks 159 E3
Kingsbury Episcopi 116 B5
Kingsbury Water Park
  Warks B76 0DY 159 E3
Kingscavil 235 E2
Kingsclere 119 G2
Kingscote 132 A3
Kingscott 113 F4
Kingscross 223 F3
Kingsdale 244 B4
Kingsdon 116 C5
Kingsdown Kent 125 F4
Kingsdown Swin 133 D4
Kingsdown Wilts 117 F1
Kingseat 243 G5
Kingsey 134 C2
Kingsfold Pembs 126 C3
Kingsfold WSuss 121 G4
Kingsford Aber 269 F6
Kingsford Aber 260 D3
Kingsford
  Aberdeen 261 G4
Kingsford EAyr 233 F5
Kingsford Worcs 158 A4
Kingsgate 125 F1
Kingshall Street 152 A1
Kingsheanton 113 F2
Kingshouse 242 A2
Kingshouse Hotel 249 D3
Kingshurst 159 D4
Kingskerswell 101 E1
Kingskettle 244 B4
Kingsland Here 144 D1
Kingsland IoA 180 A4
Kingsley ChesW&C 183 G5
Kingsley Hants 120 C4
Kingsley Staffs 172 B3
Kingsley Green 121 D4
Kingsley Holt 172 B3
Kingslow 157 G3
Kingsmoor 136 D2
Kingsmuir Angus 252 C5
Kingsmuir Fife 244 D4
Kingsnorth 124 C5
Kingsnorth Power
  Station 124 A1
Kingstanding 158 C3
Kingsteignton 102 B5
Kingsthorne 145 D4
Kingsthorpe 148 C1
Kingston Cambs 150 B2
Kingston Corn 99 D3
Kingston Devon 100 C3
Kingston Devon 103 D4
Kingston Dorset 104 C1
Kingston Dorset 105 F5
Kingston ELoth 236 C1

Kingston GtMan 184 D3
Kingston Hants 106 A2
Kingston IoW 107 D4
Kingston Kent 125 D3
Kingston MK 148 D3
Kingston Moray 268 B4
Kingston WSuss 108 C3
Kingston Bagpuize 133 G3
Kingston Blount 134 C3
Kingston by Sea 109 E3
Kingston Deverill 117 F4
Kingston Gorse 108 C3
Kingston Lacy Dorset
  BH21 4EA 3 A1
Kingston Lisle 133 F4
Kingston Maurward 104 D3
Kingston near
  Lewes 109 F3
Kingston on Soar 173 G5
Kingston Russell 104 B3
Kingston St. Mary 115 F5
Kingston Seymour 116 B1
Kingston Stert 134 C2
Kingston upon Hull 196 D5
Kingston upon
  Thames 121 G1
Kingstone Here 144 D4
Kingstone Here 145 F5
Kingstone Som 103 G1
Kingstone Staffs 172 B5
Kingston Winslow 133 E4
Kingstown 209 G1
Kingswear 101 E2
Kingswell 233 G5
Kingswells 261 G4
Kingswinford 158 A4
Kingswood Bucks 134 B1
Kingswood Glos 131 G3
Kingswood Here 144 B2
Kingswood Kent 124 A3
Kingswood Powys 156 B2
Kingswood SGlos 131 F5
Kingswood Som 115 E4
Kingswood Surr 122 B3
Kingswood Warks 159 D5
Kingthorpe 188 B3
Kington Here 144 B2
Kington Worcs 146 B2
Kington Langley 132 B5
Kington Magna 117 E5
Kington St. Michael 132 B5
Kingussie 258 E4
Kingweston 116 C4
Kinharrachie 261 H1
Kinharvie 216 D4
Kinkell 234 A2
Kinkell Bridge 243 E3
Kinknockie 269 J6
Kinlet 157 G4
Kinloch Fife 244 A3
Kinloch High 273 F3
Kinloch High 247 F4
Kinloch High 255 K5
Kinloch High 266 C4
Kinloch P&K 252 A5
Kinloch P&K 251 G5
Kinloch Hourn (Ceann Loch
  Shubhairne) 257 F4
Kinloch Laggan 250 A1
Kinloch Rannoch 250 B4
Kinlochan 248 A3
Kinlochard 241 G3
Kinlocharkaig 257 F5
Kinlochbeoraid 248 B1
Kinlochbervie 272 E3
Kinlocheil 248 B2
Kinlochetive 248 D5
Kinlochewe 265 G5
Kinlochlaich 248 B3
Kinlochleven (Ceann Loch
  Liobhann) 249 D3
Kinlochmoidart 247 G5
Kinlochmorar 256 E5
Kinlochmore 249 D3
Kinlochroag (Ceann
  Lochroag) 270 D5
Kinlochspelve 239 F2
Kinloss 267 H5
Kinmel Bay
  (Bae Cinmel) 182 A4
Kinmuck 261 G3
Kinnaber 253 F3
Kinnadie 269 H6
Kinnaird 243 G2
Kinneff 253 G2
Kinnelhead 226 B3
Kinnell Angus 253 E4
Kinnell Stir 242 A1
Kinnernley 170 A1
Kinnerley 146 A3
Kinnerton 144 B1
Kinnerton Green 170 A1
Kinnesswood 243 G4
Kinnettles 252 C5
Kinninvie 211 G5
Kinnordy 252 B4
Kinoulton 174 B4
Kinrara 259 F4
Kinross 243 G4
Kinrossie 243 G1
Kinsbourne Green 136 A1
Kinsham Here 144 C1
Kinsham Worcs 146 B4
Kinsley 186 B1
Kinson 105 G3
Kintarvie 270 E6
Kintbury 119 E1
Kintessack 267 G5
Kinton Here 156 D5
Kinton Shrop 156 C1
Kintour 230 C4
Kintra A&B 230 B5
Kintra A&B 238 C2
Kintradwell 267 G1
Kintraw 240 A4
Kinuachdrachd 239 G5
Kinveachy 259 G3
Kinver 158 A4
Kinwarton 146 D2
Kiplin Croft 261 J1
Kipp 242 A1
Kippax 194 D4
Kippen P&K 243 F3

Kippen Stir 242 B5
Kippenross House 242 C4
Kippford (Scaur) 216 C5
Kipping's Cross 123 F4
Kippington 123 E3
Kirbister Ork 277 C7
Kirbister Ork 276 F5
Kirbuster 276 B5
Kirby Bedon 179 D5
Kirby Bellars 160 C1
Kirby Cane 165 E2
Kirby Corner 159 E5
Kirby Cross 152 D5
Kirby Fields 160 A2
Kirby Green 165 E2
Kirby Grindalythe 196 B1
Kirby Hill NYorks 202 B3
Kirby Hill NYorks 194 C1
Kirby Knowle 203 D4
Kirby le Soken 152 D5
Kirby Misperton 203 G5
Kirby Muxloe 160 A2
Kirby Row 165 E2
Kirby Sigston 202 D3
Kirby Underdale 196 A2
Kirby Wiske 202 C4
Kirdford 121 F5
Kirk 275 H3
Kirk Bramwith 186 D1
Kirk Deighton 194 C2
Kirk Ella 196 C5
Kirk Hallam 173 F3
Kirk Hammerton 195 D2
Kirk Ireton 172 D2
Kirk Langley 173 D4
Kirk Merrington 212 B4
Kirk Michael 190 B2
Kirk of Shotts 234 C4
Kirk Sandall 186 D2
Kirk Smeaton 186 C1
Kirk Yetholm 228 C4
Kirkabister 279 D9
Kirkandrews 207 G2
Kirkandrews-upon-
  Eden 209 G1
Kirkbampton 209 G1
Kirkbean 217 D5
Kirkbride 209 F1
Kirkbuddo 252 D5
Kirkburn ERid 196 B2
Kirkburton 185 F1
Kirkby Lincs 188 A3
Kirkby Mersey 183 F3
Kirkby NYorks 203 E2
Kirkby Fleetham 202 B3
Kirkby Green 175 F2
Kirkby in Ashfield 173 F2
Kirkby la Thorpe 175 F3
Kirkby Lonsdale 200 B5
Kirkby Malham 193 E1
Kirkby Mallory 159 G2
Kirkby Malzeard 202 B5
Kirkby on Bain 176 A1
Kirkby Overblow 194 C3
Kirkby Stephen 200 C2
Kirkby Thore 210 C5
Kirkby Underwood 175 F5
Kirkby Wharfe 195 E3
Kirkby Woodhouse 173 F2
Kirkby-in-Furness 198 D4
Kirkbymoorside 203 F4
Kirkcaldy 244 A5
Kirkcambeck 210 B1
Kirkcolm 214 B4
Kirkconnel 225 F4
Kirkconnell 217 D4
Kirkcowan 215 E4
Kirkcudbright 216 A5
Kirkdale House 215 G3
Kirkdean 235 F4
Kirkfieldbank 234 C5
Kirkgunzeon 216 C4
Kirkham Lancs 192 A4
Kirkham NYorks 195 G1
Kirkhamgate 194 C5
Kirkharle 220 C3
Kirkhaugh 210 C3
Kirkheaton N'umb 220 C4
Kirkheaton WYorks 185 F1
Kirkhill Angus 253 E3
Kirkhill High 266 C7
Kirkhill Moray 268 B5
Kirkhope 227 E3
Kirkibost High 256 B3
Kirkibost (Circebost)
  Na H-E. Siar 270 D4
Kirkinch 252 B5
Kirkinner 215 F5
Kirkintilloch 234 A2
Kirkland Cumb 210 C4
Kirkland Cumb 209 D5
Kirkland D&G 216 C1
Kirkland D&G 225 F4
Kirkland D&G 217 E2
Kirkland of
  Longcastle 207 D2
Kirkleatham 213 E5
Kirklevington 202 D2
Kirkley 165 G2
Kirklington Notts 174 B2
Kirklington NYorks 202 C4
Kirklinton 210 A1
Kirkliston 235 F2
Kirkmaiden 206 B3
Kirkmichael P&K 251 F3
Kirkmichael SAyr 224 B5
Kirkmuirhill 234 B5
Kirknewton N'umb 228 D3
Kirknewton WLoth 235 F3
Kirkney 260 D1
Kirkoswald Cumb 210 B3
Kirkoswald SAyr 224 A5
Kirkpatrick Durham 216 B3
Kirkpatrick-Fleming 218 A4
Kirksanton 198 C4
Kirkstall 194 B4
Kirkstead 175 G1
Kirkstile Aber 260 D1
Kirkstile D&G 218 B2
Kirkstyle 275 J1
Kirkthorpe 194 C5
Kirkton A&B 239 G4
Kirkton Aber 260 E2
Kirkton Aber 268 E5
Kirkton Aber 260 E3
Kirkton Angus 252 C5
Kirkton D&G 217 D2

Kirkton Fife 244 B2
Kirkton High 258 D1
Kirkton High 266 E2
Kirkton High 266 E6
Kirkton High 274 D2
Kirkton High 256 E2
Kirkton P&K 243 E3
Kirkton ScBord 227 G4
Kirkton Manor 226 D2
Kirkton of Airlie 252 B4
Kirkton of
  Auchterhouse 244 B1
Kirkton of Barevan 267 F7
Kirkton of Bourtie 261 G2
Kirkton of Collace 243 G1
Kirkton of Craig 253 F4
Kirkton of
  Culsalmond 260 E1
Kirkton of Durris 261 F5
Kirkton of
  Glenbuchat 260 B3
Kirkton of Glenisla 252 A3
Kirkton of
  Kingoldrum 252 B4
Kirkton of Lethendy 251 G5
Kirkton of Logie
  Buchan 261 H2
Kirkton of
  Maryculter 261 G5
Kirkton of Menmuir 252 D3
Kirkton of Monikie 244 D1
Kirkton of Rayne 260 E1
Kirkton of Skene 261 G4
Kirkton of Tealing 244 C1
Kirktonhill Aber 253 E3
Kirktonhill WDun 233 E2
Kirktown 269 J5
Kirktown of Alvah 268 E4
Kirktown of
  Auchterless 269 F6
Kirktown of
  Deskford 268 D4
Kirktown of
  Fetteresso 253 G1
Kirktown of Slains 261 J2
Kirkwall 277 D6
Kirkwall Airport 277 D7
Kirkwhelpington 220 B3
Kirmington 188 B1
Kirmond le Mire 188 B3
Kirn 232 C2
Kirriemuir 252 B4
Kirstead Green 165 E2
Kirtlebridge 218 A4
Kirtling 151 E2
Kirtling Green 151 E2
Kirtlington 134 A1
Kirtomy 274 C2
Kirton Lincs 176 B4
Kirton Notts 174 B1
Kirton Suff 153 D4
Kirton End 176 A3
Kirton in Lindsey 187 G3
Kirton Holme 176 A3
Kiscadale 223 F3
Kislingbury 148 B2
Kismeldon Bridge 113 D4
Kit Hill Country Park
  Corn PL17 8AX 99 D3
Kites Hardwick 147 G1
Kitley 100 B2
Kittisford 115 D5
Kittisford Barton 115 D5
Kittle 128 B4
Kitt's End 136 B3
Kitt's Green 159 D4
Kitwood 120 B4
Kivernoll 145 D4
Kiveton Park 186 B4
Klibreck 273 H5
Knabbygates 268 D5
Knaith 187 F4
Knaith Park 187 F4
Knap Corner 117 F5
Knaphill 121 E2
Knaplock 114 B4
Knapp P&K 244 A1
Knapp Som 116 A5
Knapthorpe 174 C2
Knaptoft 160 B4
Knapton Norf 179 E2
Knapton York 195 E2
Knapton Green 144 D2
Knapwell 150 B1
Knaresborough 194 C2
Knarsdale 210 C2
Knarston 276 C5
Knaven 269 G6
Knayton 202 D4
Knebworth 150 A5
Knebworth House Herts
  SG3 6PY 150 A5
Knedlington 195 G5
Kneesall 174 C1
Kneesworth 150 B3
Kneeton 174 C3
Knelston 128 A4
Knenhall 171 G4
Knettishall 164 A3
Knettishall Heath Country
  Park Suff
  IP22 2TQ 164 A3
Knightacott 113 G2
Knightcote 147 G2
Knightley 171 F5
Knightley Dale 171 F5
Knighton Devon 100 B3
Knighton Dorset 104 C1
Knighton Leic 160 A2
Knighton Poole 105 G3
Knighton (Tref-y-clawdd)
  Powys 156 B5
Knighton Som 115 E3
Knighton Staffs 171 E5
Knighton Staffs 171 E3
Knighton Wilts 133 E5
Knighton on Teme 157 F5
Knightswood 233 G3
Knightwick 145 G2
Knill 144 B1
Knipoch 240 A2
Knipton 174 D4
Knitsley 212 A3
Kniveton 172 D2
Knock A&B 239 E1
Knock Cumb 210 C4
Knock High 256 C4

Knock Moray 268 D5
Knock of
  Auchnahannet 259 H1
Knockalava 240 B5
Knockally 275 G6
Knockaloe Moar 190 A3
Knockan 272 E7
Knockandhu 259 J2
Knockando 267 J7
Knockarthur 266 E1
Knockbain 266 D6
Knockban 265 J5
Knockbreck 268 C2
Knockbrex 207 F2
Knockdamph 265 J2
Knockdee 275 G2
Knockdow 232 C2
Knockdown 132 A4
Knockenkelly 223 F3
Knockentiber 224 C2
Knockfin 257 K2
Knockgray 215 G1
Knockholt 123 D3
Knockholt Pound 123 D3
Knockin 170 A5
Knockinlaw 224 C2
Knockintorran (Cnoc an
  Torrain) 262 C5
Knocklearn 216 B3
Knockmill 123 E2
Knocknaha 222 B4
Knocknain 214 A4
Knocknalling 215 G3
Knockrome 231 D2
Knocksharry 190 A3
Knockville 215 E3
Knockvologan 238 C3
Knodishall 153 F1
Knodishall
  Common 153 F1
Knodishall Green 153 F1
Knole 116 B5
Knolls Green 184 C5
Knolton 170 A4
Knook 118 A3
Knossington 160 D2
Knott End-on-Sea 191 G3
Knotting 149 F1
Knotting Green 149 F1
Knottingley 195 E5
Knotts 193 E3
Knotty Green 135 E3
Knowbury 157 E5
Knowe 215 E3
Knowes of Elrick 268 E5
Knowesgate 220 B3
Knoweside 224 A4
Knowetownhead 227 G4
Knowhead 269 H5
Knowl Green 151 F3
Knowl Hill 134 D5
Knowl Wall 171 F4
Knowle Bristol 131 F5
Knowle Devon 102 A2
Knowle Devon 113 E2
Knowle Devon 103 D4
Knowle Shrop 157 E5
Knowle Som 114 C3
Knowle WMid 159 D5
Knowle Cross 102 C3
Knowle Green 192 C4
Knowle Hall 116 A4
Knowle St. Giles 103 G1
Knowlton Dorset 105 G1
Knowlton Kent 125 E3
Knowsley 183 F3
Knowsley Safari Park
  Mersey L34 4AN 23 E2
Knowstone 114 B5
Knox Bridge 123 G4
Knucklas (Cnwclas)
  156 B5
Knutsford 184 B5
Knypersley 171 F2
Krumlin 185 E1
Kuggar 95 E5
Kyle of Lochalsh (Caol
  Loch Aillse) 256 D2
Kyleakin
  (Caol Acain) 256 D2
Kylerhea
  (Ceol Reatha) 256 D2
Kyles Scalpay (Caolas
  Scalpaigh) 263 H2
Kylesbeg 247 F2
Kylesknoydart 256 E5
Kylesku 272 E5
Kylesmorar 256 E5
Kylestrome 272 E5
Kyloag 266 D2
Kynaston 170 A5
Kynnersley 157 F1
Kyre Park 145 F1

L
Labost 270 E3
Lacasaigh 271 F5
Lace Market Centre
  NG1 1HF 80 Nottingham
Laceby 188 C2
Lacey Green 134 D2
Lach Dennis 184 B5
Lackford 163 F4
Lacklee
  (Leac a' Li) 263 G2
Lacock 118 A1
Ladbroke 147 G2
Laddingford 123 F4
Lade Bank 176 B2
Ladies Hill 192 A3
Ladock 96 C4
Lady Hall 198 C4
Lady Lever Art Gallery
  Mersey
  CH62 5EQ 22 B4
Ladybank 244 B3
Ladycross 98 D2
Ladyfield 240 C3
Ladykirk 237 F5
Ladysford 269 H4
Ladywood 146 A1
Laga 247 F3
Lagalochan 240 A3
Lagavulin 230 C5
Lagg A&B 231 D3
Lagg NAyr 223 E3
Lagg SAyr 224 A4
Laggan A&B 230 A4

Laggan (An Lagan)
  High 257 J5
Laggan High 258 D5
Laggan Moray 260 B1
Laggan Stir 242 A3
Lagganulva 247 D5
Lagganvoulin 259 J3
Laglingarten 240 D4
Lagnalean 266 D7
Lagrae 225 F4
Laguna 243 G1
Laid 273 G3
Laide 265 F2
Laig 247 D1
Laight 225 E4
Lainchoil 259 H3
Laindon 137 F4
Laing Art Gallery T&W
  NE1 8AG
  79 Newcastle upon Tyne
Lair 251 G3
Lairg 266 C1
Lairg Lodge 266 C1
Lairigmor 248 D3
Laisterdyke 194 A4
Laithers 268 E6
Laithes 210 A4
Lake Devon 113 F2
Lake Devon 100 B1
Lake IoW 107 E4
Lake Wilts 118 C4
Lake District Visitor Centre
  at Brockhole Cumb
  LA23 1LJ 199 E2
Lakenham 178 D5
Lakenheath 163 F4
Lakes Aquarium Cumb
  LA12 8AS 199 E4
Lakes End 162 D3
Lakes Glass Centre,
  Ulverston Cumb
  LA12 7LY 199 D5
Lakeside Cumb 199 E4
Lakeside Thur 137 F5
Lakeside & Haverthwaite
  Railway Cumb
  LA12 8AL 199 E4
Laleham 151 F1
Laleston 129 E5
Lamancha 235 G4
Lamarsh 151 G4
Lamas 178 D3
Lamb Corner 152 B4
Lamb Roe 192 D4
Lambden 237 E5
Lamberhurst 123 F5
Lamberhurst
  Quarter 123 F5
Lamberton 237 G4
Lambfell Moar 190 A3
Lambley N'umb 210 C2
Lambley Notts 174 B3
Lambourn 133 F5
Lambourn
  Woodlands 133 F5
Lambourne End 137 D3
Lambs Green 122 B5
Lambston 126 C1
Lambton 212 B2
Lamellion 97 G3
Lamerton 99 E3
Lamesley 212 B2
Lamington High 266 E4
Lamington SLan 226 A2
Lamlash 223 F2
Lamloch 215 G1
Lamonby 210 A4
Lamorna 94 B4
Lamorran 96 C5
Lampert 219 E4
Lampeter (Llanbedr Pont
  Steffan) 142 B3
Lampeter Velfrey 127 E1
Lamphey 126 D2
Lamplugh 209 D4
Lamport 160 C5
Lamyatt 117 D4
Lana Devon 98 D1
Lana Devon 112 D5
Lanark 234 C5
Lanarth 95 E4
Lancaster 192 A1
Lancaster Leisure Park
  Lancs LA1 3LA 192 A1
Lancaster Priory Lancs
  LA1 1YZ 192 A1
Lanchester 212 A3
Lancing 109 D3
Landbeach 150 C1
Landcross 113 E3
Landerberry 261 F4
Landewednack 95 E5
Landford 106 A2
Landhallow 275 G5
Landican 183 D4
Landimore 128 A3
Landkey 113 F2
Landmoth 202 D3
Landore 128 C3
Landrake 99 D4
Land's End Corn
  TR19 7AA 94 A4
Land's End Airport 94 A4
Landscove 101 D1
Landshipping 126 D1
Landulph 100 A1
Landwade 151 E1
Landywood 158 B2
Lane Bottom 193 E4
Lane End Bucks 134 D3
Lane End Cumb 198 C3
Lane End Derbys 173 F1
Lane End Dorset 105 E3
Lane End Hants 119 G5
Lane End Here 131 F1
Lane End Kent 137 E5
Lane End Wilts 117 F3
Lane Ends Derbys 172 D4
Lane Ends GtMan 185 D3
Lane Ends Lancs 193 D4
Lane Ends N'Yorks 193 F3
Lane Green 158 A2
Lane Head Dur 202 A1
Lane Head Dur 211 G5
Lane Head GtMan 184 A3
Lane Head W'Yorks 185 F2
Lane Heads 192 A4
Lane Side 193 D5

Laneast 97 G1
Lane-end 97 E3
Laneham 187 F5
Lanehead Dur 211 E3
Lanehead N'umb 219 F3
Lanesend 127 E3
Lanesfield 158 B3
Laneshawbridge 193 E3
Langais 262 D5
Langamull 246 C4
Langar 174 C4
Langbank 233 E2
Langbar 193 G2
Langbaurgh 203 E1
Langcliffe 193 E1
Langdale End 204 C3
Langdon Corn 98 C1
Langdon Corn 98 D2
Langdon Beck 211 E4
Langdon Hills 137 F4
Langdon Hills Country Park
  Essex SS17 9NH 137 F4
Langdon House 102 C3
Langdyke 244 B4
Langford CenBeds 149 G3
Langford Essex 138 B2
Langford Notts 174 D2
Langford Oxon 133 E2
Langford Budville 115 E5
Langham Essex 152 B4
Langham Norf 178 B1
Langham Rut 160 D1
Langham Suff 152 A1
Langham Moor 152 B4
Langho 192 C4
Langholm 218 B3
Langland 128 C4
Langlands 216 A5
Langlee 228 A5
Langleeford 228 D4
Langley ChesE 184 D5
Langley Derbys 173 F3
Langley Essex 150 C4
Langley Glos 146 C5
Langley GtMan 184 C2
Langley Hants 106 D2
Langley Herts 150 A5
Langley Kent 124 A3
Langley N'umb 211 E1
Langley Oxon 133 F1
Langley Slo 135 F4
Langley Som 115 D5
Langley Warks 147 D1
Langley W'Suss 120 D5
Langley Burrell 132 B5
Langley Corner 135 F4
Langley Green
  Derbys 173 D4
Langley Green
  Warks 147 E1
Langley Green
  W'Suss 122 B5
Langley Heath 124 A3
Langley Marsh 115 D5
Langley Mill 173 F3
Langley Moor 212 B3
Langley Park 212 B3
Langley Park Bucks
  SL3 6DW 135 F4
Langley Street 179 E5
Langney 110 B3
Langold 186 C4
Langore 97 G1
Langport 116 B5
Langrick 176 A3
Langrick Bridge 176 A3
Langridge
  B&NESom 117 E1
Langridge Devon 113 F3
Langridgeford 113 F3
Langrigg 209 E2
Langrish 120 C5
Langsett 185 G2
Langshaw 227 G2
Langshawburn 227 D5
Langside Glas 233 G3
Langside P&K 242 C3
Langskaill 276 D3
Langstone
  Newport 130 C3
Langthorne 202 B3
Langthorpe 194 C1
Langthwaite 201 F2
Langtoft ERid 196 C1
Langtoft Lincs 161 G1
Langton Dur 202 A1
Langton Lincs 189 D5
Langton Lincs 176 A1
Langton N'Yorks 195 G1
Langton by Wragby 188 B5
Langton Green Kent 123 E5
Langton Green Suff 164 C5
Langton Herring 104 C4
Langton Long
  Blandford 105 E2
Langton Matravers 105 F5
Langtree 113 E4
Langtree Week 113 E4
Langwathby 210 B4
Langwell 266 B1
Langwell House 275 G6
Langwith 186 C5
Langworth 188 A5
Lanhydrock Corn
  PL30 5AD 97 E3
Lanivet 97 E3
Lank 97 E2
Lanlivery 97 F4
Lanner 96 B5
Lanoy 97 G2
Lanreath 97 F4
Lansallos 97 F4
Lansdown 117 E1
Lanteglos 97 E1
Lanteglos Highway 97 F4
Lanton N'umb 228 D3
Lanton ScBord 228 A4
Lanvean 96 C3
Lapford 102 A2
Laphroaig 230 B5
Lapley 158 A1
Lapworth 159 D5
Larach na Gaibhre 231 F2
Larachbeg 247 F5
Larbert 234 C1
Larbreck 192 A3
Larden Green 170 C2

Larg 215 E3
Largie 260 E1
Largiemore 232 A1
Largoward 244 C4
Largs 232 D4
Largubaan 222 B4
Largubeg 223 F3
Largumore 223 F3
Lark Hall 151 D2
Larkfield 232 D2
Larkhall 234 B4
Larkhill 118 C3
Larklands 173 F3
Larling 164 A3
Larriston 218 D2
Lary 260 B4
Lasborough 132 A3
Lasham 120 B3
Lashbrook 113 E5
Lashenden 124 A4
Lassington 145 G5
Lassintullich 250 C4
Lasswade 236 A3
Lastingham 203 G3
Latchford 184 A4
Latchingdon 138 B2
Latchley 99 E3
Lately Common 184 A3
Lathbury 149 D3
Latheron 275 G5
Latheronwheel 275 G5
Lathockar 244 C4
Lathones 244 C4
Lathrisk 244 A4
Latimer 135 F3
Latteridge 131 F4
Lattiford 117 D5
Latton 132 C2
Lauchentyre 215 G5
Lauchintilly 261 F3
Lauder 236 C5
Laugharne
  (Lacharn) 127 G1
Laughterton 187 F5
Laughton ESuss 110 A2
Laughton Leics 160 B4
Laughton Lincs 175 D4
Laughton Lincs 187 F3
Laughton en le
  Morthen 186 C4
Launcells 112 C5
Launcells Cross 112 C5
Launceston 98 D2
Launde Abbey 160 C2
Launton 148 B5
Laurencekirk 253 F2
Laurieston D&G 216 A4
Laurieston Falk 234 D2
Lavendon 149 E2
Lavenham 152 A3
Laverhay 217 F1
Lavernock 115 E1
Laversdale 210 A1
Laverstock 118 C4
Laverstoke 119 F3
Laverton Glos 146 C4
Laverton N'Yorks 202 B5
Laverton Som 117 E2
Lavister 170 A2
Law 234 C4
Lawers P&K 242 C2
Lawers P&K 242 B1
Lawford Essex 152 B4
Lawford Som 115 E4
Lawhitton 99 D2
Lawkland 193 D1
Lawkland Green 193 D1
Lawley 157 F2
Lawnhead 171 F5
Lawrence Weston 131 E5
Lawrenny 126 D2
Laws 244 C1
Lawshall 151 G2
Lawshall Green 151 G2
Lawton 144 D2
Laxdale (Lacasdal) 271 G4
Laxey 190 C3
Laxfield 165 D4
Laxfirth Shet 279 D7
Laxfirth Shet 279 D8
Laxford Bridge 272 E4
Laxo 279 D6
Laxton ERid 195 G5
Laxton N'hants 161 E3
Laxton Notts 174 C1
Laycock 193 G3
Layer Breton 138 C1
Layer de la Haye 138 C1
Layer Marney 138 C1
Layham 152 B3
Laymore 103 G2
Layter's Green 135 E3
Laytham 195 G4
Layton 191 G4
Lazenby 213 E5
Lazonby 210 B4
Lea Derbys 173 E2
Lea Here 145 F5
Lea Lincs 187 F4
Lea Shrop 156 C4
Lea Shrop 156 D2
Lea Wilts 132 B4
Lea Bridge 173 E2
Lea Green 145 F1
Lea Marston 159 E3
Lea Town 192 A4
Lea Yeat 200 C4
Leachd 240 C5
Leachkin
  (An Leacainn) 266 D7
Leadburn 235 G4
Leaden Roding 137 E1
Leadenham 175 E2
Leaderfoot 227 G2
Leadgate Cumb 210 D3
Leadgate Dur 212 A2
Leadgate N'umb 212 A2
Leadhills 225 G3
Leadingcross Green 124 A3
Leafield 133 F1
Leagrave 149 F5
Leake Commonside 176 B2
Leake Hurn's End 176 C3
Lealands 110 A2

Lealholm 203 G2
Lealt A&B 239 F5
Lealt High 264 B5
Leam 185 G5
Leamington
  Hastings 147 G1
Leamington Spa 147 F1
Leamington Spa Art Gallery
  & Museum Warks
  CV32 4AA 16 B6
Leamoor Common 156 D4
Leanach A&B 240 C5
Leanach High 266 E7
Leanaig 266 C6
Leanoch 267 J6
Leargybreck 230 D2
Leasgill 199 F4
Leasingham 175 F3
Leask 261 J1
Leason 128 A3
Leasowe 183 D3
Leat 98 C2
Leatherhead 121 G2
Leathley 194 B3
Leaton Shrop 157 D1
Leaton Tel&W 157 F1
Leaveland 124 C3
Leavenheath 152 A4
Leavening 195 G1
Leaves Green 122 D2
Leavesden Green 136 A2
Lebberston 205 D4
Lechlade-on-
  Thames 133 E3
Leck 200 B5
Leckford 119 E4
Leckfurin 274 C3
Leckgruinart 230 A3
Leckhampstead
  Bucks 148 C4
Leckhampstead
  W'Berks 133 G5
Leckhampstead
  Thicket 133 G5
Leckhampton 132 B1
Leckie High 265 G5
Leckie Stir 242 B5
Leckmelm
  (Leac Mailm) 265 H3
Leckroy 257 K5
Leckuary 240 A5
Leckwith 130 A5
Leconfield 196 C3
Ledaig (Leideag) 240 B1
Ledard 241 G4
Ledburn 149 D5
Ledbury 145 G4
Ledcharrie 242 A2
Ledgemoor 144 D2
Ledicot 144 D1
Ledmore A&B 247 E5
Ledmore High 272 E7
Lednagullin 274 D2
Ledsham ChesW&C
  183 E5
Ledsham W'Yorks 195 D5
Ledston 194 D5
Ledstone 100 D3
Ledwell 147 G5
Lee A&B 238 D2
Lee Devon 113 E1
Lee Hants 106 C1
Lee Lancs 192 B2
Lee Shrop 170 B4
Lee Brockhurst 170 C5
Lee Chapel 137 F4
Lee Clump 135 E2
Lee Mill Bridge 100 B2
Lee Moor 100 B1
Lee Valley Park Essex
  EN9 1XQ 136 C2
Leebotten 279 D10
Leebotwood 157 D3
Leece 191 F1
Leeds Kent 124 A3
Leeds W'Yorks 194 B4
Leeds Art Gallery W'Yorks
  LS1 3AA 40 E3
Leeds Bradford International
  Airport 194 B3
Leeds Castle & Gardens
  Kent ME17 1PL 124 A3
Leedstown 94 D3
Leegomery 157 F1
Leek 171 G2
Leek Wootton 147 E1
Leekbrook 171 G2
Leeming N'Yorks 202 B4
Leeming W'Yorks 193 G4
Leeming Bar 202 B4
Lee-on-the-Solent 107 E2
Lees Derbys 173 D4
Lees GtMan 185 D2
Leeswood 169 F2
Leftwich 184 A5
Legars 237 E5
Legbourne 189 D4
Legerwood 236 C5
Legoland Windsor W&M
  SL4 4AY 135 E5
Legsby 188 B4
Leicester 160 A2
Leicester Forest
  East 160 A2
Leideag 254 B5
Leigh Dorset 104 C2
Leigh Dorset 105 G3
Leigh GtMan 184 A2
Leigh Kent 123 E4
Leigh Shrop 156 C2
Leigh Surr 122 B4
Leigh Wilts 132 C3
Leigh Worcs 145 G2
Leigh Beck 138 B4
Leigh Common 117 E5
Leigh Delamere 132 A5
Leigh Green 124 B5
Leigh Park 107 G2
Leigh Sinton 145 G2
Leigh upon
  Mendip 117 D3
Leigh Woods 131 E5
Leigham 100 B2
Leighland Chapel 114 D4
Leigh-on-Sea 138 B4
Leighterton 132 A3
Leighton N'Yorks 202 A5

Leighton (Tre'r Llai)
  Powys 156 B2
Leighton Shrop 157 F2
Leighton Som 117 E3
Leighton
  Bromswold 161 G5
Leighton Buzzard 149 E5
Leinthall Earls 144 D1
Leinthall Starkes 144 D1
Leintwardine 156 D5
Leire 160 A4
Leirinmore 273 G2
Leiston 153 F1
Leitfie 252 A5
Leith 235 G2
Leitholm 237 E5
Lelant 94 C3
Lelley 197 E4
Lemington 212 A1
Lemnas 269 G4
Lempitlaw 228 B3
Lemsford 136 B1
Lenchwick 146 C3
Lendalfoot 214 C1
Lendrick Lodge 242 A4
Lenham 124 A3
Lenham Heath 124 B4
Lenie 258 C2
Lenimore 231 G5
Lennel 237 F5
Lennox Plunton 216 A5
Lennoxtown 234 A2
Lent Rise 135 E4
Lenton Lincs 175 F4
Lenton Nott 173 G4
Lenton Abbey 173 G4
Lenwade 178 B4
Lenzie 234 A2
Leoch 244 B1
Leochel-Cushnie 260 D3
Leominster 145 D2
Leonard Stanley 132 A2
Leorin 230 B5
Lepe 106 D3
Lephin 263 G7
Lephinchapel 240 B5
Lephinmore 240 B5
Leppington 195 G1
Lepton 185 G1
Lerags 240 A2
Lerryn 97 F4
Lerwick 279 D8
Lesbury 229 G5
Leschangie 261 F3
Leslie Aber 260 D2
Leslie Fife 244 A4
Lesmahagow 225 G2
Lesnewth 98 B1
Lessendrum 268 D6
Lessingham 179 E3
Lessness Heath 137 D5
Lessonhall 209 F1
Leswalt 214 B4
Letchmore Heath 136 A3
Letchworth Garden
  City 150 A4
Letcombe Bassett 133 F4
Letcombe Regis 133 F4
Leth Meadhanach 254 C3
Letham Angus 252 D5
Letham Falk 234 C1
Letham Fife 244 B3
Lethanhill 224 C4
Lethenty 269 G6
Letheringham 153 D2
Letheringsett 178 B2
Lettaford 102 A4
Letter Finlay 257 J3
Letterewe 265 F4
Letterfearn
  (Leitir Fhearna) 256 E2
Lettermorar 247 G1
Lettermore A&B 247 D5
Lettermore High 273 J4
Letters 265 H3
Lettershaws 225 G3
Letterston 140 C5
Lettoch High 259 H3
Lettoch High 259 J1
Letton Here 156 C5
Letton Here 144 C3
Letty Green 136 B1
Letwell 186 C4
Leuchars 244 C2
Leumrabhagh 271 F6
Leurbost (Liurbost) 271 F5
Leusdon 102 A5
Levaldale 158 A1
Level's Green 150 C5
Leven ERid 196 D3
Leven Fife 244 B4
Levencorroch 223 F3
Levenhall 236 A2
Levens 199 F4
Levens Green 150 B5
Levenshulme 184 C3
Levenwick 279 D10
Leverburgh
  (An T-Òb) 263 F3
Leverington 162 C1
Leverstock Green 135 F2
Leverton 176 B3
Leverton Lucasgate 176 C3
Leverton Outgate 176 C3
Levington 152 D4
Levisham 204 B3
Levishie 258 B3
Lew 133 F2
Lewannick 97 G1
Lewcombe 104 B2
Lewdown 99 E2
Lewes 109 G2
Leweston 140 C5
Lewisham 136 C5
Lewiston
  (Blàr na Maigh) 258 C2
Lewistown 129 F4
Lewknor 134 C3
Leworthy 113 G2
Lewson Street 124 C2
Lewth 192 A4
Lewtrenchard 99 E2
Ley Aber 260 D3
Ley Corn 97 F3
Ley Green 149 G5
Leybourne 123 F3
Leyburn 202 A3
Leyland 192 B5

Leylodge 261 F3
Leymoor 185 F1
Leys Aber 269 J5
Leys Aber 260 C4
Leys P&K 244 A1
Leys of Cossans 252 B5
Leysdown-on-Sea 124 C1
Leysmill 253 E5
Leysters 145 E1
Leyton 136 C4
Leytonstone 136 C4
Lezant 98 D3
Lezerea 95 D3
Lhanbryde 267 K5
Liatrie 257 J1
Libanus 143 F5
Libberton 235 D5
Libbery 146 B2
Liberton 235 G3
Liceasto 263 G2
Lichfield 158 D2
Lichfield Cathedral Staffs
  WS13 7LD 158 D2
Lickey 158 B5
Lickey End 158 B5
Lickey Hills Country Park
  Worcs B45 8ER 14 C6
Lickfold 121 E5
Liddaton Green 99 E2
Liddel 277 D9
Liddesdale 247 G4
Liddington 133 E4
Lidgate Derbys 186 A5
Lidgate Suff 151 F2
Lidgett 174 B1
Lidlington 149 E4
Lidsey 108 B3
Lidsing 123 G2
Lidstone 147 F5
Liff 244 B1
Lifton 99 D2
Liftondown 99 D2
Lightcliffe 194 A5
Lighthorne 147 F2
Lighthorne Heath 147 F2
Lighthouse, The, Glasgow
  Glas G1 3NU 39 F4
Lighthouse, The - Poole's
  Centre for the Arts
  Poole BH15 1UG 3 B4
Lightwater 121 E1
Lightwater Valley Park
  N'Yorks
  HG4 3PT 202 B5
Lightwood 171 G3
Lightwood Green
  ChesE 170 D3
Lightwood Green
  Wrex 170 A3
Lilbourne 160 A5
Lilburn Tower 229 E4
Lillesdon 116 A5
Lilleshall 157 G1
Lilley Herts 149 G5
Lilley W'Berks 133 G5
Lilliesleaf 227 G3
Lilling Green 195 F1
Lillingstone Dayrell 148 C4
Lillingstone Lovell 148 C3
Lillington Dorset 104 C1
Lillington Warks 147 F1
Lilliput 105 G4
Lilly 113 F2
Lilstock 115 E3
Lilyhurst 157 G1
Limbury 149 F5
Lime Side 184 D2
Limefield 184 C1
Limehillock 268 D5
Limehurst 184 D2
Limekilnburn 234 B4
Limekilns 235 E1
Limerigg 234 D2
Limerstone 106 D4
Limington 116 C5
Limpenhoe 179 E5
Limpley Stoke 117 E1
Limpsfield 122 D3
Limpsfield Chart 122 D3
Linaclate
  (Lionacleit) 262 C7
Linacre Reservoirs Derbys
  S42 7JW 186 A5
Linbriggs 220 A1
Linby 173 G2
Linchmere 121 D4
Lincluden 217 D3
Lincoln 187 G5
Lincoln Castle Lincs
  LN1 3AA 77 Lincoln
Lincoln Cathedral Lincs
  LN2 1PL 77 Lincoln
Lincomb 146 A1
Lincombe Devon 100 D3
Lincombe Devon 100 D3
Lindal in Furness 199 D5
Lindale 199 F4
Lindean 227 F2
Lindertis 252 B4
Lindfield 109 F1
Lindford 120 D4
Lindifferon 244 B3
Lindisfarne
  (Holy Island) 229 F2
Lindley 194 B3
Lindores 244 A3
Lindow End 184 C5
Lindridge 145 F1
Lindsaig 232 A2
Lindsell 151 E5
Lindsey 152 A3
Lindsey Tye 152 A3
Linfitts 185 D2
Linford Hants 106 A2
Linford Thur 137 F5
Linford Wood 148 D3
Lingague 190 A4
Lingards Wood 185 E1
Lingdale 203 F1
Lingen 144 C1
Lingfield 122 C4
Lingley Green 183 G4
Lingwood 179 E5
Linhead 268 D5
Linhope 227 F5
Linicro 263 J5

Linkend 146 A4
Linkenholt 119 E2
Linkhill 110 D1
Linkinhorne 98 D3
Linklater 277 D9
Linksness Ork 277 B7
Linksness Ork 277 E6
Linktown 244 A5
Linley Shrop 156 C3
Linley Shrop 157 F3
Linley Green 145 F2
Linlithgow 235 E2
Linlithgow Bridge 235 D2
Linn of Muick
  Cottage 252 B1
Linnels 211 F1
Linney 126 B3
Linshiels 220 A1
Linsidemore 266 C2
Linslade 149 E5
Linstead Parva 165 E4
Linstock 210 A2
Linthwaite 185 F1
Lintlaw 237 F4
Lintmill 268 D4
Linton Cambs 151 D3
Linton Derbys 159 E1
Linton Here 145 F5
Linton Kent 123 G3
Linton N'Yorks 193 F1
Linton ScBord 228 B4
Linton W'Yorks 194 C3
Linton-on-Ouse 195 D1
Lintzford 212 A2
Linwood Hants 106 A2
Linwood Lincs 188 B4
Linwood Renf 233 F3
Lionel (Lional) 271 H1
Liphook 120 D4
Lipley 171 E4
Liscard 183 E3
Liscombe 114 B4
Liskeard 97 G3
L'Islet 101 F4
Lismore 240 A1
Liss 120 C5
Liss Forest 120 C5
Lissett 196 D2
Lissington 188 B4
Liston 151 G3
Lisvane 130 A4
Liswerry 130 C4
Litcham 163 G1
Litchborough 148 B2
Litchfield 119 F2
Litherland 183 E3
Litlington Cambs 150 B3
Litlington ESuss 110 A3
Little Abington 150 D3
Little Addington 161 E5
Little Alne 146 D1
Little Altcar 183 E2
Little Amwell 136 C1
Little Ann 119 E3
Little Asby 200 B2
Little Assynt 272 D6
Little Aston 158 C3
Little Atherfield 107 D5
Little Ayton 203 E1
Little Baddow 137 G2
Little Badminton 132 A4
Little Ballinluig 251 E4
Little Bampton 209 F1
Little Bardfield 151 E4
Little Barford 149 G2
Little Barningham 178 C2
Little Barrington 133 E1
Little Barrow 170 B1
Little Barugh 203 G5
Little Bavington 220 B4
Little Bedwyn 119 D1
Little Bealings 152 D3
Little Bentley 152 C5
Little Berkhamsted 136 B2
Little Billing 148 D1
Little Birch 145 E4
Little Bispham 191 G3
Little Blakenham 152 B3
Little Bloxwich 158 C2
Little Bollington 184 B4
Little Bookham 121 G2
Little Bourton 147 G3
Little Bowden 160 C4
Little Bradley 151 E2
Little Brampton 156 C4
Little Braxted 138 B1
Little Brechin 253 D3
Little Brickhill 149 E4
Little Bridgeford 171 F4
Little Brington 148 B1
Little Bromley 152 B5
Little Broughton 209 D3
Little Budworth 170 C1
Little Burdon 202 C1
Little Burstead 137 F3
Little Burton 196 D3
Little Bytham 161 F1
Little Canford 105 G3
Little Carlton Lincs 189 D4
Little Carlton Notts 174 C2
Little Casterton 161 F1
Little Catwick 196 D3
Little Catworth 161 F5
Little Cawthorpe 189 D4
Little Chalfield 117 F1
Little Chalfont 135 E3
Little Chart 124 B4
Little Chesterford 150 D3
Little Chesterton 148 A5
Little Cheverell 118 A2
Little Clacton 139 E1
Little Clanfield 133 E2
Little Clifton 209 D4
Little Comberton 146 B3
Little Common 110 C3
Little Compton 147 E4
Little Corby 210 A2
Little Cornard 151 G4
Little Cowarne 145 F2
Little Coxwell 133 E3
Little Crakehall 202 B3
Little Cransley 160 D5
Little Crawley 149 E3
Little Creaton 160 C5
Little Creich 266 D3

Little Cressingham **163** G3
Little Crosby **183** E2
Little Crosthwaite **209** F4
Little Cubley **172** B5
Little Dalby **160** C1
Little Dens **269** J6
Little Dewchurch **145** E4
Little Ditton **151** E2
Little Doward **131** E1
Little Down **119** E2
Little Downham **162** D4
Little Drayton **171** D4
Little Driffield **196** C2
Little Dunham **163** G1
Little Dunkeld **251** F5
Little Dunmow **151** E5
Little Durnford **118** C4
Little Easton **151** E5
Little Eaton **173** E3
Little Eccleston **192** A4
Little Ellingham **164** B2
Little End **137** E2
Little Everdon **148** A2
Little Eversden **150** B2
Little Faringdon **133** E2
Little Fencote **202** B3
Little Fenton **195** E4
Little Finborough **152** B2
Little Fransham **178** A4
Little Gaddesden **135** E1
Little Garway **144** D5
Little Gidding **161** G4
Little Glemham **153** E2
Little Glenshee **243** E1
Little Gorsley **145** F5
Little Gransden **150** A2
Little Green Cambs **150** A3
Little Green Notts **174** C3
Little Green Suff **164** B4
Little Green Suff **164** B4
Little Green Wrex **170** B3
Little Grimsby **188** D3
Little Gringley **187** E4
Little Gruinard **265** F3
Little Habton **203** E3
Little Hadham **150** C5
Little Hale **175** G3
Little Hallingbury **137** D1
Little Hampden **135** D2
Little Haresfield **132** A2
Little Harrowden **161** D5
Little Haseley **134** B2
Little Hatfield **197** D3
Little Hautbois **179** D3
Little Haven
  Pembs **126** B1
Little Haven *WSuss* **121** G4
Little Hay **158** D2
Little Hayfield **185** E4
Little Haywood **172** B5
Little Heath **159** F4
Little Hereford **145** E1
Little Hockham **164** A2
Little Horkesley **152** A4
Little Hormead **150** C5
Little Horsted **109** G2
Little Horton **118** B1
Little Horwood **148** C4
Little Houghton **148** D2
Little Hucklow **185** F5
Little Hulton **184** B4
Little Hungerford **134** A5
Little Hutton **203** E4
Little Irchester **149** E1
Little Keyford **117** E3
Little Kimble **134** D2
Little Kineton **147** F2
Little Kingshill **135** D3
Little Langdale **199** E2
Little Langford **118** B4
Little Laver **137** E2
Little Lawford **159** G5
Little Leigh **184** A5
Little Leighs **137** G1
Little Lever **184** B2
Little Ley **260** E3
Little Linford **148** D3
Little Linton **151** D3
Little London
  Bucks **134** B1
Little London
  Essex **150** C5
Little London
  ESuss **110** A2
Little London
  Hants **119** E3
Little London
  Hants **120** B2
Little London *IoM* **190** B3
Little London *Lincs* **176** C5
Little London *Lincs* **176** A5
Little London *Lincs* **188** D5
Little London *Lincs* **188** B4
Little London *Norf* **177** D5
Little London *Norf* **163** F3
Little London
  Powys **155** G4
Little London *Suff* **152** B2
Little London
  WYorks **194** B4
Little Longstone **185** F5
Little Lyth **157** D2
Little Malvern **145** G3
Little Maplestead **151** G4
Little Marcle **145** F4
Little Marland **113** F4
Little Marlow **135** D4
Little Marsden **193** E4
Little Massingham **177** F5
Little Melton **178** C5
Little Milford **126** C1
Little Mill **130** C2
Little Milton **134** B2
Little Missenden **135** E3
Little Musgrave **200** C1
Little Ness **156** D1
Little Neston **183** D5
Little Newcastle **140** C5
Little Newsham **202** A1
Little Oakley
  Essex **152** D5
Little Oakley
  N'hants **161** D4
Little Odell **149** E2
Little Offley **149** G5
Little Onn **158** A1
Little Orton *Cumb* **209** G1

Little Orton *Leics* **159** F2
Little Ouse **163** E4
Little Ouseburn **194** D1
Little Overton **170** A3
Little Packington **159** E4
Little Parndon **136** D1
Little Paxton **149** G1
Little Petherick **96** D2
Little Plumpton **192** A4
Little Plumstead **179** E4
Little Ponton **175** E4
Little Posbrook **107** E2
Little Potheridge **113** F4
Little Preston **148** A2
Little Raveley **162** A4
Little Ribston **194** C2
Little Rissington **133** D1
Little Rogart **266** E1
Little Rollright **147** E4
Little Ryburgh **178** A3
Little Ryle **229** E5
Little Ryton **157** D2
Little Salkeld **210** B4
Little Sampford **151** E4
Little Saxham **151** G1
Little Scatwell **265** K6
Little Shelford **150** C2
Little Shrawardine **156** C1
Little Silver **102** C2
Little Singleton **191** G4
Little Smeaton
  NYorks **186** C1
Little Smeaton
  NYorks **202** C2
Little Snoring **178** A2
Little Sodbury **131** G4
Little Sodbury End **131** G4
Little Somborne **119** E4
Little Somerford **132** B4
Little Soudley **171** E5
Little Stainforth **193** E1
Little Stainton **202** C1
Little Stanney **183** F5
Little Staughton **149** G1
Little Steeping **176** C1
Little Stoke **171** G4
Little Stonham **152** C2
Little Street **162** D4
Little Stretton
  Leics **160** B2
Little Stretton
  Shrop **156** D3
Little Strickland **199** G1
Little Stukeley **162** A5
Little Sugnall **171** F4
Little Sutton **183** E5
Little Swinburne **220** B4
Little Tarrington **145** F3
Little Tew **147** E5
Little Tey **151** G5
Little Thetford **162** D5
Little Thornage **178** B2
Little Thornton **191** G3
Little Thorpe **212** D3
Little Thurlow **151** E2
Little Thurlow
  Green **151** E2
Little Thurrock **137** F5
Little Torboll **266** E2
Little Torrington **113** E4
Little Tosson **220** C1
Little Totham **138** B1
Little Town *Cumb* **209** F5
Little Town *Lancs* **192** C4
Little Town *Warr* **184** A3
Little Twycross **159** F2
Little Urswick **199** D5
Little Wakering **138** C4
Little Walden **150** D3
Little Waldingfield **152** A3
Little Walsingham **178** A2
Little Waltham **137** G1
Little Warley **137** F3
Little Washbourne **146** B4
Little Weighton **196** B4
Little Welland **146** A4
Little Welnetham **151** G1
Little Wenham **152** B4
Little Wenlock **157** F2
Little Whittington **211** F1
Little Wilbraham **150** D2
Little Wishford **118** B4
Little Witcombe **132** B1
Little Witley **145** G1
Little Wittenham **134** A3
Little Wittingham
  Green **165** D4
Little Wolford **147** E4
Little Woodcote **122** B2
Little Wratting **151** E3
Little Wymington **149** E1
Little
  Wymondley **150** A5
Little Wyrley **158** C2
Little Wytheford **157** E1
Little Yeldham **151** F4
Littlebeck **204** B2
Littleborough
  Devon **102** B1
Littleborough
  GtMan **184** D1
Littleborough
  Notts **187** F4
Littlebourne **125** E3
Littlebredy **104** B3
Littlebury **150** D4
Littlebury Green **150** C4
Littledean **131** F1
Littleferry **267** F2
Littleham *Devon* **113** E3
Littleham *Devon* **102** D4
Littlehampton **108** C3
Littlehempston **101** E1
Littlehoughton **229** G5
Littlemill *EAyr* **224** C4
Littlemill *High* **267** G6
Littlemoor *Derbys* **173** E1
Littlemoor *Dorset* **104** C4
Littlemore **134** A2
Littlemoss **184** D3
Littleover **173** E4
Littleport **163** D4
Littlestead Green **134** C5
Littlestone-on-Sea **111** F4
Littlethorpe **194** C1
Littleton *ChesW&C* **170** B1
Littleton *Hants* **119** F4
Littleton *P&K* **244** A1
Littleton *Som* **116** B4

Littleton *Surr* **121** F1
Littleton Drew **132** A4
Littleton-Panell **118** B2
Littleton-on-Severn **131** E3
Littletown *Dur* **212** C3
Littletown *IoW* **107** E3
Littlewick Green **134** D5
Littlewindsor **104** A2
Littleworth *Glos* **146** D4
Littleworth *Oxon* **133** F3
Littleworth *Staffs* **158** C1
Littleworth *SYorks* **186** D3
Littleworth *Worcs* **146** A3
Littley Green **137** F1
Litton *Derbys* **185** F5
Litton *NYorks* **201** E5
Litton *Som* **116** C2
Litton Cheney **104** B3
Liverpool **183** E3
Liverpool Cathedral
  Mersey L1 7AZ **42** E6
Liverpool John Lennon
  Airport **183** F4
Liverpool Metropolitan
  Cathedral (RC) *Mersey*
  L3 5TQ **43** E4
Liversedge **194** B5
Liverton *Devon* **102** B5
Liverton *R&C* **203** G1
Liverton Street **124** A4
Living Coasts, Torquay
  Torbay TQ1 2BG **101** F1
Livingston **235** E3
Livingston Village **235** E3
Lixwm **182** C5
Lizard **95** E5
Llaingarreglwyd **142** A2
Llaingoch **180** A4
Llaithddu **155** G4
Llampha **129** F5
Llan **155** E2
Llanaber **154** C1
Llanaelhaearn **166** C3
Llanaeron **142** A1
Llanafan **154** C5
Llanafan-fawr **143** F2
Llanafan-fechan **143** F2
Llanallgo **180** C4
Llanarmon **166** D4
Llanarmon Dyffryn
  Ceiriog **169** E4
Llanarmon-yn-lal **169** E2
Llanarth *Cere* **142** A2
Llanarth *Mon* **130** C1
Llanarthney **142** B5
Llanasa **182** C4
Llanbabo **180** B4
Llanbadarn Fawr **154** B4
Llanbadarn Fynydd **155** G5
Llanbadarn-y-
  garreg **144** A3
Llanbadoc **130** C2
Llanbadrig **180** B3
Llanbeder **130** C3
Llanbedr *Gwyn* **167** E5
Llanbedr *Powys* **144** B5
Llanbedr *Powys* **144** A3
Llanbedr-Dyffryn-
  Clwyd **169** E2
Llanbedrgoch **180** D4
Llanbedrog **166** C4
Llanbedr-y-cennin **168** A1
Llanberis **167** E2
Llanbethery **114** D1
Llanbister **156** A5
Llanblethian **129** F5
Llanboidy **141** F5
Llanbradach **130** A3
Llanbryn-mair **155** E2
Llancadle **114** D1
Llancarfan **129** G5
Llancayo **130** C2
Llancynfelyn **154** C3
Llandafal **130** A1
Llandaff **130** A5
Llandaff North **130** A5
Llandanwg **167** E5
Llandawke **127** F1
Llanddaniel Fab **180** C5
Llanddarog **128** A1
Llanddeiniol **154** B5
Llanddeiniolen **167** E1
Llandderfel **168** C4
Llanddeusant
  Carmar **143** D5
Llanddeusant *IoA* **180** B4
Llanddew **143** G4
Llanddewi **128** A4
Llanddewi
  Rhydderch **130** C1
Llanddewi
  Skirrid **130** C1
Llanddewi Velfrey **127** E1
Llanddewi
  Ystradenni **144** A1
Llanddewi-Brefi **142** C2
Llanddewi'r Cwm **143** G3
Llanddoged **168** B1
Llanddona **181** D5
Llanddowror **127** F1
Llanddulas **182** A5
Llanddwywe **167** E5
Llanddyfnan **180** C5
Llandefaelog Fach **143** G4
Llandefaelog-
  tre'r-graig **144** A5
Llandefalle **144** A4
Llandegfan **181** D5
Llandegfedd Reservoir
  Mon NP4 0TA **130** C3
Llandegla **169** E2
Llandegley **144** A1
Llandegveth **130** C3
Llandegwning **166** B4
Llandeilo **142** C5
Llandeilo
  Abercywyn **127** G1
Llandeilo Graban **143** G3
Llandeilo'r-Fan **143** E4
Llandeloy **140** B5
Llandenny **130** D2
Llandevaud **130** D3
Llandevenny **130** D4
Llandinabo **145** E5
Llandinam **155** G4
Llandissilio **141** E5
Llandogo *VGlam* **130** A5

Llandough *VGlam* **129** F5
Llandovery
  (Llanymddyfri) **143** D4
Llandow **129** F5
Llandre *Carmar* **142** C3
Llandre *Carmar* **141** E5
Llandre *Cere* **154** C4
Llandrillo **168** D4
Llandrindod Wells **143** G1
Llandrinio **156** B1
Llandudno **181** F4
Llandudno Junction **181** F5
Llandwrog **167** D2
Llandybie **128** A1
Llandyfaelog **128** A1
Llandyfan **128** C1
Llandyfriog **141** G3
Llandyfrydog **180** C4
Llandygwydd **141** F3
Llandynan **169** E1
Llandyrnog **169** E1
Llandysilio **156** B1
Llandyssil **156** A3
Llandysul **142** A3
Llanedeyrn **130** B4
Llanedy **128** B2
Llaneglwys **143** G4
Llanegryn **154** C2
Llanegwad **142** B5
Llaneilian **180** C3
Llanelian-yn-Rhos **181** G5
Llanelidan **169** E2
Llanelieu **144** A4
Llanellen **144** A5
Llanelli **128** B2
Llanelli Millennium Coastal
  Park *Carmar*
  SA15 2LF **128** A3
Llanelltyd **154** D1
Llanelly **128** B1
Llanelly Hill **130** B1
Llanelwedd **143** G2
Llanenddwyn **167** E5
Llanengan **166** B5
Llanerfyl **155** G2
Llaneuddog **180** C4
Llanfachraeth **180** B4
Llanfachreth **168** A5
Llanfaelog **180** B5
Llanfaelrhys **166** B5
Llanfaenor **130** C1
Llan-faes *IoA* **181** E5
Llanfaes *Powys* **143** G5
Llanfaethlu **180** B4
Llanfaglan **167** D1
Llanfair **167** E5
Llanfair Caereinion **156** A2
Llanfair Clydogau **142** C2
Llanfair Dyffryn
  Clwyd **169** E2
Llanfair Talhaiarn **182** A5
Llanfair Waterdine **156** B5
Llanfairfechan **181** E5
Llanfair-Nant-Gwyn **141** E4
Llanfair-Orllwyn **141** G3
Llanfairpwllgwyngyll
  180 D5
Llanfairynghornwy **180** B3
Llanfair-yn-neubwll **180** B5
Llanfallteg **127** E1
Llanfaredd **143** G2
Llanfarian **154** B5
Llanfechain **156** A1
Llanfechell **180** C3
Llanfendigaid **154** B2
Llanferres **169** E5
Llanfflewyn **180** B4
Llanfigael **180** B4
Llanfihangel Glyn
  Myfyr **168** C3
Llanfihangel Nant
  Bran **143** F4
Llanfihangel
  Rhydithon **144** A1
Llanfihangel Rogiet **130** D4
Llanfihangel
  Tal-y-llyn **144** A5
Llanfihangel-
  ar-arth **142** A3
Llanfihangel-nant-
  Melan **144** A1
Llanfihangel-uwch-
  Gwili **142** A5
Llanfihangel-y-
  Creuddyn **154** C5
Llanfihangel-yng-
  Ngwynfa **155** G1
Llanfihangel-yn-
  Nhywyn **180** B5
Llanfihangel-y-pennant
  Gwyn **167** E3
Llanfihangel-y-pennant
  Gwyn **154** C2
Llanfilo **144** A4
Llanfoist **130** B1
Llanfor **168** C4
Llanfrechfa **130** C3
Llanfrothen **167** F3
Llanfrynach **143** G5
Llanfwrog *Denb* **169** E2
Llanfwrog *IoA* **180** B4
Llanfyllin **156** A1
Llanfynydd *Carmar* **142** B5
Llanfynydd *Flints* **169** F2
Llanfyrnach **141** F4
Llangadfan **155** G1
Llangadog **142** D5
Llangadwaladr *IoA* **166** C1
Llangadwaladr
  Powys **169** E4
Llangaffo **166** D1
Llangain **127** G1
Llangammarch
  Wells **143** F3
Llangan **129** F5
Llangarron **145** E5
Llangasty-Talyllyn **144** A5
Llangathen **142** B5
Llangattock **130** B1
Llangattock
  Lingoed **130** C1
Llangattock-Vibon-
  Avel **131** D1
Llangedwyn **169** E5
Llangefni **180** C5
Llangeinor **129** F4
Llangeitho **142** C2

Llangeler **141** G4
Llangelynin **154** B2
Llangendeirne **128** A1
Llangennech **128** B2
Llangennith **128** A3
Llangenny **130** B1
Llangernyw **168** B1
Llangian **166** B5
Llangiwg **128** D2
Llangloffan **140** C4
Llanglydwen **141** E5
Llangoed **181** E5
Llangoedmor **141** E3
Llangollen **169** F3
Llangollen Railway *Denb*
  LL20 8SN **169** F3
Llangolman **141** E5
Llangorse **144** A5
Llangorwen **154** A5
Llangovan **131** D2
Llangower **168** C4
Llangranog **141** G2
Llangristiolus **180** C5
Llangrove **131** E1
Llangua **144** C5
Llangunllo **156** B5
Llangunnor **142** A5
Llangurig **155** F5
Llangwm *Conwy* **168** C3
Llangwm *Mon* **130** D2
Llangwm *Pembs* **126** C2
Llangwnnadl **166** B4
Llangwyfan **169** E1
Llangwyllog **180** C5
Llangwyryfon **154** C5
Llangybi *Cere* **142** C2
Llangybi *Gwyn* **166** D3
Llangybi *Mon* **130** C3
Llangyfelach **128** C3
Llangynhafal **169** E1
Llangynidr **130** A1
Llangyniew **156** A2
Llangynin **127** F1
Llangynllo **141** G3
Llangynog *Carmar* **127** G1
Llangynog *Powys* **169** D5
Llangynwyd **129** E4
Llanhamlach **143** G5
Llanharan **129** F4
Llanharry **129** G4
Llanhennock **130** C3
Llanhilleth **130** B2
Llanidloes **155** F4
Llaniestyn **166** B4
Llanigon **144** B4
Llanilar **154** C5
Llanilid **129** F4
Llanishen *Cardiff* **130** A4
Llanishen *Mon* **131** D2
Llanllawddog **142** A4
Llanllechid **167** F1
Llanlleonfel **143** F2
Llanllugan **155** G2
Llanllwch **127** G1
Llanllwchaiarn **156** A3
Llanllwni **142** A3
Llanllyfni **167** D2
Llanllywel **130** C2
Llanmadoc **128** A3
Llanmaes **114** C1
Llanmartin **130** C4
Llanmerewig **156** A3
Llanmihangel **129** F5
Llan-mill **127** E1
Llanmiloe **127** F2
Llanmorlais **128** B3
Llannefydd **182** A5
Llannerch Hall **182** B5
Llannerch-y-medd **180** C4
Llannerch-y-Môr **182** C5
Llannon *Carmar* **128** B2
Llan-non *Cere* **142** B1
Llannor **166** C4
Llanover **130** C2
Llanpumsaint **142** A5
Llanreithan **140** B5
Llanrhaeadr **169** D1
Llanrhaeadr-ym-
  Mochnant **169** E5
Llanrhian **140** B4
Llanrhidian **128** A3
Llanrhyddlad **180** B4
Llanrhystud **142** B1
Llanrothal **131** D1
Llanrug **167** E1
Llanrumney **130** B4
Llanrwst **168** A1
Llansadurnen **127** F1
Llansadwrn *Carmar* **142** C4
Llansadwrn *IoA* **181** D5
Llansaint **127** G2
Llansamlet **128** C3
Llansanffraid **142** B1
Llansanffraid Glan
  Conwy **181** G5
Llansannan **168** C1
Llansannor **129** F5
Llansantffraed **144** A5
Llansantffraed-
  Cwmdeuddwr **143** F1
Llansantffraed-in-
  Elwel **143** G2
Llansantffraid-ym-
  Mechain **155** F5
Llansawel **142** C4
Llansilin **169** E5
Llansoy **130** D2
Llanspyddid **143** G5
Llanstadwell **126** C2
Llansteffan **127** G1
Llanstephan **144** A3
Llantarnam **130** C3
Llanteg **127** E1
Llanthony **144** B5
Llantilio Crossenny **130** C1
Llantilio Pertholey **130** C1
Llantood **141** E3
Llantrisant *IoA* **180** B4
Llantrisant *Mon* **130** C3
Llantrisant *RCT* **129** G4
Llantrithyd **129** G5
Llantwit Fardre **129** G4
Llantwit Major **114** C1
Llantysilio **169** E3
Llanuwchllyn **168** B5
Llanvaches **130** D3
Llanvair-Discoed **130** D3
Llanvapley **130** C1

Llanvetherine **130** C1
Llanveynoe **144** C4
Llanvihangel Crucorney
  (Llanfihangel Crucornau)
  144 C5
Llanvihangel
  Gobion **130** C2
Llanvihangel-Ystern-
  Llewern **130** C1
Llanvithyn **129** G5
Llanwarne **145** E5
Llanwddyn **155** G1
Llanwenog **142** A3
Llanwern **130** C4
Llanwinio **141** F5
Llanwnda *Gwyn* **167** D2
Llanwnda *Pembs* **140** C4
Llanwnnen **142** B3
Llanwnog **155** G3
Llanwonno **129** G3
Llanwrda **142** D4
Llanwrin **155** D2
Llanwrthwl **143** F1
Llanwrtyd **143** E3
Llanwrtyd Wells **143** E3
Llanwyddelan **155** G2
Llanyblodwel **169** F5
Llanybri **127** G1
Llanybydder **142** B3
Llanycefn **141** E5
Llanychaer
  Bridge **140** C4
Llanycil **168** C4
Llanycrwys **142** C3
Llanymawddwy **155** E1
Llanymynech **169** F5
Llanynghenedl **180** B4
Llanynys **169** E1
Llan-y-pwll **170** A2
Llanyre **143** G1
Llanystumdwy **167** D4
Llanywern **144** A5
Llawhaden **127** D1
Llawndy **182** C4
Llawnt **169** F4
Llawr-y-dref **166** B5
Llawryglyn **155** F3
Llay **170** A2
Llechcynfarwy **180** B4
Llecheiddior **167** D3
Llechfaen **143** G5
Llechryd *Caerp* **130** A2
Llechryd *Cere* **141** F3
Llechrydau **169** F4
Llechwedd Slate Caverns
  Gwyn LL41 3NB **168** A3
Lledrod *Cere* **154** C5
Lledrod *Powys* **169** F5
Llethryd **128** B3
Llidiad-Nenog **142** B4
Llidiardau **168** B4
Llithfaen **166** C3
Lloc **182** C5
Llong **169** F1
Llowes **144** A3
Lloyney **156** B5
Llundain-fach **142** B2
Llwydcoed **129** F2
Llwydiarth **155** G1
Llwyn **156** B4
Llwyncelyn **142** A2
Llwyn-croes **142** A5
Llwyndafydd **141** G2
Llwynderw **156** B2
Llwyndyrys **166** C3
Llwyneinion **169** F3
Llwyngwril **154** B2
Llwynhendy **128** B3
Llwyn-Madoc **143** F2
Llwynmawr **169** F4
Llwyn-onn *Cere* **142** A2
Llwyn-onn *MTyd* **129** G1
Llwyn-y-brain
  Carmar **127** E1
Llwyn-y-brain
  Carmar **142** D4
Llwyn-y-groes **142** B2
Llwynypia **129** F3
Llyn Brenig *Conwy*
  LL21 9TT **168** C2
Llyn Llech Owain Country
  Park *Carmar*
  SA14 7NF **128** B1
Llynclys **169** F5
Llynfaes **180** C5
Llysfaen **181** G5
Llyswen **144** A4
Llysworney **129** F5
Llys-y-frân **140** D5
Llywel **143** E4
Load Brook **185** G4
Loandhu **267** F4
Loanhead *Aber* **261** H1
Loanhead *Midlo* **235** G3
Loans **224** B2
Lobb **113** E2
Loch a Charnain **262** D7
Loch an Eilein Visitor Centre
  & Forest Trail *High*
  PH22 1QT **259** F4
Loch Choire Lodge **273** J5
Loch Eil Outward
  Bound **248** C2
Loch Head *D&G* **206** D2
Loch Head *D&G* **215** F1
Loch Lomond Shores &
  Gateway Centre *WDun*
  G83 8QL **233** E1
Loch Ness Exhibition Centre
  High IV63 6TU **258** C2
Loch of the Lowes *P&K*
  PH8 0HH **251** F5
Loch Sgioport **254** D1
Lochailort (Ceann Loch
  Ailleart) **247** G1
Lochaline
  (Loch Àlainn) **247** F5
Lochans **215** B4
Locharbriggs **217** D2
Lochawe
  (Loch Obha) **240** D2
Lochboisdale (Loch
  Baghasdail) **254** C3
Lochbuie **239** F2
Lochcarron
  (Loch Carrann) **264** E7
Lochdhu Hotel **275** F4

Lochdon **239** G1
Lochdrum **265** J4
Lochearnhead (Ceann Loch
  Èireann) **242** C4
Lochee **244** B1
Lochend *High* **275** H2
Lochend (Ceann Loch)
  High **258** C4
Locheport
  (Locheuphort) **262** D5
Lochfoot **216** D3
Lochgair **240** B5
Lochgarthside **258** C3
Lochgelly **243** G5
Lochgilphead (Ceann Loch
  Gilb) **231** G1
Lochgoilhead **241** E4
Lochgoyn **233** G5
Lochhill *EAyr* **225** F4
Lochhill *Moray* **267** K5
Lochinch Castle **214** C4
Lochinver
  (Loch an Inbhir) **272** C6
Lochlair **252** D5
Lochlane **242** D2
Lochlea **224** C2
Lochluichart **265** K5
Lochmaben **217** E2
Lochmaddy (Loch na
  Madadh) **262** E5
Lochore **243** G5
Lochore Meadows Country
  Park *Fife*
  KY5 8BA **243** G5
Lochportain **262** E4
Lochranza **232** A4
Lochside *Aber* **253** F3
Lochside *High* **273** G3
Lochside *High* **274** D5
Lochside *High* **275** H2
Lochslin **267** F3
Lochton **215** D2
Lochty **244** D4
Lochuisge **247** G4
Lochurr **216** B2
Lochussie **266** B6
Lochwinnoch **233** E4
Lockengate **97** E3
Lockerbie **217** F4
Lockeridge **118** C1
Lockerley **119** D5
Lockhills **210** B3
Locking **116** A2
Lockington *ERid* **196** B3
Lockington *Leics* **173** F5
Lockleywood **171** D5
Locks Heath **107** E2
Locksbottom **122** D2
Locksgreen **106** D3
Lockton **204** B4
Locomotion: The National
  Railway Museum at
  Shildon *Dur*
  DL4 1PQ **212** B5
Loddington *Leics* **160** C2
Loddington
  N'hants **160** D5
Loddiswell **100** D3
Loddon **165** E2
Lode **150** D1
Loders **104** A3
Lodsworth **121** E5
Lofthouse *NYorks* **202** A5
Lofthouse *WYorks* **194** C5
Loftus **203** E1
Logan *D&G* **206** A2
Logan *EAyr* **225** D3
Loganlea **235** D3
Loggerheads Country Park
  Denb CH7 5LH **169** E1
Loggie (An Lagaidh) **265** H2
Logie *Angus* **253** E3
Logie *Angus* **252** B4
Logie *Fife* **244** C2
Logie *Moray* **267** H6
Logie Coldstone **260** C4
Logie Hill **266** E4
Logie Newton **260** E1
Logie Pert **253** E3
Logierait **251** E4
Login **141** E5
Lolworth **150** B1
Lonbain **264** C5
Londesborough **196** A3
London **136** C4
London Apprentice **97** E5
London Ashford
  Airport **111** F1
London Beach **124** A5
London Biggin Hill
  Airport **122** D2
London City
  Airport **136** D4
London Colney **136** A2
London Eye *GtLon*
  SE1 7PB **45** F5
London Gatwick
  Airport **122** B4
London Heathrow
  Airport **135** F4
London Luton
  Airport **149** G5
London Minstead **106** B1
London Oxford
  Airport **133** G1
London Southend
  Airport **138** B4
London Stansted
  Airport **150** D5
London Transport Museum
  GtLon WC2E 7BB **45** E3
Londonderry **202** B4
Londonthorpe **175** E4
Londubh **264** E3
Lonemore **266** E3
Long Ashton **131** E5
Long Bank **157** G5
Long Bennington **174** D3
Long Bredy **104** B3
Long Buckby **148** B1
Long Clawson **174** C5
Long Compton
  Staffs **171** F5
Long Compton
  Warks **147** E4
Long Crendon **134** B2
Long Crichel **105** F1

Long Dean 132 A5
Long Downs 95 E3
Long Drax 195 F5
Long Duckmanton 186 B5
Long Eaton 173 F4
Long Gill 193 D2
Long Green
ChesW&C 183 F5
Long Green Essex 152 A5
Long Hanborough 133 G1
Long Itchington 147 G1
Long Lane 157 F1
Long Lawford 159 G5
Long Load 116 B5
Long Marston Herts 135 D1
Long Marston
NYorks 195 E2
Long Marston
Warks 147 E3
Long Marton 210 C5
Long Meadowend 156 D4
Long Melford 151 G3
Long Newnton 132 B3
Long Preston 193 E3
Long Riston 196 D3
Long Stratton 164 C2
Long Street 148 C3
Long Sutton Hants 120 C3
Long Sutton Lincs 176 C5
Long Sutton Som 116 B5
Long Thurlow 152 B1
Long Whatton 173 F5
Long Wittenham 134 A3
Longbenton 212 B1
Longborough 147 D5
Longbridge Plym 100 B2
Longbridge Warks 147 E1
Longbridge WMid 158 C5
Longbridge Deverill 117 F3
Longburgh 209 G1
Longburton 104 C1
Longcliffe 172 D2
Longcombe 101 E2
Longcot 133 E3
Longcroft 234 B2
Longcross Devon 99 E3
Longcross Surr 121 E1
Longden 156 D2
Longdon Staffs 158 C1
Longdon Worcs 146 A4
Longdon Green 158 C1
Longdon upon Tern 157 F1
Longdown 102 B3
Longdrum 261 H3
Longfield 123 F2
Longfield Hill 123 F2
Longfleet 105 E3
Longford Derbys 172 D4
Longford Glos 146 A5
Longford GtLon 135 F5
Longford Shrop 170 D4
Longford Tel&W 157 G1
Longford WMid 159 F4
Longforgan 244 B2
Longformacus 237 D4
Longframlington 220 D1
Longham Dorset 105 G3
Longham Norf 178 A4
Longhill 269 H5
Longhirst 221 E1
Longhope Glos 131 F1
Longhope Ork 277 C8
Longhorsley 220 D2
Longhoughton 229 G5
Longlands Aber 260 C2
Longlands Cumb 209 F3
Longlands GtLon 136 D5
Longlane Derbys 173 D4
Longlane WBerks 133 G5
Longleat House Wilts
BA12 7NW 117 F3
Longleat Safari Park Wilts
BA12 7NW 117 F3
Longlevens 132 A1
Longley 185 F2
Longley Green 145 G2
Longmanhill 269 F4
Longmoor Camp 120 C4
Longmorn 267 K6
Longnewton ScBord 227 G3
Longnewton Stock 202 C1
Longney 131 G1
Longniddry 236 B2
Longniddry Bents ELoth
EH32 0PX 236 B2
Longnor Shrop 157 D2
Longnor Staffs 172 B1
Longparish 119 F3
Longridge Lancs 192 A5
Longridge Staffs 158 B1
Longridge WLoth 235 D3
Longridge End 146 A5
Longridge Towers 237 G4
Longriggend 234 C2
Longrock 94 C3
Longsdon 171 G2
Longshaw 269 J6
Longside 269 J6
Longslow 171 D4
Longsowerby 209 G1
Longstanton 150 C1
Longstock 119 E4
Longstone 94 C3
Longstowe 150 B2
Longstreet 118 C2
Longthorpe 161 G3
Longton Lancs 192 A5
Longton Stoke 170 S
Longtown Cumb 218 B5
Longtown Here 144 C5
Longville in the
Dale 157 E3
Longwell Green 131 F5
Longwick 134 C2
Longwitton 220 C3
Longworth 133 F3
Longyester 236 C3
Lonmay 269 J5
Lonmore 263 H7
Looe 97 G4
Look Out Discovery Park,
Bracknell BrackF
RG12 7QW 121 D1
Loose 123 G3
Loosebeare 102 A2
Loosegate 176 B5
Loosley Row 134 C2

Lopcombe Corner 119 D4
Lopen 104 A1
Loppington 170 B5
Lorbottle 220 C1
Lorbottle Hall 220 C1
Lordington 107 G2
Lord's Cricket Ground &
Museum GtLon
NW8 8QN 10 F4
Lord's Hill 106 C1
Lorgill 263 G7
Lorn 233 E1
Lornty 251 G5
Loscoe 173 F3
Loscombe 104 A3
Losgaintir 263 F2
Lossiemouth 267 K4
Lossit 230 A4
Lost Gardens of Heligan
Corn PL26 6EN 97 D5
Lostock Gralam 184 A5
Lostock Green 184 A5
Lostock
Junction 184 A2
Lostwithiel 97 F4
Loth 276 E7
Lothbeg 274 E7
Lothersdale 193 F3
Lotherton Hall Estate
WYorks
LS25 3EB 195 D4
Lothmore 274 E7
Loudwater 135 E3
Loughborough 160 A1
Loughor 128 B3
Loughton Essex 136 D3
Loughton MK 148 D4
Loughton Shrop 157 F4
Louis Tussaud's Waxworks
FY1 5AA 64 Blackpool
Lound Lincs 161 F1
Lound Notts 187 D4
Lound Suff 165 G2
Lount 159 F1
Louth 188 D4
Love Clough 193 E5
Lovedean 107 F1
Lover 106 B1
Loversall 186 C3
Loves Green 137 F2
Lovesome Hill 202 C3
Loveston 127 D2
Lovington 116 C4
Low Ackworth 186 B1
Low Angerton 220 C3
Low Ballevain 222 B3
Low Barlay 215 G5
Low Barlings 188 C5
Low Bentham (Lower
Bentham) 192 C1
Low Bolton 201 F3
Low Bradfield 185 G3
Low Bradley
(Bradley) 193 G3
Low Braithwaite 210 A3
Low Brunton 220 B4
Low Burnham 187 E2
Low Burton 202 B4
Low Buston 221 E1
Low Catton 195 G2
Low Coniscliffe 202 B1
Low Craighead 224 A5
Low Dinsdale 202 C1
Low Ellington 202 B4
Low Entercommon 202 C2
Low Etherley 212 A5
Low Fell 212 B2
Low Gate 211 F1
Low Grantley 202 B5
Low Green 151 G1
Low Habberley 158 A5
Low Ham 116 B5
Low Hawsker 204 C2
Low Haygarth 200 B3
Low Hesket 210 A3
Low Hesleyhurst 220 C2
Low Hutton 195 G1
Low Kingthorpe 204 B4
Low Laithe 194 A1
Low Langton 188 B5
Low Leighton 185 E4
Low Lorton 209 E4
Low Marishes 204 B5
Low Middleton 229 F3
Low Mill 203 F3
Low Moor Lancs 192 D3
Low Moor WYorks 194 A5
Low Moorsley 212 C3
Low Moresby 208 C4
Low Newton-by-
the-Sea 229 G4
Low Row Cumb 210 B1
Low Row NYorks 201 E3
Low Stillaig 232 A3
Low Street 178 B5
Low Tharston 164 C2
Low Torry 235 E2
Low Town 220 D1
Low Toynton 188 C5
Low Wood 199 E4
Low Worsall 202 C2
Lowbands 145 G4
Lowdham 174 B3
Lowe 170 C4
Lowe Hill 171 G2
Lower Achachenna 240 C2
Lower Aisholt 115 F4
Lower Apperley 146 A5
Lower Arncott 134 B1
Lower Ashtead 121 G2
Lower Ashton 102 B4
Lower Assendon 134 C4
Lower Auchalick 232 A2
Lower Ballam 191 G4
Lower Barewood 144 C2
Lower Bartle 192 A4
Lower Bayble
(Pabail Iarach) 271 H4
Lower Beeding 109 E1
Lower Benefield 161 E4
Lower Bentham (Low
Bentham) 192 C1
Lower Bentley 146 B1
Lower Berry Hill 131 E1
Lower Birchwood 173 F2
Lower Boddington 147 G2

Lower Boscaswell 94 A3
Lower Bourne 120 D3
Lower Brailes 147 F4
Lower Breakish 256 C2
Lower Bredbury 184 D3
Lower Broadheath 146 A2
Lower Brynamman 128 D1
Lower Bullingham 145 E4
Lower Bullington 119 F3
Lower Burgate 106 A1
Lower Burrow 116 B5
Lower Burton 144 D2
Lower Caldecote 149 G3
Lower Cam 131 G2
Lower Cambourne 150 B2
Lower Camster 275 H4
Lower Chapel 143 G4
Lower Cheriton 103 E2
Lower Chicksgrove 118 A4
Lower Chute 119 E2
Lower Clent 158 B4
Lower Creedy 102 B2
Lower
Cumberworth 185 G2
Lower Darwen 192 C5
Lower Dean 149 F1
Lower Diabaig 264 D5
Lower Dicker 110 A2
Lower Dinchope 157 D4
Lower Down 156 C4
Lower Drift 94 B4
Lower Dunsforth 194 D1
Lower Earley 134 C5
Lower Edmonton 136 C3
Lower Elkstone 172 B2
Lower End Bucks 134 B2
Lower End MK 149 E4
Lower End N'hants 149 D1
Lower Everleigh 118 C2
Lower Eythorne 125 E4
Lower Failand 131 E5
Lower Farringdon 120 C4
Lower Fittleworth 108 C2
Lower Foxdale 190 A4
Lower Freystrop 126 C1
Lower Froyle 120 C3
Lower Gabwell 101 F1
Lower Gledfield 266 C2
Lower Godney 116 B3
Lower Gravenhurst 149 G4
Lower Green Essex 150 C4
Lower Green Herts 149 G4
Lower Green Kent 123 F4
Lower Green Norf 178 A2
Lower Green Staffs 158 B2
Lower Green Bank 192 B2
Lower Halstock
Leigh 104 B2
Lower Halstow 124 A2
Lower Hardres 124 D3
Lower Harpton 144 B1
Lower Hartshay 173 E2
Lower Hartwell 134 C1
Lower Hawthwaite 198 D4
Lower Haysden 123 E4
Lower Hayton 157 E4
Lower Heath 171 F1
Lower Hergest 144 B2
Lower Heyford 147 G5
Lower Higham 137 G5
Lower Holbrook 152 C4
Lower Hopton 185 G1
Lower Hordley 170 A5
Lower Horncroft 108 C2
Lower Horsebridge 110 A2
Lower Houses 185 F1
Lower Howsell 145 G3
Lower Kersal 184 C2
Lower Kilchattan 238 C5
Lower Kilcott 131 G4
Lower Killeyan 230 A5
Lower Kingcombe 104 B3
Lower Kingswood 122 B3
Lower Kinnerton 170 A1
Lower Langford 116 B1
Lower Largo 244 C4
Lower Leigh 172 B4
Lower Lemington 147 E4
Lower Lovacott 113 F3
Lower Loxhore 113 G2
Lower Lydbrook 131 E1
Lower Lye 144 D1
Lower Machen 130 B4
Lower Maes-coed 144 C4
Lower Mannington 105 G2
Lower Middleton
Cheney 148 A3
Lower Milton 116 C3
Lower Moor 146 B3
Lower Morton 131 F3
Lower Nash 126 D2
Lower Nazeing 136 C2
Lower Netchwood 157 F3
Lower Nyland 117 E5
Lower Oddington 147 E5
Lower Ollach 256 B1
Lower Penarth 130 A5
Lower Penn 158 A3
Lower Pennington 106 C3
Lower Peover 184 B5
Lower Pollicott 134 C1
Lower Quinton 147 D3
Lower Race 130 B2
Lower Rainham 124 A2
Lower Roadwater 114 D4
Lower Sapey 145 F1
Lower Seagry 132 B4
Lower Shelton 149 E3
Lower Shiplake 134 C5
Lower Shuckburgh 147 G1
Lower Slaughter 147 D5
Lower Soothill 194 B5
Lower Stanton
St. Quintin 132 B4
Lower Stoke 124 A1
Lower Stondon 149 G4
Lower Stone 131 F3
Lower Stonnall 158 C2
Lower Stow Bedon 164 A2
Lower Street Dorset 105 E3
Lower Street ESuss 110 C2
Lower Street Norf 179 D2
Lower Street Norf 178 D2
Lower Street Suff 152 C2
Lower Stretton 184 A4
Lower Sundon 149 F5
Lower Swanwick 107 D2
Lower Swell 147 D5

Lower Tadmarton 147 G4
Lower Tale 103 D2
Lower Tean 172 B4
Lower Thurlton 165 F2
Lower Thurnham 192 A2
Lower Town Corn 95 D4
Lower Town Devon 102 A5
Lower Town IoS 96 B1
Lower Town Pembs 140 C4
Lower Trebullett 98 D3
Lower Tysoe 147 F3
Lower Upcott 102 B4
Lower Upham 107 E1
Lower Upnor 137 G5
Lower Vexford 115 E4
Lower Wallop 156 C2
Lower Walton 184 A4
Lower Waterhay 132 C3
Lower Weald 148 C4
Lower Wear 102 C4
Lower Weare 116 B2
Lower Welson 144 B2
Lower Whatley 117 E3
Lower Whitley 184 A5
Lower Wick 146 A2
Lower Wield 120 B3
Lower Winchendon (Nether
Winchendon) 134 C1
Lower Withington 171 F1
Lower Woodend 134 C4
Lower Woodford 118 C4
Lower Wyche 145 G3
Lowertown 277 D8
Lowesby 160 C2
Lowestoft 165 G2
Loweswater 193 E4
Lowfield Heath 122 B4
Lowgill Cumb 200 B3
Lowgill Lancs 192 C1
Lowick Cumb 199 D4
Lowick N'hants 161 E4
Lowick N'umb 229 E3
Lowick Bridge 199 D4
Lowick Green 199 D4
Lownie Moor 252 C5
Lowsonford 147 D1
Lowther 210 B5
Lowther Castle 210 B5
Lowthorpe 196 C1
Lowton Devon 113 G5
Lowton GtMan 184 A3
Lowton Som 103 E1
Lowton Common 184 A3
Loxbeare 102 C1
Loxhill 121 F4
Loxhore 113 G2
Loxley 147 E2
Loxley Green 172 B4
Loxton 116 A2
Loxwood 121 F4
Lubachoinnich 266 B2
Lubcroy 265 K1
Lubenham 160 C4
Lubfearn 265 K4
Lubmore 265 G6
Lubreoch 249 G5
Luccombe 114 C3
Luccombe Village 107 E4
Lucker 229 F3
Luckett 99 D3
Luckington 132 A4
Lucklawhill 244 C2
Luckwell Bridge 114 C4
Lucton 144 D1
Lucy Cross 202 B1
Ludag 254 C3
Ludborough 188 C3
Ludbrook 100 C2
Ludchurch 127 E1
Luddenden 193 G5
Luddenden Foot 193 G5
Luddenham Court 124 B2
Luddesdown 123 F2
Luddington NLincs 187 F1
Luddington Warks 147 D2
Luddington in the
Brook 161 G4
Ludford Lincs 188 B4
Ludford Shrop 157 E5
Ludgershall Bucks 134 B1
Ludgershall Wilts 119 D2
Ludgvan 94 C3
Ludham 179 E4
Ludlow 157 E5
Ludney 189 D3
Ludstock 145 F4
Ludstone 158 A3
Ludwell 118 A5
Ludworth 212 C3
Luffincott 98 D1
Luffness 236 B1
Lufton 104 B1
Lugar 225 D3
Luggate 236 C2
Luggate Burn 236 D2
Luggiebank 234 B2
Lugton 233 F4
Lugwardine 145 E3
Luib 256 C2
Luibeilt 249 E3
Luing 239 G3
Lulham 144 D3
Lullington Derbys 159 E1
Lullington Som 117 E2
Lulsgate Bottom 116 C1
Lulsley 145 G2
Lulworth Camp 105 E4
Lulworth Cove & Heritage
Centre Dorset
BH20 5RQ 105 E5
Lumb Lancs 193 E5
Lumb WYorks 193 G5
Lumbutts 193 F5
Lumby 195 D4
Lumphanan 260 D4
Lumphinnans 243 F5
Lumsdaine 237 F3
Lumsdale 173 E1
Lumsden 260 C2
Lunan 253 E4
Lunanhead 252 C4
Luncarty 243 F2
Lund ERid 196 B3
Lund NYorks 195 F4
Lund Shet 278 E2

Lundale 270 D4
Lundavra 248 C3
Lunderston Bay Invcly
PA16 0DN 232 C2
Lunderton 269 K6
Lundie Angus 244 A1
Lundie High 257 H3
Lundin Links 244 C4
Lundwood 186 A2
Lundy 112 B1
Lunga 240 A4
Lunna 279 D6
Lunning 279 E6
Lunnon 128 B3
Lunsford's Cross 110 C2
Lunt 183 E2
Luntley 144 C2
Luppitt 103 E2
Lupset 186 A1
Lupton 199 G4
Lurgashall 121 E5
Lurignich 248 B3
Lusby 176 B1
Luss 241 F5
Lussagiven 231 E1
Lusta 263 H6
Lustleigh 102 A4
Luston 145 D1
Luthermuir 253 E3
Luthrie 244 B3
Luton Devon 103 D3
Luton Devon 102 C5
Luton Luton 149 F5
Luton Med 123 G2
Luton Airport 149 G5
Lutterworth 160 A4
Lutton Devon 100 B2
Lutton Dorset 105 F4
Lutton Lincs 176 C5
Lutton N'hants 161 G4
Luxborough 114 C4
Luxulyan 97 E4
Maer Corn 112 C5
Maer Staffs 171 E4
Lybster High 275 F2
Lybster High 275 H5
Lydacott 113 E5
Lydbury North 156 C4
Lydcott 113 G2
Lydd 111 F1
Lydden 125 E4
Lydden
St. Lawrence 115 E4
Lyddington 161 D3
Lydd-on-Sea 111 F1
Lyde Green 131 F5
Lydeard
St. Lawrence 115 E4
Lydford 99 F2
Lydford-on-Fosse 116 C4
Lydgate GtMan 185 D1
Lydgate GtMan 185 D2
Lydgate WYorks 193 F5
Lydham 156 C3
Lydiard Millicent 132 C4
Lydiard Tregoze 132 C4
Lydiate 183 E2
Lydlinch 104 D1
Lydney 131 F2
Lydstep 127 D3
Lye 158 B4
Lye Cross 116 B1
Lye Green Bucks 135 E2
Lye Green ESuss 123 E5
Lye Green Warks 147 D1
Lye's Green 117 F3
Lyford 133 F3
Lymbridge Green 124 D4
Lyme Regis 103 G3
Lymekilns 234 A4
Lyminge 125 D4
Lymington 106 C3
Lyminster 108 C3
Lymm 184 A4
Lympne 124 D5
Lympsham 116 A2
Lympstone 102 C4
Lynaberack 258 E5
Lynch 114 B3
Lynch Green 178 C5
Lynchat 258 E4
Lyndale House 263 J6
Lyndhurst 106 B2
Lyndon 161 E2
Lyne Aber 261 F2
Lyne ScBord 235 G5
Lyne Surr 121 F1
Lyne Down 145 F4
Lyne of Gorthleck 258 C2
Lyne of Skene 261 F3
Lyne Station 235 G5
Lyneal 170 B4
Lynegar 275 H3
Lyneham Oxon 147 E5
Lyneham Wilts 132 C5
Lyneholmeford 218 D4
Lynemore High 259 H2
Lynemore Moray 259 J1
Lynemouth 221 E2
Lyness 277 C8
Lynford 163 G3
Lyng 178 B4
Lyngate 179 E3
Lynmouth 114 A3
Lynn 157 G1
Lynsted 124 B2
Lynstone 112 C5
Lynton 114 A3
Lynton & Lynmouth Cliff
Railway Devon
EX35 6EP 114 A3
Lyon's Gate 104 C2
Lyonshall 144 C2
Lyrabus 230 A3
Lytchett Matravers 105 F3
Lytchett Minster 105 F3
Lyth 275 H2
Lytham 191 G5
Lytham St. Anne's 191 G5
Lythe 204 B1
Lythes 277 D9
Lythmore 275 F2

M

M.V. Princess Pocahontas
Kent DA11 0BS 137 F5
Mabe Burnthouse 95 E3
Mabie 217 D3
Mablethorpe 189 F4
Macclesfield 184 D5

Macclesfield Forest 185 D5
Macduff 269 F4
Macedonia 244 A4
Machan 234 B4
Machany 243 D3
Machanioch 222 C5
Machen 130 B4
Machany 243 D3
Machrie A&B 230 A3
Machrie A&B 230 B5
Machrie NAyr 223 D2
Machrihanish 222 B3
Machrins 238 C5
Machynlleth 154 D2
McInroy's Point 232 D2
Mackerye End 136 A1
Mackworth 173 E4
Macmerry 236 B2
Macterry 269 F6
Madame Tussauds GtLon
NW1 5LR 12 A4
Madderty 243 E2
Maddiston 234 D2
Madehurst 108 B2
Madeley Staffs 171 E3
Madeley Tel&W 157 G2
Madeley Heath 171 E3
Maders 98 D3
Madford 103 E1
Madingley 150 B1
Madjeston 117 F5
Madley 144 D4
Madresfield 146 A3
Madron 94 B3
Maenaddwyn 180 C4
Maenclochog 141 D5
Maendy Cardiff 130 A5
Maendy VGlam 129 G5
Maenporth 95 E4
Maentwrog 167 F3
Maen-y-groes 141 G2
Maer Corn 112 C5
Maer Staffs 171 E4
Maerdy Carmar 142 C5
Maerdy Carmar 142 C5
Maerdy Conwy 168 D3
Maerdy RCT 129 F3
Maesbrook 169 F5
Maesbury Marsh 170 A5
Maes-glas 130 A5
Maesgwynne 141 F5
Maeshafn 169 F1
Maesllyn 141 G3
Maesmynis 143 G3
Maesteg 129 E3
Maes-Treylow 144 B1
Maesybont 128 B1
Maesycrugiau 142 A3
Maesycwmmer 130 A3
Magdalen Laver 137 D2
Maggieknockater 268 B6
Maggots End 150 C5
Magham Down 110 B3
Maghull 183 E2
Magna Centre, Rotherham
SYorks S60 1DX 21 C1
Magna Park 160 A4
Magor 130 D4
Magpie Green 164 B4
Maiden Bradley 117 E4
Maiden Head 116 C1
Maiden Law 212 A3
Maiden Newton 104 B3
Maiden Wells 126 C3
Maidencombe 101 F1
Maidenhayne 103 F3
Maidenhead 135 D4
Maidens 224 A5
Maiden's Green 135 D5
Maidensgrove 134 C4
Maidenwell Corn 97 F2
Maidenwell Lincs 188 D5
Maidford 148 B2
Maids' Moreton 148 C4
Maidstone 123 G3
Maidwell 160 C5
Mail 279 D10
Maindee 130 C4
Mainland Ork 277 B6
Mainland Shet 279 C7
Mains of Ardestie 244 D1
Mains of Balgavies 252 D4
Mains of Ballhall 252 D3
Mains of Ballindarg 252 C4
Mains of Burgie 267 H6
Mains of Culsh 269 G6
Mains of Dillavaird 253 F1
Mains of Drum 261 G4
Mains of Dudwick 261 H1
Mains of Faillie 258 C1
Mains of Fedderate 269 G6
Mains of Glack 261 F2
Mains of Glassaugh 268 D4
Mains of
Glenbuchat 260 B3
Mains of Linton 261 F3
Mains of Melgund 252 D4
Mains of Pitfour 269 H6
Mains of Pittrichie 261 G2
Mains of Sluie 267 H6
Mains of Tannachy 268 B4
Mains of Thornton 253 E2
Mains of Tig 214 C2
Mains of Watten 275 H3
Mainsforth 212 C4
Mainsriddle 216 D5
Mainstone 156 B4
Maisemore 146 A5
Major's Green 158 D5
Makendon 220 A1
Makeney 173 E3
Makerstoun 228 A3
Malacleit 262 C4
Malborough 100 D4
Malden Rushett 121 G1
Maldon 138 B2
Malham 193 F1
Malin Bridge 186 A4
Maligar 263 K5
Mallaig (Malaig) 256 C5
Mallaigvaig 256 C5
Malleny Mills 235 F3
Mallows Green 150 C5
Malltraeth 166 C1
Mallwyd 155 E1
Malmesbury 132 B4

Malmsmead 114 A3
Malpas ChesW&C 170 B3
Malpas Corn 96 C5
Malpas Newport 130 C3
Maltby Lincs 188 D4
Maltby Stock 203 D1
Maltby SYorks 186 C3
Maltby le Marsh 189 E4
Malting End 151 F2
Malting Green 138 C1
Maltman's Hill 124 A4
Malton 203 G5
Malvern Link 145 G3
Malvern Wells 145 G3
Mambeg 232 D1
Mamble 157 F5
Mamhead 102 C4
Mamhilad 130 C2
Manaccan 95 E4
Manadon 100 A2
Manafon 156 A2
Manaton 102 A4
Manby 189 E4
Mancetter 159 F3
Manchester 184 C3
Manchester Airport 184 C4
Manchester Apollo GtMan
M12 6AP 47 H6
Manchester Art Gallery
GtMan M2 3JL 47 E4
Manchester Central GtMan
M2 3GX 46 D5
Manchester Craft & Design
Centre GtMan
M4 5JD 47 F3
Manchester Museum
GtMan M13 9PL 47 F7
Manchester United Museum
& Stadium Tour Centre
GtMan M16 0RA 46 D5
Mancot Royal 170 A1
Mandally
(Manndalaidh) 257 J4
Manea 162 C4
Maneight 224 D5
Manfield 202 B1
Mangaster 278 C5
Mangerton 104 A3
Mangotsfield 131 F5
Mangrove Green 149 G5
Mangurstadh 270 C4
Manish (Manais) 263 G3
Mankinholes 193 F5
Manley 183 G5
Manmoel 130 A2
Mannal 246 A2
Manningford
Abbots 118 C2
Manningford
Bohune 118 C2
Manningford Bruce 118 C2
Manningham 194 A4
Mannings Amusement Park
Suff IP11 2DW 153 D4
Mannings Heath 109 E1
Mannington 105 G2
Manningtree 152 C4
Mannofield 261 H4
Manor Farm Country Park
Hants SO30 2ER 4 D3
Manor Park 135 E4
Manorbier 127 D3
Manorbier Newton 126 D2
Manordeifi 141 F3
Manordeilo 142 C5
Manorowen 140 C4
Mansell Gamage 144 C3
Mansell Lacy 144 D3
Mansergh 200 B4
Manson's Green 137 E1
Mansfield
Woodhouse 173 G1
Manson Green 178 B5
Mansriggs 199 D4
Manston Dorset 105 E1
Manston Kent 125 F2
Manston WYorks 194 C4
Manswood 105 F2
Manthorpe Lincs 161 F1
Manthorpe Lincs 175 D3
Manton NLincs 187 G2
Manton Notts 186 C5
Manton Rut 161 D2
Manton Wilts 118 C1
Manuden 150 C5
Manwood Green 137 E1
Maolachy 240 A3
Maperton 117 D5
Maple Cross 135 F3
Maplebeck 174 C1
Mapledurham 134 B5
Mapledurwell 120 B2
Maplehurst 121 G5
Maplescombe 123 E2
Mapleton 172 C3
Mapperley Derbys 173 F3
Mapperley Notts 173 G3
Mapperton Dorset 104 B3
Mapperton Dorset 105 F3
Mappleborough
Green 146 C1
Mappleton 197 E3
Mapplewell 186 A2
Mappowder 104 D2
Mar Lodge 259 H5
Maraig (Maaraig) 270 E7
Marazion 94 C3
Marbhig 271 G6
Marbury 170 C3
Marbury Country Park
ChesW&C
CW9 6AT 184 A5
March 162 C3
Marcham 133 G3
Marchamley 170 C5
Marchamley Wood 170 C4
Marchington 172 C4
Marchington
Woodlands 172 C4
Marchwiel 170 A3
Marchwood 106 C1
Marcross 114 C1
Marcus 252 D4
Marden Here 145 E3
Marden Kent 123 G4
Marden T&W 221 F4
Marden Wilts 118 B2
Marden Ash 137 E2

Marden Beech **123** G4
Marden Thorn **123** G4
Marden's Hill **123** D5
Mardon **228** D3
Mardy **130** C1
Mare Green **116** A5
Marefield **160** C2
Mareham on
the Hill **176** A1
Maresfield **109** G1
Marfleet **196** D4
Marford **170** A2
Margam **129** D4
Margam Country Park
NPT SA13 2TJ **129** E4
Margaret Marsh **105** E1
Margaret Roding **137** E1
Margaretting **137** F2
Margaretting Tye **137** F2
Margate **125** F1
Margnaheglish **223** F2
Margreig **216** C3
Margrove Park **203** F1
Marham **163** F2
Marhamchurch **112** C5
Marholm **161** G2
Marian Cwm **182** B5
Mariandyrys **181** E4
Marian-glas **180** D4
Mariansleigh **114** A5
Marine Town **124** B1
Marishader **263** K5
Maristow House **100** A1
Mark **116** A3
Mark Causeway **116** A3
Mark Cross **123** E5
Markbeech **123** D4
Markdhu **214** C3
Markeaton **173** E4
Markeaton Park Craft Village
Derby DE22 3BG **18** A3
Market Bosworth **159** G2
Market Bosworth Country
Park *Leics*
CV13 0LP **159** G2
Market Deeping **161** G1
Market Drayton **171** D4
Market Harborough **160** C4
Market Lavington **118** B2
Market Overton **161** D1
Market Rasen **188** B4
Market Stainton **188** C5
Market Street **179** D3
Market Warsop **173** G1
Market Weighton **196** A3
Market Weston **164** A4
Markethill **243** E4
Markfield **159** G1
Markham **130** C2
Markham Moor **187** E5
Markinch **244** A4
Markington **194** B1
Marks Gate **137** D3
Marks Tey **152** A5
Marksbury **117** D1
Markwell **99** D5
Markyate **135** F1
Marl Bank **145** G3
Marland **184** C1
Marlborough **118** C1
Marlbrook **158** B5
Marlcliff **146** C2
Marldon **101** E1
Marle Green **110** A2
Marlesford **153** E2
Marley Green **170** C3
Marley Hill **212** B2
Marlingford **178** C5
Marloes **126** A4
Marlow *Bucks* **135** D4
Marlow *Here* **156** D5
Marlpit Hill **122** D4
Marlpool **173** F3
Marnhull **105** D1
Marnoch **268** D5
Marple **185** D4
Marple Bridge **185** D4
Marr **186** C2
Marrel **275** F7
Marrick **201** F3
Marrister **279** E6
Marros **127** F2
Marsden *T&W* **212** C1
Marsden *WYorks* **185** E1
Marsett **201** E4
Marsh **103** F1
Marsh Baldon **134** A3
Marsh Benham **119** F1
Marsh Farm Country Park
Essex CM3 5WP **138** B3
Marsh Gibbon **148** B5
Marsh Green
Devon **102** D3
Marsh Green
GtMan **183** G2
Marsh Green
Kent **122** D4
Marsh Green
Tel&W **157** F1
Marsh Lane **186** B5
Marsh Street **114** C3
Marshall Meadows **237** G4
Marshalsea **103** G2
Marshalswick **136** A2
Marsham **178** C3
Marshaw **192** B2
Marshborough **125** F3
Marshbrook **156** D4
Marshchapel **189** D3
Marshfield
Newport **130** B4
Marshfield *SGlos* **131** G5
Marshgate **98** B1
Marshland
St. James **162** D2
Marshside **183** E1
Marshwood **103** G3
Marske **202** A2
Marske-by-the-Sea **213** F5
Marsland Green **184** A3
Marston *ChesW&C* **184** A5
Marston *Here* **144** C2
Marston *Lincs* **175** D3
Marston *Oxon* **134** A2
Marston *Staffs* **171** G5
Marston *Staffs* **158** A1

Marston *Warks* **159** E3
Marston *Wilts* **118** A2
Marston Doles **147** G2
Marston Green **159** D4
Marston Magna **116** C5
Marston Meysey **132** D3
Marston
Montgomery **172** C4
Marston Moretaine **149** E3
Marston on Dove **172** D5
Marston
St. Lawrence **148** A3
Marston Stannett **145** E2
Marston Trussell **160** B4
Marston Vale Millennium
Country Park *CenBeds*
MK43 0PR **149** F3
Marstow **131** E1
Marsworth **135** E1
Marten **119** D1
Marthall **184** B5
Martham **179** F4
Martin *Hants* **105** G1
Martin *Lincs* **175** G2
Martin *Lincs* **176** A1
Martin Drove End **118** B5
Martin Hussingtree **146** A1
Martin Mere *Lancs*
L40 0TA **183** F1
Martinhoe **113** G1
Martinscroft **184** A4
Martinstown **104** C4
Martlesham **152** D3
Martlesham Heath **152** D3
Martletwy **126** D1
Martley **145** G1
Martock **104** A4
Marton *ChesE* **171** F1
Marton *Cumb* **198** D5
Marton *ERid* **197** D4
Marton *ERid* **197** E1
Marton *Lincs* **187** F4
Marton *Middl* **203** E1
Marton *NYorks* **194** D1
Marton *NYorks* **203** G4
Marton *Shrop* **156** B2
Marton *Shrop* **170** B5
Marton *Warks* **147** G5
Marton Abbey **195** E1
Marton-in-the-
Forest **195** E1
Marton-le-Moor **202** C5
Martyr Worthy **119** G4
Martyr's Green **121** F2
Marwell Zoo *Hants*
SO21 1JH **4** D1
Marwick **276** B5
Marwood **113** F2
Mary Rose *PO1 3LX*
82 Portsmouth
Mary Tavy **99** F3
Marybank (An Lagaidh)
High **266** B6
Marybank *Na H-E. Siar*
271 G4
Maryburgh
(Baile Main) **266** C6
Maryfield *Corn* **100** A2
Maryfield *Shet* **279** D8
Marygold **237** F4
Maryhill *Aber* **269** G6
Maryhill *Glas* **233** G3
Marykirk **253** E3
Marylebone *GtLon* **136** B4
Marylebone *GtMan* **183** G2
Marypark **259** J1
Maryport *Cumb* **208** D3
Maryport *D&G* **206** B3
Marystow **99** E3
Maryton **253** E4
Marywell *Aber* **261** H5
Marywell *Aber* **260** D5
Marywell *Angus* **253** E5
Masham **202** B4
Mashbury **137** F1
Masongill **200** B5
Mastin Moor **186** B5
Mastrick **261** H4
Matchborough **146** C1
Matching **137** E1
Matching Green **137** E1
Matching Tye **137** E1
Matfen **220** C4
Matfield **123** F4
Mathern **131** E3
Mathon **145** G3
Mathry **140** B4
Matlaske **178** C2
Matlock **173** E1
Matlock Bank **173** E1
Matlock Bath **173** D2
Matson **132** A1
Matterdale End **209** G4
Mattersey **187** D4
Mattersey Thorpe **187** D4
Mattingley **120** C2
Mattishall **178** B4
Mattishall Burgh **178** B4
Mauchline **224** C3
Maud **269** H6
Maufant **100** C5
Maugersbury **147** D5
Maughold **190** C2
Mauld **257** K1
Maulden **149** F4
Maulds Meaburn **200** B1
Maunby **202** C4
Maund Bryan **145** E2
Maundown **115** D5
Mautby **179** F4
Mavesyn Ridware **158** C1
Mavis Enderby **176** B1
Maw Green **171** E2
Mawbray **209** D2
Mawdesley **183** F1
Mawdlam **129** E4
Mawgan **95** E4
Mawgan Porth **96** C3
Mawla **96** B5
Mawnan **95** E4
Mawnan Smith **95** E4
Mawsley **160** D5
Mawthorpe **189** E5
Maxey **161** G2
Maxstoke **159** E4
Maxted Street **124** D4
Maxton *Kent* **125** F4
Maxton *ScBord* **228** A3

Maxwellheugh **228** B3
Maxwelltown **217** D3
Maxworthy **98** C1
May Hill **145** G5
Mayals **128** C3
Maybole **224** B5
Maybury **121** F2
Mayen **268** D6
Mayfair **136** B4
Mayfield *ESuss* **110** A1
Mayfield *Midlo* **236** A3
Mayfield *Staffs* **172** C3
Mayford **121** E2
Mayland **138** C2
Maylandsea **138** C2
Maynard's Green **110** A2
Maypole *IoS* **96** B1
Maypole *Kent* **125** E5
Maypole *Mon* **131** D1
Maypole Green
Essex **152** A5
Maypole Green
Norf **165** F2
Maypole Green
Suff **153** D1
Maypole Green
Suff **152** A2
May's Green *NSom* **116** A1
Mays Green *Oxon* **134** C4
Maywick **279** C10
Mead **112** C4
Mead End **118** B5
Meadgate **117** D2
Meadle **134** D2
Meadow Green **145** G2
Meadowhall **186** A3
Meadowmill **236** B2
Meadowtown **156** C2
Meadwell **99** E2
Meaford **171** F4
Meal Bank **199** G3
Mealasta **270** B5
Meals **189** E3
Mealsgate **209** F2
Meanley **192** D3
Meanwood **194** B4
Mearbeck **193** E4
Meare **116** B3
Meare Green **115** F5
Mearns **233** G4
Mears Ashby **148** D1
Measham **159** F1
Meathop **199** F4
Meavy **100** B1
Medbourne **160** D3
Meddon **112** C4
Meden Vale **173** G1
Medlar **192** A4
Medmenham **134** D4
Medomsley **212** A2
Medstead **120** B4
Meer Common **144** C2
Meer End **159** E5
Meerbrook **171** G1
Meesden **150** C4
Meeson **171** D5
Meeth **113** F5
Meeting House Hill **179** E3
Meggethead **226** C3
Meidrim **141** F5
Meifod *Denb* **168** D2
Meifod *Powys* **156** A1
Meigle **252** A5
Meikle Earnock **234** B4
Meikle Grenach **232** B3
Meikle Kilmory **232** B3
Meikle Rahane **232** D1
Meikle Strath **253** E2
Meikle Tarty **261** H2
Meikle Wartle **261** F1
Meikleour **243** G1
Meikleyard **224** D2
Meinciau **128** A1
Meir **171** G3
Meirheath **171** G3
Melbost **271** G4
Melbost Borve
(Mealabost) **271** G2
Melbourn **150** C3
Melbourne *Derbys* **173** E5
Melbourne *ERid* **195** G3
Melbury **113** D4
Melbury Abbas **105** E1
Melbury Bubb **104** B2
Melbury Osmond **104** B2
Melbury Sampford **104** B2
Melby **279** A7
Melchbourne **149** F1
Melcombe
Bingham **105** D2
Melcombe Regis **104** C4
Meldon *Devon* **99** F1
Meldon *N'umb* **220** D3
Meldreth **150** B3
Meledor **96** D4
Melfort **240** A3
Melgarve **258** B5
Melgum **260** C4
Meliden
(Gallt Melyd) **182** B4
Melincourt **129** E2
Melin-y-coed **168** B1
Melin-y-ddol **155** G2
Melin-y-grug **155** G2
Melin-y-wig **168** D3
Melkinthorpe **210** B5
Melkridge **210** D1
Melksham **118** A1
Melksham Forest **118** A1
Melldalloch **232** A2
Melling *Lancs* **199** G5
Melling *Mersey* **183** E2
Melling Mount **183** F2
Mellis **164** B4
Mellon Charles **264** E2
Mellon Udrigle **264** E2
Mellor *GtMan* **185** D4
Mellor *Lancs* **192** C4
Mellor Brook **192** C4
Mells **117** E3
Melmerby *Cumb* **210** C4
Melmerby *NYorks* **201** F4
Melmerby *NYorks* **202** C5
Melplash **104** A3
Melrose *Aber* **269** F4
Melrose *ScBord* **227** G2

Meltham **185** E1
Melton *ERid* **196** B5
Melton *Suff* **153** D2
Melton Constable **178** B2
Melton Mowbray **160** C1
Melton Ross **188** A1
Meltonby **195** G2
Melvaig **264** D3
Melverley **156** C1
Melverley Green **156** C1
Melvich **274** D2
Membury **103** F2
Memsie **269** H4
Memus **262** D4
Menabilly **97** E4
Menai Bridge
(Porthaethwy) **181** D5
Mendham **165** D3
Mendlesham **152** C1
Mendlesham Green **152** B1
Menethorpe **195** G1
Menheniot **97** G3
Menithwood **145** G1
Mennock **225** G5
Menston **194** A3
Menstrie **242** D5
Mentmore **135** E1
Meoble **247** G1
Meole Brace **157** D1
Meon **107** E2
Meonstoke **107** F1
Meopham **123** F2
Meopham Green **123** F2
Mepal **162** C4
Meppershall **149** G4
Merbach **144** C3
Mercaston **173** D3
Mere *ChesE* **184** B4
Mere *Wilts* **117** F4
Mere Brow **183** F1
Mere Green **158** D3
Mere Heath **184** A5
Mereclough **193** E4
Mereside **191** G4
Meretown **171** E5
Mereworth **123** F3
Mergie **253** F1
Meriden **159** E4
Merkadale **255** J1
Merkinch **266** D7
Merkland **216** B3
Merley **105** G3
Merlin's Bridge **126** C1
Merridge **115** F4
Merrifield **101** E3
Merrington **170** B5
Merrion **126** C3
Merriott **104** A1
Merrivale **99** F3
Merrow **121** F3
Merry Hill *Herts* **136** A3
Merry Hill *WMid* **158** B4
Merry Hill *WMid* **158** A3
Merrymeet **97** G3
Mersea Island **138** D1
Mersey Ferries *Mersey*
CH44 6QY **42** A4
Merseyside Maritime
Museum *Mersey*
L3 4AQ **42** B5
Mersham **124** C5
Merstham **122** B3
Merston **108** A3
Merstone **107** E4
Merther **96** C5
Merthyr **141** G5
Merthyr Cynog **143** F4
Merthyr Dyfan **115** E1
Merthyr Mawr **129** E5
Merthyr Tydfil **129** G2
Merthyr Vale **129** G3
Merton *Devon* **113** F4
Merton *GtLon* **136** B5
Merton *Norf* **164** A2
Merton *Oxon* **134** A1
Mervinslaw **228** A5
Meshaw **102** A1
Messing **138** C1
Messingham **187** F2
Metcombe **103** D3
Metfield **165** D3
Metherell **100** A1
Metheringham **175** F1
Methil **244** B5
Methlem **166** A4
Methley **194** C5
Methley Junction **194** C5
Methlick **261** G1
Methven **243** F2
Methwold **163** F3
Methwold Hythe **163** F3
MetroCentre **212** B1
Mettingham **165** E3
Metton **178** C2
Mevagissey **97** E5
Mewith Head **192** D1
Mexborough **186** B3
Mey **275** H1
Meysey Hampton **132** D2
Miabhag *Na H-E. Siar*
263 G2
Miabhag *Na H-E. Siar*
270 C7
Mial **264** D4
Miavaig (Miabhaig) **270** C4
Michaelchurch **145** E5
Michaelchurch
Escley **144** B2
Michaelchurch-on-
Arrow **144** B2
Michaelston-le-Pit **130** A5
Michaelston-super-
Ely **130** A5
Michaelston-y-
Fedw **130** B4
Michaelstow **97** E2
Michelcombe **100** C1
Micheldever **119** G4
Michelmersh **119** E5
Mickfield **152** C1
Mickle Trafford **170** B1
Mickleby **204** B1
Micklefield **194** D4
Micklefield Green **135** F3
Mickleham **121** G3
Micklehurst **185** D2
Mickleover **173** E4

Micklethwaite
Cumb **209** F1
Micklethwaite
WYorks **193** G3
Mickleton *Dur* **211** F5
Mickleton *Glos* **147** D3
Mickletown **194** C5
Mickley *Derbys* **186** A5
Mickley *NYorks* **202** B5
Mickley Green **151** G2
Mickley Square **211** G1
Mid Ardlaw **269** H4
Mid Beltie **260** E4
Mid Calder **235** E3
Mid Clyth **275** H5
Mid Lambrook **104** A1
Mid Lavant **108** A3
Mid Letter **240** C4
Mid Lix **242** A1
Mid Mossdale **200** D3
Mid Yell **278** E3
Midbea **276** D3
Middle Assendon **134** C4
Middle Aston **147** G5
Middle Barton **147** G5
Middle
Bockhampton **106** A3
Middle Claydon **148** C5
Middle Drift **97** F3
Middle Drums **253** D4
Middle
Duntisbourne **132** B2
Middle Handley **186** B5
Middle Harling **164** A3
Middle Kames **232** A1
Middle Littleton **146** C3
Middle Maes-coed **144** C4
Middle Marwood **113** F2
Middle Mill **140** B5
Middle Quarter **124** A5
Middle Rasen **188** A4
Middle Rigg **243** F4
Middle Salter **192** C1
Middle Sontley **170** A3
Middle Stoford **115** E5
Middle Taphouse **97** F3
Middle Town **96** B1
Middle Tysoe **147** F3
Middle Wallop **119** D4
Middle Winterslow **118** D4
Middle Woodford **118** C4
Middlebie **218** A4
Middlecliff **186** B2
Middlecott **113** E5
Middleham **202** A4
Middlehill *Aber* **269** G6
Middlehill *Corn* **97** G3
Middlehope **157** E4
Middlemarsh **104** C2
Middlemoor **99** E3
Middlequarter (Ceathramh
Meadhanach) **262** D4
Middlesbrough **213** D5
Middlesceugh **210** A3
Middlestone **212** B4
Middlestone Moor **212** B4
Middlestown **185** G1
Middleton *Aber* **261** G3
Middleton *Angus* **253** D5
Middleton *Cumb* **200** B4
Middleton *Derbys* **173** D2
Middleton *Derbys* **172** C1
Middleton *Essex* **151** G3
Middleton *GtMan* **184** C2
Middleton *Hants* **119** F3
Middleton *Here* **145** E1
Middleton *Lancs* **192** A2
Middleton *Midlo* **236** A4
Middleton *N'hants* **160** D4
Middleton *N'umb* **229** E3
Middleton *Norf* **163** E1
Middleton *NYorks* **203** G4
Middleton *P&K* **243** G4
Middleton *P&K* **251** G5
Middleton *Shrop* **156** B3
Middleton *Shrop* **157** E5
Middleton *Shrop* **170** A5
Middleton *Suff* **153** F1
Middleton *Swan* **128** A4
Middleton *Warks* **159** D3
Middleton *WYorks* **194** A3
Middleton *WYorks* **194** C5
Middleton Baggot **157** F3
Middleton Bank Top **220** C3
Middleton Cheney **147** G3
Middleton Green **171** G4
Middleton Hall **229** D4
Middleton Moor **153** F1
Middleton of
Potterton **261** H3
Middleton on the
Hill **145** E1
Middleton One Row **202** C1
Middleton Park **261** H3
Middleton Priors **157** F4
Middleton
Quernhow **202** C5
Middleton
St. George **202** C1
Middleton Scriven **157** F4
Middleton Stoney **148** A5
Middleton Tyas **202** B2
Middleton-in-
Teesdale **211** F5
Middleton-on-
Leven **203** D1
Middleton-on-Sea **108** B3
Middleton-on-the-
Wolds **196** B3
Middletown *Cumb* **198** A2
Middletown *Powys* **156** C1
Middlewich **171** E1
Middlewood *ChesE* **184** D4
Middlewood *SYorks* **186** A3
Middlewood Green **152** B1
Middlezoy **116** A4
Middridge **212** B5
Midfield **273** H2
Midford **117** E1
Midge Hall **192** B5
Midgeholme **210** C2
Midgham **119** G1

Midgley *WYorks* **185** G1
Midgley *WYorks* **193** G5
Midhopestones **185** G2
Midhurst **121** D5
Midland Railway Centre
Derbys DE5 3QZ **173** F2
Midlem **227** G3
Midloe Grange **149** G1
Midpark **232** B4
Midsomer Norton **117** D2
Midthorpe **188** C5
Midton **232** C2
Midtown *High* **273** H2
Midtown *High* **264** E3
Midtown of Barras **253** G1
Midville **176** B2
Midway **173** E5
Migdale **266** D2
Migvie **260** C4
Milarrochy **241** G5
Milber **102** B5
Milbethill **268** E5
Milborne Port **104** C1
Milborne
St. Andrew **105** D3
Milborne Wick **117** D5
Milbourne
N'umb **220** D4
Milbourne *Wilts* **132** B4
Milburn **210** C5
Milbury Heath **131** F3
Milcombe **147** G4
Milden **152** A3
Mildenhall *Suff* **163** F5
Mildenhall *Wilts* **118** D1
Mile Elm **118** A1
Mile End *Essex* **152** A5
Mile End *Glos* **131** E1
Mile End Park *GtLon*
E3 4HL **12** D4
Mile Oak **123** F4
Mile Town **124** B1
Milebrook **156** C5
Milebush **123** G4
Mileham **178** A4
Miles Green **171** F3
Miles Hope **145** E1
Milesmark **235** E1
Miles's Green **119** G1
Milfield **228** D3
Milford *Derbys* **173** E3
Milford *Devon* **112** C3
Milford *Shrop* **170** B5
Milford *Staffs* **171** G5
Milford *Surr* **121** E3
Milford Haven
(Aberdaugleddau)
126 B2
Milford on Sea **106** B3
Milkwall **131** E2
Milky Way Adventure
Park *Devon*
EX39 5RY **112** D3
Mill Bank **193** G5
Mill Brow **185** D4
Mill End *Bucks* **134** C4
Mill End *Cambs* **151** E2
Mill End *Herts* **150** B4
Mill End Green **151** E5
Mill Green *Cambs* **151** E3
Mill Green *Essex* **137** F2
Mill Green *Herts* **136** B2
Mill Green *Norf* **164** C3
Mill Green *Shrop* **171** D5
Mill Green *Staffs* **172** B5
Mill Green *Suff* **153** E1
Mill Green *Suff* **152** C2
Mill Green *Suff* **152** A3
Mill Green *WMid* **158** C2
Mill Hill *B'burn* **192** C5
Mill Hill *Cambs* **150** C2
Mill Hill *GtLon* **136** B3
Mill Houses **192** C1
Mill Lane **120** C2
Mill of Camsail **233** D1
Mill of Colp **269** F6
Mill of Elrick **269** H6
Mill of Fortune **242** C2
Mill of Kingoodie **261** G2
Mill of Monquich **261** G5
Mill of Uras **253** G1
Mill Side **199** F4
Mill Street *Kent* **123** F3
Mill Street *Norf* **178** B4
Milland **120** D5
Millbank **269** J6
Millbeck **209** F4
Millbounds **276** E4
Millbreck **269** J6
Millbridge **120** D3
Millbrook *CenBeds* **149** F4
Millbrook *Corn* **100** A2
Millbrook *Devon* **103** G3
Millbrook *Soton* **106** C1
Millburn *Aber* **260** D2
Millburn *Aber* **260** E1
Millcombe **101** E3
Millcorner **110** D1
Milldale **172** C2
Milden **261** H3
Milldens **252** D4
Millearne **243** E3
Millend **147** F5
Millenheath **170** C4
Millennium Seed Bank,
Wakehurst Place *WSuss*
RH17 6TN **122** C5
Millerhill **236** A3
Miller's Dale **185** F5
Millers Green
Derbys **173** D2
Miller's Green
Essex **137** E2
Millgate **193** E5
Millhalf **144** B3
Millhayes *Devon* **103** E1
Millhayes *Devon* **103** E2
Millholme **199** G3
Millhouse *A&B* **232** A2
Millhouse *Cumb* **209** G3
Millhouse Green **185** G2
Millhousebridge **217** F2
Millikenpark **233** F3
Millin Cross **126** C1
Millington **196** A2
Millington Green **173** D3
Millmeece **171** F4
Millness **257** K1
Millom **198** C4

Millow **150** A3
Millpool **97** F2
Millport **232** C4
Millthorpe **186** A5
Millthrop **200** B3
Milltimber **261** G4
Milltown *Aber* **259** K4
Milltown *Corn* **97** F4
Milltown *D&G* **218** B4
Milltown *Derbys* **173** E1
Milltown *Devon* **113** F2
Milltown *High* **267** G7
Milltown of
Aberdalgie **243** F2
Milltown of
Auchindoun **260** B1
Milltown of
Craigston **269** F5
Milltown of
Edinvillie **267** K7
Milltown of
Kildrummy **260** C3
Milltown of
Rothiemay **268** D6
Milltown of Towie **260** C3
Milnathort **243** G4
Milners Heath **170** B1
Milngavie **233** G2
Milnrow **184** D1
Milnsbridge **185** F1
Milnthorpe **199** F4
Milovaig **263** G6
Milrig **224** D2
Milson **157** F5
Milstead **124** B3
Milston **118** C3
Milton *Angus* **252** B5
Milton *Cambs* **150** C1
Milton *Cumb* **210** B1
Milton *D&G* **216** D2
Milton *D&G* **216** C3
Milton *D&G* **214** D5
Milton *Derbys* **173** E5
Milton *High* **265** K6
Milton *High* **266** E4
Milton *High* **267** G6
Milton *High* **266** D7
Milton *High* **266** C7
Milton *High* **275** J3
Milton (Baile a' Mhuilinn)
High **258** B1
Milton *Moray* **268** D4
Milton *Newport* **130** C4
Milton *Notts* **187** E5
Milton *NSom* **116** A1
Milton *Oxon* **147** G4
Milton *Oxon* **133** G3
Milton *P&K* **243** E1
Milton *Pembs* **126** D2
Milton *Ports* **107** F3
Milton *Som* **116** B5
Milton *Stir* **242** A4
Milton *Stoke* **171** G2
Milton *WDun* **233** F2
Milton Abbas **105** D2
Milton Abbot **99** E3
Milton Bridge **235** G3
Milton Bryan **149** E4
Milton Clevedon **117** D4
Milton Combe **100** A1
Milton Country Park *Cambs*
CB24 6AZ **150** C1
Milton Damerel **113** D4
Milton End **131** G1
Milton Ernest **149** F2
Milton Green **170** B2
Milton Hill **133** G3
Milton Keynes **149** D4
Milton Keynes
Village **149** D4
Milton Lilbourne **118** C1
Milton Malsor **148** C2
Milton Morenish **242** B1
Milton of
Auchinhove **260** D4
Milton of Balgonie **244** B4
Milton of Buchanan **241** G5
Milton of
Cairnborrow **268** C6
Milton of Callander **242** A4
Milton of Campfield **260** E4
Milton of Campsie **234** A2
Milton of Coldwells **261** H1
Milton of Cullerlie **261** F4
Milton of Cushnie **260** D3
Milton of Dalcapon **251** E4
Milton of
Inveramsay **261** F2
Milton of Noth **260** D2
Milton of Tullich **260** B5
Milton on Stour **117** E5
Milton Regis **124** A2
Milton Street **110** A3
Miltonduff **267** J5
Miltonhill **267** H5
Miltonise **214** C3
Milton-Lockhart **234** C5
Milton-under-
Wychwood **133** E1
Milverton *Som* **115** E5
Milverton *Warks* **147** F1
Milwich **171** G4
Mimbridge **121** E1
Minack Theatre *Corn*
TR19 6JU **94** A4
Minard **240** B5
Minard Castle **240** B5
Minchington **105** F1
Minchinhampton **132** A2
Mindrum **228** C3
Mindrummill **228** C3
Minehead **114** C3
Minera **169** F2
Minety **132** C3
Minety Lower Moor **132** C3
Minffordd *Gwyn* **154** D1
Minffordd *Gwyn* **167** E4
Minffordd *Gwyn* **181** D5
Miningsby **176** B1
Minions **97** G2
Minishant **224** B4
Minley Manor **120** D2
Minllyn **155** E2
Minnes **261** H2
Minngearraidh **254** C2
Minnigaff **215** F4
Minnonie **269** F4
Minskip **194** C1

Minstead 106 B1
Minsted 121 D5
Minster Kent 124 B1
Minster Kent 125 F2
Minster Lovell 133 F1
Minsteracres 211 G2
Minsterley 156 C2
Minsterworth 131 G1
Minterne Magna 104 C2
Minterne Parva 104 C2
Minting 188 B3
Mintlaw 269 J6
Minto 227 G3
Minton 156 D3
Minwear 126 D1
Minworth 159 D3
Miodar 246 B1
Mirbister 277 C6
Mirehouse 208 C5
Mireland 275 J2
Mirfield 194 B5
Miserden 132 B2
Miskin RCT 129 G4
Miskin RCT 129 G3
Misselfore 118 B5
Misson 187 D3
Misterton Leics 160 A4
Misterton Notts 187 E3
Misterton Som 104 A2
Mistley 152 C4
Mitcham 122 B2
Mitchel Troy 131 D1
Mitcheldean 131 F1
Mitchell 96 C4
Mitchelland 199 F3
Mitcheltroy
   Common 131 D2
Mitford 221 D3
Mithian 96 B4
Mitton 158 A1
Mixbury 148 B4
Mixenden 193 G5
Moar 250 A5
Moat 218 C4
Moats Tye 152 B2
Mobberley ChesE 184 B5
Mobberley Staffs 172 B3
Moccas 144 C3
Mochdre Conwy 181 G5
Mochdre Powys 155 G4
Mochrum 206 D2
Mockbeggar Hants 106 A2
Mockbeggar Kent 123 G4
Mockerkin 209 D4
Modbury 100 C2
Moddershall 171 G4
Modern Art Oxford Oxon
   OX1 1BP 80 Oxford
Modsarie 273 J2
Moel Famau Country Park
   Denb LL15 1US 169 E1
Moelfre IoA 180 D4
Moelfre Powys 169 E5
Moffat 226 B5
Mogerhanger 149 G3
Moin'a'choire 230 B3
Moine House 273 H3
Moira 159 F1
Molash 124 C3
Mol-chlach 255 K3
Mold (Yr Wyddgrug) 169 F1
Molehill Green
   Essex 151 D5
Molehill Green
   Essex 151 F5
Molescroft 196 C3
Molesden 220 D3
Molesworth 161 F5
Mollance 216 B4
Molland 114 B5
Mollington
   ChesW&C 183 E5
Mollington Oxon 147 G3
Mollinsburn 234 B2
Monach Islands (Heisker
   Islands) 262 B5
Monachty 142 B1
Monachyle 241 G3
Monevechadan 241 D4
Monewden 152 D2
Moneydie 243 F2
Moneyrow Green 135 D5
Moniaive 216 B1
Monifieth 244 D1
Monikie 244 D1
Monikie Country Park
   Angus DD5 3QN 244 C1
Monimail 244 A3
Monington 141 E3
Monk Bretton 186 A2
Monk Fryston 195 E5
Monk Hesleden 213 D4
Monk Sherborne 120 B2
Monk Soham 152 D1
Monk Soham
   Green 152 D1
Monk Street 151 E5
Monken Hadley 136 B3
Monkerton 102 C3
Monkey Mates W'ham
   RG41 1JA 34 C4
Monkey World, Wareham
   Dorset
   BH20 6HH 105 E4
Monkhide 145 F3
Monkhill 209 G1
Monkhopton 157 F3
Monkland 145 D2
Monkleigh 113 E3
Monknash 129 F5
Monkokehampton 113 F5
Monks Eleigh 152 A3
Monks Eleigh Tye 152 A3
Monk's Gate 109 E1
Monk's Heath 184 C5
Monk's Hill 124 A4
Monks Horton 124 D5
Monks Kirby 159 G4
Monks Risborough 134 D2
Monkscross 99 D3
Monkseaton 221 F4
Monkshill 269 F6
Monksilver 115 D4
Monkstadt 263 J5
Monkswood 130 C2
Monkton Devon 103 E2
Monkton Kent 125 E2
Monkton Pembs 126 C2

Monkton SAyr 224 B3
Monkton T&W 212 C1
Monkton VGlam 129 F5
Monkton Combe 117 E1
Monkton Deverill 117 F4
Monkton Farleigh 117 F1
Monkton Heathfield
   115 F5
Monkton Up
   Wimborne 105 G1
Monkton Wyld 103 G3
Monkwearmouth 212 C2
Monkwood 120 B4
Monmouth
   (Trefynwy) 131 E1
Monnington Court 144 C4
Monnington on
   Wye 144 C3
Monreith 207 D2
Montacute 104 B1
Montacute House Som
   TA15 6XP 104 B1
Monteach 269 G6
Montford 156 D1
Montford Bridge 156 D1
Montgarrie 260 D3
Montgomery
   (Trefaldwyn) 156 B3
Montgreenan 233 E5
Montpellier Gallery Warks
   CV37 6EP
   85 Stratford-upon-Avon
Montrave 244 B4
Montrose 253 F4
Monxton 119 E3
Monyash 172 C1
Monymusk 260 E3
Monzie 243 D2
Moodiesburn 234 A2
Moons Moat North 146 C1
Moonzie 244 B3
Moor Allerton 194 C4
Moor Cock 192 C1
Moor Crichel 105 F2
Moor End Bed 149 F2
Moor End CenBeds 149 E5
Moor End Cumb 199 G5
Moor End ERid 196 A4
Moor End Lancs 191 G3
Moor End NYorks 195 E4
Moor End WYorks 193 G3
Moor Green Wilts 117 F1
Moor Green WMid 158 C4
Moor Head 194 A4
Moor Monkton 195 E2
Moor Row 208 D3
Moor Side Cumb 198 D5
Moor Side Lancs 192 A4
Moor Side Lancs 192 A4
Moor Side Lincs 176 A2
Moor Street 124 A2
Moorby 176 A1
Moorcot 144 C2
Moordown 105 G3
Moore 183 G4
Moorend 209 G1
Moorends 187 D1
Moorfield 185 E3
Moorgreen 173 F3
Moorhall 186 A5
Moorhampton 144 C3
Moorhouse Cumb 209 G1
Moorhouse Notts 174 C1
Moorland (Northmoor
   Green) 116 A4
Moorlinch 116 A4
Moors Centre, Danby
   NYorks
   YO21 2NB 203 G2
Moors Valley Country Park
   Dorset
   BH24 2ET 106 A2
Moors Valley Railway
   Dorset
   BH24 2ET 105 G2
Moorsholm 203 F4
Moorside Dorset 105 D1
Moorside GtMan 185 D2
Moorside WYorks 194 B4
Moorthorpe 186 B1
Moortown IoW 106 D4
Moortown Lincs 188 A3
Moortown Tel&W 157 F1
Morangie 266 E3
Morar 256 C5
Morborne 161 G3
Morchard Bishop 102 A2
Morcombelake 104 A3
Morcott 161 E2
Morda 169 F5
Morden Dorset 105 F3
Morden GtLon 122 B2
Morden Hall Park GtLon
   SM4 5JD 11 F8
Morden Park 122 B2
Mordiford 145 E4
Mordington
   Holdings 237 G4
Mordon 212 C5
More 156 C3
Morebath 114 C5
Morebattle 228 B4
Morecambe 192 A1
Morefield 265 H2
Moreleigh 101 D2
Morenish 242 B1
Moresby Parks 208 C5
Morestead 119 G5
Moreton Dorset 105 E4
Moreton Essex 137 E2
Moreton Here 145 E2
Moreton Mersey 183 D4
Moreton Oxon 134 B2
Moreton Staffs 157 G1
Moreton Staffs 157 G1
Moreton Corbet 170 C5
Moreton Jeffries 145 F3
Moreton Mill 170 C5
Moreton Morrell 147 F2
Moreton on Lugg 145 E3
Moreton Paddox 147 F2
Moreton Pinkney 148 A3
Moreton Say 170 C4
Moreton Valence 131 G2
Moretonhampstead 102 A4
Moreton-in-Marsh 147 E4
Morfa Carmar 128 B1
Morfa Cere 141 G2

Morfa Bychan 167 E4
Morfa Glas 129 E2
Morfa Nefyn 166 B3
Morgan's Vale 118 C5
Morganstown 130 A4
Mork 131 E2
Morland 210 B5
Morley Derbys 173 E3
Morley Dur 212 A5
Morley WYorks 194 B5
Morley Green 184 C4
Morley St. Botolph 164 B2
Mornick 98 D3
Morningside Edin 235 G2
Morningside NLan 234 C4
Morningthorpe 164 D2
Morpeth 221 E3
Morphie 253 F3
Morrey 158 D1
Morridge Side 172 B2
Morrilow Heath 171 G4
Morriston SAyr 224 A5
Morriston Swan 128 C3
Morristown 130 A5
Morroch 247 F1
Morston 178 B1
Mortehoe 113 E1
Morthen 186 B4
Mortimer 120 B1
Mortimer West End 120 B1
Mortimer's Cross 144 D1
Mortlake 136 B5
Morton Derbys 173 F1
Morton Lincs 175 F5
Morton Lincs 187 F3
Morton Lincs 175 D3
Morton Notts 174 C2
Morton SGlos 131 F3
Morton Shrop 169 F5
Morton Bagot 146 D1
Morton on the Hill 178 C4
Morton Tinmouth 212 A5
Morton-on-Swale 202 C3
Morvah 94 B3
Morval 97 G4
Morvich (A'Mhormhaich)
   High 257 F2
Morvich High 266 E1
Morvil 140 D4
Morville 157 F3
Morwellham 100 A1
Morwellham Quay Museum
   Devon PL19 8JL 99 E3
Morwenstow 112 C4
Morwick Hall 221 E1
Mosborough 186 B4
Moscow 233 F5
Mosedale 209 G3
Moselden Height 185 E1
Moseley WMid 158 B3
Moseley Worcs 146 A2
Moses Gate 184 B2
Moss A&B 246 A2
Moss Wrex 170 A2
Moss Bank 183 G3
Moss Houses 184 C5
Moss Nook 184 C4
Moss of
   Barmuckity 267 K5
Moss Side GtMan 184 C3
Moss Side Lancs 191 G4
Moss Side Mersey 183 E2
Mossat 260 C3
Mossbank 278 D5
Mossblown 224 B2
Mossburnford 228 A5
Mossdale 216 A3
Mossend 234 B3
Mosser 209 E4
Mossgiel 224 C2
Mosshead 260 D1
Mosside of
   Ballinshoe 252 C4
Mossley ChesE 171 F1
Mossley GtMan 185 D2
Mossley Hill 183 E4
Mosspaul Hotel 218 B2
Moss-side High 267 F6
Moss-side Moray 268 D4
Mosstodloch 268 B4
Mosston 252 D4
Mossy Lea 183 G1
Mosterton 104 A2
Moston GtMan 184 C2
Moston Shrop 170 C5
Moston Green 171 E1
Mostyn 182 C4
Motcombe 117 F5
Mothecombe 100 C3
Mother Shipton's Cave
   NYorks
   HG5 8DD 194 C2
Motherby 210 A5
Motherwell 234 B4
Mottingham 136
   D5 Mottisfont 119 E5
Mottistone 106 D4
Mottram in
   Longdendale 185 D3
Mottram
   St. Andrew 184 C5
Mouldsworth 183 G5
Moulin 251 E4
Moulscoomb 109 F3
Moulsford 134 A4
Moulsham 137 G2
Moulsoe 149 E3
Moulton ChesW&C 171 D1
Moulton Lincs 176 B5
Moulton N'hants 148 C1
Moulton NYorks 202 B2
Moulton Suff 151 E1
Moulton VGlam 129 G5
Moulton Chapel 162 A1
Moulton St. Mary 179 F5
Moulton Seas End 176 B5
Mounie Castle 261 F2
Mount Corn 96 B4
Mount Corn 97 F3
Mount High 267 G7
Mount Kent 125 D4
Mount WYorks 185 F1
Mount Ambrose 96 B5
Mount Bures 152 A4
Mount Charles 97 E4

Mount Edgcumbe Country
   Park Corn
   PL10 1HZ 2 B3
Mount Hawke 96 B5
Mount Manisty 183 E5
Mount Oliphant 224 B4
Mount Pleasant
   ChesE 171 F2
Mount Pleasant
   Derbys 173 E3
Mount Pleasant
   Derbys 159 E1
Mount Pleasant
   ESuss 109 G2
Mount Pleasant
   Flints 182 D5
Mount Pleasant
   GtLon 135 F3
Mount Pleasant
   Hants 106 C3
Mount Pleasant
   Norf 164 A2
Mount Pleasant
   Suff 151 F3
Mount Sorrel 118 B5
Mount Tabor 193 G5
Mountain 193 G4
Mountain Ash
   (Aberpennar) 129 G3
Mountain Cross 235 F5
Mountain Water 140 C5
Mountbenger 227 E3
Mountblairy 268 E5
Mountblow 233 F2
Mountfield 110 C1
Mountgerald 266 C6
Mountjoy 96 D3
Mountnessing 137 F3
Mounton 131 E3
Mountsorrel 160 A1
Mousa 279 D10
Mousehole 94 B4
Mouswald 217 E3
Mow Cop 171 F2
Mowden 202 B1
Mowhaugh 228 C4
Mowsley 160 B2
Mowtie 253 G1
Moxley 158 B3
Moy High 249 D1
Moy High 249 G1
Moy High 258 E1
Moy House 267 H6
Moylgrove 141 E3
Muasdale 231 E5
Much Birch 145 E4
Much Cowarne 145 F3
Much Dewchurch 145 D4
Much Hadham 136 D1
Much Hoole 192 A5
Much Hoole Town 192 A5
Much Marcle 145 F4
Much Wenlock 157 F2
Muchalls 261 H5
Muchelney 116 B5
Muchelney Ham 116 B5
Muchlarnick 97 G4
Muchra 226 D4
Muchrachd 257 J1
Muck 246 D2
Mucking 137 F4
Muckle Roe 279 C6
Muckleford 104 C3
Mucklestone 171 E4
Muckleton 170 C5
Muckletown 260 D2
Muckley 157 F3
Muckley Corner 158 C2
Muckton 189 D4
Mudale 273 H5
Muddiford 113 F2
Muddles Green 110 A2
Muddleswood 109 E2
Mudeford 106 A3
Mudford 104 B1
Mudgley 116 B3
Mugdock 233 G2
Mugdock Country Park
   Stir G62 8EL 30 C1
Mugeary 255 K1
Mugginton 173 D3
Muggintonlane
   End 173 D3
Muggleswick 211 G3
Mugswell 122 B3
Muie 266 D1
Muir 251 F1
Muir of Fowlis 260 D3
Muir of Lochs 268 B4
Muir of Ord
   (Am Blàr Dubh) 266 C6
Muiravonside Country Park
   Falk EH49 6LW 235 D2
Muirden 269 F5
Muirdrum 245 D1
Muiredge 244 B5
Muirhead Aber 260 D3
Muirhead Angus 244 B1
Muirhead Fife 244 A4
Muirhead Moray 267 H5
Muirhead NLan 234 A3
Muirhouses 235 E1
Muirkirk 225 E3
Muirmill 234 B1
Muirtack Aber 261 H1
Muirtack Aber 269 G6
Muirton High 266 E5
Muirton P&K 243 E3
Muirton P&K 243 G2
Muirton of Ardblair 251 G5
Muirton of Ballochy 253 E3
Muirtown 267 G6
Muiryfold 269 F5
Muker 201 E3
Mulbarton 178 C5
Mulben 268 B5
Mulhagery 271 F7
Mull 239 E1
Mullach
   Chàrlabhaigh 270 E3
Mullacott Cross 113 F1
Mullion 95 D5
Mullion Cove 95 D5
Mumby 189 F5
Munderfield Row 145 F2
Munderfield Stocks 145 F2
Mundesley 179 E2
Mundford 163 G3

Mundham 165 E2
Mundon 138 B2
Mundurno 261 H3
Munerigie 257 J4
Mungasdale 265 F2
Mungoswells 236 B2
Mungrisdale 209 G3
Munnoch 232 D5
Munsley 145 F3
Munslow 157 E4
Murchington 99 G2
Murcott Oxon 134 A1
Murcott Wilts 132 B3
Murdostoun 234 C4
Murieston 235 E3
Murkle 275 G2
Murlaganmore 242 A1
Murlaggan High 257 G5
Murlaggan High 249 F1
Murra 277 B7
Murrell Green 120 C2
Murroes 244 C1
Murrow 162 B2
Mursley 148 D5
Murston 124 B2
Murthill 252 C4
Murthly 243 F1
Murton Cumb 210 D5
Murton Dur 212 C3
Murton N'umb 237 G5
Murton Swan 128 B4
Murton York 195 F2
Musbury 103 F3
Muscliff 105 G3
Musdale (Musdáil) 240 B2
Museum in Docklands
   GtLon E14 4AL 12 D4
Museum of Childhood,
   Edinburgh Edin
   EH1 1TG 37 G4
Museum of Childhood,
   London GtLon
   E2 9PA 12 C4
Museum of Flight ELoth
   EH39 5LF 236 C2
Museum of Garden History,
   London GtLon
   SE1 7LB 45 F7
Museum of London GtLon
   EC2Y 5HN 45 J2
Museum of Science &
   Industry, Manchester
   GtMan M3 4FP 46 C4
Museum of Transport,
   Glasgow Glas
   G3 8DP 38 A2
Musselburgh 236 A2
Mustard Hyrn 179 F4
Mustard Shop Norf
   NR2 1NQ 79 Norwich
Muston Leics 174 D4
Muston NYorks 205 E5
Mustow Green 158 A5
Mutford 165 F3
Muthill 243 D3
Mutley 100 A2
Mutterton 102 D2
Muxton 157 G1
Mybster 275 G3
Myddfai 143 D4
Myddle 170 B5
Myddlewood 170 B5
Mydroilyn 142 A2
Myerscough
   College 192 A4
Myerscough Smithy 192 C4
Mylor 95 F3
Mylor Bridge 95 F3
Mynachdy 130 A5
Mynachlog-ddu 141 E4
Myndtown 156 C4
Mynydd Llandygai 167 F1
Mynydd Mechell 180 B4
Mynydd-bach Mon 131 D3
Mynydd-bach
   Swan 128 C3
Mynyddgarreg 128 A2
Mynytho 166 C4
Myrebird 261 F5
Mytchett 121 D2
Mytholm 193 F5
Mytholmroyd 193 G5
Mythop 191 G4
Myton-on-Swale 194 D1
Mytton 156 D1

N

Naast 264 E3
Nab's Head 192 C5
Na-Buirgh 263 F2
Naburn 195 E3
Nackington 125 D3
Nacton 152 D3
Nadderwater 102 B3
Nafferton 196 C2
Nailbridge 131 F1
Nailsbourne 115 F5
Nailsea 131 D5
Nailstone 159 G2
Nailsworth 132 A3
Nairn 267 F6
Nancegollan 94 D3
Nancekuke 96 A5
Nancledra 94 B3
Nanhoron 166 B4
Nannau 168 A5
Nannerch 169 E1
Nanpantan 160 A1
Nanpean 97 D4
Nanstallon 97 E3
Nant-ddu 129 G1
Nanternis 141 G2
Nantgaredig 142 A5
Nantgarw 130 A4
Nant-glas 143 G1
Nantglyn 168 D1
Nantgwyn 155 F5
Nantlle 167 E2
Nantmawr 169 F5
Nantmel 143 G1
Nantmor 167 F2
Nantwich 170 D2
Nantycaws 128 A1
Nant-y-derry 130 C2
Nant-y-dugoed 155 F1
Nantyffyllon 129 E3

Nantyglo 130 A1
Nant-y-Gollen 169 F5
Nant-y-groes 143 G1
Nant-y-moel 129 F3
Nant-y-Pandy 181 E5
Naphill 135 E2
Napley Heath 171 E4
Nappa 193 E2
Napton on the Hill
   147 G1
Narberth (Arberth) 127 E1
Narborough
   Leics 160 A3
Narborough Norf 163 F1
Narkurs 98 D5
Narrachan 240 B3
Nasareth 167 D3
Naseby 160 B5
Nash Bucks 148 C4
Nash Here 144 C1
Nash Newport 130 C4
Nash Shrop 157 F5
Nash VGlam 129 F5
Nash Street 123 F2
Nassington 161 F3
Nasty 150 B5
Nateby Cumb 200 C2
Nateby Lancs 192 A3
Nately Scures 120 C2
National Agricultural Centre,
   Stoneleigh Warks
   CV8 2LZ 16 B5
National Army Museum
   GtLon SW3 4HT 13 A5
National Botanic Garden
   of Wales Carmar
   SA32 8HG 128 B1
National Coal Mining
   Museum for England
   WYorks
   WF4 4RH 27 F6
National Exhibition Centre
   WMid B40 1NT 15 H4
National Fishing Heritage
   Centre, Grimsby NELincs
   DN31 1UZ 188 C2
National Gallery GtLon
   WC2N 5DN 44 D4
National Gallery of Scotland
   Edin EH2 2EL 37 F4
National Indoor Arena,
   Birmingham
   WMid B1 2AA 34 D4
National Marine Aquarium
   PL4 0LF 81 Plymouth
National Maritime Museum
   Cornwall Corn
   TR11 3QY 95 F3
National Maritime Museum,
   Greenwich GtLon
   SE10 9NF 13 D5
National Media Museum
   WYorks BD1 1NQ
   65 Bradford
National Memorial
   Arboretum, Alrewas
   Staffs
   DE13 7AR 159 D1
National Motorcycle
   Museum, Solihull WMid
   B92 0EJ 159 E4
National Museum Cardiff
   CF10 3NP
   67 Cardiff
National Museum of
   Scotland Edin
   EH1 1JF 37 G5
National Portrait Gallery
   GtLon
   WC2H 0HE 44 D4
National Railway Museum
   YO26 4XJ 90 York
National Sea Life Centre,
   Birmingham
   WMid B1 2JB 34 D4
National Seal Sanctuary
   Corn TR12 6UG 95 E4
National Slate Museum,
   Llanberis Gwyn
   LL55 4TY 167 E2
National Space Centre,
   Leicester Leic
   LE4 5NS 17 C4
National Wallace Monument
   Stir FK9 5LF 242 D5
National War Museum,
   Edinburgh Edin
   EH1 2NG 37 E4
National Waterfront
   Museum SA1 3RD
   86 Swansea
National Wildflower Centre,
   Liverpool Mersey
   L16 3NA 22 D3
Natland 199 G4
Natural History Museum
   at Tring Herts
   HP23 6AP 135 E1
Natural History Museum,
   London GtLon
   SW7 5BD 11 F5
Natureland Seal
   Sanctuary Lincs
   PE25 1DB 177 D1
Naughton 152 B3
Naunton Glos 146 D5
Naunton Worcs 146 A4
Naunton
   Beauchamp 146 B2
Navenby 175 E2
Navestock 137 E3
Navestock Side 137 E3
Navidale 275 F7
Navity 266 E5
Nawton 203 F4
Nayland 152 A4
Nazeing 136 D2
Neacroft 106 A3
Neal's Green 159 F4
Neap 279 E7
Neap House 187 F3
Near Sawrey 199 E3
Nearton End 148 D5
Neasden 136 B4
Neasham 202 C1
Neat Enstone 147 F5

Neatham 120 C3
Neatishead 179 E3
Nebo Cere 142 B1
Nebo Conwy 168 B1
Nebo Gwyn 167 D2
Nebo IoA 180 C3
Necton 163 G2
Nedd 272 D5
Nedderton 221 E3
Nedging 152 A3
Nedging Tye 152 B3
Needham 164 D3
Needham Lake Suff
   IP6 8NU 152 B2
Needham Market 152 B2
Needham Street 151 F1
Needingworth 162 B5
Needles Pleasure Park IoW
   PO39 0JD 106 C4
Needwood 172 C5
Neen Savage 157 F5
Neen Sollars 157 F5
Neenton 157 F4
Nefyn 166 C3
Neighbourne 116 D3
Neilston 233 F4
Neithrop 147 G3
Nelson Caerp 130 A3
Nelson Lancs 193 E4
Nelson Village 221 E4
Nemphlar 234 C5
Nempnett
   Thrubwell 116 C1
Nenthall 211 D3
Nenthead 211 D3
Nenthorn 228 A3
Neopardy 102 A3
Nerabus 230 A4
Nercwys 169 F1
Neriby 230 B3
Nerston 234 A4
Nesbit 229 D3
Nesfield 193 G3
Ness 183 E5
Ness Botanic Gardens
   ChesW&C
   CH64 4AY 183 E5
Ness of Tenston 277 B6
Nesscliffe 156 C1
Neston ChesW&C 183 D5
Neston Wilts 117 F1
Nether
   Auchendrane 224 B4
Nether Barr 215 F4
Nether Blainslie 236 C5
Nether Broughton 174 B5
Nether Burrow 200 B4
Nether Cerne 104 C3
Nether Compton 104 B1
Nether Crimond 261 G2
Nether Dalgliesh 227 D5
Nether Dallachy 268 B4
Nether Edge 186 A4
Nether End 185 G5
Nether Exe 102 C3
Nether Glasslaw 269 G5
Nether Handwick 252 B5
Nether Haugh 186 B3
Nether Heage 173 E2
Nether Heselden 201 D5
Nether Heyford 148 B2
Nether Kellet 192 B1
Nether Kinmundy 269 J6
Nether Langwith 186 C5
Nether Lenshie 268 E6
Nether Loads 173 E1
Nether Moor 173 E1
Nether Padley 185 G5
Nether Pitforthie 253 G2
Nether Poppleton 195 E2
Nether Silton 203 D3
Nether Skyborry 156 B5
Nether Stowey 115 E4
Nether Urquhart 243 G4
Nether Wallop 119 E4
Nether Wasdale 198 C2
Nether Wellwood 225 E3
Nether Welton 209 G2
Nether Westcote 147 E5
Nether Whitacre 159 E3
Nether Winchendon (Lower
   Winchendon) 134 C1
Nether Worton 147 G5
Netheravon 118 C3
Netherbrae 269 F5
Netherbrough 277 C6
Netherburn 234 C5
Netherbury 104 A3
Netherby Cumb 218 B4
Netherby NYorks 194 C3
Nethercott 148 B4
Netherend 131 E2
Netherfield ESuss 110 C2
Netherfield Notts 174 B3
Netherfield SLan 234 B5
Netherhall 232 D3
Netherhampton 118 C5
Netherhay 104 A2
Netherland Green 172 C4
Netherley 261 G5
Nethermill 217 E2
Nethermuir 269 H6
Netherseal 159 E1
Nethershield 225 D3
Netherstreet 118 A1
Netherthird D&G 216 B5
Netherthird EAyr 225 D4
Netherthong 185 F2
Netherthorpe 186 C4
Netherton Angus 252 D4
Netherton
   ChesW&C 183 G5
Netherton Devon 102 B5
Netherton Hants 119 E2
Netherton Mersey 183 E2
Netherton N'umb 220 B1
Netherton Oxon 133 G2
Netherton P&K 251 G4
Netherton SLan 234 B4
Netherton WMid 158 B4
Netherton Worcs 146 B3
Netherton WYorks 185 G1
Netherton WYorks 185 F1
Netherton
   Burnfoot 220 B1
Netherton
   Northside 220 B1

Nethertown *Cumb* 198 A2
Nethertown *Ork* 275 J1
Nethertown *Staffs* 158 D1
Netherwitton 220 D2
Netherwood *D&G* 217 D3
Netherwood *EAyr* 225 E3
Nethy Bridge 259 H2
Netley Abbey 107 D2
Netley Marsh 106 C1
Nettlebed 134 B4
Nettlebridge 116 D3
Nettlecombe
  Dorset 104 B3
Nettlecombe *IoW* 107 E5
Nettlecombe *Som* 115 D4
Nettleden 135 F1
Nettleham 188 A5
Nettlestead *Kent* 123 F3
Nettlestead *Suff* 152 B3
Nettlestead Green 123 F3
Nettlestone 107 F3
Nettlesworth 212 B3
Nettleton *Lincs* 188 B2
Nettleton *Wilts* 132 A5
Nettleton Hill 185 E1
Netton *Devon* 100 B3
Netton *Wilts* 118 C4
Neuadd *Cere* 142 A2
Neuadd *IoA* 180 B3
Neuadd *Powys* 143 F3
Nevendon 137 G3
Nevern 141 D4
Nevill Holt 160 D3
New Abbey 217 D4
New Aberdour 269 G4
New Addington 122 C2
New Alresford 119 G4
New Alyth 252 A5
New Arley 159 E3
New Arram 196 C3
New Ash Green 123 F2
New Balderton 174 D2
New Barn 123 F2
New Belses 227 G3
New Bewick 229 E4
New Bolingbroke 176 B2
New Boultham 187 G5
New Brancepeth 212 B3
New Bridge *D&G* 216 C3
New Bridge
  Devon 102 A5
New Brighton
  Flints 169 F1
New Brighton
  Hants 107 G2
New Brighton
  Mersey 183 E3
New Brighton
  Wrex 169 F2
New Brighton
  WYorks 194 B5
New Brinsley 173 F2
New Broughton 170 A2
New Buckenham 164 B2
New Byth 269 G5
New Cheriton 119 G5
New Cross *Cere* 154 C5
New Cross *GtLon* 136 C5
New Cumnock 225 E4
New Deer 269 G6
New Duston 148 C1
New Earswick 195 F2
New Edlington 186 C3
New Elgin 267 K5
New Ellerby 197 D4
New Eltham 136 D5
New End 146 C1
New England 161 G2
New Farnley 194 B4
New Ferry 183 E4
New Galloway 216 A3
New Gilston 244 C4
New Greens 136 A2
New Grimsby 96 A1
New Hartley 221 F4
New Haw 121 F1
New Heaton 228 C3
New Hedges 127 E2
New Herrington 212 C2
New Hinksey 134 A2
New Holland 196 C5
New Houghton
  Derbys 173 G1
New Houghton
  Norf 177 F5
New Houses 200 D5
New Hunwick 212 A4
New Hutton 199 G3
New Hythe 123 G3
New Inn *Carmar* 142 A4
New Inn *Fife* 244 A4
New Inn *Mon* 131 D2
New Inn *Torfaen* 130 B3
New Invention
  Shrop 156 B5
New Invention
  WMid 158 B2
New Kelso 265 F7
New Lanark 234 C5
New Lanark World Heritage
  Site *SLan*
  ML11 9DB 234 C5
New Lane 183 F1
New Lane End 184 A3
New Leake 176 C2
New Leeds 269 H5
New Leslie 260 D2
New Lodge 186 A2
New Longton 192 B5
New Luce 214 C4
New Mains 225 G2
New Mains of Ury 253 G1
New Malden 122 B2
New Marske 213 F5
New Marton 170 A4
New Mill *Corn* 94 B3
New Mill *Herts* 135 E1
New Mill *WYorks* 185 F2
New Mill End 136 A1
New Mills *Corn* 96 C4
New Mills *Derbys* 185 E4
New Mills *Glos* 131 E2
New Mills *Mon* 131 E2
New Mills (Y Felin Newydd)
  Powys 155 G2
New Milton 106 B3
New Mistley 152 C4

New Moat 141 D5
New Ollerton 174 B1
New Orleans 222 C4
New Oscott 158 C3
New Palace &
  Adventureland, New
  Brighton *Mersey*
  CH45 2JX 22 A2
New Park *Corn* 97 F1
New Park *NYorks* 194 B2
New Pitsligo 269 G5
New Polzeath 96 D2
New Quay
  (Ceinewydd) 141 G1
New Rackheath 179 D4
New Radnor
  (Maesyfed) 144 B1
New Rent 210 A4
New Ridley 211 G1
New Road Side 193 F3
New Romney 111 F1
New Rossington 186 D3
New Row *Cere* 154 D5
New Row *Lancs* 192 C4
New Sawley 173 F4
New Shoreston 229 F3
New Silksworth 212 C2
New Stevenston 234 B4
New Swannington 159 G1
New Totley 186 A5
New Town
  CenBeds 149 G3
New Town *Cere* 141 E3
New Town *Dorset* 105 F1
New Town *Dorset* 105 F2
New Town *ELoth* 236 B2
New Town *ESuss* 109 G1
New Town *Glos* 146 C4
New Tredegar 130 A2
New Tupton 173 E1
New Ulva 231 F1
New Valley 271 G4
New Village 186 C2
New Walk Museum & Art
  Gallery LE1 7EA
  77 Leicester
New Walsoken 162 C2
New Waltham 188 C2
New Walton Pier *Essex*
  CO14 8ES 153 D5
New Winton 236 B2
New World 162 B3
New Yatt 133 F1
New York *Lincs* 176 A2
New York *T&W* 221 F4
Newall 194 B3
Newark *Ork* 276 G3
Newark *Peter* 162 A2
Newark Castle, Newark-on-
  Trent *Notts*
  NG24 1BG 174 C2
Newark-on-Trent 174 D2
Newarthill 234 B4
Newball 188 A5
Newbarn 125 D5
Newbarns 198 D5
Newbattle 236 A3
Newbiggin *Cumb* 210 A5
Newbiggin *Cumb* 210 C5
Newbiggin *Cumb* 210 B3
Newbiggin *Cumb* 191 F1
Newbiggin *Cumb* 198 B3
Newbiggin *Dur* 211 F5
Newbiggin *N'umb* 211 F1
Newbiggin *NYorks* 201 F1
Newbiggin *NYorks* 201 E3
Newbiggin-by-the-
  Sea 221 F3
Newbigging *Aber* 261 G5
Newbigging *Aber* 251 G1
Newbigging *Angus* 244 C1
Newbigging *Angus* 244 C1
Newbigging *Angus* 252 A5
Newbigging *SLan* 235 E5
Newbiggin-on-Lune 200 C2
Newbold *Derbys* 186 A5
Newbold *Leics* 159 G1
Newbold on Avon 159 G5
Newbold on Stour 147 G3
Newbold Pacey 147 E2
Newbold Verdon 159 G2
Newborough
  (Niwbwrch) *IoA* 166 D1
Newborough *Peter* 162 A2
Newborough *Staffs* 172 C5
Newbottle *N'hants* 148 A4
Newbottle *T&W* 212 C2
Newbourne 153 D3
Newbridge (Cefn Bychan)
  Caerp 130 B3
Newbridge *Corn* 94 B3
Newbridge *Corn* 98 D4
Newbridge *Edin* 235 F2
Newbridge *ESuss* 123 D5
Newbridge *Hants* 106 B1
Newbridge *IoW* 106 C4
Newbridge *NYorks* 204 B4
Newbridge *Oxon* 133 G2
Newbridge *Pembs* 140 C4
Newbridge *Wrex* 169 F3
Newbridge Green 146 A4
Newbridge on Wye 143 G3
Newbridge-on-Usk 130 C3
Newbrough 211 E1
Newbuildings 102 A2
Newburgh *Aber* 269 H5
Newburgh *Aber* 261 H2
Newburgh *Fife* 244 A3
Newburgh *Lancs* 183 F1
Newburgh *ScBord* 227 E3
Newburn 212 A1
Newbury *WBerks* 119 F1
Newbury *Wilts* 117 E4
Newbury Park 136 D4
Newby *Cumb* 210 B5
Newby *Lancs* 193 E3
Newby *NYorks* 203 E1
Newby *NYorks* 192 D1
Newby *NYorks* 204 D4
Newby Bridge 199 E4
Newby Cote 200 C5
Newby Cross 209 G1
Newby East 210 A2
Newby Hall *NYorks*
  HG4 5AE 194 C1
Newby West 209 G1
Newby Wiske 202 C4

Newcastle
  Bridgend 129 E5
Newcastle *Mon* 130 D1
Newcastle *Shrop* 156 B4
Newcastle Emlyn (Castell
  Newydd Emlyn) 141 G1
Newcastle International
  Airport 221 D4
Newcastle upon
  Tyne 212 B1
Newcastleton 218 C3
Newcastle-under-
  Lyme 171 F3
Newchapel *Pembs* 141 F4
Newchapel *Staffs* 171 F2
Newchapel *Surr* 122 C4
Newchurch
  Carmar 141 G5
Newchurch *IoW* 107 E4
Newchurch *Kent* 124 C5
Newchurch *Lancs* 193 E5
Newchurch *Lancs* 193 E4
Newchurch *Mon* 131 D3
Newchurch *Powys* 144 B2
Newchurch *Staffs* 172 C5
Newcott 103 F2
Newcraighall 236 A2
Newdigate 121 G3
Newell Green 135 D5
Newenden 110 D1
Newent 145 G5
Newerne 131 F2
Newfield *Dur* 212 B2
Newfield *Dur* 212 B2
Newfield *High* 266 E4
Newfound 119 G2
Newgale 140 B5
Newgate 178 B1
Newgate Street 136 C2
Newgord 278 E2
Newhall *ChesE* 170 D3
Newhall *Derbys* 173 D5
Newham 229 F4
Newham Hall 229 F4
Newhaven 109 G3
Newhey 184 D1
Newholm 204 B1
Newhouse 234 B3
Newick 109 G1
Newingreen 124 D5
Newington *Edin* 235 G2
Newington *Kent* 125 D5
Newington *Kent* 124 A2
Newington *Notts* 187 D3
Newington *Oxon* 134 B3
Newington
  Bagpath 132 A3
Newland *Cumb* 199 E5
Newland *Glos* 131 E2
Newland *Hull* 196 C4
Newland *NYorks* 195 F5
Newland *Oxon* 133 F1
Newland *Worcs* 145 G3
Newlandrig 236 A3
Newlands *Cumb* 209 G3
Newlands *Essex* 138 B4
Newlands *N'umb* 211 G2
Newlands *ScBord* 218 C2
Newland's Corner 121 F3
Newlands of Geise 275 F2
Newlands of Tynet 268 B4
Newlyn 94 B4
Newmachar 261 G3
Newmains 234 C4
Newman's End 137 E1
Newman's Green 151 G3
Newmarket *Suff* 151 E1
Newmarket *Na H-E. Siar*
  271 G4
Newmill *Aber* 253 F1
Newmill *Aber* 269 G6
Newmill *Aber* 261 G2
Newmill *Moray* 268 C5
Newmill *ScBord* 227 F4
Newmill of
  Inshewan 252 C3
Newmillerdam 186 A1
Newmillerdam Country Park
  WYorks WF2 6QP 27 H6
Newmills 266 D5
Newmilns *P&K* 243 G1
Newmilns *P&K* 243 F2
Newmilns 224 C2
Newney Green 137 F2
Newnham *Glos* 131 F1
Newnham *Hants* 120 C2
Newnham *Herts* 150 A4
Newnham *Kent* 124 B3
Newnham *N'hants* 148 A2
Newnham Bridge 145 F1
Newnham Paddox 159 G4
Newnoth 260 D1
Newport *Corn* 98 D2
Newport *Devon* 113 F2
Newport *ERid* 196 A4
Newport *Essex* 150 D4
Newport *Glos* 131 F3
Newport *High* 275 G6
Newport *IoW* 107 E4
Newport (Casnewydd)
  Newport 130 C4
Newport *Norf* 179 G4
Newport (Trefdraeth)
  Pembs 141 D4
Newport *Som* 116 A5
Newport *Tel&W* 157 G1
Newport Pagnell 149 D3
Newport-on-Tay 244 C2
Newpound
  Common 121 F5
Newquay 96 C3
Newquay Cornwall
  International Airport 96 C3
Newquay Zoo *Corn*
  TR7 2LZ 96 C3
Newsbank 171 F1
Newseat 261 F1
Newsells 150 B4
Newsham *Lancs* 192 B4
Newsham *N'umb* 221 E4
Newsham *NYorks* 202 A1
Newsham *NYorks* 202 A1
Newsholme *ERid* 195 G5
Newsholme *Lancs* 193 E3
Newsome 185 F1
Newstead *N'umb* 229 F4
Newstead *Notts* 173 G2
Newstead *ScBord* 227 G2

Newstead Abbey *Notts*
  NG15 8NA 173 G2
Newthorpe *Notts* 173 F3
Newthorpe *NYorks* 195 D4
Newtoft 188 A4
Newton *A&B* 240 C5
Newton *Aber* 268 C6
Newton *Aber* 269 J6
Newton *Bridgend* 129 E5
Newton *Cambs* 162 C1
Newton *Cambs* 150 C3
Newton *Cardiff* 130 B5
Newton *ChesW&C* 170 C2
Newton *ChesW&C* 183 G5
Newton *Cumb* 198 D5
Newton *D&G* 217 F2
Newton *Derbys* 173 F2
Newton *GtMan* 185 D3
Newton *Here* 144 C1
Newton *Here* 145 E2
Newton *Here* 144 C4
Newton *High* 275 J3
Newton *High* 266 E7
Newton *High* 275 H3
Newton *High* 267 J2
Newton *High* 266 C6
Newton *High* 266 E7
Newton *Lancs* 192 C2
Newton *Lancs* 199 G5
Newton *Lancs* 191 E3
Newton *Lincs* 175 F4
Newton *Moray* 268 B4
Newton *N'hants* 161 D4
Newton *N'umb* 211 G1
Newton *N'umb* 220 B1
Newton *NAyr* 232 A4
Newton *Norf* 163 G1
Newton *Notts* 174 B3
Newton *P&K* 243 D1
Newton *Pembs* 140 B5
Newton *Pembs* 126 C2
Newton *ScBord* 228 A4
Newton *SGlos* 131 F3
Newton *Shrop* 170 B4
Newton *SLan* 226 A2
Newton *Som* 115 E4
Newton *Staffs* 172 B5
Newton *Suff* 152 A3
Newton *Swan* 128 C4
Newton *Warks* 160 A5
Newton *Wilts* 118 A5
Newton *Wilts* 118 B5
Newton *WYorks* 194 D5
Newton *WLoth* 235 E2
Newton Abbot 102 B5
Newton Arlosh 209 F1
Newton Aycliffe 212 B5
Newton Bewley 213 D5
Newton
  Blossomville 149 E2
Newton Bromswold 149 E1
Newton Burgoland 159 F2
Newton by Toft 188 A4
Newton Ferrers 100 B3
Newton Flotman 164 D2
Newton Green 131 E3
Newton Harcourt 160 B3
Newton Kyme 195 D3
Newton Longville 148 D4
Newton Mearns 233 G4
Newton Morrell
  NYorks 202 B2
Newton Morrell
  Oxon 148 B5
Newton Mountain 126 C2
Newton Mulgrave 203 G1
Newton of Affleck 244 C1
Newton of Ardtoe 247 F2
Newton of
  Balcanquhal 243 G3
Newton of Dalvey 267 H6
Newton of Falkland 244 A4
Newton of Leys 258 D1
Newton on the Hill 170 B5
Newton on Trent 187 F5
Newton Poppleford 103 D4
Newton Purcell 148 B4
Newton Regis 159 E2
Newton Reigny 210 A4
Newton St. Cyres 102 B3
Newton St. Faith 178 D4
Newton St. Loe 117 E1
Newton St. Petrock 113 E4
Newton Solney 173 E5
Newton Stacey 119 F3
Newton Stewart 215 F4
Newton Tony 118 D3
Newton Tracey 113 F3
Newton under
  Roseberry 203 E1
Newton
  Underwood 221 D3
Newton upon
  Derwent 195 G3
Newton Valence 120 C4
Newton with
  Scales 192 A4
Newtonairds 216 C2
Newtongrange 236 A3
Newtonhill 261 H5
Newton-le-Willows
  Mersey 183 G3
Newton-le-Willows
  NYorks 202 B3
Newtonmill 253 E3
Newtonmore (Baile Ùr
  an t-Slèibh) 258 E5
Newton-on-Ouse 195 E2
Newton-on-
  Rawcliffe 204 B3
Newton-on-the-
  Moor 221 D1
Newtown *Bucks* 135 E2
Newtown
  ChesW&C 170 C2
Newtown *Corn* 97 G2
Newtown *Corn* 94 C4
Newtown *Cumb* 210 B1
Newtown *Derbys* 185 E4
Newtown *Devon* 114 A5
Newtown *Devon* 103 D3
Newtown *Dorset* 105 D1
Newtown *Glos* 131 F2
Newtown *GtMan* 183 G2
Newtown *GtMan* 184 B2
Newtown *Hants* 107 F1
Newtown *Hants* 119 E5
Newtown *Hants* 106 B1
Newtown *Hants* 119 E5

Newtown *Hants* 107 E1
Newtown *Here* 145 F3
Newtown *Here* 145 D2
Newtown *High* 257 K4
Newtown *IoM* 190 B4
Newtown *IoW* 106 C3
Newtown (Y Drenewydd)
  Powys 156 A3
Newtown *RCT* 129 G3
Newtown *Shrop* 170 B4
Newtown *Som* 115 F4
Newtown *Staffs* 171 G1
Newtown *Staffs* 172 B1
Newtown *Staffs* 158 B2
Newtown *Wilts* 118 A5
Newtown *Wilts* 119 E1
Newtown Linford 160 A2
Newtown
  St. Boswells 227 G2
Newtown Unthank 159 G2
Newtown-in-Saint-
  Martin 95 E4
Newtyle 252 A5
Newyears Green 135 F4
Neyland 126 C2
Nibley *Glos* 131 F2
Nibley *SGlos* 131 F5
Nibley Green 131 G3
Nicholashayne 103 E1
Nicholaston 128 B4
Nidd 194 C1
Nigg *Aberdeen* 261 H4
Nigg *High* 267 F4
Nightcott 114 B5
Nilig 168 C2
Nilson Rigg 211 E1
Nimlet 131 G5
Nine Ashes 137 E2
Nine Elms 132 D4
Nine Mile Burn 235 F4
Ninebanks 211 D2
Ninemile Bar
  (Crocketford) 216 C3
Nineveh 145 F1
Ninfield 110 C2
Ningwood 106 C4
Nisbet 228 A4
Niton 107 E5
Nitshill 233 G3
Nizels 123 E3
No Man's Heath
  ChesW&C 170 C3
No Man's Heath
  Warks 159 E2
No Man's Land 97 G4
Noah's Ark 123 E3
Noak Hill 137 E3
Noblehill 217 D3
Noblethorpe 185 G2
Nobottle 148 B1
Nocton 175 F1
Noddsdale 232 C3
Nogdam End 179 E5
Noke 134 A1
Nolton 126 B1
Nolton Haven 126 B1
Nomansland
  Devon 102 B1
Nomansland *Wilts* 106 B1
Noneley 170 B5
Nonington 125 E3
Nook *Cumb* 218 C4
Nook *Cumb* 199 G4
Noonsbrough 279 B7
Noranside 252 C3
Norbreck 191 G3
Norbury *ChesE* 170 C3
Norbury *Derbys* 172 C3
Norbury *GtLon* 136 C5
Norbury *Shrop* 156 C3
Norbury *Staffs* 171 E5
Norbury Common 170 C3
Norbury Junction 171 E5
Norchard 127 D3
Norcott Brook 184 A4
Nordelph 163 D2
Norden *Dorset* 105 F4
Norden *GtMan* 184 C1
Nordley 157 F3
Norham 237 G5
Norland Town 193 G5
Norley 183 G5
Norleywood 106 C3
Norlington 109 G2
Norman Cross 161 G3
Normanby *NLincs* 187 F1
Normanby *NYorks* 203 G4
Normanby *R&C* 203 E1
Normanby by Stow 187 F4
Normanby Hall Country
  Park *NLincs*
  DN15 9HU 187 F1
Normanby le Wold 188 B3
Normanby-by-
  Spital 188 A4
Normandy 121 E2
Norman's Ruh 246 D5
Norman's Green 103 D2
Normann's Bay 110 B3
Normans Green 165 G2
Normanston 165 G2
Normanton *Derby* 173 E4
Normanton *Leics* 174 D3
Normanton *Lincs* 175 E3
Normanton *Notts* 174 C2
Normanton *Rut* 161 E2
Normanton
  WYorks 194 C5
Normanton le
  Heath 159 F2
Normanton on Soar 173 G5
Normanton on
  Trent 174 C1
Normanton-on-the-
  Wolds 174 B4
Normoss 191 G4
Norrington
  Common 117 F2
Norris Green 100 A1
Norris Hill 159 F1
Norristhorpe 194 B5
North Acton 136 B4
North Anston 186 C4

North Ascot 121 E1
North Aston 147 G5
North Ballachulish
  (Baile a' Chaolais a
  Tuath) 248 C3
North Balloch 215 E1
North Barrow 116 D5
North Barsham 178 A2
North Bay Miniature
  Railway *NYorks*
  YO12 6PF 204 D3
North Benfleet 137 G4
North Bersted 108 B3
North Berwick 236 C1
North Boarhunt 107 F1
North Bogbain 268 B5
North Bovey 102 A4
North Bradley 117 F2
North Brentor 99 E2
North Brewham 117 E4
North Bridge 121 E4
North Buckland 113 E1
North Burlingham 179 E4
North Cadbury 116 D5
North Cairn 214 A3
North Camp 121 D2
North Carlton
  Lincs 187 G5
North Carlton
  Notts 186 C4
North Cave 196 A4
North Cerney 132 C2
North Chailey 109 F1
North Charford 106 A1
North Charlton 229 F4
North Cheriton 117 D5
North Chideock 104 A3
North Cliffe 196 A4
North Clifton 187 F5
North Cockerington 189 D3
North Coker 104 B1
North Collafirth 278 C4
North Common
  SGlos 131 F5
North Common
  Suff 164 A4
North Commonty 269 G6
North Connel 240 B1
North Coombe 102 B2
North Cornelly 129 E4
North Corner 131 F4
North Cotes 188 D2
North Cove 165 F3
North Cowton 202 B2
North Crawley 149 E3
North Cray 137 D5
North Creake 177 G4
North Curry 116 A5
North Dallens 248 B5
North Dalton 196 B2
North Dawn 277 D7
North Deighton 194 C2
North Dell (Dail Bho
  Thuath) 271 G1
North Duffield 195 F4
North Elkington 188 C3
North Elmham 178 A3
North Elmsall 186 B1
North End *Bucks* 148 D5
North End *Dorset* 117 F5
North End *ERid* 197 D5
North End *ERid* 197 D3
North End *ERid* 197 D4
North End *Essex* 137 F1
North End *Hants* 119 G5
North End *Hants* 106 A1
North End *Leics* 160 A1
North End *N'umb* 220 D1
North End *Norf* 164 B2
North End *NSom* 116 B1
North End *Ports* 107 F2
North End *WSuss* 108 C2
North End *WSuss* 108 B3
North Erradale 264 D3
North Essie 269 J5
North Fambridge 138 B3
North Ferriby 196 B5
North Frodingham 196 D2
North Gluss 278 C5
North Gorley 106 A1
North Green *Suff* 165 E4
North Green *Suff* 153 E1
North Green *Suff* 153 E1
North Grimston 196 A1
North Halling 123 G2
North Harby 187 F5
North Hayling 107 G2
North Hazelrigg 229 E3
North Heasley 114 A4
North Heath
  WBerks 133 G5
North Heath
  WSuss 121 F5
North Hill 97 G2
North Hillingdon 135 F4
North Hinksey 133 G2
North Holmwood 121 G3
North Houghton 119 E4
North Huish 100 D2
North Hykeham 175 E1
North Johnston 126 C1
North Kelsey 188 A2
North Kessock 266 D7
North Killingholme 188 B1
North Kilvington 202 D4
North Kilworth 160 B4
North Kingston 106 A2
North Kyme 175 G2
North Lancing 109 D3
North Lee 134 D2
North Lees 202 C5
North Leigh 133 F1
North Leverton with
  Habblesthorpe 187 E4
North Littleton 146 C3
North Lopham 164 B3
North Luffenham 161 E2
North Marden 108 A2
North Marston 148 C5
North Middleton
  Midlo 236 A4
North Middleton
  N'umb 229 E4
North Millbrex 269 G6
North Molton 114 A5
North Moreton 134 A4

North Mundham 108 A3
North Muskham 174 C2
North Newbald 196 B4
North Newington 147 G4
North Newnton 118 C2
North Newton 115 F4
North Nibley 131 G3
Norfolk Railway
  Norf NR26 8RA 178 C1
North Oakley 119 G2
North Ockendon 137 E4
North Ormesby 203 E1
North Ormsby 188 C3
North Otterington 202 C4
North Owersby 188 A3
North Perrott 104 A2
North Petherton 115 F4
North Petherwin 97 G1
North Pickenham 163 G2
North Piddle 146 B2
North Plain 217 F4
North Pool 101 D3
North Poorton 104 B3
North Quarme 114 C4
North Queensferry 235 F1
North Radworthy 114 A4
North Rauceby 175 F3
North Reston 189 D4
North Riding Forest Park
  NYorks
  YO18 7LT 204 B3
North Rigton 194 B3
North Rode 171 F1
North Roe 278 C4
North Ronaldsay 276 G2
North Ronaldsay
  Airfield 276 G2
North Runcton 163 E1
North Sandwick 278 E3
North Scale 191 E1
North Seaton 221 E3
North Shian (Sithean a
  Tuath) 248 B5
North Shields 212 C1
North Shoebury 138 C4
North Side 162 A3
North Skelton 203 F1
North Somercotes 189 E3
North Stainley 202 B5
North Stainmore 200 D1
North Stifford 137 F4
North Stoke
  B&NESom 117 E1
North Stoke *Oxon* 134 B4
North Stoke *WSuss* 108 C2
North Stoneham 106 D1
North Street *Hants* 120 B4
North Street *Kent* 124 C3
North Street *Med* 124 A1
North Street
  WBerks 134 B5
North Sunderland 229 G3
North Tamerton 98 D1
North Tarbothill 261 H3
North Tawton 113 G5
North Third 234 B1
North Thoresby 188 C3
North Tidworth 118 D3
North Togston 221 E1
North Town *Devon* 113 F5
North Town *Hants* 121 D2
North Town *W&M* 135 E4
North Tuddenham 178 B4
North Uist (Uibhist a
  Tuath) 262 D4
North Walsham 179 D2
North Waltham 119 G3
North
  Warnborough 120 C2
North Water Bridge 253 E3
North Watten 275 H3
North Weald
  Bassett 137 D2
North Wembley 136 A4
North Wheatley 187 E4
North Whilborough 101 E1
North Wick 116 C1
North Widcombe 116 C2
North Willingham 188 B4
North Wingfield 173 F1
North Witham 175 E5
North Wootton
  Dorset 104 C1
North Wootton
  Norf 177 E5
North Wootton
  Som 116 C3
North Wraxall 132 A5
North Wroughton 132 D4
North Yardhope 220 B1
North Yorkshire Moors
  Railway *NYorks*
  YO18 7AJ 204 B4
Northacre 164 A2
Northall 149 E5
Northall Green 178 A4
Northallerton 202 C3
Northam *Devon* 113 E3
Northam *Soton* 106 D1
Northam Burrows Country
  Park *Devon*
  EX39 1XR 113 E2
Northampton 148 C1
Northaw 136 B2
Northay *Devon* 103 G2
Northay *Som* 103 F1
Northbay 254 C3
Northbeck 175 F3
Northborough 161 G2
Northbourne *Kent* 125 F3
Northbourne *Oxon* 134 A4
Northbridge Street 110 C3
Northbrook *Hants* 119 G4
Northbrook *Oxon* 147 G5
Northburnhill 269 G6
Northchapel 121 E5
Northchurch 135 E2
Northcote Manor 113 G4
Northcott 98 D1
Northcourt 134 A3
Northdyke 276 B5
Northedge 173 E1
Northend
  B&NESom 117 E1
Northend *Bucks* 134 C3
Northend *Warks* 147 F2
Northfield *Aber* 269 G4

Northfield
  Aberdeen 261 H4
Northfield High 275 J4
Northfield GtBord 237 G3
Northfield Hull 196 C5
Northfield Som 115 F4
Northfield WMid 158 C5
Northfields 161 F2
Northfleet 137 F5
Northhouse 227 F5
Northiam 110 D1
Northill 149 G3
Northington Glos 131 G2
Northington
  Hants 119 G4
Northlands 178 B2
Northleach 132 D1
Northleigh Devon 103 E3
Northleigh Devon 113 G4
Northlew 99 F1
Northmoor 133 G2
Northmoor Green
  (Moorland) 116 A4
Northmuir 252 B4
Northney 107 G2
Northolt 136 A4
Northop
  (Llaneurgain) 169 F1
Northop Hall 169 F1
Northorpe Lincs 176 A4
Northorpe Lincs 187 F3
Northorpe Lincs 161 F1
Northover Som 116 C5
Northover Som 116 B4
Northowram 194 A5
Northport 105 F4
Northpunds 279 D10
Northrepps 178 D2
Northton
  (Taobh Tuath) 262 E3
Northtown 277 D8
Northumberland Dark Sky
  Park N'umb 219 F4
Northumbria Craft Centre,
  Morpeth N'umb
  NE61 1PD 221 E3
Northway Glos 146 B4
Northway Som 115 E5
Northwich 184 A5
Northwick SGlos 131 E4
Northwick Som 116 A3
Northwick Worcs 146 A2
Northwold 163 F3
Northwood GtLon 135 F3
Northwood IoW 107 D3
Northwood Kent 125 F2
Northwood Mersey 183 F3
Northwood Green 131 G1
Northwood Shrop 170 C4
Northwood Hills 136 A3
Norton Glos 146 A5
Norton Halton 183 G4
Norton Herts 150 A4
Norton IoW 106 C4
Norton Mon 144 D5
Norton N'hants 148 B1
Norton Notts 186 C5
Norton NSom 116 A1
Norton NYorks 203 G5
Norton Powys 144 C1
Norton Shrop 157 E2
Norton Shrop 157 G3
Norton Shrop 157 D4
Norton Stock 212 D5
Norton Suff 152 A1
Norton Swan 128 C4
Norton SYorks 186 C1
Norton SYorks 186 A4
Norton VGlam 129 E5
Norton Wilts 132 A4
Norton WMid 158 A4
Norton Worcs 146 A2
Norton Worcs 146 C3
Norton WSuss 108 A3
Norton WSuss 108 A4
Norton Bavant 118 A3
Norton Bridge 171 F4
Norton Canes 158 C2
Norton Canon 144 C3
Norton Disney 175 D2
Norton Ferris 117 E4
Norton Fitzwarren 115 E5
Norton Green
  Herts 150 A5
Norton Green IoW 106 C4
Norton Green
  Stoke 171 G2
Norton Hawkfield 116 C1
Norton Heath 137 F2
Norton in Hales 171 E4
Norton in the
  Moors 171 F2
Norton Lindsey 147 E1
Norton Little Green 152 A1
Norton Malreward 116 D1
Norton Mandeville 137 E2
Norton St. Philip 117 E2
Norton Subcourse 165 F2
Norton Wood 144 C3
Norton Woodseats 186 A4
Norton-Juxta-
  Twycross 159 F2
Norton-le-Clay 202 D5
Norton-sub-
  Hamdon 104 A1
Norwell 174 C1
Norwell Woodhouse 174 C1
Norwich 178 D5
Norwich Castle Museum &
  Art Gallery Norf
  NR1 3JU 79 Norwich
Norwich Cathedral Norf
  NR1 4DH 79 Norwich
Norwich International
  Airport 178 D4
Norwick 278 F1
Norwood End 137 E2
Norwood Green
  GtLon 136 A5
Norwood Green
  WYorks 194 A5
Norwood Hill 122 B4
Noseley 160 C3
Noss Mayo 100 B3
Nosterfield 202 B4
Nosterfield End 151 E3
Nostie 256 E2

Notgrove 146 D5
Nottage 129 E5
Notting Hill 136 B4
Nottingham High 275 H5
Nottingham Nott 173 G3
Nottingham Castle Museum
  & Art Gallery NG1 6EL
  80 Nottingham
Nottington 104 C4
Notton Wilts 132 B5
Notton WYorks 186 A1
Nottswood Hill 131 G1
Nounsley 137 G1
Noutard's Green 145 G1
Nowton 151 G1
Nowton Park Suff
  IP29 5LU 151 G1
Nox 156 D1
Noyadd Trefawr 141 F3
Nuffield 134 B4
Nun Monkton 195 E2
Nunburnholme 196 A3
Nuneaton 159 F3
Nuneham
  Courtenay 134 A3
Nunney 117 E3
Nunnington
  NYorks 203 F5
Nunnington Park 115 D5
Nunnykirk 220 C2
Nunsthorpe 188 C2
Nunthorpe Middl 203 E1
Nunthorpe York 195 E2
Nunton 118 C5
Nunwick N'umb 220 A4
Nunwick NYorks 202 C5
Nup End 131 G2
Nupend 131 G2
Nursling 106 C1
Nursted 120 C5
Nurton 158 A3
Nutbourne WSuss 108 C2
Nutbourne WSuss 107 G2
Nutfield 122 C3
Nuthall 173 G3
Nuthampstead 150 C4
Nuthurst Warks 159 D5
Nuthurst WSuss 121 G5
Nutley ESuss 109 G1
Nutley Hants 120 B3
Nutwell 186 D2
Nyadd 242 C5
Nybster 275 J2
Nyetimber 108 A4
Nyewood 120 C5
Nymans WSuss
  RH17 6EB 109 E1
Nymet Rowland 102 A2
Nymet Tracey 102 A2
Nympsfield 132 A2
Nynehead 115 E5
Nythe 116 B4
Nyton 108 B3

O
O2, The GtLon
  SE10 0BB 13 E6
Oad Street 124 A2
Oadby 160 B2
Oak Cross 99 F1
Oak Tree 202 C1
Oakamoor 172 B3
Oakbank A&B 239 G1
Oakbank WLoth 235 E3
Oakdale Caerp 130 A3
Oakdale Poole 105 G3
Oake 115 E5
Oaken 158 A2
Oakenclough 192 B3
Oakengates 157 G1
Oakenhead 267 K5
Oakenholt 183 D5
Oakenshaw Dur 212 B4
Oakenshaw
  WYorks 194 A5
Oakerthorpe 173 E2
Oakes 185 F1
Oakfield IoW 107 E3
Oakfield Torfaen 130 B3
Oakford Cere 142 A2
Oakford Devon 114 C5
Oakfordbridge 114 C5
Oakgrove 171 G1
Oakham 161 D2
Oakhanger 120 C4
Oakhill 116 D3
Oakington 150 C1
Oaklands Conwy 168 B2
Oaklands Herts 136 B1
Oakle Street 131 G1
Oakley Bed 149 F2
Oakley Bucks 134 B1
Oakley Fife 235 E1
Oakley Hants 119 G3
Oakley Oxon 134 C2
Oakley Poole 105 G3
Oakley Suff 164 C4
Oakley Green 135 E5
Oakley Park 155 F4
Oakridge Lynch 132 B2
Oaks 156 D2
Oaks Green 172 C4
Oaksey 132 B3
Oakshaw Ford 218 D4
Oakshott 120 C5
Oakthorpe 159 F1
Oaktree Hill 202 C3
Oakwell Hall & Country Park
  WYorks
  WF17 9LG 27 E4
Oakwood Leisure Park
  Pembs
  SA67 8DE 127 D1
Oakwoodhill 121 G4
Oakworth 193 G4
Oare Kent 124 C2
Oare Som 114 B3
Oare Wilts 118 C1
Oasby 175 F4
Oatfield 222 B4
Oath 116 A5
Oathlaw 252 C4
Oatlands 194 C2
Oban
  (An t-Òban) 240 A2
Obley 156 C5
Oborne 104 C1

Obthorpe 161 F1
Occlestone Green 171 D1
Occold 164 C4
Occumster 275 H5
Oceanarium BH2 5AA
  64 Bournemouth
Ochiltree 224 D3
Ochr-y-foel 182 B5
Ochtermuthill 242 D2
Ochtertyre P&K 242 D2
Ochtertyre Stir 242 C5
Ockbrook 173 F4
Ockeridge 145 G1
Ockham 121 F2
Ockle 247 E2
Ockley 121 G4
Ocle Pychard 145 E3
Octon 204 D5
Odd Down 117 E1
Oddendale 200 B1
Oddingley 146 B2
Oddington 134 A1
Odds Farm Park Bucks
  HP10 0LX 135 E4
Odell 149 E2
Odham 113 E5
Odie 276 F5
Odsey 150 A4
Odstock 118 C5
Odstone 159 F2
Offchurch 147 F1
Offenham 146 C3
Offerton 184 D4
Offham ESuss 109 F2
Offham Kent 123 F3
Offham WSuss 108 C3
Offley Hoo 149 G5
Offleymarsh 171 E5
Offord Cluny 150 A1
Offord D'Arcy 150 A2
Offton 162 B3
Offwell 103 E3
Ogbourne Maizey 133 D5
Ogbourne
  St. Andrew 133 D5
Ogbourne
  St. George 133 D5
Ogil 252 C3
Ogle 220 D4
Oglet 183 F4
Ogmore 129 E5
Ogmore Vale 129 F3
Ogmore-by-Sea 129 E5
Ogston Reservoir Derbys
  DE55 6EL 173 E1
Oil Terminal 277 C8
Okeford Fitzpaine 105 E2
Okehampton 99 F1
Okehampton Camp 99 F1
Okraquoy 279 D9
Olchard 102 B5
Olchfa 128 C3
Old 160 C5
Old Aberdeen 261 H4
Old Alresford 119 G4
Old Arley 159 E3
Old Basford 173 G3
Old Basing 120 B2
Old Belses 227 G3
Old Bewick 229 E4
Old Bolingbroke 176 B1
Old Bramhope 194 B3
Old Brampton 186 A5
Old Bridge of Urr 216 B4
Old Buckenham 164 B2
Old Burdon 212 C2
Old Burghclere 119 F2
Old Byland 203 E4
Old Cassop 212 C4
Old Church Stoke 156 B3
Old Cleeve 114 D3
Old Clipstone 174 B1
Old Colwyn 181 G5
Old Craig 261 H2
Old Craighall 236 A2
Old Crombie 268 D5
Old Dailly 214 D1
Old Dalby 174 B5
Old Dam 185 F5
Old Deer 269 H6
Old Dilton 117 F3
Old Down SGlos 131 F4
Old Down Som 116 D2
Old Edlington 186 C3
Old Eldon 212 B5
Old Ellerby 197 D4
Old Felixstowe 153 E4
Old Fletton 161 G3
Old Ford 136 C4
Old Glossop 185 E3
Old Goginan 154 C4
Old Goole 195 G5
Old Gore 145 F5
Old Grimsby 96 A1
Old Hall 188 C1
Old Hall Green 150 B5
Old Hall Street 179 E2
Old Harlow 137 D1
Old Heath 152 B5
Old Heathfield 110 A1
Old Hill 158 B4
Old Hurst 162 B5
Old Hutton 199 G4
Old Kea 96 C5
Old Kilpatrick 233 F2
Old Kinnernie 261 F4
Old Knebworth 150 A5
Old Leake 176 C1
Old Leslie 260 D2
Old Malton 204 B5
Old Milton 106 B3
Old Milverton 147 E1
Old Montsale 138 D3
Old Netley 107 D1
Old Newton 152 B1
Old Philpstoun 235 E2
Old Poltalloch 240 A4
Old Radnor
  (Pencraig) 144 B2

Old Rattray 269 J5
Old Rayne 260 E2
Old Romney 111 F1
Old Royal Naval College,
  Greenwich GtLon
  SE10 9LW 13 E6
Old Scone 243 G2
Old Shields 234 C2
Old Sodbury 131 G4
Old Somerby 175 E4
Old Station, The, Tintern
  Parva Mon
  NP16 7NX 131 E2
Old Stratford 148 C3
Old Sunderlandwick 196 C2
Old Swarland 221 D1
Old Swinford 158 A4
Old Thirst 202 D4
Old Town Cumb 199 G4
Old Town IoS 96 B1
Old Town Farm 220 A2
Old Tupton 173 E1
Old Warden 149 G3
Old Weston 161 F5
Old Windsor 135 E5
Old Wives Lees 124 C3
Old Woking 121 F2
Old Woodhall 176 A1
Old Woods 170 B5
Oldberrow 146 D1
Oldborough 102 A2
Oldbury Kent 123 E3
Oldbury Shrop 157 G3
Oldbury Warks 159 F3
Oldbury WMid 158 B4
Oldbury Court Estate
  Bristol BS16 2JH 8 D2
Oldbury Naite 131 F3
Oldbury on the Hill 132 A4
Oldbury-on-Severn 131 F3
Oldcastle Bridgend 129 F5
Oldcastle Mon 144 C5
Oldcastle Heath 170 B3
Oldcotes 186 C4
Oldcroft 131 F2
Oldeamere 162 B3
Oldfield 146 A1
Oldford 117 E2
Oldhall Aber 260 C5
Oldhall High 275 H3
Oldham 184 D2
Oldham Edge 184 D2
Oldhamstocks 237 E2
Oldland 131 F5
Oldmeldrum 261 G2
Oldmill 260 D4
Oldpark 157 F2
Oldridge 102 B3
Oldshore Beg 272 D3
Oldshoremore 272 E3
Oldstead 203 E5
Oldtown 266 C3
Oldtown of Aigas 266 B7
Oldtown of Ord 268 E5
Oldwalls 128 A3
Oldways End 114 B5
Oldwhat 269 G5
Oldwich Lane 159 E5
Olgrinmore 275 G3
Oliver 226 C3
Oliver's Battery 119 F5
Ollaberry 278 C4
Ollerton ChesE 184 B5
Ollerton Notts 174 B1
Ollerton Shrop 170 D5
Olmstead Green 151 E3
Olney 149 D2
Olrig House 275 G2
Olton 158 D4
Olveston 131 F4
Ombersley 146 A1
Ompton 174 B1
Onchan 190 B4
Onecote 172 B2
Onehouse 152 B2
Ongar Hill 177 D5
Ongar Street 144 C1
Onibury 157 D5
Onich
  (Omhanaich) 248 C3
Onllwyn 129 E1
Onneley 171 E3
Onslow Green 137 F1
Onslow Village 121 E3
Opinan High 264 D5
Opinan High 264 D4
Orange Lane 237 E5
Orasaigh 271 F6
Orbliston 268 B5
Orbost 263 H7
Orby 176 C1
Orcadia 232 C3
Orchard 232 C1
Orchard Portman 115 F5
Orcheston 118 B3
Orcop 145 D5
Orcop Hill 145 D5
Ord 256 C3
Ordhead 260 E4
Ordie 260 C4
Ordiequish 268 B5
Ordsall 187 D5
Ore 110 D2
Oreham Common 109 E2
Oreston 100 B2
Oreton 157 F5
Orford Suff 153 F3
Orford Warr 184 A3
Organford 105 F3
Orgreave 158 D1
Orkney Islands 276 C5
Orlestone 124 B5
Orleton Here 145 D1
Orleton Worcs 145 F1
Orleton Common 145 D1
Orlingbury 161 D5
Ormacleit 254 C1
Ormesby 203 E1
Ormesby
  St. Margaret 179 F4
Ormesby
  St. Michael 179 F4
Ormidale 232 B1
Ormiscaig 264 E2
Ormiston 236 B3
Ormlie 275 G2

Ormsaigmore 247 D3
Ormsary 231 F2
Ormskirk 183 F2
Oronsay 230 B1
Orphir 277 C7
Orpington 123 D2
Orrell GtMan 183 G2
Orrell Mersey 183 E3
Orrisdale 190 B2
Orrok House 261 H3
Orroland 208 A2
Orsett 137 F4
Orsett Heath 137 F4
Orslow 158 A1
Orston 174 C3
Orton Cumb 200 B2
Orton N'hants 160 D5
Orton Longueville 161 G3
Orton Rigg 209 G1
Orton Waterville 161 G3
Orton-on-the-Hill 159 F2
Orwell 150 B2
Osbaldeston 192 C4
Osbaldwick 195 F2
Osbaston Leics 159 F2
Osbaston Shrop 170 A5
Osbaston Tel&W 157 E1
Osbaston Hollow 159 F2
Osborne 107 E3
Osborne House IoW
  PO32 6JX 107 E3
Osbournby 175 F4
Oscroft 170 C1
Ose 263 J7
Osgathorpe 159 F1
Osgodby Lincs 188 A3
Osgodby NYorks 195 F4
Osgodby NYorks 205 D4
Oskaig 256 B1
Osleston 172 D4
Osmaston Derby 173 E4
Osmaston Derbys 172 C3
Osmington 104 D4
Osmington Mills 104 D4
Osmondthorpe 194 C4
Osmotherley 203 D3
Osnaburgh (Dairsie) 244 C3
Ospringe 124 C2
Ossett 194 B5
Ossett Street Side 194 B5
Ossington 174 C1
Ostend 138 C3
Osterley 136 A5
Osterley Park & House
  GtLon TW7 4RB 11 B5
Oswaldkirk 203 F5
Oswaldtwistle 192 D5
Oswestry 169 F5
Oteley 170 B4
Otford 123 E3
Otham 123 G3
Otherton 158 B1
Othery 116 A4
Otley Suff 152 D2
Otley WYorks 194 B3
Otter 232 A2
Otter Ferry 232 A1
Otterbourne 119 F5
Otterburn N'umb 220 A2
Otterburn NYorks 193 E2
Otterburn Camp 220 A2
Otterden Place 124 B3
Otterham 98 B1
Otterham Quay 124 A2
Otterhampton 115 F3
Otternish 262 E4
Ottershaw 121 F1
Otterswick 278 E4
Otterton 103 D4
Otterton Mill Devon
  EX9 7HG 103 D4
Otterwood 106 D2
Ottery St. Mary 103 D3
Ottinge 125 D4
Ottringham 197 E5
Oughterby 209 F1
Oughtershaw 201 D4
Oughterside 209 E2
Oughtibridge 186 A3
Oulston 203 E5
Oulton Cumb 209 F1
Oulton Norf 178 C3
Oulton Staffs 171 G4
Oulton Staffs 171 F5
Oulton Suff 165 G2
Oulton WYorks 194 C5
Oulton Broad 165 G2
Oulton Grange 171 G4
Oulton Street 178 C3
Oultoncross 171 G4
Oundle 161 F4
Ousby 210 C4
Ousdale 275 F6
Ousden 151 F2
Ousefleet 196 A5
Ouston Dur 212 B2
Ouston N'umb 220 C4
Out Newton 197 F5
Out Rawcliffe 192 A3
Out Skerries
  Airstrip 278 F4
Outcast 199 E5
Outchester 229 F3
Outertown 277 B7
Outgate 199 E3
Outhgill 200 C2
Outlands 171 E5
Outlane 185 E1
Outwell 162 D2
Outwood Surr 122 C4
Outwood WYorks 194 C5
Outwoods 157 G1
Ouzlewell Green 194 C5
Ovenden 193 G5
Over Cambs 162 B5
Over ChesW&C 170 D1
Over Glos 132 A1
Over SGlos 131 E4
Over Burrows 173 D4
Over Compton 104 B1
Over Dinsdale 202 C1
Over End 185 G5
Over Green 159 D3
Over Haddon 172 D1
Over Hulton 184 A2
Over Kellet 192 B1

Over Kiddington 147 G5
Over Monnow 131 D1
Over Norton 147 F5
Over Peover 184 B5
Over Rankeilour 244 B3
Over Silton 203 D3
Over Stowey 115 E4
Over Stratton 104 A1
Over Tabley 184 B4
Over Wallop 119 D4
Over Whitacre 159 E3
Over Winchendon (Upper
  Winchendon) 134 C1
Over Worton 147 G5
Overbister 276 F3
Overbrae 269 G5
Overbury 146 B4
Overcombe 104 C4
Overgreen 186 A5
Overleigh 116 B4
Overpool 183 E5
Overscaig Hotel 273 G6
Overseal 159 E1
Overslade 159 G5
Oversland 124 C3
Oversley Green 146 C2
Overstone 148 D1
Overstrand 178 D1
Overthorpe 147 G3
Overton Aber 261 F3
Overton Aberdeen 261 G3
Overton ChesW&C 183 G5
Overton Hants 119 G3
Overton Lancs 192 A2
Overton NYorks 195 E2
Overton Shrop 157 E5
Overton Swan 128 A4
Overton (Owrtyn)
  Wrex 170 A3
Overton WYorks 185 G1
Overton Bridge 170 A3
Overtown Lancs 200 B5
Overtown NLan 234 C4
Overtown Swin 133 D5
Overy 134 C2
Oving Bucks 148 C5
Oving WSuss 108 B3
Ovingdean 109 F3
Ovingham 211 G1
Ovington Dur 202 A1
Ovington Essex 151 F3
Ovington Hants 119 G4
Ovington N'umb 211 G1
Ovington Norf 178 A5
Ower Hants 106 C1
Ower Hants 107 D2
Owermoigne 105 D4
Owler Bar 185 G5
Owlpen 131 G3
Owl's Green 153 D1
Owlswick 134 C2
Owmby 160 C2
Owmby-by-Spital 188 A4
Owslebury 119 G5
Owston 160 C2
Owston Ferry 187 F2
Owstwick 197 E4
Owthorpe 174 B4
Oxborough 163 F2
Oxcombe 188 C5
Oxen End 151 F5
Oxencombe 102 B4
Oxenhall 145 G5
Oxenholme 199 G3
Oxenhope 193 G4
Oxenpill 116 B3
Oxenton 146 B4
Oxenwood 119 E2
Oxford 134 A2
Oxford Cathedral Oxon
  OX1 1AB 80 Oxford
Oxford Story Oxon
  OX1 3AJ 80 Oxford
Oxford University Museum
  of Natural History
  Oxon OX1 3PW
  80 Oxford
Oxhey 136 A3
Oxhill 147 F3
Oxley 158 B2
Oxley Green 138 C1
Oxley's Green 110 B1
Oxnam 228 B5
Oxnead 178 D3
Oxnop Ghyll 201 E3
Oxshott 121 G1
Oxspring 185 G2
Oxted 122 C3
Oxton Mersey 183 E4
Oxton Notts 174 B2
Oxton ScBord 236 B4
Oxwich 128 A4
Oxwich Green 128 A4
Oxwick 178 A3
Oykel Bridge 265 K1
Oyne 260 E2
Ozleworth 131 G3

P
Pabbay 262 D3
Packington 159 F1
Packwood 159 D5
Padanaram 252 C4
Padarn Country Park
  Gwyn
  LL55 4TY 167 E1
Padbury 148 C4
Paddington 136 B4
Paddlesworth 125 D4
Paddock 124 B3
Paddock Wood 123 F4
Paddockhaugh 267 K6
Paddockhole 218 A3
Paddolgreen 170 C4
Padeswood 169 F1
Padfield 185 E3
Padiham 193 D4
Padside 194 A2
Padstow 96 D2
Padworth 120 B1
Paganhill 132 A2
Pagham 108 A4
Paglesham
  Churchend 138 C3
Paglesham Eastend
  138 C3

Paible 263 F2
Paignton 101 E1
Paignton & Dartmouth
  Steam Railway
  Torbay
  TQ4 6AF 101 E2
Paignton Pier
  Torbay
  TQ4 6BW 101 E1
Paignton Zoo
  Torbay
  TQ4 7EU 101 E2
Pailton 159 G4
Paine's Corner 110 B1
Painscastle 144 A3
Painshawfield 211 G1
Painswick 132 A2
Pairc 270 E2
Paisley 233 F3
Pakefield 165 G2
Pakenham 152 A1
Palace of Holyroodhouse
  Edin EH8 8DX 37 J4
Palacerigg Country Park
  NLan G67 3HU 234 B2
Pale 168 C4
Palehouse
  Common 109 G2
Palestine 119 D3
Paley Street 135 D5
Palgowan 215 E2
Palgrave 164 C4
Pallinsburn House 228 C3
Palmarsh 124 C5
Palmers Cross 121 F3
Palmers Green 136 C3
Palmerscross 267 K5
Palmerstown 130 A5
Palnackie 216 C5
Palnure 215 F4
Palterton 173 F1
Pamber End 120 B2
Pamber Green 120 B2
Pamber Heath 120 B1
Pamington 146 B4
Pamphill 105 F2
Pampisford 150 C3
Pan 277 C8
Panborough 116 B3
Panbride 245 D1
Pancrasweek 112 C5
Pancross 114 C5
Pandy Gwyn 154 C2
Pandy Mon 144 C5
Pandy Powys 155 F2
Pandy Wrex 169 E4
Pandy Tudur 168 B1
Pandy'r Capel 169 D2
Panfield 151 F5
Pangbourne 134 B5
Pannal 194 C2
Pannal Ash 194 B2
Panshanger 136 B1
Pant 169 F5
Pant Glas 167 D3
Pant Gwyn 168 B5
Pant Mawr 155 F5
Pantasaph 182 C5
Panteg 130 C2
Pantglas 155 F2
Pantgwyn Carmar 142 B5
Pantgwyn Cere 141 F3
Pant-lasau 128 C2
Panton 188 B5
Pant-pastynog 168 D1
Pantperthog 154 D2
Pant-y-dwr 155 F5
Pantyffordd 169 F2
Pant-y-ffridd 156 A2
Pantyffynnon 128 C1
Pantygasseg 130 B3
Pantygelli 130 C1
Pantymwyn 169 E1
Panxworth 179 E4
Papa Stour 279 A6
Papa Stour Airstrip 279 A6
Papa Westray 276 D2
Papa Westray
  Airfield 276 D2
Papcastle 209 E3
Papil 279 C9
Papple 236 C2
Papplewick 173 G2
Papworth Everard 150 A1
Papworth St. Agnes 150 A1
Par 97 E4
Paradise Park, Newhaven
  ESuss BN9 0DH 109 G3
Paradise Wildlife Park,
  Broxbourne Herts
  EN10 7QA 136 C2
Parbold 183 F1
Parbrook Som 116 C4
Parbrook WSuss 121 F5
Parc 168 B4
Parcllyn 141 F2
Parcrhydderch 142 C2
Parc-Seymour 130 D3
Parc-y-rhôs 142 B3
Pardshaw 209 E2
Parham 153 E1
Parish Holm 225 F3
Park 268 D5
Park Corner ESuss 123 E5
Park Corner Oxon 134 B4
Park End N'umb 220 A4
Park End Staffs 171 E2
Park End Worcs 157 G5
Park Gate Hants 107 E2
Park Gate Worcs 158 B5
Park Gate WYorks 194 A3
Park Gate WYorks 185 G1
Park Green 152 C1
Park Hill 186 A4
Park Lane 170 B4
Park Langley 122 C2
Park Rose Pottery & Leisure
  Park ERid
  YO15 3QF 196 D1
Park Street 193 E3
Parkend Cumb 209 G3
Parkend Glos 131 F2
Parker's Green 123 F4
Parkeston 152 D4
Parkfield Corn 98 D4
Parkfield SGlos 131 F5
Parkfield WMid 158 B3

Parkford **252** C4
Parkgate ChesW&C **183** D5
Parkgate D&G **217** E2
Parkgate Kent **124** A5
Parkgate Surr **122** B4
Parkgate SYorks **186** B3
Parkham **113** D3
Parkham Ash **113** D3
Parkhead **234** A3
Parkhill Angus **253** E5
Parkhill P&K **251** G5
Parkhouse **131** D2
Parkhurst **107** D3
Parkmill **128** B4
Parkmore **268** B6
Parkneuk **253** F2
Parkside **170** A2
Parkstone **105** G3
Parkway **116** C5
Parley Cross **105** G3
Parley Green **106** A3
Parlington **194** D4
Parracombe **113** G1
Parrog **140** D4
Parson Cross **186** A3
Parson Drove **162** B2
Parsonage Green **137** F1
Parsonby **209** E3
Partick **233** G3
Partington **184** B3
Partney **176** C1
Parton Cumb **208** C4
Parton D&G **216** A3
Partridge Green **109** D2
Parwich **172** C2
Paslow Wood
  Common **137** E2
Passenham **148** C4
Passfield **120** D4
Passingford Bridge **137** E3
Paston **179** E2
Paston Street **179** E2
Pasturefields **171** G5
Patchacott **99** E1
Patcham **109** F3
Patchetts Green **136** A3
Patching **108** C3
Patchole **113** G1
Patchway **131** E4
Pateley Bridge **194** A1
Path of Condie **243** F3
Pathe **116** A4
Pathfinder Village **102** B3
Pathhead Aber **253** F3
Pathhead EAyr **225** G4
Pathhead Fife **244** A5
Pathhead Midlo **236** A3
Pathlow **147** D2
Patmore Heath **150** C5
Patna **224** C4
Patney **118** B2
Patrick **190** A3
Patrick Brompton **202** B3
Patrington **197** F5
Patrington Haven **197** F5
Patrishow **144** B5
Patrixbourne **125** D3
Patterdale **209** G5
Pattingham **158** A3
Pattishall **148** B2
Pattiswick **151** G5
Paul **94** B4
Paulerspury **148** C3
Paull **197** D5
Paull Holme **197** D5
Paul's Green **94** D3
Paulton **117** D2
Paultons Park Hants
  SO51 6AL **106** C1
Pauperhaugh **220** C2
Pave Lane **157** G1
Pavenham **149** E2
Pavilion Gardens, Buxton
  Derbys
  SK17 6XN **185** E5
Pawlett **116** A4
Pawston **228** C3
Paxford **147** D4
Paxton **237** F4
Payden Street **124** B3
Payhembury **103** D2
Paythorne **193** E4
Peacehaven **109** G3
Peacemarsh **117** F5
Peachley **146** A2
Peak Dale **185** E5
Peak Forest **185** F5
Peakirk **161** G2
Pean Hill **124** D2
Pear Tree **173** E4
Pearsie **252** B4
Pearson's Green **123** F4
Peartree **136** B1
Peartree Green
  Essex **137** E3
Peartree Green
  Here **145** F4
Pease Pottage **122** B5
Peasedown
  St. John **117** E2
Peasehill **173** F3
Peaseland Green **178** B4
Peasemore **133** G3
Peasenhall **153** E1
Peaslake **121** F3
Peasley Cross **183** G3
Peasmarsh
  ESuss **111** D1
Peasmarsh Surr **121** E3
Peaston **236** B3
Peastonbank **236** B3
Peat Inn **244** C4
Peathill **269** H4
Peathrow **212** A5
Peatling Magna **160** A3
Peatling Parva **160** A4
Peaton **157** E4
Pebble Coombe **122** B3
Pebmarsh **151** G4
Pebworth **146** D3
Pecket Well **193** F5
Peckforton **170** C2
Peckham **136** C5
Peckleton **159** G2
Pedham **179** E4
Pedmore **158** B4
Pedwell **116** B4

Peebles **235** G5
Peel IoM **190** A3
Peel Lancs **191** G4
Peening Quarter **111** D1
Peggs Green **159** G1
Pegsdon **149** G4
Pegswood **221** E3
Pegwell **125** F2
Peighinn nan
  Aoireann **254** C1
Peinchorran **256** B1
Peinlich **263** K6
Pelaw **212** B1
Pelcomb **126** C1
Pelcomb Bridge **126** C1
Pelcomb Cross **126** C1
Peldon **138** C2
Pellon **193** G5
Pelsall **158** C2
Pelton **212** B2
Pelutho **209** E2
Pelynt **97** G4
Pemberton **183** G2
Pembrey (Pen-bre) **128** A2
Pembrey Country Park
  Carmar
  SA16 0EJ **128** A2
Pembridge **144** C2
Pembroke (Penfro) **126** C2
Pembroke Dock
  (Doc Penfro) **126** C2
Pembury **123** F4
Penallt **131** E1
Penally **127** E3
Penare **97** D5
Penarron **156** A4
Penarth **130** B5
Pen-bont
  Rhydybeddau **154** C4
Penboyr **141** G4
Penbryn **141** F2
Pencader **142** A4
Pen-cae **142** A3
Pen-cae-cwm **168** C1
Pencaenewydd **166** D3
Pencaitland **236** B3
Pencarreg **142** B3
Pencarrow **97** F1
Pencelli **143** G5
Pen-clawdd **128** B3
Pencoed **129** F4
Pencombe **145** E2
Pencoyd **145** E5
Pencraig Here **145** E5
Pencraig Powys **168** D5
Pendeen **94** A3
Penderyn **129** F2
Pendine
  (Pentywyn) **127** F2
Pendlebury **184** B2
Pendleton **193** D4
Pendock **145** G4
Pendoggett **97** E2
Pendomer **104** B1
Pendoylan **129** G5
Penegoes **155** D2
Penelewey **96** C5
Pen-ffordd **141** D5
Pengam **130** A3
Penge **136** C5
Pengenffordd **144** A5
Pengorffwysfa **180** C3
Pengover Green **97** G3
Pen-groes-oped **130** C2
Pengwern **182** B5
Penhale **95** D5
Penhallow **96** B4
Penhalvean **95** E3
Penhelig **154** C3
Penhill **133** D4
Penhow **130** D3
Penhurst **110** B2
Peniarth **154** C2
Penicuik **235** G3
Peniel **142** A5
Penifiler **263** K7
Peninver **222** C3
Penisa'r Waun **167** E1
Penisarcwm **155** G1
Penishawain **143** G4
Penistone **185** G2
Penjerrick **95** E3
Penketh **183** G4
Penkill **214** D1
Penkridge **158** B1
Penlean **98** C1
Penley **170** B4
Penllech **166** B4
Penllergaer **128** C3
Pen-llyn IoA **180** B4
Penllyn VGlam **129** F5
Pen-lôn **166** D1
Penmachno **168** A2
Penmaen **128** B4
Penmaenan **181** F5
Penmaenmawr **181** F5
Penmaenpool (Llyn
  Penmaen) **154** C1
Penmaen-Rhôs **181** G5
Penmark **115** D1
Penmon **181** E4
Penmorfa **167** E3
Penmynydd **180** D5
Penn Bucks **135** E3
Penn WMid **158** A3
Penn Street **135** E3
Pennal **154** C2
Pennal-isaf **154** D2
Pennan **269** G4
Pennance **96** B5
Pennant Cere **142** B1
Pennant Denb **169** D4
Pennant Powys **155** E3
Pennant Melangell **168** D5
Pennar **126** C2
Pennard **128** B4
Pennerley **156** C3
Penninghame **215** E4
Pennington Cumb **199** D5
Pennington Hants **106** C3
Pennington Flash Country
  Park GtMan
  WN7 3PA **184** A3
Pennington Green **184** A3
Pennorth **144** A5
Pennsylvania **131** G5
Penny Bridge **199** E4

Pennycross **100** A2
Pennyfuir **240** A1
Pennygate **179** E3
Pennyghael **239** E2
Pennyglen **224** A4
Pennygown **247** F5
Pennymoor **102** B1
Penny's Green **164** C3
Pennyvenie **224** C5
Penparc Cere **141** F3
Penparc Pembs **140** B4
Penparcau **154** B4
Penpedairheol **130** C2
Penpethy **97** E1
Penpillick **97** E4
Penpol **95** F3
Penpoll **97** F4
Penponds **94** D3
Penpont D&G **216** C1
Penpont Powys **143** F5
Penprysg **129** F4
Penquit **100** C2
Penrherber **141** F3
Penrhiw **141** F3
Penrhiwceiber **129** G3
Penrhiwgoch **128** B1
Penrhiw-llan **141** G3
Penrhiw-pâl **141** G3
Penrhiwtyn **128** D3
Penrhos Gwyn **166** C4
Penrhos IoA **180** A4
Penrhos Mon **130** D1
Penrhos Powys **129** E1
Penrhos-garnedd **181** D5
Penrhyn Bay
  (Bae Penrhyn) **181** G4
Penrhyn Castle Gwyn
  LL57 4HN **181** E5
Penrhyn-coch **154** C4
Penrhyndeudraeth **167** F4
Penrhyn-side **181** G4
Penrhys **129** G3
Penrice **128** A4
Penrith **210** B5
Penrose Corn **96** C2
Penrose Corn **97** E1
Penruddock **210** A5
Penryn **95** E3
Pensarn Carmar **128** A1
Pensarn Conwy **182** A5
Pen-sarn Gwyn **167** E5
Pen-sarn Gwyn **166** D3
Pensax **145** G1
Pensby **183** D4
Penselwood **117** E4
Pensford **116** D1
Pensham **146** B3
Penshaw **212** C2
Penshurst **123** E4
Pensilva **97** G3
Pensnett **158** B4
Penston **236** B2
Pentewan **97** E5
Pentir **167** E1
Pentire **96** B3
Pentireglaze **96** D2
Pentlepoir **127** E2
Pentlow **151** G3
Pentlow Street **151** G3
Pentney **163** F1
Penton Mewsey **119** E3
Pentonville **136** C4
Pentraeth **180** D5
Pentre Powys **169** D5
Pentre Powys **155** G4
Pentre Powys **144** B1
Pentre Powys **156** B3
Pentre Powys **156** A4
Pentre RCT **129** F3
Pentre Shrop **156** C2
Pentre Wrex **169** F3
Pentre Wrex **170** A3
Pentre Berw **180** C5
Pentre-ffwrndan **183** D5
Pentre Galar **141** E4
Pentre Gwenlais **128** C1
Pentre Gwynfryn **167** E5
Pentre Halkyn **182** D5
Pentre Isaf **168** B1
Pentre Llanrhaeadr **169** D1
Pentre Maelor **170** A3
Pentre Meyrick **129** F5
Pentre Poeth **128** C3
Pentre Saron **168** D1
Pentre-bach Cere **142** B3
Pentrebach MTyd **129** G2
Pentre-bach Powys **143** F4
Pentrebach RCT **129** G4
Pentrebach Swan **128** B2
Pentre-bont **168** A2
Pentre-bwlch **169** E3
Pentrecagal **141** G3
Pentre-celyn Denb **169** E2
Pentre-celyn
  Powys **155** E2
Pentre-chwyth **128** C3
Pentreclwydau **129** E2
Pentre-cwrt **141** G4
Pentre-Dolau-
  Honddu **143** F3
Pentredwr Denb **169** E3
Pentre-dwr Swan **128** C3
Pentrefelin Carmar **142** C5
Pentrefelin Cere **142** B3
Pentrefelin Conwy **181** D5
Pentrefelin Gwyn **167** E4
Pentrefelin Powys **169** E5
Pentrefoelas **168** B2
Pentregat **141** G2
Pentrehelying **156** B3
Pentre-llwyn-
  llŵyd **143** F2
Pentre-llyn **154** C5
Pentre-llyn-
  cymmer **168** C2
Pentre-piod **168** B4
Pentre-poeth **130** B4
Pentre'r beirdd **156** A1
Pentre'r Felin **168** B1
Pentre'r-felin **143** F4
Pentre-tafarn-y-
  fedw **168** A1
Pentre-ty-gwyn **143** E4
Pentrich **173** E2
Pentridge **105** G1
Pentwyn Caerp **130** A2
Pen-twyn Caerp **130** B2

Pentwyn Cardiff **130** B4
Pen-twyn Mon **131** E2
Pentwyn-mawr **130** A3
Pentyrch **130** B4
Penuwch **142** B1
Penwithick **97** E4
Penwood **119** F1
Penwortham **192** B5
Penwortham Lane **192** B5
Penwyllt **129** E1
Pen-y-banc **142** C5
Pen-y-bont
  Carmar **143** D4
Pen-y-bont
  Carmar **141** G5
Pen-y-bont Powys **155** G1
Pen-y-bont Powys **169** F5
Penybont Powys **144** A1
Penybontfawr **169** D5
Penybryn Caerp **130** A3
Pen-y-bryn Gwyn **154** C1
Pen-y-bryn Pembs **141** E3
Pen-y-bryn Wrex **169** F3
Penycae Wrex **169** F3
Pen-y-cae Powys **129** E1
Penycae-mawr **130** D3
Pen-y-cefn **182** C5
Pen-y-clawdd **130** D2
Pen-y-coedcae **129** G4
Penycwm **140** B5
Pen-y-Darren **129** G2
Pen-y-fai **129** E4
Penyffordd Flints **170** A1
Pen-y-ffordd Flints **182** C4
Penyffridd **167** E2
Pen-y-gaer **144** A5
Pen-y-garn Carmar **142** B4
Pen-y-garn Cere **154** C4
Penygarn Torfaen **130** B2
Penygarnedd **169** E5
Pen-y-garreg **143** G3
Pen-y-Graig Gwyn **166** B4
Penygraig RCT **129** G3
Penygroes Carmar **128** B1
Penygroes Gwyn **167** D2
Pen-y-Gwryd Hotel **167** F2
Pen-y-lan **130** A1
Pen-y-Mynydd
  Carmar **128** A2
Penymynydd
  Flints **170** A1
Pen-y-parc **169** F1
Pen-y-Park **144** B3
Pen-yr-englyn **129** F3
Pen-yr-heol Mon **130** D1
Penyrheol Swan **128** B3
Pen-y-sarn **180** C3
Pen-y-stryt **169** E2
Penywaun **129** F2
Penzance **94** B3
Penzance Heliport **94** B3
People's Palace & Winter
  Gardens Glas
  G40 1AT **39** H6
Peopleton **146** B2
Peover Heath **184** B5
Peper Harow **121** E3
Peplow **170** D5
Pepper Arden **202** B2
Pepper's Green **137** F1
Perceton **233** E5
Percie **260** D5
Percyhorner **269** H4
Perham Down **119** D3
Periton **114** C3
Perivale **136** A4
Perkhill **260** D4
Perkins Beach **156** C2
Perkin's Village **102** D3
Perlethorpe **186** B5
Perran Downs **94** C3
Perranarworthal **95** E3
Perranporth **96** B4
Perranuthnoe **94** C4
Perranzabuloe **96** B4
Perrott's Brook **132** C2
Perry Barr **158** C3
Perry Crofts **159** E2
Perry Green
  Essex **151** G5
Perry Green Herts **136** D1
Perry Green Wilts **132** B4
Perry Street **137** E5
Perrymead **117** E1
Pershall **171** F5
Pershore **146** B3
Persie House **251** G4
Pert **253** E3
Pertenhall **149** F1
Perth (Peairt) **243** G2
Perthcelyn **129** G3
Perthy **170** A4
Perton **158** A3
Pestalozzi Children's
  Village **110** C2
Peter Tavy **99** F3
Peterborough **161** G3
Peterburn **264** D3
Peterchurch **144** C4
Peterculter **261** G4
Peterhead **269** K6
Peterlee **212** D3
Peter's Green **136** A1
Peters Marland **113** E4
Peters Port
  (Port Pheadair) **262** D7
Petersfield **120** C5
Petersham **118** C5
Peterstone
  Wentlooge **130** B4
Peterston-super-
  Ely **129** G5
Peterstow **145** E5
Petham **124** D3
Petrockstowe **113** F5
Pett **111** D2
Pettaugh **152** C2
Petteril Green **210** A3
Pettinain **235** D1
Pettistree **153** D2
Petton Devon **114** D5
Petton Shrop **170** B5
Petts Wood **122** D2
Petty **261** F1
Petty France **131** G4
Pettymuick **261** H2
Petworth **121** E5

Pevensey **110** B3
Pen-twyn Mon **131** E2
Pevensey Bay **110** B3
Peverell **100** A2
Pewsey **118** C1
Pheasant's Hill **134** C4
Phesdo **253** E2
Philham **112** C3
Philharmonic Hall, Liverpool
  Mersey L1 9BP **43** E5
Philiphaugh **227** F3
Phillack **94** C3
Philleigh **95** F3
Philpstoun **235** E2
Phocle Green **145** F5
Phoenix Green **120** C4
Phones **260** B3
Phorp **267** H6
Photographer's Gallery, The,
  London GtLon
  WC2H 7HY **44** E3
Pibsbury **116** B5
Pica **208** D4
Piccadilly Corner **165** D3
Pickerells **137** E2
Pickering **203** G4
Pickering Nook **212** A2
Picket Piece **119** E3
Picket Post **106** A2
Pickford Green **159** E4
Pickhill **202** C4
Picklescott **156** D3
Pickletillem **244** C2
Pickmere **184** A5
Pickney **115** E5
Pickstock **171** E5
Pickston **243** E2
Pickup Bank **192** D5
Pickwell Devon **113** E1
Pickwell Leics **160** C1
Pickworth Lincs **175** F4
Pickworth Rut **161** E1
Picton ChesW&C **183** F5
Picton NYorks **202** D2
Piddington Bucks **134** D3
Piddington N'hants **148** D2
Piddington Oxon **134** B1
Piddlehinton **104** D3
Piddletrenthide **104** D3
Pidley **162** B5
Piece Hall, Halifax WYorks
  HX1 1RE **26** B4
Piercebridge **202** B1
Pierowall **276** D3
Pigdon **221** D2
Pike Hill **193** E4
Pikehall **172** C2
Pikeshill **106** B2
Pilgrims Hatch **137** E3
Pilham **187** F3
Pill **131** E5
Pillaton Corn **99** D4
Pillaton Staffs **158** B1
Pillerton Hersey **147** E3
Pillerton Priors **147** E3
Pilleth **144** B1
Pilley Hants **106** C3
Pilley SYorks **186** A2
Pilling **192** A3
Pilling Lane **191** G3
Pillowell **131** F2
Pilning **131** E4
Pilsbury **172** C1
Pilsdon **104** A3
Pilsgate **161** F2
Pilsley Derbys **173** F1
Pilsley Derbys **185** G5
Pilson Green **179** E4
Piltdown **109** G1
Pilton Devon **113** F2
Pilton N'hants **161** F4
Pilton Rut **161** E2
Pilton Som **116** C3
Pilton Swan **128** A4
Pilton Green **128** A4
Pimhole **184** C1
Pimlico **135** F2
Pimperne **105** F2
Pin Mill **152** D4
Pinchbeck **176** A5
Pinchbeck Bars **176** A5
Pinchbeck West **176** A5
Pincheon Green **187** D1
Pinchinthorpe **203** E1
Pindon End **148** C3
Pinehurst **132** D4
Pinfold **183** E1
Pinged **128** A2
Pinhay **103** G3
Pinhoe **102** C3
Pinkneys Green **135** D4
Pinley Green **147** E1
Pinminnoch **214** C1
Pinmore **214** D1
Pinn **103** E4
Pinner **136** A4
Pinner Green **136** A3
Pinvin **146** B3
Pinwherry **214** C2
Pinxton **173** F2
Pipe & Lyde **145** E3
Pipe Gate **171** E3
Pipe Ridware **158** C1
Pipehill **158** C2
Piperhall **232** B4
Piperhill **267** F6
Pipers Pool **97** G1
Pipewell **160** D4
Pippacott **113** F2
Pipton **144** A4
Pirbright **121** E2
Pirnmill **231** G5
Pirton Herts **149** G4
Pirton Worcs **146** A3
Pisgah **242** C5
Pishill **134** C4
Pistyll **166** C3
Pitagowan **250** D3
Pitblae **269** H4
Pitcairngreen **243** F2
Pitcairns **243** F3
Pitcaple **261** F2
Pitch Green **134** C2
Pitch Place Surr **121** E2
Pitch Place Surr **121** D4
Pitchcombe **132** A2
Pitchcott **148** C5
Pitchford **157** E2

Pitcombe **117** D4
Pitcot **129** E5
Pitcox **236** D2
Pitcur **244** A1
Pitfichie **260** E3
Pitgrudy **266** E2
Pitinnan **261** F1
Pitkennedy **252** D4
Pitkevy **244** A4
Pitlessie **244** B4
Pitlochry **251** E4
Pitman's Corner **152** C1
Pitmedden **261** G2
Pitminster **103** F1
Pitmuies **253** D5
Pitmunie **260** E3
Pitnacree **251** E4
Pitney **116** B5
Pitroddie **244** A2
Pitscottie **244** C3
Pitsea **137** G4
Pitsford **148** C1
Pitsford Hill **115** D4
Pitstone **135** E1
Pitt Devon **102** D1
Pitt Hants **119** F5
Pitt Rivers Museum Oxon
  OX1 3PP **80** Oxford
Pittendreich **267** J5
Pittentrail **266** E1
Pittenweem **244** D4
Pitteuchar **244** A5
Pittington **212** C3
Pittodrie House **260** E2
Pitton Swan **128** A4
Pitton Wilts **118** D4
Pittulie **269** H4
Pittville **146** B5
Pity Me **212** B3
Pityme **96** D2
Pixey Green **164** D4
Pixley **145** F4
Place Newton **204** B5
Plaidy **269** F5
Plain Dealings **127** D1
Plainfield **220** B1
Plains **234** C1
Plainsfield **115** E4
Plaish **157** E3
Plaistow GtLon **136** C4
Plaistow WSuss **121** F4
Plaitford **106** B1
Plaitford Green **119** G1
Plas **142** A5
Plas Gwynant **167** F2
Plas Isaf **169** D3
Plas Llwyd **182** A5
Plas Llwyngwern **155** D2
Plas Llysyn **155** F3
Plas Nantyr **169** E4
Plashett **127** F2
Plasisaf **168** C1
Plas-rhiw-Saeson **155** F2
Plastow Green **119** G1
Plas-yn-Cefn **182** B5
Platt **123** F3
Platt Bridge **184** A2
Platt Lane **170** C4
Platt's Heath **124** A3
Plawsworth **212** B3
Plaxtol **123** F3
Play Hatch **134** C5
Playden **111** E1
Playford **152** D3
Playing Place **96** C5
Playley Green **145** G4
Plealey **156** D2
Plean **234** C1
Pleasance **244** A3
Pleasant Valley **150** D4
Pleasington **192** C5
Pleasley **173** G1
Pleasleyhill **173** G1
Pleasure Beach, Great
  Yarmouth Norf
  NR30 3EH **179** G5
Pleasure Island Theme Park
  NELincs
  DN35 0PL **188** D2
Pleasurewood Hills Theme
  Park Suff
  NR32 5DZ **165** G2
Pleck Dorset **104** D1
Pleck WMid **158** B3
Pledgdon Green **151** D5
Pledwick **186** A1
Plemstall **183** F5
Plenmeller **210** D1
Pleshey **137** F1
Plessey Woods Country
  Park N'umb
  NE22 6AN **221** E3
Plockton (Am Ploc) **256** E1
Plocropol **263** G2
Plomer's Hill **135** D3
Plot Gate **116** C4
Plough Hill **159** F3
Plowden **156** C4
Ploxgreen **156** C2
Pluckley **124** B4
Pluckley Thorne **124** B4
Plucks Gutter **125** E2
Plumbland **209** E3
Plumbley **186** B4
Plumley **184** B5
Plumpton Cumb **210** A4
Plumpton ESuss **109** F2
Plumpton N'hants **148** B3
Plumpton Green **109** F2
Plumpton Head **210** B4
Plumstead GtLon **137** D5
Plumstead Norf **178** C2
Plumtree **174** B4
Plungar **174** C4
Plush **104** D2
Plusha **97** G1
Plushabridge **98** D3
Plwmp **141** G2
Plym Bridge **100** A3
Plymouth **100** A2
Plymouth Pavilions
  PL1 3LF **81** Plymouth
Plympton **100** B2
Plymstock **100** B2
Plymtree **103** D2
Pockley **203** F4
Pocklington **196** A3
Pockthorpe **178** B2

Pocombe Bridge **102** B3
Pode Hole **176** A5
Podimore **116** C5
Podington **149** E1
Podmore **171** E4
Podsmead **132** A1
Poffley End **133** F1
Point Clear **139** D1
Pointon **175** G4
Polanach **248** B4
Polapit Tamar **98** D2
Polbae **215** D3
Polbain **272** B7
Polbathic **98** D5
Polbeth **235** E3
Poldean **217** F1
Pole Moor **185** E1
Polebrook **161** F4
Polegate **110** A3
Poles **266** E2
Polesden Lacey Surr
  RH5 6BD **121** G2
Polesworth **159** E2
Polglass **265** G1
Polgooth **97** D4
Polgown **225** F5
Poling **108** C3
Poling Corner **108** C3
Polkemmet Country Park
  WLoth
  EH47 0AD **234** D3
Polkerris **97** E4
Poll a' Charra **254** C3
Polla **273** F3
Pollardras **94** D3
Polldubh **248** D3
Pollie **274** C7
Pollington **186** D1
Polloch **247** G3
Pollok **233** G3
Pollokshaws **233** G3
Pollokshields **233** G3
Polmassick **97** D5
Polmont **234** D2
Polnoon **233** G4
Polperro **97** G4
Polruan **97** F4
Polsham **116** C3
Polstead **152** A3
Polstead Heath **152** A3
Poltalloch **240** C5
Poltimore **102** C3
Polton **235** G3
Polwarth **237** E4
Polyphant **97** G1
Polzeath **96** C1
Pomphlett **100** B2
Pond Street **150** C4
Ponders End **136** C3
Pondersbridge **162** A3
Ponsanooth **95** E3
Ponsonby **198** B2
Ponsongath **95** E5
Ponsworthy **102** A5
Pont Aber **142** D5
Pont Aberglaslyn **167** E3
Pont ar Hydfer **143** E5
Pont Crugnant **155** E3
Pont Cyfyng **168** A2
Pont Dolgarrog **168** A1
Pont Pen-y-benglog **167** F1
Pont Rhyd-sarn **168** B5
Pont Rhyd-y-cyff **129** E4
Pont Walby **129** E2
Pont yr Alwen **168** C2
Pontamman **128** C1
Pontantwn **128** A1
Pontardawe **128** D2
Pontarddulais **128** B2
Pontargothi **142** B5
Pont-ar-llechau **142** D5
Pontarsais **142** A4
Pontblyddyn **169** F1
Pontbren Llwyd **129** F2
Pontefract **195** D5
Ponteland **221** D4
Ponterwyd **154** D4
Pontesbury **156** D2
Pontesbury Hill **156** C2
Pontesford **156** D2
Pontfadog **169** F4
Pontfaen Pembs **140** D4
Pont-faen Powys **143** F4
Pontgarreg **141** G2
Pont-Henri **128** A2
Ponthir **130** C3
Ponthirwaun **141** F3
Pontllanfraith **130** A3
Pontlliw **128** C2
Pontllyfni **166** D2
Pontlottyn **130** A2
Pontneddfechan **129** F2
Pontnewydd **130** B3
Pontrhydfendigaid **142** D1
Pontrhydyfen **129** D3
Pont-rhyd-y-groes **154** D5
Pontrhydyrun **130** B3
Pontrilas **144** C5
Pontrobert **156** A1
Pont-rug **167** E1
Ponts Green **110** B2
Pontshill **145** F5
Pont-siân **142** A3
Pontsticill **129** G1
Pontwelly **142** A4
Pontyates
  (Pont-iets) **128** A2
Pontyberem **128** B1
Pont-y-blew **170** A4
Pontybodkin **169** F2
Pontyclun **129** F4
Pontycymer **129** F3
Pontygwaith **129** G3
Pontymister **130** B3
Pontymoel **130** B2
Pontypool **130** B2
Pontypridd **129** G3
Pont-y-rhyl **129** F4
Pontywaun **130** B3
Pooksgreen **106** C1
Pool Corn **96** C4
Pool WYorks **194** B3
Pool Bank **199** F4
Pool Green **158** C2
Pool Head **145** E2
Pool of Muckhart **243** F4
Pool Quay **156** B1
Pool Street **151** F4

Poole 105 G3
Poole Keynes 132 B3
Poole Pottery Poole
  BH15 1HJ 3 B4
Poolend 171 G2
Poolewe 264 E3
Pooley Bridge 210 A5
Pooley Street 164 B3
Poolfold 171 F2
Poolhill 145 G5
Poolsbrook 186 B5
Poolthorne Farm 188 A2
Pope Hill 126 C1
Popeswood 120 D1
Popham 119 G3
Poplar 138 C4
Porchfield 106 D3
Porin 265 K6
Poringland 179 D5
Porkellis 95 D3
Porlock 114 B3
Porlock Weir 114 B3
Port Allen 244 A2
Port Appin (Port na
  h-Apainn) 248 B5
Port Askaig 230 C3
Port Bannatyne 232 B3
Port Carlisle 218 A5
Port Charlotte 230 A4
Port Clarence 213 E5
Port Driseach 232 A2
Port e Vullen 190 C2
Port Ellen 230 B5
Port Elphinstone 261 F3
Port Erin 190 A5
Port Erroll 261 J1
Port Eynon 128 A4
Port Gaverne 97 E1
Port Glasgow 233 E2
Port Henderson 264 D4
Port Isaac 97 D1
Port Logan 206 A2
Port Lympne Wild Animal
  Park Kent
  CT21 4PD 124 D5
Port Mòr 246 D2
Port Mulgrave 203 G1
Port na Craig 251 E4
Port nan Long 262 D4
Port of Menteith 242 A4
Port of Ness
  (Port Nis) 271 H1
Port o'Warren 216 C5
Port Penrhyn 181 D5
Port Quin 97 D1
Port Ramsay 248 A5
Port St. Mary 190 A5
Port Solent 107 F2
Port Sunlight 183 E4
Port Talbot 128 C3
Port Tennant 128 C3
Port Wemyss 230 A4
Port William 206 D2
Portachoillan 231 F4
Portavadie 232 A3
Portbury 131 E5
Portchester 107 F2
Portencross 232 C5
Portesham 104 C4
Portessie 268 C4
Portfield A&B 239 G2
Portfield WSuss 108 A3
Portfield Gate 126 C1
Portgate 99 E2
Portgordon 268 B4
Portgower 275 F7
Porth Corn 96 C3
Porth RCT 129 G3
Porth Colmon 166 A4
Porth Navas 95 E4
Porthallow Corn 95 E4
Porthallow Corn 97 G4
Porthcawl 129 E5
Porthcothan 96 C2
Porthcurno 94 A4
Porthgain 140 B4
Porthill 171 F3
Porthkerry 115 D1
Porthkerry Country Park
  VGlam
  CF62 3BY 115 D1
Porthleven 94 D4
Porthmadog 167 E4
Porthmeor 94 B3
Portholland 97 D5
Porthoustock 95 F4
Porthpean 97 E4
Porthtowan 96 A5
Porthyrhyd
  Carmar 142 D4
Porthyrhyd
  Carmar 128 B1
Porth-y-waen 169 F5
Portincaple 241 E5
Portington 195 G4
Portinnisherrich 240 B3
Portinscale 209 F4
Portishead 131 D5
Portknockie 268 C4
Portland Basin Museum
  GtMan
  OL7 0QA 25 H3
Portlethen 261 H5
Portlethen Village 261 H5
Portloe 95 G3
Portlooe 97 G4
Portmahomack 267 G3
Portmeirion 167 E4
Portmeirion Village Gwyn
  LL48 6ET 167 E4
Portmellon 97 E5
Portmore 106 C3
Port-na-Con 273 G2
Portnacroish
  (Port na Croise) 248 B5
Portnaguran (Port nan
  Giùran) 271 H4
Portnahaven 230 A4
Portnalong 255 J1
Portnaluchaig 247 F1
Portobello 236 A2
Porton 118 C4
Portpatrick 214 B5
Portreath 96 A5
Portree (Port Righ) 263 K7
Portscatho 95 F3
Portsea 107 F2
Portskerra 274 C2

Portskewett 131 E4
Portslade 109 E3
Portslade-by-Sea 109 E3
Portslogan 214 A5
Portsmouth 107 F3
Portsmouth Guildhall
  PO1 2AB
  82 Portsmouth
Portsmouth Historic
  Dockyard PO1 3LJ
  82 Portsmouth
Portsonachan 240 C2
Portsoy 268 D4
Portuairk 246 D3
Portvoller 271 H4
Portway Here 144 C3
Portway Here 145 D3
Portway Here 145 D4
Portway Worcs 158 C5
Portwrinkle 99 D5
Portyerrock 207 E3
Posenhall 157 F2
Poslingford 151 F3
Postbridge 99 G3
Postcombe 134 C3
Postling 124 D5
Postwick 179 D5
Potarch 260 E5
Potsgrove 149 E5
Pott Row 177 F5
Pott Shrigley 184 D5
Potten End 135 F2
Potter Brompton 204 C5
Potter Heigham 179 F4
Potter Street 137 D2
Pottergate Street 164 C2
Potterhanworth 175 F1
Potterhanworth
  Booths 175 F1
Potteries Museum & Art
  Gallery ST1 3DW
  85 Stoke-on-Trent
Potterne 118 A2
Potterne Wick 118 B2
Potternewton 194 C4
Potters Bar 136 B2
Potters Crouch 136 A2
Potter's Green 159 F4
Potters Marston 159 G3
Potterspury 148 C3
Potterton Aber 261 H3
Potterton WYorks 194 D4
Pottle Street 117 F3
Potto 203 D1
Potton 150 A3
Pott's Green 152 A5
Poughill Corn 112 C5
Poughill Devon 102 B2
Poulshot 118 A2
Poulton 132 D2
Poulton-le-Fylde 191 G4
Pound Bank 145 G3
Pound Green ESuss 110 A1
Pound Green Suff 151 F2
Pound Green
  Worcs 157 G5
Pound Hill 122 B5
Pound Street 119 F1
Poundbury 104 C3
Poundffald 128 B3
Poundfield 123 E5
Poundgate 109 G1
Poundland 214 C2
Poundon 148 B5
Poundsbridge 123 E4
Poundsgate 102 A5
Poundstock 98 C1
Povey Cross 122 B4
Pow Green 145 G3
Powburn 229 E5
Powderham 102 C4
Powderham Castle Devon
  EX6 8JQ 102 C4
Powerstock 104 B3
Powfoot 217 F4
Powick 146 A2
Powis Castle & Garden
  Powys
  SY21 8RG 156 B2
Powler's Piece 113 D4
Powmill 243 F5
Poxwell 104 D4
Poyle 135 F5
Poynings 109 E2
Poyntington 117 D5
Poynton ChesE 184 D4
Poynton Tel&W 157 E1
Poynton Green 157 E1
Poyntzfield 266 E5
Poys Street 165 E4
Poyston 126 C1
Poyston Cross 126 C1
Poystreet Green 152 A2
Praa Sands 94 C4
Pratis 244 B4
Pratt's Bottom 123 D2
Praze-an-Beeble 94 D3
Predannack Wollas 95 D5
Prees 170 C4
Prees Green 170 C4
Prees Heath 170 C4
Prees Higher Heath 170 C4
Prees Lower Heath 170 C4
Preesall 191 G3
Preesgweene 169 F4
Prenbrigog 169 F1
Prendergast 126 C1
Prendwick 229 E5
Pren-gwyn 142 A3
Prenteg 167 E4
Prenton 183 E4
Prescot 183 F3
Prescott Devon 103 D1
Prescott Shrop 170 B5
Presley 267 H6
Pressen 228 C3
Prestatyn 182 B4
Prestbury ChesE 184 D5
Prestbury Glos 146 B5
Presteigne
  (Llanandras) 144 C1
Presthope 157 E3
Prestleigh 116 D3
Prestolee 184 B2
Preston B&H 109 F3
Preston Devon 102 B5
Preston Dorset 104 D4
Preston ELoth 236 C2

Preston ERid 197 D4
Preston Glos 145 F4
Preston Glos 132 C2
Preston Herts 149 G5
Preston Kent 124 C2
Preston Kent 125 E2
Preston Lancs 192 B5
Preston N'umb 229 F4
Preston Rut 161 D2
Preston ScBord 237 E4
Preston Shrop 157 E1
Preston Som 115 D4
Preston Suff 152 A2
Preston Torbay 101 E1
Preston Wilts 132 C5
Preston Bagot 147 D1
Preston Bissett 148 B4
Preston Bowyer 115 E5
Preston Brockhurst 170 C5
Preston Brook 183 G4
Preston Candover 120 B3
Preston Capes 148 A2
Preston Deanery 148 C2
Preston Gubbals 157 D1
Preston Guildhall Lancs
  PR1 1HT 192 B5
Preston on Stour 147 E3
Preston on the Hill 183 G4
Preston on Wye 144 C3
Preston Plucknett 104 B1
Preston upon the Weald
  Moors 157 F1
Preston Wynne 145 E3
Preston-le-Skerne 212 C5
Prestonpans 236 A2
Preston-under-Scar 201 F3
Prestwich 184 B2
Prestwick N'umb 221 D4
Prestwick SAyr 224 B3
Prestwold 173 G5
Prestwood Bucks 135 D2
Prestwood Staffs 172 C3
Price Town 129 F3
Prickly Ball Farm &
  Hedgehog Hospital
  Devon
  TQ12 6BZ 101 E1
Prickwillow 163 D4
Priddy 116 C2
Priest Hill 192 C4
Priest Hutton 199 G5
Priest Weston 156 B3
Priestcliffe 185 F5
Priestland 225 D2
Priestwood 123 F2
Primethorpe 160 A3
Primrose Green 178 B4
Primrose Hill 136 B4
Princes End 158 B3
Princes Gate 127 E1
Princes Risborough 134 D2
Princetown Caerp 130 A1
Princetown Devon 99 F3
Prior Muir 244 D3
Prior's Frome 145 E4
Priors Halton 157 D5
Priors Hardwick 147 G2
Priors Marston 147 G2
Prior's Norton 146 A5
Priorslee 157 G1
Priory Country Park Bed
  MK41 9SH 149 F2
Priory Wood 144 B3
Priston 117 D1
Pristow Green 164 C3
Prittlewell 138 B4
Privett 120 B5
Prixford 113 F2
Proaig 230 C4
Probus 96 C5
Protstonhill 269 G4
Provand's Lordship Glas
  G4 0RH 39 H3
Prudhoe 211 G1
Prussia Cove 94 C4
Pubil 249 G5
Publow 116 D1
Puckeridge 150 B5
Puckington 103 G1
Pucklechurch 131 F5
Pucknall 119 E5
Puckrup 146 A4
Puddinglake 171 E1
Puddington
  ChesW&C 183 E5
Puddington
  Devon 102 B1
Puddlebrook 131 F1
Puddledock 164 B2
Puddletown 105 D3
Pudleston 145 E2
Pudsey 194 B4
Pugneys Country Park
  WYorks
  WF2 7EQ 27 G6
Pulborough 108 C2
Pulborough Brooks RSPB
  Nature Reserve WSuss
  RH20 2EL 108 C2
Puldagon 275 J4
Puleston 171 E5
Pulford 170 A2
Pulham 104 D2
Pulham Market 164 C3
Pulham St. Mary 164 D3
Pulley 157 D2
Pulloxhill 149 F4
Pulrossie 266 E3
Pulverbatch 156 D2
Pumpherston 235 E3
Pumsaint 142 C3
Puncheston 140 D5
Puncknowle 104 B4
Punnett's Town 110 B1
Purbrook 107 F2
Purewell 106 A3
Purfleet 137 E5
Puriton 116 A3
Purleigh 138 B2
Purley 122 C2
Purley on Thames 134 B5
Purlogue 156 B5
Purlpit 117 F1
Purls Bridge 162 C4
Purse Caundle 104 C1
Purslow 156 C4

Purston Jaglin 186 B1
Purtington 103 G2
Purton Glos 131 F2
Purton Glos 131 F2
Purton Wilts 132 C4
Purton Stoke 132 C3
Purves Hall 237 E5
Pury End 148 C3
Pusey 133 F3
Putley 145 F4
Putley Green 145 F4
Putney 136 B5
Putsborough 113 E1
Puttenham Herts 135 D1
Puttenham Surr 121 D3
Puttock End 151 G3
Putts Corner 103 E3
Puxton 116 B1
Pwll 128 A2
Pwllcrochan 126 C2
Pwll-du 130 B5
Pwllgloyw 143 G4
Pwll-glas 169 E2
Pwllheli 166 C4
Pwll-Mawr 130 B5
Pwllmeyric 131 E3
Pwll-trap 127 F1
Pwll-y-glaw 129 D3
Pye Corner Herts 137 D1
Pye Corner Kent 124 A4
Pye Corner
  Newport 130 C4
Pye Green 158 B1
Pyecombe 109 E2
Pyle Bridgend 129 E4
Pyle IoW 107 D5
Pyleigh 115 E4
Pylle 116 D4
Pymoor (Pymore) 162 C4
Pymore (Pymoor)
  Cambs 162 C4
Pymore Dorset 104 A3
Pyrford 121 F2
Pyrford Green 121 F2
Pyrton 134 B3
Pytchley 161 D5
Pyworthy 112 D5

Quoig 242 D2
Quoigigs House 242 D4
Quoisley 170 C3
Quorn (Quorndon) 160 A1
Quorndon (Quorn) 160 A1
Quothquan 226 A2
Quoyloo 276 B5
Quoys 278 F1
Quoys of Reiss 275 J3

R

R.A.F. Museum, Cosford
  Shrop TF11 8UP 157 G2
R.A.F. Museum, Hendon
  GtLon
  NW9 5LL 10 D1
R.H.S. Garden Harlow Carr
  NYorks
  HG3 1QB 194 B2
R.H.S. Garden Hyde Hall
  Essex
  CM3 8ET 137 G3
R.H.S. Garden Rosemoor
  Devon EX38 8PH 113 F4
R.H.S. Garden Wisley Surr
  GU23 6QB 121 F2
Raasay 264 B7
Raby 183 E5
Rachan 226 C2
Rachub 167 F1
Rackenford 102 B1
Rackham 108 C2
Rackheath 179 D4
Racks 217 E3
Rackwick Ork 277 B8
Rackwick Ork 276 D3
Radbourne 173 D4
Radcliffe GtMan 184 B2
Radcliffe N'umb 221 E1
Radcliffe on Trent 174 B4
Radclive 148 B4
Radcot 133 E3
Raddington 114 D5
Raddery 266 E6
Radernie 244 C4
Radford B&NESom 117 D2
Radford Nott 173 G3
Radford Oxon 147 G5
Radford WMid 159 F4
Radford Semele 147 F1
Radipole 104 C4
Radlett 136 A2
Radley 134 A3
Radley Green 137 F2
Radmore Green 170 C2
Radnage 134 C3
Radstock 117 D2
Radstone 148 A3
Radway 147 F3
Radway Green 171 E2
Radwell Bed 149 F2
Radwell Herts 150 A4
Radwinter 151 E4
Radyr 130 A4
Raechester 220 B3
Raemoir House 260 E5
Raffin 272 C5
Rafford 267 H6
Ragdale 160 B1
Ragged Appleshaw 119 E3
Raglan 130 D2
Ragnall 187 F5
Rahoy 247 F4
Rain Shore 184 C1
Rainford 183 F2
Rainham GtLon 137 E4
Rainham Med 124 A2
Rainhill 183 F3
Rainhill Stoops 183 G3
Rainow 184 D5
Rainsough 184 B2
Rainton 202 C5
Rainworth 173 G2
Raisbeck 200 B2
Raise 210 D3
Rait 244 A2
Raithby Lincs 176 B1
Raithby Lincs 188 D4
Rake 120 D4
Raleigh's Cross 114 D4
Ram 142 B3
Ram Alley 118 D1
Ram Lane 124 B4
Ramasaig 263 G7
Rame Corn 95 E3
Rame Corn 100 A3
Rampisham 104 B2
Rampside 191 F1
Rampton Cambs 150 C1
Rampton Notts 187 F5
Ramsbottom 184 B1
Ramsburn 268 C5
Ramsbury 133 F5
Ramscraigs 275 G6
Ramsdean 120 C5
Ramsdell 120 B2
Ramsden 133 F1
Ramsden Bellhouse 137 G3
Ramsden Heath 137 G3
Ramsey Cambs 162 A4
Ramsey Essex 152 D4
Ramsey IoM 190 C2
Ramsey Forty Foot 162 B4
Ramsey Heights 162 A4
Ramsey Island
  Essex 138 C2
Ramsey Island
  Pembs 140 A5
Ramsey Mereside 162 A4
Ramsey St. Mary's 162 A4
Ramsgate 125 F2
Ramsgate Street 178 B2
Ramsgill 202 A5
Ramsholt 153 E3
Ramshorn 172 B3
Ramsnest Common 121 E4
Ranby Lincs 188 C5
Ranby Notts 187 D4
Rand 188 B5
Rand Farm Park Lincs
  LN8 5NJ 188 B5
Randwick 132 A2
Rangemore 172 C5
Rangeworthy 131 F4
Ranish (Ranais) 271 G5
Rankinston 224 C4
Rank's Green 137 G1
Ranmoor 186 A4
Rannoch School 250 A4

Ranochan 248 A1
Ranscombe 114 C3
Ranskill 187 D4
Ranton 171 F5
Ranton Green 171 F5
Ranworth 179 E4
Rapness 276 E3
Rapps 183 G1
Rascarrel 208 A2
Rash 200 B4
Rashwood 146 B1
Raskelf 203 D5
Rassau 130 A1
Rastrick 194 A5
Ratagan 257 F3
Ratby 160 A2
Ratcliffe Culey 159 F3
Ratcliffe on Soar 173 F5
Ratcliffe on the
  Wreake 160 B1
Ratford Bridge 126 B1
Ratfyn 118 C3
Rathen 269 H4
Rathillet 244 B2
Rathliesbeag 249 E1
Rathmell 193 E1
Ratho 235 F2
Ratho Station 235 F2
Rathven 268 C4
Ratley 147 F3
Ratling 125 E3
Ratlinghope 156 D3
Ratsloe 102 C3
Rattar 275 H1
Ratten Row Cumb 209 G2
Ratten Row Lancs 192 A3
Rattery 100 D1
Rattlesden 152 A2
Rattray 251 E5
Raughton Head 209 G2
Raunds 161 E5
Ravenfield 186 B3
Ravenglass 198 B3
Ravenglass & Eskdale
  Railway Cumb
  CA18 1SW 198 C3
Raveningham 165 E2
Raven's Green 152 C5
Ravenscar 204 C2
Ravensdale 190 B2
Ravensden 149 F2
Ravenshaw 193 F3
Ravenshayes 102 C2
Ravenshead 173 G2
Ravensmoor 170 D2
Ravensthorpe
  N'hants 160 B5
Ravensthorpe
  WYorks 194 B5
Ravenstone Leics 159 G1
Ravenstone MK 149 D2
Ravenstonedale 200 C2
Ravenstruther 234 C3
Ravensworth 202 A2
Raw 204 C2
Rawcliffe ERid 195 F5
Rawcliffe York 195 E2
Rawcliffe Bridge 195 F5
Rawdon 194 B4
Rawmarsh 186 B3
Rawnsley 158 C1
Rawreth 137 G3
Rawridge 103 F2
Rawson Green 173 E3
Rawtenstall 193 E5
Rawyards 234 B3
Raxton 261 G1
Raydon 152 B4
Raylees 220 B2
Rayleigh 138 B3
Raymond's Hill 103 G3
Rayne 151 F5
Rayners Lane 136 A4
Raynes Park 122 B2
Reach 151 D1
Read 193 D4
Reading 134 C5
Reading Green 164 C4
Reading Street 124 B5
Reagill 200 B1
Real Mary King's Close, The
  Edin EH1 1PG 37 F4
Rearquhar 266 E2
Rearsby 160 B1
Rease Heath 170 C2
Reaster 275 H2
Reaveley 229 E5
Reawick 279 C8
Reay 274 E2
Reculver 125 E2
Red Ball 103 D1
Red Bull 171 F2
Red Dial 209 F2
Red Hill Hants 107 G1
Red Hill Warks 146 D2
Red Lodge 163 E5
Red Lumb 184 C1
Red Oaks Hill 151 D4
Red Point Aber 261 H2
Red Post Corn 112 C5
Red Post Devon 101 E1
Red Rail 145 E5
Red Rock 183 G2
Red Roses 127 F1
Red Row 221 E2
Red Street 171 F2
Red Wharf Bay
  (Traeth Coch) 180 D4
Redberth 127 D2
Redbourn 136 A1
Redbourne 187 G3
Redbrook Glos 131 E1
Redbrook Wrex 170 C3
Redbrook Street 124 B5
Redburn High 266 C5
Redburn High 267 G7
Redburn N'umb 211 D1
Redcar 213 E5
Redcastle Angus 253 E4
Redcastle High 266 C7
Redcliff Bay 130 D5
Reddingmuirhead 234 D2
Reddish 184 C3
Redditch 146 C1
Rede 151 G2
Redenhall 165 D3
Redesmouth 220 B3

Redford Aber 253 F2
Redford Angus 253 D5
Redford Dur 211 G4
Redford WSuss 121 D5
Redgrave 164 B4
Redheugh 252 C3
Redhill Aber 260 E1
Redhill Aber 261 F4
Redhill Moray 268 D6
Redhill Notts 173 G3
Redhill NSom 116 B1
Redhill Surr 122 B3
Redhill Aerodrome &
  Heliport 122 B3
Redhouse A&B 231 G3
Redhouse Aber 260 D2
Redhouses 230 B3
Redisham 165 F3
Redland Bristol 131 E5
Redland Ork 276 C5
Redlingfield 164 C4
Redlynch Som 117 E4
Redlynch Wilts 118 D5
Redmarley D'Abitot 145 G4
Redmarshall 212 C5
Redmile 174 C4
Redmire 201 F3
Redmoor 97 E3
Rednal 170 A5
Redpath 227 G2
Redruth 96 A5
Redscarhead 235 G5
Redshaw 225 G3
Redstone Bank 127 E1
Redwick Newport 130 D4
Redwick SGlos 131 E4
Redworth 212 B5
Reed 150 B4
Reed End 150 B4
Reedham 179 F5
Reedley 193 E4
Reedness 195 G5
Reef (Riof) 270 D4
Reepham Lincs 188 A5
Reepham Norf 178 B3
Reeth 201 F3
Regaby 190 C2
Regil 116 C1
Regoul 267 F6
Reiff 272 B7
Reigate 122 B3
Reighton 205 E5
Reisgill 275 H5
Reiss 275 J3
Rejerrah 96 C4
Releath 95 D3
Relubbus 94 C3
Relugas 267 G7
Remenham 134 C4
Remenham Hill 134 C4
Remony 250 C5
Rempstone 173 G5
Rendcomb 132 C1
Rendham 153 E1
Rendlesham 153 E2
Renfrew 233 G3
Renhold 149 F2
Renishaw 186 B5
Rennington 229 G5
Renton 233 E2
Renwick 210 B3
Repps 179 F4
Repton 173 E5
Rescobie 252 D4
Rescorla 97 E4
Resipole 247 G3
Resolis 266 D5
Resolven 129 E2
Resourie 248 A2
Respryn 97 F3
Reston 237 F3
Restormel 97 F3
Reswallie 252 D4
Reterth 96 D3
Retford
  (East Retford) 187 E4
Rettendon 137 G3
Rettendon Place 137 G3
Retyn 96 C4
Revesby 176 A1
Revesby Bridge 176 B1
Rew 102 A5
Rew Street 107 D3
Rewe Devon 102 C3
Rewe Devon 102 B3
Reybridge 118 A1
Reydon 165 F4
Reydon Smear 165 G4
Reymerston 178 B5
Reynalton 127 D2
Reynoldston 128 A4
Rezare 99 D3
Rhadyr 130 C2
Rhandirmwyn 143 D3
Rhaoine 266 D1
Rhayader
  (Rhaeadr Gwy) 143 F1
Rhedyn 166 B4
Rheged - the Village in the
  Hill Cumb
  CA11 0DQ 210 A5
Rhegreanoch 272 C7
Rheindown 266 C7
Rhelonie 266 C2
Rhemore 247 E4
Rhenigidale
  (Reinigeadal) 270 E7
Rheola 129 E2
Rhes-y-cae 169 E1
Rhewl Denb 169 E3
Rhewl Denb 169 E1
Rhewl Shrop 170 A4
Rhian 273 H7
Rhicarn 272 C6
Rhiconich 272 E3
Rhicullen 266 D4
Rhidorroch 265 H2
Rhifail 274 C4
Rhigos 129 F2
Rhilochan 266 E1
Rhireavach 265 G2
Rhiroy 265 H3
Rhiston 156 B3
Rhiw 166 B5
Rhiwargor 168 C5
Rhiwbina 130 A4

Rhiwbryfdir 167 F3
Rhiwderin 130 B4
Rhiwinder 129 G4
Rhiwlas *Gwyn* 167 E1
Rhiwlas *Gwyn* 168 C4
Rhiwlas *Powys* 169 F4
Rhode 115 F4
Rhodes Minnis 124 D4
Rhodesia 186 C5
Rhodiad-y-brenin 140 A5
Rhodmad 154 B5
Rhonadale 222 C2
Rhonehouse
(Kelton Hill) 216 B5
Rhoose 115 D1
Rhos *Carmar* 141 G4
Rhos *NPT* 128 C2
Rhos Common 156 B1
Rhosaman 128 C1
Rhoscolyn 180 A5
Rhoscrowther 126 C2
Rhosesmor 169 F4
Rhos-fawr 166 C4
Rhosgadfan 167 E2
Rhosgoch *IoA* 180 C4
Rhosgoch *Powys* 144 B3
Rhos-hill 141 E3
Rhoshirwaun 166 A5
Rhoslan 167 E2
Rhoslefain 154 B2
Rhosllanerchrugog 169 F3
Rhosligwy 180 C4
Rhosmaen 142 C5
Rhosmeirch 180 C5
Rhosneigr 180 B5
Rhosnesni 170 A2
Rhôs-on-Sea 181 G4
Rhossili 128 A4
Rhosson 140 A5
Rhostrehwfa 180 C5
Rhostryfan 167 D2
Rhostyllen 170 A3
Rhos-y-bol 180 C4
Rhos-y-brithdir 169 E2
Rhosycaerau 140 C4
Rhos-y-garth 154 C5
Rhos-y-gwaliau 168 C4
Rhos-y-llan 166 B4
Rhos-y-mawn 168 B1
Rhos-y-Meirch 144 B1
Rhu 233 D1
Rhuallt 182 B5
Rhubodach 232 B2
Rhuddall Heath 170 C1
Rhuddlan 182 B5
Rhue 265 H2
Rhulen 144 A3
Rhumach 247 F1
Rhunahaorine 231 F5
Rhyd *Gwyn* 167 F3
Rhyd *Powys* 155 F2
Rhydargaeau 142 A5
Rhydcymerau 142 B4
Rhyd-Ddu 167 E2
Rhydding 128 D3
Rhydgaled 168 C1
Rhydlanfair 168 B2
Rhydlewis 141 G3
Rhydlios 166 A4
Rhydlydan *Conwy* 168 B2
Rhydlydan *Powys* 155 G3
Rhydolion 166 B5
Rhydowen 142 A3
Rhyd-Rosser 142 B1
Rhydspence 144 B3
Rhydtalog 169 F2
Rhyd-uchaf 168 B4
Rhyd-wen 168 C5
Rhyd-wyn 180 B4
Rhyd-y-ceirw 169 F2
Rhyd-y-clafdy 166 C4
Rhydycroesau 169 F4
Rhydyfelin *Cere* 154 B5
Rhydyfelin *RCT* 129 G4
Rhyd-y-foel 182 A5
Rhyd-y-fro 128 D2
Rhyd-y-groes 167 E1
Rhydymain 168 B5
Rhydymwyn 169 F1
Rhyd-yr-onnen 154 C2
Rhyd-y-sarn 167 F3
Rhydywrach 127 E1
Rhyl 182 B4
Rhyl Sun Centre *Denb*
LL18 3AQ 182 B4
Rhymney 130 A2
Rhyn 170 A4
Rhynd 243 G2
Rhynie *Aber* 260 C2
Rhynie *High* 267 F4
Ribbesford 157 G5
Ribchester 192 C4
Ribigill 273 H3
Riby 188 B2
Riccall 195 F4
Riccarton 224 C2
Richards Castle 145 D1
Richings Park 135 F5
Richmond *GtLon* 136 A3
Richmond *NYorks* 202 A2
Richmond *SYorks* 186 B4
Rich's Holford 115 E4
Rickarton 253 G1
Rickerscote 171 G5
Rickford 116 B2
Rickinghall 164 B4
Rickleton 212 B2
Rickling 150 C4
Rickling Green 150 D5
Rickmansworth 135 F3
Riddell 227 G3
Riddings 173 K7
Riddlecombe 113 G4
Riddlesden 193 G3
Ridge *Dorset* 105 F4
Ridge *Herts* 136 B2
Ridge *Wilts* 118 A4
Ridge Green 122 C4
Ridge Lane 159 E3
Ridgebourne 143 G1
Ridgeway 186 B4
Ridgeway Cross 145 G3
Ridgeway Moor 186 B4
Ridgewell 151 F2
Ridgewood 109 G2
Ridgmont 149 E4
Ridham Dock 124 B2
Riding Gate 117 E5

Riding Mill 211 G1
Ridley 123 F2
Ridleywood 170 A2
Ridlington *Norf* 179 E2
Ridlington *Rut* 160 D2
Ridsdale 211 F4
Riechip 251 F5
Rievaulx 203 E4
Rift House 213 D4
Rigg *D&G* 218 A5
Rigg *High* 264 B6
Riggend 234 B3
Rigifa 275 J1
Rigmaden Park 200 B4
Rigsby 189 E5
Rigside 225 G2
Riley Green 192 C5
Rileyhill 158 D1
Rilla Mill 97 G2
Rillaton 97 G2
Rillington 204 B5
Rimington 193 E3
Rimpton 116 D2
Rimswell 197 F5
Rinaston 140 C5
Ring o' Bells 183 F1
Ringford 216 A5
Ringinglow 185 G4
Ringland 178 C4
Ringles Cross 109 G1
Ringmer 109 G2
Ringmore *Devon* 100 C3
Ringmore *Devon* 102 C5
Ringorm 267 K7
Ring's End 162 B2
Ringsfield 165 F3
Ringsfield Corner 165 F3
Ringshall *Herts* 135 E1
Ringshall *Suff* 152 B2
Ringshall Stocks 152 B2
Ringstead *N'hants* 161 E5
Ringstead *Norf* 177 F3
Ringwood 106 A2
Ringwould 125 F4
Rinloan 259 K4
Rinmore 260 C3
Rinnigill 277 C8
Rinsey 94 C4
Ripe 110 A3
Ripley *Derbys* 173 E2
Ripley *Hants* 106 A3
Ripley *NYorks* 194 B1
Ripley *Surr* 121 F2
Riplingham 196 B4
Ripon 202 C5
Rippingale 175 G5
Ripple *Kent* 125 F4
Ripple *Worcs* 146 A4
Ripponden 185 E5
Risabus 230 B5
Risbury 145 E2
Risby *ERid* 196 C4
Risby *Suff* 151 F1
Risca 130 B3
Rise 197 D3
Riseden 123 G5
Risegate 176 A5
Riseholme 187 G5
Riseley *Bed* 149 F1
Riseley *W'ham* 120 C1
Rishangles 152 C1
Rishton 192 D4
Rishworth 185 E1
Risinghurst 134 A2
Risley *Derbys* 173 F4
Risley *Warr* 184 A3
Risplith 194 B1
Rispond 273 G2
Rivar 119 E1
Rivenhall 138 B1
Rivenhall End 138 B1
River *Kent* 125 F4
River *WSuss* 121 E5
River Bank 150 D1
River Bridge 116 A3
River Link Boat Cruises
Devon TQ6 9AJ 101 E3
Riverford Bridge 101 D1
Riverhead 123 E3
Riverside 130 A5
Riverside Country Park *Med*
ME7 2XH 124 A2
Riverside Museum &
Tall Ship Glenlee
Glas G3 8RS 30 C3
Riverton 113 G2
Riverview Park 137 F5
Riviera International Centre
Torbay TQ2 5LZ
87 Torquay
Rivington 184 A1
Roa Island 191 F1
Roach Bridge 192 B5
Road Green 165 D2
Road Weedon 148 B2
Roade 148 C2
Roadhead 218 D4
Roadside *High* 275 G2
Roadside *Ork* 276 F3
Roadside of Kinneff 253 G2
Roadwater 114 D4
Roag 263 H7
Roast Green 150 C4
Roath 130 A5
Robert Burns Birthplace
Museum *SAyr*
KA7 4PQ 224 B4
Roberton *ScBord* 227 F4
Roberton *SLan* 226 A3
Robertsbridge 110 C1
Robertstown
Moray 267 K7
Robertstown *RCT* 129 G2
Roberttown 194 A5
Robeston Cross 126 B2
Robeston Wathen 127 D1
Robeston West 126 B2
Robin Hill Countryside
Adventure Park *IoW*
PO30 2NU 107 E4
Robin Hood
Derbys 185 G5
Robin Hood *Lancs* 183 G1
Robin Hood *WYorks* 194 C5
Robin Hood Doncaster
Sheffield Airport 187 D3
Robin Hood's Bay 204 C2
Robinhood End 151 F4

Robins 120 D5
Robinswood Hill Country
Park *Glos*
GL4 6SX 132 A1
Roborough *Devon* 113 F4
Roborough *Plym* 100 B1
Roby 183 F3
Roby Mill 183 G2
Rocester 172 C4
Roch 140 B5
Roch Bridge 140 B5
Roch Gate 140 B5
Rochallie 251 G4
Rochdale 184 C1
Roche 97 D3
Rochester *Med* 123 G2
Rochester *N'umb* 220 A2
Rochester Cathedral *Med*
ME1 1SX 123 G2
Rochford *Essex* 138 B3
Rochford *Worcs* 145 F1
Rock *Corn* 96 D2
Rock *N'umb* 229 G5
Rock *Worcs* 157 G5
Rock Ferry 183 E4
Rockbeare 102 D3
Rockbourne 106 A1
Rockcliffe *Cumb* 218 B5
Rockcliffe *D&G* 216 C5
Rockcliffe Cross 218 B5
Rockfield *A&B* 231 G4
Rockfield *High* 267 G3
Rockfield *Mon* 131 D1
Rockford 106 A2
Rockhampton 131 F3
Rockhead 97 E1
Rockingham 161 D2
Rockland All Saints 164 A2
Rockland St. Mary 179 E5
Rockland St. Peter 164 A2
Rockley 133 D5
Rockside 230 A3
Rockwell End 134 C4
Rockwell Green 103 E1
Rodborough 132 A2
Rodbourne 132 B4
Rodbourne Corner 151 G3
Rodd 144 C1
Roddam 229 E4
Rodden 104 C4
Rode 117 F2
Rode Heath 171 F2
Rodeheath 171 F1
Rodel (Roghadal) 263 F3
Roden 157 E1
Rodhuish 114 D4
Rodington 157 E1
Rodington Heath 157 E1
Rodley 131 G1
Rodmarton 132 B3
Rodmell 109 G3
Rodmersham 124 B2
Rodmersham Green 124 B2
Rodney Stoke 116 B2
Rodsley 172 D3
Rodway 115 F3
Roe Cross 185 D3
Roe Green 150 B4
Roecliffe 194 C1
Roehampton 136 B5
Roesound 279 C6
Roffey 121 G4
Rogart 266 E1
Rogate 120 D5
Rogerstone 130 B4
Rogiet 131 D4
Rokemarsh 134 B3
Roker 212 D2
Rollesby 179 F4
Rolleston *Leics* 160 C2
Rolleston *N'hants* 174 C2
Rollestone 118 B3
Rolleston-on-Dove 172 D5
Rolston 116 A1
Rolstone 116 A3
Rolvenden 124 A5
Rolvenden Layne 124 A5
Romaldkirk 211 F5
Roman Baths & Pump Room
B&NESom BA1 1LZ
63 Bath
Romanby 202 C3
Romanno Bridge 235 F5
Romansleigh 114 A5
Romesdal 263 K6
Romford *Dorset* 105 G2
Romford *GtLon* 137 E4
Romiley 184 D3
Romney, Hythe &
Dymchurch Railway
Kent TN28 8PL 124 D4
Romney Street 123 E2
Romsey 119 E5
Romsley *Shrop* 157 G4
Romsley *Worcs* 158 B5
Rona 264 C6
Ronachan 231 F4
Ronague 190 A4
Ronnachmore 230 B4
Rood End 158 C4
Rookhope 211 F3
Rookley 107 E4
Rookley Green 107 E4
Rooks Bridge 116 A2
Rook's Nest 115 D4
Rookwith 202 B4
Roos 197 E4
Roose 191 F1
Roosebeck 191 F1
Roosecote 191 F1
Rootham's Green 149 F2
Rootpark 235 D4
Ropley 120 B4
Ropley Dean 120 B4
Ropley Soke 120 B4
Ropsley 175 E4
Rora 269 J5
Rorandale 260 E3
Rorrington 156 C2
Rosarie 268 B6
Rose 96 B4
Rose Ash 114 A5
Rose Green *Essex* 152 A5
Rose Green *WSuss* 108 B4
Rose Hill 109 G2
Roseacre *Kent* 123 G3
Roseacre *Lancs* 192 A4
Rosebank 234 C5

Rosebrough 229 F4
Rosebush 141 D5
Rosecare 98 B1
Rosecliston 96 C4
Rosedale Abbey 203 G3
Roseden 229 E4
Rosehall 266 B1
Rosehearty 269 H4
Rosehill *Aber* 260 D5
Rosehill *Shrop* 157 E1
Roseisle 267 J5
Roselands 110 B3
Rosemarket 126 C2
Rosemarkie 266 E6
Rosemary Lane 103 E1
Rosemount *P&K* 251 G5
Rosemount *SAyr* 224 B3
Rosenannon 97 D3
Rosenithon 95 F4
Rosepool 126 B1
Rosevean 97 E4
Roseville 158 B3
Rosewell 235 G3
Roseworth 212 D5
Roseworthy 94 C4
Rosgill 199 G1
Roshven 247 G2
Roskhill 263 H7
Roskorwell 95 F4
Rosley 209 G2
Roslin 235 G3
Rosliston 159 E1
Rosliston Forestry Centre
Derbys
DE12 8JX 159 E1
Rosneath 233 D1
Ross *D&G* 207 G2
Ross *N'umb* 229 F3
Ross *P&K* 242 C2
Ross Priory 233 F1
Rossdhu House 233 E1
Rossett 170 A2
Rossett Green 194 C2
Rosside 199 D5
Rossie Farm School 253 E4
Rossie Ochill 243 F3
Rossie Priory 244 A1
Rossington 186 D3
Rosskeen 266 D5
Rosslyn Chapel *Midlo*
EH25 9PU 32 D4
Rossmore 105 G3
Ross-on-Wye 145 F5
Roster 275 H5
Rostherne 184 B4
Rosthwaite *Cumb* 209 F5
Rosthwaite *Cumb* 198 D4
Roston 172 C3
Rosudgeon 94 C4
Rosyth 235 F1
Rothbury 220 C1
Rotherby 160 B1
Rotherfield 123 E5
Rotherfield Greys 134 C4
Rotherfield Peppard 134 C4
Rotherham 186 B3
Rotherosthorpe 148 C2
Rotherwick 120 C2
Rothes 267 K7
Rothesay 232 B3
Rothiebrisbane 261 F1
Rothiemurchus *High*
PH22 1QH 259 G4
Rothienorman 261 F1
Rothiesholm 276 F5
Rothley *Leics* 160 A1
Rothley *N'umb* 220 C3
Rotney 260 E2
Rothwell *Lincs* 188 B3
Rothwell *N'hants* 160 D4
Rothwell *WYorks* 194 C5
Rotsea 196 C2
Rottal 252 B3
Rotten Row *Bucks* 134 C4
Rotten Row *WMid* 159 D5
Rottingdean 109 F3
Rottington 208 C5
Roud 107 E4
Roudham 164 A3
Rough Close 171 G4
Rough Common 124 D3
Rougham *Norf* 177 G5
Rougham *Suff* 152 A1
Rougham Green 152 A1
Roughburn 249 F1
Roughlee 193 E3
Roughley 158 D5
Roughton *Lincs* 176 A1
Roughton *Norf* 178 D2
Roughton *Shrop* 157 G3
Round Bush 136 A3
Roundbush Green 137 E1
Roundham 104 A2
Roundhay 194 C4
Roundstreet
Common 121 F5
Roundway 118 B1
Rous Lench 146 C2
Rousay 276 D4
Rousdon 103 F3
Rousham 147 G5
Rousham Gap 147 G5
Routenburn 232 C3
Routh 196 C3
Rout's Green 134 C3
Row *Corn* 97 E2
Row *Cumb* 199 F4
Row *Cumb* 210 C4
Row Heath 139 E1
Row Town 111 F1
Rowanburn 218 C4
Rowardennan
Lodge 241 F5
Rowarth 185 E4
Rowbarton 115 F5
Rowberrow 116 B2
Rowchoish 241 F4
Rowde 118 A1
Rowden 99 G1
Rowen 181 F5
Rowfields 172 C3
Rowfoot 210 C1
Rowhedge 152 B5
Rowhook 121 G4
Rowington 147 E1
Rowland 185 G5
Rowland's Castle 107 G1

Rowlands Gill 212 A2
Rowledge 120 D3
Rowlestone 144 C5
Rowley *Devon* 102 A1
Rowley *Dur* 211 G3
Rowley *Shrop* 156 C2
Rowley Park 171 G5
Rowley Regis 158 B4
Rowly 121 F3
Rowner 107 E2
Rowney Green 158 C5
Rownhams 106 C1
Rowrah 209 D2
Rowsham 135 D1
Rowstock 133 G4
Rowston 175 G2
Rowthorne 173 F1
Rowton
ChesW&C 170 B1
Rowton *Shrop* 156 C1
Rowton *Tel&W* 157 F1
Roxburgh 228 B3
Roxby *NLincs* 187 G1
Roxby *NYorks* 203 G5
Roxton 149 G2
Roxwell 137 F2
Royal Academy of Arts
GtLon W1J 0BD 44 C4
Royal Albert Hall *GtLon*
SW7 2AP 11 F5
Royal Albert Memorial
Museum & Art Gallery
Devon EX4 3RX
72 Exeter
Royal Armouries Museum,
Leeds *WYorks*
LS10 1LT 41 G5
Royal Artillery Barracks
GtLon SE18 5DP 13 F5
Royal Bath & West
Showground *Som*
BA4 6QN 116 D2
Royal Botanic Garden,
Edinburgh *Edin*
EH3 5LR 36 D1
Royal Botanic Gardens,
Kew *GtLon*
TW9 3AB 11 C6
Royal British Legion
Village 123 G3
Royal Centre NG1 5ND
80 Nottingham
Royal Cornwall Museum
Corn TR1 2SJ 96 C5
Royal Devon 99 E3
Royal Festival Hall *GtLon*
SE1 8XX 45 F5
Royal Highland Showground
Edin EH28 8NB 32 A2
Royal Horticultural Halls
GtLon SW1P 2PB 44 D7
Royal Hospital Chelsea
GtLon SW3 4SR 13 A5
Royal Leamington
Spa 147 F1
Royal Mews, Buckingham
Palace *GtLon*
SW1W 0QH 44 B6
Royal Naval Museum
PO1 3NH
82 Portsmouth
Royal Oak 183 F2
Royal Observatory
Greenwich *GtLon*
SE10 8XJ 13 D5
Royal Opera House *GtLon*
WC2E 9DD 45 E3
Royal Pavilion *B&H*
BN1 1EE 65 Brighton
Royal Scots Regimental
Museum, The *Edin*
EH1 2YT 37 F5
Royal Scottish Academy
Edin EH2 2EL 37 F4
Royal Tunbridge
Wells 123 E5
Royal Victoria Country Park
Hants SO31 5GA 4 C4
Royal Welch Fusiliers
Regimental Museum
Gwyn LL55 2AY 167 D1
Royal Wootton
Bassett 132 C4
Royal Yacht Britannia
Edin EH6 6JJ 32 C1
Roybridge (Drochaid
Ruaidh) 249 E1
Roydon *Essex* 136 D1
Roydon *Norf* 164 B3
Roydon *Norf* 177 F5
Roydon Hamlet 136 D2
Royston *Herts* 150 B3
Royston *SYorks* 186 A1
Royton 184 D2
Rozel 100 C4
Ruabon (Rhiwabon) 170 A3
Ruaig 246 B2
Ruan Lanihorne 96 C5
Ruan Major 95 E5
Ruan Minor 95 E5
Ruanaich 238 B2
Ruardean 131 F1
Ruardean Hill 131 F1
Ruardean Woodside 131 F1
Rubery 158 B5
Ruckcroft 210 B3
Ruckinge 124 C5
Ruckland 188 D5
Rucklers Lane 135 F2
Ruckley 157 E2
Rudbaxton 140 C5
Rudby 203 D2
Rudchester 212 A1
Ruddington 173 E4
Ruddlemoor 97 E4
Rudford 145 G5
Rudge 117 F2
Rudgeway 131 F4
Rudgwick 121 F4
Rudhall 145 F5
Rudheath 184 A5
Rudley Green 138 B2
Rudloe 117 F1
Rudry 130 A4
Rudston 196 C1
Rudyard 171 G2
Rudyard Lake *Staffs*
ST13 8RT 171 G2

Rufford 183 F1
Rufford Country Park *Notts*
NG22 9DF 174 B1
Rufforth 195 E2
Ruffside 211 F2
Rugby 160 A5
Rugby Football Union,
Twickenham *GtLon*
TW1 1DZ 11 B6
Rugeley 158 C1
Ruilick 266 C7
Ruishton 115 F5
Ruisigearraidh 262 E3
Ruislip 135 F4
Ruislip Gardens 135 F4
Ruislip Manor 136 A4
Rum 255 J5
Rumbling Bridge 243 F5
Rumburgh 165 E3
Rumford 96 C2
Rumleigh 100 A1
Rumney 130 B5
Rumwell 115 E5
Runacraig 242 A3
Runcorn 183 G4
Runcton 108 A3
Runcton Holme 163 E2
Rundlestone 99 F3
Runfold 121 D3
Runhall 178 B5
Runham *Norf* 179 F4
Runham *Norf* 179 G5
Runnington 115 E5
Runsell Green 137 G2
Runshaw Moor 183 G1
Runswick Bay 204 B1
Runtaleave 252 A3
Runwell 137 G3
Ruscombe *Glos* 132 A2
Ruscombe
W'ham 134 C5
Rush Green
GtLon 137 E4
Rush Green *Herts* 150 A5
Rushall *Here* 145 F4
Rushall *Norf* 164 C3
Rushall *Wilts* 118 C2
Rushall *WMid* 158 C2
Rushbrooke 151 G1
Rushbury 157 E3
Rushden *Herts* 150 B4
Rushden *N'hants* 149 E1
Rushford *Devon* 99 E3
Rushford *Norf* 164 A3
Rushgreen 184 A4
Rushlake Green 110 B2
Rushmere 165 F3
Rushmere
St. Andrew 152 D3
Rushmoor 121 D3
Rushock 158 A5
Rusholme 184 C3
Rushton
ChesW&C 170 C1
Rushton *N'hants* 160 D4
Rushton *Shrop* 157 F2
Rushton Spencer 171 G1
Rushwick 146 A2
Rushy Green 109 G2
Rushyford 212 B5
Ruskie 242 B4
Ruskington 175 F2
Rusko 215 G5
Rusland 199 E4
Rusper 122 B5
Ruspidge 131 F1
Russ Hill 122 B4
Russel 264 E7
Russell Green 137 G1
Russell's Green 110 C2
Russell's Water 134 C3
Russel's Green 165 D4
Rusthall 123 E5
Rustington 108 C3
Ruston 204 C4
Ruston Parva 196 C1
Ruswarp 204 B2
Rutherend 234 A4
Rutherford 228 A3
Rutherglen 234 A3
Ruthernbridge 97 E3
Ruthers of Howe 275 J2
Ruthin (Rhuthun)
Denb 169 E2
Ruthin *VGlam* 129 F5
Ruthrieston 261 H4
Ruthven *Aber* 268 D6
Ruthven *Angus* 252 A5
Ruthven *High* 259 F1
Ruthven *High* 258 E5
Ruthvoes 96 D3
Ruthwaite 209 F3
Ruthwell 217 E4
Rutland Water *Rut*
LE15 8QL 161 D2
Ruyton-XI-Towns 170 A5
Ryal 220 C4
Ryal Fold 192 C5
Ryall *Dorset* 104 A3
Ryall *Worcs* 146 A3
Ryarsh 123 F3
Rydal 199 E2
Ryde 107 E3
Rydon 112 D5
Rye 111 E1
Rye Foreign 111 D1
Rye Harbour 111 E2
Rye Harbour *ESuss*
TN31 7TX 111 E2
Rye Park 136 C2
Rye Street 145 G4
Ryebank 170 C4
Ryeford 145 F5
Ryehill *Aber* 260 E2
Ryehill *ERid* 197 E5
Ryhall 161 F1
Ryhill 186 A1
Ryhope 212 D2
Rylands 173 E4
Rylstone 193 F2
Ryme Intrinseca 104 B1
Ryther 195 E4
Ryton *Glos* 145 G4
Ryton *NYorks* 203 G5
Ryton *Shrop* 157 G2
Ryton *T&W* 212 A1
Ryton-on-
Dunsmore 159 F5

S

S.S. Great Britain *Bristol*
BS1 6TY 8 B3
Saasaig 256 C4
Sabden 193 D4
Sabden Fold 193 E4
Sackers Green 152 A4
Sacombe 136 C1
Sacombe Green 136 C1
Sacriston 212 B3
Sadberge 202 C1
Saddell 222 C2
Saddington 160 B3
Saddle Bow 163 E1
Sadgill 199 F2
Saffron Walden 150 D4
Sageston 127 D2
Saham Hills 178 A5
Saham Toney 163 G2
Saighdinis 262 D5
Saighton 170 B1
St. Abbs 237 G3
St. Agnes 96 B4
St. Aidan's Winery *N'umb*
TD15 2RX 229 F2
St. Albans 136 A2
St. Albans Cathedral *Herts*
AL1 1BY 136 A2
St. Allen 96 C4
St. Andrews 244 D3
St. Andrew's & Blackfriars
Halls *Norf* NR3 1AU
79 Norwich
St. Andrews Major 130 A5
St. Anne 101 C4
St. Anne's 191 G5
St. Ann's 217 E1
St. Ann's Chapel
Corn 99 E3
St. Ann's Chapel
Devon 100 C3
St. Anthony 95 F3
St. Anthony-in-
Meneage 95 E4
St. Anthony's Hill 110 B3
St. Arvans 131 E3
St. Asaph
(Llanelwy) 182 B5
St. Athan 114 D1
St. Aubin 100 C4
St. Audries 115 E3
St. Austell 97 E4
St. Bees 208 C5
St. Blazey 97 E4
St. Blazey Gate 97 E4
St. Boswells 227 G2
St. Botolph's Church, Boston
Lincs PE21 6NP 176 B3
St. Brelade 100 C4
St. Breock 97 D2
St. Breward 97 E2
St. Briavels 131 E2
St. Brides 126 B1
St. Brides Major 129 E5
St. Brides
Netherwent 130 D4
St. Bride's
Wentlooge 130 B4
St. Bride's-super-
Ely 129 G5
St. Budeaux 100 A2
St. Buryan 94 B4
St. Catherine 117 E1
St. Catherines 240 D4
St. Clears (Sanclêr) 127 F1
St. Cleer 97 G3
St. Clement *Chanl* 100 C5
St. Clement *Corn* 96 C5
St. Clether 97 G1
St. Colmac 232 B3
St. Columb Major 96 D3
St. Columb Minor 96 C3
St. Columb Road 96 D4
St. Combs 269 J4
St. Cross South
Elmham 165 D3
St. Cyrus 253 F3
St. Davids *Fife* 235 F1
St. David's *P&K* 243 E2
St. David's (Tyddewi)
Pembs 140 A5
St. David's Hall CF10 1AH
67 Cardiff
St. Day 96 B5
St. Decumans 115 D3
St. Dennis 97 D4
St. Denys 106 D1
St. Dogmaels
(Llandudoch) 141 E3
St. Dogwells 140 C5
St. Dominick 100 A1
St. Donats 114 C1
St. Edith's Marsh 118 A1
St. Endellion 97 D1
St. Enoder 96 C4
St. Erme 96 C5
St. Erney 99 D5
St. Erth 94 C3
St. Erth Praze 94 C3
St. Ervan 96 C2
St. Eval 96 C3
St. Ewe 97 D5
St. Fagans 130 A5
St. Fagans National History
Museum *Cardiff*
CF5 6XB 7 A4
St. Fergus 269 J5
St. Fillans 242 B2
St. Florence 127 D2
St. Gennys 98 B1
St. George *Bristol* 131 F5
St. George *Conwy* 182 A5
St. Georges *NSom* 116 A1
St. George's *Tel&W* 157 G1
St. George's *VGlam* 129 G5
St. George's Hall, Liverpool
Mersey L1 1JJ 42 D3
St. Germans 99 D5
St. Giles' Cathedral,
Edinburgh *Edin*
EH1 1RE 37 F4
St. Giles in the
Wood 113 F4
St. Giles on the
Heath 99 D1
St. Harmon 155 F5
St. Helen Auckland 212 A5

St. Helena 178 C4
St. Helen's ESuss 110 D2
St. Helens IoW 107 F4
St. Helens Mersey 183 G3
St. Helier Chanl 100 C5
St. Helier GtLon 122 B2
St. Hilary Corn 94 C3
St. Hilary VGlam 129 G5
St. Hill 122 C5
St. Ibbs 149 G5
St. Illtyd 130 B2
St. Ippollitts 149 G5
St. Ishmael 127 G2
St. Ishmael's 126 B2
St. Issey 96 D2
St. Ive 98 D4
St. Ives Cambs 162 B5
St. Ives Corn 94 C2
St. Ives Dorset 106 A2
St. James South
Elmham 165 E3
St. John Chanl 100 C4
St. John Corn 100 A2
St. John the Baptist Church, Cirencester Glos GL7 2NX 132 C2
St. John's GtLon 136 C5
St. John's IoM 190 A3
St. John's Surr 121 E2
St. John's Worcs 146 A2
St. John's Chapel
Devon 113 F3
St. John's Chapel
Dur 211 E4
St. John's Fen End 162 D1
St. John's Hall 211 G4
St. John's Highway 162 D1
St. John's Kirk 226 A2
St. John's Town of
Dalry 216 A2
St. Judes 190 B2
St. Just 94 A3
St. Just in Roseland 95 F3
St. Katherines 261 F1
St. Keverne 95 E4
St. Kew 97 E2
St. Kew Highway 97 E2
St. Keyne 97 G3
St. Lawrence Corn 97 E3
St. Lawrence Essex 138 C2
St. Lawrence IoW 107 E5
St. Lawrence's Church, Eyam Derbys S32 5QH 185 G5
St. Leonards Bucks 135 E2
St. Leonards
Dorset 106 A2
St. Leonards
ESuss 110 D3
St. Leonards
Grange 106 D3
St. Leonard's Street 123 F3
St. Levan 94 A4
St. Lythans 130 A5
St. Mabyn 97 E2
St. Madoes 243 G2
St. Margaret South
Elmham 165 E3
St. Margarets
Here 144 C4
St. Margarets
Herts 136 C1
St. Margarets
Wilts 118 D1
St. Margaret's at
Cliffe 125 F4
St. Margaret's Hope 277 D8
St. Mark's 190 A4
St. Martin Chanl 101 F5
St. Martin Chanl 100 C5
St. Martin Corn 97 G4
St. Martin Corn 95 E4
St. Martin-in-the-Fields Church GtLon WC2N 4JH 44 E4
St. Martin's IoS 96 B1
St. Martins P&K 243 G1
St. Martin's Shrop 170 A4
St. Mary 100 C5
St. Mary Bourne 119 F2
St. Mary Church 129 G5
St. Mary Cray 123 D2
St. Mary Hill 129 F5
St. Mary Hoo 137 G5
St. Mary in the
Marsh 111 F1
St. Mary Magdalene Chapel, Sandringham Norf PE35 6EH 177 E5
St. Mary the Virgin Church, Holy Island N'umb TD15 2RX 229 F2
St. Mary the Virgin Church, Oxford Oxon OX1 4AH 134 A2
St. Mary the Virgin Church, Rye ESuss TN31 7HE 111 E2
St. Marychurch 101 F1
St. Mary's IoS 96 B1
St. Mary's Ork 277 D7
St. Mary's Airport 96 B1
St. Mary's Bay 111 F1
St. Mary's Church, Whitby NYorks YO22 4JT 204 C1
St. Mary's Grove 116 B1
St. Maughans
Green 131 D1
St. Mawes 95 F3
St. Mawgan 96 C3
St. Mellion 99 D4
St. Mellons 130 B4
St. Merryn 96 C2
St. Mewan 97 D4
St. Michael Caerhays 97 D5
St. Michael Church 116 A4
St. Michael Penkevil 96 C5
St. Michael South
Elmham 165 E3
St. Michaels Fife 244 C2
St. Michaels Kent 124 A5
St. Michaels Worcs 145 E1
St. Michael's Church, Hathersage Derbys S32 1AJ 185 G4
St. Michael's Mount Corn TR17 0HT 94 C3
St. Michael's on
Wyre 192 A3
St. Mildred's Church, Whippingham IoW PO32 6LP 107 E3
St. Minver 97 D2
St. Monans 244 D4
St. Mungo Museum of Religious Life & Art Glas G4 0RH 39 H3
St. Mungo's Cathedral, Glasgow Glas G4 0QZ 39 J3
St. Neot 97 F3
St. Neots 149 G1
St. Newlyn East 96 C4
St. Nicholas Pembs 140 C4
St. Nicholas VGlam 129 G5
St. Nicholas at
Wade 125 E2
St. Ninians 242 C5
St. Osyth 139 E1
St. Ouen 100 B5
St. Owen's Cross 145 E5
St. Paul's Cathedral, London GtLon EC4M 8AD 45 J3
St. Paul's Cray 123 D2
St. Paul's Walden 149 G5
St. Peter 100 C5
St. Peter Port 101 F5
St. Peter's 125 F2
St. Petrox 126 C3
St. Pinnock 97 G3
St. Quivox 224 B3
St. Ruan 95 E5
St. Sampson 101 F4
St. Saviour Chanl 101 E5
St. Saviour Chanl 100 C5
St. Stephen 96 D4
St. Stephens Corn 100 A2
St. Stephens Corn 98 D2
St. Stephens Herts 136 A2
St. Teath 97 E1
St. Thomas 102 C3
St. Tudy 97 E2
St. Twynnells 126 C3
St. Veep 97 F4
St. Vigeans 253 E5
St. Wenn 97 D3
St. Weonards 145 D5
St. Winnow 97 F4
St. Winwaloe's Church, Gunwalloe Corn TR12 7QE 95 D4
Saintbury 146 D4
Salachail 248 C4
Salcombe 100 D4
Salcombe Regis 103 E4
Salcott 138 C1
Sale 184 B3
Sale Green 146 B2
Saleby 189 E5
Salehurst 110 C1
Salem Carmar 142 C5
Salem Cere 154 C4
Salem Gwyn 167 E2
Salen A&B 247 E5
Salen High 247 F3
Salendine Nook 185 F1
Salesbury 192 C4
Saleway 146 B2
Salford CenBeds 149 E4
Salford GtMan 184 C3
Salford Oxon 147 E5
Salford Priors 146 C2
Salfords 122 B4
Salhouse 179 E4
Saline 243 F5
Salisbury 118 C5
Salisbury Cathedral Wilts SP1 2EF
83 Salisbury
Salkeld Dykes 210 B4
Sallachan 248 B3
Sallachry 240 C3
Sallachy High 266 C1
Sallachy High 257 F1
Salle 178 C3
Sally Lunn's House B&NESom BA1 1NX
63 Bath
Salmonby 188 D5
Salmond's Muir 245 D1
Salperton 146 C5
Salph End 149 F2
Salsburgh 234 C3
Salt 171 G5
Salt Hill 135 E4
Salt Holme 213 D5
Saltaire 194 A4
Saltash 100 A2
Saltburn 266 E4
Saltburn-by-the-
Sea 213 F5
Saltburn Cliff Lift R&C TS12 1DP 213 F5
Saltby 175 D5
Saltcoats Cumb 198 B3
Saltcoats NAyr 232 D5
Saltcotes 191 G5
Saltdean 109 F3
Salterbeck 208 C4
Salterforth 193 E3
Saltergate 204 B3
Salterhill 267 K5
Salterswall 170 D1
Saltfleet 189 E3
Saltfleetby All
Saints 189 E3
Saltfleetby
St. Clements 189 E3
Saltfleetby St. Peter 189 E4
Saltford 117 D1
Salthaugh Grange 197 E5
Salthouse 178 B1
Saltley 158 C4
Saltmarshe 195 G5
Saltness 277 B8
Saltney 170 A1
Salton 203 G4
Saltrens 113 E3
Saltwell Park, Gateshead T&W NE9 5AX 28 B3
Saltwick 221 D4
Saltwood 125 D5
Salum 246 B2
Salvington 108 D3
Salwarpe 146 A1
Salwayash 104 A3
Sambourne 146 C1
Sambrook 171 E5
Samhla 262 C5
Samlesbury 192 C4
Sampford Arundel 103 E1
Sampford Brett 115 D3
Sampford
Courtenay 113 G5
Sampford Moor 103 E1
Sampford Peverell 102 D1
Sampford Spiney 99 F3
Samuelston 236 B2
Sanaigmore 230 A2
Sancreed 94 B4
Sancton 196 B4
Sand Shet 279 C8
Sand Som 116 B3
Sand Hutton 195 F2
Sandaig A&B 246 A2
Sandaig High 256 D4
Sandaig High 256 D3
Sandal Magna 186 A1
Sanday 276 F3
Sanday Airfield 276 F3
Sandbach 171 E1
Sandbank 232 C1
Sandbanks 105 G4
Sandend 268 D4
Sanderstead 122 C2
Sandford Cumb 200 C1
Sandford Devon 102 B2
Sandford Dorset 105 F4
Sandford IoW 107 E4
Sandford NSom 116 B2
Sandford Shrop 170 C4
Sandford Shrop 170 A5
Sandford SLan 234 B5
Sandford Orcas 116 D5
Sandford St. Martin 147 G5
Sandfordhill 269 K6
Sandford-on-
Thames 134 A2
Sandgarth 277 E6
Sandgate 125 E5
Sandgreen 215 G5
Sandhaven 269 H4
Sandhead 214 B5
Sandhills Dorset 104 C1
Sandhills Dorset 104 B2
Sandhills Surr 121 E4
Sandhills WYorks 194 C4
Sandhoe 211 F1
Sandholme ERid 196 A4
Sandholme Lincs 176 B4
Sandhurst BrackF 120 D1
Sandhurst Glos 146 A5
Sandhurst Kent 110 C1
Sandhurst Cross 110 C1
Sandhutton 202 C4
Sandiacre 173 F4
Sandilands 189 F4
Sandiway 184 A5
Sandleheath 106 A1
Sandleigh 133 G2
Sandling 123 G3
Sandlow Green 171 E1
Sandness 279 A7
Sandon Essex 137 G2
Sandon Herts 150 B4
Sandon Staffs 171 G5
Sandown 107 F4
Sandplace 97 G4
Sandquoy 276 G3
Sandridge Devon 101 E2
Sandridge Herts 136 A1
Sandridge Wilts 118 A1
Sandringham 177 E5
Sandrocks 109 F1
Sandsend 204 B1
Sandside 199 F4
Sandside House 274 E2
Sandsound 279 C8
Sandtoft 187 E2
Sanduck 102 A4
Sandway 124 A3
Sandwell 158 C4
Sandwell Park Farm WMid B71 4BG 14 D2
Sandwell Valley Country Park WMid B71 4BG 14 D2
Sandwich 125 F3
Sandwick Cumb 199 F1
Sandwick Shet 279 D10
Sandwick (Sanndabhaig) Na H-E. Siar 271 G4
Sandwith 208 C5
Sandy Carmar 128 A2
Sandy CenBeds 149 G3
Sandy Bank 176 A2
Sandy Haven 126 B2
Sandy Lane Wilts 118 A1
Sandy Lane Wrex 170 B3
Sandy Lane
WYorks 194 A4
Sandy Way 107 D4
Sandycroft 170 A1
Sandygate Devon 102 B5
Sandygate IoM 190 B2
Sandyhills 216 C5
Sandylands 192 A1
Sandypark 102 A4
Sandyway 145 D5
Sangobeg 273 G2
Sankyn's Green 145 G1
Sanna 247 D3
Sannaig 230 D3
Sannox 232 B5
Sanquhar 225 F5
Santon Bridge 198 C2
Santon Downham 163 G4
Sant-y-Nyll 129 G5
Sapcote 159 G3
Sapey Common 145 G1
Sapiston 164 A4
Sapperton Derbys 172 C4
Sapperton Glos 132 B2
Sapperton Lincs 175 F4
Saracen's Head 176 B5
Sarclet 275 J4
Sardis 126 C2
Sarisbury 107 E2
Sark 101 G5
Sark Dark Sky Island 101 G5
Sarn Bridgend 129 F4
Sarn Powys 156 B3
Sarn Bach 166 C5
Sarn Meyllteyrn 166 B4
Sarnau Carmar 127 G1
Sarnau Cere 141 G2
Sarnau Gwyn 168 C4
Sarnau Powys 156 B1
Sarnau Powys 143 G4
Sarnesfield 144 C2
Saron Carmar 128 C1
Saron Carmar 141 G4
Saron Gwyn 167 E1
Saron Gwyn 167 D2
Sarratt 135 F3
Sarre 125 E2
Sarsden 147 E5
Sarsgrum 273 F2
Sartfield 190 B2
Satley 212 A3
Satron 201 E3
Satterleigh 113 G3
Satterthwaite 199 E3
Sauchen 260 E3
Saucher 243 G1
Sauchie 243 D5
Sauchieburn 253 E3
Sauchrie 224 B4
Saughall 183 E5
Saughall Massie 183 D4
Saughtree 219 D2
Saul 131 G2
Saundby 187 E4
Saundersfoot 127 E2
Saunderton 134 C2
Saunton 113 E2
Sausthorpe 176 B1
Saval 266 C1
Savalbeg 266 C1
Saverley Green 171 G4
Savile Town 194 B5
Sawbridge 148 A1
Sawbridgeworth 137 D1
Sawdon 204 C4
Sawley Derbys 173 F4
Sawley Lancs 193 D3
Sawley NYorks 194 B1
Sawston 150 C3
Sawtry 161 G4
Saxby Leics 160 D1
Saxby Lincs 188 A4
Saxby All Saints 187 G1
Saxelbye 174 B5
Saxham Street 152 B1
Saxilby 187 F5
Saxlingham 178 B2
Saxlingham Green 164 D2
Saxlingham
Nethergate 164 D2
Saxlingham
Thorpe 164 D2
Saxmundham 153 E1
Saxon Street 151 E2
Saxondale 174 B4
Saxtead 153 D1
Saxtead Green 153 D1
Saxtead Little
Green 153 D1
Saxthorpe 178 C2
Saxton 195 D4
Sayers Common 109 E2
Scackleton 203 F5
Scadabhagh 263 G2
Scaftworth 187 D3
Scagglethorpe 204 B5
Scaitcliffe 193 D5
Scalasaig 238 C5
Scalby ERid 196 A5
Scalby NYorks 204 D3
Scaldwell 160 C5
Scale Houses 210 B3
Scaleby 210 A1
Scalebyhill 210 A1
Scales Cumb 209 G4
Scales Cumb 199 D5
Scalford 174 C5
Scaling 203 G1
Scallasaig 256 E3
Scallastle 239 G1
Scalloway 279 C9
Scalpay (Eilean
Scalpaigh) 263 H2
Scamblesby 188 C5
Scammadale 240 A2
Scamodale 248 A2
Scampston 204 B5
Scampton 187 G5
Scaniport 258 D1
Scapa 277 D7
Scapegoat Hill 185 E1
Scar 276 F3
Scarborough 204 D4
Scarborough Sea Life & Marine Sanctuary NYorks YO12 6RP 204 D3
Scarcewater 96 D4
Scarcliffe 173 F1
Scarcroft 194 C3
Scardroy 265 J6
Scarff 278 B4
Scarfskerry 275 H1
Scargill 201 F1
Scarinish 246 B2
Scarisbrick 183 E1
Scarning 178 A4
Scarrington 174 C3
Scarrowhill 210 B2
Scarth Hill 183 F2
Scarthingwell 195 D4
Scartho 188 C2
Scarwell 276 B5
Scatraig 258 E1
Scaur (Kippford)
D&G 216 C5
Scaur D&G 216 C3
Scawby 187 G2
Scawby Brook 187 G2
Scawton 203 E4
Scayne's Hill 109 F1
Scealascro 270 D5
Scethrog 144 A5
Schaw 224 C3
Scholar Green 171 F2
Scholes SYorks 186 A3
Scholes WYorks 194 C4
Scholes WYorks 185 F2
Scholes WYorks 194 A5
School Green 170 D1
School House 103 G2
Schoose 208 D4
Sciberscross 266 E1
Science Museum GtLon SW7 2DD 11 F5
Scilly Isles
(Isles of Scilly) 96 B1
Scissett 185 G1
Scleddau 140 C4
Sco Ruston 179 D3
Scofton 186 D4
Scole 164 C4
Scolpaig 262 C4
Scone 243 G2
Scones Lethendy 243 G2
Sconser 256 B1
Scoor 238 D3
Scopwick 175 F2
Scoraig 265 G2
Scorborough 196 C3
Scorrier 96 B5
Scorriton 100 D1
Scorton Lancs 192 B3
Scorton NYorks 202 B2
Scot Hay 171 E3
Scotby 210 A2
Scotch Corner 202 B2
Scotch Whisky Heritage Centre Edin EH1 2NE 37 F4
Scotforth 192 A2
Scothern 188 A5
Scotland 175 F4
Scotland End 147 F4
Scotland Street 152 A4
Scotland Street School Museum of Education Glas G5 8QB 38 C6
Scotlandwell 243 G4
Scotnish 231 F1
Scots' Gap 220 C3
Scotsburn 266 E4
Scotston Aber 253 F2
Scotston P&K 251 E5
Scotstoun 233 G3
Scotstown 248 A3
Scott Willoughby 175 F4
Scotter 187 F2
Scotterthorpe 187 F2
Scottish Exhibition & Conference Centre (S.E.C.C.) Glas G3 8YW 38 B4
Scottish National Gallery of Modern Art Edin EH4 3DR 36 B4
Scottish National Portrait Gallery Edin EH2 1JD 37 F3
Scottish Parliament Edin EH99 1SP 37 H4
Scottish Seabird Centre, North Berwick ELoth EH39 4SS 236 C1
Scottish Wool Centre, Aberfoyle Stir FK8 3UQ 242 A4
Scottlethorpe 175 F5
Scotton Lincs 187 F3
Scotton NYorks 202 A3
Scotton NYorks 194 C2
Scottow 179 D3
Scoughall 236 D1
Scoulton 178 A5
Scounslow Green 172 B5
Scourie 272 D4
Scourie More 272 D4
Scousburgh 279 F9
Scouthead 185 D2
Scrabster 275 G1
Scrafield 176 B1
Scrainwood 220 B1
Scrane End 176 B3
Scraptoft 160 B2
Scratby 179 G4
Scrayingham 195 G2
Scredington 175 F3
Scremby 176 C1
Scremerston 229 E2
Screveton 174 C3
Scriven 194 C2
Scronkey 192 A3
Scrooby 187 D3
Scropton 172 C4
Scrub Hill 176 A2
Scruton 202 C3
Sculthorpe 177 G4
Scunthorpe 187 F1
Scurlage 128 A4
Sea 103 G1
Sea Life Centre, Blackpool FY1 5AA 64 Blackpool
Sea Life Centre, Brighton B&H BN2 1TB
65 Brighton
Sea Life Centre, Great Yarmouth Norf NR30 3AH 179 G5
Sea Life London Aquarium GtLon SE1 7PD 45 F5
Sea Life Sanctuary, Hunstanton Norf PE36 5BH 177 E3
Sea Mills 131 E5
Sea Palling 179 F3
Seabank 248 B5
Seaborough 104 A2
Seaburn 212 D1
Seacombe 183 E3
Seacroft Lincs 177 D1
Seacroft WYorks 194 C4
Seadyke 176 B4
Seafield A&B 231 F1
Seafield SAyr 224 B3
Seafield WLoth 235 E3
Seaford 109 G4
Seaforth 183 E3
Seagrave 160 B1
Seagry Heath 132 B4
Seaham 212 D3
Seaham Grange 212 D2
Seahouses 229 G3
Seal 123 E3
Sealand 170 A1
Seale 121 D3
Sea-Life Adventure, Southend-on-Sea S'end SS1 2ER 138 B4
Sealyham 140 C5
Seamer NYorks 203 D1
Seamer NYorks 204 D4
Seamill 232 C5
SeaQuarium, Rhyl Denb LL18 3AF 182 B4
Searby 188 A2
Seasalter 124 C2
Seascale 198 B2
Seathorne 177 D1
Seathwaite Cumb 209 F5
Seathwaite Cumb 198 D3
Seatle 199 E4
Seatoller 209 F5
Seaton Corn 98 D5
Seaton Cumb 208 D3
Seaton Devon 103 F3
Seaton Dur 212 C2
Seaton ERid 197 D3
Seaton N'umb 221 F4
Seaton Rut 161 E3
Seaton Burn 221 E4
Seaton Carew 213 E5
Seaton Delaval 221 F4
Seaton Junction 103 F3
Seaton Ross 195 G3
Seaton Sluice 221 F4
Seaton Tramway Devon EX12 2NQ 103 F3
Seatown Aber 269 J5
Seatown Dorset 104 A3
Seatown Moray 268 D4
Seave Green 203 E2
Seaview 107 F3
Seaville 209 E1
Seavington
St. Mary 104 A1
Seavington
St. Michael 104 A1
Seawick 139 E1
Sebastopol 130 B3
Sebergham 209 G2
Seckington 159 E2
Second Coast 265 F2
Sedbergh 200 B3
Sedbury 131 E3
Sedbusk 201 D3
Seddington 149 G3
Sedgeberrow 146 C4
Sedgebrook 175 D4
Sedgefield 212 C5
Sedgeford 177 F4
Sedgehill 117 F5
Sedgemere 159 E5
Sedgley 158 B3
Sedgwick 199 G4
Sedlescombe 110 C2
Sedlescombe
Street 110 C2
Seend 118 A1
Seend Cleeve 118 A1
Seer Green 135 E3
Seething 165 E2
Sefton 183 E2
Seghill 221 E4
Seifton 157 D4
Seighford 171 F5
Seil 239 G3
Seilebost 263 F2
Seion 167 E1
Seisdon 158 A3
Seisiadar 271 H4
Seized! Revenue & Customs Uncovered Mersey L3 4AQ
42 B5
Selattyn 169 F4
Selborne 120 C4
Selby 195 F4
Selham 121 E5
Selhurst 122 C2
Selkirk 227 F3
Sellack 145 E5
Sellafield 198 B2
Sellafield Visitors Centre Cumb CA20 1PG
198 B2
Sellafirth 278 E3
Sellindge 124 D5
Selling 124 C3
Sells Green 118 A1
Selly Oak 158 C4
Selmeston 110 A3
Selsdon 122 C2
Selsey 108 A4
Selsfield Common 122 C5
Selside Cumb 199 G3
Selside NYorks 200 C5
Selsley 132 A2
Selstead 125 E4
Selston 173 F2
Selworthy 114 C3
Semblister 279 C7
Semer 152 A3
Semington 117 F1
Semley 117 F5
Send 121 F2
Send Marsh 121 F2
Senghenydd 130 A3
Sennen 94 A4
Sennen Cove 94 A4
Sennybridge 143 F5
Senwick 207 G2
Sequer's Bridge 100 C2
Serlby 186 D4
Serpentine Gallery GtLon W2 3XA 11 F5
Serrington 118 B4
Sessay 203 D5
Setchey 163 E1
Setley 106 C2
Setter Shet 279 E8
Setter Shet 279 C7
Settiscarth 277 C6
Settle 193 E1
Settrington 204 B5
Seven Ash 115 E4
Seven Bridges 132 D3
Seven Kings 137 D4
Seven Sisters 129 E2
Seven Springs 132 B1
Sevenhampton
Glos 146 C5
Sevenhampton
Swin 133 E3
Sevenoaks 123 E3
Sevenoaks Weald 123 E3
Severn Beach 131 E4
Severn Stoke 146 A3
Severn Valley Railway Shrop DY12 1BG 157 G4
Sevick End 149 F2
Sevington 124 C4
Sewards End 151 D4
Sewardstone 136 C3
Sewerby 197 D1
Sewerby Hall & Gardens ERid YO15 1EA 197 E1
Seworgan 95 E3
Sewstern 175 D5
Seymour Villas 113 E1
Sezincote 147 D4
Sgarasta Mhòr 263 F2
Sgiogarstaigh 271 H1
Sgodachail 266 B2
Shabbington 134 B2
Shackerley 158 A2
Shackerstone 159 F2
Shackleford 121 E3
Shadfen 221 E3
Shadforth 212 C3
Shadingfield 165 F3
Shadoxhurst 124 B5
Shadsworth 192 D5
Shadwell Norf 164 A3
Shadwell WYorks 194 C3
Shaftenhoe End 150 C4
Shaftesbury 117 F5
Shafton 186 A1
Shakespeare's Birthplace Warks CV37 6QW
85 Stratford-upon-Avon
Shakespeare's Globe Theatre GtLon SE1 9DT 45 J4
Shalbourne 119 E1
Shalcombe 106 C4
Shalden 120 B3
Shalden Green 120 C3
Shaldon 102 C5
Shalfleet 106 D4
Shalford Essex 151 F5
Shalford Surr 121 F3
Shalford Green 151 F5
Shallowford Devon 114 A3
Shallowford Staffs 171 F5
Shalmsford Street 124 C3
Shalmstry 275 G2
Shalstone 148 B4
Shalunt 232 B2
Shambellie 217 D4
Shamley Green 121 F3
Shandon 233 D1
Shandwick 267 F4
Shangton 160 C3
Shankend 227 G5
Shankhouse 221 E4
Shanklin 107 E4
Shanklin Chine IoW PO37 6BW 107 E4
Shannochie 223 E3
Shantron 233 E1
Shantullich 266 D6
Shanzie 252 A4
Shap 199 G1
Shapinsay 277 E6
Shapwick Dorset 105 F2
Shapwick Som 116 B4
Sharcott 118 C2
Shard End 159 D4
Shardlow 173 F4
Shareshill 158 B2
Sharlston 186 A1
Sharlston Common 186 A1
Sharnal Street 137 G5
Sharnbrook 149 E2
Sharneyford 193 E5
Sharnford 159 G3
Sharnhill Green 104 D2
Sharow 202 C5
Sharp Street 179 E3
Sharpenhoe 149 F4
Sharperton 220 B1
Sharpham House 101 E2
Sharpness 131 F2
Sharpthorne 122 C5
Sharrington 178 B2
Shatterford 157 G4
Shatterling 125 E3
Shaugh Prior 100 B1
Shave Cross 104 A3
Shavington 171 E2
Shaw GtMan 184 D2
Shaw Swin 132 D4
Shaw WBerks 119 F1
Shaw Wilts 117 F1
Shaw Green Herts 150 A4
Shaw Green
NYorks 194 B2
Shaw Mills 194 B1
Shaw Side 184 D2
Shawbost
(Siabost) 270 E3
Shawbury 170 C5
Shawell 160 A4
Shawfield GtMan 184 C1
Shawfield Staffs 172 B1
Shawford 119 F5
Shawforth 193 E5
Shawhead 216 C3
Shawtonhill 234 A5
Sheanachie 222 C4
Sheandow 259 K1
Shearington 217 E4
Shearsby 160 B3
Shebbear 113 E5
Shebdon 171 E5
Shebster 275 F2
Shedfield 107 E1
Sheen 172 C1
Sheepridge 185 F1
Sheepscombe 132 A1
Sheepstor 100 B1
Sheepwash Devon 113 E5
Sheepwash N'umb 221 E3
Sheepway 131 D5
Sheepy Magna 159 F2
Sheepy Parva 159 F2
Sheering 137 E1
Sheerness 124 B1
Sheet 120 C5
Sheffield 186 A4
Sheffield Botanic Gardens SYorks S10 2LN 21 B3
Sheffield Bottom 120 B1
Sheffield Green 109 G1

Sheffield Park Garden
  ESuss
  TN22 3QX **109** G1
Shefford **149** G4
Shefford Woodlands **133** F5
Sheigra **272** D2
Sheinton **157** F2
Shelderton **156** D5
Sheldon *Derbys* **172** C1
Sheldon *Devon* **103** E2
Sheldon *WMid* **158** D4
Sheldwich **124** C3
Sheldwich Lees **124** C3
Shelf *Bridgend* **129** F4
Shelf *WYorks* **194** A5
Shelfanger **164** C3
Shelfield *Warks* **146** D1
Shelfield *WMid* **158** C2
Shelfield Green **146** D1
Shelford **174** B3
Shellachan *A&B* **240** A2
Shellachan *A&B* **240** C2
Shellbrook **159** F1
Shellbrook Hill **170** A3
Shelley *Essex* **137** E2
Shelley *Suff* **152** B4
Shelley *WYorks* **185** G1
Shellingford **133** F3
Shellow Bowells **137** F2
Shelsley
  Beauchamp **145** G1
Shelsley Walsh **145** G1
Shelswell **148** B4
Shelthorpe **160** A1
Shelton *Bed* **149** F1
Shelton *Norf* **164** D2
Shelton *Notts* **174** C3
Shelton *Shrop* **157** D1
Shelve **156** C3
Shelwick **145** E3
Shelwick Green **145** E3
Shenfield **137** F3
Shenley **136** A2
Shenley Brook End **148** D4
Shenley Church End **148** D4
Shenleybury **136** A2
Shenmore **144** C4
Shennanton **215** E4
Shenstone *Staffs* **158** D2
Shenstone *Worcs* **158** A5
Shenstone
  Woodend **158** D2
Shenton **159** F2
Shenval **259** K2
Shepeau Stow **162** B1
Shephall **150** A3
Shepherd's Bush **136** B5
Shepherd's Green **134** C4
Shepherd's Patch **131** G2
Shepherdswell
  (Sibertswold) **125** E4
Shepley **185** F2
Sheppardstown **275** H5
Shepperdine **131** F3
Shepperton **121** F1
Shepreth **150** B3
Shepreth Wildlife Park
  Cambs SG8 6PZ **150** B3
Shepshed **159** G1
Shepton
  Beauchamp **104** A1
Shepton Mallet **116** D3
Shepton Montague **117** D4
Shepway **123** G3
Sheraton **212** D4
Sherborne *Dorset* **104** C1
Sherborne *Glos* **133** D1
Sherborne St. John **120** B2
Sherbourne **147** E1
Sherbourne Street **152** A3
Sherburn *Dur* **212** C3
Sherburn *NYorks* **204** C5
Sherburn Hill **212** C3
Sherburn in Elmet **195** D4
Shere **121** F3
Shereford **177** G5
Sherfield English **119** D5
Sherfield on oddon **120** B2
Sherford *Devon* **101** D3
Sherford *Som* **115** F5
Sheriff Hutton **195** F1
Sheriffhales **157** G1
Sheringham **178** C1
Sheringham Park *Norf*
  NR26 8TL **178** C1
Sherington **149** D3
Shernal Green **146** B1
Shernborne **177** F4
Sherramore **258** C5
Sherrington **118** A4
Sherston **132** A4
Sherwood **173** G3
Sherwood Forest Country
  Park *Notts*
  NG21 9HN **174** B1
Sherwood Forest Fun Park
  Notts
  NG21 9QA **174** B1
Sherwood Green **113** F3
Sherwood Pines Forest
  Park *Notts*
  NG21 9JL **174** B1
Shetland Islands **279** B7
Shevington **183** G2
Shevington Moor **183** G1
Sheviock **99** D5
Shide **107** E4
Shiel Bridge
  (Drochaid Sheile) **257** F3
Shieldaig *High* **264** E6
Shieldaig *High* **264** E4
Shieldhill **234** C2
Shielfoot **247** F2
Shielhill **252** C4
Shiels **260** E4
Shifford **133** F2
Shifnal **157** G2
Shilbottle **221** D1
Shildon **212** B5
Shillingford *Devon* **114** C1
Shillingford *Oxon* **134** A3
Shillingford Abbot **102** C4
Shillingford
  St. George **102** C4
Shillingstone **105** E1
Shillington **149** G4
Shillmoor **220** A1

Shilstone **113** F5
Shilton *Oxon* **133** E2
Shilton *Warks* **159** G4
Shimpling *Norf* **164** C3
Shimpling *Suff* **151** G2
Shimpling Street **151** G2
Shincliffe **212** B3
Shinfield **120** C1
Shingay **150** B3
Shingham **163** F2
Shingle Street **153** E3
Shinness Lodge **273** H7
Shipbourne **123** E3
Shipbrookhill **184** A5
Shipdham **178** A5
Shipham **116** B2
Shiphay **101** E1
Shiplake **134** C5
Shiplake Row **134** C5
Shipley *N'umb* **229** F5
Shipley *Shrop* **158** A3
Shipley *WSuss* **121** G5
Shipley *WYorks* **194** A4
Shipley Bridge
  Devon **100** C4
Shipley Bridge *Surr* **122** C4
Shipley Common **173** F3
Shipley Country Park
  Derbys DE75 7GX **18** D2
Shipmeadow **165** E2
Shippea Hill **163** E4
Shippon **133** G3
Shipston on Stour **147** E3
Shipton *Glos* **132** C1
Shipton *NYorks* **195** E2
Shipton *Shrop* **157** E3
Shipton Bellinger **118** D3
Shipton Gorge **104** A3
Shipton Green **108** A3
Shipton Moyne **132** A4
Shipton Oliffe **132** C1
Shipton Solers **132** C1
Shipton-on-
  Cherwell **133** G1
Shiptonthorpe **196** A3
Shipton-under-
  Wychwood **133** E1
Shira **241** D3
Shirburn **134** B3
Shirdley Hill **183** E1
Shire Oak **158** C2
Shirebrook **173** G1
Shirecliffe **186** A3
Shiregreen **186** A3
Shirehampton **131** E5
Shiremoor **221** F4
Shirenewton **131** D3
Shireoaks **186** C4
Shirl Heath **144** D2
Shirland **173** E1
Shirley *Derbys* **172** D3
Shirley *GtLon* **122** C2
Shirley *Hants* **106** A3
Shirley *Soton* **106** D1
Shirley *WMid* **158** D5
Shirley Heath **158** D5
Shirley Warren **106** C1
Shirleywich **171** G5
Shirrell Heath **107** E1
Shirwell **113** F2
Shirwell Cross **113** F2
Shiskine **223** E3
Shittlehope **211** G4
Shobdon **144** C1
Shobley **106** A2
Shobrooke **102** B2
Shocklach **170** B3
Shocklach Green **170** B3
Shoeburyness **138** C4
Sholden **125** F3
Sholing **107** D1
Shoot Hill **156** D1
Shooter's Hill **136** D5
Shop *Corn* **96** D4
Shop *Corn* **112** C4
Shop Corner **152** D4
Shopnoller **115** E4
Shore **184** D1
Shoreditch **136** C4
Shoreham **136** D2
Shoreham-by-Sea **109** E3
Shoremill **266** E5
Shoresdean **237** G5
Shoreswood **237** G5
Shoreton **266** D5
Shorley **119** G5
Shorncote **132** C3
Shorne **137** F5
Shorne Ridgeway **137** F5
Short Cross **156** B2
Short Green **164** B3
Short Heath *Derbys* **159** F1
Short Heath *WMid* **158** C3
Shortacombe **99** F2
Shortbridge **109** G1
Shortfield Common **120** D3
Shortgate **109** G2
Shortgrove **150** D4
Shorthampton **147** F5
Shortlands **122** C2
Shortlanesend **96** C5
Shorton **101** E1
Shorwell **107** D4
Shoscombe **117** E2
Shotatton **170** A5
Shotesham **164** D2
Shotgate **137** G2
Shotley *N'hants* **161** E3
Shotley *Suff* **152** D4
Shotley Bridge **211** G2
Shotley Gate **152** D4
Shotleyfield **211** G2
Shottenden **124** C3
Shottermill **121** D4
Shottery **147** D2
Shotteswell **147** G3
Shottisham **153** E3
Shottle **173** E2
Shottlegate **173** E2
Shotton *Dur* **212** D4
Shotton *Dur* **212** C5
Shotton *Flints* **170** A1
Shotton *N'umb* **221** E4
Shotton Colliery **212** D3
Shotts **234** C3

Shotwick **183** E5
Shouldham **163** E2
Shouldham Thorpe **163** E2
Shoulton **146** A2
Shover's Green **123** F5
Shrawardine **156** C1
Shrawley **146** A1
Shreding Green **135** F4
Shrewley **147** E1
Shrewsbury **157** D1
Shrewton **118** B3
Shri Venkateswara (Balaji)
  Temple of the United
  Kingdom *WMid*
  B69 3DU **14** C1
Shrine of Our Lady of
  Walsingham (Anglican)
  Norf NR22 6EF **178** A2
Shripney **108** B3
Shrivenham **133** E4
Shropham **164** A2
Shroton (Iwerne
  Courtney) **105** E1
Shrub End **152** A5
Shucknall **145** E3
Shudy Camps **151** E3
Shugborough Estate *Staffs*
  ST17 0XB **171** G5
Shurdington **132** B1
Shurlock Row **134** D5
Shurnock **146** C1
Shurrery **275** F3
Shurrery Lodge **275** F3
Shurton **115** F3
Shustoke **159** E3
Shut Heath **171** F5
Shute *Devon* **103** F3
Shute *Devon* **102** B2
Shutford **147** F3
Shuthonger **146** A4
Shutlanger **148** C3
Shutt Green **158** A2
Shuttington **159** E2
Shuttlewood **186** B5
Shuttleworth **184** B1
Siabost Bho Dheas **270** E3
Siabost Bho Thuath **270** E3
Siadar Iarach **271** F2
Siadar Uarach **271** F2
Sibbaldbie **217** F2
Sibbertoft **160** B4
Sibdon Carwood **156** D4
Sibertswold
  (Shepherdswell) **125** E4
Sibford Ferris **147** F4
Sibford Gower **147** F4
Sible Hedingham **151** F4
Sibley's Green **151** E5
Sibsey **176** B2
Sibson *Cambs* **161** F3
Sibson *Leics* **159** F2
Sibster **275** J3
Sibthorpe **174** C3
Sibton **153** E1
Sibton Green **165** E4
Sicklesmere **151** G1
Sicklinghall **194** C3
Sidbury *Devon* **103** E3
Sidbury *Shrop* **157** F4
Sidcot **116** B2
Sidcup **137** D5
Siddal **194** A5
Siddington *ChesE* **184** C5
Siddington *Glos* **132** C3
Sidemoor **158** B5
Sidestrand **179** D2
Sidford **103** E3
Sidlesham **108** A4
Sidley **110** C3
Sidlow **122** B4
Sidmouth **103** E4
Sigford **102** A5
Sigglesthorne **197** D3
Sigingstone **129** F5
Signet **133** E1
Silchester **120** B1
Sildinis **270** E6
Sileby **160** B1
Silecroft **198** C4
Silfield **164** C2
Silian **142** B2
Silk Willoughby **175** F3
Silkstead **119** F5
Silksworth **212** D2
Silkstone **185** G2
Silkstone Common **185** G2
Sill Field **199** G4
Silloth **209** E1
Sills **220** A1
Sillyearn **268** C5
Silpho **204** C3
Silsden **193** G3
Silsoe **149** F4
Silver End *CenBeds*
  149 G3
Silver End *Essex* **151** G5
Silver Green **165** D2
Silver Street *Kent* **124** A2
Silver Street *Som* **116** C4
Silverburn **235** G3
Silvercraigs **231** G1
Silverdale *Lancs* **199** F5
Silverdale *Staffs* **171** F3
Silvergate **178** C3
Silverhill **110** C2
Silverlace Green **153** E2
Silverley's Green **165** D4
Silvermoss **261** G1
Silverstone **148** B3
Silverton **102** C2
Silvington **157** F5
Silwick **279** B8
Simister **184** C2
Simmondley **185** E3
Simonburn **220** A4
Simonsbath **114** A4
Simonside **212** C1
Simonstone
  Bridgend **129** F4
Simonstone
  Lancs **193** D4
Simprim **237** F5
Simpson **149** D4
Sinclair's Hill **237** F4
Sinclairston **224** C4
Sinderby **202** C4
Sinderhope **211** E2
Sindlesham **120** C1
Sinfin **173** E4

Singdean **227** G5
Singleton *Lancs* **191** G4
Singleton *WSuss* **108** A2
Singlewell **137** F5
Singret **170** A2
Sinkhurst Green **124** A4
Sinnahard **260** C3
Sinnington **203** G4
Sinton Green **146** A1
Sipson **135** F4
Sirhowy **130** A1
Sirhowy Valley Country
  Park *Caerp*
  NP11 7BD **130** A3
Sisland **165** E2
Sissinghurst **123** G5
Sissinghurst Castle Garden
  Kent TN17 2AB **124** A5
Siston **131** F5
Sithney **94** D4
Sittingbourne **124** B2
Siulaisiadar **271** H4
Six Ashes **157** G4
Six Hills **174** B5
Six Mile Bottom **151** D2
Six Roads End **172** C5
Sixhills **188** B4
Sixmile **124** D4
Sixpenny Handley **105** G1
Sizewell **153** F1
Skail **274** C4
Skaill *Ork* **277** B6
Skaill *Ork* **277** E7
Skaill *Ork* **276** D4
Skares *Aber* **260** E1
Skares *EAyr* **224** D4
Skarpigarth **279** A7
Skateraw **237** E2
Skaw **279** E6
Skeabost **263** K7
Skeabrae **276** B5
Skeeby **202** B2
Skeffington **160** C2
Skeffling **197** D5
Skegby **173** G1
Skegness **177** E1
Skegness Water Leisure
  Park *Lincs*
  PE25 1JF **177** D1
Skelberry *Shet* **279** F9
Skelberry *Shet* **279** D6
Skelbo **266** E2
Skelbo Street **266** E2
Skelbrooke **186** C1
Skeld (Easter Skeld)
  279 C8
Skeldon **224** B4
Skeldyke **176** B4
Skellingthorpe **187** G5
Skellister **279** D7
Skellow **186** C1
Skelmanthorpe **185** G1
Skelmersdale **183** F2
Skelmonae **261** G1
Skelmorlie **232** C3
Skelmuir **269** H6
Skelpick **273** K3
Skelton *Cumb* **210** A4
Skelton *ERid* **195** G5
Skelton *NYorks* **201** F2
Skelton (Skelton-in-
  Cleveland) *R&C* **203** F1
Skelton *York* **195** E2
Skelton-in-Cleveland
  (Skelton) **203** F1
Skelton-on-Ure **194** C1
Skelwick **276** D3
Skelwith Bridge **199** E2
Skendleby **176** C1
Skendleby Psalter **189** E5
Skenfrith **145** D5
Skerne **196** C2
Skeroblingarry **222** C3
Skerray **273** J2
Skerton **192** A1
Sketchley **159** G3
Sketty **128** C3
Skewen **128** D3
Skewsby **203** F5
Skeyton **178** D3
Skeyton Corner **179** D3
Skidbrooke **189** E3
Skidbrooke North
  End **189** E3
Skidby **196** C4
Skilgate **114** C5
Skillington **175** D5
Skinburness **209** E1
Skinflats **234** D1
Skinidin **263** H7
Skinnet **275** G2
Skinningrove **203** G1
Skipness **231** G4
Skippool **191** G3
Skipsea **197** D2
Skipsea Brough **197** D2
Skipton **193** F2
Skipton Castle *NYorks*
  BD23 1AW **193** F2
Skipton-on-Swale **202** C5
Skipwith **195** F4
Skirbeck **176** B3
Skirbeck Quarter **176** B3
Skirethorns **193** F1
Skirlaugh **196** D4
Skirling **226** B2
Skirmett **134** C4
Skirpenbeck **195** G2
Skirwith *Cumb* **210** C4
Skirwith *NYorks* **200** C5
Skirza **275** J2
Skittle Green **134** C2
Skomer Island **126** A2
Skulamus **256** C2
Skullomie **273** J2
Skyborry Green **156** B5
Skye **255** K1
Skye Green **151** G5
Skye of Curr **259** G2
Skyreholme **193** G1
Slack *Aber* **260** D1
Slack *Derbys* **173** E1
Slack *WYorks* **193** F5
Slackhall **185** E4
Slackhead **268** C4
Slad **132** A2
Slade *Devon* **113** F1
Slade *Devon* **103** E2

Slade *Pembs* **126** C1
Slade *Swan* **128** A4
Slade Green **137** E5
Slade Hooton **186** C4
Sladesbridge **97** E2
Slaggyford **210** C2
Slaidburn **192** D2
Slains Park **253** G2
Slaithwaite **185** E1
Slaley **211** F2
Slamannan **234** C2
Slapton *Bucks* **149** E5
Slapton *Devon* **101** E3
Slapton *N'hants* **148** B3
Slate Haugh **268** C4
Slatepit Dale **173** E1
Slattadale **264** E4
Slaugham **109** E1
Slaughden **153** F2
Slaughterford **132** A5
Slawston **160** C3
Sleaford *Hants* **120** D4
Sleaford *Lincs* **175** F3
Sleagill **199** G1
Sleap **170** B5
Sledge Green **146** A4
Sledmere **196** B1
Sleights **204** B2
Slepe **105** F3
Slerra **112** D3
Slickly **275** H2
Sliddery **223** E3
Sliemore **259** H2
Sligachan **255** K2
Slimbridge **131** G2
Slimbridge Wildfowl &
  Wetlands Trust *Glos*
  GL2 7BT **131** G2
Slindon *Staffs* **171** F4
Slindon *WSuss* **108** B3
Slinfold **121** G4
Sling **131** E2
Slingsby **203** F5
Slioch **260** D1
Slip End *CenBeds* **135** F1
Slip End *Herts* **150** A4
Slipper Chapel, Houghton
  St. Giles *Norf*
  NR22 6AL **178** A2
Slipton **161** E5
Slitting Mill **158** C1
Slochd **259** F2
Slockavullin **240** A5
Sloley **179** D3
Sloncombe **102** B4
Sloothby **189** E5
Slough **135** E4
Slough Green
  Som **115** F3
Slough Green
  WSuss **109** E1
Sluggan **259** F2
Slyne **192** A1
Smailholm **228** A3
Small Dole **109** E2
Small Hythe **124** A5
Smallbridge **184** D1
Smallbrook **102** B3
Smallburgh **179** E3
Smallburn *Aber* **269** J6
Smallburn *EAyr* **225** E3
Smalldale **185** E5
Smalley **173** F3
Smallfield **122** C4
Smallford **136** A2
Smallridge **103** F2
Smallthorne **171** F2
Smallworth **164** B3
Smannell **119** E3
Smardale **200** C2
Smarden **124** A4
Smaull **230** A3
Smeatharpe **103** E1
Smeeth **124** C5
Smeeton
  Westerby **160** B3
Smerclet **254** C3
Smerral **275** G5
Smestow **158** A3
Smethwick **158** C4
Smethwick Green **171** F1
Sminisary **247** F2
Smisby **159** F1
Smith End Green **145** G2
Smithfield **210** A1
Smithies **186** A2
Smithincott **103** D1
Smith's End **150** B4
Smith's Green
  Essex **151** D5
Smith's Green
  Essex **151** E3
Smithstown **264** D7
Smithton **266** E7
Smithy Green **184** B5
Smockington **159** G4
Smyrton **214** C2
Smythe's Green **138** C1
Snailbeach **156** C2
Snailwell **151** E1
Snainton **204** C3
Snaith **195** F5
Snape *NYorks* **202** B4
Snape *Suff* **153** E2
Snape Green **183** E1
Snape Watering **153** E2
Snarestone **159** F2
Snarford **188** A4
Snargate **111** E1
Snave **111** F1
Sneachill **146** B2
Snead **156** C3
Snead's Green **146** A1
Sneath Common **164** C3
Sneaton **204** B2
Sneatonthorpe **204** C2
Snelland **188** A4
Snellings **198** A2
Snelston **172** C3
Snetterton **164** B2
Snettisham **177** E4
Snipeshill **124** B2
Snishival
  (Sniseabhal) **254** C1

Snitter **220** C1
Snitterby **187** G3
Snitterfield **147** E2
Snitterton **173** D1
Snittlegarth **209** F3
Snitton **157** F5
Snodhill **144** C3
Snodland **123** G2
Snow End **150** C4
Snow Street **164** B3
Snowden Hill **185** G2
Snowdon Mountain Railway
  Gwyn
  LL55 4TY **167** E2
Snowshill **146** C4
Snowshill Manor *Glos*
  WR12 7JU **146** C4
Soar *Cardiff* **129** G4
Soar *Carmar* **142** C5
Soar *Devon* **100** D4
Soay **255** K3
Soberton **107** F1
Soberton Heath **107** F1
Sockbridge **210** B5
Sockburn **202** C2
Sodom **182** B5
Sodylt Bank **170** A2
Softley **211** G5
Soham **163** D5
Soham Cotes **163** D5
Soldon **112** D4
Soldon Cross **112** D4
Soldridge **120** B4
Sole Street *Kent* **124** C4
Sole Street *Kent* **123** F2
Soleburn **214** B4
Solihull **159** D5
Solihull Lodge **158** C5
Sollas (Solas) **262** D4
Sollers Dilwyn **144** D2
Sollers Hope **145** F4
Sollom **183** F1
Solomon's Tump **131** G1
Solsgirth **243** E5
Solva **140** A5
Solwaybank **218** A4
Somerby *Leics* **160** C1
Somerby *Lincs* **188** A2
Somercotes **173** F2
Somerford **158** B2
Somerford Keynes **132** C3
Somerley **108** A4
Somerleyton **165** F2
Somersal Herbert **172** C4
Somersby **188** D5
Somerset House *GtLon*
  WC2R 1LA **45** F3
Somersham
  Cambs **162** B5
Somersham *Suff* **152** B3
Somerton *Newport* **130** C4
Somerton *Oxon* **147** G5
Somerton *Som* **116** B5
Somerton *Suff* **151** G2
Sompting **109** D3
Sompting Abbotts **109** D3
Sonning **134** C5
Sonning Common **134** C4
Sonning Eye **134** C5
Sontley **170** A3
Sookholme **173** G1
Sopley **106** A3
Sopworth **132** A4
Sorbie **207** E2
Sordale **275** G2
Sorisdale **246** B3
Sorn **225** D3
Sornhill **224** D2
Soroba **240** A2
Sortat **275** H2
Sotby **188** C5
Sots Hole **175** G1
Sotterley **165** F3
Soudley **171** E5
Soughton **169** F1
Soulbury **149** D5
Soulby **200** C1
Souldern **148** A4
Souldrop **149** E1
Sound *ChesE* **170** D3
Sound *Shet* **279** D8
Sound *Shet* **279** C7
Sourhope **228** C4
Sourin **276** D4
Sourton **99** F1
Soutergate **198** D4
South Acre **163** G1
South Acton **136** A5
South Alkham **125** E4
South Allington **101** D4
South Alloa **243** D5
South Ambersham **121** E5
South Ascot **121** E1
South Baddesley **106** C3
South Ballachulish (Baile a'
  Chaolais a Deas) **248** C4
South Balloch **215** E1
South Bank **213** E1
South Barrow **116** D5
South Bellsdyke **234** D1
South Benfleet **137** G4
South Bersted **108** B3
South Blackbog **261** F1
South
  Bockhampton **106** A3
South Bowood **104** A3
South Brent **100** C4
South Brentor **99** E2
South Brewham **117** E4
South Broomhill **221** E2
South Burlingham **179** E5
South Cadbury **116** D5
South Cairn **214** A4
South Carlton **187** G5
South Cave **196** B4
South Cerney **132** C3
South Chard **103** G2
South Charlton **229** F4
South Cheriton **117** D5
South Church **212** B5
South Cliffe **196** A4
South Clifton **187** F5
South Cockerington **189** D4
South Collafirth **278** C4
South Common **109** F2
South Cornelly **129** E4
South Cornelly **129** E4
South Corriegills **223** F2

South Cove **165** F3
South Creagan **248** B5
South Creake **177** G4
South Crosland **185** F1
South Croxton **160** B1
South Dalton **196** B3
South Darenth **137** E5
South Dell
  (Dail Bho Dheas) **271** G1
South Duffield **195** F4
South Elkington **188** D4
South Elmsall **186** B1
South End *Bucks* **149** D5
South End *Cumb* **191** F1
South End *Hants* **106** A1
South End *NLincs* **196** D5
South Erradale **264** D4
South Fambridge **138** B3
South Fawley **133** F4
South Ferriby **196** B5
South Field **196** C5
South Flobbets **261** F1
South Garth **278** E3
South Godstone **122** C4
South Gorley **106** A1
South Green *Essex* **137** F3
South Green *Essex* **138** D3
South Green *Norf* **178** B4
South Green *Suff* **164** C4
South Gyle **235** F2
South Hall **232** B2
South Hanningfield **137** G3
South Harefield **135** F4
South Harting **107** G1
South Hayling **107** G3
South Hazelrigg **229** E3
South Heath **135** E2
South Heighton **109** G3
South Hetton **212** C3
South Hiendley **186** A1
South Hill **98** D3
South Hinksey **134** A2
South Hole **112** C4
South Holme **203** F5
South Holmwood **121** G3
South Hornchurch **137** E4
South Hourat **233** D4
South Huish **100** C3
South Hykeham **175** E1
South Hylton **212** C2
South Kelsey **188** A3
South Kessock (Ceasag a
  Deas) **266** D7
South Killingholme **188** B1
South Kilvington **202** D4
South Kilworth **160** B4
South Kirkby **186** B1
South Kirkton **261** F4
South Knighton **102** B5
South Kyme **175** G3
South Lakes Wild Animal
  Park *Cumb*
  LA15 8JR **198** D5
South Lancing **109** D3
South Ledaig **240** B1
South Leigh **133** F2
South Leverton **187** E4
South Littleton **146** C3
South Lopham **164** B3
South Luffenham **161** E2
South Malling **109** G2
South Marston **133** D4
South Middleton **229** D3
South Milford **195** D4
South Milton **100** C3
South Mimms **136** B2
South Molton **114** A5
South Moor **212** A2
South Moreton **134** A4
South Mundham **108** A3
South Muskham **174** C2
South Newbald **196** B4
South Newington **147** G4
South Newton **118** B4
South Normanton **173** F2
South Norwood **122** C2
South Nutfield **122** C4
South Ockendon **137** E4
South Ormsby **189** D5
South Ossett **185** G1
South Otterington **202** C4
South Owersby **188** A3
South Oxhey **136** A3
South Park **122** B4
South Parks **244** A4
South Perrott **104** A2
South Petherton **104** A1
South Petherwin **98** D2
South Pickenham **163** G2
South Pool **101** D3
South Queensferry
  (Queensferry) **235** F2
South Radworthy **114** A4
South Raceby **175** F3
South Raynham **177** G5
South Redbriggs **269** F6
South Reston **189** E4
South Ronaldsay **277** D9
South Ruislip **136** A4
South Runcton **163** E2
South Scarle **174** D1
South Shian
  (Sithean a Deas) **248** B5
South Shields **212** C1
South Shields Museum &
  Art Gallery *T&W*
  NE33 2JA **28** E2
South Somercotes **189** E3
South Somercotes Fen
  Houses **189** E3
South Stainley **194** C1
South Stoke
  B&NESom **117** E1
South Stoke *Oxon* **134** B4
South Stoke *WSuss* **108** C3
South Street *ESuss* **109** F2
South Street
  GtLon **122** D3
South Street *Kent* **123** F2
South Street *Kent* **124** C3
South Street *Kent* **124** C4
South Tawton **99** G1
South Thoresby **189** E5
South Tidworth **118** D3
South Tottenham **136** C4
South Town *Devon* **102** C4
South Town *Hants* **120** B4

South Uist
(Uibhist a Deas) **254** C1
South Upper
Barrack **269** H6
South View **120** B2
South Walsham **179** E4
South Warnborough **120** C3
South Weald **137** E3
South Weston **134** C3
South Wheatley
Corn **98** C1
South Wheatley
Notts **187** E4
South Whiteness **279** C8
South Wigston **160** A3
South Willingham **188** B4
South Wingfield **173** E2
South Witham **161** E1
South Wonston **119** F4
South Woodham
Ferrers **138** B3
South Wootton **177** E5
South Wraxall **117** F1
South Yardle **158** D4
South Zeal **99** G1
Southall **136** A4
Southam Glos **146** B5
Southam Warks **147** G1
Southampton **106** D1
Southampton
Airport **107** D1
Southbar **233** F3
Southborough
GtLon **122** D2
Southborough Kent **123** E4
Southbourne
Bourne **106** A3
Southbourne
WSuss **107** G2
Southbrook **102** D3
Southburgh **178** B5
Southburn **196** B2
Southchurch **138** C4
Southcott Devon **99** F1
Southcott Wilts **118** C2
Southcourt **134** D1
Southdean **219** E1
Southdene **183** F3
Southease **109** G3
Southend A&B **222** B5
Southend Aber **269** F6
Southend Bucks **134** C4
Southend (Bradfield
Southend)
WBerks **134** A5
Southend Wilts **133** D5
Southend Airport **138** B4
Southend Pier S'end
SS1 1EE **138** B4
Southend-on-Sea **138** B4
Southerfield **209** E2
Southerly **99** F2
Southern Green **150** B4
Southerndown **129** E5
Southerness **217** D5
Southery **163** E3
Southfield **244** A5
Southfields **136** B5
Southfleet **137** F5
Southgate Cere **154** B4
Southgate GtLon **136** C3
Southgate Norf **178** C3
Southgate Norf **177** E4
Southgate Swan **128** B4
Southill **149** G3
Southington **119** G3
Southleigh **103** F3
Southmarsh **117** E4
Southminster **138** C4
Southmoor **133** F3
Southmuir **252** B4
Southoe **149** G1
Southolt **152** C1
Southorpe **161** F2
Southowram **194** A5
Southport **183** E1
Southport Pier Mersey
PR8 1QX **183** E1
Southrepps **179** D2
Southrey **175** G1
Southrop **133** D2
Southrope **120** B3
Southsea Ports **107** F3
Southsea Wrex **169** F2
Southtown Norf **179** G5
Southtown Ork **277** D8
Southwaite Cumb **200** D4
Southwaite Cumb **210** C3
Southwark Cathedral GtLon
SE1 9DA **12** B4
Southwater **121** G5
Southwater Street **121** G5
Southway **116** C3
Southwell Dorset **104** C5
Southwell Notts **174** B2
Southwell Minster Notts
NG25 0HD **174** C2
Southwick D&G **216** D5
Southwick Hants **107** F2
Southwick N'hants **161** F3
Southwick Som **116** A3
Southwick T&W **212** C2
Southwick Wilts **117** F2
Southwick WSuss **109** E3
Southwold **165** G4
Southwood **116** C4
Sowden **102** C4
Sower Carr **191** G3
Sowerby NYorks **202** D4
Sowerby WYorks **193** G5
Sowerby Bridge **193** G5
Sowerby Row **209** G2
Sowerhill **114** B5
Sowley Green **151** F2
Sowood **185** E1
Sowton **102** C3
Soyal **266** C2
Spa Common **179** D2
Spa Complex NYorks
YO11 2PW
83 Scarborough
Spadeadam **219** D4
Spalding **176** A5
Spaldington **195** G4
Spaldwick **161** G5
Spalefield **245** D4
Spanby **175** F4

Sparham **178** B4
Spark Bridge **199** E4
Sparkford **116** C5
Sparkhill **158** C4
Sparkwell **100** B2
Sparrow Green **178** A4
Sparrowpit **185** E4
Sparrow's Green **123** F5
Sparsholt Hants **119** F4
Sparsholt Oxon **133** F4
Spartylea **211** E3
Spath **172** B4
Spaunton **203** G4
Spaxton **115** F4
Spean Bridge (Drochaid an
Aonachain) **249** E1
Spean Bridge Woollen Mill
High PH34 4EP **249** E1
Spear Hill **108** D2
Speddoch **216** C2
Speedwell **131** F5
Speen Bucks **134** D2
Speen WBerks **119** F1
Speeton **205** E5
Speke **183** F4
Speldhurst **123** E4
Spellbrook **137** D1
Spelsbury **147** F5
Spen Green **171** F1
Spencers Wood **120** C1
Spennithorne **202** A4
Spennymoor **212** B4
Spernall **146** C1
Spetchley **146** A2
Spetisbury **105** F2
Spexhall **165** E3
Spey Bay **268** B4
Speybridge **259** H2
Speyview **267** K7
Spilsby **176** B1
Spindlestone **229** F3
Spinkhill **186** B5
Spinnaker Tower PO1 3TN
82 Portsmouth
Spinningdale **266** D3
Spirthill **132** B5
Spital High **275** G3
Spital W&M **135** E5
Spital in the Street **187** G3
Spitalbrook **136** C2
Spitfire & Hurricane
Memorial, R.A.F. Manston
Kent CT12 5DF **125** F2
Spithurst **109** G2
Spittal D&G **215** F4
Spittal D&G **215** E5
Spittal ELoth **236** B2
Spittal N'umb **229** E1
Spittal Pembs **140** C5
Spittal of
Glenmuick **252** B1
Spittal of
Glenshee **251** G3
Spittalfield **251** G5
Spixworth **178** D4
Splayne's Green **109** G1
Splott **130** B5
Spofforth **194** C2
Spondon **173** F4
Spooner Row **164** B2
Spoonley **171** D4
Sporle **163** G1
Sportsman's Arms **168** C2
Spott **237** D2
Spratton **160** C5
Spreakley **120** D3
Spreyton **99** G1
Spriddlestone **100** B2
Spridlington **188** A4
Spring Grove **136** A5
Spring Vale **107** F3
Springburn **234** A3
Springfield A&B **232** B2
Springfield D&G **218** B5
Springfield Fife **244** B3
Springfield Moray **267** H6
Springfield P&K **243** G1
Springfield WMid **158** C4
Springhill Staffs **158** C2
Springhill Staffs **158** B2
Springholm **216** C4
Springkell **218** A4
Springleys **261** F1
Springside **224** B2
Springthorpe **187** F4
Springwell **212** B2
Sproatley **197** D4
Sproston Green **171** E1
Sprotbrough **186** C2
Sproughton **152** C3
Sprouston **228** B3
Sprowston **178** D4
Sproxton Leics **175** D5
Sproxton NYorks **203** F4
Sprytown **99** E2
Spurlands End **135** D3
Spurstow **170** C2
Spyway **104** B3
Square Point **216** B3
Squires Gate **191** G4
Sròndoire **231** G2
Sronphadruig Lodge **250** C2
Stableford Shrop **157** G3
Stableford Staffs **171** F4
Stacey Bank **185** G3
Stackhouse **193** E1
Stackpole **116** C2
Stacksteads **193** E5
Staddiscombe **100** B2
Staddlethorpe **196** A5
Staden **185** E3
Stadhampton **134** B3
Staffin **263** K5
Stafford **171** G5
Stagden Cross **137** F1
Stagsden **149** E3
Stagshaw Bank **211** F1
Stain **275** J2
Stainburn Cumb **208** D4
Stainburn NYorks **194** B3
Stainby **175** E5
Staincross **186** A1
Staindrop **212** A5
Staines-upon-Thames
135 F5
Stainfield Lincs **175** F5
Stainfield Lincs **188** B5

Stainforth NYorks **193** E1
Stainforth SYorks **186** D1
Staining **191** G4
Stainland **185** E1
Stainsacre **204** C2
Stainsby Derbys **173** F1
Stainsby Lincs **188** D5
Stainton Cumb **199** G4
Stainton Cumb **210** A5
Stainton Dur **201** F1
Stainton Middl **203** D1
Stainton NYorks **202** A3
Stainton SYorks **186** C3
Stainton by
Langworth **188** A5
Stainton le Vale **188** B3
Stainton with
Adgarley **199** D5
Staintondale **204** C3
Stair Cumb **209** F4
Stair EAyr **224** C3
Stairfoot **186** A2
Staithes **203** G1
Stake Pool **192** A3
Stakeford **221** E3
Stakes **107** F2
Stalbridge **104** D1
Stalbridge Weston **104** D1
Stalham **179** E3
Stalham Green **179** E3
Stalisfield Green **124** B3
Stalling Busk **201** E4
Stallingborough **188** B1
Stallington **171** G4
Stalmine **191** G3
Stalybridge **185** D3
Stambourne **151** F4
Stamford Lincs **161** F2
Stamford N'umb **229** G5
Stamford Bridge
ChesW&C **170** B1
Stamford Bridge
ERid **195** G2
Stamfordham **220** C4
Stanah **191** G3
Stanborough **136** B1
Stanborough Park Herts
AL8 6XF **136** B1
Stanbridge
CenBeds **149** E5
Stanbridge
Dorset **105** G2
Stanbridge Earls **119** E5
Stanbury **193** G4
Stand **234** B3
Standalone Farm,
Letchworth Garden City
Herts SG6 4JN **150** A4
Standburn **234** D2
Standeford **158** B2
Standen **124** A4
Standen Street **124** A5
Standerwick **117** F2
Standford **120** D4
Standford Bridge **171** E5
Standish Glos **132** A2
Standish GtMan **183** G1
Standlake **133** F2
Standon Hants **119** F5
Standon Herts **150** B5
Standon Staffs **171** F4
Standon Green End **136** C1
Stane **234** C4
Stanecastle **224** B2
Stanfield **178** A3
Stanford CenBeds **149** G3
Stanford Kent **124** D5
Stanford Shrop **156** C1
Stanford Bishop **145** F2
Stanford Bridge **145** G1
Stanford Dingley **134** A5
Stanford End **120** C1
Stanford in the Vale **133** F3
Stanford on Avon **160** A5
Stanford on Soar **173** G5
Stanford on Teme **145** G1
Stanford Rivers **137** E2
Stanford-le-Hope **137** F4
Stanfree **186** B5
Stanghow **203** F1
Stanground **162** A3
Stanhoe **177** G4
Stanhope Dur **211** F4
Stanhope ScBord **226** C3
Stanion **161** E4
Stanklyn **158** A5
Stanley Derbys **173** F3
Stanley Dur **212** A2
Stanley Notts **173** F1
Stanley P&K **243** G1
Stanley Staffs **171** G2
Stanley Wilts **132** B5
Stanley WYorks **194** C5
Stanley Common **173** F3
Stanley Crook **212** A4
Stanley Gate **183** F2
Stanley Hill **145** F3
Stanleygreen **170** C3
Stanlow ChesW&C **183** F5
Stanlow Shrop **157** G3
Stanmer **109** F2
Stanmore GtLon **136** A3
Stanmore WBerks **133** G5
Stannersburn **219** F3
Stanningfield **151** G2
Stannington
N'umb **221** E4
Stannington
SYorks **186** A4
Stansbatch **144** C1
Stansfield **151** F2
Stanshope **172** C2
Stanstead **151** G3
Stanstead Abbotts **136** C1
Stansted **123** F2
Stansted Airport **150** D5
Stansted
Mountfitchet **150** D4
Stanton Derbys **159** E1
Stanton Glos **146** C4
Stanton N'umb **220** D2
Stanton Staffs **172** C3
Stanton Suff **164** A4
Stanton by Bridge **173** E5
Stanton by Dale **173** F4

Stanton Drew **116** C1
Stanton Fitzwarren **133** D3
Stanton Harcourt **133** G2
Stanton Hill **173** F1
Stanton in Peak **172** D1
Stanton Lacy **157** D5
Stanton Lees **173** D1
Stanton Long **157** E3
Stanton St. Bernard **118** B1
Stanton St. John **134** A2
Stanton St. Quintin **132** B5
Stanton Street **152** A1
Stanton under
Bardon **159** G1
Stanton upon Hine
Heath **170** C5
Stanton Wick **116** D1
Stanton-on-the-
Wolds **174** B4
Stanwardine in the
Fields **170** B5
Stanwardine in the
Wood **170** B5
Stanway Essex **152** A5
Stanway Glos **146** C4
Stanway Green
Essex **152** A5
Stanway Green
Suff **164** D4
Stanwell **135** F5
Stanwell Moor **135** F5
Stanwick **161** E5
Stanwix **210** A2
Staoinebrig **254** C1
Stapeley **171** D3
Stapeley **173** D5
Staple Kent **125** E3
Staple Som **115** E3
Staple Cross **114** D5
Staple Fitzpaine **103** F1
Staplecross **110** C1
Staplefield **109** E1
Stapleford Cambs **150** C2
Stapleford Herts **136** C1
Stapleford Leics **160** D1
Stapleford Lincs **175** D2
Stapleford Notts **173** F4
Stapleford Wilts **118** B4
Stapleford Abbotts **137** D3
Stapleford Tawney **137** E3
Staplegrove **115** F5
Staplehay **115** F5
Staplehurst **123** G4
Staplers **107** E4
Staplestreet **124** C2
Stapleton Cumb **218** D4
Stapleton Here **144** C1
Stapleton Leics **159** G3
Stapleton NYorks **202** B1
Stapleton Shrop **157** D2
Stapleton Som **116** B5
Stapley **103** E1
Staploe **149** G1
Staplow **145** F3
Star Fife **244** B4
Star Pembs **141** F4
Star Som **116** B2
Starbotton **201** E5
Starcross **102** C4
Stareton **159** F5
Starkholmes **173** E2
Starling **184** B1
Starling's Green **150** C4
Starr **215** F1
Starston **164** D3
Startforth **201** F1
Startley **132** B4
Statham **184** A4
Stathe **116** A5
Stathern **174** C4
Station Town **212** D4
Staughton Green **149** G1
Staughton
Highway **149** G1
Staunton Glos **131** E1
Staunton Glos **145** G5
Staunton Harold
Hall **173** E5
Staunton Harold Reservoir
Derbys
DE73 8DN **173** E5
Staunton in the Vale **174** D3
Staunton on Arrow **144** C1
Staunton on Wye **144** C3
Staveley Cumb **199** F3
Staveley Derbys **186** B5
Staveley NYorks **194** C1
Staveley-in-Cartmel **199** E4
Staverton Devon **101** D1
Staverton Glos **146** A5
Staverton N'hants **148** A1
Staverton Wilts **117** F1
Staverton Bridge **146** A5
Stawell **116** A4
Stawley **115** D5
Staxigoe **275** J3
Staxton **204** D5
Staylittle
(Penffordd-las) **155** F3
Staynall **191** G3
Staythorpe **174** C2
Stean **201** F5
Steane **148** A4
Stearsby **203** F5
Steart **115** F3
Stebbing **151** E5
Stebbing Green **151** E5
Stechford **158** D4
Stedham **121** D5
Steel Cross **123** E5
Steel Green **198** C5
Steele Road **218** D2
Steen's Bridge **145** E2
Steep **120** C5
Steep Marsh **120** C5
Steeple Dorset **105** F4
Steeple Essex **138** C2
Steeple Ashton **118** A2
Steeple Aston **147** G5
Steeple Barton **147** G5
Steeple Bumpstead **151** E3
Steeple Gidding **161** G4
Steeple Langford **118** B4
Steeple Morden **150** A3
Steeraway **157** F2

Steeton **193** G3
Stein **263** H6
Steinis **271** G4
Steinmanhill **269** F6
Stella **102** B1
Stelling Minnis **124** D4
Stembridge **116** B5
Stemster High **275** G3
Stemster High **275** G4
Stemster House **275** G2
Stenalees **97** E4
Stenhill **103** D1
Stenhousemuir **234** C1
Stenigot **188** C4
Stenness **278** B5
Stenscholl **263** K5
Stenson **173** E5
Stenton ELoth **236** D2
Stenton P&K **251** F5
Stepaside Pembs **127** E2
Stepaside Powys **155** G4
Stepney **136** C4
Steppingley **149** F4
Stepps **234** A3
Sternfield **153** E1
Sterridge **113** F1
Stert **118** B2
Stetchworth **151** E2
Stevenage **150** A5
Stevenston **233** D5
Steventon Hants **119** G3
Steventon Oxon **133** G3
Steventon End **151** E3
Stevington **149** E2
Stewartby **149** F3
Stewart Park, Middlesbrough
Middl TS7 8AR **29** C4
Stewartby **149** F3
Stewarton D&G **207** E2
Stewarton EAyr **233** F5
Stewkley **149** D5
Stewton **189** D4
Steynton **126** C2
Steyning **109** D2
Stibb **112** C4
Stibb Cross **113** E4
Stibb Green **118** D1
Stibbard **178** A3
Stibbington **161** F3
Stichill **228** B3
Sticker **97** D4
Stickford **176** B1
Sticklepath Devon **99** G1
Sticklepath Som **103** G1
Stickling Green **150** C4
Stickney **176** B2
Stiff Street **124** A2
Stiffkey **178** A1
Stifford's Bridge **145** G3
Stileway **116** B3
Stilligarry (Stadhlaigearraidh)
254 C1
Stillingfleet **195** E3
Stillington NYorks **195** E1
Stillington Stock **212** C5
Stilton **161** G4
Stinchcombe **131** G3
Stinsford **104** D3
Stirchley Tel&W **157** G2
Stirchley WMid **158** C4
Stirkoke House **275** J3
Stirling Aber **269** K6
Stirling (Sruighlea)
Stir **242** C5
Stirling Castle Stir
FK8 1EJ **242** C5
Stirling Visitor Centre Stir
FK8 1EH **242** C5
Stirton **193** F2
Stisted **151** G5
Stitchcombe **118** D1
Stithians **95** E3
Stittenham **266** D4
Stivichall **159** F5
Stix **250** C5
Stixwould **175** G1
Stoak **183** F5
Stobo **226** C2
Stoborough **105** F4
Stoborough Green **105** F4
Stobwood **235** D4
Stock **137** F3
Stock Green **146** B2
Stock Lane **133** E5
Stock Wood **146** C2
Stockbridge Hants **119** E4
Stockbridge Stir **242** C4
Stockbridge WSuss **108** A3
Stockbury **124** A2
Stockcross **119** F1
Stockdale **95** E3
Stockdalewath **209** G2
Stockerston **160** D3
Stockgrove Country Park
CenBeds
LU7 0BA **149** E5
Stocking Green Essex
151 E4
Stocking Green MK **148** D3
Stocking Pelham **150** C5
Stockingford **159** F3
Stockinish (Stocinis) **263** G2
Stockland Cardiff **130** A5
Stockland Devon **103** F2
Stockland Bristol **115** F3
Stockleigh English **102** B2
Stockleigh Pomeroy **102** B2
Stockley **118** B1
Stocklinch **103** G1
Stockport **184** C3
Stocksbridge **185** G3
Stocksfield **211** G1
Stockton Here **145** E1
Stockton Norf **165** E2
Stockton Shrop **157** G3
Stockton Shrop **156** B2
Stockton Tel&W **157** G1
Stockton Warks **147** G1
Stockton Wilts **118** A4
Stockton Heath **184** A4
Stockton on Teme **145** G1
Stockton on the
Forest **195** F2
Stockton-on-Tees **202** D1
Stockwell **103** D1
Stockwell Heath **172** B5
Stockwood Bristol **116** D1
Stockwood Dorset **104** B2

Stodday **192** A2
Stodmarsh **125** E2
Stody **178** B2
Stoer **272** C6
Stoford Devon **104** B1
Stoford Wilts **118** B4
Stogumber **115** D4
Stogursey **115** F3
Stoke Devon **112** C3
Stoke Hants **119** F2
Stoke Hants **107** G2
Stoke Med **124** A1
Stoke Plym **100** A2
Stoke WMid **159** F5
Stoke Abbott **104** A2
Stoke Albany **160** D4
Stoke Ash **164** C4
Stoke Bardolph **174** B3
Stoke Bishop **131** E5
Stoke Bliss **145** F1
Stoke Bruerne **148** C2
Stoke by Clare **151** F3
Stoke Canon **102** C3
Stoke Charity **119** F4
Stoke Climsland **99** D3
Stoke D'Abernon **121** G2
Stoke Doyle **161** F4
Stoke Dry **161** D3
Stoke Edith **145** F3
Stoke Farthing **118** B5
Stoke Ferry **163** F3
Stoke Fleming **101** E3
Stoke Gabriel **101** E2
Stoke Gifford **131** F5
Stoke Golding **159** F3
Stoke Goldington **148** D3
Stoke Green **135** E4
Stoke Hammond **149** D5
Stoke Heath Shrop **171** D5
Stoke Heath Worcs **146** B1
Stoke Holy Cross **178** D5
Stoke Lacy **145** F3
Stoke Lyne **148** A5
Stoke Mandeville **134** D1
Stoke Newington **136** C4
Stoke on Tern **170** D5
Stoke Orchard **146** B5
Stoke Pero **114** B3
Stoke Poges **135** E4
Stoke Pound **146** B1
Stoke Prior Here **145** E2
Stoke Prior Worcs **146** B1
Stoke Rivers **113** G2
Stoke Rochford **175** E5
Stoke Row **134** B4
Stoke St. Gregory **116** A5
Stoke St. Mary **115** F5
Stoke St. Michael **117** D3
Stoke St.
Milborough **157** E4
Stoke sub Hamdon
104 A1
Stoke Talmage **134** B3
Stoke Trister **117** E5
Stoke Villice **116** C1
Stoke Wake **105** D2
Stoke-by-Nayland **152** A4
Stokeford **105** E4
Stokeham **187** E5
Stokeinteignhead **102** C5
Stokenchurch **134** C3
Stokenham **101** E3
Stoke-on-Trent **171** F3
Stokesay **156** D4
Stokesby **179** E4
Stokesley **203** E2
Stolford **115** F3
Ston Easton **116** D2
Stonar Cut **125** F2
Stondon Massey **137** E2
Stone Bucks **134** C1
Stone Glos **131** F3
Stone Kent **137** E5
Stone Kent **111** E3
Stone Som **116** C4
Stone Staffs **171** G4
Stone SYorks **186** C4
Stone Worcs **158** A5
Stone Allerton **116** B2
Stone Cross Dur **201** F1
Stone Cross ESuss **110** B3
Stone Cross ESuss **110** A1
Stone Cross Kent **124** C5
Stone Cross Kent **123** E5
Stone House **200** C4
Stone Street Kent **123** E3
Stone Street Suff **165** E3
Stone Street Suff **152** A4
Stonea **162** C3
Stonebridge ESuss **110** A1
Stonebridge NSom **116** A2
Stonebridge Warks **159** E4
Stonebroom **173** F2
Stonecross Green **151** G2
Stonefield A&B **231** G2
Stonefield Staffs **171** G4
Stonegate ESuss **110** B1
Stonegate NYorks **203** G2
Stonegrave **203** F5
Stonehaugh **219** F4
Stonehaven **253** G1
Stonehenge Wilts
SP4 7DE **118** C3
Stonehouse
ChesW&C **183** G5
Stonehouse D&G **216** C4
Stonehouse Glos **132** A2
Stonehouse N'umb **210** C2
Stonehouse Plym **100** A2
Stonehouse SLan **234** B5
Stoneleigh Surr **122** B2
Stoneleigh Warks **159** F5
Stoneley Green **170** D2
Stonely **149** G1
Stoner Hill **120** C5
Stones **193** F5
Stones Green **152** C5
Stonesby **174** D5
Stonesfield **133** F1
Stonestreet Green **124** C5
Stonethwaite **209** F5
Stoney Cross **106** B1
Stoney Middleton **185** G5
Stoney Stanton **159** G3
Stoney Stoke **117** E4
Stoney Stratton **117** D4
Stoney Stretton **156** C2

Stoneyburn **235** D3
Stoneyford **103** D4
Stoneygate **180** B2
Stoneyhills **138** C3
Stoneykirk **214** B5
Stoneywood **261** G3
Stonganess **278** E2
Stonham Aspal **152** C2
Stonham Barns–Suff
IP14 6AT **152** C2
Stonnall **158** C2
Stonor **134** C4
Stonton Wyville **160** C3
Stony Houghton **173** F1
Stony Stratford **148** C3
Stonybreck **278** A1
Stoodleigh Devon **102** C1
Stoodleigh Devon **113** G2
Stopham **108** C2
Stopsley **149** G5
Stoptide **96** D2
Storeton **183** E4
Stormontfield **243** G2
Stornoway
(Steornabhagh) **271** G4
Stornoway Airport **271** G4
Storridge **145** G3
Storrington **108** C2
Storrs **185** G4
Storth **199** F4
Storwood **195** G3
Stotfield **267** K4
Stotfold **150** A4
Stottesdon **157** F4
Stoughton Leics **160** B2
Stoughton Surr **121** E2
Stoughton WSuss **107** G1
Stoughton Cross **116** B3
Stoul **256** D5
Stoulton **146** B3
Stour Provost **117** E5
Stour Row **117** F5
Stourbridge **158** A4
Stourhead Wilts
BA12 6QD **117** E4
Stourpaine **105** E2
Stourport-on-Severn **158** A5
Stourton Staffs **158** A4
Stourton Warks **147** E4
Stourton Wilts **117** E4
Stourton Caundle **104** D1
Stove **276** F2
Stoven **165** F3
Stow Lincs **187** F4
Stow ScBord **236** B5
Stow Bardolph **163** E2
Stow Bedon **164** A2
Stow cum Quy **150** D1
Stow Longa **161** G5
Stow Maries **138** B3
Stow Pasture **187** F4
Stowbridge **163** D2
Stowe Glos **131** E2
Stowe Shrop **156** C5
Stowe Staffs **158** D1
Stowe Landscape Gardens
Bucks
MK18 5DQ **148** B4
Stowe-by-Chartley **172** B5
Stowehill **148** B2
Stowell Glos **132** C1
Stowell Som **117** D5
Stowey **116** C2
Stowford Devon **99** E2
Stowford Devon **113** G3
Stowford Devon **103** E4
Stowlangtoft **152** A1
Stowmarket **152** B2
Stow-on-the-Wold **147** D5
Stowting **124** D4
Stowupland **152** B2
Straad **232** B3
Stracathro **253** E3
Strachan **260** E5
Strachur (Clachan
Strachur) **240** C4
Stradbroke **164** D4
Stradishall **151** F2
Stradsett **163** E2
Stragglethorpe **175** E2
Straight Soley **133** F5
Straiton Edin **235** G3
Straiton SAyr **224** B5
Straloch Aber **261** G2
Straloch P&K **251** F3
Stramshall **172** B4
Strands **198** C4
Strang **190** B4
Strangford **145** E5
Strannda **263** F3
Stranraer **214** B4
Strata Florida **142** D1
Stratfield Mortimer **120** B1
Stratfield Saye **120** B1
Stratfield Turgis **120** B2
Stratford CenBeds **149** G3
Stratford Glos **146** B4
Stratford GtLon **136** C4
Stratford St. Andrew **153** E2
Stratford St. Mary **152** B4
Stratford sub Castle **118** C4
Stratford Tony **118** B5
Stratford-upon-Avon **147** E2
Stratford-upon-Avon
Butterfly Farm
Warks CV37 7LS
85 Stratford-upon-Avon
Strath **275** H3
Strathan High **272** C6
Strathan High **257** F5
Strathaven **234** B5
Strathblane **233** G2
Strathcanaird **265** H1
Strathcarron **265** F7
Strathclyde Country Park
NLan ML1 3ED **31** G3
Strathdon **260** B3
Strathgirnock **260** B5
Strathkinness **244** C3
Strathmiglo **244** A3
Strathpeffer (Strath
Pheofhair) **266** B6
Strathrannoch **265** K4
Strathtay **251** E4
Strathwhillan **223** F2
Strathy **274** D2
Strathyre **242** A3
Stratton Corn **112** C5

Stratton *Dorset* 104 C3
Stratton *Glos* 132 C2
Stratton Audley 148 B5
Stratton Hall 152 D4
Stratton St.
  Margaret 133 D4
Stratton St. Michael 164 D2
Stratton Strawless 178 D3
Stratton-on-the-Fosse
  117 D2
Stravanan 232 B4
Stravithie 244 D3
Strawberry Hill 136 A5
Stream 115 D4
Streat 109 F2
Streatham 136 B5
Streatham Ice and Leisure
  Centre *GtLon*
  SW16 6HX 13 B7
Streatham Vale 136 B5
Streatley *CenBeds* 149 F5
Streatley *WBerks* 134 A4
Street *Devon* 103 E4
Street *Lancs* 192 B2
Street *NYorks* 203 G3
Street *Som* 116 B4
Street *Som* 103 G2
Street Ashton 159 G4
Street Dinas 170 A4
Street End 108 A4
Street Gate 212 B2
Street Houses 195 E3
Street Lane 173 F1
Street on the Fosse 116 D4
Streethay 158 D1
Streethouse 194 C5
Streetlam 202 C3
Streetly 158 C3
Streetly End 151 E3
Strefford 156 D4
Strelley 173 G3
Strensall 195 F1
Strensham 146 B3
Stretcholt 115 F3
Strete 101 E3
Stretford *GtMan* 184 B3
Stretford *Here* 144 D2
Stretford *Here* 145 E2
Strethall 150 C4
Stretham 162 D5
Strettington 108 A3
Stretton *ChesW&C* 170 B2
Stretton *Derbys* 173 E1
Stretton *Rut* 161 E1
Stretton *Staffs* 158 A1
Stretton *Staffs* 173 D5
Stretton *Warr* 184 A4
Stretton en le Field 159 F1
Stretton Grandison 145 F3
Stretton Heath 156 C1
Stretton Sugwas 145 D3
Stretton under
  Fosse 159 G4
Stretton Westwood 157 E3
Stretton-on-
  Dunsmore 159 G5
Stretton-on-Fosse 147 E4
Stribers 199 E4
Strichen 269 H5
Strines 185 D4
Strinesdale Countryside
  Area *GtMan*
  OL4 2JJ 25 H1
Stringston 115 E3
Strixton 149 E1
Stroat 131 E3
Stromeferry 256 E1
Stromemore 256 E1
Stromness 277 B7
Stronaba 249 E1
Stronachlachar 241 G3
Strone *A&B* 232 C1
Strone *High* 258 C2
Strone *High* 248 D1
Strone *Stir* 241 G3
Stronechrubie 272 E7
Stronlonag 232 C1
Stronmilchan (Sròn nam
  Mialchon) 241 D2
Stronsay 276 F5
Stronsay Airfield 276 F5
Strontian (Sròn an
  t-Sithein) 248 A3
Strontoiller 240 B2
Stronvar 242 A2
Strood 123 G2
Strood Green *Surr* 122 B4
Strood Green *WSuss* 121 F5
Strood Green
  WSuss 121 G4
Stroquhan 216 C2
Stroud *Glos* 132 A2
Stroud *Hants* 120 C5
Stroud Common 121 F3
Stroud Green *Essex* 138 B3
Stroud Green *Glos* 132 A2
Stroude 121 F1
Stroul 232 D1
Stroxton 175 E4
Struan *High* 255 J1
Struan *P&K* 250 C3
Strubby *Lincs* 189 E4
Strubby *Lincs* 188 B5
Strumpshaw 179 E5
Struthers 244 B4
Struy 258 B1
Stryd y Facsen 180 B4
Stryt-cae-rhedyn 169 F1
Stryt-issa 169 F3
Stuart & Waterford Crystal
  Factory Shop, Crieff *P&K*
  PH7 4HQ 243 D2
Stuart Line Cruises, Exmouth
  Devon EX8 1EJ 102 D4
Stuartfield 269 H6
Stub Place 198 B3
Stubber's Green 158 C2
Stubbington 107 E2
Stubbins 184 B1
Stubbs Green 165 E2
Stubhampton 105 F1
Stubley 186 A5
Stubshaw Cross 183 G2
Stubton 175 D3
Stuck *A&B* 232 B3
Stuck *A&B* 240 D5
Stuckbeg 241 E5
Stuckgowan 241 F4

Stuckindroin 241 F3
Stuckreoch 240 C5
Stuckton 106 A1
Stud Green 135 D5
Studdon 211 E2
Studfold 200 D5
Studham 185 E1
Studholme 209 F1
Studland 105 G4
Studland & Godlingston
  Heath NNR *Dorset*
  BH19 3AX 105 G4
Studley *Warks* 146 C1
Studley *Wilts* 132 B5
Studley Common 146 C1
Studley Green 134 C3
Studley Roger 202 B5
Studley Royal Park & ruins of
  Fountains Abbey *NYorks*
  HG4 3DY 194 B1
Stuggadhoo 190 B4
Stump Cross *Essex* 150 D3
Stump Cross *Lancs* 192 B4
Stuntney 163 D5
Stunts Green 110 B2
Sturbridge 171 F4
Sturgate 187 F4
Sturmer 151 E3
Sturminster
  Common 105 D1
Sturminster
  Marshall 105 F2
Sturminster
  Newton 105 D1
Sturry 125 D2
Sturton by Stow 187 F4
Sturton le Steeple 187 E4
Stuston 164 C4
Stutton *NYorks* 195 D3
Stutton *Suff* 152 C4
Styal 184 C4
Styrrup 186 D3
Suardail 271 G4
Succoth *A&B* 241 E4
Succoth *Aber* 260 C1
Succothmore 240 D4
Suckley 145 G2
Suckley Green 145 G2
Suckley Knowl 145 G2
Sudborough 161 E4
Sudbourne 153 F2
Sudbrook *Lincs* 175 E3
Sudbrook *Mon* 131 E4
Sudbrooke 188 A5
Sudbury *Derbys* 172 C4
Sudbury *GtLon* 136 A4
Sudbury *Suff* 151 G3
Sudbury Hall *Derbys*
  DE6 5HT 172 C4
Sudden 184 C1
Sudgrove 132 B2
Suffield *Norf* 178 D2
Suffield *NYorks* 204 C3
Sugarloaf 124 B5
Sugnall 171 E4
Sugwas Pool 145 D3
Suie Lodge Hotel 241 G2
Suisnish 256 B3
Sulby *IoM* 190 B2
Sulby *IoM* 190 B2
Sulgrave 148 A3
Sulham 134 B5
Sulhamstead 120 B1
Sullington 108 C2
Sullom 278 C5
Sullom Voe Oil
  Terminal 278 C5
Sully 115 E1
Sumburgh 279 F10
Sumburgh Airport 279 F9
Summer Bridge 194 B1
Summer Isles 265 F1
Summer Lodge 201 E3
Summercourt 96 C4
Summerfield *Norf* 177 F4
Summerfield *Worcs* 158 A5
Summerhill 170 A2
Summerhouse 202 B1
Summerlands 199 G4
Summerleaze 130 D4
Summertown 134 A2
Summit 184 D1
Sun Green 185 D3
Sunadale 231 G5
Sunbiggin 200 B2
Sunbury 121 G1
Sundaywell 216 C2
Sunderland *Cumb* 209 E3
Sunderland *Lancs* 192 A2
Sunderland *T&W* 212 C2
Sunderland Bridge 212 B4
Sunderland Museum &
  Winter Gardens
  T&W SR1 1PP
  86 Sunderland
Sundhope 227 E3
Sundon Park 149 F5
Sundown Adventure Land
  Notts
  DN22 0HX 187 E5
Sundridge 123 D3
Sundrum Mains 224 C3
Sunhill 132 D2
Sunipol 246 C4
Sunk Island 188 C1
Sunningdale 121 E1
Sunninghill 121 E1
Sunningwell 133 G2
Sunniside *Dur* 212 A4
Sunniside *T&W* 212 B2
Sunny Bank 199 D3
Sunny Brow 212 A4
Sunnylaw 242 A5
Sunnyside *Aber* 261 G5
Sunnyside *N'umb* 211 F1
Sunnyside *SYorks* 186 B3
Sunnyside *WSuss* 122 C5
Sunton 118 D2
Sunwick 237 F4
Surbiton 121 G1
Surfleet 176 A5
Surfleet Seas End 176 A5
Surlingham 179 E5
Sustead 178 C2
Susworth 187 F2
Sutcombe 112 D4
Sutcombemill 112 D4
Suton 164 B2

Sutors of Cromarty 267 F5
Sutterby 189 D5
Sutterton 176 A4
Sutton *Cambs* 162 C5
Sutton *CenBeds* 150 A3
Sutton *Devon* 102 A4
Sutton *Devon* 100 D3
Sutton *GtLon* 122 B2
Sutton *Kent* 125 F4
Sutton *Lincs* 175 D2
Sutton *Norf* 179 E3
Sutton *Notts* 174 C4
Sutton *Notts* 187 D4
Sutton *Oxon* 133 G2
Sutton *Pembs* 126 C1
Sutton *Peter* 161 F3
Sutton *Shrop* 157 G4
Sutton *Shrop* 171 D4
Sutton *Shrop* 157 E1
Sutton *Shrop* 170 A5
Sutton *Staffs* 171 E5
Sutton *Suff* 153 E3
Sutton *SYorks* 186 C5
Sutton *WSuss* 108 B2
Sutton Abinger 121 G3
Sutton Bank National Park
  Centre *NYorks*
  YO7 2EH 203 E4
Sutton Bassett 160 C4
Sutton Benger 132 B5
Sutton Bingham 104 B1
Sutton Bonington 173 G5
Sutton Bridge 176 C5
Sutton Cheney 159 G2
Sutton Coldfield 158 D3
Sutton Courtenay 134 A3
Sutton Crosses 176 C4
Sutton Grange 202 B5
Sutton Green *Oxon* 133 G2
Sutton Green *Surr* 121 F2
Sutton Green *Wrex* 170 B3
Sutton Holms 105 G2
Sutton Howgrave 202 C5
Sutton in Ashfield 173 F2
Sutton in the Elms 160 A3
Sutton Ings 196 C4
Sutton Lane Ends 184 D5
Sutton le Marsh 189 F4
Sutton Leach 183 G3
Sutton Maddock 157 G2
Sutton Mallet 116 A4
Sutton Mandeville 118 A5
Sutton Montis 116 D5
Sutton on Sea 189 F4
Sutton on the Hill 172 D4
Sutton on Trent 174 C1
Sutton Poyntz 104 D4
Sutton St. Edmund 162 B2
Sutton St. James 162 C1
Sutton St. Nicholas 145 E3
Sutton Scarsdale 173 F1
Sutton Scotney 119 F4
Sutton upon Derwent
  195 G3
Sutton Valence 124 A4
Sutton Veny 117 F3
Sutton Waldron 105 E1
Sutton Weaver 183 G5
Sutton Wick
  B&NESom 116 C2
Sutton Wick *Oxon* 133 G3
Sutton-in-Craven 193 G3
Sutton-on-Hull 196 D4
Sutton-on-the-Forest
  195 E1
Sutton-under-Brailes
  147 F4
Sutton-under-
  Whitestonecliffe 203 D4
Swaby 189 D5
Swadlincote 159 F1
Swaffham 163 G2
Swaffham Bulbeck 151 D1
Swaffham Prior 151 D1
Swafield 179 D2
Swainbost
  (Suainebost) 271 H1
Swainby 203 D2
Swainshill 145 D3
Swainsthorpe 178 D5
Swainswick 117 E1
Swalcliffe 147 F4
Swalecliffe 124 D2
Swallow 188 B2
Swallow Beck 175 E1
Swallowcliffe 118 A5
Swallowfield 120 C1
Swallows Cross 137 F3
Swampton 119 F2
Swan Green
  ChesW&C 184 B5
Swan Green *Suff* 165 D4
Swan Street 151 G5
Swanage 105 G5
Swanage Railway *Dorset*
  BH19 1HB 105 G5
Swanbach 171 D3
Swanbourne 148 D5
Swanbridge 115 E1
Swancote 157 G3
Swanland 196 B5
Swanlaws 228 B5
Swanley 123 E2
Swanley Village 123 E2
Swanmore *Hants* 107 E1
Swanmore *IoW* 107 E3
Swannington *Leics* 159 G1
Swannington *Norf* 178 C4
Swanscombe 137 F5
Swansea
  (Abertawe) 128 C3
Swansea Museum SA1 1SN
  86 Swansea
Swanston 235 G3
Swanton Abbot 179 D3
Swanton Morley 178 B4
Swanton Novers 178 B2
Swanton Street 124 A3
Swanwick *Derbys* 173 F2
Swanwick *Hants* 107 E2
Swanwick Green 170 C3
Swarby 175 F3
Swardeston 178 D5
Swarkestone 173 E5
Swarland 221 D1

Swarraton 119 G4
Swarthmoor 199 D5
Swaton 175 G4
Swavesey 150 B1
Sway 106 B3
Swayfield 175 E5
Swaythling 106 D1
Swaythorpe 196 C1
Sweetham 102 B3
Sweethay 115 F5
Sweetshouse 97 E3
Sweffling 153 E1
Swell 116 A3
Swepstone 159 F1
Swerford 147 F5
Swettenham 171 F1
Swffryd 130 B3
Swift's Green 124 A4
Swiftsden 110 C1
Swilland 152 C2
Swillington 194 C4
Swimbridge 113 G3
Swimbridge Newland
  113 F2
Swinbrook 133 E1
Swincliffe 194 B2
Swincombe 113 G1
Swinden 193 E2
Swinderby 175 D1
Swindon *Staffs* 158 A3
Swindon *Swin* 133 D4
Swindon Village 146 B5
Swine 196 D4
Swinefleet 195 G5
Swineford 117 E1
Swineshead *Bed* 149 F1
Swineshead *Lincs* 176 A3
Swineshead Bridge 176 A3
Swineside 201 F4
Swiney 275 H5
Swinford *Leics* 160 A5
Swinford *Oxon* 133 G2
Swingate 173 G3
Swingfield Minnis 125 E4
Swingleton Green 152 A3
Swinhoe 229 G4
Swinhope 188 C3
Swining 279 D6
Swinithwaite 201 F4
Swinscoe 172 C3
Swinside Hall 228 B5
Swinstead 175 F5
Swinton *GtMan* 184 B2
Swinton *NYorks* 203 G5
Swinton *NYorks* 202 B5
Swinton *ScBord* 237 F5
Swinton *SYorks* 186 B3
Swinton Quarter 237 F5
Swintonmill 237 F5
Swithland 160 A1
Swordale 266 C5
Swordland 256 D5
Swordle 247 E2
Swordly 274 C2
Sworton Heath 184 A4
Swyddffynnon 142 C1
Swyncombe 134 B3
Swynnerton 171 F4
Swyre 104 B4
Sychnant 155 F5
Syde 132 B1
Sydenham *GtLon* 136 C5
Sydenham *Oxon* 134 C2
Sydenham Damerel 99 E3
Syderstone 177 G4
Sydling St. Nicholas
  104 C3
Sydmonton 119 F2
Sydney 171 E2
Syerston 174 C3
Sykehouse 186 D1
Sykes 192 C2
Sylen 128 B2
Symbister 279 E6
Symington *SAyr* 224 B2
Symington *SLan* 226 A2
Symonds Yat 131 E1
Symondsbury 104 A3
Synod Inn
  (Post-mawr) 142 A2
Syre 273 J4
Syreford 146 C5
Syresham 148 B3
Syston *Leics* 160 B1
Syston *Lincs* 175 E3
Sytchampton 146 A1
Sywell 148 D1

T

Taagan 265 G5
Tableyhill 184 B5
Tabost 271 F6
Tachbrook Mallory 147 F1
Tacher 275 G4
Tackley 147 G5
Tacolneston 164 C2
Tadcaster 195 D3
Tadden 105 F2
Taddington *Derbys* 185 F5
Taddington *Glos* 146 C4
Taddiport 113 E4
Tadley 120 B1
Tadlow 150 A3
Tadmarton 147 F4
Tadpole Bridge 133 F2
Tadworth 122 B3
Tafarnaubach 130 A1
Tafarn-y-bwlch 141 D4
Tafarn-y-Gelyn 169 E1
Taff Merthyr Garden
  Village 130 A3
Taff's Well
  (Ffynnon Taf) 130 A4
Tafolwern 155 E2
Taibach *NPT* 129 D4
Tai-bach *Powys* 169 E5
Taicynhaeaf 154 C1
Tain *High* 275 H2
Tain *High* 266 E3
Tai'n Lôn 166 D3
Tai'r Bull 143 F5
Tairgwaith 128 D1
Tai'r-heol 130 A3
Tairlaw 224 C5
Tai'r-ysgol 128 C3
Takeley 151 D5

Takeley Street 150 D5
Talachddu 143 G4
Talacre 182 C4
Talardd 168 B5
Talaton 103 D3
Talbenny 126 B1
Talbot Green 129 G4
Talbot Village 105 G3
Talerddig 155 F2
Talgarreg 142 A2
Talgarth 144 A4
Taliesin 154 C3
Talisker 255 J1
Talke 171 F2
Talke Pits 171 F2
Talkin 210 B2
Talkin Tarn Country Park
  Cumb CA8 1HN 210 B2
Talla Linnfoots 226 C3
Talladale 265 F3
Talladh-a-Bheithe 250 A4
Talland 97 G4
Tallarn Green 170 B3
Tallentire 209 E3
Talley (Talyllychau) 142 C4
Tallington 161 F2
Talmine 273 H2
Talog 142 A4
Tal-sarn 142 B2
Talsarnau 167 F4
Talskiddy 96 D3
Talwrn *IoA* 180 C5
Talwrn *Wrex* 169 F3
Talwrn *Wrex* 170 A3
Talybont *Cere* 154 C4
Tal-y-bont *Conwy* 168 A1
Tal-y-bont *Gwyn* 167 E1
Tal-y-bont *Gwyn* 181 E5
Talybont-on-Usk 144 A4
Tal-y-Cae 167 F1
Tal-y-cafn 181 F5
Tal-y-coed 130 D1
Talygarn 129 G4
Tal-y-llyn *Gwyn* 154 D2
Talyllyn *Powys* 144 A5
Talysarn 167 D2
Tal-y-wern 155 E2
Tamavoid 242 A5
Tamerton Foliot 100 A1
Tamworth 159 E2
Tamworth Green 176 B3
Tan Office Green 151 F2
Tandem 185 E2
Tandridge 122 C3
Tanerdy 142 A5
Tanfield 212 A2
Tanfield Lea 212 A2
Tang 194 B2
Tang Hall 195 F2
Tangiers 126 C1
Tanglandford 261 G1
Tangley 119 E2
Tangmere 108 B3
Tangwick 278 B5
Tangy 222 B3
Tank Museum, Bovington
  Dorset
  BH20 6JG 105 E4
Tankerness 277 E7
Tankersley 186 A2
Tankerton 124 D2
Tan-lan 167 F3
Tannach 275 J4
Tannachy 266 E1
Tannadice 252 C4
Tannington 152 D1
Tannochside 234 A3
Tansley 173 E2
Tansley Knoll 173 E2
Tansor 161 F3
Tantobie 212 A2
Tanton 203 E1
Tanworth in Arden 158 D5
Tan-y-fron 168 C1
Tan-y-graig 166 C4
Tanygrisiau 167 F3
Tan-y-groes 141 F3
Tan-y-pistyll 169 D5
Tan-yr-allt 182 B4
Taobh a' Deas Loch
  Baghasdail 254 C3
Taobh Siar 270 D7
Tapeley 113 E3
Taplow 135 E4
Tapton Grove 186 B5
Taransay
  (Tarasaigh) 270 C7
Taraphocain 248 C5
Tarbat House 266 E4
Tarbert *A&B* 231 G3
Tarbert *A&B* 231 E3
Tarbert *A&B* 231 E1
Tarbert *High* 247 F3
Tarbert (Tairbeart)
  Na H-E. Siar 270 D7
Tarbet *A&B* 241 F4
Tarbet *High* 256 D5
Tarbet *High* 272 D4
Tarbock Green 183 F4
Tarbolton 224 C3
Tarbrax 235 F4
Tardebigge 146 B1
Tardy Gate 192 B5
Tarfside 252 C2
Tarland 260 C4
Tarleton 192 A5
Tarlscough 183 F1
Tarlton 132 B3
Tarnbrook 192 B2
Tarnock 116 A2
Tarporley 170 C1
Tarr 115 E4
Tarrant Crawford 105 F2
Tarrant Gunville 105 F1
Tarrant Hinton 105 F1
Tarrant Keyneston 105 F2
Tarrant
  Launceston 105 F2
Tarrant Monkton 105 F2
Tarrant Rawston 105 F2
Tarrant Rushton 105 F2
Tarrel 267 F3
Tarring Neville 109 G3
Tarrington 145 F3
Tarrnacraig 223 E2
Tarsappie 243 G2
Tarskavaig 256 B4

Tarves 261 G1
Tarvie (Tairbhidh)
  High 266 B6
Tarvie *P&K* 251 F3
Tarvin 170 B1
Tarvin Sands 170 B1
Tasburgh 164 D2
Tasley 157 F3
Taston 147 F5
Tate Britain *GtLon*
  SW1P 4RG 13 B5
Tate Liverpool
  Mersey L3 4BB 42 B5
Tate Modern *GtLon*
  SE1 9TG 45 H4
Tate St. Ives *Corn*
  TR26 1TG 94 C2
Tatenhill 158 D6
Tathall End 148 D3
Tatham 192 C1
Tathwell 188 D4
Tatsfield 122 D3
Tattenhall 170 B2
Tattenhoe 148 D4
Tatterford 177 G5
Tattersett 177 G4
Tattershall 176 A2
Tattershall Bridge 175 G2
Tattershall
  Thorpe 176 A2
Tattingstone 152 C4
Tatton Park *ChesE*
  WA16 6QN 184 B4
Tatworth 103 G2
Tauchers 268 B6
Taunton 115 F5
Tavelty 261 F3
Taverham 178 C4
Tavernspite 127 E1
Tavistock 99 E3
Taw Bridge 113 G5
Taw Green 99 G1
Tawstock 113 F3
Taxal 185 E5
Tayburn 233 G5
Taychreggan 240 C2
Tayinloan 231 E5
Taylors Cross 112 C4
Taynafead 240 C3
Taynish 231 F1
Taynton *Glos* 145 G5
Taynton *Oxon* 133 E1
Taynuilt
  (Taigh an Uillt) 240 C1
Tayock 253 E4
Tayovullin 230 A2
Tayport 244 C2
Tayvallich 231 F1
Tealby 188 B3
Tealing 244 C1
Team Valley 212 B1
Teanamachar 262 C5
Teangue 256 C4
Teasses 244 C4
Tebay 200 B2
Tebworth 149 E5
Techniquest, Cardiff *Cardiff*
  CF10 5BW 7 B4
Tedburn St. Mary 102 B3
Teddington *Glos* 146 B4
Teddington *GtLon* 136 A5
Tedstone Delamere 145 F2
Tedstone Wafre 145 F2
Teeton 160 B5
Teffont Evias 118 A4
Teffont Magna 118 A4
Tegryn 141 F4
Tehidy Country Park *Corn*
  TR14 0HA 96 A5
Teifi Marshes Nature Reserve
  Pembs SA43 2TB
  141 E3
Teigh 161 D1
Teign Village 102 B4
Teigngrace 102 B5
Teignmouth 102 C5
Telford 157 F2
Telford Wonderland *Tel&W*
  TF3 4AY 157 G2
Telham 110 C2
Tellisford 117 F2
Telscombe 109 G3
Telscombe Cliffs 109 G3
Tempar 250 B4
Templand 217 E2
Temple *Corn* 97 F2
Temple *Midlo* 236 A4
Temple Balsall 159 E5
Temple Bar 142 B2
Temple Cloud 116 D2
Temple End 151 E2
Temple Ewell 125 E4
Temple Grafton 146 D2
Temple Guiting 146 C5
Temple Herdewyke 147 F2
Temple Hirst 195 F5
Temple Newsam *WYorks*
  LS15 0AE 27 H2
Temple Normanton 173 F1
Temple Sowerby 210 C5
Templecombe 117 E5
Templeton *Devon* 102 B1
Templeton *Pembs* 127 E1
Templeton Bridge 102 B1
Templewood 253 E3
Tempsford 149 G2
Ten Mile Bank 163 E3
Tenbury Wells 145 E1
Tenby (Dinbych-y-
  pysgod) 127 E2
Tendring 152 C5
Tendring Green 152 C5
Tenga 247 E5
Tenterden 124 A5
Tepersie Castle 260 D2
Terally 206 B2
Terling 137 G1
Tern 157 F1
Ternhill 170 D4
Terregles 216 D3
Terriers 135 D3
Terrington 203 F5
Terrington
  St. Clement 177 D5
Terrington St. John 162 D1
Terry's Green 158 D5
Tervieside 259 K1

Teston 123 G3
Testwood 106 C1
Tetbury 132 A3
Tetbury Upton 132 A3
Tetchill 170 A4
Tetcott 98 D1
Tetford 188 D5
Tetney 188 D2
Tetney Lock 188 D2
Tetsworth 134 B2
Tettenhall 158 A2
Tettenhall Wood 158 A3
Tetworth 150 A2
Teuchan 261 J1
Teversal 173 F1
Teversham 150 C2
Teviot Water Gardens
  ScBord TD5 8LE 228 B3
Tewel 253 G1
Tewin 136 B1
Tewkesbury 146 A4
Tewkesbury Abbey *Glos*
  GL20 5RZ 146 A4
Teynham 124 B2
Thackley 194 A4
Thainston 253 E2
Thainstone 261 F3
Thakeham 108 D2
Thame 134 B2
Thames Ditton 121 G1
Thames Haven 137 G4
Thamesmead 137 D4
Thanington 124 C2
Thankerton 226 A2
Tharston 164 C2
Thatcham 119 G1
Thatto Heath 183 G3
Thaxted 151 E4
The Apes Hall 163 D3
The Bage 144 B3
The Balloch 242 D3
The Banking 261 F1
The Bar 121 G5
The Birks 261 F4
The Bog 156 C3
The Bourne 120 D3
The Bratch 158 A3
The Broad 145 D1
The Bryn 130 C2
The Burf 146 A1
The Burn 253 D2
The Butts 117 E3
The Camp 132 B2
The Chequer 170 B3
The City *Bucks* 134 C3
The City *Suff* 165 E3
The Common *Wilts* 118 D4
The Common *Wilts* 132 C4
The Craigs 266 B2
The Cronk 190 B2
The Delves 158 C3
The Den 233 E4
The Den & The Glen *Aber*
  AB12 5FT 261 G5
The Dicker 110 A3
The Down 157 F3
The Drums 252 B3
The Eaves 131 F2
The Flatt 219 D4
The Folly 136 A1
The Forge 144 C2
The Forstal *ESuss* 123 E4
The Forstal *Kent* 124 C5
The Grange *Lincs* 189 E4
The Grange *Shrop* 170 A4
The Grange *Surr* 122 C4
The Green *A&B* 246 A2
The Green *Cumb* 198 C5
The Green *Essex* 137 G1
The Green *Flints* 169 F5
The Green *Wilts* 117 F4
The Grove 146 A3
The Haven 121 F4
The Headland 213 E4
The Heath 172 B4
The Herberts 129 F5
The Hermitage 122 B3
The Hill 198 C4
The Holme 194 B2
The Howe 190 A5
The Isle 157 D1
The Laurels 165 E2
The Leacon 124 B5
The Lee 135 D2
The Leigh 146 A5
The Lhen 190 B1
The Lodge 241 G5
The Marsh 156 C3
The Moor *ESuss* 110 D2
The Moor *Kent* 110 C1
The Mumbles 128 C4
The Murray 234 A4
The Mythe 146 A4
The Narth 131 E2
The Neuk 261 F5
The Node 136 B1
The Oval 117 E1
The Polchar 259 G4
The Quarter 124 A4
The Reddings 146 B5
The Rhos 126 D1
The Rookery 171 F2
The Rowe 171 F4
The Sale 159 D1
The Sands 121 D3
The Shoe 132 A5
The Slade 134 A5
The Smithies 157 F3
The Stocks 111 E1
The Swillett 135 F3
The Thrift 150 B4
The Vauld 145 E3
The Wern 169 F2
The Wyke 157 G2
Theakston 202 C4
Thealby 187 F1
Theale *Som* 116 B3
Theale *WBerks* 134 B5
Thearne 196 C4
Theberton 153 F1
Thedden Grange 120 B4
Theddingworth 160 B4
Theddlethorpe
  All Saints 189 E4
Theddlethorpe
  St. Helen 189 E4
Thelbridge Barton 102 A1

Thelbridge Cross 102 A1
Thelnetham 164 B4
Thelveton 164 C3
Thelwall 184 A4
Themelthorpe 178 B3
Thenford 148 A3
Therfield 150 B4
Thermae Bath Spa *B&NESom* BA1 1SJ 63 Bath
Thetford *Lincs* 161 G1
Thetford *Norf* 163 G4
Thetford Forest Park *Norf* IP27 0TJ 163 G4
Thethwaite 209 G2
Theydon Bois 136 D3
Theydon Garnon 137 D3
Theydon Mount 137 D3
Thickwood 132 A5
Thimbleby *Lincs* 176 A1
Thimbleby *NYorks* 202 D3
Thingley 117 F1
Thirkleby 203 D5
Thirlby 203 D4
Thirlestane 236 C5
Thirn 202 B4
Thirsk 202 D4
Thirston New Houses 221 D2
Thirtleby 197 D4
Thistleton *Lancs* 192 A4
Thistleton *Rut* 161 E1
Thistley Green 163 E5
Thixendale 196 A1
Thockrington 220 B4
Tholomas Drove 162 B2
Tholthorpe 195 D1
Thomas Chapel 127 E2
Thomas Close 210 A3
Thomastown 260 D1
Thompson 164 A2
Thomshill 267 K6
Thong 137 F5
Thongsbridge 185 F2
Thoralby 201 F4
Thoresby 186 D5
Thoresthorpe 189 E5
Thoresway 188 B3
Thorganby *Lincs* 188 C3
Thorganby *NYorks* 195 F3
Thorgill 203 G3
Thorington 165 F4
Thorington Street 152 B4
Thorley 137 D1
Thorley Houses 150 C5
Thorley Street *Herts* 137 D1
Thorley Street *IoW* 106 C4
Thormanby 203 D5
Thornaby-on-Tees 203 D1
Thornage 178 B2
Thornborough *Bucks* 148 C4
Thornborough *NYorks* 202 B5
Thornbury *Devon* 113 D5
Thornbury *Here* 145 F2
Thornbury *SGlos* 131 F3
Thornbury *WYorks* 194 A4
Thornby 160 B5
Thorncliff 185 G1
Thorncliffe 172 B2
Thorncombe 103 G2
Thorncombe Street 121 F3
Thorncote Green 149 G3
Thorncross 106 D4
Thorndon 152 C1
Thorndon Country Park *Essex* CM13 3RZ 137 F3
Thorndon Cross 99 F1
Thorne 187 D1
Thorne St. Margaret 115 D5
Thorner 194 C4
Thorney *Bucks* 135 F5
Thorney *Notts* 187 F5
Thorney *Peter* 162 A2
Thorney *Som* 116 B5
Thorney Close 212 C2
Thorney Hill 106 B3
Thornfalcon 115 F5
Thornford 104 C1
Thorngrafton 211 D1
Thorngrove 116 A4
Thorngumbald 197 E5
Thornham 177 F3
Thornham Magna 164 C4
Thornham Parva 164 C4
Thornhaugh 161 F2
Thornhill *Cardiff* 130 A4
Thornhill *Cumb* 198 B2
Thornhill *D&G* 216 C1
Thornhill *Derbys* 185 F4
Thornhill *Soton* 107 D1
Thornhill *Stir* 242 B4
Thornhill *WYorks* 185 G1
Thornhill Lees 185 G1
Thornholme 196 D1
Thornicombe 105 E2
Thornley *Dur* 212 C4
Thornley *Dur* 212 A4
Thornley Gate 211 E2
Thornliebank 233 G4
Thornroan 261 G1
Thorns 151 F2
Thorns Green 184 B4
Thornsett 185 E4
Thornthwaite *Cumb* 209 F4
Thornthwaite *NYorks* 194 A2
Thornton *Angus* 252 B5
Thornton *Bucks* 148 C4
Thornton *ERid* 195 G3
Thornton *Fife* 244 A5
Thornton *Lancs* 191 G3
Thornton *Leics* 159 G2
Thornton *Lincs* 176 A1
Thornton *Mersey* 183 E2
Thornton *Middl* 203 D1
Thornton *N'umb* 237 G5
Thornton *P&K* 251 F5
Thornton *Pembs* 126 C2
Thornton *WYorks* 194 A4
Thornton Bridge 202 D5
Thornton Curtis 188 A1
Thornton Heath 122 C2
Thornton Hough 183 E4
Thornton in Lonsdale 200 B5
Thornton le Moor 188 A3
Thornton Park 237 G5
Thornton Rust 201 E4
Thornton Steward 202 A4
Thornton Watlass 202 B4
Thorntonhall 233 G4
Thornton-in-Craven 193 F3
Thornton-le-Beans 202 D3
Thornton-le-Clay 195 F1
Thornton-le-Dale 204 B4
Thornton-le-Moor 202 C4
Thornton-le-Moors 183 F5
Thornton-le-Street 202 D4
Thorntonloch 237 E2
Thornwood 137 D2
Thornyhill 253 E2
Thornylee 227 F2
Thoroton 174 C3
Thorp Arch 194 D3
Thorpe *Derbys* 172 C2
Thorpe *ERid* 196 B3
Thorpe *Lincs* 189 E4
Thorpe *Norf* 165 F2
Thorpe *Notts* 174 C2
Thorpe *NYorks* 193 G1
Thorpe *Surr* 121 F1
Thorpe Abbotts 164 C3
Thorpe Acre 173 G5
Thorpe Arnold 174 C5
Thorpe Audlin 186 B1
Thorpe Bassett 204 B5
Thorpe Bay 138 C4
Thorpe by Water 161 D3
Thorpe Constantine 159 E2
Thorpe Culvert 176 C1
Thorpe End 179 D4
Thorpe Green *Essex* 152 C5
Thorpe Green *Lancs* 192 B5
Thorpe Green *Suff* 152 A2
Thorpe Hall 203 E5
Thorpe Hesley 186 A3
Thorpe in Balne 186 C1
Thorpe in the Fallows 187 G4
Thorpe Langton 160 C3
Thorpe Larches 212 C5
Thorpe le Street 196 A3
Thorpe Malsor 160 D5
Thorpe Mandeville 148 A3
Thorpe Market 178 D2
Thorpe Morieux 152 A2
Thorpe on the Hill *Lincs* 175 E1
Thorpe on the Hill *WYorks* 194 C5
Thorpe Park *Surr* KT16 8PN 121 F1
Thorpe Row 178 A5
Thorpe St. Andrew 179 D5
Thorpe St. Peter 176 C1
Thorpe Salvin 186 C4
Thorpe Satchville 160 C1
Thorpe Street 164 B4
Thorpe Thewles 212 D5
Thorpe Tilney Dales 175 G2
Thorpe Underwood *N'hants* 160 C4
Thorpe Underwood *NYorks* 195 D2
Thorpe Waterville 161 F4
Thorpe Willoughby 195 E4
Thorpefield 202 D5
Thorpe-le-Soken 152 C5
Thorpeness 153 F1
Thorpland 163 E2
Thorrington 152 B5
Thorverton 102 C2
Thrandeston 164 C4
Thrapston 161 E5
Threapland 193 F1
Threapwood 170 B3
Threapwood Head 172 B3
Three Ashes 117 D3
Three Bridges 122 B5
Three Burrows 96 B5
Three Chimneys 124 A5
Three Cocks (Aberllynfi) 144 A4
Three Counties Showground *Worcs* WR13 6NW 145 G3
Three Crosses 128 B3
Three Cups Corner 110 B1
Three Hammers 97 G1
Three Holes 162 D2
Three Leg Cross 123 F5
Three Legged Cross 105 G2
Three Mile Cross 120 C1
Three Oaks 110 D2
Threehammer Common 179 E4
Threekingham 175 F4
Threemilestone 96 B5
Threlkeld 209 G4
Threshfield 193 F1
Threxton Hill 163 G2
Thriepley 244 B1
Thrigby 179 F4
Thrigby Hall Wildlife Gardens *Norf* NR29 3DR 179 F4
Thringarth 211 F5
Thringstone 159 G1
Thrintoft 202 C3
Thriplow 150 C3
Throapham 186 C4
Throckenholt 162 B2
Throcking 150 B4
Throckley 212 A1
Throckmorton 146 B3
Throop 105 E3
Throphill 220 D3
Thropton 220 C1
Througham 132 B2
Throwleigh 99 G1
Throwley 124 B3
Throws 151 E5
Thrumpton *Notts* 173 G4
Thrumpton *Notts* 187 E5
Thrumster 275 J4
Thrunton 229 E5
Thrupp *Glos* 132 A2
Thrupp *Oxon* 133 G1
Thrupp *Oxon* 133 E3
Thruscross 194 A2
Thrushelton 99 E2
Thrussington 160 B1
Thruxton *Hants* 119 D3
Thruxton *Here* 144 D4
Thrybergh 186 B3
Thrybergh Country Park *SYorks* S65 4NU 186 B3
Thulston 173 F4
Thunder Bridge 185 F1
Thundergay 231 G5
Thundersley 138 B4
Thunderton 269 J6
Thundridge 136 C1
Thurcaston 160 A1
Thurcroft 186 B4
Thurdistoft 275 H2
Thurdon 112 C4
Thurgarton *Norf* 178 C2
Thurgarton *Notts* 174 B3
Thurgoland 185 G2
Thurlaston *Leics* 160 A3
Thurlaston *Warks* 159 G5
Thurlbear 115 F5
Thurlby *Lincs* 161 G1
Thurlby *Lincs* 175 E1
Thurlby *Lincs* 189 E5
Thurleigh 149 F2
Thurlestone 100 C3
Thurloxton 115 F4
Thurlstone 185 G2
Thurlton 165 F2
Thurlwood 171 F2
Thurmaston 160 B2
Thurnby 160 B2
Thurne 179 F4
Thurnham 124 A3
Thurning *N'hants* 161 F4
Thurning *Norf* 178 B3
Thurnscoe 186 B2
Thursby 209 G1
Thursden 193 F4
Thursford 178 A2
Thursford Collection *Norf* NR21 0AS 178 A2
Thursley 121 E4
Thurso (Inbhir Theòrsa) 275 G2
Thurstaston 182 D4
Thurston 152 A1
Thurston Clough 185 D2
Thurstonfield 209 G1
Thurstonland 185 F1
Thurton 179 E5
Thurvaston *Derbys* 172 D4
Thurvaston *Derbys* 172 C4
Thuster 275 H3
Thuxton 178 B5
Thwaite *NYorks* 201 D3
Thwaite *Suff* 152 C1
Thwaite Head 199 E3
Thwaite St. Mary 165 E2
Thwaites 193 G3
Thwaites Brow 193 G3
Thwing 205 D5
Tibbermore 243 F2
Tibberton *Glos* 145 G5
Tibberton *Tel&W* 171 D5
Tibberton *Worcs* 146 B2
Tibbie Shiels Inn 226 D3
Tibenham 164 C2
Tibertich 240 A4
Tibshelf 173 F1
Tibthorpe 196 B2
Ticehurst 123 F5
Tichborne 119 G4
Tickencote 161 E2
Tickenham 131 D5
Tickford End 149 D3
Tickhill 186 C3
Ticklerton 157 D3
Ticknall 173 E5
Tickton 196 C3
Tidbury Green 158 D5
Tidcombe 119 D2
Tiddington *Oxon* 134 B2
Tiddington *Warks* 147 E2
Tiddleywink 132 A5
Tidebrook 110 B1
Tideford 98 D5
Tideford Cross 98 D4
Tidenham 131 E3
Tidenham Chase 131 E3
Tideswell 185 F5
Tidmarsh 134 B5
Tidmington 147 E4
Tidpit 105 G1
Tidworth 118 D3
Tiers Cross 126 C1
Tiffield 148 B2
Tifty 269 F6
Tigerton 252 D3
Tigh a' Gearraidh 262 C4
Tighachnoic 247 F5
Tighnablair 242 C3
Tighnabruaich 232 A2
Tighnacomaire 248 B3
Tigley 101 D1
Tilbrook 149 F1
Tilbury 137 F5
Tilbury Green 151 F3
Tile Hill 159 E5
Tilehurst 134 B5
Tilford 121 D3
Tilgate 122 B5
Tilgate Forest Row 122 B5
Tilgate Park *WSuss* RH10 5PQ 122 B5
Tillathrowie 260 C1
Tillers' Green 145 F4
Tillery 261 H2
Tilley 170 C5
Tillicoultry 243 E5
Tillietudlem 225 G1
Tillingham 138 C2
Tillington *Here* 145 D3
Tillington *WSuss* 121 E5
Tillington Common 145 D3
Tillyarblet 252 D3
Tillybirloch 260 E4
Tillycairn Castle 260 E3
Tillycorthie 261 H2
Tillydrine 260 E5
Tillyfar 269 G6
Tillyfour 260 D3
Tillyfourie 260 E3
Tillygreig 261 G2
Tillypronie 260 C4
Tilmanstone 125 F3
Tiln 187 E4
Tilney All Saints 163 D1
Tilney Fen End 162 D1
Tilney High End 163 D1
Tilney St. Lawrence 162 D1
Tilshead 118 B3
Tilstock 170 C4
Tilston 170 B2
Tilstone Fearnall 170 C1
Tilsworth 149 E5
Tilton on the Hill 160 C2
Tiltups End 132 A3
Timberland 175 G2
Timberland Dales 175 G1
Timbersbrook 171 F1
Timberscombe 114 C3
Timble 194 A2
Timewell 114 C5
Timperley 184 B4
Timsbury *B&NESom* 117 D2
Timsbury *Hants* 119 E5
Timsgearraidh 270 C4
Timworth 151 G1
Timworth Green 151 G1
Tincleton 105 D3
Tindale 210 C2
Tindon End 151 E4
Tingewick 148 B4
Tingley 194 B5
Tingrith 149 F4
Tingwall 276 D5
Tingwall (Lerwick) Airport 279 D8
Tinhay 99 D2
Tinney 98 C1
Tinshill 194 B4
Tinsley 186 B3
Tinsley Green 122 B5
Tintagel 97 E1
Tintagel Castle *Corn* PL34 0HE 97 E1
Tintern Parva 131 E2
Tintinhull 104 A1
Tintwistle 185 E3
Tinwald 217 E2
Tinwell 161 F2
Tippacott 114 A3
Tipperty *Aber* 253 F1
Tipperty *Aber* 261 H2
Tipps End 162 C3
Tiptoe 106 B3
Tipton 158 B3
Tipton St. John 103 D3
Tiptree 138 B1
Tiptree Heath 138 B1
Tiptree Museum *Essex* CO5 0RF 138 C1
Tirabad 143 E3
Tiree 246 A2
Tiree Airport 246 B2
Tirindrish 249 E1
Tirley 146 A5
Tirphil 130 A2
Tirril 210 B5
Tir-y-dail 128 C1
Tisbury 118 A5
Tisman's Common 121 F4
Tissington 172 C2
Tister 275 G2
Titchberry 112 C3
Titchfield 107 E2
Titchmarsh 161 F5
Titchwell 177 F3
Titchwell Marsh *Norf* PE31 8BB 177 F3
Tithby 174 B4
Titley 144 C1
Titlington 229 F5
Titmore Green 150 A5
Titsey 122 D3
Titson 112 C5
Tittensor 171 F4
Tittesworth Reservoir & Visitor Centre *Staffs* ST13 8TQ 171 G2
Tittleshall 177 G5
Tiverton *ChesW&C* 170 C1
Tiverton *Devon* 102 C1
Tivetshall St. Margaret 164 C3
Tivetshall St. Mary 164 C3
Tivington 114 C3
Tixall 171 G5
Tixover 161 E2
Toab *Ork* 277 E7
Toab *Shet* 279 F9
Tobermory 247 E4
Toberonochy 239 G4
Tobson 270 D4
Tocher 260 E1
Tockenham 132 C5
Tockenham Wick 132 C4
Tockholes 192 C5
Tockington 131 F4
Tockwith 195 D2
Todber 117 E5
Toddington *CenBeds* 149 F5
Toddington *Glos* 146 C4
Todenham 147 E4
Todhills *Angus* 244 C1
Todhills *Cumb* 218 B5
Todlachie 260 E3
Todmorden 193 F5
Todwick 186 B4
Toft *Cambs* 150 B2
Toft *Lincs* 161 F1
Toft *Shet* 278 D5
Toft Hill 212 A5
Toft Monks 165 F2
Toft next Newton 188 A4
Toftcarl 275 J4
Toftrees 177 G5
Tofts 275 J2
Toftwood 178 A4
Togston 221 E1
Tokavaig 256 C3
Tokers Green 134 B5
Tolastadh 271 H3
Tolastadh a' Chaolais 270 D4
Tolastadh Ur 271 H3
Toll Bar 186 C2
Toll of Birness 261 J1
Tolland 115 E4
Tollard Farnham 105 F1
Tollard Royal 105 F1
Tollcross 234 A3
Toller Down Gate 104 B2
Toller Fratrum 104 B3
Toller Porcorum 104 B3
Toller Whelme 104 B2
Tollerton *Notts* 174 B4
Tollerton *NYorks* 195 E1
Tollesbury 138 C1
Tollesby 203 E1
Tolleshunt D'Arcy 138 C1
Tolleshunt Knights 138 C1
Tolleshunt Major 138 B1
Tolmachan 270 C7
Tolpuddle 105 D3
Tolvah 259 F5
Tolworth 121 G1
Tom an Fhuadain 271 F6
Tomatin 259 F2
Tombreck 258 D1
Tomchrasky (Tom Chrasgaidh) 257 J3
Tomdoun 257 H4
Tomdow 267 H7
Tomich *High* 257 K2
Tomich *High* 266 E4
Tomich *High* 266 D1
Tomintoul 259 J3
Tomnacross 266 C7
Tomnamoon 267 H6
Tomnaven 260 C1
Tomnavoulin 259 K2
Tomvaich 259 H1
Ton Pentre 129 F3
Tonbridge 123 E4
Tondu 129 E4
Tonedale 115 E5
Tonfanau 154 B2
Tong *Kent* 124 A4
Tong *Shrop* 157 G2
Tong *WYorks* 194 B4
Tong Norton 157 G2
Tong Street 194 A4
Tonge 173 F5
Tongham 121 D3
Tongland 216 A5
Tongue 273 H3
Tongue House 273 H3
Tongwynlais 130 A4
Tonmawr 129 E3
Tonna 129 D3
Tonwell 136 C1
Tonypandy 129 F3
Tonyrefail 129 G4
Toot Baldon 134 A2
Toot Hill 137 E2
Toothill *Hants* 106 C1
Toothill *Swin* 132 D4
Tooting Graveney 136 B5
Top End 149 F1
Top of Hebers 184 C2
Topcliffe 202 D5
Topcroft 165 D2
Topcroft Street 165 D2
Toppesfield 151 F4
Toppings 184 B1
Toprow 164 C2
Topsham 102 C4
Topsham Bridge 100 D2
Torastan 246 B3
Torbain 259 J3
Torbeg *Aber* 260 B5
Torbeg *NAyr* 223 E3
Torbothie 234 C4
Torbryan 101 E1
Torcastle 248 D2
Torcross 101 E3
Tordarroch 258 D1
Tore (An Todhar) 266 D6
Toreduff 267 J5
Toremore *High* 259 J1
Toremore *High* 275 G5
Torfrey 97 F4
Torgyle 257 K3
Torksey 187 F5
Torlum 262 C6
Torlundy (Tòrr Lunndaidh) 248 D2
Tormarton 131 G5
Tormisdale 230 A4
Tormore 223 D2
Tormsdale 275 G3
Tornagrain 266 E6
Tornahaish 259 K4
Tornaveen 260 E4
Torness 258 C2
Toronto 212 A4
Torpenhow 209 F3
Torphichen 235 D2
Torphins 260 E4
Torpoint 100 A2
Torquay 101 F1
Torquhan 236 B5
Torr 100 B2
Torran *A&B* 240 A4
Torran *High* 266 E4
Torran *High* 264 B7
Torrance 234 A2
Torrance House 234 A4
Torrancroy 260 B3
Torre *Som* 114 D3
Torre *Torbay* 101 F1
Torrich 267 F6
Torridon 264 E6
Torrin 256 B2
Torrisdale *A&B* 222 C2
Torrisdale *High* 273 J2
Torrish 274 E7
Torrisholme 192 A1
Torroble 266 C1
Torry *Aber* 268 C6
Torry *Aberdeen* 261 H4
Torryburn 235 E1
Torsonce 236 B5
Torterston 269 J6
Torthorwald 217 E3
Tortington 108 B3
Torton 158 A5
Tortworth 131 G3
Torvaig 263 K7
Torver 199 D3
Torwood 234 C1
Torworth 187 D4
Tosberry 112 C3
Toscaig 256 D1
Toseland 150 A1
Tosside 193 D2
Tostarie 246 C5
Tostock 152 A1
Totaig 263 G6
Totamore 246 A4
Tote 263 K7
Tote Hill 121 D5
Totegan 274 D2
Totford 119 G4
Totham Hill 138 B1
Tothill 189 E4
Totland 106 C4
Totley 186 A5
Totnes 101 E1
Toton 173 G4
Totronald 246 A4
Totscore 263 J5
Tottenham 136 C3
Tottenhill 163 E1
Tottenhill Row 163 E1
Totteridge *Bucks* 135 D3
Totteridge *GtLon* 136 B3
Totternhoe 149 E5
Tottington *GtMan* 184 B1
Tottington *Norf* 163 G3
Totton 106 C1
Toulton 115 E4
Tournaig 264 E3
Toux 269 H5
Tovil 123 G3
Tow Law 212 A4
Towan Cross 96 B5
Toward 232 C3
Towcester 148 B3
Towednack 94 B3
Tower Bridge Exhibition *GtLon* SE1 2UP 12 C4
Tower End 163 E1
Tower of London *GtLon* EC3N 4AB 12 C4
Towersey 134 C2
Towie *Aber* 269 G4
Towie *Aber* 260 D2
Towie *Aber* 260 C3
Towiemore 268 B6
Town End *Cambs* 162 C3
Town End *Cumb* 199 F4
Town End *Mersey* 183 F4
Town Green *Lancs* 183 F2
Town Green *Norf* 179 E4
Town of Lowton 184 A3
Town Row 123 E5
Town Street 163 F4
Town Yetholm 228 C4
Towneley Hall Art Gallery & Museum *Lancs* BB11 3RQ 193 E4
Townfield 211 F3
Townhead *D&G* 207 G2
Townhead *SYorks* 185 F2
Townhead of Greenlaw 216 B4
Townhill *Fife* 235 F1
Townhill *Swan* 128 C3
Towns End 119 G2
Towns Green 170 D1
Townshend 94 C3
Towthorpe *ERid* 196 B1
Towthorpe *York* 195 F2
Towton 195 D4
Towyn 182 A5
Toynton All Saints 176 B1
Toynton Fen Side 176 B1
Toynton St. Peter 176 C1
Toy's Hill 123 D3
Trabboch 224 C3
Traboe 95 E4
Tradespark *High* 267 F6
Tradespark *Ork* 277 D7
Trafford Centre 184 B3
Trafford Park 184 B3
Trago Mills, Newton Abbot *Devon* TQ12 6JD 102 B5
Trallong 143 F5
Trallwn 128 C3
Tram Inn 145 D4
Tranent 236 B2
Tranmere 183 E4
Trantlebeg 274 D3
Trantlemore 274 D3
Tranwell 221 D3
Trap 128 C1
Trap Street 171 F1
Traprain 236 C2
Trap's Green 146 D1
Traquair 227 E2
Trawden 193 F4
Trawscoed (Crosswood) 154 C5
Trawsfynydd 168 A4
Trealaw 129 G3
Treales 192 A4
Trearddur 180 A5
Treaslane 263 J6
Tre-Aubrey 129 G5
Trebah Garden *Corn* TR11 5JZ 95 E4
Trebanog 129 G3
Trebanos 128 D2
Trebarrow 98 C1
Trebartha 97 G2
Trebarvah 95 E3
Trebarwith 97 E1
Trebeath 97 G1
Trebetherick 96 D2
Trebister 279 D9
Tre-boeth 128 C3
Treborough 114 D4
Trebudannon 96 C3
Trebullett 98 D3
Treburley 98 D3
Treburrick 96 C2
Trebyan 97 E3
Trecastle 143 E5
Trecott 113 G5
Trecrogo 98 D2
Trecwn 140 C4
Trecynon 129 F2
Tredaule 97 G1
Tredavoe 94 B4
Treddiog 140 B5
Tredegar 130 A2
Tredington *Glos* 146 B5
Tredington *Warks* 147 E3
Tredinnick *Corn* 96 D3
Tredinnick *Corn* 97 G4
Tredogan 115 D1
Tredomen 144 A4
Tredrissi 141 D3
Tredunnock 130 C3
Tredustan 144 A4
Tredworth 132 A1
Treen *Corn* 94 A4
Treen *Corn* 94 B3
Treesmill 97 E4
Treeton 186 B4
Trefasser 140 B4
Trefdraeth 180 C5
Trefecca 144 A4
Trefechan 129 G2
Trefeglwys 155 F3
Trefenter 142 C1
Treffgarne 140 C5
Treffynnon 140 B5
Trefgarn Owen 140 B5
Trefil 130 A1
Trefilan 142 B2
Trefin 140 B4
Treflach 169 F5
Trefnanney 156 B1
Trefnant 182 B5
Trefonen 169 F5
Trefor *Gwyn* 166 C3
Trefor *IoA* 180 B4
Treforest 129 G4
Treforest Industrial Estate 130 A4
Trefriw 168 A1
Tregadillett 97 G1
Tregaian 180 C5
Tregare 130 D1
Tregarland 97 G4
Tregarne 95 E4
Tregaron 142 C2
Tregarth 167 F1
Tregaswith 96 C3
Tregavethan 96 B5.
Tregear 96 C4
Tregeare 97 G1
Tregeiriog 169 E4
Tregele 180 B3
Tregidden 95 E4
Tregiskey 97 E5
Treglemais 140 B5
Tregolds 96 C2
Tregole 98 B1
Tregonetha 97 D3
Tregony 96 D5
Tregoodwell 97 F1
Tregoss 97 D3
Tregowris 95 E4
Tregoyd 144 A4
Tregrehan Mills 97 E4
Tre-groes 142 A3
Treguff 129 G5
Tregullon 97 E3
Tregunnon 97 G1
Tregurrian 96 C3
Tregynon 155 G3
Trehafod 129 G3
Trehan 100 A2
Treharris 129 G3
Treherbert 129 F3
Tre-hill 129 G5
Trekenner 98 D3
Treknow 97 E1
Trelan 95 E5
Trelash 98 B1
Trelassick 96 C4
Trelawnyd 182 B5
Trelech 141 F4
Treleddyd-fawr 140 A5
Trelewis 130 A3
Treligga 97 E1
Trelights 97 D2
Trelill 97 E2
Trelissick 95 F3
Trelissick *Corn* TR3 6QL 95 F3
Trelleck 131 E2
Trelleck Grange 131 D2
Trelogan 182 C4
Trelowla 97 G4
Trelystan 156 B2
Tremadog 167 E3
Tremail 97 F1
Tremain 141 F3
Tremaine 97 G1
Tremar 97 G3
Trematon 99 D5
Tremeirchion 182 B5
Tremethick Cross 94 B3
Tremore 97 E3
Trenance *Corn* 96 C3
Trenance *Corn* 96 D2
Trenarren 97 E5
Trench *Tel&W* 157 F1
Trench *Wrex* 170 A4
Trencreek 96 C3
Trenear 95 D3
Treneglos 97 G1
Trenewan 97 F4
Trengune 98 B1
Trent 104 B1
Trent Port 187 F4
Trent Vale 171 F3
Trentham 171 F3
Trentishoe 113 G1
Trenwheal 94 D3
Treoes 129 F5
Treorchy 129 F3
Treowen 130 B3
Trequite 97 E2
Tre'r-ddol 154 C3
Trerhyngyll 129 G5
Tre-Rhys 141 E3
Trerulefoot 98 D5
Tresaith 141 F2
Tresco 96 A1
Trescott' 158 A3
Trescowe 94 C3
Tresean 96 B4
Tresham 131 G3
Treshnish 246 C5
Tresillian 96 C5
Tresinney 97 F1
Tresinwen 140 B3
Treskinnick Cross 98 C1
Treslea 97 F3
Tresmeer 97 G1
Tresowes Green 94 D4
Tresparrett 98 B1
Tresparrett Posts 98 B1
Tressait 250 D3
Tresta *Shet* 278 F3
Tresta *Shet* 279 C7
Treswell 187 E5
Trethewey 94 A4
Trethomas 130 A4
Trethurgy 97 E4
Tretio 140 A5
Tretire 145 E5
Tretower 144 A5
Treuddyn 169 F2
Trevadlock 97 G2
Trevalga 98 A1
Trevalyn 170 A2
Trevanson 97 D2
Trevarnon 94 C3
Trevarrack 94 B3
Trevarren 96 D3

Trevarrian **96** C3
Trevarrick **97** D5
Tre-vaughan *Carmar* **141** G5
Tre-vaughan *Carmar* **127** E1
Treveighan **97** E2
Trevellas **96** B4
Trevenen **94** D4
Treverva **95** E3
Trevescan **94** A4
Trevethin **130** B2
Trevigro **98** D4
Treviscoe **96** D4
Trevivian **97** F1
Trevone **96** C2
Trevor **169** F3
Trewalder **97** E2
Trewarmett **97** E1
Trewassa **97** F1
Trewellard **94** A3
Trewen *Corn* **97** G1
Trewen *Here* **131** E1
Trewennack **95** D4
Trewent **126** D3
Trewern **156** B1
Trewethern **97** E2
Trewidland **97** G4
Trewilym **141** E3
Trewint *Corn* **98** B1
Trewint *Corn* **97** G1
Trewithian **95** F3
Trewoon **97** D4
Treworga **96** C5
Treworlas **95** F3
Treworthal **95** F3
Tre-wyn **144** C5
Treyarnon **96** C2
Treyford **108** A2
Trezaise **97** D4
Triangle **193** G5
Trickett's Cross **105** G2
Triermain **210** B1
Trimdon **212** C4
Trimdon Colliery **212** C4
Trimdon Grange **212** C4
Trimingham **179** D2
Trimley Lower Street **153** D4
Trimley St. Martin **153** D4
Trimley St. Mary **153** D4
Trimpley **157** G5
Trimsaran **128** A2
Trimstone **113** E1
Trinafour **250** C3
Trinant **130** B3
Tring **135** E1
Trinity *Angus* **253** E3
Trinity *Chanl* **100** C5
Trinity *Edin* **235** G2
Trisant **154** D5
Triscombe *Som* **114** C4
Triscombe *Som* **115** E4
Trislaig **248** C3
Trispen **96** C4
Tritlington **221** E2
Trochry **243** E1
Troedyraur **141** G3
Troedyrhiw **129** G2
Trofarth **181** G5
Trondavoe **278** C5
Troon *Corn* **95** D3
Troon *SAyr* **224** B2
Tropical Butterfly House,
  Wildlife & Falconry Centre
  SYorks S25 4EQ **21** F3
Tropical World, Roundhay
  WYorks LS8 2ER **27** G1
Trosaraidh **254** C3
Troston **163** G5
Troswell **98** C1
Trottick **244** C1
Trottiscliffe **123** F2
Trotton **120** D5
Trough Gate **193** E5
Troughend **220** A2
Troustan **232** B2
Troutbeck *Cumb* **199** F2
Troutbeck *Cumb* **209** G4
Troutbeck Bridge **199** F2
Trow Green **131** E2
Troway **186** A5
Trowbridge *Cardiff* **130** B4
Trowbridge *Wilts* **117** F2
Trowell **173** F4
Trowle Common **117** F2
Trowley Bottom **135** F1
Trows **228** A3
Trowse Newton **178** D5
Troy **194** B4
Trudernish **230** C4
Trudoxhill **117** E3
Trull **115** F5
Trumaisgearraidh **262** D4
Trumpan **263** H5
Trumpet **145** F4
Trumpington **150** C2
Trumps Green **121** E1
Trunch **179** D2
Trunnah **191** G3
Truro **96** C5
Truro Cathedral *Corn*
  TR1 2AF **96** C5
Truscott **98** D2
Trusham **102** B4
Trusley **173** D4
Trusthorpe **189** F4
Truthan **96** C4
Trysull **158** A3
Tubney **133** G3
Tuckenhay **101** E2
Tuckhill **157** G4
Tuckingmill **96** A4
Tuddenham *Suff* **152** C3
Tuddenham *Suff* **163** F5
Tudeley **123** F4
Tudeley Hale **123** F4
Tudhoe **212** B4
Tudweiliog **166** B4
Tuesley **121** E3
Tuffley **132** A1
Tufton *Hants* **119** F3
Tufton *Pembs* **140** D5
Tugby **160** C2
Tugford **157** E4
Tughall **229** G4
Tulchan **243** E2

Tulleys Farm *WSuss*
  RH10 4PE **122** C5
Tullibardine Distillery *P&K*
  PH4 1QG **243** E2
Tullibody **242** A5
Tullich *A&B* **240** C3
Tullich *A&B* **240** A3
Tullich *High* **267** F4
Tullich *High* **258** D2
Tullich *Moray* **268** B6
Tullich *Stir* **242** A1
Tullich Muir **266** E4
Tulliemet **251** E4
Tulloch *Aber* **261** G1
Tulloch *High* **266** D2
Tulloch *Moray* **267** H6
Tullochgorm **240** B5
Tullochgribban High **259** G2
Tullochvenus **260** D4
Tulloes **252** D5
Tumble (Y Tumbl) **128** B1
Tumby **176** A2
Tumby Woodside **176** A2
Tummel Bridge **250** C4
Tunbridge Wells **123** E5
Tundergarth Mains **217** F2
Tunga **271** G4
Tungate **179** D3
Tunley **117** E2
Tunstall *ERid* **197** F4
Tunstall *Kent* **124** A2
Tunstall *Lancs* **200** B5
Tunstall *Norf* **179** F5
Tunstall *NYorks* **202** B3
Tunstall *Stoke* **171** F2
Tunstall *Suff* **153** E2
Tunstall *T&W* **212** C2
Tunstead *GtMan* **185** E2
Tunstead *Norf* **179** E3
Tunstead Milton **185** E4
Tunworth **120** B3
Tupholme **175** E1
Tupsley **145** E4
Tupton **173** E1
Tur Langton **160** C3
Turbiskill **231** F1
Turclossie **269** G5
Turgis Green **120** B2
Turin **252** D4
Turkdean **132** D1
Turleigh **117** F1
Turn **184** C1
Turnastone **144** C4
Turnberry **224** A5
Turnchapel **100** A2
Turnditch **173** D3
Turner's Green **147** D1
Turners Hill **122** C5
Turners Puddle **105** E3
Turnford **136** C2
Turnworth **105** E2
Turret Bridge **257** K5
Turriff **269** G5
Turton Bottoms **184** B1
Turvey **149** E2
Turville **134** C3
Turville Heath **134** C3
Turweston **148** B4
Tutankhamun Exhibition,
  Dorchester *Dorset*
  DT1 1UW **104** C3
Tutbury **172** D5
Tutbury Castle *Staffs* DE13
  9JF **172** D5
Tutnall **158** B5
Tutshill **131** E3
Tuttington **178** D3
Tutts Clump **134** A5
Tutwell **99** D3
Tuxford **187** E5
Twatt *Ork* **276** B5
Twatt *Shet* **279** C7
Twechar **234** B2
Tweedbank **227** G2
Tweedmouth **237** G4
Tweedsmuir **226** B3
Twelve Oaks **110** B1
Twelveheads **96** B5
Twemlow Green **171** E2
Twenty **175** G5
Twickenham **136** A5
Twigworth **146** A5
Twineham **109** E1
Twineham Green **109** E1
Twinhoe **117** E2
Twinstead **151** G4
Twiss Green **184** A3
Twiston **193** E3
Twitchen *Devon* **114** A4
Twitchen *Shrop* **156** C5
Twitton **123** E3
Twizell House **229** F4
Two Bridges *Devon* **99** G3
Two Bridges *Glos* **131** F2
Two Dales **173** D1
Two Gates **159** E2
Two Mills **183** E5
Twycross **159** F2
Twycross Zoo *Leics*
  CV9 3PX **159** F2
Twyford *Bucks* **148** B5
Twyford *Derbys* **173** D5
Twyford *Dorset* **105** E1
Twyford *Hants* **119** F5
Twyford *Leics* **160** C1
Twyford *Norf* **178** B3
Twyford *Oxon* **147** G4
Twyford *W'ham* **134** C5
Twyford Common **145** E4
Twyn Shôn-Ifan **130** A4
Twynholm **216** A5
Twyning **146** A4
Twynllanan **143** D5
Twyn-yr-odyn **130** A5
Twyn-y-Sheriff **130** D2
Twywell **161** E5
Ty Croes **180** B5
Tyberton **144** C4
Tycroes **128** C1

Tycrwyn **156** A1
Tydd Gote **162** C1
Tydd St. Giles **162** C1
Tydd St. Mary **162** C1
Tye Green *Essex* **151** F5
Tye Green *Essex* **150** D5
Tye Green *Essex* **137** F1
Tye Green *Essex* **136** D2
Tyersal **194** A4
Tyldesley **184** A2
Tyler Hill **124** D2
Tylers Green *Bucks* **135** E3
Tyler's Green *Essex* **137** E2
Tylorstown **129** G3
Tylwch **155** F5
Tyndrum **241** F4
  (Taigh an Droma)
Tyneham **105** E4
Tynehead **236** A4
Tynemouth **212** C1
Tynewydd **129** F3
Ty Hatherley **146** B5
Tyninghame **236** D2
Tynron **216** C1
Tyntesfield **131** E5
Ty-n-y-cefn **169** D3
Ty'n-y-coedcae **130** A4
Tyn-y-cwm **155** E4
Ty'n-y-ffridd **169** E4
Ty'n-y-garn **124** F4
Ty-n-y-gongl **180** D4
Tynygraig *Cere* **142** C1
Tyn-y-graig
  Powys **143** G3
Ty'n-y-groes **181** F5
Tyrie **269** H4
Tyringham **149** D3
Tyseley **158** D4
Tythegston **129** E5
Tytherington *ChesE* **184** D5
Tytherington *SGlos* **131** F4
Tytherington *Som* **117** E3
Tytherington *Wilts* **118** A3
Tytherton Lucas **132** B5
Tyttenhanger **136** A2
Ty-uchaf **168** C5
Tywardreath **97** E4
Tywardreath Highway **97** E4
Tywyn **154** B2

U

Uachdar **262** D6
Uags **256** D1
Ubberley **171** G3
Ubbeston Green **165** E4
Ubley **116** C2
Uckerby **202** B2
Uckfield **109** G1
Uckington *Glos* **146** A4
Uckington *Shrop* **157** E2
Uddingston **234** A3
Uddington **225** G2
Udimore **111** D2
Udley **116** B1
Udny Green **261** G3
Udny Station **261** H2
Udston **234** B4
Udstonhead **234** B5
Uffcott **132** D5
Uffculme **103** D1
Uffington *Lincs* **161** F2
Uffington *Oxon* **133** F3
Uffington *Shrop* **157** E1
Ufford *Peter* **161** F2
Ufford *Suff* **153** D2
Ufton **147** F1
Ufton Green **120** B1
Ufton Nervet **120** B1
Ugborough **100** C2
Ugford **118** B4
Uggeshall **165** F3
Ugglebarnby **204** B2
Ugley **150** D5
Ugley Green **150** D5
Ugthorpe **203** G1
Uidh **254** B5
Uig *A&B* **246** A4
Uig *A&B* **232** C1
Uig (Uige) **270** C4
Uig *High* **263** H7
Uig *High* **263** J5
Uig *High* **263** G6
Uigen **270** C4
Uiginish **263** H7
Uigshader **263** K7
Uisken **238** C3
Uiskevagh
  (Uisgebhagh) **262** D6
Ulbster **275** J4
Ulcat Row **210** A5
Ulceby *Lincs* **189** E5
Ulceby *NLincs* **188** B1
Ulceby Cross **189** E5
Ulceby Skitter **188** B1
Ulcombe **124** A4
Uldale **209** F3
Uldale House **200** C3
Uley **131** G3
Ulgham **221** E2
Ullapool (Ullapul) **265** H2
Ullenhall **146** D1
Ullenwood **132** B1
Ulleskelf **195** E4
Ullesthorpe **160** A4
Ulley **186** B4
Ulley Reservoir Country Park
  SYorks S26 3XL **21** E2
Ullingswick **145** E3
Ullinish **255** J1
Ullock **209** D4
Ulpha *Cumb* **198** C3
Ulpha *Cumb* **199** F4
Ulrome **197** D2
Ulsta **278** D4
Ulting **138** B2
Ulva **238** D1
Ulverston **199** D5
Ulwell **105** G4
Ulzieside **225** F5

Umberleigh **113** G3
Unapool **272** E5
Underbarrow **199** F3
Undercliffe **194** A4
Underhill **136** B3
Underhoull **278** D2
Underling Green **123** G4
Underriver **123** E3
Underwood *Newport* **130** C4
Underwood *Notts* **173** F2
Underwood *Plym* **100** B2
Undley **163** E4
Undy **130** D4
Ungisiadar **270** D5
Unifirth **279** B7
Union Croft **261** G5
Union Mills **190** B4
Union Street **123** G5
University of Glasgow Visitor
  Centre *Glas*
  G12 8QQ **38** B1
Unst **278** F1
Unst Airport **278** F2
Unstone **186** A5
Unstone Green **186** A5
Unsworth **184** C2
Unthank *Cumb* **210** A4
Unthank *Derbys* **186** A5
Up Cerne **104** C2
Up Exe **102** C2
Up Hatherley **146** B5
Up Holland **183** G2
Up Marden **107** G1
Up Mudford **104** B1
Up Nately **120** B2
Up Somborne **119** E4
Up Sydling **104** C2
Upavon **118** C2
Upchurch **124** A2
Upcott *Devon* **99** E1
Upcott *Devon* **113** F2
Upcott *Here* **144** C2
Upcott *Som* **114** C5
Upend **151** E2
Upgate **178** C4
Upgate Street *Norf* **164** D2
Upgate Street *Norf* **165** D2
Uphall *Dorset* **104** B2
Uphall *WLoth* **235** E2
Uphall Station **235** E3
Upham *Devon* **102** B2
Upham *Hants* **119** G5
Uphampton *Here* **144** C1
Uphampton *Worcs* **146** A1
Uphempston **101** E1
Uphill **116** A2
Uplands *Glos* **132** A2
Uplands *Swan* **128** C3
Uplawmoor **233** F4
Upleadon **145** G5
Upleatham **203** F1
Uplees **124** C2
Uploders **104** B3
Uplowman **102** D1
Uplyme **103** F2
Upminster **137** E4
Upottery **103** F2
Upper Affcot **156** D4
Upper Ardroscadale **232** B3
Upper Arley **157** G4
Upper Arncott **134** B1
Upper Astley **157** E1
Upper Astrop **148** A4
Upper Barvas **271** F2
Upper Basildon **134** B5
Upper Bayble
  (Pabail Uarach) **271** H4
Upper Beeding **109** D2
Upper Benefield **161** E4
Upper Bentley **146** B1
Upper Berwick **157** D1
Upper Bighouse **274** D3
Upper Boat **130** A4
Upper Boddam **260** E1
Upper Boddington **147** G2
Upper Borth **154** C4
Upper Boyndlie **269** H4
Upper Brailes **147** F4
Upper Breakish **256** C2
Upper Breinton **145** D3
Upper Broadheath **146** A2
Upper Broughton **174** B5
Upper Brynamman **128** D1
Upper Bucklebury **119** G1
Upper Burgate **106** A1
Upper Burnhaugh **261** G5
Upper Caldecote **149** G3
Upper Camster **275** H4
Upper Canada **116** A2
Upper Catesby **148** A2
Upper Catshill **158** B5
Upper Chapel **143** G3
Upper Chicksgrove **118** A4
Upper Chute **119** D2
Upper Clatford **119** E3
Upper Coberley **132** B1
Upper Colwall **145** G3
Upper Cotton **172** B3
Upper Cound **157** E2
Upper Cumberworth **185** G2
Upper Cwmbran **130** B3
Upper Dallachy **268** B4
Upper Dean **149** F1
Upper Denby **185** G2
Upper Denton **210** C1
Upper Derraid **259** H1
Upper Derwent Reservoirs
  Derbys S33 0AQ **185** F4
Upper Diabaig **264** E5
Upper Dicker **110** A2
Upper Dovercourt **152** D4
Upper Dunsley **135** E1
Upper Eastern Green **159** E4
Upper Eathie **266** E5
Upper Egleton **145** F3
Upper Elkstone **172** B2
Upper End **185** E5
Upper Enham **119** E3
Upper Farringdon **120** C4
Upper Framilode **131** G1
Upper Froyle **120** C3
Upper Gills **275** J1
Upper Glendessarry **257** F5
Upper Godney **116** B3
Upper Gornal **158** B3

Upper Gravenhurst **149** G4
Upper Green *Essex* **150** C4
Upper Green *Essex* **151** D4
Upper Green *Mon* **130** C1
Upper Green *WBerks* **119** E1
Upper Grove Common **145** E5
Upper Gylen **240** A2
Upper Hackney **173** D1
Upper Halliford **121** F1
Upper Halling **123** F2
Upper Hambleton **161** E2
Upper Hardres Court **125** D3
Upper Hardwick **145** D1
Upper Hartfield **123** D5
Upper Hatton **171** F4
Upper Hawkhillock **261** J1
Upper Hayesden **123** E4
Upper Hayton **157** E4
Upper Heath **157** E4
Upper Heaton **185** F1
Upper Helmsley **195** F2
Upper Hellesdon **178** D4
Upper Hengoed **169** F4
Upper Hergest **144** B2
Upper Heyford
  N'hants **148** B2
Upper Heyford
  Oxon **147** G5
Upper Hill *Here* **145** D2
Upper Hill *SGlos* **131** F3
Upper Horsebridge **110** A2
Upper Howsell **145** G3
Upper Hulme **172** B1
Upper Inglesham **133** E3
Upper Kilchattan **238** C5
Upper Killay **128** B3
Upper Knockando **267** J7
Upper Lambourn **133** F4
Upper Langford **116** B2
Upper Langwith **173** G1
Upper Largo **244** C4
Upper Leigh **172** B4
Upper Ley **131** G1
Upper Loads **173** E1
Upper Lochton **260** E5
Upper Longdon **158** C1
Upper Longwood **157** F2
Upper Ludstone **158** A3
Upper Lybster **275** H5
Upper Lydbrook **131** F1
Upper Lyde **145** D3
Upper Lye **144** C1
Upper Maes-coed **144** C4
Upper Midhope **185** G3
Upper Milovaig **263** G7
Upper Milton **133** E1
Upper Minety **132** C3
Upper Moor **146** B3
Upper Morton **131** F3
Upper Muirskie **261** G5
Upper Nash **126** D2
Upper Newbold **186** A5
Upper North Dean **135** D3
Upper Norwood **136** C5
Upper Obney **243** F1
Upper Oddington **147** E5
Upper Ollach **256** B1
Upper Padley **185** G5
Upper Pennington **106** B3
Upper Pollicott **134** C1
Upper Poppleton **195** E2
Upper Quinton **147** D3
Upper Ratley **119** E5
Upper Ridinghill **269** J5
Upper Rissington **147** E5
Upper Rochford **145** F1
Upper Sanday **277** E7
Upper Sapey **145** F1
Upper Scolton **140** C5
Upper Seagry **132** B4
Upper Shelton **149** E3
Upper Sheringham **178** C1
Upper Shuckburgh **147** G1
Upper Siddington **132** C3
Upper Skelmorlie **232** D3
Upper Slaughter **147** D5
Upper Sonachan **240** C2
Upper Soudley **131** F1
Upper Staploe **149** G2
Upper Stoke **179** D5
Upper Stondon **149** G4
Upper Stowe **148** B2
Upper Street *Hants* **106** A1
Upper Street *Norf* **179** E4
Upper Street *Norf* **164** C4
Upper Street *Suff* **153** D3
Upper Street *Suff* **152** C2
Upper Strensham **146** B4
Upper Sundon **149** F5
Upper Swanmore **107** E1
Upper Swell **147** D5
Upper Tean **172** B4
Upper Thurnham **192** A2
Upper Tillyrie **243** G3
Upper Tooting **136** B5
Upper Town *Derbys* **172** D1
Upper Town *Derbys* **173** D2
Upper Town *Derbys* **172** D2
Upper Town *Here* **145** E3
Upper Town *NSom* **116** C1
Upper Tysoe **147** F3
Upper Upham **133** E5
Upper Upnor **137** G5
Upper Victoria **244** C1
Upper Vobster **117** E3
Upper Wardington **147** G3
Upper Waterhay **132** C3
Upper Weald **148** D4
Upper Weedon **148** B2
Upper Welson **144** B2
Upper Weston **117** E1
Upper Whiston **186** B4
Upper Wick **146** A2
Upper Wield **120** B4
Upper Winchendon (Over
  Winchendon) **134** C1
Upper Witton **158** C3
Upper Woodford **118** C4
Upper Woolhampton **119** G1
Upper Wootton **119** G2
Upper Wraxall **132** A5
Upper Wyche **145** G3
Upperby **210** A2
Uppermill **185** D2
Upperthong **185** F2
Upperton **121** E5
Uppertown *Derbys* **173** E1
Uppertown *Ork* **275** J1

Uppingham **161** D2
Uppington **157** E2
Upsall **203** D4
Upsettlington **237** F5
Upshire **136** D2
Upstreet **125** D2
Upthorpe **164** A4
Upton *Bucks* **134** C1
Upton *Cambs* **161** G5
Upton *ChesW&C* **170** B1
Upton *Corn* **97** G2
Upton *Corn* **112** C5
Upton *Devon* **103** D2
Upton *Devon* **100** D3
Upton *Dorset* **105** F3
Upton *Dorset* **105** G3
Upton *Hants* **119** D2
Upton *Hants* **106** C1
Upton *Leics* **159** F3
Upton *Lincs* **187** F4
Upton *Mersey* **183** D4
Upton *N'hants* **148** C1
Upton *Norf* **179** E4
Upton *Notts* **187** E5
Upton *Notts* **174** C2
Upton *Oxon* **134** A4
Upton *Oxon* **133** E1
Upton *Pembs* **126** D2
Upton *Peter* **161** G2
Upton *Slo* **135** E5
Upton *Som* **114** C5
Upton *Som* **116** B5
Upton *Wilts* **117** F4
Upton *WYorks* **186** B1
Upton Bishop **145** F5
Upton Cheyney **117** D1
Upton Country Park *Poole*
  BH17 7BJ **3** A3
Upton Cressett **157** F3
Upton Crews **145** F5
Upton Cross **97** G2
Upton End **149** G4
Upton Grey **120** B3
Upton Hellions **102** B2
Upton Lovell **118** A3
Upton Magna **157** E1
Upton Noble **117** E4
Upton Park **136** D4
Upton Pyne **102** C3
Upton St. Leonards **132** A1
Upton Scudamore **117** F3
Upton Snodsbury **146** B2
Upton upon Severn **146** A3
Upton Warren **146** B1
Upwaltham **108** B2
Upware **162** D5
Upwell **162** D2
Upwey **104** C4
Upwick Green **150** C5
Upwood **162** A4
Uradale **279** D9
Urafirth **278** C5
Urchany **267** F7
Urchfont **118** C2
Urdimarsh **145** E3
Ure **278** B5
Urgha **263** G2
Urlay Nook **202** D1
Urmston **184** B3
Urpeth **212** B2
Urquhart *High* **266** C6
Urquhart *Moray* **267** K5
Urquhart Castle *High*
  IV63 6XJ **258** C2
Urra **203** E2
Urray **266** C6
Ushaw Moor **212** B3
Usher Hall, Edinburgh *Edin*
  EH1 2EA **36** E5
Usk (Brynbuga) **130** C2
Usselby **188** A3
Usworth **212** C2
Utley **193** G3
Uton **102** B3
Utterby **188** D3
Uttoxeter **172** B4
Uwchmynydd **166** A5
Uxbridge **135** F4
Uyeasound **278** E2
Uzmaston **126** C1

V

Valley (Y Fali) **180** A5
Valley Truckle **97** F1
Valleyfield *D&G* **216** A5
Valleyfield *Fife* **235** E1
Valsgarth **278** F1
Vange **137** G4
Vardre **128** C2
Varteg **130** B2
Vatersay (Bhatarsaigh)
  254 B5
Vatsetter **278** E4
Vatten **263** H7
Vaul **246** B2
Vaynor **129** G1
Vaynor Park **156** A2
Veaullt **144** A2
Veensgarth **279** D8
Velindre *Pembs* **141** D4
Velindre *Powys* **144** A4
Vellow **115** D4
Veness **276** E5
Venn **100** D3
Venn Ottery **103** D3
Venngreen **113** D4
Vennington **156** C1
Venny Tedburn **102** B3
Venterdon **99** D3
Ventnor **107** E5
Ventnor Botanic Gardens *IoW*
  PO38 1UL **107** E5
Venton **100** B2
Venue Cymru, Llandudno
  Conwy LL30 1BB **181** F4
Vernham Dean **119** E2
Vernham Street **119** E2
Vernolds Common **157** D4
Verwood **105** G2
Veryan **95** G3
Veryan Green **96** D5
Vickerstown **191** E1
Victoria **97** D3
Victoria & Albert Museum
  GtLon SW7 2RL **11** F5

Victoria Art Gallery *B&NESom*
  BA2 4AT **63** Bath
Vidlin **279** D6
Viewfield **275** F2
Viewpark **234** B3
Vigo **158** C3
Vigo Village **123** F2
Villavin **113** F4
Vinehall Street **110** C1
Vine's Cross **110** A2
Viney Hill **131** F2
Virginia Water **121** E1
Virginstow **99** D1
Virley **138** C1
Vobster **117** E3
Voe *Shet* **279** D6
Voe *Shet* **278** C4
Vogrie Country Park *Midlo*
  EH23 4NU **32** D4
Voirrey Embroidery *Mersey*
  CH63 6JA **22** A5
Volks Electric Railway *B&H*
  BN21 1EN **109** F3
Vowchurch **144** C4
Voy **277** B6
Vron Gate **156** C2

W

W.R. Outhwaite & Son
  Ropemakers *NYorks*
  DL8 3NT **201** D4
Waberthwaite **198** C3
Wackerfield **212** A5
Wacton **164** C2
Wadbister **279** D8
Wadborough **146** B3
Waddesdon **134** C1
Waddesdon Manor *Bucks*
  HP18 0JH **134** C1
Waddeton **101** E2
Waddicar **183** E3
Waddingham **187** G2
Waddington *Lancs* **192** D3
Waddington *Lincs* **175** E3
Waddingworth **188** B5
Waddon *Devon* **102** B5
Waddon *GtLon* **122** C2
Wadebridge **97** D2
Wadeford **103** G2
Wadenhoe **161** F4
Wadesmill **136** C1
Wadhurst **123** F5
Wadshelf **186** A5
Wadworth **186** C3
Wadworth Hill **197** E5
Waen *Denb* **169** E1
Waen *Denb* **168** C1
Waen Aberwheeler **169** D1
Waen-fâch **156** B1
Waen-wen **167** E1
Wag **275** F6
Wainfleet All Saints **176** C2
Wainfleet Bank **176** C2
Wainfleet St. Mary **176** C2
Wainford **165** E2
Waingroves **173** F3
Wainhouse Corner **98** B1
Wainscott **137** G5
Wainstalls **193** G5
Waitby **200** C2
Wakefield **194** C5
Wakehurst Place *WSuss*
  RH17 6TN **122** C5
Wakerley **161** E3
Wakes Colne **151** G5
Walberswick **165** F4
Walberton **108** B3
Walbottle **212** A1
Walcot *Lincs* **175** F4
Walcot *Lincs* **175** G2
Walcot *NLincs* **196** A5
Walcot *Shrop* **156** C4
Walcot *Tel&W* **157** E1
Walcot Green **164** C3
Walcote *Leics* **160** A4
Walcote *Warks* **146** D2
Walcott **179** E2
Walcott Dales **175** G2
Walden **201** F4
Walden Head **201** E4
Walden Stubbs **186** C1
Walderslade **123** G2
Walderton **107** G1
Walditch **104** A3
Waldley **172** C4
Waldridge **212** B3
Waldron **110** A2
Wales **186** B4
Wales Millennium Centre,
  Cardiff *Cardiff*
  CF10 5AL **130** A5
Walesby *Lincs* **188** B3
Walesby *Notts* **187** D5
Waleswood **186** B4
Walford *Here* **156** C5
Walford *Here* **145** E5
Walford *Shrop* **170** B5
Walford *Staffs* **171** F4
Walford Heath **156** D1
Walgherton **171** D3
Walgrave **160** D5
Walhampton **106** C3
Walk Mill **193** E5
Walkden **184** B2
Walker **212** B1
Walker Art Gallery, Liverpool
  Mersey L3 8EL **42** D3
Walker Fold **192** C3
Walkerburn **227** E2
Walkeringham **187** E3
Walkerith **187** E3
Walkern **150** A5
Walker's Green **145** E3
Walkford **106** B3
Walkhampton **100** B1
Walkington **196** B4
Walkwood **146** C1
Wall *Corn* **94** D3
Wall *N'umb* **211** F1
Wall *Staffs* **158** D2
Wall End **198** D4
Wall Heath **158** A4
Wall Houses **211** G1
Wall under Heywood **157** E3
Wallace Collection, London
  GtLon W1U 3BN **44** A2

315

Wallacehall 218 A4
Wallacetown 224 A5
Wallasey 183 D3
Wallend 124 A1
Waller's Green 145 F4
Wallingford 134 B4
Wallington GtLon 122 B2
Wallington Hants 107 E2
Wallington Herts 150 A4
Wallingwells 186 C4
Wallis 140 D5
Wallisdown 105 G3
Walliswood 121 G4
Walls 279 B8
Wallsend 212 C1
Wallyford 236 A2
Walmer 125 F3
Walmer Bridge 192 A5
Walmersley 184 C1
Walmley 158 D3
Walmsgate 189 D5
Walpole 165 E4
Walpole Cross Keys 162 D1
Walpole Highway 162 D1
Walpole Marsh 162 C1
Walpole St. Andrew 162 D1
Walpole St. Peter 162 D1
Walrond's Park 116 A5
Walrow 116 A3
Walsall 158 C3
Walsall Arboretum Illuminations WMid WS1 2AB 14 D1
Walsall Wood 158 C2
Walsden 184 B1
Walsgrave on Sowe 159 F4
Walsham le Willows 164 B4
Walshford 194 D2
Walsoken 162 C1
Walston 235 E5
Walsworth 149 G4
Walter's Ash 134 D3
Walterston 129 G5
Walterstone 144 C5
Waltham Kent 124 D4
Waltham NELincs 188 C2
Waltham Abbey 136 C2
Waltham Chase 107 E1
Waltham Cross 136 C2
Waltham on the Wolds 174 C5
Waltham St. Lawrence 134 D5
Walthamstow 136 C4
Walton Bucks 134 D1
Walton Cumb 210 B1
Walton Derbys 173 E1
Walton Leics 160 A4
Walton Mersey 183 E3
Walton MK 149 D4
Walton Peter 161 G2
Walton Powys 144 B2
Walton Shrop 157 D5
Walton Som 116 B4
Walton Staffs 171 F4
Walton Suff 153 E4
Walton Tel&W 157 E1
Walton Warks 147 E2
Walton WYorks 186 A1
Walton WYorks 194 D3
Walton Cardiff 146 B4
Walton East 140 D5
Walton Elm 105 D1
Walton Hall Gardens Warr WA4 6SN 23 H4
Walton Highway 162 C1
Walton Lower Street 153 E4
Walton on the Hill 122 B3
Walton on the Naze 153 D5
Walton on the Wolds 160 A4
Walton Park D&G 216 B3
Walton Park NSom 130 D5
Walton West 152 B5
Walton-in-Gordano 130 D5
Walton-le-Dale 192 B5
Walton-on-Thames 121 G1
Walton-on-the-Hill 172 B1
Walton-on-Trent 159 E1
Walwen Flints 182 C5
Walwen Flints 182 D5
Walwick 220 B4
Walworth 202 B1
Walworth Gate 212 B5
Walwyn's Castle 126 B1
Wambrook 103 F2
Wanborough Surr 121 E3
Wanborough Swin 133 E4
Wandel 226 A3
Wandon 229 E4
Wandon End 149 G5
Wandsworth 136 B5
Wandylaw 229 F4
Wangford Suff 165 F3
Wangford Suff 163 F4
Wanlip 160 A1
Wanlockhead 225 G4
Wannock 110 A3
Wansbeck Riverside Park N'umb NE63 8TX 221 E3
Wansford ERid 196 C2
Wansford Peter 161 F3
Wanshurst Green 123 G4
Wanstrow 117 E3
Wanswell 131 F2
Wantage 133 F4
Wapley 131 G5
Wappenbury 147 F1
Wappenham 148 B3
Warblebank 209 F2
Warbleton 110 B2
Warblington 107 G2
Warborough 133 G3
Warboys 162 B4
Warbreck 191 G4
Warburton 184 A4
Warcop 200 C1
Ward End 158 D4
Ward Green 152 B1
Warden Kent 124 C1
Warden N'umb 211 F1
Warden Hill 146 B5
Warden Street 149 G3
Wardhouse 260 D1
Wardle ChesE 170 C1

Wardle GtMan 184 D1
Wardley GtMan 184 B2
Wardley Rut 160 D2
Wardley T&W 212 C1
Wardlow 185 F5
Wardsend 184 D4
Wardy Hill 162 C4
Ware Herts 136 C1
Ware Kent 125 E2
Wareham 105 F4
Warehorne 124 B5
Waren Mill 229 F3
Warenford 229 F4
Warenton 229 F3
Wareside 136 C1
Waresley Cambs 150 A2
Waresley Worcs 158 A5
Warfield 135 D5
Wargrave Mersey 183 G3
Wargrave W'ham 134 C5
Warham Here 145 D4
Warham Norf 178 A1
Warkleigh 113 G3
Warkton 161 D5
Warkworth N'hants 147 G3
Warkworth N'umb 221 E1
Warland 193 F5
Warleggan 97 F3
Warley Essex 137 E3
Warley WMid 158 C4
Warley Town 193 G5
Warlingham 122 C3
Warmfield 194 C5
Warmingham 171 E1
Warminghurst 108 D2
Warmington N'hants 161 F3
Warmington Warks 147 G3
Warminster 117 F3
Warmlake 124 A4
Warmley 131 F5
Warmley Hill 131 F5
Warmsworth 186 C2
Warmwell 105 D4
Warndon 146 A2
Warners End 135 F2
Warnford 120 B5
Warnham 121 G4
Warningcamp 108 C3
Warninglid 109 E1
Warren ChesE 184 C5
Warren Pembs 126 C3
Warren House 99 E3
Warren Row 134 D4
Warren Street 124 B3
Warrenby 213 E5
Warren's Green 150 A5
Warrington MK 149 D2
Warrington Warr 184 A4
Warroch 243 F4
Warsash 107 D2
Warslow 172 B2
Warsop Vale 173 G1
Warter 196 A2
Warthill 195 F2
Wartle 260 D4
Wartling 110 B3
Wartnaby 174 C5
Warton Lancs 199 G5
Warton Lancs 192 A5
Warton N'umb 220 C1
Warton Warks 159 E2
Warton Bank 192 A5
Warwick 147 E1
Warwick Bridge 210 A2
Warwick Wold 122 C3
Warwick Castle Works CV34 4QU 16 A6
Warwick-on-Eden 210 A2
Wasbister 276 C4
Wasdale Head 198 C2
Wash 185 E4
Wash Common 119 F1
Washall Green 150 C4
Washaway 97 E3
Washbourne 101 D2
Washbrook 116 B3
Washfield 102 C1
Washfold 201 F2
Washford Som 114 D3
Washford Warks 146 C1
Washford Pyne 102 B1
Washingborough 188 A5
Washington T&W 212 C2
Washington WSuss 108 D2
Washmere Green 152 A3
Wasing 119 G1
Waskerley 211 G3
Wasperton 147 E2
Wasps Nest 175 F1
Wass 203 E5
Wat Tyler Country Park Essex SS16 4UH 137 G4
Watchet 115 D3
Watchfield Oxon 133 E3
Watchfield Som 116 A3
Watchgate 199 G3
Watcombe 101 F1
Watendlath 209 F5
Water 193 E5
Water Eaton MK 149 D4
Water Eaton Oxon 134 A2
Water End Bed 149 G3
Water End CenBeds 149 G4
Water End Essex 151 D3
Water End ERid 195 G4
Water End Herts 136 B2
Water End Herts 135 F1
Water Newton 161 G3
Water Orton 159 D3
Water Stratford 148 B4
Water Yeat 199 E4
Waterbeach 150 C1
Waterbeck 218 A4
Watercombe 105 D4
Waterend 134 C3
Waterfall 172 B2
Waterfoot ERenf 233 G4
Waterfoot Lancs 193 E5
Waterford 136 C1
Watergate 97 F1
Waterhead Cumb 199 E2
Waterhead D&G 216 B2
Waterheath 165 F2
Waterhill of Bruxie 269 H6

Waterhouses Dur 212 A3
Waterhouses Staffs 172 B2
Wateringbury 123 F3
Waterlane 132 B2
Waterloo Aber 261 J1
Waterloo Derbys 173 F1
Waterloo GtMan 184 D2
Waterloo High 256 C2
Waterloo Mersey 183 E3
Waterloo NLan 234 C4
Waterloo Norf 178 D4
Waterloo P&K 243 F1
Waterloo Pembs 126 C2
Waterloo Poole 105 G3
Waterloo Port 167 D1
Waterloo Cross 103 D1
Waterlooville 107 F1
Watermead Country Park Leics LE7 4PF 17 C2
Watermeetings 226 A4
Watermillock 210 A2
Waterperry 134 B2
Waterperry Oxon OX33 1JZ 134 B2
Waterrow 115 D5
Waters Upton 157 F1
Watersfield 108 C2
Watershedings 184 D2
Waterside Aber 260 B3
Waterside Aber 261 J2
Waterside B'burn 192 D5
Waterside Bucks 135 E2
Waterside EAyr 224 C5
Waterside EAyr 233 F5
Waterside EDun 234 A2
Watersmeet House Devon EX35 6NT 114 A3
Waterstock 134 B2
Waterston 126 C2
Waterthorpe 186 B4
Waterworld, Hanley ST1 5PU 85 Stoke-on-Trent
Watford Herts 136 A3
Watford N'hants 148 B1
Watford Park 130 A4
Wath NYorks 202 C5
Wath NYorks 194 A1
Wath upon Dearne 186 B2
Watley's End 131 F4
Watlington Norf 163 E1
Watlington Oxon 134 B3
Watnall 173 G3
Watten 275 H3
Wattisfield 164 B4
Wattisham 152 B2
Watton Dorset 104 A3
Watton ERid 196 C3
Watton Norf 178 A5
Watton at Stone 136 C1
Watton Green 178 A5
Watton's Green 137 E3
Wattston 234 B3
Wattstown 129 G3
Wattsville 130 B3
Waughtonhill 269 H5
Waun Fawr 154 C4
Waun y Clyn 128 A2
Waunarlwydd 128 C3
Waunclunda 142 C4
Waunfawr 167 E2
Waun-Lwyd 130 A2
Wavendon 149 E4
Waverbridge 209 F2
Waverton ChesW&C 170 B1
Waverton Cumb 209 F2
Wavertree 183 E4
Wawne 196 C4
Waxham 179 F3
Waxholme 197 F5
Way Gill 193 F1
Way Village 102 B1
Way Wick 116 A1
Wayford 104 A2
Waytown 104 A3
Weachyburn 268 E5
Weacombe 115 E3
Weald 133 F2
Weald & Downland Open Air Museum WSuss PO18 0EU 108 A2
Weald Country Park Essex CM14 5QS 137 E3
Wealdstone 136 A3
Weardley 194 B3
Weare 116 B2
Weare Giffard 113 E3
Wearhead 211 E4
Wearne 116 B5
Weasenham All Saints 177 G5
Weasenham St. Peter 177 G5
Weatheroak Hill 158 C5
Weathercote 200 C5
Weaverham 184 A5
Weaverthorpe 204 C5
Webheath 146 C1
Webton 144 D4
Wedderlairs 261 G1
Weddington 159 F3
Wedhampton 118 B2
Wedmore 116 B3
Wednesbury 158 B3
Wednesfield 158 B3
Weedon 134 D1
Weedon Bec 148 B2
Weedon Lois 148 B3
Weeford 158 D2
Week Devon 102 A1
Week Devon 101 D1
Week Som 114 C4
Week Orchard 112 C5
Week St. Mary 98 C1
Weeke 119 F4
Weekley 161 D4
Weel 196 C4
Weeley 152 C5
Weeley Heath 152 C5
Weem 250 B4
Weeping Cross 171 G5
Weethley 146 C2
Weeting 163 F4
Weeton ERid 197 F5
Weeton Lancs 191 G4

Weeton NYorks 194 B3
Weetwood 194 B4
Weir Essex 138 B4
Weir Lancs 193 E5
Weir Quay 100 A1
Weirbrook 170 A5
Weisdale 279 C7
Welborne 178 B5
Welburn 175 E2
Welburn NYorks 195 G1
Welburn NYorks 203 F4
Welbury 202 C2
Welby 175 E4
Welches Dam 162 C3
Welcombe 112 C4
Weldon 161 E4
Welford N'hants 160 B4
Welford WBerks 133 G5
Welford-on-Avon 146 D2
Welham Leics 160 C3
Welham Notts 187 E4
Welham Green 136 B2
Well Hants 120 C3
Well Lincs 189 E5
Well NYorks 202 B4
Well End Bucks 135 E4
Well End Herts 136 B3
Well Hill 123 D2
Well Street 123 F3
Well Town 102 C2
Welland 145 G3
Wellbank 244 C1
Wellesbourne 147 E2
Wellhill 267 G5
Wellhouse WBerks 134 A5
Wellhouse WYorks 185 E1
Welling 137 D5
Wellingborough 149 D1
Wellingham 177 G5
Wellingore 175 E2
Wellington Cumb 198 B2
Wellington Here 145 D3
Wellington Som 115 E5
Wellington Tel&W 157 F1
Wellington Heath 145 G3
Wellington Marsh 145 D3
Wellow B&NESom 117 E2
Wellow IoW 106 C4
Wellow Notts 174 B1
Wells 116 C3
Wells Cathedral Som BA5 2UE 116 C3
Wells Green 158 D4
Wellsborough 159 F2
Wells-next-the-Sea 178 A1
Wellstye Green 137 F1
Wellwood 235 E1
Welney 162 D3
Welsh Bicknor 131 E1
Welsh End 170 C4
Welsh Frankton 170 A4
Welsh Hook 140 C5
Welsh Mountain Zoo Conwy LL28 5UY 181 G5
Welsh Newton 131 D1
Welsh St. Donats 129 G5
Welshampton 170 B4
Welshpool (Y Trallwng) 156 B2
Welton B&NESom 117 D2
Welton Cumb 209 G2
Welton ERid 196 B5
Welton Lincs 188 A4
Welton N'hants 148 A1
Welton le Marsh 176 C1
Welton le Wold 188 C4
Welwick 197 F5
Welwyn 136 B1
Welwyn Garden City 136 B1
Wem 170 C5
Wembdon 115 F4
Wembley 136 A4
Wembley GtLon HA9 0WS 10 C3
Wembley Park 136 A4
Wembury 100 B3
Wembworthy 113 G4
Wemyss Bay 232 C3
Wenallt Cere 154 C5
Wenallt Gwyn 168 C3
Wendens Ambo 150 D4
Wendlebury 134 A1
Wendling 178 A4
Wendover 135 D2
Wendover Dean 135 D2
Wendron 95 D3
Wendy 150 B3
Wenfordbridge 97 E2
Wenhaston 165 F4
Wenlli 168 B1
Wennington Cambs 162 A5
Wennington GtLon 137 E4
Wennington Lancs 200 B5
Wensley Derbys 173 D1
Wensley NYorks 201 F4
Wensleydale Cheese Visitor Centre, Hawes NYorks DL8 3RN 201 D4
Wentbridge 186 B1
Wentnor 156 C3
Wentworth Cambs 162 C5
Wentworth SYorks 186 A3
Wenvoe 130 A5
Weobley 144 C2
Weobley Marsh 144 D2
Weoley Castle 158 C4
Wepham 108 C3
Wepre 169 F1
Wepre Country Park Flints CH5 4HL 169 F1
Wereham 163 E2
Wergs 158 A2
Wern Gwyn 167 D4
Wern Powys 156 B1
Wern Powys 156 A2
Wern Shrop 169 F4
Wernffrwd 128 B3
Wern-olau 128 B3
Wernrheolydd 130 C1
Wern-y-cwrt 130 C2
Werrington Corn 98 C2
Werrington Peter 161 G2
Werrington Staffs 171 G3
Wervil Grange 141 G2
Wervin 183 F5
Wesham 192 A4
Wessington 173 E2

West Aberthaw 114 D1
West Acre 163 F1
West Acton 136 A4
West Allerdean 237 G5
West Alvington 100 D3
West Amesbury 118 C3
West Anstey 114 B5
West Ashby 188 C5
West Ashford 113 F2
West Ashling 108 A3
West Ashton 117 F2
West Auckland 212 A5
West Ayton 204 C4
West Bagborough 115 E4
West Barkwith 188 B4
West Barnby 204 B1
West Barns 237 D2
West Barsham 178 A2
West Bay 104 A3
West Beckham 178 C2
West Benhar 234 C3
West Bergholt 152 A5
West Bexington 104 B4
West Bilney 163 F1
West Blatchington 109 E3
West Boldon 212 C1
West Bourton 117 E5
West Bowling 194 B4
West Brabourne 124 C4
West Bradford 192 D3
West Bradley 116 C4
West Bretton 185 G1
West Bridgford 173 G4
West Bromwich 158 C3
West Buckland Devon 113 G2
West Buckland Som 115 E5
West Burrafirth 279 B7
West Burton NYorks 201 F4
West Burton WSuss 108 B2
West Butsfield 211 G3
West Butterwick 187 F2
West Byfleet 121 F1
West Cairncake 269 G6
West Caister 179 G4
West Calder 235 E3
West Carbeth 233 G2
West Carr Houses 187 E2
West Cauldcoats 234 A5
West Chaldon 105 D4
West Challow 133 F4
West Charleton 101 D3
West Chevington 221 E2
West Chiltington 108 C2
West Chiltington Common 108 C2
West Chinnock 104 A1
West Chisenbury 118 C2
West Clandon 121 F2
West Cliffe 125 F4
West Clyne 267 F1
West Coker 104 B1
West Compton Dorset 104 B3
West Compton Som 116 C3
West Cowick 195 F5
West Cross 128 C4
West Crudwell 132 B3
West Curry 98 C1
West Curthwaite 209 G2
West Dean Wilts 119 D5
West Dean WSuss 108 A2
West Deeping 161 G2
West Derby 183 E3
West Dereham 163 E2
West Ditchburn 229 F4
West Down 113 F1
West Drayton GtLon 135 F5
West Drayton Notts 187 E5
West Dullater 242 A4
West Dunnet 275 H1
West Edington 221 D3
West Ella 196 B5
West End Bed 149 E2
West End BrackF 135 D5
West End Caerp 130 B3
West End Cambs 162 C3
West End ERid 196 C1
West End Hants 107 D1
West End Herts 136 B2
West End Kent 125 D2
West End Lancs 192 A1
West End Lincs 189 D3
West End Norf 179 F4
West End Norf 178 A5
West End NSom 116 B1
West End NYorks 194 A2
West End Oxon 134 A4
West End Oxon 133 G5
West End SLan 235 D5
West End Suff 165 F3
West End Surr 121 G1
West End Surr 121 E1
West End Wilts 132 B5
West End Wilts 118 A5
West End Wilts 118 B5
West End Green 120 B1
West Farleigh 123 G3
West Farndon 148 A2
West Felton 170 A5
West Firle 109 G3
West Fleetham 229 F4
West Flotmanby 205 D5
West Garforth 194 C4
West Ginge 133 G5
West Glen 232 A2
West Grafton 118 D1
West Green GtLon 136 C4
West Green Hants 120 C2
West Grimstead 118 D5
West Grinstead 121 G5
West Haddlesey 195 E5
West Haddon 160 B5
West Hagbourne 134 A4
West Hagley 158 B4
West Hall 210 B1
West Hallam 173 F3
West Halton 196 B5
West Ham 136 C4
West Handley 186 A5
West Hanney 133 G3
West Hanningfield 137 G2
West Hardwick 186 B1
West Harnham 118 C5
West Harptree 116 C2
West Harrow 136 A4
West Harting 120 C5

West Hatch Som 115 F5
West Hatch Wilts 118 A5
West Head 163 D2
West Heath ChesE 171 F1
West Heath GtLon 137 D5
West Heath Hants 121 D2
West Heath Hants 119 G2
West Heath WMid 158 C5
West Helmsdale 275 F7
West Hendon 136 B4
West Hendred 133 G4
West Heslerton 204 C5
West Hewish 116 A1
West Hill ERid 197 D1
West Hill Devon 103 D3
West Hill NSom 131 D5
West Hoathly 122 C5
West Holme 105 E4
West Horndon 137 F4
West Horrington 116 C3
West Horsley 121 F2
West Horton 229 E3
West Hougham 125 E5
West Howe 105 G3
West Howetown 114 C4
West Huntspill 116 A3
West Hyde 135 F3
West Hythe 124 D5
West Ilsley 133 G4
West Itchenor 107 G2
West Keal 176 B1
West Kennett 118 C1
West Kilbride 232 D5
West Kingsdown 123 E2
West Kington 132 A5
West Kington Wick 132 A5
West Kirby 182 D4
West Knapton 204 B5
West Knighton 104 D4
West Knoyle 117 F4
West Kyloe 229 E2
West Lambrook 104 A1
West Langdon 125 F4
West Langwell 266 C2
West Lavington Wilts 118 B2
West Lavington WSuss 121 D5
West Layton 202 A2
West Leake 173 G5
West Learmouth 228 C3
West Lees 203 D3
West Leigh Devon 113 G5
West Leigh Devon 101 G5
West Leigh Som 115 E4
West Leith 135 E2
West Lexham 163 G1
West Lilling 195 F1
West Lingo 244 C4
West Linton 235 F4
West Liss 120 C5
West Littleton 131 G5
West Lockinge 133 G4
West Looe 97 G4
West Lulworth 105 E4
West Lutton 196 B1
West Lydford 116 C4
West Lyford 116 C4
West Lyn 114 A3
West Lyng 116 A5
West Lynn 163 E1
West Mains 229 E2
West Malling 123 F3
West Malvern 145 G3
West Marden 107 G1
West Markham 187 E5
West Marsh 188 C2
West Marton 193 E2
West Melbury 117 F5
West Melton 186 B2
West Meon 120 B5
West Meon Hut 120 B5
West Mersea 138 D1
West Midland Safari Park & Leisure Park Worcs DY12 1LF 158 A5
West Milton 104 A3
West Minster 124 B1
West Molesey 121 G1
West Monkton 115 F5
West Moors 105 G2
West Morriston 236 D5
West Morton 193 G3
West Mostard 200 C3
West Mudford 116 C5
West Muir 253 D3
West Ness 203 F5
West Newbiggin 202 C1
West Newton ERid 197 D4
West Newton Norf 177 E5
West Norwood 136 C5
West Ogwell 101 E1
West Orchard 105 E1
West Overton 118 C1
West Panson 98 C1
West Park Aber 261 F5
West Park Mersey 183 G3
West Parley 105 G3
West Peckham 123 F3
West Pelton 212 B2
West Pennard 116 C4
West Pentire 96 B3
West Perry 149 G1
West Porlock 114 B3
West Prawle 101 D4
West Preston 108 C3
West Pulham 104 D2
West Putford 113 D4
West Quantoxhead 115 E3
West Raddon 102 B2
West Rainton 212 C3
West Rasen 188 A4
West Raynham 177 G5
West Retford 187 D4
West Rounton 202 D2
West Row 163 E5
West Rudham 177 G5
West Runton 178 C1
West Saltoun 236 B3
West Sandford 102 B2
West Sandwick 278 D4
West Scrafton 201 F4
West Shepton 116 D3
West Shinness Lodge 273 H7
West Somerset Railway Som TA24 5BG 115 E4
West Somerton 179 F4

West Stafford 104 D4
West Stockwith 187 E3
West Stoke 108 A3
West Stonesdale 201 D3
West Stoughton 116 B3
West Stour 117 E5
West Stourmouth 125 E2
West Stow 163 G5
West Stow Country Park Suff IP28 6HG 163 F5
West Stowell 118 C1
West Stratton 119 G3
West Street Kent 124 C3
West Street Med 137 G5
West Street Suff 164 A4
West Tanfield 202 B5
West Taphouse 97 F3
West Tarbert 231 G3
West Tarring 108 D3
West Thirston 221 D1
West Thorney 107 G2
West Thurrock 137 E5
West Tilbury 137 F5
West Tisted 120 B5
West Tofts Norf 163 G3
West Tofts P&K 243 G1
West Torrington 188 B4
West Town B&NESom 116 C1
West Town Hants 107 G3
West Town NSom 116 B1
West Town Som 116 C4
West Tytherley 119 D5
West Walton 162 C1
West Wellow 106 B1
West Wembury 100 B3
West Wemyss 244 B5
West Wick 116 A1
West Wickham Cambs 151 E3
West Wickham GtLon 122 C2
West Williamston 126 D2
West Winch 163 E1
West Winterslow 118 D4
West Wittering 107 G3
West Witton 201 F4
West Woodburn 220 A3
West Woodhay 119 E1
West Woodlands 117 E3
West Worldham 120 C4
West Worlington 102 A1
West Worthing 108 D3
West Wratting 151 E2
West Wycombe 134 D3
West Yatton 132 A5
West Yell 278 D4
West Youlstone 112 C4
Westbere 125 D2
Westborough 174 D2
Westbourne Bourne 105 G3
Westbourne WSuss 107 G3
Westbourne Green 136 B4
Westbrook Kent 125 F1
Westbrook WBerks 133 G5
Westbrook Wilts 118 A1
Westbury Bucks 148 B4
Westbury Shrop 156 C2
Westbury Wilts 117 F2
Westbury Leigh 117 F2
Westbury on Trym 131 E5
Westbury-on-Severn 131 G1
Westbury-sub-Mendip 116 C3
Westby Lancs 191 G4
Westby Lincs 175 E5
Westcliff-on-Sea 138 B4
Westcombe 117 D4
Westcot 133 F4
Westcott Bucks 134 C1
Westcott Devon 102 D2
Westcott Surr 121 G3
Westcott Barton 147 G5
Westcourt 118 D1
Westcroft 148 D4
Westdean 110 A4
Westdowns 97 E1
Westend Town 131 G5
Wester Aberchalder 258 C2
Wester Badentyre 269 F5
Wester Balgedie 243 G4
Wester Culbeuchly 268 E4
Wester Dechmont 235 E2
Wester Fintray 261 G3
Wester Foffarty 252 C5
Wester Greenskares 269 F4
Wester Gruinards 266 C2
Wester Hailes 235 G3
Wester Lealty 266 D4
Wester Lonvine 266 E4
Wester Newburn 244 C4
Wester Ord 261 G4
Wester Quarff 279 D9
Wester Skeld 279 B8
Westerdale High 275 G3
Westerdale NYorks 203 F2
Westerfield Shet 279 C7
Westerfield Suff 152 C3
Westergate 108 B3
Westerham 122 D3
Westerhope 212 A1
Westerleigh 131 G5
Westerloch 275 J3
Westerton Aber 261 F5
Westerton Angus 253 E4
Westerton Dur 212 B4
Westerton P&K 243 D3
Westerwick 279 B8
Westfield Cumb 208 C4
Westfield ESuss 110 D2
Westfield High 275 F2
Westfield NLan 234 B2
Westfield Norf 178 A5
Westfield WYorks 194 B5
Westfield Sole 123 G2
Westgate Dur 211 F4
Westgate N'umb 220 D1
Westgate NLincs 187 E2
Westgate Norf 178 A1
Westgate Hill 194 B5
Westgate on Sea 125 F1
Westhall Aber 260 E2
Westhall Suff 165 F3
Westham Dorset 104 C5
Westham ESuss 110 B3
Westham Som 116 B3
Westhampnett 108 A3
Westhay Devon 103 G2
Westhay Som 116 B3
Westhead 183 F2

Westhide 145 E3
Westhill Aber 261 G4
Westhill High 266 E7
Westhope Here 145 D2
Westhope Shrop 157 D4
Westhorp 148 A2
Westhorpe Lincs 176 A4
Westhorpe Notts 174 B2
Westhorpe Suff 152 B1
Westhoughton 184 A2
Westhouse 200 B5
Westhouses 173 F2
Westhumble 121 G2
Westing 278 E2
Westlake 100 C2
Westlands 171 F3
Westlea 132 D4
Westleigh Devon 113 E3
Westleigh Devon 103 D1
Westleigh GtMan 184 A2
Westleton 153 F1
Westley Shrop 156 C2
Westley Suff 151 G1
Westley Heights 137 F4
Westley Waterless 151 E2
Westlington 134 C1
Westlinton 218 B5
Westloch 235 G4
Westmancote 146 B4
Westmarsh 125 D4
Westmeston 109 F2
Westmill 180 B5
Westminster 136 B5
Westminster Abbey GtLon
SW1P 3PA 44 E6
Westminster Abbey - Chapter
House & Pyx Chamber
GtLon SW1P 3PA 44 E6
Westminster Cathedral
GtLon SW1P 2QW 44 C7
Westmuir 252 B2
Westness 276 C5
Westnewton Cumb 209 E2
Westnewton
N'umb 228 D3
Westoe 212 C1
Weston B&NESom 117 E1
Weston ChesE 171 E2
Weston Devon 103 E4
Weston Devon 103 D3
Weston Dorset 104 C5
Weston Halton 183 G4
Weston Hants 120 C5
Weston Here 144 C2
Weston Herts 150 A4
Weston Moray 268 C4
Weston N'hants 148 A3
Weston Notts 174 C1
Weston NYorks 194 A3
Weston Shrop 170 C5
Weston Shrop 157 E3
Weston Shrop 156 C5
Weston Soton 107 D1
Weston Staffs 171 G5
Weston WBerks 133 G5
Weston Bampfylde 116 D5
Weston Beggard 145 E3
Weston by Welland 160 C3
Weston Colville 151 E2
Weston Corbett 120 B3
Weston Coyney 171 G3
Weston Favell 148 C1
Weston Green Cambs 151 E2
Weston Green Norf 178 C4
Weston Heath 157 G1
Weston Hills 176 A5
Weston in Arden 159 F4
Weston Jones 171 E5
Weston Longville 178 C4
Weston Lullingfields 170 B5
Weston Park Staffs
TF11 8LE 158 A1
Weston Patrick 120 B4
Weston Point 183 F4
Weston Rhyn 169 F4
Weston Subedge 146 D3
Weston Town 117 E3
Weston Turville 135 D1
Weston under
Penyard 145 F5
Weston under
Wetherley 147 F1
Weston Underwood
Derbys 173 D3
Weston Underwood
MK 149 D2
Westonbirt 132 A4
Westonbirt - The National
Arboretum Glos
GL8 8QS 132 A4
Westoning 149 F4
Weston-in-Gordano 131 D5
Weston-on-Avon 147 D2
Weston-on-the-Green 134 A1
Weston-on-Trent 173 F5
Weston-super-Mare 116 A2
Weston-under-Lizard 158 A1
Westonzoyland 116 A4
Westow 195 G1
Westpoint Arena, Clyst St.
Mary Devon
EX5 1DJ 102 C3
Westport A&B 222 B3
Westport Som 116 A5
Westra 130 A5
Westray 276 D3
Westray Airfield 276 D2
Westridge Green 134 A5
Westrigg 234 D3
Westruther 236 D5
Westry 162 B3
Westside 261 G5
Westvale 183 F3
Westville 173 G3
Westward 209 F2
Westward Ho! 113 E3
Westwell Kent 124 B4
Westwell Oxon 133 E2
Westwick Cambs 150 D1
Westwick Dur 201 F1
Westwick Norf 179 D3
Westwick NYorks 194 B4
Westwood Devon 102 D3
Westwood Peter 161 G2
Westwood SLan 234 A4
Westwood Wilts 117 F2

Westwood Heath 159 E5
Westwoodside 187 E3
Wetham Green 124 A2
Wetheral 210 A2
Wetherby 194 D3
Wetherden 152 B1
Wetherden Upper
Town 152 B1
Wetheringsett 152 C1
Wethersfield 151 F4
Wethersta 279 C6
Wetherup Street 152 C1
Wetley Abbey 171 G3
Wetley Rocks 171 G3
Wettenhall 170 D1
Wettenhall Green 170 D1
Wetton 172 C2
Wetwang 196 B2
Wetwood 171 E4
Wexcombe 119 D2
Wexham Street 135 E4
Weybourne Norf 178 C1
Weybourne Surr 121 D3
Weybread 164 D3
Weybread Street 165 D4
Weybridge 121 F2
Weycroft 103 G2
Weyhill 119 E3
Weymouth 104 C5
Weymouth Sea Life Adventure
Park & Marine Sanctuary
Dorset DT4 7SX 104 C4
Whaddon Bucks 148 D4
Whaddon Cambs 150 B3
Whaddon Glos 132 A1
Whaddon Glos 146 B5
Whaddon Wilts 118 C5
Whaddon Wilts 117 D1
Whaddon Gap 150 B3
Whale 210 B5
Whaley 186 C5
Whaley Bridge 185 E4
Whaley Thorns 186 C5
Whaligoe 275 J4
Whalley 192 D4
Whalsay 279 E6
Whalsay Airport 279 E6
Whalton 220 D3
Wham 193 D2
Whaplode 176 B5
Whaplode Drove 162 B1
Whaplode
St. Catherine 162 B1
Wharfe 193 D1
Wharles 192 A4
Wharley End 149 E3
Wharncliffe Side 185 G3
Wharram le Street 196 A1
Wharram Percy 196 A1
Wharton
ChesW&C 171 D1
Wharton Here 145 E2
Whashton 202 A2
Whatcote 147 F3
Whateley 159 E3
Whatfield 152 B3
Whatley 117 E3
Whatlington 110 C2
Whatsole Street 124 D4
Whatstandwell 173 E2
Whatton 174 C4
Whauphill 207 E2
Whaw 201 E2
Wheatacre 165 F2
Wheatcroft 173 E2
Wheatenhurst 131 G2
Wheatfield 134 B3
Wheathampstead 136 A1
Wheathill Shrop 157 F4
Wheathill Som 116 C4
Wheatley Hants 120 C4
Wheatley Oxon 134 B2
Wheatley WYorks 193 G5
Wheatley Hill 212 C4
Wheatley Lane 193 E4
Wheatley Park 186 C2
Wheaton Aston 158 A1
Wheddon Cross 114 C4
Wheedlemont 260 C2
Wheelerstreet 121 E3
Wheelock 171 E2
Wheelock Heath 171 E2
Wheelton 192 C5
Wheen 252 B2
Wheldale 195 D5
Wheldrake 195 F3
Whelford 133 D3
Whelley 183 G2
Whelpley Hill 135 E2
Whelpo 209 G3
Whelston 182 D5
Whenby 195 F1
Whepstead 151 G2
Wherstead 152 C3
Wherwell 119 E3
Wheston 185 F5
Whetley Cross 104 A2
Whetsted 123 F4
Whetstone GtLon 136 B3
Whetstone Leics 160 A3
Whicham 198 C4
Whichford 147 F4
Whickham 212 B1
Whiddon 113 E5
Whiddon Down 99 G1
Whifflet 234 B3
Whigstreet 252 C5
Whilton 148 B1
Whim 235 G4
Whimble 112 D5
Whimple 102 D3
Whimpwell Green 179 E3
Whin Lane End 191 G3
Whinburgh 178 B5
Whinlatter Forest Cumb
CA12 5TW 209 E4
Whinny Hill 202 C1
Whinnyfold 261 J1
Whippingham 107 E3
Whipsnade 135 F1
Whipsnade Zoo CenBeds
LU6 2LF 135 F1
Whipton 102 C3
Whirlow 186 A4
Whisby 175 E1

Whisterfield 184 C5
Whistley Green 134 C5
Whiston Mersey 183 F3
Whiston N'hants 148 D1
Whiston Staffs 172 B3
Whiston Staffs 158 A1
Whiston SYorks 186 B5
Whiston Cross 157 G2
Whiston Eaves 172 B3
Whitacre Fields 159 E3
Whitacre Heath 159 E3
Whitbeck 198 C4
Whitbourne 145 G2
Whitburn T&W 212 D1
Whitburn WLoth 234 D3
Whitby ChesW&C 183 E5
Whitby NYorks 204 B1
Whitby Abbey NYorks
YO22 4JT 204 C1
Whitby Lifeboat Museum
NYorks YO21 3PU 204 B1
Whitbyheath 183 E5
Whitchurch
B&NESom 116 D1
Whitchurch Bucks 148 D5
Whitchurch Cardiff 130 A4
Whitchurch Devon 99 E3
Whitchurch Hants 119 F3
Whitchurch Here 131 E1
Whitchurch Pembs 140 A5
Whitchurch Shrop 170 C3
Whitchurch Warks 147 E3
Whitchurch
Canonicorum 103 G3
Whitchurch Hill 134 B5
Whitchurch-on-
Thames 134 B5
Whitcombe 104 D4
Whitcott Keysett 156 B4
White Ball 103 D1
White Colne 151 G5
White Coppice 184 A4
White Cross Corn 96 C4
White Cross Devon 102 D4
White Cross Here 145 D3
White Cross Wilts 117 E4
White Cube GtLon
N1 6PB 12 C4
White End 146 A5
White Hill 117 F4
White Houses 187 E5
White Kirkley 211 G4
White Lackington 104 D4
White Ladies Aston 146 B2
White Lund 192 A1
White Mill 142 A4
White Moor 173 E3
White Notley 137 G1
White Ox Mead 117 E2
White Pit 189 D5
White Post Farm Centre,
Farnsfield Notts
NG22 8HL 174 B2
White Rocks 144 D5
White Roding 137 E1
White Waltham 134 D5
Whiteacen 267 K7
Whiteash Green 151 F4
Whitebirk 192 D5
Whitebog 269 H5
Whitebridge 131 E2
Whitebridge (An Drochaid
Bhàn) High 258 B3
Whitebrook 131 E2
Whiteburn 236 C5
Whitecairn 214 D5
Whitecairns 261 H3
Whitecastle 235 E5
Whitechapel 192 B3
Whitechurch 141 E4
Whitecote 194 B4
Whitecraig 236 A2
Whitecroft 131 F2
Whitecross 214 C5
Whitecross Corn 94 C3
Whitecross Corn 97 D2
Whitecross Dorset 104 A3
Whitecross Falk 235 D2
Whiteface 266 E3
Whitefarland 261 F2
Whitefield Devon 114 A4
Whitefield Dorset 105 F3
Whitefield GtMan 184 C2
Whitefield High 258 C2
Whitefield High 275 H3
Whitefield P&K 243 G2
Whiteford 261 F2
Whitegate 170 D1
Whitehall Devon 103 E1
Whitehall Hants 120 C2
Whitehall Ork 276 F5
Whitehall WSuss 121 G5
Whitehaven 208 C5
Whitehill Aber 269 H5
Whitehill Hants 120 C4
Whitehill Kent 124 B3
Whitehill Midlo 236 A3
Whitehill NAyr 233 D4
Whitehills 268 F4
Whitehouse A&B 231 G3
Whitehouse Aber 260 E3
Whitehouse Common 158 D3
Whitekirk 236 C1
Whitelackington 103 G1
Whitelaw 237 F4
Whiteleen 275 J4
Whitelees 224 B2
Whiteley 107 E2
Whiteley Bank 107 E4
Whiteley Green 184 D5
Whiteley Village 121 F1
Whiteleys 214 B5
Whitemans Green 109 F1
Whitemire 267 G6
Whitemoor 97 D4
Whiteness 279 C8
Whiteoak Green 133 F1
Whiteparish 118 D5
Whiterashes 261 G2
Whiterow 275 J4
Whiteshill 132 A2
Whiteside N'umb 210 D1
Whiteside WLoth 235 D3
Whitesmith 110 A2
Whitestaunton 103 F1
Whitestone A&B 222 C3
Whitestone Aber 260 E5
Whitestone Devon 102 B3

Whitestreet Green 152 A4
Whitestripe 269 H5
Whiteway 132 B1
Whitewell Aber 269 H4
Whitewell Lancs 192 C3
Whitewell Wrex 170 B3
Whiteworks 99 G3
Whitewreath 267 K6
Whitfield Here 144 D4
Whitfield Kent 125 F4
Whitfield N'umb 211 D2
Whitfield SGlos 131 F3
Whitford Devon 103 F3
Whitford (Chwitffordd)
Flints 182 C5
Whitgift 196 A5
Whitgreave 171 F5
Whithorn 207 E2
Whiting Bay 223 F3
Whitkirk 194 C4
Whitlam 261 G2
Whitland
(Hendy-Gwyn) 127 F1
Whitland Abbey 127 F1
Whitleigh 100 A1
Whitletts 224 B3
Whitley NYorks 195 E5
Whitley Read 120 C1
Whitley Wilts 117 F1
Whitley WMid 159 F5
Whitley Bay 221 F4
Whitley Chapel 211 F2
Whitley Heath 171 F5
Whitley Lower 185 G1
Whitley Row 123 D3
Whitlock's End 158 D5
Whitminster 131 G2
Whitmore Dorset 105 G2
Whitmore Staffs 171 F3
Whitnage 102 D1
Whitnash 147 F1
Whitnell 115 F3
Whitney-on-Wye 144 B3
Whitrigg Cumb 209 F1
Whitrigg Cumb 209 F3
Whitsbury 106 A1
Whitsome 237 F4
Whitson 130 C4
Whitstable 124 D2
Whitstone 98 C1
Whittingham 229 E5
Whittingslow 156 C4
Whittington Derbys 186 A5
Whittington Glos 146 C5
Whittington Lancs 200 B5
Whittington Norf 163 F3
Whittington Shrop 170 A4
Whittington Staffs 158 D2
Whittington Staffs 159 D2
Whittington Worcs 146 A2
Whittlebury 148 B3
Whittle-le-Woods 192 B5
Whittlesey 162 A3
Whittlesford 150 C3
Whittlestone Head 184 B1
Whitton GtLon 136 A5
Whitton N'umb 220 C1
Whitton NLincs 196 B5
Whitton Powys 144 B1
Whitton Shrop 157 E5
Whitton Stock 212 C5
Whitton Suff 152 C3
Whittonditch 133 E5
Whittonstall 211 G2
Whitway 119 F2
Whitwell Derbys 186 C5
Whitwell Herts 149 G5
Whitwell IoW 107 E5
Whitwell NYorks 202 B3
Whitwell Rut 161 E2
Whitwell Street 178 C3
Whitwell-on-the-Hill 195 G1
Whitwick 159 G1
Whitwood 194 D5
Whitworth 184 C1
Whitworth Art Gallery,
Manchester GtMan
M15 6ER 25 E4
Whixall 170 C4
Whixley 194 D2
Whorlton Dur 202 A1
Whorlton NYorks 203 D2
Whygate 219 F4
Whyle 145 E1
Whyteleafe 122 C3
Wibdon 131 E3
Wibsey 194 A4
Wibtoft 159 G4
Wichenford 145 G1
Wichling 124 B3
Wick Bourne 106 A3
Wick Devon 103 E1
Wick (Inbhir Uige)
High 275 J3
Wick SGlos 131 G5
Wick Som 115 F3
Wick Som 116 C4
Wick VGlam 129 F5
Wick Wilts 118 C5
Wick Worcs 146 B3
Wick WSuss 108 C3
Wick John O'Groats Airport
275 J3
Wick Hill Kent 124 A4
Wick Hill W'ham 120 C1
Wick St. Lawrence 116 A1
Wicken Cambs 163 D5
Wicken N'hants 148 C4
Wicken Bonhunt 150 C4
Wickenby 188 A4
Wicker Street Green 152 A3
Wickersley 186 B3
Wicketwood Hill 174 B3
Wickford 137 G3
Wickham Hants 107 E1
Wickham WBerks 133 F5
Wickham Bishops 138 B1
Wickham Heath 119 F1
Wickham Market 153 E2
Wickham St. Paul 151 G4
Wickham Skeith 152 B1
Wickham Street Suff 151 F2
Wickham Street Suff 152 B1
Wickhambreaux 125 E3
Wickhambrook 151 F2
Wickhamford 146 C3

Wickhampton 179 F5
Wicklewood 178 B5
Wickmere 178 C2
Wicksteed Park N'hants
NN15 6NJ 161 D5
Wickstreet 110 A3
Wickwar 131 G4
Widcombe 117 E1
Widdington 150 D4
Widdop 193 F4
Widdrington 221 E2
Widdrington Station 221 E2
Wide Open 221 E4
Widecombe in the
Moor 102 A5
Widegates 97 G4
Widemouth Bay 112 C5
Widewall 277 D8
Widford Essex 137 F2
Widford Herts 136 D1
Widford Oxon 133 E1
Widgham Green 151 E2
Widmer End 135 D3
Widmerpool 174 B5
Widnes 183 G4
Widworthy 103 F3
Wigan 183 G2
Wigan Pier GtMan
WN3 4EU 183 G2
Wiganthorpe 203 F5
Wigborough 104 A1
Wiggaton 103 E3
Wiggenhall
St. Germans 163 D1
Wiggenhall St. Mary
Magdalen 163 D1
Wiggenhall St. Mary the
Virgin 163 D1
Wiggenhall St. Peter 163 E1
Wiggens Green 151 E3
Wigginton Herts 135 E1
Wigginton Oxon 147 F4
Wigginton Shrop 170 A4
Wigginton Staffs 159 E2
Wigginton York 195 F2
Wigglesworth 193 E2
Wiggonby 209 G1
Wiggonholt 108 C2
Wighill 195 D3
Wighton 178 A2
Wightwizzle 185 G3
Wigley 106 C1
Wigmore Here 144 D1
Wigmore Med 124 A2
Wigsley 187 F5
Wigsthorpe 161 F4
Wigston 160 B3
Wigston Parva 159 G4
Wigthorpe 186 C4
Wigtoft 176 A4
Wigton 209 F2
Wigtown 215 F5
Wike 194 B3
Wilbarston 160 D4
Wilberfoss 195 G2
Wilburton 162 C5
Wilby N'hants 149 D1
Wilby Norf 164 B2
Wilby Suff 164 D4
Wilcot 118 C1
Wilcott 156 C1
Wilcrick 130 D4
Wilday Green 186 A5
Wildboarclough 171 G1
Wilde Street 163 F5
Wilden Bed 149 F2
Wilden Worcs 158 A5
Wildern 119 E2
Wildhill 136 B2
Wildmoor 158 B5
Wildsworth 187 F3
Wilford 173 G4
Wilkesley 170 D3
Wilkhaven 267 G3
Wilkieston 235 F3
Wilksby 176 A1
Willand Devon 102 D1
Willand Som 103 E1
Willaston ChesE 171 D2
Willaston ChesW&C 183 E5
Willaston Shrop 170 C4
Willen 149 D3
Willen Lakeside Park MK
MK15 9HQ 9 D2
Willenhall WMid 158 B3
Willenhall WMid 159 F5
Willerby ERid 196 C3
Willerby NYorks 204 D5
Willersey 146 D4
Willersley 144 C3
Willesborough 124 C4
Willesborough Lees 124 C4
Willesden 136 B4
Willesleigh 113 F2
Willesley 132 A4
Willett 115 E4
Willey Shrop 157 F3
Willey Warks 159 G4
Willey Green 121 E2
William's Green 152 A3
Williamscot 147 G3
Williamson Park, Lancaster
Lancs LA1 1UX 192 A1
Williamthorpe 173 F1
Willian 150 A4
Willimontswick 211 D1
Willingale 137 E2
Willingdon 110 A3
Willingham 162 C5
Willingham by Stow 187 F4
Willingham Green 151 E2
Willington Bed 149 F2
Willington Derbys 173 D5
Willington Dur 212 A4
Willington Kent 123 G3
Willington T&W 212 C1
Willington Warks 147 E4
Willington Corner 170 C1
Willisham 152 B2
Willitoft 195 G4
Williton 115 E3
Willoughbridge 171 E3
Willoughby Lincs 189 E5
Willoughby Warks 148 A1
Willoughby Waterleys 160 A3
Willoughby-on-the-
Wolds 174 B5
Willoughton 187 G3

Willow Green 184 A5
Willows Farm Village Herts
AL2 1BB 136 A2
Willows Green 137 G1
Willsbridge 131 F5
Willslock 172 B4
Willsworthy 99 F2
Willtown 116 A5
Wilmcote 147 D2
Wilmington
B&NESom 117 D1
Wilmington Devon 103 F2
Wilmington ESuss 110 A3
Wilmington Kent 137 E5
Wilmslow 184 C4
Wilnecote 159 E2
Wilney Green 164 B3
Wilpshire 192 C4
Wilsden 193 G4
Wilsford Lincs 175 F3
Wilsford Wilts 118 C1
Wilsford Wilts 118 C2
Wilsham 114 A3
Wilsill 194 A1
Wilsley Green 123 G5
Wilsley Pound 123 G5
Wilson 173 F5
Wilstead 149 F3
Wilsthorpe ERid 197 D1
Wilsthorpe Lincs 161 F1
Wilstone 135 E1
Wilton Cumb 208 D5
Wilton Here 145 E5
Wilton NYorks 204 B4
Wilton R&C 203 E1
Wilton ScBord 227 F4
Wilton Wilts 119 D1
Wilton Wilts 118 B4
Wilton House Wilts
SP2 0BJ 118 B4
Wiltown 103 E1
Wimbish 151 D4
Wimbish Green 151 E4
Wimblebury 158 C1
Wimbledon 136 B5
Wimbledon All England Lawn
Tennis & Croquet Club
GtLon SW19 5AG 11 E7
Wimblington 162 C3
Wimborne Minster Dorset
BH21 1HT 3 B2
Wimborne Minster Dorset
BH21 1HT 3 B2
Wimborne St. Giles 105 G1
Wimbotsham 163 E2
Wimpole 150 B3
Wimpole Home Farm Cambs
SG8 0BW 150 B3
Wimpole Lodge 150 B3
Wimpstone 147 E3
Wincanton 117 E5
Winceby 176 B1
Wincham 184 A5
Winchburgh 235 E2
Winchcombe 146 C5
Winchelsea 111 E2
Winchelsea Beach 111 E2
Winchester 119 F5
Winchester Cathedral
Hants SO23 9LS
89 Winchester
Winchet Hill 123 G4
Winchfield 120 C2
Winchmore Hill
Bucks 135 E3
Winchmore Hill
GtLon 136 C3
Wincle 171 G1
Wincobank 186 A3
Windermere 199 F3
Windermere Lake Cruises
Cumb LA12 8AS 199 E3
Winderton 147 F3
Windhill 266 C7
Windle Hill 183 E5
Windlehurst 185 D4
Windlesham 121 E1
Windley 173 E3
Windmill 185 F5
Windmill Hill ESuss 110 B2
Windmill Hill Som 103 G1
Windmill Hill Worcs 146 B3
Windrush 133 D1
Windsor 135 E5
Windsor Castle W&M
SL4 1NJ 89 Windsor
Windsor Green 151 G2
Windy Nook 212 B1
Windygates 244 B4
Windy-Yett 233 F4
Wineham 109 E1
Winestead 197 E5
Winewall 193 F4
Winfarthing 164 C3
Winford IoW 107 E4
Winford NSom 116 C1
Winforton 144 B3
Winfrith Newburgh 105 E4
Wing Bucks 149 D5
Wing Rut 161 D2
Wingate 212 C4
Wingates GtMan 184 A2
Wingates N'umb 220 D1
Wingerworth 173 E1
Wingfield CenBeds 149 F5
Wingfield Suff 164 D4
Wingfield Wilts 117 F2
Wingfield Green 164 D4
Wingham 125 E3
Wingham Well 125 E3
Wingmore 125 D4
Wingrave 135 D1
Winkburn 174 C2
Winkfield 135 E5
Winkfield Row 135 D5
Winkhill 172 B2
Winkleigh 113 G5
Winksley 202 B5
Winkton 106 A3
Winlaton 212 A1
Winlaton Mill 212 A1
Winless 275 J3
Winmarleigh 192 A3
Winnard's Perch 96 D3
Winnersh 134 C5
Winnington 184 A5
Winscombe 116 B2
Winsford ChesW&C 171 D1

Winsford Som 114 C4
Winsham Devon 113 E2
Winsham Som 103 G2
Winshill 173 D5
Winsh-wen 128 C3
Winskill 210 B4
Winslade 120 B3
Winsley 117 F1
Winslow 148 C5
Winson 132 C2
Winsor 106 C1
Winster Cumb 199 F3
Winster Derbys 172 D1
Winston Dur 202 A1
Winston Suff 152 C1
Winston Green 152 C1
Winstone 132 B2
Winswell 113 E4
Winter Gardens FY1 1HW
64 Blackpool
Winter Gardens NSom
BS23 1AJ
88 Weston-super-Mare
Winterborne Came 104 D4
Winterborne Clenston 105 E2
Winterborne
Herringston 104 C4
Winterborne
Houghton 105 E2
Winterborne Kingston 105 E3
Winterborne Monkton 104 C4
Winterborne Stickland 105 E2
Winterborne
Whitechurch 105 E2
Winterborne Zelston 105 E3
Winterbourne SGlos 131 F4
Winterbourne WBerks 133 G5
Winterbourne Abbas 104 C3
Winterbourne Bassett 132 D5
Winterbourne
Dauntsey 118 C4
Winterbourne Earls 118 C4
Winterbourne Gunner 118 C4
Winterbourne
Monkton 132 D5
Winterbourne
Steepleton 104 C4
Winterbourne Stoke 118 B3
Winterbrook 134 B4
Winterburn 193 F2
Wintercleugh 226 A4
Winteringham 196 B5
Winterley 171 E2
Wintersett 186 A1
Wintershill 107 E1
Winterslow 118 D4
Winterton 187 G1
Winterton-on-Sea 179 F4
Winthorpe Lincs 177 D1
Winthorpe Notts 174 D2
Winton Bourne 105 G3
Winton Cumb 200 C1
Wintringham 204 B5
Winwick Cambs 161 G4
Winwick N'hants 160 B5
Winwick Warr 184 A3
Wirksworth 173 D2
Wirksworth Moor 173 E2
Wirral Country Park Mersey
CH61 0HN 182 D4
Wirswall 170 C3
Wisbech 162 C2
Wisbech St. Mary 162 C2
Wisborough Green 121 F5
Wiseton 187 E4
Wishaw NLan 234 B4
Wishaw Warks 159 D3
Wisley 121 F2
Wispington 188 C5
Wissett 165 E4
Wissington 152 A4
Wistanstow 156 D4
Wistanswick 171 D5
Wistaston 171 D2
Wiston Pembs 126 D1
Wiston SLan 226 A2
Wiston WSuss 108 D2
Wistow Cambs 162 A4
Wistow NYorks 195 E4
Wiswell 192 D4
Witcham 162 C5
Witchampton 105 F2
Witchburn 222 C3
Witchford 162 D5
Witcombe 116 B5
Witham 138 B1
Witham Friary 117 E3
Witham on the Hill 161 F1
Withcall 188 C4
Withcote 160 C2
Withdean 109 F3
Witherenden Hill 110 B1
Witherhurst 110 B1
Witheridge 102 B1
Witherley 159 F3
Withern 189 E4
Withernsea 197 F5
Withernwick 197 D3
Withersdale Street 165 D3
Withersfield 151 E3
Witherslack 199 F4
Witherslack Hall 199 F4
Withiel 97 D3
Withiel Florey 114 C4
Withielgoose 97 E3
Withington Glos 132 C1
Withington GtMan 184 C3
Withington Here 145 E3
Withington Shrop 157 E1
Withington Staffs 172 B4
Withington Green 184 C5
Withington Marsh 145 E3
Withleigh 102 C1
Withnell 192 C5
Withnell Fold 192 C5
Withybrook Som 117 D3
Withybrook Warks 159 G4
Withycombe 114 D3
Withycombe Raleigh 102 D4
Withyham 123 D5
Withypool 114 B4
Witley 121 E4
Witnesham 152 C2
Witney 133 F2
Wittering 161 F2
Wittersham 111 D1
Witton Angus 253 D2
Witton Norf 179 E5

317

Witton *Worcs* **146** A1
Witton Bridge **179** E2
Witton Gilbert **212** B3
Witton Park **212** A4
Witton-le-Wear **212** A4
Wiveliscombe **115** D5
Wivelsfield **109** F1
Wivelsfield Green **109** F2
Wivenhoe **152** B5
Wiveton **178** B1
Wix **152** C5
Wixford **146** C2
Wixhill **170** C5
Wixoe **151** F3
Woburn **149** E4
Woburn Safari Park *CenBeds*
  MK17 9QN **9** F3
Woburn Sands **149** E4
Wokefield Park **120** B1
Woking **121** F2
Wokingham **120** D1
Wolborough **102** B5
Wold Newton *ERid* **204** D5
Wold Newton
  NELincs **188** C3
Woldingham **122** C3
Wolds Village, Bainton *ERid*
  YO25 9EF **196** D4
Wolfelee **227** G5
Wolferlow **145** F1
Wolferton **177** E5
Wolfhampcote **148** A1
Wolfhill **243** G1
Wolfpits **144** B2
Wolf's Castle **140** C5
Wolfsdale **140** C5
Woll **227** F3
Wollaston *N'hants* **149** E1
Wollaston *Shrop* **156** C1
Wollaston *WMid* **158** A4
Wollaton **173** G4
Wollerton **170** D5
Wollescote **158** B4
Wolsingham **211** G4
Wolston **159** G5
Wolsty **209** E1
Wolvercote **134** A2
Wolverhampton **158** B3
Wolverhampton Art Gallery
  WMid WV1 1DU **14** A1
Wolverley *Shrop* **170** B4
Wolverley *Worcs* **158** A5
Wolvers Hill **116** A1
Wolverton *Hants* **119** G2
Wolverton *MK* **148** D3
Wolverton *Warks* **147** E1
Wolverton *Wilts* **117** E4
Wolverton Common **119** G2
Wolvesnewton **131** D3
Wolvey **159** G4
Wolvey Heath **159** G4
Wolviston **213** D5
Womaston **144** B1
Wombleton **203** F4
Wombourne **158** A3
Wombwell **186** A2
Womenswold **125** E3
Womersley **186** C1
Wonastow **131** D1
Wonersh **121** F3
Wonford **102** C3
Wonson **99** G2
Wonston **119** F4
Wooburn **135** E4
Wooburn Green **135** E4
Wood Bevington **146** C2
Wood Burcote **148** B3
Wood Dalling **178** B3
Wood Eaton **158** A1
Wood End *Bed* **149** F3
Wood End *Bed* **149** F3
Wood End *Bucks* **148** C4
Wood End *Herts* **150** B5
Wood End *Warks* **159** E4
Wood End *Warks* **159** E4
Wood End *Warks* **159** E4
Wood End *WMid* **158** B2
Wood Enderby **176** A1
Wood Green *GtLon* **136** C3
Wood Green *Norf* **164** D2
Wood Green Animal Shelter,
  Godmanchester *Cambs*
  PE29 2NH **150** A1
Wood Lane **170** B4
Wood Norton **178** B3
Wood Seats **186** A3
Wood Stanway **146** C4
Wood Street **179** E3
Wood Street Village **121** E2
Woodacott **113** D5
Woodale **201** F5
Woodall **186** B4
Woodbastwick **179** E4
Woodbeck **187** E5
Woodborough *Notts* **174** B3
Woodborough *Wilts* **118** C2
Woodbridge *Devon* **103** E3
Woodbridge *Dorset* **104** D1
Woodbridge *Suff* **153** D3
Woodbury *Devon* **102** D4
Woodbury *Som* **116** C3
Woodbury Salterton **102** D4
Woodchester **132** A2
Woodchurch *Kent* **124** B5
Woodchurch
  Mersey **183** D4
Woodcombe **114** C3
Woodcote *Oxon* **134** B4
Woodcote *Tel&W* **157** G1
Woodcote Green **158** B5
Woodcott **119** F2
Woodcroft **131** E3
Woodcutts **105** F1
Woodditton **151** E2
Woodeaton **134** A1
Woodend *Aber* **260** E3
Woodend *Cumb* **198** C3
Woodend *High* **258** C4
Woodend *High* **247** G3
Woodend *N'hants* **148** B3
Woodend *WSuss* **108** A3
Woodfalls **118** C5
Woodfield *Oxon* **148** A5
Woodfield *SAyr* **224** B3
Woodfoot **200** B1
Woodford *Corn* **112** C4

Woodford *Devon* **101** D2
Woodford *Glos* **131** F3
Woodford *GtLon* **136** D3
Woodford *GtMan* **184** C4
Woodford *N'hants* **161** E5
Woodford *Som* **115** D4
Woodford Bridge **136** D3
Woodford Green **136** D3
Woodford Halse **148** A2
Woodgate *Devon* **103** E1
Woodgate *Norf* **178** B4
Woodgate *WMid* **158** B4
Woodgate *Worcs* **146** B1
Woodgate *WSuss* **108** B3
Woodgreen **106** A1
Woodhall *Invcly* **233** E2
Woodhall *NYorks* **201** E3
Woodhall Hills **194** A4
Woodhall Spa **175** G1
Woodham *Bucks* **134** B1
Woodham *Dur* **212** B5
Woodham *Surr* **121** F1
Woodham Ferrers **137** G3
Woodham Mortimer **138** B2
Woodham Walter **138** B2
Woodhaven **244** C2
Woodhead *Aber* **261** F1
Woodhead *Staffs* **172** B3
Woodhey **183** E4
Woodhey Green **170** C2
Woodhill *Shrop* **157** G4
Woodhill *Som* **116** A5
Woodhorn **221** E3
Woodhouse *Cumb* **199** G4
Woodhouse *Leics* **160** A1
Woodhouse *SYorks* **186** B4
Woodhouse *WYorks* **194** B4
Woodhouse *WYorks* **194** C5
Woodhouse *WYorks* **194** A5
Woodhouse Down **131** F4
Woodhouse Eaves **160** A1
Woodhouse Green **171** G1
Woodhouses *GtMan* **184** C2
Woodhouses *Staffs* **159** D1
Woodhouses *Staffs* **158** C2
Woodhuish **101** F2
Woodhurst **162** B5
Woodingdean **109** F3
Woodington **119** E5
Woodland *Devon* **101** D1
Woodland *Dur* **211** G5
Woodland *Kent* **124** D4
Woodland Head **102** A3
Woodlands *Dorset* **105** G2
Woodlands *Hants* **106** C1
Woodlands *NYorks* **194** C4
Woodlands *Shrop* **157** G4
Woodlands *Som* **115** E3
Woodlands Leisure Park,
  Dartmouth *Devon*
  TQ9 7DQ **101** E2
Woodlands Park **135** D5
Woodlands St. Mary **133** F5
Woodlane **172** C5
Woodleigh **100** D3
Woodlesford **194** C5
Woodley *GtMan* **184** D3
Woodley *W'ham* **134** C5
Woodmancote *Glos* **132** C2
Woodmancote *Glos* **146** B5
Woodmancote *Glos* **131** G3
Woodmancote
  WSuss **109** E2
Woodmancote
  WSuss **107** G2
Woodmancott **119** G3
Woodmansey **196** C4
Woodmansterne **122** B3
Woodmanton **102** D4
Woodmill **172** C5
Woodminton **118** B5
Woodmoor **156** B2
Woodnesborough **125** F3
Woodnewton **161** F3
Woodperry **134** A1
Woodplumpton **192** B4
Woodrising **178** A5
Woodrow **105** D1
Wood's Corner **110** B2
Woods Eaves **144** B3
Wood's Green **123** F5
Woodseaves *Shrop* **171** D4
Woodseaves *Staffs* **171** E5
Woodsend **133** E5
Woodsetts **186** C4
Woodsford **105** D3
Woodside *Aberdeen* **261** H4
Woodside *BrackF* **135** E5
Woodside *CenBeds* **135** F1
Woodside *Cumb* **208** D3
Woodside *D&G* **217** E3
Woodside *Fife* **244** C4
Woodside *Fife* **244** A4
Woodside *GtLon* **122** C2
Woodside *Hants* **106** C3
Woodside *Herts* **136** B2
Woodside *NAyr* **233** E4
Woodside *P&K* **243** G1
Woodside *Shrop* **156** C4
Woodside *WMid* **158** B4
Woodside Animal Farm &
  Leisure Park *CenBeds*
  LU1 4DG **135** F1
Woodside Green **124** B3
Woodstock *Oxon* **133** G1
Woodstock *Pembs* **140** D5
Woodthorpe *Derbys* **186** B5
Woodthorpe *Leics* **160** A1
Woodthorpe *Lincs* **189** E4
Woodthorpe *SYorks* **186** A4
Woodthorpe *York* **195** E3
Woodton **165** D2
Woodtown **113** E3
Woodvale **183** E1
Woodville **159** F1
Woodwall Green **171** E4
Woodwalton **162** A4
Woodwick **276** C5
Woodworth Green **170** C2
Woodyates **105** G1
Woofferton **145** E1
Wookey **116** C3
Wookey Hole **116** C3
Wookey Hole Caves &
  Papermill *Som*
  BA5 1BB **116** C3
Wool **105** E4
Woolacombe **113** E1

Woolage Green **125** E4
Woolage Village **125** E3
Woolaston **131** E2
Woolaston Slade **131** E2
Woolavington **116** A3
Woolbeding **121** D5
Woolcotts **114** C4
Wooldale **185** F2
Wooler **229** D4
Woolfardisworthy
  Devon **102** A2
Woolfardisworthy
  Devon **112** D3
Woolfold **184** B1
Woolfords Cottages **235** E4
Woolgarston **105** F4
Woolgreaves **186** A4
Woolhampton **119** G1
Woolhope **145** F4
Woolland **105** D2
Woollard **116** D1
Woollaton **113** E4
Woolley *B&NESom* **117** E1
Woolley *Cambs* **161** G5
Woolley *Corn* **112** C4
Woolley *Derbys* **173** E1
Woolley *WYorks* **186** A1
Woolley Green *W&M* **135** D5
Woolley Green *Wilts* **117** F1
Woolmer Green **136** B1
Woolmere Green **146** B1
Woolmersdon **115** F4
Woolpit **152** A1
Woolpit Green **152** A1
Woolscott **147** G1
Woolstaston **157** D3
Woolsthorpe **174** D4
Woolsthorpe by
  Colsterworth **175** E5
Woolston *Devon* **100** D3
Woolston *Shrop* **170** A5
Woolston *Shrop* **156** D4
Woolston *Soton* **106** D1
Woolston *Warr* **184** A4
Woolstone *Glos* **146** B4
Woolstone *MK* **149** D3
Woolstone *Oxon* **133** E4
Woolton **183** F4
Woolton Hill **119** F1
Woolverstone **152** C4
Woolverton **117** E2
Woolwich **136** D5
Woonton **144** C2
Wooperton **229** E5
Woore **171** E3
Wootten Green **164** D4
Wootton *Bed* **149** F3
Wootton *Hants* **106** B3
Wootton *IoW* **107** E3
Wootton *Kent* **125** E4
Wootton *N'hants* **148** C2
Wootton *NLincs* **188** A1
Wootton *Oxon* **133** G1
Wootton *Oxon* **133** G2
Wootton *Shrop* **157** D5
Wootton *Shrop* **170** A5
Wootton *Staffs* **171** F5
Wootton *Staffs* **172** C3
Wootton Bassett **132** C4
Wootton Bridge **107** E3
Wootton Common **107** E3
Wootton Courtenay **114** C3
Wootton Fitzpaine **103** G3
Wootton Green **149** F3
Wootton Rivers **118** C1
Wootton St. Lawrence **119** G2
Wootton Wawen **147** D1
Worcester **146** A2
Worcester Cathedral *Worcs*
  WR1 2LH **90** Worcester
Worcester Park **122** B2
Worcester Woods Country Park
  Worcs WR5 2LG **146** A2
Wordsley **158** A4
Wordwell **163** G5
Worfield **157** G3
Worgret **105** F4
Work **277** D6
Workhouse End **149** G2
Workington **208** D4
Worksop **186** C5
Worlaby *Lincs* **188** D5
Worlaby *NLincs* **188** A1
World Museum Liverpool
  Mersey L3 8EN **42** D3
World of Beatrix Potter
  Attraction *Cumb*
  LA23 3BX **199** F3
World of James Herriot, Thirsk
  NYorks YO7 1PL **202** D4
World's End *Bucks* **135** D2
Worlds End *Hants* **107** F1
World's End
  WBerks **133** G5
Worlds End *WMid* **158** D4
Worle **116** A1
Worleston **171** D2
Worlingham **165** F3
Worlington **163** E5
Worlingworth **152** D1
Wormald Green **194** C1
Wormbridge **144** D4
Wormegay **163** E1
Wormelow Tump **145** D4
Wormhill **185** F5
Wormingford **152** A4
Worminghall **134** B2
Wormington **146** C4
Worminster **116** C3
Wormiston **245** E4
Wormit **244** B2
Wormleighton **147** G2
Wormley *Herts* **136** C2
Wormley *Surr* **121** E4
Wormley West End **136** C2
Wormshill **124** A3
Wormsley **144** D3
Worplesdon **121** E2
Worrall **186** A3
Worsbrough **186** A2
Worsley **184** B2
Worstead **179** E3
Worsted Lodge **150** D2
Worsthorne **193** E4
Worston **193** D3

Worswell **100** B3
Worth *Kent* **125** F3
Worth *WSuss* **122** B5
Worth Matravers **105** F5
Wortham **164** B4
Worthen **156** C2
Worthenbury **170** B3
Worthing *Norf* **178** A4
Worthing *WSuss* **108** D3
Worthington **173** F5
Worting **120** B2
Wortley *Glos* **131** G3
Wortley *SYorks* **186** A3
Wortwell **165** D3
Wotherton **156** B2
Wotton **100** B1
Wotton **121** G3
Wotton Underwood **134** B1
Wotton-under-Edge **131** G3
Woughton on the
  Green **149** D4
Wouldham **123** G2
Wrabness **152** C4
Wrae **269** F5
Wrafton **113** E2
Wragby **188** B5
Wragholme **189** D3
Wramplingham **178** C5
Wrangaton **100** C2
Wrangham **260** E1
Wrangle **176** C2
Wrangle Lowgate **176** C2
Wrangway **103** E1
Wrantage **116** A5
Wrawby **188** A2
Wraxall *NSom* **131** D5
Wraxall *Som* **116** D4
Wray **192** C1
Wray Castle **199** E2
Wrays **122** B4
Wraysbury **135** F5
Wrayton **200** B5
Wrea Green **191** G4
Wreay *Cumb* **210** A5
Wreay *Cumb* **210** A3
Wrecclesham **120** D3
Wrekenton **212** B2
Wrelton **203** G4
Wrenbury **170** C3
Wrench Green **204** C3
Wreningham **164** C2
Wrentham **165** F3
Wrenthorpe **194** C5
Wrentnall **156** D2
Wressle *ERid* **195** G4
Wressle *NLincs* **187** G2
Wrestlingworth **150** A3
Wretham **164** A2
Wretton **163** E2
Wrexham (Wrecsam) **170** A3
Wrexham Arts Centre *Wrex*
  LL11 1AU **170** A3
Wrexham Industrial
  Estate **170** A3
Wribbenhall **157** G5
Wrightington Bar **183** G1
Wrightpark **242** B5
Wright's Green **137** E1
Wrinehill **171** E3
Wrington **116** B1
Writhlington **117** D2
Writtle **137** F2
Wrockwardine **157** F1
Wroot **187** G2
Wrose **194** A4
Wrotham **123** F3
Wrotham Heath **123** F3
Wrotham Hill Park **123** F2
Wrottesley **158** A2
Wroughton **132** D4
Wroxall *IoW* **107** E5
Wroxall *Warks* **159** E5
Wroxeter **157** E2
Wroxham **179** E4
Wroxham Barns *Norf*
  NR12 8QU **179** E3
Wroxton **147** G3
Wstrws **141** G4
Wyaston **172** C4
Wyberton **176** B3
Wyboston **149** G2
Wybunbury **171** D3
Wych Cross **122** D5
Wychbold **146** B1
Wychnor **159** D1
Wychnor Bridges **159** D1
Wyck **120** C4
Wyck Rissington **147** D5
Wycliffe **202** A1
Wycoller **193** F4
Wycoller Country Park
  Lancs BB8 8SY **193** F4
Wycomb **174** C5
Wycombe Marsh **135** D3
Wyddial **150** B4
Wye **124** C4
Wyesham **131** E1
Wyfordby **160** C1
Wyke *Devon* **102** B3
Wyke *Dorset* **117** E5
Wyke *Shrop* **157** F2
Wyke *Surr* **121** E2
Wyke *WYorks* **194** A5
Wyke Champflower **117** D4
Wyke Regis **104** C5
Wykeham *NYorks* **204** C4
Wykeham *NYorks* **204** B5
Wyken *Shrop* **157** G3
Wyken *WMid* **159** F4
Wykey **170** A5
Wylam **212** A1
Wylde Green **158** D3
Wyllie **130** A3
Wylye **118** B4
Wymering **107** F2
Wymeswold **174** B5
Wymington **149** E1
Wymondham *Leics* **161** D1
Wymondham *Norf* **178** C5
Wyndham **129** F3
Wynford Eagle **104** B3
Wynnstay Park **170** A3

Wynyard **212** D5
Wynyard Woodland Park
  Stock TS21 3JG **212** C5
Wyre Forest *Worcs*
  DY14 9XQ **157** G5
Wyre Piddle **146** B3
Wyresdale Tower **192** C2
Wysall **174** B5
Wyson **145** E1
Wythall **158** C5
Wytham **133** G2
Wythburn **209** G5
Wythenshawe **184** C4
Wyton *Cambs* **162** A5
Wyton *ERid* **197** D3
Wyverstone **152** B1
Wyverstone Street **152** B1
Wyville **175** D5
Wyvis Lodge **266** B4

X

Xscape Castleford *WYorks*
  WF10 4DA **194** D5

Y

Y Bryn **168** B5
Y Fan **155** F4
Y Felinheli **167** E1
Y Ffôr **166** C4
Y Fron (Upper
  Llandwrog) **167** E2
Yaddlethorpe **187** F2
Yafford **106** D4
Yafforth **202** C3
Yalberton **101** E2
Yalding **123** F4
Yanley **116** C1
Yanwath **210** B5
Yanworth **132** C1
Yapham **195** G2
Yapton **108** B3
Yarburgh **188** D3
Yarcombe **103** F2
Yardley **158** D4
Yardley Gobion **148** C3
Yardley Hastings **149** D2
Yardro **144** B2
Yarford **115** F5
Yarkhill **145** F3
Yarlet **171** G5
Yarley **116** C3
Yarlington **117** D5
Yarm **202** D1
Yarmouth **106** C4
Yarnacott **113** G2
Yarnbrook **117** F2
Yarnfield **171** F4
Yarnscombe **113** F3
Yarnton **133** G1
Yarpole **145** D1
Yarrow *ScBord* **227** E3
Yarrow *Som* **116** A3
Yarrow Feus **227** E3
Yarrowford **227** F3
Yarsop **144** D3
Yarwell **161** F3
Yate **131** G4
Yatehouse Green **171** E1
Yateley **120** D1
Yatesbury **132** C5
Yattendon **134** A5
Yatton *Here* **144** D1
Yatton *NSom* **116** B1
Yatton Keynell **132** A5
Yaverland **107** F4
Yawl **103** G3
Yaxham **178** B4
Yaxley *Cambs* **161** G3
Yaxley *Suff* **164** C4
Yazor **144** D3
Ye Olde Pork Pie Shoppe,
  Melton Mowbray *Leics*
  LE13 1NW **160** C2
Yeabridge **104** A1
Yeading **136** A4
Yeadon **194** B3
Yealand Conyers **199** G5
Yealand Redmayne **199** G5
Yealand Storrs **199** G5
Yealmbridge **100** B2
Yealmpton **100** B2
Yearby **213** F5
Yearsley **203** E5
Yeaton **156** D1
Yeavering **228** D3
Yedingham **204** B5
Yelford **133** F2
Yell **278** D4
Yelland *Devon* **113** E2
Yelland *Devon* **99** F1
Yelling **150** A1
Yellowcraig *ELoth*
  EH39 5DS **236** C1
Yelvertoft **160** A5
Yelverton *Devon* **100** B1
Yelverton *Norf* **179** D5
Yenston **117** E5
Yeo Mill **114** B5
Yeo Vale **113** E3
Yeoford **102** A3
Yeolmbridge **98** D2
Yeomadon **112** D5
Yeovil **104** B1
Yeovil Country Park *Som*
  BA20 1QZ **104** B1
Yeovil Marsh **104** B1
Yeovilton **116** C5
Yerbeston **127** D2
Yesnaby **277** B6
Yesterday's World, Battle
  ESuss TN33 0AQ **110** C2
Yetholm Mains **228** C4
Yetlington **229** E5
Yetminster **104** B1
Yettington **103** D4
Yetts o'Muckhart **243** F4
Yew Green **147** E1
Yielden **149** F1
Yieldshields **234** C4
Ynys **167** E4
Ynys Tachwedd **154** C3
Ynysboeth **129** G3
Ynysddu **130** A3
Ynyshir **129** G3
Ynyslas **154** C3
Ynysmaerdy **129** G4

Ynysmeudwy **128** D2
Ynystawe **128** C2
Ynyswen **129** F3
Ynysybwl **129** G3
Yockenthwaite **201** E5
Yockleton **156** C1
Yokefleet **196** A5
Yoker **233** G3
Yonder Bognie **268** E6
York **195** F2
York Castle Museum
  YO1 9SA **90** York
York Dungeon
  YO1 9RD **90** York
York Minster
  YO1 7HH **90** York
Yorkshire Museum
  YO1 7FR **90** York
Yorkshire Sculpture Park
  WYorks WF4 4LG **185** G1
Yorton **170** C5
Yorton Heath **170** C5
Youldon **112** D5
Youldonmoor Cross **112** D5
Youlgreave **172** D1
Youlthorpe **195** G2
Youlton **195** D1
Young's End **137** G1
Yoxall **158** D1
Yoxford **153** E1
Ysbyty Cynfyn **155** D5
Ysbyty Ifan **168** B3
Ysbyty Ystwyth **154** D5
Ysceifiog **182** C5
Ysgubor-y-coed **154** C3
Ystalyfera **129** D2
Ystrad **129** F3
Ystrad Aeron **142** B2
Ystrad Meurig **142** D1
Ystrad Mynach **130** A3
Ystradfellte **129** F1
Ystradffin **143** D3
Ystradgynlais **129** D1
Ystradowen *Carmar* **128** D1
Ystradowen *VGlam* **129** G5
Ystumtuen **154** D5
Ythanwells **260** E1
Ythsie **261** G1

Z

Zeal Monachorum **102** A2
Zeals **117** E4
Zelah **96** C4
Zennor **94** B3
Zouch **173** G4
ZSL London Zoo *GtLon*
  NW1 4RY **12** A3

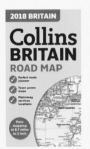
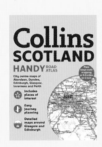

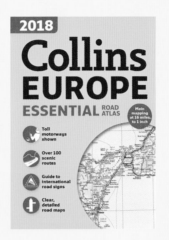
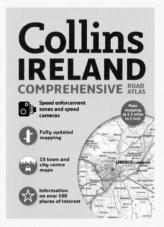

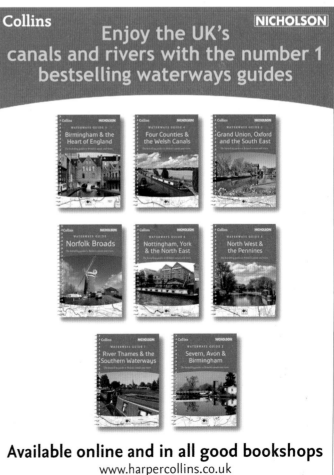

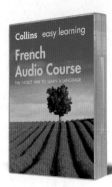

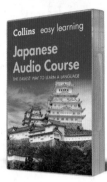

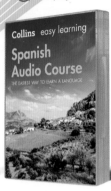